# CHAM...
# STUDENT
# GUIDE

Published by Chambers and Partners Publishing
(a division of Orbach & Chambers Ltd)
Saville House, 23 Long Lane, London EC1A 9HL
Tel: (020) 7606 1300 Fax: (020) 7600 3191
email: info@ChambersandPartners.co.uk
www.ChambersandPartners.com

Our thanks to the many students, trainees, pupils,
solicitors, barristers and graduate recruitment
personnel who assisted us in our research. Also to
Chambers and Partners recruitment team for their
knowledge and assistance and to the researchers of
Chambers UK 2006 from which all firm rankings
are drawn.

**Publisher:** Michael Chambers
**Managing Editor:** Fiona Boxall
**Editor:** Anna Williams
**Writer:** Richard Easton, Michael Lovatt, Helen Lyle,
John Lucarotti, James Plummer, Anna Saunders
**Editorial assistant:** Joanne Grote
**Database:** Andrew Taylor
**A-Z Co-ordinator:** Jill Tugwell
**Production:** Jasper John, Paul Effeny
**Business Development Manager:** Brad D. Sirott
**Business Development Team:** Neil Murphy,
Richard Ramsay
**Proofreaders:** Sarah Weise, John Bradley,
Nicholas Widdows, Sally Cope, William Cederwell
Sarah Reardon, Tom Stevens

**Printed by:** Polestar Wheatons Limited

# CONTENTS

## first steps

## solicitors

# the true picture

why do all law firm recruitment brochures look the same? the true picture is the antidote. it is the product of six months spent interviewing hundreds of trainees and newly qualified solicitors at 120 firms in england and wales. we asked them to tell us about their training contracts in their own words... and they did!

# solicitors a-z    491

the phone numbers, addresses and e-mails you need to make your applications. plus loads of really useful facts and figures on the top law firms. all in simple easy to follow a-z format

# barristers

## chambers reports

impeneterable, incomprehensible and in another world...it's too easy to stereotype the bar. we banged on the doors of 44 chambers to have a nose around and quiz the inhabitants

# STUDENT GUIDE

## 2005 | 2006

## november

**1** law fair:
university of leicester
cardiff university

**2** law fair:
university of sussex

**4** law fair:
university of
east anglia

**7** law fair:
university of leeds

**8** law fair:
university of leeds
qmu, london

**10** law fair:
university of reading

**11** vacation scheme
application
deadline:
herbert smith
(christmas)
lovells (christmas)

**12** law fair:
university of oxford

**15** law fair:
university of liverpool
university of essex
lse

**16** law fair:
lse
university of bristol

**17** law fair:
university of bristol
university of
southampton

**18** vacation scheme
application
deadline:
clifford chance
(christmas)

**21** law fair:
university of
newcastle-upon-tyne

**22** law fair:
university of durham
university of warwick

**23** law fair:
university of
birmingham
queen's university,
belfast

**24** law fair:
university of
manchester

**28** law fair:
ucl

**29** law fair:
ucl

**30** law fair:
university of sheffield

## december

**1** law fair:
university of
cambridge

**2** law fair:
university of
cambridge

**31** vacation scheme
application
deadline:
dickinson dees
(easter)

**jan 4** training contract
application
deadline:
dmh stallard

> *"All the careers
> support and
> hard work with
> my application
> reviews and
> mock interview
> has helped me
> secure my train-
> ing contract."*
>
> **Christian Fahey,
> LPC Student**

## january

**17** law fair:
university of exeter
kngs college, london

**18** law fair:
kngs college, london

**27** vacation scheme
application
deadline:
pannone & partners
slaughter and may

**31** training contract
application
deadline:
allen & overy (cpe)
bristows (feb interviews)

vacation scheme
application deadline:
allen & overy
ashurst
barlow lyde & gilbert
baker & mckenzie
bird & bird
clifford chance
(easter/summer)
clyde & co
davenport lyons
dla piper
dmh stallard
eversheds
farrer & co
field fisher waterhouse
freshfields
hammonds
herbert smith
lawrence graham
lewis silkin
manches
norton rose
olswang
osborne clarke
pinsent masons
reed smith
richards butler
simmons & simmons
sj berwin
travers smith
white & case
withers
wragge & co

# CALENDAR OF EVENTS

## ebruary

**10** vacation scheme application deadline:
addleshaw goddard
denton wilde sapte
lovells (easter/summer)
nabarro nathanson
taylor wessing

**11** vacation scheme application deadline:
gateley wareing

**14** vacation scheme application deadline:
cleary gottlieb steen & hamilton
holman fenwick & willan
ince & co
jones day
speechly bircham
weil, gotshal & manges

**15** law fair:
university of northumbria
university of wales, swansea
vacation scheme application deadline:
kirkpatrick & lockhart nicholson graham

**18** vacation scheme application deadline:
stephenson harwood

training contract application deadline:
baker & mckenzie (non-law)

**24** vacation scheme application deadline:
mccormicks
watson, farley & williams

**26** vacation scheme application deadline:
walker morris

**28** vacation scheme application deadline:
berwin leighton paisner
bristows (easter and summer)
capsticks
covington & burling
dechert
dickinson dees (summer)
kendall freeman
macfarlanes
reynolds porter chamberlain
shadbolt & co
shoosmiths
ward hadaway
wedlake bell

> *"The facilities at BPP are first class."*
>
> **Ellie Vance, GDL Student**

## march

**1** vacation scheme application deadline:
mills & reeve
trowers & hamlins

**15** vacation scheme application deadline:
mishcon de reya

**30** vacation scheme application deadline:
taylor walton

**31** vacation scheme application deadline:
bevan brittan
coffin mew & clover
foot anstey
government legal service
halliwells
hugh james
laytons
lester aldridge
morgan cole
penningtons
thomas eggar
tlt solicitors

## april

**28** vacation scheme application deadline:
pannone & partners (summer)

**30** vacation scheme application deadline:
hill dickinson
howes percival

> *"I'm sure that my success in securing pupillage is in no small way due to the quality of the BPP BVC and the commitment of the staff who teach it."*
>
> **Ian Cassie, BVC Student**

## may

**1** vacation scheme application deadline:

beachcroft wansbroughs

## june

**30** training contract application deadline:

bp collins

## july

**14** training contract application deadline:

cobbetts

**28** training contract application deadline:

mccormicks

sidley austin brown & wood

**30** training contract application deadline:

finers stephen innocent

martineau johnson

taylor walton

watson, farley & williams

**31** training contract application deadline:

addleshaw goddard

asb

ashurst

baker & mckenzie (law)

barlow lyde & gilbert

berwin leighton paisner

bevan brittan

bircham dyson bell

bird & bird

boodle hatfield

brabners chaffe street

brachers

browne jacobson

burges salmon

capsticks

charles russell

cleary gottlieb steen & hamilton

clyde & co

cms cameron mckenna

coffin mew & clover

covington & burling

cripps harries hall

davenport lyons

dechert

denton wilde sapte

dickinson dees

dla piper

dwf

eversheds

farrer & co

fladgate fielder

foot anstey

forbes

freeth cartwright

freshfields

gateley wareing

gov. legal service

halliwells

hammonds

harbottle & lewis

henmans

herbert smith

hill dickinson

holman fenwick & willan

howes percival

hugh james

ince & co

irwin mitchell

kendall freeman

kirkpatrick & lockhart

nicholson graham

lawrence graham

leboeuf, lamb, green & macrae

lester aldridge

lewis silkin

lovells

lupton fawcett

mace & jones

macfarlanes

manches

mayer, brown, rowe & maw

## august

## september

mcdermott, will & emery
mcgrigors
mills & reeve
mishcon de reya
morgan cole
nabarro nathanson
norton rose
olswang
orrick herrington & sutcliffe
osborne clarke
pannone & partners
penningtons
pinsent masons
prettys
pritchard englefield
reed smith
richards butler
salans
shadbolt & co
shearman & sterling
shoosmiths
simmons & simmons
sj berwin
speechly bircham
stephenson harwood
taylor wessing
teacher stern selby
thomson snell & passmore
tlt solicitors
travers smith
walker morris
ward hadaway
watson burton
wedlake bell
weightmans
weil, gotshal & manges
white & case
wiggin
withers
wragge & co

**1** training contract application deadline:

beachcroft wansbroughs
payne hicks beach
thomas eggar
trowers & hamlins

**4** training contract application deadline:

tarlo lyons

**11** training contract application deadline:

reynolds porter chamberlain

**26** training contract application deadline:

hodge jones & allen (for 2007)

**31** training contract application deadline:

allen & overy (law students)
bristows (for september interviews)
field fisher waterhouse
ford & warren
hewitsons
jones day
laytons

**30** training contract application deadline:

dorsey & whitney
stevens & bolton

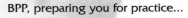

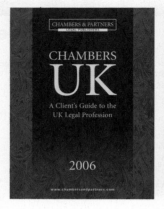
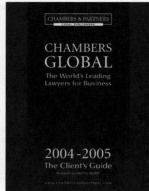
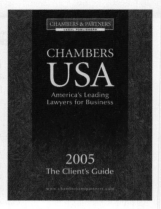

Chambers and Partners publishes a suite of legal guides that you should find helpful in your search for a training contract or pupillage.

- **Chambers UK** is the product of over 12,000 interviews with solicitors, barristers and their clients. It identifies the leading firms, sets and players across the full sweep of legal practice in the UK.

- **Chambers Global** sets out the results of our research into legal jurisdictions worldwide from Australia to Zambia. If you are considering a training contract with an international law firm, it's a must-read book.

- **Chambers USA** provides a more detailed analysis of the performance of the best firms across all US states.

These guides are available for reference in your university careers service or law library and can all be read online:

**www.chambersandpartners.com**.

# so you want to be a lawyer...

Right now you may have no more than a hunch that you want to be a lawyer. It's only natural that your knowledge at this very early stage will be limited, and our first piece of advice is simple: Don't worry! We've written this book with the specific aim of giving you the information, tools and confidence with which to make a sound career decision. You may decide to become a solicitor or a barrister, or follow one of the other career options that are covered in the following pages. You may decide to give the law a wide berth after reading this book! Whatever you decide, take things steady, plan the road to qualification carefully and make the most of the vast quantity of information that's available, if you look in the right places.

Let's start with one of the most basic questions: Do you want to be a barrister or a solicitor?

## barrister

Ask a solicitor about the key difference between the two sides of the profession and they will probably tell you it's the size of your average barrister's ego. At first sight the role of a barrister certainly looks a lot cooler than that of a solicitor. Even if you've only ever seen fictitious ones in TV dramas, you know the deal - it's all about striding into courtrooms, robes flowing; tense moments waiting for missing witnesses and razor-sharp cross-examinations that save the client's bacon and/or liberty. Glamorous? It's downright sexy!

If only. The sad truth is that there's a great deal more to the job than looking good in a wig and gown. Essentially barristers do two things. First, they go to court and present cases on behalf of others. This is the hired-gun side of the job. Second, they give specialised legal advice. This is the side of the job that requires a good deal of grey matter. How much of either of these a barrister does depends on which part of the Bar they practice and, many would say, how much of a brainiac they are. A criminal practitioner will be

on their feet most of the time, advocating in cases they may have only been given an hour or two beforehand. By contrast, a member of the Chancery Bar will spend most of their time in chambers writing tricky opinions on complicated law. Because of their detailed knowledge of the litigation process, solicitors value barristers for their ability to assess and advise on the merits and demerits of a case.

It is widely known that candidates for the Bar should be clever. They also need to be highly persuasive in their style of argument because advocacy is the name of the game both in court and back in chambers when writing opinions. Barristers must display the skill and clarity to make complex or arcane legal arguments accessible to lay clients, juries and the judiciary. But it goes beyond these two things: a good barrister will be able to understand the client's perspective - certainly in the area of commercial law - and they will be able to help construct a solution that makes business or common sense as well as legal sense. If you're hoping a career as a barrister will allow you to remain at the top of an ivory tower, you might wish to consider life as an academic.

Of course, it has been some time since barristers have had exclusive rights of audience in the courts. Solicitors can, and some have, become accredited advocates in even the higher courts. Many people thought this blurring of the distinction between the two halves of the profession would sound the death knell for the Bar. So far, so wrong. What has happened is that solicitor advocates are undertaking a lot of straightforward cases and the more complicated and lengthy matters are still going to the Bar. If only because this is often the most cost-effective way of managing the case. As a point of interest, solicitor advocates do not wear the wig and gown and are referred to as 'my friend' rather than 'my learned friend'.

Now we've dealt with what barristers do, let's take a quick look at how they run their careers, because here too there are notable differences. While solicitors are employed by law firms (perhaps eventually becoming a partner and owning a share of the business) most barristers are self-employed. This is why you hear the expression 'independent Bar'. The reason why the vast majority of the Bar remains independent is because one of the basic tenets of professional ethics is that a barrister should be able to fight for his or her client and fulfil an overriding duty to the court without fear of sanction from an employer. Actually, a minority of barristers end up being employed by companies or law firms and they make up the 'employed Bar'.

To prevent independence from turning into isolation, barristers work in groups called sets, sharing premises and professional managers etc. Barristers do not work for their sets, just at them, and as 'tenants' they contribute to the upkeep of their chambers and give a percentage of their earnings to their clerks and administrators. Unlike employed barristers and solicitors, those at the independent Bar get no sickness pay, holiday pay, maternity leave or monthly salary. What they do get is a good accountant!

Being a barrister is a great job, but the competition is fierce. If your appetite has been whetted you will find much more information in the final, orange section of this book. There we have detailed the recruitment process and laid bare some of the more obscure practices and terminology of the Bar. We have also tried to give a fair assessment of some of the difficulties that young hopefuls may encounter when trying to get on the first few rungs of the ladder. The **Chambers Reports** section gives an invaluable insight into the lives of pupils and junior barristers at some of the best sets. If you are unsure how you are going to pay for your foray into the Bar then check out the Funding section on page 46. Information about Bar School at the BVC course is to be found on page 42.

## solicitor

Hands up who knows how many solicitors there are in England and Wales. At the last count it was a whopping 121,165. And how many law firms? Around 9,200, nearly half of which are sole practitioners. Now we all know that there are some huge law firms, but who knew that less than 500 firms had more than ten partners? If nothing else, what these statistics should tell you is that becoming a solicitor will not mean the same thing for everyone.

Most budding lawyers qualify as solicitors rather than as barristers. In 2003, some 5,708 trainees started contracts, and we trust that the majority of them will now, two years later, have qualified as fully-fledged solicitors. We know that more than half of them are women and that approaching a fifth come from ethnic minority groups. What we also know is that the career path of a solicitor is more certain than that of a barrister. Yes, it's true that over 10,000 people start full or part-time Legal Practice Courses (LPC see page 30) and must compete for the available training places, but the potential for disappointment is nowhere near that with which Bar hopefuls must contend.

If you are reading this while still at university then, unless you plan to take a year out for travel or other experience, you may need to start making applications for a training contract sooner than you had imagined. If you are studying for a law degree and you want to work in a commercial firm, the crucial time for research and applications is your penultimate year. If you are a non-law student intending to take a law conversion course before going to a commercial firm then you'll have to juggle exams and career considerations in your final year. Students wanting to enter general or high street practice need not worry about training contracts until later, and the reason for this is that commercial firms generally offer training contracts two years in advance and other types of firms do so only rarely. Leave it too late and your preferred commercial firms will no longer be recruiting for the year you want to start your training. Needless to say, your choice of training contract is crucial, as it will determine the path (and perhaps also location) of your future career.

Most readers will be well aware that after the degree, law school awaits. Law grads spend one year on the LPC (or two if taking it part-time). Non-law grads must also complete the CPE/PgDL before being eligible for the LPC. Larger commercial firms commonly offer scholarships to cover course fees and some maintenance for the LPC and, if necessary, the CPE/PgDL. A handful of big City firms require students to attend specific law schools that offer specialised, City-oriented courses. Most smaller firms - those in general or 'high street' practice - tend not to offer any financial assistance and recruit closer to the start date of the training contract. Students headed for this type of firm can find the CPE and LPC years to be uncertain and expensive. We have given some guidance on how to select a law school in our LPC feature.

Even more crucial is to select the right firm for your training because its client base, work and reputation will determine the experience you gain and also have a bearing on your future marketability as a lawyer. In addition to finding out about the size and location of a firm, and the work it handles, you should learn something about the quality of its reputation and its culture. At Chambers and Partners, we've made it our business to know who does what, how well they do it and what it might be like working at a particular firm. In the Practice Areas section of this book, you'll find the core results of the research carried out for our parent publication *Chambers UK* and we'd recommend that you use it as a springboard for further research. Our league tables show which firms command greatest respect from clients and other professionals in different areas of practice. An enormous amount of additional information

is available in *Chambers UK*, including details of law firms' top clients and deals. Copies of the book should be available in your university careers office or law department library, or you can read the whole thing online at www.chambersandpartners.com. If you want to throw your research net even wider, you can find out about a firm's international work and reputation in *Chambers Global* and *Chambers USA*.

In the True Picture section of this book we've profiled 120 of the leading firms in England and Wales. This section of the book should help you understand what kind of firm might suit you and the kind of work you can expect to receive when you get there. Law firms come in all shapes and sizes. Do your research, do a bit of navel-gazing and work out what is best for you. If you look on our website www.chambersandpartners.com/chambersstudent you should find features on even more firms.

It will probably help you to envisage the legal market as one in which firms can be grouped into different categories and then you can consider which types you want to learn more about before making applications. When it comes to securing a training contract, a targeted approach beats a scattergun approach hands down.

**Magic Circle:** This group is seen by many as the elite. The firms pay big salaries to hard-working trainees and are very corporate and/or finance-oriented in their practice focus. The prestige that attaches to a magic circle training is undeniable and, to that end, there are many students who consider nowhere else. Whether this is because of the advice they are given by course directors, careers advisers, friends or family, or plain herd mentality, the fact is these firms do have the pick of the best and offer a superb but mass-scale training. Their size and big-money deals will definitely not appeal to all students and it's important that those who'd fare better in a different type of environment recognise this. For most niche practice areas, the magic circle is rarely ever the most logical choice. The other thing to note about this type of firm is the high volume of international deals. The magic circle includes Slaughter and May, Clifford Chance, Freshfields Bruckhaus Deringer, Allen & Overy and Linklaters.

**London - large commercial:** The top-ten City of London firms (including the magic circle) account for around 1,000 training contracts between them, representing approximately a fifth of all training contracts registered with the Law Society. There's not a huge difference between the magic circle and firms such as Herbert Smith, Lovells, Norton Rose, Ashurst and others of their ilk. In such large firms, work is almost entirely centred on business law, although a tiny number retain specialists in private client practice. Just as in the magic circle the money is very good. Expect to work on high-profile matters (though not always conducting particularly challenging duties). Expect to be pushed and, at times, be prepared to give 110%. If you are working against a deadline on a deal then you will be expected to stay until it is finished. This can mean working through the night and coming in at weekends from time to time.

You will need a consistently excellent academic record, from A-levels through to your first and second-year exam results or final degree. Unfortunately you'll need to go right to the back of a very long queue if you failed to gain at least a 2:1. Recruitment personnel in City firms are also keen to ensure that prospective trainees possess commercial awareness. In other words, understanding what businesses want, how they work and what lawyers can do to help them. You need to show that you have an interest in law, an interest in business and an interest in the firm you are going to. If you can't... there's something wrong with your decision.

**Regionals:** The City of London may be the beating heart of blue-chip, international business, but there's more to life than an EC postcode. Out in the regions, firms such as Dickinson Dees, Burges Salmon, Wragge & Co, Walker Morris and Halliwells offer top-notch clients and some international work. Some might as well be top London firms which just happen to be based in the regions; others focus on regional clients and work.

Regional firms can be every bit as difficult to get into as their City rivals. In some cases you are statistically more likely to be picked up by the magic circle, so if the magic circle has refused you, don't assume you'll walk into a top regional firm... they are unimpressed by sloppy-seconds applications. If you are applying to join a firm in Bristol, for example, and have studied and lived in London all your life, be prepared to be asked why you want to move to the area. The last thing firms want is to spend a fortune training you, only to have to sign your leaving card when you swan off to the capital on qualification. Recruitment personnel at the top regional practices are looking for exactly the same qualities in applicants as their peers at the top City firms.

Salaries are lower outside London, in some cases significantly so, but the cost of living is much more reasonable. You are also quite likely to benefit from less frenetic hours than many City-based practices and there's plenty of anecdotal evidence suggesting that regional firms are a bit friendlier. As you will see in the True Picture, however, it is all about finding a firm that suits you.

**Nationals:** These are multi-site firms with offices in different UK cities. Eversheds has ten branches in England and Wales; DLA has eight in England and Scotland. Hammonds has four in London, Birmingham, Leeds and Manchester, while Addleshaw Goddard skips the Birmingham option. Some nationals avoid the major cities: Shoosmiths operates in smaller cities and towns from the South Coast up to Nottingham (though it recently opened in Birmingham). These, and the other nationals, have differing approaches to recruitment and whether or not trainees move around the country, so make sure you know the policy adopted by your chosen firm.

**Niche:** Particularly in London, there are scores of niche firms to choose from. Construction, entertainment, IP, insurance litigation, shipping, family... the list goes on. If you are absolutely certain that you want to specialise in a particular field - especially if you have already worked in the relevant industry - a niche firm is a sound choice. Be aware that many firms described as niche practices actually offer other types of work. Be aware also that some niche firms do try to woo students by talking a little too much about their other areas of practice.

**General practice/ 'high street':** These range from substantial, long-established firms in large town centres to sole practitioners working above shops in the suburbs. They act for legally aided clients, individuals funding themselves and local businesses. Staple work includes matrimonial, landlord and tenant, personal injury, employment, family, wills and probate, and crime. It's increasingly likely that firms have an additional specialism in small-ticket commercial work for local businesses. Be prepared to earn considerably less than your peers in commercial practice. Commonly, you'll receive at or around the minimum salary stipulated by the Law Society (£16,450 for central London and £14,720 elsewhere). The hours can be unsociable in criminal practice, but in this kind of firm you will get to handle clients and real work from a very early stage. If you want to grow up fast as a lawyer and see how the law actually affects individuals and the community in which you practice then this is the kind of firm to go for. Unlike commercial firms, most do not recruit two years in advance and most do not sponsor students through the LPC. Larger firms may take on four or five trainees a year; the smallest will recruit on an ad hoc basis.

## law centres

From its roots in North Kensington in 1970, the network of UK Law Centres has grown to around 60 today, each set up as either a registered charity or a not-for-profit company and run by its own local management committee. Advice is given to the public without charge, with funding coming from local government grants (approximately 60%) and the Legal Services Commission (LSC) by way of 'Legal Help' certificated payments. The legal problems handled may vary from one Law Centre to another, but those who work in Law Centres can all be described as social welfare law specialists. Employment, discrimination, disability, housing, immigration, asylum and public law (eg education and community care) form the main diet. In a recent development, crime has become a speciality for one Law Centre.

Law Centres see themselves as more than just providers of legal advice to the public; their horizons are broader than those of the Citizens Advice Bureau and they tend to take on cases with a wider social impact. A client with a consumer dispute is less likely to be taken on than someone who is affected by, say, a local authority's decision on rent arrears because Law Centres have noted an alarming trend for social landlords to bring ever increasing numbers of rent arrears cases (now some 30,000 per year). Identifying such trends is part of their job. From there, it's a case of using little matters to change the big picture, perhaps by way of a test case that makes it to the House of Lords, the European Court of Justice and the broadsheets. And because Law Centres are also eager to involve the community they operate within, providing legal training and education, a job in this field can also take you down the local comprehensive to offer up your legal know-how to a row of scowling teenagers. Highlights from the past year include the newly established Enfield Law Centre's streetlegal programme that ensures that young people have access to justice; Hammersmith and Fulham Law

Centre's successful challenge brought under the Human Rights Act against the controversial section 55 of the Asylum and Immigration Act; and Lewisham Law Centre's 'Quids for Kids' campaign that informed parents of disabled children of their right to assistance via the Disability Living Allowance benefit.

Most Law Centres employ 10-15 lawyers and, if you're attracted to working with colleagues who share your ideals and social conscience, you may want to investigate a career in the sector. Routes to a career are as varied as the work. Trainee solicitors from private firms with experience of working on pro bono cases are attractive upon qualification. So too are those who have worked as paralegals for non-profit agencies and have gained supervisor level status. A career may also begin at a Law Centre itself. Every year the LSC funds 15-20 training contracts in 14 Law Centres. Mirroring a training contract in private practice, the trainee will experience different branches of law, learning from specialists in each area.

Concern with the Greater Good comes with a caveat. At junior level your salary will roughly match private practice on the high street - £24-30,000 or more in London - at senior level the gap widens. Without wishing to sound trite, what you lose in the bank you gain in the soul. Law Centres operate along different lines to private practices: less hierarchy, more of an equal say for staff at all levels (some even operate as collectives with all staff drawing the same salary). Terms and conditions at work emulate those in local government and, as such, pension and holiday provisions, etc. are good, while flexible and part-time working is common.

Law Centres are keen Equal Opportunities employers and encourage trainees from black and minority ethnic groups in order to reflect the position of Law Centres in minority communities. This commitment has led to the creation of a 'Black Trainee Solicitor Scheme'. Before you go rushing down to the postbox with your CV, take note: candidates will only be considered if they respond to an advertisement. Look for these in *The Guardian* (Wednesdays), local newspapers, a bi-monthly publication called *Legal Action* (your university law library should have it), and the Law Centres Federation website www.lawcentres .org.uk (updated daily).

To enhance your prospects you should be able to demonstrate your interest in social justice. Earn some stripes on committees or community groups; working in a Local Authority while studying a CPE/LPC part-time will give you a taste of the fields Law Centres plough. While at law school take advantage of any schemes that bring you closer to working for social justice. Some volunteers are accepted by Law Centres to help with administration and (if accredited) translation work. Volunteers usually come via other non-profit agencies so don't expect to just walk in to a Law Centre and be accepted as a volunteer. A voluntary role with a Citizens Advice Bureau is easier to get hold of and would prepare you well for the type of clients served by Law Centres.

With the Law Centre Federation setting a benchmark of opening at least two centres a year, more work and more openings are to be expected in the future. And if there isn't a Law Centre in your area, the LCF is happy to hear from those who have identified a need to establish one. Try getting on to the local authority about the need for a Law Centre - you might be making a job for yourself in the future!

## working in-house with a company

Ready for some more statistics? More than a fifth of practising solicitors are employed to work 'in-house' for a company or public sector organisation. A number of large companies and banks offer training contracts and/or pupillages. For information on in-house legal teams registered to take trainees check the Law Society's website and for pupillages, refer to the Bar Coun-

# first steps

cil. *Chambers UK* lists contact details for the legal teams of FTSE 100 companies.

We spoke to one recently qualified solicitor who trained in-house with an international bank. He had already built up experience of the financial sector through working as a transaction manager, and eventually asked the head of the legal department in the bank he worked at if they would be willing to fund him through part-time CPE and LPC courses. A training contract with the bank was the other vital piece of the jigsaw, and the bank agreed to this too. The proposal was feasible as the bank was already an accredited training provider and had a solicitor with sufficient experience (and interest) who was happy to take on the role of training supervisor. The only thing the bank couldn't provide was sufficient contentious training and so it arranged a secondment to one of the law firms on its legal panel.

Our source felt his training was as good as, if not better than, anything available in private practice. *"I was given my own work to manage and had a great deal more latitude than in a conventional training contract. I got responsibility earlier and a lot less grunt work to do."* In-house trainees certainly develop very marketable skills because almost everything they do has a practical application and their sector knowledge is immense.

So who would suit this type of training? *"Generally speaking people are more mature than private practice trainees. They are not usually recent graduates who have to be spoon-fed for a time; you can't expect a 20-year-old to opine on issues that a senior associate would opine on, and in an in-house training contract you will generally be expected to have prior banking experience."* Cold calling heads of legal at banks or companies you're interested in might not be the best way forward. Usually a trainee will be recruited after having already worked within the organisation in some other capacity, and even then *"you have to exercise discretion in trying to obtain a contract."* A softly softly approach usually works best.

## local government

Some 3,500 solicitors are employed in local authorities and there are hundreds of local authority legal departments in the UK. Some of them offer training contracts, but there's no easy-to-access centralised list of vacancies and no single recruitment office, so you must contact each legal department separately and keep an eye open for advertisements in the local, legal and national press. The website www.lgcareers.com is the best place to start your research. There are opportunities for both vacation work experience and/or paralegalling but law school sponsorship is rare. The typical salary for a local authority solicitor is £28,900 - £35,000.

Because the activities of local authorities are so varied, training contracts involve a real breadth of work. You're quite likely to undertake property, planning and environmental law; litigation and prosecution work; consumer protection, housing, education and childcare; employment, personal injury, administrative and commercial/contracts. Usually trainees follow the same seat system that prevails in private practice but for local authority trainees there is the added bonus of having rights of audience in civil and criminal courts and tribunals that outstrip those of peers in private practice. In all seats, your clients will be officers from different departments of the local authority.

For many, the real appeal is working for a public sector organisation that's concerned with the local environment and community. For others, it's the excellent working conditions and benefits; part-time working, flexi-time and job sharing are not uncommon. Most local government lawyers remain in the public sector, but the job is portable across the UK, and lawyers can also transfer to the GLS or CPS or even go into private practice. Some local authorities operate their legal departments along commercial principles and all must adhere to the principle of 'Best Value'. If ever you doubt whether a career in local government can be high flying, you might wish to consider the fact that many current local authority chief executives trained as solicitors.

## government legal service

Lately, between 20 and 30 trainee solicitors and pupil barristers have been recruited each year by the Government Legal Service to work within different government departments and offices. HM Revenue & Customs; the DTI; the Department for Work & Pensions/Department of Health; the Treasury Solicitor's Department; the Home Office; Department for Environment, Food and Rural Affairs; the Office of the Deputy Prime Minister and the Department for Transport have all welcomed new recruits over the past few years. The GLS recruits centrally in London (though occasionally some regional offices may have vacancies, advertising them in national and local newspapers), and to discover what sort of person it is looking to attract, we spoke to James Murphy of the recruitment team.

The first thing he told us was how varied the work can be. At one end of the scale there are full-time litigators, and at the other, people drafting new legislation or advising ministers. To satisfy such diverse needs, the GLS wants candidates with "*good legal minds... people who can get to the root of a problem very quickly.*" James also stressed the importance of working to deadlines and as part of the team.

To find out if applicants have what it takes, the GLS holds one-day assessments, involving a written problem (a general legal topic so as not to disadvantage CPE candidates), a group exercise and a board interview.

We'd recommend anyone applying to the GLS to have a long think about the role government lawyers take. Particularly consider how "*law and politics interact*" and the impact that they can have on life and society in the UK, whether this is by bringing about the prosecution of drugs smugglers or human traffickers, or drafting new sexual offences or employment legislation. If you feel you need to gain a greater awareness, you can simply start by reading a good broadsheet newspaper regularly - they always cover topics of note, such as plans for a new Supreme Court and new anti-terror legislation.

A recent tweak to the recruitment process now means that the departments with vacancies are posted on the GLS website so applicants need not waste time applying where no job exists. The website identifies whether the different vacancies are for solicitors' training contracts or barristers' pupillages. Most training positions are based in a single department with secondments to other departments or bodies highly likely. Legal teams vary in size from a single lawyer in the smaller bodies to 300 or so in larger departments and agencies, in particular the Treasury Solicitor's Department and the Department for Constitutional Affairs.

Within departments, trainee solicitors do 'seats' just like their peers in private practice. Most pupil barristers will follow the traditional "two sixes" system found at the independent Bar, whereby six months are spent in barristers' chambers and the other six within the GLS. Some departments have adopted the newer "four four four" system, starting pupils in the department then sending them out to barristers' chambers before bringing them back to the department again.

According to Mark James-Dawson, a solicitor with the Health and Safety Executive, the main attractions of the GLS are the variety of work on offer, the high level of responsibility and the opportunity to have a hand in shaping legislation and government policy. "*You get to do interesting, high-profile work from an early stage,*" he told us. "*From the start, you can be working on a case that is being defended by a partner in a big city firm.*" Lawyers are also positively encouraged to move between departments, meaning "*the potential for career development is greater than in private prac-*

tice." This is coupled with the traditional benefits of working in the public sector - a clear career structure and relative security; pension provisions and flexible hours to suit those with children. On the downside, lawyers sometimes get frustrated by budgetary constraints and bureaucracy, and at senior level, the astronomical sums enjoyed by their partners in top City firms simply aren't there. However, we sense that other compensations come in the form of job satisfaction and kinder hours. The current salary rates for newly qualified lawyers in London are within the range of £27,000 to £38,000, depending upon department.

The first stage in securing training with the GLS is to contact its recruitment team, rather than the departments themselves. Sponsorship for the LPC or BVC is available and there is a vacation scheme offering two or three-week insights into life as a government lawyer. The GLS features in the True Picture and Chambers Reports sections of this book.

## becoming a legal executive

If you haven't found one of those elusive training contracts or are thinking about moving sideways into a legal career, you could consider the Institute of Legal Executives (ILEX) course. Those who complete the course become legal executives - qualified lawyers who are sometimes known as the 'third branch' of the legal profession. There are over 22,000 legal executives and trainee legal executives across the country. No prior legal training is required to enrol on the course, which makes it suitable for school leavers, new graduates or those already engaged in a career and looking to branch out. It can be taken on a part-time basis, giving trainees an opportunity to combine study with practical experience.

Trainees initially study for a Professional Diploma in Law, which takes about two years part-time. The course includes an introduction to key legal concepts as well as legal practice and

procedure. Trainees then progress to the Professional Higher Diploma in Law, which allows specialisation in a particular area of practice, usually guided by the job the trainee is doing at the time. On completion, trainees become members of ILEX. To become a fully qualified ILEX fellow, it is necessary to gain five years of qualifying experience in a legal background and be over the age of 25.

Law graduates are exempt from the academic part of the course and can take examinations solely in legal practice, enabling the qualification to be gained in a little over twelve months. For those without a law degree, the professional qualification will usually take three or four years to complete while in full-time employment. There is no set time to complete the examinations, so trainees can work at their own pace. ILEX graduates end up in employment across the full spectrum of legal services from private practice, to government departments and the in-house legal departments of major corporations.

Some ILEX fellows continue studying and eventually become fully qualified solicitors. As they will already have been examined in some of the core subjects required by the Common Professional Exam Board, and the others can be taken as single subjects over another one or two years of part-time study, most fellows can seek exemption from the CPE and move straight on to the Legal Practice Course. ILEX fellows may also be exempted from the two-year training contract.

Although ILEX can provide a useful route to qualification as a solicitor, it is by no means the quickest. Yet, positions for trainee legal executives may be available when solicitors' training contracts are not and, crucially, the route does enable the student to earn whilst studying. A full list of colleges offering the course (including via distance learning) is available at www.ilex.org.uk.

## paralegal work

If you have time to fill before starting your training contract or you are yet to be convinced you want to spend time and money on law school, paralegal work can provide a useful introduction to legal practice. Employers regard time spent paralegalling favourably, as it demonstrates commitment to the profession and enables candidates to gain valuable experience and commercial or sector insight. Some firms and companies – though not all – offer traineeships to the most impressive of their own paralegals, but you should always keep in mind that the job is a valuable position in its own right. Guard against giving the impression that you will leave as soon as something better crops up. There is no single job description: some experienced paralegals may run their own cases; others with little to offer by way of experience may end up doing very dull document management tasks for months on end. The paralegal market is competitive, so those with no legal qualifications or practical experience may find it difficult to secure a position. Indeed, some top City firms require all paralegal applicants to have completed the LPC. When starting out, it may be necessary to work a number of short-term contracts until one firm decides it wants you on a long-term basis.

This can be a career in its own right, and experienced paralegals with specialist skills can make a very decent living. For information on current vacancies, check the legal press or register with a specialist recruitment agency. You should also find out if your law school's careers office has contacts and regularly check the websites of any firms in your area. Some firms employ paralegals from among those who write to them on spec.

## the crown prosecution service

If you have a passion for criminal law, and the idea of billable hours and contract drafting leaves you cold, the CPS may appeal. The service employs about 2,500 lawyers in England and Wales to handle cases involving more than 1.3 million cases in the magistrates' courts and about

115,000 in the Crown Courts.

CPS prosecutors review and prosecute criminal cases following investigation by the police. They also advise the police on matters of criminal and evidence law, some working from Criminal Justice Units, which have been established within police stations to combat the problem of failed prosecutions. Lawyers here advise the police on the appropriate charge for the crime, spending one day in the office preparing cases and the next in the magistrates' court, dealing with administrative matters relating to each case. Lawyers in the Trial Unit handle Crown Court cases, including murder, rape and robbery. Because Crown Court matters are more serious, prosecutors often act as instructing counsel, although they can become higher court advocates and conduct prosecutions themselves. While it may lack the grit and glamour of *Law and Order*, the work of the CPS can have its exciting moments.

Prosecutors can expect to come into contact with 30 or 40 cases each day, and although they don't have the same intense client contact as defence lawyers, they do interact with everyone from magistrates, clerks, solicitors, probation and police officers, to civilian and expert witnesses and even serving prisoners. They also liaise with racial equality and victim support agencies as well as victims themselves. For example, where a prosecution is abandoned, the prosecutor must inform the victim of the reasons. It's easy to see why one prosecutor told us: "*You must be flexible and prepared for anything*." You must also be fairly "*bulletproof*," as the service sometimes gets flak for failed prosecutions. Though you'll not be the most popular person at the party, at least you're guaranteed to have some pretty interesting anecdotes!

More recently, the CPS has brought in new initiatives such as 'Narrowing the Justice Gap' (reducing the time between arrest and trial) and 'CPS Direct', which ensures that prosecutors are on call 24 hours a day to attend police stations and charge suspects in complicated cases. A qualified prosecutor's salary ranges from £25,648 – £45,388 nationally and £26,954 – £51,082 in London.

The CPS expect all trainees to have completed the LPC/BVC before applying and are currently training 50 solicitors and 8 pupils. A trainee's salary starts in the region of £17,888 – £22,628 depending on location and is subject to annual review. The traditional LLB to LPC/BVC route is by no means the preferred route into the CPS. Many CPS trainees have juggled work and part-time study; some have entered the service 'sideways', having left school with few academic qualifications. In fact, the CPS recently ditched its national graduate recruitment campaigns for trainees, leaving opportunities to be advertised in the legal, national and local press and on its own website (**www.cps.gov.uk**). The closing date accompanying advertised traineeships is usually early and competition is tough. Illustrating this point, we heard some anecdotal evidence about there being 40 applications for an internal promotion to one of seven traineeships. Inclined to grow its own lawyers, the CPS has fertiliser in the form of a 'Law Scholarship Scheme' composed of a £4.2 million investment spread over three years. The funding pays for its recipients' full LPC or BVC course fees and expenses.

Caseworkers: With the CPS seemingly intent on turning its caseworkers into solicitors and barristers, perhaps becoming a caseworker is the way forward for future trainees. They assist prosecutors by researching cases and making recommendations on information required and charges to be brought. Beyond these duties, they liaise with counsel, witnesses, police and court staff; provide support to witnesses and victims and additionally attend court to assist counsel on a regular basis. London caseworkers will usually be able to do a three-month stint at the Old Bailey. Impressive organisational skills and an ability to relate to people are essential. Remuner-

ation runs between £18,425 nationally and £19,441 in London.

Currently you can start anywhere at the CPS and end up as a prosecuting lawyer. As CPS recruitment manager Lesley Williams told us: "*If you see your career in the CPS, come aboard with us at any level and show a commitment to the service.*" There are hints that "*the situation might change,*" and an "*external focus may be coming soon,*" but for now the easiest way up is from within.

For vacation placements and work experience your starting point should be www.cps.gov.uk

## her majesty's court service

HM Court Service is the part of the Department for Constitutional Affairs that is responsible for the daily business of the court system. On 1 April 2005 the old court service and the magistrates' courts were swept together into this one body. No April Fool's joke, HMCS is responsible for the administration of the civil, family and criminal courts in England and Wales – right up to the Court of Appeal. As well as providing ushers and dealing with timetabling, it is also engaged in modernising the physical appearance of courts.

Most jobs are administrative in nature; however, the service recruits Judicial Assistants at various times throughout the year. JA appointments are temporary, and each lasts for a three-month term. There are usually ten positions at any one time. Appointments are sometimes renewed, but only for a maximum of twelve months. JAs assist the Lord Justices in the Civil Division of the Court of Appeal at the Royal Courts of Justice, including legal research, advice and providing assistance in drafting judgments. Applicants for JA positions must be qualified lawyers who have completed pupillage or traineeship. They also need word processing skills, be able to demonstrate intellectual ability (by way of a 2:1 degree) and have the ability to work under pressure as part of a team. Positions are advertised in *The Times* weekly law supplement and the

Law Society's *Gazette* as well as on the HM Court Service website www.hmcourts-service.gov.uk.

Those looking for a longer term career might consider the roles of administrative officer, bailiff, and county and Crown Court ushers or clerks. The 91 Crown Courts and 218 county courts are presided over by members of the judiciary, so court clerks do not have a legal advisory role and do not need legal qualifications. Magistrates' clerks are slightly different in that they do give legal advice to lay magistrates and managers of the court. Approximately 381 magistrates' courts operate in England and Wales, and between them they handle the majority of the country's criminal proceedings. In a busy metropolitan court, as well as the usual TV licence and traffic offences, the clerks will encounter drug trafficking cases and other serious crimes on a reasonably regular basis. A rural court is likely to be quieter and crimes of violence less common. Court clerks need to be able to think on their feet and deal confidently with people. Those we spoke to said that the vast majority of defendants treat them with respect and only occasionally must they exercise the power to order individuals into custody for contempt of court. The magistrates need to know they can rely on the clerks for sound advice on issues like self-defence, identification of suspects, and inferences from the silence of defendants after arrest.

A shift in recruitment policy has seen the traditional route (by which those without degrees could train while studying for the Diploma in Magisterial Law) overtaken by the recruitment of LPC and BVC graduates as trainee court clerks. As the individual progresses through a structured training programme, the number and complexity of their court duties will increase until ultimately they are advising lay magistrates on points of law and procedure. Most courts operate nine or ten sessions a week and most clerks will be in court for the majority of these. The remaining time will be spent exercising powers delegated to them by the magistrates, such as issuing summonses. For more information about careers with the magistrates' courts or any other part of HMCS refer to its website.

## the law commission

Many laws are the product of political expediency and are drawn up at the will of the government of the day. However, the government is not always best placed to see where reforms could best be made. The Law Commission, which is an associated office of the Department of Constitutional Affairs, was set up by Parliament 40 years ago to keep the laws of England and Wales under review and propose reform where necessary.

Its key purpose is to ensure that the law is as fair, modern, simple and cost-effective as possible, and to do so the commission employs about 15 research assistants to help with the task. At any one time, it will be engaged in about 20 projects of law reform. As a researcher you could be dealing with both common law and statutes going back many centuries. You will analyse many different areas of law, identifying defects in the current system, examining foreign law models to see how they deal with similar problems, helping to draft consultation papers or preparing reports of recommendation for the Lord Chancellor. The commission also works on the consolidation of statutes and the repeal of obsolete statutory provisions. Recent papers were published on such diverse subjects as a partial defence to murder, violence against children and unfair terms in contracts.

The Law Commission recruits law graduates and postgraduates, those who have completed the LPC or BVC, and people who have spent some time in practice but are looking for a change. The job of research assistant involves some fascinating (and some less fascinating) subjects and is intellectually challenging. Candidates should have a First or high 2:1 at degree level plus a keen interest in current affairs and the workings of the law. The job suits those with an analytical mind and a hatred of waffle; they have also got to love research because there's a lot of it. So far, more than two-thirds of the commission's recommendations have been implemented by the government – you can see what they are on the commission's website – so you will get the satisfaction of seeing your work put into practice. Another plus point is that if you go on to be a lawyer, you will be streets ahead of your peers in terms of your research skills and knowledge of how statutes work. For more information on short and long-term careers in the field, check out www.lawcom.gov.uk. The recruitment campaign for research assistants commencing September 2006 opens in January 2006.

## legal services commission

This government body was created by the Access to Justice Act 1999 and replaced the Legal Aid Board in 2000. It employs 1,300 staff and operates from London and 12 towns and cities across England and Wales. It manages the distribution of public funds for both civil legal services and criminal defence services. In 2001 the Criminal Defence Service was set up to organise the supply of legal advice to those accused of crime through the use of local solicitors who were accredited by the service. In the same year, the Public Defender Service opened its first four offices, and has subsequently opened others. These offices employ their own lawyers to advise members of the public in what the LSC believes to be a more cost-effective and efficient way.

The work of the LSC can be broken down into differing areas:

The large Operations Division handles civil cases. Caseworkers assess the merits of applications for legal funding and means test applicants. They also assess and authorise claims for payment for legal services.

The Criminal Defence Service performs an audit role, dealing with the authorised providers of criminal legal advice. There are no financial or other limits as to who is entitled to claim free legal advice on criminal cases, so it is merely the lawyer's financial claims and the quality of their services that are scrutinised.

The Contracting Section audits claims for 'Legal Help' – the funding used for preliminary and basic advice on how individuals might be represented.

The Planning and Partnership Section employs consultants and executives in order to better understand how the LSC should spend funds and place its resources.

Within the ambit of the LSC's work is the Public Defender Service. Set up in 2001 with four offices, this has now increased to eight. The PDS offices are staffed by solicitors and accredited representatives who are directly employed by the Legal Services Commission (LSC) but provide independent advice, assistance and representation to members of the public. The PDS is the subject of a four year review so keep your eyes and ears open as to what happens next.

Jobs at the commission are advertised in local and/or national newspapers. A first point of contact is www.legalservices.gov.uk. A few work experience placements crop up, usually in the operations group and usually lasting for about six weeks.

# how will i fare in the recruitment game?

It's rarely 'who you know' and mostly 'who you are' that secures you a job these days. Clearly there are some things you can't change about yourself – your age, roots, ethnicity, gender, a disability. There are other things you shouldn't have to change – your sexual orientation, personality, values. Having said that, you can't approach the world of work without making a few nips and tucks to your identity and addressing the content of your CV to see if it can be improved upon.

## a matter of degrees

So you've not got a law degree. So what? From the top sets at the Bar to the little known solicitors firms on the high street, non-law graduates fare just as well as their LLB peers in the recruitment game. In the few cases where employers prefer law grads they will specify this, so unless you hear differently, conversion route applicants should proceed with confidence. Many recruiters tell us just how highly they regard staff with language skills and scientific and technical degrees, particularly where their clients' businesses will benefit.

And whether they admit it or not, many firms and chambers subscribe to the idea that there's a pecking order of universities.

Your degree result is perhaps the single thing on your CV that has most impact. Net a First and you'll impress all and sundry (at least on paper); walk away with a 2:1 and your path to employment will be made smoother; end up with a 2:2 and you're going to have to perform some fancy footwork. In a few cases the effect of a poor degree result can be softened by a letter from your tutor stipulating the reason why you underachieved. Alas, it's rarely relevant that you just missed a 2:1 by a percentage point or two; however, if you were a star student who suffered a serious accident or illness as finals loomed, confirmation of this (perhaps also by way of a doctor's letter) should assist.

Having spoken to a number of trainees and a couple of pupil barristers who left university with 2:2s, we would never discourage anyone from applying for a training position; nonetheless, these people all had other impressive qualities and/or CV-enhancing experiences. If you find yourself at the back of the queue in the job market, think hard about what you can do to overcome that 2:2 – a year or more in a relevant job, a further degree, a commitment to voluntary work perhaps.

Possibly unaware that they could be applying for training contracts and vacation schemes in their second year, many new students are lulled into a false sense of security concerning their academic performance in the first year. If the only marks you have to show recruiters are amazing thirds, you'll struggle to make headway. As boring as it may sound, work for good results throughout your time at university. At the very least, doing so will maximise your chances of a great final result.

## student daze

But don't become a dullard! Your first year away from home (or for some, full-time employment) is a time to explore new-found freedom and practically unlimited opportunities. Almost every uni will have a wide range of societies, meeting groups and sports clubs. At the vast majority, if your leisure pursuit of choice is not on offer, they'll give you the cash to set it up, provided you can rustle up a handful of like-minded individuals and it's not illegal. Pursuing your interests will give an extra dimension to both your university experience and, crucially, your CV.

Sometimes the flood of info from university bodies such as the students' union and careers service can be so heavy you feel like you are drowning in e-mails, flyers and posters telling you of this job vacancy, that Amnesty meeting, or the other CV workshop. Resist the temptation to let it all wash over you. Relevant work experience is vital to almost every successful job application, so keep your eyes open for suitable positions, and use them to test your own ideas of what you would like to do. Many universities run law-specific careers seminars in association with firms of solicitors or sets of chambers. Be savvy, go along and find out as much as you can by talking to trainee solicitors and recruiters.

Do remember that only a minority of law firms and chambers throw drinks parties or sponsor libraries – the legal profession is not limited to the folk who've actually bought you a drink! Build up a decent understanding of the structure of the profession before deciding what kind of lawyer you want to be and which firm you want to work for. Just because your friends seem to know what they want doesn't mean their choices are right for you. Similarly, your tutors and family can only help you so far. Research, research and research some more until you are confident of your preferences. Demonstrating your understanding of what the work will entail and being able to explain honestly and realistically why you want to do it will be one of the most important things to get across to recruiters.

If you want to become a commercial lawyer, you'll need this thing they call commercial awareness. We're not suggesting you become an Alan Sugar, rather that you should gain a sense of what's going on in the commercial world. Stock market down, a boom in China, hurricane Katrina – do you see how they're all connected to rising oil prices? If you have zero interest in all this stuff, what makes you think commercial law will interest you? Why not read the FT now and again, or find an internet site that will give you headline bulletins in bite-sized chunks. Keep up to date in a way that suits you, just don't be oblivious to the events going on around you at national and international level.

## ahh...those tuareg camp fires

It's official! Travel does broaden the mind. Recruiters know this too, so don't feel that you need to play down the time you've spent exploring the world. If you've itchy feet and if you haven't already been out there for a look-see, what's stopping you?

## you're not from round here are you?

London attracts young professionals from all over the world, so you can skip this bit if you're a Brit intending to work in the capital. If you hold an EU passport or have a pre-existing right to live and work in the UK and you are following the appropriate path to qualification, you can probably also proceed with optimism. Applicants who tick none of these boxes may find doors are easier to push open if they apply to firms with business interests in the country or region from which they come. This is because law firms have to show sound reasons why an overseas applicant is worth employing over someone who needs no work permit. Generally, the people we encountered who were neither EU nationals nor had a permanent right to live and work in the UK were training in the largest City firms or with specialist shipping practices. Additionally, a number of barristers chambers will take pupils who intend to return to practice in their home jurisdiction. In all cases, excellent written and spoken English is essential and you will need a convincing reason why you have chosen to commence your career in Ol' Blighty.

Regional firms and sets are often most comfortable recruiting candidates with a local connection, be this through family or education. Quite simply, they want to know that whoever they take on will be committed to a long-term career with them; they are wary of having their brightest and best skipping off to London after qualifying. The picture across the UK is a variable one: some firms clearly state their preferences for local lads and lasses; others tell us that most of their applicants do have links with the region, but that they are happy to consider anyone. Over the years we've found Irish trainees in Staffordshire, Londoners in Exeter and Scots in Birmingham, but we've also found that law firms in certain cities tend to pick people with strong ties – ever-popular Bristol is the most obvious example.

## grey matter

Older applicants often worry needlessly that they are at a disadvantage. Far from it! So long as you have something to show for your extra years, you may find it easier to impress recruiters. You already know how to work, your people/client-handling skills are doubtlessly better developed, and you may even have relevant industry-specific experience. We've chatted with successful barristers and solicitors who've done everything from secretarial work, pub management and film production to police work and PR. Certain past-life work experiences – healthcare, the armed forces, accountancy and engineering – make candidates particularly interesting.

But when is old too old? If you're still in your 20s, get over yourself – you're still a baby! If you're in your 30s, ask what it is you can offer a law firm. And if you're older still? Never say never. We have run into a small number of 40-something trainees. Given that each year after qualification a certain percentage of the UK's lawyers move firms or even drop out of the profession for good, we don't buy the argument that employers expect 30 years of service from all new recruits. More relevant is the adage concerning old dogs and new tricks, so if your coat is greying, consider carefully how you'd cope with being asked to revert to puppyhood.

## breaking down barriers

Despite the legal profession being more diverse than ever before, for students with mental or physical disabilities, things are not straightforward. In the experience of the Group for Solicitors with Disabilities, many students with disabilities have great difficulty in securing work placements and training contracts. The good news is that there are sources of advice and assistance available and the GSD has been actively involved in approaching law firms to set up designated work placement schemes for disabled students. The group also provides a forum in which students and practitioners can meet in order to share experiences and provide one another with guidance and support. Would-be barristers should refer to the Equal Opportunities (Disability) Committee of the Bar Council.

## single white male

An apt description for the legal profession 30 years ago maybe. In the course of our research, around 150 firms provided us with lists identifying their trainees. In most firms the girls outnumber the boys. The names reflect a healthy spread of ethnic backgrounds. It is worth mentioning, however, that female and non-white trainees still have too few senior-level role models and there are always a small number of law firm sex or race discrimination claims going through the employment tribunals. For the record, we know scores of gay and lesbian lawyers for whom sexual orientation is entirely a non-career matter.

In the USA, diversity has been a hot topic for longer than it has in the UK, and as with other things that have travelled east across the Atlantic (including higher salaries and a greater commitment to pro bono work) the Brits are now paying more attention to it.

## balancing act

What with studying hard, reading the FT, helping out at the local CAB, canoeing and playing hockey (you could try combining them), debating, acting as student law society president, acting on stage and attending all the careers events that crop up throughout the year, you'll hardly have time for a pint, let alone the ten that students supposedly put away in between lectures. Your mum and dad may tell you university is supposed to be a fun, carefree time, but frankly back in their day the job market was less competitive and no one built up a small mortgage in debt before the age of 21... well, only if they had a really wild time. Besides, what do the olds know? They were too busy listening to Backman Turner Overdrive and having sit-down protests.

Of course you must have fun, and you absolutely must develop your interests and friendships because these, in many cases, last far longer and can be more rewarding than any career. Ultimately, it all comes down to finding the right balance.

## help!

Did someone mention pro bono? In case you've been on the moon for the last couple of years and haven't noticed the flurry of interest in the topic, pro bono means working for free for the good of others. The benefits for those who receive pro bono assistance – and for those who give it – are so great that we've devoted the following section (overleaf) to how students can get involved.

# pro bono opportunities

Even if your idea of a dream come true is handling mergers and acquisitions in a City firm, it's time to dig deep into the corners of your soul and find your inner altruist. Recruiters are always looking for candidates with practical experience of working in a legal environment. As Kara Irwin, Director of the BPP Pro Bono Centre puts it: "*Lawyers always see this as the most interesting thing on a candidate's CV. As well as being something tangible that students can contribute to the community, it gives them the opportunity to really develop important legal skills.*" Volunteering can often be the best way to gain such skills, and there are plenty of available options for students who are willing to give up some of their spare time.

Every little bit counts, whether it's a half day a week helping out at your local CAB or six months overseas working as an intern on death row appeals, as long as you can offer some kind of long-term commitment. If you're just doing something to add a notch to your CV bedpost, it's going to look pretty obvious. We've spoken to some of the law schools and pro bono organisations to find out about the sort of things on offer. We've also put together a non-exhaustive list of other organisations involved in pro bono to get you started in your quest to save the world.

## make the most of your law school

Most post-graduate law schools, and increasingly university law departments, now have pro bono initiatives in place. At some colleges, pro bono is not just an option; it's a compulsory element of the course. At the Student Law Office of Northumbria University, which has achieved Legal Services Commission Quality Marks for its housing and employment advice, all LPC and BVC students advise real clients, from the initial interview through to advocacy before tribunals and the small claims courts.

Many law schools engage in outreach work in the local community. Take the Streetlaw Plus programme at the York branch of the College of Law. Here, students are actively helping local residents in Doncaster to address their concerns about dilapidated housing and planning through regular letter-writing surgeries.

Pro bono is not necessarily just about providing advice to individuals; it can involve carrying out research for pressure groups and international organisations. At BPP's Pro Bono Centre students have set up an intellectual property group, and recently helped to conduct research in association with a leading IP firm giving advice to the International Chamber of Commerce. Its human rights unit provided research support to the International Bar Association's Human Rights Institute in a review of the Somali legal system.

For undergraduates, it can often be more difficult to find a centrally organised pro bono initiative at university. If this is the case where you are studying, use your initiative to seek out work of your own. If you're young and inexperienced, don't worry; providing administrative support to an over-worked legal charity still looks great on your CV, and may well lead on to other things later on.

## the free representation unit (fru)

Becoming a ratified member of the FRU is a really good idea if you're thinking of going to the Bar, but it's an equally good idea if you are intending to be a solicitor specialising in any contentious area of law because chances are you'll be doing at least some of the advocacy yourself.

FRU representatives offer free advice and representation to clients who are not eligible for legal aid, appearing on their behalf before employment and social security tribunals. There is also a limited amount of work in criminal injuries compensation appeals and some immigration matters. Law students can train to become a social security representative in the final year of an LLB, or alternatively non-law graduates can do this in their CPE year. The employment option is only open to LPC and BVC students, and it should also be noted that FRU only operates in and around London, though several of the regional BVC and LPC providers have advice clinics that allow students to gain experience of tribunal advocacy.

To qualify, you'll need to attend an induction day and satisfactorily complete a legal opinion exercise. Once that's done, you'll be able to take on a case after discussing it with one of the caseworkers. Once a case is yours, you must see it through from beginning to end. A pupil barrister with a series of employment tribunal wins behind her told us: *"As a rep you'll get experience in using a whole bundle of practical legal skills. You'll conference with your client, conduct legal research, draft submissions, negotiate with your opponent, and if the case doesn't settle, you'll make oral submissions to the tribunal and get to examine and cross-examine witnesses."* From time to time, seasoned FRU reps have been known to take cases to the Employment Appeal Tribunal or the Social Security Commissioners and it's not unheard of for their names to appear in the reported decision.

If we haven't sold it to you already, it might also be pointed out that a very high number of the pupils and junior barristers that we interviewed for our Chambers Reports had worked for FRU or another similar organisation at some time in their training. It could well be the thing that saves your application from the shredder.

## some other ideas to get you started

Below is a sample of the many pro bono opportunities on offer for students. For more information on other schemes, it's worth doing some research of your own.

**the student pro bono group:** This runs in conjunction with the Solicitors Pro Bono Group and is a good source of advice and information. Students can join the group for free by registering on its website at www.students.probonogroup.org.uk

**advice on individual rights in europe:** AIRE provides information and advice throughout Europe on international human rights law, including the rights of individuals under the provisions of European Community law. It also offers direct legal advice and assistance on a case-by-case basis to legal practitioners or advisers. Internships are available for students who have a good working knowledge of international human rights law and EU law. Students must be able to commit a minimum of one day per week. A second European language is an advantage. Contact: Gabi Schlick on 020 7831 4276 or gschlick@airecentre.org.

**amicus:** Amicus is a charity providing assistance to US attorneys working on death-row cases. It gives training and arranges internships in the USA for UK post-graduate students. As internships are unpaid (though a limited number of scholarships do exist), interested applicants should have a plan for funding the placement. Contact: Sophie Garner sophiegarner@amicus-alj.org.

**the bar pro bono unit:** Established in 1996 by Attorney-General Lord Goldsmith QC, the unit matches individuals in need of legal representation with barristers in private practice willing to undertake work on a pro bono basis. Opportunities are available for students to provide administrative support to the unit on a part-time basis. This could mean anything from envelope stuffing to allocating cases to members of the panel. Contact: **www.barprobono.org.uk**

**citizens advice bureaux:** We spoke to the Citizens Advice service, which has over 22,000 volunteers in over 2,000 bureaux. Those with real commitment and enough time can train with the CAB on its Adviser Training Programme, which is a widely recognised qualification that may subsequently enable the period of your law firm training contract to be reduced by up to six months. Not all volunteers have the time or the inclination to train as advisers, and if admin, IT or reception work is enough for you, why not request one of these roles, or perhaps even help out with publicity and media activities? Debt, benefits, housing, employment, consumer issues, family matters and immigration are the most commonly raised problems, some six million of which are handled each year. Contact: **www.citizensadvice.org.uk/join-us**

**independent custody visiting:** A good idea for anyone interested in a criminal practice. Independent custody visiting began in the wake of the Scarman Report following the Brixton riots of 1981. Independent custody visitors (ICVs) work in pairs, conducting regular unannounced checks on police stations in their area to monitor the welfare of the detainees. Anyone over the age of 18 can apply to become an ICV. Applications are made to the local police authority. To download an application form, visit the Independent Custody Visiting Association website **www.icva. org.uk**

**law centres:** Law centres provide free and independent legal services to people who live or work in their catchment areas, typically covering areas where legal aid is not available such as employment and immigration. Working at a law centre is very much a career in itself however, many centres accept student volunteers to provide administrative support and assistance with casework. The website **www.lawcentres .org.uk** provides links to individual law centres across the UK.

**liberty:** Liberty is a well-established human rights organisation providing advice and representation to groups and individuals in relation to domestic law cases involving the Human Rights Act. Liberty has opportunities for a small number of students to provide general office assistance and help with casework. Students should be able to commit at least one day a week. Apply by sending a CV and cover letter to the organisation. **www.liberty-human-rights.org.uk**

**victim support:** The Victim Support Witness Service operates in every crown court across England and Wales, providing guidance and support to witnesses, victims and their families before, during and after court proceedings. Volunteers need to be able to commit at least two hours per week. For details of the nearest local office, visit **www.victimsupport.org.uk**

Remember, these are just a few of the organisations you can become involved with. And it's worth pointing out that we've focused here on law-related matters.

# cpe/pgdl/gdl: law for non-lawyers

To explain: the Law Society determines the training required to qualify as a solicitor in England and Wales. The training process has an academic stage and a vocational one. The vocational bit is the LPC but first, the academic element must be satisfied by completing one of the following: a qualifying law degree, the Common Professional Examination (CPE), or the Institute of Legal Executives' ILEX exams (see page 17). Likewise, the Bar Council requires aspiring barristers who lack a qualifying law degree to pass the CPE.

The CPE appears in a variety of different guises and goes by different names, but don't worry – there is no real difference between the Postgraduate Diploma in Law (PgDL), the Graduate Diploma in Law (GDL) and the CPE. As far as the Law Society and the Bar Council are concerned, all are equally valid. For simplicity, we use the term CPE throughout this book.

## admission requirements

The standard requirement for admission to the CPE is a degree from a university in the UK or the Republic of Ireland. Some other non-standard qualifications are recognised, such as certain overseas degrees and degree equivalent or professional qualifications. Additionally, non-graduate mature persons who have gained considerable experience and shown exceptional ability in academic, professional, business or administrative fields may be considered. Check out the table of CPE providers on our website for more particular admission requirements: some institutions (especially in the regions) will look closely at your reason for studying in the area, while others are so heavily subscribed they tend to only consider applicants who name them as their first choice.

## the course

This is no cakewalk. Full-time CPE courses last for a minimum of 36 weeks, during which you'll be expected to undertake 45 hours of lectures, tutorials, private study and research per week. With such a rigorous timetable, you can kiss goodbye to weekday hangovers and lazy afternoons of Countdown and Fifteen-to-One. Whether done as a two-year part-time course, or one-year full-time, the course covers seven "foundations of legal knowledge":

- **Contract**
- **Tort**
- **Criminal**
- **Equity and trusts**
- **EU law**
- **Property**
- **Public law**

Assessment is usually by way of written exams – these will mostly be traditional three-hour papers – and many institutions also require you to submit coursework assignments and/or a dissertation. Typically, the teaching is a combination of lectures and classroom-based activities. Some institutions require you to write several academic essays per term, while at law schools that favour a more practical approach, you'll have to prepare topics for moots or draft solutions to problem questions.

There is no gentle introduction to the CPE. This is a fast-track course, and it is essential that you remain on top of the workload, as well as the law. While really bright students may find reams of photocopied material a little elementary, no one passes without putting in the hours. Commendations and distinctions are up for grabs, and at certain firms, these may earn you a cheeky little bonus on top of any sponsorship you've been given. But remember: if you are being sponsored, your firm won't be impressed if you just scrape through.

Good organisation, a consistent approach and commitment go a long way on the CPE, and with these it is possible to do very well without being in the library 24/7. Many people manage to squeeze in part-time jobs to keep the wolf from the door.

If you worked hard at university and got a good degree, you're perfectly capable of succeeding on the CPE. Essentially, it's a case of applying the skills you already have to industrial quantities of new material. If you do this in bite-sized chunks as you go along, the whole process is relatively palatable. However, if you are in two minds about the course, you may want to think hard before committing to it. People do the CPE for a variety of reasons, but if you are just looking for something to keep you out of trouble for a year after uni, there are considerably cheaper, easier and less demanding ways of going about it.

## the institutions

No two CPE courses are the same, so do your research. Contact institutions to request a prospectus and speak to former students to find out what course suits you best. At some institutions you will be taught by practising solicitors, while elsewhere, professors offer a more academic slant; the course may be characterised by the need to memorise great swathes of photocopied material, or it can be an exciting challenge for the intellectually astute.

Quite apart from the teaching style, you may also want to consider that different institutions attract a different type of student. For example, at providers that offer City-oriented LPC programmes you'll find a higher proportion of cut-and-thrust corporate types, while at somewhere like City Uni a more academic course attracts those looking to go to the Bar.

At most institutions you will find City slickers rubbing shoulders with champions of human rights. The course draws people of all ages and from a variety of backgrounds. Of course, there will be plenty of new and recent graduates, but there will also be those who have left other careers to train as lawyers, people who have already worked in law firms in a non-qualified capacity and people from overseas who are tailoring their qualifications to the English system. For every person who arrives at law school with training contract in hand, finances sorted, career done and dusted, and halfway to partnership already, there will be plenty of others whose CVs are still a Joycean stream of consciousness. Whichever category you fall into, the course can be tough and tiring, so you must be clear that you are doing it for your own benefit (rather than Mum and Dad's). The best advice we can give is to throw yourself into it wholeheartedly.

## applications

Those wishing to study the CPE full-time must apply through the Central Applications Board. To ensure the best chance of securing a place at your college of choice, apply early in the calendar year and in the first round of applications. It is possible to apply for a place in the second round in the late spring but popular, oversubscribed schools are unlikely to still have places. If you are hoping to do your LPC at a very popular school it is really worthwhile trying to get a CPE place there because most schools guarantee LPC places to those of their students who are successful at the CPE.

The course is now offered at over 30 different universities and colleges in England and Wales. Check our website for a full list of course providers, fees and other details.

# the legal practice course

The LPC is a one-year course that falls between the academic stage of training (a qualifying law degree or the CPE) and the training contract. Rather than a second helping of black letter law, the LPC provides prospective solicitors with the skills required for the world of work. Essays are replaced with letters of advice; mooting with advocacy; textbooks with precedents, as students get to grips with the practical tasks they will face every day in the office. Yes, you may well be reminded of when to use 'Yours sincerely', or instructed as to the politest way to stop a chatty client mid-flow, or schooled on how to dress for a district judge, but, the LPC is no Lucy Clayton finishing school. The course also introduces students to essential practical issues and procedural techniques they are unlikely to have previously encountered, for example, professional conduct, accounts and tax.

The first part of the year is spent on certain compulsory elements. Students are assessed on legal skills such as interviewing, advocacy, drafting, letter writing and legal research. They also cover knowledge areas including civil and criminal litigation, conveyancing and business law. These are examined in February. The remaining months are devoted to three elective subjects which are examined in the summer. The range of options available to students varies from one course provider to another. For a full list of who offers what, refer to our website: **www.chambersandpartners.com.**

## studying for a city career

Students who have signed up to training contracts with eight City firms – Allen & Overy, Clifford Chance, Linklaters, Freshfields, Herbert Smith, Lovells, Norton Rose, and Slaughter and May – must study at prescribed institutions. The first three firms will send their students to the College of Law in London where they will take courses with a notable firm-specific component; the others will direct students to BPP in London for a souped-up course that is heavy on MBA-style commercial awareness. These

students will have no choice over elective subjects and are required to choose the private acquisitions, debt finance and equity finance options.

Much attention has been focused on these eight firms and the LPC providers they have climbed into bed with, but students should be aware that there are other institutions offering City-style electives, and studying at one of these others is no bar to gaining a City-compatible LPC. Equally, at BPP and COL London there are ample places for students wanting non-City electives.

## studying for a legal aid career

But what of developments at the other end of the spectrum? In the wake of the Access to Justice Act 1999, publicly funded legal advice has been high on the agenda. Reforms are promised to fill the gaps in the UK's legal coverage, holes so wide they have earned the name 'legal aid deserts'. Over the past two years the number of high street firms taking on publicly funded work has dropped by 14%, decreasing the number of people helped by legal aid by 28%. A mere 0.45% of public spending goes on legal advice.

But it's not all bad news. The Legal Services Commission (LSC) has set aside £3 million to fund the training of solicitors who agree to go into legally aided practice for at least two years after qualification. Supporting this cash injection, the LSC and the College of Law have created a bespoke LPC course – The Public Legal Services Pathway – available from 2005. It comprises the core commercial subjects in the College of Law's normal LPC program, targeting the issues of small to medium-sized firms, the high street and local authorities. The biggest change comes in the available electives – six in all, each with direct applicability to publicly funded practice. They include: advanced criminal practice; employment law; family law; housing law; personal injury and clinical negligence litigation; welfare benefits and immigration law.

There is much chatter about reforming the current system of legal training entirely. The Law Society's Training Framework Review Committee has come up with proposals to broaden entry to the profession, which, if implemented, could enable students to bypass the LPC altogether. However, the proposals are far from set and have many detractors. Most importantly, nothing will come into effect before September 2006, so we recommend reading on to decide where to study...

## how do you choose a law school?

The LPC Applications Board administers all LPC applications centrally. **www.lawcabs.ac.uk** contains both the application form and information on all course providers. There are plenty of things to consider when choosing a law school, so be sure to arm yourself with as much information as possible. Request prospectuses, attend open days, chat to representatives visiting your university, talk to current students and decide what your priorities are.

career issues: Your future employer (if you have one) may well have a preferred list of schools. At the very least, they should be able to give you advice, based on the experiences of its current trainees. If you don't yet have a training contract, look into the range of extra-curricular activities, clubs and societies on offer that may help you improve your CV. Also think about the quality of careers advice available at each institution. Have they got a good record of getting students placements and training contracts with the kind of firms you want to work for?

electives: If you have a training contract already, find out if your future employer wants you to take any particular electives. Otherwise, find out which course providers offer the electives best suited to the type of practice you want to move into. Some may have restrictions on elective combinations or run electives only when there is sufficient demand. For a full run down on who offers what, see our website.

assessment grades and pass rates: Pass rates are published on the Law Society's website each autumn, but be aware that direct comparisons are impossible as each institution examines and marks independently of the others. The Law Society visits and inspects each institution and then publishes an 'Ofsted-style' report along with an assessment grade. Though we have set out the current grades in the following table, the picture is about to become confused as the Law Society is changing the way it assesses institutions and the old and new systems will run together for up to three years making direct comparisons difficult.

teaching methods: Most institutions timetable around 14 hours of classes per week, but there uniformity ends. If you have travel plans, you may want to check term dates, as these can vary between institutions by a good couple of weeks. Similarly, if you are going to have a long commute to classes, or are hoping to fit in some part-time work, check the timetabling of classes – some places will fix you up with neat morning or afternoon timetables and a day off mid-week; others will expect you to hang around between classes that are spread throughout the day. Examination and assessment methods vary too, with some schools expecting more coursework, others placing greater emphasis on exams. Whereas some institutions only permit a modest statute book and practitioner text to be taken into the exam room, others hold entirely open-book exams leading to students precariously balancing files and books Jenga-style on tiny exam desks.

facilities: For every school where students must shoehorn themselves into flip-up seats in vast lecture theatres, there is another where they can lounge on a swivel seat in their own mock office. Take the LPC course at a university and you can expect to feel like you belong to a proper law faculty (complete with Klix coffee machine and last week's *Independent*); elsewhere, orchids and acres of plate glass may convince you that you've strayed into the offices of a City firm. For some students, a large institution is nothing less than a giant speed-dating opportunity; for others it will offer desired anonymity. Conversely, the intimacy of smaller classes in a smaller school may appeal.

tactics: Some of the most popular institutions require you to put them as first choice on the Law-Cabs application form for them to even consider you. We have included this type of information on the LPC providers table on our website. Check also whether your university, CPE provider or law firm has an agreement or relationship with a provider.

money and fees: Fees vary and so do the institutions' policies on the inclusion of the cost of textbooks and Law Society membership, etc. Even if you have sponsorship from a law firm, living expenses still need to be taken into account, and London especially can be a nasty shock if you haven't lived there before. Alas, not all firms offer the whopping £7K maintenance now being paid by Linklaters and some others. The latest available information about the scale of fees for each course is on our website.

location: Plenty of students find that tight finances restrict their choice of school. Living at home will save you a packet... if you can stand it! Be sure to include the cost of travel when totting up your budget though. If you're lucky enough to be able to strike out on your own, it's worth considering what you like or don't like about your university or CPE provider, and whether you want to prolong your undergraduate experience or escape it. And remember, certain LPC providers are dominated by graduates of local universities.

social mix and social life: Would you prefer to be somewhere with students following a similar career path or would you prefer to mix it up with a wider cross-section of people? Studenty cities such as Nottingham and Bristol are always a lot of fun, but the bright lights of the Big Smoke may be irresistible. However, experience tells us that compared to other cities students in London tend to slink off the moment classes end.

In the following pages we've highlighted the 13 LPC providers that currently boast an Excellent or Very Good rating from the Law Society. The reports have been written with assistance from current and former students.

| LAW SOCIETY ASSESSMENT GRADES | |
|---|---|
| Anglia Polytechnic University | Good |
| Bournemouth University | Good |
| BPP Law School, London | Very Good |
| BPP Law School, Manchester | Not yet graded |
| BPP Law School, Leeds | Very Good |
| Bristol Institute of Legal Practice at UWE | Excellent |
| Cardiff Law School | Excellent |
| College of Law at Birmingham | Very Good |
| College of Law at Chester | Very Good |
| College of Law at Guildford | Very Good |
| College of Law at London | Very Good |
| College of Law at York | Very Good |
| De Montfort University | Very Good |
| Inns of Court School of Law | Excellent |
| Leeds Metropolitan University | Satisfactory |
| Liverpool John Moores University (p/t) | Good |
| London Metropolitan University | Good |
| Manchester Metropolitan University | Good |
| Nottingham Law School | Excellent |
| Oxford Institute of Legal Practice | Very Good |
| Staffordshire University | Excellent |
| Thames Valley University | Good |
| University of Central England | Good |
| University of Central Lancashire | Very Good |
| University of Exeter | Good |
| University of Glamorgan | Good |
| University of Hertfordshire (p/t) | Good |
| University of Huddersfield | Good |
| University of Northumbria | Very Good |
| University of Sheffield | Very Good |
| University of Wales, Swansea | Good |
| University of Westminster | Very Good |
| University of Wolverhampton | Good |

*These grades were accurate at the time of going to press. Please check our website for any updates.*

# lpc providers: the inside story

## BPP Law School, London, Leeds, Manchester

**Number of places:** London: 1,296; Manchester: 252; Leeds: 432 (full and part-time)

BPP Law School is part of a worldwide professional education network. The law school has grown exponentially since opening in London and now operates in Leeds and Manchester as well as its main location in London, in Holborn. Another indicator of growth is the removal of the London GDL course and some LPC students to a separate site in Waterloo. This year we have concentrated on feedback from London LPC students, as the Leeds and Manchester courses are still new.

First impressions of "*a slick organisation*" are helped along by "*impressive leather couches, flat screens in the library and a lot of ex-professionals*" on the teaching staff. It makes the school feel "*professional and organised, like a work environment.*" Indeed, students quickly learn that "*the LPC has nothing to do with the pursuit of academic knowledge,*" several pointing out that by contrast with their university studies, "*if it's not on the syllabus then you won't cover it.*" So, "*if you asked any additional questions, the tutors simply said, 'We don't have time and it's not in the exam.'*"

BPP has been a key driver behind changes in the delivery and content of the LPC. It demands much of its students, and the timetabling is consequently full and regimented. This has the added advantage of allowing three separate cohorts to be taught simultaneously without overstressing facilities and staff. However, the scale of the operation does not go unnoticed. "*The cohorts have different days off, but it still feels like so many people... Ironically though, you don't really get to see anyone outside your small group sessions.*"

Approximately 15 hours of classes per week are weighted towards two-hour sessions for groups of 18. "*The teaching was on the whole very good, with the odd exception,*" a source reported. Ferocious exploitation of PowerPoint and Smartboards is typical of the school's no-expense-spared approach. The first indication of this is the stack of textbooks waiting in your locker on the first day.

Constant closed-book examining culminates in the compulsory assessments in April. Then follows the "*less-hectic*" electives. And here we find the lines drawn as to what kind of school this is. Many say you would only choose BPP if you are headed for the City. Certainly, this fits with the exclusive relationship BPP has with Slaughter and May, Herbert Smith, Lovells, Norton Rose and Freshfields, whose students will all attend BPP in London. However, a wide range of other non-commercial options are on offer to those with different career ambitions. When we asked BPP's dean, Peter Crisp, if the school had ignored non-City students, he pointed out that even in the London branches, only 75% of students go to City or commercial firms, with another 15-20% joining private client or general practices. And what of those with no job lined up? "*Our careers service can really target the minority, the ten to 15% that need training contracts.*" His final word: "*We aim for our students to have the best possible experience of law school. Whether they are going to the magic circle or the high street makes no difference.*"

Future students can expect increased emphasis on bringing the LPC out of its legal vacuum and arming students with more business know how, to help them better understand the needs of commercial clients as well as the law firms at which they will be employed.

With so many students coming from the top universities, there is an element of cliqueyness about BPP. Two nearby bars are popular – The Square Pig and Sway – but after happy hour people tend to drift away. BPP has not so far been known as a touchy-feely institution, but there are signs that more attention will be paid to such things as mentoring and personal tutors. Certainly its pro bono initiative has come on leaps and bounds and the careers service now has more oomph. As the most expensive school, this is still the place for those with the deepest pockets.

# first steps

## bristol institute of legal practice at uwe

**number of places:** 340 full-time, 80 part-time

Stamped with the "Excellent" hallmark by the Law Society as early as 1995, UWE remains "*fantastic, academically and socially.*" Described as "*highly organised*" and "*well-structured,*" the LPC had left those we interviewed more than satisfied. "*The quality was extremely high and the material and course prepared me seamlessly for work in the real world,*" one recalled. "*Approachable*" teaching staff create a positive vibe, so too does the decent staff-to-student ratio. Even if "*there are the odd one or two who could have given better tuition,*" the majority were "*great teachers, and always there for a chat.*" Organised "*almost along school lines*" students are grouped together in small numbers (around 12) and primarily taught by a dedicated group tutor in a set location via three-and-a-half-hour group sessions. Lectures are an occasional extra. For the most part students love this method because "*it teaches you the compulsories in depth.*" They also appreciated the "*mini-library – CPR plus textbooks all in the room* " – and "*clusters of four computers per room.*" For many, Bristol's broad spread of electives were an important factor. "*The media and entertainment module was a fantastic match for the firm I was going on to,*" said one satisfied customer. There is also the option of supplementing your LPC with an LLM.

A year in Bristol can only be a good thing, although UWE's location does leave something to be desired. Sure, "*the facilities are great*" but at some distance from the centre of town, "*there is not much going on beyond the campus café and two bars.*" The solution is a short bus, car or bike ride away in the city centre. Here there is "*an array of bars and clubs*" and established pockets of student housing in lovely areas like Redlands, Cotham and Clifton. You'll never be short of somewhere to live, nor a group of likeminded people with whom to explore the city. The only problem is, would you ever want to leave?

## cardiff law school

**Number of places:** 180 full-time

Cardiff is stuffed full of Welsh students, both those who are taking advantage of their parents' hospitality and support for one final year and those who are committed to a career in Wales. A third category is comprised of "*an awful lot of people who aren't Welsh but were Cardiff and Swansea grads who wanted to stay around in South Wales.*" Many find Cardiff as a city far friendlier and more cost-effective than living in London, and the view is that you can have "*a bit more of the student life than in London.*" The only hint of a caveat came from the past student who told us: "*My only reservation would be that people's final destination is regional not central London usually so you will not meet many other London-bound trainees.*" If your tastes run to all things truly Welsh, you might be interested in the short course on advocacy in the Welsh language.

So, you're over the fact that Cardiff is not London (you're probably delighted to learn this), why pick this particular regional provider? The school has boasted an "Excellent" rating ever since first acquiring the accolade in 1997, which explains why students report that "*the course was run really well*" and recall having "*a very, very good year.*" As in most schools, it's a case of planning your time and keeping on top of things. Said one student: "*I didn't find the course too hard, there's just a lot of it and a lot of admin.*" Overall, teaching staff get the thumbs-up: "*The tutors were really good and the course has prepared me well for what I've experienced in practice.*" The fact that all have been practising solicitors may explain why.

Most teaching rooms, the spacious library and IT facilities are situated in a modern extension of the law school, and there is also a mock courtroom with audio-visual facilities and a common room. The school's links with local firms mean guaranteed work placements for any student without a training contract, and the university's careers service is also on hand to assist. Teaching staff additionally take on the role of personal tutors to provide one-on-one advice and support. At more than £8,000, the course is not the cheapest available, but we've never heard any complaints from those who have completed it.

## college of law

**Number of places:** 3,612 full-time, 1,053 part-time

The College of Law has branches on every street corner. Okay, so that's not quite true, but with five schools across the country it does have good coverage. As the longest running provider of vocational education to prospective solicitors, COL guarantees uniformly high-quality teaching and has earned itself a "Very Good" rating in all locations. Last year's highlight was winning the exclusive mandade to deliver the LPC to future trainees of three magic circle firms – Allen & Overy, Clifford Chance and Linklaters – each of them requiring a specially tailored course that will include firm-specific elements. Students embark on these bespoke courses for the first time in September 2006.

Proud of its reputation for pushing the boundaries of legal education, COL isn't content to innovate in only the commercial sphere. Even as this book goes to print students destined for legal aid practice will be taking up places on the new and unique Public Services Pathway LPC. Furthermore, the addition of Advanced Criminal Practice to a long list of electives reinforces COL's reputation for diversity in training.

Whichever branch they attend, students are taught according to the same principles, using the same materials and based on very similar timetables. Roughly 14 hours a week are spent in formal teaching settings – large group sessions or lectures plus workshops for smaller groups – and students enjoy the privilege of being able to chose whether they take classes in the morning or the afternoon. Certainly everyone we spoke to had been kept busy in "*quite an intense year*" where even if "*most*

of the work is easily manageable in terms of content" sometimes "*the volume can be a problem.*" Students told us "*it is well structured but intellectually less challenging*" than they had expected, advising that this means "*you've got to go in with your eyes open and you may struggle to catch up if you miss things.*" Assessments take place throughout the year, but one much-appreciated feature of the COL course is that "*exams are open book – that allows you to apply your knowledge and it's a better reflection of what you will do in practice.*" It also means just a little memorising of facts, leaving you to focus on organising your "*reams of notes.*" Students were largely "*impressed by the level of teaching,*" from "*people who communicate very well*" and are "*still interested in listening to opinions.*"

Another way in which COL offers good support is in the help given to those still seeking a training contract when they begin… or even earlier. Sessions for future students on CVs and training contract applications can be "*a godsend if you're getting bogged down with what to write and past failure.*" Once in situ there is also plenty to enhance students' practical legal experience, including the prestigious Streetlaw project and other pro-bono initiatives.

## store street, london

**Number of places:** 1,260 full-time, 352 part-time

The largest law school in the UK, the sheer size and numbers at Store Street can leave students feeling a little cold. "*There's a definite feel of a factory about it,*" said one, with others adding: "*It's a bit of a charmless place*" and "*you get a feeling that you just go in, get everything done and leave.*" However, with students departing for all manner of legal careers, as an institution it is felt to be "*more interested in a broader spectrum of things than elsewhere,*" and generally speaking the course is "*taught well*" and "*what is undeniably a dry year is made bearable.*" The number of students at Store Street "*stretch facilities thin sometimes,*" but its location just off Tottenham Court Road, is "*pretty good.*" So too is the social life, even if "*you only really get to know your tutor group well.*"

## guildford

**Number of places:** 720 full-time, 220 part-time

Situated in a manor house in "*fantastic grounds,*" the "*picturesque*" college has "*a lovely campus atmosphere.*" Several students noted a "*Surrey-esque*" or "*Home-Counties vibe*" which others went further to name as "*very much Sloane Ranger territory,*" and with "*lots of people living at home*" perhaps that isn't surprising. Guildford can sometimes be "*as expensive as London, without the benefits of living in the city;*" however, with good sports and leisure facilities on site and "*a thriving social scene,*" there are still plenty of diversions to eat into your private study time and the capital is just a short train ride away. Students generally reflect on "*good teaching*" from "*interested and interesting teachers*" who "*always make time for you.*"

## chester

**Number of places:** 600 full-time, 160 part-time

Way back when, the Venerable Bede took religion to the heathen northerners. In historic Chester, COL is displaying similarly missionary intentions with regards to legal eduction, serving "*lots of student who go on to firms in Manchester, Liverpool or Leeds.*" Appropriately enough it is located in what was once a seminary, and although this doesn't result in any sort of legal fundamentalism, the students we spoke to had truly enjoyed their time at "*a relatively small but perfectly formed*" institution. "*The facilities are great*" and "*highly professional tutors*" are on hand to "*get you through everything you need to cover*" with "*grace and good humour.*"

The small campus is a short distance from the town centre. No problem if you have a car or a friend with wheels. Making these friends, if you're new to the area, shouldn't be a problem because the COL's dinky size means "*you have the same classes and so see the same people day in, day*

*out.*" Some find life "*too small and villagy, too like a Cambridge College;*" others revel in "*a really intimate atmosphere that makes a good social scene.*" The "*beautiful*" town centre is equally miniature and the relative paucity of nightspots is perhaps more of a hindrance to "*people who previously led more of a university lifestyle.*" On the other hand, "*if you want to get really stuck into studying it's a nice place to live.*"

## york

**Number of places:** 504 full-time , 160 part-time

"*York law school is great.*" We heard more positive comments regarding York than any other branch, and undoubtedly it does provide "*a well-worked programme*" with "*very nice lecturers,*" "*great continuity of staff,*" "*high standards*" and "*a relaxed atmosphere.*" Equally, there is a "*collegiate feel*" to what is "*quite a small place*" and the facilities themselves include "*good IT and a cool canteen where everyone sits together.*" As for the city: "*York is just a fabulous place to spend some time,*" students enthused. "*It's absolutely gorgeous*" and "*a brilliant place to study.*" The school is located next to the racecourse (great unless you're a recovering gambling addict or allergic to horses) with the historic town centre just minutes away. Still ringed by its original Roman walls, with the mighty River Ouse running through it (over it at some times of the year), York has a tumultuous history of Viking pillaging and religious significance (not least when the Minster was set alight by lightning during the contentious sermon of a Bishop during the late 80s). Lest we give the impression that COL students are all refined, culturally sensitive souls, we should add that one raved about "*the three or four nightclubs in town – we made them our own.*" Plenty of students pitch up without a training contract, but receive the necessary TLC from the careers service. Most students are ultimately destined for northern firms, with only a few heading for London or other southern destinations.

## birmingham

**Number of places:** 528 full-time, 160 part-time

The Birmingham branch belies its relatively tender age and boasts a strong reputation and "*intense, no-nonsense*" atmosphere. Its building was purpose built and has "*loads of computers and a good library,*" "*excellent teaching rooms and tiny group rooms with lots of white boards – it's all very well designed.*" Admittedly, increasing numbers can sometimes put pressure on these resources, but in the main students had "*few complaints*" on this score. Nor did they about the quality of teaching, which was described as "*generally good, occasionally excellent,*" even if the highest praise was reserved for "*Jill, the lady at the café who bakes really good cakes.*"

Birmingham itself has plenty to offer, with students mainly based near to the university around Selley Oak or Edgebaston. In the centre of town the mighty Bullring Centre has everything one could possibly need for life, death or entertainment, and the Mailbox and the canal are abuzz with waterside cafés and bars. All in all, students' verdict on Birmingham is that it's "*a more exciting place to be than you might think.*"

## de montfort university

**Number of places:** 100 full-time, 80 part-time/open learning

The Leicester-based De Montfort University LPC has made it into this feature for the first time having scooped an upgrade to "Very Good" at the last Law Society visit. The Law School is located close to the city centre and the city's legal heartland. Its facilities include a mock courtroom and new library plus special resource rooms that are set aside for use by LPC students only.

A notable feature of De Montfort is that around half of the students who sign up to the course each year do so on a part-time basis, many through distance learning. This is in part because of the law school's ties with the Ilex Tutorial College. The distance learning mode of study relies heavily on the school's so-called eLearning programme, an online resource that enables students to interact virtually with each other as well as teachers. Lecture notes, handouts and timetables, etc are also online. Full-time students are taught through both large groups and workshops of approximately 16 people. Whether taking the LPC full-time or by any other method, all examinations are open book except Solicitors Accounts and Business Accounts. There is a reasonable range of electives suitable for commercial or private client practice.

The course is reasonably priced and part-time students can opt to pay in up to six instalments. Places are guaranteed for successful LLB graduates of De Montfort University.

## inns of court law school

**Number of places:** 176 full-time

"*I'm doing the ICSL LPC*" is a legal tongue twister you may never quite perfect, but at least the course itself has all the prestige you'd expect from a institution recognised as a top education establishment for barristers since the dawn of time. Well, okay, since 1852. At only six years young, the ICSL LPC boasts an "Excellent" rating.

ICSL is often criticised for the factory style of its BVC provision; however, the LPC does not suffer in the same way. Students told us they "*really valued being at one of the smaller providers – there's an intimate community feel.*" Being part of a relatively small cohort (small for a London provider anyway) means "*good access to and support from staff,*" and the relative newness of the course was additionally viewed by some as allowing it to still feel "*innovative and dynamic*" in its teaching. Sessions come in 90-minute morsels, coupled with meatier three-hour group seminars plus large-scale lectures. Some 15% of the course is taught in groups of eight or less. It is true that ICSL offers less diversity in its elective choices than many other institutions ("*I could have done with a private client one,*" said somebody who had perhaps not researched fully before accepting their offer), but the choice certainly isn't restrictive.

Would-be solicitors are significantly outnumbered by prospective barristers at ICSL, and some said "*you could feel second place to the BVC in terms of facilities and events.*" Perhaps the lack of overlap between LPC and BVC students contributed to this feeling. Nonetheless, plenty of LPC students had "*really enjoyed*" their time here, and the upsides to the close proximity with the parallel world of the Bar include a superb location in the heart of Gray's Inn and the truly 'ye olde' feeling that comes from spending time in such an historic part of legal London. If you are concerned with more practical matters, an association with City University's Faculty of Law means that ICLS students benefit from Islington-based sports, social, counselling and accommodation facilities.

## university of northumbria

**Number of places:** 160
The School of Law at the University of Northumbria is the North of England's largest law department. The LPC is just one of a number of academic and vocational law courses offered and, uniquely, the university is authorised by the Law Society and the Bar Council to offer four-year exempting degrees which incorporate the vocational year of either the LPC or the BVC in the degree course. Students explained why you might want to study law this way. Firstly: "*It's worth bearing in mind that your LPC fees are included in the course so your tuition fees are paid as with a normal four-year degree.*" In terms of the teaching method: "*You are not taught in an excessively academic way. You do drafting practice as early as your first year and you cover the LPC elements across the years.*"

Don't worry if these wise words come too late, the university's straight LPC gets rave reviews too. Said one student: "*I really enjoyed it even though I hadn't studied for years. The university had absolutely excellent lecturers and tutors and we worked mainly in quite small groups.*" IT facilities

exclusively for use by law students, plus three mock courtrooms with video equipment, are part of the on-site provisions. "*Resources were never a problem,*" we were told, "*and I had no difficulties getting on a computer.*" Another agreed: "*The library and computers were good, as were the course materials.*" A very compelling reason to choose Northumbria is its nationally renowned Student Law Office, through which students take on real cases for real people. "*The SLO was one of the best aspects,*" said one past student. "*It's really good to have on your CV and I certainly had an idea about how to work as a solicitor.*"

There's something about Newcastle. Maybe it's the rejuvenation of the city and the civic pride that has developed as a result. Certainly the warmth of the place has rubbed off on the university. One past student recalled his decision to come to Northumbria: "*I was made to feel welcome when I went to look at the university. I spoke to one of the deans and she took a couple of hours out of her day and walked me round the place. The LPC course is not too large – and it costs less than most, which is really important if you haven't got a training contract at the time.*" You can't argue with that! There is also an opportunity to attain an LLM at a discounted rate when studied alongside the LPC.

## nottingham law school

**Number of places:** 648 full-time, 70 part-time
No longer one of the preferred providers since the eight consortium firms decided to switch to using only London schools, Nottingham Law School (which is part of Nottingham Trent University) now has many more places free for students headed elsewhere. Its star certainly remains undimmed amongst students, and with a truly fantastic social scene, a long-established reputation for quality legal education at all levels and an "Excellent" hallmark from the Law Society for its LPC, it's not hard to see why. The City consortium may have gone elsewhere but you can confidently rely on two facts at NLS: first, there will still be "*a*

distinct commercial focus;" and second, getting a place here will be as competitive as ever.

Students agreed: *"You really have to work hard"* in an institution that is *"very focused on tuning people for the working world."* Though some felt the approach was *"overly spoon-feeding,"* others reflected that *"there is a lot of work and they do very much guide you through it."* Students require stamina because weeks are long with mostly 9am to 5pm days of teaching focused around classes of 18 people or so. This means *"you get a lot of one-to-one attention"* and sometimes *"you can be picked on – scary if you haven't done the work!"* Anonymity is to be found in the smaller number of *"lectures for a couple of hundred people"* but, in general, *"your personal tutor knows your name as do many others."* Students praised the *"bright,"* *"switched-on"* and *"very helpful"* staff. The *"clearly laid-out"* course includes frequent closed-book exams before final assessments on the compulsory part of the course in April, perhaps explaining why many we spoke to found *"the elective part of the course is much more interesting and relaxed."*

The law school has *"everything in one building"* on the relatively intimate Nottingham Trent campus. Students can take advantage of all the university's facilities, while at the same time enjoying the *"cracking"* social life of Nottingham itself. Masses of bars, restaurants and nightclubs, and a sizeable student population make for *"a great social environment"* and there's plenty of cheap housing to be had. However, quite why it's cheap remains a perpetual gripe amongst students – *"Certain areas of the city possess a bad reputation for gang violence and drugs."* We heard this year, as last, of muggings and burglaries, but more streetwise characters advised, *"there are some rough areas but you stay out of trouble by keeping your head down."* So, choose where you live carefully and we reckon you can expect *"a fantastic year."*

## oxford institute of legal practice
**Number of places:** 353 full-time

One of the newer LPC providers, OXILP has weathered a few teething problems and retained its "Very Good" rating. No longer linked with the consortium of eight City firms, it now offers a straightforward, commercially focused LPC from a well-equipped prime location in Oxford.

Opinions were divergent about the course, but at the positive end of the spectrum we heard about *"a really practical approach,"* and *"fantastic one-on-one relations with lecturers."* Certainly the methodology is nothing unusual, with delivery via roughly 14 hours per week of 90-minute small group sessions and lectures. Though the range of electives is not the broadest and remains commercial in its orientation, there is enough to satisfy those with a taste for the high street as well. However, despite being *"a very well-organised course,"* a number of students had observed *"some average, even patchy"* and *"uninterested teaching,"* leaving them distinctly uninspired.

OXILP's location close to the centre of *"one of the most beautiful cities in the world"* sets it slightly apart from the university heartland. There is *"a good library and computer room on site"* and students additionally have access to the university's law faculty and top-drawer libraries. Many students are already familiar with the geography of the city, having spent their undergraduate days there. Newcomers told us: *"There were lots of little groups who all knew each other at the beginning. It is intimidating at first, but in the end it means you get to know more people."* Whether it's the delights of townie George Street, the culturally diverse Cowley Road, the historic city centre or the more restrained pleasures of North Oxford, there is a social scene and a setting for all personality types.

## university of sheffield
**Number of places:** 216 full-time and part-time
A law school that simultaneously benefits from being part of the greater whole of Sheffield University and its various facilities – it seems you can have your cake and eat it here. A small LPC intake guar-

antees "*a friendly atmosphere*" and "*plenty of attention from staff.*" Indeed, the "*excellent quality of teaching*" was roundly praised, based as it is around one-hour lectures and three-hour workshops in groups of 16-18. Workshops account for 80% of teaching and in these classes "*you learn in a lot of detail*" because tutors are willing to "*give you individual support.*" The course places a heavy emphasis on practitioner texts rather than course manuals.

The Sheffield LPC remains a generalist one with an array of options, so there's no danger of emerging a pure-bred corporate type unless you absolutely want to. Students go on to a very broad range of firms, from the Sheffield big guns (DLA, Irwin Mitchell, Nabarros) to smaller practices. Many students begin the course without a training contract, but there's plenty of support on offer through the university-calibre careers service and via close links with local firms. Solicitors get involved with the teaching programme and can be useful links to the real world of practice. Students can get involved with the community-based Freelaw project run by the school, or immerse themselves in the social distractions of what is now increasingly regarded as a reinvigorated city. Sheffield is catching up with Leeds in terms of vibrancy; certainly it has a top-notch theatre, bars aplenty, culture and an endless supply of industrial history. And let's not forget the dramatic countryside right on your doorstep. No surprise that although the north may be a grim prospect to some, the LPC at Sheffield is "*very, very sociable and great fun*" in the eyes of the students we interviewed. Tip: Sheffield prefers applicants to put it as their first choice on the LawCabs form. It also guarantees places to graduates of some universities.

## university of central lancashire

**Number of places:** 60 full-time, 48 part-time
Situated in Preston, UCLan certainly keeps it in the family. A good number of its students come to the LPC directly from its LLB course and a high proportion are locals eager to prove that many a

mickel macks a muckel by living chez parents. If you find yourself alone in a new town, one of the benefits of UCLan is the facilities on offer, among them the opportunity to shack up in student accommodation. However it is you end up here, "*you're guaranteed a good welcome.*"

It may not be Harvard but the law faculty at UCLan is certainly stately. Don't be misled by the olde worlde charm: the faculty has a dedicated LPC computer room and an "*excellent library.*" Students spoke positively of "*a good course,*" which though "*quite difficult*" was made more manageable by the efforts of solid tutors with "*plenty of time for you.*" The course is delivered by a punchy one-two of lectures for the entire year group and workshops for groups of around 12. The small-group focus of workshops makes them particularly good for getting to know your fellow classmates and swapping notes on hunting down a training contract. The majority of students arrive on the course without one and are glad of the services of a "*well-developed*" and "*proactive*" careers advice team. It runs an excellent work-experience programme based on week-long placements at a variety of local firms. The school was graded as "Very Good" in 2002 and at the time of writing we were awaiting the results of the inspectors' latest visit.

Socially, Preston is your oyster. Even if you pitch up on day one to find a bunch of grizzled Lancashire graduates trading university-daze stories, you'll soon ease your way into the local dialect, local beers and the local scene. We recommend an evening in with a Peter Kay DVD if you want to test your proclivity for any of the above.

## university of staffordshire

**Number of places:** 125 full-time
Having offered the LPC since 1993, the University of Staffordshire knows a thing or two about legal education, a fact reflected in the "Excellent" rating it continues to enjoy. Sitting pretty in a state-of-the-art £3 million building boasting facilities which include mock courtrooms, fantastic IT and

simulations of solicitors' offices. Classes are kept to a maximum of 16, there is a well-stocked library, a conscientious careers service and the school's strong links with local firms mean there is a practitioner-mentor for every student. Oodles of extra support is on offer via the university, not forgetting the sports, social, accommodation and other resources. What particularly caught our eye was the 'work bank' scheme that assists students in finding gainful employment to fit around their studies. The school additionally participates in the Streetlaw pro bono programme.

As well as the full-time course, there are part-time options in the daytime and the evening. Authorised to take 150 students; last year Staffs enrolled 110 full-time and 40 part-time. The breadth of commercial and non-commercial options reflects the intended career paths of students. Many on the LPC course graduated from Staffs University or have returned to the area to take advantage of mum and dad's hospitality and save on living expenses. The course fees are at the more affordable end of the scale and represent good value for money given the "Excellent" rating.

The social scene can't be described as full-on but the locale has its appeal. With the centre of Stafford close by, Hanley's shopping delights a short hop, and Festival Park, Alton Towers, walks and rugged countryside but a drive from the university, there's plenty to keep you happy. And if you really like the place, you could always hang about to top up your LPC with an LLM.

## university of westminster

**Number of places:** 120 full-time, 60 part-time

Nestled behind Oxford Circus in the heart of London's West End, the "Excellent" law school at the University of Westminster has more than just a fabulous location to recommend it. The relatively small intake of students is the perfect antidote to the factory farming elsewhere in the capital, leading students to describe it as "*very much a personal place.*" A second major consider-

ation is that the course fees are significantly cheaper than the majority of London schools (and we're not talking pocket change here unless you have huge pockets). Given that most students begin the course without a training contract, these financial savings are a big deal.

Students are split into small groups of more than 16 for the compulsories. They told us the course is "*very well structured*" and were happy with its delivery via one-hour lectures coupled with classes. Westminster offers a spread of electives that puts some other schools to shame, and with more leftfield choices like media and entertainment, international commercial arbitration and e-commerce on offer, there really is something for every taste. Many of the electives are taught by practitioners. On a similarly varied note, the school has a diverse student population, with plenty of people coming from previous careers or less usual backgrounds. Most aim for general practice or smaller commercial firms, which explains why a significant proportion of them are grateful for the "*fantastic support for those without training contracts.*" But with the school boasting excellent relationships with local law firms, a prized training contract might not be that far away.

"*The teachers are incredibly friendly,*" students told us, adding: "*They really are serious about what they do here – it's not just a fill-in year from the staff's point of view.*" The fact that around a third of each year's new students start the part-time course – commonly while working full-time – should also be a fair indication that most have considered this career seriously. Membership of the University of Westminster gives access to some pretty good facilities in the law faculty and beyond. However, avoiding the lure of the shops, bars, nightspots and theatres of Oxford Street, Soho and the West End is enough to test the patience of the most piously budget-minded individual. All in all, it's small wonder students can "*wholeheartedly recommend coming here.*"

# bar vocational course

The BVC is the vocational stage of a barrister's training. It is taught at eight law schools, with a new one – BPP Leeds – being added for 2006. Through www.bvconline.co.uk, students are permitted to apply to as many schools as they like. In an initial round they will be considered by their first three choices; they will then automatically enter a second, clearing round if necessary. There are many more applicants than places, and if you don't believe us then check out the Bar Council's statistics in the **pupillage and tenancy** section. The application process starts in October, first-round applications close in mid-January, and clearing runs from March to July. Remember: you must be a member of an Inn of Court.

The BVC teaches vocational, not academic, subjects, and it is directed towards the development of oral skills. This will include conferencing and negotiation as well as advocacy. Practical classes are given in legal research, remedies, opinion writing and drafting, and civil and criminal litigation classes will cram into your head more procedural rules than you ever thought possible. The closest thing to academia on the BVC is the training in civil and criminal evidence: here at least there is some room for the philosophical issues behind the rules. Towards the end of the course, students take two electives in areas that most interest them.

The timing of assessments varies between schools, though generally they are spread out fairly evenly. Practical skills are commonly examined using professional actors to play recalcitrant criminals and garrulous complainants during oral exams. These exams will normally have seen and unseen elements. Civil and criminal litigation may be examined by problem questions, multiple-choice tests (MCTs), or a mixture of both. Professional ethics and conduct are not usually examined as discrete subjects and could be slipped into any of the practical exams.

The BVC divides opinion. It is either *"a hugely enjoyable course that gets young lawyers fully geared up for practice"* or *"a barely necessary evil."* Wise students understand that it will be nothing like university or the CPE; nonetheless, there are common and persistent complaints. The first is the yawning gulf between the numbers enrolling and those who will end up with a career at the Bar. There will always be some students who do not intend to practice at the English Bar; some others become academics. Yet this does not account for enough people to make the statistics any more comfortable. From the outset this can make for a strained relationship between students who have not secured pupillage and course providers. *"BVC providers need to take some responsibility,"* one student told us. *"They should tighten up the entry requirements; it's better to be rejected by them before forking out eleven grand than being rejected by chambers at the other end."* Remember, these are private institutions, and if the demand exists they will meet it. BPP, for example, is a company with shareholders to answer to. Before you think about committing time and money to the BVC, understand just how competitive the hunt for pupillage and tenancy will be.

Another common criticism is that the BVC is too long and expensive: *"There is no reason why it should take nine months, it's really not very hard and all the skills covered could be taught to the same standard in six months, easily. It felt like it had been artificially stretched to fit into a convenient academic year."* In fact, the Bar Council has a working party reviewing the length and format of the course. A supporter of the full year told us: *"It allowed us all to adjust to the idea of being barristers. The BVC isn't only about increasing knowledge and developing skills, it is also about growing into a role, and for that you need time."* Also, the opinion that the BVC is a walk in the park is not held by all. Some find the transition from academe to vocation initially awkward. Developing the ability to turn flawless argument on paper into a piece of compelling advocacy can take time.

It is widely accepted that there is a certain artificiality to the course that is both inevitable and grating: "*I grew weary of the scenarios. It is difficult to work hard on behalf of a fictional person who, in a fictional world, may or may not have punched another creation in the made-up loos of a made-up pub.*" Others viewed the electives as "*a complete waste of time: they neither extended our knowledge base in any real way, nor did they truly augment the skills we had already developed.*" Nevertheless, others we spoke to had thoroughly enjoyed the BVC. "*This was one of the most interesting years of my life,*" said one, who found that the practical focus gave them pertinent skills and confidence for pupillage. Another told us: "*Undertaking the BVC really confirmed my commitment to the Bar.*"

With the advent of more providers than ever before, the received wisdom about the best place to do your BVC no longer stands up. If you are looking for pupillage on the circuits, then doing the BVC at a regional provider can be a distinct advantage. If you want to come away having enjoyed your BVC year, you may be better off at one of the smaller course providers. Read prospectuses, attend open days and chat to past and current students to get a feel for the different providers. And remember, while the core subject areas are common to all, there are differences in the electives offered, as well as course structures and fees. See **www.chambersandpartners.com**

# bvc providers: the inside story

## bpp law school, london
**Number of places:** 276 full-time, 96 part-time
In the heart of legal London, BPP Law School is one part of a worldwide professional education company. Step through the doors and you can't help but be reminded that you've left university far behind you – a shrine to glass and steel, BPP plc has a distinctly corporate feel to it. It refers to its students as clients and no expense is spared in keeping them in line, on track and focused on the years of practice ahead of them.

Expect the usual compulsory knowledge subjects and practical skills, plus a plump list of options. Advocacy classes are taken in groups of six and mock courtrooms are fully kitted out with video, PowerPoint, smartboards and actors. The majority of teaching is done in small groups of 12. The school's active pro bono centre guarantees all committed students work experience in a variety of projects ranging from legal advice clinics to research for human rights charities.

BPP also trains prospective solicitors on the LPC and CPE. The BVC cohort is the smallest of the three and has its own dedicated communal area, lockers and classrooms. Students share other facilities, including a subsidised canteen and a library with opening hours verging on 24/7. Past students speak well of BPP, saying that lectures and classes are planned to the last detail and that the quality of the teaching is excellent. With such high course fees, so they should be! BPP is now applying for permission to teach the BVC in Leeds.

## bristol institute of legal practice, uwe
**Number of places:** 120 full-time, 36 part-time
Bristol is home to many of the best sets on the western circuit, so if you're aiming for a pupillage in the South West, consider taking your BVC at UWE. The school has strong links with local practitioners and judges, several of whom play an active and continuing role in teaching the course. One of the highlights is the compulsory work experience; one week spent marshalling with a High Court, circuit or district judge, and another placing students in a working legal environment, eg chambers, the CPS or a CAB. For all you *Bad Girls* fans, prison visiting is also possible.

The small BVC cohort enables staff to build

good relationships with students, who are divided into groups of 12, each with its own base room. Much of the teaching and learning is carried out in these rooms, with larger groups assembling for knowledge-based subjects. Option subjects include alternative dispute resolution, clinical negligence and Mercantile Court matters.

UWE's campus location on the edge of Bristol is best described as dreary, so make sure you find yourself accommodation in one of the city's vibrant student areas for maximum fun.

## cardiff law school

**Number of places:** 60 full-time
Low fees and a small intake of students make Cardiff a good option, especially when you factor in the high ratio of staff to students and the many University facilities. Advocacy, conferencing and negotiation skills are all taught in small groups of six, with remaining subjects delivered to groups of 12. Two weeks of work experience includes a week spent in a local chambers and a week's marshalling with a circuit or district judge. Though not vast, a very decent number of options are available given the small size of the intake.

Cardiff has recently been voted one of the best places to work and study, and it is certainly popular with students intending to practice overseas, making the student body a diverse one. For those looking for pupillage in the UK, the law school has fostered close links with sets on the Wales and Chester circuit. If you're looking elsewhere, be assured that a number of past students have also found pupillage further afield. Cardiff's BVC is one of the most oversubscribed, so you should put the school first in your list of preferences.

## the college of law, store street, london

**Number of places:** 180 full-time
COL is smaller and cheaper than its London rivals. Students report a close and supportive working relationship between students and staff, and rarely pass negative comments about the structure of the course. Most teaching is delivered to groups of six, with skills teaching employing recurring case studies and using the same set of facts to develop a variety of oral and written skills. The range of elective subjects offered is excellent. There are plenty of opportunities for extra advocacy experience, including a pro bono elective in the third term in which students can represent clients before the London Residential Property Tribunals. Externally judged mock trials are part of the course and 'practitioner evenings' are opportunities to participate in advocacy in front of barristers. There is also an annual mooting competition.

Store Street's packed and busy environment is often likened to a factory by CPE and LPC students. The fact that BVC students do not say the same is a credit to those who run the course. The central location off Tottenham Court Road is ideal should you need to buy a sofa or a laptop.

## the inns of court school of law

**Number of places:** 575 full-time, 75 part-time
The biggest of them all, ICSL used to be the only Bar School. Located off Gray's Inn Square, it has a distinctly barristerial air about it, a beautiful setting, excellent library access and an interactive IT-heavy lecture theatre. A response to previous feedback concerning the diseconomies of scale, the student body is now divided into cohorts, each with its own course director.

Students are taught in large-group lectures of around 100 and small-group classes of 12. Advocacy is taught to groups of six. As well as the usual compulsory and option subjects, there are weekly practitioner classes delivered by barristers and judges and the possibility of doing work for the Free Representation Unit as an option.

Verdicts on the BVC at ICSL are mixed. There's a general notion that there are too many people without a shot at tenancy and who are struggling with the course. Some people express concern that course assessment criteria do not correspond well with what will be expected of a pupil in real-life practice. Others say that although some tutors are really well respected, there is an element of despondency among others on the teaching staff. Yet it must be remembered that ICSL has years of experience with the BVC and its manuals are used by a number of the other providers. It is one of the pricier providers but you will get a shed-load of books as part of the deal. For many students this is the IBM choice, but perhaps they should consider carefully whether bigger really does mean better.

## manchester metropolitan university
Number of places: 108 full-time
A space-age building and lecture theatre complete with interactive whiteboards, Manchester Met certainly looks the part. Students are assigned to a syndicate group of 12 and perform regularly in front of their colleagues. This gives them a good, realistic idea of their strengths and weaknesses from early on. There is a long list of option subjects.

Anyone looking for pupillage will benefit from strong links with chambers on the northern circuit. Practising barristers regularly deliver masterclasses, providing excellent opportunities for students to interact and impress. All students have a chance to undertake a mini-pupillage with a local chambers, and a pro bono advice clinic is new on the agenda. Around 30% of UK students obtain pupillage, mostly on the northern circuit. Course fees are relatively low, but if you're considering applying, make sure you give clear and articulate reasons as to why this is the right school because Manchester Met receives at least 300 applications per year from students selecting it as their first choice.

## university of northumbria at newcastle
Number of places: 130 f/t , 20 on exempting LLB
The BVC is just one of a number of academic and vocational courses offered at Northumbria and, uniquely, the university is authorised to offer four-year exempting degrees incorporating the BVC into the LLB. Why study the courses together in this way? First, *"you do the practical side as you do the more theoretical things. This has to the most useful thing for your future career."* Second, the cost of the BVC is scooped up into the cost of the LLB and this works out to be far more economical. Finally, the university is home to the nationally renowned Student Law Office, where students get to take on real cases for real people. If that doesn't set you apart from most students then we don't know what will. Northumbria's conventional BVC is a good choice too, and you won't miss out on vital first-hand experience at the SLO.

Back in class, the law school occupies a new building with three fully equipped mock courtrooms. Teaching is mostly in small groups in dedicated rooms. The school has good links with practitioners on the northern circuit and barristers and judges pop in to give lectures or judge moots. There are also visits from police and forensics experts and an established court visits programme. An LLM can be studied at a discounted rate while on the BVC.

## nottingham law school
**Number of places:** 90-100 full-time
Nottingham has built a name for excellence in legal education. So popular is its BVC course, it will now only take students who have a fighting chance of getting pupillage. The admissions strategy must be paying off because at least 50% of the BVC graduates go straight into pupillage.

Teaching is delivered to groups of 12, with advocacy training taken by groups of six in the old Guildhall Courtroom. The range of optional subjects is excellent. Students receive their own copy of Archbold's Criminal Practice and the civil procedure text, The White Book. As well as being a vital tool for any practitioner, they also make an effective doorstop. To keep them in touch with the London Bar, regular buses are laid on to take students to dine at their Inns. With fairly competitive course fees and reasonable accommodation costs, Nottingham is a smart choice financially and in terms of quality.

# funding

Training a lawyer is an expensive caper. Some students secure training contracts or pupillages before commencing their studies and will receive funding to cover their course fees and some living expenses. In a stealth move that caught rivals unawares, Linklaters announced in September 2005 that it was bouncing its maintenance grant up to £7,000 pa. Some others quickly followed. Full details of who offers what are set out on our **Salaries and Benefits** table. For other students, money worries can make law school stressful.

## taken for granted

There's a very slim chance your Local Education Authority may come to the rescue with a grant or allowance if you make it past the rainforest of application forms. Funds are sometimes available to applicants with physical or other difficulties, carers or those with children.
See **www.dfes. gov.uk/studentsupport**.

An organisation called the Educational Grants Advisory Service (EGAS) can carry out a charity and trust search on your behalf. Their really useful website is **www.egas-online.org.uk**. Also see **www.support4learning .org.uk**.

The internet is a brilliant source of information, and check your university or local library for reference books such as The Educational Grants Directory. Here are some of the funds we found:
• **BPP Law School** scholarships awarded by seven of the key staff, each set their own criteria, eg the applicant is the first lawyer in their family.
• **The Law Society Bursary** scheme is open to GDL or LPC students.
• **The Law Society Diversity Access Scheme** supports talented people who face obstacles to qualification.
• **Inderpal Rahal Memorial Trust** supports women from an immigrant or refugee background.
• **The Kalisher Scholarship and Bursary** is for a BVC student who intends to practise at the criminal Bar.
• Loans from the **Leonard Sainer Foundation**.
• **The Student Disability Assistance Fund** – see **www.bahshe.demon.co.uk**.
• Universities and publicly funded colleges have discretionary **College Access Funds** available to assist especially hard-up students.

## career development loans

Barclays Bank, the Co-operative Bank and the Royal Bank of Scotland provide these on behalf of the DfES. Full details are at **www.lifelonglearning .co.uk/cdl**. You can borrow up to £8,000 to fund up to two years' study.

## bank loans

Already got a huge overdraft? No problem! You could still qualify for a special package from a high street bank. Interest rates are low and the repayment terms usually favourable, but sniff around to see what the different banks are offering. Many banks have graduate loan schemes tailored to the needs of the legal profession, and will, for example, regard pupillage as a formal part of the training when it comes to determining the time for repayment.

Scott Jago, manager of Legal Student Services at NatWest's Legal Centre, advises students to arrange any required loan as soon as they have been accepted onto a course. *"Law students need to plan their expenditure carefully,"* he told us. Scott also recommends that students stick to a budget, drawing down against their loan on a monthly basis. *"If you want a manageable student debt when you start work, then monthly budgeting during your studies is essential."*

## barristers

Pupils and CPE or BVC students can apply for a range of scholarships from the four Inns of Court and many base their choice of Inn on the likelihood of getting some of the £3 million plus that is paid out each year. Some awards are merit-based, others consider financial hardship. All pupillages come with a minimum chambers award of £10,000. Some sets pay far more and allow students to draw on these awards while on the BVC.

## part-timing and the four-letter word

If a decade of loan repayments doesn't appeal then you must do as fools and horses do: work! Full-time study and work are uncomfortable bedfellows so consider seriously whether you ought to be studying part-time. Doing so may allow you to work a more rewarding job while also performing better at college. Part-time study may initially seem an affront to fresh undergraduates. You may have to mingle with mature students, men and women with wives, husbands, kids, mortgages... bald spots even. We say revel in the difference – it will be good practice for when you are a lawyer.

For LLB grads or students who have completed the CPE, paralegalling may be an option. And there are myriad of other options on the periphery of the profession, from commercial contracts negotiation and transaction management to social policy or other research. Whatever job you do, working whilst studying brings with it a commodity to be traded on – respect.

## benefits, benefactors, begging...

Living at home while you study may not sound that appealing but sometimes needs must. And as for a loophole in the law that almost begs students to declare bankruptcy and evade student debt, we do not recommend this unless you want to make the job of qualifying even harder. Why not con-sider other creative ways to ease the debt burden:

• A student card will get you cheap travel, discount haircuts, cinema tickets and drinks in some places. If nothing else, you will be a cheap date.

• Law books are pricey so don't go on a spending spree before term starts. College libraries will have the core texts and we guarantee you'll find former students with books for sale. Check out notice boards for second-hand tomes.

• A number of law schools, chambers and solicitors firms run competitions. Do a Google search.

• Market research focus groups pay decent money for an hour or two of your time. Or, how about being a human guinea pig – medical establishments will pay for the privilege of giving you the flu or a few electric shocks. Just don't do anything too scary and think carefully about how you'll feel when a stranger knocks on your door in 2026 and calls you dad.

## capital concerns

Newsflash: London streets aren't paved with gold – just concrete, pigeon droppings and chewing gum. Rent and living costs in cities like Sheffield, Nottingham and Cardiff are far lower. But don't assume that out of London means within your price range – Guildford, for example, is as pricey as it is pretty.

Before taking any steps, sit down and add up what you think you'll need and then add some more. If you need to study for the CPE and LPC or BVC and you do so at the most expensive places, course fees could cost you up to £18,000 (CPE/BVC) or £15,000 (CPE/LPC). Do so at the least expensive schools and these figures could be reduced to around £10,000 and £8,000 respectively. Worth thinking about if money is the main sticking point.

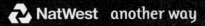

# universities
# and law schools
# a-z

# A-Z Universities and Law Schools

# BPP Law School

68-70 Red Lion Street, London, WC1R 4NY
Tel: (0845) 070 2882
Email: law@bpp.com
Website: www.bpp.com/law

## college profile

BPP is the leading provider of professional legal education in the country with over 4,000 students based across four specially designed and highly equipped Law Schools. As the leading provider, they have the skills and resources to offer you the individual support needed to prepare you for the realities of legal practice. This is achieved using a unique mix of academic and practitioner lecturers, first rate facilities, award winning pro bono projects and an unrivalled careers service.

BPP's careers service comprises not only specialist careers advisors, but also careers tutors, who have worked in practice and sat on recruitment selection panels. This distinctive blend of knowledge and experience ensures you are fully equipped with the knowledge and support needed to secure a training contract or pupillage.

## graduate diploma in law (full-time, part-time, and distance learning)

BPP's GDL is taught with a practical, student-centred approach to not only familiarise you with the basic principles of law, but to also introduce you to legal practice. You will be taught using a combination of large and small group sessions, allowing you to develop your knowledge and skills fully by receiving maximum support and individual feedback. Although competition for places at BPP is intense, graduates from BPP's GDL are guaranteed a place on the school's LPC and intending barristers can apply to join their BVC.

If you are unsure whether a career in law is for you, BPP's popular taster course, the BPP Summer School, is available to give you an insight into the legal world.

## legal practice course (full-time and part-time)

BPP's LPC is designed to prepare you for real life as a trainee solicitor. Taught by experienced solicitors from a variety of practice backgrounds, you will benefit from a course designed in close collaboration with the top legal firms in the country and the widest range of electives ensuring you can study the area of legal practice most important to you.

## bar vocational course (full-time and part-time)

BPP's BVC is highly regarded by the profession and is the only course in London to be unconditionally validated by the Bar Council for the full six-year term. Studying the BVC at BPP will allow you to concentrate on developing your essential barristerial skills of drafting, opinion writing, advocacy, conference and negotiation. These skills will be refined using groups as small as six students alongside practising barristers, who will become your opponents in mock trials and final assessments.

BPP Law School operates an exclusive scholarship programme for selected BPP students. Applications must be received by the beginning of April prior to you commencing your course. Please visit the website www.bpp.com/law for more information.

# Cardiff Law School

Cardiff Law School, Cardiff University, Museum Avenue, Cardiff CF10 3UX
Tel: (029) 2087 4941/6660  Fax: (029) 2087 4984
Email: law-lpc@cf.ac.uk or law-bvc@cf.ac.uk
Website: www.law.cardiff.ac.uk/cpls

**contact**
LPC: Byron Jones
Tel: (029) 2087 4941/6660
Email: law-lpc@cf.ac.uk

BVC: Lucy Burns
Tel: (029) 2087 4964
Email: law-bvc@cf.ac.uk

**other postgraduate law courses:**
The Postgraduate Secretary
Tel: (029) 2087 6102

## university profile

Cardiff Law School is long established, well-resourced and enjoys an international reputation for its teaching and research. In the most recent assessment of research quality conducted by the Higher Education Funding Council, Cardiff achieved a grade 5 rating, placing it in the top law schools in the country. Cardiff offers opportunities for students to pursue postgraduate study by research leading to the degrees of M.Phil and Ph.D. In addition, taught Masters degrees in the areas of canon, commercial, European legal studies and medical law are offered in full and part-time mode.

## legal practice course and bar vocational course

Within the Law School, the Centre for Professional Legal Studies is validated to offer both the Legal Practice Course and the Bar Vocational Course. Students are taught by experienced solicitors and barristers who have been specifically recruited for this purpose. The Centre prides itself on its friendly and supportive teaching environment and its strong links with the legal profession. Placements with solicitors' firms or sets of Chambers are available to students pursuing the vocational courses, while students studying the Bar Vocational Course additionally enjoy placements with Circuit and District Judges. Cardiff's Legal Practice Course has consistently been rated 'Excellent' by the Law Society; one of the few providers of this course to hold the top ranking.

## facilities

Recent developments within the Law School include extensive IT provision together with dedicated accommodation for the vocational courses which house a practitioner library, courtroom facilities, and fixed and movable audio visual equipment for recording inter-active practitioner skills activities. In addition, the main law library contains one of the largest collections of primary and secondary material within the UK. The Law School is housed in its own building at the heart of the campus, itself located in one of the finest civic centres in Britain and only a short walk from the main shopping area. The University has its own postgraduate centre, together with a full range of sporting and social facilities.

# University of Central England in Birmingham

School of Law, Franchise Street, Perry Barr, Birmingham B42 2SU
Tel: (0121) 331 6600  Fax: (0121) 331 6622

## college profile

UCE School of Law has been a major centre for legal education and training in the city for over 30 years. UCE is committed to providing a service that meets your needs – whether academic, professional or personal. It can be seen in the distinctly informal staff-student relationships, in the extensive support provision and learning facilities that you would expect to find in a large university such as UCE, including a legal practice resource centre, IT workrooms and mock courtroom, and of course in the quality and relevance of its courses.

## postgraduate diploma in legal practice/lpc (full or part-time)

UCE's LPC maintains a generalist approach, reflecting the fact that the majority of students progress to general practice in small and medium sized firms. However, UCE is also committed to making sure that this is not at the cost of those students who aim for commercial practice – UCE offers distinctive electives for this sector including mergers and acquisitions, commercial property and commercial law. UCE aims to develop the problem-solving skills, commercial awareness and self-sufficiency that a trainee solicitor needs. Small class sizes and accessible staff ensure that individual study needs are met and that you receive the support you need to maximize personal development.

## graduate diploma in law/gdl (full or part-time)

The GDL course is designed for non-law graduates wishing to enter the profession as solicitors or barristers. The purpose of the GDL is to provide legal training, which although primarily academic in nature, also reflects the demands that legal practice will place on that academic knowledge. UCE's teaching emphasises participation and student-centred learning. A variety of teaching methods are employed in order to develop the legal skills which form the basis of a successful career in law. An 'open door' policy and a commitment to individual personal development ensures you receive the support needed to maximize your potential.

## pgcert/pgdip/llm corporate and business law (full or part-time)

Explores relevant and topical legal issues relating to the corporate and business world.

## pgdip/llm international human rights (full or part-time)

**USA Pathway:** Explores the conflict between the US Death Penalty and international standards. Students may undertake a semester's internship in the USA.
**European Pathway:** Studies the increasing importance of Human Rights in the UK and European law, including international environmental law and conflict, and refugees.

## pgdip/ma criminal justice policy & practice (full or part-time)

Studies how criminal justice policy is formulated and how criminological theory relates to practice.

**contact**
Apply to:
**full-time GDL and LPC courses**
Central Applictions Board
**part-time GDL and LPC courses**
Direct to university
**other courses**
Direct to university

**contact names**
GDL        Keith Gompertz
LPC        Martyn Packer

**other postgraduate courses**
The Faculty Office

Email: lhds@uce.ac.uk
Website: www.lhds.uce.ac.uk
Website: www.uce.ac.uk

**UCE BIRMINGHAM**
Faculty of Law, Humanities,
Development and Society

# The College of Law

Braboeuf Manor, Portsmouth Road, Guildford GU3 1HA
Freephone: (0800) 328 0153 Fax: (01483) 460460
Email: admissions@lawcol.co.uk
Website: www.college-of-law.co.uk

**contact**
Freephone:
(0800) 328 0153
If calling from overseas:
+44 (0) 1483 460382
Email:
admissions@lawcol.co.uk
Website:
www.college-of-law.co.uk

## college profile

The College of Law is the UK's largest provider of postgraduate legal education, with six centres in five different cities: Birmingham, Chester, Guildford, London (2) and York. They combine an international reputation with long-standing success and educational innovation and offer variety with flexibility, with more course choices in more locations than any other provider.

Training more than 5300 students every year, the College has the depth of resources and flexibility to offer legal education, training and experience tailored to an individual's needs. They also have the largest and best-resourced careers and recruitment service in legal education, with links to hundreds of legal recruiters. Students are provided with practical, relevant and up-to-date support maximising their chances of securing a training contract or pupillage.

## graduate diploma in law (GDL) full-time/part-time/ distance learning

Specifically designed to give you legal expertise that more than matches a law degree. Ensures the development of a thorough understanding of the challenges of practice taught by lawyers with real practice experience.

Study full-time, part-time or by distance learning.

## legal practice course (LPC) full-time/part-time/weekend

Choose from 4 specialist routes - no other provider offers this flexibility. Over 90% of teaching is in small, student-centred workshops.

Study full-time, part-time or by weekend learning.

## bar vocational course (BVC) full-time and weekend* London centre only

Practice-focused course, structured around case-work at the Bar. Benefit from an unrivalled programme of course-related activities, including award-winning pro bono.

Study full-time or by weekend learning.

*subject to Bar Council approval

The College runs open days at all its centres. Visit the website, www.college-of-law.co.uk for details and to book a place.

# Manchester Metropolitan University

School of Law, All Saints West, Lower Ormond Street, Manchester M15 6HB
Tel: (0161) 247 3050   Fax: (0161) 247 6309
Email: law@mmu.ac.uk

**contact**
CPE/GDL: Harriet Roche
LPC: Paul Duffy
BVC: Wanda Clarke

## college profile
The School of Law is one of the largest providers of legal education in the UK, and enjoys an excellent reputation for the quality and range of its courses. It is one of six providers that offer the full range of law courses LLB, GDipL, LPC and BVC. The School's courses are well designed and taught, combining rigorous academic standards with practical application. In September 2003, the School moved into a brand new, state of the art building, in the heart of Manchester.

## bar vocational course (full-time)
This course provides the vocational stage of training for intending practising barristers. However, skills learnt on the course such as advocacy and drafting are transferable to other professions. The BVC is skills based and interactive with particular emphasis on advocacy which is taught in groups of six. The course adopts a syndicate (mini-chambers) approach. Students are allocated to a particular group which has its own base room which contains extensive practitioner legal resources both in hard copy and online form. Each room has the latest in IT and AV equipment. There is also a BVC court room and a separate BVC resource room. Excellent student support is provided including careers advice and an additional professional programme that is designed to bridge the gap between student and professional life. A particular feature of the course is the close links it enjoys with the Northern Circuit whose members are involved in Advocacy Master Classes, the teaching of professional conduct and in a student mentoring scheme.

## legal practice course
## (full-time or part-time: part-time = attendance on Thursdays over two years)
The legal practice course provides the vocational stage of training for those wishing to qualify as a solicitor. Offering a full range of private client and commercial electives, the school aims to cater to students who are looking to practice in specialised areas (eg entertainment law or advanced criminal litigation) as well as students who wish to develop a broad subject base. A mentor scheme operates to put students in touch with local practitioners. Consistently recommended for its state of the art resources, student support and careers guidance and staffed by approachable and knowledgeable teaching staff, the LPC at Manchester Metropolitan University will provide a sound foundation for your legal career.

## graduate diploma in law/cpe
## (full-time or part-time or distance learning)
An increasing number of graduates enter the legal profession this way, with employers attracted by the applicant's maturity and transferable skills. The course places emphasis on the acquisition of legal research and other relevant legal skills. On completion students normally join the School's LPC or BVC Course. This means that if the full-time mode is followed a non-law graduate can become professionally qualified in two years. There is a guaranteed place for CPE students on the school's LPC course.

# Nottingham Law School

Nottingham Law School, Belgrave Centre, Nottingham NG1 5LP
Tel: (0115) 848 6871 Fax: (0115) 848 6878
Email: linda.green2@ntu.ac.uk
Website: www.ntu.ac.uk/nls

**contact**

Nottingham Law School
Belgrave Centre
Nottingham NG1 5LP
Tel: (0115) 848 6871
Fax: (0115) 848 6878
Email:linda.green2@ntu.ac.uk
Website:www.ntu.ac.uk/nls

## bar vocational course

Nottingham Law School has designed its BVC to develop to a high standard a range of core practical skills, and to equip students to succeed in the fast-changing environment of practice at the Bar. Particular emphasis is placed on the skill of advocacy. Advocacy sessions are conducted in groups of six and the School uses the Guildhall courtrooms for most sessions. The BVC is taught entirely by qualified practitioners, and utilises the same integrated and interactive teaching methods as all of the School's other professional courses. Essentially, students learn by doing and Nottingham Law School provides an environment in which students are encouraged to realise, through practice and feedback, their full potential.

## legal practice course

The LPC is offered by full-time and part-time block study. This course has been designed to be challenging and stimulating for students and responsive to the needs of firms, varying from large commercial to smaller high street practices, and it still carries the endorsement of a large cross section of firms from major corporate through to high street.

Nottingham Law School's LPC features: integration of the transactions and skills, so that each advances the other, whilst ensuring the transferability of skills between different subject areas. Carefully structured interactive group work which develops an ability to handle skills and legal transactions effectively, and in an integrated way. A rigorous assessment process that nevertheless avoids 'assessment overload', to maintain a teaching and learning emphasis to the course. A professionally qualified team, retaining substantial links with practice. An excellent rating from The Law Society's Assessment Panel in every year of its operation.

## the graduate diploma in law (full-time)

The Nottingham Law School GDL is a one year conversion course designed for any non-law graduate who intends to become a solicitor or barrister in the UK. The intensive course effectively covers the seven core subjects of an undergraduate law degree in one go. It is the stepping stone to the LPC or the BVC, and a legal career thereafter. It is a graduate Diploma (Dip Law) in its own right and operates on a similar basis to the LPC (see above), though inevitably it has a more academic basis.

NOTTINGHAM
LAW SCHOOL

# University of Wolverhampton

School of Legal Studies, Molineux Street, Wolverhampton WV1 1SB
Tel: (01902) 321000  Fax: (01902) 321570

**contact**
Ms Loraine Houlton
Head of Corporate &
Professional Division
Tel: (01902) 321999
Fax: (01902) 321567

## college profile

Based in Wolverhampton and offers courses for students intending to follow a variety of careers within the legal profession. The law school has been offering these courses for over 20 years. Its LPC programme has had consistently good ratings. The lecturers are drawn from experienced solicitors, barristers, academics and individuals from business and industry. There are excellent IT facilities, a well-stocked library, bookshop and a sports centre. The School also offers an LLM in International Corporate and Financial Law, which draws together a number of legal issues with an international dimension such as the regulation of financial services and financial crime. It also deals with matters such as international banking law and international corporate finance. The School also offers an MA in Practice Management, a course developed in connection with the management section of the Law Society. It is taught on a flexible, part-time, block-delivery basis and is designed to provide an outlet to complex managerial and organisational issues facing practice managers.

## legal practice course (full/part-time)

The vocational training course for those intending to practise as solicitors, the University's LPC offers a sound basis for a professional career. The core subjects of Business, Litigation and Conveyancing are taught, together with a range of commercial and private client options. Professional skills courses, practical workshops and seminars are all part of the training. Additional benefits include close links with local practitioners, mentoring, CV distribution and group social activities. The Legal Practice Course is housed in modern purpose-built dedicated accommodation which includes LPC Resources room and video suites. The course is taught by experienced professionally-qualified staff with close links with the local profession. It has active personal tutor support, in-house and guest practitioners, a Practitioner Liaison Committee and a careers tutor.

## common professional examination (full/part-time)

The academic stage of training for non-law graduates wishing to become solicitors or barristers. A full programme of lectures and tutorials is offered on this demanding course. Students are taught by experienced practitioners. Places on the LPC are guaranteed for successful students. New flexible studying choices are under discussion. Teaching methods on the CPE are varied and include lectures, group-led discussion and debate, workshops, oral presentations and independent research. The course includes an intensive induction programme involving use of library, methodology and an introduction to IT. The course as a whole is designed to provide the essential skills necessary for a successful career in law.

UNIVERSITY OF
WOLVERHAMPTON
The real choice

# solicitors

# solicitors timetable

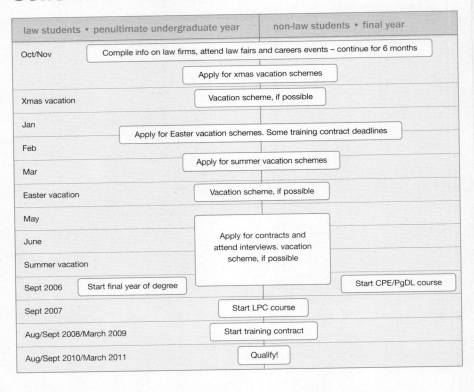

| law students • penultimate undergraduate year | non-law students • final year |
|---|---|
| **Oct/Nov** | Compile info on law firms, attend law fairs and careers events – continue for 6 months |
| | Apply for xmas vacation schemes |
| **Xmas vacation** | Vacation scheme, if possible |
| **Jan** | Apply for Easter vacation schemes. Some training contract deadlines |
| **Feb** | |
| **Mar** | Apply for summer vacation schemes |
| **Easter vacation** | Vacation scheme, if possible |
| **May** | |
| **June** | Apply for contracts and attend interviews. vacation scheme, if possible |
| **Summer vacation** | |
| **Sept 2006** | Start final year of degree          Start CPE/PgDL course |
| **Sept 2007** | Start LPC course |
| **Aug/Sept 2008/March 2009** | Start training contract |
| **Aug/Sept 2010/March 2011** | Qualify! |

*Notes*

*1   It is important to check application closing dates for each firm as these will vary.*

*2   Some firms will only accept applications for vacation schemes from penultimate year students whether law or non-law. See A-Z pages for further information.*

*3   Some firms require very early applications from non-law graduates. See A-Z pages for further information.*

*4   The timetable refers primarily to those firms that recruit two years in advance. Smaller firms often recruit just one year in advance or for immediate vacancies.*

# vacation schemes

Vacation schemes provide a valuable insight into life as a solicitor and can be an important first step to gaining a training contract. If you spend your time wisely, you can discover a lot about a firm's character. Of course you might also discover that you don't want to be a solicitor after all, in which case you're going to save yourself a good deal of time and money.

According to Tom Purton, recruitment partner at Travers Smith: *"Vacation schemes are important for both students and the firm. In essence they greatly reduce the risk of recruitment going wrong on both sides."* Some firms place great weight on their schemes, viewing them as integral to the recruitment process. Don't overestimate their importance though – having a couple of placements under your belt doesn't miraculously transform you into a better candidate. As Tom says: *"If a person has done a vacation scheme it demonstrates their commitment to obtaining a training contract, but is only one of the factors that we consider when making an offer."*

Although some firms offer more vac scheme places than training contracts, they are still hard to get because of the huge number of applicants, and it's a sad fact that spaces are often filled by students doing multiple schemes. The key to success is to take the application process seriously – the firms certainly do. It's also worth taking your time to research the firms you want to apply to, and if you do want to go on more than one scheme, consider applying to different styles of firm to see where you feel most at home.

So you've got a place! Well done, but don't raise your expectations too high concerning the work you'll be doing. Firms will not expect you to spot a hole in their precedent documents or wow their biggest client. What they are looking for are keen, attentive, polite and punctual students, who *"grab every opportunity that is presented to them."* If there is a cricket match after work, ask if you can go along (who knows, they might need you to play). If you are put on the firm's intranet, resist the temptation to e-mail your mates and do not indulge in sending around funnies, even if other members of staff do. In a less formal scheme, if you are introduced to people in the department and you have spare capacity, there's nothing to stop you making an offer of help, but if you have a minder, always check with them first as there may be a full programme of events and jobs to keep you busy. Get to know the trainees and ask them questions about what they like about the firm. This will be useful for you and will show them that you're interested.

Always take a written note when someone asks you to do a job. If necessary, recap what they've asked of you and clarify whether they envisaged a timescale or if they have a deadline. Keep a notebook with you and list the tasks you have been given, by whom, and when they need to be done by. If someone then asks you to do something else, you'll have a better idea of your capacity and priorities. Finally, if there's anyone who seems important and with whom you've had dealings, do remember to say goodbye and thank them for any help they've given you.

The experience is as much about your personality as your work, so make sure you speak to as many people as possible. Tom advises: *"Enjoy yourself, but also take it seriously. Although firms are looking for characters rather than drones, there is a balance to be struck."* Blinded by a hectic schedule of social events and copious quantities of alcohol, students have been known to return to the office drunk, fall asleep in the library or even give up and go shopping for the day. And although the trainees might be a lot of fun, they're probably keeping an eye on you, and will report back if you criticise the partners or fail to suppress your raging hormones on the big night out. There's always one.

If you don't get on a scheme, it's not the end of the world. Most firms state that they will consider candidates for training contracts, even if they didn't get on their vac scheme. Firms also run open days, which can be almost as useful for getting a feel for the firm and speaking to trainees. Remember, too, that other work experience will set you out from the crowd just as effectively – helping a high street solicitor, a summer job in an office environment or voluntary work with a charity.

# solicitors

## vacation schemes

| firm name | number of places | duration | remuneration | deadline |
|---|---|---|---|---|
| Addleshaw Goddard | 75 | 2 weeks | Not known | 10 February 2006 |
| Allen & Overy | 95 | 10 days or 3 weeks | £250 p.w. | 31 January 2006 |
| Ashurst | Easter (grads & final year non-law); summer (penult year law) | Easter: 2 weeks summer: 3 weeks | £250 p.w. | 31 January 2006 |
| Baker & McKenzie | London: 30 international: 3-5* | 3 weeks/*6-12 weeks in Lon/o'seas office | £270 p.w. | 31 January 2006 |
| Barlow Lyde & Gilbert | Yes, plus open days and drop in days | Not known | Not known | 31 January 2006 |
| Beachcroft Wansbroughs | Yes | Not known | Not known | 1 May 2006 |
| Berwin Leighton Paisner | 50 | 2 weeks | Not known | 28 February 2006 |
| Bevan Brittan | 60 | Not known | Not known | 31 March 2006 |
| Bird & Bird | 20 | 3 weeks | £240 p.w. | 31 January 2006 |
| Boodle Hatfield | 10 | 2 weeks | Not known | 1 January 2006 |
| Bristows | Yes | Christmas/Easter: 1 week summer: 2 weeks | £200 p.w. | Christmas: 26 Nov 05; Easter/summer: 28 Feb 06 |
| Burges Salmon | 40 | 2 weeks | £200 p.w. | Not known |
| Capsticks | Yes | 2 weeks | Not known | 28th February 2006 |
| Cleary Gottlieb Stein & Hamilton | Yes | Easter: 2 weeks summer: 3 weeks | Not known | 14th February 2006 |
| Clifford Chance | Christmas, Easter and summer (some overseas) | 2-4 weeks | £270 p.w. | Christmas: 18 Nov 2005 Easter/summer: 31 Jan 2006 |
| Clyde & Co | 15 | 2 weeks | Not known | 31 January 2006 |
| CMS Cameron McKenna | 55 | 2 weeks | £225 p.w. | Not known |
| Coffin Mew & Clover | Open week in July | Not known | Not known | 31 January 2006 |
| Covington & Burling | 16 | Not known | Not known | 28 February 2006 |
| Davenport Lyons | 12 | 2 weeks | £175 p.w. | January 2006 |
| Dechert | Up to 16, plus 20-30 assessment days in April and October | 2 weeks | min. £225 p.w. | Vac scheme: 28 February 2005 |
| Denton Wilde Sapte | Yes, plus open days | Not known | Not known | (OD: 25 nov. 2005) 10 February 2006 |
| Dickinson Dees | 40 | 1 week | £125 p.w. | Easter: 31 Dec 05 summer: 28 February 06 |
| DLA Piper Rudnick Gray Cary | 200 | 2 weeks | £210 p.w (Lon) £170 p.w (Ors) | 31 January 2006 |
| DMH Stallard | Yes | 1 week | Unpaid | 31 January 2006 |

# solicitors

## vacation schemes

| firm name | number of places | duration | remuneration | deadline |
|-----------|-----------------|----------|--------------|----------|
| Eversheds | 250 | 2 weeks summer, 1 week Easter | regional variations | 31 January 2006 |
| Farrer & Co | 30: Easter and summer | 2 weeks | £240 p.w. | 31 January 2006 |
| Field Fisher Waterhouse | Yes | Not known | Not known | 31 January 2006 |
| Foot Anstey | Yes | Not known | Not known | 31 March 2006 |
| Freshfields Bruckhaus Deringer | 125 | 2 weeks | £550 total | 31 January 2006 (apply asap after 1 december 2005) |
| Gateley Wareing | Yes | 1 week | Not known | 11 February 2006 |
| Government Legal Service | 60 | 2-3 weeks | £200-250pw | 31 March 2006 |
| Halliwells | 60 | 2 weeks | £150 p.w. | 31 March 2006 |
| Hammonds | 64 | 2 weeks | £230 p.w. (Lon) £180 p.w. (Ors) | 31 January 2006 |
| Herbert Smith | 115 (Christmas: non-law; Easter/summer: law and non-law) some o/seas | Not known | Not known | Christmas: 11 Nov 05 Easter/summer: 31 Jan 06 |
| Hewitsons | Yes | 1 week | Not known | Not known |
| Hill Dickinson | Yes | 1 week | Not known | 30th April 2006 |
| Holman Fenwick & Willan | Yes | 2 weeks | £250 p.w. | 1 January to 14 February 2006 |
| Howes Percival | Yes | Not known | Not known | 30 April 2006 |
| Hugh James | Yes | Not known | Not known | Not known |
| Ince & Co | 15 | 2 weeks | £250 p.w. | 14 February 2006 |
| Irwin Mitchell | Yes | Not known | Not known | Not known |
| Jones Day | 20 at Christmas: non-law 10 at Easter: non-law 40 in summer: law | 2 weeks | £300 p.w. | Christmas: 31 Oct 05 Easter/summer: 14 Feb 06 |
| Kendall Freeman | Yes | Not known | Not known | 28 February 2006 |
| Kirkpatrick & Lockhart Nicholson Graham | Yes | Not known | Not known | 15 February 2006 |
| Lawrence Graham | 32 in Easter & summer | 2 weeks | £220 p.w. | 31 January 2006 |
| Laytons | 6 | 1 week | Not known | 31 March 2006 |
| Lester Aldridge | 8 | 2 weeks | £75 p.w. | 31 March 2006 |

## vacation schemes

| firm name | number of places | duration | remuneration | deadline |
|---|---|---|---|---|
| Lewis Silkin | 16 | 1 or 2 weeks | Not known | 31 January 2006 |
| Linklaters | 30 in Christmas (non-law), 60 in summer (law), some o/seas | Not known | £275 p.w. | Not known |
| Lovells | 90 Christmas, Easter and summer | Not known | Not known | Christmas: 11 Nov 05 Easter/summer: 10 Feb 06 |
| Macfarlanes | 36 | 2 weeks | £250 p.w. | 28 February 2006 |
| Manches | 24 | 1 week | £200 | 31 January 2006 |
| Mayer, Brown, Rowe & Maw | 32 Easter and summer | 2 weeks | Not known | Not known |
| McCormicks | Yes | Not known | Not known | 24 February 2006 |
| Mills & Reeve | Yes | 2 weeks | Not known | 1 March 2006 |
| Mishcon de Reya | 12 | 2 weeks | £200 p.w. | 15 March 2006 |
| Morgan Cole | 6 open days | n/a | n/a | 31 March 2006 |
| Nabarro Nathanson | 60 | 3 weeks | Not known | 10 February 2006 |
| Norton Rose | 15 in Christmas 45 in summer | 2 weeks | £250 p.w. | 31 October 2005 31 January 2006 |
| Olswang | Yes | 2 weeks | £250 p.w. | 31 January 2006 |
| Osborne Clarke | 20 Easter and summer | 1 week | £175-200 p.w. | 31 January 2006 |
| Pannone & Partners | 50 Easter and summer | 1 week | none | Easter: 27 Jan 06 summer: 29 April 06 |
| Penningtons | open day places + vac scheme | Not known | Not known | 31 March 2006 |
| Pinsent Masons | 120 | 2 weeks | Not known | 31 January 2006 |
| Reed Smith | 12 | 3 weeks (Lon) 2 weeks (Mids) | £600 (Lon) £300 (Mids) | 31 January 2006 |
| Reynolds Porter Chamberlain | 18 | 2 weeks | £250 p.w. | 28 February 2006 |
| Richards Butler | 30 in London plus overseas placements | 2 weeks | £220 p.w. | 31 January 2006 |

## vacation schemes

| firm name | number of places | duration | remuneration | deadline |
|---|---|---|---|---|
| Shadbolt & Co | 6 | 2 weeks | £188 p.w. | 28 February 2006 |
| Shoosmiths | 30 | 2 weeks | £230 p.w. | 28 February 2006 |
| Simmons & Simmons | Not known | Not known | Not known | 31 January 2006 |
| SJ Berwin | 60 | 2 weeks | £225 p.w. | 31 January 2006 |
| Slaughter and May | 60 (penult. year of degree) | 2 weeks | £275 p.w. | 27 January 2006 |
| Speechly Bircham | 12 | 3 weeks | £250 p.w. | 14 February 2006 |
| Stephenson Harwood | 18 | 2 weeks | £250 p.w. | 18 February 2006 |
| Taylor Walton | 8 | up to 3 weeks | £176 p.w. | 30 March 2006 |
| Taylor Wessing | 30 | 2 weeks | £225 p.w. | 10 February 2006 |
| Teacher Stern Selby | 20 | Not known | Not known | Not known |
| Thomas Eggar | Yes | 1 week | travel expenses | 31 March 2006 |
| TLT Solicitors | 12 | 1 week | Not known | 31 March 2006 |
| Travers Smith | 45 +15 Christmas places | 2 weeks | £250 | 31 January 2006 |
| Trowers & Hamlins | 25-30 plus open days | 2 weeks | £225 p.w. | 1 March 2006 |
| Walker Morris | 45 | 1 week | £170 p.w. | 26 February 2006 |
| Ward Hadaway | Yes | 1 week | Not known | 28 February 2006 |
| Watson, Farley& Williams | 30 | 2 weeks | £200 p.w. | 24 February 2006 |
| Wedlake Bell | 6 | 3 weeks | £200 pw | 28 February 2006 |
| Weil, Gotshal & Manges | 12 | Not known | Not known | 14 February 2006 |
| White & Case | 40-50 | 2 weeks | £300 p.w. | 31 January 2006 |
| Withers | 6 in Easter and 24 in summer + Milan opportunities | 2 weeks | Not known | 31 January 2006 |
| Wragge & Co | Easter and summer | Not known | Not known | 31 January 2006 |

# applications and selection

The race to find a training contract attracts an increasingly crowded field of candidates and, consequently, law firms can be ever more selective about who they invite to join their stable. The following guide to the applications procedure has been compiled by a panel of expert tipsters.

## studying the form

Your first step is to find out which firms you want to apply to, and why. Consider which practice areas you might find interesting and work out who does them well. The **Solicitors Practice Areas** section summarises some of the main types of work and includes ranking tables showing the best firms. For more information on these runners and riders, or to learn about more specialist areas, consult our parent publication *Chambers UK*, which is available online or in your university or law school careers office. You should also consult law firms' own websites and any promotional material they produce. Because each firm is different in size, practice orientation and culture, you'll probably find reading the *True Picture* section of this guide helpful in deciding which ones appeal. Once you've made your choices (we cannot tell you how many to make), consider how your skills, qualifications and interests are relevant to these firms.

Remember, most commercial firms recruit two years in advance of the start of the training contract. Miss the starting gun and you'll probably have to wait another year to join the race. If they want to go straight from their LPC to their training contract with no time out, law students should apply before or during the summer vacation between the second and third years of their degree, and non-law degree candidates before starting their CPE. However, be aware that a few of the big City firms have early application deadlines – some even earlier than the spring of the year in which the CPE course starts. Smaller firms recruit one year in advance or even closer to the start of the contract; some will test ride applicants by offering paralegal work to see how they perform, only then allowing the prospect of a training contract to be discussed.

As a rule, it's far better to make fewer, targeted applications and to tailor them to individual firms than to send off hundreds of one-size-fits-all covering letters and CVs. Recruiters can always spot blanket applications, and rather than hedging your bets, this tactic could turn you into a non-runner. Here are a few basic tips:

* Don't put anything in your CV unless you can expand on it at interview. Your professed passion for sailing will ring hollow if you can't tell your aft from your anchor.
* Avoid chronological gaps in your experience. If you've taken time off, put it down and be prepared to explain why.
* Your CV gives you an opportunity to make your achievements shine, so keep it to two or three pages max and make the most of your strengths by effective use of headings or bold text.
* Don't make your application gimmicky - photos, bizarre fonts and lurid colours should be avoided. One recruiter recalled the time when one bright spark sent a piece of fruit with their application, accompanied by a note instructing them not to be a lemon and to pick her for a training contract. Of course, it didn't work.

Unless stated otherwise, CVs should be accompanied by a covering letter. This gives you a chance to expand on why you want to work for that particular firm, and maybe what you usefully learned from that expedition to Borneo. The letter should convey why you and the firm are a good fit, and give the reader a more personal insight into your qualities. Keep it to one page in length. Recruiters won't be impressed by waffle or padding, and certainly don't want to read a treatise on how amazing their firm is. Finally, make sure that someone checks it over for you – one of the major reasons for rejecting applicants is that they haven't managed to spell the name of the firm correctly, or even their own in some cases.

If the firm doesn't ask for a CV, it will require you to complete a dreaded application form. These forms can take a surprising amount of time to fill in, so get started early. Most firms adhere to strict deadlines, and we've heard stories about candidates sending off electronic applications at two minutes past midnight and being told that they cannot be accepted. If the form is to be hand-written, take a photocopy and practise writing on that first. A form covered in Tipp-ex and three different colours of ink will get attention for all the wrong reasons. Also, make sure you don't leave gaps: if you are struggling to complete a box, write slightly bigger to make sure there are no glaring empty spaces. Plan what you want to say in each section and make sure the form covers your whole range of skills and attributes. Read each question carefully to work out what the firm is really asking. Unless you do there's a danger you'll only give half an answer. Again, unless asked not to, you can include a short covering letter to highlight the best aspects of your application, include experiences you couldn't fit in and confirm your dedication to the cause. Finally, make sure you keep a copy of the form to read over should you be invited for interview.

## getting ahead of the field

Almost all firms now demand a uniformly high level of academic achievement – a minimum 2:1 degree and excellent A-levels. As always, some thoroughbred applicants will gallop away with a host of offers, but for the rest, a little attention to what firms are looking for could save a trip to the knacker's yard. According to Sally Carthy from DLA Piper: "*Academics are only a starting point. You have to be able to market yourself better than your contemporaries. Applicants should be able to demonstrate a broad range of interests, show commitment to the profession, and have done their research on the firm.*" Look at what else

you can do to demonstrate your teamwork and problem-solving skills, as well as your business acumen. If you can get work experience or a vacation scheme place this will really help you understand the reality of practice. And if you can't, try and speak to lawyers at every opportunity. Ask family and friends if they know someone you can chat to, or perhaps there is someone at university or law school who can give you advice or contacts.

When it comes to interviews, anyone can get nervous or flustered, but effective preparation should boost your confidence and give your performance added credibility. As Sally Carthy says: "*Interviews are an oral examination. If you don't prepare for an examination, you prepare to fail.*" First things first, it always pays to be up to date with news and current affairs by reading both mainstream quality newspapers and the legal press. For the latter, try Tuesday's law supplement in *The Times* as well as *The Lawyer* or *Legal Week* and The Law Society's *Gazette*. These mags are all online. According to Sally, it's not so much about the opinions you form on various topics, but "*how you stand by your convictions and put forward a reasoned response.*"

Make sure you have studied the firm's own literature just prior to interview. If you know which partner will be interviewing you, find out as much as you can about him or her from the firm's website, or they may even be profiled in *Chambers UK*.

Think about how you would answer the most obvious questions. Amazing as it may seem, we are regularly told that candidates seem incapable of explaining why they want to be a lawyer.

Some firms use reasoning tests, and although it's not possible to prepare for these as such, your careers service may well have something similar so that you can get an idea of what sort of questions might be posed. And don't forget to ask around; friends of friends may have attended the same firm's assessment day just a week before, and may be willing to pass on a few tips.

## race day

When the big day comes, aim to turn up an hour early and find a café somewhere nearby to sit down and have a cup of tea. Then you can have a last look through a copy of the application you sent and any crib notes you've made. If you're rushing to make it on time, you won't be thinking clearly. Worse still, you might get sweaty. If you are travelling a long way, make sure that you take the firm's number with you in case you are delayed. Both partners and HR people are very busy and will not appreciate being kept waiting, especially without warning. Whilst waiting in reception for your interview, make sure that you are polite to everyone you meet. Recruiters will quickly find out if you've been rude or arrogant to receptionists or secretaries.

If more than one person interviews you, try to speak to everyone on the panel. Listen carefully and think clearly before answering questions. Sally Brewis from Dickinson Dees has a word of advice: "*Don't try to dodge a question as experienced interviewers will always come back to it. Hardly surprisingly; lawyers are quite good at doing that.*" Keep an eye on your body language, don't fidget and maintain eye contact as far as possible without scaring anyone. V. important: prepare a couple of sensible questions for the end of the interview, but make sure you couldn't easily have found the answers on the firm's website.

## falling at the first fence

Do try to dress appropriately. Jeans and trainers, however smart, won't convey the right impression, nor will anything too racy or alternative. Whether you see yourself as a suit person or not, you should probably wear one (or something equally formal if you're female).

Even strong candidates can ruin their chances by trying too hard to impress. Sally Carthy advises people to "*remember that the legal profession is a conservative one, and so your style should be in keeping with that.*" It's probably best to avoid making too many wise cracks because even the most amiable partners won't appreciate you horsing around.

## reaching the winner's enclosure

It's now relatively rare to be offered a training contract after one simple interview. These days, many firms employ a variety of psychometric tests, group exercises and case studies to weed out the also-rans. Non-law students can take comfort from the fact that these exercises and tests are designed to be completed by those without prior legal training. When embarking on a group exercise, remember that the aim is to determine how well you work in a team rather than how quickly you start jockeying for position. Listening to others in the group does not simply mean being quiet when they're talking: pick up on what they have said and make your own comments on their suggestions. According to Sally Brewis: "*Firms are not necessarily looking for the person who shouts the loudest, but the one who is making the most sense. It's good to show that you can organise people, but make sure that you're not leading them down the wrong path.*" If there is a social event at lunchtime or at the end of the day, remember that you are still being watched. Even the friendly trainee who adopts you as you hide by the buffet table may comment on your performance once you've gone home.

You have been invited to meet recruiters because they are genuinely interested in you. As Sally Brewis says: "*Interviewers usually want to give you the best opportunity to shine, not trip you up.*" Finally, don't forget that an interview or assessment day is a two-way thing. Make sure you take the opportunity to find out more about the place – for example, what the atmosphere is like, which departments are popular to train in, and what kind of client contact trainees have. Remind yourself that you're on a fact-finding mission as you walk through the door of the office. This thought should help you keep things in perspective.

# solicitors

## applications and selection

| firm name | method of application | selection process | degree class | number of contracts | number of applications |
|---|---|---|---|---|---|
| Addleshaw Goddard | See website | Interview + assessment centre | 2:1 | 50 | 2,000 |
| Allen & Overy | Online | Interview | 2:1 | 120 | 2,700 |
| asb law | See website | Interviews + assessments | 2:1 | 5 | 500 |
| Ashurst | Online | Interviews | 2:1 | 45-50 | 2,500 |
| B P Collins | Handwritten letter & CV | Interview + selection day | 2:1 | Not known | Not known |
| Baker & McKenzie | Online | Oral presentation+ interview | 2:1 | 30 | 2,000 |
| Barlow Lyde & Gilbert | Online | Interview day | Not known | 16-18 | 2,000 |
| Beachcroft Wansbroughs | Online | Interview + assessment | 2:1 preferred | 30+ | Not known |
| Berwin Leighton Paisner | Online | Assessment day + interview | 2:1 | 35 | 2,000 |
| Bevan Brittan | Online | Not known | Not known | Not known | Not known |
| Bircham Dyson Bell | CV + covering letter | Interviews | 2:1 preferred | 8 | 450 |
| Bird & Bird | Online | Assessment morning | 2:1 | 14 | 850 |
| Boodle Hatfield | Online | Interviews + assessment | 2:1 | 6-8 | Not known |
| Brabners Chaffe Street | Application form | Interview + assessment day | 2:1/post-grad | 7 | Not known |
| Brachers | Online | Interviews | 2:1 | 6 | 400 |
| Bristows | Application form | Interviews | 2.1 preferred | up to 10 | 3,500 |
| Browne Jacobson | Online | Assessment centre | 2:1 | 10 | 800 |
| Burges Salmon | Application form | Not known | 2:1 | 20-25 | 1,500 |
| Capsticks | Application form | Summer placement then interview | 2:1 or above | 4-5 | 150 |
| Charles Russell | Online | Assessment day | 2:1 | 16 | 2,000 |

# solicitors

## applications and selection

| firm Name | method of application | selection Process | degree class | number of contracts | number of applications |
|---|---|---|---|---|---|
| Cleary Gottlieb Steen & Hamilton | cover letter & CV | Interviews | 2:1 | 5 | 2,250 |
| Clifford Chance | Online | Assessment day | 2:1 | 120 | 2,000 |
| Clyde & Co | Online | Interview + assessments | 2:1 | 20 | 1,200+ |
| CMS Cameron McKenna | Online | Interview + assessment centre | 2:1 | 60 | 1,500 |
| Cobbetts | Online | Assessment day | 2:1 | 25-30 | 1,000 |
| Coffin Mew & Clover | CV & covering letter | Interview | 2:1 (usually) | 5 | 400+ |
| Covington & Burling | See website | 2 interviews | 2:1 | 4 | Not known |
| Cripps Harries Hall | Application form | Interview | 2.1 | 7 | 750 |
| Davenport Lyons | CV & covering letter | Interviews | 2:1 | 6 | 2,000 |
| Davies Arnold Cooper | Application form | Not known | 2:1 (usually) | 5 | Not known |
| Dechert | Online | Interview + assessments | 2:1 | 12-15 | Approx 1,500 |
| Denton Wilde Sapte | Application form | Interview + assessments | 2:1 | 30 | 1,500 |
| Devonshires | Online | Not known | 2:1 and higher | 5 | 500 |
| Dickinson Dees | Online | Interview + assessment | 2:1 | 12 – 15 | 800 |
| DLA Piper Rudnick Gray Cary | Online | Interviews + assessments | 2:1 | 85+ | 2,500 |
| DMH Stallard | Application form | Interviews, assessments + work placement | 2:1 | 6-7 | 115 |
| Dorsey & Whitney | letter & CV | Not known | 2:1 | 4 | Not known |
| DWF | Online | Interviews | 2:1 | 8 | 500 |
| Eversheds | Online | Selection day + interview | 2:1 | 80 | 4,000 |
| Farrer & Co | Online | Interviews | 2:1 | 8-10 | 800 |
| Field Fisher Water-house | Online | Interviews + assessments | 2:1 | 17 | 1,200 |
| Finers Stephens Innocent | Online | Interviews | 2:1 | 5 | 800 |
| Fladgate Fielder | Application form | Assessment day + interview | 2:1 | 3 | Not known |

# solicitors

| firm name | method of application | selection process | degree class | number of contracts | number of applications |
|---|---|---|---|---|---|
| Foot Anstey | Letter & CV or online form | Assessment day | 2:1 preferred | 12 | Not known |
| Forbes | Handwritten letter & CV | Interview | 2:1 | 4 | 350+ |
| Ford & Warren | Handwritten letter & CV | Interviews + exercise | 2:1 | 6 | 700 |
| Forsters | Application form | Interviews | Not known | Not known | Not known |
| Freeth Cartwright | Online | Interview + selection day | Not known | Not known | Not known |
| Freshfields Bruckhaus Deringer | Online | Interviews + written test | 2:1 | 100 | c.2,500 |
| Government Legal Service | Online | Assessment day | 2:2 | 22-30 | 1,200+ |
| Gateley Wareing | See website | Not known | 2:1 | Not known | Not known |
| Halliwells | Online | Interview + assessments | 2:1 | 31 | 1,500 |
| Hammonds | Online | Assessment + interview | 2:1 | 40 | 1,200 |
| Harbottle & Lewis | CV & letter | Interview | 2:1 | 4 | 800 |
| Henmans | Application form | Interview | Not known | 3 | 450 |
| Herbert Smith | Online | case study + interview | 2:1 | 100 | 2,000 |
| Hewitsons | Application form | Interview | 2:1 | 10 | 850 |
| Hill Dickinson | CV & letter online | Assessment day | Not known | Not known | Not known |
| Hodge Jones & Allen | Application form | Interview | 2:1 | 6-7 | 500 |
| Holman Fenwick & Willan | Online | Interviews + written exercise | 2:1 | 8 | 1,000 |
| Howes Percival | Online | assess. centre + interview | 2:1 | 8 | 300 |
| Hugh James | Application form | Interview + presentation | 2:1 (usually) | 8 | 500 |
| Ince & Co | letter & CV | Interviews + written test | 2:1 | 8-10 | 1,500 |
| Irwin Mitchell | Application form & covering letter | Assessment centre + interview | None specified | 20-25 | 1,200 |
| Jones Day | CV & letter | Interviews | 2:1 | 15-20 | 1,500 |
| Kendall Freeman | Online | Interviews | 2:1 | 8 | Not known |
| Kirkpatrick & Lockhart Nicholson Graham | Online | Interview + assessment | 2:1 | 20 | 800 |

# solicitors

## applications and selection

| firm name | method of application | selection process | degree class | number of contracts | number of applications |
|---|---|---|---|---|---|
| Lawrence Graham | Application form | Interview | 2:1 | 24 | 800 |
| Laytons | Application form | Interviews | 1 or 2:1 | 8 | 2,000 |
| LeBoeuf, Lamb, Greene & MacRae | CV & covering letter | 2 interviews | 2:1 | 6 | 700 |
| Lester Aldridge | Letter, CV & application form | Interview | 2:1 | 10 | 300 |
| Lewis Silkin | Application form | Assessment day | 2:1 | 5 | 800 |
| Linklaters | Application form | 2 interviews + case study | 2:1 | 130 | 4,000 |
| Lovells | Online | Assessment day | 2:1 | 90 | 2,500 |
| Lupton Fawcett | Application form & handwritten letter | Interview + assessment day | 2:1 preferred | 2-3 | 300 |
| Mace & Jones | Online | Interview | 2:1 | Varies | 1,500 |
| Macfarlanes | Online application | Assessment day | 2:1 | 25 | 1,000 |
| Manches | Application form | Interviews | 2:1 | 10 | 860 |
| Martineau Johnson | Online | Half-day assessment centre | 2:1 | 10-12 | 500 |
| Mayer, Brown, Rowe & Maw | Online | Interview + assessments | 2:1 | 25-30 | 720 |
| McCormicks | Application form | Interview + assessments | 2:1 | 4 | 500 |
| McDermott, Will & Emery | CV & covering letter | Not known | Not known | Not known | Not known |
| McGrigors | Online | Assessment day | 2:1 | 10-15 | Not known |
| Mills & Reeve | Application form | one-day assessment centre | 2:1 | 20 | Approx 600 |
| Mishcon de Reya | Application form | Not known | 2:1 | 6 | 900+ |
| Morgan Cole | Online | Assessment centre + interview | 2:1 preferred | Not known | Not known |
| Nabarro Nathanson | Online | Interview + assessment day | 2:1 | 25 | 1,500 |
| Norton Rose | Online Application form | Interview + group exercise | 2:1 | 60 | 3,000+ |

# solicitors

| firm name | method of application | selection process | degree class | number of contracts | number of applications |
|---|---|---|---|---|---|
| Olswang | Online | Interview + assessments | 2:1 | 20 | 2,000 |
| Orrick, Herrington & Sutcliffe | Letter & CV | Interviews | 2:1 | 6 | Not known |
| Osborne Clarke | Online | Assessment day | 2:1 | 20 | 1,000-1,500 |
| Pannone & Partners | Online | Interviews | 2:1 | 14 | 1,200 |
| Payne Hicks Beach | Letter & CV | Interview | 2:1 | 3 | 1,000 |
| Penningtons | Online | Not known | 2:1 | 12 | 1,000 |
| Pinsent Masons | Online | Assessment day + interview | 2:1 | 55 | 2,000+ |
| Prettys | Letter & CV | Not known | 2:1 preferred | 5 | Not known |
| Pritchard Englefield | Application form | Interview | generally 2:1 | 3 | 300-400 |
| Reed Smith | Online | Assessment day | 2:1 | 8 | 700 |
| Reynolds Porter Chamberlain | Online | Assessment day | 2.1 | 15 | 900 |
| Richards Butler | Online | Assessment + interview | 2:1 | 20 | 2,000 |
| Salans | handwritten letter & CV | Interviews + workshop | 2:1 | 3-4 | 500+ |
| Shadbolt & Co | Online | Interview + assessment | Usually 2:1 | 4 | 100 |
| Shearman & Sterling | Application form | Interviews | 2:1 | 15 | Not known |
| Shoosmiths | Application form | Full-day selection centre | 2:1 | 14 | 1,000 |
| Sidley Austin Brown & Wood | covering letter & application form | Interview(s) | 2:1 | 6-8 | 500 |
| Simmons & Simmons | Online | Assessment day | 2:1 | 50 | 2,500 |
| SJ Berwin | Online | 2 interviews | 2:1 | 38 | 2,000 |
| Slaughter and May | covering letter + CV or online | Interview | 2:1 | 85 | 2,500+ |
| Speechly Bircham | Application form | Interview | 2:1 | 6 | 500 |
| Stephenson Harwood | Online | Assessment centre | 2:1 | 12 | Not known |

# solicitors

| firm name | method of application | selection process | degree class | number of contracts | number of applications |
|---|---|---|---|---|---|
| Stevens & Bolton | Letter & application form | Interviews | 2:1 | 3 | 250 |
| Tarlo Lyons | Application form | Interviews | 2:1 | 3 | 200 |
| Taylor Walton | CV & covering letter | Interviews | 2:1 or above | Not known | Not known |
| Taylor Wessing | Online | 2 interviews | 2:1 | 20 | 1,150 |
| Teacher Stern Selby | Letter & application form | 2 interviews | 2:1 (not absolute) | 3-6 | 1,000 |
| Thomas Eggar | Letter & CV | Assessment centre + interview | 2:1 | Not known | Not known |
| Thomson Snell & Passmore | Letter & application form | Assessment Interview | 2:1 | 4 | approx 500 |
| TLT Solicitors | Application form | Assessment centre | 2:1 preferred | 8 | 500+ |
| Travers Smith | CV and covering letter | Interviews | 2:1 | up to 25 | 2,000 |
| Trowers & Hamlins | letter, application form & CV | Interview(s), essay + practical test | 2:1+ | 18 | 1,600 |
| Walker Morris | Application form | Interviews | 2:1 | 15 | approx 800 |
| Ward Hadaway | Application form & letter | Interview | 2:1 | 10 | 400+ |
| Watson Burton | Application form & covering letter | Not known | 2:1 | 5 | 1,000 |
| Watson, Farley & Williams | Online | Assessment centre + interview | 2:1 min | 10 | 1,000 |
| Wedlake Bell | Application form | Interviews | 2:1 | 7 | Not known |
| Weightmans | Online | Not known | Not known | Not known | Not known |
| Weil, Gotshal & Manges | Online | Not known | 2:1 | 12 | Not known |
| White & Case | Online | Interview | 2:1 | 20-25 | 1,600 |
| Wiggin and Co | Online | Two-day selection | 2:1 | 3 | 500 |
| Withers | Application form | 2 interviews + exercise | 2:1 | 14 | 1,000 |
| Wollastons | CV & application form | Interviews | 2:1 | 2 | 500 |
| Wragge & Co | Online | Telephone discussion + assessment day | 2:1 | 25 | 1,000 |

# offer and acceptance

After the hard work of securing a training contract, you'll need to know what to do when you actually land one. Law students will already know all about offer and acceptance; if you haven't yet been introduced to the timeless delights of the well-known case of Carlill v The Carbolic Smokeball Company, what better time to learn!

By accepting a training contract offer you enter into a legally binding contract with the law firm, so accept the right offer. Appreciating the minefield into which inexperienced students step, the Society publishes good practice guidelines by which law firms should manage the recruitment process. The guidelines are detailed and we advise anyone who is unsure about their position to read them. They are on the Law Society's website, **www.lawsociety.org.uk**. To give you a feel for things, we've summarised them here.

If you're still an undergraduate, training contract interviews can only be scheduled for 1 September onwards in your final undergraduate year. If you've impressed the firm while on a vacation scheme or after work experience, the firm must wait until this date before interviewing you or offering a contract. At interview, you will be told if there is a further stage to the process. You should also be told within two weeks of reaching the end of the process whether or not you have been successful. An offer should be made in writing. However, we've found that many recruiters now seem to be making initial offers to students by phone. You need not accept a verbal offer unless you want to; be polite and confirm with them that they will send the formal offer in writing for you to consider.

No deadline for acceptance of an offer should expire earlier than four weeks from the date of the offer. If you need more time to consider an offer, firms are supposed to consider your request 'sympathetically' provided you have a good reason. No definition of 'good reason' is given in the guidelines. If a firm is going to pay your law school fees, it should set out the terms and conditions of the arrangement in the training contract offer letter. The firm's willingness to provide financial assistance should not affect the time limit for accepting the contract.

We get calls from students who want to hang on to an offer from one firm while they pursue applications with others. Too many trainees just take the first offer they receive because the firm has a decent enough reputation and is prepared to fund law school. If your top choice firm offers you a job, and you're confident it's the one for you, then go for it. Otherwise, feel free to continue with other applications to see how they will play out. It goes without saying that you must guard against allowing an acceptance deadline to elapse.

Students are supposed to respond promptly to a firm that's made an offer, either by accepting or rejecting it. If you feel you need more time, you will have to enter into diplomatic discussions with the law firm, telling them how much longer you need. Make sure you get written confirmation of any extension to the deadline.

You can hold only two offers at a time. Accept your preferred offer in writing and confirm to everyone else that you are withdrawing your application. This is only fair to recruiters, who are really busy at this time of year, and other applicants who may suffer if you are still hogging the shortlist.

# salaries and benefits

## salaries and benefits

| firm name | 1st year salary | 2nd year salary | sponsorship/ awards | other benefits | qualification salary |
|---|---|---|---|---|---|
| Addleshaw Goddard | £20,000 (Manch/Leeds) £28,000 (London) | £22,000 (Manch/Leeds) £30,000 (London) | CPE & LPC: fees + £4,500 maintenance | Corporate gym m'ship, STL, subsd restaurant, pension, pte healthcare | £33,000 (Manch/Leeds) £48,000 (London) |
| Allen & Overy | £29,000 | £33,000 | LPC: fees + £7,000 CPE: fees +£6,000 (London), £5,000 (elsewhere) | Pte healthcare scheme, PMI, STL, subsd restaurant, gym m'ship, 6 weeks unpaid leave on qual | £51,000 |
| asb law | £18,000 | Not known | Interest-free loan | Not known | Not known |
| Ashurst | £28,000-29,000 | £31,000-32,000 | CPE & LPC: fees + maintenance, £500 LPC distinction award, language tuition bursaries | PHI, pension, life ass, STL, gym m'ship | £48,000 |
| Baker & McKenzie | £29,000 + £3,000 'joining bonus' | £32,000 | LPC: fees + £7,000 CPE: fees + £6,000 | PHI, life ins, PMI, pension, subsd gym m'ship, STL, subsd restaurant | £50,000 |
| Barlow Lyde & Gilbert | £28,000 | £30,000 | CPE & LPC: fees + maintenance | Not known | £47,000 |
| Beachcroft Wansbroughs | £28,000 (London) £20,000 (regions) | £30,000 (London) £22,500 (regions) | CPE & LPC fees + £3,500 bursary | Flexible scheme inc. holiday, pension, pte healthcare | Not known |
| Berwin Leighton Paisner | £28,000 | £32,000 | CPE & LPC: fees + £4,500 p.a. maintenance | Flexible package inc. PHI, PMI, subsd conveyancing, subsd gym m'ship | £50,000 |
| Bevan Brittan | Not known | Not known | CPE & LPC: yes | Not known | Not known |
| Bircham Dyson Bell | £27,500 | £28,500 | CPE & LPC: Yes | PMI, life ass, PHI, pension | £44,000 |
| Bird & Bird | £28,000 | £30,000 | CPE & LPC: fees + £3,500 p.a. maintenance | BUPA, STL, subsd sports club m'ship, life cover, PHI, pension, childcare vouchers | £48,000 |
| Boodle Hatfield | £27,500 | £29,500 | CPE & LPC: fees + maintenance | Pte healthcare, life ass, STL, pension, PHI, conveyancing grant | £44,000 |
| BP Collins | £19,000 | £20,000 | 50% LPC costs refund when TC starts | Not known | Not known |
| Brabners Chaffe Street | £19,000 | Not known | LPC: yes | Not known | Not known |

*Notes: PHI = Permanent Health Insurance; STL = Season Travel Ticket Loan; PMI = Private Medical Insurance*

# solicitors

## salaries and benefits

| firm name | 1st year salary | 2nd year salary | sponsorship/ awards | other benefits | qualification salary |
|---|---|---|---|---|---|
| Brachers | £17,400 | £19,030 | LPC/CPE: £6,000 discretionary award | Not known | £31,000 |
| Bristows | £26,000 | £28,000 | CPE & LPC: fees + £5,000 p.a. maintenance | Pension, life ass & health ins | £43,000 |
| Browne Jacobson | £21,500 | Not known | CPE & LPC: fees + maintenance | Not known | Regional variations |
| Burges Salmon | £21,500 | £22,500 | CPE & LPC: fees + £4,500 p.a maintenance | Bonus, pension, PMI, mobile phone, laptop, gym m'ship, social club, xmas gift | £35,000 |
| Capsticks | Not known | Not known | CPE & LPC: scholarship contributions | Bonus, pension, PHI, death in service, STL | £41,500 |
| Charles Russell | £28,000 | £30,500 | CPE & LPC: fees + maintenanc £4,500 p.a. (Lon/Guild) £3,500 (Chelt) | BUPA, PHI, life ass, pension, STL | £46,000 |
| Cleary Gottlieb Steen & Hamilton | £35,000 | £40,000 | LPC: fees + £8,000 maintenance | Pension, PHI, disability ins. health club | £74,000 |
| Clifford Chance | £29,000 | £33,000 | LPC: fees + £7,000 CPE: fees + £6,000 (Lon) or £5,000 elsewhere), prizes for first class degree & top LPC performers | Interest-free loan, PMI, subsd restaurant, fitness centre, life ass, occupational health service, PHI | £50,000 |
| Clyde & Co | £28,000 | £31,000 | CPE & LPC: fees + maintenance | Subsd sports club, STL, staff restaurant | £46,000 |
| CMS Cameron McKenna | £28,500 | £32,000 | CPE & LPC: fees + £5,000 p.a. maintenance (Lon/Guild/Oxf), £4,500 (elsewhere) | Bonus, gym m'ship, life ass, pension, pte healthcare, STL, counselling, subs'd rest. | £50,000 |
| Cobbetts | £21,000 | £22,000 | CPE & LPC: fees + £3,000 p.a. maintenance | BUPA, gym m'ship, pension, STL, death in service, counselling | £33,000 |
| Coffin Mew & Clover | Competitive | Competitive | CPE & LPC: discussed with candidates | Not known | £29,000 |
| Covington & Burling | £30,000 | £33,000 | CPE & LPC: fees + £5,000 p.a. maintenance | Pension, PHI, pmi, life ass, STL | Not known |
| Cripps Harries Hall | £17,500 | £20,000 | LPC fees: 50% interest-free loan, 50% bursary | Not known | £31,000 |

*Notes: PHI = Permanent Health Insurance; STL = Season Travel Ticket Loan; PMI = Private Medical Insurance*

# solicitors

## salaries and benefits

| firm name | 1st year salary | 2nd year salary | sponsorship/ awards | other benefits | qualification salary |
|---|---|---|---|---|---|
| Davenport Lyons | £28,000 - £28,666 | £29,332 - £30,000 | No | STL, client intro bonus, contrib to gym m'ship, discretionary bonus | Not known |
| Davies Arnold Cooper | £26,000 | Not known | CPE & LPC: fees + maintenance | PMI, STL | Not known |
| Dechert | £28,000 | £32,000 | LPC: fees + £7,000 p.a. maintenance | PHI, life ass, subsd gym m'ship, STL | £50,000 |
| Denton Wilde Sapte | £28,000 | £31,000 | CPE & LPC: fees + £4,500 p.a. maintenance (£5,000 in London) | Flexible benefit scheme | £48,000 |
| Devonshires | £25,500 | £26,500 | Under review | STL, healthcare scheme, subsd health-club m'ship | Competitive |
| Dickinson Dees | £18,500 | £19,500 | CPE & LPC: fees + £4,000 interest-free loan | Not known | £30,500 |
| DLA Piper Rudnick Gray Cary | £29,000 (London) £20,000 (regions) | £32,000 (London) £22,000 (regions) | CPE & LPC: fees + maintenance | Not known | £50,000 (London) £34,000 (Birmingham) £32,500 (other English) |
| DMH Stallard | £19,000 | £21,000 | Not known | Not known | £31,000 |
| Dorsey & Whitney | £28,500 | £31,500 | Not known | Pension, health ins, life ass | £55,000 |
| DWF | £20,000 | Not known | LPC: fees | Life ass, pension | Not known |
| Eversheds | £29,000 (London) | £32,000 (London) | CPE & LPC: fees + maintenance | Regional variations | £50,000 (London) |
| Farrer & Co | £27,500 | £30,000 | CPE & LPC: fees + £4,500 p.a. maintenance | Health & life ins, subsd gym m'ship, STL | £43,000 |
| Field Fisher Waterhouse | £28,000 | £31,000 | CPE & LPC: fees + £4,500 maintenance | STL, medical ins, life ass, pension, gp service | £47,000 |
| Finers Stephens Innocent | highly competitive | highly competitive | LPC & CPE: fees | Pension, PMI, life ins, long-term disability ins, STL | highly competitive |

*Notes: PHI = Permanent Health Insurance;  STL = Season Travel Ticket Loan;  PMI = Private Medical Insurance*

## salaries and benefits

| firm name | 1st year salary | 2nd year salary | sponsorship/ awards | other benefits | qualification salary |
|---|---|---|---|---|---|
| Fladgate Fielder | £27,000 | £28,000 | Not known | Pension, PHI, life ass, STL, sports club, bonus | Not known |
| Foot Anstey | £16,750 | £19,000 | LPC: £8,000 | Contributory pension | £30,500 |
| Forbes | At least Law Soc min | £17,720 | Not known | Not known | highly competitive |
| Forsters | £26,000 | £28,000 | CPE & LPC: fees | STL, PHI, life ins, subsd gym m'ship | £43,000 |
| Freeth Cartwright | £18,000 | Not known | Not known | Not known | Not known |
| Freshfields Bruckhaus Deringer | £29,500 | £33,500 | LPC: fees + £7,250 CPE: fees + £6,250 | Life ass, PHI, pension, interest-free loan, STL, PMI, subsd staff restaurant, gym | £52,000 |
| Gateley Wareing | £20,000 | £22,000 | LPC: fees + £4,000 maintenance CPE: fees | Not known | £33,000 |
| Government Legal Service | over £20,000 (London) | Not known | LPC fees + £5–7,000 CPE: possibly | Pension, subsd canteen | £27,000–£38,000 |
| Halliwells | £22,145 | £23,175 | CPE & LPC: fees + £4,500 p.a. maintenance | Pension, subsd gym m'ship | £34,000 |
| Hammonds | £27,000 (London) £20,500 (other) | £30,000 (London) £23,000 (other) | CPE & LPC: fees + £4,500 maintenance | Flexible benefits scheme | £46,000 (London) £34,000 (other) |
| Harbottle & Lewis | £25,900 | £26,900 | LPC: fees + interest-free loan | Lunch, STL | £44,000 |
| Henmans | £17,750 | £19,000 | Not known | Not known | £31,000 |
| Herbert Smith | £29,000 | £33,000 | CPE & LPC: fees + up to £7,000 p.a. maintenance | Profit share, PHI, PMI, STL, life ass, gym, group personal accident ins, matched contrib. pension | £50,000 |
| Hewitsons | £18,000 | £19,000 | None | Not known | £31,500 |
| Hill Dickinson | £19,500 | £21,000 | Not known | Not known | Not known |
| Hodge Jones & Allen | £20,000 | Not known | Not known | Pension, life ass, disability ins | £25,750 |
| Holman Fenwick & Willan | £28,000 | £30,000 | CPE & LPC: fees + £5,000 p.a. maintenance | PMI, PHI, accident ins, subsd gym m'ship, STL | £47,500 |
| Howes Percival | £21,000 | £23,000 | CPE & LPC: funding + maintenance grant | Pension, PHI | Not known |

Notes: PHI = Permanent Health Insurance; STL = Season Travel Ticket Loan; PMI = Private Medical Insurance

## salaries and benefits

| firm name | 1st year salary | 2nd year salary | sponsorship/ awards | other benefits | qualification salary |
|---|---|---|---|---|---|
| Hugh James | Competitive | Competitive | Not known | Contribution to stake-holder pension | Not known |
| Ince & Co | £27,000 | £30,000 | LPC: fees + £4,750 grant (London), £4,000 (elsewhere), CPE: dis-cretionary | STL, PMI, PHI, pension | £47,000 |
| Irwin Mitchell | £18,540 (outside Lon-don) | £20,600 (out-side London) | CPE & LPC: fees + £3,000 maintenance | Healthcare, pension, sub'd gym m'ship | Not known |
| Jones Day | £36,000 | £40,000 | CPE & LPC: fees + £8,000 p.a. maintenance | Pte healthcare sports club m'ship, group life cover | £55,000 |
| Kendall Freeman | £29,000 | £32,500 | CPE & LPC: fees + maintenance of £5,000 (London) or £4,500 (elsewhere) | Not known | £50,000 |
| Kirkpatrick & Lockhart Nicholson Graham | £28,000 | £31,000 | CPE & LPC: fees + £4,500 maintenance | PHI, life ass, STL, gym, pension, BUPA | £49,000 |
| Lawrence Graham | £28,000 | £32,000 | CPE & LPC: fees + £4,000 p.a. maintenance | STL, on-site gym, life ass | £48,000 |
| Laytons | market rate | market rate | CPE & LPC: funding considered | Not known | market rate |
| LeBoeuf, Lamb, Greene & MacRae | £33,000 | £37,000 | CPE & LPC: fees + £7,000 maintenance | Health, life & disability insurance contribs, STL | £65,000 + bonus |
| Lester Aldridge | £16,500-17,000 | £17,500-18,000 | LPC: yes | Life ass, pension | £31,000 |
| Lewis Silkin | £29,000 | £31,000 | LPC: fees + £4,500 maintenance CPE: fees | Life ass, critical illness cover, PMI, STL, pen-sion, subsd gym m'ship, bonus scheme | £43,000 |
| Linklaters | £29,700 | Not known | CPE: fees + £5-£6,000 LPC: fees + £7,000 | Bonus schemes, health & w'wide travel ins, life ass, pension, STL, subsd gym m'ship | £52,000 + bonus |
| Lovells | £29,000 | £32,000 | CPE & LPC: fees + £7,450 p.a. maintenance (Lon) or £6,450 for GDL elsewhere, £500 bonus & £1,000 salary advance on joining, £500 prize for first class degree | PPP med ins, life ass, PHI, STL, in-house gym, staff restaurant, in-house dentist, doctor & physio, local retail discounts | £50,000 |

*Notes: PHI = Permanent Health Insurance;  STL = Season Travel Ticket Loan;  PMI = Private Medical Insurance*

# solicitors

## salaries and benefits

| firm name | 1st year salary | 2nd year salary | sponsorship/ awards | other benefits | qualification salary |
|---|---|---|---|---|---|
| Lupton Fawcett | Competitive | Competitive | LPC: interest-free loan | PMI, STL | Competitive |
| Mace & Jones | £16,000 | £16,500 | Not known | Not known | Negotiable |
| Macfarlanes | £29,000 | £33,000 | CPE & LPC: fees + £5,000 p.a. mainte-nance (Lon/Guild/Oxf), £4,500 (elsewhere), prizes for LPC distinc-tion or commendation | Comprehensive package | £50,000 |
| Manches | £27,500 (London) | £31,000 (London) | CPE & LPC: fees + £4,000 p.a. mainte-nance | STL, BUPA, PHI, PMI, pension, life ass | £45,000 (London) |
| Martineau Johnson | £20,000 | £21,500 | Not known | Not known | £34,000 |
| Mayer, Brown, Rowe & Maw | £29,000 | Not known | CPE & LPC: + £4,500 p.a. maintenance (£5,000 for Lon/Guild) | STL, subsd sports club m'ship, PMI | £50,000 |
| McCormicks | Highly com-petitive | Highly com-petitive | Not known | Not known | Highly competitive |
| McDermott, Will & Emery | £31,500 | £35,000 | CPE & LPC: fees + maintenance | PMI, life ass, PHI, STL, subsidised gym m'ship, employee assistance programme | £60,000 |
| McGrigors | £28,000 | £32,000 | CPE & LPC: fees + £4,500 p.a. mainte-nance | Life ass, pension, lunch allowance, income protection | £48,000 |
| Mills & Reeve | £21,000 | £22,000 | CPE & LPC: fees + maintenance | Life ass, pension, bonus, subsd gym, BUPA discount | Not known |
| Mishcon de Reya | £27,000 | £29,000 | CPE & LPC: fees + bur-sary | PMI, subsd gym m'ship, STL, PHI, life ass, pension | Not known |
| Morgan Cole | Competitive | Competitive | CPE & LPC: fees + maintenance | Not known | Not known |
| Nabarro Nathanson | £28,000 (Lond) £20,000 (Sheffield) | £32,000 (Lond) £22,000 (Sheffield) | CPE & LPC: fees + £5,000 p.a. mainte-nance (Lon/Guild), £4,500 (elsewhere) | PMI, pension, STL, subsd restaurant, subsd corporate gym m'ship | £50,000 (London) £32,000 (Sheffield) |

*Notes: PHI = Permanent Health Insurance;  STL = Season Travel Ticket Loan;  PMI = Private Medical Insurance*

# solicitors

## salaries and benefits

| firm name | 1st year salary | 2nd year salary | sponsorship/ awards | other benefits | qualification salary |
|---|---|---|---|---|---|
| Norton Rose | £28,500 | £32,000 | CPE & LPC: fees + up to £7,000 p.a. maintenance, £1,000 travel scholarship | £800 loan on arrival, life ass, pte health ins, STL, subsd gym m'ship | Not known |
| Olswang | £28,000 | £32,000 | CPE & LPC: fees + £4,500 maintenance, (London) or £4,000 (o/s London) | Pension, PMI, life cover, dental scheme, STL, subsd gym m'ship and staff restaurant, PHI | £48,000 |
| Orrick, Herrington & Sutcliffe | £28,000 | £32,000 | CPE & LPC: fees + £4,500 maintenance | Pension, PHI, gym STL, PMI, dental care | Not known |
| Osborne Clarke | £28,000 (London/TV) £21,000 (Bristol) | Not known | CPE & LPC: fees + maintenance grant | Pension PMI, STL, PHI, life ass | £48,000 (London) £43,000 (TV) £35,000 (Bristol) |
| Pannone & Partners | £21,000 | £23,000 | LPC: fees | Not known | £32,000 |
| Payne Hicks Beach | £27,500 | £29,500 | CPE & LPC: fees | STL, life ass, PHI, pension | Not known |
| Penningtons | £27,000 (London) | £29,000 (London) | LPC: fees + £4,000 maintenance | Pension, life ass, PMI, STL, crit ill cover | Not known |
| Pinsent Masons | £28,000 (London) | £32,000 (London) | CPE & LPC: fees + maintenance | Not known | £48,000 |
| Prettys | Not known | Not known | LPC: yes | Not known | Not known |
| Pritchard Englefield | £21,750 | £22,250 | LPC: fees | Subsd training, luncheon vouchers, PMI, STL | Approx £40,000 |
| Reed Smith | £28,000 (London) £19,500 (Coventry) | £32,000 (London) £22,000 (Coventry) | CPE: fees + £4,000; LPC: fees + £5,000 | BUPA, STL, life ass, PHI, pension | £49,000 (London) |
| Reynolds Porter Chamberlain | £28,000 | £30,000 | CPE & LPC: fees + £4,500 p.a. maintenance | Bonus, PMI, income protection, STL, subsd gym m'ship | £48,000 |
| Richards Butler | £29,000 | £32,000 | CPE & LPC: fees + £6,000 p.a maintenance | Bonus, life ins, BUPA, STL, subsd staff restaurant, conveyancing allowance | £48,000 + bonus |
| Salans | £27,000 | £29,000 | LPC: fees | PMI, pension, STL, crit ill cover | Variable |

*Notes: PHI = Permanent Health Insurance; STL = Season Travel Ticket Loan; PMI = Private Medical Insurance*

# solicitors

## salaries and benefits

| firm name | 1st year salary | 2nd year salary | sponsorship/ awards | other benefits | qualification salary |
|---|---|---|---|---|---|
| Shadbolt & Co | £25,000 | £29,000 | LPC: 50% fee refund when TC starts | PMI, PHI, life ass, paid study leave, STL, bonus, prof m'ships + subs | £43,000 |
| Shearman & Sterling | £35,000 | £37,500 | CPE & LPC: fees + £5,000 maintenance | Not known | £60,000 |
| Shoosmiths | Market rate | Market rate | LPC: £13,000 | Life ass, pension, staff discounts, Christmas bonus | Market rate |
| Sidley Austin Brown & Wood | £29,000 | £33,000 | CPE & LPC: fees + maintenance | PMI, disability cover, life ass, contrib to gym m'ship, STL | Not known |
| SJ Berwin | £28,000 | £32,000 | CPE & LPC: fees + £5,000-£7,000 maintenance | Not known | £50,000 |
| Simmons & Simmons | £28,000 | £32,000 | CPE & LPC: fees + maintenance | STL, fitness loan, trav ins, accident ins, death in service, PMI, staff restaurant | £50,000 |
| Slaughter and May | £29,500 | £33,000 | CPE & LPC: fees + maintenance | BUPA, STL, pension, subsd health club m'ship, 24-hour accident cover | £51,000 |
| Speechly Bircham | £28,000-£29,000 | £30,000-£31,000 | CPE & LPC: fees + maintenance | STL, PMI, life ass | £47,000 |
| Stephenson Harwood | £28,000 | £32,000 | CPE & LPC: fees + maintenance | Subsd health club m'ship, PMI, BUPA, STL | £49,000 |
| Stevens & Bolton | £23,000 | £25,000 | CPE & LPC: fees + £4,000 p.a. maintenance | PMI, life ass, pension, STL, PHI | £39,000 |
| Tarlo Lyons | £27,000 (on average) | £29,000 (on average) | LPC: fees | Bonus, PMI, pension plan, gym m'ship | £42,000 |
| Taylor Walton | Not known | Not known | LPC: full sponsorship | Not known | Not known |
| Taylor Wessing | £28,000 | £31,000 | CPE & LPC: fees + £4,500 p.a. maintenance | PMI, PHI, STL, subsd staff restaurant, pension | £50,000 |
| Teacher Stern Selby | £25,000 | Not known | LPC: occasional funding | Not known | £40,000 |
| Thomas Eggar | Not known | Not known | LPC: 50% grant, 50% loan | Not known | Not known |
| Thomson Snell & Passmore | Competitive | Competitive | LPC: grant & interest free loan | Not known | Not known |

*Notes: PHI = Permanent Health Insurance; STL = Season Travel Ticket Loan; PMI = Private Medical Insurance*

## salaries and benefits

| firm name | 1st year salary | 2nd year salary | sponsorship/ awards | other benefits | qualification salary |
|---|---|---|---|---|---|
| TLT Solicitors | Not known | Not known | LPC: fees + maintenance | Pension, subsd sports & health club m'ship, life ass | Market rate |
| Travers Smith | £28,000 | £32,000 | LPC & CPE: fees + 5,000 p.a. maintenance (£4,500 o/side Lon) | PHI, permanent sickness cover, life ass, STL, subsd bistro, health club m'ship | £50,000 |
| Trowers & Hamlins | £28,000 | £30,500 | CPE & LPC: fees + £4,250–£4,500 p.a. maintenance | STL, PMI, employee assistance programme, bonus, death in service | £47,000 |
| Walker Morris | £20,000 | £22,000 | CPE & LPC: fees + £4,500 maintenance | Not known | £33,000 |
| Ward Hadaway | £18,000 | £19,500 | LPC: fees + £2,000 int-free loan | Death in service insurance, pension | £32,500 |
| Watson Burton | £16,750 | £18,250 | LPC: fees | Not known | £32,500 |
| Watson, Farley & Williams | £16,750 | £18,250 | LPC: fees | Not known | £32,500 |
| Wedlake Bell | £26,000 | £28,000 | LPC & CPE: fees + £2,500 p.a. mainte-nance (if no LEA grant) | Pension, STL, subsd gym m'ship. life ass, PHI | Not known |
| Weightmans | Competitive | Competitive | CPE & LPC: fees | Pension, PHI, life ass | Not known |
| Weil, Gotshal & Manges | £35,000 | Not known | Not known | Not known | Not known |
| White & Case | £36,000-£37,000 | £38,000-£39,000 | CPE & LPC: fees + £5,500 p.a. maintenance, prize for LPC commen-dation or distinction | BUPA, gym m'ship contrib, life ins, pension, PHI, STL, bonuses | £63,000 |
| Wiggin and Co | £26,500 | £31,500 | CPE & LPC: fees + £3,500 p.a. maintenance | Life ass, pte health cover, pension scheme, PHI | £44,000 |
| Withers | £28,000 | £30,000 | CPE & LPC: fees + £4,500 p.a. maintenance, prize for CPE/LPC dis-tinction or commendation | STL, PMI, life ass, Christmas bonus, subsd cafe | £46,000 |
| Wollastons | £21,000 | £22,000 | LPC: fees | Not known | Not known |
| Wragge & Co | £21,500 (Birmingham) £28,500 (London) | £24,500 (Birmingham) £31,500 (London) | CPE & LPC: fees + £4,500 p.a. mainte-nance, prizes for LPC distinction | £1,000 int-free loan, pen-sion, life ass, PHI, travel schemes, PMI, sports & social club, indep fin advice, subsd gym m'ship, Christmas gift | £34,500 (Birmingham) £49,000 (London) |

*Notes: PHI = Permanent Health Insurance; STL = Season Travel Ticket Loan; PMI = Private Medical Insurance*

# solicitors

# banking & finance

Banking and finance covers a multitude of specialist areas, but in essence it is the management and documentation of the movement of money. From straightforward bank loans, through property finance, project finance, capital markets, securitisations and structured loans to leveraged finance involving complex cross-border structures, there's a mass of terminology and concepts that will, at this stage, leave you dazed and confused. But in time, and after exposure to different styles of transaction, you'll soon know your equity from your elbow.

## type of work

Some deals follow a well-worn path, never veering from standard-form documentation; others require a great deal more brainpower and break new ground. Here, at the pointy end of finance, lawyers actually assist with the structuring of the deal, as well as ensuring compliance with relevant laws. The job is intellectually challenging, but commercial awareness is just as important. As Richard Kendall, a partner at Ashurst, told us: "*You need an understanding of where the client wants to get to and an understanding of the legal risks involved in getting there.*" This may involve taking security in several jurisdictions and the movement of money across borders, through different currencies and financial products.

Most of the day you'll be at your desk, working on documentation or managing deals; the rest of the time is spent in meetings with clients or other lawyers, either familiarising yourself with the commercial context of the deal, getting involved in the cut and thrust of negotiating its terms, or bringing it to completion. During negotiations, the lawyer must understand when he can compromise and when he must hold out on a point – he will be guided by the client and by a good understanding of market standards.

The type and location of the firm you join will determine your experiences. City firms act for international banks whereas regional firms' work is of a more domestic nature, usually for UK banks and building societies, or the companies they lend to. If you want to be a hotshot in international finance then it's the City for you, and if you want international travel, you're likely to be able to find a job that caters to your wanderlust – though you'll rarely have time to explore the places you visit.

## skills needed

...an interest in the City...initiative and quick thinking...comfortable with complex documentation...attention to detail...teamworking...good communicator...stamina...
Richard likes the fact that clients are "*smart, dynamic and demandin*g." It's a challenge working with them and it requires "*intellectual rigour.*" He also enjoys building up longer-term relationships with investment bank clients.

The volume and complexity of the work requires a diligent, organised approach. As for having to be a genius with numbers, Richard told us: "*You'll get the odd have-a-go finance lawyer who'll try and check the formula, but it's best to let the experts do the checkin*g." With some types of finance the hours have peaks and troughs; when a deal is building up you might work every weekend for three or four weeks with some all-nighters, but you can see the deals coming and plan for them. With other types, the diet is more regular, and a junior solicitor in a top firm might work 12-hour days with only occasional all-nighters. It's important to pick the right group or department to suit your preferred work pattern, but in all areas you'll have to work hard and you'll need physical stamina.

## career options

In City firms there's a greater chance that you'll become specialised early on in your career. This may or may not appeal to you, and if it doesn't then a smaller or regional firm may be a better choice. Secondments to international banks are available from City firms – even for trainees – and, as Richard pointed out, are "*an excellent opportunity to view things from a client's perspective.*" Subsequent moves in-house are common, especially for capital markets work or compliance roles to ensure that banks work within financial services regulations. Finally, banking law can be an ideal platform for a career in the financial markets; however, if you already know you want to be a banker, don't waste time training as a lawyer.

## leading firms from Chambers uk 2005-6

### Banking & Finance: Acquisition Finance
London

1. Allen & Overy LLP
   Clifford Chance LLP
2. Ashurst
   Linklaters
3. Freshfields Bruckhaus Deringer
   Lovells
   Shearman & Sterling LLP
4. Denton Wilde Sapte
   Latham & Watkins
   Macfarlanes
   Simpson Thacher & Bartlett
   White & Case
5. DLA Piper Rudnick Gray Cary
   Herbert Smith LLP
   Slaughter and May
   Travers Smith
   Weil, Gotshal & Manges
6. Addleshaw Goddard
   Berwin Leighton Paisner
   Cleary Gottlieb Steen
   CMS Cameron McKenna LLP

### Banking & Finance: Bank Lending
London

1. Allen & Overy LLP
   Clifford Chance LLP
2. Linklaters
3. Denton Wilde Sapte
   Slaughter and May
   White & Case
4. Ashurst
   Cleary Gottlieb Steen
   CMS Cameron McKenna
   Freshfields Bruckhaus Deringer
   Lovells
   Norton Rose
5. Addleshaw Goddard
   Baker & McKenzie LLP
   Berwin Leighton Paisner
   Herbert Smith LLP
   SJ Berwin
6. Bird & Bird
   Dechert LLP
   Jones Day
   Simmons & Simmons
   Stephenson Harwood
   Taylor Wessing

## Banking & Finance
### South

1. **Blake Lapthorn Linnell** *Southampton*
   **Bond Pearce** *Southampton*
2. **asb law** *Crawley*
   **Paris Smith & Randall** *Southampton*

## Banking & Finance
### Thames Valley

1. **Osborne Clarke** *Reading*
2. **Boyes Turner** *Reading*
   **Pitmans** *Reading*
3. **Clarkslegal LLP** *Reading*
   **EMW Law** *Milton Keynes*
   **Howes Percival** *Milton Keynes*
   **Matthew Arnold & Baldwin** *Watford*
   **Morgan Cole** *Oxford*
   **Shoosmiths** *Reading*

## Banking & Finance
### South West

1. **Burges Salmon** *Bristol*
   **Osborne Clarke** *Bristol*
2. **Bond Pearce** *Bristol*
3. **Bevan Brittan** *Bristol*
   **Rickerbys** *Cheltenham*
4. **Clarke Willmott** *Bristol*
   **Foot Anstey Sargent** *Plymouth*
   **TLT** *Bristol*

## Banking & Finance
### Wales

1. **Eversheds LLP** *Cardiff*
   **Morgan Cole** *Cardiff*
2. **Geldards** *Cardiff*
3. **Berry Smith** *Cardiff*

## Banking & Finance
### Midlands

1. **Eversheds LLP** *Birmingham*
   **Pinsent Masons** *Birmingham*
   **Wragge & Co LLP** *Birmingham*
2. **DLA** *Birmingham*
   **Martineau Johnson** *Birmingham*
3. **Browne Jacobson** *Nottingham*
   **Gateley Wareing** *Birmingham*
4. **Cobbetts** *Birmingham*
   **Freeth Cartwright** *Birmingham*
   **Hammonds** *Birmingham*

## Banking & Finance
### East Anglia

1. **Eversheds LLP** *Cambridge*
   **Mills & Reeve** *Norwich*
2. **Taylor Vinters** *Cambridge*
3. **Birketts** *Ipswich*
   **Wollastons** *Cambridge*

## Banking & Finance
### North West

1. **Addleshaw Goddard** *Manchester*
   **DLA** *Manchester*
   **Eversheds LLP** *Manchester*
2. **Halliwells LLP** *Manchester*
   **Hammonds** *Manchester*
3. **Cobbetts** *Manchester*
   **DWF** *Manchester*
   **Pinsent Masons** *Manchester*
4. **Brabners Chaffe Street** *Liverpool*
   **George Davies** *Manchester*
   **Hill Dickinson** *Liverpool*
   **Kuit Steinart Levy** *Manchester*

## Banking & Finance
### Yorkshire

1. **Addleshaw Goddard** *Leeds*
   **DLA** *Leeds*
   **Eversheds** *Leeds*
2. **Hammonds** *Leeds*
   **Pinsents** *Leeds*
   **Walker Morris** *Leeds*

## Banking & Finance
### North East

1. **Dickinson Dees** *Newcastle*
   **Eversheds** *Newcastle upon Tyne*
2. **Robert Muckle** *Newcastle upon Tyne*
   **Ward Hadaway** *Newcastle upon Tyne*
3. **Watson Burton** *Newcastle upon Tyne*

# competition

The basic aim of both the UK and EU regulatory authorities is to ensure that markets function effectively on the basis of fair and open competition. According to Herbert Smith partner James Quinney, the Competition Act 1998 revolutionised UK domestic competition law. "*Before it came into effect, domestic law was toothless and many companies could safely ignore it. Under the new regime, regulatory bodies have extensive investigation powers – such as carrying out dawn raids – and can impose hefty fines. Now all parts of British business have had to sit up and take notice.*" Recently there have been huge fines for a cartel that kept the price of vitamins artificially high, companies alleged to be involved in the price-fixing of replica football shirts, and Argos/Littlewoods, which the OFT found to have fixed the prices of Hasbro toys and games.

## type of work

The work can be divided into three main areas: negotiating clearance from the appropriate authorities for acquisitions, mergers and joint ventures; advising on the structuring of commercial or co-operation agreements to ensure they withstand a competition challenge; and dealing with investigations by the regulators into the way a client conducts business (eg, alleged exploitation of customers or cartels). Most lawyers engage in work across all three areas, and typically a mixture of both contentious and non-contentious matters. There are also opportunities to work in more specialised areas such as cross-border trade or anti-dumping (preventing companies exporting a product at a lower price than it normally charges in its home market).

EU and UK competition rules are substantially similar, but the UK bodies concentrate on those rules that have their greatest effect domestically, while the EU authorities deal with matters where the rules affect more than one member state. However, unlike the EU position, individu-als can be sent to prison for five years for certain breaches of the UK competition regime. In the UK, the main competition institutions are the Office of Fair Trade (OFT), the Competition Commission and the Competition Appeal Tribunal; on matters also affecting other EU countries it is the European Commission. Additionally, there are industry-specific regulatory bodies, such as Ofcom for the media and telecoms industry. The recently introduced EU Modernisation Programme will allow national bodies to apply EU provisions, a development that may shift the focus from the Commission towards the national regulators.

As a trainee you will conduct plenty of research, perhaps into a particular market or how the authorities have approached a certain type of agreement in the past. It is unlikely that you'll get much independence and even junior lawyers usually work under the close supervision of a partner. As James says: "*It can be a difficult area of the law to dip into. You need a degree of practical day-to-day experience to provide good competition advice, but there are lots of interesting points to latch onto.*"

## skills needed

... clear, analytical mind...good judgement and confidence...articulate, both orally and on paper... mediation and lobbying skills...attention to detail...numeracy...decisiveness...

As competition law is so diverse, lawyers constantly need to keep on their toes. Says James: "*You need an ability to think laterally. Competition is a broad discipline involving an interesting mix of law, economics and politics. You have to be prepared to learn, and be engaged in more serious academic thought than there would be in a standard corporate law job, where the emphasis is more on doing the deal.*"

Competition lawyers also need a high level of business acumen. As James says: "*You need to have a close relationship with your client, because you have to understand their business. And clients really appreciate it if you can speak their language."* Indeed, one of the attractions of the job is that you get to find out about a range of different industries.

Students who want to learn more about competition law could think about enrolling on a course or possibly studying for a master's degree. James also recommends reading either *The Economics of EC Competition Law* by Simon Bishop and Mike Walker or periodicals such as *EU Competition Law Review* or *Competition Law Journal*. It is also desirable to have a good understanding of economics. As a great deal of business is done in Brussels, fluency in another language can also be useful.

## career options

This is a highly competitive area and there will never be as many opportunities available as qualifying trainees wanting jobs. However, it would appear that the government sees the development of competition law as a priority in order to promote UK and EU productivity, so the increase in regulation – and legal work – is set to continue. Moreover, there might be a need for specialist competition advocates to conduct the more important cases before the High Court or Competition Appeal Tribunal. In international law firms, the potential to travel or to be posted abroad is also increasing as more governments across the world are adopting competition and merger laws. As for the regulatory authorities, OFT, for example, has doubled its number of investigators in recent years, so the potential for in-house roles is increasing.

# solicitors

## Leading firms from Chambers UK 2005-6

### Competition/ European Law
#### London

[1] Freshfields Bruckhaus Deringer
Herbert Smith LLP
Linklaters
Slaughter and May

[2] Allen & Overy LLP
Ashurst
Clifford Chance LLP
Lovells
Simmons & Simmons
SJ Berwin LLP

[3] Addleshaw Goddard
Baker & McKenzie LLP
CMS Cameron McKenna LLP
Eversheds LLP
Macfarlanes
Mayer, Brown, Rowe & Maw LLP
Norton Rose
Richards Butler

[4] Bird & Bird
Bristows
Denton Wilde Sapte
DLA Piper Rudnick Gray Cary UK
Field Fisher Waterhouse
Latham & Watkins
McDermott Will & Emery UK LLP
Shearman & Sterling LLP
Wilmer Cutler Pickering Hale

### Competition/ European Law
#### The South

[1] Burges Salmon LLP
[2] Bond Pearce LLP *Plymouth*
Osborne Clarke *Bristol*
TLT Solicitors *Bristol*

### Competition/ European Law
#### Wales

[1] Eversheds LLP *Cardiff*
[2] Morgan Cole *Cardiff*

### Competition/ European Law
#### Midlands

[1] Pinsent Masons *Birmingham*
[2] Eversheds LLP *Birmingham*
Martineau Johnson *Birmingham*
Shoosmiths *Nottingham*
Wragge & Co LLP *Birmingham*

### Competition/ European Law
#### The North

[1] Addleshaw Goddard *Manchester*
Eversheds LLP *Leeds*
[2] Dickinson Dees *Newcastle*
[3] Cobbetts *Manchester*
Pinsent Masons *Leeds*

# construction & projects

While some lawyers are happy to deal with intangibles like share offerings and Eurobonds, construction lawyers prefer to spend their time working on the things that actually exist in the real world, be they skyscrapers, shopping centres or sewerage treatment plants. One person for whom the real world holds greater appeal is Bob Maynard, a partner at Berwin Leighton Paisner. *"Sewerage systems may not sound that glamorous, but bad sanitation is the world's biggest killer,"* Bob told us. *"And you can see what a difference something like, say, a bridge can make to people's lives – whether they are driving cattle or a Cadillac across it."* We can indeed...

## type of work

Our subject lawyers assist their clients at both the 'procurement end' of construction and engineering projects – ie developing the contractual arrangements that allow things to be built – and the dispute end – picking up the pieces when things go wrong. It is because these arrangements involve so many different parties and continue for a far longer period of time than your average contractual relationship that there is so much scope for difficulties. No wonder, then, that construction features so prominently in contract and tort case law.

Perhaps as a consequence of the amount of time and money spent on resolving disputes, over the last decade the industry has set about adopting a new philosophy, whereby parties work in partnership with each other rather than expecting to have to sue each other at some stage. Furthermore, instead of mammoth, drawn-out court battles, adjudication of disputes has become the industry norm and all contracts now contain mandatory provisions detailing how any dispute will be resolved.

Normally people have a natural bias for contentious or non-contentious work, so if you want to concentrate on one rather than the other, be aware that some firms like their construction

lawyers to handle both aspects. *Chambers UK* outlines the nature of the leading construction practices across the country.

## skills needed

...attention to detail... excellent drafting... good judgement... down-to-earth attitude... comfortable with technical information... industry background a major boon... stamina... imagination... team worker... good interpersonal skills...

Those who take the non-contentious path will, according to Bob, be faced with *"the challenge of getting the contractual arrangements right,"* something which requires a clear understanding of how construction projects work and the interrelationships between parties. You will draft documents that need to account for all the potential problems in a complex, and reasonably long-term, arrangement between a number of parties.

On the contentious side, *"you need particularly good analytical skills as there is always a lot of information to sift through."* You need to have an affinity with case law and be prepared to keep up to date with the reports as well as industry trends and thinking. Since the Technology and Construction Court introduced its Pre-action Protocol, many more disputes have been resolved through mediation and this, in turn, means more time spent negotiating.

Perhaps more so than in other areas you should expect to spend more of your time with non-lawyers and non-City people. *"I like the clients,"* Bob said; *"they are down-to-earth, unstuffy people. They are people who build things."* You could be dealing with technical individuals, such as geotechnical and structural engineers, or creative types – architects and designers – or even the owners of small construction companies who have been on and off building sites since their first day as an apprentice brickie. As a lawyer, you'll probably never be regarded as 'one of them', but relationship building is frequently as important as legal knowledge for winning and keeping clients.

## career options

Nearly all international construction and engineering projects are governed (to varying degrees) by English or New York law, which means that experience in this field is internationally marketable. Those who make a name for themselves in top-end arbitration may get the chance to take on work in places like Hong Kong and Singapore.

Back on home turf, and for those looking to get out of private practice, many companies in the construction industry have lawyers working in-house, be this as a general corporate counsel or as a litigator.

Construction law isn't a subject that bewitches many students – certainly not like environment or competition law – but it can become rather appealing once they've sampled it in practice. Anyone coming from a science or engineering academic background, or those who've had some direct experience of the construction industry, tend to see the potential of the area more readily, and these people are certainly very attractive to the profession.

## leading firms from chambers uk 2004-2005

### Projects: International Infrastructure
### London

1. Allen & Overy LLP
   Clifford Chance LLP
   CMS Cameron McKenna LLP
   Freshfields Bruckhaus Deringer
   Linklaters
   Lovells
2. Ashurst
   Baker & McKenzie LLP
   Berwin Leighton Paisner
   Debevoise & Plimpton LLP
   Dewey Ballantine

### Projects: Energy
### London

| 1 Allen & Overy LLP | Clifford Chance LLP |
| Linklaters | Shearman & Sterling LLP |
| White & Case | |
| 2 Freshfields Bruckhaus Deringer | Latham & Watkins |
| Milbank, Tweed, Hadley LLP | Norton Rose |
| 3 Baker & McKenzie LLP | Denton Wilde Sapte |
| Trowers & Hamlins | |
| 4 Cadwalader, Wickersham & Taft | Chadbourne & Parke |
| LeBoeuf, Lamb, Greene & MacRae | Slaughter and May |
| Sullivan & Cromwell | Vinson & Elkins LLP |

### Construction: Purchaser-led
### London

| 1 Allen & Overy LLP | Ashurst | Berwin Leighton Paisner |
| Clifford Chance LLP | Linklaters | |
| 2 Freshfields Bruckhaus Deringer | Herbert Smith LLP | Lovells |
| Norton Rose | Trowers & Hamlins | |
| 3 Addleshaw Goddard | Baker & McKenzie LLP | Campbell Hooper |
| Denton Wilde Sapte | Eversheds LLP | Kirkpatrick & Lockhart Nicholson |
| Macfarlanes | Nabarro Nathanson | Taylor Wessing |
| 4 Clyde & Co | Field Fisher Waterhouse | Fladgate Fielder |
| Hammonds | Lawrence Graham LLP | Lewis Silkin |
| Simmons & Simmons | SJ Berwin LLP | Slaughter and May |
| Wedlake Bell | | |

# solicitors

## Construction: General
## London

1. Pinsent Masons
2. Berwin Leighton Paisner
   Clifford Chance LLP
   CMS Cameron McKenna LLP
   Lovells
   Mayer, Brown, Rowe & Maw LLP
3. Campbell Hooper
   Eversheds LLP
   Hammonds
   Kirkpatrick & Lockhart Nicholson
   Taylor Wessing

## Construction: Supplier-led
## London

1. Pinsent Masons
2. CMS Cameron McKenna LLP
   Fenwick Elliott LLP
   Mayer, Brown, Rowe & Maw LLP
   Shadbolt & Co
3. Berrymans Lace Mawer
   Kennedys
   Reynolds Porter Chamberlain
4. Barlow Lyde & Gilbert
   Beale and Company Solicitors
   Davies Arnold Cooper
   Glovers
   Lane & Partners
   Winward Fearon
5. Corbett & Co
   Kingsley Napley
   Speechly Bircham

## Construction
## The South

1. Shadbolt & Co LLP *Reigate*
2. Blake Lapthorn Linnell *So'ton*
   Cripps Harries Hall LLP *Tunbridge*
   Lester Aldridge Bournemouth
3. Charles Russell *Guildford*
   DMH Stallard *Brighton*
   Thomas Eggar *Reigate*

## Construction
## South West

1. Bevan Brittan LLP *Bristol*
   Burges Salmon LLP *Bristol*
   Osborne Clarke *Bristol*
2. Ashfords *Exeter*
   Beachcroft Wansbroughs *Bristol*
   Pinsent Masons *Bristol*
3. Bond Pearce LLP *Plymouth*
   Clarke Willmott *Bristol*
   Veale Wasbrough Lawyers *Bristol*
   Withy King *Bath*

## Construction
## Wales

1. Eversheds LLP *Cardiff*
2. Hugh James *Cardiff*
   Morgan Cole *Cardiff*

## Construction
## Midlands

1. Wragge & Co LLP *Birmingham*
2. Gateley Wareing *Birmingham*
3. Eversheds LLP *Birmingham*
   Hammonds *Birmingham*
   Pinsent Masons *Birmingham*
4. Beachcroft Wansbroughs *B'ham*
   Cobbetts *Birmingham*
   DLA Piper *Birmingham*
   Freeth Cartwright *Nottingham*
   Shoosmiths *Birmingham*
5. Browne Jacobson *Nottingham*
   Geldards LLP *Derby*
   Martineau Johnson *Birmingham*
   Nelsons *Nottingham*
   Wright Hassall *Leamington Spa*

## Construction
## Thames Valley

1. Blake Lapthorn Linnell *Oxford*
   Clarkslegal LLP *Reading*
   Morgan Cole *Reading*
2. Boyes Turner *Reading*
   Henmans *Oxford*

## Construction
## East Anglia

1. Mills & Reeve *Cambridge*
2. Eversheds LLP *Cambridge*
   Hewitsons *Cambridge*
3. Greenwoods LLP *Peterbrough*
   Taylor Vinters *Cambridge*

## Construction
## North West

1. Pinsent Masons *Manchester*
2. Addleshaw Goddard *Manchester*
   Halliwells LLP *Manchester*
   Hammonds *Manchester*
   Hill Dickinson *Liverpool*
   Mace & Jones *Manchester*
3. DLA Piper
   Eversheds LLP *Manchester*
4. Beachcroft Wansbroughs *Man*
   Cobbetts *Manchester*
   DWF *Manchester*
   Pannone & Partners *Manchester*

## Construction
## Yorkshire

1. Addleshaw Goddard *Leeds*
2. Pinsent Masons *Leeds*
3. DLA Piper *Leeds*
   Eversheds LLP *Leeds*
   Hawkswell Kilvington P'ship *Leeds*
   Walker Morris *Leeds*
4. Denison Till *York*

## Construction
## North East

1. Dickinson Dees *Newcastle*
   Watson Burton LLP *Newcastle*
2. Ward Hadaway *Newcastle*
3. Eversheds LLP *Newcastle*
   Hay & Kilner *Newcastle*

# corporate law

It's the beating heart of most commercial firms, but in corporate departments top salaries and big deals accompany long hours. Large City firms act for companies listed on stock exchanges, while smaller City and regional firms tend to advise leading regional private companies and a handful of the FTSE 250. There are other differences, most notably extended hours and reduced chances for junior lawyers to take on significant responsibility in the largest City firms.

## type of work

You'll have heard many of the terms: mergers and acquisitions (M&A); corporate restructurings; going public; rights issues; venture capital; MBOs. Soon enough this foreign lexicon will become familiar – at base, it all relates to the buying, selling and financing of businesses. And because all deals are interlinked with finance we have the umbrella term 'corporate finance'.

Here's an example. A company wants to buy a smaller competitor's business and needs to get the money together to do so. It might restructure its own business, disposing of certain assets it no longer requires. If it is a privately owned company (not listed on a stock exchange), it could raise money by becoming listed and offering shares to the public and institutional investors. If it is already a publicly listed company, it could offer new shares for sale. Alternatively it could raise money via debt – eg loans from the market (bonds) or from banks.

Or how about a company that hasn't been performing as well as it could. Let's say its management team believe they could do a better job if they owned the company. Bring on the private equity lawyer, a breed of corporate lawyer that helps his client to complete a management buyout (MBO). Most of the time the management team doesn't actually have enough money to do the deal, hence the involvement of a private equity company – an investor looking to back the business for a healthy return and usually an influence in decision making.

The key phases to any type of deal are: negotiating and drafting the agreements; arranging financing; and carrying out 'due diligence', which is an investigation exercise to verify the accuracy of information passed from the purchase target to the buyer, or from the company raising money to the funder. We spoke to one of the City's top corporate lawyers, Charles Martin of Macfarlanes. He told us that transaction management was increasingly being influenced by US practices, particularly the due diligence phase, which he likened to "*carpet-bombing – everything is looked at now and documentation is longer.*" To put this in context, Charles believes that after Enron, the dot.com crash and scandals involving City analysts, the role of the legal adviser in business transactions and corporate affairs has never been more important.

## skills needed

...good all-rounder...stamina...can handle demanding, intelligent clients...commercially savvy... decisive and confident...tact and clear communication...eye for detail...organised...
The role is mainly transactional, but you may also be the first port of call for the client. And what of the idea that corporate lawyers are deal doers who know little 'pure' law? Actually, you need to be conversant in a variety of disciplines, and know when to refer matters to a specialist in, say, merger control, employment or tax.

Contrast the transactional lawyer's job with that of a litigator. The litigator is instructed only when a client has a problem, which he then has to resolve by relying on technical legal issues and procedures. Those who gain greater satisfaction from enabling a venture to reach fruition might find the idea of a life spent resolving disputes about as appealing as a career in an aspirin-packing factory.

Team spirit is essential and it will get you through a deal. Working three 20-hour days in a row may be rare, but it does happen. "*The hours are very lumpy,*" Charles admitted, "*but there's no point in fighting it; you just have to enjoy the peaks and troughs.*" The long hours arise through client demand, and their expectations have risen as instant communication via mobile phones, e-mail and now BlackBerry has exploded. But being surrounded by busy, intelligent, high-achieving people is half of the appeal, Charles explained.

A robust and confident manner is typical in this field. Softies take note: stamina and good health are a must because you simply can't duck off home or pull a sicky whenever you need to; you have to keep pushing yourself because the deals wait for no one.

## career options

As the new millennium fireworks fizzled, corporate departments became unnervingly quiet. The oomph had gone from the market. Jobs were lost. It was a reminder that the fortunes of corporate lawyers are tied to the general economy. There's a sense that things are picking up now but, even so, keep your fingers crossed for a boom when you qualify in 2010.

Many trainee lawyers head for the City, assuming that there is nothing of worth in the regions. While regional firms do usually work on lower-value matters, the best ones are winning a number of important instructions, some with a cross-border element. If you do want international work in the regions or a smaller London firm then judge a practice by its overseas offices, associations and client base. *Chambers UK* should give you a few pointers.

A sound grounding in corporate finance makes an excellent springboard for working in industry. Lawyers move in-house to major companies, tempted by decent hours and salaries. Some go to banks, usually as in-house lawyers, occasionally as corporate finance execs or analysts. Company secretarial positions suit lawyers with a taste for internal management and compliance issues.

If you have a hunch that you want to be a corporate lawyer, why not try Charles' foolproof home-testing method: "*Read the City pages in your newspaper. It's not going to do it for you in the first two weeks, but if after six to nine months you are still basically not interested, then this job is not for you.*" Simple.

## leading firms from Chambers UK 2006

| Corporate Finance: Larger Deals/Larger Resources London | Corporate Finance: Larger Deals/ Medium Resources London | |
|---|---|---|
| [1] Freshfields Bruckhaus Deringer | [1] Ashurst | |
| Linklaters | [2] Lovells | Macfarlanes |
| Slaughter and May | [3] CMS Cameron McKenna | Norton Rose |
| [2] Clifford Chance LLP | Shearman & Sterling LLP | Skadden, Arps, Slate, Meagher |
| Herbert Smith LLP | Weil, Gotshal & Manges | |
| [3] Allen & Overy LLP | [4] Simmons & Simmons | Travers Smith |
| | [5] Baker & McKenzie LLP | Mayer, Brown, Rowe & Maw LLP |
| | [6] Jones Day | McDermott Will & Emery UK LLP |
| | White & Case | |

# solicitors

## Corporate Finance: Mid-Market Deals/ Medium Resources
London

[1] **Bird & Bird**
  **Faegre & Benson LLP**
  **Lewis Silkin**
  **Memery Crystal**
  **Osborne Clarke**
[2] **Barlow Lyde & Gilbert**
  **Fox Williams**
  **Harbottle & Lewis LLP**
  **Marriott Harrison**
  **Reed Smith**
  **Reynolds Porter Chamberlain**
  **Richards Butler**
[3] **Beachcroft Wansbroughs**
  **Covington & Burling**
  **Finers Stephens Innocent**
  **Morrison & Foerster MNP**
  **Watson, Farley & Williams**
[4] **Bates Wells & Braithwaite**
  **Holman Fenwick & Willan**
  **Howard Kennedy**
  **Manches LLP**
  **Salans**
  **Withers LLP**

## Corporate Finance The South: Kent & Sussex

[1] **asb law** *Crawley*
  **Rawlison Butler** *Crawley*
  **Thomas Eggar** *Worthing*
[2] **DMH Stallard** *Crawley*
  **Thomson Snell** *Tunbridge Wells*
  **Vertex Law LLP** *West Malling*
[3] **Brachers** *Maidstone*
  **Clarkson Wright & Jakes** *Orpington*
  **Cripps Harries Hall** *Tunbridge Wells*
  **Steele Raymond** *Bournemouth*

## Corporate Finance: Mid-Market Deals/ Larger Resources
London

[1] **Addleshaw Goddard**
  **Berwin Leighton Paisner**
  **Denton Wilde Sapte**
  **DLA Piper Rudnick Gray Cary**
  **Lawrence Graham LLP**
[2] **Eversheds LLP**
  **Field Fisher Waterhouse**
  **Kirkpatrick & Lockhart Nicholson**
  **LeBoeuf, Lamb, Greene & MacRae**
  **Nabarro Nathanson**
  **SJ Berwin LLP**
  **Taylor Wessing**
[3] **Charles Russell**
  **Clyde & Co**
  **Dechert LLP**
  **Hammonds**
  **Olswang**
  **Pinsent Masons**
  **Stephenson Harwood**

## Corporate Finance The South: Surrey, Hampshire & Dorset

[1] **Blake Lapthorn Linnell** *Fareham*
  **Bond Pearce LLP** *Southampton*
  **Stevens & Bolton LLP** *Guildford*
[2] **Clyde & Co** *Guildford*
  **Paris Smith & Randall** *Southampton*
  **Shoosmiths** *Fareham*
[3] **Lamport Bassitt** *Southampton*
  **Lester Aldridge** *Southampton*
  **Penningtons Solicitors** *Basingstoke*
  **Shadbolt & Co LLP** *Reigate*
[4] **Charles Russell** *Guildford*
  **Clarke Willmott** *Southampton*
  **Coffin Mew & Clover** *Southampton*
  **Moore & Blatch** *Southampton*

## Corporate Finance Thames Valley

[1] **Manches** *Oxford*
  **Osborne Clarke** *Reading*
[2] **Boyes Turner** *Reading*
  **Clarkslegal LLP** *Reading*
  **Pitmans** *Reading*
  **Shoosmiths** *Reading*
[3] **Blake Lapthorn Linnell** *Oxford*
  **EMW Law** *Milton Keynes*
  **Field Seymour Parkes** *Reading*
  **Howes Percival** *Milton Keynes*
  **Kimbells LLP** *Milton Keynes*
  **Wilmer Cutler Pickering** *Oxford*
[4] **Blandy & Blandy** *Reading*
  **Darbys** *Oxford*
  **Matthew Arnold & Baldwin** *Watford*
  **Moorcrofts LLP** *Marlow*
  **Morgan Cole** *Reading*
  **Olswang Thames Valley** *Reading*

## Corporate Finance South West: Bristol & Surround

[1] **Burges Salmon LLP** *Bristol*
  **Osborne Clarke** *Bristol*
[2] **TLT Solicitors** *Bristol*
[3] **Bond Pearce** *Bristol*
  **BPE Solicitors** *Cheltenham*
  **Charles Russell** *Cheltenham*
  **Clark Holt** *Swindon*
[4] **Rickerbys** *Cheltenham*
  **Roxburgh & Milkins LLP** *Bristol*
  **Veale Wasbrough Lawyers** *Bristol*
[5] **Bevan Brittan LLP** *Bristol*
  **Clarke Willmott** *Bristol*
  **Lyons Davidson** *Bristol*
  **Thring Townsend** *Bath*
[6] **Ashfords** *Bristol*
  **Withy King** *Bath*

# solicitors

## Corporate Finance South West:
### Devon & Cornwall

1. **Bond Pearce LLP** *Exeter*
2. **Ashfords** *Exeter*
3. **Foot Anstey** *Plymouth*
   **Michelmores** *Exeter*
4. **Stephens & Scown** *St Austell*

## Corporate Finance Wales

1. **Eversheds LLP** *Cardiff*
   **Geldards** *Cardiff*
   **M & A Solicitors LLP** *Cardiff*
2. **Morgan Cole** *Cardiff*
3. **Berry Smith** *Cardiff*
   **Capital Law** *Cardiff Bay*
   **Dolmans** *Cardiff*

## Corporate Finance West Midlands

1. **Wragge & Co LLP** *Birmingham*
2. **DLA Piper Rudnick** *Birmingham*
   **Eversheds LLP** *Birmingham*
   **Pinsent Masons** *Birmingham*
3. **Cobbetts** *Birmingham*
   **Gateley Wareing LLP** *Birmingham*
4. **Bevan Brittan LLP** *Birmingham*
   **Browne Jacobson** *Birmingham*
   **Hammonds** *Birmingham*
   **Heatons** *Birmingham*
   **Martineau Johnson** *Birmingham*

## Corporate Finance East Midlands

1. **Browne Jacobson LLP** *Nottingham*
   **Eversheds LLP** *Nottingham*
2. **Freeth Cartwright LLP** *Nottingham*
   **Gateley Wareing LLP** *Nottingham*
   **Geldards** *Derby*
   **Shoosmiths** *Nottingham*
3. **Hewitsons** *Northampton*
   **Howes Percival** *Northampton*

## Corporate Finance East Anglia

1. **Mills & Reeve** *Norwich*
2. **Birketts** *Ipswich*
   **Eversheds LLP** *Norwich*
3. **Hewitsons** *Cambridge*
   **Taylor Vinters** *Cambridge*
4. **Prettys** *Ipswich*
   **Taylor Wessing** *Cambridge*
5. **Greene & Greene** *Bury St Edmunds*
   **Greenwoods** *Peterborough*
   **Howes Percival** *Norwich*
6. **Kester Cunningham John** *Thetford*
   **Steeles (Law) LLP** *Norwich*

## Corporate Finance North West

1. **Addleshaw Goddard** *Manchester*
   **DLA Piper Rudnick** *Manchester*
   **Eversheds LLP** *Manchester*
2. **Halliwells LLP** *Manchester*
   **Hammonds** *Manchester*
3. **Cobbetts** *Manchester*
   **DWF** *Liverpool, Manchester*
   **Kuit Steinart Levy** *Manchester*
   **Pannone & Partners** *Manchester*
   **Pinsent Masons** *Manchester*
4. **Beachcroft W'broughs** *Manchester*
   **Brabners Chaffe** *Liverpool, Manchester*
5. **Nexus Solicitors** *Manchester*
   **Wacks Caller** *Manchester*

## Corporate Finance Yorkshire

1. **Addleshaw Goddard** *Leeds*
   **DLA Piper Rudnick** *Leeds, Sheffield*
   **Eversheds LLP** *Leeds*
2. **Hammonds** *Leeds*
   **Pinsent Masons** *Leeds*
   **Walker Morris** *Leeds*
3. **Cobbetts** *Leeds*
   **Gordons** *Bradford*
4. **Irwin Mitchell** *Leeds*
   **Keeble Hawson** *Sheffield*
   **Lee & Priestley** *Leeds*
   **Lupton Fawcett** *Leeds*
   **McCormicks** *Leeds*
   **Rollits** *Hull*
5. **Andrew M Jackson** *Hull*
   **Denison Till** *York*
   **Gosschalks** *Hull*
   **HLW** *Sheffield*
   **Schofield Sweeney** *Bradford*
   **Wake Smith** *Sheffield*

## Corporate Finance North East

1. **Dickinson Dees** *Newcastle upon Tyne*
2. **Eversheds LLP** *Newcastle upon Tyne*
   **Ward Hadaway** *Newcastle upon Tyne*
3. **Robert Muckle** *Newcastle upon Tyne*
4. **Hay & Kilner** *Newcastle upon Tyne*
   **Watson Burton LLP** *Newcastle*

# crime

Criminal solicitors act for defendants in cases brought before the criminal courts. Lesser offences are usually dealt with exclusively by solicitors in the magistrates' courts, while for more serious charges in the Crown Courts, most defendants still prefer a barrister to conduct the advocacy.

## type of work

**general crime:** For most lawyers, 'everyday crime' is their staple. Jae Carwardine at London firm Russell-Cooke, says: "*Diversity is the appeal of the job – you really don't know what each day is going to present you with.*" A hectic schedule of visits to police stations, prisons and magistrates' courts, plenty of face-to-face client meetings and advocacy means this is definitely not a desk job. The work is date-driven and cases have a fast turnover; lawyers who are accredited to work as Duty Solicitors in the magistrates' courts are certainly likely to see the fruits of their labour quickly.

Criminal law has evolved rapidly over the past decade, evidenced by a succession of Crime Bills. With changes in mode of trial issues, the handling of youth work, sexual offences, a new Proceeds of Crime Act and of course the Human Rights Act, Jae says it is essential that you keep up to date on changes. She also notes that "*the abolition of means testing is diminishing private work greatly – the number of people eligible for legal aid has significantly increased.*"

**criminal fraud:** Jae explained the difference between this and everyday crime: "*It involves mountains of paperwork and analysis of figures – you need to understand business operations.*" Fraud specialists usually have a much smaller caseload, but cases can run for years. A limited number of firms undertake this work.

## skills needed...

...an eye for detail...sharp and resolute on your feet...excellent people skills...empathy...good organisational and IT skills...100% commitment...

Trainees used to be thrown in at the deep end, but the Law Society's accreditation process now means that, until accredited, they cannot attend police station interviews by themselves, nor make magistrates' court appearances. Once accredited, they will start with simple hearings to build confidence. Jae says: "*You have to be confident because it is nerve-racking – no one ever forgets their first bail application!*"

In court or at the station, the ability to think on one's feet, analyse matters quickly and deal with last-minute evidence or unexpected changes is key. And when handling casework, you will be looking for the things others have missed, so a questioning mind is essential, especially when faced with forensic or medical evidence, or a number of expert witnesses.

Criminal clients can be challenging: they may come from deprived backgrounds or have drink, drug and/or psychiatric problems, so "*accomplished people skills*" are essential. The need to maintain a professional stance is also vital, but Jae notes: "*You build very strong relationships with clients; you get to know the whole family, and receive Christmas cards. People never forget you because you are their lifeline.*"

There's a certain camaraderie amongst criminal solicitors as they're always meeting in police stations and courts, and they have a 'common enemy', so to speak, in the CPS. However, Jae warns: "*You do have to be quite thick-skinned; be prepared to be humiliated in public, and take it.*" This is not law for the faint-hearted; "*If you are desperately shy, it probably won't work for you.*"

Criminal lawyers need to be able to deal with stress. Jae advised: "*This is a job for someone who really enjoys hard work and is committed. There is huge job satisfaction, but without great remuneration."* If a fat-cat salary is your biggest priority, reconsider now before it's too late...

## career options

In 2001, the Legal Services Commission introduced a franchise system limiting the number of firms that handle publicly funded criminal defence. It also introduced the first Public Defender Services. To find the best criminal firms, look at our parent publication, *Chambers UK*, or alternatively ask a Citizens Advice Bureau or your local Law Society to recommend crime specialists. Training contracts at firms handling specialist or high-profile work are rare, but general crime firms will have more openings. Some lawyers actively promote the idea of trying paralegal work or outdoor clerking before applying for a training contract. Various government bodies such as the Serious Fraud Office or Customs provide a more prosecution-based approach, while work in the voluntary sector is a practical way to gain a realistic view of people and real life. Refer to page 14 for info on the CPS.

## leading firms from Chambers UK 2006

### Crime
London

| | |
|---|---|
| [1] BCL Burton Copeland | Bindman & Partners |
| Birnberg Peirce & Partners | Edward Fail Bradshaw & Waterson |
| Kingsley Napley | Taylor Nichol |
| Tuckers | |
| [2] Corker Binning Solicitors | Edwards Duthie |
| Fisher Meredith | Hickman & Rose |
| Hodge Jones & Allen | Iliffes Booth Bennett (IBB) |
| Powell Spencer & Partners | Saunders Solicitors LLP |
| Simons Muirhead & Burton | Stokoe Partnership |
| TNT Solicitors (Thanki Novy Taube) | TV Edwards |
| [3] Andrew Keenan & Co | Birds Solicitors |
| Hallinan, Blackburn, Gittings & Nott | Henry Milner & Co |
| Kaim Todner | Meldrum & Young |
| Russell Jones & Walker | Venters Solicitors |
| Victor Lissack, Roscoe & Coleman | |
| [4] Claude Hornby & Cox | Galbraith Branley |
| Goldkorns | Hughmans |
| J D Spicer & Co | McCormacks |
| Reynolds Dawson | Russell-Cooke |

### Crime
The South

| | |
|---|---|
| [1] Blake Lapthorn Linnell *Fareham* | |
| Clarke Kiernan *Tunbridge Wells* | |
| Coffin Mew & Clover *Fareham* | |
| [2] Bishop & Light *Brighton* | |
| Hamnett Osborne *Haywards Heath* | |
| Knights *Tunbridge Wells* | |
| White & Bowker *Winchester* | |

### Crime
Thames Valley

| | |
|---|---|
| [1] Blake Lapthorn Linnell *Oxford* | |
| Darbys *Oxford* | |
| Macnab Clarke *Abingdon* | |
| Morgan Cole *Oxford* | |

# solicitors

## Crime
### South West

[1] **Bobbetts Mackan** *Bristol*
**Douglas & Partners** *Bristol*
**Kelcey & Hall** *Bristol*
**Sansbury Campbell** *Bristol*
[2] **Nunn Rickard Solicitor** *Exeter*
**Russell Jones & Walker** *Bristol*
**St James Solicitors** *Exeter*
**Stone King Solicitors** *Bath*
**Walker Lahive** *Plymouth*
[3] **Aidan Woods & Co** *Bristol*
**Allen & Partners** *Bristol*
**Ashfords** *Tiverton*
**Bay Advocates** *Torquay*
**Dunn & Baker** *Exeter*
**Foot Anstey** *Plymouth*
**Stones** *Exeter*
**WBW Solicitors** *Newton Abbot*

## Crime
### Wales

[1] **Gamlins** *Rhyl*
**Huttons** *Cardiff*
**Martyn Prowel Solicitors** *Cardiff*
[2] **Clarke & Hartland** *Cardiff*
**Colin Jones** *Barry*
**Douglas-Jones Mercer** *Swansea*
**Goldstones** *Swansea*
**Graham Evans & Partners** *Swansea*
**Harding Evans** *Newport*
**Howe & Spender** *Port Talbot*
**Hugh James** *Blackwood*
**Robertsons** *Cardiff*
**Savery Pennington** *Cardiff*
**Spiro Grech & Harding** *Cardiff*
**Wilson Devonald** *Swansea*

## Crime
### Wales

[1] **Martyn Prowel Solicitors Cardiff**
**Roy Morgan & Co Cardiff**

## Crime
### West Midlands

[1] **Glaisyers** *Birmingham*
**Jonas Roy Bloom** *Birmingham*
[2] **Carvers Solicitors** *Birmingham*
**Lanyon Bowdler** *Telford*
**Purcell Parker** *Birmingham*
**Tuckers** *Birmingham*
**Tyndallwoods** *Birmingham*

## Crime
### East Midlands

[1] **Cartwright King** *Nottingham*
**The Johnson P'nship** *Nottingham*
[2] **Fletchers** *Nottingham*
**Kieran Clarke Solicitors** *Chesterfield*
**Nelsons** *Nottingham*
**The Smith Partnership** *Derby*
[3] **Banner Jones Midd'ton** *Chesterfield*
**Elliot Mather** *Matlock*
**Varley Hadley Siddall** *Nottingham*
**Ward & Griffiths** *Nottingham*
**Woodford-Robinson** *Northampton*

## Crime
### East Anglia

[1] **Belmores** *Norwich*
**Hatch Brenner** *Norwich*
**TMK Solicitors** *Southend-on-Sea*
[2] **David Charnley & Co** *Romford*
**Hunt & Coombs** *Peterborough*
**Lucas & Wyllys** *Great Yarmouth*
**Norton Peskett** *Lowestoft*
**TNT Solicitors** *Harlow*
[3] **Cole Bentley & Co** *Great Yarmouth*
**Copleys** *Huntingdon*
**Fosters** *Norwich*
**Gepp & Sons** *Chelmsford*
**Hegarty & Co** *Peterborough*

## Crime
### North West

[1] **Brian Koffman & Co** *Manchester*
**Burton Copeland** *Manchester*
**Draycott Browne** *Manchester*
**JMW Solicitors** *Manchester*
**Tuckers** *Manchester*
[2] **Cunninghams** *Manchester*
**Farleys** *Blackburn*
**Forbes** *Blackburn*
**Maidments** *Manchester*
**Olliers** *Manchester*
[3] **Cobleys** *Salford*
**Cuttle & Co** *Manchester*
**Kristina Harrison Solicitors** *Salford*
**Pearson Fielding P'ship** *Liverpool*
**RM Broudie & Co** *Liverpool*
**Rowlands** *Manchester*
**Russell & Russell** *Bolton*

## Crime
### North East

[1] **David Gray Solicitors** *Newcastle*
**Irwin Mitchell** *Sheffield*
**McCormicks** *Leeds*
**Sugaré & Co** *Leeds*
[2] **Grahame Stowe, Bateson** *Leeds*
**Henry Hyams** *Leeds*
**Howells** *Cardiff*
**Lester Morrill** *Leeds*
**Levi & Co** *Leeds*
**The Max Gold Partnership** *Hull*
**Williamsons Solicitors** *Hull*

# employment law

It's a current hot favourite with trainees, but is employment law the tamagotchi craze of the profession or is it destined to endure as one of the most engaging areas of legal practice? If the rapidity with which the body of law is changing and expanding means anything, then it is likely that employment lawyers will have plenty of work to keep them busy and interested for a long time to come.

## type of work

Employment lawyers are intimately involved in the relationships between employers and employees. For employers they offer precautionary advice, negotiate senior level staff exits, and limit the damage when things go wrong and disgruntled ex-employees bring claims for, say, unfair dismissal or discrimination. For employees they can be pillars of strength, helping to secure sometimes life-changing tribunal decisions or assisting in contract negotiations. Some lawyers have particularly close ties with trade unions, or act for employers dealing with broader labour issues.

When picking a firm, decide whether you have a strong preference for acting for employees (applicants) or employers (respondents), or perhaps unions. Similarly, do you want your work to be primarily contentious or non-contentious? Certain firms work along partisan lines; others like Mike Burd's firm Lewis Silkin believe that the best employment lawyers become well rounded through exposure to all aspects of practice. Mike puts much of the appeal of the job down to "*shifting gears between hugely differing roles.*" Additionally, "*every case is a drama with its own cast of characters – it's like going to the theatre every time.*" But, a word of warning: some (although not all) of the very big commercial firms offer a heavy diet of 'corporate support' work to their employment lawyers, effectively rendering them mere ancillaries to the gun-slinging deal doers of the corporate department.

## skills needed

...being a 'people' person...emotional intelligence tempered by commerciality...communication and negotiation skills...a talent for advocacy...practicality... quick assimilation of changes in strategy and advice...detailed knowledge of relevant law...

Flexibility and rapid response are vital. Mike explained that on the contentious side problems flare up unpredictably and need to be resolved quickly. "*It's a rare day when my plans are not blown out of the water. I might be drafting complex bonus provisions for an executive and end up on the phone to the chief exec of a company who has just been sacked and wants to see me urgently.*" Of course you have to be good with people, but it's more than that: "*You have to be sanguine about the foibles of human beings...which can be endless!*" You also need to know when to be tough, particularly in negotiations with other lawyers. As for advocacy, this is where bared teeth and hardball tactics will work against you: employment tribunals are less formal and less legalistic in their language and procedure than normal court hearings.

## career options

After a hard-core trainee seat in corporate, where one's role is essentially that of a remora fish, employment can be a reminder of what you thought the law was all about when still an idealistic student. It's usually easier to relate to the case scenario – by then you'll have been an employee yourself – and lawyers in this field are amongst the most pleasant in the profession. Factor in the never-a-dull-day aspect to the job and it's no wonder NQs are queuing around the block for the few jobs that crop up. Unless you can cast a spell over the head of department, you'd be well advised to steal a march on peers by ensuring that your training is fulsome, and perhaps supplemented by voluntary work at a CAB, law centre or FRU. With these organisations there's even a chance

# solicitors

you might get some tribunal experience. If your employment seat combines pensions and employment law, and the emphasis is on the P and not the E, then this extra-curricular activity could make all the difference.

In the dozen or so years since employment law has become a specialist practice area, the number of practitioners has mushroomed, both in private practice and in-house at larger companies – eg Warner Bros, M&S and Shell, for example. And if the law doesn't do it for you, you could sidestep into HR. If it's just fee earning that you've had enough of, a know-how position could see you collating and explaining the avalanche of new legislation and regulations to your colleagues in a law firm, a task Mike likens to *"playing 30 games of chess, blindfold, every day!"*

*Chambers UK* will give you information about the nature of the work and the clients of the best employment law practices across the country.

## leading firms from Chambers UK 2006

| Employment: Mainly Defendant London | |
| --- | --- |
| [1] Allen & Overy LLP | Baker & McKenzie LLP |
| Herbert Smith LLP | Simmons & Simmons |
| [2] Eversheds LLP | Lewis Silkin |
| Lovells | Mayer, Brown, Rowe & Maw |
| McDermott Will & Emery UK LLP | |
| [3] Beachcroft Wansbroughs | Charles Russell |
| Clifford Chance LLP | CMS Cameron McKenna LLP |
| Dechert LLP | Fox Williams |
| Freshfields Bruckhaus Deringer | Hammonds |
| Linklaters | Macfarlanes |
| Olswang | Pinsent Masons |
| [4] Addleshaw Goddard | Denton Wilde Sapte |
| DLA Piper Rudnick Gray Cary UK LLP | Farrer & Co |
| Nabarro Nathanson | Slaughter and May |
| Taylor Wessing | Travers Smith |
| [5] Ashurst | Barlow Lyde & Gilbert |
| Berwin Leighton Paisner | Bird & Bird |
| Mishcon de Reya | Norton Rose |
| Osborne Clarke | Salans |
| SJ Berwin LLP | Speechly Bircham |
| Stephenson Harwood | Withers LLP |
| [6] Aldridge Parker | Archon |
| Doyle Clayton | Finers Stephens Innocent |
| Harbottle & Lewis LLP | Kemp Little LLP |
| Lawrence Graham LLP | Manches LLP |
| Reynolds Porter Chamberlain | Richards Butler |
| Tarlo Lyons | Watson, Farley & Williams |

| Employment The South |
| --- |
| [1] Blake Lapthorn Linnell *Fareham* |
| DMH Stallard *Crawley* |
| [2] Bond Pearce LLP *Southampton* |
| Charles Russell *Guildford* |
| Clarkson Wright & Jakes *Orpington* |
| Clyde & Co *Guildford* |
| Cripps Harries Hall *Tunbridge Wells* |
| Paris Smith & Randall *Southampton* |
| Stevens & Bolton LLP *Guildford* |
| Thomson Snell *Tunbridge Wells* |
| [3] asb law *Crawley* |
| Brachers *Maidstone* |
| Coffin Mew & Clover *Southampton* |
| Lamport Bassitt *Southampton* |
| Lester Aldridge *Southampton* |
| Moore & Blatch *Southampton* |
| Sherrards Employment Law and Human Resources *Haywards Heath* |
| [4] Furley Page *Canterbury* |
| Mundays *Cobham* |
| Rawlison Butler *Crawley* |
| Thomas Eggar *Chichester* |

# specialist areas

## Employment
### South West

1. **Bevan Brittan LLP** *Bristol*
   **Burges Salmon LLP** *Bristol*
   **Osborne Clarke** *Bristol*
2. **Ashfords**
   **Bond Pearce LLP** *Plymouth*
   **TLT Solicitors** *Bristol*
   **Veale Wasbrough Lawyers** *Bristol*
3. **Beachcroft Wansbroughs** *Bristol*
   **Burroughs Day** *Bristol*
   **Clarke Willmott** *Taunton*
   **Foot Anstey** *Bridgewater*
   **Michelmores** *Exeter*
   **Rickerbys** *Cheltenham*
   **Stephens & Scown** *Exeter*
   **Withy King** *Bath*
4. **Bevans** *Bristol*
   **BPE Solicitors** *Cheltenham*
   **Charles Russell** *Cheltenham*
   **Lyons Davidson** *Bristol*
   **Pattinson & Brewer** *Bristol*
   **Thompsons** *Bristol*
   **Thring Townsend** *Bath*
   **Wolferstans** *Plymouth*

## Employment:
### Mainly Applicant
#### London

1. **Russell Jones & Walker**
2. **Pattinson & Brewer**
   **Thompsons**
3. **Bindman & Partners**
   **Irwin Mitchell**
   **Rowley Ashworth**
   **Simpson Millar**
   **Webster Dixon**

## Employment
### Thames Valley

1. **Clarkslegal LLP** *Reading*
2. **Olswang Thames Valley** *Reading*
   **Osborne Clarke** *Reading*
3. **Boyes Turner** *Reading*
   **Henmans** *Oxford*
   **Manches** *Oxford*
   **Pitmans** *Reading*
   **Shoosmiths** *Reading*
4. **BPC Business Lawyers** *Beaconsfield*
   **Cater Leydon Millard Ltd** *Abingdon*
   **Matthew Arnold & Baldwin** *Watford*
   **Morgan Cole** *Reading*
   **Penningtons Solicitors LLP** *Newbury*
   **Pictons** *St Albans*

## Employment
### Wales

1. **Eversheds LLP** *Cardiff*
2. **Geldards** *Cardiff*
   **Hugh James** *Cardiff*
   **Morgan Cole** *Cardiff*
   **Russell Jones & Walker** *Cardiff*
3. **Capital Law** *Cardiff Bay*
   **Dolmans** *Cardiff*
   **Harding Evans** *Newport*

## Employment
### East Anglia

1. **Eversheds LLP** *Cambridge*
   **Mills & Reeve** *Cambridge*
2. **Greenwoods Solicitors** *Peterborough*
   **Hewitsons** *Cambridge*
   **Taylor Vinters** *Cambridge*
3. **Hegarty & Co** *Peterborough*
   **Steeles (Law) LLP** *Norwich*
4. **Ashton Graham** *Ipswich*
   **Prettys** *Ipswich*
   **Wollastons** *Chelmsford*

## Employment
### Midlands

1. **Eversheds LLP** *Nottingham*
   **Wragge & Co LLP** *Birmingham*
2. **Hammonds** *Birmingham*
   **Martineau Johnson** *Birmingham*
   **Pinsent Masons** *Birmingham*
3. **Bevan Brittan LLP** *Birmingham*
   **Browne Jacobson LLP** *Nottingham*
   **Cobbetts** *Birmingham*
   **DLA Piper Rudnick** *Birmingham*
   **Gateley Wareing LLP** *Birmingham*
4. **Geldards** *Nottingham*
   **Howes Percival** *Leicester*
   **Irwin Mitchell** *Birmingham*
   **Mills & Reeve** *Birmingham*
   **Shakespeares** *Birmingham*
5. **Averta Employment** *Solihull*
   **BPE Solicitors** *Birmingham*
   **Freeth Cartwright LLP** *Nottingham*
   **George Green** *Halesowen*
   **Higgs & Sons** *Brierley Hill*

# specialist areas

## Employment
### North West

1. **Addleshaw Goddard** *Manchester*
   **DLA Piper Rudnick** *Manchester*
   **Eversheds LLP** *Manchester*
2. **Cobbetts** *Manchester*
   **DWF** *Manchester*
   **Halliwells LLP** *Manchester*
   **Hammonds** *Manchester*
   **Mace & Jones** *Manchester*
3. **Pannone & Partners** *Manchester*
   **Thompsons** *Manchester*
4. **Berg Legal** *Manchester*
   **Brabners Chaffe Street** *Manchester*
   **Burnetts** *Carlisle*
   **James Chapman and Co** *Manchester*
   **Ricksons** *Manchester*
   **Weightmans** *Liverpool*
5. **Aaron & Partners LLP** *Chester*
   **Baines Wilson** *Carlisle*
   **Hill Dickinson** *Liverpool*
   **Keoghs** *Bolton*
   **Kuit Steinart Levy** *Manchester*
   **Russell Jones & Walker** *Manchester*
   **Whittles** *Manchester*

## Employment
### Yorkshire

1. **DLA Piper Rudnick Gray** *Leeds*
   **Eversheds LLP** *Leeds*
   **Pinsent Masons** *Leeds*
2. **Addleshaw Goddard** *Leeds*
   **Cobbetts** *Leeds*
3. **Ford & Warren** *Leeds*
   **Hammonds** *Leeds*
   **Irwin Mitchell** *Sheffield*
   **Walker Morris** *Leeds*
4. **Gordons** *Leeds*
   **Lupton Fawcett** *Leeds*
   **McCormicks** *Leeds*
   **Morrish & Co** *Leeds*
   **Rollits** *Hull*
   **Wake Smith** *Sheffield*

## Employment
### North East

1. **Dickinson Dees** *Newcastle*
   **Eversheds LLP** *Newcastle upon Tyne*
2. **Short Richardson** *Newcastle*
   **Thompsons** *Newcastle upon Tyne*
   **Ward Hadaway** *Newcastle upon Tyne*
3. **Crutes Law Firm** *Newcastle*
   **Jacksons** *Stockton on Tees*
   **Robert Muckle** *Newcastle upon Tyne*
   **Samuel Phillips Law Firm** *Newcastle*
4. **Archers** *Stockton on Tees*
   **Hay & Kilner** *Newcastle upon Tyne*
   **Watson Burton LLP** *Newcastle*

# environmental law

Typically acting for corporate clients seeking damage limitation, pre-emptive advice and defence from prosecution, few environmental lawyers fit the whale-saving stereotype.

## type of work

Head of environmental law at City practice Simmons & Simmons, Kathy Mylrea says: "*The beauty of environmental law is that it is extremely varied.*" Overlapping with property law, criminal matters and European legislation, the work breaks down into three broad areas:

- transactional, project and property support;
- compliance and regulatory advice; and
- litigation, including criminal and civil disputes, judicial reviews and statutory appeals.

With such diversity, it is unsurprising that a single day can see a solicitor handle matters as assorted as health and safety prosecutions, corporate transactions and environmental permit applications. We heard that "*job satisfaction is generally high because environmental law is relevant – it is there every day when you have a drink of water or put the rubbish out.*" The work isn't as desk-bound as many areas of law and, while "*visiting a rubbish tip is not everybody's idea of a great day out,*" if you prefer a real breeze to aircon, and river beds to sleeping pods, welcome to the great outdoors. That said, the whole sector is constantly evolving, and, back at the office, there is plenty of paperwork: trainees and junior solicitors find that there are always new areas to be researched, legislation to be untangled, and manuals to be updated.

## skills needed

...deal with intellectual problems commercially... be an all-rounder...understand corporate structures...awareness of environmental issues...basic grasp of science...research, interpretation and presentation skills...

Kathy says that above all "*you need strong basic legal skills*" – simply because environmental law is so broad, overlapping with so many other areas. A genuine interest in a specialist area such as renewable energy, conservation or water pollution is also vital, because "*no one gets on in environmental law unless they are really interested in it.*" Bags of research and complex legislation means academic skills are crucial, but Kathy warns: "*You can't be too purist – environment law is largely about looking for solutions,*" so sound judgement, pragmatism and commercial nous are all equally important. Expect lots of client contact, often over many years. Indeed, the ability to establish strong relationships is crucial, and as environmental risks are inherently difficult to quantify, you must develop a good gut instinct about matters and learn to think laterally to find appropriate solutions.

## career options

Environmental law is increasingly integrated into other areas: legal developments in related fields such as the Utility Bill and the review of EC chemicals legislation all generate activity, yet environmental lawyers are quite a rare breed. You won't find a team of 20 or 30 lawyers, even in the largest practice, and this means that it is a competitive area to break into as an NQ. Kathy explained that environmental lawyers often have another string to their bow "*in case the need for legal advice in the area shrinks in the long term, or there is a reduction of environment work in the shorter term.*"

Genuine interest, commitment and a willingness to be flexible are essential to private practice, but there are other options. Kathy says: "*Private practice doesn't have a monopoly,*" and while it shouldn't be dismissed, she notes that "*if your objective is to change environment law, you should consider the other routes too.*" In a local authority legal department you'll handle regulatory work, planning issues, waste management and air pollution prosecutions, and have a role in advising the authority on its own liability. In-house positions are rarer, except in large organisations such as Greenpeace, Friends of the Earth and the RSPB.

The Department for Environment, Food and Rural Affairs employs over 80 lawyers, including trainees on GLS-funded schemes. Work here includes litigation, drafting of subordinate legislation, advisory work and contract drafting.

The Environment Agency has lawyers in Bristol and eight regional offices, and is responsible for protecting and enhancing the environment through regulation of those corporate activities that have the greatest potential to pollute. The scope of work is vast, extending from waste management to flood defence, contaminated land to environmental impact assessment. Further, the agency is the prosecution body for environmental crimes, so there is plenty of prosecution work as well as enforcement activity and close involvement with government lawyers on the drafting and implementation of legislation.

# specialist areas

## leading firms from Chambers UK 2006

### Environment
Nationwide

1. Freshfields Bruckhaus Deringer

2. Allen & Overy LLP — Ashurst
   Barlow Lyde & Gilbert — Burges Salmon LLP
   Clifford Chance LLP — CMS Cameron McKenna LLP
   Linklaters — Simmons & Simmons

3. Baker & McKenzie LLP — Berwin Leighton Paisner
   Denton Wilde Sapte — Jones Day
   Mayer, Brown, Rowe & Maw LLP — Slaughter and May

4. Addleshaw Goddard — Eversheds LLP
   Hammonds — Kirkpatrick & Lockhart Nicholson
   Graham LLP — Lovells
   Macfarlanes — Nabarro Nathanson
   Trowers & Hamlins

5. Herbert Smith LLP — Lawrence Graham LLP
   Norton Rose — SJ Berwin LLP

6. Bircham Dyson Bell — Blake Lapthorn Linnell
   Bond Pearce LLP — Davies Arnold Cooper
   DLA Piper Rudnick Gray Cary UK — Dundas & Wilson
   Osborne Clarke — Stephenson Harwood
   Taylor Wessing — Wragge & Co LLP

### Environment
Midlands

1. Eversheds LLP *Nottingham*
   Wragge & Co LLP *Birmingham*

2. Browne Jacobson LLP *Nottingham*
   Hammonds *Birmingham*
   Pinsent Masons *Birmingham*

### Environment
Wales

1. Eversheds LLP *Cardiff*
   Geldards *Cardiff*

2. Hugh James *Cardiff*
   Morgan Cole *Cardiff*

### Environment
East Anglia

1. Mills & Reeve *Cambridge*

2. Eversheds LLP *Norwich*
   Hewitsons *Cambridge*
   Taylor Vinters *Cambridge*

### Environment
The South

1. Blake Lapthorn Linnell *Southampton*
   Bond Pearce LLP *Southampton*

2. DMH Stallard *Brighton*

3. Brachers *Maidstone*
   Stevens & Bolton LLP *Guildford*

### Environment
Thames Valley

1. Clarkslegal LLP *Reading*
   Manches *Oxford*

2. B P Collins *Gerrards Cross*

### Environment
South West

1. Burges Salmon LLP *Bristol*

2. Bond Pearce LLP *Plymouth*
   Osborne Clarke *Bristol*

3. Clarke Willmott *Bristol*

4. Bevan Brittan LLP *Bristol*
   Veale Wasbrough Lawyers *Bristol*

5. Ashfords
   Thring Townsend *Bath*

### Environment
North East

1. DLA Piper Rudnick Gray *Sheffield*
   Eversheds LLP *Leeds*
   Nabarro Nathanson *Sheffield*

2. Addleshaw Goddard *Leeds*
   Dickinson Dees *Newcastle*
   Hammonds *Leeds*
   Pinsent Masons *Leeds*

### Environment
North West

1. Eversheds LLP *Manchester*

2. Addleshaw Goddard *Manchester*
   Cobbetts *Manchester*
   Hammonds *Manchester*

3. Aaron & Partners LLP *Chester*
   Halliwells LLP *Manchester*

# family law

Family lawyers handle divorce, disputes between cohabitants, inheritance disputes between family members, prenuptial and cohabitation agreements, and all matters relating to children. They will also deal with issues arising from registration of same-sex relationships, following Civil Partnership legislation.

## type of work

Your experience as a family lawyer will depend on whether you opt for general practice on the high street or one of the specialist practices that deal more with higher-value divorces and complex child or international matters. The former may be less glamorous but in general practice you'll be thrown in at the deep end. So which route is best? James Pirrie at Family Law in Partnership points out that in general practice you are more likely to have your own caseload from the start, which will increase your client skills. If you start in a specialist practice, you're more likely to be consigned to *back-room duties – drafting documents and form-filling as part of a team.*

Whichever route you take, the ambit of your work will be wider than you'd expect as family law cases may involve inheritance and wills issues, conveyancing knowledge, judicial review (especially in connection with public funding, formerly legal aid) welfare benefits and the CSA, corporate law, tax, trusts and pensions – and that's before we start taking into account foreign jurisdictions. According to James, *"a good family lawyer's career profile should look more like Ayers Rock than Nelson's Column!"*

Clients will be husbands, wives, cohabitants, local authorities, children's guardians and, occasionally, children in their own right. You will also regularly encounter social workers, psychologists, probation officers and medical professionals, accountants, financial and pensions advisers, family lawyers from foreign jurisdictions and a wide variety of other experts. It is helpful to have some experience of people, relationships and the ways of the world in order to handle what can sometimes be distressing case scenarios. No two clients are ever the same, and neither are their stories; however, one thing that remains a constant is the need to keep the interests of any children paramount.

The first meeting with a client is crucial. At this stage you must *"try to understand what they want to achieve, help them understand the process options (and crucially, which of them are afford-able), explain how the court might approach the issue, and do the sums to see what is sensible."* Subsequent tasks include drafting petitions, putting together skeleton arguments for court, and negotiating settlements. As a junior, you'll prepare bundles of case documentation and attend court to take notes. The more experienced you become, the greater the advocacy opportunities.

James thinks it is fairly easy to become immersed in the work and to take on responsibility. He reassures us that *"there isn't the same burnout in family law as in City work."* Family law is not a static area of practice – the Human Rights Act has opened up new possibilities; how children are dealt with has moved under the spotlight with the activities of men's groups such as Fathers For Justice, and acquiring psychological insights and negotiation skills is a never ending process

## skills needed

...good listener...life experience... professional distance...interest in human relationships...commercial acumen...enjoy advocacy...carrying your clients' confidence.

Empathy and sensitivity are invaluable traits; but James stresses: *"It is not important to have been through the wringer yourself. You can be very good contextually, or technically brilliant."* One of the first things you'll learn is that *"it is no good to just act like a sponge, absorbing all your client's emotions."* Instead, *"you need to have a clear focus and strong communication skills because you are the conduit for your client's realities and concerns."*

While family law may sound soft around the edges, at the negotiating table when your client's home, children or livelihood are at stake, "*you need to be tough, and able to look someone in the eye and not blink for as long as it takes.*"

## career options

Most family lawyers opt for private practice, be this tough litigation, negotiation, mediation or the new kid on the block – collaborative family law. This is a new model where the lawyers act for their clients in round-table negotiations but contract out of subsequently litigating the case. Others may pursue in-house positions with local authorities instead of private practice.

## leading firms from Chambers UK 2006

### Family/Matrimonial
#### South West
[1] **Burges Salmon LLP** *Bristol*
**Clarke Willmott** *Bristol*
**Foot Anstey** *Plymouth*
**Stephens & Scown** *Exeter*
**TLT Solicitors** *Bristol*
**Tozers** *Exeter*
[2] **Act Family Law Practice** *Plymouth*
**Hartnell Chanot Law Practice** *Exeter*
**Wolferstans** *Plymouth*
[3] **Ford Simey** *Exeter*
**Gill Akaster** *Plymouth*
**Hooper & Wollen** *Torquay*
**Rickerbys** *Cheltenham*
**Stone King Solicitors** *Bath*
**Stones** *Exeter*
**Thring Townsend** *Bath*
**WBW Solicitors** *Torquay*
**Withy King** *Bath*

### Family/Matrimonial
#### Wales
[1] **Harding Evans** *Newport*
**Hugh James** *Cardiff*
**Larby Williams, Gwyn & Gwyn** *Cardiff*
**Nicol Denvir & Purnell** *Cardiff*
**Wendy Hopkins Family Law** *Cardiff*
[2] **Avery Naylor** *Swansea*
**Howells** *Cardiff*
**Leo Abse & Cohen** *Cardiff*
**Martyn Prowel Solicitors** *Cardiff*
**Robertsons** *Cardiff*

### Family/Matrimonial
#### East Anglia
[1] **Mills & Reeve** *Cambridge, Norwich*
[2] **Buckles** *Peterborough*
**Hunt & Coombs** *Peterborough*
**Silver Fitzgerald** *Cambridge*
**Taylor Vinters** *Cambridge*
[3] **Cozens-Hardy & Jewson** *Norwich*
**Gotelee & Goldsmith** *Ipswich*
**Hansells** *Norwich*
**Hatch Brenner** *Norwich*
**Hewitsons** *Cambridge*
**Kester Cunningham John** *Cambridge*
**Leonard Gray** *Chelmsford*
**Marchant-Daisley** *Cambridge*
**Overburys** *Norwich*
**Prettys** *Ipswich*
**Rudlings & Wakelam** *Thetford*

### Family/Matrimonial
#### Midlands
[1] **Blair Allison & Co** *Birmingham*
**Challinors** *Birmingham, West Brom.*
**Rupert Bear Murray** *Nottingham*
[2] **Anthony Collins** *Birmingham*
**Divorce and Family** *Birmingham*
[3] **Benussi & Co** *Birmingham*
**Cartwright & Lewis** *Birmingham*
**Freeth Cartwright LLP** *Nottingham*
**Hadens (fmly Haden Stretton)** *Walsall*
**Harrison Clark** *Worcester*
**Lanyon Bowdler** *Shrewsbury*
**Nelsons** *Nottingham*
**Osborne & Co** *Birmingham*
**Turnbull Garrard** *Shrewsbury*
**Tyndallwoods** *Birmingham*
**Wace Morgan** *Shrewsbury*
**Young & Lee** *Birmingham*

### Family/Matrimonial
#### Thames Valley
[1] **Blandy & Blandy** *Reading*
**Manches** *Oxford*
[2] **Boodle Hatfield** *Oxford*
**Darbys** *Oxford*
**Henmans** *Oxford*
**Morgan Cole** *Reading*
[3] **Bower & Bailey** *Oxford*
**Horsey Lightly Fynn** *Newbury*
**Iliffes Booth Bennett (IBB)** *Uxbridge*

# specialist areas

## Family/Matrimonial
### London

1. Manches LLP
   Withers LLP
2. Alexiou Fisher Philipps
   Charles Russell
   Farrer & Co
   Hughes Fowler Carruthers
   Levison Meltzer Pigott
   Miles Preston & Co
   Payne Hicks Beach
   Sears Tooth
3. Clintons
   Collyer-Bristow
   Dawson Cornwell
   Kingsley Napley
   Mishcon de Reya
4. Bindman & Partners
   Goodman Ray
   Gordon Dadds
   Reynolds Porter Chamberlain
5. Anthony Gold
   CKFT
   Family Law In Partnership
   Forsters LLP
   Harcus Sinclair
   International Family Law Chambers
   Osbornes
6. Ambrose Appelbe
   Bross Bennett
   Dawsons
   Fisher Meredith
   Hodge Jones & Allen
   Rooks Rider
   Russell-Cooke

## Family/Matrimonial
### North West

1. Pannone & Partners *Manchester*
2. Addleshaw Goddard *Manchester*
   Cobbetts *Manchester*
   Green & Co *Manchester*
   Halliwells *Liverpool*
   Mace & Jones *Liverpool, Knutsford*
3. Brabners Chaffe Street *Liverpool*
   Hill Dickinson *Liverpool*
   JMW Solicitors *Manchester*
   Laytons *Manchester*
   Morecrofts *Liverpool*
   Stephensons *Leigh*

## Family/Matrimonial
### Yorkshire

1. Addleshaw Goddard *Leeds*
2. Andrew M Jackson *Hull*
   Gordons *Bradford*
   Grahame Stowe Bateson *Harrogate*
   Irwin Mitchell *Leeds*
   Jones Myers Partnership *Leeds*
3. Lupton Fawcett *Leeds*
   Walker Morris *Leeds*
   Zermansky & Partners *Leeds.*

## Family/Matrimonial
### The South

1. Lester Aldridge *Bournemouth*
2. Brachers *Maidstone*
   Charles Russell *Guildford*
   Paris Smith & Randall *Southampton*
   Thomson Snell *Tunbridge Wells*
3. Blake Lapthorn Linnell *Portsmouth*
   Coffin Mew & Clover *Portsmouth*
   Cripps Harries Hall *Tunbridge Wells*
   Ellis Jones *Bournemouth*
   Max Barford & Co *Tunbridge Wells*
   Watson Nevill Solicitors *Maidstone*
   Williams Thompson *Christchurch*

## Family/Matrimonial
### North East

1. Dickinson Dees *Newcastle*
2. Hay & Kilner *Newcastle upon Tyne*
   Mincoffs *Newcastle upon Tyne*
   Samuel Phillips *Newcastle upon Tyne*
   Sintons *Newcastle upon Tyne*
   Ward Hadaway *Newcastle upon Tyne*
   Watson Burton LLP *Newcastle*

# intellectual property

Intellectual property law is commonly divided into hard IP (patents) and soft IP (trade marks, design rights, copyright, passing off, anti-counterfeiting and confidential information). Unless a firm is very specialist, it will deal with both types of work.

## type of work

Patents protect new, industrially applicable inventions, providing the proprietor with a monopoly to work the invention for a certain period. A trade mark provides a limited monopoly to use that mark on certain goods or services; and a registered design gives the owner an exclusive right to use the design. IP can be contentious or non-contentious and patent litigation, in particular, can be very complex, often with high stakes. The IP lawyer's role ranges from simple advice on the results of trade mark searches to trade mark opposition work, advice on a worldwide trade mark filing strategy and drafting sponsorship, endorsement and merchandising contracts.

James Love, head of IP at Pinsents, explained what this means on a day-to-day basis: "*A large proportion of time is spent letter writing, as disputes often don't go beyond a letter to the other side.*" And the rest of the time? "*Reading the patents once a case has taken off means wading through lots of material, seeking the smoking guns that are going to help your case.*" It isn't all paper-based: James described the typical IP lawyer's office as "*littered with the kind of products you find on supermarket shelves.*"

And rather like UN weapons inspectors, patent lawyers get out and about – perhaps visiting factories to learn about production processes. The work is increasingly international (not least because of the internet) and is set to become more so as the European Community gets up to speed on trans-EC rights.

IP lawyers might be stuck into trade mark infringement proceedings, or they could just as easily be called upon to work as a part of a multidisciplinary team on a large corporate transaction. Trainees and NQs usually have a decent number of smaller, discrete matters to work on, but there are times when they might feel like an insignificant cog in a vast machine when a high-value dispute takes off.

Clients include manufacturers and suppliers of hi-tech, engineering, pharmaceutical and agrochemical products, leading brand owners, universities, scientific institutions and media organisations. Lawyers must be able to handle a diverse range of individuals from the "*sophisticated, dynamic and pushy director of a big company to the mad inventor type who is pernickety and convinced his invention will make him millions.*"

## skills needed

**patent law** ...a basic understanding of science (min. A-levels; ideally a degree)...aptitude for technical matters...well-organised...precise drafting...

**general ip** ...curiosity for all things creative, artistic and technological...handle quirky/artistic types...interest in the internet...up with consumer trends...

James stressed the importance of attention to detail, precision and accuracy: "*You need to be able to think in a very accurate, concentrated way – words are very important, and you have to analyse them in meticulous detail.*" Good drafting skills are absolutely critical, particularly in patent work; but beyond this, and especially in general IP matters, you'll need to have a good sense of commercial strategy and branding issues, and be innovative in the way you think.

Many lawyers have a science background. While this is going to be a huge bonus, James was quick to counsel young hopefuls against putting themselves through science A-Levels to bolster their CV. Some large firms do send NQs on a course in Bristol run by the Intellectual Property Lawyers Association, but James assured us that students would do better to "*hone their legal skills than become an armchair scientist*." Equally, while a science background may help you keep up when people start discussing the intricacies of electrode potential, "*if you are too much of a techy, you may leave the judge swamped; however, if you have had to go through the mental gymnastics yourself it can be helpful when it comes to explaining it all to someone else*."

## career options

The Thames Valley has a concentration of IT companies and Cambridge's 'Silicon Fen' has grown on the back of the hi-tech and biotech companies that have spun out of the university.

*Chambers UK* identifies the leading IP practices and gives details of their particular specialisms and clients.

Manufacturing, pharmaceutical and research companies employ patent specialists and there are in-house legal teams at all the large pharmaceutical companies, for example Procter & Gamble, Reckitt Benckiser and Unilever. Non-patent lawyers find their way into the media world: all major publishers and television companies have in-house IP lawyers. Many broadcasting companies now employ lawyers in positions such as head of business and legal affairs. Additionally, there is a visible drift of lawyers into firms of trade mark agents and patent attorneys where a good living is to be made. Equally, there is a drift in the other direction too.

## leading firms from Chambers UK 2006

| Intellectual Property: General London | |
|---|---|
| 1 Bird & Bird | Bristows |
| Taylor Wessing | |
| 2 Ashurst | Field Fisher Waterhouse |
| Herbert Smith LLP | Linklaters |
| Lovells | Willoughby & Partners |
| 3 Baker & McKenzie LLP | DLA Piper Rudnick Gray Cary |
| Freshfields Bruckhaus Deringer | Olswang |
| Simmons & Simmons | Wragge & Co LLP |
| 4 Allen & Overy LLP | Clifford Chance LLP |
| Mayer, Brown, Rowe & Maw LLP | Roiter Zucker |
| SJ Berwin LLP | Slaughter and May |
| 5 Addleshaw Goddard | Briffa |
| Collyer-Bristow | Finers Stephens Innocent |
| Howrey LLP | Lewis Silkin |
| Marks & Clerk Solicitors | McDermott Will & Emery UK LLP |
| Redd | Richards Butler |
| White & Case | |
| 6 Harbottle & Lewis LLP | Jones Day |
| Kilpatrick Stockton | Orchard |

| Intellectual Property: Patent Litigation London |
|---|
| 1 Bird & Bird |
| Bristows |
| 2 Herbert Smith LLP |
| Taylor Wessing |
| 3 Linklaters |
| Simmons & Simmons |
| 4 Baker & McKenzie LLP |
| Clifford Chance LLP |
| DLA Piper Rudnick Gray Cary |
| Field Fisher Waterhouse |
| Freshfields Bruckhaus Deringer |
| Lovells |
| Wragge & Co LLP |
| 5 McDermott Will & Emery UK LLP |
| Olswang |
| Roiter Zucker |

# specialist areas

## Intellectual Property
### The South
[1] **Blake Lapthorn Linnell** *Fareham*
[2] **DMH Stallard** *Crawley*
[3] **Bond Pearce LLP** *Southampton*
**Lester Aldridge** *Bournemouth*
**Shadbolt & Co LLP** *Reigate*

## Intellectual Property
### Thames Valley
[1] **Willoughby & Partners** *Oxford*
[2] **Olswang Thames Valley** *Reading*
**Shoosmiths** *Milton Keynes*
[3] **Manches** *Oxford*
**Matthew Arnold & Baldwin** *Watford*
**Osborne Clarke** *Reading*
**Marcus J O'Leary** *Wokingham*

## Intellectual Property
### South West
[1] **Bevan Brittan LLP** *Bristol*
**Osborne Clarke** *Bristol*
[2] **Bond Pearce LLP** *Bristol, Plymouth*
**Burges Salmon LLP** *Bristol*
[3] **Ashfords** *Bristol*
**Beachcroft Wansbroughs** *Bristol*
**Humphreys & Co Solicitors** *Bristol*

## Intellectual Property
### Wales
[1] **Geldards LLP** *Cardiff*
[2] **Eversheds LLP** *Cardiff*
**Morgan Cole** *Cardiff*

## Intellectual Property
### Midlands
[1] **Wragge & Co LLP** *Birmingham*
[2] **Browne Jacobson LLP** *Nottingham*
**Eversheds LLP** *Nottingham*
**Martineau Johnson** *Birmingham*
**Pinsent Masons** *Birmingham*
[3] **Cobbetts** *Birmingham*
**Putsmans Solicitors** *Birmingham*

## Intellectual Property
### North East
[1] **Addleshaw Goddard** *Leeds*
[2] **DLA Piper Rudnick Gray** *Leeds*
**Pinsent Masons** *Leeds*
**Walker Morris** *Leeds*
[3] **Dickinson Dees** *Newcastle*
**Eversheds LLP** *Leeds*
**Hammonds** *Leeds*
**Irwin Mitchell** *Leeds*
**Lupton Fawcett** *Leeds*
**Sanderson Lumber** *Leeds*
**Ward Hadaway** *Newcastle upon Tyne*

## Intellectual Property
### East Anglia
[1] **Mills & Reeve** *Norwich*
**Taylor Vinters** *Cambridge*
[2] **Greenwoods** *Peterborough*
**Hewitsons** *Cambridge*
**Taylor Wessing** *Cambridge*

## Intellectual Property
### North West
[1] **Addleshaw Goddard** *Manchester*
**Halliwells LLP** *Manchester*
[2] **DLA Piper Rudnick Gray** *Manchester*
**Eversheds LLP** *Manchester*
**Hill Dickinson** *Liverpool*
[3] **Cobbetts** *Manchester*
**Hammonds** *Manchester*
[4] **Berg Legal** *Manchester*
**Kuit Steinart Levy** *Manchester*
**Pannone & Partners** *Manchester*
**Taylors** *Blackburn*

# litigation/dispute resolution

You probably think litigators live for protracted courtroom battles and entertain the idea of an early case settlement in much the same way as a mortician would view his latest masterpiece sitting up and asking for the Sunday papers. You'd be wrong. It's a grim fact of commercial reality that clients rarely wish to emerge from the courtroom to pose triumphantly on the steps for photographers. On the contrary, clients generally hope to reach a commercial settlement as quickly, cheaply and unobtrusively as possible. Result? Most cases never reach trial.

Unless they can be settled by correspondence, disputes are often concluded in one of three ways. The first is through litigation itself – the issue and pursuit of court proceedings, which can be expensive and time-consuming. For this reason, contracts often provide for disputes between the parties to be referred to the second method: binding arbitration. Arbitration is usually conducted by an expert in the subject matter if it is particularly specialised and, unlike court proceedings, arbitration is confidential. The third method is alternative dispute resolution (ADR). Although it can take various forms, the most common form of ADR is mediation. This involves structured negotiations between the parties, which are overseen and directed by an independent mediator. The parties retain the right to litigate if they find it impossible to reach an agreement.

## type of work

Put simply, litigation is a process. Once a case has been commenced, it follows a predetermined course laid down by the rules of court: statement of case; disclosure of documents; witness statements; various procedural applications; and in a small number of cases, trial. Managing this process is the litigator's primary role, and this requires not only a mastery of the rules, but also a keen appreciation of tactics and attention to

detail. The Civil Procedure Rules (CPR) introduced in 1999 were intended to speed up the exchange of information between the parties and cut the number of cases reaching the courts. Simon Willis, a partner at Barlow Lyde & Gilbert, believes that the CPR have made a difference: *"Parties are generally more inclined to be reasonable in their approach to litigation, and there is more emphasis on resolving disputes without resorting to trial. The reforms have got rid of some of the worst excesses under the old rules – there is less litigation by numbers."*

Commercial litigation covers a multitude of business disputes, ranging from a skirmish over a tenancy agreement to full-scale combat over the terms of a multimillion-dollar contract. Some litigators specialise, for example, in insurance, construction, media or shipping cases – for more information, look at the other relevant practice area sections in this guide. Specialisation usually has more to do with acquiring market knowledge than learning different skills or procedures; many litigators will tell you that it's better to start off as a generalist, so you can develop the requisite core skills and make yourself more marketable.

As a trainee, your workload will depend entirely on the type of firm you go to. Magic circle firms are unlikely to give eager young recruits free rein on the latest international banking dispute, but they will get an opportunity to observe experienced lawyers at work on headline-grabbing cases, even if their own role is far from glamorous. By contrast, in firms that handle much smaller matters, trainees are given the opportunity to deal with all aspects of a case, from drafting correspondence and conducting meetings with clients and counsel to trotting along to court to make small procedural applications. While we're on the subject of court appearances, let's examine the role of the solicitor advocate following the extension of High Court rights of audience to solicitors. Some see this as natural evolution of the legal market, a visible erosion of the artificial barriers between solicitors and barristers. Yet, while many firms do offer advocacy training to their solicitors, it is not always as high up on the list of priorities as you might think. As Simon explains: "*Although it is growing, it is a gradual process. The business case is not there for bringing all advocacy in house. While firms are placing less reliance on counsel generally, the Bar still has an important role to play.*" When it comes to the crunch and there's a compelling need for someone to display an encyclopaedic knowledge of complex procedural rules, or demonstrate a mesmerising talent for cross-examination, clients and solicitors still feel more comfortable turning to the Bar.

Despite there not being a flood of solicitors seeking rights of audience in the higher courts, many firms are aiming to keep more advocacy in-house and draft more of their own pleadings. Students can certainly ask a firm to outline its policy on this issue: Will becoming a solicitor advocate be possible at all, purely optional, actively encouraged or mandatory? Students should also bear in mind that specialist litigation firms and those handling smaller cases may provide greater scope for advocacy than large City firms.

## skills needed

...drive...commercial awareness...tactical thinking...enjoy formulating and articulating arguments...a need to win...assimilate information quickly...think laterally...good negotiator...thick-skinned but sensitive to clients' needs...

This is, in essence, an adversarial area of practice, which will suit those who relish a good old battle of wits. As Simon says: "*It's a good choice if you enjoy an intellectual challenge and want to get close to the law – if you can see yourself exercising your judgement, taking a view, and then having the confidence to stand by it.*" This is still a relevant insight even if the current trend for ADR contin-

ues. "*A mediation requires many of the same skills as the litigation process: you still have to understand and present your case and identify the weaknesses in your opponent's. Equally, litigation is not always daggers drawn, and good litigators will be looking for opportunities to negotiate and compromise – whether or not a formal mediation is in progress.*"

According to Simon, some of the most important skills for a litigator are "*the ability to assimilate complex facts, to identify the important issues in a dispute, and to explain those issues, and your view, in a way your clients can understand.*" You need to be able to speak and write both concisely and precisely, especially when a high degree of legal analysis is involved. As you will not always be the sole lawyer working on a case it is also important to be able to work effectively as part of a team and earn the trust of those around you.

Litigators also need an ability to understand the commercial pressures facing clients at what can be a particularly taxing time. Simon explains: "*You have to look beyond the legal issues in a case and take account of your client's commercial position and objectives.*" On the other hand it does not pay to get too carried away. "*You not only have to manage the case, but also your client's expectations in terms of their realistic position, and what would be the likely cost of pursuing or defending an action.*"

## career options

The Law Society requires all trainee solicitors to undertake contentious work, and in almost all cases you tend to discover fairly quickly whether you are suited to litigation. If you want to get a feel for advocacy prior to applying for training contracts, we'd recommend you join your local mooting or debating society.

Once qualified, litigation skills are less transferable than the other professional and business skills that you will have developed. As such, it may not be as easy to take up an in-house role as it would be for transactional lawyers. Better make sure private practice suits you...

# specialist areas

## leading firms from Chambers UK 2006

### Litigation:
### General Commercial
### (Larger Teams)
London

1. Herbert Smith LLP
2. Clifford Chance LLP
   Freshfields Bruckhaus Deringer
   Lovells
3. Allen & Overy LLP
   Linklaters
   Slaughter and May
4. Ashurst
   Barlow Lyde & Gilbert
   Norton Rose
   Simmons & Simmons
   SJ Berwin LLP
5. Baker & McKenzie LLP
   Clyde & Co
   CMS Cameron McKenna LLP
   Denton Wilde Sapte
   Richards Butler

### Litigation:
### General Commercial
The South: Surrey,
Hampshire & Dorset

1. Blake Lapthorn Linnell *Fareham*
   Bond Pearce LLP *Southampton*
   Clyde & Co *Guildford*
2. Charles Russell *Guildford*
   Lester Aldridge *Southampton*
   Stevens & Bolton LLP *Guildford*
   Thomas Eggar *Reigate*
3. Barlow Robbins *Guildford*
   Clarke Willmott *Southampton*
   Moore & Blatch *Southampton*
   Paris Smith & Randall *So'ton*
   Shadbolt & Co LLP *Reigate*
   Shoosmiths *Fareham*

### Litigation:
### General Commercial
### (Medium Teams)
London

1. Eversheds LLP
   Jones Day
   Macfarlanes
   Mayer, Brown, Rowe & Maw LLP
   Pinsent Masons
   Stephenson Harwood
2. Berwin Leighton Paisner
   Dechert LLP
   Ince & Co
   Morgan, Lewis & Bockius
   Nabarro Nathanson
   Reynolds Porter Chamberlain
   Taylor Wessing
3. Addleshaw Goddard
   DLA Piper Rudnick Gray Cary UK
   Hammonds
   Kendall Freeman
   Kirkpatrick & Lockhart Nicholson
   Olswang
   White & Case
4. Charles Russell
   Davies Arnold Cooper
   Howrey LLP
   Lawrence Graham LLP
   Lewis Silkin
   McDermott Will & Emery UK LLP
   Memery Crystal
   Mishcon de Reya
   Travers Smith
   Watson, Farley & Williams

### Litigation:
### General Commercial
The South: Kent & Sussex

1. Cripps Harries *Tunbridge Wells*
   DMH Stallard *Brighton*
   Thomson Snell *Tunbridge Wells*
2. asb law *Crawley*
   Brachers *Maidstone*
   Rawlison Butler *Crawley*

### Litigation:
### General Commercial
Thames Valley
Leading firms

1. Clarkslegal LLP *Reading*
   Nabarro Nathanson *Reading*
2. B P Collins *Gerrards Cross*
   Boyes Turner *Reading*
   Manches *Oxford*
   Olswang Thames Valley *Reading*
   Pitmans *Reading*
3. Henmans *Oxford*
   Iliffes Booth Bennett *Uxbridge*
   Matthew Arnold *Watford*
   Morgan Cole *Oxford*
   Shoosmiths *Reading*

### Litigation:
### General Commercial
South West
Leading firms

1. Burges Salmon LLP *Bristol*
   Osborne Clarke *Bristol*
2. Ashfords
   Beachcroft Wansbroughs *Bristol*
   Bevan Brittan LLP *Bristol*
   Bond Pearce LLP *Exeter*
   Clarke Willmott *Taunton*
   TLT Solicitors *Bristol*
   Veale Wasbrough Lawyers *Bristol*
3. BPE Solicitors *Cheltenham*
   Charles Russell *Cheltenham*
   Foot Anstey *Exeter*
4. Bevans *Bristol*
   Laytons *Bristol*
   Michelmores *Exeter*
   Rickerbys *Cheltenham*
   Stephens & Scown *Exeter*

# specialist areas

## Litigation: General Commercial
### Wales
Leading firms

[1] **Eversheds LLP** *Cardiff*
**Geldards** *Cardiff*
**Hugh James** *Cardiff*

[2] **Capital Law** *Cardiff Bay*
**Morgan Cole** *Cardiff*

## Litigation: General Commercial
### Midlands

[1] **Eversheds LLP** *Birmingham*
**Pinsent Masons** *Birmingham*
**Wragge & Co LLP** *Birmingham*

[2] **Cobbetts** *Birmingham*
**DLA Piper Rudnick Gray** *Birmingham*
**Gateley Wareing LLP** *Birmingham*
**Hammonds** *Birmingham*
**Martineau Johnson** *Birmingham*

[3] **Browne Jacobson LLP** *Nottingham*
**Freeth Cartwright LLP** *Nottingham*
**Shoosmiths** *Northampton*

[4] **Anthony Collins** *Birmingham*
**Challinors** *West Bromwich*
**George Green** *Cradley Heath*
**Heatons** *Birmingham*
**Kent Jones and Done** *Stoke-on-Trent*
**Moran & Co** *Tamworth*
**Shakespeares** *Birmingham*

## Litigation: General Commercial
### East Anglia

[1] **Mills & Reeve** *Cambridge*

[2] **Birketts** *Ipswich*
**Eversheds LLP** *Cambridge*
**Hewitsons** *Cambridge*
**Taylor Vinters** *Cambridge*

[3] **Howes Percival** *Norwich*
**Prettys** *Ipswich*

[4] **Greenwoods Solicitors** *Peterborough*
**Steeles (Law) LLP** *Norwich*

## Litigation: General Commercial
### North West

[1] **Addleshaw Goddard** *Manchester*
**DLA Piper Rudnick** *Manchester*
**Eversheds LLP** *Manchester*

[2] **Brabners Chaffe Street** *Liverpool*
**Cobbetts** *Manchester*
**Halliwells LLP** *Manchester*
**Hammonds** *Manchester*
**Hill Dickinson** *Liverpool*
**Pannone & Partners** *Manchester*

[3] **Beachcroft Wansbroughs** *Manchester*
**DWF** *Manchester*
**Kuit Steinart Levy** *Manchester*
**Wacks Caller** *Manchester*

[4] **Berg Legal** *Manchester*
**Kershaw Abbott** *Manchester*
**Mace & Jones** *Manchester*
**Rowe Cohen** *Manchester*

## Litigation: General Commercial
### Yorkshire

[1] **Addleshaw Goddard** *Leeds*
**DLA Piper Rudnick Gray** *Leeds*
**Eversheds LLP** *Leeds*
**Hammonds** *Leeds*
**Pinsent Masons** *Leeds*
**Walker Morris** *Leeds*

[2] **Cobbetts** *Leeds*
**Gordons** *Leeds*
**Irwin Mitchell** *Sheffield*
**Keeble Hawson** *Leeds*
**Lupton Fawcett** *Leeds*
**Nabarro Nathanson** *Sheffield*

[3] **Andrew M Jackson** *Hull*
**Beachcroft Wansbroughs** *Leeds*
**Ford & Warren** *Leeds*
**Gosschalks** *Hull*
**McCormicks** *Leeds*
**Rollits** *Hull*

## Litigation: General Commercial
### North East

[1] **Dickinson Dees** *Newcastle upon Tyne*
**Eversheds LLP** *Newcastle upon Tyne*
**Ward Hadaway** *Newcastle upon Tyne*

[2] **Robert Muckle** *Newcastle upon Tyne*
**Watson Burton** *Newcastle upon Tyne*

[3] **Crutes Law Firm** *Newcastle u-Tyne*
**Gibson & Co** *Newcastle upon Tyne*
**Hay & Kilner** *Newcastle upon Tyne*
**Sintons** *Newcastle upon Tyne*

# media & entertainment

## advertising and marketing

Advertising and marketing law is split into pure and general work. Pure advertising law focuses on the client's products or advertisements, ensuring the content is legal and appropriate. General work encompasses commercial contracts with suppliers, clients and the media, plus corporate transactions, litigation and employment issues.

**type of work:** Copy clearance lawyers advise clients on issues such as comparative advertising, unauthorised references to living individuals and parodies of films or TV shows. A solid grasp of defamation and intellectual property law is essential. Legislation such as the Lotteries and Amusements Act and the Consumer Protection Act feature, and copy clearance work is further governed by regulatory codes such as those of the Advertising Standards Authority (ASA) and Ofcom. The lawyer must help the client to say exactly what he or she wants to say without falling foul of these regulations.

Sometimes you will be defending the client against allegations that their work has infringed the rights of third parties or advising on whether an ad should be pulled. At other times you will go on the offensive, helping clients to bring complaints about competitors' advertising, for example if a competitor is 'knocking copy' (making disparaging references to your client's products) or making claims that your client wouldn't be allowed to make.

As clients are often already committed to a course of action before they speak to you, the answer to a query is rarely a straightforward 'no'. Instead, advice is often about damage limitation or risk management and it's up to the lawyer to identify the risks and, if not eliminate them, manage them as best they can. Rather than a slow wade through turgid legal documents, advertising law is fast-moving and refreshing, with immediate results. Clients are similarly creative and lively, and always looking for fast, practical advice.

## reputation management

Reputation management work oozes sex appeal, celebrity and intrigue. Until recently, libel cases were the order of the day; now the planetary alignment of the Human Rights Act (particularly Article 8, the right to privacy, and Article 10, the right to freedom of expression) and the nation's unhealthy obsession with celeb gossip and pics has opened up a whole new galaxy of claims. Naomi Campbell, Sara Cox, and Catherine and Michael are the vanguard and their lawyers are also fast becoming 'names' in their own right.

**type of work:** We spoke with Caroline Kean of media boutique Wiggin LLP about a life in libel and reputation management. She told us there were fundamental differences between acting for defendants (newspapers, other publishers and broadcasters) and claimants (commonly celebrities and politicians). "*Defendants instruct you as a part of their business. They have commercial nous, and a budget, and they don't usually have hysterics.*" By contrast, the individual claimants probably feel they are going through the worst episode of their life and will need a good deal of handholding. Claimant lawyers need a heck of a lot of patience and the ability to get clients to really open up and expose their weaknesses.

When libel claims are made or threatened, the burden of proof switches to the defendant and, as such, their lawyers have to think and act strategically to prove that there has been no libel. Caroline says: "*At times you get to be an investigative journalist,*" and she's even been to meetings wired up. Less dramatic, maybe, but no less important to the client, are the non-contentious elements of the job including pre-publication or pre-broadcast advice to authors, editors and TV companies.

Caroline believes those destined to build a career in this field need "*an affinity with publishing matters*" and must be up to date with the news and gossip in the media world. In short, listen to the radio, watch TV, and read newspapers and magazines. "*One of my first jobs in the morning is to read The Mirror's celebrity and sports pages,*" Caroline chuckled. But she reminded us that "*you are first and foremost a lawyer – and not a failed luvvie.*" In a similar vein, while it won't hurt to have edited your student newspaper or to have had some media experience, recruiters are aware that some applicants would indeed be better suited to journalism than the law. Ultimately, issues like freedom of speech and the right to privacy must matter to you as legal concepts and, to best serve your clients' interests, you'll need to build an armoury of legal tools. If you have your heart set on this kind of work, try reading a monthly magazine called *Media Lawyer.*

Jobs exist in-house at larger publishing and broadcasting concerns and it is relatively common for lawyers to hop over the fence from private practice... and back again. Even in private practice, regular office hours don't really apply. "*Near to a copy deadline your phone is going all the time, and you're likely to get calls late on a Friday or on a Sunday. If the client needs you, you have to be there.*" The upside, Caroline reports, is that the job is "*the most enormous fun.*" Sounds like great work, if you can get it!

## entertainment

At parties, when asked what they do, many lawyers kill conversations. Not entertainment specialists.

**type of work:** Lawyers handle film and broadcasting, music, theatre and publishing work. We spoke to The Simkins Partnership's Robin Hilton and Julian Bentley, who explained that, while these areas of the entertainment industry each have different demands, with all of them "*you*

*need to know how to give commercial advice in a legal context.*" Essentially, all clients need contract, employment and litigation advice, and intellectual property is also very relevant.

When it comes to film and TV work, Robin says: "*Like any industrial process, you have to research and develop the product, make it and market it.*" Legal advice is required at each stage, particularly those involving contractual arrangements (including banking and secured lending) and the law of copyright. "*You have to hold the producer's hand and take them through it; engaging artists, dealing with the director, putting together a patchwork of finance and then going through production.*" A film lawyer may have to manage the contractual relationships with tax funds, banks, studios and several producers as well as giving clearance and classification advice.

Television lawyers only tend to be drafted in when issues or problems arise relating to the content of a programme, defamation claims, engaging talent or negotiating deal terms and contracts. Robin described film and TV work as "*reasonably office-bound*" and warned that "*people who think being a TV lawyer is a form of the entertainment business will be in for a shock. First and foremost, you're a lawyer not a showbiz person.*" In fact, "*clients look to you to apply the rigour they often don't apply*" and expect an awareness of compliance, defamation, privacy, confidence and finance law. Robin added: "*You do need a passion for the industry itself, but that comes second to understanding the commercial framework – you can't just say 'I love watching telly' or 'I'm a film buff'.*"

Music law divides evenly between work for major companies, the independent sector and talent, including record producers, songwriters and artists. Contract, copyright and competition law are key. Litigation can arise when there is a dispute over contract terms or ownership of rights in a composition, or if there is a split in a band or with management. Even when there are no musical differences, clients need help in negotiating contracts and so Julian warns that potential music lawyers *"need to be aware that it is document intensive – you have to be able to write well."* Julian also stressed that *"you really have to be ensconced in the business – live it and breathe it."*

Just a handful of London lawyers work for theatre and opera companies, producers, theatrical agents and actors, negotiating contracts and arranging funding. Publishing law is also a pocket-sized area of practice, as much of the contractual, licensing, copyright and libel advice for newspapers and publishers is carried out in-house.

## skills needed

...people skills...patience...prepared to immerse yourself in the industry...a thorough knowledge of contract and copyright law...creativity in problem solving...commercial aptitude...methodical nature...being inquisitive...

## career options

For all the industry's apparently laid-back approach, competition for legal positions is ferocious, and that applies to training contracts too.

There are two basic routes in: train at a niche entertainment firm or at a large City firm with a specialism in entertainment. In either case, a demonstrable commitment to the field and an understanding of industry trends and new technology will really help. Try and get some relevant work experience, read the trade press and the media pages of the general press and watch lots of TV. Julian said: *"A lot of people in the music industry who aren't frontline musicians probably once were, and that includes lawyers...to say we're all failed musicians is not quite right, but music was top of our list of hobbies!"* Turning your hand to a bit of DJing, music journalism or booking bands at university will go down well as *"it demonstrates you might know people and can work the industry."*

Lawyers can quite easily transfer between private practice and jobs with media and entertainment organisations. The hours and regularity of in-house jobs appeal to some, as does the perception that you are closer to the production process. There are fewer in-house positions available in the music sector; in television they are plentiful, with all the big names such as BBC, Warners, Channel 5, Clear Channel and Endemol employing their own lawyers.

## leading firms from Chambers UK 2006

| Media & Entertainment: Film & TV Production Nationwide | |
|---|---|
| [1] Olswang | |
| [2] Davenport Lyons | Harbottle & Lewis LLP |
| Lee & Thompson | |
| [3] DLA Piper Rudnick Gray Cary UK | Richards Butler |
| Sheridans | SJ Berwin LLP |
| [4] Addleshaw Goddard | Bates Wells & Braithwaite |
| Bird & Bird | Charles Russell |
| Howard Kennedy | Russell-Cooke |
| Salans | Simons Muirhead & Burton |
| Wiggin LLP | |
| [5] MLM *Cardiff* | Morgan Cole *Cardiff* |

| Media & Entertainment: Film Finance Nationwide |
|---|
| [1] Richards Butler |
| SJ Berwin LLP |
| [2] Davenport Lyons |
| DLA Piper Rudnick Gray Cary UK |
| Olswang |
| [3] Addleshaw Goddard |
| Howard Kennedy |
| Salans |

# specialist areas

## Media & Entertainment: Broadcasting
### Nationwide

[1] DLA Piper Rudnick Gray Cary UK
Olswang
[2] Goodman Derrick
Wiggin LLP
[3] Field Fisher Waterhouse
Herbert Smith LLP
Lovells
Richards Butler
[4] Bird & Bird
Clifford Chance LLP
Davenport Lyons
Linklaters
Norton Rose
Taylor Wessing
Travers Smith
Wragge & Co LLP *Birmingham*

## Media & Entertainment: Computer Games
### Nationwide

[1] Harbottle & Lewis LLP
Osborne Clarke
[2] Ashurst
Bird & Bird
Briffa
Bristows
Lewis Silkin
Lovells

## Media & Entertainment: Music
### Nationwide

[1] Russells
[2] Clintons
Lee & Thompson
[3] Addleshaw Goddard
Bray & Krais Solicitors
Eversheds LLP
Sheridans
[4] Forbes Anderson Free
Hamlins
Harbottle & Lewis LLP
Mayer, Brown, Rowe & Maw LLP
Olswang
The Simkins Partnership
[5] Collyer-Bristow
Davenport Lyons
Engel Monjack
Marriott Harrison
Northrop McNaughtan Deller
Russell-Cooke
Spraggon Stennett Brabyn

## Media & Entertainment: Publishing
### Nationwide

[1] DLA Piper Rudnick Gray Cary UK
[2] Finers Stephens Innocent
Harbottle & Lewis LLP
Taylor Wessing
[3] Arnold & Porter UK LLP
Davenport Lyons
Farrer & Co
Lovells
Olswang
Reynolds Porter Chamberlain
The Simkins Partnership
[4] Blake Lapthorn Linnell *Oxford*
Lewis Silkin
Manches *Oxford*
Wiggin LLP

## Media & Entertainment: Theatre
### Nationwide

[1] Clintons
[2] Addleshaw Goddard
Bates Wells & Braithwaite
Harbottle & Lewis LLP
Russell-Cooke
The Simkins Partnership

# personal injury and clinical negligence

From simple pavement trippers to those suffering from industrial diseases, members of the public call upon personal injury lawyers to help them bring claims. In the majority of cases, it will be an insurance company that is liable to pay compensation and, accordingly, they too instruct PI lawyers. Some lawyers act for both claimant and defendant clients, but most concentrate on one or the other.

Clinical negligence claims are made where individuals have suffered injury or illness as a result of medical treatment that has gone wrong. Examples include orthopaedic surgery, cerebral palsy caused by birth trauma, incorrect dental treatment and delay in diagnosis by GPs. In all cases, the defendant will be a medical professional or body, usually the NHS, but sometimes the Medical Defence Union or insurance companies. As with PI, lawyers tend to act for either claimants or defendants.

## type of work

We spoke to Rod Findlay, a partner specialising in clinical negligence at Newcastle firm Samuel Phillips & Co, who told us just how much work had to be done before a claim could be issued. After hearing the client's story, the lawyer spends several months obtaining and considering the medical records to see if they support what the client is saying and can provide the basis for a good claim. *"Some cases are really simple and some are a right old mess! You can have a huge volume of records, several different specialists and different hospitals. One client of mine had 14 sets of records."* Only after the initial review period is complete will the lawyer know whether there's a good chance of success for the claimant and be in a position to issue proceedings. At this stage he can also begin to prepare the case for a possible trial, although this may be a couple of years down the line. The basic procedural steps of litigation include taking witness statements, instructing experts to prepare reports, disclosure of documentary evidence and, inevitably, negotiations with the other party. As with any type of litigation, most cases never reach trial and are settled.

Legal aid is still available for clinical negligence work – although practitioners do worry for how much longer – and the government is promoting schemes whereby legal work and costs are minimised. For example, its Chief Medical Officer has suggested that all claims below £30,000 and brain-damaged baby cases should be concluded by reference to a single expert's report. The PI scene has already undergone huge changes since the loss of legal aid, the rise and demise of various claims companies, and the predominance of 'no win, no fee' agreements.

## skills needed

...a good bedside manner...sympathetic but detached...patience...tact...organised and methodical...logical thinker...good negotiator... interest in medical matters...

This kind of work, particularly clinical negligence, is especially suited to those with experience in the healthcare sector or who have studied medicine, although most young lawyers have no such background. *"The first thing I did when I qualified was buy a medical dictionary,"* Rod said, adding that clin neg can be a difficult area for those starting out and that good guidance is essential. *"It's because you're not just dealing with an injury, you're criticising another professional. You're just out of law school and you just about know about your own profession. But as you progress, you see cases crop up again and again, and you are better able to make experienced-based judgement calls."*

A trap for young players is *"listening to the story without picking up on the legal issues."* No matter how tragic or awful the client's experience, you have to remember to stick to your role — you are neither a medical adviser nor a best friend. Some of the facts in these cases can be quite gruesome, so this is not a job for the squeamish, or indeed for those overly sensitive to human misery. Defendant lawyers also have to accept that their role is to minimise their client's liability to the claimant, and this requires faith in the fairness and integrity of the legal process.

The job as a whole is very paper-based, although there is the odd court hearing or home visit to a client. Be prepared to knuckle down to a lot of perusing and summarising of medical reports.

## career options

Most lawyers stay in private practice for their whole careers, but don't assume that defendant lawyers never switch to working for claimants, and vice versa. Rod doubts there are differences in the type of person working on either side, although he suggests that those interested in PI and clinical negligence should pick their firm carefully. Some have specialisms (asbestos-related diseases, head and spine injuries, dental malpractice) and their lawyers become niche players; at others, lawyers remain generalists. On the defendant side, the NHS Litigation Authority has a near monopoly when it comes to issuing instructions, and every three years it reviews its panel of law firms. The review in January 2004 should have fixed the market until 2007. Interested students can choose PI and medical law options at university and law school, and the super-keen may find a publication called *Healthcare Risk Report* edifying.

## leading firms from Chambers UK 2006

### Personal Injury: Mainly Claimant
London

1 Irwin Mitchell
Leigh Day & Co
Stewarts

2 Anthony Gold
Field Fisher Waterhouse
Rowley Ashworth
Thompsons

3 Alexander Harris
O.H. Parsons & Partners
Pattinson & Brewer
Russell Jones & Walker
Russell-Cooke

4 Bindman & Partners
Bolt Burdon Kemp
Hodge Jones & Allen
Iliffes Booth Bennett (IBB) *Uxbridge*
Levenes
McMillan Williams
Prince Evans

### Personal Injury: Mainly Defendant
London

1 Barlow Lyde & Gilbert
Beachcroft Wansbroughs
Berrymans Lace Mawer

2 Greenwoods
Kennedys

3 Davies Arnold Cooper
Plexus Law
Vizards Wyeth

4 Badhams Law *Croydon*
Davies Lavery
Norton Rose
Reynolds Porter Chamberlain
Watmores
Weightmans

### Personal Injury: Mainly Claimant
The South

1 Blake Lapthorn Linnell *Southampton*
George Ide, Phillips *Chichester*
Lamport Bassitt *Southampton*
Moore & Blatch *Southampton*
Shoosmiths *Basingstoke*

2 Coffin Mew & Clover *Southampton*
Colemans-ctts *Kingston-upon-Thames*
DMH Stallard *Brighton*
Penningtons Solicitors *Godalming*
Thomson Snell *Tunbridge Wells*

# specialist areas

## Personal Injury: Mainly Defendant
### The South

1. Beachcroft W'broughs *Winchester*
   Berrymans Lace *Southampton*
   Davies Lavery *Maidstone*
   Vizards Wyeth *Dartford*
2. Bond Pearce LLP *Southampton*
   Clarke Willmott *Southampton*
3. Capital Law *Southampton*
   Lamport Bassitt *Southampton*

## Personal Injury: Mainly Claimant
### Thames Valley
### Leading firms

1. Boyes Turner *Reading*
   Harris Cartier LLP *Slough*
   Osborne Morris *Leighton Buzzard*
   Thring Townsend *Swindon*
2. Blake Lapthorn Linnell *Oxford*
   Fennemores *Milton Keynes*
   Field Seymour Parkes *Reading*
   Henmans *Oxford*

## Personal Injury: Mainly Defendant
### Thames Valley

1. Henmans *Oxford*
   Morgan Cole *Oxford*
2. Eldridge & Co *Oxford*
   Pitmans *Reading*
   Thring Townsend *Swindon*

## Personal Injury: Mainly Claimant
### South West

1. Bond Pearce LLP *Plymouth*
   Clarke Willmott *Bristol*
   Lyons Davidson *Bristol*
   Thompsons *Bristol*
   Augustines Injury Law *Bristol*
2. BPE Solicitors *Cheltenham*
   David Gist Solicitors *Bristol*
   Rowley Ashworth *Exeter*
   Veitch Penny *Exeter*
   Withy King *Bath*

## Personal Injury: Mainly Defendant
### South West
### Leading firms

1. Beachcroft Wansbroughs *Bristol*
2. Bond Pearce LLP *Bristol*
   Cartwrights Insurance *Bristol*
   Lyons Davidson *Bristol*
   Veitch Penny *Exeter*
3. Bevan Brittan LLP *Bristol*
   Morris Orman *Cheltenham*
   Wansbroughs *Devizes*
4. Foot Anstey *Bridgwater*
   Stephens & Scown *Exeter*

## Personal Injury: Mainly Claimant
### Wales

1. Hugh James *Cardiff*
2. John Collins & Partners *Swansea*
   Leo Abse & Cohen *Cardiff*
   Russell Jones & Walker *Cardiff*
   Thompsons *Cardiff*
3. Loosemores *Cardiff*
   MLM *Cardiff*

## Personal Injury: Mainly Defendant
### Wales

1. Dolmans *Cardiff*
   Douglas-Jones Mercer *Swansea*
   Hugh James *Cardiff*
   Morgan Cole *Cardiff*
2. Capital Law *Cardiff Bay*
   Cartwright Black Solicitors *Cardiff*
   Eversheds LLP *Cardiff*

## Personal Injury: Mainly Claimant
### Midlands
### Leading firms

1. Irwin Mitchell *Birmingham*
2. Barratt, Goff *Nottingham*
3. Alexander Harris *Solihull*
   Freeth Cartwright LLP *Nottingham*
   Rowley Ashworth *Birmingham*
   Thompsons *Birmingham*
4. Anthony Collins *Birmingham*
   Flint, Bishop & Barnett *Derby*
   Higgs & Sons *Stourbridge*
   Russell Jones *Birmingham*

## Personal Injury: Mainly Defendant
### Midlands

1. Beachcroft W'broughs *Birmingham*
   Browne Jacobson LLP *Nottingham*
   Buller Jeffries *Birmingham*
2. Berrymans Lace *Birmingham*
   Davies Lavery *Birmingham*
   DLA Piper Rudnick *Birmingham*
   Everatt & Company *Evesham*
   Weightmans *Birmingham*
3. Keoghs *Coventry*
   Wragge & Co LLP *Birmingham*

# specialist areas

## Personal Injury: Mainly Claimant
### East Anglia
[1] **Taylor Vinters** *Cambridge*
[2] **Ashton Graham** *Ipswich*
**Edwards Duthie** *Ilford*
**Kester Cunningham John** *Thetford*
**Morgan Jones & Pett** *Norwich*

## Personal Injury: Mainly Defendant
### East Anglia
[1] **Edwards Duthie** *Ilford*
**Eversheds LLP** *Ipswich*
**Kennedys** *Chelmsford*
**Mills & Reeve** *Norwich*
**Prettys** *Ipswich*

## Personal Injury: Mainly Claimant
### North West
[1] **Pannone & Partners** *Manchester*
[2] **John Pickering & Partners** *Oldham*
[3] **Colemans-ctts** *Manchester*
**Donns Solicitors** *Manchester*
**Linder Myers** *Manchester*
**Mace & Jones** *Liverpool*
**McCool Patterson** *Manchester*
**Potter Rees** *Manchester*
**Russell Jones** *Manchester*
**Thompsons** *Liverpool*

## Personal Injury: Mainly Defendant
### North West
[1] **James Chapman** *Manchester*
[2] **Beachcroft W'broughs** *Manchester*
**Berrymans Lace Mawer** *Liverpool*
[3] **DWF** *Liverpool*
**Halliwells LLP** *Manchester*
**Hill Dickinson** *Liverpool*
**Horwich Farrelly** *Manchester*
**Keoghs** *Bolton*
**Ricksons** *Manchester*
**Weightmans** *Liverpool*

## Personal Injury: Mainly Claimant
### Yorkshire
[1] **Irwin Mitchell** *Leeds, Sheffield*
[2] **Keeble Hawson** *Sheffield*
**Morrish & Co** *Leeds*
**Stewarts** *Leeds*
[3] **AMS Law** *Sheffield*
**Bridge McFarland** *Grimsby*
**Pattinson & Brewer** *York*
**Rowley Ashworth** *Leeds*
**Russell Jones & Walker** *Sheffield*

## Personal Injury: Mainly Defendant
### Yorkshire
[1] **Beachcroft Wansbroughs** *Leeds*
**Berrymans Lace Mawer** *Leeds*
**DLA Piper Rudnick Gray** *Sheffield*
**Nabarro Nathanson** *Sheffield*
[2] **Ford & Warren** *Leeds*
**Halliwells LLP** *Sheffield*
**Irwin Mitchell** *Sheffield*
**Langleys** *York*
**Praxis Partners** *Leeds*

## Personal Injury: Mainly Claimant
### North East
[1] **Thompsons** *Newcastle upon Tyne*
[2] **Browell Smith & Co** *Newcastle*
**Marrons** *Newcastle upon Tyne*
**Sintons** *Newcastle upon Tyne*
[3] **Gorman Hamilton** *Newcastle*
**Hay & Kilner** *Newcastle upon Tyne*
**Irwin Mitchell** *Newcastle*
**Russell Jones** *Newcastle*

## Personal Injury: Mainly Defendant
### North East
[1] **Berrymans Lace** *Stockton on Tees*
**Crutes Law Firm** *Newcastle*
**Eversheds LLP** *Newcastle*
[2] **Hay & Kilner** *Newcastle upon Tyne*
**Sintons** *Newcastle upon Tyne*

# specialist areas

## Clinical Negligence: Mainly Claimant
### London

[1] **Irwin Mitchell**
**Leigh Day & Co**
[2] **Kingsley Napley**
**Parlett Kent**
[3] **Charles Russell**
**Field Fisher Waterhouse**
**Russell-Cooke**
**Stewarts**
[4] **Alexander Harris**
**Anthony Gold**
**Bindman & Partners**
**Pattinson & Brewer**

## Clinical Negligence: Mainly Defendant
### London

[1] **Capsticks**
**Hempsons**
[2] **Barlow Lyde & Gilbert**
**Bevan Brittan LLP**
**Kennedys**
**RadcliffesLeBrasseur**
**Weightmans**
[3] **Berrymans Lace Mawer**
**Reynolds Porter Chamberlain**
**Trowers & Hamlins**

## Clinical Negligence: Mainly Claimant
### The South

[1] **Blake Lapthorn Linnell** *Fareham*
**Penningtons Solicitors** *Godalming*
**Thomson Snell** *Tunbridge Wells*
[2] **Coffin Mew & Clover** *Fareham*
**George Ide, Phillips** *Chichester*
**Moore & Blatch** *Southampton*
**Wynne Baxter** *Brighton*

## Clinical Negligence: Mainly Claimant
### Thames Valley

[1] **Boyes Turner** *Reading*
**Harris Cartier LLP** *Slough*
[2] **Henmans** *Oxford*
**Osborne Morris** *Leighton Buzzard*

## Clinical Negligence: Mainly Defendant
### The South

[1] **Beachcroft W'broughs** *Winchester*
[2] **Brachers** *Maidstone*

## Clinical Negligence: Mainly Claimant
### South West

[1] **Barcan Woodward** *Bristol*
**Foot Anstey** *Bridgewater*
**Parlett Kent** *Exeter*
[2] **Bond Pearce** *Bristol*
**John Hodge** *Weston-super-Mare*
**Michelmores** *Exeter*
**Over Taylor Biggs** *Exeter*
**Preston Goldburn** *Falmouth*
**Russell Jones** *Bristol*
**Withy King** *Bath*
**Wolferstans** *Plymouth*

## Clinical Negligence: Mainly Defendant
### South West

[1] **Bevan Brittan LLP** *Bristol*
[2] **Beachcroft W'broughs** *Bristol*

## Clinical Negligence: Mainly Claimant
### Wales

[1] **Hugh James** *Cardiff*
**Huttons** *Cardiff*
**John Collins & Partners** *Swansea*
[2] **Harding Evans** *Newport*

## Clinical Negligence: Mainly Defendant
### Wales

[1] **RadcliffesLeBrasseur** *Cardiff*

# specialist areas

## Clinical Negligence: Mainly Claimant
Midlands

[1] **Alexander Harris** *Solihull*
**Challinors** *Birmingham*
**Freeth Cartwright** *Nottingham*
**Irwin Mitchell** *Birmingham*
[2] **Anthony Collins** *Birmingham*
**Brindley Twist Tafft** *Coventry*

## Clinical Negligence: Mainly Defendant
Midlands

[1] **Browne Jacobson** *Birmingham*
[2] **Bevan Brittan LLP** *Birmingham*
**Weightmans** *Leicester*

## Clinical Negligence: Mainly Claimant
East Anglia

[1] **Kester Cunningham** *Thetford*
[2] **Attwater & Liell** *Harlow*
**Gadsby Wicks** *Chelmsford*
**Morgan Jones & Pett** *Norwich*
**Scrivenger Seabrook** *St Neots*

## Clinical Negligence: Mainly Defendant
East Anglia

[1] **Kennedys** *Cambridge*
[2] **Mills & Reeve** *Norwich*

## Clinical Negligence: Mainly Claimant
North West

[1] **Alexander Harris** *Altrincham*
**Pannone** *Manchester*
[2] **Edwards Abrams** *Liverpool*
**JMW Solicitors** *Manchester*
**McCool Patterson** *Manchester*
[3] **Donns Solicitors** *Manchester*
**Lees & Partners** *Birkenhead*
**Linder Myers** *Manchester*
**Maxwell Gillott** *Lancaster*
**Walker Smith Way** *Chester*

## Clinical Negligence: Mainly Defendant
North West

[1] **Hempsons** *Manchester*
**Hill Dickinson** *Liverpool*
[2] **Weightmans** *Liverpool*

## Clinical Negligence: Mainly Claimant
Yorkshire

[1] **Irwin Mitchell** *Sheffield*
[2] **Heptonstalls** *Goole*
**Lester Morrill** *Leeds*

## Clinical Negligence: Mainly Defendant
Yorkshire

[1] **Hempsons** *Harrogate*
[2] **Eversheds LLP** *Leeds*
[3] **DLA Piper Rudnick** *Sheffield*

## Clinical Negligence: Mainly Claimant
North East

[1] **Ben Hoare Bell** *Sunderland*
**Hay & Kilner** *Newcastle*
**Irwin Mitchell** *Newcastle*
**Mincoffs** *Newcastle upon Tyne*
**Peter Maughan & Co** *Gateshead*
**Samuel Phillips** *Newcastle*

## Clinical Negligence: Mainly Defendant
North East

[1] **Eversheds LLP** *Newcastle*
**Ward Hadaway** *Newcastle*

# private client

Private client lawyers give advice on wealth management to individuals, families and trusts. Some additionally handle matrimonial matters or provide small-scale commercial advice; others focus on specialist tax and trusts or wills and probate. A few work in related areas such as heritage property and charities.

## type of work

Trust law can be a bit turgid, but those who are best suited to private client practice tend to develop a real interest in it. Trusts are a means of holding assets and avoiding tax, allowing family members or other beneficiaries to access funds without the donor losing all control. Often trusts are held in an offshore jurisdiction, in which case these lawyers must ensure their client understands any foreign law implications. Increasingly, lawyers advise overseas clients wanting to invest in the UK, and banks whose overseas clients have UK interests.

In an average private client department, will drafting and probate forms a significant part of the work and can provide young lawyers with a hands-on role from day one. While your friends in the corporate department might be paginating and bundling rooms full of documents, you will be drafting wills or even organising house clearances.

Specialist charities lawyers work for national charities and local private charitable trusts on matters such as charity registrations and reorganisations, Charity Commission investigations or the development of trading subsidiaries. Such organisations also require mainstream commercial advice.

## skills needed

...common sense...lateral thinking...communi-cation and 'people' skills...pragmatism.. objectivity...organised mind...natural curiosity...eye for detail...a desire to help people...a good bedside manner...

If other people's personal affairs make you sit up and listen you'll be in your element. Private client solicitors necessarily become party to very personal information, so impartiality is essential. Chris Belcher at Farrer & Co points out: "*You have to be able to step back and maintain a professional, objective point of view.*" Fear not, the client list is unlikely to be exclusively made up of little old ladies; some clients will be famous, perhaps even super rich. Yet, the job is never going to be as spicy as a position in the offices of *Heat* or *Hello*! and you must always bear in mind that the highly confidential nature of your work means you won't be able to name-drop with your mates in the pub.

Private client practice may lack the fast and furious pace of corporate work, but it does make other demands: the work can be technical and you have to be interested in the academic side. For example, with all that tax and accounts work, it helps to be numerate, though fortunately "*you don't have to be Einstein!*"

Chris is very clear that "*there is no typical lawyer, as there is no typical client.*" Despite the green-welly image of specialist private client practices, more and more of their clients have made their money through property, business or even a lottery win, so a public school education and country retreat are not essential. Clients instruct lawyers for their technical legal knowledge not their pedigree, and they are even more inclined to instruct those who can combine know-how with practical skills and a personable approach.

## career options

After a lull in the 1990s the field is experiencing a period of growth. Along with more wealth and more clients, the passing of three new Trustee Acts has seen the sector evolving. General social trends and greater life expectancy are also having an impact.

# specialist areas

In-house opportunities are rare so most lawyers remain in private practice. While few City firms offer private client services, there are a number of small and medium-sized London firms with an established reputation, and plenty of excellent practices nationwide. Moves between high street firms and those servicing wealthy individuals are rare, so try and get a training contract with the right type of firm for you.

There is less scope for charity lawyers in terms of specialist law firms, but working at one will enable you to make good client contacts, which could lead to a move into the charities sector itself. For an overview of the leading private client and charities law practices refer to *Chambers UK*.

## leading firms from Chambers UK 2006

### Trusts & Personal Tax
London

[1] Macfarlanes
Withers LLP
[1] Allen & Overy LLP
Baker & McKenzie LLP
Boodle Hatfield
Charles Russell
Lawrence Graham LLP
[1] Bircham Dyson Bell
Currey & Co
Farrer & Co
Forsters LLP
Hunters
Payne Hicks Beach
Speechly Bircham
Taylor Wessing
[1] Berwin Leighton Paisner
Collyer-Bristow
Finers Stephens Innocent
Harcus Sinclair
Herbert Smith LLP
Linklaters
RadcliffesLeBrasseur
Trowers & Hamlins
[1] Davenport Lyons
Dawsons
Harbottle & Lewis LLP
Howard Kennedy
Lee & Pembertons
Penningtons Solicitors LLP
Simmons & Simmons
Smyth Barkham
Wedlake Bell

### Trusts & Personal Tax: Contentious
London

[1] Allen & Overy LLP
Herbert Smith LLP
Withers LLP
[2] Baker & McKenzie LLP
Berwin Leighton Paisner
Boodle Hatfield
Charles Russell
Clifford Chance LLP
Harcus Sinclair
Lawrence Graham LLP
Macfarlanes
Speechly Bircham
[3] Laytons
Norton Rose

### Trusts & Personal Tax
Thames Valley

[1] B P Collins *Gerrards Cross*
Boodle Hatfield *Oxford*
[2] Boyes Turner *Reading*
Henmans *Oxford*
Penningtons *Newbury*
[3] Blandy & Blandy *Reading*
Iliffes Booth *Uxbridge*
Matthew Arnold *Watford*
[4] Clarkslegal LLP *Reading*
Pictons *Hemel Hempstead*
Stanley Tee *Bishops Stortford*

### Trusts & Personal Tax
The South

[1] Cripps Harries *Tunbridge Wells*
Thomas Eggar *Chichester*
[2] Blake Lapthorn *Fareham*
Charles Russell *Guildford*
Lester Aldridge *Bournemouth*
Paris Smith *Southampton*
Penningtons *Godalming*
Stevens & Bolton LLP *Guildford*
Thomson Snell *Tunbridge Wells*
White & Bowker *Winchester*
[3] Adams & Remers *Lewes*
asb law *Horsham*
Brachers *Maidstone*
Buss Murton *Tunbridge Wells*
DMH Stallard *Brighton*
Godwins *Winchester*
Lamport Bassitt *Southampton*
Moore & Blatch *Lymington*
Mundays LLP *Cobham*
Rawlison Butler *Crawley*
Whitehead Monckton *Maidstone*

# specialist areas

## Trusts & Personal Tax
### South West

[1] **Burges Salmon LLP** *Bristol*
**Wilsons** *Salisbury*

[2] **Bond Pearce LLP** *Plymouth*
**Charles Russell** *Cheltenham*
**Foot Anstey** *Plymouth*
**Osborne Clarke** *Bristol*
**Wiggin Osborne** *Cheltenham*

[3] **Ashfords** *Exeter*
**Clarke Willmott** *Bristol*
**Coodes** *St Austell*
**Hooper & Wollen** *Torquay*
**Michelmores** *Exeter*
**Rickerbys** *Cheltenham*
**TLT Solicitors** *Bristol*
**Veale Wasbrough** *Bristol*

## Trusts & Personal Tax
### Wales

[1] **Geldards LLP** *Cardiff*
**Hugh James** *Cardiff*

[2] **Margraves** *Llandrindod Wells*

## Trusts & Personal Tax
### Midlands

[1] **Browne Jacobson** *Nottingham*
**Martineau Johnson** *Birmingham*

[2] **Hewitsons** *Northampton*
**Higgs & Sons** *Brierley Hill*
**Mills & Reeve** *Birmingham*

[3] **Cobbetts** *Birmingham*
**Freeth Cartwright** *Nottingham*
**Lodders** *Stratford-upon-Avon*

[4] **Gateley Wareing** *Birmingham*
**Geldards LLP** *Derby*
**Hallmarks** *Worcester*
**Pinsent Masons** *Birmingham*
**Shakespeares** *Birmingham*

## Trusts & Personal Tax
### East Anglia

[1] **Mills & Reeve** *Norwich*

[2] **Greene & Greene** *Bury St Edmunds*
**Hewitsons** *Cambridge*
**Taylor Vinters** *Cambridge*
**Willcox & Lewis** *Norwich*

[3] **Birketts** *Ipswich*
**Howes Percival** *Norwich*

[4] **Ashton Graham** *Ipswich*
**Barker Gotelee** *Ipswich*
**Buckles** *Peterborough*
**Cozens-Hardy** *Norwich*
**Hansells** *Norwich*
**Hood Vores** *Dereham*
**Hunt & Coombs** *Peterborough*
**Prettys** *Ipswich*
**Roythorne & Co** *Spalding*
**Wollastons** *Chelmsford*

## Trusts & Personal Tax
### North West

[1] **Addleshaw** *Manchester*
**Halliwells LLP** *Manchester*

[2] **Birch Cullimore** *Chester*
**Brabners Chaffe** *Liverpool*
**Cobbetts** *Manchester*
**Pannone & Partners** *Manchester*

## Trusts & Personal Tax
### North East

[1] **Dickinson Dees** *Newcastle*
**Wrigleys** *Leeds*

[2] **Addleshaw Goddard** *Leeds*
**Andrew M Jackson** *Hull*
**Gordons** *Leeds*
**Irwin Mitchell** *Sheffield*
**Rollits** *Hull*

[3] **Grays** *York*
**Lupton Fawcett** *Leeds*
**McCormicks** *Leeds*
**Ward Hadaway** *Newcastle*
**Watson Burton LLP** *Newcastle*

# specialist areas

## Charities
### London

1. **Bates Wells & Braithwaite**
   **Farrer & Co**
2. **Nabarro Nathanson**
   **Stone King Solicitors**
   **Withers LLP**
3. **Allen & Overy LLP**
   **Bircham Dyson Bell**
   **Charles Russell**
   **RadcliffesLeBrasseur**
   **Russell-Cooke**
4. **Berwin Leighton Paisner**
   **Claricoat Phillips**
   **Harbottle & Lewis LLP**
   **Hempsons**
   **Herbert Smith LLP**
   **Lawrence Graham LLP**
   **Speechly Bircham**
   **Trowers & Hamlins**
5. **Campbell Hooper**
   **Devonshires**
   **Gordon Dadds**
   **Howard Kennedy**
   **Macfarlanes**
   **Winckworth Sherwood**

## Charities
### The South

1. **Blake Lapthorn** *Portsmouth*
2. **Cripps Harries** *Tunbridge Wells*
   **Griffith Smith** *Brighton*
   **Thomas Eggar** *Chichester*
3. **Lester Aldridge** *Bournemouth*
   **Thomson Snell** *Tunbridge Wells*
4. **DMH Stallard** *Brighton*

## Charities
### Thames Valley

1. **Blake Lapthorn Linnell** *Oxford*
   **Henmans** *Oxford*
2. **B P Collins** *Gerrards Cross*
   **BrookStreet** *Witney*
   **Iliffes Booth** *Ingatestone*
   **Manches** *Oxford*
   **Morgan Cole** *Oxford*
   **Winckworth Sherwood** *Oxford*

## Charities
### South West

1. **Stone King Solicitors** *Bath*
2. **Wilsons** *Salisbury*
3. **Burges Salmon LLP** *Bristol*
   **Osborne Clarke** *Bristol*
4. **Bond Pearce LLP** *Plymouth*
   **Foot Anstey** *Bridgewater*
   **Rickerbys** *Cheltenham*
   **Thring Townsend** *Bath*
   **Tozers** *Exeter*
   **Veale Wasbrough** *Bristol*

## Charities
### Midlands

1. **Anthony Collins** *Birmingham*
   **Martineau Johnson** *Birmingham*
2. **Cobbetts** *Birmingham*
   **Mills & Reeve** *Birmingham*
3. **Band Hatton** *Coventry*
   **Pinsent Masons** *Birmingham*
   **Shakespeares** *Birmingham*

## Charities
### East Anglia

1. **Hewitsons** *Cambridge*
   **Mills & Reeve** *Norwich*
   **Taylor Vinters** *Cambridge*
2. **Greenwoods** *Peterborough*
   **Hegarty & Co** *Peterborough*

## Charities
### North West

1. **Addleshaw** *Manchester*
   **Brabners Chaffe** *Liverpool*
   **Halliwells LLP** *Manchester*
2. **Birch Cullimore** *Chester*
   **Blackhurst Swainson** *Preston*
   **Bremners Solicitors** *Liverpool*
   **Cobbetts** *Manchester*
   **Kuit Steinart Levy** *Manchester*
   **Pannone** *Manchester*

## Charities
### North East

1. **Wrigleys** *Leeds*
2. **Addleshaw Goddard** *Leeds*
   **Dickinson Dees** *Newcastle*
   **McCormicks** *Leeds*
   **Rollits** *York*
3. **Grays** *York*
   **Irwin Mitchell** *Sheffield*
   **Robert Muckle** *Newcastle*
   **Ward Hadaway** *Newcastle*
   **Watson Burton LLP** *Newcastle*

# property/real estate

It's a conundrum: the UK population watches property development shows on TV 24/7, yet few law students aspire to be property lawyers. Admittedly land law lectures at uni or law school usually baffle and bore in equal measure, but it's worth digging a little deeper because the reality of practice is very different.

## type of work

We spoke to Mike Bothamley, head of Beachcroft Wansbroughs' property practice, and asked him to tell us what gets property lawyers out of bed in the mornings. "*The deals – I love deals!*" he explained, adding that buildings and the built environment "*and what they can do for peoples' quality of life*" were also important to him. Factor in the ongoing relationships with clients and various other professionals and you begin to see that daily life in practice is no snooze in the lecture theatre.

Mike, who concentrates on large-scale developments, talked about the life cycle of deals. They start with site assembly (buying all the required land) and planning permissions, progress through the funding and construction stages, and culminate in the sale or letting of completed buildings. The clients you act for will determine the sort of work you do. Developers tend to be more entrepreneurial and risk-taking than, for example, banks, which operate within narrower parameters and require more i-dotting and t-crossing from their lawyers. You might want to bear this in mind when choosing a firm. Many of the lawyers we speak to find the development side of the job the most interesting; others specialise in particular types of property: retail premises, agricultural land or offices, for example.

Whatever specialisation you end up in, the law and, more importantly, the market both keep evolving. Recently, for instance, the government has introduced the concept of commonhold land ownership, and there's a growing trend for 'out-sourcing', whereby companies divest themselves of real estate ownership and management functions so they can concentrate on their core business. Mike also explained that the pensions crisis has led to greater interest in development and investment. He's right – you can see this at either end of the scale: the bloke down the road who's just taken out a buy-to-let mortgage and the fact that there's hardly a city centre in the UK that's not already been, or is currently being, redeveloped. Apparently, "*lowest common denominator development is a thing of the past,*" and there's a greater emphasis on the impact the built environment has on the business and residential communities that use it, in particular upon good design and sustainable development.

## skills needed

cool-headed and unflappable...collaborative nature...lead others or work alone...analytical mind...grasp commercial and practical realities...see big picture while delving into detail...good drafter and negotiator...

One of the most satisfying aspects of the job is the co-operative process between all the parties to a deal – clients, opposite numbers, builders, surveyors, banks, planners, etc. Basically, "*everybody is after the same result;*" so if writing nasty letters and threatening court action leaves you cold, this could be your field. Yet you can't be a pushover; your client will expect you to negotiate favourable terms for them and you'll need to be firm. Happily, as you progress, industry knowledge becomes second nature, and it becomes easier to understand the commercial logic of a transaction, so that – as Mike puts it – "*you only expend powder and shot on the points that really matter.*"

Property lawyers are jugglers. Usually they have several transactions on the go at any one time and, to stay on top of things, they need to be organised, proactive and fully aware of the consequences of each move in a transaction. But no matter how exciting things are for experienced lawyers, they all had to earn their stripes by doing their fair share of drafting and negotiating bog-standard leases and contracts. There are times when this can be tedious, but there are now more standardised documents in use, a development which makes life easier.

## career options

There are several allied career options for lawyers – planning, environmental, local authority, banks and funders, contractors, surveyors, property companies – and ex-property lawyers often make good developers themselves. There's also been a rise in the number of openings for professional support lawyers – ideal for those with less interest in doing deals than in the documentation or the legal principles holding them together.

## leading firms from Chambers UK 2006

### Real Estate: Larger Deals
London

[1] Berwin Leighton Paisner
Clifford Chance LLP
Linklaters
[2] Ashurst
Herbert Smith LLP
Lovells
Nabarro Nathanson
[3] Freshfields Bruckhaus Deringer
Macfarlanes
SJ Berwin LLP
Slaughter and May
[4] Allen & Overy LLP
CMS Cameron McKenna LLP
DLA Piper Rudnick Gray Cary
Jones Day
Lawrence Graham LLP
Olswang
[5] Dechert LLP
Denton Wilde Sapte
Mayer, Brown, Rowe & Maw
Norton Rose
Paul, Hastings, Janofsky & Walker
Simmons & Simmons

### Real Estate: Hotels & Leisure
London

[1] Berwin Leighton Paisner
Clifford Chance LLP
[2] CMS Cameron McKenna LLP
Freshfields Bruckhaus Deringer
SJ Berwin LLP
[3] Allen & Overy LLP
Davies Arnold Cooper
Denton Wilde Sapte
Field Fisher Waterhouse
Linklaters
Lovells
Richards Butler
[4] Davenport Lyons
DLA Piper Rudnick Gray Cary
Douglas Wignall & Co
Fladgate Fielder
Herbert Smith LLP
Taylor Wessing
Wragge & Co LLP

### Real Estate: Medium Deals
London

[1] Addleshaw Goddard
Forsters LLP
Travers Smith
[2] Boodle Hatfield
Eversheds LLP
Field Fisher Waterhouse
Maxwell Batley
Richards Butler
Taylor Wessing
Wragge & Co LLP
[3] Clyde & Co
Davies Arnold Cooper
Farrer & Co
Finers Stephens Innocent
Fladgate Fielder
Howard Kennedy
Kirkpatrick & Lockhart Nicholson
Lewis Silkin
Osborne Clarke
Speechly Bircham
Trowers & Hamlins
[4] Bird & Bird
Hammonds
Harbottle & Lewis LLP
Manches LLP
Mishcon de Reya
Penningtons Solicitors LLP
Reed Smith
Solomon Taylor & Shaw

# specialist areas

## Real Estate
### The South

[1] **Blake Lapthorn** *Fareham*
**Bond Pearce LLP** *Southampton*
**Cripps Harries** *Tunbridge Wells*
[2] **Clyde & Co** *Guildford*
**DMH Stallard** *Crawley*
**Paris Smith** *Southampton*
**Shoosmiths** *Fareham*
**Stevens & Bolton LLP** *Guildford*
**Thomas Eggar** *Chichester*
[3] **Coffin Mew** *Southampton*
**GCL Solicitors** *Guildford*
**Lester Aldridge** *Bournemouth*
**Mundays LLP** *Cobham*
**Rawlison Butler** *Crawley*
**Thomson Snell** *Tunbridge Wells*
[4] **Brachers** *Maidstone*
**Charles Russell** *Guildford*
**Clarke Willmott** *Southampton*
**Lamport Bassitt** *Southampton*
**Penningtons** *Basingstoke*
[5] **asb law** *Crawley*
**Clarkson Wright** *Orpington*
**Laytons** *Guildford*
**Moore & Blatch** *Southampton*
**Shadbolt & Co** *Reigate*
**Steele Raymond** *Bournemouth*

## Real Estate
### Thames Valley

[1] **Pitmans** *Reading*
[2] **Boyes Turner** *Reading*
**BrookStreet** *Witney*
**Clarkslegal LLP** *Reading*
**Denton Wilde** *Milton Keynes*
**Iliffes Booth Bennett** *Uxbridge*
[3] **Blake Lapthorn Linnell** *Oxford*
**Harold Benjamin** *Harrow*
**Manches** *Oxford*
**Matthew Arnold** *Watford*
[4] **B P Collins** *Gerrards Cross*
**Blandy & Blandy** *Reading*
**Darbys** *Oxford*
**Fennemores** *Milton Keynes*
**Field Seymour** *Reading*
**Morgan Cole** *Reading*
**Olswang** *Reading*
**Owen White** *Slough*
**Penningtons** *Newbury*
**Pictons** *Luton*
**Shoosmiths** *Reading*
**Thring Townsend** *Newbury*

## Real Estate
### South West

[1] **Burges Salmon LLP** *Bristol*
[2] **Ashfords**
**Beachcroft Wansbroughs** *Bristol*
**Bevan Brittan LLP** *Bristol*
**Bond Pearce LLP** *Plymouth*
**Clarke Willmott** *Bristol*
**Davitt Jones Bould** *Taunton*
**Michelmores** *Exeter*
[3] **BPE Solicitors** *Cheltenham*
**Charles Russell** *Cheltenham*
**Foot Anstey** *Plymouth*
**Osborne Clarke** *Bristol*
**Rickerbys** *Cheltenham*
**Stephens & Scown** *Exeter*
**TLT Solicitors** *Bristol*
**Veale Wasbrough** *Bristol*
[4] **Clark Holt** *Swindon*
**Davies and Partners** *Gloucester*
**Thring Townsend** *Swindon*
**Withy King** *Bath*

## Real Estate
### Wales

[1] **Eversheds LLP** *Cardiff*
**Geldards LLP** *Cardiff*
[2] **Berry Smith** *Cardiff*
**Morgan LaRoche** *Swansea*
[3] **Hugh James** *Cardiff*
**Morgan Cole** *Cardiff*
[4] **Capital Law** *Cardiff Bay*
**M & A Solicitors LLP** *Cardiff*
**Robertsons** *Cardiff*

# specialist areas

## Real Estate
### East Midlands

1. **Browne Jacobson** *Nottingham*
   **Eversheds LLP** *Nottingham*
   **Freeth Cartwright** *Nottingham*
2. **Geldards** *Derby*
   **Harvey Ingram LLP** *Leicester*
   **Shoosmiths** *Nottingham*

## Real Estate
### West Midlands

1. **Eversheds LLP** *Birmingham*
   **Wragge & Co LLP** *Birmingham*
2. **Cobbetts** *Birmingham*
   **DLA Piper Rudnick** *Birmingham*
   **Pinsent Masons** *Birmingham*
3. **Hammonds** *Birmingham*
   **Shoosmiths** *Northampton*
4. **Knight** *Newcastle-under-Lyme*
   **Martineau J'son** *Birmingham*
   **Reed Smith** *Coventry*
   **Wright Hassall** *Leamington Spa*

## Real Estate
### East Anglia

1. **Birketts** *Ipswich*
   **Hewitsons** *Cambridge*
   **Mills & Reeve** *Cambridge*
   **Taylor Vinters** *Cambridge*
2. **Ashton** *Bury St Edmunds*
   **Eversheds LLP** *Cambridge*
   **Greene&Greene** *Bury St Edmunds*
   **Greenwoods** *Peterborough*
   **Kester Cunningham** *Cambridge*
   **Prettys** *Ipswich*

## Real Estate
### North West

1. **Addleshaw** *Manchester*
   **Cobbetts** *Manchester*
   **DLA Piper Rudnick** *Liverpool*
   **Eversheds LLP** *Manchester*
2. **Halliwells** *Liver, Manchester*
   **Hill Dickinson** *Liverpool*
3. **Beachcroft** *Manchester*
   **Brabners** *Liverpool*
   **DWF** *Liverpool, Manchester*
   **Hammonds** *Manchester*
   **Mace & Jones** *Manchester*
   **Pannone & Partners** *Manchester*
4. **Field Cunn'ham** *Manchester*
   **JMW Solicitors** *Manchester*
   **Land Law** *Altrincham*
   **Pinsent Masons** *Manchester*

## Real Estate
### North East

1. **Dickinson Dees** *Newcastle*
2. **Eversheds LLP** *Newcastle*
3. **Robert Muckle** *Newcastle*
   **Ward Hadaway** *Newcastle*
   **Watson Burton** *Newcastle*

## Real Estate
### Yorkshire

1. **Addleshaw Goddard** *Leeds*
   **Walker Morris** *Leeds*
2. **DLA Piper** *Leeds, Sheffield*
   **Pinsent Masons** *Leeds*
3. **Cobbetts** *Leeds*
   **Eversheds LLP** *Leeds*
   **Hammonds** *Leeds*
   **Nabarro Nathanson** *Sheffield*
4. **Andrew M Jackson** *Hull*
   **Gordons** *Leeds*
5. **Gosschalks** *Hull*
   **Irwin Mitchell** *Sheffield*
   **Keeble Hawson** *Sheffield*
   **Lupton Fawcett** *Leeds*
   **Rollits** *Hull*
   **Shulmans** *Leeds*
6. **Beachcroft** *Leeds*
   **Denison Till** *York*
   **Langleys** *York*
   **McCormicks** *Leeds*
   **Wake Smith** *Sheffield*

# public interest

Are you the kind of person who won't shrug their shoulders and allow an injustice to continue unchallenged simply because it is lawful? This field is incredibly popular with students, yet academic argument and the rigours of practice are worlds apart...

## civil liberties and human rights

Human rights issues crop up in both civil and criminal cases. On the civil side examples include claims of rights to education and community care under the Mental Health Act, or cases of discrimination at work, where people are unfairly passed over for promotion, or miss out on benefits or equal pay. The right to family life is enshrined in the HRA and family lawyers have to consider human rights in relation to child access and residency. In housing cases, the issue might be a gay or lesbian partner's right to succeed to a tenancy previously held by their deceased partner.

Danny Simpson, head of the criminal and civil liberties department at Howells in Sheffield, explained how "*a lot of human rights issues relate to people's interactions with the state*" and judicial review is a key tool by which the decisions of public bodies can be challenged. A "*tidal wave of legislation*" spanning terrorism and antisocial behaviour intersects with the Public Order Acts and the Human Rights Act to throw up a multitude of issues in relation to asylum seekers' rights, treatment of people in police custody and local authorities' obligations towards people who are mentally ill, all of which have been the subject of recent cases.

Danny's caseload contains miscarriages of justice and files relating to public order convictions arising out of demonstrations and confrontations with the police. He also handles a wide range of police complaints and prisoners' issues.

In July 2004, the House of Lords made a ruling on whether the fingerprints of a detainee in police custody could be retained even if no charges were laid against them. And consider for a moment the fact that the Home Secretary decides whether or not prisoners serving life sentences may be released. The European Court of Human Rights says it is wrong that a politician should make a decision based on whether or not a person has been sufficiently punished or the likelihood that their imprisonment has acted as a deterrent to others. The only valid criterion for a politician, says the court, is whether or not the person is a continuing danger.

## skills needed

...passion...determination...demonstrated commitment...creativity...initiative... communicate well with Joe Public and with the court...love of advocacy...

Danny is clear that "*there is no point in doing this work for the money – you will be considerably worse paid than in other areas.*" Instead, "*you do it because you have a desire or a vocation to improve another's situation.*" As you'll have extensive contact with people who are mentally ill or "*don't appreciate the full extent of their legal predicament,*" empathy and sympathy are required in equal measure. Strong analytical skills are also vital because it's your job to "*identify the legal issues you can do something about, and those economic or political situations that, as a lawyer, you can't help with.*" Organisational skills will serve you well, and you will need patience to battle against bureaucracy and red tape. Importantly, you must be able to manage a client's expectations; it will not help them if your idealism clouds a situation.

## career options

The number of people who tell us they are looking for training contracts in this field outstrips the number of contracts available by some margin. However, as the work is largely legally aided (or done for free if no funding is available) the firms that specialise cannot offer trainees attractive salaries and certainly don't sponsor them through law school. "*In one respect there is a bottomless pit of work; in another it is difficult for practices to do the work at all without going bust.*"

"*Firms distinguish between those applicants who say they are interested and those who really are interested,*" so carrying out voluntary work for a law centre or specialist voluntary organisation such as the Howard League for Penal Reform or the Children's Legal Centre, or joining a relevant organisation such as Liberty or Justice, will improve your chances. The *Legal Action Group Bulletin* is an accessible publication covering the area and you'll find it enormously helpful in gaining a better understanding of the issues that concern lawyers in this field. It also goes without saying that regularly reading good quality newspapers is important, if only to keep track of Mr Clarke's new measures.

Law centres and the voluntary sector pick up from where private practice leaves off, and it is not uncommon for dedicated lawyers to move between the two arenas during their careers. For more information on life inside law centres, see page 13.

## immigration law

The subject of immigration is close to the hearts of many, not least among them the Home Secretary and readers of the *Daily Mail*. For better or worse, politics and public opinion are inexorably linked to the practice of immigration law. There are two strands of practice: business and personal, the latter being the one that motivates most students to enter the field, as it addresses one of the most fundamental issues in a person's life – the question of whether they will be permitted to live and work or study in the country they choose. For some clients, this will determine whether they can be together with their spouse/partner and family. For others, who have fled from persecution in their countries of origin, removal could mean torture or death.

Last year saw a further reduction in the number of firms undertaking legal aid immigration work, following a new set of cuts to legal aid funding. Publicly funded work has always been the preserve of the most committed of practitioners, and so it is sad to see a number of excellent firms now bowing out because the work is becoming uneconomic. Twinned with financial cutbacks is the continuing raft of restrictive legislative activity in the linked areas of immigration and asylum, such as the recently overturned policy to refuse accommodation and assistance to destitute asylum seekers. Those entering practice must be more committed than ever.

On the business side, things are looking rosier. Until recently, there was a vilification of economic migrants, now the government has a new approach – managed migration. It is trying to cut down on asylum seekers and those seeking leave to remain on other human rights grounds, and instead ensure that those who come to the UK are coming to work and bringing skills. Business immigration lawyers advise and assist on work permits for employers and employees, and related schemes for Highly Skilled Migrants and investors. Dealing with corporate clients and businessmen requires a particular set of skills, in particular managing client expectations. You have to be able to see their commercial concerns. At worst, a businessman might need to travel abroad for a high-level meeting, yet the Home Office wants their passport. By contrast, for an asylum client, nothing is more important than getting leave to remain in the UK.

## skills needed

...sensitivity...compassion and commitment ...able to deal with emotional clients... tenacity...willing to question the authorities...language skills...an understanding of the broader commercial context...

Unless you're organised, you'll find the job impossible. It's the nature of the game. Everything has a deadline and you've got to meet them, one lawyer told us. Furthermore, publicly funded work is accompanied by a mountain of unremunerated form filling and red tape, which you just can't ignore. You'll need to be familiar with several different sources of law – UK law and Home Office policy, European law, human rights legislation – and you'll need to know which will be most advantageous to your client. If advocacy is important to you, the good news is there's plenty of opportunity to develop this skill. Certainly it means an enormous amount to the client to have the same person take their case from start to finish. If you do end up working with asylum seekers, there's a delicate balance to be struck. You will hear some horrific stories and you'll have to be tough enough to elicit the right information, while also being sensitive towards the client.

## career options

Of those who have quit private practice recently, some went into the administrative side, becoming immigration adjudicators; others headed for the voluntary sector. Generally speaking immigration lawyers are motivated by higher ideals than money; in fact, working in the voluntary sector can be more satisfying as there are less funding constraints than in private practice. There are branches of the Refugee Legal Centre and the Immigration Advisory Service across the country and these organisations, and others like them, will doubtless continue to be very busy and offer employment opportunities.

As a student it is important to test your commitment to the field and to keep up to date by becoming a student member of the Immigration Law Practitioners Association. Consider joining organisations like the Joint Council for the Welfare of Immigrants, Amnesty or the Medical Foundation (which helps torture victims). Wherever possible, take immigration law subjects at law school or uni.

# solicitors

## leading firms from Chambers UK 2006

### Human Rights
London

1. Bindman & Partners
2. Bhatt Murphy
   Birnberg Peirce & Partners
   Christian Khan
   Hickman & Rose
   Leigh Day & Co
3. Scott-Moncrieff, Harbour & Sinclair
   Simons Muirhead & Burton
4. Deighton Guedalla
   Hodge Jones & Allen
   Palmer Wade

### Immigration: Business
London

1. CMS Cameron McKenna LLP
   Kingsley Napley
   Laura Devine Solicitors
   Magrath & Co
2. Bates Wells & Braithwaite
   Reed Smith
3. Baker & McKenzie LLP
   Gherson & Co
   Mishcon de Reya
   Penningtons Solicitors LLP
   Sturtivant & Co
4. DJ Webb & Co
   Fox Williams
   H2O Law LLP
   Harbottle & Lewis LLP
   Lovells
   Taylor Wessing

### Human Rights: Commercial
London

1. Clifford Chance LLP
   Freshfields Bruckhaus Deringer
   Herbert Smith LLP

### Immigration: Personal
London

1. Bindman & Partners
   Birnberg Peirce & Partners
   Wesley Gryk
2. Bates Wells & Braithwaite
   Deighton Guedalla
   Glazer Delmar
   Luqmani Thompson & Partners
   Wilson & Co
3. Bartram & Co
   DJ Webb & Co
   Elder Rahimi

### Immigration
Thames Valley

1. Darbys *Oxford*
   Turpin Miller & Higgins *Oxford*

### Human Rights
Midlands

1. Public Interest Lawyers *Birmingham*
2. Public Law Solicitors *Birmingham*
   Tyndallwoods *Birmingham*

### Human Rights
The North

1. Harrison Bundey *Leeds*
   Howells *Sheffield*
   Irwin Mitchell *Sheffield*
2. A S Law *Liverpool*
3. Ben Hoare Bell *Sunderland*
   Robert Lizar *Manchester*

### Immigration
Midlands

1. The Rights Partnership *Birmingham*
2. Tyndallwoods *Birmingham*

### Immigration
The North

1. A S Law *Liverpool*
   David Gray Solicitors *Newcastle*
   Harrison Bundey *Leeds*
   Howells *Sheffield*
2. Henry Hyams *Leeds*
   Jackson & Canter *Liverpool*

### Immigration
East Anglia

1. Gross & Co *Bury St Edmunds*
   Wollastons *Chelmsford*

# shipping

**p&i club:** Protection and Indemnity Club – a marine insurance club run mutually by and for shipowners.

**charter party:** a commercial instrument; essentially a contract for the hire of the whole or a part of a ship.

**bill of lading:** a receipt given by the master of the ship for goods loaded, a contract of carriage between the owners of the ships and the owners of the goods and a negotiable certificate of title to the goods themselves.

**salvage:** reward payable by owners of recovered ships; goods saved at sea by 'salvors'.

Do you dream of being a master and commander like Russell Crowe, or cavorting with pirates in the Caribbean? Careers in shipping law are diverse, unpredictable and truly international. For a landlocked nine-to-five desk job, look elsewhere.

## type of work

Shipping law concerns the carriage of goods or people by sea. Contentious work is divided into wet ('Admiralty') work and dry ('marine') work. Wet work is broadly tortious, and concerns disputes arising from accidents or misadventure at sea (collision, salvage, total loss or modern-day piracy). It often attracts former naval officers or ex-mariners. In this area, lawyers need to act fast: delays cost money, and clients expect quick analysis and sensible answers. Dry work, on the other hand, concerns disputes related to contracts made on dry land, such as charter parties, bills of lading, and sale of goods contracts.

Non-contentious work primarily concerns ship finance and ship-building contracts, sale and purchase agreements, employment contracts for crew members, affreightment contracts, and the registration and re-flagging of ships. Further niche areas include yachting or fishing, which usually involve regulatory matters. Be under no illusion – ship finance is nowhere near as exciting as casualty work, nor does it offer the same opportunities for travel.

Dry shipping specialist Tony Rooth of Watson, Farley & Williams divides his time between court and arbitration appearances, conferences with counsel, client meetings, giving internal advice and taking witness statements – a caseload that is nothing if not diverse. While shipping law does not have a work-all-night culture, there is often an element of unpredictability about it. Wet lawyers, especially, may have to jet off to Panama or Piraeus at short notice to take a witness statement or deal with a casualty. Tony tells us it's a case of "*have passport, will travel.*" And when you consider that you'll often be dealing with people or problems located in a different time zone, it becomes clear why shipping law doesn't suit the routine junkie. "*In a worst-case scenario, you'll have a client in the East, and a ship in the West.*"

In spite of headline-hitting cases – such as the Herald of Free Enterprise or Exxon Valdez disasters, "*shipping may not be as sexy or remunerative as some other areas of the law.*" Yet all is not lost; globalisation and industry consolidation mean that the area is far from static, and one can't really envisage world trade grinding to a halt. Trainees and NQs must expect to get chucked in at the deep end fairly early on. Research, client meetings, taking witness statements and drafting basic documents all mean "*lots of devilling, lots of exposure and certainly no photocopying.*" Devilling, by the way, means doing work for someone more senior (and busier) than you.

## skills needed

...always up to speed on legal developments/ industry trends...firm grip on contract, tort and court procedure...available to travel at short notice...good communicator... team spirit and self motivation...

Dry lawyers need to develop a good knowledge of conflicts, contract and tort. Wet lawyers need to be bold, as they will face adversity and the unexpected. All shipping lawyers will be interacting with people from different cultures and countries and at different ends of the social scale; many of them will have been schooled in the university of life and, as Tony notes, are strong characters who can sometimes be *"suspicious or difficult to handle."* From shipowners, operators, traders and charterers through to P&I clubs and hull underwriters – it's a really mixed bag, so people skills and good communication are crucial.

In wet work, naval or marine experience is common, but this is not to say you can't build a career without it. Most shipping lawyers start out with little industry knowledge, but soon acquire it. As Tony explained: *"It does help if you know your port from your starboard, especially when dealing with navigation matters."*

## career options

The majority of UK-based jobs are to be found in London, with the remainder in larger port cities. In international firms, assistants can choose to work abroad, something that is generally considered to be a good career move. If, following qualification, you decide shipping is not for you, as a contentious shipping lawyer you'll have gained a solid grounding in commercial litigation. If you've taken the non-contentious route, you should be able to shift relatively seamlessly into general finance or corporate work. And if private practice disappoints, then P&I clubs, shipowners, operators and marine insurers all have openings for lawyers, but the financial rewards will be less than in private practice, as will the legal component of the position. Failing all else, there's always piracy...

## leading firms from Chambers UK 2006

| Shipping London | |
|---|---|
| 1 Holman Fenwick & Willan | Ince & Co |
| 2 Clyde & Co | |
| 3 Hill Taylor Dickinson | Richards Butler |
| 4 Barlow Lyde & Gilbert | Bentleys, Stokes & Lowless |
| Jackson Parton | More Fisher Brown |
| Waltons & Morse | Winter Scott |
| 5 Clifford Chance LLP | Curtis Davis Garrard Uxbridge |
| Lawrence Graham LLP | Middleton Potts |
| Shaw and Croft | Stephenson Harwood |
| Thomas Cooper & Stibbard | Waterson Hicks |
| 6 Davies Arnold Cooper | Fishers |
| Hill Dickinson | Mays Brown, Solicitors |
| Norton Rose | Watson, Farley & Williams |

| Shipping The Regions |
|---|
| 1 Eversheds LLP Newcastle upon Tyne |
| 2 Andrew M Jackson Hull |
| Davies, Johnson & Co Plymouth |
| Mills & Co Newcastle upon Tyne |
| Rayfield Mills Newcastle upon Tyne |
| 3 DLA Piper Rudnick Gray Manchester |
| Hill Dickinson Liverpool |
| Lester Aldridge Southampton |
| 4 Bond Pearce LLP Plymouth |
| Dale & Stevens LLP Felixstowe |
| Foot Anstey Plymouth |
| John Weston & Co Felixstowe |
| Prettys Ipswich |

# sports law

Rather than being a discipline in its own right, sports law is an industry focus. Consequently, many of the firms that offer this kind of service do so by drawing upon the services of lawyers from other practice groups, and only a few have a team of dedicated sports lawyers. Broadly speaking, sports law encompasses:

• regulatory advice to teams and ruling bodies;
• advice on media, advertising and sponsorship;
• general corporate and commercial advice.

## type of work

Like it or not, sport is a business. What this means for the sports lawyer is that advice must always be given in a commercial context. As Stephen Hornsby of The Simkins Partnership notes: "*Ultimately the most important things are the contracts. It is better to be a good contract lawyer than a good sports lawyer.*" On top of this, the lawyer needs to develop an understanding of intellectual property, sponsorship and broadcasting issues. On occasion, they may also need to tackle crime, personal injury and employment matters and, of late, some have been at the forefront of developments in the law regarding image rights and privacy.

Consider the juxtaposition of commercial considerations with sports regulations and domestic and EU law. The Bosman case, which concerned player transfer fees, is a prime example of where industry-specific and EU laws can collide. EU employment law prevailed, resulting in a tremendous knock-on effect in the football industry. The same can be said about the attempt by the Inland Revenue to abolish football's 'super creditor' rule. That rule requires a club in administration to pay other clubs and its own players before creditors, on pain of expulsion from the league. If the challenge succeeds, clubs will tighten up on the amount of money and players they are willing to lend to each other, perhaps leading to reductions in players' wages and a restricted transfer market. However, as Stephen notes: "*Sport, and especially football, will shortly be run as any other business. As the legal immunities begin to collapse, and the false liquidity in the market comes to an end, this will result in greater legal involvement.*"

Both the globalisation and commercialisation of sport have brought new issues that the legal framework must encompass. Intrusive press coverage has resulted in concerns over the accuracy of reports and potential claims for defamation or breach of privacy. The interests of broadcasters and sponsors often compete with those of the players and spectators – should players have to undertake rounds of press interviews after completing a match, rather than going home to their families? Should teams have to play late at night to maximise TV viewing figures? Does the ubiquitous sponsor's logo projected across the pitch detract from the enjoyment of the paying spectator? These are all conflicting interests that sports lawyers must face when negotiating the next round of broadcasting rights.

## skills needed

...strong on contract law...commercial nous...interpersonal skills...entrepreneurial approach...innovation... passion for the subject...ability to see the other side of the argument...

It's important that you have a genuine interest in the industry. You've don't need to have read every edition of *The Racing Post* since the age of nine or be able to recite the names of past winners of the FA Cup, but if you want to work for a particular client, you ought to know a bit about the sport's relevant governing body and its professional organisation.

In this industry, perhaps more so than any other, you've got to be able to impress clients with your personality and passion. As well as executing the technical aspects of the job, you must be prepared to run what may in fact be closer to a consultancy service to help your client to manage his image. As Stephen says: "*The idea is to be a trusted adviser. If you have an idea, you pick up the phone and tell them about it, and give them a plan how to action it. It's not about just waiting for the phone to ring.*" If emotions are running high, you must stay cool and rational and consider the merits of an alternative game plan. "*You must always understand that the opposition have a valid point of view themselves, and it is usually well thought out and sincerely held.*" It's at this point that a sports lawyer needs that extra bit of imagination to make sure the ball stays in play.

## career options

Lawyers move into this area by both accident and design. Some leading practitioners specialised in a field that affects sport, say IP or competition law, and then realised that their efforts had earned them a reputation on the sports field. Others had actively sought employment as a junior lawyer in one of the dedicated sports law practices. Stephen believes that opportunities in private practice will grow, especially if more lawyers take on work that was previously the preserve of agents.

Some lawyers find they are more satisfied working in-house at one of the governing bodies such as the RFU, MCC or FA. There are also roles within media organisations, say negotiating broadcasting rights on behalf of terrestrial or satellite broadcasters.

## leading firms from Chambers UK 2006

### Sport: Regulatory
London

[1] **DLA Piper Rudnick Gray Cary UK**
Hammonds
[2] **Charles Russell**
Farrer & Co
Max Bitel Greene
[3] **Freshfields Bruckhaus Deringer**
Teacher Stern Selby
The Simkins Partnership

### Sport
The Regions

[1] **James Chapman and Co** *Manchester*
[2] **Clarke Willmott** *Southampton, Bristol*
McCormicks *Leeds*
[3] **Addleshaw G'dard** *Leeds, Manchester*
George Davies *Manchester*
Walker Morris *Leeds*
[4] **Cramer Richards** *Leeds*
Hill Dickinson *Liverpool*
Kuit Steinart Levy *Manchester*
Osborne Clarke *Bristol*

### Sport: Commercial/Media
London

[1] **Bird & Bird**
Hammonds
[2] **Couchman Harrington Associates**
DLA Piper Rudnick Gray Cary UK
[3] **Denton Wilde Sapte**
Harbottle & Lewis LLP
Kirkpatrick & Lockhart Nicholson
Olswang
The Simkins Partnership
[4] **Addleshaw Goddard**
athletes1 Legal
Field Fisher Waterhouse
Fladgate Fielder
Herbert Smith LLP
Macfarlanes
Simmons & Simmons
Withers LLP
[5] **Clintons**
Collyer-Bristow
Farrer & Co
Freshfields Bruckhaus Deringer
Slaughter and May

### Sport: Horse Racing & Equestrian
The Regions

[1] **Ashfords** *Exeter*
Edmondson Hall *Newmarket*
Taylor Vinters *Cambridge*
Whatley Lane *Newmarket*
Withy King *Marlborough*

### Sport
Wales

[1] **Hugh James** *Cardiff*
[2] **Loosemores** *Cardiff*

# tax

The tax lawyer's primary role is to advise on the most tax-efficient means of structuring and running a business. If you thought tax was all dusty books and dull conversation, think again!

## type of work

The work comes in three main varieties: tax planning; transactional advice; and litigation. Nigel Popplewell, head of corporate tax at Burges Salmon in Bristol, told us: "*Some tax lawyers are happiest with planning, others like the rough and tumble of negotiation, and there are some who like the crack of court work and investigations – and a good fight with the Revenue.*" Sounds like there's something for everyone.

Tax law evolves with incredible speed, so you need to have your finger on the pulse when it comes to judicial decisions and new legislation. The simple fact is that there's a lot of tax law and you must make a commitment to learning it. Although qualifying into tax can "*be a bit like starting all over again,*" Nigel stressed that a junior lawyer can get up to speed on the technical aspects of the work relatively quickly: "*After 18 months you can do a huge amount. You may not be able to make judgement calls, but you can stand your ground and deal with the tax authorities.*" Taking the Chartered Tax Adviser exams will help, but a few more years of investment in your career may be required before your instincts become fully tuned and you have the requisite experience to handle any situation solo.

Much of a tax lawyer's work comes from other departments in the firm – perhaps a question from the property department on how VAT applies to a land purchase and construction project, or maybe assistance required by corporate colleagues in structuring a joint venture or a company reorganisation. The role is a blend of advisory work on large projects and ad hoc queries that require immediate answers. Tax lawyers are key to corporate deals, but generally they do not take a seat alongside their M&A counterparts on the all-night, deal-closing roller coaster. Nigel pointed out that "*no one wants to argue about tax at 2am,*" and so the tax points tend to be covered early on in a deal. Moreover, "*as soon as someone says 'tax', people say 'over to you', which gives you more control over your hours and environment.*"

## skills needed

...excellent academics...analytical mind...willing to challenge and test...technical excellence...good on interpretation of black letter law...clear communication...commerciality...

While there is always room for the tax lawyer with an academic leaning and "*there is an element of truth in the anorak stereotype,*" if you have the hermit-like tendencies of a Howard Hughes and would hate being wheeled out in front of clients, you may have a problem. An essential element of your job will be to distil difficult principles into palatable, client-friendly language. In this sense, your job is just like that of any other corporate lawyer except your subject matter can be much more impenetrable and convoluted. In short, knowing the rules isn't enough: "*If you haven't got the communication skills, you won't be terribly good.*"

## career options

Nigel observed that "*it can be difficult to get people involved in tax,*" but a career in this field should ensure you are well treated. "*Tax lawyers are highly thought of, and firms guard their employees very jealously.*" Despite these specialists being hugely in demand, tax lawyers tend not to move around much, and firms must ensure they "*grow their own.*" Moves to the Bar are not unheard of; indeed, some of the most respected tax barristers first achieved success as tax solicitors.

Outside private practice, you can work in-house in the tax department of a large corporation or financial institution, or you can work for the government in the Inland Revenue or Customs & Excise. Occasionally solicitors move to accountancy firms in a tax consultancy role. Overall, the skills and knowledge gained in private practice are transferable at all levels of qualification. We heartily agree with Nigel's parting shot: "*You are probably amongst the most employable lawyers in the world.*"

## leading firms from Chambers UK 2006

### Tax
### London

[1] Freshfields Bruckhaus Deringer
Linklaters
Slaughter and May
[2] Allen & Overy LLP
Clifford Chance LLP
[3] Ashurst
Herbert Smith LLP
Lovells
Macfarlanes
[4] Berwin Leighton Paisner
CMS Cameron McKenna LLP
Denton Wilde Sapte
Norton Rose
Simmons & Simmons
SJ Berwin LLP
Travers Smith
[5] Nabarro Nathanson
Olswang
Shearman & Sterling LLP
Watson, Farley & Williams
[6] Addleshaw Goddard
Cleary Gottlieb Steen & Hamilton
Clyde & Co
Field Fisher Waterhouse
Fried, Frank, Harris, Shriver
Jones Day
McDermott Will & Emery UK LLP
Weil, Gotshal & Manges

### Tax
### The South

[1] Burges Salmon LLP *Bristol*
Osborne Clarke *Bristol*
[2] Blake Lapthorn Linnell *Fareham*
TLT Solicitors *Bristol*

### Tax
### Midlands
### Leading firms

[1] Pinsent Masons *Birmingham*
Wragge & Co LLP *Birmingham*
[2] DLA Piper Rudnick Gray *Birmingham*
Eversheds LLP *Nottingham*
Hammonds *Birmingham*
[3] Bevan Brittan LLP *Birmingham*
Mills & Reeve *Cambridge*

### Tax
### The North

[1] Addleshaw Goddard *Leeds*
Pinsent Masons *Leeds*
[2] Eversheds LLP *Leeds*
Hammonds *Leeds*
[3] Dickinson Dees *Newcastle*
Walker Morris *Leeds*

Lawyers who specialise in Technology, Media & Telecoms must keep up to date with both changes in the law and developments in this ever-changing sector. And thanks to the concept of 'convergence', they are increasingly advising clients from a number of media. It's no longer sufficient to be, say, a broadcasting specialist or an internet specialist – as these two technologies fuse, lawyers need to be familiar with both strands.

## type of work

The average TMT lawyer spends much of their time advising on commercial transactions and drafting the requisite agreements. However, according to Mark O'Conor, an IT partner at Bird & Bird: *"You need to differentiate yourself from a standard commercial lawyer so that you can add value."* To achieve this you need to be familiar with the latest industry know-how and understand how the most recent set of regulations is going to impact your client's business. You will be frequently applying your legal knowledge to new commercial situations: Does your client need a disclaimer on its website? Is a contract made online legally enforceable? Does your client's marketing e-mail count as unsolicited spam? How can you ascertain whether someone is abusing your client's software licence by allowing too many users of their product? What are the consequences of the change of the media regulator from Oftel to Ofcom? If these issues press your buttons, read on...

Large commercial companies commonly have their own in-house lawyers. Mark explained: *"You have to be able to deal with a real mix of people – some want you to stay in the back room, whereas others may want you to write the hymn sheet for them."* The prevalence of in-house legal teams is good news for junior solicitors and trainees keen on a secondment. Whether or not clients have their own advisers, *"part of your job is to keep one eye on the latest cases and trade journals and to keep your clients informed. It is always good practice to send out a quick e-mail or bulletin; even if they don't read it, it lets them know that you're still on their case."*

## skills needed

...grounding in corporate and contractual law...understanding regulations and their application to real situations... comfortable with technical jargon...innovative...knowledge of competition and copyright matters...

It's not necessary to know absolutely everything about computers and technology. As Mark says: *"What you need is a real interest in the industry. You don't have to know what goes on when you take the cover off every gadget, but you should have an idea of the jargon. When you're presented with a schedule of things in a contract, you have to know what they're talking about. It always helps if you know your LAN from your WAN."* Mark recommends reading *Wired* (*"a men's lifestyle magazine with computers in it"*) or more serious publications such as *Computer Weekly* or *New Scientist*.

More generally, you'll need to be in possession of a full set of commercial skills. One minute you could be working on a plan to charge for online music; the next you'll be called away because an ISP has a domain name issue. For much of your work there may be no direct precedent, so it will be necessary to demonstrate innovative thinking and logical analysis. Yet, you'll still need to be prepared to spend time in the library researching black letter law.

## career options

Although the market is competitive, there is still room for a few more junior lawyers. *"The work can be quite collegiate or team-based. I would expect trainees to be doing the raw research and attending meetings and negotiation sessions with the client. They may have to be the person making the notes, but why not let them also prepare the first draft of the contract?"* And more good news – British TMT lawyers are well respected elsewhere: *"IT law in the UK is at the forefront, so US companies won't hesitate to fly you over there. If you get big Silicon Valley companies or large users as clients, you can expect to travel anywhere."*

It's reasonably easy to join the in-house legal team of a telecoms or IT company. Or, because the tools of a TMT lawyer's trade are honed in general commercial law (albeit with a technology slant), any large organisation with a serious IT component would be happy to log you on.

# solicitors

## leading firms from Chambers UK 2006

### Information Technology
London

1. Allen & Overy LLP
   Baker & McKenzie LLP
   Bird & Bird
   Field Fisher Waterhouse
   Linklaters
2. Clifford Chance LLP
   DLA Piper Rudnick Gray Cary UK
   Herbert Smith LLP
   Kemp Little LLP
   Lovells
   Osborne Clarke
   Pinsent Masons
3. Barlow Lyde & Gilbert
   Denton Wilde Sapte
   Freshfields Bruckhaus Deringer
   Latham & Watkins
   Mayer, Brown, Rowe & Maw LLP
   Norton Rose
   Olswang
   Simmons & Simmons
   Slaughter and May
   Taylor Wessing
4. Berwin Leighton Paisner
   Eversheds LLP
   Kirkpatrick & Lockhart Nicholson
   Milbank, Tweed, Hadley & McCloy
   Morrison & Foerster MNP
   Nabarro Nathanson
   Pillsbury Winthrop Shaw Pittman
5. Addleshaw Goddard
   Bristows
   Harbottle & Lewis LLP

### Information Technology
The South

1. Blake Lapthorn Linnell *Southampton*
   Bond Pearce LLP *Southampton*
   DMH Stallard *Crawley*
2. Clyde & Co *Guildford*
   Shadbolt & Co LLP *Reigate*

### Information Technology
Thames Valley

1. Boyes Turner *Reading*
   Manches *Oxford*
   Moorcrofts LLP *Marlow*
   Olswang Thames Valley *Reading*
   Osborne Clarke *Reading*
   Marcus J O'Leary *Wokingham*
2. Clark Holt *Swindon*
   Shoosmiths *Northampton*
   Willoughby & Partners *Oxford*

### Information Technology
South West

1. Beachcroft Wansbroughs *Bristol*
   Osborne Clarke *Bristol*
2. Bevan Brittan LLP *Bristol*
   Burges Salmon LLP *Bristol*
   Foot Anstey *Exeter*
3. Ashfords *Bristol*
   Rickerbys *Cheltenham*

### Information Technology
Wales

1. Eversheds LLP *Cardiff*
   Geldards LLP *Cardiff*
   Morgan Cole *Cardiff*
2. Hugh James *Cardiff*

### Information Technology
Midlands

1. Eversheds LLP *Nottingham*
   Wragge & Co LLP *Birmingham*
2. Technology Law Alliance *B'ham*
   v-lex limited *Sheffield*
3. Martineau Johnson *Birmingham*
   Mills & Reeve *Birmingham*
   Pinsent Masons *Birmingham*

### Information Technology
The North
Leading firms

1. Addleshaw G'dard *Leeds, Man.*
2. Eversheds LLP *Leeds*
   Pinsent Masons *Leeds, Manchester*
3. Halliwells LLP *Manchester*
   Irwin Mitchell *Leeds*

### Telecommunications
Nationwide

1. Allen & Overy LLP
   Baker & McKenzie LLP
   Bird & Bird
   Clifford Chance LLP
   Linklaters
2. Field Fisher Waterhouse
   Freshfields Bruckhaus Deringer
   Herbert Smith LLP
   Mayer, Brown, Rowe & Maw LLP
   Olswang
3. Addleshaw Goddard
   Ashurst
   Charles Russell
   Simmons & Simmons
   Taylor Wessing
   Wilmer Cutler Pickering Hale
4. Denton Wilde Sapte
   DLA Piper Rudnick Gray Cary UK
   Eversheds LLP
   Kemp Little LLP
   Kirkpatrick & Lockhart Nicholson
   Lovells
   Norton Rose
   Osborne Clarke
   Slaughter and May
   White & Case
   Wragge & Co LLP

# international opportunities

The idea of the international law firm is far from new: UK law firms have ventured overseas since the 19th century. What has changed in recent times is the number of firms with offices overseas and the desire on the part of the largest firms to plant flags all over the globe. The Brits weren't the first in the game but they've certainly made up for lost time, and the largest firm worldwide is now our very own Clifford Chance. It still has some way to go though to catch up with Baker & McKenzie for the prize for most offices in most countries.

There are so many UK and US firms with overseas networks that students are spoiled for choice. Keeping track of which firms are opening or closing offices in different countries is almost a full-time occupation, but wherever possible we have mentioned the main changes of the past year in our **True Picture** reports. What we can never predict though is exactly who is going to merge with who. The last five years have been characterised by European mergers and alliances as well as transatlantic tie-ups.

If you are determined to spend part of your training contract overseas then you need to do a bit of research into the overseas activities of the firms that most interest you. A good place to start might be Chambers Global, which you can read online at **www.chambersandpartners.com**or your university's careers library or law department may have its own copy.

## let's get out of here!

Although time abroad gives you experience of working in another jurisdiction, you'll not normally practise foreign law. An overseas seat is without doubt a very rewarding and challenging experience. It will usually be taken in an office that is smaller than your firm's UK office, and you will normally have greater responsibilities. The trick to securing the most popular overseas seats is to wage an effective campaign of self-promotion and to get the prerequisite experience in the UK office before you go. The key to getting a particular seat may be as simple as having the right second language, but remember that language skills may also act as a handcuff. Quite simply, if the firm has a Moscow office and you are the only Russian-speaking trainee you won't be going to New York. Each year we chat to trainees who are overseas or have recently come back from time abroad. Here are their postcards...

## brussels

Brussels plays host to the headquarters of many EU institutions. Nearly 160 embassies are based there, in addition to 120 IGOs and 1,400 NGOs. Political powerhouse it may be, but it is probably fair to say that you can cram most of Brussels' attractions into a weekend. So what about spending a whole six months out there? One fan of the city said: *"Brussels gets a slating, but I thought it was cool. All those cobbley streets and bars and cafes - it was quite quirky."* It's also worth pointing out that this could be one of the most cosmopolitan places on the planet: *"I don't think there were any Belgian people in Brussels!"*

**work:** For EU or competition law, Brussels is **the** place. If you speak French and want to improve it, great but language skills are not essential. *"Competition law can be quite intense at times,"* but all-nighters and Saturdays in the office are *"very rare."* In addition to EU law, *"there is also a lot of quality trade work coming through the city."* A DLA trainee said her work was characterised by *"big deals, lots of research and lots of responsibility."* Much of her day was spent monitoring public affairs and reviewing EU publications and websites. Don't underestimate the volume of research-based tasks that will come your way. *"You won't get much client contact but there are a lot more conferences and seminars to attend."* Litigation also rears its head, not only in the court of first instance but also the European Court of Justice.

**rest and play:** Most law firms have apartments close to their office. UK trainees live in an enclave in the Schumann area near to the Commission buildings and flock together on arrival for tours and events laid on by the firms. Brussels is only two and a half hours from London, so persuading friends and family to visit won't prove difficult. Brussels is a manageable city with a pleasant pace of life, though one trainee found it "*a bit too catholic - all the shops shut on Sundays, so everyone goes to the cinema.*" Its most famous symbol is the Mannekin Pis, though we suspect the excitement wears off after a couple of visits.

## hong kong

An island of capitalism within a communist state, despite having returned to the tight embrace of China in 1997, Hong Kong is still "*beyond fabulous.*" From the moment you arrive at Chek Lap Kok Airport the island city will tire, amaze and entertain you in equal measure. Hong Kong exists for people to make money and shop, and its inspiration is more Ronald McDonald than Chairman Mao. The crowds, noise and smog could send your blood pressure soaring, so take a leaf out of the locals' book and take a free T'ai Chi class in the park or visit the region's Buddhist temples and remote islands. It must work, as HK residents enjoy very high life expectancy. September to March is mild; otherwise it gets exceedingly hot and sweaty.

**work:** With the bonded zone of Guangzhou so close, the city's law firms have found plenty to occupy themselves on trade agreements. Mostly trainees deal with general commercial work, but corporate transactions do crop up and there is also some litigation and IP. You must be ready to master a whole new set of traditions and etiquette before you can deal effectively with clients and colleagues. One trainee reported on the long hours local lawyers put in: "*They have an obsession with working and that was very very hard for me to adjust to. Usually I did 9.30am until 7pm, but the locals stayed later.*"

**rest and play:** Trainees' apartments are on The Levels, a residential hill where your relative altitude reflects your wealth. "*At the top is The Peak where the temperature is always a couple of degrees cooler so that became the popular place to live. Plus it has fantastic views.*" Most trainees live halfway up with the expats, where there's a pleasant village feel. Full of clubs, Wanchai is the old sailors' hangout, just ten minutes from the CBD and "*never feels threatening.*" Clubs stay open until 4am and sometimes 8am; many supply free drinks for girls on Wednesdays. Less crazy is Lan Kwai Fong, with its concentration of expat bars. The Chinese tend not to drink as often; indeed, one source thought "*the opportunities to meet local people socially are limited,*" so make sure you make friends in the office. Go to mainland China for a round of golf, black market shopping or to visit trainees in Shanghai. One trainee managed to do so much travelling that he likened his time in HK to "*the life of an international playboy.*" You may laugh... we heard his stories!

## new york

Manhattan, is 24/7. Of course, you'll already know that if you watched SATC. What you'll also know is that NY is a sassy, smoke-free, carb-free, cab-honking, cosmopolitan-drinking, style-conscious, your-name's-not-on-the-list kinda of town. At least, it is if you're doing it right. Despite overseas allowances and cheap taxis, even trainees coming from London find the city extremely expensive, if only because everyone needs tipping. Don't accept a posting unless you're prepared to spend big and make the most of everything the city has to offer. The best time to visit is in the fall, when the New York is "*absolutely beautiful*" and you don't have to put up with intense heat or cold.

**work:** New York law is reasonably similar to UK law but similarities can be deceptive, and there can be times where you feel like an Englishman in New York: "*I did a lot of bankruptcy work which functions in a very different way to the English system of insolvency.*" Banking and capital markets are high on the agenda, and a lot of work from Latin America comes through the city. New York offices can feel more formal than their counterparts in the UK; yet in spite of this, US firms often have better developed diversity and pro bono programmes. During a busy period, you might be in the office until the wee hours, but generally 9am to 8pm are typical.

**rest and play:** Trainees get apartments with fantastic views on the Upper East and Upper West sides. Beyond the daily cost of living, the main expense is weekend travel, be this for skiing upstate in the winter or trips to the Hamptons in the summer. Culturally, New York is in a league of its own and between them the Whitney, the Met, the Guggenheim and the Moma contain some of the most important art of the last century. By the same token, with big brash musicals on Broadway and a decent, if not always ground-breaking selection of work off-Broadway, off-off-Broadway and off-off-off Broadway, neither would you want to miss a trip to theatre. Sustained by a potent mix of cwaffee and cocktails, you could keep going for the entire six months without sleep, though you're likely to be exhausted long before the possibilities. And if you've got any time to spare, walks in an autumnal Central Park or a skinny latte at your local bookstore/coffee house are clichés to tick off in your Eye Spy NY.

## paris

"*If your life is rubbish, at least you are in a beautiful place!*" So said one trainee of the city of romance, style, art and haughty grandeur. Whether you feel more at home in the cafés of the Left Bank or on the leather sofas at the National Bank, there is everything a young bourgeois or bohemian could wish for, from haute couture to basement jazz clubs. May is the perfect time to invite friends across as it's not too hot and there are no tourists around. There's no need to be one of les miserables if there's no 'special friend' with whom you can stroll, hand in hand, along the Champs Elisee, "*it's a great place to be single; you can fall in love with Paris.*"

**work:** Paris seats range from broad-based finance options through asset finance, capital markets, corporate and even international arbitration as the ICA is based in the city. Trainees find they are given considerably more responsibility than they are used to as "*the concept of supervisor isn't really there.*" One trainee told us: "*I grew up in the Paris office.*" French speakers will blend in with the locals rather than the tourists, and in the office much of your work can involve translating documents from English into French or vice versa. There's a notional 9.00am-5.30pm work schedule with an hour or two for a proper sit-down lunch. "*They're a bit keen on their food,*" said one trainee, while another admitted to leaving Paris "*double the size*" she'd been when she arrived. Most lawyers usually leave the office by seven PM.

**rest and play:** Whether it's a 30th-floor apartment in the 15th arrondissement in the south west of the city or a pad in Le Marais you'll probably end up walking to work. A readymade, e-mail-based social scene awaits new arrivals and you have to make an effort not to fall into the ex-pat scene. Bars and restaurants stay open until late, even on school nights. "*You can be eating at midnight and then still go on somewhere else as nothing closes.*" Your tastes may become distinctly French, even in the space of six months – "*everyone drinks champagne!*" Weekend travel options are endless. Depending on the time of year, you can be on the slopes or the sands within a few hours thanks to the high speed TGV.

# overseas seats – who goes there?

| location | firm |
|---|---|
| Abu Dhabi | Richards Butler, Shearman & Sterling, Simmons & Simmons, Trowers & Hamlins |
| Amsterdam | Allen & Overy, Baker & McKenzie, Clifford Chance, Baker & McKenzie, Clifford Chance, CMS Cameron McKenna, Freshfields Bruckhaus Deringer, Herbert Smith, Linklaters, Norton Rose, Slaughter and May |
| Athens | Norton Rose |
| Australia | Baker & McKenzie |
| Bahrain | Norton Rose, Trowers & Hamlins |
| Bangkok | Allen & Overy, Herbert Smith, Linklaters Watson Farley & Williams, |
| Beijing | Bird & Bird, Freshfields Bruckhaus Deringer, Herbert Smith, Linklaters |
| Berlin | Hammonds, Linklaters |
| Boston | Dechert |
| Bratislava (Slovakia) | Allen & Overy, Linklaters |
| Brussels | Allen & Overy, Ashurst, Baker & McKenzie, Bird & Bird, Cleary Gottlieb Steen & Hamilton, CMS Cameron McKenna, Clifford Chance, Cobbetts, Dechert, Dickinson Dees, Eversheds, Freshfields Bruckhaus Deringer, Hammonds, Herbert Smith, Linklaters, Lovells, Mayer Brown Rowe & Maw, McGrigors, Nabarro Nathanson, Norton Rose, Olswang, Pinsent Masons, Shearman & Sterling, Simmons & Simmons, SJ Berwin, Slaughter and May, Taylor Vinters, White & Case, Weil Gotshal & Manges. |
| Bucharest | Linklaters |
| Budapest | Allen & Overy, CMS Cameron McKenna, Linklaters, Weil, Gotshal & Manges |
| California | Osborne Clarke, Weil Gotshal & Manges |
| Chicago | Baker & McKenzie |
| Cologne | Freshfields Bruckhaus Deringer, Linklaters |

| location | firm |
|---|---|
| Copenhagen | Slaughter and May |
| Dubai | Allen & Overy, Clifford Chance, Clyde & Co, Denton Wilde Sapte, Norton Rose, Trowers & Hamlins |
| Düsseldorf | Bird & Bird, Simmons & Simmons, Slaughter and May |
| Frankfurt | Allen & Overy, Ashurst, Bird & Bird, Clifford Chance, Freshfields Bruckhaus Deringer, Herbert Smith, Linklaters, Lovells, Norton Rose, SJ Berwin, Slaughter and May, White & Case, Weil, Gotshal & Manges |
| Geneva | Slaughter and May |
| The Hague | Bird & Bird |
| Hamburg | Allen & Overy, CMS Cameron McKenna |
| Helsinki | Slaughter and May |
| Hong Kong | Allen & Overy, Baker & McKenzie, Bird & Bird, Clifford Chance, Clyde & Co, CMS Cameron McKenna, Freshfields Bruckhaus Deringer, Hammonds, Herbert Smith, Holman Fenwick & Willan, Linklaters, Lovells, Norton Rose, Richards Butler, Simmons & Simmons, Slaughter and May, Stephenson Harwood, White & Case |
| Johannesburg | White & Case |
| Lisbon | Linklaters, Simmons & Simmons |
| Luxembourg | Allen & Overy, Linklaters, Slaughter and May |
| Madrid | Allen & Overy, Ashurst, Clifford Chance, Denton Wilde Sapte, Freshfields Bruckhaus Deringer, Hammonds, Linklaters, SJ Berwin, Simmons & Simmons, Slaughter and May |

# the true picture

| location | firm |
|----------|------|
| Milan | Allen & Overy, Ashurst, Bird & Bird, Clifford Chance, Freshfields Bruckhaus Deringer, Linklaters, Lovells, Norton Rose, Simmons & Simmons, Slaughter and May, White & Case, Withers |
| Moscow | Allen & Overy, Baker & McKenzie, Clifford Chance, CMS Cameron McKenna, Denton Wilde Sapte, Freshfields Bruckhaus Deringer, Herbert Smith, LeBoeuf Lamb Greene & McRae, Linklaters, Norton Rose, White & Case |
| Munich | Ashurst, Bird & Bird, Clifford Chance, Dechert, Linklaters, Norton Rose, Weil, Gotshal & Manges |
| New York | Allen & Overy, Baker & McKenzie, Cleary Gottlieb Steen & Hamilton, Clifford Chance, Dechert, Freshfields Bruckhaus Deringer, Linklaters, Lovells, Shearman & Sterling, Slaughter and May, Weil Gotshal & Manges |
| Oman | Trowers & Hamlins |
| Oslo | Slaughter and May |
| Paris | Allen & Overy, Ashurst, Bird & Bird, Clifford Chance, CMS Cameron McKenna, Denton Wilde Sapte, Eversheds, Freshfields Bruckhaus Deringer, Hammonds, Herbert Smith, Holman Fenwick & Willan, LeBoeuf Lamb Greene & McRae, Linklaters, Lovells, Norton Rose, Richards Butler, Shadbolt & Co, Simmons & Simmons, Slaughter and May, SJ Berwin, Taylor Wessing, Travers Smith, Watson, Farley & Williams, White & Case, Weil, Gotshal & Manges |
| Philadelphia | Dechert |
| Piraeus | Clyde & Co, Holman Fenwick & Willan, Ince & Co, Norton Rose, Richards Butler, Watson, Farley & Williams |

| location | firm |
|----------|------|
| Prague | Allen & Overy, Baker & McKenzie, Clifford Chance, CMS Cameron McKenna, Linklaters, Norton Rose, Slaughter and May, Weil Gotshal & Manges, White & Case, |
| Rome | Allen & Overy, Bird & Bird, Clifford Chance, CMS, Denton Wilde Sapte, Linklaters |
| Rotterdam | Denton Wilde Sapte, Simmons & Simmons |
| Sao Paulo | Clifford Chance, Linklaters |
| Shanghai | Clifford Chance, Freshfields Bruckhaus Deringer, Herbert Smith, Linklaters |
| Singapore | Allen & Overy, Baker & McKenzie, Clifford Chance, Clyde & Co, Freshfields Bruckhaus Deringer, Herbert Smith, Linklaters, Lovells, Norton Rose, Shearman & Sterling, Stephenson Harwood, Watson, Farley & Williams, White & Case |
| Stockholm | Bird & Bird, Linklaters, Slaughter and May, White & Case |
| Tokyo | Allen & Overy, Clifford Chance, Lovells, Freshfields Bruckhaus Deringer, Herbert Smith, Linklaters, Simmons & Simmons, Slaughter and May, White & Case |
| Turin | Hammonds |
| Utrecht | CMS Cameron McKenna |
| Vienna | CMS Cameron McKenna, Freshfields Bruckhaus Deringer |
| Warsaw | Allen & Overy, Clifford Chance, CMS Cameron McKenna, Linklaters, Weil, Gotshal & Manges |
| Washington | Baker & McKenzie, Dechert, Freshfields Bruckhaus Deringer |

# the true picture

# introduction

The True Picture reports on 120 English and Welsh firms, ranging from the international giants to small regional practices. Most handle commercial law, although many of these also offer private client experience. Others are what is termed 'general practice' firms.

## how we do our research

The firms in the following table all agreed to provide complete lists of their trainees. After checking the lists are complete, we randomly select a sample of individuals to interview over the phone. Our sources are guaranteed anonymity, as we feel this is the best way to give them the confidence to say exactly what they want. The True Picture is not forwarded to the law firms prior to publication; they see it for the first time when this book is published.

Trainees tell us why they chose their firm and why others might want to. We talk about seat allocation and the character and work of different departments. We ask about the hours and the after-hours fun, and we ascertain what happens to people on qualification. We look for the things trainees agree upon, or present both sides of the argument if they do not agree.

We're bored by the tired lines used in many recruitment brochures. You know the ones that tell you Smashing, Great & Partners is a standout firm because of its 'friendly culture' where everybody is 'down to earth' and 'approachable partners' operate an 'open-door policy'. Take it from us: these traits are not the preserve of a few firms. We try to focus on the detail of what builds a firm's character.

## our findings

In recent years, with the NQ job market in pretty dire health, we sensed many trainees were either world-weary or eternally grateful to have a job on qualification. This year most were aware of their improved prospects, and this encouraged many to be more picky about what area of law they wanted to specialise in. With the deals market improving, corporate departments have become busier and the hours worked are now longer. Perhaps as a direct result, there has been a resurgence of interest in non-transactional departments for qualification. The reality is there are not enough litigation jobs to satisify demand.

We try not to concentrate too much on current market conditions when writing the True Picture, as we recognise that things will probably have changed by the time our readers start their training. However, we also recognise that the climate of 2005 affects the fortunes and market positions of law firms, and this in turn may have a bearing on what firms will be like in 2008 and beyond.

The other thing we just can't predict is law firm mergers or closures. Thankfully the latter are rare, but the mergers crop up regularly. When firms merge, trainees' contracts are honoured, though of course it does mean they end up working at a different firm to the one they signed up to.

## across the board:

• Some seats are more popular than others. The perfect example is employment law.

• Levels of responsibility vary between departments. In property you might have your own small files. In corporate you will generally work in a very junior capacity as part of a team.

• The experience in litigation depends entirely on the type of cases your firm handles; usually a trainee's responsibility is inversely proportionate to the value and complexity of a case. If your firm handles personal injury claims, you may have conduct of matters yourself. If your firm goes in for long-running financial services litigation or multi-jurisdictional matters, you could be stuck for months on document management jobs.

• In times of plenty, corporate and finance seats mean long hours, commonly climaxing in all-nighters. Again, the size and complexity of a deal will determine your role, but corporate and finance usually require the most teamwork.

• Most firms offer four six-month seats; some

six four-month seats and others their own unique systems. Trainees switch departments and supervisors for each seat. Most share a room and work with a partner or senior assistant; others sit open-plan either with the rest of the team or with other trainees. Occasionally a trainee will even have their own room.

- All firms conduct appraisals, a minimum of one at the conclusion of each seat, and often halfway through as well.

- Client secondments, where offered, are a great way to find out how to be a better lawyer by learning to understand a client's needs. Often they turn out to be the highlight of a training contract.

- The Law Society requires all trainees to gain experience of both contentious and non-contentious work. Additionally, most firms have certain seats they require or prefer trainees to try. Some firms are very prescriptive, others flexible. The important thing to remember is that a training contract is a time to explore legal practice to see what you're best at and most enjoy. You will probably surprise yourself!

- See the Chambers Student website for statistics detailing law firms NQ retention since 2000.

The following terms will be useful when reading the True Picture

- **agency work** – making a court appearance for another firm that can't get to court
- **all-nighter** – working through the night
- **cmc** – case management conference
- **coco** – company-commercial department or work
- **dispute resolution** – litigation, mediation, arbitration etc
- **grunt work** – also known as donkey work, monkey work or even document jockeying. Administrative (and boring), yet essential, tasks including photocopying, paginating, compiling court bundles and scheduling documents, bibling (putting together sets of all the relevant documents for a transaction), data room duty (supervising visitors to rooms full of important documents, helping them find things and making sure they don't steal them!) and proof-reading or checking that documents are intact.

- **high net worth individuals** – rich people
- **NQ** – a newly-qualified solicitor
- **PQE** – post-qualification experience
- **trainee partner** – a trainee who acts like a partner
- **mentor partner** – much better, the kind of partner who will guide you and buy you lunch
- **supervising partner** – you'll get one of these each seat, or you may be allocated a senior assistant
- **training partner** – the lucky partner who over sees the whole training scheme
- **real estate** – the newer name for property

## what kind of firm do I choose?

Your choice of firm will be based on location, size and the practice areas available... then it's a matter of chemistry. Some firms are stuffier; some are more industrious and some are very brand-aware and involve trainees heavily in marketing. Some have a strong sense of identity and others allow more freedom of expression. Some work open-plan; others occupy premises long past their sell-by date! Some focus on international business; others are at the heart of their local business communities. Some concentrate on contentious work, others transactional. The combinations of these variables are endless.

## and finally...

We hope the True Picture will help you decide what sort of firms you want to target. No matter how hard or how easy securing a training contract turns out to be, you'll want to end up with the right one.

| SIZE | FIRM NAME | CITY | TOTAL TRAINEES | PAGE |
|------|-----------|------|----------------|------|
| 1 | Government Legal Service | London* | 50 | 294 |
| 2 | Eversheds LLP | London* | 193 | 259 |
| 3 | DLA Piper Rudnick Gray Cary US LLP | London* | 153 | 250 |
| 4 | Clifford Chance LLP | London | 240 | 222 |
| 5 | Allen & Overy LLP | London | 240 | 161 |
| 6 | Linklaters | London | 250 | 344 |
| 7 | Pinsent Masons | London* | 105 | 399 |
| 8 | Freshfields Bruckhaus Deringer | London | 208 | 288 |
| 9 | Addleshaw Goddard | Manchester* | 90 | 159 |
| 10 | Herbert Smith LLP | London | 151 | 306 |
| 11 | CMS Cameron McKenna LLP | London* | 120 | 229 |
| 12 | Denton Wilde Sapte | London* | 73 | 244 |
| 13 | Slaughter and May | London | 185 | 435 |
| 14 | Lovells | London | 138 | 348 |
| 15 | Hammonds | London* | 79 | 300 |
| 16 | Norton Rose | London | 129 | 381 |
| 17 | Ashurst | London | 89 | 172 |
| 18 | Wragge & Co LLP | Brirmingham | 48 | 484 |
| 19 | Barlow Lyde & Gilbert | London | 34 | 177 |
| 19 | Beachcroft Wansbroughs | London* | 58 | 180 |
| 19 | SJ Berwin LLP | London | 72 | 432 |
| 22 | Berwin Leighton Paisner | London | 70 | 183 |
| 23 | Nabarro Nathanson | London* | 56 | 378 |
| 24 | Simmons & Simmons | London | 104 | 429 |
| 25 | Halliwells LLP | Manchester* | 50 | 298 |
| 26 | Mills & Reeve | Cambridge* | 37 | 372 |
| 27 | Shoosmiths | Northampton* | 27 | 423 |
| 28 | Clyde & Co | London* | 44 | 226 |
| 29 | Irwin Mitchell | Sheffield* | 42 | 322 |
| 30 | Cobbetts | Manchester* | 50 | 232 |
| 31 | Baker & McKenzie | London | 70 | 175 |
| 32 | Taylor Wessing | London* | 44 | 449 |
| 33 | Bevan Brittan LLP | Bristol* | 42 | 186 |
| 33 | Olswang | London* | 40 | 384 |
| 35 | Mayer, Brown, Rowe & Maw LLP | London | 54 | 362 |
| 36 | Burges Salmon LLP | Bristol | 37 | 208 |
| 37 | Hill Dickinson | Liverpool* | 20 | 309 |
| 38 | Morgan Cole | Cardiff* | 28 | 375 |
| 39 | Trowers & Hamlins | London* | 33 | 460 |
| 40 | Field Fisher Waterhouse | London | 32 | 266 |

*firms are listed in order of size as measured by partner and assistant figures provided to Chambers UK. *Head or primary UK office*

# THE TRUE PICTURE 120 FIRMS TABLE

| SIZE | FIRM NAME | CITY | TOTAL TRAINEES | PAGE |
|------|-----------|------|----------------|------|
| 40 | Charles Russell LLP | London* | 29 | 216 |
| 40 | Osborne Clarke | Bristol* | 47 | 386 |
| 43 | Reynolds Porter Chaimberlain | London* | 22 | 408 |
| 44 | Lawrence Graham LLP | London | 36 | 333 |
| 45 | Richards Butler | London | 40 | 410 |
| 46 | Travers Smith | London | 40 | 457 |
| 47 | Dickinson Dees | Newcastle* | 28 | 247 |
| 48 | Macfarlanes | London | 49 | 354 |
| 48 | White & Case | London | 50 | 476 |
| 50 | Penningtons Solicitors LLP | London* | 27 | 396 |
| 51 | DWF | Liverpool* | 16 | 257 |
| 52 | Pannone & Partners | Manchester | 25 | 389 |
| 53 | Browne Jacobson LLP | Nottingham* | 20 | 203 |
| 54 | Stephenson Harwood | London | 34 | 444 |
| 55 | McGrigors | London* | 65 | 369 |
| 56 | Freeth Cartwright LLP | Nottingham* | 15 | 286 |
| 57 | Walker Morris | Leeds | 30 | 463 |
| 58 | TLT Solicititors | Bristol* | 14 | 452 |
| 59 | Withers LLP | London | 26 | 482 |
| 60 | Martineau Johnson | Birmingham* | 21 | 359 |
| 61 | Bird & Bird | London | 25 | 191 |
| 62 | Speechly Bircham | London | 10 | 439 |
| 63 | Kirkpatrick & Lockhart Nicholson Graham | London | 21 | 330 |
| 64 | Shearman & Sterling LLP | London | 16 | 421 |
| 65 | Jones Day | London | 42 | 325 |
| 66 | Ashfords | Exeter* | 22 | 169 |
| 67 | Farrer & Co | London | 17 | 263 |
| 68 | Holman Fenwick & Willan | London | 16 | 314 |
| 69 | Lewis Silkin | London* | 14 | 341 |
| 69 | Ward Hadaway | Newcastle* | 16 | 465 |
| 71 | Ford & Warren | Leeds | 12 | 279 |
| 72 | Manches LLP | London* | 20 | 356 |
| 72 | Gateley Wareing | Birmingham* | 14 | 292 |
| 74 | Bircham Dyson Bell | London* | 15 | 188 |
| 75 | Hugh James | Cardiff* | 19 | 317 |
| 76 | Watson, Farley & Williams | London | 22 | 468 |
| 77 | Ince & Co | London | 17 | 319 |
| 77 | Weil, Gotshal & Manges | London | 18 | 473 |
| 79 | Dechert | London | 24 | 241 |
| 80 | Sidley Austin Brown & Wood LLP | London | 13 | 427 |

*firms are listed in order of size as measured by partner and assistant figures provided to Chambers UK. *Head or primary UK office*

# THE TRUE PICTURE 120 FIRMS TABLE

| SIZE | FIRM NAME | CITY | TOTAL TRAINEES | PAGE |
|------|-----------|------|----------------|------|
| 81 | Lester Aldridge | Bournemouth* | 14 | 339 |
| 82 | Russell-Cooke | London | 9 | 413 |
| 83 | Foot Anstey | Exeter* | 20 | 274 |
| 84 | Bristows | London | 14 | 201 |
| 85 | Mace & Jones | Liverpool* | 8 | 351 |
| 86 | Anthony Collins | Birmingham | 13 | 167 |
| 87 | Cripps Harries Hall | Tunbridge Wells* | 14 | 239 |
| 88 | Wedlake Bell | London | 12 | 470 |
| 89 | Capsticks | London | 9 | 211 |
| 90 | Forsters LLP | London | 7 | 281 |
| 91 | Forbes | Blackburn* | 16 | 276 |
| 92 | Brabners Chaffe Street | Liverpool* | 19 | 196 |
| 92 | Reed Smith LLP | London* | 12 | 405 |
| 94 | DMH Stallard | Brighton* | 15 | 254 |
| 94 | Taylor Vinters | Cambridge | 14 | 447 |
| 96 | McDermott Will & Emery LLP | London | 4 | 367 |
| 97 | Boodle Hatfield | London* | 10 | 193 |
| 98 | Finers Stephens Innocent | London | 10 | 269 |
| 98 | LeBoeuf, Lamb, Greene & MacRae | London | 9 | 336 |
| 100 | Harbottle & Lewis LLP | London | 8 | 303 |
| 101 | Cleary Gotlieb Steen & Hamilton | London | 4 | 219 |
| 101 | Andrew M Jackson | Hull | 12 | 165 |
| 103 | Salans | London | 8 | 416 |
| 103 | Stevens & Bolton LLP | Guildford | 6 | 442 |
| 105 | Kendall Freeman | London | 16 | 328 |
| 106 | Hodge Jones & Allen | London | 13 | 312 |
| 107 | Paris Smith & Randall | Southampton | 6 | 392 |
| 108 | Coffin Mew & Clover | Southampton* | 11 | 235 |
| 109 | Collyer-Bristow | London | 6 | 237 |
| 110 | Fox Williams | London | 8 | 284 |
| 111 | Challinors | West Bromwich* | 9 | 214 |
| 112 | Fisher Meredith | London | 15 | 271 |
| 112 | Payne Hicks Beach | London | 5 | 394 |
| 112 | Brachers | Maidstone | 8 | 198 |
| 115 | Prettys | Ipswich | 10 | 403 |
| 115 | Teacher Stern Selby | London | 10 | 455 |
| 117 | McCormicks | Leeds* | 9 | 365 |
| 117 | Shadbolt & Co LLP | Reigate* | 11 | 418 |
| 119 | BTMK LLP | Southend* | 6 | 206 |
| 119 | Wiggin LLP | Cheltenham* | 6 | 479 |

*firms are listed in order of size as measured by partner and assistant figures provided to Chambers UK. *Head or primary UK office*

# the true picture

## Addleshaw Goddard

### the facts

**Location:** Leeds, London, Manchester
**Number of partners/assistants:** 170/500
**Total number of trainees:** 90
**Seats:** 4x6 months
**Alternative seats:** Secondments
**Extras:** Pro-bono – Manchester Uni and Springfield legal advice centres

Like a big jigsaw puzzle, Addleshaw Goddard is a whole greater than the sum of its parts.

### up up and away

In 2003, top dog of Leeds and Manchester Addleshaw Booth contemplated its underachieving London office. It also caught sight of drooping City player Theodore Goddard and scented a strategic merger. In a spirit of politeness the resulting outfit was named Addleshaw Goddard. Since the merger, AG has done its level best to reinvigorate the concept of the mid-market law firm: core practice areas have been nurtured and grown – a promising finance team was imported from Nicholson Graham & Jones – but most importantly, AG has done well to fend off most of the usual post-merger integration problems that can lay a new firm low. Instead, it paid off an £11 million overdraft, increased its profitability hugely and saved up for future expansion in London. As any experienced commercial lawyer will tell you, that's the best way to keep existing talent happy and draw new talent to the firm. It really does seem that the simple logic of the merger is paying off: extra clout in the capital for the northerners, a new sense of purpose and tougher management for the old TG. There is no mind-bending strategy here, it is merely *"ambition, increased focus on winning FTSE 350 clients and a real focus on productivity."* At the back of it all is a strategy designed to attain status as one of the lead firms behind the magic circle by 2009.

Yet this ambition is unlikely to lead to extremes. Ever-sensible Addleshaws is consolidating existing strengths, managing well and using extended reach when the time is right. Our sources tell us *"banking and finance is the thing for London."* This year the new improved London office added Allied Irish Bank to a finance client roster that already included Barclays, RBS and HSBC. It also scooped instructions from existing Leeds and Manchester client NM Rothschild & Sons, which clearly felt the firm was now worth its time in the City. Conversely, northern offices with lower overheads and cheaper rates can also be a good way to attract and retain London clients. The business-minded amongst those we spoke to noted that *"London is a substantial focus of strategy; we are able to leverage off work to Manchester and Leeds at regional prices."*

All eyes may be on London, but Addleshaws is still dominating its regional bases like it has done for years. PFI and construction strengths were boosted by hires from key rivals in the north (including an entire contentious construction team from Hammonds in Leeds) and the firm welcomed its appointment to the Partnerships for Schools legal panel in order to work on the £2.2 billion Building Schools for the Future project. The MoD, Department of Health and English Partnerships also remain important clients, but it's not all bricks and mortar as regular instructions from the likes of BA and Abbey indicate. This year northern corporate and private equity teams scooped a lead role on the complex £23 million demutualisation of Interflora and also advised Maplin Electronics on its £244 million purchase by Montagu Private Equity.

### who's wearing the trousers?

All the external indicators point to management having handled the business side of the merger almost perfectly, but how does it feel for staff? By all accounts, most decision making comes from the legacy Addleshaw Booth, and our sources (both northern and southern) were unanimous that

# the true picture

*"London is fitting in and doing well – it now feels like an equally important part of the firm."* Plenty is being done to prevent a north-south divide from developing. Increasingly *"trainees swap offices for seats"* and teams work nationally, so that if you're in projects in Manchester you might easily find yourself at a meeting in London. Training sessions in Leeds also see people converging from all points of the compass, meaning *"cross-site integration is a social fact as well as a buzz term!"*

We did hear a few gripes that the firm's single-minded, post-merger business model – *"wanting more, better work"* – lacks a human element. Said one trainee: *"It pushes utilisation and productivity over quality of life."* But despite this, and some pretty testing hours across the offices in the bigger departments, we mostly heard positive noises from trainees. A common theme was that *"it's a very tolerant, open place to work."* Recent attempts to *"define shared cultural values for the entire firm"* reminded us of Addleshaw Booth's old 'ABC Way' which attempted to enshrine the values and culture of the firm.

## lucky dip

Trainees rotate through four six-month seats and must spend time in each of the firm's transactions, real estate and litigation divisions. Those with a taste for the niche need not despair, because these compulsory postings don't all have to be mainstream seats. To explain, IP and employment both count as litigation, whilst property lit, construction and planning all fulfil the property requirement. But be aware of one important fact: if you do want to secure a niche seat, *"scheming and strategy"* are the way forward in a *"competitive and sometimes lottery-like rotation process."* Summing up seat allocation one trainee laughed: *"You put down your choices and it depends on a) how competitive the seat is and b) if HR would prefer to see you elsewhere."* By accepting that *"getting your last choice once is par for the course,"* most trainees learn to be either satisfied or even quite happy with the results.

A seat in one of the larger departments like corporate recovery or corporate finance is a common way to begin the training contract, not least because these departments initiate greenhorns more gently. Obviously this can lead to *"a glut of what I'd call the standard trainee tasks – a phrase I've come to loathe – bibling, bundling, scheduling."* Administrative rites of passage are balanced out by *"research on more unusual corporate matters"* or even more pleasantly challenging roles such as *"co-ordinating several overseas firms on a multinational deal."* PFI is another department where the size of the clients (MoD, etc) and the scale of deals can mean *"a lot of admin"* and make it *"difficult to get involved even though the work is interesting."* By contrast, although the firm's excellent reputation for property can mean playing a minor role on a big deal for a client such as Sainsbury's, one of the attractions of a seat in the department is *"running a caseload of smaller files, planning your next moves and representing all manner of clients, including city and borough councils, estate trustees, agricultural estates or just residential clients."* Commercial litigation seats also provide a range of experiences and clients *"from plcs and large retailers to much smaller companies where you can run the files yourself."*

## be keen, get ahead

The appeal of the smaller departments like employment, planning and IP is undeniable and the lucky trainees who experience these areas speak enthusiastically. Regional variations include the trendy media and sports litigation seats in London (*"celebrities and Internet work for main names"*) and one or two private client seats covering either family or trusts and probate matters in the northern offices. No matter what seats they discussed with us, trainees were pretty pleased with the quality of support received. *"It's amazing really, you can ask anyone anything, you never feel intimidated by asking the stupid trainee questions,"* confessed one; others were quick to praise *"the balance you get between autonomy, responsibility and support."* Respecting those you work for is central to such a happy equilibrium, and we suspect that the trainee who joked about "*the awe and wonder of associates and partners complimenting me on good work*" was secretly a lot more pleased than he was letting on.

When pushed to self-description trainees give a clear picture of a self-possessed group at ease with themselves and each other. "*We're pragmatic, realistic people*," they admitted, "*with heads sensibly screwed on*." They are "*eager to get ahead but not by trampling over others*." This summary is a familiar one after our many years of reporting on Addleshaw Booth, but what of the new Addleshaws-bred London trainees? "*There is definitely a little bit more of the City about them*," said one northerner, "*but get us all in a room together*," chipped in a Londoner, "*and it becomes quite difficult to tell us apart*."

## what's in a name?
Given its position in the pecking order up north, Addleshaws will continue to be an obvious choice for students seeking a top-class commercial training in either Leeds or Manchester, especially when new-found City success and the possibility of seats in the capital are added into the bargain. But why would a London-bound applicant choose the firm? Clearly the firm's record of recent success will be part of the equation, as will a preference for joining a mid-sized office where trainees can still be recognised by name. But what of the name Addleshaw Goddard? After all, it hasn't yet acquired the same prestige value amongst students as the City establishment. Why Addleshaws over Lovells or Macfarlanes? We suspect the firm will attract those for whom a "*no-nonsense approach*" and other values imported from the north are a refreshing change from the City norm. And for those who still believe working for a national firm is not quite City enough, well, they have plenty of other options. As for those finishing their training contracts in September 2005, across the network 36 out of 46 were offered jobs and chose to stay with the firm.

On a material level, the two London premises are "*good to adequate*," with the Canon Street office

good and the larger Aldersgate office getting some much needed attention. The London social life centres on monthly drinks in the Aldersgate atrium and a modest scene in Smithfield bars including the Red Cow and Bed. The two northern offices seemingly have more to offer. The "*large and quite self-sufficient*" Leeds office is pleasantly situated on the canal front with "*a lovely atrium and an outside bit beside the canal*." An on-site café is popular, as are the wealth of city-centre bars within easy reach, among them Arch 54, Elbow Rooms and Ma Maison. Across the Pennines in Manchester, they enjoy the same-dress down Friday as everyone else in the firm which makes life all the easier for "*Friday night drinks at the Pitcher and Piano or Rain Bar then on to some hideous club*." There's also the once-monthly "*Project Café*" where the firm picks up the bar tab. Call a drink a drink, we say.

## and finally...
Having played a blinder in the merger, Addleshaw Goddard is sitting pretty and well positioned to keep on growing. If management can keep up the momentum while also keeping everyone sweet, this firm looks like the ideal choice for students intent on a quality commercial training and a bright future.

# Allen & Overy LLP

## the facts
**Location:** London
**Number of partners/assistants:** 195/683
**Total number of trainees:** 240
**Seats:** 3 or 6 months long
**Alternative seats:** Overseas seats, secondments
**Extras:** Pro bono – Liberty, RCJ CAB, Battersea Legal Advice Centre, death row appeals; language training

A reputation as the gentlest of magic circle firms doesn't fool applicants to this legal behemoth.

Signing on the dotted line gets them a super salary, a superb training, easy access to some of the best commercial departments around and guaranteed seats in a finance practice that's a world beater. And if they risk the flames of long hours and fierce competition for niche seats, it's worth it to emerge newly forged as a qualified solicitor with an Allen & Overy hallmark.

## magic numbers

Born in 1930, A&O first cantered to prominence working on behalf of King Edward VIII during his controversial abdication from the throne – quite a client we have to admit. But those dim and distant days are now dwarfed by the sheer scale of a firm that has elevated banking and finance practice to an art form and runs with the elite of the magic circle. The original Mr Allen and Mr Overy would surely applaud the success of a firm whose profits per equity partner rose 10% to £670,000 last year, but the firm is definitely a different animal to the courtly thoroughbred they raised. These days nearly half of the firm's efforts are focused on banking and international capital markets (ICM) and trainees eager to take on such work see it as "*the pre-eminent practice in the field – I had to come here.*"

Not to mince words, A&O operates at the very top of the international loans market and counts many of the foremost investment banks amongst its satisfied customers. In no particular order: Citibank, HSBC, Bank of America, Barclays Capital, Deutsche Bank, ABN AMRO, Merrill Lynch, BNP Paribas, Société Générale and RBS. Its deal credentials are impeccable: lawyers advised Apax Partners and Cinven on the financing of their €2.1 billion acquisition of VNU World Directories, one of the largest deals in Europe in 2004. Proving that big is obviously best for A&O, its lawyers also received instructions on Deutsche Bank's $2.345 billion senior debt and $300 million second lien facilities for a subsidiary of engineering outfit Invensys plc.

The status and size of the firm's capital markets teams, notably distinct from its general finance practice, are perhaps the best measure of A&O's stranglehold in this field. Long-time pioneers of bond issues (the firm assisted in issuing the first Eurobond in 1963), notable recent innovations include advising Anglo Irish Bank on the first 'alternative capital instrument' under the new rules of the Irish Financial Services Regulatory Authority concerning regulatory capital eligibility; helping Collins Stewart Tullett plc on the first ever capital raising by a UK investment firm in public bond format; and assisting Sampo Bank on the first tier one deal for a Finnish bank since the introduction of Finnish FSA. Don't worry if the deals seem as incomprehensible as they are notable – we'd be surprised if they didn't.

## mind your step

Truly a bronzed Olympian God of finance, A&O's slight Achilles' heel is a corporate department that has trodden on a few upturned drawing pins in the last year. Leaked details of an explosive dressing-down dished out by banking types peeved at the corporate department's financial results, and a distinct lack of corporate partners being made up in the last round of promotions left the corporate team hobbling. But it has picked out the splinters and made strides – corporate lawyers held their own in advising Malcolm Glazer on his successful bid for Manchester United and scooped instructions from Shell Chemicals on the £2.4 billion sale of the energy giant's plastics division. While firmly on its feet, trainees told us: "*The department isn't massively expanding but happy to consolidate recent improvements.*"

The dominance of finance, ICM and corporate translates simply at trainee level. "*At least a year*" must be spent in any of the departments coming under these broad headings, and some spend upwards of 85% of their time in such seats. Described as an experience that can "*whack the life out of you,*" banking seats, whether in global loans, financial services regulatory, leveraged finance, restructuring or projects, left their mark on our sources. Just like a cold front, deals can move in and hang around for ages, bringing inclement experiences with them. "*Transactions are massive and six months might not see you through to a closure,*" explained our sources, reflecting on how "*there can be a lot of crummy work like proof-reading, especially in your first seat.*" Even though they are not running transactions, trainees can nevertheless see "*plenty of scope for getting responsibility.*" On a large deal, for example, "*there are so many novation agreements to be drafted that the partners will let you draft them and e-mail them out to clients.*" Furthermore, "*being responsible for the conditions precedent can involve six boxes of documents,*" not forgetting the associated delights of "*getting to know lawyers by telephone across different jurisdictions.*"

Corporate was described as equally "*hardcore,*" with a similar opposition between more menial work and "*getting involved with drafting bits of sales and purchases.*" The recent bumpy ride "*does not compute at trainee level because you've always got work to do.*" Both finance and corporate departments "*have their quieter times – if your trainer is hunting for work it can leave you a bit high and dry.*" In such situations, our sources recommend "*being proactive and asking for work.*" Apparently "*e-mailing across the department is frowned upon in banking and corporate*" but "*being clear to your trainer can produce results.*"

## here comes the sun

The sun shines more brightly for trainees in ICM seats, not least because of "*a brilliant atmosphere*" that is "*relaxed,*" "*enjoyable*" and founded on "*an amazing team spirit.*" What also helps is "*an army of paralegals*" and "*a fast-paced turnover of work*" resulting in "*a tonne of drafting of offering circulars and financial documents.*" Trainees refer to a "*less laborious approach... not like corporate where you search for a missing comma for hours.*" The ebb and flow of work also makes the long hours come and go, except in ICM Securitisation, where "*they were dreadfully long all the time.*" A scrap of cloud on an otherwise clear vista.

Unlike some firms, A&O hasn't resorted to a college course to fulfil the contentious requirement of the training contract and all trainees complete three months in a litigation seat. Those with a taste for it can seek a full six months but should bear in mind the "*enormous popularity of the department for qualification.*" Again this year, we heard mixed views: some trainees relished "*research on things like corruption or financial regulation*" and "*following multiple cases through the courts,*" whilst others bemoaned "*tedious tasks*" and an "*administrative flavour.*" The keenest trainees clearly get the most out it and "*people who are there for six months tend to be given the best work... the three-monthers can be treated as an afterthought.*"

The model of the three-month litigation seat looks to be a contagious one that is dissolving the hard walls of A&O's four-seat structure and we learned of plenty of trainees who had taken five or even six seats. In negotiating the vagaries of the "*rotation lottery,*" current trainees advise that "*you've got to make it clear exactly what you want to do or the numbers mean you won't get it.*" You need to exercise your 'priority seat request' – effectively a trump card guaranteeing a desired seat – especially if you fancy a long spell in litigation or time in a niche department like IP, employment, real estate, competition, employment or tax. Sources recommend "*identifying a specific partner in a specific area and telling HR you want to work with them.*"

Niche departments have a substantial corporate support function and their seats often tend to be viewed as a way to give "*variety to training*" rather than "*genuine areas for qualification.*" Adding further zest to the two years, there are many overseas seats and client secondments. "*Hong Kong and New York are always popular,*" but it seems that each intake has its own preferences: "*In our year,*" explained one trainee, "*lots of people had partners, so HR had to work hard to give away some of the overseas seats. There was no one for Dubai or Singapore whereas the client secondments were competitive.*"

# the true picture

Whether scoffing "*aperitivos after work*" and "*dealing with formidable partners*" in Milan, "*coping with ridiculous amounts of autonomy*" at a leading bank or "*working my ass off*" in Amsterdam, trainees seemed equally pleased with their adventures.

## you winsome, you lose some

Straying from A&O is, for the majority, a short-lived adventure. In September 2005, 52 of the 62 qualifiers stayed on, with many qualifying into the firm's core practice areas. Among our interviewees there were also some who had negotiated their way into more exclusive departments and others who were moving to pastures new for niche work. "*I didn't get what I wanted but you take that risk,*" said one of them. And if the gamble doesn't pay off, the glow of the A&O brand on your CV will take you far. The following words say it all: "*Initially it felt worrying being on the job market again, but you realise that having been here you can go anywhere because the training is so good. The agencies are falling over themselves to get you a job.*"

One of the consequences of choosing a magic circle firm is that "*you are one in several hundred trainees.*" This guarantees a great schedule of classroom style training sessions but "*can sometimes be alienating.*" Certainly all those we interviewed were adamant that "*there really isn't an A&O type.*" One remarked: "*Realistically, how much difference is there between the different magic circle firms?*" For the most part we agree, but we did notice that those who seemed to have best negotiated the ups and downs of training on a mass scale were unafraid to "*make a stand and get [their] voice heard.*" The more driven of our sources suggested: "*Some people are just too willing to be deferent;*" the timorous or fainthearted definitely run the risk of "*falling between the cracks.*"

Getting feedback is a matter in point. On the one hand some told us: "*There isn't always a great culture of responsiveness,*" whilst others suggested: "*Of course you don't get feedback on everything, but if you ask you'll be told. I'm not worried about walking into anyone's office to ask a question.*" All the evidence suggests that those who "*put a lot in, get a lot out.*" Such an attitude explains the pleasure one nearly qualified found in "*realising you're comfortable giving advice to clients – even telling them they are wrong – without that niggling fear that you're wrong.*" This achievement doesn't come without effort and our sources had put in long hours over the two years. All had experienced "*hellish periods*" and "*being in until the wee small hours repeatedly,*" as well as the more normal slog of "*8am to 9pm or 10pm.*" True to form, most told us: "*It's just par for the course.*"

## going to market

Socially, we can only hope we stumbled upon an unusual year group as some trainees were all too aware of the downside of being "*part of a massive, impersonal intake, which can be bitchy, cliquey and gossipy.*" We should stress that this was not the view of all we interviewed and even the least happy had "*four or five friends who are close.*" Interestingly, one second-year trainee commented: "*The year below has some very sociable people and they've gathered big groups around them. In contrast, my year was quite diffuse.*" Everyone is welcome in any one of the firm's many sports teams – "*cricket, football, wakeboarding, netball, you name it*" – and regular trainee-organised events see large groups come together for "*alcohol, dancing and good company.*" Departmental drinks are "*especially common in corporate*" but also on offer across the firm. Some of our sources preferred these events, describing them as "*more relaxing – you're chatting with associates or partners as people and there's no element of competition.*"

By the time you make it to A&O the firm will be residing in "*spectacular*" new offices next to Spitalfields Market. Still under construction, trainees' descriptions relied on an artist's impression showing three glass cubes replete with all mod cons plus roof terrace and gym. We're looking forward to an invite just as soon as it opens for business.

## and finally...

There's no question that if you are attracted to the finance end of international law you will find no better alternative to Allen & Overy in the City of London... whether you're in it for the long haul or whether you're simply after the firm's sterling name for your CV.

# Andrew M Jackson

## the facts

**Location:** Hull
**Number of partners/assistants:** 31/32
**Total number of trainees:** 12
**Seats:** : 4x6 months
**Alternative seats:** None

In its first hundred years, Hull firm Andrew M Jackson rode out the gradual decline in shipping, the industry that made its reputation, as well as the more sudden crash in the local fishing industry. While both still play a part in the AMJ story, broader commercial success is the vision for the next hundred years.

## frying bigger fish

Hull is neither quaint like the Dales, nor historic like York. It's too mainstream and post-industrial to be rustic, yet it's always playing catch up in the status stakes with Sheffield and Leeds. So when trainees told us that AMJ's senior partner has set his sights on *"equalling the level of the big Leeds firms,"* we applauded but wondered at the realism of the ambition. The January 2005 defection of head of corporate to a new practice in Leeds does suggest that there is some way to go, although an excellent national client roster including MFI, Northern Foods, Express Dairies, Road Haulage Association, Associated British Ports, AXA Insurance, Seven Seas and Carpetright, stamps authority on *"the clear aim to be competitive in Yorkshire and Humberside, even nationally."*

Trainees also told us: *"The firm placed adverts in a Times newspaper supplement on Hull recently."* And whilst fishing industry litigation has traditionally constituted the bulk of AMJ's international work, there have been increasing numbers of instructions from French and Dutch insurers on transport matters lately.

Clearly top dog in Hull and proud of an *"all-rounder reputation,"* AMJ nevertheless retains a strong marine department. It advises on everything from Admiralty matters to marine P&I and regulatory issues for clients like Sunderland Marine to contractual issues for shipping and freight forwarding companies. In terms of the fishing industry and its providers and distributors, lawyers recently represented a client in an action brought by Defra relating to 500 tonnes of fish meal. Trainees who work in the shipping department engage in *"an area of law [they] hadn't come into contact with at law school"* and are exposed to cases as diverse as *"on-board accidents, cargo matters and purchases of vessels."*

Beyond this salty surprise, what attracted our interviewees to the firm was the breadth of work on offer: *"Although ostensibly a commercial firm, there's a completely non-commercial side too."* A strong private client practice with domestic conveyancing and civil litigation (*"lots of PI and neighbour disputes"*) combines with a tax and trusts department advising over 150 substantial trusts. Not forgetting the highly rated family department – it offers *"so much client contact. I handled mediations, ancillary relief and domestic violence cases, both for wealthy clients and on a legal aid basis."* Yet the commercial side of the firm is where the bulk of the lawyers are employed and the commercial property department is now the largest in the firm. Trainees work on *"large retail developments"* as well as care home provider HICA's retirement village sites. They also have exposure to big commercial deals like Northern Foods' headquarters relocation to Leeds and smaller scale work for local owner-managed businesses on which they can draft leases and licences themselves. There are also seats on offer in employment ("*really good – I was at tribunal in my first week*"), commercial litigation and coco, all of which "*tend to be very popular.*"

## a dab of tcp

Those with more defined commercial tastes did feel greater "*pressure on options at rotation time*" than those with a private eye, but in general, seat changing is a relaxed affair with trainees happy to recognise "*the second years take priority.*" The fact that there are two seats in both employment and commercial property also helps relieve any pressure. But should there be complications, not only can trainees raise issues with their current supervisor, but also their delightfully named Training Contact Partner or TCP. Just like that brown bottle of strange-smelling stuff that your mum used for anything from cut knees and salving hurt pride to kitchen cleaning and vermin extermination, a TCP has many functions. Supervisors offer "*monthly or daily feedback, depending on how closely you work for them,*" whereas a TCP fulfils an overarching pastoral role, being "*there for a moan and to sort out general issues or specific ones... like a tutor at college really.*" Last year we heard a few gripes about uneven quality amongst those selected to be TCPs, but we're pleased to say no one had a bad word to say this year. "*It's an almost perfect system.*"

Our sources were equally impressed with the character of the firm, which they described as "*robust,*" "*inclusive*" and "*definitely going places... and they want you to go with them.*" As well as a more upwardly mobile cross-Yorkshire presence, going places includes a posh new website, a recent rebrand and a hoped-for move from a "*terrible 60s office block*" when the current lease expires. Said one trainee: "*You just can't feel proud to bring clients into the current building; our logo isn't even on the outside.*" Despite such concerns, it is clear that trainees feel involved in the life of the firm, whether at fee earner lunches once a week ("*you get the chance to earwig a bit on the latest*

*developments*"), helping out at marketing events or more simply reading the monthly newsletter, 'The Marvell.' Named after famous 17th century local poet Andrew Marvell, this august publication features "*all the news, arrivals, promotions and other tittle-tattle.*"

Naming the mag after a local lad made good is also symptomatic of another truth about AMJ: "*They really value [trainees with] a link to the local area.*" Admittedly "*this year there are several people from Lincolnshire and even someone from Leeds,*" the vast majority have family, friends or fiancés in the city, with almost all having lived in Hull for much of their lives. This is not to say that they haven't studied elsewhere, or that applications from outside the region won't be welcomed, but you definitely need a dash of Hull-centricity by birth or inclination to make it into and stay the course at AMJ.

## fire in the hull

Hull is enjoying something of a renaissance at present, which is all the more reason for those from further afield to consider it a possibility. New development, new investment and a new marketing focus emphasising Hull's position as a 'gateway to Europe' can be seen in concrete form in the rise of Hull City Football Club. Two promotions in two seasons and a swanky new home at the KC stadium are emblematic of new optimism in a city that is continually given a kicking in various national surveys. Last year trainees enjoyed a TSG ball "*in the beautiful banqueting suite at the KC stadium,*" but "*the fact that everyone's got family and friends in Hull cripples the social scene a bit.*" We've heard this before and the trainees themselves admit that "*each year the new intake think they'll be the ones to change it, but it never seems to work.*" All is not lost: there are organised events at Christmas and "*there'll often be an e-mail on a Friday asking who fancies a drink, and partners are generous with the rounds.*" Revolution and Jaz are the venues of choice before people make the "*20-minute walk home*" to the suburbs, or head further out to places like

Beverley or Cottingham. With hours of 9am to 5.30pm, cheap housing and *"pleasant country-side close by,"* the phrase 'quality of life' has more pertinence than might be imagined. Clearly satisfied with the whole package, four of the five trainees accepted NQ positions with the firm in 2005.

## and finally...

A quality firm that is a beacon to those seeking a solid commercial training in the flatlands of Holderness and the wider East Riding, Andrew M Jackson deserves a closer look from those further afield. If you like the sound of ambitious, steady and upcoming, then to Hull with you.

# Anthony Collins

## the facts

**Location:** Birmingham
**Number of partners/assistants:** 20/66
**Total number of trainees:** 13
**Seats:** 4x6 months
**Alternative seats:** None
**Extras:** Pro Bono – St Basils (Legal Advice)

In 1973 Mr Anthony Collins set up shop as a licensing specialist. Today, far from luring lost souls out of law school with the promise of 24-hour boozing and a trip to the bookies, the Anthony Collins creed is built around a purer kind of spirit.

## good work

The firm's work can be divided into three main branches: commercial services, private client and 'Transformation'. The commercial services branch includes commercial property, dispute resolution, employment and coco. It is also the guardian of Mr Collins' superb licensing legacy. The private client branch covers family and probate work and houses the firm's powerful clinical negligence team, revered for its representation of claimants in high-profile

cases of birth injuries, brain-damaged children, orthopaedic and psychiatric injuries. Finally, the Transformation group handles such matters as charities, community regeneration, housing management and property litigation. Despite the obvious differences between the three areas, the outlook of lawyers is the same firm wide: *"Everybody is in the firm to do good things; everybody here contributes to making everything better."* AC's self image is one of a firm that *"deals with a lot of issues that have an element of justice in them."* A social conscience is evident throughout the firm: *"Even the commercial services department does work for charities and housing associations."* A dedicated charities team has a committed following among children's and Christian charities such as Tearfund, The Bible Society and Baptist Union. Meanwhile, the highly rated social housing group commands considerable respect among housing associations and other registered social landlords.

Our sources assured us that despite any do-gooding appearances, *"there is absolutely no patting each other on the back for doing something wonderful."* Instead, the firm takes its ethical approach in its stride and keeps its eye on the commercial prize. This year it is leaving its old *"cramped"* and *"shabby"* retreat for *"very swish, professional-looking"* offices with *"a glass front, a big shiny floor and glass lifts"* that give the impression of *"more of a City firm."* Is Anthony Collins turning to the dark side? No, *"it is the people and their ethics that make us different, not the building. We won't lose anything."*

## teaching the lame to walk

And what of the training? In the past, the contract has followed the firm's three branches of work, giving those with a clear interest in one particular branch the opportunity to develop it. This year we heard how trainees mixed commercial seats with spells in transformation or private client. All our sources concurred with the trainee who commented that *"the boundaries haven't constrained my training."* Seats in clin neg are much sought after,

167

and a quick look at the firm's successes in the field reveals why. The team recently achieved a £1 million settlement in a complex wrongful birth claim. It was also involved in obtaining an £800,000 result for a client who had to have a below-knee amputation after doctors failed to diagnose vascular problems. High-value claims are the norm, according to trainees: "*There is hardly any slip-and-trip work.*" What this means for trainees though is less autonomy, which seems to be well counteracted by decent involvement in cases, meeting experts, attending hearings and "*the adrenaline rush of court deadlines, the cut and thrust of litigation and the adversarial approach.*" Exciting? "*It's tremendous!*"

The firm's Transformation work undoubtedly "*adds a really new dimension*" to the training contract, and "*the whole new spin*" it puts on the firm's charity, housing association and local authority clients is "*a strong draw*" for trainees. The dedicated social housing team acts for a multitude of registered social landlords on both management and litigation matters. On the management side, that includes transferring ownership of properties between local authorities and housing associations, which was described by one trainee as "*conveyancing on an unbelievable scale.*" On the litigation side, the team acts on issues of disrepair and nuisance. This year lawyers obtained an Asbo excluding a tenant from his home-town for five years, the longest Asbo yet granted. The team has also been involved in setting up one of the UK's first arm's length management organisations (ALMO), whereby the management of vast numbers of council homes is effectively outsourced to a third party. The firm's charity team combines general charity matters, such as charity commission registrations for mainly "*faith-based charities,*" with more commercial work such as mergers and acquisitions and technically complex "*internal shuffle-arounds*" for health sector charities and RSLs.

And so to the work of the regeneration team. If you were hoping for Charlie Dimmock types planting jolly geraniums and building pergola to evoke memories of that last holiday in Halkidiki, you'll be disappointed to discover that it is slightly more technical than this. Usually acting for community and residents' associations in conjunction with consultants, the team advises on the strategic planning of regeneration schemes, which involve a variety of property, local government, commercial and charities law, such as the £66million wholesale regeneration of Stonebridge Estate in North London. Or as one flippant source put it: "*Basically they take a scrubby, crappy council estate somewhere and turn it into a nice place to live.*"

## love thy neighbour

Throughout the training contract, where the nature of the work permits, autonomy and responsibility are plentiful. Trainees manage their own files in commercial property and family, do their own advocacy in social housing and get to draft witness statements, attend court and meet clients till the cows come home. One weary soul even confessed: "*I would be happy to do more grunt work!*" No such luck! The firm has a host of office angels and paralegals who get "*the slightly more boring tasks,*" making a training contract a near bundle-free experience and our sources all the better for it.

In largely open-plan offices trainees are usually seated within earshot of their supervisor. To ensure that any cries for help are heard, in addition to the usual three-monthly review there is a monthly trainee forum "*for voicing your opinion on how to improve things*" and have prayers answered by the training partner and HR personnel. There are also 'best practice lunches' every couple of months where all the trainees sit down with the supervisors and "*go through how we can make things better.*"

This caring-sharing, all-inclusive attitude is indicative of a firm that lauds social values and community spirit. Again this year we heard that "*the whole ethos of the firm is Christian based.*" However, while it was observed that in some departments "*partners have Bibles on their desks,*" the general consensus was that "*you're not really aware of it on a*

# the true picture

daily basis. It's certainly not an inhibitor and it does-n't hold you back if you're not a Christian." One source neatly summarised the firm's position by saying: "Don't rip anyone off, be a good business, be caring, show responsibility."

We didn't have to chat for long to realise that AC recruits in its own image. "Basically we are happy people who like helping each other out, who want to advocate the type of work that we do. We aren't moti-vated by huge, big-money deals; we are motivated by making a difference." In September 2005, one of the two qualifiers stayed with the firm.

## doing a dimmock

Perhaps taking a leaf out of the firm's book, Birm-ingham has also undergone some serious regeneration. Again, more than a few hanging bas-kets and a bit of bunting, the city now boasts the £800 million transformed Bull Ring, the new Self-ridges building, a completely reconstructed city centre, Europe's largest cinema complex at Star City and a £42 million glass-roofed 'lifestyle' complex at Fort Dunlop. Anthony Collins' trainees know how to make the most of all this, and we heard of both planned and spontaneous drinks after work, nights at the dogs and trips to the cinema and theatre. There are also a good number of lunches at the thankfully untransformed local greasy spoon.

A "real family atmosphere" drives the annual summer day out, drinks evenings and office lunches laid on by different departments each month, and of course there's the annual Christmas bash. Sadly, the trainees' annual day of canal boating for charity was called off this year because "the boat is too old." Instead trainees went off to a local homeless shelter to "do a Ground Force." Their horticultural skills did not stretch to water features or decking, but after a day of "planting flowers and painting fences" every-one seemed rather happy with the results. With so much going on, it is a good thing that "there is a mass exodus at 5.15pm" and "you really don't get slated for going home on time." More than that, we heard that "late nights happen hardly ever."

## and finally...

"Anybody that wants to make a difference should come here; anybody who isn't really bothered should-n't, because they wouldn't last." We think you'll figure out if you 'get' this firm pretty quickly so if you see it at a law fair, make a beeline for its stand.

# Ashfords

## the facts

**Location:** Bristol, Tiverton, Taunton, Plymouth, Exeter, London
**Number of partners/assistants:** 44/74
**Total number of trainees:** 22
**Seats:** 4x6 months
**Alternative seats:** Secondments
**Extras:** Pro bono – eg Tiverton Saturday Surgery

Ashfords has five offices spread from Taunton to Plymouth offering a full range of commercial, matrimonial, criminal and personal injury serv-ices to clients ranging from individuals to local authorities and international plcs.

## the single life

In 2004 Ashfords ended what was ultimately judged a marriage of inconvenience with the firm that is now known as Bevan Brittan. For 20 years it was separate beds and little exchanged beyond that which was legally required. Following the split there were no dark nights of the soul spent moping over old pho-tos; Ashfords handled things with perfect equanimity, and why not considering that divvying up the possessions was so simple. The firms' shared client list reportedly stretched only 12 names long. For their part, our sources unanimously confirmed of the split: "To be honest it has made no difference at all."

Newly single and independently minded, Ash-fords is fully in control of its own show. Though it now pitches for work without the added oomph of the Bevan Ashford brand, a factor that was signifi-

169

cant in relation to the public sector, it has already won a notable victory in a tender battle for the role as litigation adviser to the London Borough of Wandsworth. This is not only a feather in the cap of the firm's public law team, but also underlines Ashfords' ability to operate anywhere from London to darkest Devon and Cornwall. Furthermore, the confident opening of a small Bristol office on the day of the demerger clearly indicates Ashfords' outgoing intentions. It has already added a corporate insolvency team in the City. And although profit figures weren't in when we went to press, the firm had recorded five consecutive years of healthy turnover increase and high profits.

Apart from a new moniker, a flashy new corporate identity and the small problem of "*making sure you answer the phone without saying Bevan Ashford,*" the lives of trainees haven't been much affected by the demerger. However, we were keen to hear their thoughts on where the firm might be headed, wondering whether Ashfords might follow the pattern of some other regionals with aspirations and close down smaller branches to focus on more profitable work in bigger commercial centres. Apparently not. "*We've been assured that Taunton and Tiverton will be staying open,*" trainees said of the two smallest branches, adding that while much of the work in these offices may be private client and family/crime for clients including landed estates and farmers, "*both are well-established, have a very wealthy client base and are integral to the firm.*"

## hungry for more

Nevertheless, we did detect signs that Ashfords "*is trying to strike a balance between regional dominance and a more national profile.*" One only needs to look at the Exeter coco practice ("*the chairman of the firm is also the head of corporate, that says it all*") to see that Ashfords' appetite for bigger and better national work is a driving force. A solid reputation for mid-range M&A is evidenced by advice to regular international client Schlumberger on the megabucks sale to IBM of its business continuity

and disaster recovery operation, serving governments, banks and major corporations from 40 sites globally. Instructions from Pittards on the sale of its raw materials division in Dumfries, Scotland also prove the point. Other clients from beyond the West Country include the MoD, North Yorkshire County Council, English Heritage and BT. Not forgetting those closer to home, "*a strong regional client base*" includes the South West of England Regional Development Agency, South West Water, Teignbridge Propellers, Dartington Food Company and several local authorities including Devon CC and Exeter and Plymouth city councils.

In addition to its coco team, the Exeter office possesses very well-regarded IP, employment, commercial litigation and real estate teams and these, together with the "*entirely commercial*" new Bristol office, are spearheading Ashfords' national ambitions. For now, the London office is "*merely a place for meeting clients, it's not staffed,*" though maybe the firm will consider extending its toehold at some point, not least because "*the Wandsworth connection is bringing work in for property, for public law and for commercial litigation.*"

Ashfords is mindful that it can't rest easy on its West Country laurels, a fact emphasised by rival firm Foot Anstey's recent opening of a new Taunton office. Trainees tell us that Ashfords' approach is a cross-regional one, such that "*partners move around a lot between offices; it often feels more like departments operating across the South West rather than separate offices of the same firm.*" For example, an Exeter-based public law partner frequently spends time in Plymouth "*servicing lots of Devon and Cornish local authority clients.*" Meanwhile, "*Plymouth is probably getting a coco lawyer to enhance our ability to operate down there,*" and Bristol also enjoys the occasional attendance of "*IP and planning lawyers.*" Just to emphasise regional flexibility, we're told: "*PI lawyers recently moved from Tiverton to Exeter because of a new client win.*"

## tour of duty

Working their way through four six-month seats requires trainees to be equally flexible. Seats are currently available in all offices and trainees tell us that exactly where and when they go is *"largely up to us in negotiation with HR."* Aside from stiff competition for the IP seat at Exeter (which includes a secondment to the University), *"most people get what they want, and even if a seat's not on the list to begin with you can usually negotiate about it."* We noticed a tendency for most to spend the first two seats in one office before moving elsewhere, but in theory *"there's no reason why you shouldn't move for every seat."* If you wanted to, of course.

Undoubtedly the *"busiest and most commercial"* branch is the one in Exeter. Here the *"bustling, noisy open-plan offices"* are located in a new building on a business park *"next to junction 25 of the M5."* The on-site gym and canteen just about make up for *"the electricity substation outside the window and the dismal chain pub nearby."* Not least because there's nowhere to go for lunch offsite, *"people tend to take shorter lunch breaks"* and the commercial flavour does mean the working day can be longer than elsewhere in the network. However, 'longer' means, *"once having to stay until 8.30pm, and boy was I pissed off."* Otherwise, a working day of 9am to 5.30pm really is the norm across the firm.

The offices in Tiverton and Taunton are all smaller and share a *"family-like atmosphere. In Tiverton all the support staff are local, have been there forever and everyone goes to each other's weddings and birthdays."* Tiverton's *"beautiful Regency buildings with sash windows and lots of light"* are a contrast to the Taunton office in its *"modern, 60s premises in the centre of town,"* but the seats here are very similar with *"matrimonial, commercial property, wills/trusts/probate and employment"* all on offer. Out west in Plymouth, the *"prefab concrete 60s/70s"* building is *"slightly empty after the BBL [now Bevan Brittan] healthcare team left,"* but there are still *"excellent seats."*

Wherever they had wandered, trainees spoke enthusiastically about the *"variety of work that lets you find your legal tastes."* They valued, too, *"the determination to give you responsibility if you prove yourself"* and the *"good quality of work that the firm does."* Whether it was *"digging out deeds for the land registry," "getting integrally involved on a share buy-back"* or *"attending meetings with clients and counsel,"* no matter what their work tastes, trainees seemed satisfied. Admittedly, we did hear some mixed messages over the quality of feedback: this was applauded by some but more equivocally judged by others. *"It entirely depends on the person you get – some are very good and detailed in their notes, with others you do work and then never hear about it again."* More uniformly reliable are formal appraisals, which *"really tell you how you're doing and what to work on."* Indeed, with a one-month-in appraisal added for first-seaters, and mentors (*"associates or juniors in the department"*) in every seat, Ashfords certainly provides trainees with a good support network.

## natural beauties

Given that *"almost everyone has a connection to the South West by virtue of family or university,"* the region holds few surprises for Ashfords' trainees. Those we spoke to had chosen the firm for *"the balance it offers between life and work"* and enjoyed *"a perfect compromise between quality of work and a reasonable size."* As a group, trainees encompass a broad age range, a variety of universities and a fair few previous careers, but all apparently share *"a good sense of humour"* and *"confidence to a point."* They stress that applicants should possess *"a quality of not taking yourself too seriously"* and remain *"relaxed in outlook."* Sounds like the best kind of regional stereotyping to us!

Wherever they are based, trainees' social lives *"seem to centre on Exeter."* They enjoy drinks in Chumleys and Chaplins, often heading on to *"one of the many lovely nightclubs."* If you detect sarcasm in relation to the nite spots of Exeter, none such is in evidence when it comes to The Summer Games, which pits trainees against employees from various Exeter businesses in beach-bound high jinks. No sarcasm either when it comes to "*relaxed summer and Christmas parties.*" And when all is done, there's the incidental pleasure of going home through some of the loveliest countryside in the UK. "*You're only ever ten minutes from somewhere beautiful – one girl lives in a village near the beach and Dartmoor, you can't beat that.*" Wooed by the lifestyle and working environment, five of the eight NQs stayed with the firm in 2005.

## and finally...

If you didn't already want to train in the South West, perhaps you do now. Ashfords offers a full spectrum of work and it looks as if there's ample scope to grow with the firm.

# Ashurst

## the facts

**Location:** London
**Number of partners/assistants:** 108/296
**Total number of trainees:** 89
**Seats:** 4x6 months
**Alternative seats:** Overseas seats, secondments
**Extras:** Pro bono – Islington and Toynbee Hall legal advice centres; Disability Law Service, Business in the Community, death row appeals; language training

Nudging its way into the £200 million turnover bracket in 2005, established City firm Ashurst offers one of the most rounded training experiences in the Square Mile.

## survival of the fittest

With a renewed confidence and a fleet of colourful, striped cabs bearing the Ashurst brand charging around the capital, Ashurst lawyers have become London's new Rainbow Warriors. Image-wise this is a major departure from the Ashurst Morris Crisp of yesteryear, whose founding fathers were a 19th

century radical and reformer (Mr A), one of the original subscribers to the telephone (Mr M) and a well-known eccentric and collector of garden gnomes (Mr C). Apparently it was good to lose Morris and Crisp – "*they were a bit blue-blooded. That's not the image that the firm wants to portray,*" said one trainee. "*We were laughing today about some of our old Victorian-style drafting! Now it's much more colloquial – there's a push towards plain English.*" Another told us: "*There is a genuine keenness to get away from the old-fashioned fuddy-duddy stuff. Now we have brightly coloured carpets everywhere... There's no crazy installation art but the lawyers now have six different colours of business cards.*" Someone else considered that "*the image before was very Oxbridge Rah! Rah! Now it's more pan-European.*"

## box office smash

By all accounts Ashurst is enjoying something of a renaissance. A recent survey of 2,400 listed companies (including those listed on AIM) showed the firm had the highest number of clients across the stock market as a whole. Some of these only recently instructed Ashurst for the first time, among them Abbey, African Copper, Biofusion, Phytopharm and Reuters. The firm has certainly worked on some big, bold deals lately, among them Deutsche Börse's proposed cash offer for the London Stock Exchange and Taylor & Francis Group's merger with Informa Group. Another high-profile deal was the acquisition, on the same day, of both the Odeon cinema chain for approximately £400 million and the UCI cinema chain for approximately £150 million on behalf of venture capital firm Terra Firma. Ashurst also advised Blackstone Capital Partners on its €375 million acquisition of Legoland Parks and Merlin Entertainments, the operator of visitor attractions including Sea Life and the London Dungeon.

According to our colleagues on *Chambers UK*, the firm has won impressive corporate work from much bigger firms with conflicts of interest. The best example of this was when Freshfields was prevented from acting for Philip Green's company Revival Acquisitions in its well-publicised bid to acquire Marks & Spencer through hostile takeover. Because it had previously given legal advice to M&S, Freshfields was barred from acting for Green's company and in stepped our subject firm to save the day. Ashurst, though not always the first choice on such megadeals, is increasingly recognised as a safe pair of hands, ready, willing and perfectly able to carry the load.

You might think that a corporate seat would be mandatory at Ashurst; in fact, the only stipulations are that trainees do a contentious seat and a transactional seat. The latter is usually taken in corporate and M&A or international finance, but can equally be spent in real estate or energy, transport and infrastructure. Some of the trainees who had done a seat in corporate loved the experience, while others remained less enthusiastic. One fan with an eye on a post-qualification job told us: "*To a degree, the corporate department is split into areas – I was in capital markets and corporate finance doing lots of public company work. They've got a good system of annual rotation for junior corporate assistants which enables you to look at the different focuses of the department.*" This seems to fit with the firm's philosophy of keeping things reasonably general during the training contract. Another of our sources had developed an affection for finance work: "*The transactional side is more for me,*" they announced. "*I like the speed of deals and also you get more contact with clients and more responsibility.*"

## the geek shall inherit the earth

Praise too for the tax team. "*It's fantastic – there's a great spirit and trainees are given lots of responsibility.*" Partners were particularly applauded for the guidance they give to their charges. To fit in with the team you need a similar mindset: "*It's a bubbly team and quite academic, though not as geeky as you'd expect!*" Litigation was also described as "*very welcoming.*" This popular department is known for its

consistent hours and appeals to people who may have toyed with the idea of a career as a barrister. At least one of our sources had realised it wasn't their cup of tea: "*You need to be patient with research and give a lot of attention to detail. It is very slow.*"

Trainees say that seat allocation "*evens out,*" even if you can't always get what you want at the time you want it. More important, apparently, is who you end up sharing an office with. "*If you sit with a partner and you want to qualify into that department it's a clear advantage.*" Whether this is wholly true we're not sure but what we do believe is that Ashurt offers the classic, rounded City training, not too heavy in one area or another. As well as the seats on offer in the London office, secondments to banks and large corporates like IBM provide valuable alternative experiences, and although Ashurst is not especially well known for its overseas seats, "*there are always people in Paris and Germany.*" In fact, the firm has nine other offices in Europe and Asia (unusually in India and Japan as well as Singapore) as well as a New York outpost, and many of the European offices can offer trainee seats. Projects and private equity deals seem to account for a fair share of the overseas work, among the most important being the Perpignan to Figueras high-speed rail link, which has seen Ashurst's UK and European lawyers working together.

One thing many students want to ask is 'What about the hours?' At Ashurst 9am to 7pm is standard, but expect to work longer in certain transactional departments. Said one trainee: "*In finance I was doing 50 to 60 hour weeks, nine in the morning to nine at night was probably a good average.*" In any large City firm the demands placed on lawyers and trainees can be higher than students imagine, but learning to take it in one's stride and thrive on the buzz is all part of the training experience. "*All the highs I've had relate to the deals. If someone pops in to say thank you it can really make a difference,*" confirmed one interviewee. "*On one deal I worked flat out from Monday morning to Wednesday evening and the partner in charge gave me a case of champagne to acknowledge my contribution. It's nice when you're recognised. It makes you more likely to help next time."*

It's not always wine and roses. Another trainee spoke of a clash with a supervisor. *"He was a difficult man,"* they explained, before stressing that *"with a couple of exceptions, generally supervisors get picked quite well."* They come from amongst the ranks of partners and senior assistants, with trainees always sharing their room. The system of appraisals was described as *"standard – a little chat half the way through the seat, a written review at the end and then another review with partner on training committee and an HR person to go over that review."*

## catch of the day

For many, the Ashurts name is closely associated with sport, and the firm fields decent teams in several games. One particularly candid interviewee revealed how *"traditionally the place attracted blue blazers and sporty bimbos; people who had a good profile but were not so good academically. I don't think that's true now."* Another source told us how these days you won't find *"the real public schoolboy Oxbridge type – there's no really competitive go-getter atmosphere."* As for who we did find, along with long-term students and those who had come from previous careers, we also had the pleasure of a conversation with a self-confessed *"serial dosser"* (though whether their claim holds water is debatable!). We learned that *"people are good humoured. The dress code is casual and I think that that reflects people's attitude."* One trainee put their finger firmly on the firm's pulse when they said: *"There is a lot of socialising and lots of friendships are formed during the training. This is not a plodder's firm; it wouldn't suit the 'bury your nose in the books' type."* Someone else said much the same: *"You need technical expertise but you also need to be sociable. Most people here are outgoing – people with good chat. Some of the vac schemers we had recently were far too timid to get on here."* No such problems for the majority of 2005 qualifiers:

36 of the 44 who completed their training contracts took positions with the firm, spreading themselves across all the different departments.

In this *"collegiate"* atmosphere, *"everyone supports each other."* One source said, charmingly: *"I wanted to work somewhere where I wasn't just an extra fish in the pond."* There are plenty of opportunities for socialising with fellow trainees. In addition to the usual nights out in the pub, *"we have good pool nights – snooker not swimming – and karaoke nights."* The corporate department upholds an age-old tradition called 'Sundowners' in which a partner leaves an envelope stuffed with money with one of the secretaries. Trainees have to track down the envelope and the person who finds it takes the others out for drinks. Not to be outdone, the litigation department also hosts regular post-work drinks on the terrace of their building over the road. Though offering up *"nothing scandalous"* for our sources to gossip about, Christmas parties are *"always good fun and everyone gets involved. The partners in litigation are hilarious."* At one Ashurst ball the heroes and heroines dress code inspired a Robin Hood, a Cleopatra and a character from 'The Matrix'. Isn't that standard lawyer attire these days?

## and finally...

Trainees are keen to sell the message that *"the firm is going places"* and that it is *"a bit more punchy!"* But they want it both ways, telling us: *"If you are very serious and overtly ambitious then this is probably not the place for you."* Despite their confident (and colourful) new stride, there was an appealingly relaxed side to the trainees we spoke to. We've a hunch that this side of Ashurst's character will last well after the stripy cabs have been mothballed with the gnome collection and the antique telephones.

# Baker & McKenzie

## the facts

**Location:** London
**Number of partners/assistants:** 76/183
**Total number of trainees:** 70
**Seats:** 4x6 months
**Alternative seats:** Overseas seats, secondments
**Extras:** Pro bono – Waterloo Legal Advice Centre, UN High Commission for Refugees, death row appeals; language training

The original global law firm, Baker & McKenzie is a proud member of the exclusive $1 billion revenue club and has a heritage that is both illustrious and characterful.

## on a roll

Since its early days in Chicago, Bakers has championed the notion of international practice. With 8,000 staff scattered across more than 65 offices in nearly 40 countries over three continents, it's fair to say that the firm is living up to its ideals. It is probably also fair for the firm's graduate recruitment literature to suggest that the annual meeting of partners is akin to a UN summit, albeit one with profit on its delegates' minds. Together the offices have a mighty clout and a seriously impressive client list of major multinationals. Among those of great relevance to the UK lawyers: BP, Estée Lauder, Sony, Fujitsu, Levi Strauss & Co and Daimler-Chrysler. Yet, having grown on a franchise principle, each office enjoys autonomy and a character all of its own.

The London office, having been around since 1961, is an excellent example of the Baker & McKenzie Way. Now one of the largest offices, "*it does not feel part of what was once an American firm – there are no typically US characteristics and no hours culture.*" In fact trainees tell us: "*The defining feature is that you feel like you're in an international firm, always dealing with offices around the world whether it's in Europe, Asia or the Americas.*" What's

more, London this year turned in a stunning performance involving a massive 35% hike in profits, comfortably outstripping global growth of 3.3%. Backing up "*the feeling that corporate is where the real money is made,*" much of the growth is attributable to a great run in the corporate and banking departments and deals for the likes of BP, United Business Media, ING, France Télécom and the Development Bank of Singapore. Perhaps attracted by the prospect of healthy bank balances, a team of four securistisation partners recently joined the firm from the highly regarded finance division of Norton Rose. London's recent success owes something to good housekeeping too. A 2005 review of stationery and other paper procurement saw the firm save almost £250,000 on notepaper and toilet rolls.

## you shall go to the ball

The plurality and diversity of B&M has undoubtedly helped it to prosper in each new country where it has set up shop. Indeed, trainees have told us for many years that there is little danger of the firm embracing a "*single corporate persona,*" even if they do note "*a working tension between international cohesion and the disparate nature of offices.*" Over the last few years, a 'Visual Identity Programme' has been phased in to create greater continuity across the network – in the main relating to cosmetic matters like "*branding and templates*" – though we did hear this year that a new assessment criteria for fee earners has been introduced, "*setting the standards by which lawers are supposed to be judged worldwide.*" The trainees tell us it is "*too early to say*" whether this will have a significant effect on the London office culture, or if it is part of a wider trend towards homogeneity. What is certain is that trainees will continue to enjoy the breadth of seat options which has long been "*a key factor*" in attracting them to the firm.

The training scheme is based on the bog-standard four-seat model with the usual options of corporate, commercial, banking and property given

# the true picture

a fresh flavour by way of easy access to seats in employment, IP and IT, pensions, tax, dispute resolution, and competition and trade. The firm's excellent reputation in many of these more niche fields means trainees are more likely than most of their City peers to enjoy extended periods of good-quality niche work. This is definitely not a firm where you will spend two years simply propping up corporate and finance transactions. One source who'd relished their time in an employment seat offered this illustrative insight: "*Within two weeks of joining I was the only person representing the firm at an employment tribunal. I got a broad range of associate-level work and was given as much responsibility as I could handle.*"

IP/IT and employment are the departments that most attract trainees, yet they seem content to do their turn in the others and generally people seem happy with the efforts of HR in arranging rotation. "*I've been very impressed with the way they have managed it,*" admitted one satisfied customer. "*At each seat move they do try and accommodate everyone and maybe a few people have to compromise, but not often.*" The only "*hot topic*" is that the firm's general preference for the compulsory corporate stint to be taken in the second or third seat doesn't necessarily match up with how trainees would like to play it. Oddly, the corporate department has a fiercesome, ugly sister reputation among the trainees, and perhaps it is because this is where long hours will be most likely to crop up. That said: "*Everyone who's been says it is nowhere near as bad as they thought it would be.*" That said, the annual trainee revue at the 2004 Christmas party was a version of Cinderella in which a poor trainee "*couldn't go to the ball because her evil supervisor in corporate gave her due diligence to do.*" Perhaps predictably, Cinders was rescued by "*her fairy godfather, who was an IT partner.*" Was this panto merely a vehicle for "*taking the piss out of partners*" or did it reflect home truths? Perhaps we'll never know...

## then again...

... maybe we will. Overall, those we interviewed were very happy with the type of work and responsibility they'd experienced over the two years. "*I was given quite a lot early on,*" said one source, while another concluded: "*It is sometimes the luck of the draw, but if you demonstrate you're good enough people will give you quality work.*" Across all seats we heard from trainees who had been "*entirely responsible for one aspect of the case,*" or had conducted "*over-the-phone negotiations with the partner from the other side,*" or had "*rarely felt that you weren't being challenged.*" Several spoke of being awed by "*very high standards*" which were initially "*a shock*" and "*daunting,*" but which they had soon come "*to relish.*" Of huge appeal was the fact that "*you're actively discouraged from doing photocopying.*"

A good training contract is a delicate balance of responsibility against supervision. Trainees all sit with a supervisor and there is also a partner allocated in each department to keep a careful eye on how each trainee is performing and how much they are being asked to do. This structure enables trainees to "*get work from everybody in the department*" and pursue "*the work you're interested in. For example, in dispute resolution I got on public law matters that interested me.*" Fortunately, "*feedback is constant: some people go out of their way to e-mail you or phone you or come to tell you how you are doing.*" On a more formal basis, gathering together all feedback for three-monthly reviews means "*it's a three-way process, between you, your supervisor and everyone you've worked for.*" Who needs a fairy godfather!

## you shall go abroad

If you tire of London life, there's a galaxy of overseas seats to select from. This means that "*generally if you want to go abroad you will go,*" though "*you might have to be flexible about where you go.*" In recent years trainees have visited Chicago, Sydney, New York, Hong Kong, Tokyo, Madrid, Moscow, Brussels, Prague, Toronto and Brazil. Before you've mentally begun to pack and plan your weekend trips in Asia or Australia, be advised that each overseas office tends to offer very specific seats, so in Washington and Brussels it is competition law, in Chicago it is tax or corporate, and in Moscow you can select from finance or corporate. It is these specifics that heighten the pressure on particular seats. For example, the Sidney placement offers the double whammy of life in Oz and litigation or employment experience. Of course it is hot property!

Even students can get a taste of life in an overseas B&M office. Check the firm's website for details of its summer programme. If you want to sample life as a lawyer and you are attracted to international law, this has got to be one of the best vac adventures going.

## why are we here?

The firm sits prettily in a modern building close to Blackfriars on New Bridge Street. It may be relatively compact, but it is packed with facilities including a new staff restaurant on the first floor and a subsidised Starbucks on ground floor. And let's not forget the infamous artwork in the meeting rooms. Doubtless these works probe the nature of modernity, human existence and our relationship with the world, but "*it's a weird collection of work and it keeps you awake in meetings pondering what they might mean.*"

Unless you are in corporate or stuck into a weighty transaction elsewhere, the hours are a none-too-arduous 9.30am to 6.30pm most days. A Friday-only dress-down policy goes full-time in the summer. Trainees spoke of "*a very sociable atmosphere, where you develop a big network of friends, both trainees and associates in the UK and beyond.*" A monthly, firm-wide "*meal and free bar*" helps to fuel conviviality, with local pubs such as The Blackfriar or The Evangelist good places to carry on after work. "*Some intakes are more sociable than others,*" we heard, but the majority of the trainees we spoke to seemed to have a pretty full social agenda. For those into their sports, there are work teams from women's rugby to netball, cricket, football and sailing.

Our interviewees confirmed what we have known about the firm for many years: staff are "*positive about and loyal to the firm.*" Of themselves, trainees say they are an "*interested and go-getting*" group who are "*diverse in interests, sociable and down-to-earth.*" At the same time: "*The firm tends to shy away from recruiting from traditional universities like Oxford and Cambridge,*" but whether this actually reflects "*less importance being placed on purely academic ability*" or simply "*a commitment to diversity*" we're not sure. What we do know is that in September 2005, 15 of the 17 qualifiers accepted NQ jobs.

## and finally...

Baker & McKenzie offers international opportunities, an international perspective and a broad range of practice areas within a sound training contract. The firm clearly works for everyone we spoke to, and we suspect there are few commercially minded types for whom it wouldn't work.

# Barlow Lyde & Gilbert

## the facts

**Location:** London
**Number of partners/assistants:** 75/180
**Total number of trainees:** 34
**Seats:** 4x6 months
**Alternative seats:** Secondments
**Extras:** Pro bono – St Botolph's Project and Toynbee Hall Legal Advice Centre

Barlow Lyde & Gilbert is one of the most prominent litigation firms in the UK and is a best known for handling top-grade professional indemnity and insurance cases.

# the true picture

## saving your bacon

The firm litigates, arbitrates, mediates and counsels on a huge variety of disputes and other sticky situations. Recent examples include everything from wise words to Shell in relation to the Financial Services Authority's investigation into the recent re-statement of its oil reserves; injunctive proceedings on behalf of UPS aimed to curb the activities of animal rights protestors; and a £24 million claim on behalf of an insurance company against the manufacturer and installer of a smoker following a fire at a bacon warehouse near Bury St Edmunds.

No trainee escapes litigation at BLG so don't apply here if this is your intention. The mammoth professional liability and commercial litigation (PLCL) department is engine room of the firm and, for trainees, "the trend is for two seats in PLCL." And not always through choice. PLCL is made up of five groups: commercial litigation; financial institutions; professional indemnity; accountants' negligence; and solicitors' negligence. The work handled by these last four groups has a common theme – cases in which advisers fail to meet required service standards and losses are incurred as a result. The client list is truly impressive: from accountancy, PricewaterhouseCoopers, Baker Tilly and BDO Stoy Hayward; from the world of property, the surveyors and valuers Jones Lang LaSalle, DTZ and Cluttons; key actuaries, engineers and players in the financial services arena; firms of solicitors from the magic circle to the high street. BLG is without doubt the professionals' choice, and should you ever find yourself in a tight corner professionally maybe you'll give the firm a ring.

Several of the trainees we spoke to had encountered one particular case in PLCL – the massive Equitable Life litigation, which was probably the biggest case to hit the UK courts for eons. The trial was scheduled to run for eight months from April 2005 but settled in September. BLG was representing the accountancy firm Ernst & Young, helping it to fend off a claim from Equitable Life worth a massive £2.6 billion. Now that's what we call high stakes!

## edge of your seat

When working on any big case, a trainee's contribution, although important, is modest. "My role was attending meetings and helping with witness statements; reviewing documents and classic document management work," confirmed one source. Another described "pounding away through the night" preparing bundles on urgent matters including injunctions. At such times, high-tension drama makes up for the fact that the task itself can be "as dull as dishwater." Paralegals share the load, and as trainees become more experienced they also learn to delegate the jobs they love to hate. "The stuff I delegate is photocopying and checking, proof-reading and going to court to issue applications," revealed a savvy second-year. A seat in general claims (mostly PI and clin neg) is quite a contrast because trainees are allowed to run several of their own files. The seat teaches them how to correspond with other solicitors, draft witness statements and even attend court alone for case management conferences and infant approval hearings (where payments to minors are rubberstamped by the court).

In addition to defending clin neg cases for the NHSLA, there is PI defence work for insurance companies and local authorities. According to BLG's own material, it acts for virtually every major local authority in the South East, and takes on all manner of cases from property damage to personal injury and failure to educate claims. In addition to this swathe of local authorities, BLG acts for a line-up of police forces, defending them – usually via their insurers – from claims ranging from assault and false imprisonment to misfeasance (in layman's terms, turning a blind eye).

The common thread running through the majority of the litigation at BLG is the nature of the client – insurance companies. You'll recognise the names: Direct Line, Churchill, Norwich Union, Zurich, Lloyd's... we could go on and on... and on.

A seat in the market-leading reinsurance department really puts trainees to the test. This is where a brain the size of a small planet comes in really handy because the cases are so complicated. Not all insurance cases are mind boggling in their complexity though, and some even manage a bit of entertainment industry glamour. One partner has a nice line in claims concerning the cancellation of concert tours – among them tours by Limp Bizkit, David Bowie and Shirley Bassey. The film industry is a further source of insurance litigation, with cases including financing shortfalls and damaged film stock on 'Bridget Jones – The Edge of Reason'.

## baggage claim

Seats are also available with teams specialising in aerospace and shipping work. Regulatory, commercial and litigation advice is administered to major aviation industry names (BAE Systems, Cathay Pacific, Qantas) and an equally healthy client list in the shipping sector. The shipping work involves everything from ship sales and purchases to charterparty and cargo disputes, salvage, collisions, insurance and international trade issues. Over the years BLG has represented insurance companies in relation to many of the biggest maritime disasters (Exxon Valdez, Marchioness, Piper Alpha), yet the seat manages to also provide trainees with their own small files. By all accounts, the experience here is "*more challenging*" than PLCL and "*you get involved in the cases a lot more.*" Among the more unusual matters that land in the aviation department are "*passenger claims, including one concerning a guy whose wife's dowry got lost on a plane.*" Wherever cases have an international angle, trainees find themselves liaising with foreign 'correspondent' law firms to ensure that "*the advice is dispensed in accordance with the laws of that country.*"

If you come here wanting to litigate, you're laughing all the way to qualification; if you come here for a transactional training it's not the most natural choice and you run the risk that you may only have six months non-contentious experience.

In short, when it comes to a fifty-fifty contentious/non-contentious balance in training, some people get it, some don't, and others never wanted it in the first place. All we'll say is just be aware of this. Another fact to be aware of is that the firm's offices in Hong Kong, Shanghai and Singapore are almost never visited by trainees so don't come here with the specific intention of bagging an overseas seat.

Let's now look at the transactional side of the firm. The corporate department is newly divided into distinct teams – property, tax, commercial technology (which handles multimillion-pound outsourcing deals), employment and straight corporate. In 2004 the banking team waved goodbye and joined US firm Winston & Strawn, apparently so as to feel less of a sideline to the main action. The view of some people we spoke to was that BLG is "*more of a litigation firm than it ever was*" and that changes and departures in the corporate/banking divisions arose because of "*pressure from the litigation side of the partnership.*" The new salami-sliced corporate department will "*make it more transparent as to how much the different parts of the non-contentious arm are making.*"

All trainees undertake a non-contentious seat; some wangle two. Trainees told us one of the hottest seats was 'comm tech', which one described as "*the best kept secret in London.*" Here, a trainee's remit includes "*a lot of proof-reading, referring to precedents and drafting clauses, research for associates, sitting in on client meetings*" and the all important "*maintaining version control of documents*" so as to ensure that the right updates are sent through to all parties in a negotiation. Alas, the team was far from a secret and in July 2005 its much-vaunted head was lured by DLA Piper.

## yee-ha!

At BLG a typical day runs from 9am to 6pm and only rarely do trainees end up working late into the night. This is the beauty of litigation-led firms: the hours are more regular and predictable. The

# the true picture

schedule allows for plenty of socialising, especially in the summer vac season when the after-work scene moves up a gear. Don't plan on taking up a new hobby in June or July, we say. One trainee admitted: "*It is a well-travelled idea that Barlows is a heavy drinking firm, but in fact it depends on the department... there is a reasonable amount of drinking that goes on but departmental social budgets don't all go straight behind a bar.*" Barbecues, games nights, birthday drinks, leaving drinks, departmental parties ("*the last PLCL party had a wild west theme with bucking broncos*") go-karting and indoor golf in the firm's splendid marble lobby – BLG certainly enjoys its fun and games and as often as not chooses to involve clients. You will be pleased to learn that "*as a trainee you get a fair amount of client contact and you are encouraged to go to client events.*"

BLG trainees tend to be sociable types who get to know each other quickly and then keep up contact throughout the two years, not least through time spent in the Slug and lettuce and the more upmarket Dion in Leadenhall. The majority of them stay firm friends after qualification too; in September 2005, 11 of the 16 qualifiers took jobs with the firm, distributing themselves across the departments.

## and finally...

BLG recruits a high proportion of its trainees from its vac scheme, so if you have your heart set on the firm you know what to do. If you have a hunch that you might be a natural born litigator, we can't think of anywhere more appropriate.

# Beachcroft Wansbroughs

## the facts

**Location:** Bristol, London, Leeds, Manchester, Birmingham, Winchester
**Number of partners/assistants:** 139/259
**Total number of trainees:** 58
**Seats:** 4x6 months
**Alternative seats:** Secondments

Beachcroft Wansbroughs is one of the UK's larger firms, occupying a position in the top 25. Its focus on insurance work and public sector clients marks it out from most of its peers.

## public interest

BW sits on the panels of FedEx, insurance giant AXA and the £2.2 billion Partnerships for Schools (PfS) project. These three panel positions reflect its strengths well: for FedEx it provides employment support; the PfS role is a good example of its public sector expertise; and AXA takes advantage of its vast insurance litigation capability. "*One of the most interesting things about the firm is the mix of public and private sector work,*" remarked one of our sources. In the private sector, clients include Bank of India, Citibank and a phalanx of AIM clients. In the public sector, the firm's primary interests lie in health, where it is a preferred adviser to an avalanche of NHS trusts and the NHS Litigation Authority, which manages the defence of actions brought by or on behalf of disgruntled patients. Away from litigation, advice and representation is given in relation to all manner of health sector issues, including public inquiries such as the Shipman Inquiry.

Unlike some firms you'll encounter in your search for a training contract, BW is not given to fits of self-importance. In fact, it could be accused of being a little too modest. "*We're in the top 25, but annoyingly we're not a household name,*" said one source. Another's frustration is summed up as follows: "*We're the only firm on all six of Zurich's legal*

# the true picture

panels – *that's a testament to our strength – and we're still not that well known.*" The firm's great hope, new managing partner Simon Hodson, promises to raise its profile in line with its achievements. "*There will be a big marketing drive soon,*" one trainee assured us, predicting that "*if the firm decides to become an LLP, a facelift may mean a complete rebrand.*"

With large offices in Leeds, Manchester, London and Bristol, plus tiddlers in Winchester, Birmingham and Brussels, BW trainees are spoilt in their choice of location – all but Brussels are open to them for at least one seat. When deciding which of the firm's offices you want to make your base, choosing where you want to live should not be the only key consideration. Different parts of the BW network specialise in different types of law, so if commercial transactions tickle your fancy, head for London, while Bristol boasts the firm's coveted health litigation and health advice seats. Leeds and Manchester are both litigation-heavy offices. With only a small minority of trainees moving to another office for one of their four seats (a switch from Leeds to Birmingham for construction, for example), it is important to pick the right location for your work preferences.

## mind the loophole

In London, BW's six-floor office in Fetter Lane near the Royal Courts of Justice offers the trainee a mix of employment, technology and commerce, construction, projects, corporate, financial services, property and several breeds of litigation. The firm has one of the finest employment teams in the country, and it has lately flexed its legal muscle in some of the UK's largest tribunal cases. It was successful in its defence of Kent & Medway Towns Fire Authority in a claim relating to part-time working brought on behalf of more than 16,000 firefighters. The employment team introduces trainees to a plethora of work experiences, compromise agreements being a favourite as "*trainees can take a lead on these.*" Such agreements are used when a senior employee is removed from a company and the parties are able to work together to avoid litigation. In cases where the parties do end up in tribunal proceedings, trainees learn how to juggle drafting witness statements with regular client meetings and research. Learning to devise case strategies comes as an eye-opener; said one trainee: "*It's fun trying to find the loopholes where an employer has slipped up.*"

At a second London office in Eastcheap, trainees can try professional indemnity or other types of insurance litigation. Some of the larger cases are long running, leaving trainees "*mainly assisting*" their superiors. To give an example, when "*a hotel goes up in flames leaving a deficit of millions,*" it will be you "*scouring Halsbury's and performing desktop research for case law and checking legal points.*" One past occupant of a litigation seat told us: "*The research is very intellectual and, looking back, I quite impressed myself.*" At times there will be the unenviable task of preparing bundles of documents for court and other paper-heavy chores, but suffice to say "*you won't be stuck away behind a photocopier all the time.*" A seat in Maryland Gardens, the diminutive personal injury satellite office, also means assisting a partner, this time in defending "*big multimillion-pound claims.*" The kind of case for which BW has earned a name includes Allport v Wilbraham, a sports injury case in which the firm successfully defended a rugby referee alleged to have been negligent when he failed to ensure a scrum had properly engaged. A young player was paralysed from the neck down, however, the Court of Appeal decided no compensation was due. Other matters have included accidents at work, stress and asbestos claims.

Any prospective trainee keen on corporate or finance transactions for private sector entities might wish to note that this is probably the best office to go for, given the seats available. It is also the office from which trainees are selected for a client secondment to Unilever.

# the true picture

## healthy ambition

Down the M4, the Bristol office can in some respects claim to be the firm's nerve centre, and certainly it is the home of the graduate recruitment team. Again, a large number of contentious seats are available here, one such being in personal injury. Trainees are given their very own caseload on their first day in the department – plenty of *"health and safety claims worth less than £10,000"* and a range of other smaller matters *"can involve quite a bit of advocacy, especially if the partners sense you like it."* Said one source: *"Applications in chambers are really awful the first time; then it just becomes second nature. It's nice being trusted on your own and not having someone holding your hand."* Other seats include clin neg, professional indemnity, projects and construction.

Bristol is where the largest of BW's three health teams is to be found (the others are in Winchester and Leeds). Winchester is, at most, a six-month stop-off for trainees and has something of the Bermuda Triangle about it. Said one source: *"Someone has been there, but I'm not sure who or when – they just go off the radar."* Health advice in Bristol is very wide in scope: everything from hospital mergers to challenges to treatment decisions made by local Primary Care Trusts. In particular, the firm has used its judicial review experience in relation to the proposed closure of a hospital, the resourcing of IVF treatment and the alleged unlawful detention of a psychiatric patient.

## northern highlights

Leeds and Manchester are the two northern outposts in the BW Empire. Leeds provides a window on the world of public sector development, with trainees able to undertake a projects seat that introduces them to myriad health sector organisations and local authorities, *"mainly on PFI and PPP projects."* Here, their role is to assist on mammoth deals such as the NHS LIFT projects for Doncaster; Tees Valley and South Durham; Bradford and Airedale; and Liverpool and Sefton. The work is not all health-related: the firm is advising Liverpool City Council

on the £42 million Central Library redevelopment and Doncaster MBC on a project to build two new secondary schools. *"There is a lot of procurement law,"* involving *"very technical wrangling about how public bodies interact,"* reported one old hand. Naturally, on vast deals that go on for years a trainee's input is limited to research combined with document management chores – *"reviewing, amending and advising on contracts, proof reading and drafting things like variation deeds."* As well as projects, there are seats in property, construction, employment and professional indemnity litigation.

A trip across the Pennines brings us to Manchester where insurance litigation awaits the majority of new recruits. *"It's not compulsory, but most trainees do it first,"* we heard. Trainees manage some of their own small cases, *"predominantly road traffic accidents, employers liability and product liability,"* and the seat is *"a good confidence builder,"* requiring them to *"hit the ground running."* Varied tasks range from making applications and sitting in on hearings to drafting witness statements and researching on the quantum of damages. Other seats include commercial and professional indemnity litigation, corporate plus commercial and technology.

## shiny happy people

Whichever office they worked in, our sources attested to good-quality work and positive training experiences. Mid and end-of-seat appraisals come as standard, with some seats including even more regular check-ups with supervisors. As with training, when it comes to social matters it is the department that dictates. There is no annual firm-wide jamboree; instead, the various departments have become adept at mixing business and pleasure, most congregating annually. *"All the projects teams, say, will come together. There will be lessons, then a meal, then a drink."* The employment lawyers' training day resulted in an easyJet flight to Barcelona – *"Bizarrely it was cheaper to go there than to meet up in England."*

# the true picture

There are social committees in each of the offices, and by all accounts the most fun-fuelled locations are Leeds and Manchester. Trainees spoke of treasure-hunt pub crawls weaving their way around Leeds and ending up in Greek Street. In Manchester, each month at something called 'The Hundred Club' a member of staff wins £100 in a prize draw and there is a seemingly endless list of organised trips and nights out.

Just like the firm, the typical BW trainee is not showy or brash. They come from reputable universities and although they are *"quite ambitious, they don't want to be in work at 8am and leave at 8pm."* Trainees saw themselves as *"team players with not really much competiveness"* between them, rather than the type who would *"stamp over people as you attempt to shine."* Fittingly, they regarded the firm as *"a supportive environment"* in which *"people are genuinely interested in the law."* In September 2005, 22 of the 25 qualifyers chose to stay with the firm.

## and finally...

While Beachcroft Wansbrough covers an appealing range of disciplines, there's no getting away from the dominance of insurance litigation – particularly PI and clin neg – and public sector clients.

# Berwin Leighton Paisner

## the facts

**Location:** London
**Number of partners/assistants:** 140/233
**Total number of trainees:** 70
**Seats:** 4x6 months
**Alternative seats:** Secondments
**Extras:** Various pro bono initiatives

The trophy cabinet at Berwin Leighton Paisner is as crowded as Peter Jackson's mantelpiece. In the past three years this top-15 UK firm has wowed the legal pundits, won several important new clients and seen turnover and profits skyrocket.

## raising the stakes?

Once known primarily for its stellar property and planning practices, old Berwin Leighton has rung the changes. Retaining the loyalty of a swathe of public sector bodies and key client Tesco, the firm used its 2001 merger with Paisner & Co to add expertise in the corporate and technology spheres. This in turn became an effective springboard to further diversification for the new BLP. *"This is a very important period in the firm's history,"* explained one trainee, *"we're seeing a total restructuring of the business."* Perhaps not total, though certainly the firm has made noticeable strides in finance and mid-market corporate deals. Last year, for example, it advised Bonaire Investment Holdings on the $372.5 million sale of Internet poker business Paradise Poker (as advertised by Caprice) to the AIM-listed company Sportingbet. On the finance side of the deal, BLP steered Barclays Capital and Barclays Bank in the provision of £75 million of debt finance. In another deal, it helped Allergy Therapeutics on its AIM admission, raising £16 million in the process. And proving that every little helps, last year the firm facilitated an increase in Tesco's Euro Note Programme from £5 billion to £10 billion. Such is the new face of BLP.

With the corporate department now a recognised player, *"you'd think most trainees would be very interested in a corporate seat,"* opined one source, *"but it is not always the case. Many are still eager to put down core real estate as their first-choice seat."* Given that real estate and related areas (construction, planning and real estate finance and litigation) still account for a fair whack of the qualification jobs, this is perhaps no bad thing. In September 2005, 22 of the 27 qualifiers stayed with the firm. If you were wondering about how the rise of corporate and finance will affect job numbers in the future, we can't say for sure. What we can tell you is that the real estate department is not standing still – it recently won a major new instruction from Canary Wharf Group less than six months after nabbing the company's favourite lawyer, Robert MacGregor from Clifford Chance.

## the realty deal

A seat in the real estate department is all but certain. For most it will be a 'core' real estate posting to one of four work groups: leisure, hotels and public sector; Tesco/general real estate; real estate finance/institutions and general development; and real estate finance/entrepreneurial clients. *"The partner in charge of training wants to see us become well rounded and believes that real estate is essential to that. If you really don't want to touch real estate in your training, this is perhaps not the firm for you."*

In the hotels and leisure group trainees find themselves working both independently on smaller files and giving general assistance on bigger projects. *"On the small files I had quite a lot of autonomy,"* said one trainee. *"A cupboard of my own files meant a world of freedom."* Planning sounds like a good first seat as the team is supportive and *"the work is fairly research based so it's not a massive leap from law school. The firm knows it's very unlikely to get someone who has studied a lot of planning law so they know whoever comes in they will have to bring them up to speed."* On major developments and disputed planning applications trainees assist more senior fee earners, but when it comes to less contentious issues, they are able to practice their drafting, say on the Section 106 agreements by which developers bargain with planning authorities and include public amenities or infrastructure in their proposals.

Entering the real estate finance department can feel like *"going to a different firm"* as the pace and working pattern contrast sharply with other real estate seats. Trainees quickly realise how the demands of bankers differ from those of local authorities whose staff *"aren't always going to be at their desks when you ring them at 4.55pm."* In finance and corporate seats, the *"structured 9am until 6pm or 7pm day"* is likely to go AWOL. One of our interviewees spoke of finishing at 5.30pm some weeks and then *"not going home until 4pm the following day"* during others.

All trainees must complete a contentious seat, many of them choosing construction, real estate litigation or corporate recovery options rather than straight commercial litigation. As before, we sensed no widespread enthusiasm for litigation though this is great news for the minority who do take to it.

## one in eight

Secondments to clients, including Tesco's HQ in Hertfordshire and RAC (during a business and technology seat), London Underground (during a construction seat) and investment bank Schroders (during a finance seat) allow a taste of the real world. A Tesco secondment brings all manner of commercial work: drafting contracts, Internet-related matters, managing debts owed to the company, even defamation cases. For those who take up a Tesco secondment or who are placed with the real estate team that services the retail giant, the training experience can be very Tesco-centric. So we had to ask an obvious question of trainees, the answer to which was frequently: *"Yes, I shop at Tesco."* From one convert, we learned: *"You can also get your car insurance and landline telephone from them... they will eventually take over the world!"* Perhaps this is no wild claim: if a food supplier like McDonald's can do it, why not a supermarket? Look at the rise of Wal-Mart in the US and its subsequent invasion of other countries. Tesco, too, has stores overseas. In Asia alone it operates in Thailand, Malaysia, South Korea and Taiwan, owns a retail chain in Japan and is negotiating deals in China. In the UK, one pound in every eight spent in our shops goes into Tesco's tills. Think what this means for BLP.

Said one trainee of his attraction to the firm: *"BLP is getting high-quality work that is challenging and demanding."* 2004 saw the uncaging of Project Leo, a programme of self-examination and goal setting for the firm. The aim, explained one trainee, *"is to become the most respected law firm in the City. It's a target that people can work towards. We don't want to be the biggest; we're just happy to be a high-quality, respected firm."* Winning several awards over the past 18 months, including *Chambers Global's* 'UK Law

# the true picture

Firm of the Year', has made this goal seem all the more achievable.

## domestic bliss

The trainees we spoke to saw themselves as *"normal people who are happy to work hard for a decent wage."* Among the things that motivate them are *"positive feedback from a client who has read a letter or a research note that I've done and it has been useful for their transaction."* We've always viewed BLP trainees as a very sensible lot – they seem to know where they're going in life and just get on with the business of getting there without making a big drama out of things. Again this year we noted that a higher than usual proportion of the trainee group is either married or in a settled relationship even before starting at the firm. We view them as decisive people who have considered their life choices quite early on, made decisions and stuck to them. A number of our sources saw something in this idea. Said one: *"They do tend to recruit people who seem more in tune with what they will be doing in the future."* The firm is well known for its strong connections to the Jewish community, which leads some to wonder if it is a Jewish firm. The answer to this question is simple: it is not, but if the observation of faith requirements is important in your daily life then at BLP it will be very easy to manage as a good number of your colleagues will also wish to do the same thing.

Several of those we spoke to said they had turned their backs on the magic circle from the outset: *"I didn't like them when they were doing presentations; the trainees were showing off... how many hours they worked, how many all-nighters they did. I just knew I was not a magic circle person."* Typically we heard: *"I wanted to know everybody in my year group and be recognised within the firm. I didn't want to get lost."* One trainee added: *"My friends at magic circle firms have become so specialised and I wonder if they have really learned that much."*

Adelaide House and Magnus House just behind it together make up the BLP Empire at London Bridge. The firm has alliances with firms in New York, Paris, Milan and Rome, a new friend in Germany, and even a small outpost of its own in Brussels, yet it remains a distinctly British institution at heart. *"I don't care too much about going abroad,"* said one typical homebody, adding: *"I have dealt with some clients abroad though."* Of greater importance to the trainees we spoke to was the idea of winning in the game of personal life/work life roulette. This attitude undoubtedly promotes an environment in which *"no one is pushing and elbowing others out of the way."*

## silence in the back row!

After work the Sports Bar over the road offers *"lots of candles and free prawn crackers,"* though rarely, it seems, sports coverage. FOB underneath the office is the regular venue for monthly firm drinks and, despite being billed as *"an un-classy old man's Wetherspoon pub,"* local boozer The Monument still pulls them in. This year's Russian Christmas party at the Grosvenor Hotel on Park Lane was a fairly lavish affair featuring Cossack dancers (joined on stage by the partners who'd consumed sufficient vodka) and a motivational after-dinner speech by BLP's hired gun/mascot Laurence Dallaglio. We polled our interviewees on the quality of 73-times-capped Dallaglio's speaking talents. Depending on who you ask, he is either *"just eye candy, fine as the face of the firm but don't get him to speak"* or *"a far better speaker than [managing partner] Neville Eisenberg."*

## and finally...

Motivation is very much the name of the game at the moment, and doubtless you'll pick up on the firm's energy and pride if you get to meet any of its trainees or recruiters. Yet, there's no sense of complacency. As one trainee, quoting Tesco Chief Exec Terry Leahy, told it: *"Tesco currently has 12.5% of the UK retail market, and that means there's 87.5% to go."* The parallel with Berwin Leighton Paisner's current thinking is undeniable.

# the true picture

## Bevan Brittan LLP

### the facts
**Location:** Bristol, London, Birmingham
**Number of partners/assistants:** 68/175
**Total number of trainees:** 42
**Seats:** 4x6 months
**Alternative seats:** Secondments

Inexorably linked with the public sector, most notably the health service, Bevan Brittan is a three-office firm that is coming into its own.

### back to the future
Almost 20 years ago, two west of England firms, Bevan Hancock and Ashford Sparkes & Harward merged to form Bevan Ashford. In Autumn 2004, the two firms put an end to their long-running experiment and demerged. One limb became Bevan Brittan and the other Ashfords. But our job is to tell the Bevan Brittan story...

It starts in Bristol, where the firm's original work revolved around healthcare and clinical negligence litigation. From this, a whole world of public sector legal services emerged. In essence the firm has grown by thoroughly immersing itself in the sea changes that have affected healthcare, education and other public services, at times even helping to bring about these changes. In the dominant sphere of health, the firm's work spans everything from defending hospitals in claims arising out of difficult births to providing key advice to the government on the NHS LIFT project, which will see the development of 500 new one-stop health centres and the refurbishment of over 3,000 GP practices up and down the country. The experience gained on LIFT is also being used in relation to advice to DfES and Partnerships for Schools, the body which will implement the 'Building Schools for the Future' programme which over the next 10-15 years aims to provide new facilities for every secondary school-age child.

### an inspector calls
Recruited specifically for each of BB's three offices in Bristol, London and Birmingham, trainees will encounter this core work. Beyond this, the Bristol office offers the greatest number of contracts and seat options (though all three offices are growing) and so it is here that we first interviewed trainees to learn what else was keeping them busy.

Taking full advantage of its deep understanding of the health and education sectors, BB administers regulatory advice to numerous public bodies, including Partnerships for Health, the National Care Standards Commission, and the Commission for Patient and Public Involvement in Health. Trainees tell us that a healthcare regulatory seat is hot property: "*We act for the bodies that regulate everything from child minders and nurseries to old people's homes so, for instance, Ofsted regulates child minders and the Commission for Social Care regulates children's homes. We deal a lot with registrations, refusals to register, complaints, and the inspections which show when things are not up to standard. Some of the things you hear about can be quite horrible.*" The work particularly appeals to trainees with an interest in the human condition. Said one: "*I want to do good and help people and by stopping bad practices you can.*" No wonder the seat is so popular. It also exposes trainees to "*work on inquests and best-interest cases where treatment is being refused ... Jehovah's Witnesses and gravely ill babies, that kind of thing.*"

One step closer to clinical practice and its problems, seats with BB's clinical negligence teams are to be found in each location, and are compulsory in at least the Birmingham office (where there is still a relatively limited list of seats on offer). Always acting for the defendant, the trainee is able to maintain a degree of detachment from individual claimants, but the work can still have its "*gruesome*" moments. Said one source: "*Every other week at an education lunch there will be a consultant who will flash up some horrid picture of someone's face or body.*" Perhaps lunch isn't the best time for these sessions after all! The cases BB takes from the NHS Litigation

Authority and the Medical Defence Union tend to be worth a fair bit of money, and so it is rare for trainees to run their own files. One trainee rattled off his experiences thus: "*Every time my supervisor goes to interview a witness I go along. I have had a go at drafting instructions to counsel and witness statements and core documents. I sort out medical records, organise witnesses and track down documents. I also go to all the case management conferences and infant approval hearings.*" By the time you've done all that you should have a fair idea of whether the work is for you.

## easy does it

In answer to our question about whether working for the public sector felt any different to working for the private sector, one source told us: "*They seem more grateful!*" There are costs implications too. "*If you are doing property work for the NHS they want to know how much it will cost to do things... after all it is the tax payers' money. And they have different reasons for doing things, it's not just monetary reasons, it's because they need a new hospital or a GP's surgery.*" But if you thought the firm only represented the public sector you'd be wrong. Indeed, its commercial focus is stronger than ever. On its list of private companies – easyGroup, insurance company Zurich, various banks, Balfour Beatty and several others in the construction industry. Some of these clients offer secondment opportunities for trainees.

Essentially, the key to understanding BB is to understand its relationship with both public and private sectors, more particularly the "*interface between them*" which, in turn, is "*the driving force for the firm.*" In the field of projects/PFI/PPP, blending traditional public sector expertise with newer commercial skills has enabled BB to stand out from the crowd. To prove the point, it has accepted eight instructions from major international construction company Hochtief and work on international projects is becoming commonplace. Lately it assisted Partnerships British Columbia on a $400 million PFI hospital project (the first in Canada). It has also advised on proposed schemes in Finland and the Czech Republic. Said one source without hesitation: "*The firm is definitely trying to sell itself as a projects firm.*"

Projects seats bring their own demands born out of the complexity of the work. "*We do have special training sessions,*" assured one trainee, "*but to be fair, when you first start it is quite daunting. You get an induction pack to read and it explains the basics. The expectation isn't too heavy, you can have a go at drafting things and it's great if they say, 'That's fine' and not too demoralising if they put red pen all over it.*" Construction and property seats provide good vantage points for projects work and allow those people who click with the big stuff to build further on their initial experiences.

## it's good to talk

In most offices, and most seats, trainees reported regular hours of 8.30 or 9am until 6 or 6.30pm, with just a few late nights or lost weekends. The regime led one source to take the view that "*it's fun being under pressure with everyone driving towards a collective goal, a couple of late nights never hurt anybody!*" But it's not 100% harmony, 100% of the time, for 100% of the people. The issue of poor communication was raised by a number of sources. Said one: "*There have been various sessions where it has become apparent that it is a problem.*" Another told us: "*The biggest issue is the cultural side of things; some people have different ideas of what working life should be, different ways of working. I think the old views are being lost along the way and there are no coherent new views.*" It sounds as if BB is learning a very simple lesson – growth needs to be carefully managed.

At least trainees have no difficulty communicating with their supervisors; open-plan working puts them in close proximity to each other. Said one: "*I know everyone in the office and really feel a part of the firm. Partners all know your name.*" Monthly video-conferenced seminars connect the trainees and from time to time they meet up for in-the-flesh training (though hopefully not too many more of those gruesome photos!). These dedicated training days have the added advantage of allowing them to cast an eye over each other's digs. The Bristol office moves in 2006 to swanky new premises at King's Orchard and, when we interviewed them, Birmingham trainees were also eagerly anticipating a move at the end of August 2005. Said one from Brum: "*This office had just opened when I came to the firm and now we're having to hold back on further recruiting as there's not enough room. They have added a pensions team and tax and a licensing team. The planning team is getting bigger... all the departments seem to be growing. And recently three new people started in the healthcare team and are looking to develop work coming from the north of Birmingham.*" A sign of things to come perhaps? "*Who knows! If we start getting claims from up there we might get more projects work and then in the very long term we might look at becoming more northern focused.*" Walk before you run though: just before we went to press we learned that one of the Birmingham healthcare partners had left for rival firm Mills & Reeve. At the junior end, nine of the 12 September 2005 qualifiers stayed with the firm.

## projecting into the future

Our sources further suggested the firm might now be concentrating on recruiting people with more commercial leanings than most of their predecessors, saying: "*The seats on offer now are more commercial and not what people in my intake joined for.*" Yet it looks to us as if BB maintains an interest in non-standard applicants. The firm has for some time taken on a number of trainees for three-year training contracts run in tandem with part-time LPC study. However, not everyone recommended this route to qualification, telling us it was tough to combine full-time work with evening and weekend study.

In times of change, at least there's always one constant – unwinding with colleagues after work. Monthly drinks parties at each office coincide with dress-down Fridays. In between, colleagues pop out together whenever the fancy takes them. The favourite venue in Birmingham being Bar One Ten. In London, "*trips to the pub used to be an office-wide thing, but now we are bigger it's more a case of groups of friends meeting up, usually in The Puzzle downstairs, Corney & Barrow or The Magpie & Stump.*" In Bristol, staff will doubtless settle on a favoured watering hole after their move in 2006.

## and finally...

Bevan Brittan has its eye on the big projects prize, and if you think you might be interested in giving this weighty work a go, it's a splendid choice. Contrasting work in clinical negligence provides a human-interest angle, and an increasing range of mainstream commercial work ensures the experience does not become overly specialised.

# Bircham Dyson Bell

## the facts

**Location:** London, Cardiff, Edinburgh
**Number of partners/assistants:** 45/65
**Total number of trainees:** 15
**Seats**: 4x6 months
**Alternative seats:** Secondments,
**Extras:** Pro Bono – Paddington Law Centre

The Fun Powder Plot, enraged hunt protestors, night-long stand-offs: you'd think the Westminster of the noughties was a hotbed of flour-bombing, mud-slinging, rabble-rousing civil unrest? Not entirely. While goings-on within the Houses of Parliament may resemble the more colourful pages of the Ladybird Book of British History, round the corner Bircham Dyson Bell's activities are far from elementary.

## trains, planes and automobiles

To cut to the chase, Birchams is one of a handful of firms offering work of a parliamentary nature. The core of the parliamentary team's work is the promotion of and opposition to legislation, which means that it ends up advising on some of the country's biggest projects. One source explained in a little more detail: *"It is driven by big infrastructure matters; there is lots of public transport... trains, trams, roads and buses."* Unsurprisingly, *"Crossrail is the big buzzword at the moment."* If you are perusing these pages to pass time while waiting for your bus to arrive/train to depart/Tube train to extract itself from a tunnel and you feel driven to action – hop on!

The parliamentary department is certainly winning trainee votes at the moment and new lawyers from Macfarlanes and Richards Butler have brought additional projects experience to the firm, which has recently added Thames Water's massive Upper Thames Reservoir project to its portfolio. Other work includes the London Gateway Port project, Docklands Light Railway extensions and proposed tram systems in London, Merseyside, Nottingham and Edinburgh. If this is a world away from your current experience, fear not. When quizzed on the subject our sources were sufficiently vague to convince us that they too had no real knowledge of the issues before they started at the firm. Despite this handicap, trainees find they can assist on *"drafting petitions against private bills and a range of fairly eclectic matters like harbour revision orders, compulsory purchases and historic byelaws."* A seat here definitely provides *"something a bit different to talk about, something beyond the more run-of-the-mill seats."* There is a downside of course. With *"massive national infrastructure projects that go on for years,"* a seat here can be a backbench experience, although that's *"great if you like research."*

## swing seats

If instead you feel driven to distraction by transport issues, Birchams offers plenty of diversions. There are no compulsory areas in the four-seat arrangement, and trainees can also choose season tickets for private client, company/commercial, litigation, real

estate, charities and employment law seats. Last year, second-year trainees got stuck in *"a real bottleneck around litigation,"* but being as varied in their interests as the firm is in its departments, generally our sources had not been disappointed. The private client department is still the firm's largest. Offering three seats, it is the last bastion of Birchams' traditional roots. In hushed tones, trainees described a cloistered, *"quite other-worldly"* department that is *"traditional and proper"* in its approach to *"a cerebral discipline."* Although bespoke tax planning and foreign matters for wealthy individuals are largely beyond their reach, with the help of *"great teachers"* and *"a lot of hand-holding,"* trainees are left to their own devices drafting simple wills and attending to less complex matters. Nevertheless the department's size, reputation and gravitas haven't prevented it from *"becoming less influential in the firm."* Sources told us that *"commercial and parliamentary are really growing – it is beginning to swing a bit."*

Indeed it would not take Peter Snow with a large dangly arrow and some cunning computer graphics to tell you that the mood at Birchams is swinging in a different direction. Compared to private client, a seat in real estate sees trainees casting off mothbally tweeds and rolling up pinstriped-sleeves. *"Suddenly you have 30-50 files to get on with yourself and you are on the phone to the other side every day."* Trainees are given approximately the time it takes to inhale deeply to get their heads round commercial leases, acquisitions, licences, portfolio refinancings and construction matters. While one source confessed: *"It is terrifying actually,"* our interviewees generally viewed the *"full-on 'Let's do it!' attitude"* of the department positively. In an interesting development, Birchams has enticed two of the country's top social housing lawyers to join the firm, bringing their entire team of solicitors and a top-notch portfolio of local authority and housing clients with them.

A seat in litigation brings matters as diverse as family, contentious probate and debt recovery, which work-wise means *"tons of stuff"* like drafting witness statements, meeting clients, attending conferences with counsel and even conducting low-level advocacy. Ask a Birchams trainee for the high point of their training contract and the answer is likely to be akin to: *"winning my first court case, then celebrating with the client afterwards."* A stark contrast with a company/commercial seat, which is a much more humdrum affair. A stint here means helping out on day-to-day commercial advice as well as assisting partners with the more exciting deals such as Falkland Islands Holdings on its hostile bid for The Portsmouth Harbour Ferry Company.

## wall of noise

Neatly addressing both the firm's recent expansion and its lately adopted commercial outlook, Birchams has embarked on an office reorganisation of the *"taking down a lot of walls"* and becoming open-plan variety. In an attempt to be *"a lot more modern"* and *"update itself,"* the firm has a new website and *"new coloured pens."* Behind the traditional Georgian façade now lurks a contemporary office space described by one wit as "like a call centre." However, Birchams is not about to leave its long-time party faithfuls in the lurch, and it continues to *"work hard to retain the distinctive, civilised, pleasant culture"* that sets it apart. The new *"utilitarian"* look makes space for the firm's old traditional image in one meeting room decked out in antique furniture and oil paintings. Likewise, despite the trendy graphics on the new website, one source admitted relief that *"much of the old text remains."*

Birchams trainees are not about to throw off their suits for a dress-down policy, nor indulge in some trans-hierarchical boozy bonding session. Instead, our sources were happy to endorse the benefits of a more traditional working culture, reflected by the *"very sensible hours."* A standard day is a sedate 9.15am-6pm, and though property may keep you until sevenish, *"there is no compulsion."* A parliamentary seat is the main contender for keeping people late to box-up paperwork, but *"we call for pizzas and just get on with it."* Generally, grunt work is minimal across the seats and even in departments

where the work does not readily lend itself to the shaky hand of a new trainee, recruits are given responsibility and supervision in careful measures. By all accounts, a Birchams training is *"a very proper preparation"* with mid and end-of-seat appraisals and plenty of firm-wide lunchtime seminars. Little wonder our sources spoke with confidence in their own ability. In September 2005, three of the six qualifiers stayed with the firm.

## lawyers who lunch

An air of maturity in part derives from the type of people Birchams recruits. As one source explained: *"The application process for City firms doesn't suit people who are older. Here, it is just a letter and your CV, and you won't get thrown in the bin for being too old."* A consequence of recruiting life's grown-ups is that the social scene lacks a certain something in terms of scandalous goings-on. *"We lunch a lot,"* our sources confessed, *"we are quite happy to slope off for a drink after work, but we could never make a profession out of it!"* So lunch it is then – a fry-up in the greasy spoon round the corner in the winter, sarnies in St James' park in the summer. For unadulterated sophistication *"the girls go to Zanders."* Alas, *"the boys don't understand the point of cocktails so they don't come."* The pubs of Victoria offer a more gentlemanly pint.

Christmas parties fall into the *"very classy black-tie"* category and last year partners tried to encourage trainees to perform a sketch to enliven the proceedings. After much resistance in the junior ranks there was a change of plan – *"we had speeches and a raffle instead."* Needless to say, the *"champagne and canapés"* format for the annual summer party is far less controversial. In short, if you can't enjoy your Chateauneuf du Pape without donning a Big Bird outfit and doing the funky chicken, Birchams may not be your best bet.

## and finally...

This is one for those with a distinctive taste for parliamentary affairs... in fact, it is one for those with distinctive taste, full stop.

# Bird & Bird

## the facts

**Location:** London
**Number of partners/assistants:** 53/82
**Total number of trainees:** 25
**Seats:** 4x6 months
**Alternative seats:** Overseas seats, secondments
**Extras:** Language training

Bird & Bird represents a mountain of technology-led businesses and organisations, has nine international offices and fields leading specialists in IP, IT, telecommunications, e-commerce and sports. Interested in checking out its plumage?

## bird brains

Knowledge is business. If this isn't a learned proverb then it should be. And if it isn't then a Bird & Bird lawyer has probably filed an application to trademark it even before you've finished reading this sentence. All over the world people are coming up with new inventions, miracle cures and better technologies. These all need to be developed, protected, exploited, sold, implemented and improved. And where knowledge is business it is also legal business, which is where the Birds come into the picture. The firm's lawyers are involved in the legal side of everything from helping the smallest internet start-up off its feet to ensuring pharmaceutical giants patent their latest drugs to cracking down on infringements on a mighty telecommunications company's intellectual property. If life sciences, aviation, sports, public and private sector IT, media, communications or any kind of Internet business appeals, then ditch those magic circle application forms and dig out that Letts GCSE Combined Sciences revision guide.

Now we say that, but actually, although "*many partners at the firm have PhDs* " and possess "*frankly scary intellects,*" in some years there have been relatively few new recruits with science backgrounds. Whether the Birds had widened their search, whether rivals stole the march on them and snapped up all the boffins, or whether the thin science years were an aberration; we're not quite sure, but what can be said for certain is that if you lack a scientific or technical background you'll want to think carefully about why the firm's work appeals to you. Of course, given the massive potential in these markets, if you have "*a life sciences or genetics interest,*" step on up!

## lip smackin' pill poppin' polo suckin'

Patent litigation is a major part of Bird & Bird's worldwide reputation. Covering pharmaceutical, mechanical and biotech cases that non-science trainees may struggle to get their heads around, the department excels in representing some of the biggest multinational companies in the world. Long-term clients include Ericsson, Nokia, Intel, Cisco Systems, ExxonMobil, Interbrew, Nestlé, Pfizer and Transkaryotic Therapies, but B&B is not a firm to rest on its laurels. By the time this book has gone to print the Birds will have taken a case on appeal to the House of Lords for long-standing client Synthon concerning the validity of a patent owned by SmithKline Beecham relating to an anti-depressant called paroxetine mesylate. This will be the first time for nearly ten years that the Lords have considered a UK test for novelty and enablement, so as well as being complex scientifically, the firm's work also pushes the law to its limits. If all that seems too complex, then suck on this: the IP department has also recently represented Nestlé in a High Court appeal against a ruling which asserted that the food giant could not trademark the circular shape and embossed writing of the Polo mint.

The Polo case represents the soft side of IP, the side that pretty much any trainee can chew on. Here the matters involve the enforcement of trade marks, such as the instruction from the FA over IP rights for the Three Lions shield and England shirt designs during Euro 2004. Trainees perhaps have slightly more responsibility here, with several we spoke to enjoying experiences like this: "*I've been working for Nokia on copyright infringement work, writing to ISPs to close down websites that contain infringing material.*" However, a more common theme across the department is to be "*entirely engrossed in huge cases where you do the background work like interviewing experts or disclosure exercises and your exposure to clients or a wider range of work is limited.*"

## technically hitched

Trainees are enthusiastic about "*working with and learning from incredibly bright people at the top of their field*" and they speak of a definite "*intellectual atmosphere.*" "*You'll spend more time discussing issues or a technical point informally to try and solve a problem,*" one trainee confirmed. A not dissimilar experience (in terms of scale, if not the niceties of refined intellectual debate) is to be had in the general commercial litigation department, which has significant cross-border expertise and represents companies such as BT, T-Mobile, O2, Primus Telecommunications, SilverStone, Verizon, Kawasaki and American Media.

However, our sources did observe a somewhat different atmosphere and working culture in the non-contentious departments. Real estate, coco, employment, banking, property, tax, communications and surprisingly even IT and e-commerce were all described as "*more conservative, suited and booted*" and "*like a different firm to IP.*" With some of those departments being quite small and having mainly "*a corporate support role,*" extra responsibility is on offer for trainees. Here, too, some noted a distinct technology bent. Said one: "*In banking I worked on an EBRD case worth several million pounds, but I was also doing a lot of Internet banking matters.*" Corporate deals commonly reflect the leanings of the IP department; for example, the firm won a lead role on a major joint venture between AstraZeneca and Cambridge Antibody Technology (CAT) that will see the two companies fund a minimum of 25 antibody development programmes in

an investment worth nearly £100 million. Perhaps this recurring theme explains why the class of 2005 told us: "*Most people know where they want to qualify by the third seat, so the fourth is used to diversify your experience.*" Eight of the 12 qualifiers stayed on with the firm in September 2005, and although they faced the usual six-month probationary period, presumably they took comfort in the knowledge that "*no one ever seems to have fallen at that hurdle.*" The race for NQ jobs seemed like a marathon for some who told us that "*the process can drag on,*" but others breezed through. And just to prove that non-boffins can come first at Bird & Bird, those eight NQs took jobs in employment, banking, tax and commercial.

## big birds

The commercial teams are "*incredibly popular*" with trainees. Commercial 1 deals with IT projects and has "*more of a public sector focus,*" giving trainees the chance to "*draft software licensing agreements and freedom of information terms, and do work on bigger stuff like a major procurement process for a government department renewing its IT system.*" Comm1 lawyers have recently been supporting BT in its largest ever project, the implementation of a £2.6 billion NHS National Programme for IT. Comm 2 handles telecoms, general commercial and sports work. Here too the work is of a substantial nature, not least in the case of the firm's advice to Airbus on EU-related legal issues pertaining to the encrypted ground-to-air communications system for the company's A380 project. In case you're not an aviation nut, that's one of the new generation of super-sized passenger jets. Now that's what we call a big bird.

Every trainee we spoke to used the F-word to describe the firm's self-image. "*It definitely thinks of itself as being a little bit funky;*" "*oh yes, every effort is made to seem funky and progressive.*" Not exactly what you'd expect from a firm established in 1846. Our sources confessed: "*It's definitely a marketing slant, the reality is more professional and conservative.*" We say, steady on Birds – there's nothing more pathetic than a middle-aged man desperately trying to recapture his youth and disguise a beer belly and thinning hair with trendy clothes and an iPod. Perhaps sensing this, trainees say: "*We don't want to be trend setters or hangers-on, or be seen to be faddish, but we do want to be more cutting edge than the average firm.*"

## pale and interesting

Turning their eagle eyes on each other, our sources concluded: "*Every one of us definitely has a bit of character and a willingness to embrace change.*" "*We are ambitious but not to the extent that we'd tread on each other to achieve what we want.*" Trainees tend to find themselves either working very closely with a supervisor on one particular matter, or "*walking around the department getting work,*" dependent on the variables of seat, supervisor and deal-load. As such, this is definitely a training that favours those who are more self-sufficient. Those with the confidence to look further afield may angle for one of the regular client secondments, or if they "*make enough noise*" trainees might even be allowed to visit one of the overseas offices in Brussels, The Hague, Stockholm, Milan, Rome, Paris, Düsseldorf, Munich, Frankfurt, Beijing and Hong Kong. No one chose to fly the nest last year, perhaps because they found themselves with "*a predominantly UK focus in work.*"

The Birds occupy three buildings, with the bulk of the firm nesting down over the four floors of 90 Fetter Lane. Until now the IP department has resided in splendid isolation in adjacent Furnival Street premises but is shortly to be joined by other lawyers. The gradual expansion of the firm is confirmed by the movement of one of the commercial groups to join a back office team in another Fetter Lane property. The latter is "*not as bright and airy as the rest,*" but, light levels aside, the buildings are "*all much of a muchness.*" Down in the basement of 90 Fetter Lane on a given Friday every couple of months, employees can expect to be entertained with "*drinks in the partners' dining room.*" Emerging

pale and blinking into the light from these underground festivities, trainees stumble blindly into Walkers, which is universally acknowledged to be "*a dirty hole,*" yet, amazingly, is still popular. Trainees tell us they "*make it out for drinks every Friday without fail,*" and if a combination of vitamin D deficiency and alcohol doesn't leave them too listless, they can join any or all of the firm's active cricket, rugby, football, hockey, softball and rounders teams.

## and finally...

Like a good wine, Bird & Bird should be chosen to suit the palate. If you have a nose for IP and technology, then this firm is an ideal choice, offering an excellent training and the reliability of a big name.

# Boodle Hatfield

## the facts

**Location:** London, Oxford
**Number of partners/assistants:** 27/39
**Total number of trainees:** 10
**Seats:** 4x6 months
**Alternative seats:** None

With nearly 280 years of practice behind it, Boodle Hatfield is as much a Mayfair institution as the trilling nightingale in Berkeley Square. A spanking new des res at the top of new Bond Street is ringing a few changes, but property and private client work remain the key notes.

## extreme makeovers

Back in 1730, a young chap named Robert Andrews had for several years been plying his trade as a legal clerk and estate manager for the Grosvenor family when legal reforms allowed him to become a solicitor and set up his own practice. Fast-forward to 2005 and the product of Robert's labours is Boodle Hatfield, a firm whose fortunes in the intervening 275 years have been inextricably bound up with the

Duke of Westminster's Grosvenor Estate. This long acquaintance does not mean stagnation or sleepiness, however; Grosvenor's London estate comprises 120 hectares of prime Mayfair and Belgravia territory, including a mixture of offices, five-star hotels, embassies, international retailers, exclusive apartments and houses. It all adds up to a demanding variety of property matters for Boodles. It has also received instructions on more distant parts of Grosvenor's empire, including the £800 million Paradise Street development in Liverpool which is one of the largest mixed-use developments in Europe, extending over 42 acres with 30 individually designed buildings. That's 1.5 million sq ft of retail, 230,000 sq ft of leisure and 465 residential units, two department stores, two hotels, parking and five acres of open space. Phew! Such is the firm's expertise in property development, property finance and construction that many other landed estates and busy companies have turned to the firm over the years. The firm must be rather excited about snagging new client ILVA (Denmark's answer to IKEA) as it plans the opening of its first four UK stores.

## what is a house?

As they rotate through their four seats, trainees *"almost inevitably"* spend time in the property department, and will likely also experience tax, funds and pensions (TFP), corporate and litigation. There is *"a lot more flexibility than you might imagine"* within this basic pattern because of the variety of work that the different departments take on. A seat in property, for example, could be in *"construction, leasehold enfranchisement, commercial property, or residential conveyancing,"* and if you are really keen on experiencing more than one type of property *"you can do two seats, several people have."* By the same token, litigation can encompass family and employment as well as commercial cases.

Property is a very common first seat, a trend that is appreciated by trainees *"because you get your own files immediately and are thrown into work."*

Unanimously praised as *"a great learning experience,"* we couldn't help but notice a touch of the Sesame Street about the department. Trainees learn their property ABCs on leases and licences for the Grosvenor Estate and other clients with large portfolios. Of course, sometimes relationships between landlords and tenants become strained and disputes lead them to either the courts or the Land Valuation Tribunal. Working with property specialists in the litigation department, trainees are exposed to all manner of subjects from rent arrears to the lexicon of property law and practice. As we write, Boodles' litigators are steering two separate High Court challenges to definitions in the established landlord and tenant legislation. The first case asks 'What is a House?' and the second 'What is a Building?' Existential questions indeed! Where are Big Bird and Mr Snuffalepagus when you need them?

## pesticides and poisonous families

Having acknowledged that *"property is the mainstay,"* our sources quickly pointed to *"vigour in the other areas of the firm's practice."* *"Knocking on the door of property in terms of size,"* private client is definitely alive and kicking. Covering tax, trusts and family work between the London HQ and an Oxford outpost, the TFP team possesses a stellar reputation for both contentious and non-contentious work. Clients tend to be rather wealthy and trainees inform us that the firm not only does its best *"to help them manage their personal matters but also serve their business and property matters."* To wit, the litigation department is currently advising on a familial dispute over the division and disposal of a hotel business.

Our interviewees detected *"renewed activity and a broadening of the work base in litigation,"* a department which tackles everything from employment and family matters to general commercial cases. To prove the point, this year Boodles received instructions from a prominent media company concerning the dismissal and subsequent prosecution of an employee who it believed had fiddled the books, advised a large chemical company on the EU review of pesticides, and assisted Kershaws Quality Foods and other members of the cockle industry on disputes concerning FSA cockle-testing methods. How unshellfish of them! A litigation seat comes complete with "*a base level of bread and butter work*" (to go with the cockles) and "*you can ask for a particular focus, for example family law or employment.*" Those with a desire to immerse themselves more fully in family (or TFP) can request a seat in the Worcester Street office in Oxford. Such "*flexibility and responsiveness*" from the firm leaves almost everyone satisfied.

## gushing praise

Trainees were full of praise for "*excellent quality of work and supervision,*" telling us "*you do a bit of pagination from time to time, especially in litigation, but they mainly steer you away from such work.*" Property litigation is "*massively popular*" because "*you get your own files,*" but trainees equally enjoy the commercial cases in litigation. TFP is "*very busy*" with trainees "*drafting wills and trusts for wealthy individuals*" and "*getting involved in contentious work for overseas and UK private investors.*" Here, as in a corporate seat, they are "*generally used by the entire department so the work is varied*" and, because "*the corporate team is smaller,*" trainees are "*involved in most deals,*" albeit that "*there's less direct client contact and your role is more administrative.*"

"*A good culture of getting feedback,*" a "*very positive learning environment*" and "*effective mid and end-of-seat appraisals*" seem entirely to vindicate one of the core reasons why trainees chose Boodles. "*I wanted to be one in eight not one in a hundred,*" said one typical source. "*Here you know everyone from the senior partner to the post room staff and you're valued for your contribution.*" Most important of all, "*you're not an extra paralegal: you're part of the team and the firm makes you feel like an ongoing investment in its future.*"

## oils well that ends well

In the past we've interpreted Boodles' venerable age and awareness of heritage as being at the heart of a slight conservatism, but trainees this year were adamant that this isn't the case. "*There's a really young, fresh feel to the firm, lots of younger partners and an exciting atmosphere,*" they insisted. Undoubtedly, a major factor behind this new energetic feel is the firm's recent move to "*beautiful new premises*" at 89 New Bond Street above a branch of Zara and not too distant from Tiffany. "*Being just off Oxford Street*" there are the obvious benefits/dangers of the neighbourhood, an aspect of the firm shopaholics may wish to consider before applying. "*Fresh, open-plan, glass-walled offices*" and "*flat screens and all the latest technology*" have not taken over entirely. "*All the oil paintings of the firm founders and a history of the firm are upstairs in the open-plan area outside the meeting rooms.*" Lest we forget.

With hours averaging 8.30am to 6.30pm, the new location hasn't changed the tenor of the firm's social life and trainees still enjoy evening drinks or lunches together. When we conducted interviews, opinion was divided as to whether the nearby Loop ("*it's a bar, a restaurant and a disco downstairs*") or the even-more-proximate Hogshead ("*it's alright for a Hogshead*") has assumed the mantle of firm local. Judging by the mixture of antipathy and affection in describing it, we'll say the Hogshead. As for other activities, there are football and netball teams, regular games evenings and an annual dragon boat racing competition. "*It takes place at Bisham Abbey, where the England team train, but that's about as far as the comparisons go. We're not very good.*" The trainees we interviewed hailed from "*traditional or traditional redbrick universities*" and were glad to have found "*quality of work and work-life balance.*" In 2005, all four qualifiers stayed on with the firm, going into property and litigation.

## and finally...

A nice slice of property and private client work in a prime location.

# Brabners Chaffe Street

## the facts
**Location:** Liverpool, Manchester, Preston
**Number of partners/assistants:** 46/63
**Total number of trainees:** 19
**Seats:** 4x6 months
**Alternative seats:** Secondments

Buoyant after its landmark House of Lords victory for the *Liverpool Echo* making it harder to obtain gagging orders against the press, North West firm Brabners Chaffe Street may regret that decision after letting the *Student Guide* all over its trainees.

## all your eggs in one basket
In 2001, 200-year-old Brabners of Liverpool fused with Manchester firm Chaffe Street to create a three-site firm (Brabners already had a Preston office) with its sights set on becoming one of the best in the North West. The firm's profits look healthy and turnover is growing, with corporate and property the main drivers (their departmental turnover last year increasing by 30% and 22% respectively). 200 years old? Brabners is fresh in its salad days. It advised instamatic bamboo shoot suppliers Simply Fresh Foods on its management buyout and assisted Derbyshire's Starcross Foods on its £17 million acquisition of Dairy Crest. When not dealing with England's food producers, Brabners indulges its taste for the finer things in life. Next time you drool longingly over a sterling silver giraffe or Empress Alexandra letter holder and pen rest, remember that it was probably a Brabners' lawyer who did the legal work behind the glistening gift items – darling of Russian tsars, Fabergé is on the firm's client list.

In each of the three offices trainees sit with a partner and are "*privy to information the open-planned will never hear.*" "*The idea is to be close to a partner*" and assimilate as much as possible. In so doing "*you learn how to handle the other side and can pick up tips on how to massage clients.*" The only downside is the inhibition of a trainee's mischief gene. "*The golden rule is no naughtiness because you're always on show. As well as ear wigging on them they're ear wigging on you.*" Earwigs aside, despite one trainee implying it was a case of Masonic lot drawing for seat allocation, the divvying up of departmental postings seems to run reasonably smoothly. Everyone does litigation (or employment) to fulfil the law Society's contentious requirement; most do commercial property, reflecting the importance of this work to the firm, and then there are other options including corporate, banking and private client. The training contract can best be described as commercial law with few frills. That said, litigation seats can include helpings of construction, IP and media law amongst other gems and even the most mainstream of seats has variety built in. One trainee put it well: "*If you want to go to a North West firm with a corporate focus and no messing, then apply to Brabners.*"

The other thing we should point out is that for now at least the training will keep you in a single city. For most this is currently Liverpool (12 trainees). Manchester is the second office (five trainees) and Preston the smallest (two trainees). Last year we reported that inter-office secondments were "*in the pipeline,*" and it sounds as if they are still there. "*The offices are beginning to work closer together and they're still promising a North West seat beyond discretionary secondments.*" Watch this space, we say.

## mink coats and dusty deeds
Let's start our tour of training in Liverpool with the "*pervasive*" commercial property department. With Ireland's construction boom waning, its property developers have sought out moneymaking ventures on the UK mainland, and they've come just in time for an influx of European regeneration funding into Liverpool. Brabners has been quick to draw in these clients. It is also an indication of the size and strength of the Liverpool property team that it is acting on Manchester deals, lately the sale of the

# the true picture

SAS Radisson Hotel for nearly £50 million and the purchase and redevelopment of Eagle Star House – a project valued at over £40 million. Assisting with buying and selling large pieces of commercial land, trainees can expect some *"truly random"* tasks. One partner specialises in unregistered land, *"meaning lots of unregistered plots in Wales with not a postcode between them."* You'll trawl through deed upon deed and thank the pre-Land Registration Act 2002 world for giving you such complicated files. *"None are as straightforward as your city-centre commercial conveyance – they're all far more interesting."*

A litigation seat may also throw up obscure issues. Research into compensation schemes for asbestosis sufferers goes hand in hand with *"thoroughly random"* assignments relating to everything from mink farming to Cornwall's mundic walls. Preparing documents – aka bundling – advising clients, drafting letters of claim and statements of case, and appearing before district judges are all part of the role in litigation. The office offers the full range of seats, and if you're still not satisfied, then client Mersey Docks is happy to take seconded trainees for a brew of corporate, property and employment. *"I wished I'd done it,"* grumbled one stay-at-home.

## happy mondays to fridays

Litigation in Manchester covers a multitude of different things and at times you may feel you've been seconded onto the set of The Sweeney. You and the office's fraud expert get to raid properties screaming: *"If you weren't who you are I'd kick your arse up to your shoulder blades."* *"Everything except the last bit is true,"* our source soberly corrected us. *"It's a lot like detective work."* A property seat may lack the same thrill of the chase, but one trainee was quick to defend it from the brat pack over in corporate. *"People over-glamorise corporate and see commercial property as its poorer cousin – it's just not true."* While not as hectic a seat as in Liverpool, *"the training in the department is great – people invest in your career and show you a bit of enthusiasm. It can be a thrill when*

*you begin to fully understand how large conveyances work."* Manchester offers all seats bar private client and family at the moment.

The legal hub of the Lakes and Borders, Preston is home to Brabners' most northerly office. Lying just off the Georgian Winckley Square (*"lovely name that – like wrinkly with a lisp"*) the firm occupies a building with interiors *"slightly resembling a bomb site."* Needless to say such disrepair is temporary. *"We're being refurbished,"* a trainee assured us. *"Brabners is challenging to be one of the big firms, so we need to look the part."* On the drawing board, the plans look *"fantastic – what you'd expect from DLA or Pinsents... much needed if you want to attract bigger clients."* For now, clients include the landed gentry of the far North West and trainees' work experiences reflect this. In a property seat in Preston, they are likely to encounter their share of wayleaves and easements for the wealthy farmers of Cumbria (definitely more Ralphs than Teds). Trainees get their own files, even if it is just *"acting on a small case for a bank putting charges over a borrower's property."* At the same time they will be assisting on bigger projects for developers and *"dealing with the relevant local authority, which can get quite complex sometimes."* Lest we leave you thinking the property team deals only with farmland, we should point out that there is also a lawyer specialising in brownfield redevelopments.

## gagging for it

The Liverpool office occupies one of your *"typical Liverpool buildings."* Relatively good on the outside and unremarkable on the inside. Suffice to say the interiors were pronounced as *"not cluttered"* and finished in a *"nasty yellow-patterned scheme."* Travel eastward to Barbners in Manchester and you'll enter *"the warren."* *"There's no open plan, just two floors of five or six boardrooms with offices all around and a warren of walkways."* (Sounds like Strangeways to us.) A move is sorely needed: *"We want to consolidate our new ID but from the outside and on the inside the office is too old school."* The good news is that both Liverpool and Manchester staff can look forward to new digs by 2007. Of the ten September 2005 qualifiers only five chose to stay on, in part because very specific preferences could not be satisfied by more general job offers to some of the others.

Better marks for Brabners' social calendar which amounts to a *"very unpretentious"* schedule of football matches and Friday night trainee marches to the local for a *"gossip-fest and shots."* The Merseyside Trainee Solicitor Group (MTSG) and other professional groups (*"mostly accountants and construction bods"*) keep the Liverpudlian trainees entertained. Since their town became a city, the Preston staff have been able to enjoy Hartley's Wine Bar and the Vodoo Lounge. *"Preston's not Manchester or Liverpool,"* one keen geographer acknowledged, *"but it's up and coming."* Over in Manchester, Piccolino's remains the main hang. Here Corrie *"stars"* are to be spotted hobnobbing with the likes of Rio Ferndinand. *"I could smell the money,"* said one source without a trace of disdain. You may even get a gander at pop Svengali Tony Wilson.

It sounds as if Brabners' Christmas celebrations are enough to twist most melons: simply substitute *'partner'* for *'celebrity'* and you have the perfect party entertainment. *"I'm a Partner, Get Me Out of Here!"* included *"office-based rather than jungle-based challenges."* Instead of munching fish eyes and dung beetles, senior partners instead got into a Paul Burrell flap about flat-pack furniture assembly. After a royal *"leg-pulling,"* the undefeated partners were then subjected to heats of *"skivvy duties."* For added authenticity, *"someone dressed up as a kangaroo and jumped all over the partners,"* and another anon slipped into a gorilla costume to cause more mayhem. Plans for this year's monster raving loony Operation Xmas may begin with an invasion of Brabners' neighbour, Liverpool's Town Hall. *"It's all hush-hush, so don't tell."* We won't. Gagging order, schmagging order...

## and finally...

With Brabners Chaffe Street its definitely a case of WYSIWYG and with post-merger consolidation the name of the game for the foreseeable future, there's every chance that what you see now is what you'll get when you start your training in 2008. Definitely one for the spirited applicant.

# Brachers

## the facts

**Location:** Maidstone, London
**Number of partners/assistants:** 21/28
**Total number of trainees:** 8
**Seats:** 4x6 months
**Alternative seats:** Occasionally Lille

One of Kent's finest, Brachers is a broad-based regional firm with clients of all shapes and sizes from the NHS to hop-growing farmers.

## in good healthcare

Brachers has a number of strings to its bow but one of the most notable is its superior healthcare team. The team is a major pull for trainees and clients alike: the firm's coveted place on the NHS Litigation Authority legal panel ensures it a steady flow of clinical negligence cases. Broader clinical and policy advice is also sought by around 30 NHS trusts and primary care trusts, all looking for wise counsel on data protection, pensions and other problematic areas. The clin neg team is beloved by trainees, most of whom are more than eager to spend six months there. *"It's a lovely team,"* explained one. *"Everyone pitches in to give you work, so long as task requests are okayed by your supervisor."* Trainees prefer this system because it leads to variety in a department in which cases can go on for years... if they ever make it to court. Trainees soon learn that, just as in most areas of litigation, the main aim is *"to go for settlement."* Working on a *"patchwork quilt"* of files, you eventually build up a full sense of how litigation runs from start to finish. The trainee's job takes in *"anything from letters of claim and instructing experts through to settling cases and negotiation costs."*

As well as a dose of clin neg, trainees get experience of the employers' liability claims that filter through from NHS trusts. So, if someone falls over and stubs a toe on a dialysis machine, it'll come their way. Lately trainees were mobilised for research tasks, *"as the NHSLA recently got quite keen on the reporting done for all their cases."* All in all, there's *"not much minion-work"* in clin neg; *"the nightmare stories of filing and photocopying forever aren't here. We've got helpful secretaries who don't mind working for a trainee."*

## my family and other animals

If clin neg gets trainees thinking nationally about clients, then the family, private client, property and agricultural affairs departments are the most Kentish aspects of the firm. The client base includes a number of major agricultural concerns and families with deep roots in the South East. You'd probably be surprised at the different things farmers get up to beyond milking cows and driving tractors. Before your imagination runs away with you, what we mean is the diverse purposes to which their land is used. Last year, lawyers advised on the reorganisation of a family farming company. This involved advice concerning the directors' pension funds, the transfer of leasehold and freehold property to a family member who wanted to establish a new farm, and advice on the tax implications of the eventual sale of land worth millions of pounds, if redeveloped. In another deal, lawyers sold a large former dairy farm for £3.4 million, including making provision for employees, dealing with occupied cottages and disposing of milking equipment, a herd of cows and the EC milk quota that was attached to the land.

The family team deals with all manner of people, and when it is rushed off its feet with divorces and public law child cases, trainees are delegated tasks including drafting divorce petitions and letters to the other side. The seat can sometimes turn into a festival of bundling, however, with some of our sources recalling seemingly never-ending case management duties. Intriguingly, the family team also handles RSPCA criminal prosecutions. A rarity, animal welfare law gives trainees *"a lot of joint responsibility on files... You are involved in everything to do with the animals; you're not just asked to do little bits of work and then never discover the big picture, you are central to cases."* The prosecution work takes trainees to the magistrates' court – and the Crown Court for appeals – but even when in the office they are less likely to be spending time loading the printer and more likely to be rifling through case law concerning *"starved horses, mistreated kittens and beaten dogs." "It can be traumatic,"* confided one source, *"but I've learnt one thing in my time here – people take their animals seriously."*

Perhaps some take their animals a tad too seriously: *"There are no drowned kittens in the private client team, but there is a Jack Russell!"* Pardon? *"Has no one told you about the Jack Russell? The head of department brings his dog to work – she, Holly, is kind of the firm dog."* The pet-friendly private client team is certainly trainee friendly: awaiting new recruits is a *"drafting-heavy"* six months of wills and trusts in which they learn a heck of a lot. One source who had loved their time in the seat told us: *"It's fun, technical, challenging, interesting"* – and it's got the dog! *"Yes, the dog helps out on cases, provides entertainment and is an all-round muse."* And just in case you thought tax law couldn't be exciting, the firm recently ended up in the House of Lords fending off the Inland Revenue in a landmark capital gains tax case.

## tales from the underground

Kentish does not have to mean provincial. The property team is busy trawling through deeds and harassing the land registry over water easements affecting the new Channel Tunnel Rail Link in an attempt to negotiate a global easement on behalf of Union Rail. Such big commercial clients provide a good contrast to the residential conveyancing that can end up as the foundation of a trainee's own caseload, even in a first seat. Thankfully, "*you're never thrown in at the deep end*" if you do run files solo. "*It's always just a straightforward conveyance or drafting a few small leases for one of the commercial clients.*" The emergency cord is always close at hand by way of supervisors or other friendly fee earners ready to help out "*if you hit a problem.*"

Major client Eurotunnel relies on Brachers for employment advice, and puppy lovers and sniffle experts Kimberley-Clark also instruct the employment lawyers, along with the National Gallery, First Assist and endless NHS bodies. The Maidstone employment seat covers everything from beer-and-sandwiches trade union disputes through maternity rights to race, sex and disability discrimination claims. The seat introduces trainees to both claimant and defendant work.

Though it has a smaller office in London, Maidstone is the firm's principal location. Here it is spread across two sites – Medway House is an old Victorian building with a flower-filled courtyard and Sommerfield House is a lovely Kentish stone building. Whichever they work in, trainees either get their own office ("*it can be a bit boring on your own though*") or they bunk-up with a fellow trainee.

"*Everyone is so friendly*" that the office can feel like a home away from home – especially if you rent the cottage located in its grounds. Last year our sources put on their best estate agent voices to tell us the cottage was "*a great starter place.*" This year their descriptions took on a decidedly gothic tone: "*Ah, the dreaded cottage – I think they've sorted the damp out now.*" The property is in fact "*a listed toll booth keeper's cottage,*" in which two first-years get to set their alarm clocks to snooze as their second-year comrades sit in traffic on the way to work. Another architectural oddity is the firm's very own bunker, a remnant from WWII that was inherited from the Royal Observer Corps. It is suitable only for storing deeds, the local fire brigade's training

equipment and a ghost (apparently). In the event of nuclear war the RAF get the bunker back (and presumably the ghost too). Some firms offer super-annuation plans, gym memberships and even company cars – how many can offer survival after Armageddon?

Another rather unusual thing for the southern Home Counties is Brachers' affiliation with a law firm in the French town of Lille. This has evolved into an exchange programme that sometimes brings a young French lawyer over to spend time with the Brits and sometimes sees a trainee popping over the channel for three months. Another important association for trainees is Brachers' membership of Law South, a group of firms which pools its resources for training purposes. It all points to a firm that can see further than the county borders.

## shaken not stirred

All this makes the Maidstone HQ sound much more exciting than Brachers' London branch on New Fetter Lane, which only has a Marks & Spencer behind it. An employment seat is currently available in the capital though frankly our sources were more interested in the firm's Maidstone operations. So what is the appeal of Maidstone? At first we were told it is "*a culture shock you quickly acclimatise to,*" but quickly learned of a welcoming, if not rug-cutting, social scene. "*Trainees get a budget to spend on going out*" and last year it bought them a trip to the bright lights of Leicester Square. Every year there are firm-wide parties in the summer and at Christmas, the last of which had a James Bond theme with all the trimmings. Amongst the bow-tied Bonds and sparkly gowned Moneypennies, things took a decidedly Austin Powers turn when the "*male partners turned up dressed as women.*" "*One partner came to the party as Jaws' girlfriend – the one with pigtails.*" Bizarre!

Perhaps unable to contemplate a Christmas without a Brachers party, two of the three qualifiers chose to stay with the firm in September 2005.

## and finally...

Brachers' offers a charmingly quirky, yet great-quality training contract. From its four-legged friends to its plc clients, if you can't find something that's right up your street we'd be very surprised.

# Bristows

### the facts

**Location:** London
**Number of partners/assistants:** 29/61
**Total number of trainees:** 14
**Seats:** 3 or 6 months long
**Alternative seats:** Secondments
**Extras:** Language training

With over 160 years' experience at the forefront of intellectual property law, Bristows has litigated over patents since before patent legislation was even invented.

### science in action

Bristows' clients include the biggest names in pharmaceuticals, IT and telecommunications, consumer products and television; the current trainee crop includes biochemists, microbiologists, natural and physical scientists, and engineers. A happy coincidence? We suspect not. With stellar patent litigation, life sciences and commercial IP work under the microscope, "*the nature of the work encourages scientists to apply.*" Bristows' provides the perfect solution to the quandary: "*I didn't want to be a research scientist in a lab, but I didn't want the knowledge to go away.*"

The advantage to Bristows of recruiting those who have thus far viewed life through the scratched lenses of Perspex protective goggles is clear. When the matters involve heavy-duty patent documents and complex expert evidence, "*there is a benefit to having people who can readily understand what is thrown at them,*" and relevant academic training "*gives you a head start in terms of interpreting things.*" We should stress that "*they aren't looking for every lawyer to have a science background*" and in departments such as corporate and property it makes little difference.

Illustrating the extent of the firm's specialist focus, a full six months in IP litigation is "*compulsory for all.*" Once this is dispatched, a system of three-month seats exposes trainees to many other areas of practice, usually including a spell in the 'commercial' team dealing with non-contentious IP topics. The trainees we spoke to had encountered up to seven different seats and had views on this. "*Originally three-month seats were meant to be an occasional thing and it has gone too much one way,*" thought one; for another the advantage of the current system was obvious – "*You can say that I really know the firm. There is only one department I haven't been in!*" But the inevitable problem that "*you are just getting into something and it is time to pack your bags*" has prompted a shift "*back to a more traditional six-month system,*" and we heard rumours of a move to make property and corporate each compulsory for six months. What is absolutely certain is that IP is the clear favourite. "*It just depends whether people prefer the contentious or non-contentious stuff.*"

### avoiding spills

Contentious IP includes trademark, copyright and design litigation, but it is the celebrated patent litigation that really gets heads spinning. In this sphere the firm has recently acted for Cooper Cameron Corporation (providers of systems and project management to the oil and gas industry) in proceedings relating to the infringement of its patents for complex underwater valves, known in the vernacular as 'horizontal Christmas trees.' It has also brought patent infringement proceedings against Procter & Gamble in relation to their Easy Ups training pants. Little wonder Bristows' client Kimberley-Clark was getting its knickers in a twist – in the UK alone sales of Easy Ups are estimated to be worth around £50 million. If you've got your head round that, you might want to grapple with the really complex case being handled for Affymetrix, the multimillion-dollar name behind GeneChip microarrays and other systems used in genomics and human health research.

We suspect that new recruits across the country relate to the idea of being "*only a trainee,*" but at Bristows standing on the bottom rung of the legal ladder can equally place you at the top of a specific field of knowledge. "*You can joke that a PhD is not a novelty at Bristows,*" but while "*the partners may have done a PhD ten years ago,*" it is accepted that "*they will bow to the fact that the trainees may know more about it.*" As a result, "*everyone is quietly confident in everyone's ability,*" regardless of their seniority, and there is an acknowledgement that "*people might be able to contribute more than photocopying or bundling.*" Describing their roles in various matters, one trainee said: "*I was looking at it with a scientific eye to make sure the right language was being used in relation to the science.*" Another had prepared a briefing for colleagues on the science involved in a new case. Bless them, our sources were keen to stay modest, with one assuring us: "*We are not working above our station!*" Indeed not, with powerful bodies and volatile matters in the Bristows flask, trainees are rarely put in charge of the bunsen burner for very long and readily admitted that "*if there is a load of bundling to be done, the secretaries will be doing some of it but so will the trainee.*" Equally, they may find themselves "*doing disclosure on hundreds and hundreds of documents.*" Away from the large cases "*you do actually get reasonable responsibility*" – attending client meetings, case management conferences and court. You might even get to try your hand at minor advocacy.

## good for you

A non-contentious IP seat brings exposure to "*anything and everything*" for clients including the BBC, British American Tobacco, Tetley and Freeview. Bristows has advised Diageo (the drinks giant that includes Smirnoff, Guinness and Baileys among its many brands) on matters ranging from the contracting of leading model Lisa Snowdon in relation to a Guinness advertising campaign to a new range of Johnnie Walker clothing and the manufacture and supply of widgets. In this seat, you will be "*drafting small matters and doing pieces of research;*" alas, there can also be "*quite a lot of proof-reading.*" In the small trade mark team trainees are involved throughout, from "*procedural filing to drafting oppositions to why another person's trade mark shouldn't be granted.*"

Away from IP, there are seats in commercial litigation, competition, employment, corporate and property. "*People generally dread corporate,*" we were told. Perhaps it is because "*this is often where the later nights come in;*" however, we suspect it is more a case that "*it is not what people came here for.*" At least working for "*a nice bunch of people*" makes the experience more pleasant, though the location of the department in a different building means "*it does seem a bit separate.*" We hear that efforts are made to keep everyone as connected as possible and "*there is a lot of cross-referral, a lot of liaison*" and "*the client base is similar – technologically based and offshoots of labs.*"

Of property, too, we heard how "*people are sometimes a little apprehensive,*" but soon discover that "*it is a really good, fun seat because you get to run your own files.*" As well as assisting on the team's commercial transactions, trainees also take the reins on residential conveyancing for partners and members of staff. Trainees spoke about how much they enjoyed "*seeing a transaction through from start to finish and handling it yourself,*" so much so that one committed scientist ventured: "*It has made me much more open minded about what I want to qualify into.*" Another popular way to spend a seat is with the in-house legal department of a key client. Those we spoke to who had been away relished the opportunity to "*see through the looking glass*" and learn how to "*build commercial awareness.*" Back in the office, trainees' preparation for the world of work is aided by end-of-seat appraisals and supervisors who are "*very keen to explain things.*" Certainly our sources appreciated that "*feedback is always very constructive and you feel quite valued.*"

## pub-lic debate

"*Charming would be the word*" to describe the four Georgian premises that Bristows occupies on Lincoln's Inn Fields near the Royal Courts of Justice. "*You could say there is a traditional feel,*" one trainee conceded of both the firm's residence and its persona. We're told "*an inherent conservatism*" translates into a formal dress code and an intense focus on professionalism. While "*it is certainly not traditional in terms of partners being superior,*" we did learn that "*everyone respects the partners as being experts.*" Trainees emphasised that the firm's focus was "*the more hard academic patent side of things, not the glitzy things*" and perhaps this explains the "*productive, academic environment.*" Interestingly, we heard that "*it is not like a library, but it is a bit like tutorials.*" Consequently, "*somebody who sat with a book and only interacted with the book*" might struggle to survive because "*chipping in*" and pooling knowledge is the norm.

Amazingly, in this "*very focused and very driven*" environment, "*no one would bat an eyelid if you came in at 9.15am and left at 6pm, as long as you weren't running away from someone who really needs help.*" More often than not "*the building is emptying out by 6.30pm,*" after which, on certain nights of the week, "*trainees can normally be found in the pub.*" The trouble is deciding on which one to visit. While "*The Square Pig attracts some custom,*" we also hear that "*The Seven Stars is good – the landlady is a bit mental and there is a cat.*" There are some who say: "*Let's go to All Bar One!*" and others who respond: "*No let's not!*" Happily the firm's sporting endeavours prompt less debate – there is a "*no-skills-required*" approach to football, netball and cricket matches and they usually end up in the pub. Of course, we have no idea which one. As ever, the highlight on Bristows' calendar is its black-tie dinner dance in March, and for the bulk of the September 2005 qualifiers there will be plenty more of these to come. Six of the eight stayed on with the firm, three of them qualifying into IP litigation.

## and finally...

An annual intake of brilliant minds helps Bristows maintain its position at the cutting edge of IP litigation... and they don't go amiss in other departments either!

# Browne Jacobson LLP

## the facts

**Location:** Nottingham, Birmingham, London
**Number of partners/assistants:** 57/108
**Total number of trainees:** 20
**Seats:** 4x6 months
**Alternative seats:** None
**Extras:** Pro bono – CAB, ProHelp, Prince's Trust, Criminal Injuries Compensation Scheme

Something is happening at Midlands premier league litigation firm Browne Jacobson. Its latest annual profit figures reveal a 37% jump based on a 12% turnover increase to a sturdy £27 million.

## plaint by numbers

Browne Jacobson is a highly colour-sensitive firm, starting with its name and moving on to its various teams. Trainees have the chance to visit all four business groups: property, business services, business and professional risk (BPR) and insurance and public risk (IPR). The first two are transactional, the second two contentious. While BPR remains "*colourless,*" IPR is a rainbow of teams. Medical negligence is defended by the purple team, public authority work is conducted by the red team, straightforward RTAs and slips and trips are tackled in gold, and environmental cases are appropriately dealt with by the green team. The palette then extends to indigo, violet and other obscure shades. Said one trainee: "*I can always put a name to someone, but I can't always put a nuance to them!*"

With a large proportion of all revenue generated by litigation, it should come as no surprise that if you train here you'll become fully inducted into the dark arts of dispute resolution. This is not to say that there isn't ample transactional and advisory work for trainees to try. Judging by the experiences of those we interviewed, it's perfectly possible to get an even balance of contentious and non-contentious work in your training. The seats available in the main Nottingham office include commercial litigation, corporate, property, employment, construction and insolvency, as well as all the kaleidoscope of choice offered by the rainbow warriors in BPR and IPR. Sometimes you can create your own seat if you put forward a good enough argument and it makes business sense. By way of example, "*split seats like construction/commercial litigation have been approved before.*" Trainees say the firm "*really tries to accommodate you if you've already done your mandatory contentious and non-contentious seats.*"

At this firm the hands-on training is exemplary. "*You're one of only ten trainees [per year] so you're bound to get your own files. You definitely won't be doing just grunt work.*" Trainees "*mostly sit with partners,*" either in their room or open plan. "*They will always conference you in on calls, so you're always involved in a negotiation by hearing it.*" "*Ideal for contextualising your small piece on a big case,*" listening to a partner in action is sometimes as valuable as the answers to the direct questions you can ask at any time. "*There is no need for everything you do to be billable,*" we were assured.

## look away now!

One of the 12 firms on the NHS Litigation Authority panel, and one of the best clinical negligence practices in the country, Browne Jacobson receives a steady flow of defence work on cases involving medical foul-ups. May we recommend a strict TV diet of *Casualty* and *CSI* for a few weeks before starting this seat because as one strong-stomached source pointed out, interviews with doctors and nurses can often have "*plenty of gore.*" We're talking about "*eye injuries, horrid stuff. They went into gross detail – it was great!*" As well as an ability to hang on to your breakfast, "*you have to be quite confident to work in the department.*" Trainees become closely involved in large cases rather than hopping "*here, there and everywhere like elsewhere in the firm.*" Their role is to conduct background research, draft witness statements and attend conferences with counsel, all of it leading up to the trial date. The complexities of the cases are explained by the partners they work for, and these individuals are praised for being "*willing to take the time to go through everything.*" Other work stems from the NHS relationship: acting for a consortium of five NHS trusts, lawyers have been assembling the evidence in the public inquiry following the guilty verdicts returned against consultant psychiatrists Kerr and Haslam, who had sexually assaulted a string of female patients.

Another highly regarded department, environment and regulatory provides a mix of health and safety, corporate manslaughter and countryside authorities' panel work. Prosecutions for the Countryside Council of Wales and English Nature will take you to the magistrates' court where you might witness a downcast dry-stone wall vandal or sheep defacer (remember Cambrian sheep graffiti artists?) receiving their dues. Environmental and regulatory law is introduced to you by the seat's departing trainee, who will have prepared a helpful pack consisting of a department Who's Who and client list. "*It even had cases to look at and recommended books – it was wonderful,*" a source effused. The environmental experts have taken on some really interesting work lately. For example, advising the Countryside Council for Wales on its concerns over a proposal by the Port of Mostyn to extend the harbour area in the Dee Estuary. Expansion will allow the shipping of aircraft wings (the UK's contribution to the European Airbus project), but there are major concerns because the Dee Estuary is an important area for birdlife and grey seals. The

Department for Transport will most likely hold a public inquiry and Browne Jacobson lawyers will most likely be there.

Perhaps you recall news stories about investigations into abuse in children's homes. These lead not only to criminal prosecutions but also to civil claims against the local authorities charged with responsibility for the welfare of the victims. Browne Jacobson represents the local authorities and their insurance companies in such cases. "*The topic is not nice,*" one trainee confirmed, "*so you deal with it in a pragmatic way. The court sets out values and sees how much the person is due... It is very specialised work and we are one of the leaders in the field; the insurers will only go to a few firms.*" One of the trainee's main jobs is to read through social services files and pull out all the relevant information. The separate police investigation also kicks up a stack of records. The trainee prepares a case summary and manages the vast amount of collated documentation. And when we say vast, a final agreed court bundle can end up with thousands of documents in it, especially on a large case such as recent litigation involving 20 claimants who were residents in various South Wales children's homes in the 1980s.

## in the bag

If you think it's all public sector work here at Browne Jacobson then think again. When Arla Foods needed character licensing agreements for Postman Pat, Scooby Doo and Bob the Builder, the firm's IP lawyers fixed it. The corporate group has a growing profile in private equity and on deals for Midlands-based owner-managed businesses. Work has even come from European clients such as Louis Vuitton and Christian Dior. One of the firm's top deals last year was the acquisition of Charcol, the UK's leading mortgage broker, by Advantage Capital. Over in the property team they're also going great guns: clients here include Wilkinson hardware (for which it worked on 20 new stores), East Midlands Development Agency, Derby City Council, Fendi, Kenzo and Nottingham Forest FC.

And what of the two smaller offices – Birmingham and London? Well, the six-year-old Brum office currently offers seats in corporate, employment, medical negligence, plus blue-team RTAs and insurance liability. Property and construction seats will be coming soon. The office has reached critical mass and "*they're now recruiting for trainees in Birmingham.*" One Nottingham trainee had been only too happy to be seconded to Birmingham for corporate work. The seat had involved "*typical trainee stuff... disclosure, board minutes, meetings – shadowing on sales and purchasing mainly.*" To stoke the engine in Brum, trainees are encouraged to participate in networking and marketing activities: "*Because Browne Jacobson is quite new to the city, it's fun being part of the growth,*" our source concluded. Apparently, "*our aim is to go from being one of the best in the East Midlands to having a presence across the Midlands.*" Fortune is smiling on this design, and so is Birmingham City Council on whose revamped legal panel the firm now sits.

Trainees tell us the London office is simmering gently: "*It's tough down there,*" one admitted. Aware that a London outpost is a good client-gatherer for the Midlands offices, the location is viewed as important, particularly for the French inward investment practice that has been carefully nurtured. Six-month secondments are available to London, mostly for professional indemnity litigation spiced up with assistance to other teams, both transactional and contentious. As the trainee in London, "*you're the person all the lower-level work comes to.*" This means you get to open and run your own files and conduct "*any kind of small hearing before masters... you're in court all the time here.*"

## savage behaviour

So who would fit in at this firm? Someone without too many airs and graces: "*We have a laugh and there's nothing pretentious about us.*" A good first degree is expected (of course), but a good academic record won't suffice "*if you can't speak up for yourself.*" To clarify, "*that's not loud and lairy, but quietly*" *confident with who you are."* In 2005, eight of the ten qualifiers chose to stay with the firm.

Although *"very active,"* the firm's social scene is *"thankfully not forced down your throat,"* and so *"it's not looked down on if you don't turn up to the intra-firm things."* The sports and social committee organises everything from an It's a Knockout-style day out to a much-anticipated pub crawl/treasure hunt and drinks parties in Nottingham Castle. The popular pub next to the office is called The Royal Children but everyone at the firm just calls it The Kids.

Browne Jacobson has an interesting article on its website warning clients of the potential employment law dangers that lie in wait at the office Christmas party. For companies intent on replicating scenes from Alex Gilmore's *Fish Sunday Thinking*, the article has plenty of advice, including the simple act of appointing a master of revels to umpire proceedings. Is such a position filled at the firm's own Christmas bash? *"No, we just have partners in drag!"* The *Student Guide* has diagnosed an epidemic of partner cross-dressing at several firms this year, regional firms suffering most acutely from bouts of Lily Savageitis. *"They're in drag most years,"* sighed one source. As cringeworthy as it sounds, we are pleased to report that the fake boobs and fishnets are all part of the partners' efforts to entertain the troops with skits. This is in stark contrast with the Christmas distractions at some other firms, where it is the trainees who are tarred, feathered and pushed onto the stage in the name of pantomime. *"They entertain us for the hard work we've put in during the year,"* our sources reported.

## and finally...

Browne Jacobson can offer top-grade litigation training in a rainbow of different hues plus very decent commercial work for an increasingly impressive national clientele. This could be the Midlands training you're looking for... especially if you fancy being privy to saving a few seals along the way.

# BTMK LLP

## the facts

**Location:** Southend-on-Sea, Chelmsford
**Number of partners/assistants:** 15/15
**Total number of trainees:** 6
**Seats:** varying in length
**Alternative seats:** None

Leading Essex firm TMK cast a roving eye over commercial work and ended up in a merger with a local commercial/general practice Bates Travell. We decided to have a look-see at what this means for trainees.

## start spreading the news

*"Crime and family will always be the centre of the firm and both are based on publicly funded cases,"* one source surmised. Nonetheless, Southend's finest is planning to drop some legally aided work in an attempt to move into largely uncharted waters. The closure of its Basildon branch and the removal of its Chelmsford satellite to newer, *"swankier"* premises, suggested a firm consolidating resources for a regional push. And then we learned of TMK's merger. *"You haven't heard?"* reproached one trainee: *"It's been in all the local papers. Why didn't you know?"* The merger with Southend's Bates Travell has not only put the B in BTMK, but also spurred the firm on in its campaign for *"domination of Essex and East Anglia."*

## get shirty

BTMK has a fairly idiosyncratic seat system. In the first year you'll spend either four months in each of three seats, or three months in each of four. The second year is then a single seat long so *"you can guide yourself nicely into where you want to qualify."* On offer to trainees are seats in crime, family and civil litigation (though the merger may bring a commercial option for future trainees). As for location, everyone spends at least a seat in Chelmsford, two trainees being accommodated in

# the true picture

either crime or family seats at each rotation.

Clients range from those in cuffs down the local nick to those in cuff-links running local businesses. As a trainee you'll encounter clients on the phone and face-to-face straight away; our sources described being "*dropped right in*" in their first week. BTMK tries to "*pace*" advocacy, so "*if you feel ready, they'll let you do it from day one. If not, they won't make you do anything you're not comfortable with.*" Trainees get to know the courts well; in civil matters often "*the cases are short and sweet and unopposed; it's just you and a judge. You get to know the inside of the county court pretty quickly, the judges and ushers get to know your face.*"

It is easy to identify ever-increasing freedom and responsibility in a BTMK traineeship. You are "*rarely stuck behind a photocopier – they only give you work to improve you.*" After a customary "*intensive training period*" at the start of your year-long fourth seat, "*you'll be able to cover the work of a fee earner and open new files.*" The support on offer in the first year is still there and "*you can always bounce problems or ideas off other fee earners.*" What lessen, however, are supervisor meetings, which go from fortnightly to monthly. Supervision becomes more "*ad hoc and rolling*" as the primed second-year trainee prepares for qualification.

## waylaid at wayland

Let's look more closely at the individual seats. Before you've even worked out where the kettle is in the crime department, you'll be down the mags' court taking instructions from clients. A trainee's mags' caseload includes "*committals to Crown, theft, driving offences, lower-end assaults – that sort of thing.*" On Crown Court files, they brief counsel and advise on sentencing and appeals. The BTMK life of crime is certainly a varied one: off to court on a bail variation in the morning, inside HMP Wayland to see an appealing (though possibly unappealing) client in the afternoon. "*Prison is not too bad,*" one source remarked, "*but only for a short stay!*" Maybe so, but a visit to Belmarsh, where terror suspects are interned, is "*fairly intimidating.*" "*At the first checkpoint they take your photo, at the second they take your prints, the third is the metal detector, on the fourth they let the dog have a sniff at you, and then there's just five and six to go and you're in.*" So what's the inside of inside like? "*I don't know – our client refused to speak to us and we had to go back through all six checkpoints with nothing.*"

In family seats, trainees get the chance to run a file or two solo, "*as long as it is not your first seat.*" Time in the office is spent drafting divorce proceedings and helping the lay client fill out a Form E, which is "*basically the document that divvies up the money.*" Trainees spend much of their time at court, sitting behind counsel and assisting one day, advocacy in the county court the next. When assisting a supervisor or barrister, trainees will concentrate on looking after the client, "*who often doesn't quite know what's going on. For this you need empathy and professionalism.*" When it comes to their own court appearances, trainees cut their teeth advocating at smaller, ex parte non-molestation hearings, which are usually "*quick and come in at the last minute.*"

The skills learned in family are most transferable to a seat in civil litigation, which turns out to be a hotchpotch of PI, employment and housing with the emphasis usually determined by trainees' desires. "*If you ask to do more employment they'll try and accommodate you,*" one source related. "*Fairly large*" contract disputes and larger personal injury claims may mean a temporary backseat for the trainee, but often supervisors will oversee the opening of a file and then hand it to a trainee, staying in the wings for advice. Even a first-year can run a case from beginning to end. Our sources stressed that in this seat there's a "*good chunk*" of housing. Typical cases are "*matters ranging from housing disputes to Asbo and nuisance defences; no full-blown contested trials, mainly applications for interim possession orders and possession order hearings.*"

## your starter for ten

BTMK sources unanimously declare: "*The training is superb!*" and it begins before you've even landed the contract. At interview a gladiatorial spelling bee sorts the weak from the strong contenders. "*I seem to remember having to spell 'amendment' and 'judgment' – bit of a cheeky one that, you'd think it had another E.*" If you make it through "*the red faces and giggles*" of the maths and current affairs test in the induction weeks, formal training moves into the realm of fortnightly supervision meetings. These involve a thorough discussion of the constituent parts of the Law Society's checklist of activities for your particular seat and also enable your supervisor to issue you with your first of many projects. These could be to produce a summary of, say, road traffic offences – "*like an idiot's guide which keeps you abreast of the law and can be used for clients when they phone up.*"

Trainees reported working a healthy 8.15am until 6.30pm day, and sometimes longer if they complete the Police Station Accreditation during a twelve-month crime seat and are signed up to the police station duty rota. Budding criminal lawyers should also beware of shrinking weekends – courts open on Saturdays now. Trainees say that if you put in the hours it will pay off: "*You'll get what you want if you show your enthusiasm.*" Two out of four trainees managed to do just that this year, going into the crime and family departments respectively.

## bingoing mad

The laws of HR dictate that a healthy office social life is the perfect bonding mechanism. At BTMK you're also quids in on the deal. The social committee hires a charabanc to take staff to Romford dog track and Newmarket races; "*someone won £200!*" revealed one green-eyed source. Trips to France and barbecues are also on the cards, as are drinks evenings in local pubs when partners' credit cards end up behind the bar. "*The majority of the fee earners are not originally from the area and have moved here for the job, which means they're always up for a*

*drink,*" we heard. Chelmsford is uniformly ignored by trainees ("*the night life isn't great there*"), who far prefer the bright lights of Southend: "*You've got all the bars and clubs you want there.*"

The Christmas party is "*always in the same place – the Ancora restaurant in one of the towns outside Southend.*" An aperitif or two is followed by "*a blow-out, sit-down dinner.*" At this point, trainees take centre stage for a spot of singing, miming "*and taking the piss out of partners.*" "*We played pop songs and people had to guess which song matched which partner. We called it partner bingo.*"

## and finally...

Every time we speak to BTMK trainees we encounter a committed bunch of young lawyers that exude a level of professionalism any magic circle firm would be proud of. But "*great training*" comes at a price – BTMK doesn't contribute a penny toward your LPC. Remember, too, that the firm "only recruits a few months in advance," so keep your eyes peeled.

# Burges Salmon LLP

## the facts

**Location:** Bristol
**Number of partners/assistants:** 62/171
**Total number of trainees:** 37
**Seats:** 6x4 months
**Alternative seats:** Secondments
**Extras:** Pro bono – Bristol University Law Clinic, Bristol Neurological Unit, Drug Addiction & Recovery Agency, Bristol & Avon Enterprise Agency

Burges Salmon is a law firm in the pink, and not just because of its trademark roseate stationery. Bristol born and bred it has the healthy flush of the countryside about it, yet nearly three-quarters of its work originates beyond the South West. Sure, the firm may blush at regular compliments and nomina-

# the true picture

tions for awards, but a 300% increase in turnover in the last decade hardly warrants such modesty. Sounds like a bed of roses...

## mainly mighty

The naturally wary will be looking for a catch. If there is one then we've not found it. Burges Salmon continues to live up to its reputation as a City law firm outside the Big Smoke, with a national and international client roster that includes EMI, Virgin, Ofgem, CompuServe, Reuters, Orange, Honda, Coca-Cola, BAE Systems, First Group, MoD and the Association of Train Operating Companies. Proving its Mighty Mouse ability to take on a scale and type of work seemingly beyond its reach, BS enjoyed an excellent year in 2004/5, with a 16% increase in turnover to over £42 million, instructions to advise on the sale of Jordan Formula One Racing, instructions from Argos on a landmark OFT competition case, and a call from the very foreign sounding Pfalz-flugzeugwerke Gmbh (PFW) to handle its acquisition of a substantial aerospace tooling manufacturer. And to mention just one more deal, First Group used the firm on a competitive tender bid for the GNER rail franchise, the largest in European rail history.

Although its 'City firm in the provinces' aspirations have a genuine basis, BS can't quite match the gargantuan clout of the big London firms. BS has less than 200 lawyers while the likes of Linklaters and A&O, for example, have over 800 in London alone. So although BS last year advised the MoD on a £2.5 billion military satellite PFI scheme, you won't regularly find it working the truly stratospheric deals. Let's just say even Mighty Mouse couldn't last ten rounds with the Incredible Hulk, though on the right day he could score a knockout in the third.

## fancy footwork

As any gardener knows, good soil and deep roots mean a healthy plant, and with BS such a prize specimen, it should come as no surprise that the South West's agribusiness is the traditional core of the firm. Trainees acknowledge that *"it's one of the reasons why the firm is here and it is still important."* The firm is retained by the National Trust and the Crown Estate and frequently acts on the most complex cases in the field. For example, lawyers are presently advising on litigation against the government in relation to environmental issues arising from the disposal of carcasses in the Foot and Mouth crisis. The firm's established client list includes *"farm tenants, farming co-operatives, clients anxious to keep the farm that's been in the family for generations, landed gentry and big corporations."* Those big corporations include Shell and P&O (both working to recover of possession of farmland to enable the development of a proposed deep-water freight terminal), as well as banks such as HSBC, which is involved in agricultural financing.

Though its feet are rooted in pasture, the firm's head and heart are corporate, yet trainees admit they'd noticed the trademark aroma of the farmyard even in their corporate seats. "*I did a lot of bread and milk work*" said one, referring to deals like the Milk Link joint venture, which created the second largest cheese producer in the UK, or the restructuring of Centaur Grain Limited. Bread, milk and cheese – sounds like the perfect late-night deal completion snack. Lest we give the impression that BS offers a straight choice between cows and corporations, we should stress that the firm has a genuinely broad practice and highly respected departments across the spectrum of private and commercial work. Our colleagues on *Chambers UK* rank BS lawyers in the top band of some 24 sections of their guide and they recognise the firm's significant strength in such diverse fields as transportation, environmental law, competition and employment. For any prospective trainee, this quality across the board has got to be a real pull.

## catch of the day

Everyone we spoke to enthused about the firm's trademark six by four-month seat system; many recognised that *"it's much more in our interest than the firm's. The firm basically makes a sacrifice for us."* Far from feeling that four months is too short, trainees believe *"it gives you the perfect amount of exposure to an area and broad experience."* They also point out the option to *"return to a seat you've enjoyed and really test it out."* In simple terms, three seats are compulsory: company/commercial, property, and a commercial litigation/CDC (commercial disputes and construction) seat. Trainees then choose between either employment and pensions or tax and trusts. Having ticked off these four, the fifth seat is a free choice, and the sixth and final seat is taken in the area in which the trainee hopes to qualify. In addition to the options within the office, client secondments are available to Babcock, Nirex and GMAC. And after qualification, more secondments are available to the MoD (no uniform required), Orange, Ofgem and US firm Thompson Hine.

In the past we've found that the fifth seat was used to test a preference for qualification, but trainees this year were evidently more decisive: *"I knew where I wanted to qualify after the first four, so took my fifth in a complimentary area to broaden my legal knowledge."* We spoke to trainees just before decision time for NQ jobs this year, but there was little or no tension in the air. Everyone seemed to have the feeling they were going to be kept on in the department of their choice, and in the event 16 of the 18 were. It all goes to support the oft-made suggestion that *"there's a clear route through to partnership at the firm and they recruit potential partners not bodies to be trainees."* As one source explained, the traditionally high retention rate *"takes the pressure off us so there's little competition between trainees."*

Resisting the temptation to open offices elsewhere, and sticking to the single-site policy, BS is perfectly happy to strut its national stuff from Bristol. Trainees told us: *"Our firm identity is cohesive and there are close links to the local community."* The firm's waterfront offices *"right in the middle of town"* really are home sweet home for the entire firm. Bristol is undoubtedly a fantastic city and every year trainees enthuse about the *"quality of life"* they enjoy in tandem with *"the best quality, City-level work."* When trainees tell of *"a ten-minute walk to work along the river, bacon sandwich in hand, and in for 9.15am,"* it's hard not to feel the lure. But as one trainee observed: *"You could go to any firm in Bristol, have quality of life and leave the office by 5.30pm. We definitely work harder here and we do longer hours than others in the city."*

## the muppet show

Trainees also confirm there is *"a slight but widespread conservative streak"* that makes them occasionally wish for some of the *"marketing aggression of other local firms like Osborne Clarke."* However, our sources weren't under any illusion that the grass is greener elsewhere, recognising that their firm is *"a fairly conservatively run place with the focus on sensible development."* What this also means though is *"there wasn't any dot.com flurry,"* nor any of the problems of international over expansion and over-reliance on the technology sector as was experienced by Osborne Clarke. The firm's policy of *"careful organic growth"* has paid off and it continues to grow at a steady pace. A recent recruitment drive has focused on luring three to four-year qualified lawyers away from their City jobs to the fresh air and good living of Bristol. The ads feature hotshot associates in open top cars and weekend surfers... and yes, the grass really is greener in a BS marketing campaign.

The typical BS trainee has a family or educational connection to the South West, though we suspect this is no longer as vital as it once was. The trainees we spoke to were quick to admit: *"We're outgoing,"* *"we've all got a certain natural confidence"* and *"you'd want to be friends with all these people if you met them outside work."* Between them there's a lot of *"banter"* (alright, one less articulate individual called it *"happy teasing"*) and we finished our interviews with a clear impression of a well-matched

# the true picture

group of intelligent and sparky people with the capacity to do most things well while not taking themselves too seriously. Last year's *"assault course charity fundraiser dressed as pigs"* is a good example. It stuck in the minds of some of our sources for a particular reason – *"seeing one female trainee dressed as Miss Piggy writhing in mud is a memory I will cherish."* Mud baths aside, the *"vibrant trainee social life"* is as full as can be handled. There are bags of sporting opportunities including sailing, football, climbing, mountain biking, cricket, hockey and netball (hands up who'd be surprised to learn that BS is *"the best at most sports in Bristol?"*) – and trainees are always out together, taking advantage of the city's many bars and pubs. Favourites? Well, *"there's the waterfront near the office... that's glass fronted bars to the left, more pubby places to the right... then there's Clifton, but also all the places in what we call the triangle..."* We get the picture. Organised events include departmental drinks and annual summer and Christmas bashes. *"The summer do was in a marquee with a bar and dodgems and human table football and a horrific spinning thing."* Horrific? *"Yes, well, it was after six pints."*

## and finally...

If you're top of the class and want a training to match, then Burges Salmon will give you breadth of experience and high-quality work, all while enjoying the benefits of a Bristol lifestyle. But here's two things to think about: getting a training contract will be no mean feat as your competitors will also be the best of the best, and if you do make it in the door you'll have to work rather hard.

# Capsticks

## the facts

**Location:** London
**Number of partners/assistants:** 29/48
**Total number of trainees:** 9
**Seats:** 6x4 months
**Alternative seats:** Secondments
**Extras:** Pro bono – Putney Law Centre

Capsticks is a niche firm targeting the health sector. But don't assume every day in the office will be as clinical as an episode of ER because the range of services on offer has spread faster than MRSA.

## clinical impression

In 1980 a clinical negligence lawyer called Brian Capstick started in practice with a fellow specialist. Over the course of the following decade Mr Capstick turned his firm into one of the most respected names in the field and won the NHS as its main client. The NHS is still the firm's lifeblood today, despite the client roster now also including several private sector health organisations (BUPA among them). As well as the central NHS Litigation Authority, the firm acts for around 200 NHS trusts and primary healthcare trusts.

Clinical law still accounts for over 50% of the firm's work, whether defending individual claims from patients concerning allegations of flawed medical treatment, or providing policy and other advice designed to circumvent litigation. Life being what it is, problems arise during treatment and, sadly, complications in childbirth are far from uncommon. Recent medical malpractice claims include the case of a mother who alleged that a London NHS trust failed to give proper information on the risks of amniocentesis during the pregnancy of her severely disabled son, and a case against Epsom & St Helier NHS Trust brought by a patient who claimed she was inadequately counselled before spinal surgery. Capsticks successfully defended

# the true picture

both cases. Trainees acknowledge that patients' stories can sometimes be upsetting, but they presumably factor this into their decision to come to the firm. One typical trainee told us: "*I knew I wanted to do clinical negligence work and that's usually what people coming here think it's all about.*"

Trainees sit with a supervisor and become heavily involved in a small number of their cases, perhaps drafting instructions to counsel or letters of instruction to experts. "*You have to get a handle on the medical side of things and you'll be looking at medical records to see what happened and when. From that you'll prepare a chronology.*" Although most cases settle, one of the trainees we spoke to had been lucky enough to go to a trial and had conducted a number of small applications before masters in the High Court. This is when you learn that it is vital to "*know your case inside out and be completely prepared.*"

## professional distance

On the clinical advisory side, lawyers handle a multitude of topics from child protection and consent to treatment cases through to mental health issues, judicial reviews and hospital closures. A flurry of queries has arisen under the Data Protection Act and the new Freedom of Information Act (many relating to patient records), while on the mental health side there are interesting cases concerning Mental Health Review Tribunals. In one such case, the firm successfully represented Mersey Care NHS Trust when it asked the High Court to overturn a decision to make moors murderer Ian Brady's tribunal hearing public. You may also be aware of cases in which parents have challenged a hospital's decision to not resuscitate their gravely ill baby. Again, these cases can be emotionally demanding, although as one trainee rightly pointed out: "*Reading about it on paper is different to being there and experiencing it first hand – you are much more distant. Our clients are the hospital trusts, and the people we deal with, well, it's their job to deal with these cases as rational professionals.*"

## upLIFTing experiences

The NHS is Europe's largest employer and it wrestles with the same issues as any private sector employer. As such, Capsticks' employment team handles the standard sex and race discrimination claims, dismissals and transfer obligations, and from time to time it also has to tackle some very large-scale cases. On behalf of North Cumbria Acute NHS Trust, the firm recently settled an equal pay claim initiated eight years ago by 1,500 female employees. When trainees told us of their experiences in the employment department they sounded identical to those of a trainee in any firm acting for plc clients. One added: "*It's nice to work with clients who know what they are doing. You call up a director of HR in an NHS Trust and you both know what you are talking about. Everyone you are dealing with is a professional; they are always available and it's their job to help you. It's a reciprocal relationship and it works.*"

The NHS owns a massive portfolio of property and it buys and sells land and buildings just like any other large landowner. "*My year and the people in the years above all wanted to do clinical negligence seats and to go into a department like property was 'Oh god, I've just got to get through it'. But the people who work there are incredibly bright and intelligent and you realise that property is not just a sideline here.*" Capsticks is heavily involved in PFI and PPP projects up and down the country, particularly the LIFT projects that are regenerating primary care facilities across the UK. Trainees encounter these projects in several departments – property, employment and, especially, commercial. The commercial seat is possibly the most difficult to settle into as these projects are so large and complicated. They run for such long periods of time that a stint of just four months usually means a trainee only sees a small slice of the matter.

With a few reservations, the firm's six-seat system does win trainees' approval. Said one: "*Four months goes quickly, especially if you have a holiday in the middle, but if it hadn't been for the six seats I wouldn't have done employment or litigation and I have learned different skills in each seat."* Some trainees also get to experience life in a hospital by going on part-time secondments one or two days per week. Wherever they are located, trainees find their time is split between work that challenges them and less inspiring but essential tasks. All our sources accepted this with good grace and confirmed that overall the downtimes were more than compensated for. To use a clinical analogy, even brain surgeons have to start by learning how to suture cut fingers.

## be there or be square

The day shift in the office is over by 5.30pm or 6pm, although at peak times in transactional departments it can run on later. Those seeking out company can pop over the road to one of two favoured bars, Le Piaf and Putney Station. But which is better? *"That's a contentious question,"* laughed one source, *"I am a Piaf fan, but the Putney Station people say wine is better over there. Perhaps it is, but it's easier to sit in a big group in the Piaf and it's more cosy, less clinical."*

Alas, there is something of the clinical about the firm's seven-storey office building on Upper Richmond Road in the heart of Putney. We have it on good authority that from the outside the building is *"like an NHS hospital,"* while the inside reveals *"offices that are huge by London standards, and from the top two floors you can see all across London including the London Eye."* As for the location, *"Putney is great!"* Shopping and lunching opportunities abound, and to work off those lunchtime calories how about a spot of five-a-side football? As we interviewed, teams were about to be picked for the hard-fought annual intra-firm tournament.

For the past three years since the firm gave itself a new website and red square logo, we've been tracking the whereabouts of a four-foot-high red plastic cube, though it doesn't seem that popular judging by the verbal equivalents of rolled eyes we heard during our interviews. Its symbolism is lost on most, but our thanks go to the trainee who knew that the cube represented *"dynamism, passion and energy."* No, we don't get it either...

## life of brian

It was good to hear trainees speak with passion about their jobs though. It doesn't surprise us given that everyone does a vac scheme before starting their contracts so they know what they are letting themselves in for. Considering the quality and interesting nature of the day-to-day work on offer at the firm, you can see why the firm receives applications from people with or without prior experience of healthcare. That said, when you speak to trainees, you learn that the majority did have a prior interest, even if only through having a medical practitioner in the family. This is how one of our interviewees saw it: *"There are some former doctors here but you can do absolutely fine with little or no understanding of medicine. It just adds an extra context to the work. A lot of the experiences would be easily transferable to other law firms; for example, in dispute resolution, where the work is mostly contract and even includes defamation, often very media sensitive. All that would be useful in other firms."* Indeed, in 2005, three of the seven qualifiers took their skills to NQ jobs elsewhere.

We sensed that the clear purpose of the firm filters through to the way trainees feel about themselves as young lawyers; they speak with a level of confidence that is lacking at some of the more directionless firms. *"Our ethos is one of enormous pride in working for the public sector,"* offered one source, adding: *"I think the firm has a progressive and cosmopolitan atmosphere."* As another put it: *"Most people would see the benefits of having a good public health service. Most people come here with views which are supportive of it."* Most are Guardian readers we're guessing!

As an aside, we should warn applicants of a romantic disposition that they are highly likely to find love, even a spouse, at the firm. A third Captsicks wedding is on the cards, as well as a Capsticks baby due later in 2005. Rumour has it that, whatever the child's sex, it will be called Brian.

## and finally...

Recommending Capsticks is easy. If you want to be involved with the NHS or other healthcare organisations, either on clinical matters or large-scale structural or policy issues, then you can't do better.

# Challinors

## the facts

**Location:** West Bromwich, Birmingham
**Number of partners/assistants:** 26/24
**Total number of trainees:** 9
**Seats:** 4x6 months
**Alternative seats:** None

Challinors is a 200-strong firm forged through the merger of Messrs Lyon & Clark with Challinors in 1996. Following the merger, it was left with offices in Smethwick, the leafy Birmingham suburb of Edgbaston, the city's centre and West Bromwich in the Black Country.

## snow laughing matter

After ringing in the millennium, Challinors promptly closed shop in Smethwick and relocated staff to West Bromwich and Birmingham. Lured by the promise of commercial expansion, it continues to transplant lawyers to the city, recently uprooting its commercial litigation team from West Bromwich. It's what we might call law firm gentrification. And the pay off? Challinors at present deals with some mid-range players including 4D Telecom and the West Bromwich Building Society and it hopes that other larger clients will come knocking. Rest assured, the firm is not wholly abandoning its Black Country base. Far from it – its legally aided crime and family departments are as busy as ever, but like many firms Challinors has been seduced by privately funded work. Said one trainee of the firm's

commercial push: "*It shouldn't put someone off, we're still a large general practice.*" Large maybe, general definitely. The firm also has a few specialist areas of practice – for instance, charities and licensing law – and it is "*looking to set up more.*" We hear that an imminent rebranding exercise will draw attention to the firm's diversity.

While its business strategy accords with current trends among mid-sized regional firms, Challinors is a pioneer according to marketing manager Beverley Weston. "*We're very unique,*" Bev assured us, "*you won't find another firm who have taken surveyors in.*" She was referring to the legal-surveying hybrid Challinors Blizzard, a "*one-stop shop*" for technical and legal services to the construction industry. One has to applaud the firm's agility in noticing a niche and filling it, a gamble that paid off when a series of contracts amounting to £14 million for Pritchards Construction Ltd came in. If local building firms or clients such as the West Bromwich Building Society don't tickle your fancy there's always Challinors' employment client Wiggles and Giggles. What fancy Wiggles and Giggles' tickle is, however, a moot point. Intrigued by the company name we endeavoured to find out more about the business and were left with two possibilities: Staffordshire's premier supplier of childminders or the North Midlands' family-run, premier supplier of adult intimates. We leave it to you, the budding Challinors trainee to find out, though perhaps not during interview.

## going going gone

The large West Bromwich HQ has lawyers working in all of the firm's key areas. Here the majority of trainees can be found working in a communal space shared with paralegals and other junior fee earners. Based purely on the number of seats available in each office, all trainees visit West Brom and Edmund House in Brum; only some end up in Edgbaston. In the central Birmingham office at Edmund House clients are met and greeted in a "*refurbished, quite modern,*" "*blue and light coloured* wood" reception area on the tenth floor. While waiting they might sit and leaf through Brum's own broadsheet *The Birmingham Post, which Challinors try and get in through marketing events*." The city centre lawyers specialise in clinical negligence, construction, licensing and commercial services. The tiddler of the three, the Edgbaston office in a Grade II listed building, which apparently once served as a hospital, has a wills and probate team and a dinky property team.

According to trainees, "*you usually get property as your non-contentious seat*." This seat means a stint in either Edgbaston or West Bromwich, and in the former location trainees work closely with a partner, initially just assisting but gradually building up to their own files. In West Bromwich they handle lower value residential conveyancing and encounter the excitement of the auction room. Auctioneering is not as antiquarian as it sounds – there are no piles of mouldy deeds, instead "*hi-tech computer presentations*" are co-ordinated under the gabble's strike. Trainees produce auction packs of official copies of deeds and searches and distribute them on the day. They "*have to think on their feet*" as it is incumbent on them to ensure that all runs smoothly, a duty difficult to discharge "*when your purchaser doesn't have a deposit, hasn't signed the contract and may well be in London not Birmingham*." Sounds like a classic case of build a stile and get over it.

Family seats in either Edmund House or West Brom are popular. You'll need a car to enjoy the experience in West Brom as the county court is quite far from the office. By contrast, "*everyone*" at Edmund House "*uses public transport because parking is a joke in the city centre*" and the county court is only round the corner. Sometimes a case may end up in Coventry, although we have been assured "*you're only rarely sent to Coventry!*" In both offices a trainee's time is split between divorces and children cases, divorces being the commoner of the two. Expect to handle your own files and learn to cope in a professional manner with clients' specific grievances. Often this means listening to gripes in meetings and then repeating them – *sans* expletives – when drafting instructions to counsel and letters to the opposition. "*People literally argue over teaspoons*," one source balefully sighed.

## mean streets

In West Brom's civil litigation seat "*you get your own office*," no bad thing as "*you have a lot more drafting to concentrate on*." Expect to Xeroxicise in the department: there are no paralegals so menial duties are shared between trainees and juniors. Reparation for pushing the big green button is found in your own caseload, albeit that this includes "*walk-in-off-the-street*" cases with clients bleating about "*me ex-partner who's got me TV*." The disputes may be petty and the merits of cases dubious, nonetheless for the trainee this is valuable practice in handling small claims (and claimants) alone. Notably, while the litigation department this year decided to "*turn away low-value work*," trainees are free to take cases on for the experience.

A PI seat in West Bromwich will enmesh a trainee in the entangled compound "*trip-and-slip, quick-turn-over, no-win-no-fee claims*." A high yield of agency work "*for advertised-off-the-telly firms*" means a full caseload for the department. Challinors is also part of a seven-strong Midlands consortium – the Midlands Accident Lawyers, abbreviated to MAL (though we feel the brain behind this name should have realised that the particle is all too easily coupled in the mind with the words 'practice' and 'ingerer'). MAL seeks work on local television and radio and the constituent law firms have even resourced a call centre between them. In the PI department trainees have the day-to-day running of smaller files, including "*correspondence to clients and solicitors for the opposition, taking statements and that sort of thing*." Don't expect too much court time as almost all small cases are settled out of court on modest terms. Some don't even make it to the negotiating table, as in one example where a claimant had fallen foul of the jogger's curse twice, first by tripping on a crack and second by coming violently into contact with the path. It later transpired that he had neglected to mention two salient features of his exercise regime: the incident took place around 2am and he had been drinking in the pub until 1.30am. Of course, you will also assist on "*proper negligence – people who have been hit by cars and have brain damage,*" claims "*for millions that drag on for years.*"

## yam yow are yow brummie?

The Midlands is riven by regional divides largely unknown to outsiders. One such fault line exists between the Brummie and the Yam Yam; the former are infamous, the latter not famous. The Black Country's Yam Yams are so called because of a unique dialect that lies somewhere between Chaucer and Noddy Holder and produces idioms such as 'Yam yow are yow?' (Are you?). Despite being headquartered in the Yam Yam zone (West Bromwich), "*there are lots of Brummie accents at Challinors.*" We're told that roots in Birmingham or the vicinity is "*not a requisite*" but is definitely "*preferred*" as "*it shows your commitment to the area and that you wouldn't up and leave for London.*" Challinors' trainees usually come straight from self-funded LPCs though the firm offers a modest* interest-free loan. If you end up with a year to spare between your LPC and training contract you might even take a paralegal position there to get a head start on repayments. In 2005, two of the four qualifying trainees stayed on with the firm going into crime and family.

According to our sources West Bromwich is a social vacuum and of late the pulse of the firm's social life seems to have flatlined. "*We don't have a social committee, it died off. We tried to resurrect it, things would be organised but people wouldn't turn up.*" Never fear, the Birmingham Trainee Solicitors Society (BTSS) is there to wheel in the crash cart and spark life into them. This organisation has a full calendar and never fails to come up with the goods socially. For its own part, the firm has lately organised "*a night out at the Glee Club*" and a beano to

London. "*The whole firm gets to go. You have lunch on a Thames boat, then do what you want.*" It sounds like a school trip except "*you spend most of it in the pub.*" At Christmas, trainees attend departmental, office and firm-wide parties. The firm-wide gathering sounds a hoot – "*You go to the AGM in the morning, there is an awards ceremony, then lunch, then the bar opens.*" After all that you probably need a drink!

## and finally...

Challinors offers a varied traineeship across a solid general practice. If unsure whether to commit to publicly funded work, private clients or a commercial career, it will allow you to pursue all three until you decide which best suits you.

# Charles Russell LLP

## the facts

**Location:** London, Cheltenham, Guildford, Oxford
**Number of partners/assistants:** 93/197
**Total number of trainees:** 29
**Seats:** 4x6 months (L/C); 6x4 months (G)
**Alternative seats:** Secondments

Charles Russell is a mid-sized general commercial firm with offices in London, Guildford and Cheltenham. In August 2005 it opened up a tiny Oxford branch.

## it takes all sorts

CR takes trainees in London, Cheltenham and Guildford. Alas, it is too soon for us to say when and if Oxford will be drawn into the training scheme but what we do know is that it has been set up to focus on IT, bioscience, publishing and higher education issues. Across its three more-established offices, 70% of the firm's work is commercial, covering property, corporate finance, commercial litigation, insolvency, employment, and other more specialist areas.

The remainder is geared for private individuals and covers trusts, probate and family affairs. The blend is "*ideal if you're not entirely sure what kind of work would suit you*" and a standard four-seat rotation in London and Cheltenham allows an unusual level of flexibility should you want to shorten or extend a seat. In Guildford a similar flexibility applies to a six-seat system.

No particular seats were considered best avoided but one of the jewels in its crown is a sparkling private client practice that has been advising the great and good for hundreds of years, and others are cutting-edge media and communications departments that keep the cobwebs at bay. The firm takes on a sufficiently varied group of people to cover its many bases so each intake contains those who prefer dealing with "*personal issues*" for individuals, those who are "*pugnacious*" born litigators and those who are drawn to the clients of the corporate department because "*they are commercial people who understand business issues.*"

In recent times the corporate team has acted for Select Appointments in a £1.1 billion takeover by Dutch employment agency Vedior, a huge deal creating the world's third largest employment group. Such megabucks deals are not the norm here; more common are transactions for companies listed or about to be listed on the Alternative Investment Market. In 2005, CR made its way up the list of the top-ten legal advisers on AIM flotations, finishing second only to a specialist practice. Not bad going, we say! From a trainee's perspective the typical CR deal – ie mid-market – gives them a distinct advantage over their peers at the biggest firms. Said one source: "*You get to do work that you wouldn't get at magic circle firms where you are constantly bogged down in admin.*" Be warned though, you will still find yourself shuffling a fair bit of paper because, no matter what the size of the deal, someone has to do it.

## a local shop for local people?

IP/media is a terribly popular seat "*because of*" as one trainee joked, "*the possibility of meeting famous people.*" CR has bags of experience acting for media organisations, both on the corporate side – it advised Faber Music on its acquisition of International Music Publications, the European printed music business of Warner Bros – and on the financing and production of films. CR lawyers recently assisted regular client Universal Pictures UK in connection with the financing of The League of Gentlemen's film 'Royston Vasey', and assisted on the production work for 'Head in the Clouds' and 'The Merchant of Venice'.

Also favoured is the litigation department, which breaks down into smaller groups – communications, IT, commercial, insurance and contentious trusts and probate. On the commercial property side, the firm has helped Eton College develop a 2,000 metre rowing lake, acted for Guildford Council in redeveloping the enormous Friary Shopping Centre and worked on the regeneration of the Brighton Pavilion Theatre and an adjoining casino development for The Trevor Osbourne Group. If a spin around the office still leaves you wanting, secondments are "*a great learning experience*" and trainees have gone to production companies, government agencies and big corporates like Cable & Wireless.

It seems that the firm's smaller size allows trainees to sidestep hierarchy in work matters. One commented that "*you can always bounce ideas off people; if you're doing research you can go from one of the NQs to the head of department.*" Furthermore, "*it's nice that the partners do still muck in. If you're in the office at ten o'clock the partner generally will be as well. It's like a group of friends pulling together.*" On hours, our sources were unanimous: "*It is not an easy ride but it's better than many other firms.*" The average hours for a trainee are probably 8.30am to 6.30pm or 7pm. "*Occasionally you have to put in the late hours but the adrenaline takes you through.*"

## animal house

When one trainee told us that at CR "*people are very important – you're going to be spending a lot of time here,*" we decided to find out what type the firm went for via an application form that demands to know who your favourite inventor is, and what animal your best friend would describe you as. "*There is a mix of non-law and law graduates,*" the youngest of whom are straight from university with the rest having travelled or come from different careers. "*It's not stuffy or posh,*" our sources assured us. "*People come from all sorts of backgrounds.*" The characteristics that will stand you in good stead are "*confidence and enthusiasm,*" and the firm's recruitment brochure features an appropriately wide-eyed young executive couple who look like they've just been busted emerging from the stationary cupboard. Still, an improvement on one we found from a couple of years back, which featured a trainee with a brown paper bag over their head and another image of a young lady bound in rope, biting down on a pencil. Very odd.

Trainees also say, "*you need to be sociable and adaptable. Further up the ladder there is an old-school-tie tradition, but the younger lawyers are outgoing and unaffected.*" Be aware that "*people skills are rated quite highly, not just pure academic ability. Here you get to work on marketing and go to drinks parties so if you just want to do your work and leave you might not fit in so well.*"

## maxwell house

The London office is looking for a new home after several years in one of Robert Maxwell's old abodes. "*The building itself isn't great – I think we could do with a move,*" confessed a source. In terms of interior design, "*there's nothing too horrendous on the art front,*" though another announced: "*I wouldn't want it in my house!*" The location is great; "*it's on the edge of the City and close to the West End*" and apparently on the ninth floor there is an under-used helipad. Who knows, maybe if you're working really late and all the taxis are booked...

"*You might not want to come here if you want a magic circle environment. You wouldn't fit in – the ethos here is different,*" concluded one trainee. Another agreed: "*We're all quite chilled and sociable.*" When discussing their social lives, our sources were generally tight lipped about office party indiscretions, although we heard that "*one partner did do stand-up comedy and it was actually quite funny!*" Probably best to wait until post-qualification before trying the old squirt-in-your-face-flower trick on your head of department. The annual sports dinner in November, at which "*the whole firm goes out and gets drunk,*" provides a telling snapshot of the different departments. "*There are awards for sports people – corporate people get the most drunk. No one in private client gets any prizes!*" Perhaps this is because "*people in private client are genii whereas the corporate department is younger and has a reputation for going out a lot.*"

## we're so surrey

Guildford's six seats are "*great if you don't know what you want to do or don't want to get stuck in something you don't enjoy.*" The office was described as "*dynamic and growing*" but has so far managed to retain a close-knit feel and is "*still of a size that means you don't get lost; you are known.*" Apparently, "*the managing partner knows everyone – I can't praise him highly enough.*" Another trainee agreed that he did an excellent job of keeping all the offices informed of the firm's business, adding: "*There's a one-firm approach.*" Social events are good for getting everyone to intermingle and there seems to have been other attempts at standardisation – "*There are more perks to the job now – we even have sandwiches in meetings.*" If a few sangers fail to impress you, perhaps you'll be swayed by CR's summer ball or its cocktail and casino night. Unfortunately at the latter, the only thing changing hands was monopoly money.

Guildford trainees explained that "*the partners are not old fuddy duddies and the facilities are completely bang up to date, but the firm is traditional in* terms of its values. It believes in family values and in looking after its people." People do seem to stay loyal to the firm, with many shunning the temptations of London to build a life and career in Surrey. "*There are several people who have gone all the way from trainee to partner here and that's encouraging*," said one source. Guildford trainees keen to develop strong roots themselves can take on a marketing role by joining the Surrey Young Executives group.

## 'nam

The "*lovely*" Cheltenham office is a relatively small-scale operation and takes only one trainee each year. A typical rotation moves through property, commercial litigation, coco and then a private client seat. Again, the mix of private client and commercial work was what appealed to our source. Reports suggest you'll find yourself handling a reasonable mix of international and local work. In terms of feedback and appraisals, it's the same system as London and Guildford – there's a mid-seat review and then a more in-depth appraisal at the end of each seat.

Occupying a classic Regency building, the office is "*spacious and close to the town centre, the bars and restaurants.*" It's nice to hear that "*partners do recognise that people have a life outside the office and they lead by example. There are no weekends in the office although late nights are possible in coco.*" Perhaps concerned they had made the place sound too quiet, our source hastily added: "*You can work late if you want – it's not like a ghost town.*" Certainly not during the week of the various Cheltenham festivals (literature, music, jazz) which the firm sponsors.

The firm had a pretty successful year for NQ retention. In September 2005, 12 of the 14 qualifiers stayed on.

## and finally...

Charles Russell is the perfect place to start a legal career if unsure about what kind of law you want to practice. Judging from the buildings occupied by each office, the choice between London, Chel-tenham and Guildford could depend on whether you feel most comfortable in an airport departure lounge, a country mansion, or a grammar school. Just be sure to brush up on your mad inventors.

# Cleary Gottlieb Steen & Hamilton

## the facts

**Location:** London
**Number of partners/assistants:** 15/48
**Total number of trainees:** 4
**Seats:** 4x6 months
**Alternative seats:** Overseas seats, secondments
**Extras:** Pro bono – various projects including assistance to LawWorks, Liberty and Devon & Exeter Racial Equality Council

Cleary Gottlieb Steen & Hamilton is a distinctive US outfit with over 50 years of European presence and 12 international offices from Cologne to New York and Moscow to Hong Kong. Students with equally broad vision may wish to consider a training contract at its independent-minded London office.

## the founding fathers

Back in 1949 a fresh-faced Cleary Gottlieb performed what we might call a reverse Mayflower. The firm sent a boatload of lawyers across unknown waters to confront restless natives and open an office in Paris. The move followed naturally from advising the post-war French government on the implementation of the Marshall Plan. The intervening years have seen exponential increase in both the capacity and the desire of US firms to operate worldwide, and Clearys has been a major player. Recent instructions by the French government on the €20 billion privatisation of utilities companies such as Electricité de France and Gaz de France has seen Cleary working alongside counterparts like Shearman & Sterling and Sullivan &

Cromwell. However, its long and broad experience of European practice gives it a competitive advantage, one that is nowhere better illustrated than in its 2005 representation of some of Europe's biggest business groups in lobbying the US Securities and Exchange Commission to reform delisting procedures for foreign companies. Stick that in your peace pipe and smoke it.

Offices in Hong Kong, Tokyo and Moscow underline the fact that 'International' isn't a euphemism for 'European'. A combined New York and Hong Kong team recently scored a lead role on Standard Chartered Bank's $3.3 billion acquisition of Korea First Bank, the largest ever single overseas investment in the country. Slightly further west, the firm acted as US, English and Russian counsel to Gazprom in a $1.25 billion investment-grade bond offering, another notable deal in that it was the first export receivables-backed bond of a Russian company with contract-related security arrangements for gas sales across Europe.

London trainees told us their office is not merely a part of Cleary's international network, but *"an office with a heartbeat independent of the Americans."* As one put it: *"The people from Paris are distinct personalities; they feel that they work for a French law firm, we feel that we work for an English law firm."* Makes sense really, but it isn't always the case with big US firms abroad. Wondering whether this view was really on the money, we looked for harder evidence and found that of the firm's 171 partners, 70 are based outside the USA and more than a third have worked in two or more offices.

## ever so slightly blighty

The London practice is *"basically divided in two. There's finance, which is banking and capital markets, and then there's M&A, which is large corporate acquisitions."* This is a fair summary, although it can't be overemphasised quite how much a trainee's experience will involve international work. Said one source: *"On day one I was researching Cypriot law, and by the end of the week speaking*

*to clients in Russia and Greece."* To prove the point, let us mention that the corporate side of the London practice recently acted as counsel to LN Holdings in its $13.3 billion share sale to Ispat International, which formed the world's largest steel company, Mittal Steel. Not to be outshone the London office's capital markets practice last year advised Goldman Sachs as manager in an overnight £150 million convertible bond offering by Luxembourg client QIAGEN, and was counsel to the underwriters led by BNP Paribas on a €1.4 billion warrants offering by Arcelor. Nevertheless, *"the English practice is strong and growing in stature within the firm"* and at least half of Clearys' London lawyers are Britishers.

## boundless enthusiasm

When discussing the best reasons for choosing the firm, trainees pointed to its unique training contract and its self-proclaimed collegiate atmosphere. You'll notice that we haven't used the word department when referring to practice areas, and that is for a very simple reason – Clearys doesn't have any. In any of its offices. Anywhere in the world. This policy is based on the view that specialisation isn't a necessity and that even senior lawyers may have very diverse practice interests. For their part trainees say: *"Hopefully it means you're a more rounded lawyer,"* with one telling us: *" I chose this firm because I didn't want to specialise too early."* Then again, they did cut off the litigation option, which Clearys' London office doesn't touch.

Sharp readers will realise that a department-free firm equals a very fluid training contract. To be clear, trainees do rotate around the firm, working with four different training partners, the specialisms of whom will, to a degree, dictate the type of work they receive. For example, one told us: *"In my private equity seat I probably did about 70% private equity work."* And what of the other 30%? Well, that depends on the trainee's individual tastes and what needs to be done in a relatively small office where *"there is always the need for another helping hand."* In essence "*you get a bit of everything.*" Although there was the comment along the lines of "*sometimes it would be nice to finish a seat and feel that you'd perfected one discipline,*" the majority view is that "*if you want something, ask and you'll get it.*" Another consequence of being in a departmentless firm is that you end up with major responsibility and considerable client contact early on, whether it's "*finding unconventional soft options for Russian private equity clients*" or "*drafting a financing agreement in only my second seat.*"

What really oils the wheels of this unconventional working model is an "*accommodating atmosphere*" in which "*you can ask any partner for help and they'll give you as much time as it takes, even if they're not working on the matter.*" Describing "*a very informal environment with no real set way of doing anything,*" trainees' enthusiasm for The Clearys Way was perfectly evident and they couldn't help returning to one simple concept – "*collegiality is pervasive.*"

## want to be a part of it?

For the adventurous trainee the hotshot Brussels office offers an antitrust seat as well as the chance to sample "*180 varieties of Belgian beer*" (though not in the office). Indeed, it looks as if trainees do their fair share of jet setting on business trips from London – some lucky so-and-sos recently went to Russia and South Africa. And whether it's by the miracle of digital videoconferencing, a brief encounter or something more meaningful, "*a trip to the mothership of New York is recommended, even encouraged.*" If you want to make more than a flying visit, there are two options.

The first is to top up your LLB with an LLM at a major American law school, then study for the New York Bar at the firm's expense, train on its foreign lawyer programme for nine months (replete with mighty salary and excellent social life) and return to London to complete your training. The second entails qualifying in the UK before heading to the Big Apple to take the New York Bar exam. The majority

of those we spoke to this year considered the latter to be preferable, with New York a serious career option "*for two or three years after qualification*" rather than a mere training contract junket. There's no doubt that Clearys London is one of the best places to join if you really fancy becoming a fully-fledged American lawyer. However, be aware that both options require a UK law degree rather than a CPE/GDL conversion qualification.

Successful training contract applicants will quite likely have an LLB and possibly even a Master's degree. The reasons for this are not least to do with the firm's discerning approach to recruitment, in which quality and compatibility with The Clearys Way are paramount. Said one source (still not quite able to believe their luck): "*When they took me on they'd already taken three for the year and they said they'd have been quite happy to leave it at that if no one worthwhile came along.*" To back up the anecdotal with hard facts, we might as well tell you that over 2,000 would-be trainees applied to the firm in 2005. Better make your application a good one!

Trainees emphasised the fact that the firm recruits "*for the long haul – they spoke of the possibilities of partnership when they rang to offer me my training contract!*" It is almost unheard of for trainees not to be offered NQ positions (all four were offered jobs and accepted in 2005) and "*this breeds a security and commitment which enhances your training.*" That commitment is sometimes put to the test, with hours of 9.30am to 7pm commonly stretching to "*10pm when you're busy and even midnight when you're very busy.*" To compensate there are taxis and meals when you do work late, not forgetting those must-have tools of the trade – Amex, BlackBerry, laptop and big leather chair.

## london pride

As they swivel in the chair, in their standard dress-down attire, contemplating the pleasant London Wall offices, trainees can also debate whether to pop down to the cafeteria for a latte or a subsidised meal ("*one pound for an entire dinner!*"). But choice breeds choice: *"Should you have the homemade burger cooked rare, medium or well done?"*

After-work socialising offers less diversity with *"comparatively few organised events"* and infrequent pub trips reflecting the fact that *"people have family and university friends in London."* However, a silly season is effectively announced in the summer months when the arrival of associates from New York prompts *"a frenzy of events almost every day from theatre trips to meals out to nights on the town."*

## and finally...

In the words of one trainee, Cleary Gottlieb Steen & Hamilton offers *"international work of an excellent quality, high levels of responsibility and an intimate working environment."* Add top-drawer salary to that list and it becomes pretty comprehensive. If you've got an eye on dual US/UK qualification, this is your firm, but even if not we reckon it to be a refined choice for those with a discerning corporate appetite.

# Clifford Chance LLP

## the facts

**Location:** London
**Number of partners/assistants:** 222/681
**Total number of trainees:** 240
**Seats:** 4x6 months
**Alternative seats:** Overseas seats, secondments
**Extras:** Pro bono – various law centres; language training

Say the word 'big.' Say it again and this time drop your voice an octave. And again, but really go for the ful-blown, movie-trailer 'It was a time of war and destiny' bass vibrato. That's still not quite it. Imagine how a blue whale with a 200-a-day Marlboro Red habit would say big. Nope. How Zeus would say it, shaking the very foundations of the earth. That's it. Clifford Chance: it's big and it rocks the legal world.

## coward? hardly!

Ever since the 1987 unification of London firms Clifford Turner and Coward Chance *"a driving expansion"* has seen our subject open 28 offices in 19 countries and muscle into every emerging market and field of practice. Now centred around six main worldwide divisions – banking and finance, capital markets, corporate finance, litigation, real estate and TPE (tax, pensions and employment) – CC's practice is characterised by breadth and quality. The firm is ranked highly by our colleagues on *Chambers UK* in everything from administrative and public law to capital markets, Islamic finance and PFI. The rise and rise of Clifford Chance has been an almost unmitigated story of success.

Almost. The firm's American adventure has been beset with problems by way of office closures and law suits in California and a haemorrhaging of partners in New York. Closer to home, the Berlin project was wrapped up this year, contributing to the firm's static financial returns for 2004/5. It all begs the question, has CC's expansionist phase come to an end? On this point, some trainees told us: *"The focus now seems to be on cementing our position as global leader,"* mentioning *"a push for seamless standards across offices worldwide."* Others, particularly those who had taken overseas seats, beg to differ. *"Yes, there's an element of consolidation, but having seen how we are in Hong Kong, we're getting more deals from India than ever before, we're expanding in Tokyo and Singapore and doing our best to get in on the massively growing Chinese economy."* In fact, together with its own São Paulo office (incidentally the largest non-Brazilian law firm in the country), Clifford Chance looks excellently placed to maximise the profits to be made out of the rapidly emerging BRIC economies (Brazil, Russia, India and China). All part of the simple little plan for world domination, you might say.

## phat finance

That plan was originally developed around a stellar finance capacity which, even today, remains one of the mainstays of CC's practice. Truly financial heavyweights (although we're not saying they eat too much), CC lawyers advised the banks supporting Philip Green's much-publicised hostile bid for M&S. They also received instructions from CVC Capital Partners and the Permira Funds on a £1.75 billion joint offer made for The AA, advised Barclays Capital on its role in the consortium making a £1.1 billion bid for Somerfield, and took a lead role on the €800 million refinancing of steel producer Corus Group. Not to be outdone, CC capital markets lawyers advised Czech pharmaceutical company Zentiva on its $200 million IPO (the first dual listing in London and Prague combined with a US offering), assisted the underwriters on the £776 million IPO of Admiral Group including a US offering under Rule 144A, and similarly helped satellite telecommunications company Inmarsat in connection with an aggregate $927.5 million high-yield senior notes issuance.

The firm's finance bent translates into at least one compulsory finance seat for every trainee, with some eager for more. "*You have to be either masochistic or unlucky to do two seats there*," said one trainee, clearly no fan. Perhaps this slight antipathy results from the fact that it can be "*massively hard work*," "*demanding and notorious for long hours*" in "*departments that are at the top of their game*." Nevertheless, plenty of our interviewees had worked through the pain barrier and "*really enjoyed*" their time in finance. General banking seats were appreciated most; strangely their "*up and down hours*" turn out to be a plus point ("*sometimes you're leaving at 5am, at others you can walk out at 4pm and no one bats an eyelid*") as does the chance to take on "*smaller scale drafting.*" Much of a trainee's time is spent on transaction management, among other things simple tasks such as "*getting the documents there and signed on time.*" This may sound like small beer, but our interviewees recognised that responsibility comes in all shapes and sizes. If something more specialised appeals, try one of the seats concentrating on regulatory advice or project finance.

The former suits those drawn to research; the latter involves large projects including the largest MoD PFI ever, advising the consortium supplying £13 billion worth of in-flight refuelling jets to the RAF.

Life can be "*hard-core*" in certain other finance departments. "*Securitisation and asset finance are the worst, in that order.*" Securitisation means "*long hours, everybody knows it,*" and as trainees peer up at junior associates they observe that "*the burn-out rate is phenomenal.*" One commented: "*Photos are taken of new people when they start, and it's shocking trying to match them up to the grey faces around you.*" Asset finance, meanwhile, "*gives the impression that it's funding the rest of the firm, lots of swagger and very male-oriented.*" Some lucky trainees, mainly third or fourth-seaters, had "*taken a much more central role on the smaller transactions,*" even doing closings by themselves.

## dealicious

Not satisfied with its dominance in finance, CC has worked up a massive capacity for corporate work that has seen it race to the summit of M&A deal tables across Europe. Corporate lately advised Barclays Bank on its £29 billion recommended acquisition of a majority stake in South African bank ABSA, and acted for Macquarie Capital Alliance Group on its £1.2 billion purchase of YBR Group. Across the department, lawyers also added Reuters to an extensive list of clients that already included the likes of British Energy, Banco Santander, GE, Canary Wharf plc, Standard Life, Aviva, Accenture and Daily Mail & General Trust. Here, as elsewhere, breadth of practice is the watchword, such that in addition to the core teams in corporate finance and private equity, trainees can also take seats in financial institutions, CMT (communications, media and technology), competition, commercial and funds. No matter where they are, trainees tend to take on "*massive amounts of due diligence, reviewing data and document management,*" and all this with minimal drafting opportunities due to the "*scale and complexity of deals*." It is the "*peripheral*" nature of transaction management which some find dispiriting ("*it's harrowing stuff – all the clichés of long hours and data rooms*"), though admittedly others find pleasure in "*the brilliantly social people*" and the opportunity to work closely with "*incredibly skilled lawyers*" on "*transactions that are making the news*."

## dark nights of the soul

Across the firm it is generally true that "*you progress from logistical, data-management work in your early seats to getting more responsibility in your third and fourth seats*." Even the earlier period can bring satisfaction because "*you have to understand what's happened in the deals to do your job properly*." But if the majority had experienced moments of "*mind-numbing boredom*," almost all had been "*pushed hard to take on more when it's possible and if you show you're capable*." Mid-seat appraisals were picked out by many as a useful exercise that "*gives you confidence about the way you're doing work and how people perceive you*," but also the chance "*to emphasise the work you want to do*." Admittedly, trainees are unlikely to be running deals themselves, but the experience of "*drafting agreements*," "*spending positive time with clients*" and "*engaging in really interesting work*" had been there for our sources. Responsibility seems closely linked to the relative quality of supervisor, with the presence of "*some who view you as an inconvenience*" leading several interviewees to suggest that "*the firm needs to challenge the perception that trainees should be treated like grunts*." Others had less patience with this viewpoint, one saying: "*Some people need a lot of affirmation, but if you're doing badly you'll be told... isn't that enough?*" We choose to underline the advice of the perceptive individual who told us: "*It's easy to spot the ones who want to teach you as opposed to have you do their donkey work. Gravitate towards them.*" Luckily the seat allocation system allows you to specify your preferred supervisor, not merely your preferred area of practice.

Hours, too, have the potential to be "*dreadful*," with almost all our interviewees picking out a period of late nights or 'all-nighters' as the low point of their two years. "*I hit rock bottom when I put on my coat, hoping to leave at 2am in corporate, and was asked if I was cold*." Long days from 9am until 8pm are common, with nothing but pure luck determining the number of nights or weekends that must be endured. "*I've had two in two years, others have had weeks on end*," admitted one source. Apparently, "*it's never so bad that you can't see light at the end of the tunnel*" (even if it is the sun rising), and although "*no one likes to stay awake all night*," most recognise it as "*the compromise you make when you come to Clifford Chance*."

## litigation: a thorn in your side?

Bearing in mind the predominance of corporate and finance work, we did wonder if trainees felt the two years of training turned them into rounded lawyers or specialised transactionalists. Whether by luck or not, this year we spoke to a group that was diverse in terms of its legal interests. Few interviewees felt they had been forced into a transactional mould. Beyond the endless list of finance and corporate seats, there are other options, among them real estate, competition, tax, IP, construction and employment. And what of straight litigation seats? "*Those who think they might want to qualify there*" are most likely to complete a full six months in general commercial litigation, arbitration or shipping, where they can engage with matters such as the representation of Thistle Hotels on £100 million worth of pleaded claims against 18 defendants. To clear the path for the eager, the firm has a couple of alternatives to offer the disinterested. One is an 18-month commitment to the firm's Free Law pro bono scheme, the other a three-month secondment to charities such as Law4All and Liberty, often taken in conjunction with a three-month litigation seat at the firm. All trainees attend a short, but intensive, litigation course. Even fiercely transactional types had to admit that "*the chance to do advocacy and engage with individuals was cool*."

# the true picture

When it comes to seat allocation, CC does have a slight reputation for "*putting the firm first,*" and frankly this can leave some trainees in the mire at rotation time. Pinning your hopes on one specific path through training is a recipe for disappointment because "*although you mostly get your first or second choice, you might not.*" What has developed is a generally accepted state of agreeable compromise that leaves the majority uncomplaining. A good many trainees come to the firm hoping for a seat in their preferred overseas destination, and with options as varied as Brussels, Paris, Warsaw, Frankfurt, Prague, New York, Singapore and Hong Kong amongst others you can understand why. However, overseas postings can also be a source of disquiet, with "*people forced to fill the less popular ones.*" If you're dying for New York but speak Russian, beware. "*Language capabilities do dictate where people go as this serves the firm's interests.*" CC can justifiably claim to be one of the most international of law firms offering UK training and if a seat overseas is a priority for you this has to be one of the best firms to consider.

## probably the best training...

CC is headquartered in a skyscraper that towers thirty floors above Canary Wharf and features so many facilities, shops and bars that one trainee described it as "*like coming to work in a Carlsberg advert.*" Whilst a number of our sources hankered for a return to the City and an EC postcode, none failed to recognise that "*the gym, the bar, the restaurant, the space – everything about it here is top-class.*" A relatively relaxed attitude to dress ("*you can be in trousers and shirt, no tie, most days*") also helps to establish an atmosphere that led one trainee to sum up thus: "*I came through the door on the first day and just knew I would progress and learn more here.*" Of course, you can't put the quality of the learning experience entirely down to a lack of starchiness: a wealth of "*excellent-quality formal training*" is delivered through "*internal seminars and talks from outside lecturers.*"

We had to chuckle when one of our interviewees whispered: "*You know, some people are partners the moment they walk in.*" You mustn't assume this leads to an overly competitive atmosphere amongst trainees, however. The same source added: "*Most of us know it's a fantastic brand on the CV and a great stepping stone... it got me my new job no problem.*" Unlike this individual, the majority of CC qualifiers remain at the firm, for a while at least. A very respectable 57 of the 61 September 2005 qualifiers decided to stay, even if it is common to think "*two to three years down the line I'll be looking around.*"

While they're there, trainees value "*the scale and internationalism*" of what they view as "*a real worldwide legal powerhouse.*" The firm's multicultural flavour is reflected in the trainee population, and not merely in their national origins. As a group they are "*catholic in the sense of being eclectic*" and "*not defined by any specific personality trait.*" The variety of backgrounds, universities and ages is "*refreshing,*" and ties into a broader notion that "*there really isn't a prescriptive culture, there's no one way it's demanded you be.*" The flipside of the coin is that the vastness of the trainee population can leave some feeling lost. "*Pockets develop, so some people go out together, whilst others are a bit cynical and go straight home,*" commented one source. From another we heard how "*the size and independence of the departments means you can go without seeing people for months.*" In short, this is such a big place that "*it's common to walk into the canteen and know no one.*" Post-work socialising usually means "*drinks in the chainy pubs around Canary Wharf,*" mainly "*with friends from your intake.*" Additionally, there is "*a mass of sport*" from football and rugby to cricket and hockey. Really motivated types find themselves co-opted onto the trainees' social committee which is charged with organising annual summer and winter events. The committee's trade mark is "*going to town with the budget and really going for the wow factor with lots of champagne and freebies.*" We like their style...

## and finally...

*"Inclusive, international and enormous"* is how one trainee summed up Clifford Chance. The giant is not letting up in its quest to be the biggest and best law firm in the world, so you might want to ask yourself if your career aspirations are equally bold.

# Clyde & Co

## the facts

**Location:** London, Guildford
**Number of partners/assistants:** 110/158
**Total number of trainees:** 44
**Seats:** 4x6 months
**Alternative seats:** Overseas seats, secondments
**Extras:** Pro bono – Kingston, Lambeth and Mary Ward law centres, Brent and RCJ CABs

Offices in the Middle East, Western and Eastern Europe, Asia and South America evidence the international nature of litigation goliath Clyde & Co. The firm has been battling it out on the high seas since the 1930s and is still known today for its superb shipping and international trade practices. Another core strand is insurance litigation and in June 2005 it merged with crack aviation firm Beaumont & Sons.

## military manoeuvres

Shipping is *"one of the mainstays of the firm."* Around 150 specialist marine lawyers handle the entire range of wet and dry matters: collisions, salvage and pollution liabilities; bill of lading and charterparty disputes; trading and freight derivatives disputes; shipbuilding and repair; marine insurance; finance disputes and criminal prosecutions. The firm is ranked top for the number of reported shipping cases heard by the English courts. On the non-contentious side, Clydes handles ship finance, regulatory issues and general commercial work, and is well known for acting for cargo owners and insurers, shipbuilders, shipowners, charterers, traders and air carriers, freight forwarders and hauliers. On top of all this, the firm acts for the organisations that insure all of the above activities and clients.

According to our cabin boy sources, shipping litigation is *"quite a sociable department. They organise lots of drinks with clients – brokers and traders – you'll work in a small team and you'll be invited out with the partners."* On the work front, *"it was both dry and wet matters, so there was variety. I got to handle cases about contracts of sale, bills of lading and charterparties. And there were demurrage (that's when a ship is waiting in port and accrues costs) and collision cases. I had a couple of smaller files of my own and I also did very small things on bigger files."* Naturally there are times when trainees are *"stuck on admin"* such as *"writing the narratives for bills,"* but one can hardly expect more on complex high-value cases. Yet some readers may be interested to hear that only some of our sources had visited court, and then only in a 'hands-off' role to observe a barrister. Indeed, one of our sources was horrified by the idea of standing up in front of a master and making an application himself..

## boozing and cruising

Just as the shipping industry is new territory for most trainees, the world of insurance is also a law unto itself. *"There's distinct terminology and you are dealing with Lloyd's of London a lot. We're working on the glamorous side of insurance not the boring personal injury side."* In insurance litigation, trainees are exposed to some mammoth cases and with so much money at stake, *"this is about as litigious as it gets."* *"I am doing a fair amount of disclosure,"* confessed one source, though another spoke of drafting a court application and letters to other solicitors. Lately the firm has defended insurers in respect of property damage at Canary Wharf following the collapse of a crane, and it has also acted for the insurers to Damien Hirst and other artists who saw their works lost in the Momart warehouse fire which destroyed over £20 million of old mattresses and tents. Further afield, Clydes is defending reinsurers in both the Venezuelan Supreme Court and the London Commercial Court on a $51 million claim following an explosion at a power station in Venezuela.

If insurance can be complex, then reinsurance is even more so. Again, Clydes recognises the need for guidance and education and offers basic training sessions at the start of each seat. The ideal trainee is *"willing to learn and sponge-like in picking things up quickly, otherwise your value is limited."* And, *"as well as being flexible and keen, you've also got to be resilient because not all jobs will be interesting ones."* Though the cases frequently are. Take, for example, the representation of the UK government on a misfeasance in public office action brought by shareholders in relation to the collapse of Railtrack. Some students may wish to think carefully about how they will feel when representing giant commercial interests against the little people. For instance, the firm is defending drinks manufacturers Bacardi, Diageo and Allied Domecq in US class action claims that their marketing campaigns encourage underage drinking. Thankfully, Clydes recognises the importance of including lower value cases in their workload and all our sources had taken charge of *"a couple of smaller debt claims where I am actually drafting the claims and running the files."*

## political intrigue

Without question the firm is *"primarily in the contentious realm, although it has diversified a lot."* Yet in spite of this heavy litigation leaning, some of our sources believed Clyde & Co to be as good a choice for transactional work as any other in London. While we're not entirely sure we agree with such a proposition, it is true that not every trainee will limit themselves to one non-contentious seat and the firm has acted on some noteworthy transactions.

As well as seats in corporate, insolvency, tax, property and employment, the firm offers options such as healthcare and medical negligence defence, commercial dispute resolution and a seat in international trade and energy, which involves *"financing trade transactions, joint ventures between different companies, some fraud and bribery and, on the energy side, some work on power plants."* One trainee spoke of having to research the complicated rules of extradition and international arrest warrants: *"They were good at talking me through stuff and they broke me in quite nicely."* In the areas of war and political risk the firm is the key litigation adviser to the government's Export Credit Guarantee Department.

From the second seat onwards, trainees have a fair amount of say in which seats they get. If a seat is popular, the trick is to wage a good campaign and have a word with the relevant partners. Curiously, our interviews revealed a general lack of understanding as to how seat allocation works, the extent to which partners determine trainees' movements and the extent to which campaigning and quiet chats are required or effective.

## palmed off

Trainees work in both London and Guildford; for most this means three seats in their chosen location and one in the other. *"This current intake of first years were a bit surprised by the policy, but the firm pays your travel costs and Guildford is just 40 minutes on the train from London."* It's *"a bit of a slog"* unless you live close to Waterloo so some trainees do relocate for the duration of the seat. The office premises in Surrey are more modern than in London, and as to which office has the best atmosphere, it depends on who you speak to. Most seats are on offer in each location.

Secondments to Hong Kong, Singapore, Piraeus and Dubai can be taken in the second or third seat, and there's now also a Dubai client secondment to Motorola. In these *"you'll get a lot of responsibility and a lot of client contact at an early stage."* Corporate trainees in Dubai set up new companies for people investing in the Gulf, including Iraq. Much of their time is spent liaising with foreign correspondent firms and *"with all the problems going on in Iraq, and Saudi too, I felt I was dealing with really topical issues."* One topographical issue on which Clydes has been involved is The Palm project, a man-made island in the shape of a palm tree. We'd suggest Googling for some pretty stunning graphics of the island as it emerges from the sea. Litigation trainees, meanwhile, have to come to terms with the absence of the concept of legal precedent in Dubai. It can make research somewhat complicated! Out of the office, they can look forward to desert trips, days spent diving or nights in ex-pat bars and restaurants. The firm provides an apartment and a car, and it has been known for some trainees to be accompanied by their spouse or partner. Back in the UK other secondments crop up to clients including the FSA and major insurers.

## dancing with dad

*"It doesn't try to be as crazy and it can be fairly traditional."* So said one trainee of the firm. We found certain traditions rather charming – for instance *"all the partners' files are different colours."* Then again, *"this sometimes leads to a bit of an issue over whose colour a new matter will go under."* Another charming feature of daily life is the treats trolley that roams the corridors in London. *"The first time I came across it I just heard it rumbling down the corridor,"* laughed one source. *"In the mornings it does breakfast rolls, at lunchtime it has salad boxes and sandwiches, and then cakes plus the usual snacks in the afternoon."* Clydes, like many firms, has been granted a licence to brew Starbucks coffee in its staff canteen, but some 21st century trappings have been a long time in coming. In April 2005 we were told: *"We've still got no intranet here and that is frustrating. But on the positive side you are not treated like an automaton. A firm that has a lot of technology and gives everyone a BlackBerry is great in that it is modern, but the flipside is that you are treated less humanely."* Well, that's one theory. Another fact readers may wish to consider concerns something

that is common to firms with shipping roots – men do tend to vastly outnumber women at senior levels. In Clyde's case just 10% of the senior figures profiled on its website are female. No shortage of ladies at trainee level – the firm recruits a good, even balance of men and women. On qualification in September 2005, 14 of the 16 took jobs with the firm, distributing themselves throughout the different departments.

Clydes' international work, clients and offices attract an international group of trainees as well as UK-born trainees who speak foreign languages. They also have a shared interest in becoming litigators, and as one wise individual put it: *"If I'd had a preference for finance, I would have joined a bank."* In terms of hours, the firm's litigation leanings seem to keep trainees on a steady 9am until 6-6.30pm course with few late nights. After work The Ship and Balls Bros. are the drinking venues of choice for London staff, with Fuego's being *"the bar that everyone says they're not going to end up in, but every now and then they do. It's where partners are seen to dance sometimes. It's slightly more cringeworthy than watching your dad dancing. More like dancing with your dad – that level of cringeworthiness."* And for fancy footwork of a different kind, how about football? Clydes' team is *"quite good"* and sensitive enough *"not to take out clients' legs or be over competitive."*

## and finally...

Shipping and insurance are still the name of Clyde & Co's game and, such is the weight of the firm's influence here, we believe it always will be. If you are interested in training at one of the UK's major litigation firms, or you want a top-level firm in Guildford, this is where the smart money goes.

# CMS Cameron McKenna

## the facts

**Location:** London, Bristol, Aberdeen, Edinburgh
**Number of partners/assistants:** 117/456
**Total number of trainees:** 120
**Seats:** 4x6 months
**Alternative seats:** Overseas seats, secondments
**Extras:** Pro bono – Islington Law Centre; travel bursaries; cultural/language training

Trainees who'd prefer their training with a little TLC just can't wait to give CMS Cameron McKenna a big ol' hug. But with corporate and banking work aplenty, a plethora of overseas offices and a flair for energy practice, is it really so touchy-feely at this top-20 firm?

## energised

The trainees we interviewed had moderately divergent views on whether or not the firm is pursuing a transformation into a raw-meat-eating corporate playa. Some felt that "*ramping up corporate to compete with big boys*" is a definite aim, whilst others reflected on a more even approach to matters based on "*our breadth of strength in niche areas*" and "*the Camerons ethos of being a little bit more balanced and lacking the bigger dick complex.*" Since we're in the business of making comparisons, we'll point out that Camerons' corporate and M&A lawyers advised long-term client HSBC on the financing of Morrisons' £2.9 billion acquisition of Safeway, FTSE 100 company Enterprise Inns on a £2.3 billion purchase of over 3,000 pubs and National Australia Bank on the sale of its two Irish banks to Danske Bank for £967 million. Other notable clients include the lottery people Camelot, Royal Mail and Pfizer. However, as impressive as those billion-pound deals are, they definitely represent the firm's highlights; matters in the tens and hundreds of millions band are much more the norm.

Where it truly does knock rivals into a cocked hat is in the fields of energy and natural resources work, a fact illustrated by the many high-profile power and utilities companies instructing the firm, among them National Grid and Thames Water. In oil and gas, in the past year the firm has assisted BP in the sale of its Ormen Lange gas field assets, received joint instructions from Shell and Esso on a similar £200 million divesting of North Sea oilfield assets, and advised Cairn Energy on negotiations over long-term sales contracts to the Indian government for oil discovered by Cairn in Rajasthan. Indeed, such is the firm's expertise that to a degree the corporate teams rely on clients lured in through this aspect of the firm's practice. Proving this point, one of its flagship M&A transaction of late was National Grid's £5.8 billion disposal of its four regional gas distribution networks.

## internationalised

Cameron's energy has fuelled its approach to Eastern Europe where it has developed one of the most extensive networks of law offices. It has branches or associate offices in the Czech Republic, Hungary, Poland, Romania, Russia, Serbia and Montenegro and Bulgaria and our *Chambers Global* colleagues were sufficiently impressed with its achievements to name it 'Eastern European Firm of the Year 2005' at a recent awards ceremony. It is currently engaged on the proposed sale of a majority interest in the Slovak generator company, Slovenské elektrárne, a ground-breaking corporate sale/privatisation in Central Europe. Just as in the UK, where energy lawyers tread others soon follow. A team of Camerons private equity lawyers recently advised Advent International on the €730 million privatisation of the Bulgarian telecoms operator, and the firm's strong PPP/PFI expertise (clients back home in the UK include Metronet) is being used to exploit the nascent Russian market, having recently snatched five experienced projects/finance lawyers for its Moscow office from floundering international firm Coudert.

Our sources inform us that many trainees are

keen to visit an overseas office for a seat. Those who do go abroad "*really get to grips with the international nature of the firm,*" and tell us the experience proves "*an eye-opener.*" Excepting understandable competition for seats in Prague and Hong Kong, most people seem to get what they want. Even those who visit less exotic places find it worth the trip: "*No one ever really wants to go to Bristol or Aberdeen, but they come back having loved it.*" We do not suggest that the 25% who prefer to stay home in London are dullards; plenty of them take the "*absolutely invaluable*" opportunity to sample life in-house by spending a seat with one of a number of clients including Nestlé, Exxon, AIG and National Australia Bank.

## lucky number three

Trainees complete four six-month seats with nothing strictly compulsory beyond the standard law Society requirements. That said, the firm is broadly keen for them to spend time in three of the main practice groups: corporate; banking; property; energy, projects and construction; commercial; and insurance. We did hear a few gripes about "*rotation glitches*" and one or two comments suggested that "*the formula isn't set in stone, you could do three commercial seats if you wanted.*" A host of specialist departments such as employment, financial services, IP, health and safety, insurance litigation and tax mean that many trainees have strong views about the range of work they'd like to sample and feelings can sometimes run high. "*Grad recruitment tends to promise that you'll get your first choice in your third seat but it didn't work that way for me,*" said one trainee at the same time reminding us of the Camerons trainees' ongoing obsession with 'seat three'. However, we'd put that complaint in the context that the majority of those we spoke to were satisfied with their four seats and even those who'd been disappointed recognised the HR people had "*a difficult job to do.*" The soundest advice we heard was that "*It's best to take a strategic attitude and minimise any fuss... it won't help later.*"

If they do sometimes have to bite their lips then by contrast a stint in the real estate department has trainees singing out loud. "*You get a lot of responsibility early on with 30-40 files of your own to run,*" trilled one. Another chimed in: "*It's terrifying to begin with, you think 'How will I manage?' but then you realise [the files are] all slow burners, you send out a letter then wait a week.*" Recognised as a "*good learning experience,*" the responsibility real estate offers finds an echo in the banking seat, which often means getting wrapped around PFI funding issues in a department that acts for funder groups on big projects like the National Air Traffic services project or the recent advice to a consortium of banks led by DEPFA on the €80 million A4 toll motorway project in Poland. (There's that Eastern European link again.)

## more than this?

Across in a straight projects seat, trainees help out on mammoth matters such as continuing advice to the Department for Transport in relation to the restructuring of the cross-channel rail industry and the Channel Tunnel Rail Link. Then of course there's big client Metronet which the firm advises in relation to implementation aspects of the London Underground PPP. In both banking and projects "*the bigger transactions mean more menial work*" but "*there is responsibility to be had.*" By contrast, the smaller size of the majority of niche departments left trainees enthusing about "*the broad spectrum of regulatory and research work*" they got in financial services or "*having your finger in every pie*" in IP where they encounter "*disputes, data protection issues and IP licences.*"

Everyone we interviewed had spent time in corporate, where "*depending on luck and the size of transactions you get you can even be doing some secretarial-style work.*" The majority of our sources had focused on "*one or two mighty deals*" and experienced a life of "*little bits of research, admin letters, indexing and bibling.*" Some had fared better. "*I got involved with four or five deals of a smaller nature so I was drafting letters, writing the due diligence reports and talking through advice with clients."* Here, as elsewhere in the firm, the advice offered by our sources was that *"you have to cultivate people. If you do the small stuff well and show your capability then you get noticed."* Wise words, but we noticed again this year that relatively few trainees have a long-term view of the corporate department. Most do their time and then look elsewhere for qualification. So would the M&A-minded be better off at the magic circle? Over to one trainee with corporate on their mind – *"So what if there are a few less zeroes on the end of deals, I've had more responsibility than any of my friends at other firms. On one AIM float I was working with the MD and company directors, I knew the business and the transaction inside out. Who'd want more than that?"* It got us thinking...

## a nicely run concern

Most trainees perceive Cameron McKenna as being a perfect halfway house between the hardcore rigours of the magic circle and a gentle training option. Very typically we hear comments like: *"I work on big deals for household names and see those deals in the newspaper, but I don't have hideous hours or expectations. There are no weekend calls for me. Maybe it's not the number-one ranking name in the industry but it's big enough for me."* Satisfaction for Camerons trainees is found in *"the fact that we're a good firm, we don't need to be Clifford Chance or A&O, we're not hard-nosed, posturing or inscrutable."* We've heard similar things from trainees at the firm for many years and it accords with the reputation the firm possesses for being more *"approachable, human and balanced"* than many top firms. Our sources believed they had all experienced reasonable hours for a City firm, citing *"9am to 7pm or 8pm"* as common and the bad times *"rarely awful for very long."* One lucky source had managed only one all-nighter over two corporate seats. And if you *"sometimes have to chase up the busier partners for mid-seat appraisals"* then you'll also find that *"the majority are very good at giving*

*feedback,"* or you could take the chance to point out the failing when you *"fill out a feedback form on your supervisor."*

However, in the last few years another 'friendly face of the City' type firm, Lovells, has done its damnedest to shed a nicey-nice image that was perceived to be having a negative impact on recruitment and business. So far as we can tell, no such thoughts are on Cameron McKenna's mind, but in that context it seems reasonable to ask whether Camerons trainees lack the hunger of some of their contemporaries. *"We're all confident rather than arrogant,"* thought one source. Another suggested: *"We're reasonable, nice people; able and clever."* A third put it like this: *"I paralegalled at a magic circle firm and felt like it would take me months to find the five pleasant people amongst 60 trainees, many quite odd. Here you all seem to be on the same wavelength."* Weighing everything up, we have to conclude that Camerons trainees aren't the most career-driven types we encounter in our annual interviews across the City, but they are intelligent, pleasant and doubtless great to work with. Clearly satisfied with life, in March 2005 24 of the 29 qualifiers accepted jobs with the firm and in September 2005 the figure was 23 out of 27.

Trainee socialising is done en masse, although the baton is handed over to younger hands as qualification approaches. *"We were out three nights a week in the first year, but now it's more like lunch or drinks weekly."* *"A grotty old man's pub,"* The Hand & Shears, remains the centre of their social life, although why this should be the case when there are oodles of fab bars just five minutes beyond is a mystery to us. There are also *"poor-quality but fun"* sports teams (their words not ours!), trainee-organised trips *"to do things like bowling,"* a book club, a yearly trainee ball, *"regular departmental drinks"* and a *"monumental annual party that absolutely everyone attends."* With so much going on, if you can't find fun then there's clearly no helping you!

## and finally...

If you want to be trained in a large City firm without getting killed in the process, then remember the name CMS Cameron McKenna. We'd also point to a broad spread of work marked out by a truly stellar projects and energy practice, particularly in relation to Eastern Europe.

# Cobbetts

### the facts

**Location:** Manchester, Birmingham, Leeds
**Number of partners/assistants:** 146/117
**Total number of trainees:** 50
**Seats:** 4x6 months
**Alternative seats:** Brussels, secondments

Five years ago Cobbetts languished behind its larger Mancunian peers, lavishing much attention on its property practice and little else. Five years on and Cobbetts took a £15 million turnover and turned it into last year's £50 million, a 300% jump. How did the firm do this? Murders and executions? No – mergers and acquisitions.

### rural rides

Like its namesake, the 19th century radical William Cobbett, Cobbetts has been on a rural ride around the shires capturing five other firms and a swag bag of poached partners. It now has a second office in Manchester plus others in Leeds and Birmingham. The first firm to be co-opted, or rather Cobbetted, was Leeds-based Read Hind Stewart in 2003. Then came Walker Charlesworth & Forster, specialising in planning and social housing. Its foray into Yorkshire triumphantly completed, Cobbetts picked up the scent of Manchester corporate specialist Fox Brooks Marshall, whose clients include the AIM-listed Russian mining company Highland Gold which mines in unpronounceable places like Mnogovershinnoe, Novoshirokinskoye and Taseevskoye. The Midas touch inherited from Fox,

Cobbetts has recently done a sparkling deal with Sunrise Diamonds, advising the company in connection with a series of explorations in Finland. Facing south, Cobbetts then cried havoc and let slip the dogs at Birmingham's commercial generalists Lee Crowder. This was welcome news for Lee Crowder trainees; one confessed to have come to Cobbetts "*through the back door*" and knew of the merger before taking the contract with LC. Before you scour the legal journals searching for insider tips, it appears as though Cobbetts' merging spree ended with Leeds planning specialists Wilbraham & Co in 2004.

### virtual reality

Property being the firm's forte, it naturally looked at its own offices and began indulging in a spot of Lawrence Llewellyn-Bowening. "*The old offices were becoming very cramped*;" accordingly new open-plan offices have been designed to complement the new Cobbetts. Trainees love the new Birmingham building with its pods and "*low partitions to allow for more communication*." "*It is aesthetically more pleasing*," effused one critic who continued to stroke his chin at the "*modern art in grey-ey-blue, quite clean, crisp and professional meeting rooms*." While mergers and growth have necessitated the moves, a desire to homogenise the rapidly expanded and disparate firm may explain why Cobbetts commissioned brand new premises. The same architects behind Birmingham have been busy brainstorming for Leeds and Manchester. Having signature architecture across the firm is a realisation of Cobbetts' patented "*One Virtual Office*" vision. The One Virtual Office has already harmonised work flowing through the network, something trainees noticed when "*doing a bit of pensions work for Manchester whilst in Birmingham*." However, whilst Leeds and Manchester trainees do their PSC together, one Manchester Cobbetteer said: "*I don't have a clue what goes on in Birmingham and I don't know any trainees there*." Time will tell how real the One Virtual Office will prove to be, but the new Leeds office

# the true picture

is definitely real, will be ready in 2006, closely followed by new digs in Manchester. For now staff have not only *"a simulation-thingy with a view from the street"* and full permission to *"sticky beak at the plans,"* but also two committees to debate the detail. Apparently, *"they are handpicking door handles at the moment."*

As well as seeing where the firm will live, trainees also have a good idea where it is going. Said one: *"The firm wants us to see the bigger picture."* Preferred, therefore, are *"the commercially aware not straight academics;"* trainees who are *"keen to understand what goes on in practiee."* A caveat: come here and you may begin to Cobbett away like there's no tomorrow. One source was unnervingly adamant *"everyone knows where the firm is going and wants to go there too."* Apart from a degree of de-individuation in speech and unquestioning appreciation for the firm's master plan, the Cobbetts trainee appears *"balanced, down to earth, and not at all full of themselves."* The One Virtual Office, uniform architecture and the odd lapse into Cobbettese may indicate a firm intent on destroying difference, but so far at least the quest for a single identity has not destroyed all individuality. To illustrate, the tasks allocated to trainees *"depend on who you are – if you're not up to it you won't get it."*

## urban adventures

Trainees are not shunted around the network for their four seats, so if you're hired for Birmingham you train in Birmingham and so on. When we interviewed, there were 24 trainees working in Manchester, 13 in Birmingham and nine in Leeds, which gives a fair indication of the relative-size of each office. As might be expected, the range of seats on offer is greatest in Manchester, though even Leeds' trainees have all the basics plus access to a crack pensions team. Commercial litigation, property, banking, corporate, commercial and employment are available across the firm, with Manchester and Birmingham getting an extra helping of private client. If you're lucky you may get to

go on one of a number of client secondments or even spend some time in an affiliated firm in Brussels called Stanbrook & Hopper.

Property is the new black and everyone wears it for a season. Someone told us: *"If you really don't want to do property you could get out of it,"* but we suspect you'd have to have quite a hissy fit to achieve this as around half of all the firm's work is property based. Trainee trepidation often appears unfounded, and once the seat begins they appreciate that *"it's not as dry as land law on the LPC."* And indeed, why wouldn't you want a first seat where *"you won't be restrained doing mundane things."* Assisting on big development project while regularly on the phone to the Land Registry and sorting through deeds is *"not as boring as it sounds."* And you'll get to put all your knowledge into practice when *"reviewing leases and then reporting back to the client."* Trainees also handle a little residential conveyancing solo: *"they try to get you at least one"* because it's good practice for bigger deals...

... of which there are many. The firm represents some 20 housing associations and 90 other registered social landlords and has built up a superb client base amongst local authorities, several of which are engaged in massive urban regeneration projects. Lawyers have been involved with the InPartnership regeneration scheme for Higher Broughton (Salford CC) and various aspects of the regeneration of Langworthy/Seedley. Turning around declining areas is clearly Cobbetts' thing: it is acting for the Ancoats Buildings Preservation Trust on the £14 million repair of Murrays' Mill funded by the Heritage Lottery Fund and the North West Development Agency. From the old to the new; Cobbetts worked on the formation of a joint venture between Lancashire County Developments, Burnley Borough Council, Northern Technologies and Burnley College in relation to a new Technology Centre in Burnley to be developed at the old Michelin tyre factory.

# the true picture

## a little help from your friends

A deluge of insolvency work has hit the Birmingham office so the quasi-mandatory property seat can turn into propinsolvency, with a trainee spending three months in each department. However, ever-lengthening client lists led one trainee to predict that insolvency will soon be a seat in its own right. As they do in insolvency, bundling duties can sit high on the agenda in commercial litigation, where the complexity of cases goes some way to explaining why trainees don't get to run their own show. If intent on dealing with your own cases the family seat is for you, though be aware: it is hard fought over by trainees. For a "*simple divorce*" (for 'simple' read 'not involving much money') "*clients want trainees instead of partners because we're cheaper.*" At the other end of the spectrum, sitting in on a valuable divorce hearing is an eye opener; "*there are huge amounts of money involved. Sitting behind counsel or with a solicitor in court it is interesting to see how counsel works and how the judge decides.*"

The free range in family is unlikely to carry on in employment seats, where a "*to-do list*" from your supervisor "*itemises all the draft tribunal documents, research and bundles*" you must contend with. You "*may get to have a go at more complex stuff*" – letters to the other side and briefs for counsel – although some moaned about "*limited responsibility.*" The vagaries of different departments accepted, the general rule is that "*partners won't mollycoddle you,*" instead "*they go through your mistakes and then let you get on with things.*" But it's also worth pointing out that if you do get deluged you won't be left drowning by your peers. "*E-mails fly around and people are always helping each other out.*"

## curtain calls

For a mere two pounds a month, Cobbetteers have an entire social scene laid on for them. Weekends in Madrid, trips to Alton Towers and a host of smaller jollies are available across the network. Expect "*Thai meals rounded off with clubbing*" and monthly drinks in most departments. Bacchic revelry outside the firm is provided by various professional organisations at whose events Cobbetteers can sup with solicitors and surveyors and imbibe with barristers and accountants. At this year's Birmingham Trainee Solicitors Society soiree in the city's Victorian Botanical Gardens, trainees got to heckle guest speaker Clive Anderson who was asked by one cheeky Cobbetteer whether he would "*prefer a romantic evening with Tony Blair or George Bush.*" To quote our source, jester Anderson replied with his usual brand of wit: "*Erm... well... I think you need to define romantic.*" More fun is promised in the future "*and after the merger is bedded down there will be a lot more cross-office stuff.*" It may be that Manchester and Birmingham could learn a trick from Leeds, where trainees tend to thank God it's Friday more enthusiastically than their Brummie and Mancunian peers. Among the regular haunts for Leeds' Cobbleteers is Plush, a "*swanky, trendy, leather sofa place where a lot of trainees cram in.*" A "*quirky*" Friday may be whiled away in Indie Joze, where "*you go into a deserted building and behind a curtain is revealed a bar.*" After a few behind the curtain you'll be moving in mysterious ways down to Greek Street or the Corn Exchange. In Birmingham trainees head for Digress, Metro and the Old Joint Stock, "*a converted bank that looks like a bank inside.*" In Manchester Le Figaro is currently drawing them in. And long may it do so. In all locations the retention rates for 2005 qualifiers was as good as it has always been. In September 2005, 16 of the 21 qualifiers took jobs, five of them in property, the remainder spread across several departments.

## and finally...

With so many new branches, Cobbetts' skyline has become as crowded as Manhattan's. Rather than merging with even more firms, we suspect it will now concentrate on bedding down the new arrivals and reshaping its own real estate portfolio. What you see now is probably what you'll get when you start your training contract.

# the true picture

## Coffin, Mew and Clover

### the facts

**Location:** Southampton, Fareham, Gosport, Portsmouth
**Number of partners/assistants:** 20/34
**Total number of trainees:** 11
**Seats:** 6x4 mouths
**Alternative seats:** None

SOUTHAMPTON. Michaelmas term lately over, the mists on the Hampshire downs were massing; underneath the neon glow of Sainsbury's a fingerless gloved hand ran across its latest trial bundle...

### done and dusted

Coffin, Mew and Clover's necrotic Dickensian name cannot but conjure up teetering piles of dusty, red ribbon-bound affidavits. It is then with much regret that we must inform readers that while the firm's roots date back to the 1800s, the firm has moved on. Upon asking trainees 'How did you climb into the coffin?' the *Student Guide* was told in no uncertain terms "*We refer to the firm as CMC.*"

These initials could be said to be reflective of the firm's burgeoning CoMmerCial focus. After several years of felling dead wood amongst the partnership and consolidating a sprawl of high street offices into the present trim four, the leaner firm has a new, hungry look. "*The firm is progressive,*" said a source keen to suggest an aim to create "*London by the coast.*" Other trainees resisted such blue-sky thoughts, assuring us that "*while other firms in the region are going commercial, CMC are willing to maintain a balance between private and commercial.*" They pitched the balance at "*50/50,*" with different offices focusing on different work. In the Gosport branch you'll deal with private clients who walk in off the street. Southampton and Fareham service commercial clients "*in town.*" North Harbour is on a business park strategically located by Junction 12 of the M27. During your traineeship you should see the inside of all these offices.

### pic 'n' mix

Added to the private and commercial mix, CMC operates a six-seat scheme that allows the undecided trainee to sample from the candy shop that is the law. Some trainees cited the six seats as a prime reason for joining the firm and noted the "*jealousy*" of friends elsewhere. Undoubtedly the diversity of a contract that allows you to roam has much to commend it; however, there are limitations placed upon trainees who pander to their uncertainty. Unless they have already paralegalled at the firm, new trainees find family and crime are typical starter seats designed to prepare them for the paperwork and face-to-face interaction needed in legal practice. They also find that a property seat is effectively compulsory given the firm's reliance on this work, be it for residential, commercial or social housing clients. In effect, private clients dominate the first year.

Seats can sometimes turn into amorphous "*amalgamations.*" A crime seat at North Harbour can fuse with family so one day you're attending "*pleadings*" in the mags' court, the next "*you're sitting behind counsel in a family matter.*" Preparatory weeks sifting through property registration forms in the residential team morph into a commercial property seat a few weeks later. A mini-clinical negligence seat comes free with every PI seat as both teams occupy the same floor in the office.

### in the navy

To its credit CMC has a stellar crime team, and as a trainee helping out on the duty rota you'll be in and out of the mags' "*never knowing what you're going to get.*" Add in time spent shadowing barristers at the crown court and you have a seat where you're constantly on the move. A car is a must – ditto in family – so if you don't have your own, you'll need to rely on someone who'll let you "*hitch a lift.*" More movement comes from splitting your time "*half-and-half*" between Fareham and Southampton in a family seat. Private cases range from divorces amongst the South Downs' nouveau riche and retirees to "*average Joe Bloggs off the street.*" Trainees also assist on matrimonial files from "*our clients in the forces, off the naval bases.*" When sat in court behind counsel, your job is to explain proceedings to bemused clients and to "*mop up the tears – nothing that a cup of tea and a sympathetic ear can't fix.*" The public side of family may be more emotionally demanding, however. Children proceedings can be "*heart wrenching,*" so you quickly learn to "*step away from it. You won't go home in tears; it's just a fact of life.*"

In Southampton the firm's employment lawyers represent both employees and employers. With employee work "*you feel a sense of justice when you argue for one worker up against a huge firm.*" But our sources had no qualms when acting "*on the flip side*" for university and social housing organisations. CMC is additionally renowned for its representation of police and military personnel, especially those in the navy.

More naval work crops up in the PI department where lawyers' caseloads include dock-related asbestos claims. Trainees may also handle files in CMC's forte, major head injuries. Referrals from the cranial trauma charity Headway are usually complex and sometimes unfortunately require attendance at inquests – "*Morbid? Yes, but something you have to do.*" Assisting a partner or associate allows "*active involvement in cases,*" but with seats lasting only four months it isn't possible to strike out on your own as a trainee. Here, as in other departments, the brevity of seats (and the splintering of some into "*mini-seats*") can work against the trainee's interests.

## smiles for sale

CMC has built a fine name for itself in the world of social housing and acts for the likes of Portsmouth Housing Association, the Town and Country Housing Group plus new acquisitions Saxon Weald Housing Association and South Oxfordshire Housing Association. Two seats are available in the housing department, one contentious and the other non-contentious. In the former, trainees deal with nuisance cases, drafting demotion notices for problem families who breach tenancy agreements or the conditions to be attached to an ASBO. As human rights issues are live throughout these procedures, a trainee learns that "*gently-gently is the best approach.*"

Commercial property in Fareham and Southampton brings client meetings to bash out lease agreements, lease drafting and detailed searches for hidden rights of way and easements. Commercial property for local businesses is, therefore, a little more "*hands-on*" than some other seats. Finally, in a corporate seat you will nose around in the business of a range of clients from "*one-man bands to something a bit more substantial.*" These more substantial clients bring larger deals, such as the arrangement of a £92 million loan facility for Southampton University and the sale of the entire issued share capital of a dental laboratory by dental prosthetics company, Quality Smiles Ltd.

## creole lady branston pickle

CMC is under the jackboot of the irresistible march of supermarkets... "*they just keep following us.*" The Fareham office has Sainsbury's looming over it; North Harbour sits next to Tesco; and lawyers in Southampton stare out at our personal favourite, Waitrose. Perhaps this is why every month trainees take turns on a dinner party rota, a long-standing tradition that usually produces grub with a far greater nutritional value than the typical Friday's dinner of "*a chip bowl*" down the pub. "*It's all quite studenty;*" it is apt therefore that their local chilli-cheese 'n' beanz boozer is called The Varsity. To work it all off the firm has the usual trio of sports teams: football; cricket and netball. Further on the trainee-only front, a few frustrated Pop Idols seem to have infiltrated the firm. Karaoke nights are just an excuse for trainees to indulge in Rogers and Hammerstein numbers and belt out bits from Grease. Worse still, one trainee has succumbed to the 'My Way' virus and purchased her own karaoke set.

Despite all this trainee-only fun, the youngsters are certainly not sealed off from partners. At 8:30am each day they get to open the post with partners, who pull rank by date stamping it. You'll get to know them all through this activity and *"meeting people first thing in the morning is a good way to judge them."* At the other end of the day, trainees are often invited to wine-tasting events and pub quizzes with clients. CMC's main firm-wide extravaganza is the Christmas party, last time themed on 'Moulin Rouge'. Two senior male lawyers donned *"nasty-looking wigs"* and fishnet stockings, pouted for an application of lippy and clambered into red dresses. In the end they looked like *"dockers in drag."* Could this be the same pair who during CMC's Red Nose Day event this year waxed their legs in the name of charity?

## and finally...

Coffin Mew & Clover is a promising firm for those looking for a well-supervised and varied – if slightly inconsistent – traineeship in the South. Fingerless gloves optional.

# Collyer-Bristow

## the facts

**Location:** London
**Number of partners/assistants:** 33/20
**Total number of trainees:** 6
**Seats:** 4x6 months
**Alternative seats:** None

The Collyer-Bristow portrait is built on base coats of corporate/commercial, litigation and property. A strong outline is added by respected family and private client teams, and arresting detail is found in the strokes of *"seductive media, technology and sports work"* for the likes of Damien Rice, Ben Ainslie, Ernie Els, Jane Macdonald and Status Quo.

## painting by numbers

At least six months in the litigation department is the only stipulation for trainees who join this small London mid-sizer. Their other three seats are picked from the four remaining departments in an amicable process in which they just *"sit down as a group and find a combination that works."*

Litigation is C-B's largest department and *"you can spend a year there as it's a very busy seat and there is plenty to do."* Basically, the firm just *"throws you in there!"* Cases relating to employment, property, construction, insolvency and IP are *"all very much up for grabs"* and at any one time you may be *"issuing claims, following them through, going to court with counsel and making your own application in the RCJ."* The flipside to *"the chance to stand up on your own"* is *"a fair share of bundling."* At least *"you can farm out the unnecessary photocopying."* Recently the department represented the League Against Cruel Sports who sought leave to intervene in the Countryside Alliance's attempts to overturn the anti-hunting legislation that was squeezed through using the Parliament Act. With so many different types of case going on, *"if you want experience in a particular area, you have got to shout for it, or you can end up just doing whatever needs doing."* A loud voice may earn you a place assisting C-B consultant Clive Woolf, who represents people on death row in the Carribbean. *"How many trainees get to go to the Privy Council?"* one source challenged.

A seat in coco is felt to be *"the most demanding in terms of time,"* and with work coming at you from a number of different partners, *"you have to learn how to say no."* Standard duties amount to incorporating new businesses and drafting various agreements for *"a mixed bag"* of clients *"from very big, well-known companies right down to start-ups and individuals."* The coco lawyers take on some media, IT and sports work and, again, trainees have to *"shout quite hard"* if they want some of this action. In recent times, C-B has negotiated for Vodafone in connection with endorsements by David Beckham, on behalf of

Damien Rice in relation to the soundtrack for the film 'Closer' and in connection with the music for 'Little Britain'.

## valley deep, mountain high

Beyond the end of Llanddewi Brefi High Street those fine folk at C-B spotted *"a hole in the market for English lawyers practicing in Switzerland."* Without hesitation they filled it with a partner in late 2004 and are now the proud owners of a Geneva office offering commercial advice for Swiss-based multinationals such as existing client Philip Morris International. It is also perfectly placed to support an ample private client practice in London which acts for *"lords and ladies, top QCs and judges, newsreaders and other people in the media, musicians and actors... "* Trainees were bursting with enthusiasm for this *"essentially old-school"* team; one said: *"On paper it doesn't sound exciting at all, but it is strangely addictive."* Perhaps this is because *"you are expected to contribute usefully"* from the outset – *"you are given a pile of files and told 'here you are'. It's the best experience you can get."*

The family team is especially well regarded both inside the firm and out. Coveted among trainees, a seat here gives them exposure to their own small divorce files, including the financial side and private law children's work. Trainees tell us supervisors *"let you do quite a lot at quite an early stage."* Such as? *"Outdoor clerking at the Principle Registry, filing court documents, going before the district judge of the day, seeing clients on your own, conferences with counsel... "* All in all the experiences in this seat are described as *"brilliant!"* By contrast, *"property is not so popular."* There is both commercial work for developers such as Willmott Dixon and Cadugan Developments and residential conveyancing for a varied clientele. Though they failed to muster anywhere near the same enthusiasm for the experience in property, trainees did admit that *"people who have done it have got more out of it than they thought they would."*

## potty

The firm's Bedford Row offices are home to an art gallery that holds regular exhibitions. The Christmas exhibition, where 200 pieces of art go on sale at £200 *"can be pretty mental."* Trainees are drafted in to man the sales desk, but only after they have identified their own personal favourites. Among the most memorable pieces from recent years, *"a really hideous ceramic bulldog"* and *"a really rough-looking polka dot teapot. It was just an absolute abomination."* The firm's interest in the arts also runs to commissioning an artistic Christmas tree each year. Apparently *"the garage is absolutely chock-a-block with old Christmas trees,"* including last year's *"very strange but quite cool"* effort. Having seen a picture of it, we would agree with one trainee's description – *"a toilet brush... kind of red with a kind of tail wrapped round it."*

The garage is not the only place that is chock-a-block. In cramped offices in Bedford Row, trainees have been sitting *"wherever there is space."* Hopefully the September 2005 expansion into adjoining buildings will have given them a little more elbow-room. The firm has occupied its premises in Bedford Row for 180 years and we wondered if its long history in one of the capital's most famous legal neighbourhoods was indicative of other things cobwebby. *"It is pretty traditional,"* one trainee told us. *"The senior partner has a big leather desk, and you do have to wear a suit, except when it is boiling"* (and on one Friday a month). An old-school approach may also lie behind a system that allows trainees to seek out work that interests them from across departments, and receive appraisals halfway through each seat from whoever is most familiar with their work.

## dancing bears

When asked why they chose the firm, one trainee voiced a common sentiment – *"I knew I'd be like a square peg in a round hole in a large City firm."* Our sources were unabashed about their decision to train somewhere *"a bit quirky and a bit different, somewhere that respected individualism.*" Far from a collection of freak show acts, the firm is a place for those who shun the homogeneity of City firms and "*want some balance in their lives.*" When things are busy "*staying late is part of the deal,*" but these late nights are a rarity and most people down tools around 6.30pm. Trainees get on well together and frequent a pub called The Enterprise of an evening. There are regular trainee dinners and they spend "*quite a bit of time sitting in Gray's Inn Gardens drinking Frappucinos and eating sandwiches.*" A rather staid black-tie Christmas bash was overshadowed by this year's summer barbecue overlooking the bear enclosure at London Zoo. Apparently the polar bears were especially fond of the steel band.

C-B is proud of its many "*slightly artistic types,*" including "*an associate who has written a book, a partner who is an artist on the side, a few art lovers, a couple of musicians and another partner who writes comedy for Radio 4.*" There are no artists among the current trainee group; some come straight from law school, one had a previous career in research, another is ex-RAF and one used to be a surgeon. Our sources also stressed the importance of strong academic credentials, adding: "*You've got to be able to stand your own and have a bit about you.*" In 2005, two of the three qualifiers took jobs with the firm.

## and finally...

For a colourful legal landscape, a tableau of interesting clients and some engaging portraits, you'll definitely want to go and view the Collyer-Bristow gallery.

# Cripps Harries Hall

## the facts

**Location:** Tunbridge Wells, London
**Number of partners/assistants:** 35/50
**Total number of trainees:** 14
**Seats:** Usually 6 of varying length
**Alternative seats:** None

With 38 partners and an annual turnover of nearly £20 million, there's much more to Cripps Harries Hall than its ultra middle-class location might suggest. Pretty, but City, you might say.

## a spa is born

In 1606 a hung-over young Kentish nobleman, Lord North, while looking for a drink of water, happened upon a reddish iron-rich pool. Its contents hit the spot. Suitably refreshed, he declared the spring to have healing properties. Some 400 years and hundreds of thousands of thirsty ladies and gentlemen later, we have Royal Tunbridge Wells, and for the last 173 years Cripps Harries Hall has represented the great, good and plain old wealthy of this most English of towns. A traditional private client base still plays its part, particularly on the "*landed gentry, high-value estates and farms*" side of things, although "*not all have been with the firm since 1832!*"

These days it is commercial practice that propels Cripps forwards and the firm has recently reorganised itself along the suitably watery lines of "*business streams.*" We're told "*they're all about giving commercial clients the sense of being our total obsession, so you don't have a corporate department with lawyers who do charities work, you have a specific charities stream.*" Although still "*too early to tell whether it will make a massive difference,*" what the reorganisation definitely reflects is the exacting standards of a client list that includes central government and local authority departments, police authorities, housing associations, utilities, regional businesses and some plcs, as well as charities such as the Royal Geographical Society, Paignton Zoo and Living Coasts. The 2005 hire of a dual-qualified UK/French lawyer to target French companies setting up in the South East is another indication of Cripps' corporate ambitions, through the loss of other corporate partners to rival firms must have stung.

At present, commercial property and litigation/dispute resolution (LDR) constitute "*the lion's share*" of the firm's work. In recent times Cripps massively boosted its property profile through involvement in Lovells' innovative Mexican-Wave scheme for PruPIM, the property investment group of Prudential. The scheme involves Cripps being fed less complex aspects of the group's real estate management by main lawyers Lovells, and it works well for everyone: the City player's lawyers are freed up for more complex work, PruPIM pays less on simpler matters and Cripps enjoys a mass of new instructions. What's more, this work breeds other work. In the last year, Lovells also subcontracted the due diligence element of a £2.1 billion PFI project to the firm. And Cripps has been independently successful, retaining a place on the legal panel of property giant Land Securities and scooping its own instructions from well-known developers and government agencies. A place on Kent County Council's major projects panel was a notable achievement last year.

Property dispute resolution is *"a fresh young department"* thriving on the PruPIM injection, but also taking on plenty of its own work. Trainees spoke of *"lots of Channel Tunnel Rail Link matters."* Commercial LDR acts for a range of regional, national and international clients including RBS, a Malaysian can manufacturer, an Indian steel company and a notable utility company. Recent cases include a global logistics company in disputation with an international car manufacturer, and advice to Creative Resins International in a libel action against Glasslam Europe. Admittedly, not as glamorous as Gary Lineker and Harry Kewell's recent bust-up, but it doubtless sent ripples though the world of decorative glass technology.

## speak up!

Cripps possesses a petite London premises, the primary purpose of which is *"to provide a place to meet London or national clients"* and *"give you a base for a few days."* However, Kent is *"the heartland"* of the firm's practice and the one definite in the life of a Cripps trainee is two years based in Tunbridge Wells. We say one definite because a training here

necessitates more flexibility than a troupe of Romanian gymnasts. The usual arrangement is for trainees to take six seats, the length of which varies according to the area of law and the popularity of the seat. For example, because family and employment are *"incredibly popular,"* trainees can only expect to notch up three months in either.

Nevertheless, even this trend is not certain because *"you can ask to extend your stay and they'll do what they can to help you."* Though *"you have to be very clear about your preferences along the way,"* those who do shout up can sometimes get what they want. We learned of people spending brief stints in corporate and much longer periods in litigation, and people who had cut six seats to just four so as to embrace a much-loved field. However, the firm's needs and areas of expertise will often call the shots; for example, because of its size a commercial property seat is *"almost inevitable."* Apart from this trainees can choose from planning, dispute resolution (either commercial or private client-themed), property litigation, residential conveyancing, farms & estates, construction, corporate, family, employment and tax, wills and probate. This wealth of choice suits anyone *"not certain where their legal interests lie,"* and the six-seat system *"gives excellent breadth of experience."* Naturally there are a few qualifications on the grounds that *"three months isn't always enough time pick up a seat,"* but overall the scheme ticks along remarkably well.

## purple prose

Cripps' near-legendary 'Purple Pages' intranet isn't the only aspect of the firm's support structure that is more than comprehensive. Weekly training sessions are administered via *"in-house seminars and lectures from external experts,"* informal feedback is plenteous because *"you talk with your supervisor a lot to judge work levels and get comments,"* and trainees speak admiringly of *"supervisors' ability to ensure that as you progress you get more and more involved in things."* Perhaps we wouldn't go as far as one trainee who announced with high drama: *"We are appraised to within an inch of our lives,"* but the structure of formal feedback certainly has a lot to do with this nurturing *"but not limiting"* support. Trainees submit themselves to lower-key monthly appraisals with supervisors and a grander final appraisal at the end of each seat. This is swiftly followed up by *"a meeting with the head of HR and the managing partner."* No wonder *"you always have a clear sense of how you are doing."*

In the past we have been moved to wax lyrical about the firm's contracted working day of 9am to 5.15pm with a 75-minute lunch break, but this year's interviewees punctured our hyperbole. *"To be honest you don't often leave on the dot of 5.15pm,"* *"my normal day is 8.30am-6pm."* Matters demanding a trip to Lun'on town can also involve *"getting back late at 10pm or even 12pm,"* albeit *"not too often."* In short, the hours are just off unbelievably good and definitely *"not those that friends do in the City."* All our sources valued *"the chance to do City-type work at a regional firm with presence,"* and had been attracted by *"the variety of experience in training, from residential conveyancing to private client to corporate."* For them *"ambition," "a progressive outlook," "ongoing growth"* and *"a great reputation"* were all reason enough to give the City a miss and hitch themselves to Cripps' rising star. In 2005, all seven qualifiers once again ignored the temptations of the City and took NQ jobs with the firm.

## shaken not stirred

Many trainees enjoy *"a leisurely walk into work and no battle with the tube."* Virtually everyone we interviewed had chosen the firm to avoid *"the London lifestyle, the London hours,"* but one thing they cannot avoid is *"the high cost of living,"* which when negotiated on a relatively low salary means *"your training contract is a matter of surviving financially."* One way of side-stepping the issue is to live at home, and with *"three or four trainees per year having a family connection to the local area"* that is an option for several in the group. Those who arrive in Tunbridge Wells as strangers suggest *"it is an easy*

*transition"* aided by *"the supportive atmosphere at the firm"* and the pleasant environs of the town. *"It's a beautiful town and it's really easy to get into the country."* The firm is based in decorous Georgian offices in the heart, and appropriately the dress code is described as *"conservative."*

Those who choose to socialise with work colleagues enjoy end-of-month drinks, sports teams (cricket, football, netball or racquets) and an annual summer ball organised by second-year trainees. When we conducted our interviews plans were afoot for a James Bond-styled extravaganza, including *"a Las Vegas casino and a top secret quiz."* London is only a *"40-minute train ride away,"* so it's easy enough to keep City friendships or socialise in the Big Smoke. Nights out in Tunbridge Wells usually mean Sankey's wine bar and/or *"dreadful"* club Davinchi's (sic), where trainees will *"often see the same faces from the town"* though *"you'd have to be fantastically sociable to strike up acquaintance that way."* Some people do live Tunbridge life to the full – *"One girl's got really into the local salsa scene."* You go girl!

## and finally...

Cripps Harries Hall will give you *"quality, diversity and responsibility"* in the most serene of surroundings. Wells, what are you waiting for?

# Dechert LLP

## the facts

**Location:** London
**Number of partners/assistants:** 38/62
**Total number of trainees:** 24
**Seats:** 6x4 months
**Alternative seats:** Overseas seats, secondments
**Extras:** Pro bono – comprehensive in-house programme and North Kensington Law Centre

Once True Brit, it's been more True Grit at Dechert of late. After initial post-merger wobbles this Anglo-American mid-sizer is shaping up nicely.

# the true picture

## setting up shop

In last year's guide while paying homage to Dechert's American roots, we gave readers a taste of the rich history of the city of Philadelphia. In 2005, the year in which Dechert's London office moves from its old home near the Temple, we've chosen to honour its English roots. The story started in 1938 when young solicitors Leonard Sainer and Alfred Webb joined forces with Frank Titmuss. The resulting firm, Titmuss, Sainer & Webb became one of the best in the market for property deals, especially ones involving retail premises. This leaning was in part due to Leonard Sainer's connection to the chap who set up Sears, and indeed Sainer eventually became chairman of the retail giant. Mr Sainer was a bit of a star all round it seems; not only did he invent a clever type of property deal called the 'sale and leaseback', he also conjured up the concept of the 'hostile takeover'. After learning all this we were amazed the firm was ever willing to give up its original name when it tied the knot with the Americans from Philly. It certainly makes you wonder if the latest chapters of the firm's story can match up to the early ones...

In 1994, the firm entered into an alliance with US firm Dechert Price & Rhoads. As each year passed, their relationship became stronger until eventually in 2000 the parties merged fully. Ever since, the English office has been increasingly easily swayed by the Americans, and in the eyes of some people, subsumed by them. What resulted was a shrinkage in London – trainees made no bones about the fact that some partners had gone (taking associates with them) because they didn't like the changes. Other partners departed because their specialist practices no longer fitted in with the firm's plans. For a while it looked a touch wobbly, but for their part, current trainees are unconcerned with these developments. The definite view of one source was that *"over the last 18 months the firm became an even friendlier place as some of the older, less friendly partners left."*

## reit good

What Dechert has seen in London is a shift in emphasis, *"a swing towards corporate and financial services."* One wise source explained how this has had *"a knock-on effect on other departments. The property department is looking to become more involved in investments, for example REITS rather than straightforward deals."* Trainees spoke enthusiastically of *"great experiences"* in the corporate department. Because it is not an overly fragmented group, trainees get to try M&A, private equity, share transfers and even partnership matters. *"I did one big deal for two and a half months,"* said a source, *"and the other month and a half was a variety of matters. I saw four or five completions in that time."* From drafting board minutes to managing online data rooms and attending meetings, *"it's certainly not just crappy photocopying jobs."* In the past year the firm has sold the Early Learning Centre chain to the boss of Waterstones, a former MD of Ocado and a senior M&S exec, for £62 million. It also took on the massive £1 billion sale of Travelex, the foreign exchange company that features Jonny Wilkinson in its sticks and stones TV advertising campaign. The majority of our sources sensed *"there's definitely more of a feeling that the firm is competing at a higher level and there's better work. The Travelex deal shows that."*

Speaking of big-money matters, Dechert's UK financial services team has grown from a standing start in 1997 to one of the country's top departments, billing over £9 million in 2004. It helps to set up funds, management companies and distribution operations in jurisdictions around the world, and advises on the creation of domestic and offshore funds, collateralised debt obligations and membership applications to the FSA and other regulators as well as pursuing activities in the main cash and derivatives markets. *"It is without doubt the scariest seat you can do. With everything else you have had some experience of it at law school or in everyday life, but financial services is a bit of a mystery."* At each rotation there are three or four seats here so it is well worth the firm laying on an induction and specific training sessions. "*Not a lot makes sense in the first month*," admitted one past occupant, "*it was a very, very difficult first month*." A word of advice: "*People who have no real interest in corporate should not go there*," but "*it is looked on very favourably if you do a seat in FS*."

To mirror the US operation, the real estate department has been fused with the finance department. Trainees spoke of "*a lot of landlord & tenant work – both points of view – quite a lot of research and also a residential house sale*" (presumably just for the experience of running a deal solo). Though Dechert has been accused of allowing elements of its real estate practice to wither, it is still very strong on the finance side. Among its many international bank clients are GMAC and Royal Bank of Scotland. Other real estate clients include Tate & Lyle, Bhs, Freeport Leisure and Frogmore Estates.

## it's a group thing

A six-seat system is fully exploited by trainees, and most repeat favourite seats. Said one: "*I am incredibly pleased I chose a firm that let me do six seats. It helped me make up my mind and allowed me to be sure my qualification choice is the correct one*." On the seat list: corporate; financial services; banking; tax; real estate; property litigation; commercial litigation; employment and contentious IP. Everyone does a corporate-type seat, a property-type seat and a litigation-type seat. The allocations seem scrupulously fair, and we encountered people who had concentrated on corporate and financial services and people who had taken a mainly contentious route. The scheme seems brilliantly organised.

At the start of their training contracts, new recruits visit the head office in Philadelphia, which is fittingly known as the city of brotherly love. "*The Philly jaunt was great*," reported one trainee. "*It was good to meet the American folk in the same position as us and excellent for us as a group to get to know each*

other. *We really gelled*." A competition law seat in Brussels gives another chance to leave the office behind, as does a new Munich seat for a German-speaking trainee. Additionally, some of those qualifying into transactional seats get to spend the last two months of the training contract in Philadelphia, Boston, New York or Washington. Sadly, qualification did not bring good news for all at Dechert in 2005. Eight jobs were offered to 14 people: two each in FS, corporate and real estate plus one each in tax and litigation.

Of the Americanisation process, one source told us: "*When I first joined the firm seemed like an outpost of an American firm that was run like a British firm, now we are a real part of an American firm and our billing and IT services come from the US. The IT helpdesk is in Philly; you call up and a guy proxies into your computer from there. It works well though!*" The general view is that "*Philly tells London precisely what is happening*," yet many trainees still speak of a relatively relaxed British environment: "*We're not all working 70 hours a week and coming in at the weekend*." One was quick to stress that "*there are no bean bags here and we're not all sitting round drinking Starbucks coffee*." The biggest effect of the American management is noted in relation to the work – larger deals, more transatlantic matters and there are even four or five US partners in the London office these days. On the downside, staff in London still get annoying communiqués from America addressed to 'All Attorneys'. Said one trainee: "*I sometimes think the US lawyers forget the firm has a European element, especially when you get an e-mail asking you if you know of a lawyer in Rapid Falls, Michigan*."

## saint bernard

Trainees have nothing but praise for both the quality of their work experiences and the volume, content and quality of classroom-style training. "*We're trained up to our eyeballs*," joked one. All attribute their satisfaction to the hard work of director of training Bernard George, who just happens to be a former head of the College of Law. *"Bernard is a god in terms of training and mentoring and just checking that you are OK. He is the man, there is no other like him."* Bernard's watchful eye is backed up by a 'panel partner' for each trainee. These individuals commit to sitting in on every end-of-seat appraisal and some trainees maintain regular contact with them, periodically meeting to discuss their progress. At the grindstone, of course there will be times you'll be stuck proof-reading or bundling documents, but such chores do not dominate. Rise to the challenge and good work should follow; return to a seat and the work will become more challenging.

Trainees share much of their socialising with partners, associates and support staff, and spoke warmly of their seniors. *"I would have no problem in speaking to partners,"* confirmed one typical source. The firm's associates organise social events, sometimes for no reason other than *"to get rid of their budget!"* The calendar reaches its peak during the summer when American summer interns get to spend a few days in London. Next year they will visit the firm's new *"shiny and angular"* office at Times Square – *"that's Times Square London, not New York, unfortunately."* Although they will miss out on the tinkling fountain and show of blooms in the courtyard next to the firm's old offices in Inner Temple, there will be ample mod cons to compensate.

The sporting life of the firm is worth a mention, if only because the football team came third in the legal league last year. When we spoke to them, trainees were warming up for the annual partners v staff cricket match in Dulwich. Said one: *"I don't know anything about cricket, I am just showing up for the barbecue. They do let the girls have a go though."* Trainees can also enter a five-a-side footie tournament (*"from what I can gather it is quite competitive"*) and get involved with the mixed hockey and softball teams. Doubtless they're all good sports at this place.

## and finally...

If anyone recommends Dechert to you based on experiences dating back more than, say, three years, we suggest you seek a fresher second opinion. Dechert is definitely not the firm it used to be. But do we hesitate to recommend it? Absolutely not!

# Denton Wilde Sapte

## the facts

**Location:** London, Milton Keynes
**Number of partners/assistants:** 122/419
**Total number of trainees:** 73
**Seats:** 4x6 months
**Alternative seats:** Overseas seats, secondments
**Extras:** Pro bono – RCJ CAB, The Prince's Youth Business Trust; language training

Denton Wilde Sapte is a firm with a long history in London. It has all the appeal one expects of a broad-based, mid-sized player, but there have been some twists and turns in its tale of late.

## a walk on the wilde side

It's not unfair to say that Dentons has had a rough ride recently – imagine rodeo riding with no trousers and a sandpaper saddle. To give you the back story, 2003 saw the firm cut 70 jobs, let 50% of its qualifying trainees go and say arrivederci and adieu to its European network, Denton International (not to be confused with Dana International, the transvestite Israeli champion of Eurovision 98). In 2004 it pulled out of Asia, cutting off Beijing, Singapore, Hong Kong and Tokyo. You would have thought it was due a break after that lot, but profits and partners continued to roll out of Dentons' door. A further blow came with the resignation of 40 people from its media and IP team last year and the relocation of a five-partner insurance and reinsurance litigation group to Chadbourne & Parke. Turnover is also down more than 10% on last year and, as we were researching for this feature, the head of Dentons' much-trumpeted Africa practice was also poached by DLA. Again, this must have stung because Dentons had invested heavily in Africa in recent times, securing formal associations with local firms in Botswana, Ghana, Tanzania, Uganda and Zambia.

Having spilled the beans on the bad news, we need to commend the firm for the way in which it has responded. Instead of moping around or indulging in a festival of bitching and recriminations, the partners have invested in a fresh new look, installed new managers and devised a plan to take them forward. You can see the new look for yourself on the firm's website; a slick, polished affair with plenty of orange (the corporate colour and a selection of inspirational quotes from the likes of Benjamin Franklin, WH Auden and Nobel physicist Werner Heisenberg. On the grad recruitment part of the site you'll also find some fun puzzles and pretty bog-standard interview tips – turn up on time, be positive, don't forget to smile, trim unruly nose hairs, etc. The site frequently returns to the concept of knowledge and so, naturally, we wondered about the firm's newly acquired self-knowledge.

In early 2005 the current chief exec Howard Morris took the reins, promising to make the management more transparent and more flexible. Trainees told us: "*He sends regular e-mails and there's also a suggestions box*" for any thoughts they wish to share. We're not sure what has been collected in the box, but we can pass on a couple of the suggestions that came out of our interviews. "*The work we do is good and we have the ability, but I'm not sure why that's not transferred into profit levels,*" pondered one trainee. Another trainee would "*get everyone together in one place and work together a bit more – people work in separate offices [and separate buildings] and no one is sure what people do in other departments. There must be a degree of internal marketing to each other.*"

## fantastic four

The firm is now structured around four key industry sectors: financial institutions; real estate and retail; energy, transport and infrastructure; and technology, media and telecoms (TMT). The latter remains important despite the defection of 40 lawyers to DLA; indeed the firm is doing rather well in the field of IT outsourcing for clients like GE Capital, Toshiba, and Teletext, and this year advised the MoD on a huge £4 billion IT outsourcing contract. TMT lawyers also worked on the settlement of a dispute between Virgin Mobile, Virgin Management and T-Mobile, plus Virgin's £198 million buy-back of T-Mobile's 50% shareholding in its mobile operator. And no doubt they shared in the England team's joy last summer, having advised the England Cricket Board on a further four-year sponsorship deal with Vodafone.

The energy, transport and infrastructure group advised the listed Spanish electricity company UniÛn Fenosa on the sale of Cambridge Water plc to Cheung Kong Infrastructure, a listed Hong Kong-based company. Lawyers were active, too, on the first round of government wind farm concessions, advising Irish wind farm developer Airtricity Holdings in relation to the establishment of a joint venture with US leader Fluor International for the construction and operation of a wind farm in the Thames Estuary. On the transport side, lawyers advised Stagecoach and Virgin Rail on their joint bid for the new InterCity East Coast franchise, a deal initially wrapped up in a joint venture with Deutsche Bahn.

When it comes to advising financial institutions the firm has a great profile and recently joined GE Capital's new M&A panel. Clients such as HSBC, National Australia Bank, Barclays, Citibank and Société Générale are also firmly on board. Dentons is especially known for its acquisition finance capability as well as boasting more focused expertise in areas such as trade finance, asset finance and Islamic finance. It recently advised ABN AMRO on the £1.75 billion facility for Morrison's in relation to

# the true picture

the acquisition of Safeway shares. And in the field of syndicated lending it has advised BayernLB and the other mandated lead arrangers on a facility involving some 63 international banks. The real estate and retail practice continues to handle large-scale property transactions, acting recently for London & Regional Properties on its disposal of 280 pubs to the Laurel Pub Co. Dentons also boasts an impressive real estate litigation practice, acting on behalf of both landlords and tenants. Last year it represented both HSBC and Argos in relation to large leasehold disputes.

## tax evasion

But what can you expect to contribute as a wet-nosed trainee? And which areas of the firm's work will you encounter? These days *the general policy is that you will end up in real estate and in banking.* Trainees say *a few feathers were ruffled by being forced to do these seats,* but simply suggest *you must get on with it.* When we checked we learned from HR that, yes indeed, banking and finance seats are central to the training experience at the firm and they advise trainees to do both, but not all do so. Finance trainees can expect to be having a go at *first drafts of loan agreements and legal opinions* as well as *running lists of conditions precedent with lots of autonomy, and client contact with overseas lawyers and banks.* The general feeling is that in this part of the firm *they're good at giving you decent work and a fair amount of client contact,* although it is here you are likely to encounter the worst hours – said one trainee: *I wasn't getting home until 11 at night.* To get on in one of these seats, *you must be excited by big numbers and large transactions.* A stint in corporate also brings *transaction management, attending meetings and first drafts* of sections of agreements, or even entire documents if small enough. Though the hours are generally more regular, the experiences on offer in property are essentially pretty similar.

Tax, meanwhile, involves *far more research, but the work style wasn't for me, I like the transactional* side of things,* one source mused. When we asked another past occupant of the seat how they had found it, they cleverly replied: *Tax is something that finds you.* Perhaps they were more suited to the *sense of autonomy and independence* in real estate, which prompted the comments: *I was negotiating highway agreements off my own bat. I wasn't just a small atom in a greater whole.* By contrast, a trainee reporting on a project finance seat spoke of less responsibility, mainly because *the details of the loan documents are very technical, so it doesn't even come down to junior solicitors. I was responsible for looking at conditions precedent and liaising with other parties and solicitors... and post-completion I was putting the bibles together. It was very administrative, but everyone knows that before they go in.*

Some say litigation is where the real law lies – *I like the adversarial nature,* declared one trainee. *I enjoy the dynamic between the solicitor and the client, managing client expectations and so on.* One of our sources assisted on a large arbitration, *taking witness statements and managing documents... there was lots of checking cross-references and proof-reading, and lots of interpreting spreadsheets.* And to make up for the document pushing, there is occasional advocacy, such as in property lit where on a squatters proceeding one trainee had *appeared before a master with the clients in the background.* Property lit is mostly hands-on work – *It's a small team so I was involved in quite high-level matters and also running my own files,* typically *debt collection and rent arrears.* Employment seats take trainees *to employment tribunals for various hearings* and introduce them to *negotiations for high-level dismissals.* Frankly, the list of different experiences goes on and on... rather like the list of different seat options.

## lacuna matata

Usually, 9.30am until 6pm is *normal;* real estate can be *hectic,* though *late nights are rare,* and a busy time in litigation is defined as *until 7pm most nights.* As is to be expected, banking is the killer, and here "*you can be in until one or two in the morning.*" When asked about low points, trainees' most common grumble concerned hours. "*It's tough when you're stuck on a deal and you see your friends leaving on time,*" said one.

Dentons no longer has the same international capability that had inspired some trainees to apply to the firm, but we did hear that "*after the lacuna of the last 18 months there is now an increased opportunity to go abroad,*" be this in one of the firm's own offices – Paris, Moscow or Dubai – or to a 'best friend' firm in, say Rome or Madrid. Alas, anyone hoping to tack an African safari onto their training may have to think again... though we hear Paris has an excellent zoo. Time out of the office can also be achieved through a secondment to an energy client or one of the banks with which the firm has long-standing relationships.

Our sources had thought deeply about the kind of training they wanted before taking the leap. "*What grabbed me about the firm was that I knew a couple of people who had been taken on and they were both completely different; one was older and had been working at something else before, the other hadn't studied law at university.*" Another trainee judged the firm to be "*broad-minded in recruitment.*" The clear message is that "*there is no set standard of what a trainee should be.*" Dentons' style was considered to be down the middle, "*not old school but not cutting edge.*" Like listening to Dire Straits on your iPod, maybe. One trainee said: "*My general impression is that it's not too hierarchical, there's never any sense that trainees can't pipe up.*" There are "*no prima donnas*" we hear; "*it's always easy to find people to give you a hand.*" Be warned that you probably won't fit in if "*you're someone who is too strong a character – and if you don't want to dig in and work.*" The training on offer is of a very decent standard and mostly takes place in-house.

Less cheery news: Dentons has been plagued by relatively low retention rates on qualification in the last couple of years and 2005 was unfortunately no turnaround year. Final score: 31 of the 43 qualifiers stayed on.

The social life depends very much on the intake and the department you're stationed in. One trainee we spoke to reported it as "*scorching,*" another as "*a little underwhelming.*" Rest assured that there are plenty of watering holes nearby in which to drown your sorrows or celebrate triumphs, including the ubiquitous Corney & Barrow (although "*you have to watch out for partners*"), and a quick e-mail around the office will "*always throw up a few stragglers who'll join you for a half.*"

## and finally...

By all accounts Denton Wilde Sapte is ready for a new relationship after recent dramas. Apparently the managing partner has appointed someone to draw up a list of potential merger suitors, most likely to be a mid-sized UK firm. Definitely a firm worth watching.

# Dickinson Dees

## the facts

**Location:** Newcastle, Stockton-on-Tees
**Number of partners/assistants:** 65/128
**Total number of trainees:** 28
**Seats:** 4x6 months
**Alternative seats:** Brussels, secondments

Two hundred years old and the cornerstone of Newcastle's legal landscape, Dickinson Dees shows no sign of complacency. Without doubt, this is one of the finest regional firms in the UK and if you're even considering a commercial career in the North East, it has got to be right up there on your shortlist.

## convoy!

Before packing your suitcase and heading to London to see if the streets are paved with gold, do yourself a favour and pause for thought over the North East. Large commercial clients are also paying heed to the region now that they've realised they can get their work done up there perfectly well and for a fraction of City prices.

With offices in Newcastle and Stockton-on-Tees, DD has a packed quiver of commercial departments. At the risk of boring readers by listing the areas of practice in which our parent publication *Chambers UK* ranks the firm top in the North East, we're going to do it anyway – agriculture and rural affairs, banking and finance, charities, competition law, construction, corporate finance, education, employment, energy, family, financial services, IT, IP, insolvency, licensing, litigation, local government, pensions, planning, private client, real estate, social housing, tax and transport. Did we miss anything? Ah yes, client secondments to the likes of Durham City Council and Reg Vardy.

Dickie Dees' reputation has allowed it to take a swipe at the big national firms, recently pipping Eversheds and Pinsent Masons to the post on a tender to oversee Cumbria County Council's £200 million outsourcing of road maintenance operations. These two firms also had to budge up and make room on the English Partnerships panel after an exhaustive eight-month review ended with our subject firm earning a coveted place. Other new public sector clients including Leeds City Council have come flocking, as have clients in the private sector – Sainsbury's and US chemical group Huntsman were recently herded in. When boarding a bus in London your conditions of carriage have been overseen by our friends in the North East ever since Arriva got wise to DD. Indeed, there's a veritable convoy of transportation clients now shunning the lawyers in the capital and heading to Newcastle for legal advice – Thameslink Rail, the London Central bus company and London General Transport Service.

## until the cows come home

The training contract has four seats, three of which are restricted to seats within the coco and property groupings, and one of which must be contentious. On day one of the compulsory property seat your new desk will be covered in files, testament to the "*extra responsibility*" given to trainees in property. Everyone gets to see a property purchase all the way through, as well as assisting partners on enormous transactions that may cover hundreds of sites. An alternative to straight property is the secured lending seat where, working for the banks, trainees learn how companies use property assets as security for loans in much the same way that people mortgage their homes. A construction seat would be a natural complement for anyone considering qualification into property, and here a mixture of non-contentious and contentious work provides "*enjoyable variety*" – everything from drafting building contracts, warranties and framework agreements to note taking and observation at client meetings.

The coco department brings trainees into contact with "*all types of clients from small businesses and limited companies to plcs.*" Always assisting partners and assistants, their work is similarly varied in scope depending on what breed of seat they end up with. A commercial seat means "*drafting contract terms and conditions, licences for IT and software, data protection policies etc.*" A seat working on private equity deals was felt to have "*a very steep learning curve.*" Corporate seats are the usual culprits for longer hours. Said one source: "*I stayed until 3am for a completion and it was good to see something through to closure... quite exciting and a bit of a buzz.*" Overall, our sources appreciated being taken to client meetings, if only to note-take and listen, though "*if you have anything of value to say, you say it.*"

In commercial litigation, you may get a small file of your own, but mostly training will come through smaller tasks for the clients which partners and associates are representing. You should get to practise drafting applications and taking witness statements as well as paper chasing. The highlight has to be "*advocacy, usually before a district judge.*" At first a "*nerve-wracking experience,*" soon it becomes just another day in court. If your seat is in property litigation, you'll see "*a mixture of run-of-the-mill*" landlord and tenant disputes, termination of leases, rent arrears recovery and kicking tenants out." If all that sounds quite hard-nosed, you might prefer the cases relating to "*more esoteric stuff and weird, little-used land law.*" Believe it or not we even heard about a case of some cows being evicted from their field, though admittedly this was a tale from the firm's agriculture department.

## rescue workers

In an insolvency seat, as well as winding up applications ("*applying for a company to be killed off*"), you'll work on "*company rescue.*" Alas we can't back up the trainee who tried to convince us this meant "*wearing overalls and jumping out of a van!*" Here, you'll assist partners as they attempt to "*shore up a company's resources so it gets as much money as possible out of the financial mess it got itself into.*" For those interested in seeing how companies can get into such messes, a stint in secured lending will reveal all. Working for banks, say on a deal to lend money to a company looking to expand, "*you investigate and snoop into the company's present assets – it's like being a detective.*"

Other seats include private client ("*more tax-based than expected*"), family ("*mainly rich people*"), employment, planning and environmental law. A few lucky trainees get to spend three months at the other end of the Eurostar tracks in Brussels doing EU competition law with Crosby Renouf, "*a quaint little practice that deals with everyone from trade associations to whole countries.*" Backseat driving is the curse of working for big clients, but who cares when the Merc takes you to lobbying meetings at the Commission with clients of all nationalities. "*If you pick up the phone you won't be replying in English,*" chuckled one trainee before confirming that the rest of the conversation usually did take place in the trainee's mother tongue.

## at the ambassador's residence

In all seats, appraisals every three months and constant supervision are combined with departmental training. When, where and what "*all varies according to the department; some are training-heavy and law-specific and some just give refresher courses.*" Lawyers from around the firm sometimes don mortarboards to teach their peers, so the pensions team will impart relevant pearls of wisdom to the insolvency team, and the environment lawyers will make pertinent presentations for the property lawyers. When not cramming new law, trainees are no strangers to hard graft: "*Beware of thinking you'll have an easy ride here,*" warned one source. "*London people think it's all play up here, but there are no jollies and beers at five – you're here to work.*" As we indicated earlier, late nights and weekends are not unknown, though "*you'll never be left late in front of a photocopier.*"

The firm will shortly be moving some staff into a new office at Trinity Gardens behind Newcastle's law courts. Its other building, St Anne's, occupies a waterfront location. The "*state-of-the-art*" Trinity Gardens has a roof terrace overlooking the Tyne "*and may even have a Tesco Metro at the bottom of it. We're quite thrilled about that.*" Trainees viewed the move as wholly appropriate for "*a firm continuing to change from a traditional regional to a modern corporate organisation.*" A smaller Teesdale office offers seats in family, commercial litigation, property and corporate. If any of these appeal, a posting to the Tees Valley is sweetened with a company car – "*a Peugeot 307*" which you'll "*miss like mad*" afterwards.

Rather like their firm, DD trainees exude professionalism. They are encouraged into the mindset that everyone is an ambassador for the firm, and we were certainly given the Ferrero Rocher treatment. "*It's part of learning about business development,*" explained one source. "*We're encouraged to get involved in that early on… it's not just down to partners to drum up clients and raise the firm's profile, it's up to all in the firm.*" In case you were wondering, the DD trainee is not a corporate clone – a recent intake included an ex-English lecturer, an adjourned journo, a former farmer and a sometime soldier. Varied backgrounds are coupled with fine academic credentials. Vital, too, is "*a commitment to the job and the area;*" though you needn't have been suckled on Newcastle Brown and nourished with pease pudding, the firm will want to be certain you'll stay longer than qualification. In 2005, ten of the 14 qualifiers were offered jobs and stayed on.

## decaf-lon

After-work haunts include the Pitcher and Piano and retro hang-out Stereo. Those who find bags under eyes unfashionable prefer civilised lunches at the Baltic. Last year's formal black-tie Christmas bash saw a whopping 1,000 people "*sipping on champers*" during serious speeches. Sounds too stuffy? Don't worry, there followed a lively awards ceremony including "*The Order of the Flash Harry going to he who wears the loudest shirt, and Outstanding Lunch Time Achiever for whoever takes the longest lunch.*" A pantomime planned for the 2005 Christmas party was shrouded in mystery when we rang, though we were told that "*some people take it really quite seriously – rehearsals, full costumes, that sort of thing.*" If it's bad cruise ship performances you crave, last year's dinner dance morphed into a Stars in their Eyes extravaganza. "*The entries were quite good, especially Will Young and Robert Palmer... and five finance lawyers did Steps.*" Eeuw!

After a recent lull, sport received "*a kickstart*" when the firm decided to compete in a regional "*corporate decathlon – ten matches over ten months.*" Our sources were currently training for event number five on the calendar, the Highland Games. We also heard of a strange trainee weekend away that revolved around the intriguing sport of bicycle polo. More conventional tastes can be satisfied by a cricket team ("*with one girl in it*"), a football team ("*without a girl in it*") and a hockey team ("*without a boy in it*").

It seems the *Student Guide* has become something of "*an unofficial forum*" for trainees and their beefs. Last year we reported complaints about "*the blasted coffee machines,*" and how people had to

walk at least "*half a mile*" for a decent cappuccino. Since then the firm has installed "*glowing orange machines you can get lattes and all sorts of drinks from.*" A "*mutiny*" has been prevented! Yet amid the cheers, some dissenters claim "*the coffee is still horrible.*" Ever the vox populi of trainees, we must exhort the firm to "*put kettles and fridges*" into the new Trinity Gardens office. The people have spoken.

## and finally...

With such a huge reputation in the North East, and as one of the most respected firms in the country, if you're thinking of training in Dickinson Dees' neck of the woods you'd be mad not to check it out.

# DLA Piper Rudnick Gray Cary LLP

## the facts

**Location:** Birmingham, Leeds, Liverpool, London, Manchester, Sheffield, Scotland, Ireland.
**Number of partners/assistants:** 342/790
**Total number of trainees:** 153
**Seats:** 4x6 months
**Alternative seats:** Secondments
**Extras:** Pro bono – The Prince's Trust and other regional schemes

Spreading across the globe as fast as bird flu, DLA Piper has had another record-breaking, earth-shattering year, having emerged from a successful union with American firm Piper Rudnick Gray Cary.

## trading places

Although the firms are united under the infamous DLA Piper blue square logo, by their own admission it's still very much a global association rather than a full merger. That said, the cross-pond hook-up has gone swimmingly and, six months on, the organisation posted a 13% profit rise for Europe and Asia off the back of an 18% increase in income. And with global turnover having broken through the three-quarters of a billion pound mark, DLA Piper has good reason to feel bullish.

DLA Piper hasn't finished its expansion programme. At the time of writing it was in advanced talks to acquire the entire CIS network of accountancy-tied Ernst & Young Law, consisting of offices in Moscow, St Petersburg, Tbilisi and Kyiv. If it comes off, it will mean the addition of 100 lawyers, new coverage in Georgia and Ukraine and extra firepower in Russia. DLA Piper is also thought to be looking for an Australian partner. Earlier in 2005 it delivered a hard blow to London firm Denton Wilde Sapte by taking more than 40 lawyers from its well-established TMT department. It seems they were attracted by the international network and the tie-in with the Americans. Again taking a swipe at Dentons, DLA Piper snagged the head of that firm's Africa practice recently.

An increasing number of new clients acknowledge that the firm has the firepower to work on significant deals. Last year it piloted GNER through a competitive tender to win the largest franchise in European rail history. And to give you a flavour of the work being done stateside, recently DLA Piper beat the big boys of New York real estate law to advise the city's Port Authority on the estimated $7 billion redevelopment of the site of the former World Trade Center.

## field of dreams

Trainees' views on the firm's 'build it and they will come' approach to growth are interesting. "*We're dynamic and strong and we know where we're going,*" said one, though another added: "*It has become a bit of a monster, taking over the world. Every time they announce another merger it's like, here we go again.*" A third agreed: "*I'm not sure what the latest vision is. We've conquered the US so I suppose it is Asia next…*" "*Maybe go to the moon,*" suggested a fourth. It's hard to deny that "*there is no other firm like this and a lot of it is down to Nigel Knowles and the firm's northern*

roots. *There's a real appetite for success, and I think we're going out there looking for it instead of expecting it in our lap.*" All the trainees we spoke to expressed admiration for the firm's joint CEO Nigel Knowles (who shows up each year to the trainee induction in Nottingham). "*He genuinely sees the future of the firm in us,*" said one admirer. At regular roadshow appearances, Knowles explains to the assembled crowds "*where we're from and where we're going to. Nigel has a great ability to enthuse everybody – he's very charismatic and likeable.*" Evangelical zeal is a running theme. Last year's Christmas presentation included film footage of the firm's charity walk from Lands End to John O'Groats and "*the music in the background was a bit OTT.*"

If you balk at the idea of joining a cult, you'll be relieved to hear that "*people don't buy into it all when he's not around. I think people can be a bit cynical about some of the aspirations and the sugar coating.*" Someone who dared to look behind the Wizard of Oz's curtain whispered: "*The slogan is 'A different kind of law firm' but of course it's not going to revolutionise the way legal services are provided.*" Another said: "*It's gained loads of momentum, but the problem is what happens when you stop?*" Good question.

## capital ideas

For now the London office continues to bulk up. Though still in essence a mid-market player, the office has secured some very respectable work. Witness the £750 million disposal by The Blackstone Group of the Savoy hotel chain comprising Claridges, the Berkeley, the Connaught and the Savoy plus its theatre. London trainees spoke of their experiences in various departments, mostly transactional. A commercial and projects seat was "*hard because it involved quite complex PFI deals;*" banking meanwhile involved "*all manner of leveraged deals, which were very asset-based. The hours were long but there was a real sense of reward.*" In a banking seat, "*when you work your arse off, the week after they'll take you out for lunch and you won't find you way back to the office afterwards!*" A stint in the regulatory department brings work on "*corporate defence and tax investigation.*" Here, a trainee's role might be to "*review files and flag up suspicious documents,*" and then, if they're lucky, to apprise the client of their findings. Our sources definitely believed that even a small amount of recognition made up for hard graft. "*When the partner was sent a case of champagne, he sent two bottles down to me.*"

The London office occupies impressive new premises on London Wall. Trainees considered the atmosphere to be more formal than in the northern offices, and also spoke of very long hours in certain transactional seats. On the plus side, supervisors are deemed to have "*really pushed to get the best out of me.*" The social scene in the City involves "*the regular stuff*" ie nights in local pubs, more particularly The City Pipe (known affectionately as The Shitty Pipe). Adventurous trainees have even been known to go as far afield as Smithfield in pursuit of pleasure. There are parties at Christmas and to mark the end of the financial year, and we hear the real estate department has a penchant for "*raucous*" karaoke. At trainee level the London office is "*slightly more of the private school breed, but we're still much more down-to-earth and unstuffy than magic circle trainees I've met. You know, the types who rebuilt a Romanian orphanage in their gap year.*"

Trainees say that now DLA Piper has become so international in its focus, the UK emphasis has shifted to London. According to one: "*There is some resentment from the regions that London is now seen as the centre of the firm. After all, it originated in Sheffield all those years ago.*" A different view from the regions is that everyone is "*pretty chuffed with the London office and they ship everyone down as often as possible to visit.*"

## where DLA Piper leeds...

The firm is one of the strongest half dozen in Leeds, a tough market in which it grabs its share of the best work. Back in 2003, lawyers advised Deloitte & Touche on a £130 million-disposal via administrative receivership of Teesside power station. Even now they continue to act for the receivers on a range of issues, including various cross-border derivative transactions. In other insolvency matters, lawyers advised PwC on the distressed sale of the UK's second-largest independent kitchen manufacturer, and also for Leeds United FC regarding its well-publicised financial difficulties, moving it from the brink of extinction through a restructuring of its £100 million debt and disposal to its current owners. We've focused here on the firm's insolvency and corporate recovery work because trainees recommended the seat so highly. In litigation seats trainees spoke of "*a lot of court-based work... I was making applications myself as well as doing a lot of drafting.*"

As you'd expect, trainees are committed to working in Leeds. "*I wanted to stay in Yorkshire,*" said one. "*I think that the quality of work is second only to London; in fact, sometimes it is shipped up from London.*" Another draw is the Leeds office building, "*a pointed, tall glass tower*" judged to knock spots off anything offered by the other firms. The majority of trainees already knew each other from law school and maintain active friendships and social lives while at the firm. Generally our sources thought that they'd been "*very lucky with the hours. An average day would be 8.30am to 6.30pm – later for completions.*" Said one: "*I don't think I'll ever get used to the morning starts though!*"

## supermanchester

The Manchester office is big in DLA Piper's traditionally strong areas of banking, litigation, real estate and insolvency. They also handled the £880 million public-to-private transfer of The Big Food Group. In real estate, Manchester lawyers acted on one of the largest UK investment deals of 2004 – the sale of a property investment portfolio for more than £150 million. It involved 11 separate firms of solicitors and required multi-jurisdictional advice. Of their seat choices, trainees told us: "*There's no compulsory requirement – they like you to do corporate or commercial, but other than that they are flexible.*"

# the true picture

"*Real estate is very popular because it's friendly, big and there's a good quality of work.*" "*We're booming in real estate,*" we heard. "*There's lots of property development in the middle of Manchester and it's nice to walk past a building and feel personally connected to work.*" Someone who had sampled a commercial projects seat ended up doing bags of research for Building Schools for the Future, a big PFI project through which hundreds of millions of pounds will be invested in secondary education. "*There's a good mix of rail, transport and schools work. They do try to get you into the high-level stuff and you'll get the opportunity to try discreet drafting tasks.*" The Manchester insurance department is mainly busy with PI and professional negligence cases. Here "*you're dealing with your own workload all the way up to small hearings. It's very good for your confidence.*" Trainees spoke of a friendly, easy-going team and very good hours of 9am until 5.30pm. "*The work tends to be simple and digestible, and things tend to move at a set pace.*" Corporate is a huge contrast but also offers good experiences. One past occupant proudly announced: "*I handled a couple of my own completions... If they see the opportunity for someone to run with something they'll let you do it.*"

In most seats in Manchester the average hours are 9am until 6.30pm or 7pm and you may have to come in on the odd weekend. There are good summer and Christmas parties and quiz nights whenever possible. "*The Christmas before last we had associates on the stage grabbing the mic. They were a bit red-faced the next day.*" In fairness, they were probably only trying to emulate the great leader!

## basket cases

Elsewhere in the regions, the Birmingham office is particularly well known in the health and safety market; Liverpool is in pole position for regional real estate; and Sheffield is renowned for personal injury and environmental work. In Sheffield, where the DLA Piper story started, the working day

is not as long as in London, Leeds or Manchester – basically you work as and when required and "*the emphasis is on teamwork.*" This office is viewed as being "*smaller and more friendly when you walk in – the receptionists aren't afraid to have a giggle.*" Trainees make an effort to socialise together, be this "*down the pub after work, bowling or on picnics.*" It's no picnic in the office though. Our sources told us: "*Other trainees in Sheffield think we are worked a lot harder than them. Whether or not that's true, we always have a laugh with it.*"

In Liverpool a corporate trainee was hard at work on a company acquisition when we called. "*There was a fair bit of drafting, but I just rolled my sleeves up and got stuck in. I also worked on a prospectus for a plc.*" Real estate is the biggest department and a seat here offers exposure to "*big clients and lots of work.*" This is a particularly down-to-earth office where everyone works hard and there are no airs and graces. "*The social life is good. There was a corporate cup this week, which involved a 5 km race around Liverpool, and last week a bunch of us went to the Chester races.*" Every Friday "*at 5.30pm everyone downs tools and goes across the road to the Newz Bar.*"

## i'd like to teach the world to bill...

Since so much attention had been paid to the DLA Piper brand we asked trainees which household name they felt their firm was like. The most common answers: "*Coca-Cola – recognised all round the world,*" and "*Heinz baked beans – solid, been around for a long time and everyone knows them.*" Someone else thought the most apt comparison was "*the Dyson hoover (sic) – a new, distinctive brand that's different from what's out there; constantly innovating.*" Sounds exhausting!

As does the formal training regime. "*I can't fault the training. They have it down to a fine art,*" confirmed one source. Much of it is residential and outsourced, "*which is great because if it's in the office it lends itself to running back to the desk in the breaks.*" Soft skills training on topics such as networking and confidence boosting is advertised on the intranet and is generally open to everyone. The appraisal system is "*very good, but heavily dependent on your supervisor.*" One trainee reported: "*All four have been honest and they're not afraid to tell you to pull your boots up!*" In terms of potential improvements on the part of the firm, one trainee spoke for their comrades everywhere when they announced: "*Maybe there are a few communication and admin problems. It is possible to melt down into paperwork because there are so many processes and people. Ten hours later your computer may still be broken.*" Aside from that, the only common grumble we heard was that "*the NQ job process was not handled in a way that makes it easy for trainees. Not knowing what's going on breeds jealousy and suspicion.*" As it turns out, 62 of the 78 English qualifiers stayed on in September 2005, distributing themselves fairly evenly across the different offices and departments.

With a large intake of trainees across its many UK offices, it is hard to define a single DLA Piper type though some of our sources were happy to try. Said one: "*I've found that you will get on with the partners if you have a bit of personality and can engage in some cheeky banter. They like having a bit of a joke. If you can maintain a sense of humour at 3am you will do well.*" Another confirmed: "*One-dimensional people are not liked. You need to have confidence and character.*" As befits DLA Piper's meritocratic ideals: "*Your background doesn't matter; it feels like they look for personalities, though you must work hard and gain your reputation.*" Paying homage to the firm's Sheffield roots, trainees described themselves as "*grafters – self-reliant people used to sorting things out for themselves.*" That sounds about right to us.

## and finally...

DLA Piper is an optimistic and at times pugnacious firm with an appealingly no-nonsense approach both to the law and its own business. If you fancy yourself as a true believer, pull up a pew.

# DMH Stallard

## the facts

**Location:** Brighton, Crawley, London
**Number of partners/assistants:** 46/65
**Total number of trainees:** 15
**Seats:** 4x6 months
**Alternative seats:** None

From small acorns great oaks grow. DMH Stallard has swelled from Brighton high street practice to broad-based commercial outfit through a potent mixture of mergers and unbridled ambition. Along the way it's gained offices in Crawley and London and is now operating with a turnover of £20 million.

## fishtales

Back in the swingin' 70s, a threesome of Sussex firms came together to form Donne Mileham & Haddock, developing a much-respected private client practice that was complemented by considerable strength in property and litigation. So far, so regional. But come the nineties the firm shifted its priorities and began to cast acquisitive and expansionist eyes further afield. A new office in Crawley near Gatwick Airport, together with a trendy new moniker – DMH – were the first steps in the evolution of the commercial practice, particularly insofar as it was servicing a growing base of technology clients. The firm then acquired a London office.

Given that the firm now represents retail banks (Allied Irish; RBS) and local authorities (LB Croydon; Surrey County Council) as well as companies such as retail giant Arcadia, SEEBOARD, Amlin plc and Fender Musical Instruments, plus the Greater London Magistrates' Courts Association and venture capital outfit South East Growth Fund, you'd think the growth strategy was reaping dividends. Not quickly enough for DMH's tastes it seems. Earlier in 2005 it merged with niche London corporate practice Stallard, creating a combined City presence of nearly 20 partners. The merger propelled the newly christened DMH Stallard into the mid tier. After launching a London employment team, the firm then went on to test its newfound strength by acting on seven AIM admissions, advised Wyndeham Press Group plc on its £6.2 million purchase of the Graphics Facilities Group, and beat off competition from 16 other firms (DLA Piper and Prettys amongst them) to become the sole adviser for Shoreham Port, currently in the midst of a £250 million regeneration programme. Not bad for what was once just a small South Coast player.

## icescapades

Despite retaining separate premises in London, the firm is apparently *"doing its utmost to achieve a seamless integration,"* with *"emphasis on it being a merger not a takeover."* Admittedly, Stallards' shipping litigation team chose to join another firm – Hextalls – rather than stay within the new partnership, but overall the post-merger picture looks rosy. *"It's changed completely the way the firm is running and the direction it's heading in,"* enthused one trainee. *"We've gone from being a Brighton-based firm with a presence in Crawley, to a London and South East firm with three equally important offices."* True enough, DMH Stallard is now well positioned to serve clients in both the capital and across the Southern region. Its various teams cover the gamut of law, from corporate finance to property and planning, from litigation and employment to technology and IP, insolvency and private client.

This also means *"excellent breadth of experience"* for trainees, who can choose to take their four six-month seats pretty much wherever they like. Stallards had a very small trainee programme, which means that even after merger the trainee year groups will continue to be a modest 15 or so for the forseeable future. This will presumably mean that the firm's ability to satisfy trainees at rotation time (*"we always get the seat choices we want"*) will continue. Though nothing is strictly compulsory in the programme, the firm's emphasis on property work

and clients effectively makes it impossible to side-step a seat in either a straight property, planning or property litigation. But when you consider that the client list features Brighton and Hove Albion FC, Sussex County Cricket Club and Reigate & Banstead Housing Trust (which owns nearly 7,000 properties), and that recent projects include the Brighton International Ice Arena, these are hardly undesirable tenancies.

With each office possessing distinct specialist groups, trainees are certain to shuttle between offices. The combined London offices offer insolvency, commercial litigation, commercial property and coco seats, whilst Crawley has positions available in coco, commercial property, commercial litigation (including innovation/media – *"basically IP"*) and employment. Down in Brighton, there are commercial property, planning, property litigation, personal injury and 'private office' departments. Private office seats give exposure to *"anything from tax, trusts and pensions to family work"* for a client base largely made up of *"wealthy regional individuals"* and *"referrals from elsewhere within the firm."* In short, don't come here if what you're really looking for is legal aid work. Just as a PS, we should also tell you that property litigation has a small crime team within it. We're not entirely sure why, and we don't recommend you bank on getting crime work in your training.

## situation comedy

Quite how the new equilibrium between London, Brighton and Crawley will affect the trainees remains to be seen. At present, most of them live in or close to Brighton and make the 45-minute commute to Crawley by car when stationed there. Three trainees were sharing a house in Brighton when we rang: *"The running joke was that it was a bad comedy pilot. We were going to let the firm put a camera in for an experiment until we realised it would be a sure-fire way to lose your job!"* The appearance of new seats in London has forced trainees into an hour-and-twenty-minute train journey to and from the capital, but whether the day will come when they live in London and reverse commute only time can tell. For now they are grinning like Cheshire cats, telling us: "*You can have your cake and eat it – the fantastic social life, great living conditions and decent hours*" of Brighton, and "*the chance to do corporate seats in London.*" Again, we can only speculate quite how the equation of hours, location, quality of life and calibre of work will compute. What we can tell you is that trainees think Brighton is "*a fantastic place to be,*" and that's in spite of receiving regional salaries in a town where rents are as pricey as in many parts of London. Even so, trainees assure us you can live relatively comfortably and still afford a social life. "*We mainly go to places on the seafront in Hove,*" one source revealed. "*There's a bar called Audio and there's also a terrible club called Casablanca.*"

The working day in Brighton is the epitome of reasonableness, with 8.30am or 9am until 5.30pm the norm (though "*you do work hard while you're there*"). In Crawley and London the days can be longer – even before adding in the commute – but seemingly never dreadful. Clocking-off time will be "*7.30pm or 8pm at worst.*" It is probably fair to say that the majority of readers will be unfamiliar with the appeal of Crawley. Our interviewees told us we maligned the town in last year's *Student Guide*: "*It's not horrible, in fact the old cobbled part of town where our offices are is lovely. It's the 1970s new-build bit of town that's awful.*" Though we stand corrected on our unfair description of the not-horrible bits of Crawley, suffice it to say you won't find us moving there. In London, the legacy Stallard office is situated in übertrendy Clerkenwell close to Smithfield meat market and some of London's best bars and restaurants (especially if you like the offal bits of cow and pigs). The legacy DMH office is in Aldgate, a short stroll from the Thames and the Tower of London.

## counting your chickens

Socially, the firm responds well to geographical separation. From a trainee's perspective, visits by future recruits are always welcome as "*the firm gives you a fat wad of cash to blow on a social event.*" The big date in the calendar is the annual AGM, "*where the entire firm gets together for speeches from the managing partner and dinner in the evening.*" Staff also get a summer party, this year aboard a boat on the Thames. The Crawley and Brighton offices double up as gallery spaces, and the art in their receptions was a big talking point in our interviews. One wry source explained: "*The collections vary week by week. We've had picturesque scenes and giant chickens – they're all on sale, but I've never bought one yet.*" Who knows, maybe after they start getting their NQ salary...

Traditionally DMH trainees were "*lured by the outdoor life or Brighton's social scene.*" Typically they had "*a strong local connection*" with the South Coast. The fact that "*several people have really relished getting to work in London*" suggests a sea change in recruitment might be in order so as to match the firm's changing appeal. When we asked trainees to sum up their colleagues, they told us how people were "*really quite clever,*" "*fun personalities*" who can "*take a bit of stick and laugh about it.*" Being one of only a dozen or so trainees has its challenges and it demands a certain robustness. Although they heaped praise on their supervisors, our sources noted that "*you get work from everybody, all the time; it can be hectic and you've got to be able to deal with it or learn to say no.*" The upside of this is that "*if you prove you're capable, you get more and more responsibility.*" In short, no one's going to forget you exist and you're going to gain a huge amount of confidence over the two years. Clearly ready for more, in September 2005, four of the seven qualifying trainees accepted NQ positions with the firm.

## and finally...

With a growing profile and an increasingly commercial strategy to match its geographical shift, DMH Stallard looks like a shrewd choice. How important the Brighton lifestyle will continue to be remains to be seen, but for now at least if you want to chase that particular dream this is still your number-one firm.

# DWF

## the facts

**Location:** Liverpool, Manchester, Warrington
**Number of partners/assistants:** 67/119
**Total number of trainees:** 16
**Seats:** 4x4 + 1x8 months
**Alternative seats:** None

Commercial firm DWF started life as an insurance litigation practice in Liverpool in 1977. Since then it has evolved into a broader-based commercial player that has made its mark in both Manchester and Liverpool. The firm offers training contracts in both cities.

## a tale of two cities

Successful applicants opt for one or other of DWF's main offices, usually blissfully ignorant of a third branch in Warrington that handles vast quantities of low-value insurance claims. Unlike their peers at some other rival firms, trainees are not expected to sample both Manchester and Liverpool. And with the same range of seats available at each location, there seems little reason to do so. All trainees complete five seats, the first four being four months long and the final being a massive eight-monther in the area into which they intend to qualify. Commonly, seats are taken in insurance litigation, corporate, commercial property and commercial dispute resolution/professional negligence. Additionally, there are a few less standard options including health and safety, employment, IP, construction, pensions, planning and insolvency.

## day trippers

An insurance litigation seat is all but guaranteed as the firm is "*known first and foremost for this work and it's the biggest department.*" One trainee admitted: "*I knew this firm had based its business growth on that work and I went into it with some trepidation. As it turned out it was all defendant work, acting for Royal & SunAlliance and the Motor Insurance Bureau and I enjoyed it, although I am still not sure how I would feel about doing claimant work.*" Though defence lawyers can usually remain distanced from the emotional side of cases, there is always drama in the background. "*One nasty case involved the loss of an eye on a farm, and there were RTAs where the issue of liability was very complex. In one a girl was run over and there was a question about whether she had been playing chicken.*" As well as road traffic accidents and mishaps at work, the insurance defence lawyers also take on professional negligence cases concerning accountants' and lawyers' botches. If you did fancy seeing things from the claimant's side, there is a team working in a separate "*plush*" office in Liverpool called Cavern Court. "*It is named after the club where the Beatles played, which means you have to dodge the Japanese tourists at lunchtime and stop to take pictures of people by the John Lennon statue.*"

Litigation trainees assist partners on higher value cases while also looking after their own smaller matters. Though four months isn't long enough to see a case through from beginning to end, these smaller files can teach trainees about the litigation process and enable them to "*go to court alone for case management conferences and the odd small hearing.*" In Liverpool, one insurance lit supervisor was described as "*absolutely fantastic... great at managing your workload and the types of work you were doing; adept at letting you write letters or undertake your own phone calls; adjusting his supervision to your ability and informally making you aware of the ground rules so you're not running to him every five minutes. He was just the most skilful person for managing work.*" High praise indeed.

Manchester trainees can accompany the firm's in-house barrister to court. One told us: "*I tagged along with Mark quite a few times. He's good with trainees; he will pop round and say 'I have a hearing in half an hour, does anyone want to come along?'*" As the office is conveniently located "*just over the road from court,*" disappearing for an hour to carry the barrister's bags is no drama. Time in court also provides a break from what is generally accepted to be a "*heads-down*" environment.

## the commercial diet

Away from the contentious realm, DWF's commercial property department has grown to 11 partners and is looking to win more of the region's bigger deals. Recent successes includes earning a place on Manchester Airport Group's legal panel and acting on St Modwen Group's recent £12.5 million purchase of a half share in the Kirkby Shopping Centre. Property trainees divide their time between their own smaller files and bigger projects run by partners.

By comparison with the steadiness of property, the workload in corporate can be "*very up and down.*" As one source explained: "*When I started it was quiet so I had the time to review things. I was really encouraged to read around... and then it went mad.*" Another told us: "*I had a very good supervising partner and worked as his assistant all the time. If I could do the drafting I would, and if he had the time to show me how to do something then he did. Of course I also did the traditional board minutes and company filing and the more mundane stuff.*"

The corporate department regularly works for a number of food producers, including Princes, Inter Link and Burton's. In one of its more significant deals, the Manchester office advised Inter Link in its placement of shares on AIM and its acquisition of Soreen. "*On medium-sized deals you are more likely to do useful work than trainees working on a really big deal where they're at the bottom of the food chain,*" concluded one source. Sadly, not everyone enjoyed the corporate experience – "*I was really looking forward to it being over because as a junior you can get*

some rubbish jobs which are tedious but important at the same time. The trainees cop for those... things like page-turning on bundles of documents when they're about to complete a deal. Doing 12 hours of that is as dull as anything.*" Which just goes to prove you can't please all of the people all of the time.

## get off my land

The banking team acts for a number of well-known lenders (Bank of Scotland, RBS, Lloyds TSB, Yorkshire Bank, Skipton Building Society), typically on deals worth up to £30 million, often to fund management buyouts or buyins. On asset finance work, trainees help to mortgage aeroplanes and helicopters by liaising with the Civil Aviation Authority, the banks and the borrowers. Other smaller departments include a health and safety team that defends criminal prosecutions, and an IP team that provides support for transactions and advice on trade marks and licensing. The employment and pensions group works mainly for employers such as Burton's Foods and Liverpool John Moore's University, although its relationship with the DAS legal expenses insurer also brings some claimant work. These insurers also make their presence felt in the comlit department in Liverpool, where trainees advise members of the general public on boundary disputes, professional negligence and consumer claims.

Some trainees were happy with their seats; others thought the "*luck of the draw*" system could be improved upon. Said one: "*People need to know whether the system is flexible and open to debate or if seats are predetermined and fixed. There should definitely be more consultation.*" Whatever the negatives, the end results are to be applauded. Yet again, in 2005 five of the six qualifiers got NQ jobs in their preferred departments.

## sunny jim

DWF would suit someone with a good academic background and their "*feet firmly on the ground.*" They should be "*the type who doesn't need everything set out for them in a rigid career structure. You have to be adaptable as well as ambitious."* All our sources spoke about the hours they worked. Said one: "*I know I am working at one of the North West's biggest players and there's kudos in that, but I don't have to be here for Addleshaws' hours – the balance is right.*" For another this balance was "*critical.*"

We must mention the infectious and positive influence of managing partner Jim Davies, given the frequency with which his name popped up in our interviews. You may hear that he is "*the name and the front man at the firm*" though in truth he is just one of a tight pool of important equity partners. Nevertheless, popular opinion says that "*Jim has been influential on the way DWF's personality has developed. He likes a collegiate approach to business.*" Of course, "*that becomes more and more difficult as the firm gets bigger and it needs a more traditional line management structure. The collegiality is still here now though and it's one of the things I like most about the firm.*"

DWF aspires to keep growing, even if the pace of growth has slowed lately. One sage told us: "*It has to ask itself, does it want to be a DLA or just stay as one of the biggest in the North West.*" And from another we heard: "*It's very difficult for a firm to grow just by generating new business, and it may merge as others have done recently.*" Indeed, the Liverpool and Manchester markets have been alive with law firm mergers lately: Hill Dickinson, Brabners, Halliwells, Cobbetts – they've all been at it. We'll be watching with interest.

## when parties get political

In Liverpool, Friday nights mean The Living Room; in Manchester a somewhat quieter scene revolves around Bar 38 and 14 Lloyd Street. Liverpool trainees organise 'Young Professionals' evenings at which hordes of... um, young professionals, get together to make merry. In 2004, the 80s-themed event even made the pages of *The Daily Post*. Some of our Manchester contacts dismissed these events as "*a waste of money*" and little more than an opportunity for great gangs of youngsters to "*come, get leathered and go home.*" Manchester trainees are now combining forces with qualified solicitors and organising their own more select events. Whatever the pros and cons of these differing approaches, at least DWF recognises the importance of getting trainees involved in marketing activities.

## and finally...

The North West legal market is a crowded one, but we reckon DWF has to be one of the best natured of the commercial firms in the region. It's also a very sensible choice if you have no desire for a long commute for months on end.

# Eversheds LLP

## the facts

**Location:** Leeds, Manchester, Newcastle, Birmingham, Nottingham, Cardiff, London, Cambridge, Ipswich, Norwich
**Number of partners/assistants:** 322/948
**Total number of trainees:** 193
**Seats:** 4x6 months
**Alternative seats:** Overseas seats, secondments
**Extras:** Pro bono – various projects

With ten offices across England and Wales and more legal staff than any other firm, Eversheds is the UK's biggest private practice legal services provider. Its name is recognised by business clients up and down the country and increasingly beyond our borders.

## redrawing the map

In the 1980s the Eversheds network grew as a franchise. The brand was stamped onto a number of good commercial firms from Bristol to Newcastle. In the 1990s the franchise phase gave way to centralised thinking: one firm, one voice, etc. In the last five years a process of rationalisation and consolidation has caused less profitable offices to close and seen three distinct geographical groups form. Eversheds North encompasses Leeds, Manchester and Newcastle; Eversheds Central brings Birmingham, Nottingham and Cardiff together; Eversheds London & South East ties Cambridge, Norwich and Ipswich together with the capital.

Though each office is physically separate and each regional group operates as a single unit for management purposes, the idea is that lawyers everywhere regard themselves as a part of national practice groups. The approach is most effective and most easily observed with smaller more niche practice areas such as tax or pensions. Among corporate and real estate lawyers the impetus to work in tandem with colleagues on the other side of the country is weaker.

## same same but different

With standardisation now the order of the day, you might assume an identical training experience will be found in all Eversheds locations. This is true to the extent that great efforts have been made to shape a single culture and recruit the classic down-to-earth *"normal"* Eversheds type into all offices. Yet in certain respects differences are patently clear even to an outsider. To take one example raised by an East Anglian source, a London trainee will be paid roughly the same salary as an East Anglian newly qualified lawyer, something which irks anyone who lives with the expense of Cambridge and works on deals sent up from the London office. Another issue, perhaps less contentious, is that different offices offer variations in seat menus. A Cardiff trainee could spend six months in the 'Legal Services' department doing high-volume, low-value, low-cost trip-and-slip PI cases; in London or Birmingham such a thing would never be countenanced. In Newcastle, the firm defends clinical negligence cases for the NHS Litigation Authority and handles shipping work; Manchester and Cardiff have the best employment teams; Leeds boasts hot consumer finance lawyers; London gets the biggest corporate deals; very little goes on in Ipswich these days other than projects, construction litigation and PI; in Birmingham there's very little that doesn't go on. In essence, Eversheds is as diverse as it is big.

Trainees are recruited into a single office, or in the case of East Anglia a trio of offices. Shared PSC training gives them an opportunity to meet, make friends and compare notes, and as is to be expected in any group of nearly a hundred people, *"there are definite characters who mix easily and quieter trainees who stick within their own office groups."* One London trainee was very complimentary about her regional peers: *"There are some very impressive trainees in other offices,"* she said before relating a story about a Manchester recruit who met a prominent businessman on one of his trains and talked him into supporting a charity with which she was involved. But beyond the PSC and periodic practice area training sessions – sometimes via annoying... two-second delay... videoconferencing – there isn't a great deal of national trainee interaction.

## supervision orders

Beyond London, the typical Eversheds trainee tends to choose the firm for its leader status in their home or adoptive region. In London its more a case of feeling good about the place on your interview day – "everyone was polite and it seemed that people genuinely did have time for you." London trainees readily accept that they are not motivated to work on the biggest multibillion-pound international deals; they are instead searching for a reasonable balance between the hours spent in the office and the hours spent outside it. Contrary to popular belief, we suspect the most ambitious of Eversheds' trainees may reside elsewhere.

Wherever they work, all trainees are supposed to undertake seats in corporate, real estate and litigation and our mini seat survey confirms that real estate is the one key variable that almost never varies. Common ground is also to be found in the quality and nature of supervision. It seems that

# the true picture

Eversheds has tied the task of trainee supervising into the mechanism for reaching partnership and, as such, the senior solicitors who take on the role do so with an appropriate degree of seriousness. All that said, core corporate seats commonly disappointed our sources. "*It didn't turn my world upside down,*" said one, "*basically the bigger the deal and the more important the clients the less contact you have. Unless I attended meetings as a note taker I felt I was missing out.*" Another source analysed the breed: "*As a corporate lawyer you haven't got your head stuck in a book all day; it is very very practical and the lawyer's role is to project manage the deal.*" Many trainees end up preferring their time in smaller specialist departments because they offer more law-based tasks and greater responsibility. This can lead to supply and demand issues on qualification.

Readers wondering about Eversheds' client list may wish to note a trend for bigger and bigger clients that can be serviced from whichever part of the network best fits the bill. This trend is most noticeable in Ipswich and Norwich where the offices no longer service a predominantly local client base. Indeed, the Norwich corporate team recently defected to rival firm Mills & Reeve because that firm has maintained its commitment to Norfolk companies. Two big fish that have been caught in Eversheds' nets are international chemical giant DuPont and Internet leader Cisco. With each of these companies the firm has entered into a 'partnering' arrangement whereby it services all of its UK legal requirements from wherever it chooses. Yet the 'national not local' approach has not hit home everywhere just yet. One Nottingham trainee, for example, told us: "*Here we're acting for big companies like Boots and then a lot of other local clients. It suits the firm and it's profitable.*" In Newcastle, one source amusingly pointed out: "*You could pay a partner in Newcastle to do proof-reading for the same price as say a Denton Wilde Sapte trainee in London.*" Obviously you wouldn't, but you could if you wanted to.

## northern highlights

Up in Eversheds' 'Northern' region, Leeds and Manchester have finally abandoned their six-seat training to come into line with the rest of the firm's four-seat system. Though possible, trans-Pennine seat swaps are rare, usually occurring only if a department is oversubscribed in one or other office. We heard of no switches to or from Newcastle. Beyond mainstream areas of practice (litigation, banking, corporate and, of course, real estate) the Leeds office particularly impresses with its competition, environment and local government work, while Manchester is doing great things in planning, pensions and employment. Trainees tell us the Leeds office is on a roll at the moment so heaven knows how positive the atmosphere will be when everyone decamps to a sparkly new skyscraper in 2006. The Manchester contingent already occupies pretty impressive offices though it is Eversheds' Newcastle abode that turns most heads. You'll see it as you approach the city on the train from Durham, though from the outside you'll miss the comedy of the floor-level water feature in reception. Apparently even at close quarters it's easily missed so you might want to take a spare pair of dry socks if you visit. Social events in each city have ranged from go-karting and the theatre to murder mystery weekends and trips to theme parks. Local bars – The Apartment in Newcastle, Rain Bar in Manchester and various places in Leeds' Greek Street – take up any slack in the social calendar. "*Strangely in Leeds trainees go out with trainees, but in Manchester you also go out with your supervisors.*"

## the workshop of the world

Birmingham and Nottingham have operated as a close pair for long enough to feel like one unit. In May 2005 Eversheds redrew the UK map to incorporate Cardiff into the Midlands or 'Central' region. Indeed the two Midlands' offices are now managed from the super-efficient Cardiff office. Trainees in Brum and Nottingham have become familiar with each other through working on ad hoc days or weeks in the other office, but switches with the Cardiff office look unlikely given the distance and such moves are left to partners and qualified solicitors. Interestingly, a Nottingham source thought the arrival of Cardiff and the choice of a Welsh managing partner for the group strengthened the position of the smaller Notts office. "*Birmingham was the head office, now it feels like we're on the same footing again.*"

According to trainees up and down the network, the firm's greatest strength is real estate. In the Midlands, lawyers have shown their worth on deals including the £600 million mixed-use development of a 14-acre site in the centre of Birmingham and the £550 million regeneration of Bristol's Broadmead area. But proving that it's not all real estate, the corporate department has pulled off the £160 million flotation of photographic retailer Jessops and a number of acquisitions, disposals and international joint ventures for Rolls-Royce.

Life in Brum sounds pretty good for trainees. The BTSS continues to organise excellent balls, sports tournaments, networking evenings, plus educational and charitable events which all serve to cement relationships among the city's young professionals who handily "*all work in a small area in central Birmingham.*" Almost all seem to live in Five Ways, Harborne, Edgbaston or the Jewellery Quarter. "*If they had a big fire in one of those places it would shut down half the law firms in Birmingham,*" mused one chirpy source. Eversheds' Colmore Row office gets the thumbs-up: "*The design is great, the reception is brilliant – all light and airy with big sofas – and the canteen has a great chef who does fish and chips on Friday.*" For nights out they choose Bar One Ten because they are "*too posh for Digress these days!*" Over in Nottingham "*there has been a revolution*" and trainees now shun the regular haunt The Castle as "*it is overpriced and on a Friday it is full of all the local business people in suits swapping business cards.*" (Psst... that's called networking.)

In Cardiff a purpose-built open-plan office close to the train station and overlooking the Mil-

lennium Stadium seems to sum up 21st century Cardiff and 21st century Eversheds. "*When I decided to do law,*" said one source, "*this was the obvious choice. Everyone knows it is the biggest, best and most well known in the area in size and presence. Even if you are not going into law you know of Eversheds, and if you really want to work for a top law firm in Wales its your goal all along.*" Like Birmingham, the professional community is a tight one and after work local bar The Yard is as good a place as any to catch up with Wales' movers and shakers.

## capital and counties

The Cambridge, Norwich and Ipswich offices play host to a rotating group of approximately 20 trainees. The basic rule on seats is that they get either their first choice of department or their choice location, and thankfully sometimes both. Cambridge packs the biggest punch; Ipswich by comparison is an outpost and Norwich recently suffered the defection of its corporate team to its regional archrival and the Cambridge IP boffins moved to local IP hotshot Taylor Vinters last year. Such moves do highlight the potential vulnerability of smaller, less influential offices within national firms.

And so to Eversheds' office in the capital, which is smaller than many other big-name firms in the City though similar in size to most of the other national firms' London offerings. For big corporate deals try the £244 million acquisition of Maplin Electronics by a private equity house and Adidas' disposal of its Salomon division to Amer for £329 million. London has corporate and finance lawyers with specialisms too rarefied for most of the firm's regional offices so leading to trainee seats unavailable elsewhere. A financial services seat, for example, involves a mix of UK authorised funds and offshore funds. We detected a certain air of independence from the rest of the network among the London trainees; yet, as in every office, the classic "*normal*" type is to be found. "*It's shocking when you come to Eversheds and you realise that lots of people like you work here!"*

We mustn't forget to mention that there are three seats in Paris and an opening in Brussels. The firm has a wider network of associated offices and firms, but for now just these two locations are on offer. A couple of client secondments are also available, including one to Asda.

## visionaries

'Vision and Values' is a new code by which staff and partners are required to operate. *"I think Vision and Values is a great scheme,"* said one source; *"everyone in the firm from partners down to support staff can say if someone is acting in a way they don't think is right."* If you want to read them in detail look on the firm's website but to summarise: people should be nice to each other and put the client first. Perhaps believing the carrot to be more effective than the stick, the firm has tied the code to a system of gold, silver and bronze awards, each accompanied by a modest cash payment. A Nottingham lawyer who gave a stranded client a bed on a frozen January night won a gold award and has become a firm-wide legend. Sadly though it's more common for people to receive awards for busting a gut and good old-fashioned overtime. Is this really putting a specific value into action, trainees ask? As one pointed out: *"No one has ever got an award for having a fab weekend away."* Another difficulty stems from the fact that *"some departments nominate lawyers all the time and others never do."*

The stick, by the way, is there if needed. Performance reviews for all staff and partners call for 360° feedback and several sources confirmed the departure of a partner specifically because he couldn't comply with the values. Criticisms aside, the overall view is that the firm's heart is in the right place with the values, even though they can't make the hours any shorter when you're up to your neck in due diligence or trial bundling. We rather liked the honesty of the trainee who effectively told us keenness and hard graft are everything at the firm. *"You've got to want to work very hard and be chal-*

*lenged to work in a prestigious law firm. You have to understand that Eversheds has spent all these years building up a reputation. If you step up to the mark they reward you, but there are also some people with bad attitudes towards working here, those who are not prepared to work that extra hour or put themselves out."* Unsurprisingly this comment came from the "*model*" Cardiff office.

Eversheds markets hard to students and certain of its recruiters have talents that would shame the Pied Piper into retirement. And having led a hundred or so students to the firm each year, the HR folk go to great lengths to try and fix everyone up with jobs on qualification. This year the firm was not as successful as previously, and although there were more jobs available than qualifying trainees, just 62 of the 81 qualifiers stayed on.

## and finally...

Although Eversheds is unlikely to want to grow much more in size in the UK, it will want to develop its international contacts, push for larger clients and win more valuable work. This monster firm says that big does not have to mean impersonal, and while we agree, we would point out that working for Eversheds no longer necessarily means involvement in your local business community. If this is important to you, pick a regional name not this national one. The other message coming through from trainees is don't view Eversheds as a soft option.

# Farrer & Co

## the facts

**Location:** London
**Number of partners/assistants:** 62/55
**Total number of trainees:** 17
**Seats:** 6x4 months
**Alternative seats:** Secondments

We've said it before and we'll say it again: two things define Farrer & Co – character and history. It has bags of each and they are what makes the firm such a unique institution.

## meet the ancestors

Check out Farrers' website for a very entertaining history lesson on the firm's early years when two men – each called Tempest Slinger – joined together in practice in Lincoln's Inn. If this aspect of the firm's persona appeals then you'll love the grandeur of its premises. Just inside the entrance to No. 66 Lincoln's Inn Fields hang the family trees of one-time resident the Duke of Newcastle and his in-laws the Marlboroughs. They act as a reminder of the importance still placed on the people and private client work that have long been central to Farrers' existence.

So far so grand, but then, stuck behind the impressive frontage, is a bog-standard, modern office block that backs onto Kingsway. As to which is more representative of the firm it is hard to say, but it is important to understand that Farrers is committed to both its past and its future. As one trainee put it: "*Neither dominates, both co-exist happily.*" Chandeliers and 300 years of history no doubt appeal to certain clients – those whose forebears have entrusted the security of their lineage and family heirlooms to the firm. Perhaps they are also impressed by snippets of information about how the Charter of the Bank of England was sealed in the main boardroom in 1694, or the fact that the Queen uses Farrers. With such a treasure trove of history to draw upon, it is hard to imagine the firm ever playing down its glorious past or indeed ever leaving its prestigious address. Yet at the same time it has recognised the need to develop new interests beyond private client work and new client relationships beyond the Establishment. In this respect, Farrers has met with some of its greatest successes in the media world, specifically in the field of publishing. The firm enjoys, for example, a long and fruitful relationship with the likes of News Group and Emap.

## you will, you will, you will

The six-seat training scheme scores full marks with trainees, who are thankful for the opportunity to range over the firm's varied landscape. One seat must be taken in each of the following four groupings: charities or private client; commercial (including banking and employment); property (commercial and private/estates options); and litigation (family, media or general disputes). Then follows a 'wild-card' seat of the trainee's choice before the final four months is spent in the department into which they hope to qualify.

Our first visit should be to the private client department. It looks after clients from all over the world, including old-money families, businessmen who have made their own fortunes and even some celebrities. According to trainees, "*the only common factor is that they all have enough money.*" As well as drafting wills while clients are still alive, trainees get busy after they die, completing inheritance tax probate forms to send to the capital taxes office, writing to banks and companies in which the deceased had shares in order to realise their assets, and advising on tax issues, for example if the executors wanted to sell the deceased's house. "*A lot of the work is about tax,*" concluded one trainee.

A seat in estates and private property (EPP) means agricultural advice for the Historic Houses Association, the Duchies of Cornwall and Lancaster and other large landed estates. "*I was conveying bits of land – a lot of it unregistered – and drawing up leases. I had a brilliant supervisor, sharing a room with him and an assistant, and he was very good at teaching me, often taking a few minutes to explain the vagaries of property law.*" Such one-on-one experiences are mirrored right around the firm, with all our interviewees reporting good relationships with their supervisors and overall principals. Indeed, relationships are what Farrers does best...

... unlike the clients of the family department, where there are "*quite a few anxious people who can sometimes be quite demanding.*" Again, generally they are "*quite rich,*" though with clients who want

# the true picture

to keep costs down, trainees might edge towards their own spotlight moments, such as attending a final court hearing with a barrister. As with any litigation seat, here there is scope for administrative chores such as preparing bundles for court. Compensation can be found in drafting instructions to counsel, particulars of divorce petitions and attending client meetings. Combining the demands of clients with unavoidable court deadlines means the hours in family can be slightly longer than elsewhere in the firm. Not that these are particularly onerous: most trainees reported leaving by 6pm on a regular basis. Said one: "*I am in the majority in my opinion on hours – I don't want to spend my whole day working so I come in at 9am and leave at 6pm.*"

## you are what you EAT

Proving that the pen is mightier than the sword, Farrers' superb defamation practice group has long been involved in many of the highest profile disputes and sticky situations involving the press and other parts of the media. Much of its work involves keeping the newspapers out of trouble by providing pre-publication advice, though there are always times when matters career headlong into the courtroom. For the *Financial Times* it successfully applied to strike out most of a £230 million special damages claim brought by Collins Stewart, which alleged that the newspaper had libelled the company and damaged its share price. For News Group it has been involved in libel actions brought by David and Victoria Beckham, Justin Timberlake, Kieren Fallon and Gillian McKeith of 'You Are What You Eat' fame. Lawyers also represented Andrew Gilligan in the Hutton Inquiry.

Farrers additionally advises some of its media clients on corporate and commercial matters, such as the £3.25 million sale of the books division of British Medical Journal Publishing Group to Blackwell's. Students should be aware that the corporate experience here is a far cry from that to be had with the City giants. Deals do not come with price tags in the billions or even the hundreds of millions; they are smaller transactions, often conducted by individual investors. We would have loved to have worked on the recent £22 million sale of Green & Black's to Cadbury Schweppes. If there weren't a few free bars kicking around on that deal then there's no justice in the world.

In various fields, Farrers lawyers work on matters that hit the headlines. Take employment law, for example. Here the firm represented Eton College on the Harrygate case that arose following the bullying-related unfair dismissal of art teacher Sarah Forsyth. Another case concerning the royals was that of the employment claim brought by Elaine Day, a former member of the Prince of Wales' household. And speaking of esteemed institutions, some seats come with attached secondments – in past years the Science Museum, the British Olympic Association and Christie's the auctioneers have all featured.

## oh no it isn't!

Some people believe Farrers struggles with an image as a traditional, tweedy firm acting for blue-blooded, tweedy clients. It's not that this reputation is entirely misplaced – certainly not in the past – but there is a divergence of opinion as to whether the image is accurate today. One trainee neatly summed it up as follows: "*To a certain extent the stereotype fits, and although it's not fair to categorise the entire firm, some people do fit the description.*" That trainee went on to describe a variety of different characters across the firm, adding: "*Actually it's great having different styles and types here as there's so much to learn from them.*"

Invariably, the trainees who end up at Farrers also applied to the same group of law firms, ie Macfarlanes, Withers and Charles Russell. It confirms to us that they ran a targeted campaign when looking for a job. Said one: "*I don't have an interest in the City type of law and I didn't apply to any of those firms. Possibly one or two would have applied and got training contract offers from the magic circle as a back up; they seem easier to get as those firms offer so many."* In stark contrast, an emotional attachment to Farrers is often made early on in the recruitment process. Said one interviewee: "*I ended the vac scheme thinking I would be so upset if I had to go somewhere else to train."*

Or perform. Each year at the Christmas party the trainees put on a revue based on the more colourful elements of the partnership. They, in turn, are not permitted to take offence. "*They love the attention,"* we were told, and none more so, it seems, than senior partner and defamation supremo Robert Clinton who offers pre-performance advice on the script. Last Christmas the performance had an Olympic theme and was hosted by a trainee attempting a Des Lynam/Robert Clinton hybrid character. "*Whilst it is very nerve- wracking, it is a great way for partners to get to know us and vice versa,"* reasoned one source when we asked why the tradition endured. We're not sure how many years the revue has been running, but through our unique brand of research we did learn that, by remarkable coincidence, the good old British pantomime has its roots in Lincoln's Inn Fields. It was here in 1717 that the so-called father of English pantomime, John Rich, first performed what eventually became the thigh-slapping, cross-dressing, high-camp performances we know today.

Less grease paint and more war paint, Farrers staff are pretty serious when it comes to sport, be it rugby sevens or a weekend cricket fixture against the *News of the World*. We're not sure how important the class of 2005 were to each of the sports teams, but we do know that all seven stayed on with the firm to take qualification jobs in employment, corporate, media, IP and litigation.

## and finally...

Farrer & Co must surely be one of the UK's most characterful law firms, and it has a canny knack for spotting the type of characters that will fit in to its culture. The message for any student hopeful is simple: do you have a strong interest in any of the firm's specialist areas? If the answer is yes then start practising your best "He's behind you!"

# Field Fisher Waterhouse

## the facts
**Location:** London
**Number of partners/assistants:** 87/134
**Total number of trainees:** 32
**Seats:** 6x4 months
**Alternative seats:** Secondments
**Extras:** Pro bono – various, eg asbestos cases

Mid-sizer Field Fisher Waterhouse ranks high in the London mix-and-match league. Its blend of interesting niches and mainstream practice makes it perfect for any student unwilling to gamble on a particular area of law before even trying it. If you want five different kinds of banking, go elsewhere!

## all together now

In November 2004 the firm devised a new strategy and set itself the ambitious goal of increasing profitability by 50% in three years. Financial results published in summer 2005 showed a very decent start – turnover up by more than 10% on the previous year and profit up by 19%. If we're to put FW's strategy in the simplest way we can, it is to get serious, get organised, be clear about what the firm does best and carry on doing more of it. It follows a period when its many specialist groups were all doing well individually but not working with any great sense of common identity. Said one trainee: "*They realised communication was not the best. Now people are more aware of what is going on outside their own department."*

One of the firm's core teams – brands, technology, media and telecoms (BTMT) – has enjoyed a high profile since the days of the dot.com boom. Its old client base of technology start-ups, e-commerce businesses and software companies have stepped aside to allow room for government departments (Cabinet Office, Home Office, National Probation Directorate, Insolvency Service) and large private sector names (Accenture, Deloitte Consulting, Dell, Tesco, Marks & Spencer and Blockbuster). Recognising the importance of the BTMT lawyers and their new focus on big projects, FFW's goal is to build the UK's top team for technology work and, incidentally, one of the top four teams for IP.

Of his IT seat one trainee told us: "*It is a trusting group and so I was able to help by drafting agreements or bits of agreements. I'd be allowed to go to a meeting to understand how the client wanted an agreement to change and then they let me have a go. They take the trainees seriously.*" And the process of training them – "*IT asked me to e-mail round my diary to all the partners. If I was doing too much research, they'd say we can take you to more meetings. In IT you always knew what you were doing and why.*" One of the team's flagship public sector instructions is a role advising the Home Office on the delivery of the proposed national identity cards programme. If the liveliness of political debate and the enormous potential for technical glitches are anything to go by then this project will run and run. One trainee explained how tough it was to "*walk in half way through a project that has been going on for years.*" Though you have to work hard to get your head around the big picture, some of the work can be parcelled up into trainee-sized "*little chunks.*" In short, "*it's hard work in there and a lot of trainees are put off it... if you're not very organised it would ruin you!*"

## professional naughtiness

One of the most sought-after trainee destinations is the professional regulatory team which handles "*a lot of healthcare work and prosecutes cases on behalf of the General Medical Council. There's also a bit of an interest in sports regulation but it's not massive. Trainees do get quite involved in the work and this is one of the departments where you get your own smaller files. You also get to go to court quite a bit*

because when there's a prosecution, someone has to cover each day of the hearing. One case went on for months.*" As well as making notes in hearings – which take place all over the country – trainees draft instructions to counsel, take witness statements and prepare bundles of documents. You'll be well aware of some of the team's work – the Shipman Inquiry and the disciplining of the Chief Constable of Humberside after the Soham murders are just two examples. In the case of Dr Andrew Wakefield, who alleged a link between the MMR vaccination and autism, the team represent the GMC in its decision to prosecute based on misuse of public funds and fraudulent clinical research. The outcome of the prosecution will undoubtedly impact on the public's confidence in the national vaccination programme. So great is the appeal of this work, "*there are always people climbing over each other to get the seat.*"

There are two medical litigation seats, one handling clinical negligence claims and the other asbestos claims, an area in which FFW is a leading claimant firm. Trainees do get to sample each type of work and are given one or two smaller files to look after under supervision. Asbestos cases come in three grades of nastiness: pleural plaques, asbestosis and mesothelioma, a form of lung cancer. "*It was upsetting when I had to go and interview a guy dying of mesothelioma as he was too sick to travel. It did make me feel really angry towards the company that had exposed him to asbestos,*" one trainee told us. People enjoy these seats because they feel "*more real, more personal*" than commercial work. "*You just get really sad about the asbestos cases... The employers who are at fault just turn to their insurance company but the claimants really need the money for care and to know their widow has financial security. You feel doing the work is worthwhile.*" The seats are a perfect training ground: "*A lot of taking witness statements – that's good from a confidence point of view – conferences with counsel at which you take notes, drafting pleadings, particulars and schedules of loss, attending hearings and doing a few interim hearings yourself, which is scary but good once you have done your first one... "* (Deep intake of breath) Of course there is also *"bad stuff such as paginating but even that's great for a Friday afternoon."*

## package deal

The travel and aviation team has divided into two, and seats here bring more PI cases, this time on the defendant as well as the claimant side. Expect cases from tour operators concerning trips and slips, mass food poisonings and people diving into shallow swimming pools and breaking their necks. In one especially tragic case the firm represented the tour operator involved with a major coach crash in South Africa, and another unusual matter involved the vandalisation of an aircraft. On the non-contentious side clients call with all manner of commercial questions and need help with things such as ATOL registration. *"I got a lot of client contact in that seat,"* one trainee reported. *"They really rely on the trainee to get stuck into the work and it felt like I was making a difference."*

The usual real estate, commercial litigation, banking and corporate departments feature too. *"Real estate is quite good for having your own files so I wasn't just doing proofing and photocopying. I did a lot of telecoms work for a mobile network operator and had about ten phone mast files."* The working pattern in corporate is pretty hardcore: *"The hours are really horrific,"* revealed one source. *"I have never done an all-nighter, but I have had a couple of 3am completions."* The workflow dictates how busy trainees become and what they get up to. Said one: *"I walked into an enormous deal which really took off and then died and then resurrected again. It was a £60 million sale of a company and I was collating the information sent on from the client and fielding any questions from the other side. It was quite a lot of work at the time and the deal was in all the papers. I read about it in the FT."* As a rule you should not expect to be in the office *"much after 8pm"* and *"if you're not at all busy then it's 6pm."* FFW's corporate territory is the mid-market and AIM league; not

huge deals but very decent work nonetheless. Though we did find trainees who enjoyed corporate, it's probably fair to say that the typical FFW trainee has their head turned by one or more of the specialist seats. In part this is because they are given greater independence and responsibility in these other parts of the firm... and by and large the hours are better.

## buried treasures

FFW's treasure trove of seats can be plundered through its new six-seat rotation. Previously alternate years brought either two six-month seats or three four-month seats, but after trainees asked the firm to consider a six-seat model it decided to give it a go. The firm requires trainees to spend time in corporate (commercial or banking and finance count) and litigation (many varieties to choose from). Everything else is up for grabs. Such a varied training is all well and good but can lead to bottlenecks and a few pouts when it comes to doing the compulsory corporate seat. The only other thing that leads to murmurs of discontent is the difficulty of accessing secretarial support in certain departments where trainees suffer from back-of-the-queue syndrome. If in need of TLC, trainees can turn to their mentor since a new scheme was put in place to twin them with a four-to-five year qualified solicitor.

To match its cultural and strategic changes, FFW has been *"tarting up the building. The problem before was lack of space and so they've opened up two additional floors which used to be flats."* There has been renovation, too, in the basement where a portion of the Roman-built London Wall runs through. Though technically open to public view, none of our sources had ever seen a tourist or an archaeologist snooping around. After work on a Friday night The Hog's Head and The Chancellor play host to trainees and other staff. Other socialising revolves around sport, namely an annual interdepartmental football tournament, softball and netball, squash and tennis.

FFW tends to recruit people who've attended good universities and have perhaps had a year of travel or work before starting their career. The big news at the moment is that the firm is looking for even more of them. In the summer of 2005 it recruited additional people to start that September and in 2006. Those qualifying in 2005 were delighted to learn there were more jobs than qualifiers and as a result all eleven stayed on. Clearly the firm is serious about its growth strategy.

## and finally...

If you don't want to have to spend your entire training contract digging in vain for interesting pieces of work, Field Fisher Waterhouse might be the unusual find you've been looking for.

# Finers Stephens Innocent

## the facts

**Location:** London
**Number of partners/assistants:** 33/32
**Total number of trainees:** 10
**Seats:** 4x6 months
**Alternative seats:** None

The pairing in 1999 of general commercial and property specialists Finers and media firm Stephens Innocent has survived the test of time to prove that unlikely combinations can also be winning ones.

## banana split

Laurel and Hardy, Tom and Jerry, the much loved Richard Whiteley and Carol Vorderman... a litany of unlikely pairings that have carried off the chalk-and-cheese effect to great acclaim. Okay, so the relationship between the two sides of FSI may lack a certain something in terms of slapstick humour and comic timing, but when it comes to the happy union of commercial property and media matters, neither of them is slipping on a banana skin.

So here's the deal: FSI has six core areas of practice – commercial property, litigation, coco, media/IP, private client and employment. The firm is also a member of Meritas – an international association of independent law firms. Sadly this does not mean glamorous foreign postings for trainees, but with household brands and famous names on the client list, a spell on Great Portland Street should be far from humdrum.

In the four-seat training contract, the first seat is picked for you and there is one compulsory seat: "*You will do property, and that is a matter of fact.*" As the firm's largest department, the property team has a huge demand for trainees; as a firm with "*quite a few sexy departments*" property seats are often viewed with a sense of impending doom. One source likened juggling 40-50 files in a "*pressured and fast-moving*" team to a "*baptism of fire.*" Another concurred: "*That is completely fair – it has been a bit of a personal struggle.*" However, for every wannabe meeja lawyer who spoke of their time in property negatively, we found another trainee who viewed the pace and work on offer more positively. Said one: "*The stuff they do is high profile and it is attractive*" and because "*partners don't have time to spoon-feed you,*" this means supersize portions of responsibility.

Trainees spending their lunch break on nearby Oxford Street cannot fail to notice the results of the commercial property team's labours. Monsoon, Boxfresh, LK Bennett, LA Fitness and Virgin Group are all clients of the firm. And if after all that shopping they've worked up an appetite, they can always pop in to Pizza Hut, which the firm advised on the creation of its 600th restaurant. For those who know their cavity walls from their stuffed crust, the department's construction and projects work ranges from development of West India Quay to a project to provide permanent housing for homeless refugee families.

## do you want fries with that?

After tramping around the Lea Valley in wellies, a spell with the media/IP team is quite a change. It carries out a range of work in film finance and publishing, but it is defamation cases that really get the bulbs popping. Last year FSI was heavily involved in the ECHR submission for Dave Morris and Helen Steel, the two environmentalists sued by McDonald's in 1990 for producing a leaflet entitled 'What's wrong with McDonald's?' Alas, our sources were suitably discreet (ie cagey) about their time in here; suffice to say they claim to have worked on "*quite hot stuff.*" Typical trainee tasks include attending client meetings and conferences with counsel, taking witness statements and drafting orders for court directions. As one source explained: "*A lot of it is general assistant stuff for trainees because we have some big, high-profile cases. When they kick off it can be frantic, and there are tantrums and stuff.*" As in the past, media/IP is the iPod mini of seats. Okay, so the waiting list isn't quite so long, it won't cost you quite so much, and you are unlikely to be mugged down a dark alley as a result, but the clamour is there, and the kudos. Last year the firm managed to meet the demand for the seat; however, as one sage voice warned: "*People apply to FSI because media sounds cool, but you aren't guaranteed a media seat.*"

In general commercial litigation seats there are fewer drama queens and trainees can run their own small debt collection files, even trying their hand at making applications before masters in the High Court. Less likely to earn you column inches in *Hello!*, but at least "*you're not always on the outskirts of a big thing.*" Trainees were buzzed up on the corporate department's recent successes: "*It is going from strength to strength*" we heard. "*I had an absolute stormer,*" another chipped in. Filing Companies House forms, updating registers, managing documents, contract drafting and research are all standard fodder, but when there's something big on the table "*it is quite exciting.*" The work of the coco team is also no joking matter. It advised on the sale of the Café Rouge and Bella Italia chains and has made a name for deals on the AIM market for clients such as Hill Station (the ice cream of choice amongst celebrities). If this veritable sundae of work doesn't entice, how about a squirt of private client and a sprinkling of family?

## keeping it real estate

The harsh facts of life are up for grabs in these seats, with divorce, maintenance suits and estate planning the order of the day. Occupying space in Clipstone Street, over the road, these departments are "*quite separate*" from the frenzy of the main office. Trainees speak of a "*close-knit, friendly team*" with a more relaxed atmosphere. "*It's not that things are less urgent,*" one trainee qualified, "*it's just that it's a very strong team and you feel more backed up.*"

Trainees described a training system where people worked hard to accommodate their interests and where three-monthly appraisals kept everyone on track. All our sources had been given plenty of responsibility, and where the size of the matter made this impossible, supervisors had at the very least nudged them forward to get a better view. FSI is not shy about appealing to mature applicants – it requests a CV rather than requiring the completion of an application form, an approach which is better for those who cannot neatly pack their life into little tick-boxes. Trainees confirmed: "*They appreciate life experience and contacts. They don't use age and qualifications as an initial filter.*"

The fact that certain FSI partners make regular TV and radio appearances appears to have rubbed off on trainees, who scattered our interviews with references to networking, profile-raising and client wins. Such an outlook is invaluable in a smaller firm where, to an extent, you make your own luck. In the past, the firm's retention figures have been decidedly under par, and a closer look would suggest that this is more to do with a divergence between the firm's needs and trainees' interests than anything else. It is the same story again in September 2005, with only one of the firm's four qualifiers staying on at the firm, this year taking a place in the family team.

## fancy dress and other odd looks

FSI's building on Great Portland Street is wrapped around a central atrium complete with palm trees and artwork (rumour has it "*media partner Mark Stephens used to accept payment in art*"). Lawyers' offices are more conventional with nothing more quirky than "*a few exhibits from IP cases lying around – shoes, a cuddly toy and things.*" The social scene is similarly understated. Last year the annual shindig was a Caribbean-themed summer party at Kensington Roof Gardens with "*theoretical fancy dress*"... "*if you wanted to.*" For the rest of the year, there are monthly 'wind-down' drinks and nibbles. Friday nights see trainees and solicitors heading to Villandry's, The Crown & Sceptre or The Masons Arms for "*spit and sawdust,*" and with three members of staff in separate bands, no one's short of a gig to go to.

Civilised hours mean a normal day ends at about 6pm. Naturally there will be the odd twilight shift, and during a trial you may find yourself "*working like the clappers – all hours, evenings, weekends, bank holidays.*" On the whole though "*people look at you oddly if you come in at the weekends... they don't really get it.*" Equally liberating, formal dress is abandoned every Friday and for the whole of August. Only jeans and t-shirts are off limits, though one member of staff effortlessly carries off leather trousers. A media type we presume? "*Oh no, it's someone in property.*"

## and finally...

This quintessentially West End firm spices up property practice with the streetload of well-known retailers on its client roster. And for those who just don't get the appeal of real estate, front-page media involvement should do the trick.

# Fisher Meredith

## the facts

**Location:** London
**Number of partners/assistants:** 9/40
**Total number of trainees:** 15
**Seats:** 4x6 months
**Alternative seats:** None

Cross the Thames at Vauxhall Bridge, bear left up Kennington Lane and in five minutes you'll be a stone's throw from Fisher Meredith, a legal aid firm with a broad practice. This is a firm with its feet in the local community and its head way above the high street.

## leaving stockwell, taking stock

Traditionally the age for taking stock and getting serious, FM is handling its 30th birthday with impressive equanimity. True the world has changed since its inception: we're guessing senior partner Eileen Pembridge wears business casual when she guests on Radio 4's 'Points of Law' these days, but in 1975 championing the excluded, the abused and the wronged probably demanded serious flares. But while fashions come and go, ideals are forever and the firm's commitment to championing individuals' rights is as enduring as the classic little black dress. In the words of one trainee: "*The core ethos is still about general access to justice for members of the community, civil liberties, and family and crime practice.*" The London bombings on 21st July 2005 are a perfect case in point. Although the attempt to detonate explosives at Oval tube station was very close to home, the firm is representing one of several suspects charged with involvement in the failed plot. The firm knows that the times when the police are under public pressure to produce quick results, are the very times it is most important to ensure the rights and liberties of the individual are not compromised.

A year ago FM moved to a new, four-storey office that came complete with "*a wall of glass down*

# the true picture

*one side."* On taking possession of the unfortunately named Blue Sky House, the firm rebranded in a distinctly slick manner, its website showing charming pictures of the Scottish coast, Devon moorland and Kentish hayfields. But we're left wondering quite what these images have to do with representing a 16-year-old repeat offender, visits to Brixton prison or domestic violence injunctions. Had we stumbled on a looming identity crisis? Apparently not, according to the trainees we interviewed this year. They say the slicker identity and new premises are a proactive step at a time of instability in the world of publicly funded law. *"With competitive tendering coming into legal aid work, all the firms like us are under pressure, so we need a way of marking ourselves out and attracting new clients,"* said one source. Another stressed: *"It's not a betrayal of values, it's about survival."*

## practically ideal

The firm has been one of the Legal Services Commission's 'preferred suppliers', but no one makes assumptions about the future. One trainee summed up the balance of old and new perfectly, saying: *"We're a business and we have to keep running in order to be able to serve those clients who need our help. That means more privately paying clients, but we haven't gone corporate."* All our sources were pragmatic about this trend: *"No one's shocked that we have to earn money, but as a group of trainees we're all committed to civil liberties and human rights."*

Shoring up the publicly funded practice with private work and a raised profile has meant an increase in *"wealthy individual clients. We get more and more crime and family referrals from big city firms."* It has also stimulated an existing area of business – local authorities, voluntary sector agencies and charities, both in and beyond London. So, in addition to representing some of the accused in the Damilola Taylor case last year (a quintessential FM instruction), the firm also received instruction from the likes of Age Concern, Mencap, the Refugee Council and the Royal Embassy of Saudi Arabia.

## save lives not tax

Trainees choose FM *"because its size, reputation and range of departments is unusual for a firm that predominantly deals with publicly funded work."* One has to admit that their jobs are hard won; almost all have acres of experience behind them, be it temping at criminal firms or voluntary work for human rights' charities. *"The firm is very keen on people with a background in the field or substantial evidence of commitment and interest in civil liberties."* So if you're fired to make an application start accruing those pro bono brownie points. And hit the books while you're at it because *"everyone is academically strong with plenty of distinctions from law school."*

As for idealism, well, that takes you a long way when you're dealing with demanding clients on a seventeen and a half grand salary while managing a stack of law school debts as high as a house. *"Most of us still need support from family or partners,"* one trainee revealed. But if you choose this kind of legal career, satisfaction isn't sought or found in your pay packet. *"I didn't want to do a job where you help big corporations reduce their tax bill. This job can be hard work, but when you present an application to a judge that you've prepared, you get an order that means your client's abusive husband can't come near her any more and you see the client's relief... that's what it is about."*

## nursing them through it

Not every day of the four six-month seats is quite so dramatic or satisfying, not least because *"legal aid work means a lot of bureaucracy and wranglings with the LSC."* It is *"generally understood that crime and family are effectively compulsory,"* but seats are also on offer in immigration, child law, housing, public services, fraud and business crime, police and prison law and employment. Most trainees find their way to qualification by taking a preferred path and we even heard of one trainee who was doing a conveyancing seat *"because they'd really wanted it."*

# the true picture

Across all departments trainees take on what they refer to as "*triage responsibility*," which basically means "*being first point of contact for new walk-in or telephone clients, assessing their needs and either taking the matter further or referring them to the local authority or a charity if we can't help.*" It allows trainees to practice their people skills and can be "*emotionally draining when someone's crying down the phone that their husband has walked off with everything. You've got to be empathetic but also objective about the legal case.*" Thankfully, there are less intense tasks too: clerking, selecting and instructing counsel, contacting witnesses, sourcing evidence and liaising with clients over court appearances. The "*9ish to 5.30ish*" hours are scarcely onerous, but trainees do have an additional responsibility to be "*trainee of the day doing the urgent tasks and errands or even scarier stuff like going before the district judge.*"

It all adds up to an "*excellent training, but you have to be organised and proactive, be willing to take responsibility and have the ability to communicate effectively with clients with different levels of understanding.*" Our sources were generally happy with the feedback and support they received, but admitted "*the emphasis is on the trainee as much as the supervisor to get the most out of each seat and supervisors can vary in approach quite substantially.*"

## a life of crime

Entertaining three trainees at a time, the crime department offers "*a faster pace of work than the civil seats. You run cases under supervision from taking instructions from clients at arrest to gathering evidence, contacting witnesses, liaising with the courts and instructing barristers.*" Expect anything from benefit scams and shoplifting to rape, murder or serious fraud such as the R v Green £6.8 million money laundering case. Naturally trainees have "*far less autonomy on the more serious cases.*" The police and prison law team works on actions against the police for unlawful detention or treatment.

The family department sees perhaps the greatest number of privately paying clients, but also plenty of "*divorces for people in prison*" (not that we're suggesting rich people don't also go to prison sometimes). Family law can be "*a harrowing and interesting area of work which tests various skills in dealing with vulnerable and sometimes unstable clients.*" There's also a separate children's law team where care proceedings and residence matters are the staple. A typical matter might be "*representing parents against a local authority which is trying to take their children into care due to accusations of drug abuse.*"

The public services law team has a particular flair for combining educational and community care issues. For example, "*cases advising parents in response to [a school] exclusion on special education needs grounds.*" Here as elsewhere in the firm, satisfaction can be found in "*dynamic work that challenges existing law.*" One trainee worked on a case involving the forced separation of two OAPs who had been married for 60 years when one partner was taken into care. There was no legislation to cover the matter.

## running with the pack

Increased trainee numbers have not diluted the bond among them. "*We made an effort to meet up before arriving at the firm and it's carried on. We're encouraging next year's lot to do the same.*" They lunch together regularly and slip to The Doghouse for drinks after work. And if they feel like chasing a stick, Kennington Park is but a dash away. Last year's firm-wide summer outing was a trip to Brighton, and the Christmas party was a "*let-your-hair-down*" affair that took place at a members only club just off the Strand. Several sources alluded to salacious gossip "*involving management,*" but for want of hard evidence we thought it best to let sleeping dogs lie.

It remains to be seen what impact increased trainee numbers will have on the retention rate for NQs, but in 2005 one of the two qualifiers took a job at the firm, specialising in police and prison law.

## and finally...

If you have passion, commitment, stomach and fortitude for publicly funded work then Fisher Meredith should be high on your shortlist. As a classy, well-managed practice it is well placed to ride out the legal aid storm.

# Foot Anstey

## the facts

**Location:** Plymouth, Exeter, Taunton
**Number of partners/assistants:** 32/61
**Total number of trainees:** 20
**Seats:** 4x6 months
**Alternative seats:** None

Devon-based Foot Anstey Sargent ditched the military bit of its name just as it was gearing up for a full offensive on the legal market. These leaders in media and family work, bolstered by ranks of litigators and transactional lawyers, are crusading in the western shires. Let battle commence!

## foot soldiers

In the 5th century, when Germanic invaders pinned the native Britons in the bottom corner of the British Isles, they probably didn't envisage Alfred the Great popping up 400 years later to conquer the Danes and spread the word of clotted cream teas and morris dancing. Some 1200 years on another uprising is afoot now that Foot Anstey, having enjoyed a long reign from its Plymouth and Exeter strongholds, has chosen to fulfil its ambitions for greater influence in the South West.

The firm's two main offices are in Plymouth in an old TV studio with "*a plush glass front*" and "*tinted windows,*" and some 38 miles away in Exeter. At the time of writing the Exeter contingent was brandishing the bubble wrap and parcel tape in anticipation of its impending move to Senate House, a new "*big red building right in the town centre.*" Across the two offices, the firm handles an impressive breadth of work for nationally known clients such as Wrigley, NatWest and The Beer Seller, as well as regional concerns including Plymouth Marine Laboratory, Cornwall County Council, South West Arts and Cornish Homes. For trainees, experiences range from marine litigation to medical negligence, private client and planning.

Foot Anstey trainees share the firm's conquering spirit, and news that the firm had planted its flag in Taunton and Bridgwater was received with a cheer... plus requests for relocation to Taunton. The new offices resulted from a merger in May 2005 with Somerset firm Alms & Young, which offered residential conveyancing, family and "*other less commercial stuff,*" though we did hear that "*one partner is going to take commercial law to Somerset.*" That's the spirit! The merger, we're told, is phase one of the firm's "*aim to double in size*" and dominate all the lands west of Bristol. "*We are focused on that area. We are going to take over all the really pretty areas,*" said one without a hint of irony. Another announced: "*We want to attack somewhere like Cornwall.*" Next stop Truro perhaps?

## tough as old boots

Signing up for the Foot Anstey campaign requires nerves of steel as the application day itself is "*hard core.*" Quite apart from a rigorous round of interviews, written assessments and psychometric tests, "*halfway through they call you all in and send some people home, Pop Idol-stylee.*" If you're lucky, you emerge starry-eyed and make a heart-rending speech about your wonderful parents and the other talented competitors. If not, you slink back to your law firm short list in the uncomfortable knowledge that there aren't that many other good commercial options in the region.

A cunning mix of "*weird people who love talking about their Table As*" (don't worry, you'll learn what this is at law school) and "*those who like trawling through documents*" plus a number who are happy "*dealing with emotional people*" ensures that none of the four six-month seats are oversubscribed. The firm also does its best to allow trainees to return to a favoured department for the final seat before quali-fication. In short, "*the firm really bends over backwards to accommodate you*" if you have a prefer-ence of location (though crime and personal injury seats are only available in Plymouth and IP, clin neg and property litigation are only available in Exeter). If you do have to travel for one seat, chances are you'll get travel expenses and a parking space for your trouble.

## i want to be alone

As in past years, the "*superb*" family department was a hot favourite with trainees, and we can see why. The family finance team handles everything from "*legal aid up to multimillion-pound cases,*" while childcare specialists take care of adoption, surrogacy and education matters as well as private children law. The Living Together team specialises in cohabitation issues, including the rights of gay couples. For trainees, a spell here means "*responsi-bility thrown at you from the moment you step through the door.*" Despite receiving "*a bit of a shock at the sheer volume of work,*" trainees enjoyed the "*really hands-on*" nature of the seat and the auton-omy that comes with running your own smaller divorce files and legal aid cases.

Equally compelling is the firm's defamation and reputation management work. Such work outside London is rare, but at Foot Anstey it is well done, ranking among the very best in the regions. The team acts for clients such as Trinity Mirror and Associated Newspapers (*The Mail, Evening Stan-dard, Metro*) on a broad spread of defamation, IP and media matters, and it also represents individu-als who have been libelled. This year the team got a look in on Catherine Zeta-Jones' one-woman pri-vacy campaign when it advised regional UK papers on claims by her US attorneys of misuse of her image rights.

## step outside the safety zone

"*In seats like private client, crime and family*" the work lends itself to trainees receiving their own caseload. However, for some of our sources there had been spells where they felt less involved in the commercial seats, occasionally adopting "*quite a background role,*" especially on "*very large deals that have been going on for five years or so.*" In such cir-cumstances they felt it was "*impossible to pick up on the ins and outs*" of the deals. Thankfully, opportu-nities to help out on much smaller transactions do arise, and at times sources had found themselves "*doing everything from sending out the contract pack up to the point of completion.*"

Similarly in litigation seats "*you are much more in the background as the matters are high value,*" but Foot Anstey is "*not impressed if you do monkey work. If you've got 200 pages of photocopying they tell you to take it to general admin.*" Again, where there are smaller cases, trainees get to take on more demand-ing roles, including heading off to chambers and the small claims court to test their advocacy skills. As if reading our thoughts, one trainee told us: "*They are always pushing you a little bit further outside your safety zone.*"

While "*trainees are high in demand*" and may receive work from across the department, "*if your supervisor needs you, you do their work first.*" In return, they play ball by giving three-monthly appraisals, though "*you also get feedback on the day-to-day stuff. You get constructive advice after everything... just not necessarily a pat on the head.*"

## you're not from round 'ere

"*It being Devon,*" one sage source observed, "*there is not really a reputation for long hours.*" Trainees get in at 8.30am and tend to be gone by 5.30pm or 6pm at a push. Hideous tales of twilight woe are "*few and far between.*" Moreover, anyone who does stay beyond midnight "*feels really proud about it and has to tell everyone.*" In fact, a trainee who once stayed until 2am has since acquired legendary sta-tus. Such neat hours are conducive to post-work socialising, and in Plymouth that means the Walk-about *"because it's 25 metres from the front door."* In Exeter the local is a nearby wine bar. Plymouth is probably the more lively location; one source even ventured to speak of *"a city buzz."* In Exeter meanwhile *"you see the same people every day. It's a bit like living in The Truman Show."*

With both locations, open countryside at the end of the street and the coast on the doorstep means there is always plenty to keep people entertained. Unfazed by the distance between the two offices, trainees arrange regular nights out and even get together at the weekends. There are also football and netball teams, quiz nights and TSG social events. For its last Christmas bash the firm hired a hotel in Torquay, everyone stayed over, and those who missed breakfast stumbled off to a greasy cafe to compare hangovers and injuries.

Our sources spanned the twenty-nothing-thirty-something age band and the straight-through-uni-versus-previous-career divide. So where is the common ground? At the end of the A303, of course. Everyone we spoke to was clear that *"they will ask you about it at interview if you have no apparent link with the area."* The reason why is simple, *"they don't want you to just run off to the bright lights of London after training."* Slim chance of that with the *"career-oriented"* trainees we interviewed; cheerful, chatty and enthusiastic, they were evidently *"quite settled in the South West."* Foot Anstey, it seems, recruits in its own image – loyal to the region and walking with a confident stride. In 2005 five of the six second-years stayed on at the end of their training to carry on putting their best foot forward.

## and finally...

If the only thing you're decided on is the South West, Foot Anstey's range of practice areas and ambitious spirit could be just what you need.

# Forbes

## the facts

**Location:** Blackburn, Accrington, Clitheroe, Preston, Chorley, Leeds, Manchester
**Number of partners/assistants:** 24/50
**Total number of trainees:** 16
**Seats:** 4x6 months
**Alternative seats:** Secondments
**Extras:** Pro bono – CAB

Forbes is a firm with a century's past in Lancashire, and a willingness to adapt to the challenges of legal practice in the region.

## accrington stanley: who are they? exactly!

With branches across the county, the firm is deeply rooted in Lancashire but is not insular. You needn't be from Lancashire for Forbes as long as you're bred north of the Watford Gap from a place that also begins with 'L'- the firm has an office in Leeds and one trainee is from Leicester. As for the clients, the firm's Lancashire focus has ensured that its commercial client list is similarly regional with a smattering of larger national business in the insurance sector. Most of its private clients, meanwhile, step in off the street or are waiting patiently in a cell.

Forbes' sprawl of offices across the North West results from the amalgamation of smaller local practices over the years. A five-storey Preston office contains the widest array of departments dealing with both commercial and publicly funded clients. *"You could work there for ages and would never meet someone on the first floor if you worked on the fourth."* Chorley, on the other hand, is *"two terraces stuck together"* dealing only with two sorts of law – family and crime. There you see everyone daily and it feels *"like a family and is more informal."* While all offices (except Leeds and Manchester) do some crime work, all cases bound for crown go to Preston.

Accrington is home to an office charmingly named Gothic House. *"I've gone over to the dark*

# the true picture

side," giggled one trainee. "*It's not black with devils hanging off the corners*," though the former Lancashire municipal building is next to a churchyard. Blackburn's Rutherford House has none of the Edgar Allen Poes; instead, like Chorley, it is a group of terraced houses. It is bigger overall than Accrington but space is meanly apportioned to tiny offices. Rutherford House is the hub of Forbes' PI, employment, civil litigation and property departments. Blackburn's other offices, Northgate House and Marsden House service legal aid and defendant insurance clients respectively. The two couldn't be more different – trainees at Northgate take clients fresh from the road, whilst a seat at Marsden involves little face-to-face client contact. Far away on the wrong side of the Pennines, the Leeds office deals exclusively with defendant insurance. This type of litigation is also the raison d'être for the new Manchester office, which should eventually broaden in the scope of its commercial activities. Any trainee whose attention is captured by this work could ask for a secondment to client Millgate Insurance (the Co-op's claims arm).

## the world on your shoulders

The trainee group was summed up as follows: "*Red-brick graduates are recruited as trainees, ex-poly grads become paralegals.*" Whether the lines are quite so sharply drawn we'd hesitate to say, but it is clear that non-traditional routes into a legal career are commonplace, with the ILEX to LPC an oft trodden path. A current senior fee-earner, we're told, was with the firm for ten years slowly working his way along this path. "*At the moment there are a lot of internal applicants for traineeships,*" though, as in other firms, the harsh reality is that a paralegal hoping to turn trainee has to "*shine.*" Some trainees commit to the Herculean task of a part-time LPC course running concurrent with a training contract, which means the usual four-seat traineeship is stretched across three as opposed to two years. Forbes allows time off for lectures but a "*misconception exists in the department that afternoons off are*

study time as opposed to lecture time.*" Annual leave must be used if you want to revise; only examinations mean days off. This type of training experience can be tough, especially when doing a crime seat. The roster may show a 5pm finish but you may end up staying in the station until 11pm if a big police operation is under way.

Despite the presence of criminal lawyers in every office, it is possible to complete a training contract consisting entirely of commercial seats. Those who have completed the LPC before joining the firm may be preferred for commercial work. Conversely, trainees thrust straight into crime seats at the start of their contracts tend to have already completed the necessary Police Station Accreditation scheme whilst working as paralegals. First-years have little choice about what they do and crime and family are likely contenders for first and second seats respectively. Officially there are no compulsory seats in the second year when trainees' own views play a bigger part. Seat allocation produces tetchiness amongst trainees in many firms and we sensed the exacerbation of such petty discontents may arise at Forbes because "*some trainees are told their seat in advance and then told not to tell others.*" Regardless of such seat allocation woes, something must be working as all the 2004 qualifiers stayed with the firm and four of the five stayed in 2005.

## the con ate my homework...

Family law will always involve emotionally testing moments from the 'd-i-v-o-r-c-e' and 'c-u-s-t-o-d-y' tantrums to a large volume of care proceedings that can leave you feeling "*more like a social worker.*" Prepare for the realisation that "*it's people's lives you're dealing with,*" perhaps solo – trainees deemed sufficiently experienced are given their own cases.

Over time the firm's criminal lawyers become familiar with the patrons of Lancashire's many magistrates' and Crown Courts. "*You meet a lot of the same people again and again,*" and with recidivism rates so high trainees come to appreciate the distraction of a first-time offender – "*It's nice to deal with a nice normal client who hasn't already been to the crown court and who isn't a drug dealer."* Now, 'normal' is an awkward objective gauge (all manner of people have all manner of hobby-horsical notions); nevertheless the following behaviour has to be far from normal, even by custody suite standards. During an unsupervised interview in the police station a suspected car thief told the trainee advising him that he had changed his previously pliant mind. The system had failed him and he 'an't done notin'. Assenting to her client's wish, our trainee dutifully drew a line through her instruction notes and requested the aforementioned twoccer to be so kind as to authenticate the correction with a signature. He was not so kind. He ate the notepad.

## rover's return

In recent years the firm has sought out white-collar or corporate crime, a move consistent with its keener interest in commercial work. Yet Forbes' interests remain varied, disparate one might even say, which is perhaps why the firm spent time and money to create a brand – new logo, new letterhead etc, all in corporate colours. The future is now not only bright but also orange and blue.

Forbes' commercial clients include first division Burnley FC and giants Blackburn Rovers FC. For schmoozing purposes, Forbes makes the most of its premiership connection and its luxury box at Blackburn. The corporate and commercial deals handled by the firm may not be the largest kicking around but trainees end up with a good assortment of tasks including drafting and research assignments. Defendant insurance, too, is a varied seat with trainees getting involved with pre-action files, interim applications and case-management conferences. In many of the private client areas of work you speak to the uninitiated: *"Insurance companies know what they're talking about, make a mistake and they'll know."* Even your *"two-line letters will be checked."* Nevertheless trainees reported of their supervisors, *"they let you have a go"* at most things.

Solo appearances before district judges at infant approval hearings are balanced with backroom tasks such as brief preparation on larger cases. Comparing her training with that of a friend at a big Manchester firm, one trainee said: *"With such big clients all she does is photocopying."* At Forbes you do everything qualified solicitors do, just *"on a smaller scale."*

The firm's social calendar is far from full. If it's someone's birthday expect Friday night drinks, otherwise social events seem limited to training days in Preston. There are sports teams, although some of the firm's netballers have recently gone into retirement, one of them with a pretty good excuse. Last year we reported a marriage in the firm – this year it's a Forbes baby.

Despite the rebranding, we sense that Forbes has yet to forge tight links between its offices. The firm's intranet and in-house magazine *Forbes Focus* may be spreading the word, but perhaps not loudly enough – *"Things are often shrouded in secrecy,"* one source concluded. A trainee is lucky enough to see the inside of quite a few offices, other staff are less likely to have this overarching view of their employer. How the network is to be more firmly connected perhaps lies in the future, a future in which the firm is intent on taking a bigger share of the region's defendant insurance work while steadily developing its commercial departments. It sounds like an exciting time to be joining... if you think so too, you might be interested to learn that the firm now runs a paid vacation scheme.

## and finally...

For those heading for a wide-ranging, challenging traineeship, possibly one that begins on a lower rung of the legal ladder, Forbes looks to be a good destination. Oh, and if you're from Accrington, you're laughing!

# Ford & Warren

## the facts
**Location:** Leeds
**Number of partners/assistants:** 21/92
**Total number of trainees:** 12
**Seats:** 4x6 months
**Alternative seats:** None

Ford & Warren is a Yorkshire firm, and how. Gruffer than your gruff granddad with a chest cold and more straightforward than two slide rules in a row. So, in that spirit: it's in Leeds, it does its best work in employment, transport law, defendant PI and commercial litigation.

## wheely good

The core of the firm's expertise is in transport law and it possesses a hearty client roster that includes Travel West Midlands, First Group, National Express, First Great Western, Hydro Aluminium Motorcast and Scotrail. In a road regulatory capacity the firm advises such clients on contracts for carriage, acquisitions and disposals, environmental problems and prosecutions, tachograph fraud and even corporate manslaughter in relation to major road accidents. Bearing in mind the 'big engines and wheels' theme of these clients, it isn't surprising that the firm's reputation for employment is extensively transport based. It is experienced in industrial relations, for example advising on the rules for ballots before strike action. It also has a history of representing Leeds City Council, regional educational establishments and NHS trusts. Both transport and employment are popular seats with trainees, particularly the latter because of *"extremely well-respected partners and a really varied workload."* The only caveat is that *"the scale of the work means you don't see many cases through from start to finish."* Specific work for NHS trusts has included defending part-time pension claims, drafting new contracts under the 'Agenda for Change' initiative and resolving immigration prob-

lems arising out of the recruitment of overseas medical staff.

A stint in commercial litigation, another of the firm's hotbeds of activity, offers yet more transport-flavoured work, including regulatory matters with a leaning towards corporate crime. There's also a licensing and leisure strain to be enjoyed, giving trainees exposure to clients such as the Punch Pub Company, Greene King, Heritage Inns and Thomas Cook Retail. Proof then that F&W fee earners are not merely wheeled warriors.

## off road

When F&W lawyers do go by Shank's pony, they are sure to plant their feet firmly, a care bred of expertise in defending large insurers like Saga, Ecclesiastical and Royal & Sun Alliance against everything from slip and trip claims right through to more catastrophic injuries. Described as *"a really enjoyable seat"* trainees get stuck into a steady diet of *"drafting defences and reports to clients on RTAs and employer's liability claims."* Or how about assisting on the defence of a school caught up in an assault at work case. Two particularly interesting cases from the past year share a common outcome: claimants choosing to discontinue their claim after meeting stiff opposition from the F&W lawyers. In the first case, a college lecturer who was seeking over £300,000 from his ex-employer for stress, decided to pull out ten days into the trial. He ended up having to pay 80% of the defendant's costs. The second case involved a driving examiner who sued a learner driver for severe personal injury and psychological damage caused by an accident during a driving test. The defence claimed there was no accident and brought in a psychiatrist who concluded the driving instructor was either a malingerer or perhaps even a bit bonkers. Eventually after F&W lawyers unearthed a heap of discrepancies in the claimant's evidence, she discontinued her claim.

Beyond its four specialist areas, F&W offers trainees seats in commercial property, insolvency, family, trusts and probate, residential conveyancing and corporate. Much maligned by trainees when we last reported on F&W, this year our sources felt a greater affinity with commercial property. Said one: "*I had varied work for decent clients from plcs and limited companies to private business individuals and charities.*" Whilst some admitted to periods of boredom, there were others who enthused about "*effectively running cases myself – in one instance I ran a land transfer from start to finish.*" Private client and family work is F&W's road less travelled: "*I think most people try for a commercial route through training here.*"

## self-help

In case you are wondering what has led us to characterise the firm as bluff and no-nonsense, you need look no further than the F&W website, which makes the graphics on our antique ZX Spectrum 48K (with rubber keys) look like the latest Xbox release. A deliberately low-tech affair, the website features emphatic statements like "We could take shooting parties to Lombardy and put up our fees to pay for them. We don't." Having been beaten around the head with the F&W philosophy on value for money, we turned to our interviewees for an explanation. "*The website has none of the glitz or falseness of big London firms,*" they told us. "*We don't try to curry favour by false promises, we provide an excellent legal service and our clients value the fact that we charge them only for the services that they need.*" Gotcha. Loud and clear.

Our impression of an almost ascetic client-facing profile was underscored by the website's recruitment pages, which, in the manner of a self-made Yorkshire businessman-turned-self-help-guru demands "*self-discipline, self-motivation and self-development.*" However, trainees were quick to dispel any idea that faint hearts should steer clear. "*The F&W type of person is quietly determined to do a good job and reap the rewards of working hard, but the atmosphere is incredibly friendly,*" they said. Are they sure? "*Yes, if I meet the managing partner in the lift we'll chat as if he was another trainee, it's the same with everybody.*"

## no-door policy

Trainees elsewhere often speak proudly of their firm's open-door policy. At F&W there are as few doors and walls as possible, with the entire firm sitting open plan. "*Even the more senior partners don't have their own dedicated offices.*" The set-up is designed to "*foster a community atmosphere*" and trainees were emphatic that it is successful in this – "*you really can ask anyone a question.*" It also means that the seven floors of the office in central Leeds are "*light, airy and mainly done in the company colours of blue, black and white.*" A top-floor social area is open to all and trainees also like the fact that they are physically bundled together in the office. "*We don't sit with our supervisors, but in trainee banks on each floor.*" Perfect for passing crib notes and "*getting help on difficult points.*" There must have been a heck of a lot of banter on the day that all six 2005 qualifying trainees learned they had secured jobs with the firm.

Our interviewees were also right pleased with the format for appraisals – three formal reviews for each six-month seat. "*You get a flavour of how things are going and the points you raise are actually acted on.*" One source also added: "*If you do get day to day work back without feedback, then you just go and ask for it.*" While there's not an abundance of formal training sessions, we still got the impression that the two-year training is a comprehensive one. When it comes to seat rotation there's no intrigue, "*you send in an e-mail listing your preferences and giving your reasons and the firm then decides.*" Our sources were largely happy with the way things had panned out, with the smartest of them revealing the best tip for working the system was "*to make the reasons justifying your choices compelling.*"

## say what you mean

A strong work ethic is underlined by a "*strict and formal dress code*" and regimented hours of 9am to 6pm. The easy conclusion to draw is that it's a northern thing, but that would be to ignore the fact that "*although a few [trainees] have a Leeds or*

West Yorkshire link, three out of five in my year came from much further afield." So while you don't need local roots to win a training contract at the firm, we reckon that identification with what it stands for might be crucial. As one trainee said: "From the website and interview I got the impression this was a firm in sync with how I feel. I think it's a lawyer's job to be a lawyer"... as opposed to holiday rep or marketing exec, we assume they mean. As a group, trainees are generally "not fresh faced and straight out of law school" but have had a few years of experience of life to give them "the wisdom and wrinkles of the late twenties." Perhaps it is this maturity that keeps the social life "low key" and limited to birthday lunches at "old reliable Pizza Express" or Friday night drinks in Baroque, Bar Med or Browns. Or other places beginning with B. Sports teams and a Christmas bash (last time at the Leeds Hilton) are the highlights of the calendar.

## and finally...

Ford & Warren gives its trainees exposure to good quality mid-market Leeds work and a straightforward training. Dig out that sober suit for the interview and keep in mind that this firm "doesn't scream and shout; it just gets the job done."

# Forsters LLP

## the facts

**Location:** London
**Number of partners/assistants:** 29/46
**Total number of trainees:** 7
**Seats:** 6x4 months
**Alternative seats:** None

The Forsters' name is synonymous with stellar property work, which makes up 55% of the firm's turnover. Forsters has it all – expertise, an impressive client base, charm and stylish new accommodation.

## the forsters saga

In 1998, the management of highly respected firm Frere Cholmeley Bischoff signed over the fruits of their labours to the developing Eversheds franchise. As in all the best period dramas, there were some dissenters, in this case the property department. It chose to make its own way in the world under the name of Frere Cholmeley's 19th century founder, John Forster. Happily, unlike the Forsyte Saga, the Forsters story lacks dark intrigue, emotional despair and disastrous marriages; Forsters also manages property and personal affairs with greater aplomb than the ill-fated Forsytes.

The firm's superb reputation stems from its success on medium-sized real estate deals. Among its recent projects are the redevelopment of the King Edward Court shopping centre in Windsor, and the development of 'eco homes' on a 1.7-acre greenfield site near Sudbury. On both of these matters it advised the local authority, but its client list includes commercial giants such as McDonald's and large landowners such as the Portman Estate. In the excellent private client department, the clientele runs from "big, old landed estates to new money."

## retail therapy

Trainees undertake six seats, spending their last four months in the area they want to specialise in after qualification. "You don't come to a firm like Forsters and expect to be able to avoid property;" it is "the blood of the firm." Some trainees choose to spend considerable chunks of their two years doing property work, but if you feel one seat is as much as you want, "it is not something you get railroaded into going back to." The other seats on offer are commercial, construction, employment, private client and family.

The vast and busy commercial property team has particular expertise in the retail sector and a track record of involvement in shopping centre projects right across the British Isles, from the £31 million Aberfan Shopping Centre in Port Talbot to the £42 million North Point Shopping Centre in

Hull, plus others in Torquay, Hyde and Accrington. With so many bags to carry, the team is more than willing to delegate to trainees, not least "*because they need to.*" Property seats are consequently "*very hands-on*" and at times risk becoming "*stressful.*" Trainees are "*definitely a cog in the wheel of bigger transactions,*" but find plenty of scope to tick away on their own negotiating leases and licences. Indicative of the calibre of work handled by Forsters, even seats in residential property were lauded by our sources. Here you can "*run your own files and follow things through from start to finish.*" It's all a far cry from the humdrum textbook conveyances of the LPC; these are sales of "*very grand residential properties*" such as the Octagon, an appropriately shaped 19th century Chelsea home valued at £3 million.

For a variation on the property theme, a property litigation seat exposes trainees to everything from "*bread-and-butter lease renewals*" to "*little old grannies moaning about the dog barking next door.*" The team's work includes commercial and residential landlord and tenant disputes, dilapidations claims, title disputes, rent review interpretation and property-related professional negligence. There is also variety in the trainee's role: in addition to running their own files, our sources had issued proceedings for larger matters and attended trials. Also linked to the property practice is the fast-growing construction team, where trainees encounter warranties, and various building and engineering agreements. On the downside, "*you don't do construction on the LPC so you have a very sketchy understanding of how things work,*" but on the upside the small group is ideal and "*you are the third or fourth highest person in the team.*"

## a spoonful of sugar

Of the firm's property bent, trainees told us: "*It is certainly not the lead department with everyone else toeing the line.*" "*Other departments have established themselves quite well*" and the burgeoning private client team is a prime example. Explaining the way

the team works, one source told us: "*The partners and clients tend to be very close, and the partner knows the client's business, life and family inside out.*" It is only to be expected that "*you are never going to develop that relationship in a four-month seat.*" Work-wise, "*the emphasis is very much on trusts*" and "*tax is also a core of our work.*" However, "*from a trainee's point of view you can get involved in probate and basic will drafting. You go along to trustees' meetings, draft deeds of appointment and retirement, and settlements.*" All in all, "*you are given really quite a lot of responsibility.*"

"*Corporate is not a massive focus of the firm, and it doesn't profess it to be,*" but for trainees mindful of the value of some corporate experience, a seat in this area is a real variety show. Said one source: "*A lot of work is connected to property – you can't get away from that, but they also have their own work which is unconnected.*" The type of transaction trainees had experienced included listing companies on the AIM index, shareholder agreements and "*work for companies that have been struck off – getting them back on their feet and reinstated.*" And of course there's a steady diet of company secretarial tasks including attending meetings, drafting minutes and resolutions, and preparing Companies House filings.

At Forsters, "*you have to be prepared to muck in and you are expected to be part of the team from day one.*" Thankfully, "*photocopying and proof-reading is a rarity,*" with trainees more likely to be juggling files, communicating with clients and heading off to court. In short, "*if you like responsibility and are keen to have a go, you will survive at Forsters. If you need to be nannied, maybe not.*" Even without Mary Poppins as their role model, "*none of the partners make you quiver*" and there are plenty of kindly folk to help out "*if you are running around with a panicked look on your face.*" Certainly "*they won't let you loose on clients without adult supervision.*" Trainees tend to share an office with their supervisor and find the first six months of their training are "*crammed full*" of weekly lunchtime training sessions. Throughout the two years, supervisors *"let you assume responsibility at your own pace"* and *"point you in the right direction."* There are also thorough mid and end-of-seat appraisals and trainees told us: *"You are made to feel that what you are doing is actually worth something."*

## you, me, some monkeys...

In February 2005 Forsters relocated to a new abode on Hill St in Mayfair to allow for further expansion and to bring the whole firm under one roof. The office is ideally situated for the property agents based around Berkeley Square and the firm's private clients who *"much prefer coming into Mayfair as they can sneak to Claridges for lunch."* The office occupies an 18th century townhouse, originally commissioned by Elizabeth Montagu, 'The Queen of the Bluestockings' and author of the snappily titled *An Essay on the Writings and Genius of Shakespear compared with the Greek and French Dramatic Poets, with some Remarks upon the Misrepresentations of Monsieur De Voltaire*. Ms Montagu's pronounced tastes are still in evidence in the form of *"amazing cornices"* and Robert Adam features that are outshone only by the listed James Stuart painted ceiling in the firm's library. Still overwhelmed with excitement for the move, trainees shared our enthusiasm for such finer features, and were equally impressed by *"all the latest mod cons."* One exclaimed: *"Everything works here! In the last offices we sweltered in the summer and froze in the winter."* If a well-behaved thermostat doesn't cut the mustard with you, brand new showers, a super kitchen and a stunning terrace, just might.

Elizabeth Montagu is quoted to have once said *"I never invite idiots to my house."* It seems that Forsters has the same philosophy when it comes to recruitment. The astute and discerning trainees we spoke to had selected the firm fully aware of its private client and property expertise. Some trainees had spent time working as paralegals, others had come straight from law school, but together they made for a young group with a mature approach to

their careers. Socially, they enjoy *"knocking around together,"* and happily for them, Elizabeth Montagu's traditional 'conversation parties' have fallen by the wayside. Blue stockings have also been replaced by suits Monday to Thursday, with dress-down Fridays. When it comes to hours, *"it is not the psyche of the firm for you to work needlessly until midnight;"* trainees reported regular days of 9am till 6.30pm, leaving plenty of time for drinks on the terrace or in nearby Shepherd's Market. Other diversions include quiz nights, greyhound racing, mixed softball in Hyde Park, the odd cricket match and a five-a-side football team. Sadly *"there aren't enough chaps to play rugby."*

The summer party in 2005 followed a classic Pimms and barbecue format in the choice location of London Zoo's Monkey Kingdom. It was a far cry from the 'Hollywood Bling' Christmas bash in *"a chichi bar"* in Victoria. We suspect Ms Montagu would have looked less kindly on those who *"turned up in hoodies and medallions"* than those who opted for *"glamorous frocks, fancy hair dos and sparkly jewellery."* It is probably safe to say that she would have approved of the firm's decision to invite all four of the 2005 qualifiers to stay on at Hill Street.

## and finally...

Outstanding property and private client work in a firm that *"understands the past as well as being able to show a very commercial face"* – Forsters affords the best of both worlds.

# Fox Williams

## the facts

**Location:** London
**Number of partners/assistants:** 15/37
**Total number of trainees:** 8
**Seats:** 5x21 weeks
**Alternative seats:** None

According to its website Fox Williams is a firm of listeners. "How many times have you come across lawyers who did not really listen to you?" it asks. We thought we'd reciprocate by offering the firm's trainees our ears.

## wooster sauce

Sixteen years of listening to clients have taken FW from a six-partner operation to the chunky 50-partnered commercial practice it is today. Specialising in five areas, the firm does not spread itself thinly: employment work figures prominently, it has a stellar partnership team and its corporate, property and com-tech departments work in close cohesion. We suspect no recommendation can be heartier than the custom of other solicitors – FW recently advised on the creation of the Anglo-American law partnership Kirkpatrick & Lockhart, Nicholson Graham LLP, a 1,000-lawyer operation with a $500 million turnover. It also does break-ups. When four partners at the accountancy firm Deloitte & Touche defected to KPMG, the Foxes handled the equity muddles and soothed the acrimony. The partnership team isn't the only one privy to professional gossip – FW has been representing the Law Society in its legal hopscotch from an Employment Tribunal to the Employment Appeals Tribunal and eventually the Court of Appeal after former vice president Kamlesh Bahl brought 71 separate claims of sex and race discrimination, harassment and victimisation against her old employer. Proving that nobody outfoxes the Foxes, her claims were reduced from 71 to seven.

Employment work ranges from claimant repre-

sentations for the GMB (Britain's fourth-largest union) to defending Dulwich College (alma mater of Raymond Chandler and Bertie and Jeeves creator P.G. Wodehouse). The firm even dabbles in immigration law, though this is less asylum and more business and USA-focused. Clients include leading multinationals and West Coast technology companies requiring work-permits, visitor rights and changes of status for employees and their families. Helping to put the bacon back into Britain, FW's corporate finance client list contains advertising agency Mustoes, the company responsible for flogging what apparently is our nation-defining condiment – HP Sauce.

## what not to where

Foxy Fox has cut quite a dash with the fashionistas. Mambo, Cult Clothing, Karen Millen, Firetrap, Sonneti and Full Circle are all on its books. "*Fashion work is being pushed very hard*," one trainee explained. "*It's a booming area of business.*" Not content with high street fashion, the firm advises on the purchase of the high street itself. A £10 million retail parade in Scunthorpe went under the hammer with FW lawyers advising the syndicate of private investors who bought it. All this work must be making one of the firm's founders, the inimitable Ronnie Fox, somewhat style conscious. Apparently he drives to work in either his Lexus or his Mercedes, both sporting registration plate anagrams of Fox.

On the style stakes it all falls down when you learn that the Foxes den is at the back of Marks & Spencer in Moorgate. "*A fairly standard office block*," the building screams "*mid-Eighties*," and yet not a man or woman is still wearing shoulder pads. Then again, "*there are some traders on the fifth floor so you might find some red braces up there.*" Below the greed-is-good brigade, FW has four floors, each "*mirroring the other, so once you know one you know them all.*" Helpfully, all are colour coded: less Wall Street, more Quality Street from the sounds of it. The first floor is blue and contains employment and property. It offsets the second floor's green perfectly, where more employment lawyers and an administrative team reside. The third floor's walls display the most contentious colour in the office, salmon pink – not a shade immediately called to mind when commerce/technology and dispute resolution are involved. Finally, the yellow fourth floor houses the corporate and partnership teams. The *Student Guide* must be careful when doling out architectural fashion tips, however: we occupy a five-storey art deco affair displaying mint julep, bottle green and cream walls with red windows.

## full employment

With just five departments in the firm, you'd think that trainees would have a five in five chance of sitting in all of them. This is true for some, while others may elect to repeat a favourite seat. According to trainees the system produces "*a wide range of experiences – elsewhere you might get a choice, but they'll probably shove you into three different versions of corporate before your time is up.*"

Roundly praised as "*a good experience,*" employment law at FW is a mixture of contentious and non-contentious cases for claimant and respondent clients (mostly the latter). With a grounding in employment law guaranteed, the firm seems a far better option than any of the big City giants if this is the field that most appeals. Expect "*a lot of research,*" especially into unfair and other types of dismissals. Supervisors don't skimp on the "*juicy stuff*" for trainees: "*You're well informed as to what is going on and are brought in on teleconferences and conferences with counsel.*" If employment falls later in your training contract, you can expect to have a few smaller matters of your own, say the compilation of employers' equal ops handbooks and the drafting of employment contracts. Over in dispute resolution what you loose in drafting experience you gain in court time. "*A couple of claim forms and consent orders came my way in terms of drafting,*" one source said, "*but I was always in and out of court.*" Delivering documents and getting orders stamped

allows you to clock up enough court miles to fly your own applications before masters – "*It was fine, if slightly unexpected,*" one source recalled.

One of the smaller departments, property is the place for running your own files. Trainees take on licences to assign or alter leasehold property plus "*smaller post-completion matters,*" and on the larger deals they help out with more administrative tasks. "*A lot of money changes hands, so you just take the spin-offs and push them forward on your own without crossing over into the meat of the rest of the file.*" The property team has work coming out its ears at the moment, meaning there's "*a lot to be done by the trainees – you just have to dive in!*" By comparison, corporate was described as "*quite quiet*" at present. Consequently, "*if you don't sit close to the action you won't get the work, because it tends to get farmed out immediately and whichever trainee is visible will land the file.*"

Our last visit is to the commerce & technology department, which is "*split in two.*" Wait for it... "*There's commerce and then there's technology.*" The commercial bods prepare "*distribution agreements*" and technology bods work on "*software agreements.*" Both types take on IP work, an area that produces files trainees can run themselves – usually trademark registrations or disputing other companies' use of FW clients' trademarks. The trainee's remit includes attending negotiations to take notes and having a stab at the first drafts on letters, plus "*a load of research as per usual*" – no bad thing when doggy paddling in the uncharted waters of technology.

In all departments, trainees sit with an associate ("*sometimes even a partner*") sharing their office. They see it as "*a great way of learning things through osmosis.*" Additional learning comes from the legal updates and seminars that punctuate the two years – everything from standard PSC topics and black letter law to "*things like how to collect digital evidence from PCs and mobiles.*" As the months pass, trainees are given "*incrementally more responsibility,*" although we did hear one complaint from someone who argued FW "*can be a very risk-averse firm, so you're heavily supervised.*" And what of the hours? No complaints there; weekends and late nights in the office are unusual.

## the lion the fox and the wardrobe

The social and charities committee organises netball, football and rounders matches as well as the formal firm-wide get-togethers. On an informal note, Fridays see some of the younger Foxes holed up in the Red Lion. One trainee revealed that, when it comes to socialising, "*it is fairly hierarchical here – partners won't come to the ad hoc drinks, just the official ones.*" The Christmas party includes a trainee revue: "*Always a highly embarrassing moment when you have to lampoon others in the firm.*" The favoured technique of the cub jesters is to produce "*an interesting take on life at Fox without having a P45 land on you doormat.*" The performance usually incorporates "*wigs and cracking gags.*"

In September 2005, one of the three qualifying trainees stayed at the firm.

## and finally...

The firm's prowess in employment law tends to lead to a perception that it is a niche firm, yet Fox Williams actually offers a broad training contract. Its sense of style is evident from its website and office décor, as well as its client list, making it a great pick for anyone keen to avoid regulation City grey.

# Freeth Cartwright LLP

## the facts

**Location:** Nottingham, Leicester, Derby
**Number of partners/assistants:** 60/41
**Total number of trainees:** 15
**Seats:** 4x6 months
**Alternative seats:** None
**Extras:** Pro bono – Hyson Green Law Centre

Freeth Cartwright is one of the East Midlands'

strongest players and has offices in Nottingham, Derby and Leicester. Its growth and evolution over the past decade is nothing short of impressive, especially when it comes to commercial services. At the same time, nationally it has one of the finest reputations for group litigation and clinical negligence litigation.

## people in glass houses...

Commercial property is the big story at FC and the majority of trainees spend six months in this department, some with reluctance, others finding they have an affinity for the work. One convert told us: "*It's not that I had an enormous epiphany... but I found it really interesting to relearn everything about easements and covenants and to put the knowledge in context and implement it.*" Flagship deals for the firm include the mixed-use Trinity Square development in Nottingham, the Riverlights development in Derby and a £100 million redevelopment in Leicester city centre. Depending on which office you were working in, you could pop out at lunchtime to monitor progress on one of them. Said one trainee: "*I like it when you go around the city spotting bits of land and wondering what it will become and if we will be involved.*" Yet not all the deals are located on FC's doorstep: in a key social housing matter, it is advising Derwent Housing Association on the 600-bed Glass House student accommodation project in Birmingham's Loveday Road, and in the area of PFI and large-scale projects, it has involvement in matters as far flung as Moscow, Prague and Paris.

## ... shouldn't count their chickens

The corporate department operates in the world of SMEs (small to medium-sized enterprises), private equity and AIM. As one of our interviewees explained: "*Because of the nature of the firm and its location it is acting for local chicken farmers and valve and widget makers on industrial sites around the Midlands. There are a lot of old staples and I was surprised how old-fashioned the client base was.*" But

# the true picture

there is more to the story and "*two areas of growth are nursing homes and biotech spinouts*." This year's deals have included the spinout from the University of Nottingham and subsequent funding of biotech company Critical Pharmaceuticals, plus the £5.3 million management buyout of Paul Holdings, an engineering company that works in the aerospace and nuclear industries. In fact, well-known companies instruct the firm on all manner of things from trademark filing to litigation and construction, among them Coors Breweries, HMV Media, Waterstones, Paul Smith, The Tanning Shop, Arriva plc and ntl. Hardly chicken feed.

## in demand

Trainees spend most or all of their time in Nottingham, while Derby offers seats in commercial, property and commercial litigation, and Leicester has commercial lit, insolvency, employment and clin neg seats. In addition to these options, Nottingham offers private client, personal injury, corporate, tax, IP, property lit and business services options. The only caveat is that it is only the busiest departments that get trainees and so not all seats are available at every rotation. "*Because partners have to specifically request a trainee it means they don't see you as just an overhead.*"

Before it made a big commercial push a few short years ago, it was clinical negligence and PI practice for which the firm was best known. Product liability litigation over the MMR vaccine and Trilucent soya breast implants kept the firm in the news and the firm's clin neg partners regularly achieve multimillion pound results for their clients. One recent birth injury case was settled for over £5.5 million, and in an ongoing case lawyers in Leicester are acting for 206 patients who were wrongly diagnosed or treated for epilepsy. This is a key firm for applicants interested in clin neg work, but they should be aware that they cannot escape commercial work and must do at least one seat on that side of the firm. On the flipside, no one is forced to do a non-commercial seat. As for location,

the firm will expect trainees to work in Derby or Leicester for a seat, if asked to do so. Those who do move around have a quick 30-minute train journey from Nottingham to either of the other cities and the firm pays the fare. The Derby office, for example, has grown at a brisk pace since it opened in 1995 and now has around 50 staff in new premises in Cardinal Square. As a whole the firm employs 450 people.

## lawless?

All three offices work open plan with trainees sitting near to, if not next to, their supervisor. Apparently the trick is to try and get a seat near the window, though on your first day at the firm we don't recommend using the same rush-for-the-back strategy that you might have at the start of a new school year. In each location the system for end-of-seat appraisals is the same, with "*most partners giving several appraisals throughout the seat. With my current one we meet once a week to go through all my files and see how I am getting on.*" We had great reports from trainees on the work they'd done in their various seats, be this trips to court for possession hearings in property lit or drafting documents in transactional departments.

In Nottingham, staff enjoy working in the Cumberland Court office, particularly since the "*rude and disinterested*" catering contractor in the canteen was replaced. Getting the majority of staff together under one roof has meant that the firm feels more connected and more sociable than previously, and as an added bonus, "*if you need to speak to someone, say in employment, you just stroll down a floor rather than fire off an e-mail.*" The Castle pub is the firm's preferred venue for end-of-week drinks, and trainees often slip out midweek for a cheeky pint together. Some live centrally in the Lace Market; others choose the burbs. And if you were wondering how far a trainee salary stretches in the east Midlands, about half the second-years had ventured into property ownership when we rang them. Of course, Nottingham has well-documented violent crime and antisocial behaviour problems, which according to our sources have not been over hyped by the media. "*I've seen fights in the street, midweek on my way home from work. Nottingham is definitely not as nice as it was; and there are simply not enough police to deal with the 70-80,000 people who flock to the late bars, and all the stag and hen weekends.*"

## waste not, want not

The hours in some commercial groups may extend beyond the standard 9am to 5pm, and some of our sources reported starting work far earlier in the mornings just to make inroads into a heavy workload. The fact that at times the hours are no different to what is standard in London is perhaps a reflection of the firm's growing success. The first profit figures released since it became a Limited Liability Partnership showed a 10% increase on the previous year. Maybe people have been spurred on by FC's motivational slogan 'Only your best is good enough' which appears on everyone's screensaver. We have it on good authority that "*you can get off during the day, but it re-establishes itself during the night. The only way to deal with it is to set the monitor to go onto sleep mode when screensaver kicks in. See how much we all hate it!*" Not all. "*One of my bosses used to sing it... I think he's become institutionalised.*" Speaking of which, this may be the appropriate course of action for the partners who dress up (usually in drag) and perform a humorous musical sketch at the Christmas party each year.

Earlier in 2005, a number of FC lawyers gave it their best at a charity cricket tournament at Trent Bridge featuring Nottinghamshire County Cricket Club captain Jason Gallian as the star turn. We'd also like to give a mention to the staff who raised money for a school for the deaf in Ghana by participating in a marathon. And while we're at it, here's a pat on the back to whoever keeps the firm on the straight and narrow when it comes to recycling.

## fishing off the company peer

As the prominence of the commercial practice areas grow, the tendency for trainees to have strong East Midlands connections lessens. As we were pondering on what kind of person works at the firm, we stumbled upon some interesting family connections. Among the partners and staff there are several clans: two brothers and one of their wives; a husband and wife and his dad; an uncle and nephew; and no less than four some-time members of the same family. We take this phenomenon both as a measure of the small size of the pool of top-end firms in Nottingham and the number of shared Sunday lunches between FC-ers.

As it happens, group meals and social events start even before new trainees begin their contracts. It means there are reassuringly familiar faces on day one of the training contract and encourages a strong bond between intakes. Sometimes the bond is so strong that, as last year, it leads to the altar. In September 2005, six of the seven qualifiers stayed on with the firm – the same great result as in the previous year.

## and finally...

If the East Midlands is your intended patch and you want to sign up with one of the region's hotshot firms, then Freeth Cartwright has got to be a key target. If the pace of change continues, who knows where it'll be by the time you arrive.

# Freshfields Bruckhaus Deringer

## the facts

**Location:** London
**Number of partners/assistants:** 181/520
**Total number of trainees:** 208
**Seats:** between 3 and 6 months long
**Alternative seats:** Overseas seats, secondments
**Extras:** Pro bono – RCJ CAB, Tower Hamlets Law Centre, FRU, death row appeals; language training

# the true picture

If international corporate law is what excites you, you'll no doubt be putting Freshfields Bruckhaus Deringer right at the top of your hit list. Rarely out of the headlines, you can be sure the firm will have one of its well-manicured fingers in any pie that's in town.

## golden ticket

A member of the magic circle, the firm's name on your CV is like a Blue Angel hallmark of quality branded on your backside. It may be painful at times but whatever your plans for the future, no one can remove it from you. You may find more responsibility as a trainee at a mid-sized firm, but here you will work on the biggest deals in the City. A Freshfields training will take you far – look at it as Charlie's golden ticket in the Wonka world of law. Even if you find all that chocolate too much after a while, there will always be huddled masses of keen young students waiting to get in to the factory.

The past year provided a good harvest of deals for the firm's corporate lawyers. By way of example, they advised Brascan (a North American real estate, power generation and asset management group) and a linked consortium in relation to the contested £5.29 billion takeover offer for Canary Wharf Group. They also acted for a company called Novar (which deals with systems and training relating to fire, security and communications) on its defence of a hostile cash and share bid from Melrose, and on the recommended £960 million cash offer from Honeywell International. Freshfields' finance lawyers have had a similarly busy time. The firm was the lead adviser to Debenhams on the company's £2 billion refinancing, bringing a crack team of finance and corporate lawyers together to advise on the complex recapitalisation of the high street giant with a view to its flotation. More good news came when the firm landed a place on Barclays' general advisory panel after the conclusion of the bank's review of external legal advisers. This appointment was a coup for Freshfields, as it narrowly missed out on winning a place

on the coveted panel when it was last reviewed in 2003. It also landed a major role advising Lehman Brothers on its acquisition of Le Meridien, the troubled London-based hotel group. In the area of asset finance, the firm acted for the three European export credit agencies and a large syndicate of banks with respect to the restructuring of the financing of 38 Airbus aircraft following Air Canada's filing for CCAA protection both at home and in the US. In another asset finance deal, lawyers advised Babcock & Brown on setting up CBRail, a new rolling stock operating lessor which is a joint venture between Babcock & Brown and HBOS. It then advised CBRail on acquiring Porterbrook's European rail lease portfolio.

If all of the above make your eyes glaze over then Freshfields, and City law generally, probably isn't for you. If it makes you want to dust down your pinstriped suit, pop a cork and punch the air, read on.

## safari so good

In a firm of this size you can expect the different departments to have developed their own microclimates, each supporting different species. Where you make your home depends on whether you are more *"transactional or legally minded"*... a lion or an owl, so to speak.

Corporate is the chest-pounding king of the jungle where, trainees say, *"the hierarchy is well developed and there is a positive sense of who does what. People have a clear idea of where they fit in."* As in finance teams, trainees say working in corporate means *"huge hours,"* often overnight and at weekends. There is *"a lot of testosterone and a lot of swearing!"* Naturally when assisting on the mammoth deals that are handled by the firm, trainees have a lowly position on the team. It's difficult to see how it could be otherwise and we sensed that our sources knew this. It was interesting that despite finding it tough going at times, many trainees considered corporate to have been their best seat. Said one: *"There's lots of planning and resources. You feel very well looked after."*

It's not just corporate where the stakes and the adrenaline levels are high. One trainee reported a frightening first day on safari in "*manic*" banking. "*I was in until 3am in the morning!*" The finance department offers "*long hours but stimulating work,*" although our sources concluded that the training wasn't quite up to corporate's very high standards. Said one source: "*There are lots of people leaving. It's partly to do with the nature of work – I once spent 39 hours at my desk – but it's also the lack of partners taking control.*" Again, corporate fans won the day: "*The recent news is that they're trying to build up finance, but they've got a long way to go. When compared to corporate it pales in comparison.*"

## global village people

Away from the powerhouses of international corporate and finance, real estate is a popular choice for a seat. Apparently this lot are "*very friendly but a little bit strange.*" When asked to explain this comment, one source told us: "*It's a bit like being in a village hall with people wearing cardigans – but they're very lovely. Everything is a bit slower and on average they have better hours.*" Another trainee agreed for the most part with this synopsis, adding that "*real estate offers good work and good people. You get more legal work rather than just shuffling paper.*" Should these descriptions leave you in any doubt as to the importance of the department's work, you might wish to note that in the past year it acted for Land Securities on the sale of Building 1, at Bankside, EC1 to IPC Magazines, and on a number of real estate portfolio transactions.

Secondments to nearly a dozen clients including IBM and Morgan Stanley come highly recommended for the end of the training contract and give a hint at what the future might hold for those people who will eventually jump the fence to become in-house lawyers. Overseas seats are another option for the tail end of training. On the departures board are terrifically popular slots in the Far East (eg Beijing, Singapore and Tokyo) and loads of European cities (eg Amsterdam, Brussels and Frankfurt).

The offices and technology on offer are described as second to none. "*IT support is brilliant; Freshfields doesn't scrimp on support services.*" Nor fruit. A firm believer in five a day, Freshfields provides complementary "*apples and oranges, sometimes figs and plums.*" However, some people did have the odd grape, sorry gripe, concerning an element of old-fashioned hierarchy felt to still linger in certain quarters. As one trainee put it: "*Some partners will stare at the ceiling rather than acknowledge your existence. It's not really appreciated. Some of the senior partners are like that.*" Of course they are the minority, and with most "*you can walk in and ask things.*" As in any of these huge City firms, "*you must be prepared to take the rough with the smooth. People will assume you're up to speed and you're good so you must stay on the ball.*" You also need to be robust. Someone told us that after a personality clash with a supervisor, "*the review was so bad that the partner concluded, 'You don't belong here.'*" Clearly they did because they are one of the vast majority of trainees that remain with the firm after qualification each year. In 2005, 89 out of 101 stayed.

Our interviewees' views on the future were borne of "*pragmatism mingled with indecision. Some people know they want to be a partner, others only sit it out for a few years.*" Following the pattern at all similar firms, in time "*people move on for personal reasons like wanting to start a family, or else for financial reasons – maybe to an American firm. You rarely hear of someone who moves on because it is unbearable.*" The work can certainly take its toll – one of the trainees we spoke to had been burning the midnight oil the night before and gave us his girlfriend's telephone number instead of his office line. She was surprisingly good on the intricacies of debt finance (and delighted to hear from us).

When it came to suggesting some improvements, one trainee told us: "*I would make the qualification process more transparent. Most of us are* quite nosy; they recruit people who want to get on in their career." Another trainee felt that what was really lacking was a standardised ethos across the departments, citing finance as a less stable environment than other departments. Leaving these issues aside, one experienced source told us: "*As a professional practice, I don't think it gets any better than Freshfields.*"

## pearls of wisdom

So you've narrowed down your hunt to big London firms, and you've got the brains and the brawn to breach the magic circle. So what makes Freshfields different from its rivals? After all, the UK's big five slug it out for the same deals, look for the same kinds of people to man the decks, and have a similar standing in the eyes of the legal community. Firstly, at Freshfields we heard that the recruitment process was appealingly "*low-key and well handled*" compared to certain others. Secondly, once on the inside, our interviewees reported that the flexibility built into the seat system was a real boon. You'll be expected to cover corporate, finance and litigation, but the seats vary in length between three and six months. Thirdly, from the point of view of our sources, "*the place tends to attract good people.*" Said one: "*Of the 50 people in my intake I get on with about 90%.*"

Yet there is still something of the old school about Freshfields and we think it is embodied in the personal style session that trainees are subjected to as part of the induction week. Believe it or not, an external style consultant is hired to get new recruits looking shipshape. "*She told us how to dress, how to choose cuts and colours, and tie up your hair,*" revealed one source. Advice was also given about how to match a tie with your jaw line and how to maintain good levels of personal hygiene. Sounds like they got Kim, Aggie, Trinny and Susannah all rolled into one. While responses to the session varied between "*annoying*" and "*very helpful,*" what is clear is that the firm's sartorial aspirations are more Saville Row than M&S. Purple shirts, butcher's knots and the latest Toni & Guy barnet probably won't go down that well.

The style consultant reminded trainees that it only takes five seconds to form an impression of someone. So, what would you glean from five seconds with a Freshfielder? Apparently "*each year is different,*" though apparently some factors are a given these days. For instance, "*the whole blondes and blues image is outmoded*" and, like its contemporaries, Freshfields is looking further afield to attract talent. Some 47 universities from around the world are represented amongst trainee alma maters, even if the Oxbridge proportion is 49%. In any trainee population of over 200 people, it's going to be hard to find any glaring similarities, and we were pleasantly surprised to note the firm's attitude towards mature applicants and second-jobbers. "*In my year we have everything from ex-bankers to an ex-bricklayer,*" revealed one trainee; another advised us that nine of the 45 people in their intake had earned themselves a doctorate before starting at the firm. "*The firm shows an understanding towards people who want a career change – there's no fuss. The recruitment department knows what it is doing.*"

## the wholesome truth

On a Friday night you can always guarantee someone will be in The Witness Box, a favourite watering hole, and numerous other social events grace the trainee calendar – charity nights, quizzes, theatre trips, bowling and meals out. Once in a while, there will be departmental jollies and one trainee spoke of banking lawyers heading off to the races (presumably to 'invest' a bit of cash). Of course, "*socialising is optional – it really doesn't matter if you do or don't join in. After a while you want to see your friends after work rather than other trainees.*" And anyway, not everyone's definition of good fun is the same: "*You always hear about people doing extraordinary things out of work, like walking the length of Ireland.*"

Freshfields loves its sport and is more than big enough to field good-quality teams for most games.

"*We've been on a big netball tour, and a mixed netball team just started, playing in Lincoln's Inn against other law firms.*" And if team games don't do it for you, you can always become the loner that haunts the office gym. Though we suspect there aren't too many of this type... it's just not very Freshfields. One trainee summed things up nicely when they told us: "*We are all outgoing – we do speak up for ourselves but don't push our ideas on others. We try and have fun and not take ourselves too seriously. We slot into whatever we should be like in that situation.*"

## and finally...

If you're dead set on a top City training and if you're prepared to make corporate work your life, either for a few years or the rest of your career, Freshfields will give a first-rate training in a consummately professional environment. Just be sure to floss your teeth, moisturise and ditch that bow tie for the interview.

# Gateley Wareing LLP

## the facts

**Location:** Birmingham, Leicester, Nottingham
**Number of partners/assistants:** 30/82
**Total number of trainees:** 14
**Seats:** 4x6 months
**Alternative seats:** None

After a few years of swift growth, Midlands commercial firm Gateley Wareing has settled into a more measured phase of its development. Its current tactic is a period of consolidation while keeping an eye on a second growth spurt.

## super, smashing great

Gateley Wareing comprises a main office in Birmingham with an annual intake of six trainees and two smaller branches in Leicester and Nottingham each offering a single traineeship. The firm has organised itself into two main divisions – property services (construction, commercial property and environmental) and corporate services (corporate, commercial dispute resolution, commercial advice, private client, employment, tax, banking and insolvency) and recruits find a diversity of work ranging from litigating over timeshare scams to drafting biotech licences and selling manufacturing businesses.

Local enterprises have long been at the heart of Gateleys' business. For the most part the company names won't wow you, but at least as a trainee you'll be entrusted with regular client contact and feel you are taking an active role in things. The big names are there though: in insolvency the firm advises the accountancy firms KPMG, PwC and Ernst & Young; real estate lawyers are helping Center Parcs open a fifth village in Hertfordshire; George Wimpey and McAlpine instruct the construction team and, ladies, for all your bead bracelet and lip gloss needs Claire's Accessories is a client of the employment team. Arguably the core of the firm is the corporate department which in 2004 racked up 25 MBO and MBI transactions, 44 sales, 79 acquisitions, 18 refinancings and nine AIM flotations. Among its top deals was the £70 million Denby pottery MBO.

## give us a clue

Trainees are usually allocated their first seat, with the firm capitalising on any relevant experience. In these choice-obsessed days 'compulsory' is anathema, but as one source noted: "*If they'd asked me I wouldn't have a clue what to have asked for.*" All the main seats available to trainees in Brum are available in the other two locations and seat trading between the offices is possible. When it comes to the ever-popular employment law, "*most of the girls go for it.*" Despite our sources coyly playing down the competition for this seat, it emerges "*only one trainee was not bothered; the rest would have liked to do it.*" Indeed, employment's popularity is confirmed by news that in addition to Brum, Leicester has gained a coveted seat in this field and two trainees qualified into the department in September 2005. All up, four of the six qualifiers stayed with the firm.

As for other seats, corporate is *"damned hard work"* compared to property *"where you get to go home at a decent time every evening."* Corporate trainees get chucked into a whirl of client meetings, administration of company books, drafting board minutes and resolutions, and helping out with the documentation for acquisitions and share transfers. Basically, *"lots of team work."* Alas, some were less than enamoured with the commercial litigation experience, especially the bundling and painstaking pagination involved in case preparation. One trainee was a little disappointed to have *"only got into court on the last day of the seat."* Those hungry for more court time might choose to supplement the litigation seat with six months in insolvency where trainees appear by themselves on minor hearings and may sit behind a barrister for more serious ones.

## an offer you can't refuse

No image consultant could untangle the Gordian knot of the twee and the blokey that characterises the firm's website. Though Gateleys' cyber shopfront includes pictures of besuited partners looking like hardboiled film-noir private dicks, a reference to partners playing Brains and the Tracey boys at a Thunderbirds party for employees' children mars the hard man effect. One partner's 'desert-island discs' section on his online biog records contentment with nought but The Godfather and Tractor Tom on DVD. This coupling, awkward though it is, typifies the lack of suntan-and-a-grin pretentiousness at the firm.

Thomas De Quincey never had a nice word to say about Birmingham. He went so far as to popularise 'Birmingham' as an adjective for everything ersatz and imitative. Not so with Gateleys – there is nothing imitative or *"pretentious"* about the place and everyone has the DTEs (*"down to earths"*). It is very much a case of *"straight talkers"* with *"good*

*commercial sense"* and the wherewithal to *"practically apply"* that knowledge. Birmingham's entrepreneurs brook no nonsense and *"don't want to hear legalease;"* they *"want to be told their options clearly"* and *"can smell bullshit."* The trainees' task is to prevent them picking up the scent and achieving this relies heavily on maintaining their *"down-to-earth"* rating. We'd say DTE levels per trainee were off the scale. And if trainees are DTE, partners are especially DTE.

## in the soup

Most of the West Midlands trainees hail from Birmingham or her leafy appendages, Solihull and Sutton Coldfield. Similarly, local connections are also to be found in Gateleys' eastern outposts. The Birmingham office is a Brummagem hierarchy with its überBrummie senior partner being described as Noddy Holder by one trainee. For pedantry's sake we feel duty bound to point out former Slade front man Noddy's Wolverhamptonian rather than Brummie roots. Noddy's nativity aside, the point to be gleaned is that Gateley inclines towards Coupa Sooup rather than gazpacho. That's DTE.

Gateleys' Birmingham HQ occupies the city's former Ear Nose and Throat Hospital – a red brick remnant of Birmingham's late Victorian heyday. The firm went through a rhinoplasty of its own and glazed its terracotta home a few years back. The results are open-plan departments on several floors allowing ample snooping through the glass frontage at *"who's in and what's going-on."* The Nottingham branch's recent move from snug offices to a *"v. plush"* glass affair *"just like the Birmingham office"* corresponds with brisk growth in both East Midlands branches. Unlike the Birmingham office, however, both Nottingham and Leicester occupy a single floor so *"you get to know everything that's going on"* within a more *"communal atmosphere."*

To ease new arrivals into the community there is a buddy system. Not that they all need one as some come from among the ranks of the firm's own paralegals. If entirely new to the firm, the once-a-month post room detail is a good opportunity for trainees to get to know their peers. The subject of post duty elicited some exasperation from our sources: no one enjoyed getting in an hour early to date stamp the mail although it does at least keep you up to speed on all the firm gossip.

## modern day vikings

Earlier in 2005 a government survey into the behaviour of Brits abroad on holiday revealed that Midlanders have a tendency to party harder than people from other regions. Gateleys, too, has developed a reputation for the occasional rambunctious antics, piffle spread by fellow Brummie law firms according to one source who dismissed the image *"as true as Birmingham's own reputation for being nothing but concrete."* Nonetheless, a maxim entrenched in the firm's ethos is *"work hard, play hard"* and we'll venture that Gateley's cakes and ale infamy is not entirely unjust. One post-party incident has entered the annals of both the firm and the *Student Guide.* 'Tis the stuff of legends:

> *And it is written: on the eve of the Christ's birth mirth was to be had; and one Knight of the Scotch Egg did brave the frozen waterway of the sacred Barge; and that knight had imbibed of mead; and that knight did fall through said icy crust; and verily mirth was had by all.*

Savour such legal legends, they happen but rarely. Last year's Christmas bash was less of a health and safety issue we hear. Every September trainees are introduced to the play-hard half of the Gateley Way at a special welcome night in a local pub. *"Daunting"* it may be, but it's *"a good way to kick-off the two years."* Last year's party had a Blind Date theme, with one of the male solicitors standing in for Cilla. It seems that transvestism is rife – at the Pirates of the Caribbean themed Yuletide bash two male trainees cast off suits and donned *"those dresses that push your boobs out."* Such frolics are designed by the firm's events committee, which toils to ensure a social calendar busy enough to bind the three Gateleys offices together. A summer party and two Christmas parties (one perversely in January) also pepper the year and additional seasoning comes in the form of Friday night drinks. The Birmingham office's drinking den, Bushwackers, is conveniently located beneath the office, *"just like on Ally McBeal."* Indeed, just like Ally McBeal *sans* pouting, unisex toilets and dancing babies...

A caveat on the giggles though: the Gateley maxim also includes *"work hard"* and staying late is a regular feature of most seats. There's *"no work for work's sake"* and why would there be when there are periodic long-haul, 30-hour deal completions to manage. One source was in the office from 7am on a Wednesday until midday on the Thursday. The Reservoir Dogs-style partner pictures on the website may underline that it is only through a hard slog that the rewards of hard play are known.

## and finally...

On the couch Gateley Wareing appears to hold reasonable aspirations for greatness rather than delusions of grandeur. In the wake created by the giants of the Midlands legal scene there is plenty of profitable business to be had and the firm is adept at handling it. As one trainee saw it: *"Gateleys has identified a nice little niche and for a firm of its size it has done well."* It certainly has.

# Government Legal Service

## the facts

**Location:** London
**Number of partners/assistants:** 2,000
**Total number of trainees:** 50
**Seats:** 4x6 months
**Alternative seats:** Brussels
**Extras:** Language training

The biggest legal employer in the country with 2,000 lawyers, the Government Legal Service deals with matters ranging from personal injury at the MoD to the Hutton Inquiry. It offers a training contract that is defined by variety and responsibility on work that lies at the heart of government. If you can get your head around the idea that the Queen would effectively be your senior partner then you may wish to heed the advice of the GLS website, "You can't beat us – so join us!"

## missed opportunities

So large and established is the GLS that few students can be unaware of its existence. The fact that so many overlook the training opportunity here is doubtless due to the perceived glamour of private practice and assumptions about the greyness of the public sector. Our investigations over the last two years lead us to a very different conclusion and furthermore, as a trainee, you will notice little structural difference between working in the two sectors.

In common with many law firms, the application form itself gives plenty of room for detail, and if you get past that first hurdle, you'll be invited to attend for a day at a GLS assessment centre. Expect an individual interview, in which applicants are required to prepare a discussion on a recent topic from current affairs, and a group problem-solving exercise. The GLS website states that applicants must have at least a 2:2; the reality is that without a 2:1 or better, you'll need to impress in other ways to stand out from the competition.

## makin' the law

The civil service goes OTT on acronyms and abbreviations: DCMS, DCA, Defra, DfES, DTI DWP/H and that's just the Ds. Most sources were suitably apologetic when they slipped into civilservicespeak and deserve understanding for their affliction. For now you need only familiarise yourself with the six main departments that take trainees: the Department for Constitutional Affairs (DCA), the Department for Transport (DfT), HM Revenue & Customs (HMRC), the Office of the Deputy Prime Minister (ODPM), the Department of Trade and Industry (DTI), the Health and Safety Executive

and the Treasury Solicitors (Tsol). With an intake of seven trainees per year, the latter is your most likely destination. In all, 40 departments exist, all of which take trainees from time to time.

As in most law firms, trainees go through the mangle of four six-month seats – in the case of the GLS "*split between two litigious and two advisory seats.*" Though seat allocation is "*a bit of a mystery*" in the first year, trainees have more influence in the second year. As one source told us: "*If you do the chasing up, you'll get the seat you want.*" It seems, too, that "*there has been a big push to allow people to control their own careers*" though "*it depends on who is in control of the department and how interventionist they are.*" Trainees share a room with their supervisor (or line manager as they call them) and most find "*they are always there for you to ask questions, no matter how stupid.*" The PSC is taken at BPPP law school, and just as in private practice there are performance assessments, though in the case of the GLS these are annual and the trainee walks away with an overall grade.

While most seats are taken in the trainee's home department, all participate in intra-governmental secondments to further broaden their experiences. These moves to, say the Ministry of Defence or Department for the Environment, Fisheries and Rural Affairs should be regarded as a sign of things to come because after qualification government lawyers "*rotate departments every two or three years.*" And given that lawyers spend their careers transferring from department to department according to need, getting used to this "*may be said to be part of the training.*" Adaptability, it seems, is hardwired into the civil servant lawyer who is likely to work across many disciplines during his or her career. This is in stark contrast to the career path of the private practitioner who, once qualified, will find changing tack so arduous that they are unlikely to try. Difference also enters the equation when you consider the actual work undertaken at the GLS. In short, forget about photocopying the law, in this training you'll have a hand in writing it.

# the true picture

## terminal decline

Though you might imagine the civil service to be a heavily stratified environment, *"there's not a huge distinction between newly qualified lawyers and trainees; the only difference is that their work goes out unchecked and ours doesn't."* And now for the best bit: *"You don't do the crap work!"* Even on huge cases, only a small amount of photocopying and bundling duties are expected. One trainee confirmed: *"I only photocopied twice and expressed discontent. I didn't do it again."* Instead, on the big matters trainees assist lawyers by acting as caseworkers, taking charge of a small piece of the jigsaw. The government of the day is always susceptible to claims for breach of contract or tort and, additionally, legislation and administrative decisions may be challenged by judicial review. Trainees become familiar with not only the workings of the court system but also those of the tribunals, commissions, inquiries and quasi-judicial bodies at which the government requires legal representation. Inquiry work can be especially interesting, whether it relates to the circumstances surrounding the deaths of Dr. David Kelly or Victoria Climbie or the concreting over of the south east of England for extra airport runways.

From airport planning to by-laws affecting military encampments down your local park, the ODPM will see a trainee grappling with those *"creatures of statute – local authorities."* *"I never thought I'd say this but by-law work is amazing,"* raved one convert. Dubiously we listened on. A lot of work concerns rough sleepers, a bugbear for local authorities intent on flexing their delegated law-making function. Requiring the assent of the ODPMT, such proposals leave the trainees weeding out *"statute duplication, extant statute contravention, the discriminatory, the over-the-top and the downright ridiculous."* One source, whose respect for Georgian statute writers now clearly knows no bound, managed to dredge up the Vagrancy Act 1824. *"It's great!"* he cried. *"You get to talk about people 'wandering at large' and use lots of arcane legal terms."* Whatever shakes your tree!

## anything to declare?

The Health & Safety Executive, *"established as a statutory organ in 1974 per the Health and Safety Act of that year... if you're interested,"* has in recent times been busy with the government's overhaul of its energy policy – tending toward fissile rather than renewable sources... if you're interested. Trainees have advised on leases for new nuclear facilities as well as making unsupervised visits to future sites, *"sometimes representing the government alone."*

Is splitting atoms too much like splitting hairs for you? Would you like to handle a kilo of cocaine instead? If yes, the recently devolved HM Revenue & Customs prosecuting department will let you do just that. Drug enforcement cases see trainees working on a fast-track team dealing with *"nabbed"* minor importers, cases *"which start small but have a funny way of growing."* You might find yourself stamping a public interest immunity case for non-disclosure *"just in case someone gets murdered."* As a trainee with the prosecutors, for the first month you'll be a caseworker following trials; by the end of your seat you'll have run *"about 25 files to completion."* Over in Customs' civil litigation team, expect everything from small personal injury claims arising out of allegedly harsh stop-and-searches to *"massive judicial reviews."* You won't see the large cases all the way through and inevitably your tiny PI files will be settled out of court, but between them the little and the large build up a fascinating picture. At the lower end you'll negotiate settlements, and at the higher end you'll be at the Royal Courts of Justice, sitting behind the barrister you've just briefed, staring at *"mouldy Babylonian judges in wigs."*

## the naked civil servant

Stripped bare, the civil servant used to be a middle-class, middle-brow middling. Bowler hatted, he would arrive on platform 4 with *The Times* snugly under a wing, ready for the commute. This isn't the civil servant we found. Our sources were a multi-ethnic batch of trainees of diverse ages and from a variety of backgrounds, some fresh from university, others seasoned by previous careers. The modern civil servant is a creature impossible to caricature. One more mature interviewee had *"rejection letter after rejection letter"* come to realise that the private sector *"may advertise diversity and equal ops but the reality is if you're not from this university, not from this school and not this age, you won't get in."*

An air of the unknown citizen still lingers though; our sources seemed capable only of defining the GLS trainee by what they are not. For example, *"you shouldn't have a strong political persuasion because you don't bring partisanship to work."* Similarly, there is a vague sense that candidates might wish to be *"careful what you say and who you say it to. They will security check you so you don't want any skeletons in the closet."* Before you get the 1984 heebie-jeebies, you should be fine so long as you don't have anything really bad to hide.

While rare, situations in which lawyers define themselves as being morally compromised do crop up, *"the Home Office being the most politically divisive department."* You'll remember lawyer Elizabeth Wilmshurst whose hara-kiri was prompted by the furore surrounding the Attorney General's advice to the Government on the legality of the war in Iraq. When asked if they would be happy to defend a government action they believed to be unreasonable, one upright source declared: *"I would fall on my sword."* One cannot imagine many corporate lawyers doing the same when acting for, say, an exploitative multinational corporation.

## on yer bike

*"Don't come here to make money!"* You'll receive a comfortable salary but you won't be driving with your LITIG8 personalised plate to the airport and then flying club class to your own Caribbean retreat in a custom-made zebra zoot suit. *"No, but I don't live with stress everyday,"* grinned a contented source. Megabucks aside, the civil service has good pension and travel loan schemes, and the environmentally conscientious DEFRA even assists in the purchase of a bike for transportation purposes. You're on your own for bicycle clips, though.

On job security, one trainee reassured us: *"I've never heard of a trainee not getting a job or of one refusing a job."* *"Once you're in it's a pension and the good life,"* another confided with a wink. This is where the perks end. If you think you're heading for a honey pot at taxpayers' expense here's the sting – *"You'll not get a free beer or lunch out of the government."* Make the most of those canapés at any law firm jollies you pitch up to in your search for a training contract because once you start with the GLS they'll become a thing of the past. The tightened purse strings of government mean the party coffers have to be filled by staff themselves. *"We set up our own social committee in the end,"* said one trainee. At least over in Customs & Excise trainees are assured a good night out because they can *"sneak into gigs in the courtyard of Somerset House."* The highlight performances of 2005 were The Doves and Queens of the Stone Age. *"And if you can't sneak in, you can just open a window and sit back with a bottle of wine."*

Unless you're at a gig, civilised hours mean you'll actually see your loved ones for more than *Newsnight* and a good night kiss. *"I've never stayed later than 6.30pm,"* one trainee assured us, *"in fact, I always come in at 9am and leave at 6pm."* No weekends, no 3am completions. *"It sounds corny but the work-life balance really exists here,"* beamed one trainee. Another agreed: *"I can honestly say I enjoy going to work everyday."* You just can't argue with that!

## and finally...

Unless you're intent on a red-braces career in the City you might want to give careful consideration to the GLS. Job security with a decent salary, easy hours and a chance to shape government policy – from where we're standing that sounds like a great package.

# Halliwells LLP

## the facts

**Location:** Manchester, London, Sheffield, Liverpool
**Number of partners/assistants:** 115/190
**Total number of trainees:** 50
**Seats:** 5x21 weeks
**Alternative seats:** Secondments
**Extras:** Pro bono – Manchester Uni Advice Centre

Fast-paced, profitable, expansionist and popular with ambitious students, Halliwells is the ideal choice for those ready to have their mettle tested to its limits. Once limited to Manchester, the Halliwells training regime is now also offered in Liverpool and London.

## cuff links

One thing is certain about both Halliwells and its trainees – they are a driven lot. Three years ago, the opening of a London office confirmed the firm's designs on extra-regional success, and last year it consolidated its prominence in the North West by merging with Liverpool's Cuff Roberts, a 16-partner firm best known for commercial property, and then snapping up three of DLA Piper's Liverpool partners. A Sheffield satellite specialises in defendant personal injury and other insurance litigation, although there are signs that this office, too, will grow and diversify its activities. Will Halliwells' relentless march never end? Whether or not we have a national firm in the making, what we do know is that Halliwells has quadrupled in size in five years.

The firm is highly successful in all major areas of commercial law and stands out in several. The corporate lawyers, known for their entrepreneurial and commercially realistic style, acquit themselves well, acting on deals such as Cardpoint's £75 million acquisition of the remote ATM estate of HBOS. Involvement in the AIM market means Halliwells now boasts 31 recently floated companies on its client list and the firm has additionally been successful in winning panel positions from major companies including Barclays, Legal & General and Tesco. In a major coup for the insolvency department, the MG Rover directors instructed Halliwells after the company's financial collapse. Not content with success in established fields, the firm has set up a marine litigation practice in Manchester by hiring practitioners from a rival firm.

## sweet nothings

Unofficially, trainees have just four potential seat choices during their first year: property, insurance litigation, comlit and corporate recovery. Niche seats like IP have become the preserve of second-years, and for IP "*you have to hand your CV in to get it.*" The happy few encounter "*the nicest, most intelligent, best team players*" and "*partners who are really inspiring because they're so clever.*" When not staring in awe at these brainiacs, trainees help to fire off broadsides on behalf of companies like Swizzels Matlow, which recently took action against infringers of their Love Hearts™ sweets. The seat additionally includes some commercial work, which involves trainees drafting licensing agreements for biotech companies and observing at meetings with "*high-profile media and sports clients.*"

While you're tethered to the team in IP, life as a trainee in comlit is positively free-range. Comlit has three seats: environment, white-collar crime and debt recovery, the last being a destination for most trainees. Dealing with the debts of all manner of clients from Reebok to "*little landlords*" can seem "*a bit dull*" in comparison to other types of litigation, because "*it always ends up with us suing someone and then either bankrupting them or suing them some more.*" As well as the usual "*crappy*" tasks of photocopying and preparing bundles, trainees get a considerable amount of court time. A first appointment before a district judge will "*inspire nerves*" even in the sappers at Halliwells, but you'd better get used to the county court because "*you will go to every hearing for the team.*" One trainee reflected with amusement on how "*some judges let you get out *quick and some don't. One even asked me for my advice on the law!"*

## taxing times

Corporate seats are *"very challenging."* Thrown into the midst of company acquisitions, one trainee reported working on five completions, experiencing them from the perspective of venture capitalists, banks, buyers and sellers. *"Trainees are always part of the team and always have a good role. On the completion day, trainees check through everything and do the amendments – they are pretty vital."* The more academic tax department may not be the *"biggest barrel of laughs you ever had,"* but as with IP you'll get to bask in the glory of working with *"the most intelligent lawyers in the firm."* Here you'll grasp the nettle of black letter law in order to save clients from paying unnecessary tax bills. *"Oops! I shouldn't say tax evasion – it's more tax avoidance,"* one trainee quickly corrected a slip of the tongue. Tax involves *"little hands-on work for the trainee;"* instead they keep partners abreast of changes in current law and *"report back on new loopholes."* Beyond research, a share sale agreement or two may make it onto a trainee's desk for consideration of the tax issues.

Greater variety lies in property. Drafting away in Manchester and Liverpool, trainees are given sale and purchase files of their own. One trainee assured us: *"If you've done lots of property at university and college you'll understand everything."* A tad more confident than you'd expect? Perhaps, but that's a typical Halliwells trainee for you. From the initial information trawl to reeling in the billing, trainees do the lot with minimal supervision. Beware though, *"mundane stuff like photocopying, bundling and going to court on errands"* lurk in London's insolvency seat. A tip from one source: *"Get friendly with the admin staff and they might do the copying for you."*

Intriguingly, the firm gained a family department in the Cuff Roberts merger, *"and now it's lovin' it."* There are murmurs that Manchester will get its own team in the future. Another develop-

ment is the prospect of trainees switching offices in the North West for one of their 21-week seats. The move will be optional but 'strongly encouraged', and the trainees' view is that *"unless there were personal reasons why you couldn't go, it would be frowned upon if you turned your nose up at it."* As for Sheffield, whereas last year the branch was something of a pariah to trainees, *"a few have braved it this year"* for a seat in either insurance litigation or construction.

The London office has grown steadily since it was set up in 2002 and now employs lawyers handling corporate, property, corporate recovery, employment, insurance, comlit and property litigation. Trainees recruited to this office can do seats in any of these areas, if there is a demand for them. Another thing to bear in mind is that the firm is happy to encourage cross-fertilisation through office moves for trainees.

In true Halliwells' style the managing partner was quoted in the legal press as saying the firm was *"200% committed to London."* And committed to its trainees it seems: in September 2005, 15 of Halliwells' 18 qualifiers were awarded jobs.

## garden gekkos

Halliwells' trainees have a refreshing candour. Instead of being subjected to mantras about work-life balance and ergonomically designed work pods, we heard it straight from them. *"If you want to bide your time in life then don't come here; wall-flowers and daily routiners need not apply."* Here, it's Miracle Grow and a place in the hothouse, *"even the quiet ones are quietly assertive!"* Redbrick graduates are standard, but your academic record will only get you so far. *"What they want is drive – if you're gonna get the dollar, you've gotta put the work in,"* one Gordon Gekko in training pronounced. In addition to the academic high flyers, the firm has a good track record of awarding training contracts to those it has come to admire and trust through a period of paralegal work. Whichever route they take to a traineeship, people are *"expected to achieve for the firm.*" Some admit that the style of training – "*most of it on the job*" – can mean you "*sometimes do feel out of your depth.*" But in this no-pain, no-gain regime no one's left in any doubt as to how much they eventually gain. As you might expect, "*very few trainees escape from working late on a regular basis.*" It was interesting to hear how the atmosphere in the (ex Cuffs) Liverpool office differed from the Manchester HQ. One trainee described Liverpool as "*a bit more gentlemanly and peaceful; people take their time more and get out earlier.*"

One source offered this nugget of advice for prospective recruits: "*If you want to spend lots of time with boyfriends or girlfriends, wifie or hubby, it could be a problem,*" because this is the ultimate "*work hard but play hard*" environment. "*There's a lot going on,*" we heard. "*One marketing man looked at our social budget and was horrified by the amount spent on booze, far higher than other major law firms he had visited, so he said.*" Fridays are generally cordoned off for a pint or two after work. Ducking in and out of Le Figaro or All Bar One during your Manchester tour of duty will be the norm. In Liverpool a couple in the White Bar may precede a couple more in Andersons and by the time you get to the Newz Bar on Water Street, you'll just "*follow the crowd into the Living Room.*" You need a kebab just thinking about it! Out of kilter with the rest, Halliwells' Londoners seem more retiring – "*you can socialise as much or as little as you like,*" our source told us before outlining the "*great shopping and lunch opportunities*" in the capital.

Socially, the strongest connections exist between Liverpool and Manchester trainees. Three firm-wide social events punctuating the year ensure that the London lot aren't left out. We're reliably informed that the "*Spring Business Update*" is merely an alias for partying. According to one source, "*there was a facts-and-figures speech which started at 6.30pm and ended at 7pm, at which point six hours of drinking at the free bar commenced!*" As flippant as these comments may

sound, we did also hear that "*the AGMs make you want to be ambitious.*" In the summer, the firm gathers at a hotel for "*a nice meal, good DJ and free tot,*" and finally, "*the boundaries just melted away at the Christmas party,*" a natural corollary to watching 50-year-old partners boogying, we suspect.

## and finally...

You may be wondering about now whether you are up for being part of Halliwells' special forces. Make no mistake – training here is a challenge, but those it recruits tell us the slog is absolutely worth it.

# Hammonds

## the facts

**Location:** London, Leeds, Manchester, Birmingham
**Number of partners/assistants:** 138/278
**Total number of trainees:** 79
**Seats:** 6x4 months
**Alternative seats:** Overseas seats, secondments
**Extras:** Pro bono at all locations, eg Paddington Law Centre

Unless you've been hiding in a law-proof bunker, you'll likely know that Hammonds has had a year best described as dreadful. But as a large national firm with four UK offices and an expansive overseas presence, there are some compelling reasons to consider the firm.

## painful news

Originally a northern firm, Hammonds expanded throughout the nineties and early noughties at a phenomenal rate. It went through mergers with both niche and large firms, opened an international network of offices and made a play for status in the City. Recently the story has made for less comfortable reading – profits down 25% in 2005 (following an 18% decline the previous year); criticism of management decisions; a flood of departing partners. In 2005 the firm had to make 60 redundancies nationally and an £8.5 million 'hole' emerge in its accounts. Some basic web research will turn up a wealth of opinion as to the whys and wherefores of Hammonds' current predicament. It should also reveal some of the measures the new management has put in place to try and sort things out. In February 2005, a lock-in agreement saw the overwhelming majority of equity partners reaffirm their commitment to Hammonds for a further 14 months.

Naturally we were keen to know what trainees had made of these events, and true to form they were willing to oblige. We've grown used to Hammonds' trainees telling us exactly how it is. Not for them polite clichés, on-message dronings and the usual meek claims about how everyone's really friendly at their firm. Glue their thoughts together and they read as follows. "*It has been really hard*," "*there were times when you'd get disillusioned*," "*morale was pretty low*," "*at points we all wondered what kind of firm we might end up working for*," "*the firm hit rock bottom.*"

## reasons to be cheerful

Frank they may, but unbalanced they are not. Our trainee sources must have known something because, despite all they'd been through, out of the 31 who qualified in 2005, 27 accepted NQ positions with the firm. What gave them the confidence to sign on the dotted line? "*The problems were handled well internally*," "*we were kept informed about what was going on*," "*there's a programme aimed at addressing the difficulties*," "*the figures are already starting to look better*" and "*people are positive and focused because the right people are now at the helm to take us forward.*" An ongoing internal strategy review is a key part of this "*growing optimism*," but trainees also point out that "*[new managing partner] Peter Crossley has done a great job of getting people communicating.*" This is not to say that Hammonds has already emerged into the sunlight fully recovered, but there was definitely enough light at

the end of the tunnel to convince our sources of their future with the firm.

Trainees say what really inspired their confidence was the fact that "*we're really busy. People ask how it is to be here and I can only say, 'I'm working flat out and everyone else I know is.' That tells me what I need to know.*" Indeed, Hammonds has continued to do some excellent work across its Manchester, Leeds, Birmingham and London offices, this year winning its first major instructions from the UK's largest independent pub chain, Spirit Group, following appointment to six of its legal panels. What's more, it also won a first-time instruction from Australian investment fund Prime Infrastructure, advising on a £202 million offer for gas provider IEG. The firm then won a global role advising FTSE 250 company and maker of Durex condoms, SSL International, acted for Rensburg plc on the £150 million acquisition of Carr Sheppards Crosthwaite, advised Innovia Films on a £330 million MBO of the films business of UCB, and assisted Abbey National Treasury Services on a £758 million private equity portfolio sale. All this and a client list that stretches from Royal Mail Group to Smith & Nephew, and Royal & SunAlliance to National Grid, British Energy, Michelin, London Underground, Trinity Mirror, Aston Villa FC, Gaz de France, Müller UK, Allied Domecq and Marriott. Plenty of reasons to be cheerful.

## gone but not pawgotten

Despite looming deadlines, the *Student Guide* always makes time for the truly meaningful things in life. So it is that we ask you join us in observing a respectful silence to mark the passing of a unique animal. Just as the Littlest Hobo eventually padded its way to that great dog kennel in the sky, so too has Hammonds called time on the location-rotation training scheme that saw trainees visit more offices than the roving mutt had cherubic young owners predisposed to near-death adventuring. From this year's applicants onwards, there will only be fixed-location contracts in each of the four UK offices, although it will be possible for regional trainees to spend one seat in London. The overseas seats will remain an "*alluring prospect*" for southerners and northerners alike, and with seats in Hammonds' Madrid, Turin, Brussels, Hong Kong, Berlin and Paris offices (the latter two requiring degree-level fluency) it is scarcely surprising. Trainees in London can also try for the regular secondment to media client Clear Channel, and in Manchester there is the possibility of spending time with a major chemicals client.

Trainees reflected: "*It's a good thing that it's ending because the admin seemed to be a lot of work... but it won't change the character of the firm.*" If anything they feel "*it will strengthen the character and atmosphere of each office*" because "*people will put roots down and really invest in working life there.*" The implication is that the transient lifestyle had not always benefitted trainees. As for the suggestion that lack of rotation might affect unity across offices, our sources were dismissive: "*Departments function nationally and they communicate perfectly well. Plus IT is all integrated, so it shouldn't be a problem at trainee level.*" A fixed contract in Manchester or Leeds or Brum, together with the near guarantee of a London seat and the fairly unique possibility of an overseas seat is certainly appealing. But will Hammonds be able to get equally high-calibre London applicants? Apparently, "*the firm was a bit worried about this and has put London salaries up to match other firms.*"

## no more pain in the axis

Even if trainees will no longer spin on the office carousel, they'll still feel a little trademark Hammonds dizziness because of a six-seat scheme in which corporate (this includes banking and tax), litigation and property are the only compulsories. Trainees say the negatives of short seats are far outweighed by the available choice, pointing out that they can get through less-favoured seats "*quickly and painlessly*" while "*doubling up in an area you really enjoy.*" There's no hanging around with a four-month seat: "*Basically you spend a week or so settling in, then you go for it for the next couple of months.*" Another source added: "*It would probably help the fee earners more if we did six-month seats, but from what I've heard from friends elsewhere, we don't lose out in terms of responsibility.*" Including the compulsories we mentioned, Hammonds has a broad spread of departments for trainees to sample – commercial and IP; construction; commercial dispute resolution (CDR); corporate; real estate; banking; insolvency; tax and very highly regarded pensions and employment teams.

Hammonds continues to work hard to reinforce its national identity, with 0870 numbers across offices, departments that operate in the same way up and down the country and "*regular firm-wide departmental training sessions.*" Another constant is "*excellent quality of feedback and responsibility.*" In each seat trainees have "*a daily supervisor who tends to be an associate*" in addition to "*a supervising partner who takes an overview on your work.*" So between "*pre, mid and end-of-seat appraisals with them both,*" and "*frequent informal chats,*" trainees generally find that they "*have a clear idea of how [they're] performing.*" Similarly, the rule of thumb across offices is "*if you prove you have the capability, you'll be given the work.*" One interviewee spoke admiringly of "*never feeling out of my depth... I felt I was outside my comfort zone often, but that meant I was being stretched.*"

Unfortunately we do not have the space to anatomise each department in each office, but to give you a representative picture, the trainees we spoke to had handled their own files in property, "*drafted witness statements and went to tribunals*" in employment, "*did bibling but also drafted main share purchase agreements*" in corporate, "*attended mediations and took witness statements*" in CDR, "*worked with interesting clients and cutting-edge law*" in commercial and IP, and "*in tax... did a lot of Stamp Duty Land Tax returns, which was great for file management experience.*" Happily, the firm has "*good day and night secretaries and repro teams,*" which "*you are encouraged to use to keep grunt work to a minimum.*" Sounds good to us.

## officely speaking

Trainees meet for a residential version of the PSC at the beginning of the contract, but from there on in we imagine the experience will become increasingly office-specific. Leeds and Manchester are closest to the historical core of the firm, sharing "*a no-nonsense, anti-hierarchical*" atmosphere that is "*not so much a northern thing as to do with the people there. I know the office managing partner as well as I know the guy who delivers the post.*" Both these offices have maintained good levels of profitability and we did detect a certain "*self-assured, self-sufficient*" sense of purpose there. Nevertheless the two are distinct. On Park Lane, a short hop from the city centre and "*all the bars of Greek Street,*" the Leeds office is "*very modern with a Caffé Ritazza on site.*" Sports teams, a social committee and trips to local bar Mononi's are all part of "*a massively social atmosphere*" and "*a true sense of togetherness in the office.*" Across the Pennines, the "*smaller*" Manchester office is "*very nice, open, airy and light.*" Its size means "*there is a lot more interaction between departments than in, say, London,*" and creates "*a vibrant social scene.*" Further south, Birmingham trainees report that theirs is "*the most friendly of the offices,*" even if "*the 60s offices are a bit of a joke – we need new funky glass and silver ones, please!*" However, it has "*lots of space*" and quite a few would be happy to stay and enjoy it. What's more, its location "*close to the centre of town, near Cathedral Square,*" is not to be sniffed at. The icing on the cake is that "*Utopia is only ten paces from the front door.*" In case you are suddenly having visions of heaven on earth in Birmingham, Utopia is a bar.

All the offices share a "*Mondays to Thursdays, smart, Fridays, dress-down*" policy. All organise quarterly drinks parties and a couple of special get-togethers each year ("*Christmas was a medieval themed party with a hog roast and partners in the stocks*"). "*Off-sites – where departments meet across offices*" – are good for social integration on a wider scale. The working day averages 8.30am to 6.30pm in the regions, with "*longer days in London*" just one factor in making the operation in the capital slightly divergent from the Hammonds norm. In the words of one trainee down south, London has "*gone a bit quiet. We took quite a slating for bad performance, so it feels like we've our tail between our legs.*" Nevertheless, this same source loved "*the buzz of City work and the high-pressure atmosphere.*" The office is close to Liverpool Street and boasts "*a supportive trainee population*" that likes nothing better than to bond over drinks in the nearby Magpie & Stump. "*It looks like a dirty, old man's pub but it's good in the summer,*" we're assured. Wherever they worked, trainees were confident that the characteristic "*gritty and very determined*" Hammonds atmosphere will remain. "*It goes back to the type of person the firm hires,*" they told us – "*confident, ambitious and sociable.*"

## and finally...

Based on the testimony of our sources, we recommend giving Hammonds some serious thought. You'll want to do you own research on the firm's current business plans and its finances, but with European seats, excellent formal training and bags of character, we think it has much to offer the right candidate.

# Harbottle & Lewis LLP

## the facts

**Location:** London
**Number of partners/assistants:** 24/40
**Total number of trainees:** 8
**Seats:** 4x6 months
**Alternative seats:** Secondments

### Act 1 Scene 1

[London. 1955. Enter Mr Harbottle and Mr Lewis.]
Harbottle: Hello old friend from law school. How is

life at Allen & Overy?

Lewis: I'm enjoying it very much thank you. How about you?

Harbottle: I'm getting along wonderfully with my theatre and film clients. In fact, would you like to set up a new practice with me?

Lewis: A capital idea. Why not?

Harbottle: Great. Let's call it Harbottle & Lewis

Lewis: Hah! That's catchy.

**The End**

## strictly boardroom

... or just the beginning. With one founding partner passionate about theatre and film and the other trained in the City, it is perhaps entirely fitting that 50 years on Harbottle & Lewis still has a dedicated media practice and a highly rated corporate team adept at smaller deals. Though "*litigation and corporate/commercial are the biggest departments, they don't dominate*" and it is the firm's work in film, TV, sport, publishing, advertising, theatre and music that still earns the biggest round of applause.

Of course the script has changed since the early days when the firm knew its lines on film and theatre work. First it had to tune into television, then music, after which there was the Internet, e-commerce, interactive entertainment and computer games. As ever, Harbottles is keeping up with the latest scene changes, recently advising major mobile phone companies on ringtone deals. Thankfully, more traditional work remains centre stage, including advising on the 'Billy Elliot' musical and acting for the Prince's Trust on Party in the Park.

If a training contract at Harbottle & Lewis sounds like working the red carpet on premiere night at Leicester Square, be aware that "*it is not like that at all.*" In fact, "*only a small amount of what you do every day might have a celebrity name at the top of the paper,*" and "*you are not constantly on the phone to them.*" However, our sources were the first to admit "*the media work adds a bit of flavour to what you are doing. It is lovely to see your work in the news and think 'I helped with that',*

rather than 'Today I helped finance a dam in East Timor'.*"

Positioned on Hanover Square, just off Oxford Street and slightly stage-left of Soho, the firm's location confirms its status as a truly West End firm. Though it's an A-list media law firm "*it's not flash and swanky and it's not cool and crisp.*" This year it is treating itself to some cosmetic surgery – not a full facelift, just "*a fresh lick of paint and a bit more glass.*"

## who lives in a house like this?

The training brings seats in litigation, corporate, property, IP and media, with trainees learning which four they will get upon arrival at the firm. They are "*based on what you said at interview,*" though if that initial audition does not result in you landing the part you want, "*you can change the plan later if it doesn't affect anyone else.*" The only rule is that you can't do both IP and media. Inevitably, media is "*the most popular,*" by contrast property receives cooler reviews. The property team's client base of corporate property investors sets it apart from other departments. It does also act for theatres and carries out support work for other departments so there is at least "*a media connection.*" While we were assured that "*there is no bog-standard conveyancing*" there is "*selected residential work for rich clients.*" Sadly none of our sources were willing to play 'Through the Keyhole' with us.

The corporate department may seem an unlikely place to spot stars, but recently the team acted for Simon Fuller on the £100 million sale of 19 Entertainment. Other clients, such as Ministry of Sound, Telstar Music Group and Talkback Productions suggest that Harbottles has glitter running through its veins alongside red corporate blood in the shape of clients such as British Midland Airways, the Virgin Group, Reed Group and Merlin Financial. Spend time here and you are likely to find that "*it is just you and the partner doing the entire deal,*" giving you opportunities and exposure you might not expect at such an early stage in your career. So, you're *"not just the monkey doing the rubbish work."*

## when the bottom fell out of chaps

A coveted 'second floor' entertainment seat gives the best view in the house. Here, trainees spend *"three months sitting in the film and TV team, and three in music."* On the film and TV side *"there are no real celebrities; it is mainly financial work, tax funds and tax partnerships,"* with trainees taking a supporting role on sale and leaseback transactions for films or directors' and presenters' agreements. A stint in music means recording and management contracts and *"quite a lot of new media work: licences for mobile ringtones, digital downloads and stuff."* While one source admitted that *"you do meet a lot of bands because you have to go along to things and get artists to sign release forms,"* another lent a little closer to whisper that *"all the stars, all the juicy stuff, is down in litigation."*

Litigation seats are divided between major defamation and libel cases on the one hand and commercial matters on the other. The two types of case are *"vastly different,"* so the firm ensures that trainees *"get to do both."* Recently the litigation team was instructed by a clothing company called Basic Box to recover damages pursuant to a licence agreement that gave it the right to manufacture and market a line of clothing under Christina Aguilera's name. The business didn't look quite so appealing after she made negative comments on Oscar night about celebrities bringing out clothing labels. On the defamation side *"the clients are very important and want to avoid getting in the papers so the cases are very quick."* For trainees that means a walk-on part. On more commercial matters such as debt recovery and contract disputes trainees get a few lines of their own along with the inevitable glut of admin tasks and research. Our sources had run their own debt actions, attended directions hearings at court unaccompanied and even made their own small applications. *"You aren't arguing points, but you are as involved as you can be."*

A client secondment to Virgin means six months in Gatwick with heaps of autonomy on general commercial and contractual work. *"It is quite scary at first, but at the end you appreciate how valuable it is."* It may also offer a rare opportunity to literally rub shoulders with you know who. One source admitted: *"I did meet Richard. I held the door open for him. That was it."*

## ab fab?

Despite the *"obvious hierarchy,"* Harbottles is a *"quite inclusive firm"* and *"everyone knows your name, from the partners to the person who fills the biscuit tin."* So although *"definitely traditional in its values, they are non-traditional in how people lower down the ranks are valued."* The firm continues its tradition of providing lunch for the entire staff every day, and we can only presume that, yes, the senior partner does bunk up to make room for the post boy.

Speaking of squeezing up and making room, apart from property where trainees get an office to themselves, newbies share with *"someone who has expressed an interest in having a trainee."* This may not be your supervisor, but *"you aren't dumped on someone who doesn't want you there,"* and each trainee is assigned a mentor at associate or assistant solicitor level too. Trainees are encouraged to attend the firm's internal training sessions, and there is a formal end-of-seat appraisal system (though we heard murmurings that it is *"not particularly rigidly enforced"*). The problem, it seems, is that *"they are too nice to say if you aren't doing something right."* Fear not: on a day-to-day basis all work is checked and as time goes on *"more and more stuff comes back less and less amended."*

Usually at Harbottles it's a wrap by 7pm. Not so bad when the day doesn't start until 9.30ish. Time and again we heard how *"people here do their job and enjoy it, but on Friday night they have their other friends."* So if you're chasing that coveted 'falling out of cab and into gutter outside Soho House' shot on the front page of *Closer*, you'll have to cultivate the right friends outside work. At Harbottles there are quiz nights, tennis evenings, the odd drinks night and a cricket day, but definitely nothing involving taxis or gutters. In the humble words of one trainee: *"We're all terribly dull, there is never any gossip."* Hmmm...

In September 2005, two of the three qualifiers stayed with the firm, one to take on the honest daily toil of property, the other to stand under the bright lights of the film and TV department.

## and finale

[London. 2005. Enter Student Guide Researcher and Law Student]

Law Student: Gosh, this sounds like a jolly decent place. Should I apply?

Researcher: Well if you want to play a part in an excellent production, with an interesting script and a dedicated cast, do.

Law Student: I think I shall

**The End**

# Herbert Smith LLP

## the facts

**Location:** London
**Number of partners/assistants:** 154/448
**Total number of trainees:** 151
**Seats:** 4x6 months
**Alternative seats:** Overseas seats, secondments
**Extras:** Pro bono – Whitechapel Legal Advice Centre, death row appeals; language training

This City outfit has manoeuvred its way to the front of the grid in the UK market and pushes insistently against the magic circle, outpacing all but two of its members on profitability. Inventive and unparalleled when it comes to litigation, Herbert Smith has barged its way onto the transactional scene and is now intent on improving its finance practice. Is there any stopping the firm?

## herbies: fully loaded

Certainly, no one's putting the brakes on quite yet. In fact with profits per partner rising 14% to a record £800K in 2004/5, the word 'consolidation' appears to be absent from the Herbies lexicon. The work for which it is best known – litigation – played as strong a part as ever in this top-drawer performance, but corporate, too, enjoyed a stellar year, emphasising how integral energy, communications, financial institutions and private equity lawyers have become to the firm's fortunes. High-profile advice to Hollinger International on the £729 million sale of the Telegraph Group to the Barclay brothers was matched by instructions from the majority shareholder on the £1.35 billion MBO of Saga and from Securicor on its £1.7 billion merger with Group 4. Weighty figures indeed, and whilst they have helped boost Herbies' standing in European corporate deal tables, so too have moves this year to increase integration with the firm's excellent European allies Stibbe and Gleiss Lutz.

Typical of a firm with a self-improving itch, a perceived lack of clout in the finance arena was viewed as a challenge rather than a weakness. Having prioritised finance as a growth area in the last year, Herbies met with success when it was asked to advise ABN AMRO and Citigroup in relation to a $1 billion facility for TNK. It also advised RBS, Mizuho Corporate Bank and Bank of Scotland on a $250 million senior secured borrowing base facility for Marubeni Oil & Gas (USA + UK) and assisted Lehman Brothers on a £245 million securitised portfolio loan. So, even if it's not quite ready to lead on the finance circuit, all the signs point to Herbies becoming a good deal more race-worthy.

## bones of contention

The perennial issue for the trainees who chose Herbert Smith for its *"significant litigation expertise"* is how much litigation training can they expect and what are the chances of qualifying into a litigation job? Take note: a corporate seat is compulsory, but can be substituted for a stint in a finance department, leaving three seats in which to build up experience of contentious work. Oh that it were that simple... A problem arises in that most trainees have the same tastes and seat preferences when it comes to contentious work. With "*so many trainees wanting to do litigation rotation can be a bit of a lottery.*"

In truth, most of our interviewees had secured their preferred litigation seat at some time during their training. However, getting a second seat in this part of the firm is "*very, very difficult,*" unless it's in one of the niche departments like employment, IP or pensions, or "*you're lucky enough to get an overseas seat that is litigation-based.*" What we're left concluding is that while the quality of litigation experience on offer to trainees is good, this doesn't guarantee a heavily contentious training contract or even a contentious career at the firm afterwards. Illustrating this point, one trainee told us: "*In my intake there'll be at least twice as many applicants for litigation as jobs.*" This is the norm, year after year. In September 2005, 52 of the 57 qualifiers stayed with the firm, a fifth of whom qualified into litigation departments. As usual a number of qualifiers compromised and took transactional jobs.

Facing a legal climate in which fewer cases are making it to court, the firm has recast its Group D litigation team as a specialist arbitration/dispute resolution group, with Groups A and B ("*general litigation with a banking and finance slant*") taking on the displaced energy and public law work. Group C remains focused on *insurance* litigation. If the move reflects genuine concern that large-scale litigation can no longer be relied upon as a cash cow, reassurance came in the form of a continuing stream of high-profile litigations. Cases in point: the representation of BSkyB in its action against EDS for deceit, negligent misrepresentation and breach of contract; the representation of AWG on its claims for fraud against the individuals involved in its acquisition of the Morrison construction and asset management businesses; and the representation of the liquidating partners of Andersen UK on a wide range of matters. Herbies' lawyers recently secured victory in the High Court for Cambridge Antibody Technology against healthcare and pharmaceutical company Abbott Laboratories in a dispute over the royalty payment due on the sale of arthritis drug HUMIRA. Underlining the fact that the magic and art of advocacy is not dying, the firm has taken the innovative step of establishing its own in-house advocacy unit. Complete with "*two QCs and two associates joining later this year,*" the unit will allow Herbies to dispense with the services of outside barristers in many situations. It will also offer great experience for the lucky trainees who take a seat there. Unsurprisingly, "*there's a scramble for places already.*"

## fleshing out the picture

So what's the great appeal of litigation at Herbert Smith? Its popularity certainly isn't due to an excess of responsibility on offer to trainees. They find their hands full with "*the inevitable bundling, indexing and photocopying of documents plus disclosure tasks.*" This is the less desirable by-product of "*the vast scale of the matters you work on,*" although our sources took consolation in "*the high profile of the cases – it's a thrill to see what you're working on in the papers.*" In addition to the buzz of reading about their cases in the newspapers, trainees do find "*some high-quality work mixed in with the mundane,*" and seem to particularly enjoy "*drafting witness statements and correspondence.*" However, "*having first stab at lots of things*" can sometimes be a double-edged sword, because "*getting something back covered in red pen can be demoralising.*" All in all, the "*robust and self-righting*" seem to revel in litigation seats and we heard less of the distinctly damning reports on some supervisors that have emerged in the past. "*I had heard that litigation was more frosty,*" acknowledged one source." "*Litigation A was even called The Fridge in previous years.*" Indeed it was. Has there been change for the better in this once traditional and hierarchical department? Perhaps so, according to the source who said: "*Everyone I've worked with has been incredibly helpful. My supervisor couldn't involve me enough." "I've not come across anyone aggressive or unpleasant at all,"* added another.

## hot and cold

Mulling over the *"cooler"* reputation of litigation (shared also by some finance teams, we're told), one interviewee suggested: *"The people who find it cold are probably the people who really enjoy the boisterous atmosphere of corporate."* Indeed, *"the up-and-down"* nature of corporate life had translated into *"good fun and great experience"* for our sources, who had more often than not visited the department in their first seat. "*I sat with a senior partner and he was fantastic; he got me really involved in two good takeovers,"* said one trainee, whilst another admitted, almost shamefacedly: *"Sometimes you'd leave at 5pm, other times you'd stay all night, but everyone would stay, so I have to say it led to great camaraderie."* True, there do seem to be a good deal of *"administrative tasks"* to be taken on, but *"people are very appreciative and there's lots of drafting... and not just board minutes."*

The feast or famine nature of corporate often leads trainees *"to search out work from others in the quieter times."* Across in another common first seat – real estate – there's little danger of having a window in the schedule. "*It was a baptism of fire,"* laughed one seasoned source. *"There are lots of small matters which are easy to delegate to a trainee: licences to assign, licences to alter, plus a lot more client contact than anywhere else."* This all makes for *"a great way to learn the ropes; you learn to be organised and disciplined in the way you work."* It isn't just odds and sods on offer here because the real estate department works on sizeable property and PFI matters, including long-term projects. Of late, lawyers have been busy with the redevelopment of King's Cross Central, Stratford City, the Dome/Greenwich Peninsula and the Bracknell and Sheffield town centre regeneration schemes. In the past year real estate lawyers have also advised financiers Lehman Brothers on the

£135 million sale of 15 Westferry Circus by Canary Wharf and also won a competitive tender to advise Southwark Council on the £1.5 billion redevelopment and regeneration of Elephant and Castle. Whether assisting supervisors or assuming responsibility of their own, our interviewees had benefited from the fact that the department's lawyers *"are used to giving trainees responsibility and have a good inbuilt support network."*

## fortress herbert

The firm resides in a vast glass and steel building next to Exchange Square and Liverpool Street Station. It is presently undergoing *"a much-needed refit"* to rid it of *"early 90s decor that is starting to show its age."* About time too, we say. Some departments have moved to an adjacent building, which is linked to the main one by a *"frosted glass bridge through the air."*

Despite a *"decent"* canteen and *"regular drinks trolleys come Friday afternoon,"* we did observe that, whilst not exactly barricading themselves in, some departments do keep their drawbridges firmly up. *"There isn't massive interaction between groups,"* said one source, another adding: *"Corporate and litigation are so enormous and there's little overlap."*

Depending on the department and *"to a certain extent on luck,"* all those we interviewed had experience of *"extreme hours: 36-hour days and the like,"* as well as *"quieter times when you're out on the dot of 5.30pm."* Our sources seemed to have handled the chicanes of the contract with the fortitude that characterises Herbies' trainees. *"You've got to be robust and confident in your ability to get on,"* said one; another confiding that *"you join and are slightly awed by the calibre of person around you, what they've done educationally and socially."* Thankfully, these trends don't seem to result in *"over-the-top, over-extroverted or overly aggressive types."* Instead, people recognise *"you have to toughen up a bit"* and then *"become increasingly confident over time."* There is a smoother ride to be had in smaller departments, such as IP, pensions, employment, tax and construction, which are *"generally friendlier and allow more responsibility,"* but even in the larger departments we heard this year that, *"aside from the odd one or two who aren't approachable, most supervisors are very willing to help you out." "The majority work hard to give you constructive feedback"* and the quality of formal training is *"excellent,"* with sessions *"structured and thorough, so you really feel like they've invested massively in you."*

## herbert fountain

When it comes to socialising, trainees initially group together by intake and go for regular drinks at nearby bar Davy's. *"A rush of events"* at the beginning of the two years *"gradually becomes more lunchtime meetings as time goes by and people are busy or away on secondment."* Overseas seats are popular and can be taken at any one of the firm's several international offices or with allied firms. Location choices include Paris, Amsterdam (with Stibbe), Hong Kong and Singapore. Stay-at-homes can try for one of several client secondments to the likes of BSkyB, Coca-Cola, Cable & Wireless and Liberty amongst others. At times, the brain-drain feels very obvious; however with *"between 30 and 60 in your intake," "you're almost guaranteed to find a core group that you get on with really well."* Cliques are thrown aside for the bi-annual, black-tie trainee ball, a chance to get blinged up for a night at a glam venue. Other highlights include a *"major Christmas party"* (held last year at the Honourable Artillery Club fields) at which *"people let their hair down a bit"* and *"the senior partner got involved in some cabaret entertainment."* We're thinking less cross-dressing in smoky Berlin nightclubs, and more witty comic singing. But you never know... especially when you hear of the hedonism of *"a chocolate fountain – messy but delicious."*

## and finally...

Herbert Smith offers one of the most rounded training contracts of the City firms in the sense that you won't be restricted to finance and corporate seats for the majority of your training. Whether this translates into quite as much mainstream litigation experience as the majority of its trainees hope for is another matter.

# Hill Dickinson

## the facts

**Location:** Liverpool, Manchester, Chester, London
**Number of partners/assistants:** 115/114
**Total number of trainees:** 20
**Seats:** 4x6 months
**Alternative seats:** Secondments

Founded way back in the early 19th century, when bonkers hat-wearer Napoleon was tinkering with the political geography of Europe, Liverpudlian Hill Dickinson is still going strong. Formerly a maritime specialist with a caseload that once included the ill-fated Titanic, the firm has now branched out into insurance, healthcare, Manchester and London.

## capital of compensation culture

Though Hill Dickinson is a firm conscious of its history (*"you can't forget it, there are pictures of the Titanic everywhere"*) it is far from a museum for former glory. With a sharp focus on the future and beaming with municipal pride, HD has woven its fortune with that of home city Liverpool, becoming official solicitor to the city's upcoming European Capital of Culture year in 2008. Like Liverpool herself, the firm has market potential and is in the process of a rethink that could result in an identity rehash. To raise its profile, HD recently managed to get its name splashed on the canvas for Bolton boxing wonder Amir Khan's first professional fight, televised from Liverpool. *"It was great seeing us on telly,"* grinned one source.

In time for the Capital of Culture year, HD will have united its current four sites in Liverpool, bringing all staff together under a single, purpose-built roof. Hiring the hod carriers, foremen and architects comes with a hefty price tag, but the firm seems in a good position to foot the bill. It's been a downhill struggle of late: a merger with property specialist Bullivant Jones assisted in a 34% turnover hike, income bouncing from £14.5 million to £22 million in a year.

Not that the firm needed the merger to put it on the map: its strengths already included clinical negligence and insurance litigation as well as the heritage work in shipping. Best in the North West for clin neg, the firm is one of the chosen few on the NHS Litigation Authority's legal panel. From the Kernan inquest (the shooting of a samurai sword-wielding mental health outpatient) to judicial reviews into withholding aggressive treatments, HD lawyers have fascinating cases "*as well as the usual compensation-culture stuff.*" In addition to the NHSLA, key clients include several passenger and merchant shipping lines plus insurance companies such as Royal & SunAlliance and Norwich Union.

## grand plans

With ever larger clients on its books, HD is developing some serious ambitions. According to one cheerleader, the firm "*would like to do big things, starting with a drive to be number one in the North West and pushing out from there.*" Another more measured source concluded that "*in reality the firm is just getting used to trying for bigger things and it hasn't hit them fully how to do it yet.*" For now, the Liverpool hub is supported by offices in Manchester and London plus a titch in Chester specialising in "*children's law and legal aid.*"

Everyone knows that working life is hell accessorised with screensavers and cute kitten mugs, so in the circumstances we're happy to report that HD trainees seem a contented bunch who are blessed with the twin pillars of a good training contract – "*responsibility*" and "*support.*" Each trainee shares an office with a partner or, more often, senior solicitor. The advantage to this is that "*all your questions get answered and you get to hear about other people's cases.*" In other words, eavesdropping on desk-

thumping phone negotiations and seeing how a firm runs behind closed doors. When it comes to training, don't expect to be scribbling notes and doodling afternoons away in a lecture room, because this is a firm that values on-the-job learning. Naturally this statement comes with the usual disclaimers ("*sometimes you will get the crappy jobs like page numbering for a week, but that's part and parcel of training*"), however, in the main trainees are entrusted with everything from court applications to drafting documents and the odd client meeting.

Trainee traffic between the branches is largely restricted to Mancunian and Liverpudlian seat swaps. At any one time most trainees are in Liverpool and three are in Manchester. If you look for patterns in seat moves or swaps, the conclusion you quickly reach is that "*nothing is set in stone.*" Epitomising this attitude is a loosely defined North West construction seat that sees its Liverpool occupant commuting to Manchester a few times a week for non-contentious experiences. It is only the M62 that sees this much action; said one source: "*I'd be very surprised if someone in Liverpool was told to go to London.*" And what of Chester? "*I wouldn't know how to get to the Chester office and I've never met anyone from there.*"

## a sporting chance

The oldest of the four offices in Liverpool, Pearl Assurance House, may also be its most industrious. "*When I arrived there were 40 files on my desk,*" declared one source. "*A lot of fairly straightforward work*" is encountered in a marine seat here; defendant PI streams in from cruise ship and passenger ferry operators. Trainees also end up working on vibration white finger cases, "*a few misplaced RTAs*" and asbestos claims from sailors on merchant ships in the 1940s and 50s. On smaller cases, trainees produce instructions for counsel, organise medical examinations and handle case management conferences at court alone. Take a seat over in Dale House (home to the property/construction teams) and you'll be assisting deals relating to large property portfolios, perhaps preparing certificates on title for the refinancing of hundreds of different premises "*all at once!*" Running your own freehold sales and drafting licences to assign leases are among the other treats. HD's third office on Liverpool's Corn Exchange means insurance litigation, a "*bustling seat*" with a lot of "*responsibility*" to compensate for the inevitable "*crap*" of bundling, bibling and pagination.

HD's healthcare division is split into four parts – general advice, mental health, property and clin neg. All four teams are popular amongst trainees, though we sense that it is the first that is the most popular. Work for the National Care Standards Commission, for example, includes juicy appeals and tribunals, often relating to the cancellation of registrations for rickety old people's homes. A trainee's role, on say a judicial review case, is to "*take part in meetings with counsel and keep clients up to date.*" Coroner's inquests keep "*popping up*" Lazarus-like in this seat. As one trainee explained, death is a growth industry at HD – "*we're doing more and more inquests.*"

Tinkering with the standard four-seat training is not unknown at HD, trainees variously doubling up or shrinking and extending seats, especially in London. "*I wanted to see a big case through to conclusion and they let me stay on,*" one interviewee explained. Mixed seats also feature: in Manchester trainees sometimes work in an IP/coco/sports concoction – it's a fun hotchpotch with a theme of sorts. Manchester's growing sports practice is winning high-profile clients and cases such as Gary Lineker's defence of libel allegations following his treatise on transfer regulations in the *Sunday Telegraph*. "*It sounds very glamorous, and it is,*" one source told us of the practice, leaving us grinding our teeth with envy at tales of schmoozing with footballers and rugby players, and valiantly defending sports stars from "*exploitation of their image rights.*" Your own caseload won't be forthcoming here, but the morsels you do get will be tasty, especially when helping to draft the terms of players' transfer contracts.

## king of the cornhill

In London, the firm occupies four floors of "*old Gothic-Georgian-I-don't-know-what-it's-called*" architecture on Cornhill. It accommodates two trainees, and pursues a predominantly maritime practice. Trainees can choose from professional indemnity, PI and a variety of shipping seats. One reported experience of "*shipping finance, and a yachting-specific seat with salvage and transit work for planes, trains and automobiles.*" If shipping law sounds as appealing as a watery grave, ask yourself how many areas of legal practice could produce sentences like these: "*Frozen fish trawlers registered in St Vincent and marooned off the coast of Guinea-Bissau will go through the International Law of the Sea tribunal in Hamburg. They're just bizarre fact-pattern cases – bonkers.*" You're telling us! "*It's really fascinating work,*" our source continued, "*hilariously fascinating work.*" Take one of the firm's speciality areas – mega-yachts. For the uninitiated, these are bespoke floating palaces (Roman Abramovich is reported to have one worth over £70 million). Usually fitted out with "*amazing woods, gold and marble... they're quite kitsch. We sold Armani one, and a Saudi prince – it's quite, quite bizarre.*" Once used to the bizarreness, trainees help to draft the documents that enable these lavish craft to be bought and sold, usually liaising with a number of banks ("*or if it's a prince or king just the one bank*").

Any London trainee who wishes to pop north for a seat can do so, and they might well go in search of a stint in Liverpool's corporate department. This seat lacks the same gold-plated vibe – lately the corporate lawyers have been handling the disposal of roll-on, roll-off ferries.

## bat out of hill

Every month the trainees in Liverpool organise an evening of sober discussion. "*We agenda a debate on a topical subject... something like ID cards."* You'll be relieved to hear that monthly drinks also have their place, with the Liverpudlians traipsing to the appropriately named Trials and Mancunians to *"the nearest pub."* Firm-wide social events are non-existent, with Christmas parties and other organised jollies all organised on a departmental basis. Partners let their hair down at these events and even pick a few outings themselves. Apparently one of them persuaded colleagues to go along to a Meatloaf gig.

Whether or not they share a love for sweaty, motorcycle-riding crooners, the majority (seven out of eight) of the qualifying trainees stayed on with the firm in 2005. The fact that two journeyed south to qualify into the currently *"brisk"* Cornhill office suggests that the firm is attempting organic growth to supplement a recent raft of lateral hires in the capital.

## and finally...

The legal market in the North West is definitely hotting up, and it looks to us as if Hill Dickinson has no intention of simmering slowly on the back burner.

# Hodge Jones & Allen

## the facts

**Location:** London
**Number of partners/assistants:** 19/37
**Total number of trainees:** 13
**Seats:** 4x6 months
**Alternative seats:** None

North London community law firm Hodge Jones & Allen's superb pedigree makes it a very popular choice for aspiring trainees with issues of conscience and justice rather than pound signs in their eyes.

## three men and their baby

Back in 1977 three young solicitors met for a drink in a pub in Camden Town. Over two pints of Directors, Henry Hodge, Peter Jones and Patrick Allen hatched a plan to start their own firm to champion the concept of justice and legal advice for all in the community, irrespective of ability to pay. The three friends found office space in Camden High Street above a small finance company that offered 'Loans From A Fiver'. Henry Hodge was dispatched on his motorbike to buy a telephone and the young lawyers' bank manager sent them their first client. Nearly 30 years later, Mr Justice Hodge is one of the first solicitors to have become a High Court Judge and was recently made president of the Asylum and Immigration Tribunal; Peter Jones is Dean of Nottingham Law School; and Patrick Allen, who continues to practice at HJA, is one of the UK's best-known multiparty claimant lawyers. Still located in Camden Town, the firm itself employs around 160 people and its original aims and values are as important now as they were all those years ago.

## crime pays

In a HJA training contract trainees complete four six-month seats from a selection consisting of crime, family, property/conveyancing, wills, trusts and probate, housing, mental health, civil litigation and personal injury/clinical negligence. The criminal department is a core part of the firm and *"most people do a crime seat, although you wouldn't have to unless you really wanted to."* One of the first things trainees do is gain accreditation as a police station adviser, which entails attendance at stations to advise clients on charge. It has been known for some students to become accredited through the firm before they even commence their contract, and many trainees regard police station work as a useful source of additional income, happily staying on the police station rota even after leaving their crime seat. Because the criminal department is large, trainees end up with the firm's 'own client' pager once every three weeks and then there's an additional rota for trainees to back up the solicitors on call on the duty solicitor scheme. Being on call means 12 hours overnight and a 24-hour period at the weekend. *"I never thought about it before I started,"* said one trainee, *"people get arrested at all times of day and night."*

Obviously police station visits can be *"a little bit daunting,"* but before striking out on their own trainees will have visited on a number of prior occasions, first to observe then to be observed giving advice. *"You just have to get stuck in at some point,"* one source told us, *"and I really feel I have sufficient support back at office. Sometimes you do find yourself in a grey area and so you get a second opinion."* After a while trainees learn that the job is all about reaching *"a fine balance between being confrontational and getting what you want by being nice."* The best advice is *"be confident and really know your law. My supervisor said to me, 'When you're in a police station you are on police territory and so you must know the law better than them'."*

Crime work is demanding, not least because some clients have mental health, drug or alcohol problems. Sometimes all three. *"The people with drug problems around here are fairly representative of our clients. You have to be a compassionate person, though not a bleeding heart liberal."* Most importantly, *"you can't make judgements about your clients,"* even though it can be frustrating to see them return time and again. For better or worse, the firm has been acting for members of some families since 1977. *"You come into this job feeling idealistic,"* one trainee opined: *"but the reality is slightly different. I am interested in social justice and ensuring that everyone has access to legal representation... after a while you realise that pushing people round the system doesn't serve anyone."*

## tough love

The family department is another prime seat for full-on client contact and fast-paced days. The team covers care proceedings and domestic violence cases as well as more straightforward divorces. *"It's*

*a really good seat because even as a trainee you have rights of audience and there are loads of opportunities to do advocacy on things like domestic violence injunctions in the principal registry and [child] contact disputes in county court."*

In the housing department, trainees encounter possession proceedings and homelessness. *"The client may come in after hearing a rejection of their application by the council and want you to represent them at the review of the decision."* If the review does not go favourably there is a right to appeal in the county court on a point of law under the Housing Act. Some cases may seem hopeless at the start, but hard work and devotion can turn them around. *"It takes a lot of time and energy, but the outcome can be so worthwhile."* As for what kind of person can cope with having their heartstrings tugged every day, *"you need to be quite a strong character because what you want to know and what a client tells you can be two different things."* It's all about putting the role of lawyer to the fore, even if this means *"you can come across as quite tough."*

Both the clinical negligence and personal injury departments take trainees to assist on everything from RTAs to serious injuries. One brain injury case settled for over £3 million last year. HJA has always been a prominent name in multiparty claims and you may have read about the fate of two high-profile matters, MMR and Gulf War Syndrome where, unfortunately for the claimants, public funding was withdrawn after it was deemed unlikely that a successful legal case could be proved on the science and facts available. It's interesting to note that, in amongst the lawyers in HJA's PI and clin neg teams, there are scientifically qualified staff, including a nurse who started her training contract in September 2005.

## balancing the books

In past editions we reported on a trend towards taking on privately paying and commercial work, especially in property. There appears to have been a change of emphasis again (which pleases certain elements of the firm no end), which means the training contract experience remains purely in the sphere of publicly funded and/or private, as opposed to commercial, clients. *"The rates of legal aid have not gone up for many years but overheads have,"* yet the Legal Services Commission is keeping bellies full at HJA. Indeed, the firm has been appointed to seven of the LSC's panels ranging from Mental Health Review Tribunals to children's law.

Clients can come from distant and unlikely places. *"A great number of the housing clients come from Camden or Islington, and most of the conveyancing is local, but clients come from across London and even Edinburgh and Manchester in PI."* Trainee solicitors, too, are drawn from across the UK. And higher up in the firm there have been new arrivals in the fields of police actions, inquests, inquiries and human rights and civil liberties. We wondered if this was indicative of a more radical phase for the firm though were unable to reach a conclusion on the point. In fact, if you were wondering about whether the firm has any political/ideological leanings, it's probably fair to say that some of the older partners have been closely associated with the current Labour government, while some of the younger ones probably swing further to the left.

## regent's spark

Trainees sit with a supervisor, usually a partner, *"but are left to get on with things; they're not breathing down your neck all the time."* One source told us: *"I feel I have always been challenged and believed in. Often I've been left to run something that I didn't feel I could do at first. But then you realise that you can and you're not ever doing things that can't be undone."* In this training, it's all about finding out what you can do, not what you can't.

The firm receives many hundreds of applications and can afford to be picky: basically you need a First or a high 2:1 at degree level and then also be capable of getting a distinction at law school. On top of all that (occasionally instead of it) an impressive CV evidencing commitment to publicly funded law or charitable/social endeavours will be required to convince the firm that you are made of the right stuff. Someone also joked about applicants needing a letter from the pope. At least we think it was a joke. There are two routes to a training contract: either prove your worth as a paralegal or apply directly for a contract a year in advance of its start date. Neither route seems easier than the other. In September 2005, two of the five qualifiers stayed on at the firm, with the remainder finding alternative jobs without difficulty.

A social life is on offer if you want it, with Mac Bar over the road and The Eagle around the corner, both being popular for Friday night drinks. There are two special annual events – the Christmas party and a summer outing. The latter is usually an afternoon in nearby Regent's Park devoted to a picnic and a highly competitive interdepartmental softball tournament.

## and finally...

Leaving aside the issues of personal fulfilment, there is no escaping the fact that legal aid work is a tough gig. You must learn your craft quickly and prove your worth, and you must accept lower financial rewards than your peers in commercial practice. If you think you have the commitment required for this work, just pray you manage to hit the Hodge Jones & Allen jackpot.

# Holman Fenwick & Willan

## the facts

**Location:** London
**Number of partners/assistants:** 62/54
**Total number of trainees:** 16
**Seats:** 4x6 months
**Alternative seats:** Overseas seats, secondments
**Extras:** Language training

# the true picture

London shipping specialist Holman Fenwick & Willan has ridden the main since 1883 and is one of the most respected shipping practices afloat today.

## botan-ebay

Some of the largest marine and aviation litigation from the past two decades has washed up at Holmans' door. Its lawyers acted in the Piper Alpha and Cormorant Alpha North Sea oilrig disasters, the nautical Scandinavian Star fire and the British Midlands air crash on the M1 near Kegnorth. The headline work most recently, however, has been the immense web of insurance liability litigation spun after the Exxon Valdez Alaskan oil spillage in 1989. Some 16 years after 25 million gallons of crude oil coated the Bligh Reef, Holmans emerged victorious from the Court of Appeal for its reinsurance company Brandywine. At stake: the many many millions of dollars it cost to clean up the environment.

Despite these big cases, overall there has been a worldwide downturn in shipping work. Nonetheless, Holmans has kept a steady course to profitability, lately promoting five associates to partner and hauling aboard a ship finance expert and his small crew from rival firm Stephenson Harwood. Holmans is keen to build up this transactional work and acts for both lenders and borrowers. We note that some cases border on the bizarre, among them a tale from South America. While spring cleaning, Holmans' client the Brazilian navy noticed its biggest warship, the Minas Gerias, was looking a tad rusty, all the more so after her active service in WWII under the name HMS Vengence. The navy decided to auction the ship. Nothing out of the ordinary, you may say, except that it posted it on eBay. At which point British Royal Navy veterans launched a 'Save the Vengence' campaign to prevent a sale. Holmans won the day for the Brazilian navy, however, and the proud ship was towed into the sunset like Turner's 'Fighting Temeraire' to end its days as scrap in India. We must say we also like the sound of the work going on in Holman's superb super-yacht practice where lawyers enable the playboys of the western world to indulge their passion for big toys. Ever wondered how much a super yacht costs? Try £40+ million. Beluga caviar anyone?

## international bright young things

The clear message from trainees is that Holmans is not just a shipping firm. In the area of energy and natural resources, for example, it has picked up work following the collapse of Enron and acts for clients from all over the world. One of them, PT Kaltim Prima Coal, is being counselled on a $1.2 billion mining development in Kalimantan and a further $1 billion project in Sangatta (both in Indonesia). The same client also used the firm to refinance its $404 million worth of senior debt. Yet much of the time the "*shipping theme*" pervades not only the energy practice but also other areas of the firm's work – employment for example. Said one trainee: "*There are different seats in other departments but you can definitely still smell the sea in them.*" For the record, the full list of seats available to trainees is shipping litigation; reinsurance; employment; trade; energy; ship finance; EU; commercial property; commercial litigation and insolvency.

In their first year trainees' allocations are largely dictated by the business needs of the firm and the range of seats left over after the second-years have had their pick. Most are shanghaied into shipping litigation at some stage, no bad thing as for many it is "*by far and away the best seat.*" Larger cases often involve corrupted cargo ("*usually rats nibbling their way through whole containers of grain*") or on-board thefts. Naturally trainees can only assist on these larger cases, and when it comes to trial preparation there is inevitably a good deal of photocopying and bundling to get through. This work is less of an albatross around the neck when handling their own smaller files alone – "*fish drying machines that don't work, wonky paving and quite a bit of insolvency... it's a real mixed bag.*" Many personal injury cases involve "*injured sailors on ships,*" and when handling such matters trainees learn how to assess evidence and *"decide whether the shipowner is liable."* If they are *"then we calculate the quantum."* Instructing barristers and experts, assessing witness statements and visiting court, our sources found themselves doing *"all the meaty stuff... you can really get your teeth into things."*

Non-contentious shipping finance means poring over the specifications, histories and registrations of the cathedrals of the sea. According to one trainee: *"Selling a ship is a lot like selling a house except you might have to co-ordinate the purchase between London, Germany and Hong Kong all at the same time."* Security documents and loan agreements, a pledge of accounts and a deed of covenant or two will give you *"good drafting experience."* Here too, and indeed across the seats, there is plenty of research to keep trainees busy. *"Trainees are relied upon for research,"* we heard, *"we're newer out of school and with the computer skills that this generation has we're ready for research."* In competition work, for example, trainees immerse themselves in *"the details of an anti-competition notification and then formulate drafts – rather like essays on the transaction."* In all, *"thinking laterally and mulling over black letter law creates an exciting blend of the practical and academic."* Competition seats can also throw up some unusual titbits to trainees: an ongoing project to draft legislation for Nigeria's planned privatisation of utilities means *"trawling the legislation of developing nations."*

## getting shipshape

Shipping law is not normal fodder on either the LPC or a degree course, and new trainees soon learn that the shipping industry is a world of its own with a language of its own. One source summed up most eloquently why taking the plunge into shipping is so worthwhile. *"Rather than invisible corporate cases involving just numbers, shipping cases are real situations of navigational errors and ships crashing into each other. The law might not be different – it is still torts and contract – but it is certainly more real."*

So even if you're completely uninitiated, don't demur at demurrage, be affrighted by affreightment or barricade against barratry. Of course, a marine background or interest will help you (the firm boasts its fair share of keen sailors and *"ex-navy types"*) but is *"not a prerequisite."* More usually it is a person's international outlook that will help secure them a job. With sister offices in Paris, Nantes, Rouen, Hong Kong, Shanghai, Singapore and Piraeus, Holmans is a truly international firm. It encourages applications from polyglots and globetrotters, those who *"have been immersed in international communities,"* so if you can speak Cantonese, grew up in London, Rio and Dar-es-Salaam and came down with a good degree from a decent university then Holman will definitely look twice at you.

Should you ultimately tire of London – and Samuel Johnson was decidedly wrong in his pronouncement that only those tired of life could do so – then there's good news. *"Things are booming in the Pacific Rim at the moment. You could move there with the firm if you wanted."* Such moves generally wait until after qualification, but *"if you ask and it fits"* you might swing an overseas seat. For those who don't fancy the long haul, secondments are available to some of Holmans' UK clients.

## personality goes a long way

The Georgian-fronted London office is sparkling after its 2003 refit. *"There are no oak panels"* but the *"general tone is reserved, conservative and traditional."* We dug around to find out a little more about the tone aboard the good ship Holman and noted how one word continually cropped up in relation to the partners – *"personality."* Trainees' experiences vary from one seat to another and can often be put *"down to the personality of a partner."* Some are charming; some can be abrasive. Trainees suggest that with some *"you have to be thick skinned,"* explaining that the firm has few *"protocols and codes"* and partners tend to work and behave as they choose. In terms of the training scheme this can sometimes be an issue; for example mid-seat appraisals : "*there's supposed to be one but there often isn't.*" The impression we gained was that recruits with more dominant personalities may find little or no room for exerting them. Those with calmer, more accommodating natures seem to find things easier.

Trainees don't get up to anything really nautical out of hours. Usually it is a case of a shandy and a shanty down at the Pitcher & Piano, or "*if we feel a bit more fancy then we go to Pause.*" As for organised events, there are annual morale boosters in the summer and at Christmas. The two parties follow a pattern: "*One year the Christmas party is in a nice place and the summer one upstairs in a pub, then the next year it's vice versa.*" By all accounts you won't catch the partners ripping up the dance floor and swinging their blazers round their heads, instead "*you tend to see more secretaries enjoying the fun stuff.*" One honest source revealed that "*there's a bit of a divide: the support staff have a good old knees-up but the lawyers should really make more of an effort.*"

All we can say is this: with so many characters – one department so filled with South African lawyers that it goes by the name of Kruger National Park; a fleet of non-lawyer master mariners (actual beardy ships captains); and more weekend sailors than you can shake a yardarm at – there is never going to be a dull moment at this firm. Factor in the possibility that you could be trained up into some kind of International Rescue operative and you can see the appeal. Who needs dancing? In September 2005, seven of the nine qualifiers chose to stay with the firm.

## and finally...

For those with a true global vision, orienting their internal compass to Holman Fenwick & Willan will be a smart move.

# Hugh James

## the facts

**Location:** Cardiff, Merthyr Tydfil, Blackwood
**Number of partners/assistants:** 48/54
**Total number of trainees:** 19
**Seats:** 4x6 months
**Alternative seats:** None

Legal hybrid Hugh James is one of Wales' best-known firms. It operates in both the commercial and publicly funded spheres and also fills many of the gaps left between the two. All this adds up to a feast of experiences for trainees.

## it's a group thing

In its promotional literature the firm pares itself into quarters: claimant PI; publicly funded law; business litigation and business services. Dig around and you become aware of a gradual but deliberate move away from areas of publicly funded work in favour of private and commercial clients. Yet this shift, also evident in many other firms, does not necessarily mean an inexorable march towards the world of corporate deals. It is for litigation that we see the firm as a major force. From personal injury to commercial claims and local authority disrepair defence work, Hugh James is dominant in Wales. Its involvement in massive industrial disease cases has allowed some 35,000 claimants to recover over £200 million in compensation for illnesses such as asbestosis and Vibration White Finger. And as new types of claim arise, the firm's experience of class actions is proving to be invaluable. It is currently running cases concerning the drug Seroxat (2,000 claimants); intra-ocular lenses implanted in cataract patients (1,000 claimants) and the Quorn food product, which a group of 800 US claimants alleges can cause allergic reactions.

## broken bones

On personal injury claims, lawyers act for a substantial number of individual claimants – presently

65,000 nationally and internationally – ranging from those involved in simple pavement trips and slips to extraordinary circumstances such as the Gerona Air Crash. Yet the firm has chosen to ride two horses and also represents local authorities and certain insurers in other cases, including failure to educate, stress and bullying, deafness, RSI and catastrophic injury claims. One recent case related to an explosion at a petrol station in west Wales where ten people claimed property losses, personal injury and psychiatric damage.

## broken homes

If you find broken bones too distressing, what about dealing with tumbledown buildings in a property litigation seat instead? The team's main clients are Cardiff and Blaenau Gwent Councils for whom it handles vast numbers of housing disrepair claims. Trainees can end up with a few hundred files of their own, which ensures exposure to "*plenty of advocacy and case management conferences. When you've 30 files at a time in front of a district judge that's exhilarating.*" In a seat like this you can "*see a file at the start, at the end, and all the way through. I learned more about litigation procedure than I would have done anywhere else.*" This comment is as good a way as any to illustrate the firm's approach to training.

According to our sources, trainees are all stretched, sometimes to their limits. Said one: "*Initially in Merthyr I don't think I had quite the support I should have had... but not every seat is a baptism of fire.*" They all looked back and told us: "*I feel I have learned a heck of a lot,*" confirming that the pressure placed upon them is a good thing... "*so long as everything goes alright!*" One typical source told us: "*Although I've felt under tremendous pressure on occasions, they do listen if you say you've got too much. I know I can go into any job interview now and say, 'I can do that'.*" In many seats "*they depend on us to see a lot of clients, instruct counsel and attend court.*" It's all about "*being prepared to just throw yourself into the job and realising the more you do, the more it toughens you up.*" Whether it's in Cardiff,

Merthyr or Blackwood, trainees must quickly become self-sufficient: "*I ended up with a big caseload,*" said one, "*they don't just give you all the crap which is why I like working here.*"

## broken hearts

Though "*they have stopped doing family and crime in Merthyr,*" it is business as usual in the Cardiff family department, where there are both affluent clients and a full caseload of care work and Hague Convention child abduction cases. "*Perhaps one parent says they are going on holiday with the child and then they just never come back. Or they come along for a contact visit one day and never return with the child. We've had cases involving abduction in Libya, South Africa... all over the world.*" In the 'asset management' department (wills, probate and trusts), as in the family department, clients range from "*those who don't have a great deal of money to those who have a lot.*" Generally, poorer clients are to be found in Blackwood and Merthyr, where they just walk in off the street, while wealthier clients visit the Cardiff office having first made an appointment.

Again, if the idea of dealing with broken families makes you uncomfortable there are other less emotionally charged seats to try out. "*Property in Cardiff is a massive department and renowned for buying land for property developers and then selling off plots. They do masses of that kind of deal and have won new clients lately who are developing whole new villages.*" Barratt Homes has been the commercial property department's main client in Cardiff for the last 20 years or so.

## a moveable feast

Trainees complete four six-month seats – or at least that's the theory. In practice, it has been known for time in a seat to be cut short to just two or three months because another department has needed an extra pair of hands. Alternatively, "*if you're doing really well where you are, they like to keep you.*" No wonder trainees stress the need for flexibility. In appraisals, *"the opportunity is there to discuss seats and what you've enjoyed or not enjoyed. There are plenty of instances where people have specifically asked to stay in a department and they have been listened to, but there are others where people have left seats when requested to do so."* The flexibility in the system can be great (*"I have been very lucky: I wanted to specialise and I have had plenty of opportunity to do just that"*) or it can be a real disadvantage (*"what use is a two-month seat?"*). Seat changes can also be stressful: *"You can feel totally out of your depth, especially if you end up with a difficult partner or a demanding boss and there's no one else around your level."* From what we can tell though, it is common to latch on to an area of practice and spend a year or more in that area. Certainly, most trainees work in their preferred field in the run up to qualification. Only three of the seven 2005 qualifiers took jobs with the firm, in what was a disappointing year for a firm with normally high retention.

As to where trainees end up, *"most are put in a branch office at some point because it is such a different experience."* Because Merthyr has a commercial property department *"technically it is possible to stay on the commercial track, but most people will end up having greater variety by doing a seat in PI or conveyancing."* In Merthyr and Blackwood *"the main difference is the client base and the fact that the two branch offices are more relaxed."* By contrast, Cardiff, with its shiny, open-plan, glass office building and fabulous views of the Millennium Stadium and Cardiff Castle has *"more of a corporate image."* In this sense Hugh James is almost two firms in one, and we wondered if the two sides were in danger of dragging the partnership in opposing directions. *"I don't think you could fuse the two sides of the firm completely,"* thought one source, while another told us: *"It does all seem to work together, even though it is definitely letting go of its publicly funded work."* Trainees spoke of the firm as *"an animal that is constantly adapting to its environment."*

## better the devil you know

Though there are *"a lot of Welsh people"* among the trainee group, we have it on good authority that there are also currently a couple of people from England who were at university in Wales. We also noted several of the current crop had been recruited after a period of time working as a Hugh James paralegal, and the firm has a clear preference for taking applicants who have completed its vacation scheme.

*"We've all got the same kind of background and attitude,"* our sources told us. *"We're outgoing, confident and independent. We don't mollycoddle each other."* In Blackwood on Fridays folk wander over Market Square to have lunch together in Y Coed Deuon; in the Merthyr office their local pub is The Bellevue, and in Cardiff The Yard is still a favourite for end-of-week fun. The working day is demanding in its content, but not in its hours. One trainee was happy to report: *"They don't want you to work your arse off till ten every night. I usually come in at 8.30am and I leave at 5.30pm."*

## and finally...

Now the second largest law firm in Wales, Hugh James has got to be a top choice for trainees. No two training contracts need be alike here, and the overwhelming feeling is that *"you are not on a conveyor belt."* Remember that the summer scheme is a key part of the recruitment process, and remember too that this is not a purely commercial training.

# Ince & Co

## the facts

**Location:** London
**Number of partners/assistants:** 53/52
**Total number of trainees:** 17
**Seats:** 4x6 months
**Alternative seats:** Piraeus, occasional secondments

Just like Britannia, Ince & Co rules the waves. This 135-year-old firm's sails are filled with the winds of maritime expertise and excellent insurance litigation capability. Steady blasts of other work add a few knots' worth of speed to a shipshape outfit plotting a more than steady course.

## do you need to go to sea?

At Ince, the swell of the sea is never far away so you have to get your sea legs at some point. But if you don't know a lanyard from a halyard will you be allowed aboard? Of course – with little coverage of shipping law on the LPC or most degree courses, "*you can reasonably say at interview that shipping sounds interesting but you don't know much about it.*" In fact, "*claiming you've had a burning interest in shipping since childhood might raise a few eyebrows.*" Ultimately what's important is that at the end of two years' training you'll have probably discovered that "*shipping is fascinating.*" But lest you imagine you'll turn into a swarthy, peg-legged nautical litigator, we should stress that with an Ince training contract you really can chart your own course across the seven seas. With insurance and shipping as the historical core, naturally the training experience will be decidedly contentious. But the winds of change are being felt, and our sources hinted at "*more openings for transactional stuff, even in just the last year.*" Heck, the firm even has property and private client work!

## keeping watch

Like most trainees, young Incers change supervisors every six months. But unlike their contemporaries elsewhere, they don't undertake seats in the conventional sense, instead managing their own workload and focusing on things that excite them. Described as being "*one of the best features of the firm,*" our sources revelled in being "*allowed to choose the work you do,*" and thrilled to be "*going on the hunt and speaking to the partners you want to work for.*" It's definitely a system that suits more proactive and self-motivating types, who are best able to deal with an ebb and flow whereby "*you can't always refuse work, and it's often difficult*

with no one person judging if you're overloaded or underworked." No matter how difficult it is at first, "*you soon learn to go on the lookout when you see that in a few weeks you'll be running out of work.*" You also learn to keep a weather eye on the overall shape of your training contract, although helping keep things shipshape is the six-monthly supervisor swap. The swap allows you to "*keep your existing files to push to completion, but get a new influx of work as well.*"

Trainees don't fly along with all sheets to the wind. Trim is provided by "*a series of appraisals with the training principal,*" based on feedback from "*the associates and partners you've worked for.*" A committee of partners serves as lookout, ensuring breadth of training: "*If they observe that you're doing too much of one kind of work, they'll move you.*" We heard of several trainees who had "*been moved off matters that were taking up all of their time,*" but all appreciated that this was to "*make sure your workload is balanced.*" And if trainees did wryly admit that "*the nature of your relationship with supervisors depends on their age and personality,*" all were adamant that "*the majority do see their job as one of training.*" Said one straightforward source: "*Everyone I sat with was concerned to know what I was doing and how it was going, even the so-called aggressive ones.*"

## deeply fathomable

Cromarty, Forth, Tyne, Dogger: variable becoming north three or four. Showers. Good. If you've ever been baffled by the shipping forecast, you're not alone. Having completed the standard PSC in a two-week burst, trainees get a further two-week induction course on all things nautical. So maybe they don't learn how to splice rope or tie knots, but they are brought up to speed on "*areas that aren't covered at law school. For example, sessions on charter parties are crucial because otherwise they'd be a completely foreign language.*" What begins as arcane, swiftly becomes everyday. Eventually the only question left is 'Do you prefer your shipping wet or dry?'

Ince acts for some of the biggest cargo owners, charterers, insurers and shipowners, and has actually managed to shrug off a recent downturn in reported shipping cases to perform at its best level for several years. Wherever in the world ships encounter problems involving grounding, weather, unforeseen disasters, loss of cargo, accidental pollution or political issues, there's a fair chance Ince will be acting for interested parties. Late in 2004, lawyers represented owners and insurers of Tropic Brilliance when the fully loaded tanker ran aground and blocked the Suez canal for three days. They also received instructions from owners and P&I clubs concerning the oil tanker Prestige and the bulk cargo ship Selendang Ayu which sank off the coasts of Spain and Alaska respectively, both resulting in major pollution. In fact, Ince's emergency response team is often instructed on marine disasters within minutes of their occurrence. The excitement generated by headline matters is, as one trainee commented: "*Thrilling! We just get the best work. Every casualty or big insurance case seems to come our way. You see something on the news, come into work and it's on the books. With Piper Alpha there were two instructions, one 19 and the other 20 minutes after the event.*"

Such disasters are the so-called 'wet' side of shipping because they happen at sea. Trainees learn that the lawyer's reality when dealing with '*collisions and salvage*' involves considerable "*preparation of fact summaries and witness statements*" with a view to battling with other parties. By contrast, 'dry' shipping centres on contractual problems including charterparty and cargo disputes, plus a range of transactional work. Said one trainee: "*My supervisor had me assist on contract matters worth millions and let me run smaller dry cases almost entirely by myself.*" Diversity of experience is a major attraction, but although the opportunities for travel and the excitement of wet work (everyone loves a good disaster) has an attractive sheen ("*the wet boys think they're really*

cool*"), the reality can be somewhat different – "*you're lined up to go somewhere like Bolivia or Canada, then at the last minute the trip is cancelled.*" For an extended trip overseas, you'll want to apply for Ince's only overseas seat in the Greek port of Piraeus.

## dry berth

Despite the flotilla of shipping matters, it is possible to "*carve out a non-shipping line for yourself*" (not our pun for once). Some of our sources had done just this: "*I did a lot of specialist energy work, a fair bit of insurance and some landlord and tenant,*" declared one. If corporate practice interests you then trainees recommend "*going for a few beers with the lawyers in the business finance group who focus on non-contentious corporate work.*" It often comes with an energy or aviation slant. An even surer path to dry land is to be found in professional indemnity litigation. Ince's insurance practice handles "*some really high-quality work*" and trainees get involved with identifying cases, disclosure exercises and even drafting. Mainly because "*the cases are massive,*" the levels of responsibility can be lower here, but are nevertheless satisfying. Massive, by the way, means multimillion-pound instructions for a number of insurance companies.

All our sources recognised that "*you have to work to establish yourself and prove your worth,*" not least because "*partners do recommend trainees to each other.*" As such, it really is "*up to you to put yourself about.*" As a consequence of the "*robust*" environment in which trainees work, it perhaps isn't surprising that our sources were "*not the type that get pushed around easily, quite bullish and assertive people.*" Such personality traits allowed them to fit in at a firm that is populated by "*rugged individuals who pride themselves on a no-nonsense approach.*" However, trainees had also noticed the onset of "*a slightly more touchy-feely approach*" designed to "*engender a team atmosphere.*" And at cabin boy level? "*As a group of trainees we're close;*

*we're all mates outside work."* In work, *"if you have a problem in the office, you e-mail and everyone responds with advice."*

## merry celeste

If there is a warming of the air, then trainees put it down to the recent move from *"old and skanky"* premises to the top two floors of the positively sparkling International House in St Catherine's Dock. Still close to the firm's traditional Tower Bridge berth, the new office is *"nice and spacious with fantastic views"* thanks to *"wraparound glass walls."* The pretty vistas may be easy on the eye, but the real effect of the move has been to *"increase morale a lot,"* resulting in *"a sense of going places."* Some legacy of the past does live on – we're told *"you have to maintain the sober, conservative-shirts look,"* although trainees understand that this is key to *"Ince's serious and hardworking image, as well as clients' expectations."* Overall, there is a *"confident sense of direction about the place at present,"* and trainees happily reflect upon *"what must be one of the best pay-to-hour ratios in London: an average day is 9am to 6.30pm with the odd, unusual midnight thrown in."* In short, *"the place is like a ghost town after 8.30pm."*

Trainees enjoy nights out together, even if the office move means their traditional drinking haunts are no more. The bars and restaurants in St Catherine's Dock are being carefully examined, and this may account for *"uneven attendance at the monthly office drinks – sometimes it's packed, others not."* However, the Christmas ball was undoubtedly *"fantastic – the senior partner gave a speech and when we all went out to Charley's nightclub he was the last man standing."* Sports-wise, there is five-a-side football, rugby, sailing, golf and karting to be enjoyed. Trainees did notice that despite the lack of formal 'departments' within the firm, socially *"people group together along the lines of their specialism."* They added that in work terms *"there's a lot of going back and forth between areas on cases,"* which in turn *"does great things for social cohesion."* Such thoughts

prompted many to return to the habitual Ince theme of *"diversity and fluidity in training,"* several trainees suggesting that it is a feature that continues post qualification. Said one: *"As an NQ you carry on working out what areas you like, the partners seek you out, and somewhere in the middle you find your niche."* In September 2005, 11 of the 12 qualifying trainees stayed with the firm to discover their metier.

## and finally...

Ince & Co offers top-notch shipping and insurance work, and would particularly suit those of a litigious disposition.

# Irwin Mitchell

## the facts

**Location:** Sheffield, Leeds, Birmingham, London
**Number of partners/assistants:** 84/182
**Total number of trainees:** 42
**Seats:** 4x6 months
**Alternative seats:** Secondments
**Extras:** Pro bono – various legal projects

From humble roots in Edwardian Sheffield, Irwin Mitchell is now one of the nation's largest providers of legal services. A personal injury practice that outstrips almost all comers is just one of its many enticements.

## viva españa!

IM's tale is the stuff of legend. The firm began life as a criminal outfit representing gang members in the badlands of Sheffield. Since then it has steadily branched out and now covers everything from human rights issues in employment, healthcare and housing provision, to a £145 million bond issue for Sheffield City Council. During the 1990s the firm went national, initially through a Leeds merger and then via offices in London and Birmingham. Turning over £102 million in 2004/5, it is now taking on more trainees than ever and continually having to keep an eye on its ability to accommodate staff. A giant new purpose-built office in Sheffield is in the pipeline – naturally *"open plan to enhance our team-work environment."*

Fuelling the growth is a client base that includes charities such as Age Concern and Mensa, big companies including British Steel and AXA Sun Life, and the man on the street (often in large numbers, as class actions are one of the firm's strong suits).

After assuring its national presence, IM has opened up two new homes in Madrid and Marbella. A succession of successful claims against the likes of First Choice Holidays and Thomsons has convinced the firm that its number one travel team needed to go where the action and package holiday tummy bugs are. However, one sneaky source quipped: *"Madrid is a name – a plaque on the wall – and there were vicious rumours that the Marbella office is just a couple of sun loungers for the partners."* Surely not? *"No, not really – Irwin ate the Spanish firm Lorenzo Zurburge whole."*

The move to España is in keeping with IM's history of *"merging, consolidating, expanding and then merging again,"* a process that has continued since it ventured beyond Sheffield for the first time in 1994. Whether sunny Spain awaits future trainees is *"up in the air,"* so leave that factor 15 at home on interview day. What you might like to take with you is a decent degree from a redbrick university and *"a personable and down-to-earth character."* We note that time spent paralegalling for the firm is another common route, though IM has an absolutely vast army of paralegals, legal execs and non-qualified case handlers, so a job offer as a paralegal should not be regarded as a first step to a training contract.

## very moving

Every year, recruits from around the network descend on Sheffield for their PSC training. *"The mutual support is great,"* said one source, *"it's nice to know you can rely on other people going through the same thing."* IM's training is fulsome: there are departmental skills seminars and ample lectures on legal topics. Appraisals every three months are both a chance to set aims and *"tell you what you're good at."* Don't get us wrong, trainees do have a few significant gripes, namely seat allocation and office moves. Aside from the usual Law Society contentious/non-contentious requirements, no seats are compulsory; however, on joining the firm, a trainee will become increasingly familiar with the concept of *"business need."* *"You'll hear that phrase a lot,"* one source warned. And indeed we did. To give the term some context: *"Business need dictates where you go, and sometimes it feels like a lottery."*

Unless closely tied to an area through marriage and children, all trainees move offices at some stage of their training contract, commonly with only six weeks to prepare for relocation. We heard of some people commuting between cities and others contending with rent on two homes. *"They won't help you find a place to live,"* came a plaintive cry, *"the best you'll get is a train ticket to your new city and maybe a day off to look for lodgings."* We have to say that a number of our sources were *"a bit peeved"* at IM's disinclination to provide greater assistance, though we also heard that moving to another office for six months can be a good bargaining tool when it comes to subsequent seats. *"If they've pissed you off once then they are aware they've done that to you."* An impromptu move could be the best way of getting your bum on a coveted seat.

## all the gory details

IM's chart-topping PI work involves multi-party claims, and its caseload is bulked up by referrals from trade unions. Over the years, the firm has represented thousands of coal miners suffering from illness or injury sustained at work – everything from emphysema and silicosis to persistent knee complaints. With compensation formulae applicable to most of these mining cases, *"there is a lot of esoteric work – statistical analyses and data collection."* You'll use a calculator less on multi-party consumer claims, where part of the trainee's job is to keep abreast of trends in pharmaceutical usage. *"Through media searches you'll be keeping an eye out for test study results for drugs with a view to spotting possible negligence."* Other class actions handled by the firm include Equitable Life, dodgy timeshares and vCJD. Is it just us or is IM beginning to sound like a cross between the *Cook Report* and *Watchdog* teams?

The mainstay of a seat in the firm's equally respected clinical negligence department is *"reviewing all the medical records from GPs, hospitals and physios."* Obstetric malpractice and neuro trauma are common, so trainees quickly learn to *"talk to gynaecologists and midwives, doctors and consultants in order to pass their findings on to counsel."* Be warned: these cases are slow burners and *"after the initial instruction is received, medical records take two to three months to come through and then expert instruction takes a further two to three months. By that time the seat's over."* A strong stomach is best. Literally, in some cases – *"having to learn about colon surgery isn't always the nicest thing in the world... especially when clients send in their photos!"*

## carry on cruising

Being responsible for the day-to-day running of cases in travel litigation means *"liaising with clients on a regular basis."* You'll need to suppress any giggles when claimants describe the effects of paella-induced diarrhoea in dodgy two-star hotels. Many of the hearings take place abroad, so the trainee won't be in and out of court that often. It's more a case of providing documentary support for group food poisoning claims or other cases such as that of the ill-fated P&O cruise ship Aurora which failed to convince its round-the-world passengers that engine trouble was a sufficiently good excuse for only getting them as far as the Isle of Wight.

Away from the business of sick and injured people lies commercial litigation. The exact nature of cases differs from one office to another and, by all accounts, so does the training experience. In Birmingham, expect *"more responsibility,"* because

despite not having your own files *"you get to draft more court documents and begin to take instructions from clients."* In London, large civil fraud matters and group litigation are exciting but less likely to give trainees much responsibility. What it lacks in drafting opportunities it makes up for in glamour, with trainees getting the chance to sit behind counsel in the High Court. And it need be no less exciting back in the office where trainees assist on 'search and seizure' applications. To explain: *"You might act for the defendant when another company comes a-knocking at the door with a court order. They turn up at 6am and seize anything they want to take – people literally rifle through underwear."* Far from the dramas in the smalls drawers of London, commercial litigation in Sheffield enables trainees to run files from start to finish. Sometimes they will be worth as little as £200 to £300 each, admittedly low on the legal Richter scale, but at least they allow even first-seaters to become their own boss.

## in demand

There are corporate seats in each office, though these usually also cover other work. In Sheffield you might also touch on charities law; in Leeds the seat also covers IT and IP. This particular hybrid brought, for one trainee, *"lots of IP for the first six weeks, then the corporate team whirred into action and I became solely a corporate trainee."* The challenge in IP might include handling trade mark applications solo; in corporate, an AIM flotation could keep the trainee busy with *"verification of prospectuses and snooping around companies' shares... quite a big job."* On bigger deals, *"cancelling life for a while"* is advisable because *"you will work right through sometimes – 8am to midnight or 3am."* Generally though, trainees' hours are far more respectable, with 8.30am until 6pm being the norm.

IM trainees are difficult to type, and perhaps this is because *"Irwin Mitchell doesn't want blank canvases; they want mature trainees, though not necessarily in years. We certainly don't sing a firm song like DLA!"* For a profitable national firm, IM is also relatively free of machismo, and so *"you don't have a room full of alpha males jockeying with each other."* This clearly appealed to the September 2005 qualifiers: 11 of the 14 stayed with the firm. On the other hand, you may have noticed that it is not the most generous of the firms we cover in this book, with only modest relocation assistance, discretionary loans to its prospective trainees and a downright idiosyncratic LPC fee payment system.

A summer barbecue sums up IM's no-nonsense approach to socialising, and there are *"the odd away days"* for team building. Across the firm, one Friday each month is a dress-down day, and various teams celebrate the fact with *"first Friday drinks."* In Leeds this means moseying to Indie Joze and Plush; in Sheffield the regular haunts include *"The Wig & Pen and The Priory; we tend to stick away from All Bar One, it's full of bloody lawyers now!"* Christmas is the time for pushing the boat out; for instance, the branch Christmas party in Brum was held at the five-star Hyatt, a champagne reception melting into a meal and disco. At this point our source's memory became *"hazy... but someone did sing Summer Lovin' at the karaoke."* The pan-firm Christmas party is *"mammoth, to say the least."* Held in Sheffield's Ponds Forge Sports Centre, the real challenge for the organisers is making the venue look something other than *"a sports hall with tinsel."*

## and finally...

A training contract at Irwin Mitchell is challenging: you must be good on paper, firm in character and WTT (willing to travel). Which is undoubtedly where a GSOH will come in handy. Anyone intent on claimant personal injury or clinical litigation would be negligent to overlook the firm, though of course its appeal goes far wider than this.

# Jones Day

## the facts

**Location:** London
**Number of partners/assistants:** 40/80
**Total number of trainees:** 42
**Seats:** Non-rotational
**Alternative seats:** None
**Extras:** Pro bono – Waterloo legal Advice Centre

Our subject, Jones Day in London, was born of a 2002 merger between the American law firm of the same name and the UK-based Gouldens. The latter was famed for its radical non-rotational, seat-free training system (henceforth *"the method"*), big salaries and independent-minded lawyers. Has anything changed?

## english mustard

Headquartered in Cleveland, Jones Day employs 2,200 lawyers spread over 29 locations worldwide. Gouldens, by contrast, had 40 partners and a reputation for top-shelf (albeit smaller top-shelf) corporate work. Three years on, now that they've had time to get to know each other, what do the lawyers make of the arranged marriage? Clearly it was not to everyone's liking because the London operation has lost 11 partners in the past year, the finance group having been hit particularly hard. It has also lost its private client arm after another partner defection. But there is a decent dowry for trainees – the firm has bumped up their salaries such that second-years now take home a whopping £40k.

Despite having been brought into the Jones Day fold, trainees say there is still a strong element of the old Gouldens autonomy about the place. One told us: *"Day to day I don't feel part of a global firm. There's not much contact with trainees from other offices, and you will find no more Americans here than many other London firms."* *"It's more or less the same firm that I signed up with,"* reported another. There have been some cosmetic changes, but mainly it's "*administrative stuff.*" It seems that Cleveland has learned a lesson from past mergers; accordingly, "*London is run by London... Jones Day used to try to run things centrally. Now they rely on local partners across the world.*" Isn't that called globalisation?

## home alone?

Let's examine 'the method'. In the absence of a seat system, "*you're shown to your own office on the first day and there doesn't seem to be any rhyme or reason to where you sit. As a trainee you walk the floors and knock on people's doors, building up relationships as you go.*" Not being forced into departments enables you to build up greater experience of the work you most enjoy. "*The beauty of this place is that you can get very entrenched in your chosen department. You're not forever moving around, so you can build good contacts and good friendships.*" It is very much a case of learning by "*potential mistakes,*" or rather "*when you know there's not so much scrutiny you have to have keener eyes and be more alert. You don't have a person leaning over your shoulder.*"

Greater autonomy and independence appeal to a certain type – the archetypal hunter-gatherers, comfortable with a carcass of some corporate beast swung across their shoulders. If you want to stay back and paint the cave or de-louse your friends, or you are happier visiting a well laid-out corner shop for provisions than lurking in the bushes with a spear, this is not the place for you. All we can advise readers is this: underestimate the demands of the method at your peril.

Darwinian it may be, but the method is at least meritocratic. "*One of the best things is when you get repeat work and you're asked to come in on deals because someone trusts you rather than just because you're arbitrarily sat there.*" One warrior/trainee was pretty stoical: "*If you get slighted you pick yourself up, dust yourself off and fight another day.*" Another told us: "*With this system you can really grab training by the balls. I felt that the sky was the limit.*" But being out on the plain by yourself can be a lonely experi-

ence and "*there will be some nights when you feel that the sky is falling in.*" One trainee confessed: "*I was slightly nervous about the training system, but I decided to put myself in their hands – they have experience after all.*"

"*Because you're no one's trainee, you just have to go out and find yourself a mentor, someone you enjoy working with and someone who can teach you the craft.*" The client exposure is roundly considered to be excellent, and to prove this one source informed us: "*I have two meetings this afternoon, one on my own and another with a team member. As trainees, we're left to handle our own clients.*" Another trainee added: "*The partners don't muscle in, they're happy to leave us to negotiate settlements.*" It all adds up to a big burden, but one that is accepted readily. "*I am working harder than peers from law school but the work isn't menial so there's no resentment.*"

## flights of fantasy

To give you some idea of some of Jones Day's latest work, litigators have represented TUI Northern Europe, owners of Thomson Holidays, Britannia Airways and Lunn Poly in defending injunction proceedings brought by Warwick District Council concerning the building of an interim passenger facility at Coventry Airport. They have also advised Alfa on the litigation aspects of the $20 billion TNK-BP merger of 2003. It was the largest ever investment by an English company in Russia, and the largest ever Russian transaction. They acted, too, for Waste Recycling Group in a contractual dispute involving one of the UK's largest waste disposal sites. Other litigation clients included Motorola, Occidental Petroleum, Cardinal Health and Dell.

In property, lawyers handle high-value investment transactions including the £50 million purchase of land on behalf of Arsenal FC and the £97 million sale of Fulham Broadway Retail Centre. They are also involved in finance transactions, including a £550 million refinancing and securitisation for Arlington Business Parks Partnership and a

£432 million restructuring of the City of London Office Unit Trust. Jones Day's investment fund practice acted on IPOs for Dexion Trading and Dexion Equity Alternative, as well as for Collins Stewart on fund raisings by Westbury Property. In the burgeoning hedge fund field (clearly a side effect of the US merger) lawyers acted for Perry Capital on a significant investment in Resolution Life Group, for a major hedge fund shareholder in British Energy's restructuring, and also for US hedge funds on sovereign debt transactions in Albania, Bulgaria, Congo, Iraq, Nicaragua and North Korea. However, even with all this overseas business, as yet there are no overseas trainee postings, be it to an Outpost of Tyranny or anywhere else.

## grub's up

One side effect of the method is that "*you can build up a reputation for yourself pretty quickly.*" An annual appraisal is organised after comments have been gathered from everyone you've worked for. "*We also have to report [to the training partner and trainee co-ordinator] on a weekly basis with a work diary, which is a brief description of what you're doing. Every quarter we see Liz [the training partner] and she goes through a checklist of what you're expected to cover. You tick off what you think you've done and if it's not balanced she tells you to look elsewhere. You can't get away with missing stuff out.*"

Trainees go to Washington in September for a week of seminars washed down with "*lots of barbecues and parties.*" It helps to put things in context because London is still very much focused on London work. "*You really get a perception of how big the firm is when you meet people from Hong Kong, Milan and Madrid.*" The trip has certainly proved to be one of the most popular aspects of the merger. Back on home turf, "*in the first year you'll have two lunchtime seminars a week, going down to once a week in your second year.*" It's an excuse for a really good lunch. "*There's a kitchen upstairs with a fully trained cook – as a poor trainee, two free meals a week is not to be sniffed at!*" Over lunch with the

training partner and trainee manager once a month you can speak your mind, and this can be a helpful process. "*There are lots of administrative things which get up people's noses, but there is no problem with saying we have issues with XYZ.*" By way of example, "*someone had a gripe about some departments focusing on one trainee, leaving no opportunity for others to get involved.*"

## law and peace

"*There is very little hierarchy*" and "*trainees are treated extremely well because you're not indentured to anyone. It's an open market so people who want you to work for them will treat you well.*" However, one NQ warned that "*when you qualify you land with a bump. As a trainee you feel you're batting above your game; when you qualify you're the same as everyone else.*" Always remember, the game reserves are not endless. One trainee admitted: "*The system is quite political and competitive,*" but "*most are happy here up to five or six years after qualification.*" "*It's not a stepping stone in the way the magic circle might be;*" in fact, it's more a way of life. On the downside, "*the bureaucracy has definitely increased; there are lots of new forms flying around, but the firm has managed to keep its personality despite having been swallowed up.*"

One thing that has changed since the merger is that some of Gouldens' "*flamboyance*" has melted away. "*They always had a reputation for earning lots and spending lots... that's been tempered by merging with a cost-effective US operation.*" One trainee summed up the thoughts of several when they said: "*If I was in charge of the London office I would try and get the Americans to back off a little bit – I'd also bring back the summer party that got cancelled.*" At least there is a big Christmas party, and they even have a trainee pantomime to keep spirits up. Last year *A Christmas Carol* involved "*looking back into the past of Gouldens and the future of Jones Day. They gave us a day off to prepare it and then a meal to say thank you.*" Another trainee fired off this warning shot to their masters: "*The Americans must understand the difference – here people expect free drinks and nights out. I would reintroduce compulsory drinking!"* We could almost hear the war cries of the other trainees in the distance.

## and finally...

To stretch our caveman metaphor to within an inch of its life, be aware that you only get to eat what you kill at Jones Day in London, and if you prefer to relax in your cave all day you might not find a space round the campfire when night falls.

# Kendall Freeman

## the facts

**Location:** London
**Number of partners/assistants:** 21/37
**Total number of trainees:** 16
**Seats:** 4x6 months
**Alternative seats:** Secondments
**Extras:** Pro bono – LawWorks

Kendall Freeman is a medium-sized London firm focused on the insurance sector. Formed in 2003, it rose like a phoenix from smouldering ashes left behind after the dissolution of a broader commercial firm called DJ Freeman.

## it's knot what you know...

With profits soaring, it looks as if the Kendall Freeman project is a success. Its impressive insurance client list incorporates AXA, Direct Line, HSBC Insurance Brokers, Equitable of the United States, Chubb, new client TCRU Bermuda and various Lloyd's Names. Much of the work done for these clients is contentious, the firm recently flitting between America, France and London for AXA RE on tri-jurisdictional film finance litigation, and heading for the Commercial Court for Lumbermens Mutual's £19 million insurance spat with Glasgow's Braehead shopping centre developer, Bovis. In the complex realm of reinsurance, KF has

been instrumental in the ongoing multi-jurisdictional fallout from the bankruptcy of US reinsurers T&N, whose audit book closed leaving parent company Federal-Mogul with a £500 million muddle requiring KF to unpick the knots. When not contending in the courts, the firm's insurance lawyers like nothing better than to dole out complex regulatory advice. Worried that you know nothing of the insurance world? No need. At the beginning of an insurance seat *"they take you aside and teach you all the terms. They also give you a tour of the Lloyd's building and explain how the system operates – it's just like a big market really."*

## resistance is futile

Trainees undertake four seats and you just have to look at this firm's work profile to know that the training will lean more to the contentious side than most. Insurance litigation? *"It's gonna happen!"* is the way one source put it. How right they were. It is vital to get an early appreciation of what lies at the heart of the firm; indeed, the experience is key to understanding most of its practice areas. Even the corporate seat, for instance, was regarded as *"a kind of insurance."* Unsurprising when you consider that typical work included the recent MBO evacuation at one Lloyd's grouping and the complicated restructuring of another.

Available in two flavours – insurance/reinsurance and general commercial – litigation seats provide trainees with a relatively research-based workload. It could be *"a particular point of insurance or reinsurance, or maybe an arbitration query."* Snatches of drafting come within their reach – *"indemnity provisions, confidentiality issues, consent orders..."* Litigation seats can have a nasty habit of turning into months of drudgery, particularly when cases are high in value, but on the subject of mundane photocopying and bundling, there was good news – *"we have paralegals who do most of it."* Some cases can last *"for years,"* so while you're decoding a company's structure or preparing disclosure documents, it is unlikely you'll see a matter from start to finish. To compensate, trainees are exposed to smaller pieces of more basic litigation and even get a chance to make the odd court application.

## coalition of the billing

KF litigators have a multitude of talents and specialist areas of expertise, including one of the firm's unique selling points – a public international law practice. Just a few firms operate in this field and our subject firm is one of the most experienced of these. It is currently recovering billions of dollars worth of assets looted by former heads of state, among them Nigeria's former dictator General Sani Abacha who embezzled somewhere between $2 and $3 billion. Working alongside the UN, the Commonwealth, OECD and Transparency International, KF lawyers are intent on tracing the secreted cash, while striving for state immunity on behalf of Nigeria's government and its Central Bank. The firm is additionally working on the very definition of Nigeria, demarcating her four land and two maritime boundaries through the National Boundary Commission. Our sources were naturally reticent about their involvement in such "*sensitive matters*," limiting their comments regarding "*asset tracing*" and "*maritime boundary work*" to the bare minimum.

Fresh from law school their well-honed research skills are exercised daily. "*A handle on current affairs definitely helps*," especially when instructions are taken from the likes of Iraq's Coalition Provisional Authority. Work also comes from the governments of Somaliland, Kenya and Pakistan. Anyone who hankered after, but never signed on the dotted line for, a job as our man in Addis Ababa or Baghdad will be interested to note that the UK Foreign and Commonwealth Office and Commonwealth Secretariat are also on the firm's books.

Defamation is another interesting area of litigation. Take the saga of Sheikh Khalid bin Mahfouz, accused of links to Osama bin Laden, which has preoccupied both the press and KF for some time. After settling for substantial damages and an apology from *The Mail on Sunday*, the Sheikh then went on to win the same from Pluto Press. Most recently it was Bonus Books that was paying up and saying sorry. "*It's good to have names people recognise as a reference point for the firm*," said one trainee, although another noted: "*It can be equally rewarding working on the small unreported cases where you get more of the interesting work to do*." Another saga is that of the very rich man who owns Harrods. At the start of 2004, with KF's help Mr Al Fayed won libel damages and an apology from the contrite publishers of *The Mail on Sunday* after allegations concerning his finances. Come 2005 and KF had none other than Fulham FC on its client list, coaxing the club through its bitter employment dispute with former manager Jean Tigana. For those yet to spot the connection, Mr Al Fayed is chairman of Fulham.

"*Quite coveted and fairly popular*," the employment seat refreshes the parts other seats can't reach. "*You get the human interest element there, even though you're representing defendant companies on the whole*," revealed one source. "*Client contact is maximal*," and with a high turnover of cases you'll also get smaller files to run under supervision. Awaiting the employment trainee is a mass of varied work from drafting claim forms, taking witness statements and the odd bit of research into bonus entitlements to "*quick queries as to whether a company has to pay this person's maternity leave and stuff on the new age discrimination legislation*."

Trainees can additionally take seats in corporate, construction and insurance insolvency or be seconded to a major client where they find that working in-house is rather like private practice sans specialisms – "*you have to know a bit of everything. One day someone will ring with a sale of goods query, the next day it'll be a data protection problem and the day after that competition dilemmas*."

# the true picture

## lights out

Back in the bosom of the firm, trainees sit with their supervisors (*"usually partners"*) from whom they learn both directly and indirectly. *"Osmosis is the thing – listening to a senior partner on the phone is terrific, you learn just from that how to treat a client."* Trainees additionally have a junior lawyer as an 'aunt' or 'uncle' to buddy them through the contract, plus a mentor partner, the best of which offer careers advice.

KF's office on Fetter Lane is conveniently located *"close to the RCJ and all the barristers' chambers."* Close too, are the bars and eateries of Farringdon and Clerkenwell. At the moment the office has a view of a building site. *"It used to be a publisher's, now I can see St Paul's!"* rejoiced one source, neglecting to tell us that the firm had only recently emerged from litigation with the developer of the site. Enter stage left former DJ Freeman client Land Securities with its proposal to plonk an 18-storey tower on the land. Despite KF winning £50,000 damages in its right-to-light claim, the building will go up and the vista onto St Paul's will be no more than a memory. The right-to-light crusade is an exemplar for the firm as a whole: *"If you're interested in litigation come here!"* In fact, one source was so adamant on this point that they announced that *"only a fool"* would apply without wanting a solid grounding in litigation.

*"Enthusiasm is key,"* according to most sources. The current trainees are a group of straightforward redbrick university graduates, all of whom cited the firm's size as one of their main reasons for choosing it. *"You're not trainee number 62 here and you're not anonymous,"* asserted one. By your fourth seat everyone will know your name. Proving there is no *"them and us"* hierarchy, partners sit down to canteen grub with staff, and they don't mind stumping up for a drink or two at one of the local pubs around Fetter Lane. The firm's social committee organises trips to Walthamstow dog track and Somerset House for ice skating in winter, with tennis matches and softball in the summer. The annual summer party this year took place on board the HMS

*Belfast...* hopefully no one was lost overboard after a few too many shandies. Few are lost overboard on qualification: in September 2005 six of the eight stayed on, with the other two opting to go elsewhere for different types of practice.

## and finally...

Intriguing cases, intriguing clients, big-bucks insurers and a secure knowledge that when you buy your foie gras from Harrods just a little bit of it already belongs to you, a Kendall Freeman contract is definitely worth a gander.

# Kirkpatrick & Lockhart, Nicholson Graham LLP

## the facts

**Location:** London
**Number of partners/assistants:** 51/61
**Total number of trainees:** 21
**Seats:** 4x6 months
**Alternative seats:** Occasional secondments
**Extras:** Pro bono – Battersea Law Centre; language training

The 2005 linking of UK mid-sizer Nicholson Graham & Jones with US firm Kirkpatrick & Lockhart has created a 12-office organisation that stretches from London to LA.

## in the words of david cassidy

At the stroke of midnight on 31st December 2004, while the rest of London was distracted by fireworks and champagne corks, Nicholson Graham & Jones quietly slipped away, arm in arm with a hunky Yank. Was this a drunken festive pull it would regret in the morning? Not at all. NGJ had been flirting with Kirkpatrick & Lockhart for some months. The pair now go by the married name of Kirkpatrick & Lockhart Nicholson Graham, and despite *"a nervousness about it"* (not so much how soon to say the 'L word' but fears that *"the billable hours would go* up"), we hear that the bashful Brits are *"getting used to the Americans and have been pleasantly surprised."* Those who adopt the Hugh Grant approach to transatlantic relations will be pleased to hear that *"we are still very British... probably."* Certainly, *"there is no swearing allegiance to the American flag."* In fact, with not a baseball cap in sight, we sensed that, for many, the merger *"does seem to have passed us by. The impression was that it is not about entering an entirely new world."* In the main, it is business as usual in London, though one source muttered concerns that Kirkpatrick's stateside ban on junk food in its offices might result in Londoners being *"subjected to healthy eating and California lifestyles."* We checked: you can still get Twix and Mars bars from the vending machines.

Though *"you wouldn't notice an Americanisation as such, the firm is a bit more vibrant."* The merger seems to have kick-started ambitious plans *"to double in size over the next few years;"* already there have been new arrivals in banking, corporate and IT. There are plans to revamp the firm's Cannon Street offices, where we hear *"the edges are fraying a bit,"* and a new *"all-singing, all-dancing"* accounting system is clear evidence that the merger has given the firm a huge boost.

## survival kit

While the firm may be *"going places,"* for now at least trainees are stuck at home. *"The possibility of secondments has been raised"* (of course) though in the meanwhile there is plenty to keep trainees occupied in London. They also seem to have had high hopes for a big tailgate party in the USA to mark the start of play, but had to resign themselves to listening to others' tales. There was a 'retreat' in Boston for all the partners, and 20 assistants from London *"all went to Pittsburgh for a symposium."* The closest trainees get to the land of the brave and the home of the free is by monthly video link-up to a conference, sorry, *"town hall meeting."* So no party invite, but at least trainees came back from their Christmas hols to a goodie bag – *"a branded rucksack"* containing *"a fetching fleece, mugs and a tin with a tea bag or two in it."*

The merger has provided the London office with *"a depth of talent, money, experience and manpower that we didn't have before,"* and trainees are convinced Kirkpatrick in London will *"punch higher."* Certainly the firm's three core areas of corporate, real estate and litigation have always put up a decent fight for medium-sized work. These three departments *"balance each other out"* (although *"within each department there is a very different take on which is dominant!"*) and so it is only natural that trainees are required to spend time in each. If you think three compulsory seats sounds a little restrictive in a four-seat system, note that *"they are very flexible"* so corporate includes banking, property includes construction, and a whole host of work (including property, banking, insolvency and general commercial cases, employment, travel and IP matters) huddles under the litigation umbrella. Satisfied trainees advise that *"it is up to you to stand up and say what you want more of,"* adding that those in charge have *"an uncanny knack of putting people in the right seat."*

## the big three

The corporate department includes Kirkpatrick's small but respected partnership and private equity groups plus a strong M&A practice. One source explained: *"We don't do the billion-dollar deals, we do the £300 million deals and below, and the AIM work. Not the FTSE 100s but the FTSE 250s."* Recent transactions have included the £30 million acquisition for Air Music & Media of budget DVD supplier Music Box. Said one trainee: *"You more or less just slot into the deal,"* and if you're lucky *"you might be given your own part that you are responsible for,"* even if it is only *"filing and elements of due diligence."* Contrast that with a role on tiny transactions where you are *"actually drafting shareholders' agreements and business asset transfer agreements."* One, summing up the experience, told us: *"I felt like a proper lawyer."* However, *"some people are nervous of cor-*

# the true picture

*porate because it is perceived to have the longest hours.*" Inevitably, transactional seats can be demanding when things hot up, but despite "*the odd blip*" of weekend working and a smattering of long nights, a standard day in the office is 9am until 6.30pm.

The property team has a bias towards finance and acts for banks and financial institutions including HSBC, Lloyds TSB and Bank of Scotland. Straight property work includes disposals and acquisitions of portfolios worth in excess of £100 million for clients such as Hanson, Laing O'Rourke and Young's Brewery. Here trainees get "*a lot of responsibility very early,*" one telling us: "*On average I had 25-30 files of my own and was very much allowed to just get on with it.*" Staple trainee fare includes "*lease negotiations and licences to assign or to permit alterations.*" On such matters, "*the responsibility is on your shoulders. The letter comes in and it is for you to respond and have the first crack at drafting.*" While "*it is quite a tough first seat,*" the benefits are "*a lot of face time with clients*" and "*a chance to stand on your own two feet.*"

Litigation experiences are broad – you might tick the box by taking an insolvency seat or undergo a full-blown contentious seat in the commercial litigation department. Here, specialist cases relating to property, banking and sport are mixed in with general commercial disputes. "*Variety is also noticeable in the scale of cases.*" Larger disputes bring "*quite a bit of bundling, etc.*" though trainees reported favourably on plenty of court time, conferences with counsel, and drafting witness statements. These more interesting tasks can certainly be performed on the smaller files that trainees are permitted to manage alone.

With the three compulsory seats done, a final seat can be selected from construction, banking, tax, employment, IP, technology and sport. A first-class travel team also takes a trainee to help on work for the likes of Gullivers Travel Associates, ABTA, Carnival, Kuoni and Air Jamaica. Recent work for the team has ranged from extending Eurostar's lease

of their train sets to GNER to successfully defending a claim against Thomas Cook for damages for personal injury arising from holidays overseas.

## how much love is there?

Trainees are always "*paired up*" in a room with a supervisor, allowing them to "*learn a lot by osmosis.*" We're told: "*You'll be given as much responsibility as you want and as much or as little supervision as you need.*" Departmental training sessions and formal end-of-seat appraisals keep everyone on point, plus "*you can ask for a mini-appraisal half way through a seat.*" Chances are you won't need to ask though – supervisors are "*always willing to check over work*" and "*if you do something good people do say thank you.*" Feedback works both ways, and regular 'Ask Tony' sessions give junior staff the opportunity to have anonymously submitted questions answered in an open session by managing partner Tony Griffiths.

"*Anyone totally ruthlessly ambitious*" might not fare well in an environment where "*people aren't looking to cut others down in the process of looking out for their own career.*" As well as pockets of "*very good friends,*" we hear "*there is always a couple... Somewhere down the line there is always a romantic liaison.*" Those we spoke to came from a mix of universities, including a couple from Oxbridge; degrees ranged from theology to psychology, and ages spanned twenty-nothing to thirty-something. Not all extremes are covered. One source felt "*the überconfident and the überunconfident wouldn't do so well.*" Here it's more a case of "*being a slightly bigger fish in a slightly smaller sea,*" so applicants "*interested in working on the mega deals*" should perhaps look elsewhere. The merger has brought a wealth of qualification jobs, with 11 available to the ten qualifiers in September 2005. Nine people accepted positions.

## fine dining

In a firm that fosters open channels of communications and close relations, the existence of a partner's dining room is "*a bit of a bugbear*" for many younger staff. The consensus seems to be that *"it is not very cohesive to have partners eating in one room where food is provided and everyone else going to get a sandwich somewhere."* If the merger really has *"brought an impetus to change things"* perhaps the partners could consider opening it up as a staff deli, as they did over at Dechert when it hooked up with Americans. We trust the future of the annual country house weekend is assured for all eternity. The entire fee-earning staff decamp for a weekend of team building and revelry. Last time, in true Blue Peter fashion, the corporate challenge required everyone to make greeting cards. Apparently, *"it is a great leveller when one of the heads of department is covered from head to foot in glitter."* The fancy dress continued into the evening's London Underground party, which was attended by seven nuns and someone in an elephant suit accompanied by a cardboard castle. Warren Street was interpreted by people wearing bunny outfits, and while a number of partners took the easy option of tennis gear (Wimbledon), the trainees won a prize for representing Heathrow in handcrafted trolley dolly uniforms.

Back in London, *"within walking distance of the office there are ten good pubs,"* the choice as to which you frequent *"depends on your budget and who you are out with."* Interested in sport? Why not try out for the cricket team or either the men's or women's footie teams. Though it has been reinstated, the men's team was *"hoiked out of the league"* for a while after *"disciplinary problems on the pitch."* Perhaps they were confused about whether the US merger had changed the rules of engagement.

## and finally...

Even if the name is a mouthful, there's something wonderfully straightforward and sensible about Kirkpatrick & Lockhart Nicholson Graham. Nothing in life is certain, but we suspect that, even after the merger and its attendant changes, this firm is not going to disappoint students seeking a straightforward and sensible training contract with good job prospects at the end of it.

# Lawrence Graham LLP

## the facts

**Location:** London
**Number of partners/assistants:** 93/109
**Total number of trainees:** 36
**Seats:** 4x6 months
**Alternative seats:** None

Lawrence Graham is your classic mid-sized London law firm. It exhibits all the qualities long admired in such organisations, including good work in each of its three core commercial departments – business and finance, real estate and litigation – and a highly respected private client team. What's more, it can also boast very respectable profits and a debt-free bank balance.

## inbetweenies

Resting between the Goliaths of the City and the David's of the West End, LG has been a popular feature of the London legal landscape since Biblical times. Of its three commercial areas, the best known is property, though the firm makes a decent showing in litigation and mid-market corporate deals. For example, acting for Entertainment Rights (a company that acquires TV characters and brands) it bought Tell-Tale Productions, owner of the lucrative Tweenies brand. It performs well in AIM work, which is natural territory for firms of this size and, perhaps not surprising given LG's strength in real estate, a number of its biggest deals are sourced via that department or have real estate assets at their heart. Last year, for example, lawyers acted for Globe Pub Company, which bought 364 pubs for approximately £345 million. That's practically one pub for every day of the year!

Real estate business accounts for more than a third of the firm's entire revenue stream, and with

12 trainees at a time in the department, it is no secret that this work plays an important part in the training contract. Some people told us they had actively chosen the firm because of its reputation in this area and most had enjoyed the experience, even those of the view that *"property is not where my heart lies."* The department commonly hosts first-seaters (most of them herded into a central seating area dubbed *"the pig pen"*), and the work is relatively easy for newbies to get their heads around. *"I was pretty nervous to start but it was a great seat,"* recalled one old hand. Depending on who you sit with, your time will be spent on development projects, retail sector transactions, general property management issues or even telecoms work. There are also separate real estate litigation and real estate finance seats. Keeping several property lawyers busy of late is the proposed £3 billion regeneration of 240 hectares of derelict land in Cricklewood, North London. The project will create a new mixed-use urban centre with up to 5,500 homes and 400,000 square metres of offices. Another recent deal has seen lawyers advising two clients, the Universities Superannuation Scheme and Grosvenor Estates, on the purchase and development of a £167 million retail scheme in Cambridge city centre.

## one man's meat...

That trainees have different experiences in the real estate department is typical of the firm as a whole. Of the corporate department, we heard: *"One partner believes in doing things formulaically and he keeps all his lists of everything completely up to date – his transactions are very regimented. Others are more like 'Oh we'll do this tomorrow' and then tomorrow becomes next week. Working for the latter you have to be more independent; with the first partner you know that you'll be following things schematically."*

There is certainly ample variety in the seats on offer. Private client satisfies those who wish to try something other than commercial work and in the past some trainees have even spent three months in the firm's Monaco office. The firm acts for a raft of wealthy individuals, both old 'green-welly' money and foreign and domestic entrepreneurs. Also on the firm's books are a number of charities including Oxfam, RNIB, the Salvation Army, the British Legion and Friends of the Earth. Private client work is rare in a firm of this size, but there's no mystery in why LG retains its interest here – it has a superb reputation for both non-contentious trusts and tax planning, as well as trusts litigation.

In the local authorities seat, trainees assist a team of *"the loveliest people"* with housing and leisure transfers from the public to private sector. The seat has the added bonus of training in how to market and tender for new business, as well as the usual drafting and research tasks and meetings with clients. Litigation seats are always popular, and if there is one area where supply does not quite meet demand, then it is here. There is a single employment seat and a single IP seat sit as well as commercial litigation, plus there are reinsurance and shipping options at the smaller second office at St Mary Axe near Lloyd's of London. Again, in litigation the experiences vary: *"Some partners do massive financial cases that go on for ages and ages; working with others you'll get more smaller cases."* We heard from trainees who'd made small applications in court themselves – perhaps to wind up a company or make someone bankrupt – and those who'd observed cases in the Court of Appeal. There will always be time spent on administrative tasks such as preparing court bundles; however, no one said their time in the department had been blighted by these chores. Indeed, you get the sense that there is nothing deeply unpleasant going on in any part of LG. The hours are perfectly manageable (most trainees reported working from 9am to 6.30pm most days) and the mood is generally positive and encouraging.

## ... is another man's poison

Yet trainees need to be adaptable in order to manage relationships with supervisors. *"It's definitely the case that different partners have different mentalities when it comes to trainees and different*

# the true picture

*approaches to mentoring,"* one source confided. *"That can affect the quality of the training. A few are a little laisez-faire and will give you a bit of work when they think about it."* By contrast, others are *"incredibly helpful... 100% approachable and reassuring."* The property department came out especially well, with one partner in particular being practically canonised during our interviews. Overall, the supervision, encouragement and responsibility trainees received from the teams in which they worked struck us as one of the very best elements of this training contract.

And yet there is something about Lawrence Graham that can make defining the training experience, perhaps even the firm itself, a difficult task. In some ways, it is quite formal and regimented; in others, it lacks structure. For example, although you may be told that the firm has a dress-down policy, trainees say they need to wear suits as they never know when they are going to be whisked into a meeting or off to court. To give another example, a system for allocating NQ jobs is all but absent and the process requires considerable effort on the part of trainees. No jobs are advertised, so no one really knows what can be applied for. *"There is an onus on you to make things happen for yourself and that can be a hard position to be in,"* said one source. Why such a haphazard approach? *"They probably don't want to advertise a space in case they don't get who they want applying for it,"* thought another trainee. It all sounds rather unmanaged. Nonetheless there's no denying that in past years the process has usually resulted in very decent retention rates. By comparison, 2004 was a disaster with only 50% of the qualifiers staying at the firm. This year the qualifying trainees fared better, with jobs being offered to 12 of the 16 qualifiers and 11 accepting. Interestingly, when we asked trainees about the difficulties of the system we sensed no great will on their part to band together to push for a more transparent and trainee-friendly mechanism. In this instance their innate sense of independence does not serve them so well.

## small change

For the last few years we've bemoaned the fact that LG's stability and consistency gave us nothing unusual to report. This year the management (no change there, the existing administration has just secured a further term) has delivered a newsworthy item in the form of a tiny merger with the former accountancy-tied firm Tite & Lewis. It may not have been as dramatic as some of the other pairings of 2004, but the addition of five new partners and accompanying staff has gifted a new area of business – outsourcing – and the addition of a few new faces in corporate and property. Not exactly a revolution, this was utterly typical of LG's easy-does-it brand of change.

## more change

There's a corner of legal London that will for ever be associated with Lawrence Graham – Daly's wine bar, the hub of LG society. Trainees meet for drinks on a regular basis, and once or twice a month the firm's social committee will organise an event, perhaps bowling or a trip to Somerset House for ice skating. Each August the partners host a soiree on the roof of the office, overlooking the Thames, and then there are departmental Christmas parties and an annual firm-wide summer ball. But wait! The social map will surely change in 2007 when the firm moves from its offices near the Royal Courts of Justice on The Strand to the Foster-designed More London building near Tower Bridge. It sounds as if some hope the prestigious new address will boost the firm's profile, which is arguably lower than deserved.

The move can't come a moment too soon as LG's 70's era offices are showing their age. *"The lifts don't work,"* moaned one trainee, *"you can find yourself in the basement by accident... and they ping randomly."* The general verdict was that the firm is by nature *"not that swish,"* though it tries to make up for it in its art gallery-cum-lobby. *"Sometimes the art is peculiar. They've just had one piece which is a mattress with some paint on it... it's not going as far as*

*Tracey Emin: I mean it was just paint! And then there's another one which is a painting of some Subbuteo figures. They had a children's art competition last year and we all thought that art should have gone up in the central foyer, but they put it in the meeting rooms instead."* You might have to make an effort to get close to the art though as *"staff aren't allowed to use the main entrance – we go in and out through the side of the building."*

## and finally...

Lawrence Graham's comfort factor has undeniable appeal for students looking to enlist somewhere other than a magic circle boot camp. For a broad commercial training, exposure to some interesting work and the odd bit of weird art, this firm is a really safe bet.

# LeBoeuf, Lamb, Greene & MacRae LLP

## the facts

**Location:** London
**Number of partners/assistants:** 20/45
**Total number of trainees:** 9
**Seats:** 4x6 months
**Alternative seats:** Overseas seats, secondments
**Extras:** Language training

Grand old 86-year-old New Yorker LeBoeuf, Lamb, Greene & MacRae has coughed loudly and grabbed a few London legal headlines of late. Will it also attract your attention?

## oil you ever wanted

Part of an extensive network of 20 offices, LeBoeuf's London branch was opened in 1995. The wave of new arrivals from the USA into the London legal market in the mid-90s prompted a sullen 'overpaid and over here' response from the Brits, especially when some firms realised their best lawyers were being poached. People said the Americans would

never stay, that their investments would be short-term, but this has proved largely untrue. In fact, an American Revolution has taken place in London: City lawyers' salaries have risen and so too have partners' appetites for higher profits. In turn, this has had an effect on working practices and the demands placed on individual lawyers. What we are left with is a marketplace in which training contracts at American firms can be characterised by higher salaries, smaller offices, more limited seat options but closer contact with partners. In terms of quality of work and the number of hours worked, there is rarely any disadvantage to being at an American firm.

Perhaps we should really describe LeBoeuf as an 'international firm' because although most of its lawyers and staff are based Stateside, its activities are global. Another key point to make is that although small in London – where it has 60 lawyers – globally LeBoeuf has about 600 lawyers in a dozen offices in the USA and eight others in strategic locations around the world. And internationally there's a theme – Bishkek in the Kyrgyz Republic, Almaty in Kazakhstan, Riyadh in Saudi Arabia... have you smelled the oil yet?

Energy and insurance sector clients are at the heart of LeBoeuf's practice worldwide. Ignore this information at your peril because these two industries will be dominant influences on your training. On the insurance side, the London office acts for Zurich, Eagle Star, Royal & SunAlliance plus various Lloyd's syndicates and a host of other key names. On the energy side, it advises a considerable number of well-known oil and gas companies and various national governments.

## a cut above

LeBoeuf's transactional and projects work in London is characterised by a smaller number of high-value deals, many of them centring on Africa and Eastern Europe. Indeed, LeBoeuf has made a big impression with its Africa deals and was recently recognised by our colleagues on *Chambers Global* when they awarded it the title of 'Africa Law Firm of the Year' in 2005. The London lawyers have been involved in a raft of major work, including advice to the Government of Equatorial Guinea on a $1.4 billion liquefied natural gas project and the establishment of a national oil company. They are presently advising a consortium of oil companies including Sonangol, ChevronTexaco, BP, ExxonMobil and Total on various elements of a planned $5 billion project to process gas from Angolan offshore fields for sale to the USA. Then there's advice to the Islamic Republic of Mauritania regarding the Chinguetti offshore oil field, which is due to come on stream in 2006, and to NamPower, Namibia's state-owned electricity utility, concerning the exploitation of the Kudu offshore gas field.

Not every deal is energy-related. Last year, LeBoeuf's London and Paris offices advised Finnish company Amer Sports on its €480 million purchase of French winter sports equipment company Salomon from adidas. On the projects side, lawyers have helped construction groups Hochtief and Dragados with their bids to work on the £800 million Thessaloniki Submerged Tunnel project in Greece. Amazingly, some of the work in London is actually UK-based. The litigation department, for example, has been representing an insurance company in football injury cases brought by Premiership clubs claiming financial compensation for injured players. In the most recent example Blackburn Rovers achieved a landmark decision on appeal in a case where a player was forced to leave the club because of back problems. This case may well have opened the floodgates to other claims for injuries previously regarded as inevitable wear and tear.

On the subject of interesting cases, here's a new spin on that old favourite from land law lectures – what makes an item a fixture rather than a mere fitting? LeBoeuf has been advising a medical equipment finance company which had cause to exert its rights over something called a Gamma Knife. Unlike the incredibly useful but alas fictitious X-Ray Specs, this turns out to be an actual piece of radioactive equipment, so rare in fact that there are only three in the country. The problem was that the equipment had become an integral part of a building in Harley Street and the building's landlord, The Crown Estate, wanted to see a new tenant take over the lease... and with it the Gamma Knife.

## anyone for paris?

As engaging as these cases can be, trainees must accept that not all of their work will be fabulously exciting. Without an army of paralegals to call upon, it is trainees who carry the heavy load when it comes to document management tasks etc. but at least "*people do give you a hand when you really need it.*" To compensate there are "*little trips abroad*" which are "*indicative of the fact that almost everything we do is international.*" There are also plenty of little trips to the High Court during litigation seats. "*I got to go most days,*" said one source, "*I was lodging documents or getting things sealed and attending trials on big cases worth a lot of money.*" All trainees do a litigation seat and at least two corporate seats. Beyond this, property and tax options appeal to some, and the regularity with which trainees now take seats in Moscow and Paris leads us to conclude that these are a permanent feature of the training programme. Shorter secondments to insurance companies are also possible.

We're told the London office feels like an English firm that is governed at a distance from the United States. Trainees' day-to-day work experiences are much the same as for their peers working on international deals in UK firms, although some sources point to a relative lack of rigid structure in the training scheme. This can work both for and against trainees; sometimes it's all "*really good top-end work and training experiences,*" other times "*you are treated like labour... there's still a need for paralegals.*" Perhaps the arrival of a dedicated training manager will even things out. We're told the appraisal system could also be made more effective, as at present vocalising moans simply left people feeling "*like a whiny little child.*"

## or new york?

One thing that is definitely more American than British, however, is the size of trainees' and qualified lawyers' pay packets. LeBoeuf's NQs now earn £65,000 per year, considerably more than their counterparts at the magic circle and other large UK firms. And lest they forget where it all began for LeBoeuf, second year trainees join other European associates for a week in the New York office. Here they learn first hand what the firm wants to achieve – by all accounts a premium brand that attracts high-calibre lawyers and clients that can afford to keep the firm operating very profitably. LeBoeuf doesn't want to be all things to all clients in all places, preferring instead to focus on its key markets. Illustrating its resolve, it recently closed offices in Salt Lake City and Denver to open up in a more important commercial centre, Chicago. More regular contact between the Brits and the Yanks is maintained by way of videoconferenced training sessions; "*though not always directly relevant, it is nice to know that if you get a call from people in the US you know what they do.*" Of more use are the lectures and seminars laid on in-house in London.

The London management has been busy too. It has recruited an IP partner specialising in chemicals, pharmaceuticals and biotech matters; two energy partners from rival firm Vinson & Elkins; and an insurance expert from Dechert. Then, as if these scalps weren't enough, in May 2005 one of the most senior figures in the energy practice of Coudert Brothers leapt aboard LeBoeuf before the Coudert ship sank without trace, and the first ever solicitor to become a QC arrived from another rival US firm. Said one source: "*As a ready reckoner it has doubled in size in the time I have been here.*" Doing their bit for growth at the junior end, three of the four September 2005 qualifiers accepted jobs at the firm.

## let's get ready to rouble

Trainees tell us they have it all – the opportunity to work on massive international deals within an office where they quickly get to know everyone and, importantly, everyone gets to know them. This cuts both ways though: perform well and word gets around, mess things up or get lazy and your reputation spreads equally quickly. Undoubtedly, LeBoeuf suits those with the ability and willingness to work hard and muck in doing whatever necessary, whenever necessary. Someone who really wants to be a part of a big intake of trainees which is then pushed through a two-week induction and regular classroom training probably isn't cut out for this firm. Beyond this the firm seeks the same kind of candidate as any other good London firm – "*people with a 2.1 or First and exemplary A-levels,*" a bit of "*straightforward common sense*" and maybe even some relevant experience. Interestingly, even within the small intake of five trainees per year LeBoeuf usually manages to recruit at least a couple of people with non-UK backgrounds, especially those with Russian heritage or language skills. A word of warning though: "*People turn up and say they want to qualify as a New York lawyer but that's wrong, you've got to look at the London office as the place you want to work.*"

The firm's Thames-side office has great views and is ideally located for short strolls or lunches by the water. Friday nights mean drinks with younger associates in Agenda just downstairs or another local bar. The social scene is not frenetic because frankly most people have a life to maintain outside work, and while the average day sees trainees "*in at 9am and away at 7pm or 8pm,*" the hours can be more demanding at times. At least they know how to enjoy themselves at the Christmas black-tie bash; apparently, "*the partners are often the ones leading the shenanigans!*" The summer party is also good fun and usually held in a cool location such as London Zoo.

## and finally...

For a highly paid, internationally focused career that's heavily based on the energy and insurance sectors, LeBoeuf is an ideal choice. Though the range of its work and numbers of staff in London are growing, and this in turn points to a broader training, you need to be certain you understand the firm's business before blithely signing on the dotted line.

# Lester Aldridge

## the facts

**Location:** Bournemouth, Southampton, Milton Keynes, London
**Number of partners/assistants:** 40/57
**Total number of trainees:** 14
**Seats:** 4x6 months
**Alternative seats:** Occasional secondments

Lester Aldridge has cast off its south coast mooring and voyaged into deeper waters with new offices in Milton Keynes and London. The firm also makes waves as one of the nicest places to work in the UK.

## 'ark at them!

Lester Aldridge handles the full range of legal disciplines from private client to consumer finance, divorce and children's law to corporate restructuring, debt recovery to construction. You'd struggle to squeeze its multitude of practice areas into the streamlined shell of Ellen MacArthur's B&Q; in fact, you'd probably need something more like an ark in size. That is not to say that LA isn't a sleek-hulled operation: as one of the major players in the south, the firm commands respect for producing quality work across the board and a successful growth strategy. Though in the past year there have been reports of partner departures (some taking large clients with them and turning bitter) the overall picture remains positive.

Following a flurry of activity in 2004, LA now has five offices. Trainees spend the bulk of their time in the Bournemouth HQ, where seats in dispute resolution, real estate, employment, corporate, private client and family are on offer. In another large office in Southampton, seats can include dispute resolution, corporate, real estate, planning and corporate recovery. A smaller office at Bournemouth International Airport handles fast-track (low-value) debt recovery and fast track property work (residential conveyancing and remortgaging). In the summer of 2004, LA opened up a finance-focused Milton Keynes office, and in the autumn it added a London anchorage following a merger with property specialists from the about-to-be-disbanded Park Nelson.

## dorset rise

So why the expansion? In the past we have noted the firm's ambitious plans and were reminded again this year that "*LA like to see themselves as cutting edge and moving forwards.*" How appropriate then that LA's new London office has the address 'Dorset Rise'. Does this mean the firm feels hampered by a beach resort location? Apparently not. "*London was an opportunity that came up and they decided to take it,*" though "*there is no desire to become the next Eversheds.*" Instead "*LA still see themselves as a South Coast regional firm. They want to be the best in that area and the London office is a good card to have in the pocket in that sense.*" If anything, "*the London office reflects the fact that our clients are national and international.*" LA divides its attention between international names such as Volkswagen and Toyota, whose financial services limbs are advised by the firm, household brands like P&O Cruises and McCarthy & Stone, and Bournemouth's local businesses. And according to trainees, from "*brand names all the way down to local businesses, there is no drossy work.*"

A four-seat contract exposes them to the firm's broad raft of work. No seats are compulsory, though most trainees do a stint in commercial property or private client because of the size of those two departments. Beyond that, "*they will try* and identify what type of person you are and the area you want to be in" and "most people tend to get a go at what they want at some point." It seems that "most trainees want a corporate seat" and "the marine side of things turns heads." The corporate team offers trainees "good exposure to clients" and the opportunity to play an active role in M&A work, which last year included the acquisition of Shield soap from Unilever. A seat in the marine team is harder to come by, but for the lucky few it can involve work for London insurers handling collisions at sea. The team also deals with some personal injury work, for example "little old ladies who fall over their own feet on cruise ships."

## one knock for yes, two for no

Ah yes, those little old ladies. Bournemouth has a (justified) reputation as the UK's cotton-top capital and in a private client seat you will have ample opportunity to ponder the merits of a blue rinse. Some trainees view it as "a really lovely, gentle seat to start with before you hit commerciality." The department represents "quite a heady mix of people from those off the street to those from the higher echelons of society" and trainees get to run their own probate files, draft wills, deal with executors and handle tax questions. Plus "there are cakes and biscuits every other day." Trainees can also sample contentious probate as the firm has carved out a niche in disputes of the "Great Aunt Betty has left everything to Battersea Dogs Home and nothing to me" ilk. Similarly contentious, a spell in family entails "lots of court appearances," conferences with counsel, research and drafting. Here, the fact that the clients are actually on the other end of the phone rather than in the next life may explain why the work is faster moving, and why it can be "harder to have a file just to yourself."

There's no absence of autonomy in the debt recovery team, which can accommodate two trainees at any one time. As one source explained: "It is basically commercial litigation in the context of contractual debt." Our sources spoke of managing up to 80 of their own files, covering "anything from sign-makers operating out of their own front room all the way up to, say, a national steel manufacturer." Not to mention large international clients, finance companies, utilities and accountancy firms. The real estate team handles commercial property plus planning and environment matters and trainees enjoy being "left to run with things, not fed piecemeal work." In planning that means handling development applications and contamination cases, while a commercial property seat provides "the chance to go from the outset of a transaction right through to exchange, completion and registration."

## no stowaways

In addition to thorough end-of-seat appraisals, trainees can air their views at quarterly group meetings with the managing partner, which often culminate in drinks or dinner. "The agenda is based on what trainees put forward, plus the managing partner's input. 75% of the meeting is geared by us." More than that, e-mails from the managing partner, a staff forum, regular staff questionnaires and day-to-day feedback from supervisors leave trainees feeling "totally informed." It came as no surprise to us then that again this year LA featured in the *Sunday Times'* survey of '100 Best Companies to Work for'.

At LA there are Easter eggs for every member of staff, happy hours, dress-down Fridays and, until it became a victim of its own success, in Southampton the whole office sat down to a Full English every Friday morning. More importantly, "quite honestly they listen to every opinion in the firm; they value everyone in the organisation from the secretary with a good idea right through to the managing partner." As one trainee put it: "If you don't intend to become a positive member of your team and the firm, then you should go somewhere else." As if to prove the point that even the backroom boys step forward, this year it was Varden Ede, the firm's "chappie in the postroom," who, after being voted 'Personality of the Year' by the rest of the staff, accompanied the managing partner to the *Sunday Times* awards ceremony.

There is also a starring role for Sparkle the dog, who after years of service pacing the corridors, presiding over board meetings and keeping the kitchen free of crumbs is *"still around... just."* A less charitable source described her as *"clinging on to life,"* but she certainly isn't clinging on to her infamy: she even has her own intranet profile. As one source observed: *"Having a dog wandering around might conjure up images of an old office above a chip shop, but it is just a symptom of the firm."*

## sounds fishy

Before you ask, none of the offices are above a chippie (though rumour has it the old Park Nelson London office was above Sweeny Todd's butchery-cum-barber shop). And just in case you were wondering, the commute between Bournemouth and Southampton is 40 minutes. Recently tarted up, the Southampton office sports a marble reception, snazzy new desks and LA's new corporate colours – silver and blue. The other offices are going through a makeover *"in keeping with the blue and silver theme."* From the top-floor meeting rooms of the Bournemouth office there are *"fab views"* and, as one smug source noted: *"From my window, in one direction I can see where the town stops and the New Forest starts. In the other direction I can see where the town stops and the sea starts."* That'll do.

With such temptations on their doorstep, it is no wonder that trainees don't hang around at the end of the day. To explain the firm's relatively strict adherence to the official hours of 9.30am to 5.30pm, one source ventured: *"Well, a lot of people down here sail."* Other sporting endeavours include netball, cricket and football, and there are official team-building initiatives involving youth hostels and lots of beer. Unofficial team-building initiatives involve Downes wine bar and lots of beer. Pub quizzes, a summer ball, a summer fair (complete with donkey rides) and, of course, a Christmas party all add to the mix. At this year's Christmas party, the kings and queens theme was liberally interpreted – there were beauty queens and wise men, not to mention an entire cocktail of king prawns from the banking and finance department. Curiously, all the trainees dressed up as Britney Spears.

At LA, for every trainee who has fast-tracked through a law degree and the LPC, there is another who has taken time out or paralegalled for the firm. And for every *"back-office technical lawyer"* there is a *"more confident type."* What they do have in common is that they seem to share the easy manner of people who are sure of their decision to choose a strong regional firm over a London career. That and the fact that they *"all like beaches."* In September 2005 all four qualifiers stayed with the firm.

## and finally...

Lester Aldridge has cemented its reputation year on year, and with any luck it will get through its current choppy waters without too much drama. If the South Coast is where you want to work as a lawyer, we can think of no better place to learn the ropes.

# Lewis Silkin

## the facts

**Location:** London, Oxford
**Number of partners/assistants:** 44/70
**Total number of trainees:** 14
**Seats:** 4x6 months
**Alternative seats:** None

Although property, corporate and litigation represent the bulk of Lewis Silkin's work, its glitzy niche practices are what catch the eye. Superb social housing, excellent employment and a monumental media, brands and technology group (MBT) – all this and a self-proclaimed 'rather more human' approach. Should you believe the hype?

# the true picture

## it's in the dna

As amazing as it may seem, this firm was once as much steeped in south London legal aid work as commercial practice north of the river, and it is widely known that its origins speak of a solid commitment to social values and more than a hint of leftwards political leanings. The Lewis Silkin of 2005 is apparently *"aware of its history and the tradition of social conscience but not driven by it today."* The firm's always-bang-up-to-date website tells you *"History? Yes, we have plenty of it – over 50 years' worth … just ask when we meet,"* but tactfully declines to expand further online. This strikes us as fair enough for a firm increasingly understood as a purely commercial outfit with a diverse and much-envied clientele in the media (ad agencies like McCann-Erickson, major publishers including Haymarket, games companies such as EA), in catering (PizzaExpress and Pret A Manger to name-drop two) and in retail (Harrods and House of Fraser).

So has Lewis Silkin laid the ghosts of an illustrious past to rest and set down the burden of social conscience and political sympathies? Well, not exactly. Whilst none of the trainees we interviewed were identifiably card-carrying members of any party, they did allude to some identification with principles other than profit. *"The old ethos doesn't noticeably affect the way that work is carried out, but it is a constant in the background, part of the origin and make-up of the firm,"* confirmed one.

## hyperventilating bubbles

When considering where to spend their four six-month seats, the two places in the corporate department are an attractive proposition, not least because *"a lot of the work comes from the trendy media clients."* In 2005 its lawyers acted for top ad agencies in their corporate transactions, and advised The Moving Picture Company on its £52.7 million sale by Carlton Communications to Technicolor. Proving they have other strings to their bows, they sold refrigeration manufacturing business Jerome Engineering to German conglomerate

Bitzer and performed more than decently on a range of other mid-rank deals. Trainees reported satisfaction in *"supporting transactions from beginning to end,"* as well as taking on *"responsibility for due diligence exercises"* and sometimes a whole lot more. *"I ran a share acquisition from start to finish under supervision,"* said one. *"I was there at the opening meeting and was there at the completion."*

Lewis Silkin's advertising and marketing law ability is second to none, so the creation of a dedicated MBT department is no more surprising than the fact that *"it's sexy, or at least that's what everyone seems to think when you tell them you're doing a seat there."* The firm represents four of the five worldwide advertising and marketing groups – Omnicom, Interpublic, Publicis and Havas – and this year also won telecoms giant Hutchison 3G (now simply called 3) as a client, advising on its dispute with $O_2$ about bubble imagery in a series of adverts. No less exciting are the firm's relationships with stellar brands including Coca-Cola, Estée Lauder, Gillette, HJ Heinz, John Frieda, McCain Foods, Nissan, Powergen and Renault. Our sources breathed deeply for just long enough to tell us that *"the work is incredibly varied, one day you're doing advertising clearances with Ofcom, the next drafting a commercial agreement and doing IP law."*

## gainfully employed

This next bit may leave you drooling with anticipation of ready access to a seat that would cost both your soul and months of campaigning elsewhere. If employment is your bag, then three seats in the department per rotation mean access for all. Accounting for nearly 30% of Lewis Silkin's work, employment is not strictly a niche department any more. Augmenting organic growth in the capital, over in the firm's new Oxford office staff have now *"completely settled in."* Trainees occasionally flit to and from this second office, but the solid mass of top-notch applicant and respondent work on offer in London tends to keep them anchored in the Big Smoke. And no wonder – the firm's lawyers recently took Stephanie Villalba's multimillion-pound discrimination claim against Merrill Lynch to appeal, advised Sainsbury's on the departure of its chairman Sir Peter Davis, and received instructions from a host of household names including Viacom's UK companies (MTV, CBS, Viacom Outdoor, Simon & Schuster, Paramount), Hallmark Cards, Apple, Computacenter, Agfa, Hertz, Xerox and The Royal Academy of Dance.

From a trainee's perspective, *"great involvement"* is made possible by the firm's willingness to act both for employers and employees. On larger respondent work, trainees *"assist on matters such as drafting defences or reasons to refute;"* on the other side of the fence, they *"run applicant cases from start to finish,"* instructing counsel, accompanying a client to tribunal and possibly dabbling in *"a bit of advocacy."* It all equates to *"feeling like you're an integral part of the team."*

## social issues

In the compulsory litigation seat (often split half commercial, half construction) trainees assist on anything from bog-standard commercial contracts claims to an instruction from Mohamed Al Fayed in relation to the current UK inquest into the death of his son Dodi and Diana, Princess of Wales. They end up *"drafting witness statements"* and *"liaising with the courts"*, as well as helping out with the inevitable paper pushing. Here, too, they manage their own small files, be this *"a coroner's inquest for a social landlord"* or, as one trainee put it: *"Pursuing clients for unpaid legal bills, coercing them, getting heavy. You run the file, you are the enforcer!"*

A stint in property means either commercial transactions or social housing matters. The former brings *"landlord and tenant work for property investors and a bit of residential for high-net-worth individuals;"* the latter exposes them to the varied needs of housing associations – *"auctions and disposals, grants of easements and wayleaves, big refinancings."* Common to both is *"good client contact"* and *"running your own files,"* which helps to

explain the appeal of what trainees call *"a fantastic seat."* In a commercial environment where profit is the only bottom line, you wouldn't necessarily expect expertise in social housing to survive, let alone thrive. It is therefore worth pointing out that Lewis Silkin this year snared a social housing partner from another leading practice. Pushing large-scale finance and urban regeneration work, this prestige team acts for clients including The Cambridge Housing Society, Southern Housing Group, Notting Hill Housing Trust, London Borough of Lewisham and Abbey.

## slippery character

Our annual grapple with the conundrum that is Lewis Silkin's culture – summed up in the word 'Silkiness' – came no nearer to resolution this year. Everyone agrees that, compared to the relative roughness of many law firms, Lewis Silkin offers a smoothness to the touch that is soothing to body and mind, but no one can quite define it. Some view it simply as *"pride in giving useful advice in practical terms to clients;"* others suggest *"it's about a quality of being straightforward."* One source told us: *"It's the value placed on work-life balance;"* someone else said: *"It's to do with the firm being grounded and unstuffy."* If pushed, we'd define it as egalitarian, light-humoured and open. No matter what you call it, the fact is that *"it is tangibly there, even if you can't exactly pin it down."*

Certainly our sources' affection for the firm was barely denuded by there being only one NQ job between six qualifiers in September 2005. They appreciated that this disastrous result was not the norm and were mostly looking at NQ life beyond the firm, adding that they valued the *"excellent culture of feedback,"* *"the determination to give you broad experience of the areas you are working in,"* and the *"care and attention that your work receives."* What really impressed them was the willingness of partners and associates *"to take five minutes out to help you, no matter how busy they are."* Feedback sessions with HR no longer take place in the pub, but they nonetheless help to keep things flowing and, so too, does a relaxed dress code.

## green-eyed monsters

Lest you imagine all is harmony and prelapsarian innocence at Lewis Silkin, we should point out that a little green-eyed beastie sits on the shoulders of many in the firm's Gough Square offices. They may have a beautiful building complete with *"taps that dispense sparkling water"* and *"a computer downstairs in the canteen for checking your dodgier e-mails,"* but envy has crept into their hearts. Due to the expansion of the employment team, property has moved across the courtyard to a building that is *"more modern, very plush"* and boasting *"newer desks and better computers"*... and a whole lot more room! *"There's just so much space there, it makes the other building feel cramped,"* breathed one covetous trainee, evidently forgetting the old maxim about grass and comparative shades of greenness.

No such cardinal sins infect the pleasant interrelations of trainees. Regular evenings out have of late seen a *"hunt for more variety"* with regard to venue. The firm itself organises excellent, *"informal but not riotous"* summer and Christmas events, with *"champagne, canapés, a meal and a disco"* par for the course. None of it is exactly hedonistic excess, but if they need to work off the booze and calories, trainees can participate in a range of team sports. We're told the emphasis is definitely on participation: *"We play clients at football, but it's not so much that we lose tactfully, more that we're not able to win!"*

At least the experience offers a valuable lesson in the virtues of humility and tolerance, although from what we heard in our interviews it might not be entirely necessary. *"All the trainees are ambitious but not overly so, no one becomes unbearably competitive,"* one source told us, whilst another reflected on the paradox of *"a diverse group in terms of backgrounds and interests"* who yet *"share common characteristics."* That'll be the Silkiness then. And if we did notice that trainees here aren't the most desperately driven we've come across in the City, then

perhaps it reflects a smoothness round the edges that is pure Lewis Silkin. *"There's a real emphasis on people's relationships with each other,"* said one source straight out of the firm mould.

## and finally...

The fact that Lewis Silkin can 100% guarantee niche training experiences alongside broader commercial ones makes it fairly unique amongst mid-sized London firms. Add in that Silkiness and all you have to do is decide whether the firm rubs you up the right way.

# Linklaters

## the facts

**Location:** London
**Number of partners/assistants:** 180/640
**Total number of trainees:** 250
**Seats:** 4x6 months
**Alternative seats:** Overseas seats, secondments
**Extras:** Pro bono – Hackney law centre, Mary Ward Legal Advice Centre; language training

As part of the City's magic circle, Linklaters is a true heavyweight in all things transactional. With offices in 22 countries, we're half expecting it to announce that it's opened up on the moon. Ambitious? You betcha!

## eurobondage

Linklaters is world-renowned for its corporate practice and has worked extremely hard to put its finance practice on an equal footing. To give you some flavour, it advised on five of the ten largest IPOs completed in London over the first six months of 2005. Lawyers acted for Dresdner Kleinwort Wasserstein on the £5 billion PartyGaming listing, and for the issuers on the IG Group, Mapeley and Caliber Global Investment listings. Linklaters continues to act for all the major investment banks in the global securities market, including Citigroup,

# the true picture

Merrill Lynch, Morgan Stanley, ABN Amro, Barclays, CSFB, Deutsche Bank, HSBC, UBS and JPMorgan. The SWX Swiss Exchange turned to the firm for assistance on its new listing regime for Eurobonds and other international debt securities, making it possible for international bond issuers to obtain a Swiss listing for foreign-law governed Eurobonds, convertible and exchangeable bonds and other debt securities. The equity-linked market saw a number of landmark transactions, including the Swiss Re (of gherkin fame) mandatory convertible bond, and in the UK market, Linklaters' team maintained its record of having acted on every UK public listed convertible issue in the last three years. In the debt issuance practice, Links handled the ground-breaking and structurally complex Network Rail MTN programme, which provided the frameworks for the largest euro and sterling tranches ever made by a corporate. The strength of Linklaters' high yield practice was reflected in advice to the lead managers on both the equity and two series of high yield debt of Invensys plc. These lawyers also acted on Corus Group's high yield issuance and the offer of high yield bonds by Sistema Capital, the financing vehicle for the Russian group, Sistema.

Linklaters' M&A practice is especially dominant. Corporate lawyers advised Centrica on its £1.75 billion sale of the Automobile Association (the largest private equity M&A deal in Europe in 2004), and National Grid Transco on its billion-pound acquisition of Crown Castle UK, which changed the landscape of the UK broadcasting transmission market and included significant regulatory involvement with the OFT and Ofcom. Speaking of matters regulatory, the firm's London competition practice had a storming year; its lawyers assisted Microsoft on the EC merger clearance required for the proposed joint acquisition of ContentGuard by Microsoft and Time Warner. The team was additionally involved in a number of key cases outside merger control, and is presently advising on two out of the three current Competition

Commission market references, one pertaining to the supply of store cards and the other liquefied petroleum gas. Linklaters' projects practice covers the full range of projects, including infrastructure, PFI/PPP, energy, oil and gas, electricity and nuclear, renewables, telecoms and technology, mining, water and rail. It closed nine PFI/PPP deals in the last year, including the financing of the Oncology Wing at St James' Hospital in Leeds, where lawyers acted for the UK Treasury on the first ever Credit Guarantee Facility-financed structure project and established new precedents for future CGF deals.

Confused by most of the above? Don't worry. According to one trainee: "*It's pretty much impossible to describe to someone what the work involves until you're here.*" Then again, that's our job...

## seats you sir

The training at Linklaters is based on a traditional four-seat system, with the defining features being big companies, big banks and big numbers. The kind of work you'll be given in a corporate seat seems to depend on your ability to track it down. Some had been given "*decent responsibility*", though warned of the dangers of getting stuck on administrative work. It is inevitable that you'll encounter document management ("*taking papers to a board meeting to be signed, lots of organisation and readjustment of documents*"); indeed, one trainee spent three months doing it while working on an IPO. "*There were long hours and a lot of donkey work,*" was the report. Yet a different trainee told us: "*I was lucky to run a segment of a deal on my own, but some people can end up just doing little bits of due diligence.*" As in any top-notch corporate practice, you have to take the rough with the smooth. The rough was for one person "*doing 95 hours in five days. It was crap-quality proofing work, but it's amazing what the body can do when you push it.*" While the smooth for another was "*being the key contact on a massive deal where the client would ask for me. It was great when the client showed confidence in me.*"

The finance practice is on the rise and don't

trainees know it! "*It's not A&O*," whispered one, "*but it's up there and it's improving.*" Asset finance is "*young, dynamic, being grown and emphasised heavily... it's quite a sexy world of private jets and boats.*" A financial markets seat is more regulatory in nature: "*If the FSA is to investigate a client or run an investigation, we put together corporate governance reports, little bits of regulatory advice.*" Work on the restructuring and insolvency side of banking gives a good idea of how businesses work.

## the great leveller

Tax is a small advisory department rather than a large transactional hub. The work is research based and prompted one trainee to conclude: "*It allowed me to get back to black letter law.*" "*The only caveat is that even associates at two, three, four years post-qualification are still finding their feet because the legislation is so complex.*" However, once you get your head around the basic tenets, "*it can be very satisfying – you appreciate that the structure of a lot of the deals is tax-driven.*" Another bonus, "*the Finance Bill changes the law every year; it's a good leveller as everyone has to learn the same new stuff.*" The environment is "*very different from the rest of the firm, everyone is eccentric and relaxed and the hours are a good 9.30am to 6.30pm. By 6pm your brain is frazzled so there's not much point hanging around!*" Compared to the more administrative role played by trainees in corporate seats, "*tax opinions are like short theses; you take a specific issue and run with it.*"

The niche departments always attract interest from trainees. "*EU/competition, employment and real estate are all popular,*" confirmed one source. "*They are smaller so they're harder to get in to.*" And what of litigation? For those with minimal interest in the area, the requirement for contentious experience is met by a two-week course, so leaving them free for four full seats of non-contentious training. But as one astute trainee rightly observed: "*Across the City there is apparently a move away from the obsession with transactional work to areas with more law and better hours.*" Consequently those who do

have a desire to litigate can spend a full six-months in the department. One source spent half of their seat working on a High Court matter, "*helping to prepare court documents and liaising loads with the client.*"

## the drive of your life

Seat allocation is fairly transparent, though trainees recommend making your needs and desires well known because "*if you don't assert your preference you can end up in seats you don't want. You have to be assertive.*" Depending on the department you find yourself in, "*it's true that the perception of a trainee's value is different.*" For example, in the financial markets group, which is "*small, niche, quiet and friendly, they invite trainees on away days. In derivatives, which has a laddish drinking culture to it, they didn't take trainees on the group retreat and that didn't go down too well.*"

The trainees we spoke with were forthcoming in their opinions of themselves and of the firm's overall culture. We could almost see their hands shooting up at the front of a classroom. The one thing that unites them is that "*everyone is very bright, I haven't come across any trainees who don't know what they're doing.*" Another agreed: "*Most trainees come from an intellectual background so you can't distinguish them in that way. It's like having 3As at Oxbridge: it may set you apart from the general population, but it's nothing special when you're there.*" The current trainee group hails from 40 different universities around the world, in part because the firm now markets itself to students in places as far away as Bangalore and Australia. Besides good grades, trainees are "*driven,*" "*self-assured*" and "*made of solid stuff.*" "*I think everyone has natural, inner confidence,*" suggested one Zen master. From all we heard, it cannot be overstated that wallflowers need not apply. "*You must be outgoing and put yourself forward because good work isn't going to just come to you. People without a hierarchical mentality get on best... you must be able to talk to partners as equals.*" You've also got to have confidence in your views and not be afraid to open your mouth; *"it might be that you've got it wrong, but it is unlikely to be totally stupid by virtue of the fact that you're here in the first place."* Professionalism was regularly alluded to, as was an air of modernity. Said one trainee: *"I wanted to stay away from an old-school law firm and I liked Links' modern approach."*

## lpc you later

For the most part, our sources spoke highly of the firm's ethos and their initial impressions. *"I thought that Linklaters was less pretentious than some of its rivals,"* thought one. Another told us: *"I wanted a firm which shared my kind of drive and ambition and was full of like-minded people."* It is certainly ambition-a-go-go right now: the firm reported a 22% rise in profits for the last financial year and celebrated its best set of results for ages. This success has trickled down to the most junior lawyers, with Linklaters becoming the first magic circle firm to break through the £50,000 salary for newly qualified lawyers by adding a cool grand to the wage packet. The past year also saw the Law Society officially validate the Linklaters LPC, which will be administered to all new recruits at the College of Law. The course will focus on the kinds of transaction carried out by the firm and link in with the firm's own training programme for staff. However, some trainees weren't impressed by the proposed LPC, telling us: *"I just think it encourages exclusivity that should be discouraged."* Instances of press reports *"piss-taking about Links school uniforms"* had clearly stung.

To avoid the problem of isolation, the firm has arranged for its future trainees to take certain LPC subjects with students headed for other firms. It has also stolen a march on other firms by being first to hoik up the students' maintenance payment to £7,000 per year.

Trainee appraisals are taken very seriously, as befits a firm packed with *"results-driven people who like to know how they are performing. The firm encourages on-going appraisals and then formal mid and end-of-seat appraisals."* The firm's handling of on-the-job training was roundly praised, with few dissenting voices. Seat by seat, *"when you go into different practices you get excellent training, and the materials they give you are excellent, so well organised."* On a day-to-day basis *"the person you get as a principal makes a huge difference. I was unlucky in one seat; my supervisor was a difficult character and was throwing the same thing at me all the time. My trainee manager took me out for a glass of wine and talked to me for three hours."*

The office itself is *"a bit of a maze,"* but at least the artwork on the client floors is all *"in the best possible taste."* The same cannot be said for the engine rooms upstairs – *"the secretaries like to put up posters of Brad Pitt and David Beckham."* Similarly, while it's all minimalism and gliding waiters in the client reception, *"in most departments you get cakes in the afternoon on Thursday and Friday and a drinks trolley on Friday evening."*

## lastminute.opportunities

Seeing as the school analogy has already been made we might as well add that we've always seen Links trainees more as head boys and girls than the smart kids who sat at the back of the class, never did any work and always came top. As you might expect with so many ambitious high-flyers in a pressurised situation, *"coming up to qualification there can be lots of sitting around and grumbling. People have a bitch and wind each other up."* Nevertheless, the social life was considered to be *"excellent"* and across such a large firm you are bound to find people with similar interests. Expect typical hours to be the City average of 9.30am to 7pm, though at times you will be stretched to your limits. Said one trainee: *"For three months in corporate I was hardly out of the office."*

Few squabbles are necessary when it comes to bagging an international placement or client secondment – 90% of trainees go on one or the other. *"Some of the most popular destinations are Singapore, Hong Kong, New York and São Paulo,"* advised one jet-setter. Eastern European locations are generally viewed as less glamorous, with the trainee who said: "*I think it is fear of the unknown,*" probably spot on. Someone who had opted to stay closer to home said of their client secondment: "*I had a great variety of work and was reporting directly to a member of the board.*" Spaces are available at a number of client companies including Merrill Lynch, BP, Viacom and Liberty. Again, a go-getting attitude will always stand you in good stead – "*the firm is rife with opportunities but you must put yourself forward.*"

In 2005 the firm retained 111 of its 131 qualifiers. Having been through an unfortunate period of oversupply of trainees, the firm is settling into a phase where supply and demand on qualification are becoming better matched. Hence the fact that periods of unpaid or part-paid leave are no longer offered to qualifiers.

## and finally...

Linklaters can offer an amazing training and set the right person on their way to a glittering legal career. If you're prepared to put in the hours, pull up a seat on the front row of City law and raise your hand high. Just be sure it's what you really want.

# Lovells

## the facts

**Location:** London
**Number of partners/assistants:** 146/350
**Total number of trainees:** 138
**Seats:** 4x6 months
**Alternative seats:** Overseas seats, secondments
**Extras:** Pro bono – The Prince's Trust, Community Links

City giant Lovells blends heavyweight corporate and commercial practice with substantial litigation expertise, highly reputable specialist departments and a wealth of international offices.

## a hive of activity

Let's talk deals. Lovells' many recent corporate glories include advice to Granada on its £5.7 billion merger with Carlton Communication and the Barclay Brothers on their successful bid for the Telegraph Group. The firm also advised longstanding client Petro-Canada on its $980 million acquisition of Intrepid Energy North Sea, and helped ING on its sale of Baring Asset Management's financial services for £245 million. Having helped ING to acquire Barings in the first place, Lovells certainly knew its way around that deal. And it had no problems with Umbro's £145 million LSE flotation either. What's more, with colonies everywhere from Alicante to Zagreb, Shanghai to Chicago and Beijing to Brussels, Lovells' international capacity means it is a positive hive of cross-border activity. So if deals, including the €90 million LBO of Barcelona's leading private hospital complex Centro Medico Teknon, didn't literally taste of honey, they were certainly sweet for a firm that is just as happy sipping the nectar of exotic blossoms as UK blooms.

Alongside such eminent transactional work, the firm also boasts enviable litigation expertise that has brought involvement in many of the most prominent cases of recent times. Continuing instructions from the liquidators of BCCI in the historic and never-ending litigations against the Bank of England are illustrative, as was the firm's role in reaching a shock settlement on the liquidator's parallel action against the Bank of America. On a more workaday, but equally important scale, Lovells is currently advising Equitable Life Assurance Society against allegations of misselling. And there's yet more: the firm has stellar product liability and competition teams, which continue to defend the manufacturers of the MMR vaccine and British American Tobacco against consumer claims, and companies like $O_2$ and Mastercard on unfair trading matters.

With the firm displaying excellence in all the main areas of commercial legal practice, it's no wonder students are drawn to it like bees to honey.

# the true picture

## it ain't half hot mum

Last year, trainees told us Lovells was increasingly looking to concentrate on its corporate and finance work, moving away from the diversity that has long characterised the firm. Indeed, news in December 2004 that a major redundancy programme affecting partners worldwide was being pushed through in response to flagging profitability did smack of a new ruthlessness at a firm which has long been renowned for its friendly demeanour. Is Lovells finding its inner drill sergeant? If it is then he's got some work to do: profits fell by a stinging 21% in 2004/5.

This year, trainees told us "*there is a feeling that the firm is trying to sand off the extraneous edges and becoming more of a corporate machine.*" Nonetheless, some of our sources had trodden a diverse litigation/niche-heavy path through their two years of training, and we should also point out that our sources were far from unanimous about the extent or likely impact of the drift. "*There's such a strong and influential litigation side to the firm, likewise with property, that you can't imagine them being wiped out,*" said one, whilst another observed how "*all the specialist departments do corporate support, but are well developed and recognised in their own right as well – they are part of the firm's character.*" Like trainees, we wonder if "*the firm might lose its spot in the market if it tries to become more purely corporate.*" Bearing in mind that trainees have long chosen Lovells for "*the breadth of practice on offer,*" we suggest those now hoping to join the firm keep their ears to the ground.

A straightforward four-seat scheme requires a stint in corporate or finance and one in a contentious area of work. Bucking the trend at the magic circle firms, Lovells' trainees for the most part embrace the litigation experience. Said one non-law grad: "*I didn't have the grounding in law, so wasn't as clear as some of my friends about the area I wanted to go into and I didn't want to get pinned down in corporate work.*" This view is typical.

Thanks to a useful pie chart in the new low-key graduate recruitment literature we can state that corporate and finance currently make up 45% of the firm's work, whilst the slice of litigation accounts for a still substantial 21%. Another 13% is made up of projects, energy and property work, and 'commerce' accounts for the remaining 1%. In Lovells' case, 'commerce' incorporates a mouth-watering melange of teams such as competition, employment, pensions and IP/IT. But beware – these titbits can be hard to get. We did ask the firm for a breakdown of NQ jobs by practice area for September 2005 but it was not forthcoming, so we suggest you draw your own conclusions about the following. At this time, 30 of the 35 qualifiers stayed with the firm, although there were more vacancies than qualifying trainees.

## pass the spanner

Across departments, the general rule of thumb is that "*the larger the deal the more likely you are to do tedious grunt work and some horrendous hours.*" As a consolation "*you do get forewarned and when you slave it is genuinely appreciated.*" Corporate and banking seats have the greatest propensity for intensity and "*working solely for your supervisor on a very specific matter,*" whether in the acquisitions team working through "*the conditions precedent on large-scale transactions for major banks,*" "*drafting and proofing on public and private company work*" or "*helping with the nuts and bolts*" on a major restructuring. Trainees take pleasure in an unexpectedly large amount of client contact; "*I was always on the phone, attending meetings and even went to several closures,*" said one source.

Although popular with the majority of trainees, any of the larger litigation departments, such as insolvency litigation, offer a not dissimilar experience to those corporate seats, that is to say "*working in very high-profile groups with high-profile partners doing work that is very limited in terms of breadth.*" In layman's terms, you may well be "*doing the most humdrum tasks,*" but you will get to see big-scale litigation in action. This is a trade-off that those who train with the City giants are usually prepared to make, especially when there is the prospect of greater responsibility in "*respected niche departments.*" Broadly speaking, specialist departments like employment, competition or tax offer "*more intimate atmospheres and greater responsibility*" even if "*studious work*" means "*being quite sealed off from the world*" and "*wracking your brains to get them around the documents.*"

The real estate department provides support to the corporate lawyers and also takes the lead on major standalone property transactions for clients like Prudential, Waitrose and Nomura International. It has a reputation for "*much shorter hours,*" which means more time for extra-curricular activity such as cricket and football matches with clients or simply "*nipping home early.*" Trainees relish the prospect of "*being left largely to your own devices running 30-40 files of things like retail unit leases and licenses.*" It may not sound that exciting, but "*there's a lot of client contact and you're always on the phone to managing agents.*" The department as a whole is said to have a "*laidback, slightly older feel.*" Whichever seat they were in, all our interviewees were full of praise for the "*detailed and meticulous*" quality of the formal training they received.

## not so lovelly

When asked about the process of seat allocation, our sources were mainly philosophical, suggesting "*most people expect to get one seat in an area they don't want.*" They must also do a fair bit of form filling to help HR manage the complex task of moving scores of trainees around and we heard mixed messages about the need to be tactical. Said one source: "*I went to speak to the relevant partner about a seat I really wanted and got it.*" On hearing this, another laughed: "*I did nothing more than fill out the form and got every seat I wanted.*" Though competition for most London seats, especially mainstream ones, is not that hot, when it comes to the wealth of secondments and overseas postings, things get hairier. With seats available in Brussels, Milan, Paris, Hong Kong, New York and Tokyo to name just a few, is it surprising there's a queue?

Lovells is no longer so keen on the 'friendly face of the top ten' reputation that has attached itself to the firm over many years. As our interviewees pointed out this year, "*we don't want to be seen to be easy to walk all over, [the image] is not very high-powered.*" We are assured that internally the firm is "*strict but responsive,*" "*the dress code is suits only*" and "*there's a real quality of studiousness.*" And, according to one source keen to convince us the firm deserved the Bob Cratchit Memorial Award for Seasonal Sacrifice, "*if you have to work the hours you work them, even if it means cancelling your Christmas holidays.*" All in all, we'd say the firm knows a bullish reputation can be very useful without making a lighter touch impossible.

As Lovells' recruitment policy places high importance on academic success, "*many people are from Oxford or Cambridge, maybe as much as 70%.*" Beyond academics there is a seeming preference for candidates "*with well-rounded interests*" and an articulate and polite manner. Our interviewees tended to think before they spoke and then spoke carefully. Their self-analysis: "*We're nice, low-key and studious; amenable but not in your face;*" "*grounded and not pretentious;*" "*driven but not aggressive.*" Our thanks to the trainee who reflected thus: "*You don't always have wonderful fun working on a late-night transaction or doing drudgery, but the people make even the bad times bearable.*" It brings tears to our eyes.

## scrue that!

"*You tend to be friends with a core of people from your intake,*" we learnt. "*They're the ones you continue seeing after the fresher-style socialising dies down.*" Secondments and overseas seats from as early as the second six months undoubtedly speed its demise, though the people we interviewed who were approaching the end of their training did still enjoy the odd night out together in the bars of Farringdon. "*The Fence and The Living Room we always go*

to, *sometimes Bacchus because it is right downstairs.*"
Clearly the 2005 vintage of trainee is in the mood
for puncturing myths, because nobody volunteered
the name of The Bottlescrue, a legendary Lovells
drinking venue. When we mentioned it their
response was uniform: "*It's disgusting!*" "*I think
that's really a place for qualifieds. No, make that five
to ten-year qualifieds,*" said one horrified source.

The firm does enjoy its big blowouts. A recent
Olympic-themed fancy dress ball was a classical
hotchpotch that borrowed a little Roman Baccha-
nalian spirit. The Christmas event sees the firm take
over the Grosvenor Hotel, which has "*the only room
we'd all fit into, so it's always held there.*" Speaking of
grand spaces, Lovells' twelve-floor Atlantic House
office on Holborn Viaduct is "*very plush with a gym,
an on-site Starbucks and a good cafeteria.*" A central
atrium stretches from the ground to the top floor
and contains a massive seven-storey moving steel
sculpture that is "*impossible to miss.*" It is in fact the
largest indoor sculpture in Europe, so Tate Modern
eat your heart/turbine hall out. But size isn't everything of course; there is the small matter of
meaning, and that's where the sculpture falls down
for many. Said one trainee: "*Er... I think it's supposed
to represent the scales of justice or something.*" Whatever the heck it means, if we worked there we'd want
to climb it.

## and finally...

Lovells' quality work allied to its breadth of practice
mean a balanced training that will either equip you
for the wider world or allow you to centre your legal
self on Atlantic House. Just remember two things:
first, the increasing focus on big corporate and
finance deals, and second, this firm is no soft
option.

# Mace & Jones

## the facts

**Location:** Liverpool, Manchester, Knutsford
**Number of partners/assistants:** 38/51
**Total number of trainees:** 8
**Seats:** 4x6 months
**Alternative seats:** Secondments

Respected for its sterling employment and family
work and praised in our parent publication *Chambers UK* for a host of different commercial areas of
practice, Mace & Jones is no longer content with
mere respect.

## city or united?

A partner swap-shop has opened in the North West:
M&J scalped two apiece from Wacks Caller, DLA
and Addleshaw; Pannone in turn picked off a few
M&J partners. Tit-for-tats are all part of the region's
legal merry-go-round as workloads increase, competition accelerates and the leading names in the
market advance towards ever greater commercialisation through expansion. Quite often, growth is
accompanied by consolidation, with firms homing
in on fewer locations. This is not merely as a result
of economies of scale, but also down to a shift away
from the kind of work that is conducted in small,
less profitable, neighbourhood offices.

So it was with interest that we learnt that the
firm's small Huyton office was closing and that
trainees will no longer spend a seat in Knutsford.
Our sources told us: "*We're going for more corporate
and commercial work in order to strengthen our position; the two main cities are the focus now.*" All eyes
on Manchester and Liverpool then.

We went hunting for proof that "*the future is
more commercial and more corporate*" at M&J, starting with its largest department – property. This
department certainly does very well and has a particular forte in development/urban regeneration,
acting recently on a number of important deals in
the North West. Among them is the largest develop-

ment in Cheshire, Pochin plc's construction of a 780-bedroom student accommodation building in Crewe to be let to Manchester Metropolitan University. Over in commercial litigation, Liverpool FC swung its Mace at Middlesbrough FC, which was claiming £6.5 million loss alleged to have arisen out of Liverpool's approach to Christian Ziege. The case reached the Court of Appeal. Other well-known names that choose to spray Mace include the Manchester Ship Canal Company and Balfour Beatty. Infrastructure experts AMEC also prefer the firm, so much so that one of their in-house trainee solicitors is seconded to M&J, leaving room for one of the firm's trainees to go to AMEC for a seat. Spookily, Mace is an anagram of AMEC – hmmm... have the trainees ever been seen together in the same room?

## gainfully employed

Employment law is an M&J speciality and, as one of the more hands-on seats, it is a popular destination for trainees. Clients include Littlewoods, the Highways Agency, Shell, Merseyside Police, the Health & Safety Executive, National Probation Service and one or two others we'd love to name but absolutely can't. Plenty of drafting awaits the employment trainee, though creative expression on *"a precedent or letters of advice and response"* will eventually meet the red pen of the supervisor, who'll *"check and inevitably amend"* things. Regular tribunal hearings need a note taker to frantically scribble *"everything the chairman of the panel says"* or jot down the agreed details of a settlement negotiation. All in all it's a busy and fun six months.

By contrast, at times, corporate seats risk leaving a trainee *"not actively involved in matters,"* though the blame for this is placed firmly at the door of the pressure of work on lawyers. Land here early in your traineeship and you must be prepared to knuckle down to administrative-type tasks; second-year trainees are far more likely to get *"quite involved in even the large deals,"* preparing the due diligence file, completing the minutes for meetings and assisting with completions. One trainee loved their time in the seat, *"organising the documents, chasing people up about deadlines – it's totally hands-on all the time and you get to see a deal through from beginning to end."* Clients range from small owner-managed businesses in Liverpool to a few plcs in Manchester, which is definitely the more active office for corporate work and the preferred place to do a corporate seat. The firm's bag is primarily private limited company M&A, with developing expertise in telecommunications, pharmaceuticals and retail pharmacy-related deals. Clients include Artisan Ship Canal Developments, Auto Trader, Austin Reed, Bank of Ireland, the Co-operative Bank and NatWest.

## court in the act

On the contentious side, one of our sources who had worked on PI litigation reported with satisfaction on their experiences. *"To start with you do a lot of vetting of claims, forming opinion on whether they're worth taking on by phoning clients and getting information out of them. Then you get to draft witness statements and attend a lot of interlocutory hearings before a district judge; there's quite a bit of advocacy, but often no one on the other side shows up."*

More court time will be clocked up in family. The family departments in Manchester and Liverpool concentrate on expensive divorces and only while a trainee will you pick up the remnants of the firm's legal aid caseload. Largely due to the small financial return on these cases – usually care orders – trainees do most of the work. The rest of their time is spent assisting associates, perhaps researching a jurisdiction question in a child custody case or snooping into an offshore trust on a pricey divorce. When in court expect a fair bit of *"waiting around"* and a role getting clients through what is invariably an unfamiliar and emotional process. Said one past master: *"You have to have empathy with clients. Listening skills are a must."* If a first-seater (especially if there is also a newly qualified in your team) you should expect more monkey work, including quite a bit of photocopying and trial bundling.

## lloving your work

The firm's HR machine has been busy, and a new training regime is in place. All seats now come fitted with a work checklist, *"which gives more structure to the training; you're constantly checking against the list now."* If you notice a missing item, associates and partners are more than happy to accommodate.

Competition over seats is unlikely to lead to murder by Trainee Mustard in the boardroom with the stapler, largely due to the fact that choice is limited to six possibilities. All trainees experience four (or if they repeat a seat, three) of the following: employment, property, PI, family, corporate and commercial litigation. They must, however, be prepared to move between offices during the two years, possibly spending no more than two seats in any one office. This is something to bear in mind from a travel and/or residence point of view; live on the wrong side of Manchester and a commute to Liverpool is arduous.

You may have noticed that the firm's website appears in both English and Welsh. Asserting the Jones in Mace & Jones are two lawyers from Blaenau Ffestiniog and Llanfairpwllgwyngyllgogerychwyrndrobwllllantysiliogogogoch (and yes we can pronounce that). Suitably impressed, the University of Bangor signed up with the firm, adding to a solid list of North Wales clients. The Welsh contingent aside, regional connections are the norm at the firm. In the words of one source: *"If they have two candidates who are equally good and one is from round here and the other's from down south, they'll pick the one from round here."*

## (yet another) day at the races

Despite Liverpool having been the firm's HQ for 75 years, Manchester has had more attention lavished upon it lately. An office relocation last year places the Mancunians in the city's old Sun Alliance building, *"a ten-storey, tinted-glass office block."* *"Open-plan floors and glass-fronted meeting rooms"* lead up to *"a massive board room seating 30... all fairly grand and impressive."* Remarkably, one trainee has *"the best seat in the house with a view west across the city."* We would tell you which department it is in but have been sworn to secrecy. The move from older cramped quarters is *"a statement to Manchester."* And what is M&J mouthing at Manchester? *"Everyone had better take us seriously because we're coming through!"* Just in case you didn't quite get the message here it is again – *"We're going to be a dominant force in the Manchester legal market; we'll be up there with the Pinsents, Cobbetts and Halliwells of the world."* Over in Liverpool the firm's offices are close to the Liver Building and within walking distance of the city centre.

Some trainees let slip that the firm's culture is somewhat conservative and old school, and quite hierarchical in places. One or two of the partners prefer to be called Mr so-and-so, rather than have trainees use their first name and *"there are no dress-down days – you always wear a suit."* For the most part, partners and especially associates in most departments *"will always take an interest in you and ask what kind of work you'd like,"* and a trainee forum every six months is as much a chance to air *"any experiences and the pros and cons of each seat"* as it is to plan how to spend the social budget. The talk of the forum must have been last year's table football tournament. Annually, 40 of the region's small businesses gather to play for a hotly contested trophy, hosted by M&J.

And those who enjoy the races will definitely enjoy whiling away a summer's eve at the firm's annual barbecue at Chester racecourse. In fact, the firm has developed quite a habit of visiting the place and uses it for several events. On a more regular basis, All Bar One in Manchester is the venue of choice when trainees meet up. They do so whenever possible, *"although to be fair it's quite difficult with us all spread out over the region."* Partners, bless 'em, pay for drinks for all once a month. In between times, the Liverpool trainees catch up at the popular Newz Bar or down at the docks at the scarily titled Slaughter House.

## and finally...

Conservative with a little 'c', Mace & Jones is banking on bigger things and hoping to become commercial with a bigger 'c'. In a region that's particularly active at the moment, everything is to play for.

# Macfarlanes

## the facts

**Location:** London
**Number of partners/assistants:** 65/124
**Total number of trainees:** 49
**Seats:** 4x6 months
**Alternative seats:** Secondments
**Extras:** Pro bono – Cambridge House Advice Centre, death row appeals; language training

In a world of magic circle giants Macfarlanes proves that smaller can indeed be more beautiful.

## as you were

In the history of humankind, any group or individual defining itself against the mainstream of popular opinion guarantees itself opprobrium at the very least. You're a regular 58,000 BC ape with a notion of standing upright on two limbs instead of using all four. Conclusion: Get out of our tree! You're an observant type in 1568 with a conviction that the world is round and ideas about how to prove it. Conclusion: Expect the Spanish Inquisition. You're a member of a women's social club in 1720 whose activities include chanting, nocturnal walks and a keen interest in small mammals. Conclusion: Burn you witch! You're a normal god-fearing Amish man in 2002 and you prefer to live without modern technology. Conclusion: You luddite religious freak! Yes, 60,000 years of human evolution have proved time and again that we humans are faddish creatures who, alas, don't so much know what we like, as dislike what we don't know.

Which brings us nicely to Macfarlanes, which since the year dot has rigorously pursued a highly profitable formula of doing what it does well and ignoring all faddish changes in the legal profession. Promoting from within, largely ignoring lateral hires, no overseas offices, no trendy new premises, seeking sustained organic growth in areas of core strength – it is a decidedly non-fashionable strategy but it has enabled the firm to achieve the second highest profitability in the UK legal profession for many a year. So what conclusion does the outside world draw? Why, Macfarlanes must be insular, conservative, impenetrable, perhaps cultish and definitely weird.

Challenged with this perception, trainees quickly admit it is "*quite conservative, somewhat insular and fairly risk-averse.*" However, they were equally quick to point out that "*being conservative goes hand in hand with being very profitable: the firm doesn't take massive risks or focus on less important things like having the most up-to-date workstations.*" In simple terms "*why try to fix what isn't broken?*" A perfect example of this approach is found in the firm's "*slightly grotty*" multi-site premises. Said one trainee: "*The meeting room I'm in has new carpet and chairs, so they have made an effort, but there are marks on the wall and the wallpaper's scratched.*" Ultimately it boils down to this: "*If you ask people which they'd prefer, a bonus or swanky new offices, there'd be no competition.*"

## learning your rbv's

What consistently attracts generations of candidates to the firm is that "*it doesn't want to be or pretend to be a magic circle outfit*" and "*it is medium sized but allows you to work on really big-ticket work.*" Amongst many other high-profile matters, it recently advised Pernod Ricard on its £7 billion bid for drinks giant Allied Domecq, and Cable & Wireless on its £700 million bid for Energis. Across all of its departments, the firm acts for a wealth of household-name clients such as Trainline, Campbell Soups, Hat Trick Productions, Jaguar Racing, Fitness First, Reebok, the Ministry of Sound, Virgin Group, Anheuser-Busch, Saatchi & Saatchi and Anglian Windows. Those we interviewed all valued the feeling of "*not being a drone, one in a hundred and twenty trainees*" but recognised the concomitant – "*you often work extremely hard, especially in the mainstream corporate seats.*"

A corporate seat is "*a lull-and-storm existence: when you're incredibly busy you yearn for a quiet day, but in the quiet weeks you're desperate for some work.*" Furthermore, our interviewees enjoyed a level of responsibility that sometimes left them dreaming of dull data room management. "*You're basically treated like a junior assistant,*" enthused one, another gasping: "*I've done verification exercises, assembled documents and liaised with clients, researched complex share structures and travelled to completion meetings overseas.*" The relatively small size of the firm partly explains this trend "*with less hierarchy and structure in relation to who does what, you sometimes do the menial stuff as a trainee but just as often you get a task because you're the only one available or you've been working on a matter to date so it makes most sense.*" Some partners are especially happy to give trainees supervised autonomy on smaller deals, but as a true indication of the way Macfarlanes' size impacts on trainees, we couldn't ask for a better example than the story about a trainee who in their first seat attended a meeting with a magic circle firm and a major bank. Just before it began, the Macfarlanes partner and his assistant were called into another room leaving the trainee to take the meeting with the magic circle partner, his assistant, his trainee and the bank.

Schedules are sufficiently pressured that the corporate departments have a weekly form-based assessment to ensure that individual lawyers aren't snowed under. Tick box R if you are Ready For More, B if you are Busy, and V if so Very Busy that you can't possibly take on more work. Our hard-bitten source chuckled: "*You don't often tick less than B!*"

## voulez vous du cash?

As a general rule trainees rotate through seats in litigation, property and mainstream corporate, taking a fourth seat either in private client or another, more specialised, area of corporate law, like tax or competition. The corporate hungry among trainees (or the occasional few who can't be fitted into a litigation seat) can opt for a week-long advocacy course that fulfils the Law Society's contentious experience requirement and was described as "*adequate – the theory part was inspiring but the practical part was rotten.*" As a consequence, the firm is now reviewing its choice of course provider. Litigation itself can involve anything from mainstream commercial, to specialist IP to matters relating to private client issues and is overall "*a more protected department*"although, "*partners are still very keen to get you actively involved.*" Like commercial property "*it is more relaxed and laidback than the corporate departments... laidback in a conservative way that is!*" In commercial property, another main player in the firm, trainees enjoy the greatest diversity of work, "*running your own files, giving legal advice over the phone, always the first point of contact for clients,*" "*you do landlord and tenant stuff, licences to assign, commercial sales and purchases, development matters and get a lot of responsibility.*" In addition, seats are also available in a range of "*small and friendly*" satellites such as funds, tax, competition, commercial and employment, the latter being particularly sought after.

With all this choice and no international offices, opportunities to flee the nest are neither much in evidence nor massively desired. There's a regular secondment to 3i and a three-month posting to the Court of Appeal to act as a judge's assistant. "*Most assistants seem to go on secondment when one to two years' qualified, which makes more sense as then you're investing in your chosen field.*" However, "*a good proportion of our work is international,*" so those with language skills do find themselves using them not infrequently and occasionally to bizarre ends. "*I got called into the private client department* to translate for a client's French maid who was being made a gift of money. That was odd." Alors!

It is an experience that few contemporaries at big City firms are likely to have, not least because Macfarlanes is one of the only major firms to maintain a private client department. Currently bringing in an estimated 12–13% of the firm's turnover, the team is no stunted offshoot, a fact underlined by the making up of three private client partners this year. As well as giving "breadth to your training contract," a seat here offers trainees experience in a range of probate, trusts and personal tax matters, often including landed estates and hence "frequent overlap with the property team."

## from the castle to the priory

Our sources praised the "high quality of training" and "the close attention that supervisors pay to your work." In all seats supervisors conduct appraisals; these are then reviewed by a partner from the training committee and the trainee's own mentor partner, the latter also obliging with the odd meal out under the smoke screen of a pastoral chat. Conversely, for a firm that "isn't the biggest risk-taker, they are actually very brave with their training ethos. A partner told me there genuinely isn't any work that you wouldn't be allowed to try if you asked."

"It's intimidating quite how clever everyone else seems to be; you only hope you seem the same to them," reflected one humble source. Most possessing distinctions or commendations from the LPC, "about half" graduated from Oxbridge and the remainder from other good universities. "Everyone is an individual: there are intellectual introverts, socialising extroverts, but everyone seems happy to be themselves." We note that the typical Macfarlanes virtues of "hard work, diligence, articulacy and personability" remain strong. Proving their commitment to the distinctive cult of Macfarlanes, 13 of the 14 qualifiers stayed on with the firm in 2005. Just as their foretrainees did and their foretrainees' foretrainees...

We were struck once again by the variety of interests that trainees boast – "there are sportsmen, dancers, artsy types, musicians, you name it." Perhaps it is this factor that sometimes leaves the social scene "slightly underdeveloped... it practically died for six months when The Castle closed." Thankfully the establishment has reopened after a refurbishment and every Friday you'll find "at least a hundred Macfarlanes employees from support staff to partners drinking on the pavement outside." There are biannual trainee events and a triennial firm ball, last time a sumptuous affair at Billingsgate Fish Market featuring "Cirque Du Soleil performers, a bouncy castle, lasers and lots of champagne." Laudably, some trainees have tried to arrange "other events that don't revolve around alcohol." Appropriately enough, when we interviewed trainees, the next such dry-social was a trip to watch Ewan McGregor in Guys And Dolls. Prohibition America and The Pledge: perhaps all the trainees will be on the wagon next year. Watch this space.

## and finally...

Steady is as steady does. If you want the benefits of a big-ticket City training with improved levels of responsibility, then Macfarlanes is your pick. No fireworks, no razzamatazz, just a cast-iron guarantee of quality training and an oh-so-impressive name for your CV.

# Manches LLP

## the facts

**Location:** London, Oxford
**Number of partners/assistants:** 52/60
**Total number of trainees:** 20
**Seats:** 4x6 months
**Alternative seats:** Occasional secondments

London and Oxford-based Manches is a perennial favourite of the student seeking civilised working conditions in a mid-sized firm with varied interests.

# the true picture

## family business

Founded in 1930 by a double-glazing magnate, the firm is still very much in family hands. The founder's daughter is the present chairman and his son heads up the property department. We noticed there was even a Ms Manches among the trainee group. Fitting as it is that Manches is renowned for its world-beating family department, the people we chatted to were equally attracted to the sheer diversity of work on offer during the training contract. Recent highlights have included the arrival of the commercial litigation team from US firm Shook Hardy, bringing with them clients including Ryanair. The firm also restructured and consolidated its IP, technology and media team following the exit of two key partners, and in doing so has won clients including Gizmondo, Elle Macpherson Intimates and Karen Millen. Two or three trainees at a time get to experience this popular work. It's good news all round for the commercial property practice, which as well as adding two new partners has drawn Pizza Hut, Oasis and Heal's to an existing client list plump with such retail giants as Argos, Moss Bros, Liberty and WHSmith.

Manches' main London office occupies smart premises on the Aldwych, surrounded by hotels, theatres and various venerable national institutions. Covent Garden is on the doorstep for lunch, post-work drinks or a spot of busking in the lean days before payday. A typical training experience will involve time in property, with the remaining three seats chosen from family, corporate, employment, construction, commercial litigation and IP/tech/media. "*My main criterion was to avoid something which was bland and corporate,*" said one source. "*The idea of doing completely different seats appealed to me.*"

The London office is just about big enough so that "*every department has its own personality. The family department is good fun; it is idiosyncratic and full of quirky personalities,*" and in many respects it is the firm's crown jewel. Our parent publication *Chambers UK* ranks Manches best in

town for family, and this department certainly proved a pull to many of the trainees we spoke with. "*I felt very privileged to be working there,*" reported one. Manches' lawyers are known for their representation of the great, the good and the plain old rich and famous, and have also appeared in a number of the important reported cases of the recent past. If the litigation of the 'post-White era' means anything to you, then you'll understand how influential the firm has been. With marital finance featuring large, trainees end up "*working on big money aspects, trusts and financial vehicles... you get to work with the best counsel and spend time in court.*" As well as assisting with "*complex financial situations, dividing assets and working out settlements*" for those with pots of cash, trainees manage less complex cases for more ordinary folk, if only because less affluent clients find it easier to pay the bill when trainees have been deployed on their files. Both types of work are demanding – "*you are literally working non-stop throughout the day*" – and training is recognised as being "*of a very high standard.*" Those of our interviewees who wanted to make a career in family law fully understood that "*if you've trained in the family department of Manches, you can do anything after that.*"

## anything but monkey business

The firm's commercial work was another draw for our interviewees, one confirming that they had been looking for "*a firm which was commercial but without the broker and banker type of culture.*" If you get a buzz from business but don't want to get swamped by the hours and huge intakes of big City players, then mid-sized options such as Manches are definitely to be explored. "*Someone working here isn't going to end up on an enormous salary, but having spoken to friends in the City, the type of work they're given is nothing like the stuff I've been working on. I don't get thrown scraps, I am doing real work,*" reasoned one source. Just to prove that Manches can provide a home for all sorts, one trainee told us:

"*I wanted to do commercial work because the personal dimension of family law didn't appeal to me. I didn't want that emotional link with my work.*" FT junkies beware though: the size of deals handled in no way matches the big firms – "*We do AIM listings and mid-market M&A.*" In property, trainees reported handling a number of their own files and spoke of partners devoting a lot of time to overseeing their training. In litigation trainees were pleased to become "*very much involved in drafting, liaising with witnesses and developing strategy.*"

## enthusiastic support

Trainees praised the firm's supportive atmosphere, one telling us: "*If the supervisor is away there are always other people to speak to.*" On-the-job training experiences are supplemented by in-house know-how sessions in each department. And it's never a case of having to sneak off to attend them, "*we're encouraged to go to lectures and seminars.*" Trainees generally feel at ease, even though "*there is a definite sense of where you stand in the hierarchy. It varies from department to department, but it's not stuffy and you can voice an opinion.*" A piece of advice to those keen to get off to a good start: "*Never be afraid of asking questions, it shows enthusiasm.*"

One minor grumble is that "*the appraisal system is a little bit random. It makes me wonder if it is based on individual departments' wishes rather than a single format. But having said that I asked for informal feedback in one department and I got it.*" A couple of other people pointed out that, relative to larger firms, support systems were less comprehensive. Another suggested area for improvement would be to provide "*more soft skills training,*" though we suspect this request came as a result of appetites already being whetted by sessions on how to network ("*the key is to just go for it and not feel stupid*") and manage time (apparently a great course if you have a tendency to "*leak time*"). Overall, however, trainees had little to moan about other than the odd paper cut from

bouts of excessive photocopying. With nine out of ten qualifiers being retained in September 2005, both the trainees and the firm seem pretty happy with their respective sides of the bargain.

## a breed apart

Our sources felt they had made a more considered choice than some of their contemporaries who were lured by the big bucks and bright lights of the City giants. "*If you apply for a mid-sized firm you are generally planning to make a career for yourself there,*" thought one. "*In my year trainees opted to stay even though they didn't all get their first choice of NQ job.*" Trainees also offered some considered opinions on the kind of people that the firm attracts. Said one: "*I'd read in a previous edition of your guide that there were lots of eccentric people, which appealed.*" Someone else was relieved that they had found "*eccentrics rather than egos.*" Instead of hordes of recent graduates, "*there are lots of second jobbers, so people came with commercial experience. Of my intake only one has done an undergrad law degree.*" Trainees tell us there is a distinction between the magic circle type and the Manches type. "*Some of us are a little bit quirky. There's a sense of maturity and individualism which makes for a more interesting climate to work in.*" In terms of personality, "*we are not wallflowers but we're not arrogant. Trainees have firm ideas about things and want to have a good work-life balance. We're not ambitious to the point of having nothing else in life.*"

In terms of how you tackle your work, "*you have to be communicative and head-on in your approach. It's important to develop a good relationship with partners, and you must be able to hold your own and be willing to muck in.*" It sounds as if it's all about striking the right balance. "*It's fine to keep your head down, but if you are very introverted you might not get on so well. If you're someone who likes constant attention and reassurance you won't get on well either. You're given the opportunity to shine and if you need help it's there, but not if you need it constantly.*"

# the true picture

Though trainees say the hours are much better than at the bigger, more deal-driven firms down the road in the EC postcodes, don't think that this is a nine-to-five job. "*If there's a tight deadline you must be in whenever necessary, and you'll occasionally be in for late nights and weekends.*" Perhaps because they don't need to work in an excessive manner during the week, trainees "*don't tend to go out on Friday night and get absolutely trolleyed.*" It's not that they don't socialise, just that they do so in a more measured way. Every quarter, the firm hosts 'ten pound nights' in a local pub, and this acts as a good opportunity for staff to mingle beyond their usual groupings. Given that the firm sponsors the annual Manches Cup sailing regatta, you'd expect sport to be pretty important; interesting then that the two events we heard most about were softball and table football!

## lords of the ringroad

The smaller Oxford office boasts the winning combination of a more intimate environment and a wide and glamorous client base. Though it moved from a city centre location out to the Oxford Business Park earlier this year, it is still well placed to take work from the Oxford colleges, publishers and nearby hi-tech companies. It also handles legal matters on behalf of local writers and the Tolkien Estate, which owns the copyrights in the literary and artistic works of JRR and a large portfolio of trade marks. We have to say, from where we stand, the Oxford office represents a brilliant opportunity for any commercially minded trainee who wants to start and continue a career among the dreaming spires.

## and finally...

Manches can offer a halfway house between town and country – if you enjoy the diary pages as much as the city pages and want the chance to work with people as well as profits, take a closer look.

# Martineau Johnson

## the facts

**Location:** Birmingham, London
**Number of partners/assistants:** 39/99
**Total number of trainees:** 21
**Seats:** 6x4 months
**Alternative seats:** None

"Midlands-based firm with excellent niches WLTM solvent commercial clients (GSOH, NS pref.) for friendship and maybe more. Has London flat, will travel." This is Martineau Johnson, around since the 19th century, now breaking into the 21st century.

## i will survive

Break-ups blighted 2004 and early 2005; some of MJ's partners just wouldn't stay. The first of the defections came in May 2004 when Cobbetts hired IP specialist Mauro Paiano. MJ then lost tax and trusts chief Matthew Hansell to Mills & Reeve in October. Energy specialist Paul Brennan quit next, followed by head of pensions Simon Laight and the head of education Nicola Hart who left for Pinsents. With 2005 came the loss to Stoke-on-Trent firm Heatons of former commercial litigation head Andrew Spooner. Like any broken-hearted ex, MJ did the only thing it could: it dolled itself up

Change had to come and many thought MJ's traditional approach was in need of spin. As one source noted: "*Image is as important as doing the work.*" The firm's old offices admittedly "*had quite big windows,*" but the small client reception areas were "*not a great selling point.*" The need to market a slicker image to clients came as an epiphany to the firm with, according to trainees, a reputation for not entirely proactive client gathering. A "*brand-spanking new office*" at 1 Colmore Square is accompanied by a new telephone system, "*sort of curvy*" desks behind which staff sit in their new "*Shiatsu-like all-singing and all-dancing*" chairs of the future ("*we had to have a training session just to show us how to work them*"). And, having lost the impracticality of an office spread across two buildings, interdepartmental communication has at last been facilitated.

Formerly trainees were holed up in a room with their supervising partner – fine if you got on, less than fortuitous if you didn't – but with the new open-plan working they sit grouped with two fee earners as well as their partner. This generates a "*greater variety*" of work as files can come from three directions rather than a single source and trainees say they are no longer kept out of the loop. All in all the move has been very well received by trainees, who tell us MJ needs the extra space in the new building "*for potential expansion.*" And how will this expansion develop? "*We will continue to concentrate on niche markets and then just encourage a corporate client base.*"

## university challenges

Martineau has a wide array of departments from litigation to agricultural and rural affairs, including top-ranking private client and charities departments. Clients range from the landed gentry of Warwickshire to international NGOs. Impressively, the firm advised on the terms of an emissions reduction purchase agreement in connection with a Kyoto Protocol Clean Development Mechanism project in India last year. It also seems to have a thing for dons and deans, and across the firm you will come into contact with universities. The education department's client portfolio includes the University of Wales, Cardiff (guided through a merger with the University of Wales, College of Medicine) and recent acquisition Plymouth University. In employment matters Aston, Coventry, Plymouth, Aberystwyth, Cardiff and Warwick universities are all represented, and the firm's health and safety and IT teams deal with Birmingham and Staffordshire universities respectively.

Unlike most of the larger Brum firms MJ operates a six-seat training scheme, probably because it's the only way recruits can take full advantage of so

many specialist areas of work. A corporate and a property seat are 'preferred' but beyond these there is an almost endless list to choose from. But what about lack of experience after just four months in a seat? Experience-shmerience, what about the experience of six whole seats for the inexperienced who don't know what to choose! Plus you'll probably end up in the same seat twice, allowing you to be certain of your choice of qualification department. For MJ trainees there may also be strategic reasons for wanting to double or even triple-up on seats, as some of them do. Spending an entire year in the same department allows you to hone impressive skills, far better than "*if you have to apply somewhere else afterwards and only had four months' experience.*" The people we interviewed quite naturally had their futures in mind after watching the firm's intake of trainees drop from 13 to nine in 2004, with trainees asked to defer starting their training contracts. In 2005 the intake returned to normal and the firm has been "*keen to reassure everyone there are more jobs than trainees on qualification.*" Indeed, the final score – seven out of eight staying in 2005 – proved exactly this.

## more tea vicar?

Among the seat options is a posting to the firm's eight-lawyer satellite office in London. Trainees say they are "*quite strongly encouraged*" to go there but that "*no one is forced.*" Somewhere in between voluntary and mandatory then. The lawyers in the capital specialise in banking litigation, private client, property and environment law. As the contentious banking seat is so popular in Birmingham, going to London is sometimes "*the only option*" for a trainee intent on sampling this work. Not wishing to leave trainees stranded in the Big Smoke, the firm provides accommodation. The London office is "*fantastic – it feels like a small firm, only you step out and just happen to see St Paul's Cathedral!*" The cases in litigation, include defending banking clients from customers suing for discriminatory behaviour in the granting of loans and shaggy dog "*cases of people who fall downstairs and then say that a contract signed afterwards is invalid because they don't know what they're doing."* Trainees frequently end up in the High Court sitting behind a barrister and the odd solo appearance before a master in chambers also spices things up.

Back in Brum non-contentious insolvency seats see trainees being partner-fed tasks. Never will they run their own case, they are all *"too big and too complex;"* they will, however, be allowed to *"view the big picture."* Completion meetings can *"sometimes run into the night"* though – as across the firm – staying late is an irregularity. The corporate department was formerly *"quite quiet"* but since the office move trainees feel the work has *"picked up"* and several deal completions have been greeted with champagne, *"which is always a bonus!"* In a corporate seat, drafting board minutes, completion agendas for M&A deals and letters, updating statutory books and exhuming *"the skeletons in the cupboard"* for due diligence research are all on a trainee's to-do list. Be warned: *"Photocopying is always a trainee thing, but there is a mixture of that sort of work and good work."*

In the world of private client law, the posturing and puffery of commercial negotiations are missing; however our sources assure us the seat is positively unstilted, varied and *"not as boring as you'd think."* Trainees grapple with in-depth legal research while talking to *"very rich people"* and the *"illustrious"* of the Midlands. Over in the landed estates department there are plenty of Lords and Ladies with whom trainees do not usually speak, though the voyeurs among them will get *"quite a good look at their houses."* MJ also handles transactions on behalf of the diocese of Birmingham, so selling run-down rectories and granting leases to youth-clubs in church halls will be part of your daily bread. Phone calls to the bishop and ancient land claims aside, trainees also act as direct advisers on *"commoners'"* questions. Some thorny issues arise beyond disputed hedgerows – *"one guy wanted to know if he could bury his father in the back garden."*

The aforementioned commoner was not religious and wanted an eco-burial for his dad. The problem required much sifting through legislation, case law and disposal certification to identify potential public health issues. Was the burial to be near a watercourse? If so, did the deceased die of something contagious? Does a garden become a cemetery if someone is buried there? *"What if someone buys it? You'd have to tell them or they'd dig a corpse up and think there was a murder!"* Perpetrated by Reverend Green with the chandelier in the choirmaster's study perhaps.

## dig for victory

MJ has become community-aware. Contrary to popular opinion, Birmingham is the UK's greenest city, with trees and parks aplenty, and all of them in need of pruning and weeding. MJ lawyers have answered the call, so join the firm and you should expect to find yourself trowel-in-hand in a community project before qualification. Working for the greater good may be part of the new drive *"to bring Martineaus in line with other firms."*

More greenery was found at the Birmingham Trainee Solicitors Society (BTSS) bash at the Botanical Gardens. The theme of the 2005 summer ball was Bling, and the event culminated in a coronation for *"the king and queen of bling."* A second BTSS bash takes place each winter and – like the summer ball – MJ pays for trainees to attend. The event is seen as *"potentially good for networking"* and a chance *"to represent the firm."* The November event also includes partners (the office sort not the home sort) so *"in theory you have to behave yourself"*... not that partners would know about most trainee indiscretions as *"they leave after the dinner and speech."*

The BTSS also gave triumphant MJ trainees their own sports trophy for 2005. Excelling in a series of games intended to test the physical and mental agility of Brum's young lawyers, MJ won out in netball, water polo, the beautiful game and the venerable events of wacky racing and giant Jenga. Trips to comedy clubs, theatres, bowling and quiz nights fill out the year and Fridays are for drinks in local bars. And on the subject of awards, despite the pre-move setbacks and the stress adjusting to a new home, MJ attained a respectable debut ranking at number 71 in the *Sunday Times'* '100 Best Companies to Work For' survey in 2005. For trainees the award manifests itself in a pay rise putting them in line with the bigger firms in Birmingham.

## and finally...

With its swish premises and the promise of commercial expansion, Martineau Johnson suddenly has new appeal. The numbers are also looking good with a modest increase in profits and turnover for 2004/5.

# Mayer Brown Rowe & Maw LLP

## the facts

**Location:** London
**Number of partners/assistants:** 97/143
**Total number of trainees:** 54
**Seats:** 4x6 months
**Alternative seats:** Brussels, secondments
**Extras:** Pro bono – RCJ CAB, Bar pro Bono Unit, Liberty, Islington, Fulham and Toynbee Hall law centres; language training

One of the biggest law firms in the world, Mayer Brown Rowe & Maw stretches across the globe from the west coast of America to the east coast of China. Its operation on the meridian does more than keep things in balance: London has been an important part of the equation for nearly four years.

## the luck of the irish

Wooed by the prospect of a few Hershey bars and a couple of pairs of nylons, century-strong English rose Rowe & Maw succumbed to the charms of Chicago player Mayer Brown & Platt in 2002. Rowe & Maw had a reputation that erred on the disabling side of caution. Mayer Brown & Platt had a small but kick-ass finance-based operation in the capital. By merging, Mayer Brown Rowe & Maw became one of a growing number of transatlantic couplings and, indeed, many now hold it up as an example of how these things should be done. The merger thrust the London operation onto the worldwide stage and put within its reach clients that it would never otherwise have got its hands on. For the Americans, the London acquisition gave them instant strength in numbers in the UK and a gateway to European business.

Within the corridors of the firm's principal Pilgrim Street office in London, the merger is known colloquially as *"the combination."* And while we're on the subject of what to call things, apparently there's no more sure-fire way of attracting senior partner Paul Maher's ire than to call the firm 'American'. For the record, *"it's international not American,"* and with 13 offices around the world, you can understand why. Quite the globetrotter, MBRM has a London client list that now boasts countless multinationals: Nestlé, Easyjet, Cable & Wireless, EMI, Virgin, AT&T, Reuters, Rothschild, Société Générale, Bank of America, RBS, Dow Chemical, Volkswagen... need we say more? Recent highlights include the representation of ICI on the sale of a US, Canadian and European Vinamul Polymers business for $208 million, and Danske Bank on its agreement to buy Northern Bank and National Irish Bank from National Australia Bank for £967 million. What is it about the firm and the Irish at the moment? It has just advised Sloane Capital, the property fund of Irish horseracing tycoons John Magnier and JP McManus, on the £170 million sale and leaseback of central London offices occupied by Standard Chartered Bank.

## a sporting chance

And did someone almost mention football? Here, too, the firm is becoming ever more active, lately advising The FA in its defence of employment tribunal proceedings brought by the former PA Faria Alam, and on its £150 million negligence claim against law firm Hammonds concerning problems arising out of The FA's contract with ITV Digital. New client Midland Group confirms the sporting trend, the Canadian company instructing the firm for its acquisition of Jordan Grand Prix. Sending lawyers to the International Court of Arbitration for Sport, MBRM is now advising US track and fielders and Canadian rowers in selection and title disputes.

A growing area of practice post-merger, corporate is *"absolutely, definitely compulsory"* for trainees. From a number of interviewees we heard that time in the department offers *"nothing particularly interesting"* and the seat brings *"no responsibility, only grunt work."* Most drafting is done by associates and NQs, leaving trainees to man the data room, manage due diligence exercises, index and bible. They receive regular training sessions covering *"various aspects of corporate law,"* but regret *"the lack of opportunity to put much of it into practice."* All had sat with partners but only some were given a rare, *"quirky treat"* such as phoning a client on a small deal or writing a supervised letter. Most of our sources had been regarded as *"the team trainee"* and felt that for *"12-13 hours a day"* they were at the team's beck and call. Yet, even if waiting around into the night for a single document to surface is *"annoying,"* the golden rule is to simply *"roll up your sleeves and don't make enemies."*

## using your noodle

*"Making allies"* in finance is far more rewarding, and here it sounds as if you are treated as *"an assistant"* not photocopier fodder. *"More responsibility"* is your due after a stint in corporate and that's just what you get. Writing letters *"in your own name"* and learning how to draft security documentation, trainees say you feel closer to your supervisors and enjoy being their shadow. They particularly like the fact that *"you can have all your stupid questions answered patiently."* This seat is not admin-free, as finance work is heavily oriented towards *"the organisational side of loan transactions."* One trainee whose interests and talent clearly lay elsewhere candidly confirmed: *"I never really got beyond understanding that fact really – there was a real buzz in the department, though."* It may have been generated by the hive of US lawyers – one trainee concluded: *"They buzz around more than we do."* The *"American-heavy"* finance department is dominated by a *"strong, old Mayer Brown & Platt contingent,"* which has contributed to changing *"the work culture but not the work ethos."* At times it's just like it is in the movies: *"Sitting together and eating takeaway Chinese at three in the morning is weird!"*

A relic of the old Rowe & Maw, public law is one of the firm's most interesting areas of practice. Many view it as the best in the City for public sector disputes, and it has been involved in some of the key issues in administrative law, most famously fronting the inquiry into Tesco heiress Dame Shirley Porter's foulest hour over the Westminster 'Homes for Votes' scandal. Clients range from the Mayor of London to local authorities and the NHS. One trainee spoke wistfully of their time in the department, praising *"down-to-earth public sector clients"* and the opportunity to have *"plenty of contact"* with them. Wading in for district auditors against local councils, and acting for the parliamentary ombudsman in her investigation into the Equitable Life collapse is all in a day's work. This *"Napoleon of Notting Hill sort of thing"* is likely to appeal to some types more than others, but if you're into *"eclecticism"* and bizarre research, that type might well be you. The mix of work ranges from access-to-information wrangles for the Falklands government and the disclosure of witnesses' identities during the Stephen Lawrence Inquiry, to a House of Lords case to determine whether the entry clearance system operated by British immigration officers at Prague airport in July 2001 unlawfully discriminated against those of Romani ethnic origin. Unfortunately this treasure trove of legal thrills is only available to one trainee at a time.

## knotty problems

International arbitration is another intriguing area of work. MBRM's highly respected practice juggles jurisdictional muddles across time zones for all kinds of clients. *"You could be using English law for Portuguese and Arab parties, or French law for Brazilian and Japanese clients."* Dealing with a pick 'n' mix of common and civil laws, with reams of international cases to scour, trainees take the role of researchers into this *"slippery and complex yet fascinating"* world. Less routine than High Court litigation (which is bound by rigid and prescriptive practice rules), international arbitration allows a trainee to witness more *"fluid"* and purposive practice. Naturally, unpicking whole problems won't fall to a trainee, but the odd witness interview might. As if all this weren't enough, the other office-based seat options include pensions, employment, construction, real estate, IP, commercial litigation, insurance, tax and environmental law.

Secondments to Unilever, insurance broker Marsh & McLennan, Reuters, ICI, Cable & Wireless, AstraZeneca and National Starch are all good opportunities to spend one of your four seats out of the office. All offer the holy grail of *"autonomy,"* and although *"the pace is slower," "accountability is higher."* What's more, an *"up-front relationship"* with clients means there is no hiding behind a water cooler; *"you really get to see what clients want in a client context."* Despite the network of international offices, only the Brussels branch is open to trainees and it offers six months of EU competition, though there is another client secondment to a Belgian company. *"One day, secondments to other places will crop up – if they want the cross-fertilisation to make the firm truly international then they'll have to start them,"* a source predicted.

Last year trainees stopped short of passing judgement on the long-term effects of the merger on London's autonomy and its working practices. Though still hesitant to do so, they did allude to certain changes, saying: *"If you merge with a big American firm there's bound to be added pressures on billing."* They also told us: *"Sometimes even when you've finished your work it is not acceptable to go before 7pm."* The hours – and certainly the training styles – differ between departments; sometimes a close relationship with a supervisor is encouraged, sometimes freelancing for the team is the only option. It sounds to us as if the trainee experience mirrors the London office as a whole: *"Mayer Brown is not so much a firm as firms within a firm. Saying something about corporate would not be true of finance or litigation, and they don't really mix."*

## o'hare today...

A trainee liaison group meets to organise social things (especially for new joiners and vac students) and speak generally with HR on training-related issues. On a wider level there are others in the firm busy masterminding fun and games. The litigation department apparently hosted a softball event in Hyde Park and graciously allowed the corporate team to win. The Christmas party is a big, office-wide event, and more regularly there are departmental evenings and training days. The finance team easyJetted all the way to Berlin last year for an *"on the whole enjoyable"* training weekend. But perhaps the highlight of your training at MBRM will be in its closing act. To underline its international agenda, the firm pay for all those taking NQ jobs to hit the tarmac at O'Hare for a week of schmoozing in the firm's Windy City HQ. In 2005, some 15 of the 19 qualifying trainees did just that.

## and finally...

Blue-chip clients, increasingly international work and a nice trip to Chicago at the end of it all, it is no surprise that Mayer Brown Rowe & Maw is an ever more popular destination for aspiring City trainees. If the firm can iron out some of the remaining issues with its corporate training, it can expect beaming smiles all round.

# the true picture

# McCormicks

## the facts

**Location:** Leeds
**Number of partners/assistants:** 12/29
**Total number of trainees:** 9
**Seats:** 4x6 months
**Alternative seats:** None

Describing itself as a fearless law firm with a fearsome reputation, Leeds firm McCormicks does a lot of barking, but backs it up with one heck of a bite. With its teeth sunk firmly into a rich diet of charities, sports law and commercial practice this firm is your original Yorkshire terrier.

## fight club

Using the word fearless to describe someone is essentially a polite way of saying they are a lunatic. The fearless person is one who takes on challenges and commits to actions that the majority of us would avoid at all costs, like climbing Everest or wrestling naked with tigers. By this criterion is McCormicks really the fearless outfit it claims? Well there's evidence to suggest that if the firm is not 100% certifiably insane, then it is certainly just that little bit crazier than Average Joe law firm. First, consider McCormicks' proud self-celebration as Leeds legal scene's gutsy lightweight with the right hook of a heavyweight. Since 1983 pint-sized McCormicks has been battering its way to an excellent reputation; it is, if you will, the law firm equivalent of the whippety teenage boxing sensation Amir Khan. Trainees delighted in telling us *"you'd probably only class us a small/medium firm but the standard of employees and the nature of the clientele puts us on another level."* A crazy claim? Not when you consider that the firm represents the FA, the Premier League, Leeds United, Hull FC, charities like the Duke of Edinburgh's Award, the Outward Bound Trust and Age Concern plus a host of theatre and television companies and media personalities.

Second, we present characterful senior partner Peter McCormick OBE, a man whom trainees cannot mention without laughing and whom they cannot praise highly enough. *"Without a doubt Peter is a larger than life character and he's a huge part of the firm's success,"* gushed one admirer, whilst others described him as *"massively driven – he works harder than anyone else at the firm."* What's more *"there's no reason for him to do it all now, but he thrives on the graft and getting out there."* The presence of this *"no-nonsense, straight-talking figure"* undoubtedly informs the firm's fearless attitude and seems to be at the heart of a *"plain-speaking, direct ethos that involves a great sense of camaraderie and requires a sense of humour."* True, there was less talk this year of Monday morning reveal-your-weekend-indiscretions meetings and rubber band flicking competitions on a Friday. However, we were assured that *"a frantically busy few months"* had slowed such activity, but that *"at the monthly fee earners meetings Peter is his boisterous self,"* and *"at fee earners conferences, where we all stay in a hotel together,"* there are all the characteristic high jinks we've come to expect. *"Creme Egg-eating competitions, drinking games, drunken debauchery and even a 1,000-piece jigsaw puzzle."*

Third, note the way in which trainees take to this culture. *"You've got to be feisty and boisterous to work here,"* they tell us. *"You've got to be willing to get out there whether it be in legal or marketing terms and back yourself up." "We're all ambitious and believe in our own ability."* This self-confident, articulate bunch seem to thrive on a *"culture of independence;"* they are keen to emphasise *"individuality"* as a key McCormicks trait. They range from the urbane to the bluff but each possesses a definite touch of the fearless.

## a sporting chance

In choosing where to take their four six-month seats trainees can select from private client (including family), corporate and commercial, corporate crime and risk, corporate recovery, commercial dispute resolution (including employment) and commercial property. If you're wondering where the exciting media/broadcasting and sports law bits fit in then you'll be pleased to hear that *"although they are separate and well-developed practices, the work they generate filters across almost every department."* Hence a seat in employment might see you helping a supervisor on the transfer of players to Leeds United from AC Milan or drafting the contracts for TV's *Dream Team.* A stint in corporate might see you help with IP/IT advice to the FA regarding unofficial calendars or exploiting new media opportunities. Spend time in commercial litigation and you might assist celebrities like Nell McAndrew, Paul Merton or the cast members from Emmerdale on defamation and reputation management matters.

However, this section of the *Student Guide* isn't called the True Picture for nothing and we'd be failing in our responsibility if we didn't point out that *"the sports and celebrities work is enjoyable, but it's only one side of the firm."* The firm's main client base is composed of *"owner-managed businesses, larger local firms and smaller national firms."* Flip the starry McCormicks coin over and you end up getting your hands dirty. A seat in employment might see you *"drafting employee handbooks for a charity,"* commercial litigation could involve *"working on a termination of a distribution agreement for a small business"* and corporate might demand *"patience as you draft board minutes and resolutions."* The corporate team last year advised school supplies company TeacherBoards on a £6 million disposal and the ghd hair people Jemella Group on negotiations in relation to a proposed new business in Denmark and distribution agreements in Scandinavia.

The private side of the firm's practice is largely accounted for by the family department, which *"represents wealthy business people in respect of ancillary relief, divorce or trusts and succession planning."* A good deal of the department's work is *"referred by the corporate practice,"* which is also true of commercial property when those *"owner-managed* businesses need to arrange a lease or move premises, or charities have issues with their property portfolios."* The exception is the criminal department, which offers trainees experience of *"the full gamut of crime from Friday night beatings-up to top-end regulatory fraud matters."* Such corporate crime work is another feather in McCormicks' cap and the firm regularly defends individuals or groups against serious fraud allegations brought by the FSA.

## putting your butt into it

Trainees are highly enthusiastic about a *"rigorous and challenging"* yet *"highly supportive"* training that is focused more than anything *"on practising the skills you'll need as a qualified lawyer, rather than training for its own sake."* Regular feedback from supervisors, monthly meetings with the managing partner and six-weekly meetings with the trainee's current department head left our sources feeling *"in control of the way training is going."* That's before you factor in the benefits of working closely with expert supervisors: *"It's like watching a professional sportsman like Michael Vaughan: you admire their technique and ability and learn from them."* Sure, *"you sometimes do the garbage tasks, but it's quid pro quo, you get the chance to take on responsibility on quality work too."* Such reciprocity is also evident in trainee-founded group MyLaw, which is a forum *"for all younger members of the firm to raise issues"* as well as organising *"marketing events for young professionals in the Leeds business community so you can learn the skills of networking and make contacts for when you're qualified."* On which subject, we can report that retention rates are generally good and in 2005 all four qualifiers stayed on with the firm.

Organic growth is an oft-repeated mantra at McCormicks, and on this score the firm is as good as its word. This year it knocked through from Britannia Chambers into 5-6 Oxford Place so that *"we're not all sitting on top of each other now."* Britannia Chambers is a veritable mountain of stairs, which trainees admit *"give you buttocks of steel, you're up and down them all day long."* A far-flung

Harrogate office is important to the corporate crime department (and has good family, crime and residential conveyancing practices) but doesn't much concern trainees "*unless you've got a meeting with a Harrogate-based client.*"

Situated smack bang in the middle of Leeds, McCormicks' location gives easy access to the city's "*rejuvenated, café-bar, open-all-hours*" culture. The Vic remains the favourite pub with trainees, although the dubiously named Baby Cream is another regular haunt. A social committee takes up what little slack there is and organises trips to the dogs or local theatres; naturally the firm's summer and Christmas parties involve "*the consumption of fairly substantial amounts of liquid.*" After last year's fancy dress extravaganza, we were disappointed to learn that the 2004 Christmas do was "*a black-tie affair,*" but we're hopeful that 2005 will see a return to costumed form.

## and finally...

An unorthodox firm whose success more than justifies its modus operandi, McCormicks offers a training contract that is hard work and plenty of fun, and fully equips trainees for the cutthroat world of Leeds commercial law. As one source summed it up: "*I've been challenged massively but come September I feel like I'll be as prepared as I possibly could be for qualified life. That's the acid test of a training, surely?*"

# McDermot Will & Emery LLP

## the facts

**Location:** London
**Number of partners/assistants:** 22/45
**Total number of trainees:** 4
**Seats:** 4x6 months
**Alternative seats:** None
**Extras:** Pro bono – Sir John Cass Foundation

One of the top-20 largest law firms globally, McDermott Will & Emery's empire amounts to over 1,000 lawyers in 15 offices in five countries. The London branch has around 70 lawyers (the majority of whom are English qualified) dedicated to being a fighting-fit, full-service outpost.

## on a mission

Just one of the many US firms that arrived in London in the mid 90s, McDermotts grew by plundering "*dynamic young associates and partners from the big City firms.*" This has created what trainees describe as "*a youthful, highly motivated office*" "*without stodginess and with a thrusting atmosphere.*" In the seven years of its short London life, the firm has particularly excelled in employment and IP law. Indeed, these groups have not only attained significant market profile, but are also responsible for an impressive roster of clients that includes Balfour Beatty, British American Tobacco, Levi Strauss, Marks & Spencer, the National Theatre, Sainsbury's, Avis Europe, United Airlines, Hitachi, Oracle, United Airlines, EMI, The Diamond Trading Company (DeBeers), Formula One Management, Bradford & Bingley, $O_2$ and Motorola.

Trainees admit: "*IP and employment are still the drivers, they're where the big-name partners who you want to work with are,*" but observe that "*corporate is getting much busier.*" The firm is "*committed to the vision of a full-service US law firm in London,*" an objective worked towards "*with almost missionary zeal.*" As a result, "*tax is kicking off*" and "*litigation is developing a good reputation.*" Corporate lawyers this year advised broker Collins Stewart on Cyberscan Technology's £91.3 million AIM listing, and Beaumont Cornish on another AIM placing of mobile data services company WIN. A flair for energy work has seen finance lawyers assist on Merrill Lynch Commodities' $800 million purchase of the energy trading business of Entergy-Koch, and litigation lawyers represent Morgan Stanley in an action brought by the administrators of an Enron trading company.

Lateral hires in tax, corporate and capital markets, although partly compensating for departures last year, give credence to trainees' claims of "*the commitment to growth.*" Similarly, the hiring of Norton Rose's arbitration chief Juliet Blanch together with members of her team and the takeover of Brussels boutique Stanbrook & Hooper to strengthen the European competition/trade practice highlights McDermotts' desire to diversify.

## preaching to the converted

Bringing converts into the fold is one way to achieve such aspirations, raising your own believers is another. We weren't surprised to learn that "*trainees are a key part of organic growth,*" nor that there is near-total NQ retention year on year and both of the qualifiers stayed with the firm in 2005. High retention is due in part to "*exacting recruitment standards.*" Trainees were unequivocal that "*if you give the impression you've applied to the usual number of magic circle and City firms, you won't get in.*" Instead, they recommend "*a specific and determined application,*" detailing clearly your thoughts "*about why the firm is right for you.*" Articulate, intelligent, and possessing excellent academic results and a defined sense of humour, each of our interviewees had "*that little bit of extra spark or experience.*" Even after increasing the number of vacancies to three, with scores and scores of applications per year the firm can afford to be very choosy. Doubting Thomases need not apply.

## home on the range

Most missionaries come to proselytise, and the common assumption is that US firms preach the Gospel of St Greenback – the one where Jesus turns two fish and five loaves into a multinational food retailer. True, McDermotts does have "*well-publicised 2000-hour billing targets*" and "*a certain American flavour,*" but our sources were adamant that "*London isn't just a part of the American operation.*" One of our sources pointed to "*the amount of dealings I've had with our German and Italian*

*offices*" and "*the quantity of work that the office sources itself*" as evidence of an independence. In fact, although "*a fair amount of work has a US angle,*" our interviewees detected "*a decentralisation of power from Chicago to other offices, and a movement to a more internationalist approach.*" The firm has offices in Dusseldorf, Milan, Brussels, Rome and Munich, although these, like the US offices, are not available for trainee secondments. Going some way to compensate for this is a chance for trainees to join their contemporaries from around the world for an orientation week in the USA. Having acquired a taste for trips Stateside, they can look forward to associates 'retreats' once every two years.

Back at home in London, there is "*a boutique atmosphere that is informal and friendly.*" McDermotts occupies five floors ("*well kitted-out and plush looking*") of a Bishopsgate office building. The building possesses "*the façade of an old bank building, none of the monumentality of magic circle premises.*" In short, the kind of grand old building American firms in London think they ought to be seen in.

## calling the shots

The trainees we spoke to loved the contradiction inherent in "*training at a massive multinational firm with City-level work, but getting real responsibility and a personal experience.*" Not for these trainees the trials and tribulations of "*being forced into asset finance against your will*" or months of scheming to secure a niche seat. "*Because there are so few of us, there's almost no work you can't do.*" As well as excellent employment and IP/IT teams, trainees can also take one of their four six-month seats in banking, pensions, litigation, tax, or competition law. However, the small size of the operation means there's always "*slack to be taken up from other departments.*" So, for example, "*you could test out a bit of IP work whilst you're in corporate.*" Trainees find that being a scarce resource can sometimes lead to "*over-extension – it can be hard to say no to people who ask for your help.*" The payoff is that "*if someone gives you* grunt work they'll always push something meaty your way to keep you sweet. They know they'll need you again sometime soon." Associates and partners in competition to keep trainees happy? Now we have heard everything.

In general, trainees have a big say in their training. "If you want a second stint somewhere, or a particular seat, they'll do everything to accommodate you." It is an approach characteristic of "a supportive, non-hierarchical, non-pretentious atmosphere" in which trainees enjoy "excellent feedback" and "levels of responsibility that are almost scary sometimes." Mid and end-of-seat appraisals, together with "a general attitude that people want to help you develop," keep trainees ticking over nicely, and for the most part "partners are excellent at judging your ability." One trainee came over a little giddy remembering an event at 1am one night: "I had to close a deal myself with one associate in the US and the other in Italy. I thought, 'Can I do this?' But then, thankfully, it got delayed by a day!" This may not be an everyday experience ("inevitably there's proof-reading and the like"), but trainees at least get to spend the majority of their time drafting, researching, briefing counsel and "being encouraged to speak up at client meetings." One source even suggested: "We get work that perhaps at other firms is more associate level." Fortunately, the hours are not dissimilar to those experienced by trainees at other City firms, with "9am to 7 or 7.30pm a normal day." Yes, there are some late nights "but nothing etched indelibly in your memory for awfulness."

McDermotts would suit someone who is "proactive and self-motivating, not least when it comes to socialising. "It's okay but limited, very sociable and chatty [in the office] but there's no 'let's all go down the pub on a Friday night' mentality." In response, some years ago trainees formed a social committee named 'Pondlife' ("something to do with us being bottom of the food chain") which organises dinners and drinks for not only the trainee group but also junior associates. Wider firm events "tend to be organised around a specific thing like a pub quiz or croquet." On these occasions "everyone makes an effort to put in an appearance, even if the usual suspects are left at the end." Isn't it always the way...

## and finally...

If you have no desire to become a McDermott Will & Emery convert, we suggest you steer clear of conversation with any of the firm's trainees. "A growing international network, high-quality work, choice in your training, a massive firm but a small firm feel..." They're a pretty convincing lot.

# McGrigors

## the facts

**Location:** London
**Number of partners/assistants:** 54/109
**Total number of trainees:** 65 (UK-wide)
**Seats:** 4x6 months
**Alternative seats:** Scotland, Brussels, Belfast, secondments

A medium-sized corporate practice in a City location, some will say McGrigors' office in the English capital "has the feel of any other London mid-tier firm." What distinguishes it from the rest is its Scottishness and its close links with the accountancy giant KPMG.

## uniting the kingdom

North of Hadrian's Wall in the awfu dreich wather, McGrigors has been a dominant feature in the legal highlands for over 200 years. In 2002 it strode south to bag an office in England, scooping up the London legal experiment of worldwide accountancy practice KPMG. KLegal, as it was then known, was shortly to be cut loose by its accountant parent in the wake of US legislation (the Sarbanes-Oxley Act) following the collapse of dodgy energy company Enron and the subsequent implosion of its auditors Arthur Andersen. The whole debacle led to restrictions in the ability of accountancy firms to work in partnership (called MDP) with legal firms to perform joint services for clients. In one fell swoop, the rug was pulled from under KLegal. In walked Braveheart McGrigors to help the firm to its feet.

This year it was perfectly clear to us which of the two legacy firms was wearing the troosers and which was stirring the parritch. Some London trainees thought "*there is still a bit of an us-and-them type of feeling*" and that the pairing was "*still working on getting that combined, connected presence.*" For example, we heard how "*the London market and the Scottish market are totally different,*" and that the jarring of a well-established reputation north of the border and an "*entrepreneurial atmosphere*" in London was "*the biggest issue the firm faces.*" Nonetheless, we sensed a growing acceptance of the new living arrangements and heard trainees refer to "*one national firm, the only true UK firm... except we don't have an office in Wales!*"

## all i want for christmas

With the revolutionary concept of MDP fading but still remembered by several of our sources, we were unsurprised at a lingering undercurrent of discontent. One source lamented: "*It is not the firm that I joined. I applied to a London firm and ended up at the regional office of an Edinburgh firm.*" It sounded rather like the disappointment of a child who lies awake on Christmas night only to see his Dad, dressed in pyjamas, tiptoeing across the room to hang a lumpy sock at the foot of the bed. Those still reeling from the news that MDP won't be coming down the chimney any time soon needn't feel short-changed. A McGrigors training still comes stuffed full of work for the accountancy behemoth. Though officially there is "*no real tie*" to KPMG anymore, a 'best friend' relationship brings a wealth of work and referrals. Equally, the loosening of ties means the firm "*has been able to regain some of the clients we couldn't previously act for. We have become a lot more independent.*" If you're looking for proof, the client list includes the likes of BP, RBS, O$_2$, Royal Mail, MoD and Tarmac.

One source told us: "*The Scottish side of the firm has always been strong, now it is just a matter of London catching up a bit.*" Indeed, McGrigors sits in "*the Scottish magic circle*" and the firm's name is synonymous with "*all-pervading excellence.*" By contrast, trainees thought London "*a bit light on heavyweight expertise,*" though we did hear of "*a few gems embedded within it.*" Core work in London includes corporate, banking and real estate. An increasingly prolific projects team has provided advice to various local authorities on waste management matters, and acts on NHS LIFT projects. To give a specific example, McGrigors London advised the funders of the £127 million Bassetlaw Grouped Schools PFI project for Nottinghamshire County Council, comprising new secondary schools, centres for post-16 education, leisure centres and a new special school. It also provided advice to the principal bond guarantor and the lead managers on the first 'Building Schools for the Future' scheme entirely financed by a bond issue – a £150 million project to build 24 new schools across central Scotland.

## taxing times

Though the allocation of trainees' four six-month seats is, apparently, "*a random lottery,*" most of those we spoke to seemed happy with their lucky dips. A compulsory corporate seat can be satisfied by time in the banking department, the contentious requirement can be fulfilled in dispute resolution, construction or tax litigation, and other seats are taken from a list that includes real estate, banking, technology and people services (ie employment and pensions). "*A big beast,*" the busy corporate department "*freaks most people out.*" Indeed, time spent with a team with "*no sympathy for first-seat trainees*" can be "*very much a baptism of fire*" for brand new recruits. The combination of "*a lot of real characters*" and a high-pressure environment left some people "*quite scared.*" The seat offers "*the whole spectrum of corporate work*" so trainees lend a hand on "*everything from Companies House searches*" to due diligence on AIM flotations, share restructuring projects and share purchase agreements." Inevitably there are times when "*they just need you as a runaround*" and "*there are moments at 2am when you just want to go home and you think, 'Is this what I really want to do?'*" At least these occasions are balanced with "*very good-quality work*" and "*a fair degree of autonomy.*" On smaller matters, there is even the possibility of "*pretty much running the file.*"

Described by one source as "*a leading edge to the practice and a great experience,*" McGrigors' tax litigation team advises on claims against HM Revenue & Customs. It is without doubt a popular choice for trainees. "*All Chinese-walled off*" in KPMG's offices, the team gets trainees working alongside accountants, exposing them to such matters as the recent test case brought against the Government following an ECJ decision relating to companies' ability to recover VAT paid on the costs of their flotation or issue of shares. This is "*a relatively small team so there is a lot of scope to get involved and do more than just photocopying, bibling and indexing.*" In busy times "*they need 100%*" from trainees – note-taking in meetings, drafting witness statements, filing documents and attending court. Little wonder, one confessed, "*the summer went by and I didn't really notice!*" The specialist pensions team is another in which trainees "*worked quite closely with KPMG,*" gaining "*a lot more exposure to high-level matters.*"

## great walls

The ongoing relationship with KPMG has led to a number of secondments with the organisation, and aside from "*a fight to the death*" for one particularly popular slot, there is no shortage of seats. A KPMG secondment is an ideal way to "*get embedded with a key client.*" Trainees relished the opportunity to handle "*things you might not get your hands on at McGrigors.*" Much the same is said of a three-month spell doing competition work in Brussels. Here, "*the work is great, the nightlife is excellent and the beers are spectacularly good!*"

If your last Christmas stocking has left you with an Argyle sweater, The Proclaimers greatest hits and a hunger for a horizon that extends beyond next door's bathroom window, why not sign up for a spell in Glasgow or Edinburgh? Despite reports that "*it is always more popular to come to London than go to Scotland,*" we heard of two brave Angles who enjoyed haggis so much they were going back for a second helping. Apparently, "*it's a good gig – London salary, flat, all bills paid for, several flights down to London.*"

To promote cross-border relations, the firm organises a trainee conference for all new recruits. Last year the Scottish contingent flew down for three days in Kent and some months later, at the first gathering of the entire McGrigors clan, the whole London office flew to Edinburgh for an Olympics of "*It's a Knockout-type events.*" The day culminated in a medal ceremony and a fireworks display. Other initiatives have included a senior management roadshow bringing six-monthly presentations on the firm's progress, and monthly departmental meetings.

For trainees, mid-seat reviews are followed by "*much more detailed*" end-of-seat sessions, though one source pondered on how "*the appraisal system isn't as robust as it could be.*" At least sitting next to your supervisor in an open-plan office means close direction on a daily basis. Certainly in the smaller departments "*you will get more feedback*" because "*they delegate more responsibility and need to make sure you know what you are doing.*"

## highland ways?

At the end of 2004, McGrigors took on "*very hi-tech, very clean, very fresh,*" new offices in Old Bailey. Like any move from bachelor pad to family home, the new address is a "*a marked improvement*" on the former. While "*the old building was frankly appalling,*" the new one "*brings the London operation on a par with the Edinburgh operation.*" We prayed for wall-to-wall tartan carpet and complimentary Edinburgh Rock in reception. A quick snoop revealed sharp minimalism and little that was overtly Scottish other than a few thistley flower arrangements. It's also business casual rather than kilts, and corporate ballyhoo runs no further than a fish tank on the fourth floor and *"a flat screen TV downstairs"* that shows BBC News 24 continuously.

The offices are located next to an All Bar One, which is both convenient and dangerous as *"you literally have to walk past it on your way to the station."* Aside from occasional long nights and weekends at your desk, the working day is typically 9ish to 7ish, with the result that *"All Bar One must make a sweet fortune out of us."* Or the partners at least – one wily source revealed that *"the partners are very generous, I have only bought about five drinks in all the time I have been here!"* Those for whom the walk to the bar is insufficiently energetic can play five-aside football and rugby sevens. Budding Paula Radcliffes should note that *"quite a few people are into running,"* and a team is entered into the Great City Race. For walkers there's the Caledonian Challenge, *"a 54-mile walk across the West Highland Way in 24 hours."* And for aches in all the right places there is *"a lot of revelry, and waking up with a sore head"* from the annual Christmas party and Burns' Supper complete with Scottish dancing.

The united kingdom of McGrigors is *"welcoming to people from alternative paths;"* *"a fair chunk have done a post-grad course of some sort or another, another chunk have done time as a paralegal, others have no experience whatsoever outside the classroom."* We also heard of people arriving via first careers. Common to all were an enterprising spirit and an open mind. McGrigors' less familiar brand may not suit *"anyone with delusions of grandeur,"* and *"someone who is especially London-centric"* may not automatically gravitate towards a firm with a distinctly tartan weave. However, those willing to try a new outfit for size should listen to the trainee who told us: *"I see more and more that I am not having to explain who McGrigors are."* Of the 17 London trainees qualifying in September 2005, ten took jobs in the capital, one accepted a post in Belfast and another in Glasgow.

## and finally...

McGrigors is ideal if a long and distinguished heritage north of the border and a fresh start in London appeal in equal measure.

# Mills & Reeve

## the facts

**Location:** Birmingham, Cambridge, London, Norwich
**Number of partners/assistants:** 79/203
**Total number of trainees:** 37
**Seats:** 6x4 months
**Alternative seats:** None

*"I wanted to do things as diverse as agriculture, PFI and corporate."* If this sounds like the little voice in your head, read on...

## shoes for every occasion

Mills & Reeve first opened its doors in Norwich in 1880. In 1987 it set up shop in Cambridge, then added Birmingham and London to the list in comparatively short order. With Norwich as the firm's historic base, Cambridge a *"livelier, faster paced, heart of the firm"* and Birmingham as the *"exciting and new"* addition to the family, we were left wondering which way the blood flows through the firm. It turns out that, with distinctly different work in each office, *"there is not too much rivalry"* between them and almost endless variations on the legal theme.

In Norwich, the firm's age prompted the comment: *"We're almost in the fabric of the City."* The work here is *"centred much more on big estates"* and the office retains its reputation for weighty private client and agricultural work, engendering *"a more traditional atmosphere."* With a snazzy glass-fronted, open-plan office complete with a breakout area and in-house Starbucks, the traditional side of the firm is certainly diluted by a corporate environment and influences. Indeed, the firm is well known in the county for corporate and commercial matters, regularly acting on £5–20 million transactions. Making a dig at Norfolk's lean legal pickings, one trainee quipped: *"There's not a heck of a lot of competition."* They could not have foreseen that just one week later the Norwich corporate team of the firm's closest rival, Eversheds, announced it would be joining M&R. Presumably there are now a few more pairs of shiny black oxfords lined up with the wellies in M&R's back porch.

Expansion is the name of the game over in Cambridge too. The firm has taken over an extra floor in its city-centre building and removed walls to relieve pressure. In addition to its usual broad offering, here M&R is *"a bit more cutting edge"* in the work it handles. Home to half of the firm's corporate partners and the largest commercial services group, it is no surprise that our sources described Cambridge as *"the most corporate-y office."* On the client roster are Caterpillar (UK) Limited and Aveva Group, though the Cambridge office is also renowned for acting for *"hi-tech-Silicon Fen kind of companies."* Admittedly the turn-of-the-century hype has died down somewhat, but hi-tech and biotech matters still come in from the likes of Cambridge University, Zeus Technology and Dwight Cavendish, who the team has advised in relation to licences for electronic protection against video and DVD piracy. Private equity deals feature large, examples of which are the investments by GEIF Ventures (a £5 million early stage fund) in Novacta Biosystems and Casient Limited, which has devised state-of-the-art wireless mesh-networking technology. Novacta had previously received funding from another of M&R's clients, the Iceni Seedcorn Fund.

## nought to thirty in a year

The smallest office in the quartet is London, which undertakes public law, local government and healthcare matters. It also has a strong insurance focus and acts for the likes of Zurich and St Paul International on professional negligence matters involving solicitors, accountants and financial advisers. Trainees have the option of spending time in London, though *"if you're not interested in insurance you don't think about it."* While we heard murmurings about plans to expand the ambit of the London office, for fast, decisive moves, all eyes are on Birmingham. M&R is capitalising on the fact that Birmingham is *"a bigger place than Cambridge"* and *"offers more opportunities for growth."* A year ago, the firm offered no private client services in the Midlands; now thanks to the efforts of Martineau Johnson's former head of private client there is a department of 30, admittedly something only made possible by the arrival of Wragge & Co's entire private client team. Another unusual hire came in the form of an employment barrister from one of the city's better-known sets.

Birmingham's core public sector team continues with its busy schedule, acting on behalf of the General Medical Council in professional conduct prosecutions, involving itself in a fistful of NHS LIFT projects and a score of other PFI projects for NHS trusts. The firm also successfully acted for Portsmouth Hospital NHS Trust on the highly publicised case of Charlotte Wyatt, where it was held that doctors should not resuscitate the gravely ill premature baby when she stopped breathing. The team's growth continues, and just before we went to press the firm pinched another healthcare partner from rival Bevan Brittan. Interestingly, she had done her training with M&R years before.

As if entire new departments and prolific work weren't enough, new office premises have also helped launch Birmingham into the limelight. Decked out in *"retro interior design style"* (by all accounts more than a few G Plan bookshelves off eBay) the décor prompted one tactful source to admit *"they have been quite brave with the interior;"* another talked us through the lime green carpets, red and electric pink chairs, plus *"a whole wall of wavy wood effect."* Creature comforts for staff include a 'retreat' with *"loads of sofas and music channels projected onto the wall."*

## run trainee, run

The six-seat training means trainees *"effectively get an extra two bites of the cherry."* Any frustration felt at having their plates cleared away before they had finished was counterbalanced by the smorgasbord of legal disciplines on offer – family, agriculture, private client, insurance and healthcare litigation, technology, corporate, commercial property, commercial litigation, construction, education, charities, and regulatory and defence work. Trainees tell us: *"You can tailor things to what you want to do"* and *"it is quite usual to get eight months in something relevant"* to your intended qualification field. *"If you were dead set on doing one thing"* and it's not available in your home office *"you can do it in another."* We should stress that *"moving is not obligatory,"* though *"it is encouraged."* As an extra incentive, if you find yourself paying twice for accommodation, the firm will cover any additional expenses.

*"Employment is in vogue right now"* (when is it not?), corporate and property are also popular as *"everybody wants a bit of experience in those things."* Poor old tax *"is perceived as being dull and akin to accounting."* In some seats such as private client *"you get given things and told to just run with it and come back if you have any queries."* By contrast corporate trainees are more likely to *"get passed bits and bobs, here and there,"* though we're assured *"they do try and get you involved on most deals if they can."* Seats in commercial disputes and insurance litigation allow trainees to get *"a genuine sense of what it is like to be a solicitor."* Again, on larger cases it is more *"people handing me the work rather than me running it,"* though we did encounter trainees whose experiences included running files, handling small arbitrations, drafting orders, taking witness statements, instructing counsel and attending court hearings. We even heard of one trainee who had been chased by a pack of journalists waiting outside court.

When not sprinting down handy alleyways, trainees sit *"under the eagle eyes"* of their supervisors. Quite how eagley the eyes are depends on who they sit with. *"Some want to see every e-mail, others let you send it out unless you want it checked,"* but generally *"they work to whatever level you are at."* Formal end-of-seat reviews and informal mid-seat reviews are supplemented by *"ten-minute chats when you literally just turn around in your chair"* and *"you never give in a piece of work and never see it again."* Suitably philosophical on the subject of grunt work, one source remarked: *"Sometimes you do just have to prepare bundles because that's life,"* while another added: *"The trainee is the cheapest person after the reprographics department. You are expected to do slightly menial tasks as befits the position."* Thankfully such chores are *"ancillary to proper experience."*

## little piggy goes to market

While there are occasions when late nights are necessary; usually most of our sources sloped off home by 6pm. In Birmingham, monthly social events have included treasure hunt-style pubcrawls, go-karting and theatre trips. In Cambridge there is a book group, regular socials, a squash ladder and cricket and football teams. A recent footie match against the Norwich office ended in defeat for Cambridge because apparently *"Norwich brought in loads of secretaries' boyfriends."* With the bulk of new recruits working in Cambridge, the Christmas party here includes *"what could loosely be described as entertainment"* penned and performed by the trainees. In Norwich, too, a reasonably large trainee cohort imposes the same penalty on colleagues. When not clambering into the rear end of a pantomime horse, Norwich recruits enjoy monthly drinks evenings, bowling and boat trips (not at the same time). They also patronise The Adam and Eve, supposedly England's oldest pub, which has had its own real live ghost since 1549 when Lord Sheffield had his head hacked off with a meat cleaver. Nice. Ideal for summer picnics, the Botanic Gardens behind the Cambridge office are *"a great perk,"* and for a post-work pint and packet of pork scratchings there is the

Flying Pig next door. Sadly, despite a petition, the pub is due to be demolished to make way for luxury flats and offices.

The distances between them and the differences cultivated by their respective locations have not prevented the M&R trainees from becoming a relatively coherent group. The firm is "*conscious of not being broken up*" and "*works really hard to make it one complete unit.*" Nevertheless, there may be some truth in the notion that in the larger offices trainees "*keep their cards closer to their chest*" when it comes to career plans and seat choices, whereas in Birmingham (where there is "*hardly a mass gathering*") it is easier to "*talk openly about your plans as there are more positions available than trainees.*"

With pretty much the entirety of central England on at least one of its doorstops, M&R has plenty of scope to grow, and seems intent on doing just that. So, whether you're a southerner, a northerner, or any kind of cross-breed, if you've already written off that bit in the middle, take heed of the trainee who said: "*I expected Birmingham to be like a war zone and I was blown away. I expected Norwich to be full of farmers, yet it isn't true at all.*" M&R attracts hard-working, well-meaning types, people who are "*confident and outgoing without being cocky.*" Once source warned: "*Arrogance will definitely not be tolerated*" and suggested "*an assumption that you know what you are doing and have no need for any more guidance won't go down well.*" In September 2005, 15 out of 20 qualifiers stayed with the firm, distributing themselves fairly evenly across offices and departments.

## and finally...

Even if you're still reeling from the disappointing news that East Angular is nowhere near Tunisia you can console yourself with the knowledge that Mills & Reeve's horizons lie far beyond the Norfolk Broads. Geography aside, the firm's legal landscape is as expansive as it comes.

# Morgan Cole

## the facts

**Location:** Cardiff, Swansea, Reading, Oxford, London
**Number of partners/assistants:** 50/179
**Total number of trainees:** 28
**Seats:** 4x6 months
**Alternative seats:** Secondments

Ask many in the profession about Morgan Cole and they'll tell you it has been on the road to hell. Look at the latest profit figures and you get the sense it's on the return journey.

## i think m4 i am

In 1998, Welsh firm Morgan Bruce looked beyond Swansea and Cardiff and hit the tarmac of the eastbound M4 to merge with Oxford and Reading firm Cole & Cole somewhere around Junction 11. Six months down the road, Morgan Cole revved into the capital for a merger with insurance whizz Fishburn Boxer. But just two years on and signs of overstretch had turned into evidence of entrenched divisions within a firm that had never fully integrated. The defections began, around 100 partners dropping to 50; profits plummeted commensurately. A Shakespearean power struggle between the English and Welsh offices masked antipathies from the original merger, and MC's problems were further compounded by Fishburn Boxer's decision to disengage after just three years in the partnership. There were other unfortunate consequences: AXA, for example, jettisoned Morgan Cole's Cardiff and Croydon offices from its legal panel, precipitating the closure of MC's Croydon insurance litigation branch.

So where is the firm now? In London operations are confined to a small Fleet Street office with just one team – insurance. Our sources assure us that the firm's gear-crunching reversal ended at Reading and that the four Welsh and TV offices remain open for the long haul. Trainees also told us MC has "*weathered its storm*," and that they'd observed "*a sea change in the last few months.*" Partners are being made up from the ranks and "*there were as many NQ jobs offered as newly qualifieds this year.*" Where AXA and some other clients feared to tread, HSBC and Tesco dared: both these FTSE 100 companies appointed the firm to their legal panels. And the firm's Welsh connections have paid dividends, MC recently securing the advisory tender on the £400 million Severn Power facility in South Wales.

## finally coming together

The trainees are now divided between two camps: Wales and the Thames Valley. From September 2005, London will be no more than a one-seat appendage to the latter. At the start of the training contract all recruits meet in Oxford's Oriel and St Anthony's Colleges for the PSC and a general induction into the ways of the firm. Though they gather infrequently thereafter, interestingly this year's trainees tried hard to convince us that all offices worked in harmony with each other. Last year Welsh trainees reported a sense that the firm was run from the Thames Valley and vice versa the reports from Oxford and Reading trainees. Now they say the beginnings of departmental unity are apparent: every Monday morning, for example, a video-linked discussion beams out from Swansea to the London insurance team. Admittedly trainees don't tend to move between offices, but "*if someone in Cardiff wants to do a seat in Oxford they could swap – it's not a physical impossibility.*"

## the welsh valleys

In Wales, MC is one of the dominant commercial firms. Why would you choose to train here over the others? "*It's less cut-throat than Eversheds,*" came one reply. Its work is distinctly Welsh: corporate lawyers have been advising the likes of the University of Wales, Swansea in negotiations with IBM over a supercomputer. They have also advised the lottery grant distributor in Wales, the Welsh Language Board, Care Council for Wales, Milford Haven Port Authority and The National Assembly for Wales. The property lawyers have the pleasure of working with well-known companies such as Crabtree & Evelyn, plus energy companies, banks and developers. MC litigators have been busy with clients as diverse as universities, NHS trusts, a white goods manufacturer and a French rugby club.

Swansea's Llys Tawe branch occupies a modern building overlooking the marina. Eventually the area's cement mixers and builders' bums will be replaced by new bars and flats, but for now trainees make do with the cafés and cappuccino-dens just ten minutes away from the office. As well as a view of the sea, their workplace has so much space "*you could have your own room if you wanted.*" Why would you, however, when the "*argy bargy*" and "*bustle*" of lawyers rushing to court provides the ideal soundtrack to office-bound duties. In Swansea's commercial litigation seat trainees encounter "*good mediations*" as well as attend court themselves for "*mortgage repossessions and charging orders.*" The other seats on offer are property and corporate.

Cardiff's Bradley Court can feel comparatively "*up-tight:*" "*the work is much heavier… drafting documents in silence, you can hear a pin drop.*" The acoustic difference is easily accounted for: Swansea is the hub for the firm's Welsh insurance litigation, while the bulk of transactional work (and seats) – corporate, property, general commercial and banking – are to be found in Cardiff, along with health and professional indemnity. In this last area, trainees are exposed to "*principally PI and clinical negligence*" and cases that go to trial all over England and Wales… "*Chesterfield, London… and Swansea.*" Back in the office they get stuck into research, perhaps on freedom of information claims, and even "*dabble*" in mental health work. Employment is both popular and relatively easy to get. After the preparatory drafting, trainees accompany solicitors (with or without a barrister) to tribunals and court hearings. Observing the proceedings is a great way to get an overview of the case and tips on how to conduct negotiations.

Trainees usually move between the Welsh offices during the course of their training – something to bear in mind if, like one or two of our sources, you're likely to grumble about the commute. Traffic between Wales and the Thames Valley is minimal, although 2005 saw an emergency scramble to Cardiff to assist on liquor licensing applications under the recent new legislation.

## the thames valley

Moving east to the Thames Valley and MC's main Reading office at Apex Plaza, a "*very up-market glass building*" presiding over the town's railway station. The "*smart coffee bars, palm trees and security*" may make it sound like Palo Alto, though we suspect this is where the similarity ends. This "*bustling and busy*" office has trainee seats in commercial IT, employment and corporate, with insurance litigation available at Kennet House "*if you must.*" The corporate seat sounds the busiest – we heard reports of days stretching until 2am for deal completions. For banks alone it acted on over £25 million worth of MBO/acquisition lending in 2004. Among the most interesting of the deals handled lately was the £1.5 million MBO of Thames Cryogenics. For corporate trainees, the completions are hectic, the photocopying occasional, the drafting opportunities plentiful, and all is deemed "*useful experience.*" A steadier pace in the employment seat means fewer late nights and "*more law*" – research into the ever-shifting Rubix cube of employment legislation, updating employer handbooks and providing guidance on redundancies and disciplinary hearings.

"*Academic and quiet,*" the Buxton Court site "*off the A34*" near Oxford is described by trainees as "*just like an industrial unit.*" An Oxford original, the seat in family and matrimonial law is unusual in MC's predominantly commercial practice. The assessment of one trainee was that family work is "*very similar to property, the only difference is that you have the individual element.*" Trainees learn to deal with this aspect of the work when accompanying clients to court: "*You have to explain a lot of the procedures to them – that's the human interest bit.*" Otherwise, time is taken up in this "*nicely busy*" seat by drafting the letters that fly between solicitors and preparing evidence and court bundles. Oxford trainees can further choose between seats in commercial litigation, general commercial, IP and commercial property ("*with a bit of residential if you want*"). A regulatory health and safety seat adds 'animal interest' in that the firm takes on prosecutions for the RSPCA.

In London, a seat in the dispute management group might have seen one source minding snippets of two large and lengthy litigations, but instead they got the chance to go before masters in chambers, advocated before county court judges and had a free rein on small-scale files.

## in the fast lane

There's welcome news in that the training budget is no longer managed on a departmental basis. A centralised coffer now allows trainees to go into "*more obscure seats*" without the need for teams to fret over the audit. Secondments are also available to Fishburn, the insurance firm which demerged from MC, and select clients.

Trainees view MC as "*a nurturing firm*" in which criticism is "*constructive*" and "*has a positive spin on it.*" Minimal thumb twiddling is permitted, though "*they won't make you sit at your desk unnecessarily racking up billable hours – you're here to train.*" Indeed, a constant theme in our interviews this year was the quality of training offered. Said one source: "*You don't sit in silence; they explain things to you fully.*" Depending on the office, you'll either sit in a room with your supervisor (Swansea and Reading) or with your team open plan (Cardiff, London and Oxford). Supervisors may or may not be partners – in fact a three-year-qualified solicitor is as likely a room-mate, in part due to the many partner-level departures over the years. Said one: "*I was scared *when I first came because Morgan Cole had got a pan-ning in the press and it was pretty tough at the time."* They soon learned that one man's P45 is another's newly acquired caseload because, ironically, the departures which destabilised the firm gave many trainees more responsibility and client exposure than they might otherwise have received. Compet-ing calls on partners' time led to *"hands-off"* supervision, meaning that *"rather than learn through imitation you'd have to think about things. It wasn't just execution of tasks, you had to problem solve."* Mature readers looking for a training con-tract after a previous career may be heartened by our discovery of an ex-police officer and a hard-working mum in amongst the wide-eyed graduates in the current trainee group. As one interviewee put it: *"So long as you're intelligent, industrious and friendly you don't need to be an absolute spod to get on here."* In September 2005, six of the nine qualifiers took jobs with the firm.

## and finally...

Morgan Cole's training contract could be described as a responsive four-seater. However, the firm as a whole has until recently driven like a badly welded cut-and-shunt with its bonnet in Wales and its boot just outside the M25. From what we can tell the goggles are out and the re-welding is underway.

# Nabarro Nathanson

## the facts

**Location:** London, Sheffield
**Number of partners/assistants:** 115/225
**Total number of trainees:** 56
**Seats:** 6x4 months
**Alternative seats:** Brussels, secondments
**Extras:** Language training

A quick look at Nabarro Nathanson's lead work is enough to confirm that medium-sized the firm may be, but middling it is not.

## grand designs

At Nabarros the *"running theme"* is property. You may choose to ignore this statement and apply, go through an interview, on to a vacation scheme and land yourself a training contract in blissful igno-rance of the firm's leanings, but *"it becomes pretty clear as soon you arrive."* The firm's property lawyers act for some of the biggest names in the industry, among them British Land, Quintain and Land Securities, and they currently advise the funding consortium behind the UK's largest urban regeneration project, the vast £800 million Par-adise Street development in Liverpool. In previous years the firm has had a hand in such illustrious projects as the new Wembley Stadium, Birming-ham's Bull Ring and the 'Shard of Glass' London Bridge Tower. In spite of the firm's clear commit-ment to the property industry, some of our sources remained insistent that *"property definitely isn't dominant,"* instead turning our heads towards other key departments such as *"very, very busy"* corporate.

Trainees also worked hard to convince us that the firm's breadth of work enables *"equal training across the board,"* which in turn means *"training contracts can go off in completely different directions."* On first hearing this we were about as skeptical as Kevin McCloud when faced with a pair of deluded city dwellers intent on building their dream home out of drinking straws... on a salt marsh in West Wales. Yet, in true McCloud style, by the third commercial break, we had conceded to their assertions.

If you're now confused as to where we/you/trainees stand on the property/not property issue then all should become clear when we explain that the reference to property being a *"running theme"* is best used in relation to the client base rather than the type of law the majority of Nabarros lawyers actually practice. Departments such as cor-porate, litigation and construction would be *"mortified if they were thought of as support to prop-erty,"* but in reality find it difficult to divorce themselves entirely from property industry or property-focused deals.

## get off my land!

In the six-seat training scheme there are three compulsories – property, corporate and litigation. A trainee's first seat is allocated and thereafter they have access to an extensive list that includes energy and infrastructure, banking, insolvency, construction, employment, IT/IP and telecoms. *"Inevitably with 50 trainees, there are always going to be some who aren't perfectly happy."* However, *"you rarely hear someone whingeing"* and *"it definitely does seem to come good in the end."* True enough, we didn't hear anybody whingeing; praise was heaped on a system that provides a 'buddy' throughout law school; a mentor on arrival; a supervisor as a roommate; a comprehensive appraisal system and a graduate recruitment team that *"you can't fault."* Trainees *"never feel out on a limb, there is always someone behind you checking that you are okay"* and *"if you are enthusiastic about what you are doing, people will give you as much work as you ask for."*

No need to ask for more in property. Here, newbies *"hit the ground running"* with their own workload covering everything from *"due diligence to preparing sales packs"* plus *"drafting leases, rent reviews and bank guarantees."* Though *"there is a really steep learning curve,"* we weren't at all surprised to hear that *"the quality of the work is such that I really didn't mind working hard."* By contrast, in litigation *"you don't get your own files, you just help out."* In a commercial lit seat that may mean taking witness statements, gathering evidence and attending conferences with counsel; in a property lit seat it is likely to also entail *"an awful lot of research."* Nabarros' highly prized property litigation team undertakes *"the more unusual things that come along."* Such as? *"Squatters proceedings, rights of light and dilapidations claims are the big thing."*

## logging off

The corporate department splits into four divisions: private capital; M&A; private equity and public sector. It has won the affection of trainees with its prolific work for FTSE 350 and fast-growth companies and last year clocked up £7.2 billion worth of M&A transactions, including the £335 million sale of InnSpired Group to Punch Taverns. It acted on the Empire Online AIM flotation and has added Xerox and HMV Group to its client list. Corporate seats mean *"a lot of preparing documents and bibles,"* or as one person put it, *"being in charge of all the paper."* Generally, *"it is just a case of rolling with whatever is given to you."* Corporate seats may occasionally require trainees to stay in the office into the small hours, but *"if someone does have to do it, it is big news."* A typical trainee day is usually a sensible 9.30am until 6.30pm.

An employment law secondment to Oxford University is available to one lucky London trainee, a competition law seat can be found in Brussels, and it is also possible for Londoners to spend a seat up in the firm's smaller Sheffield office. Some bright sparks may be aware that until earlier in 2005 Nabarros had an office in Reading. The announcement that Nabarros was to close one of its offices prompted speculation that the firm was abandoning more than an out-of-town address. Don't worry – it's not the end of civilisation as we know it. The firm has merely acknowledged that it was time to log off and shut down its IT-led Reading practice because it made financial sense to do so. Or as one trainee put it: *"The clients have matured and don't need someone on their doorstep. They are bigger and can be serviced out of London."* What remains then is a Sheffield and London-based firm, and just in case you were worried about Sheffield's future, breathe easy because we learned recently that it accounts for almost a fifth of the firm's revenue.

## dancing queen

In Sheffield, one of the options open to trainees is a first-class personal injury team that defends the

DTI on claims concerning vibration white finger damage from drill use, lung diseases, noise-induced injury and other miscellaneous health problems arising from the activities of the old British Coal. It's a mammoth exercise with over 600,000 VWF and respiratory disease claimants due a share of a pot worth over £8 billion. The full range of seats is reassuringly wide and includes many of the same options as in London – corporate, employment, public sector projects and, of course, property. Nabarros' Sheffield contingent – among them eight trainees – occupies a modern building at the grand-sounding *"Gateway to the City,"* adjacent to the canal and conveniently close to the popular Blue Water pub. Corporate fluff extends to a car park and *"a lot of pictures of boats because we are next to the canal."* As lovely as it sounds, it seems a far cry from the firm's snazzy London HQ with its Starbucks-trained baristas and atrium spanned by illuminated glass bridges with *"little rainbow strip lights that make a pretty night-time scene, like a retro 70s' square-tiled illuminated dance floor…"*

In London, *"rather than just doing Friday night beer, and see you later"* the trainee social scene is conducive to *"making proper friends."* With *"no social committee as such"* trainees organise their own fun – *"karaoke, Greek dancing, salsa nights"… "nothing too extravagant!"* One brave lad explained: *"The girls like dancing and the boys get bullied into it. The salsa night was a key example of that."* Perhaps all the dancing has been inspired by last year's 70s-themed Christmas party, at which the entertainment included a Queen tribute band fronted by *"the fattest Freddie Mercury you'll ever see."* In Sheffield, the Christmas do is a civilised black-tie affair though, here too, trainees are partial to a spot of dancing *"when we feel relaxed and have no inhibitions."* Both offices have summer parties, the last London one was held at the Transport Museum, which is a *"bizarre"* choice unless your daily commute leaves you wanting for more of the same.

## is this the way to amarillo?

On the sporting front, Nabarros musters teams for football, netball, *"ad hoc rugby sevens and hockey."* It also entered teams into the recent Oxfam Trailwalker event. One trainee who had clearly not participated explained: *"They have to walk for 24 hours. They start in the Midlands and walk to London or something. It is the equivalent of climbing Ben Nevis and coming back down again. Twice"* A better-informed source confirmed: *"teams of four walking 100kms in under 30 hours without stopping."* The firm's sports day arguably does as much for north-south relations as shared work and video-linked meetings. London and Sheffield trainees also attend a joint induction when they arrive and at the start of the second year the London cohort heads off for something entitled *"Trainees in the North Weekend."* If the good humour and game approach of our sources is typical, we can only assume that the weekend is a riotous success. Back in the office, Friday is smart-casual dress day, which *"is a nightmare – you almost have to have a Friday wardrobe."* So bad is it that one trainee confessed: *"We call it 'Dress Like Your Dad' Friday."*

From what we can tell, Nabarros' trainees chose their firm because they *"wanted to do the big-type work in a place that was a little bit smaller."* The person who told us *"although I like corporate work, I didn't want to do the really hardcore corporate work"* could have spoken for the majority of her peers. What our sources described was a firm *"neither obsessively old-fashioned"* nor *"obsessively going after the newest fads;"* not *"old and traditional, nor funky and modern."* 'You can't sit on the fence!' we protested. *"Watch me. Just watch me!"* one trainee replied. In September 2005, 14 out of the 19 qualifiers chose to stay put at the firm.

## and finally...

If you want to learn the secrets of Nabarro Nathanson's success we suggest you sign up for a vacation scheme because these days over 90% of its trainees are recruited through this programme. It will also give you ample opportunity to figure out where you stand on the 'It's a property firm – It's not a property firm debate'.

# Norton Rose

## the facts

**Location:** London
**Number of partners/assistants:** 124/219
**Total number of trainees:** 129
**Seats:** 6x4 months
**Alternative seats:** Overseas seats, secondments
**Extras:** Pro bono – Tower Hamlets and Tooting law centres, FRU, death row appeals, language training

Number ten by turnover in the UK, Norton Rose is a long-established City player that is *"a finance firm first and foremost."*

## no.6 your time is up

... or as one student put it: *"Banking focused – and students need to appreciate that fact."* It goes without saying that *"most new trainees don't have a clue what the different areas of finance mean;"* however, with a little experience under their belts, *"a lot of trainees love it."* With 35% of the firm's revenue coming from finance deals, with any luck you'll love it too. The firm has an almost endless list of banking specialisms – *"BT1 is a ship finance team; BT2 does aviation finance; 3 is project finance; 4 is an acquisition finance team; 5 doesn't exist anymore and I'm not sure if it ever did. BT6 is securitisation and capital markets and derivatives..."* BT7, BT8 and BT9, we've learned, handle asset and structured finance, insolvency and restructuring, and more projects. Then, just a fortnight after completing our interviews, the rump of BT6 ran off to Baker & MacKenzie. But before we could finish pondering on why they'd packed their bags, reinforcements had been brought in from Lovells and A&O.

Asset finance is a key area for NR and there are separate teams for ships, planes and trains. Some of the deals are huge – take for instance the £120 million purchase of 30 trains by Silverlink and Central Trains for operation on the West Coast Main Line, or easyJet's acquisition of 82 Airbus A319 Aircraft for $3.6 billion. Not all our sources clicked with the work; said one: *"Ship finance was fine for just four months. I found it very document heavy. You're using similar documents each time round, just changing the parties' names."* But as we all know, one man's poison is another man's asset finance and we heard from someone else who loved the fast turnaround times of the deals: *"I've just come from litigation where they do massive cases that go on for years and years and years."* With asset finance work *"you can be involved from beginning to end and understand better what you are doing and how you are fitting in with the deals. You can get a lot of responsibility."* Readers, this is your first sniff of that lovely idiom about horses and courses...

## draw your conclusion

In project finance, trainees assist more senior lawyers and are rewarded with first drafts of bits of agreements, board minutes and resolutions. *"I never had to do huge amounts of photocopying, the print room do all that, but trainees do the proof-reading,"* one source recalled. Not terribly exciting, but once you consider the scale of the deals in hand, not terribly surprising. NR advised on a bid to the Abu Dhabi government to develop and upgrade the country's Taweelah B power and water desalination plant. At over $2.8 billion, it is the biggest ever project finance deal of its kind in the Middle East. On the £2.1 billion refinancing of London Underground's JNP (Jubilee, Northern and Piccadilly) PPP project the firm advised the European Investment Bank, 29 other banks, Ambac and several hedge providers in relation to the interface of the original financing and the refinancing. Apparently among certain partners there's a saying – *"If you can't draw it don't do it."* Consequently, *"everything runs on diagrams."*

Seats in the three corporate finance teams

(CFTs) divide trainee opinion. Managing data rooms and hours of due diligence clearly doesn't impress everyone. Corporate's detractors blame long hours and lack of responsibility. "*I wouldn't want to rate the ratio of good to bad work*," grumbled one, "*I like to be in control of the work I'm given rather than working to unrealistic timetables*." Another added: "*I had very low-responsibility tasks. Most of the time it was proof-reading and I felt like a glorified secretary. I didn't go to law school to proof-read. I'd been studying for a hundred years and I wanted to get into my job. I have letters after my name yet I was concerned that I was not able to prove myself other than by working late nights and volunteering to help out when it was busy. The quality of my work could only be judged by my proof-reading*." Ouch! Yet within CFT1 is a seat which also handles regulatory and investment funds issues. It is "*a right mixed bag with a fair amount of research on the Financial Services Act. If you want a more academic experience, in this seat you get to analyse insider dealing and abuses of market position. The advice is all about helping businesses to structure themselves so they don't fall into traps*."

Some of our sources preferred the firm's dispute resolution teams. "*DRT1 is more the corporate and banking side of litigation; DRT2 is more arbitration and construction cases*." Trainees soon learn that "*the cases we deal with are generally humungous*." Said one: "*I did get involved with a big arbitration and had to roll up my sleeves and pitch in with photocopying at times, though normally it's a case of filling in a form and sending it to the print room to be done*."

## the rules

Organising departments into teams is both beneficial for and essential to the day-to-day operation of the firm. It breaks large groups of lawyers down into manageable units that can develop an identity of their own (and unfortunately in BT6's case an exit strategy). The atmosphere and working patterns of a team are determined by the dominant personali-

ties within it, such that "*each individual team is like a firm in itself – a firm within a firm*." Beyond the team structure, International Business Groups (IBGs) bring together practitioners who share an interest in core industry sectors, eg aviation, rail or property. There are also Key Client Groups to act as a focal point for all the lawyers who work for the firm's most important clients. A trainee can volunteer to assist one of these groups, and several of our sources recommended doing just that. "*It has really benefited me*," said one, "*you can learn quite a lot about things like marketing and business development*." It also helps a trainee raise their own profile in the firm.

As well as finance, corporate and litigation, trainees can access property seats and a host of specialist areas. To get them around it all the firm runs a six-seat training scheme which appeals because "*you get to see so many different parts of the firm. When you're studying, you don't know what it will be like in practice and with only four seats you could miss the department that's for you! And besides, if you go to a seat you don't like, it is over before it has started... thank goodness!*" Why might someone dislike a seat? "*Because of a personality clash with the person they are sitting with – although teams are generally really friendly – or if you are an academic person and you learn that churning out documents is not for you, or the team is very academic and you want to spend your time closing deals*." (Can you hear those horses for courses?) The only downside is the rapidity with which four months pass in a seat you love or when working in a complicated area of law. The question then becomes whether or not you get the chance to revisit the department before you qualify.

Early in the contract, trainees undertake three 'core' seats – banking, corporate and litigation – then a free choice, perhaps in a niche area such as employment, a smaller team such as property, or even an overseas seat or client secondment (eg Exxon Mobil and Nestlé). There are plenty of overseas seats, Hong Kong and Singapore being the hottest choices, Paris and Dubai also appealing

# the true picture

greatly. Among the many opportunities, few require a second language. After the first four seats, trainees spend more time in their department of choice or home in on an industry sector by tracing it through different departments. Actual seats can be repeated unless they are really popular ones. Unfortunately, this can include litigation. When we asked about the appeal of litigation, its fans explained two things: "*They trust you more in litigation than they do in corporate and finance*" and, crucially, "*litigation has better hours.*"

## midnight express

Yes, the hours can be long, but as one source noted: "*Although I was a bit aggravated, I understood that coming here was my choice. The hours should be no shock to anyone.*" Seats in corporate and some banking teams mean working "*9am to 8pm or 10pm or 11pm or even all night,*" a regime which led one trainee to sigh: "*Transactional work is not for me.*" On qualification in September 2005, 28 of the 31 NQs took jobs with the firm, though the general view from trainees was that a number had made a compromise because "*a lot of people wanted litigation and were offered transactional jobs... the same as the previous intake.*" In light of this information, we must reiterate that NR is "*mainly focused on banking and corporate... on qualification most people go to these big departments.*"

Even though it is true to say that "*if you've worked with someone on a deal they remember you,*" NR is not one of those firms where you know absolutely everybody. Our sources were largely unfamiliar with trainees in other intakes, even though starting at the firm means "*an instant crowd of new friends.*" As well as mates, every trainee has a mentor partner who is there for them in good times and bad. Said one source: "*I can ask about overall training contract issues and how to best manoeuvre myself.*" And what of the other partners you encounter? "*There is a hierarchy but it's not like you can't interact with people at team drinks and lunches.*" We're told that NR folk are "*all quite like-minded,*" which leads to "*a fun, banter-y atmosphere.*" Trainees identified people who were "*hard-working, ambitious, clever and well rounded... friendly, not stuck up, not too jolly hockey sticks.*" Don't assume the Oxbridge quotient is especially high because it is not. Apparently, the ideal candidate has "*a high standard of intelligence and soft skills. They place great emphasis on soft skills – humour and a good professional appearance. Of course there are a couple of awkward people here, but run the percentages and they're good.*"

In 2007 the entire firm will move to More London on the south bank of the Thames and come together under one roof for the first time in a long while. A symbolic change has already taken place – staff can now ditch suits and ties when not seeing clients, though it seems our sources have a preference for wearing the suits that they shelled out for just before starting their traineeships. For those who wish to adopt the new casual look, the dress code is clear: no jeans, no trainers and always proper shirts with collars. As one trainee noted: "*Norton Rose likes to take itself quite seriously and be what a top-ten law firm should be.*"

As befits any decent top-ten law firm, NR's international profile was celebrated at its 2005 'Orient Express' summer ball held in "*a big marquee by river.*" The invitation promised "A whirlwind whistle stop tour through northern and eastern Europe, Asia and the Mediterranean regions." Another high spot on the calendar is the annual inter-office Olympics, also an ideal way to celebrate the international profile of the firm. We think it apt that the firm values sport as highly as it does. Think about it: how could it be otherwise in such a team-oriented environment?

## and finally...

One trainee declared: "*I don't need a magic circle name on my CV to know I am at a good firm,*" and he's right – Norton Rose offers the archetypal City experience. It is perfect for students seeking a finance-centred, highly paid training with international opportunities, big deals and long hours... and lots of teams with initials.

## Olswang

### the facts

**Location:** London, Reading
**Number of partners/assistants:** 80/163
**Total number of trainees:** 40
**Seats:** 4x6 months
**Alternative seats:** Brussels, secondments
**Extras:** Pro bono – LawWorks, ProHelp, Toynbee Hall and Tower Hamlets law centres, language training

Staring at its 25th birthday, Olswang has managed to maintain a reputation for being cool while becoming unashamedly mainstream in its tastes.

### the comeback kid

Born in 1981, Olswang is only slightly older than most of our readers. And just as you lot have changed over your lifetimes, so has this firm. At the height of the dot.comedy Olswang was the only place to be for a cool young lawyer whose tastes were more Slim Shady than corporate drone. Riding the crest of the technology wave, Olswang expanded by an amazing 40% in just one year. It all looked unstoppable. Until, of course, it did stop. The value of tech companies plummeted. The firm's profits slumped. Downsizing was substituted for recruitment and the doom merchants rubbed their hands in glee.

But everyone loves a fighter and, refusing to allow a mere recession to stand in its way, Olswang regrouped and reshaped. Instead of thinking small it thought big, and when the law firm Andersen Legal imploded after the Enron debacle hit the headlines Olswang took over its Reading office. If that weren't enough, when the respected London firm DJ Freeman disbanded, Olswang hired the bulk of its property team. Earlier in 2005 the firm took on eight

lawyers from niche property practice Julian Holy and also made a new American friend through a 'strategic alliance' with New York firm Greenberg Traurig. (No one's talking full merger here so stay calm for now!)

The one-time technology and media supremo, although somewhat bruised by circumstance, has transformed itself into a fit and healthy mid-market player with the wisdom of hindsight and a stack of talented lawyers. These days its client list is replete with property giants such as Green Property and Woolworths as well as media names such as MTV and Channel 4. These days press releases are just as likely to refer to lawyers advising Land Securities Trillium on a property outsourcing deal with the DVLA as involvement with successful movies like 'Closer', 'Vera Drake', 'Hotel Rwanda' and 'Finding Neverland'.

### cinematic highlights

The trainees we chatted to were acutely aware of the changes in the firm's orientation through the types of work on offer to them in the four-seat scheme. No seat is strictly compulsory and there are plenty to choose from in the main groupings of corporate (mainstream, private equity, tax and banking options), property, litigation and media, telecommunications and technology. That said, corporate is effectively guaranteed as it is the largest department.

The firm is performing well in the realm of mid-market transactions and has clocked up a number of good deals in the past year. It was especially pleased to win instructions from a new client, an active US buyout house called Blackstone, and has already advised Blackstone on its takeover of Cineworld and its £200 million purchase of the UGC cinema chain. Who doesn't love going to the pictures? Perhaps followed by a meal. Olswang acted on a deal relating to the La Tasca chain of Spanish restaurants, which placed approximately £37.5 million of shares through the firm's investment bank client Altium Capital earlier in 2005.

# the true picture

Inevitably in a corporate seat there is a risk of sinking slowly into a mire of admin tasks, but here as in other departments fortune favours the bravas and trainees can ensure their six months are not helado on earth (¡Dios mìo! – the supply of Spanish grub gags is practically limitless) by making it known they want their fair share of decent and demanding tasks. *"As well as doing things like collating disclosure bundles I was also going to meetings. I'm the sort of person who will always do the best I can and I was rewarded with responsibility. They are good at recognising effort."*

## reality bites

Most of those we chatted to had also spent time in the property department, which we are pleased to report does not hold the pariah status it has at many other firms. One source enthused about how *"you get far more responsibility than anywhere else. I had my own files and that took up most of my time... mostly leases and licences, commercial conveyancing and a bit of residential."* Trainees spoke positively about the way in which they were absorbed into departmental teams in each seat. While the media (MCT) seats are the main reason most had joined the firm in the first place, they were clearly able to connect with the work of other departments. The only slight caveat was that some who had been supervised both by partners and assistants preferred rooming with the latter. Said one: *"The partners I sat with were too busy and were doing stuff that was not relevant for a trainee. An assistant can work with you more directly and you feel more comfortable with them."*

'Is this still a media firm?' became an important topic for discussion in our interviews and trainees were refreshingly frank in their assessments. *"There is still a focus but not such a focus"* is the short answer. Far from being a standard part of the training, media seats can be devilishly hard to get: one trainee had to *"beg, steal and borrow,"* as well as do *"mini interviews to put my case."* Once you enter the department, you also learn that your life isn't going to transform, you're not going to become best buds with the Gallagher clan and you're still a plain-old lawyer. Then again, as one trainee rightly remarked: *"A lot of the stuff in the law can be quite dry so anything unusual makes it more interesting, such as a contract with Naomi Campbell at the top instead of Company X."* Divided into four teams, the MCT department is quite the variety show. Team 1 deals with internet, e-commerce and data protection issues; 2 covers broadcasting, TV, publishing and advertising; 3 is film and 4 is IP litigation. *"Teams 1 and 2 interlink,"* so broadening the experiences of trainees who sit with each. And the kind of work an MTC trainee might expect to see? *"Drafting contracts for a film client, perhaps reviewing their precedents of licence and confidentiality agreements, research and writing research reports, reviewing an advertising deal."* Secondments to clients have included the BBC, HIT Entertainment and Film Four. Other reasons to spend time away from the office are *"random short secondments for a few weeks"* and a competition seat in Brussels. The Reading office has not become a common stopping-off point, although the firm would certainly entertain a request to go there for a seat and trainees from Reading have thus far all been able to take seats in London.

## you're so 'swang

Olswang's popularity makes it one of the hardest firms to get into. So who makes the grade and who falls by the wayside? Defining the typical Olswanger is not all that hard: a large number of them have a keen interest in music or film and most were naturally attracted to the firm's media work. But do take comfort from the fact that although some of the more mature trainees have already worked in the advertising, music or TV/film industries, neither a previous media career nor a Jonathan Ross-sized knowledge of movie trivia are essential. Those outsiders who think the firm is populated entirely by trendy meeja types could not be more wrong. *"The girls tend to be quite stylish – attractive, young profes-*

sional women who look really smart in a modern way – but the blokes are just average, though they might put a bit of gel in their hair." In terms of people's work preferences, the firm has "become more discerning and has focused on the diversity of the people they take in." It is in trainees' characters that similarities are more likely to be found. One observer reported that the typical trainee was "quick and smart," and beyond this "socially superb – you can get on like a house on fire with them as they are chatty and open people, confident in a way that makes you feel very comfortable." On the other hand, "from a work point of view they are very driven but hide it very well. They have confidence in their own ability and they expect a lot from themselves and have really high standards. They will go out there and try and get the best. I think they are deceptively relaxed." After many years in this game, we'd say this assessment is spot on.

"As a student people make the mistake of thinking bigger is better. When I told my friends I didn't want to work for the magic circle they said, 'That's a really bad career move.' But I wanted to go somewhere I would be asked for my opinion. They've gone to cog-in-machine firms and become miserable. Here I feel the partners are genuinely concerned about your training, and if you kick up a fuss and say I need this or want to do that they will listen." Olswang trainees are definitely the sort who have the nerve to ask.

In September 2005, qualifiers were in the fortunate position of not having to compete so hard for the available NQ jobs. A year before, 27 of them had qualified; this year just 15 were chasing the jobs and of them 13 stayed with the firm. It seems that after a string of poorer years for retention, the firm's got everything under control.

## square pig, round hole

Olswang resides in High Holborn in an office directly above a Starbucks. The building was apparently designed to look like the sail of a ship, though you might see more similarity with a TV screen (especially if you're still watching an old-fashioned curved one). Inside it's all glass walls and peculiar art. If you've a hole to fill, the staff restaurant Ozone serves up good, subsidised food right into the evening, which is ideal if you end up working late. As you undoubtedly will from time to time.

On moderately special occasions the firm holds parties on its seventh-floor roof terrace. For the annual Christmas party they really push the boat out; last year the party had "a 70s theme with a 70s band and Scooby Doo. A lot of partners went to town with their costumes." Perhaps the best aspect of the social life is the departmental weekend away, which a very very lucky trainee could possibly get to go on in each of their four seats. Entire departments, partners, lawyers, secretaries and all decamp at the firm's expense to some European destination for a weekend of partying. Barcelona looks to be the most popular destination. With an 8.5% turnover hike to £405 million in 2004/5, it looks as if the good times are rolling once more for 'the 'Swang'. And which department has the most fun? "The property department is the most sociable; they're always in the pub, usually The Square Pig."

## and finally...

Olswang is an ambitious and hard-working law firm that acts for household-name clients in many areas, not merely its MCT department. Don't apply here simply because you think it sounds cool – the recruiters will see you coming a mile off.

# Osborne Clarke

## the facts

**Location:** Bristol, London, Reading
**Number of partners/assistants:** 99/122
**Total number of trainees:** 47
**Seats:** 4x6 months
**Alternative seats:** Overseas seats, secondments

Osborne Clarke is a three-office UK firm which grew fat on a diet of technology-led business in the

# the true picture

90s. Still operating from London, Reading and its original Bristol base, the firm's activities are more diversified these days.

## reliving the dream

OC's letterhead features the silhouette of a big cat. That's big in the dangerous, not the overfed, sense since digital liposuction shaved a millimetre or two off its tummy. In its heartland, Bristol, OC is top cat to rival firm Burges Salmon's top dog. Yet the cat is a completely different animal to the Salmon. If your mind works like ours, you're now imagining a game of rock-paper-scissors featuring a dog, a cat and a fish. Cat beats fish, dog beats cat, confusion over what happens if dog and fish face off. Needless to say, both OC and BS have their leading qualities but, of the two, OC is *a more progressive and for-ward-thinking firm.* Another point to note concerns OC's attitude towards its UK operation. Its mantra is *one firm, three offices.*

There is something altogether more predatory about OC. Differentiated by its international focus and a commitment to multi-jurisdictional legal practice, the firm opened offices or made friends with overseas firms, creating an alliance stretching from Tallinn and St Petersburg to Palo Alto in California. OC dreamed of creating a law firm on which the sun never sets. Alas, rapid expansion turned quickly to overstretch when the technology sector took a turn for the worse. Trying to maintain an alliance spanning eleven time zones inevitably led to jetlag and the beleaguered moggy was accused of neglecting its domestic interests. By the beginning of 2004, OC was in need of a shake-up. Overheads were scrutinised, the bitter fruits being lay-offs and the senatorial demise of certain part-ners.

Having used up a couple of lives in the dot.comedy, the now-leaner beast of Bristol is back with a well-calculated roar rather than a sorry meow. The firm hasn't abandoned either its inter-est in technology-led businesses or its fascination for overseas offices and friends. Its TMT practice is

on the up, the UK now being the most competitive telecoms market in the Eurozone after Sweden. In the corporate sphere, OC lawyers recently com-pleted the largest deal in the firm's history, advising 3i on its £555 million buyout of car park operator NCP. More history is to be made soon, this time on the greener side of the Irish Sea. The firm's con-struction team is currently acting for Nishimatsu Construction on the Dublin Port Tunnel, Ireland's largest ever building project.

Telecoms and dot.coms still loom large on OC's client list. As well as sitting on the Amazon.com legal panel, the OC cat also represents Vodafone, Nortel, Motorola, Carphone Warehouse and the lovely folk at Friends Reunited. The firm's IP lawyers look after the interests of a varied client base from Microsoft and Honda, to Classic FM and the bizarre-sounding Clean Ice Pig, a pipe-cleaning technology spin-off from long-standing client the University of Bristol.

## nights on the tiles

As you may recall, Top Cat lived in an alley in a dust-bin with little more than a regular supply of milk a paw's reach way. We're pleased to report, however, that OC's three residences are considerably better appointed and better equipped. The Bristol's HQ is *amazing.* *It's very modern, lots of space and it's got a nice atrium.* When working late, a waft of jazz music may beckon you to join evening cocktails with clients in said atrium, *proving you don't always have to be chained to the desk.* Breakout rooms aren't as alarming as they sound: *If you have to work quietly or take a conference call* these glass pods are an invaluable alternative to open-plan working. The advantage to a trainee of working open plan is that they are surrounded by *12 to 15 fee earners,* with their work being allocated *as and when it comes in* via any one of them. Across the different departments and seats, supervision is uni-formly described as *great,* and lunchtime seminars *informative.* The opportunity to have discretionary monthly appraisals goes beyond the required mid and end-of-seat evaluations.

A large number of seats are on offer: corporate, banking, commercial employment, pensions and incentives (a favoured destination for trainees), litigation, property, tax and private client. Second-years naturally have preferential treatment ("*especially for the third seat*"), with first-years scooping the remainder. We noted that property and corporate seats are common for first-years with the more specialised work falling to those nearing qualification. Corporate is viewed as "*a solid start*" to the training contract. The mergers and acquisitions of "*both tech and non-tech companies*" will see you attending your fair share of completion meetings. These are "*really good fun and go on into the early hours.*" Even at that time of the night "*it's really useful to see the results of a three or four-month deal.*" Bless the trainee who told us: "*You're supposed to be tired in corporate.*" Completion-day champagne is also quaffed in banking, where trainees experience yet more of "*the peaks and troughs of sequences of late nights.*" Drafting opportunities include board minutes and directors' certificates, and there are endless conditions precedent exercises to complete. If drafting is the "*highlight*" of the seat, setting up a bible of core documents is definitely "*less of a highlight.*"

More drafting is to be found in the construction seat, where one past occupant explained that, far from being "*chained to the photocopier,*" they had ample opportunity to perfect "*precise drafting skills.*" Our sources also advised that the only Bristol seat promising its own files is commercial litigation. The award for best euphemism must go to the person who spoke of managing files for "*fee-sensitive clients.*"

## carry on cruising

Anticipating better times to come, the firm recently bought the bubble wrap and boxes for a move to swanky new London digs. "*Compared with the old ones, the new ones are great,*" was one appraisal of the London Wall office. With added rooftop hangouts offering panoramas that take in the newly scrubbed St Paul's, the building is certainly "*impressive.*" And the interior? "*Very white.*" The carpet? "*Very blue.*" And the chairs? "*They're red.*" This tricolour is well lit by "*floor-to-ceiling windows,*" making the whole ensemble sound suspiciously like a cruise ship.

Clients are drawn to the London office for specialist services, such as advertising and marketing law, computer games and media advice, plus an experienced private equity team. A seat with the latter offers trainees mixed experiences. The transactional nature of the work and the size of deals leave few "*problem-solving tasks*" and instead the work can be "*very administrative.*" This translates into "*a lot of bible bashing and bundling*" and there aren't many client meetings to relieve the bundle blues. All in all "*they don't let you out much.*" In commercial litigation seats, trainees feel more involved with cases, even the mammoth ones. "*You work more closely with your supervisor and get to see just what a big client demands – it was insightful for me,*" said one fan of the seat. On smaller matters, trainees are allowed to conduct telephone conferences with clients with a supervisor sitting in for silent support. Add in "*e-mails and letters of advice*" and "*sitting in on mediations and arranging seminars*" and it all adds up to a very positive experience.

OC's small Thames Valley office – snappily abbreviated to TVO – brings trainees to Reading. Until recently, there were two other similar firms in the town – Olswang and Nabarro Nathanson. The latter announced its departure in the summer of 2005, primarily because its London lawyers were so close at hand, and it did occur to us to wonder whether OC might follow suit any time soon, especially when we heard that venture capitalist 3i, one of the OC's biggest clients has decided to leave Reading and instead run its operations from London and Manchester. But whilst the trainee population in Reading was down to two from an historical level of five (compared to 21 in Bristol and 15 in London), there was nothing to suggest that OC has any plans to retract its Reading arm.

OC looks like a firm that is in the habit of following its clients. A Munich branch opened in May 2005 to service clients such as Adobe, Invensys, Microsoft, Open Text, 3i and Yahoo!, all of which have operations there. As yet there is no Munich posting for trainees, although an EU competition seat is open in Cologne for anyone fluent in German. More people qualify for a seat in the Sunshine State and, consequently, competition for flights to California is stiff. At every seat rotation, two trainees jet off to the manicured lawns and palm trees of the utopic Palo Alto to conduct "*mostly marketing and only some fee earning.*"

## tonight matthew...

In each office, a social committee is given "*a certain amount of subsidy,*" which is put towards trainee outings, known colloquially as "*trouts.*" It's the usual round of go-karting, guffaws at comedy clubs, "*eating and drinking*" and cinema trips. Sporting life takes the form of "*cricket matches with barbecues, softball and netball tournaments.*" The most recent summer party was held at Kew Gardens and featured a five-a-side football tournament. Teams assembled from all the offices; "*this year even some of our Germans turned up.*" The firm hired red double-decker buses to ferry everyone to another party, this time featuring fancy dress. For reasons known only to himself, "*the head of litigation came as Rod Stewart.*" Yes, of course we asked if trainees thought he was sexy. No, of course we can't print their replies.

The firm's business-casual dress code doesn't usually stretch to Lycra (thankfully). It is, however, very much in keeping with an atmosphere that trainees describe as "*relaxed and warm.*" OC is famed for a certain transparency that allows staff to feel they know a fair amount about the general plan. At regular team meetings, "*you get a heads-up as to where the firm is going,*" and when the firm was redesigning its office space it sought the opinions of staff on all the issues that would affect them. The typical recruit to OC has a similarly open character

as well as being "*smart, bright and friendly with a good sense of fun,*" and the firm receives more than enough good applications to enable it to be quite picky. Once they start at the firm, trainees soon learn that OC lacks "*a conformist culture,*" and as a result, "*so long as you get the job done, you can be the person you want to be... you can be as individual as you want.*"

Across the offices, all nine qualifiers stayed with the firm in September 2005.

## and finally...

If you want a regional firm with an international outlook and a training contract with ample scope for variety, Osborne Clarke looks pretty perfect.

# Pannone & Partners

## the facts

**Location:** Manchester
**Number of partners/assistants:** 84/101
**Total number of trainees:** 25
**Seats:** 4x6 months
**Alternative seats:** Occasional secondments

Like Manchester, you've got strange ways if you're considering a quality career in the North West and you're unaware of this firm. With an arsenal of departments, an apparent commitment to so-called 'lifestyle' working and healthy profits, Pannone & Partners claims to be "the complete law firm."

## because you're worth it

With a mix of legal goodies surrounded by the bread-and-butter of personal injury and corporate work, Pannones' range of departments is more or less complete so far as trainees are concerned. Those intent on a commercial career can marvel at the firm's £33 million annual turnover (up 12% on the previous year's swelling profits) and know that the growth is indicative of an expanding client list that has transformed the corporate team into the second highest earner in the firm. Those more interested in a career advising Joe Public can be reassured that Pannones' commitment to him is backed by long expertise, a back catalogue of impressive cases and a magnum-sized PI team. Neither the private nor commercial departments have – as yet – been allowed to take precedence.

Pannones' interests range from Thalidomide sufferers to the city of Manchester itself – the firm is currently involved in a £150 million deal that will change its landscape through the ongoing renewal of the Piccadilly area. But regionally based need not mean regionally focused: national and international clients include L'Oréal for all your cosmetic needs and the Church of England for all your celestial needs. This year oil titan ChevronTexaco called upon Pannone to act on the sale of 118 service stations to Somerfield supermarkets – reputedly for £15.3 million. Not megabucks by London standards, but indicative of a growing trend for big companies to be attracted to the lower rates and guaranteed partner participation on offer at mid-tier and regional firms. Supporting the firm's international clientele is the Pannone Law Group (PLG), a network of affiliated firms in jurisdictions ranging from Andorra to Uruguay. Put down that factor 10: secondments are not available. A journey to the nearest phone and a call to an affiliated Spanish office about Iberian trade marks, or a back-and-forth run to the family department's new "*mini-office*" in Hale, is as close as you'll get.

The four-seat training scheme allows a decent amount of choice and trainees "*tend to double up the last seat,*" spending a year in their preferred area for qualification. Slipped discs must surely be an occupational hazard for partners who, intent on giving trainees the experiences they need, "*bend over backwards*" for them. No sooner does a trainee raise an area of experience that needs to be developed, than a supervisor is on the case and an e-mail flies around the department for assistants and partners to scour for a piece of work that will fill the void.

## matters of the heart

Clinical negligence is a forte, with cases ranging from Gulf War Syndrome to group actions against plastic surgeons. Such lengthy and complex cases mean trainees can only assist, say with client interviews, instructing experts and attending hearings, and unfortunately "*photocopying and bundling is not unknown.*" On a macabre note, expect to see some "*interesting photos*" and thumb through medical dictionaries looking for "*lots of long words.*"

The clients of the family department are "*a very rich lot*" who would balk at trainee representation. At least you'll get to dig around, mining for the assets about which a client's ex is being economical with the truth. This will mean company searches and time spent poring over schedules of pensions, shares and property assets. In one case valuables included "*a vintage football shirt.*" Given the danger that one can occasionally "*lose sympathy*" with clients' foibles, patience for human idiosyncrasies is a great asset to a trainee. In short, marital breakdown is never easy, and sometimes it can be very hard. Who'd have foreseen that divorce would become a side effect for the anti-impotence drug Viagra until Pannone and other pioneering firms began representing the women on the receiving end of their husband's newly re-discovered sexual appetite?

Perhaps the most disturbing work is to be found in the formerly compulsory PI seat where one partner specialises in child abuse claimant cases. Usually trainees are bombarded with work from various fee-earners but when sitting with this partner it's more of a one-on-one training. The trainee's role includes "*a fair amount of bundling and a lot of letters of instruction to medical witnesses,*" summarising evidence and preparing medical chronologies, and note taking at regular conferences with barristers and medical experts. Occasional calls from claimants can be "*hard going*" but the knowledge you are "*helping a client*" is "*very rewarding.*" Elsewhere in PI, trainees handle a lot of road traffic accidents and will shortly be taking on more work on foreign accidents referred by the National Accident Helpline. A PI seat may also bring trainees into contact with industrial diseases, which our sources tell us leaves you feeling "*genuinely proud of your work.*" One elderly widow had told a trainee: "*It's nice to speak to someone who cares about my husband, why he died and who he was.*"

## 1000-yard stare

Should a commercial career interest you, Pannone has continually bettered its commercial performance over the past five years. Commercial seats mean a supporting role for trainees so don't expect to be centre stage, especially in meetings. You need not worry about being consigned to the reprographics room though as there will always be a steady stream of board minutes and resolutions to be drafted plus small agreements and disclosure letters to prepare. Though these tasks are all "*heavily supervised,*" this is "*not constraining – it is always useful and a good opportunity to learn.*" A coco seat draws work from the corporate, banking, insolvency and commercial teams, whereas a property seat is more self-contained and, unlike corporate, trainees can run some simple files by themselves.

The business crime seat may sound like something out of a John Grisham novel but in practice it comes closer to Microserfdom. "*Nearly driven loopy*" by the experience, one trainee spent weeks inputting data and told us "*business crime means endless lever-arch folders of documents.*" Extraordinary psychopathologies have also been reported in the insolvency department. One source clearly remembered beginning an insolvency seat but has since "*blanked it out.*" In distinct contrast, another was clearly suffering from some sort of post-insolvency stress disorder, perhaps missing the adrenaline of bankruptcy hearings before a district judge in the county court. While some loved court work, others found the process "*petrifying.*" Agency work from other firms in particular can be "*pretty shit scary,*" but it does ensure you develop the thousand-yard stare so necessary for advocacy.

## training the third way

It is encouraging that swelling profits haven't been bought by disturbing Pannones' "*work-life balance.*" Indeed, the firm has gone up two places on the *Sunday Times*' '100 Best Companies to Work For' survey and now perches at number four. Increasing profitability, happy workers – can this be a law firm? Pannones' matriarchal structure is further proof of its rarity in the legal world. Women outnumber men roughly 360 to 150 and the whole operation is steered by the only female managing partner among the major firms in the North West.

The constitutions of both the firm and its trainees tend to contain an "*idealistic part.*" Asked why they did not choose high street practice, many of our sources focused on the lack of LPC funding and job certainty at such firms. One concluded: "*It's becoming the only option to go for somewhere like Pannone.*" Another factor in people's choices was "*ambition*" – these trainees appear to want social justice with healthy salaries; they intend, therefore, to tread the Third Way on offer at Pannone, where their "*idealistic part*" is allowed a tethered range. Individual trainees have brokered a merger between commercial sense and social conscience; through pro bono work they can even produce a happy medium. One trainee conducted a series of free seminars to raise awareness of gay employee rights and accompanied it with an article in *Canal Street* magazine. The lead of social justice can be turned into firm's gold, the alchemy being good business sense: "*If you can spin a pro bono for business ends it gets a better take-up.*" The Canal Street project could well "*drum up business*" for the employment department.

## let them eat cake

The influence of a powerful HR department is felt across a firm which "*tries to promote not working long hours*" as part of its commitment to work-life balance. Shopping days (last year in Edinburgh), summer barbecues and leisurely Christmas parties are among the social events coordinated with the help of the HR people. They should trademark their *"speed-networking"* events, a subtle tweaking of the tried and tested speed-date. The best technique is to nod politely and laugh where appropriate during these *"painful musical chairs,"* where you get to meet others in the firm and find out what they do.

Strategic deployment of the carrot rather than the stick sees case settlements and deal completions rewarded with cakes and chocolates. After hitting its 2004 target the whole firm was given a bonus equal to a week's pay and an extra day's holiday. Nevertheless, even in this egalitarian workplace some are more recognised than others. Individuals who perform especially well are accorded recognition for their labours: *"you're picked out"* if you *"personally shine."*

In September 2005 six of seven qualifiers stayed on with the firm.

## and finally...

This firm has struck a fine balance. The private client/commercial blend offsets a social conscience with competitiveness, and the firm's needs harmonise with those of its trainees. We'll venture to suggest that you and Pannone & Partners could make beautiful music together.

# Paris Smith & Randall

## the facts

**Location:** Southampton
**Number of partners/assistants:** 19/36
**Total number of trainees:** 6
**Seats:** 4x6 months
**Alternative seats:** None

If Southampton's history is marked by famous departures – the Pilgrim Fathers, The Titanic, Craig David – Paris Smith & Randall shows us what can be achieved by sticking around.

## founding fathers

The book *180 Years in the History of Paris Smith & Randall* was never likely to topple *Harry Potter and the Philosopher's Stone* from its number-one spot on the bestseller list, but for a Paris Smith & Randall trainee this 1998 tome has become compulsory bedtime reading... especially when some pesky *Student Guide* researcher calls up demanding a potted history of the firm, in less than 500 words, on my desk by Friday.

A quick flick through this weighty hardback will tell you that the firm's *"long and distinguished history"* dates back to 1818 and a certain Mr Bryant. However, by 1891 it was the names Paris, Smith and Randall engraved in brass above the door. The *"most recent survivor"* of the original Paris, Smith & Randall lineage to take the firm's helm was Cecil Paris, who passed away as recently as 1998. A third-generation Parisian and keen cricketer in his day, the official Hampshire Cricket Club records, Mr Paris *"captained the side with immense concentration and effort."* Now just over 180 years of similar concentration and effort have allowed Paris Smith to carve itself a reputation as *"a prestigious local firm."* Trainees acknowledged the presence of other firms on the South Coast, mainly those with *"satellite offices here,"* but proudly described themselves *"a solely Southampton firm."*

Paris Smith serves both local and national clients with a comprehensive practice divided neatly between private and commercial work: on the one hand residential property, family, tax and estate planning; on the other company/commercial, commercial property, licensing, public sector and secured lending. Straddling the two are litigation and employment teams. For trainees, this means *"a good mix of work"* in a firm that *"bridges that gap between the high street and a national firm."*

## a little of what you fancy

Despite moves to bring the training scheme in line with a more usual four-seat set-up, Paris Smith continues to afford trainees some flexibility and all our sources had squeezed in an extra spell here or there. Efforts to *"set out your seats in black and white"* early on seem almost pointless given a tendency to accommodate trainees' preferences *"as you go."* Ultimately, *"everyone who wants something gets it, though it may only be for three months."* Even if you are hell-bent on commercial work, the firm is *"keen for you to experience private client or family, even if just for three months to give a taste."* No seat is strictly compulsory *"as long as departments that need trainee cover are constantly covered,"* namely commercial property, family and litigation. Further investigation reveals that *"almost everyone does commercial property – it's the focus of the practice."*

Described as *"**the** department,"* commercial property is *"certainly the biggest and certainly expanding."* For trainees, time here means *"anything ranging from research to drafting documents"* for the likes of Rose Bowl plc (the home of Hampshire Cricket Club), Southampton City Council, Southampton FC and Portsmouth FC. The property team has also has recently scored for Pirelli on the sale of its Southampton factory.

*"Next biggest are company-commercial and commercial litigation."* The corporate lawyers' work continues the fast-cars-and-footballers theme, with deals including the £6 million disposal of dealerships for Derek Warwick Honda and the €70 million securitisation of the German bundesliga club FC Schalke 04. Despite suffering from the *"peaks and troughs"* syndrome that afflicts most corporate departments, such decent deal experience makes the Paris Smith team an interesting prospect for a young corporate hotshot intent on remaining on the South Coast. In one of its biggest deals to date the team recently worked on the reorganisation of a £50 million trading subsidiary of defence and civil contractor VT Group plc. A company/commercial seat means *"board minutes, company resolutions, shelf companies and a little IP work."* Our sources had participated in management buyouts and share sales. And in any event, *"general company work and constitutional sorts of things"* are *"a good way of getting your feet wet."*

If the division of labour is *"probably slightly biased towards commercial work,"* we were assured *"there is a lot of call for private client lawyers down here."* The ever-popular (and ever-expanding) employment team is considered *"an exciting department to be in"* and affords trainees plenty of responsibility when *"drafting policies, looking at compromise agreements, going to tribunals and taking witness statements."* The employment team represents *"a combination of private and commercial clients,"* so for a pure private client experience ask for a seat working on wills, trusts and tax planning for *"those who come in off the street, those referred from commercial side, and those who are long-standing, grand clients of the firm."* The last category sounds intriguing. A stint in family can be *"quite daunting;"* here trainees find themselves in court, at meetings with clients and conferences with counsel, and back at the office drafting divorce petitions.

## colour me crazy

You might think three months in a seat is hardly time enough to log on and check your e-mail, let alone manage your own files. Trainees confirm there is something in the idea and point out that six-month seats are far more likely to lead to autonomy. The firm likes to *"start out softly softly while you get yourself settled."* Then *"the more they trust you, the more responsibility they give you."* *"Photocopying!"* groaned one trainee when we asked about duller aspects of the job. *"It's everyone's bugbear... and the plan colouring!"* The same source did concede that actually *"most of the time you are drafting, writing to clients, attending court and doing hands-on stuff."* Another agreed: *"There will always be times when you have to muck in, but it's never very often and is usually for something you have been working on."*

There are formal appraisals every three months and on the third Wednesday of every month the training partner meets with the trainee group. Typically this is *"just to touch base,"* read the trainee clap-o-meter and feed back to the partnership but "*he will also fight your corner for you if needs be.*"

The office occupies "*quite an imposing site*" at some traffic lights on one of the main routes into Southampton, ensuring that "*everyone knows the building.*" To address the firm's current problem of being "*absolutely maxed out,*" two smaller offices "*a stone's throw away*" accommodate training facilities, admin and some of the private client departments. Trainees tell us there are "*no funny sculptures or crazy colour schemes*" and the firm's facilities are terribly conventional, perhaps no surprise for a firm that has built an excellent reputation in Southampton without resorting to razzmatazz. The secret of its success? "*Really concentrating on the [geographical] area*" and maintaining a steady focus on service standards.

## gone in sixty seconds

"*Quite an austere public front*" translates into "*proper*" office dress and a "*very professional*" approach. That said, Paris Smith trainees do like to let their hair down, and with office hours "*pretty much nine to five*" and comments like "*six o'clock is a late night for some people*" not an outrageous exaggeration, no one feels cheated of their me-time. Organised social events have included bingo, go-karting, barbecues and quiz nights. At the Christmas party there's a quaint tradition whereby one trainee must stand up in front of the entire firm and thank the managing partner for his speech. Thankfully it "*only lasts about a minute,*" but requires the unlucky 'volunteer' to "*drink lots of wine and shake a bit*" beforehand. Far less nerve wracking are casual, chatty trainee lunches at the "*funky*" Apartment 26, and when the roof garden here won't suffice, there's a park next to the office. Paris Smith fields netball and football teams and, emulating their forebears, "*the cricket team is exceptional.*" Alas, the firm has missed a trick on the sporting-slash-benefits-and-perks front. The "*exceptionally deep car park*" under the office is "*apparently below water level*" and could easily double up as a swimming pool.

Don't worry if your overarm bowling is weak: Paris Smith also recruits from silly mid off and deep cover. The current trainee side includes fast bowlers straight out of law school, good catchers who landed training contracts after previous careers, and reliable batsmen who notched up runs as para-legals. While sporting prowess is not a prerequisite, good sportsmanship probably is. Our sources were a helpful, enthusiastic and "*inclusive bunch*" and, as in many South Coast firms, the trainee group is home grown. "*The firm does prefer people with local connections and they want people to grow within the firm. They aren't completely against people who don't have connections, but you have to have a good reason for going to Southampton... you've got to really tell them why.*" Confirming their commitment to the region, in September 2005 all three qualifiers stayed with the firm.

## and finally...

If a hardback history book seems a little old-fashioned in our digital age, rest assured the latest chapter in the Paris Smith & Randall story is far from it. For anyone committed to a career in Southampton, anything you can find on the firm will be well worth a read.

# Payne Hicks Beach

## the facts

**Location:** London
**Number of partners/assistants:** 28/21
**Total number of trainees:** 5
**Seats:** 4x6 months
**Alternative seats:** None

A timeless classic, Payne Hicks Beach has been around since 1730 and is going nowhere in a hurry.

## where there's a will

If the thought of big business leaves you cold and you reckon blackberries belong in pies rather than lawyers' briefcases, PHB could be of real interest to you. A private client firm through and through, much of its work centres on tax, trusts and probate services. Its clients are in the main wealthy individuals, estates, trusts, family businesses, universities and colleges, museums and charities. This little gem is about as far from the likes of Clifford Chance and Linklaters as it is possible to go.

Despite its comparatively small size, PHB handles some fantastic work. One partner led a team supporting the Treasury Solicitor in the representation of almost 500 current and former soldiers at The Bloody Sunday Inquiry in Northern Ireland; other high-profile clients include round-the-world yachtswoman Ellen MacArthur and organisations like the Royal Yachting Association. The firm's well-known family lawyer Fiona Shackleton acted for Prince Charles in his divorce, and now works as personal solicitor to Princes William and Harry. The firm was also involved in the administration of the estate of John Edwards – close friend, minder and muse to the artist Francis Bacon, who had left him more than enough for a retirement of comfort and cocktails in Thailand. Considering the profile of some of its recent cases and clients, PHB is suitably discrete in terms of flagging up its successes and touting for business. "*It relies on word of mouth and doesn't actively market itself,*" revealed one source.

## family dramas

PHB takes just two or three trainees per year. They spend six months in four of the firm's five departments – private client; family; company and commercial (including employment); property and dispute resolution – and the training is designed to give access to a good cross-section of the firm's work. "*There is a different feel to each department,*" we heard. Tax work, for example, is considered "*very unemotional – everything is quietly controlled and calm.*" By contrast, in the matrimonial department there are "*lots of emotional clients and last-minute urgency.*" Litigation is by all accounts less urgent and frantic, being "*fairly academic and involving intricate*

*research.*" Despite its proximity to the Royal Courts and more barristers than you can shake a wig at, opportunities for advocacy are limited. "*We always use counsel,*" reported one source regretfully.

In terms of the type of work that draws people to PHB, several had been particularly keen on working in its famous matrimonial department. "*I was attracted to the human element,*" said one fan. In order to thrive there "*you need to enjoy listening to problems and must be prepared to be a shoulder to cry on.*" The seat comes replete with frequent appearances in court and "*lots of client contact,*" so if you feel short-changed on the Perry Mason moments in your litigation seat, this is where to come. If it's intellectual rigour you're after, the private client team coordinates the investments of trust funds totalling several hundred million pounds, sometimes linking through to corporate vehicles and frequently international in scope. It's definitely more than will writing for little old ladies.

## plotting your own course

One problem with smaller firms is the absence of paralegals to take care of the menial chores. "*As a trainee you are at the bottom of the food chain, which means you can find yourself doing a full day of photocopying,*" revealed one source. Across the firm "*the levels of responsibility vary between trainees. The more they trust you, the more work you get.*" According to trainees, "*the firm is excellent... for the right person.*" Colleagues are described as "*pleasant – they tend to have a good sense of humour and be self-confident.*" The firm certainly seems to look for people who are "*self-sufficient*" and who "*don't go along with the herd.*" Personality-wise, "*if you want to sit in the background, don't come here. Confidence is important. You must recognise that it's going to be challenging.*" And wise advice from one old hand: "*It's important to keep level headed when you're under stress.*" The working pattern will certainly help you in this regard and trainees see it as a real bonus that "*hours are more or less 9am to 6pm on average. You can have a life as well as work.*" All the trainees we spoke to were clear about what they were after in their training. Typically we heard: "*I didn't want to go into the City. I didn't want the hours or to work with aggressive partners. Corporate work bores me to tears. I like the fact that this firm is old and traditional.*"

The firm's premises in Lincoln's Inn's New Square, close to the Royal Courts of Justice, were originally intended to hold eight sets of barristers and ooze olde legal worlde charm. Oil portraits and open fireplaces have weathered the test of time and still fend off Bloomberg feeds and polished marble atria. How refreshing to speak to people who are unabashed in telling us their firm is "*old-school and prides itself on its traditional aspects.*" Though barely more than a breeze, the winds of change are having an effect, however. Said one source: "*It's a very old firm, but younger partners are trying to change things. We do have a lot of old family clients, but there are a lot more entrepreneurs and businesses.*"

## sail of the centuries

Regular Thursday fee earners' lunches bring teams together to sample the dishes prepared by in-house chef Fifi. On the sporting front think cricket, tennis, hockey and boating rather than pool and darts. Matches are played against teams fielded by barristers chambers and the firm's olde worlde bankers around the corner. The annual Christmas party inspires "*a reasonable turnout.*" On the bill last time a raffle with the top prize a calendar signed by Olympic sailors and donated by one of the partners who is himself an ex-Olympic sailor. We only hope he was too hung-over to scrutinise eBay the morning after.

Our interviews with trainees left us with the impression that what you see really is what you get at PHB. Seat allocation is simple and largely avoids conflict and uncertainty. The four seats provide "*a broad spread of experience with huge amounts of responsibility for everyone*" and "*lots of client exposure – you're always on the phone.*" Furthermore, the size of the deals and cases handled by the firm mean

trainees can get "*far more involved in what is going on,*" and regular training seminars keep them on point. PHB has teamed up with some other local firms for these seminars and so in term time trainees can go to weekly events run by a professional training company and held in the nearby Royal College of Surgeons. Out of term they take place on an ad hoc basis, though there are still the monthly departmental meetings in-house.

While they might have moaned about minor things, overall our sources were pleased with their lot, evidenced by the fact that both of 2005's qualifiers took NQ jobs at the firm. Indeed, trainee gripes were restricted to the infrastructure – although the building is considered to be lovely, its decor, air con and IT system are all deemed to be a bit behind the times. Any suggested improvements? "*The dried flowers wind me up,*" and "*it would be nice to have proper central heating – Monday mornings can be very cold.*" Dare we recommend a pair of those Dickensian fingerless gloves for winter months?

## and finally...

If you think you might prefer to work on the set of a costume drama rather than the latest blockbuster, Payne Hicks Beach delivers a decidedly bespoke training.

# Penningtons Solicitors LLP

## the facts

**Location:** Basingstoke, Godalming, London, Newbury
**Number of partners/assistants:** 68/120
**Total number of trainees:** 27
**Seats:** 4x6 months
**Alternative seats:** None

With commercial and private client services on offer in the capital and across the south of England, Penningtons is a good bet for anyone seeking a broad legal training.

# the true picture

## the boys are back in town

Not only does Penningtons straddle the town-country divide, it also divides its time between property, litigation, corporate/commercial and private client. Which is the dominant gene? It's hard to tell – these days Penningtons looks the picture of equilibrium. It has not always been the case: the firm's glory days as a major City player in the 1980s were followed by a run of bad luck in the 1990s, but *"all that is behind us now,"* the firm is on an even keel and *"this is definitely a very positive time for us."* The plan is simple: *"Bigger and better!"*

The London office probably takes the mantle of HQ; however, with several specialist practices and strong local identities, it is Penningtons' regional offices that lay claim to being *"the big boys in town."* Newbury, for example, is home to respected family and private client teams; Basingstoke's excellent social housing team advises some of the largest housing associations in the south; and Godalming offers a notable travel team and superb clin neg lawyers with expertise in neurosurgery, obstetrics and orthopaedics. Trainees choose one office and then stay there. Our first message, therefore, has to be to choose the right office, considering carefully the benefits of each. A typical seat list in each location includes property, private client, coco and commercial litigation, bolstered by regional variants such as professional regulation in London, family in Newbury, or travel litigation in Godalming.

## floral tributes

*"They like you to do property,"* and the reason is clear – earning the highest percentage of the firm's turnover, *"property dominates."* Among the most well known of Penningtons' property clients are Vodafone, Fyffes/Geest and Sunglass Hut. In terms of deals, the team recently agreed a lease for 'Roast' the new restaurant in the Floral Hall area of Jamie Oliver's old haunt, Borough Market. For trainees, property work covers everything from finance through to commercial leases and residential conveyancing. On commercial transactions *"most of the work involves lots of money"* so there are few opportunities for them to run their own files, but there is variety in the tasks available. Said one source: *"They deliberately give you work they haven't given you before."* Proving itself *"a huge contrast to commercial property,"* private client is acknowledged to be *"a good starter seat."* The majority of our sources had spent time here, and one told us how *"straight away on arrival I was involved in some very good work. From simple wills through to tax planning wills through to declarations of trust."* Trainees reported heaps of contact with *"predominantly wealthy aristocratic types"* and enjoyed work that is *"quite taxing... excuse the pun."*

Penningtons' commercial clients range from *"tiny little people"* (entrepreneurs not midgets) to *"well-known, substantial firms."* The deals trainees encounter tend to be for *"a lot of private companies and sometimes plcs rather than the other way round,"* but that doesn't make them any less colourful or appetising. Between them the regional offices have advised fine foods specialist Ritter Courivaud on its acquisition of a caviar business; Eurofins Laboratories on the purchase of Direct Laboratory Services; and Williamson Tea Holdings in connection with the de-listing of the plc from the OFEX market. In London, lawyers advised Alpha Hospitals (a provider of psychiatric services) on the acquisition of Mayflower Hospitals, which operates facilities in Bury and Sheffield. Our sources reported having played a genuine role in *"seeing big deals through from start to finish,"* and applauded a recent decision to move all company secretarial work (very adminny) to a dedicated team in Basingstoke, so *"freeing up fee earners to do the actual corporate work."* For trainees the decision enables them to *"focus on what interests you"* – commercial advice or employment matters, for example.

## pokey politics in london

According to London trainees, Penningtons' City office is in *"a great location."* According to those luxuriating in the vast acreage of the Home Counties, *"it is pokey and packed."* Either way, there is ample room for some fascinating litigation. Lawyers advised the Conservative Party in April 2005 on Howard Flight's claim that Michael Howard's moves to withdraw the whip and subsequent endorsement as a parliamentary candidate were unconstitutional and unlawful. If, like Flight, you miss out on a seat with the Tories, there's plenty of drama to be had in commercial litigation. Here, the firm is currently handling High Court proceedings for overseas clients involving a worldwide freezing order obtained by an Indian-based company in a dispute over the acquisition of a business in Central America.

For after-hours rabble-rousing, the local pub is the Slug and Lettuce, and staff also enjoy quiz nights, karaoke and *"regular sundowners"* plus an annual Christmas dinner dance in January.

## the mobsters of godalming

In Godalming plans are afoot to bring everyone under one roof, though for now a main office houses coco, litigation and employment lawyers, with private client and property colleagues *"just a stroll down the High Street."* For those with a taste for sun sand and sangria, a spell with the travel team may be just the ticket. Here, trainees encounter superb PI involving jurisdictional, limitation period or enforcement issues.

In 1698, Peter the Great stopped off for a pint on his way through Surrey and ended up having a riotously big night on the town. Penningtons' trainees are doing their level best to make up for this by proving that soirees in Godalming need not be uncivilised. They put on quarterly networking events for other local young professionals (Scalextric evenings, champagne tasting etc) and manage to behave impeccably at 'Penningtons' Pennies' nights, when everyone in the office receives a drinks voucher to be traded in at a local watering hole. If none of this appeals, *"just hop on the train to Clapham."* What you won't want to miss is the

office Christmas party; at last year's everyone made the most of the Gangsters and Gals theme. *"The head of property looked very dangerous with slicked back hair and shades."*

## down like a shot to basingstoke

As we have already mentioned, Basingstoke is home to excellent PI and clin neg work – *"We don't do simple PI here."* The mainly claimant caseload includes cerebral palsy cases and *"people being given the wrong drugs and problems during operations."* On a simpler claim, a trainee can *"do all the work first hand"* as well as assisting on more complex claims. Time in the property or litigation departments will expose trainees to right-to-buy issues and site acquisitions for housing associations.

The open-plan office is *"lovely because it is easy to chat and be very sociable;"* a good job too because boozy Friday nights are rare as *"most people drive to work."* Instead trainees lunch together and join other staff for curry nights and bowling trips. And come the summer party they're all set to *"end up doing shots with the partners."*

## living like kings in newbury

Newbury hangs its hat on an excellent private client team and is also home to the firm's core family team – a popular choice for trainee seats. The Newbury lawyers now occupy a part of Vodafone's old HQ and the open-plan office affords plenty of room for swelling numbers in family, private client, commercial property and coco.

*"A disproportionate number of pubs in Newbury"* lend themselves to a full social scene. The nearby King Charles alternates with the office as a venue for Friday drinks and there are regular events such as wine tastings, quiz nights, paintballing, cricket matches and a softball tournament. At the Christmas bash trainees and partners take it in turns to do *"I don't know what you'd call it... some sort of performance."* Last year, hot on the heels of the office move, the trainees appeared as partners seeking out

their ideal pied à terre in "*Lawcation Lawcation Lawcation.*"

## all together now

With four offices, it is hardly surprising that Penningtons "*does seem a little bit fragmented;*" however, some carefully considered initiatives ensure "*you always feel part of the big Penningtons picture*" and everything "*hangs together, particularly at trainee level.*" All gather in London for training one Thursday each month. 'Trainee Thursdays' ("*we have yet to come up with a snappier name*") also allow the group to spend some social time together, as does the firm's annual sports day, although as one source admitted: "*It's just rounders actually!*"

The firm adopts a common approach on day-to-day matters such as office hours. Both in the capital and the counties "*official hours are nine to five-thirty, and it is certainly not frowned upon if you stick to them.*" A typical day ends around 6pm. Across the firm smart-casual attire is standard for Fridays and throughout the summer months. And (hurrah!) the rigid IT policy which had caused much consternation has been relaxed in all offices. Similarly so have trainee reactions – "*You still can't access Hotmail, but it's not that much of a biggie.*"

Trainees are "*expected to muck in and do their best.*" Sometimes that will mean a smattering of "*cruddy tasks,*" but there are compensations and "*they aren't afraid of sending you to do advocacy.*" We even heard of one poor soul for whom mucking in meant acting as understudy for five different speaking parts in the employment team's annual role-play seminar for clients. Before you get stage fright, "*they don't expect you to be Superman*" and "*you are quite within your rights to turn around and say 'I am really snowed under.'*" In such situations you are also entitled to expect others to dig you out. "*Very patient*" supervisors offer three-monthly reviews, and there is further support from mentors and, as in past years, our sources praised HR angel Andrea Law. Happy to continue to sing from the Penningtons' hymn sheet, in September 2005 eight of the 12 qualifiers took jobs at the firm.

## and finally...

While Penningtons' regional offices are an obvious choice in their various locales, the London office must compete with scores of other similar-sized firms for students' attention. Gauge the firm by what it can offer you in terms of seats and clients. Perhaps an Indian conglomerate will be the draw, or perhaps it will be the opportunity to switch between PI/clin neg, commercial work and private clients.

# Pinsent Masons

## the facts

**Location:** Birmingham, Bristol, London, Leeds, Manchester, Scotland
**Number of partners/assistants:** 252/498
**Total number of trainees:** 105
**Seats:** 4x6 months
**Alternative seats:** Secondments
**Extras:** Pro bono – various projects including Birmingham business scheme, death row appeals

In December 2004 national construction, engineering, IT and energy firm Masons merged with full-service national outfit Pinsents. It was by no means the most obvious union to the outsider, so we looked to our sources to explain the whys and wherefores of the Pinsent Masons match.

## for all eyes only

Having grown through a number of carefully considered mergers over the previous decade, and having given a few other firms the glad eye before singling out Masons, you'd think Pinsents' management would be expert at cloak-and-dagger negotiations. Apparently not. "*All the partners at Masons were referring to 'Project Matthew' and all the partners at Pinsents kept discussing 'Project James' – it was all a bit obvious.*" How so? "*Well,*

# the true picture

*James Mason and Matthew Pinsent... it wasn't subtle. Plus someone found the domain name www.pinsentmasons.com registered in a partner's name."*

So, having cracked the not-so-secret code, what was the trainees' verdict? They told us about the merger's logic: "*The idea is we did complementary things,*" explained one. "*Pinsents was full-service corporate law,*" whilst "*Masons was energy, utilities and construction.*" Their simple conclusion: "*There was little work overlap except in projects and some IT aspects,*" so "*it's about being a more complete firm and doing everything that a client wants.*" Consider, too, that Masons brought with it a network of overseas offices stretching from Dubai to Hong Kong (and not forgetting Glasgow and Edinburgh). Certainly, this newly forged top-15 UK law firm should now be able to win work that, alone, each of the legacy firms might have missed.

## but does it add up?

In truth, Masons' specific IT and construction sector expertise fitted well with the "*sector-driven approach*" Pinsents had been championing. You'll find details of the 'chosen markets' strategy on the firm's website, but it essentially involves "*offering a client in a specific sector, say the food industry, all the legal answers they need. So the corporate lawyer gets the IP lawyer in, or the property lawyer gets the finance lawyer in, as necessary.*" You could say the merger merely gave a whopping great boost to the strategy by making the new firm the leader in another chosen market – construction. Pinsent Masons also boasts new strengths that have arisen as a direct result of the merger. For example, corporate work was one of Pinsents' key strengths, and when combined with Masons' prowess in IT, it leads to a healthy new outsourcing and technology department. Another notable area of fusion is the new firm's projects capability.

Apparently, the benefits of enhanced expertise are already being felt. In Manchester, for example: "*We're getting construction-related banking work we*

*never would have got before.*" And it's not just Manchester; other offices have noticed "*an influx of work from Scotland,*" and trainees further reflected: "*We're always being told about pitches that we could never have made pre-merger.*" Ever on the hunt for hard evidence, the *Student Guide* went looking for other client wins. We found construction giant Morrison, the Co-op and the Scottish Executive. These clients join the likes of Invensys, the London Stock Exchange, AOL Europe, Wembley National Stadium, Smith & Nephew, Barclays Private Equity, Budgens, Argos, Thistle Hotels, Mayflower and Lend Lease on the firm's books. The construction division of this last client (Bovis Lend Lease) was a legacy Masons client, but Pinsent Masons this year received its first M&A instruction from the developer – the £245 million purchase of residential property company The Crosby Group. Other post-merger deal highlights include projects lawyers advising the Government of Cyprus on a £343 million airport PPP, and corporate lawyers assisting Californian medical equipment suppliers Medex on the European aspects of its £478 million sale to FTSE 100 company Smiths Group.

## getting to know each other

Time will tell quite how perfect the union will be, but on the basis of our interviews with trainees, everyone seems to be settling down quite well. Exactly how the merger will affect the average trainee's experience also remains to be seen, as "*there is a two-year time frame within which to complete full integration.*" Some processes are slower than others; so for example: "*IT was bad to begin with but has been catching up recently.*" And in another area: "*They're just starting to begin consultation on a shared-values document.*" As it turns out, the training scheme – effectively the Pinsents model – is one of the most established aspects of the post-merger firm.

Unsurprisingly, change has been felt most in the cities with offices from both legacy firms. In Manchester, Leeds and London, the offices have either been combined or "*a one-site move is on the cards.*" Here on the front line, trainees are witness to "*efforts to unify ideologically,*" with "*lots of joint team days out and ice breakers.*" In London, for example, "*trainees have begun to take seats outside the office they joined.*" By contrast, in Bristol (ex-Masons) and Birmingham (ex-Pinsents), "*it's pretty much been business as usual... you almost feel too removed from it all.*"

One obvious way forward is to bring all new trainees together for a residential version of the PSC in a conference centre in Bedfordshire. Both firms had done this prior to merger and found it "*great for building friendships across offices.*" Another feature of the old Pinsents' training scheme that goes down well is the appraisal regime – "*The idea is you have one a month, so six per seat!*" We were told: "*Getting six is a miracle, but you'll almost certainly have three or four and sometimes even five,*" with the end result being "*you always know exactly how you're doing*" and "*any problems get turned around very quickly.*" Sitting close to their supervisor, the majority of our interviewees had found themselves being stretched at work and particularly admired supervisors' willingness to "*match your work to your abilities as you progress.*" If taken as a first seat, property may mean "*doing your own little bits of a property finance transaction and running small mortgage files.*" If taken as a third or fourth seat, a trainee might be "*on the front line of deals.*" One spoke of "*working exhaustively and actively in negotiations during the last two weeks of a major, major projects deal.*" "*Substantial client contact*" is another characteristic feature of trainee life, and if "*you're sometimes pushed outside your comfort zone,*" there is always the extra support of a designated buddy – "*someone not related to your work at all who is there for support and advice.*"

## take your pick

Seat allocation works remarkably well considering the number of trainees and offices involved. Even first-seaters are asked to list three preferences for their initial seat and this element of choice contin-

ues through to the fourth seat. Though there are no overseas opportunities until after qualification, anything up to 20% of trainees will spend some time on secondment to a client.

What's undoubtedly true is that there are differences between Pinsent Masons' several locations. Life in the tiny Bristol office (which just lost its entire property team to rival firm Clarke Willmott) will be a world away from the hustle and bustle of the large Birmingham office. Given that prospective trainees must apply to a specific office, the obvious thing to say is don't just stick a pin into a map and hope for the best. You'll need a demonstrable "*connection or commitment*" to your chosen location, and you'll also want to pick one that suits your work interests. This is best investigated through a vacation placement, if only because the firm recruits heavily off the back of the scheme.

In Leeds, two offices have already combined into what is arguably the firm's "*nicest building – shiny glass, all-singing, all dancing features like a deli and perfect waiters on hand in meetings.*" The Park Row building is close to the train station, with the bars of Greek Street and the Corn Exchange "*just a short walk away.*" Real estate litigation, tax, employment, general litigation and energy work are particular strengths of the unified Leeds offering, according to our colleagues at *Chambers UK*. In Leeds, quarterly drinks evenings, a variety of sports teams and "*cohesive trainee intakes*" make the social scene similar to that experienced across the Pennines in Manchester, where the firm is still housed in two separate premises. The Chancery is described as "*modern, open-plan and slightly friendlier,*" while "*Barbirolli Square is a more old-fashioned period building with separate offices.*" As in Leeds, "*9am to 7pm is an average day,*" although "*you can easily work longer for prolonged periods in departments like banking.*" Social events between the offices "*are doing the job*" of bonding the trainees together in the north. Work, too, seems to be dovetailing nicely, with Manchester offering complimentary excellence in pensions, pensions litigation, construction, health and safety and IT.

## cruise control

In Birmingham, a side effect of the merger has been to delay a much-needed office refit. Situated in the heart of legal Brum, an "*imposing*" if "*oddly shaped*" building with "*lots of strange pointy spaces*" hosts top-notch banking and finance, litigation, tax and competition teams. Here at the centre of the network, "*you do feel like part of a national firm,*" trainees told us. "*You travel at least once a month and the work is mainly national,*" but at the same time "*within that you feel part of a local office.*" If they sometimes feel they have "*a double existence,*" it is not an unwelcome sensation: almost all the regional trainees we spoke to cited the balance between "*the benefits of working for a national firm with quality of work, with reasonable-sized groups, plenty of responsibility and a sociable atmosphere*" as one of the firm's prime attractions.

The Birmingham social scene is "*great,*" whether it is drinks in Utopia or Bushwhackers, TSG events, sports or the office Christmas party. At the Christmas bash, "*an awful lot of people get dressed up – seeing the managing partner dressed as superman is an eye-opener!*" Across most of Pinsent Masons' offices, the day-to-day dress code is a slightly more restrained "*Monday-to-Thursday smart, Friday business casual.*"

Down in the "*small and informal*" Bristol office, we did hear a few murmurs of discontent. Not about the dress code, nor the available work, which includes excellent construction and real estate litigation practices plus health and safety and projects. No, the grumbles concern the office's location. The building is "*in a thoroughly beautiful Georgian square close to the town centre,*" but there's a slight mismatch with certain other local business, specifically "*the ladies of negotiable affection circulating around the square.*"

London is where the firm has most work to do in developing itself as a unified outfit. It was by far Masons' largest location and Pinsents' London operation was to an extent still grappling with its identity. Needless to say, the combined London operation has excellent construction and general litigation practices and, amongst other things, good corporate finance, health and safety, IT and insurance teams. Of the three office locations in the capital, the best by far is the "*very-modern, open-plan*" Aylesbury Street building in Clerkenwell. "*Ideally the offices would merge,*" but whilst this seems unlikely any time soon, integration is "*well under way.*" Playing no small part in ex-Pinsents trainees willingness to move over to Clerkenwell is the area's lunchtime and evening appeal. And if it is true that "*the vibe in the City offices is less friendly and personable than in the regions,*" we feel duty bound to point out that we hear similar things from other national firms. Unsurprisingly, the hours are typically longer, too. According to some, "*9am until 8pm or 9pm,*" is not massively uncommon.

## a league of gentlemen

Placing their confidence in the new firm, 31 of the 37 English qualifiers stayed on at Pinsent Masons in September 2005. They certainly gave us the impression that the new firm had much to offer them and we heard no one hark back to the pre-merger days, wishing things could be the same. For Masons (certainly) and for Pinsents (quite probably) this merger has been a smart decision. As to whether the firms were a good match beyond practice area coverage, opinion is currently divided. "*It was suggested that the firms had complimentary working cultures, styles and mindsets... I'll go with that,*" said one source, while another argued: "*A lot of people wouldn't agree that the cultures match up.*" Some felt "*Pinsents was probably the more modern and more relaxed firm,*" when compared to the "*more traditional functions and hierarchies of Masons.*" We have a hunch that one thing that will last as the new firm goes forward is "*the gentlemanly reputation of Pinsents*" – even if Masons' less cautious approach to change shakes things up a bit!

## and finally...

Pinsent Masons offers all the advantages of working at a top-15 national firm: consistently good training, ample resources and excellent UK and cross-border work. Combine all this with the specific appeal of each regional office, and factor in the likely benefits to be gained with time and consolidation, and maybe you're now thinking like the person who told us: "*This is a firm that's just beginning... it's got big aims.*"

# Prettys

## the facts

**Location:** Ipswich
**Number of partners/assistants:** 16/29
**Total number of trainees:** 10
**Seats:** 4x6 months
**Alternative seats:** None

Ipswich firm Prettys turns 100 in 2006. Is it sitting back with a glass of port to reflect on a long and distinguished career and await the soft flomp onto the mat of its centennial telegram? Not at all.

## pretty old

Prettys is approaching its big birthday with the exuberance of youth rather than the cynicism of age. As one trainee explained: "*We could celebrate the last 100 years by digging into the archives, but it was decided that that is not what we want. We are very much looking forward to the next 100 years.*" Why does cryogenics spring to mind?

Despite the firm's revered past and a private client heritage, trainees more readily flagged up the firm's work in corporate, litigation, shipping and employment, saying: "*The commercial departments set the tone for the firm*" and "*they very much want to expand those areas, they are very keen on marketing and developing business.*" Indeed, our interviews were peppered with references to the firm's development plans and its "*forward-looking,*" "*forward-thinking*" approach. We are told Prettys "*certainly does seem to be going through changes;*" trainees point to a new managing partner and a new business development manager.

## ports of call

In Prettys' four-seat scheme, trainees have no choice as to the first of their seats. After this, the firm "*will accommodate as many people's interests as they possibly can.*" There are no compulsory seats, nor any major restrictions, though one trainee told us: "*I think French property is out of bounds.*" But you know what, when we checked we heard that this seat was indeed possible, and learned that the firm would consider any sensible suggestion for new seats. For now, trainees' options include property, property litigation, corporate services, IT/IP, employment, commercial litigation, shipping, wills and probate, matrimonial and personal injury (both claimant and defendant seats). They seemed quite pleased with their lot; one even boasted: "*I was really trying to avoid property and they took that on board.*"

What can be said is that "*if you come to Prettys you probably have a commercial focus.*" Certainly the commercial litigation and corporate departments are very popular, the latter primarily servicing what trainees define vaguely as "*Suffolk firms.*" A spell here puts them "*very much in the thick of it*" on acquisitions, share sales and management buyouts. Yes, "*you have a role preparing bibles, doing disclosure and due diligence,*" but the team always makes the effort to "*keep you in the loop throughout the transaction.*" Among the firm's clients are Ipswich Town FC and various local horseracing studs.

The shipping lawyers cast their nets in more distant waters, acting for P&I clubs, charterers, shipowners and other elements of the transportation industry. Considering shipping to be "*quite a complex area of law,*" trainees described "*big commercial disputes for freight forwarders and hauliers,*" including "*big non-delivery of goods or defective goods cases, like some HIV testing kits sent to Kenya that were stored at the wrong temperature."* For trainees, the size and complexity of the matters can mean less of a hands-on role. One admitted: *"I haven't been to any ports!"* At least *"you are very much kept involved. You sit in on conference calls, get quite a lot of client contact and get to grips with the case quite well."*

## bicycles and boob jobs

A seat in the firm's PI department proves a complete contrast, requiring trainees to plunge head first into their own caseload. Expect to *"meet every Tom, Dick or Harry off the street"* and *"run your files more or less single-handedly."* One source said: *"I was handed seven straight away and built up to about 25."* The team's work is *"predominantly claimant"* and matters include *"cyclists getting knocked off their bikes, workplace accidents and other road traffic accidents."* On the clinical negligence side there are claims following unsuccessful breast reconstructions and complications during birth. The past year has also seen *"some quite major, six-figure clin neg cases."* The remainder of the work is for defendants including MoD, Suffolk County Council and insurers such as Royal & SunAlliance.

Work in the private client department is equally hands-on. *"The roots of the firm,"* its traditional caseload of wills, trusts and tax planning for wealthier individuals is *"pretty far removed from the huge international litigation being done in shipping."* It is not at all removed from the litigation going on in the PI department however, and in one case lawyers set up a trust to look after a £500,000 personal injury award. Another piece of work involved dealing with a £7 million international estate. Admittedly, none of our sources had pushed for a private client seat though those who had spent time there acknowledged: *"It was a lot of fun and a good for the interviewing experience and client contact."*

Across the firm, trainees praised the quality of the work they had undertaken, telling us: *"You're not just sat photocopying and proof-reading all day, you actually get involved."* Running their own files,

interviewing clients and attending court for *"applications, agency hearings and bankruptcy petitions,"* Prettys' trainees are aware of their continuing development and growing armoury of skills. They share an office with their supervisor wherever possible, and chatted about roommates with genuine admiration and respect, praising them for *"knowledge that is second to none"* and for *"making it clear that they are approachable."* We can only assume that the three-monthly appraisals are a pleasant experience.

## flat out

The firm's Georgian townhouse in the centre of Ipswich *"looks quite twee but is like a Tardis."* One trainee told us: *"It is like a cottage – it's got window boxes and is so pretty."* However, just as in Grimm tradition looks deceive. The elegance of the old street frontage hides a vast modern office block. We think it is a rather good metaphor for a firm whose more traditional areas are bolstered by an extensive commercial practice.

Official office hours are 8.45am until 5pm and our sources told us they were usually out of the door before 6pm, with late nights a rarity. With long evenings to fill, trainees immerse themselves in the firm's busy social agenda of client parties and marketing events. On the calendar in July is Ladies' Day at Newmarket racecourse. Then there is the intriguing sounding Suffolk Business Challenge, apparently *"kind of like the Krypton Factor."* We have visions of lawyers dishing out business cards while scrambling up a cargo net but it is probably nothing like that at all. Other highlights include a firm-wide summer barbecue, Christmas lunch and a hard-fought pub quiz. Perhaps in an attempt to address the fact that *"Suffolk is not the hilliest of places"* Prettys organises an annual walking weekend, this year in the Lake District. For hardened hikers, there was a walk up Scaffel Pike; for those less inclined, clay pigeon shooting, riding, sailing and ice climbing. Back on the flat, *"lively is not the word"* to describe Ipswich, which is *"basically a small town;"* however, all our sources seemed smitten with the place, particularly as the marina is undergoing major redevelopment and a planned new university promises an acceleration in the town's nightlife. For a drink after work *"the traditional haunt was Mannings, but normally it is The Curve now."*

Out of town, *"Suffolk is absolutely stunning"* and, as one sage told us: *"It will always be near London."* If you thought trainees' loyalty to Ipswich must stem from longstanding personal connections with the town, you may be surprised to learn that *"trainees come from far and wide."* Well, Essex and Lincolnshire at least... In-depth statistical analysis revealed that in 2004/5 nine of the ten trainees were female *"but that doesn't mean boys shouldn't apply."* Far from it. Just to confuse matters, the two guys who will be joining in 2005 are both called Rob. On qualification in September 2005, four of the five trainees took jobs with the firm.

## and finally...

Ipswich is a way of life; one you ought to be certain you'll appreciate before moving there. Once you've answered that question, your choice of firm should be pretty easy.

# Reed Smith LLP

## the facts

**Location:** London, Coventry
**Number of partners/assistants:** 38/34
**Total number of trainees:** 12
**Seats:** 4x6 months
**Alternative seats:** Secondments
**Extras:** Pro bono – ICSL and College of Law legal advice schemes.

Employing nearly 1,000 lawyers worldwide, but with 14 of its 17 offices stateside, Pittsburgh-based Reed Smith is a US firm through and through... except in London and Coventry, where it has a decidedly British flavour.

## made in America?

Reed Smith's is a quintessential American tale. In recent years, it has propelled itself from regional Pennsylvanian practice to gargantuan national and then international outfit through a series of strategic acquisitions, one of the largest of which was the merger with UK firm Warner Cranston in 2001. Though the dust has long settled on that union, Reed Smith is far from letting the grass grow under its feet: this year it opened its first continental European practice – in Munich – and hatched plans for a Paris office. Back across the pond, the firm acquired West Coast litigation boutique Fleming & Phillips, whilst also becoming locked in merger talks with 215-lawyer Chicago litigation and IP specialist Wildman Harold. If successful, this latest merger will create a 1,200+ lawyer outfit, which would burst into the top 25 of US firms.

And what of London and Coventry? On the one hand, a US-style billing culture is in operation and UK revenues rose a whopping 29% in 2004, outpacing firm-wide growth, itself a huge 19%. On the other, trainees tell us that those earth-shaking mergers and developments feel *"relevant but distant"* and that *"the only way you really feel you're in an American firm is when you have to enter 'vacation' instead of 'holiday' on your calendar."* Relatively pint-sized, both offices are *"defined by the working culture of a boutique City law firm which has been defended fiercely post-merger."* *"Although work does come to and fro, to their credit the Americans have respected us."* Of course, affectionate cultural stereotypes are just as pervasive in the USA as here, so we weren't surprised when we heard of US partners' tolerance of *"the annual summer party, when the entire office shuts down for the day – they didn't understand it, but it's carried on."*

What exists is *"a great balance"* between *"feeling like you're at a UK firm with a UK culture"* and simultaneously *"feeling a part of a larger entity."* There's no doubt that with *"the weight of a massive firm behind us,"* both the impetus for growth and the clout to achieve it are there. In the UK, expansion is *"steady, targeted and careful, based on existing strengths."* Finance, coco and real estate remain the core of UK practice, and with a swathe of big-name clients across these areas it is scarcely surprising. High street chains like Moss Bros have their counterpart in more exclusive retailers such as Tiffany, whilst the full gamut of dining options is encompassed, from McDonald's, Domino's and KFC franchisees to more upmarket establishments like Pizza Express and The Restaurant Group.

New clients include pharma companies like Respironics, Nations Healthcare and McNeil Nutritionals; long-standing clients include manufacturers like Tate & Lyle, Akzo Nobel and Sara Lee. Finance is *"particularly growing in the IPO area,"* with lawyers handling deals such as Global Oceanic Carriers' AIM placing and maintaining successful relationships with financial institutions such as Crédit Lyonnais and Bank of Cyprus. An interesting import from the USA is a growing life sciences practice.

## a simple formula

As one honest source put it: *"The big picture stuff is great and it's nice to know we're expanding, but you're mainly concerned with your two years of training."* True enough, and if an application to Reed Smith appeals, remember that although *"exchange between London and Coventry is good,"* as a trainee you are firmly bound to one or the other. Both benefit from their small size, creating *"an atmosphere that is relaxed, informal and fun,"* however the experience of each is distinct. Situated in *"beautiful"* glass-walled offices on the Thames at London Bridge, and possessing views of *"the river, Southwark Cathedral and Borough Market,"* the London office is undoubtedly *"more social, more cohesive and has longer working hours"* than its Midlands counterpart. Trainees here spend a year in the European corporate division (covering corporate, commercial and finance work and

changing supervisor after six months), then six months in litigation and a final seat in either real estate or employment. Combining such a simple formula with *"only four of us per year,"* rotation is rarely a problematic process.

Another function of the office's size is that *"if you have an interest and it's more than just a fancy, they'll try to accommodate you."* As such, tax, business immigration, IP and insurance are all within a trainee's reach. All up, with seats not overly specialised, *"you get a massive variety of work."* Sitting with their supervisors, trainees find that *"work comes to you from all over,"* and even if *"there are times when everyone's required to work on a big finance matter say, you are never pigeon-holed."* Those we spoke to had experienced levels of responsibility from *"the minimal to the almost complete,"* enjoying *"drafting letters and witness statements, or finishing off insolvency injunctions"* in litigation and, in employment, *"doing policy reviews, drafting contracts or taking witness statements and going to tribunal."* Over in real estate it's a case of *"running a small caseload as well as assisting on larger matters."* In all seats, if variety is the key word, the one constant is *"supervisors who are very conscious of their role and give excellent feedback"* so that *"you're very rarely surprised when it comes to evaluations."*

## back to university

Trainees do not as yet get to travel to the US *"except if you're in a department that goes on retreat to the States and they take you."* However, *"the US management committee comes over for drinks and meetings once a quarter,"* and transatlantic work, video conferencing and telephone calls had left some of our sources with *"people I'd consider as friends in the US offices."* The Reed Smith University is a scheme designed *"to unify training across the firm and centre it around core practice areas."* Only introduced in January 2005, the scheme is affiliated with the Wharton Business School and focuses on five disciplines: law; IT; professional development;

leadership; and business development. The hoped-for benefits are yet to trickle down to trainees, but those we interviewed told us: "*It does reinforce the sense of being part of a wider firm.*" There is also a scheme in place allowing junior associates in the UK to take the New York Bar exam.

Unlike us, our sources didn't perceive the idea of a US giant with a Coventry office as being hugely unusual. It is a definitively local affair with "*almost all staff and trainees [having] a local connection.*" When we interviewed, trainees took seats in litigation, real estate, coco/banking & finance and employment, and the balance between international, national and local seemed well struck. Enthusing about the variety of cases in litigation, one source told us how "*one minute you'll be working for a small regional business where you're running the matter yourself, and the next you'll be assisting on a hideously complicated matter for a multinational pharma company.*" "*Coco is developing, especially in banking,*" with clients such as Bank of Scotland and Lloyds TSB and recent instructions coming from major international aviation and manufacturing companies. Recent lateral hires have re-energised the employment department, where trainees "*see a lot of contentious work and attend big tribunals.*" However, shortly after it was announced that the local property and debt recovery departments would be leaving.

## racing colours

Coventry and London share a "*chinos and jeans dress-down culture,*" hours of "*roughly 9am-6.30pm*" and "*supervisors who are generally good at giving feedback.*" In fact the only real gripe that Coventry trainees have is their office building. Right next to the train station, the firm occupies "*what looks like a 60s building*" that is "*certainly not glamorous*" despite its good transport links. In fact, though trainees did return frequently to "*the convenient location, also close to the town centre*" the prospect of a move in two or three years was clearly a tantalising one. But what it lacks in aes-

thetic charm it makes up for in warmth of spirit and a "*practically non-existent hierarchy.*" You'd think that this "*relaxed*" atmosphere in the office would spill over into more regular post-work socialising, except that "*everyone travels in by car, so the element of spontaneity goes and everything has to be carefully planned.*" A Coventry social committee does organise events – bowling, pool nights – every so often, but undoubtedly the London office "*sees a lot of impromptu nights out drinking at The Mudlark.*" There are also a variety of sports teams in the City office. More organised socialising tends to be reserved for the "*Christmas party which some Coventry people come to*" and the summer outing "*where all the UK staff meet up.*" This year Uncle Tom Cobleigh and all enjoyed a day of corporate hospitality and Grand Prix racing car testing at Silverstone. If watching David Coulthard and Michael Schumacher deuce it out instilled a competitive spirit among trainees, they certainly hid it well, describing each other as a "*civilised bunch,*" "*keen but not wanting to take over the world*" and "*with no hot-headed arrogant types.*" We also observed a range of usual and less usual universities represented. There wasn't any lack of drive shown when it came to qualification in 2005, when six out of seven trainees raced onto the NQ circuit in Reed Smith colours.

## and finally...

A Midlands law firm with international reach, or a City boutique with big US clout, neither Reed Smith office is quite what it might at first seem. But with a small-firm atmosphere, a rounded training and international post-qualification prospects, it's definitely worth taking a second, third and fourth glance.

# the true picture

## Reynolds Porter Chamberlain

### the facts

**Location:** London, Tiverton
**Number of partners/assistants:** 65/153
**Total number of trainees:** 22
**Seats:** 4x6 months
**Alternative seats:** Secondments

Reynolds Porter Chamberlain is an insurance firm with a charming character and interesting sidelines. If you feel in your bones that you're a natural-born litigator we'd recommend you have a look-see.

### hard and seoul

Though technically no practice area is compulsory, because of the firm's "*very large litigation leaning*" at least one or two of a trainee's four seats will be in insurance litigation. Professional negligence accounts for a hefty share of this work, and the firm has divided its vast prof neg division into four distinct areas, each corresponding with a different profession. The Accountants and D&O Group acts for accountancy firms (including two of the 'Big Four') and their insurers, while the Lawyers Liability Group acts for solicitors, barristers and their insurance companies – Aon, St. Paul, Hiscox and Bar Mutual among others. The growing Regulatory and Brokers Group (viewed as least interesting by most trainees) acts for the insurers of brokers and financial advisers. Said one trainee: "*I worked on a very large case and that meant a very large document task which a junior assistant and I were looking after. It meant sorting through loads of documents, but that's just what you have to do. Having said that I would go along to meetings and speak to witnesses. And I did get an overview of the market and the mis-selling problem. These cases are really technically complicated and challenging.*" Finally, there's the Construction & Engineering Group. It takes on some truly massive cases such as the mul-timillion-pound arbitration arising out of the widening of the Songsu Bridge in Seoul, South Korea. The hearing on this case actually took place in Singapore, proving that law firms don't need to have international offices to be involved in international work... Although RPC does have a distant outpost in Tiverton, Devon.

### burning ambition

The health law team also deals with professional mishaps and blunders. Until last year the firm held a prestigious place on the legal panel of the NHS Litigation Authority, but after removing itself it now only represents the insurers of private healthcare companies. Our guess is that this boils down to how much these clients pay. Health law is popular with trainees as "*you get lots of hands-on experience.*" One source explained: "*You go to hospitals to speak with witnesses and doctors because you have to have established a rapport with the hospital and staff. I got to go to a lot of meetings and I found it really interesting reading into cases.*" The facts can be hard to swallow sometimes: "*There were a lot of babies with birth injuries, which was upsetting.*" Perhaps what trainees most like is that the seat gives "*a very good grounding in civil procedure*" and "*if the department was fairly busy they would virtually let you run a case.*" Trainees sort through "*voluminous amounts*" of claimants' medical records (sometimes "*morbid*" stuff), reading and understanding them in order to write letters of instructions to medical experts and draft instructions to counsel. They even attend small pre-trial hearings, so "*you certainly don't do photocopying every day.*"

RPC's insurance/reinsurance team handles cases of huge value and complexity, often seeking to establish the different proportions of an insurance payout that should be footed by different insurers. Put impossibly simply, reinsurance is insurance against insurance liability. Past cases have concerned the World Trade Center collapse, the Ladbroke Grove rail disaster, hurricane damage in the Caribbean and fire damage at Center Parcs. More manageable for trainees is a seat in the insurance group that deals with product liability, property and employers' and public liability cases. "*You have your standard arson fraud where Mr Landlord burns down his pub... that happens more often than you'd think with pubs and hotels that are making a loss.*" As for product liability, "*some of the research you do is so off the wall. There are a lot of experts involved and that's when cases get interesting. It's up to you to become a mini expert about a lot of things – surveying or the effects of drugs for example. It can be really challenging.*"

In several seats trainees take turns on the 'outdoor clerking' rota and end up developing an intimate relationship with courts all over London and beyond. On their appointed days they can be issuing High Court summonses, making procedural applications or taking notes. Some seats also bring real advocacy in small hearings in front of county court district judges.

## vanity case

Until mid 2005, a seat in the family department meant celebrity divorces and international child abductions. Our sources were wary of promoting the department to potential applicants, sensing that it was far from central to the firm's plans for the future. And how right they were. Within weeks the team had upped sticks to another firm, Manches. They were almost as considered in their comments about seats in the media team. "*Everyone starts off claiming they want to do one.*" Most eventually opt to stay within the firm's mainstream areas. The good news is that "*media has now got two trainees in the department so chances are you will get a seat there if you really want it.*" The team handles defamation, breach of confidence and privacy for newspapers and other publishing clients. "*I got to read lots of letters of complaint from celebrities,*" revealed one discreet source before closing the door to further questions. RPC turns out to have one of the UK's leading defamation practices and has handled some juicy libels lately. It acted, for example, for *Vanity Fair* in the action brought by Roman Polanski con-

cerning allegations about his behaviour following his wife's murder. In another case it defended Time Warner Book Group in a case brought by Doreen Lawrence, mother of murdered Stephen Lawrence.

As well as client secondments (Carillion and WS Atkins), there are just two non-contentious seat options available – coco and property. Property is bottom on the trainees' list of preferences; by contrast, they are frequently taken aback by how much they enjoy corporate. This department has a very wide remit, covering not only corporate transactions but also general commercial advice. Said one trainee: "*I wasn't really sure what to expect; I've done company secretarial work, IP and e-commerce, drafting website agreements...* " Deal wise, RPC sits in the mid-market league and its highlights from the past year have included a Danish company's £100 million purchase of 50% of the shares of SeaScape Limited, a company involved in the construction of an offshore wind farm near Liverpool, and the £35 million acquisition of Jobsite Worldwide by newspaper client Daily Mail Group. Indeed, publishing clients feature large on the firm's client roster – Associated Newspapers; Condé Nast; *Forbes Magazine*; Guardian Newspapers; Harper Collins; Random House and The National Magazine Company, which publishes *Harpers & Queen*, *Esquire*, *Country Living* and *House Beautiful* are just some of the names involved.

## a tale of two offices

RPC presently operates from two offices. Chichester House in Holborn is the larger and contains everything but the hard-core insurance work. The 'City' office near to the insurance hub at Lloyd's was once deemed an outpost by trainees but now has many fans; some even claim it has a better atmosphere than 'Chich'. "*They are hugely different,*" said one source, "*The City office works very very hard and it is constant. You knuckle down and get on with things, but the socialising is also better. You go out for drinks with your team more often and you mix between teams.*" Chich meanwhile "*has a lot more* space and that probably makes it feel more relaxed." Trainees normally share a room with an assistant, close to their supervising partner's room. In addition to a supervising partner for each seat they have a dedicated 'minder partner' to last them through the training contract and a buddy from among the second-year group to help them through the tricky first few weeks at the firm. For the most part they get two appraisals per seat though some partners are tardy with the mid-seat review and this can be unhelpful for a trainee's development. The HR folk no doubt crack the whip when they hear about this. Speaking of HR, there was considerable praise for the job they do, particularly the way in which the training contract interview day is structured and managed.

## we are sailing

Each year the firm enters the popular Manches Cup sailing regatta for a spot of cruising up and down the Solent. It's followed by a blow-out ball that's way more fun than a tot of rum followed by enforced dancing on deck to the strains of the hornpipe. In an ideal world the sailing falls on the same weekend as the partners' retreat (last time held in Venice), ensuring that no one important spots you staggering down a jetty three sheets to the wind. RPC has lively summer and Christmas parties plus two 'socials' in between. When after a quick pint or two at the end of the week there are any number of bars in the Holborn area to tempt trainees away from regular haunts The Old Nick and Penderel's Oak. Those posted to the City office also have their favourites, though apparently to get into The Abacus on a Friday night you have to start queuing from 6pm.

Because ongoing relationships are so important in the insurance world, law firms like RPC organise social events with clients in mind, and trainees reap the rewards of a policy that ensures ample client contact both in the office and out. Lunchtime drinks; quiz nights; seminars – trainees are always invited. Perhaps this explains why typically they are naturally confident and brimming with people skills. And, according to one source: "They are committed to the firm and loyal." Supporting this idea, in September 2005 nine of the ten qualifiers stayed at RPC, interestingly three of them going into corporate.

Trainees tell us their firm's somewhat traditional edge is rubbing off. The partners still dine in their exclusive dining room two or three times a week, but staff sense that change is in the air and that the firm is moving up through the gears. Our sources spoke of senior-level lateral hires, growing the firm, "mutterings about moving to a new building that's City based, not West End based, consolidating the two offices," focusing more intently on financial targets, increasing the trainee intake from ten to 15 per year, developing the corporate department, honing the insurance side of the firm into a collection of eight superteams. Though relatively subtle, change has already been noted.

## and finally...

Even with growth in the corporate department, don't come here expecting anything other than a litigation-heavy training. The main thrust of business at Reynolds Porter Chamberlain is insurance litigation and likely always will be. If that's what you're after then this is a cracking choice.

# Richards Butler

## the facts

**Location:** London
**Number of partners/assistants:** 82/118
**Total number of trainees:** 40
**Seats:** 4x6 months
**Alternative seats:** Overseas seats, secondments
**Extras:** Pro bono – Aldgate Advice Centre; language training

More international than other firms of its size; a greater emphasis on litigation than the majority of

City firms; a raft of niche areas of work – one thing's for sure, you don't choose to train at Richards Butler because it's middle of the road.

## it's all greek to me

This is a shipping specialist with bags more besides. RB's training contract is free of compulsory seats and fat with choice and, yes, it is even possible to come and train here and never enter the shipping department. That said, our sources were in agreement on one thing: contentious work is very much to the fore. Said one: "*The busiest departments are shipping and commercial disputes. The firm might not say that it is setting itself out as a litigation firm, but as it stands the corporate department isn't the one bringing in the big money, though it is picking up.*" Another agreed: "*I don't feel corporate is a driving force.*" Don't say we didn't tell you...

The majority of the firm's work is international, either because the clients come from overseas or the subject matter of the deal or case is located overseas... or on the sea. Hong Kong, for instance, has long been a major profit centre for the firm. Most interviewees struggled to recall working on matters that were purely domestic: "*It's definitely very international in London, certainly in shipping where I was dealing mostly with Greek and American clients and no English clients. You feel it most in shipping, but there's definitely some international work in corporate and the other commercial departments too.*"

## charterparty time

So let's talk ships. It seems that you either love shipping litigation or you hate it. Said one source: "*It is quite difficult, especially at first as you have a whole new industry to get to grips with as well as the law.*" Another thought the law aspects were particularly demanding: "*The level and variety of work is immense; it's everything you've ever covered in contract and tort with some conventions thrown in.*" And from another: "*I was doing various charterparty and bills of lading disputes. I think I was getting better experience than in a commercial dispute resolution*

*seat where a trainee might work on one or two big banking and insurance cases. In shipping I had between 50 and 100 cases and in six months I got to see the whole litigation process across the portfolio of cases. I was drafting witness statements, claim forms and general correspondence and I also went to court a few times.*"

Yet the commercial disputes group has its fans, even if as a trainee they must start at the bottom ("*in a dark windowless room doing disclosure*") and build up experience. The cases RB handles are often substantial in value and it has become known as a good firm for clients in dispute with big banks. As much as we want to blow a fanfare for the firm's litigation arm, we must say we're puzzled by the disappearance of two key partners in the last year to the London offices of US firms. These departures must have been a real disappointment to RB.

A separate team of litigators specialise in trade disputes, many of which are resolved by way of international arbitration. Hands up who knows anything about trade finance, credit risks, confiscating goods in transit, the futures market, commodities brokers or what to do when you're exporting South American soya beans to China and everything goes wrong? As we thought, not many hands. Here, just as in other specialist departments, the firm recognises that the sector is an unfamiliar one so young lawyers don't go short of training. And on the subject of training, a special mention goes to the library team, who are "*incredibly knowledgeable and helpful.*" Most of the research tools a trainee needs can be found on their desktops, but there are special shipping databases in the library that enable them to locate a ship anywhere in the world and find out where it is going and what it is carrying. Quite probably South American soya beans to China.

## time for bed, said zebedee

There's no risk of property being an unsung hero at RB because the majority of trainees rave about their time in the department. Unless you were too busy revising for your GCSEs at the time, you may have heard about the £1 billion proposal to redevelop Battersea Power Station as a leisure complex with bars and clubs, a cinema, restaurants and shops. Though it has been on hold for a few years, planning permission has finally come through, allowing the mammoth development to proceed. Richards Butler won the instruction to act for the owners of the site via its Hong Kong office, where lawyers were already familiar with the wealthy family in question. Undoubtedly the power station will keep the London property lawyers moving at full steam for years to come, and probably well beyond the proposed completion date of 2008. Perhaps with an eye on this work, quite a few of the second-year trainees tried to qualify into property in 2005. All told, the firm kept on 14 of its 19 qualifiers.

Transactional experience can also be gained in corporate, tax, banking and ship finance seats, and yet another type of finance work can be found in the media department. One trainee told us about film finance deals, but played down the glitz factor. *"It means acting for big banks... and it's not at all glamorous! Ultimately all the big firms act for the banks, so you are in effect doing a banking seat."* Spoilsport! We'd rather finance movies like 'The Magic Roundabout' or 'The Libertine' than a new widget factory any day. Naturally, seats in the prestigious media department are very popular and there are quite a few people in every intake who push to work there. *"There is a lot of competition,"* confirmed a successful trainee, *"particularly at qualification time as they don't offer that many jobs there."*

## yankee doodlings

Offices in Paris, Hong Kong, Abu Dhabi, Piraeus and São Paulo mean overseas secondments to be taken at either the second or third rotation. Those who prefer home soil to overseas toil may be able to substitute a secondment to a client, currently MTV, the BBC or Rank. Getting either an overseas posting or a client secondment is relatively easy as there are almost as many available as there are trainees in each of the four evenly balanced intakes. Getting precisely what you want, well that's another matter entirely.

We interviewed RB trainees in April 2005, when it was no secret that the firm was in merger talks with the larger, 600-lawyer New York firm Proskauer Rose. Proskauer boasts New York's top employment practice and possesses a good reputation for other types of litigation. The two firms had been sniffing around each other's back legs for long enough for their mutual interest to be as well kept a secret as Brad and Angelina's off-screen liaisons. By June the talks were off, leaving everyone wondering which American firm was next in line for attention.

## good vibrations

This year as in past years, a series of engaging individuals gave us clear explanations as to why they had accepted an offer from RB. They told us why they had rejected the magic circle – or not bothered to apply – and what they liked and disliked about their training. Either RB is very successful in recruiting people with the ability and confidence to stand back and analyse matters, or something about the workplace engenders this. Trainees are utterly believable when they tell you how much they like the firm's general atmosphere because they don't hold back on the caveats. For example, there was some negative comment about the culture in the shipping litigation department, to the effect that it is *"quite old fashioned"* and *"an old boys' club."* Nevertheless, one of our sources who held this view also said: *"I have had my best experiences in that department."*

And we've no reason to doubt their sincerity when they tell us they have access to some great work, because they own up to the fact that other experiences can be a disappointment. In a corporate seat, for example, *"a lot of the time it can be admin and proof-reading jobs, but then if you show initiative you can get drafting work.*" We can only presume that the frankness with which they speak to the *Student Guide* is reflected in their interactions in the office. Each trainee is assigned a mentor from among the senior assistants, who periodically takes the trainee out for lunch and an elder-sibling style chat. Trainees whose mentors remembered that they'd taken on the honour/duty seemed to find the relationship a useful one.

At the end of the week some of the trainees and younger staff retire to the nearby Slug and Lettuce or The Poet. Special nights out for the entire trainee group are far less common, much to the disappointment of some of our interviewees. In the summer staff can take their lunch up onto the office's roof terrace for a spot of sunbaking, and it's also the venue for an annual barbecue, which last year featured a Beach Boys covers band. Several floors below the firm's restaurant 'Writs' makes up for in decent grub what it lacks in fresh air and light. It also plays host to the monthly 5.31 club, a drinks evening named after the theoretical end of the working day. Our sources stressed that in practice the working day doesn't end at 5.30pm; rather, "*if you try and get up before 6pm it will look really bad. Normally people leave between 6.30pm and 7pm.*"

## and finally...

Any student who suspects they are a born litigator should put Richards Butler on their shortlist. Here, contentious opportunities crop up in more guises than Alistair McGowan on a Saturday night special. The only thing to bear in mind is that the Richards Butler you see now may not look exactly the same in 2008.

# Russell-Cooke

## the facts

**Location:** London, Kingston-upon-Thames
**Number of partners/assistants:** 38/58
**Total number of trainees:** 9
**Seats:** 4x6 months
**Alternative seats:** None

With a list of specialisms as long as your arm, Russell-Cooke remains intent on stretching its own limbs. Merging with three boutique firms in three years has only lengthened the firm's already respectable range of commercial, family, crime and professional discipline teams. Let's hope they don't dislocate something.

## more boutiques than rodeo drive

In 2003 R-C assimilated charity specialists Sinclair Taylor & Martin. It then realised its selfish gene and co-opted Evill & Coleman in March 2005. "*We used to call them Evil then we were told not to;*" the correct pronunciation is, in fact, Evill not Evil – but the former is no fun. Two months after eating Evill and R-C weren't yet sated. It quaffed niche media and entertainment firm Harrison Curtis whole, slurping up the latter's stellar client list. With a smile on its face, the newly merged firm advised advertising giants DDB London on its campaign for Volkswagen featuring the body-popping remix of 'Singin' in the Rain'. R-C's new entertainment lawyers were also in the wings for the launch of the Old Vic Theatre Company with Kevin Spacey as artistic director. They have worked with the National Film Trustee Company on the finance and production of the frankly bonkers indie movie 'The Piano Tuner of Earthquakes' and for clients in Royston Vasey (Channel 4) they provided legal advice concerning 'The League of Gentlemen's Apocalypse'.

Celebrity and infamy also attaches itself to the employment and crime departments. Following claims of unfair dismissal and sex discrimination against Eton College, teacher Sarah Forsyth was thrust into the tabloid glare because of her alleged 'assistance' on Prince Harry's AS level art coursework. High-profile criminal cases have included R v Dalton in which R-C represented a defendant who allegedly murdered then dismembered his Korean wife, storing the pieces in a freezer. The firm also took on a succession of football hooliganism trials. Meanwhile R-C's professional regulation team represent the prettier people of the beautiful game, namely former Chelsea star Adrian Mutu after his drugs ban, and have advised on commissions dealing with the footballing phenomenon 'tapping-up'. Just to recap, the firm's work ranges from Papa Lazarou to Eton schoolmarms, Chelsea Headhunters to children in care – an incredible portfolio we think you'll agree.

The firm maintains its breadth through a commitment to both commercial and private clients, making it an ideal place for the undecided student. Yes, future commercial expansion seems likely but the firm appears intent on combining a "*high-streety element*" with "*a big-firm side.*" In sound-bite style, one trainee portrayed the future as: "*People-oriented rather than money-oriented.*" They could run for office on that comment!

## bite the bullet

R-C occupies five buildings, three in Putney (known as 'No2', 'No113' and 'The Crescent'), a diminutive Kingston-upon-Thames office and a central London office in Bedford Row in Bloomsbury. While Putney is the traditional home, no individual office exerts dominion; not only are individual offices quite independent, departments themselves function like fiefdoms – "*mini-firms within the firm.*" Accordingly, each department "*budgets itself and decides whether a trainee is needed or not.*" And little homogeneity exists across the firm. A rumoured "*big centralised office*" in Putney may be a distant curative but for now it appears that the mergers may have accentuated the federal as opposed to centralised governance of the firm.

As one source noted: "*Russells is expanding rapidly but has not adapted well to the changes.*" The "*tight, jaunty and angular*" Crescent offices seem an apt architectural symbol of the firm's "*intrigue and interest.*" One trainee described being "*lost*" in the Crescent – apposite in a firm where "*you don't always know where you are.*" It's tempting to draw a parallel with the lack of transparency some trainees feel over the structure of their traineeships – "*They don't officially tell you anything... it's not cloak and dagger but it's not open.*" Seat allocation does indeed have its mysteries: the lesser-spotted crime seat, for instance, is rare, so too the family seat. In previous years these have been unavailable; this year both have been open. The bottom line remains consistent – seat allocation is a compromise between trainees' desires and the firm's financial considerations, with money having the bigger say.

One thing is "*a dead cert:*" you will begin your traineeship in commercial property, the firm's only quasi-compulsory seat. Busy commercial property may also be a trainee's second seat – whether wanted or not – because R-C's three commercial property teams in Bedford Row, Putney and Kingston have "*a lot of work*" and consequently need helping hands. Rumour has it that trainees "*play Russian roulette for doing a second seat in property.*" This seat will throw up portfolio properties requiring investigation into title, drafting contracts for sale, licences and lease renewals. Always working from a precedent, "*you never draft from scratch.*" Finding a bullet in the chamber has its plus point: you are likely to get a first-choice seat later in your contract. Indeed we were told of two trainees who both spent 12 months in commercial property and then found themselves in hotly contested seats. Can anyone smell a trade-off?

## charity begins at home

Charity law is another of the possibly-maybe seats open to a trainee. Thanks to the Sinclair merger, trainees may now get to meet and greet "*lots of nice* clients" from Battersea Dogs Home, War on Want and Barnardo's. Charity is *"a good place if you want to dip your toe in a lot of different areas of law;"* the seat includes property, employment, IP, *"coco-like stuff,"* setting up companies through incorporation, trusts and *"fairly hefty applications to the charity commission registry."* Such diversity comes with five partners who can all supply a trainee with work at any one time.

A trainee in No 113's PI seat will sit with a single partner. Trainees handle the day-to-day running of small trip-and-slip cases but rarely see the conclusion of the larger files on which they assist as *"cases can drag on for years."* The future looks brighter for those interested in family law, an area we previously reported as a no-go for trainees. This year two seats – *"along with tensions over those seats"* – exist in Kingston and at No 113. It is unlikely you will handle your own files while in family, though you will draft divorce petitions, obtain domestic violence injunctions and accompany clients and barristers to court. Copious client contact defines this seat, some of it more welcome than others. *"We have quite demanding clients who are emotional and can ring up quite a lot. It is the trainee who will deal with the emotional phone calls."* You have been warned.

## going clubbing

Last year we reported on the insolvency of the firm's netball team due to excessive expenditure. Thankfully the same fate has not befallen the firm's cricket team. The gentle knock of willow on leather provides the soundtrack to a trainee's opportunity to mingle with partners as you each cast long shadows fielding into the evening. Halcyon days can also be whiled away aside the Thames playing rounders, or on the Solent sailing competitively against the likes of Clifford Chance and Allen & Overy in the Manches Cup. Back to the Thames, one summer's day each year a party is held alternately in Putney or Kingston and functions as *"a rather relaxed AGM."* Our tip is to bring

a brolly: *"Last year's was an absolute wash-out because of torrential rain."* Unlike the summer do, the Christmas party is *"a much more formal affair."* Until now it was always held at the Edwardian RAC clubhouse in Mayfair, which we've learned has the only fully functioning Turkish bath in the area. Despite the potential for steamy antics, trainees tell us the party has always been far from steamy. Next year staff will be scrubbed and starched for The Hurlingham Club in west London, *"your typical private members club: quite reserved and a bit stuffy."* Two of the four September 2005 qualifiers will be in attendance, one having opted for a private client NQ job and the other for an NQ position with the charities team.

For a *"disparate"* firm spread from Gray's Inn to Kingston-upon-Thames cohesion is difficult. Newsletters land on desks and e-mails circulate; departmental functions succeed but firm-wide meets are harder to effect. Trainees seem as unconcerned about their work social life as the firm is – they are simply *"not very good at getting together as trainees"* and *"don't really function as a group"* perhaps because all *"have their own lives."* The past two intakes of trainees were almost exclusively female and trainee outings have tended to be for ladies who lunch or simply want to *"grab a coffee together."* Dutifully we must report that the Blue Pumpkin and Pizza Express remain their favoured haunts.

## and finally...

If undecided whether to go for commercial or private client work, or for the City or the suburbs, Russell-Cooke is a clever choice. The addition of three new boutique firms in the past three years has brought even greater variety to what was already a varied training experience... just don't forget the property element.

# Salans

## the facts
**Location:** London, Bromley
**Number of partners/assistants:** 30/32
**Total number of trainees:** 8
**Seats:** 4x6 months
**Alternative seats:** Secondments

Salans is the very definition of an international law firm. Pick a continent, any continent (don't pick Australasia or Africa) and Salans is sure to have an office. The firm has been steadily adding branches across the globe for over two decades and the result is a mutually supportive network of local experts working for global clients everywhere from the relative obscurity of Kazakhstan's largest city Almaty to the buzz of downtown New York.

## oil in a day's work
Originating in Paris, French firm Salans merged with London banking practice Harris, Rosenblatt & Kramer to make an Anglo-French axis that was soon heading both west and east to find more merger-fodder. The London operation is just one of 14 worldwide that make up this Anglo-Franco-American-Sino-Russo-Turko-Kazakh-Czecho-Slovakian monster of a law firm. While Salans' list of offices reads like the departure board at Heathrow, jet-setting is not written into the Salans training contract. "*Generally the firm doesn't offer seats abroad; a request might be granted but I don't know anyone who's been abroad,*" a source explained.

Even if you can't make it to Kazakhstan, Almaty will come to you in the form of involvement in cross-border transactions. London lawyers have been working on banking transactions for arrangers, lenders and security trustees BNP Paribas in its dealings with the unpronounceable Kazmunaigaz – Kazakhstan's premier mineral exploration and production company. The financing of the company's $600 million crude oil facility was the largest oil-related deal in Kazakhstan last year. The BNP Paribas work perfectly illustrates the interconnectedness of Salans' international operations: experienced local practitioners in Almaty provided on-the-ground support, while the transaction was led from London. Take another example – a recent case handled by Salans' international arbitration group in which Vivendi Universal claimed, counterclaimed and counter-counter-claimed its way into a wrangle after its well-publicised joint venture with a Polish telecoms entity. The seat of the arbitration was London, the law governing the dispute Polish and the client French.

The ideal trainee is someone who will be thoroughly motivated by international business, even if they must wait until after qualification to work in another country. One such recruit told us: "*The Eastern European and ex-Soviet stuff is exciting – it's probably the most vibrant market in the world right now.*" And all credit to the firm: Salans has a reputation in the City amongst those looking to profit from the opening markets in the thawing remnants of the Soviet bloc.

## without pride or prejudice
Eastern European mineral exploitation isn't the only thing you'll see. Salans' finance client list bulges like Gordon Gekko's money clip: banks, investment funds, credit card companies, building societies, insurance companies, finance houses and export credit agencies – you name it, if there's a finance client to be represented then Salans wants to represent it. Perhaps this is what is driving the firm to expand its banking clientele further by drawing a former Lester Aldridge partner into the fold, despite his old firm threatening to sue him for a king's ransom. There is also an office in Bromley dealing with high-volume, low-value work for mortgage lenders, but trainees do not spend any time there.

Last year's calculator-destroying deal for the corporate finance team was the acquisition by Germany's Klüber Lubrication of the worldwide chemicals arm of Britain's Foseco Group, which comprised 19 companies spread over five continents. If anyone could empathise with the multi-jurisdictional logistics involved in such a deal it would be Salans' client Alsop, an architecture and design practice with projects in China, North America, Russia, Poland and throughout the rest of Europe. When Alsop hit money troubles after the £500 million collapse of a project called Fourth Grace, the law firm was there for the recovery and restructuring of its business.

If you want a little glitter to go with your finance or restructuring, how about introducing yourself to the firm's very respectable film/TV production and finance teams. You might find yourself working with Ulster TV one week, Sony Pictures, Twentieth Century Fox and Universal Studios the next. Best of all you can feel suitably sanctimonious at dinner parties when the topic is the demise of the British film industry. Salans acts for the likes of Richard Attenborough Productions and Working Title Films on such ambassadorial features as 'Pride and Prejudice', 'Notting Hill', 'Four Weddings and a Funeral', plus 'Bridget Jones' Diary' and her 'Edge of Reason'.

## waterloo sunsets

With clients like these you need an office to match. The firm came to the same conclusion last year and its shiny new digs overlook London's finest architectural folly, the Millennium Bridge. The move is, according to trainees, in keeping with "*aspirations to grow and be prestigious.*" Trainees work at close quarters with fee earners, sharing their rooms, although in most seats they find that tasks come in from the entire team, not just a single supervisor. As to the quality of work they get, this depends largely on how visible they choose to be. "*You have to make yourself known to get the work,*" explained one source. "*If you demonstrate skill then you'll get the work – simple.*" Hiding in the secretarial pool behind the photocopier or a plant – each proven techniques of work minimisation at

larger firms – is not an option here. "*Responsibility*" is perhaps what separates this training from that on offer at a City giant. "*I'd just be angry if I ended up without any responsibility,*" said one suitably keen interviewee.

## wound up

There are no compulsory seats beyond the Law Society's minimum requirements, though for most trainees these result in a trip to the litigation department. Our sources' recollections of litigation ranged from "*very hectic*" to "*cushioned,*" perhaps because their experiences were determined by the numbers of junior staff available at the time. Said one: "*There were no paralegals when I got there*" – not a good sign for anyone allergic to the photocopier or those dinky paginators. Certainly, "*document management is a feature of the seat*" whether it takes up little or much of your time. The more interesting fare on offer includes drafting letters, witness statements or statements of claim, and research on subjects as varied as seizures by HM Revenue & Customs or anti-suit injunctions to prevent cases being brought in other jurisdictions. "*I did a six-page memo on that – I must say it was enjoyable,*" one trainee recalled. Though unable to contribute much to large arbitrations, trainees find that smaller scale litigations are ideal for them. How about a trip to the court for a registrar's hearing to wind-up a company? "*That can be scary, as sometimes the respondent turns up and you have to handle a counter argument. It's quite a challenge but it toughens you up.*"

When in the litigation department you're "*pretty much everyone's;*" in corporate you belong much more to one associate, dealing with "*one or two big clients who generate a lot of work.*" For AIM-listed companies, plcs and "*large mineral exploitation outfits,*" you'll "*have an input*" in prepping companies for flotation or "*helping them in terms of requests into share issues.*" The requests can be complex, so don't expect to be negotiating with CEOs and company directors on day one; instead, be willing to settle for a role as chief gopher. For anyone who is interested, the corporate seat can include some insolvency matters. "*The insolvency team is small so you can't do a pure seat there, but you can handle some of the work.*" This is the chance for corporate trainees to "*take a file forward with supervision but without so many constraints.*"

Employment law is one of the firm's real strengths in London, and it acts for a string of blue-chip clients, many in the finance sector. Naturally, the seat is a popular one with trainees. A client secondment could occupy you for six months, or how about property, where you'll gain "*a good overview of conveyancing*" through the residential files that are entrusted to you. They may not be the most valuable deals you'll ever work on but at least the deals will be yours from drafting the contracts for sale to dealing with title issues and completion. "*That independence is great,*" recalled one source.

## led astray

"*It is not uncommon for people to go for drinks on a Friday night,*" a trainee revealed, allowing us to prise out of them the names of the two most frequented bars – Fullers and The Red Herring. However, this is "*not a social club – we don't spend all our time with one another.*" Anyone worried about developing early middle-aged spread in a desk job can join the football team, which plays against other law firms. Christmas means parties, of course; last year the firm took over a Mayfair club for "*a very nice dinner and dancing at the end of the night.*"

By now you'll have gathered that this is the sort of firm that will suit someone willing to stand on their own two feet from an early stage in their career. In smaller firms like this, an ambitious trainee can make a big impression, but the corollary is that there is nowhere to hide. And it seems they don't want to – in September 2005 the firm almost managed to continue its record of 100% retention, when three of the four qualifying trainees accepted jobs.

## and finally...

It may not be a name on the lips of students everywhere, but Salans is an ideal place for anyone who wants to be thrust into international practice from the off.

# Shadbolt & Co

## the facts

**Location:** London, Reigate
**Number of partners/assistants:** 24/17
**Total number of trainees:** 11
**Seats:** 4x6 months
**Alternative seats:** Paris, secondments

Shadbolt & Co is an attractive proposition for anyone with leanings towards the construction and engineering industry.

## firm foundations

The firm's origins go back to the early 90s when Dick Shadbolt, the former head of construction at what is now CMS Cameron McKenna, 'retired' from City life but made the mistake of retaining a few cases in order to finish them off. Before he knew it he'd rented office space near his home in Reigate, hired some lawyers and had a growing practice on his hands.

Apart from one dissenter who argued that the firm had grown and developed into a mainstream law firm, the general view of our interviewees was that Shadbolts should still be regarded as a construction specialist. "*Most of the work is construction related, and although all the departments are expanding, because of the Shadbolts name and the firm's origins, they are swamped by the construction side of things.*" One trainee confided: "*The firm would probably like to be described as less niche than it is, but construction is where most of the work and profits come from. Having said that they do have good satellite departments. As a trainee, realistically speaking, you'll do one construction seat at least.*"

# the true picture

## road gang

Clients come from the construction industry and beyond, including organisations as well known as the BBC. Most cases relate to delayed or defective premises and many have huge amounts of money at stake. In one of the biggest cases to be heard by the UK's Technology and Construction Court in 2004, Shadbolt represented one of a number of companies that had participated in the development of a wastewater treatment facility in West Yorkshire. Over the ten weeks of the trial, a considerable volume of technical information and evidence was examined in a bid to determine liability for aspects of the poor operation of the plant. The case illustrates how construction litigation can be extremely complex when it comes to the facts, which in turn requires lawyers to be extremely detail-conscious. They must also be unafraid of large volumes of documentary evidence, much of it written in terms that are the preserve of technical experts. New trainees can be shocked by how detailed cases can be: "*You can't just apply the black letter law, you have to have an appetite for rolling your sleeves up. It can be difficult work, a defects claim, for example, is quite a daunting thing to do.*"

On the non-contentious side, trainees get involved in construction work relating to projects and PFI/PPP. "*It is really complicated,*" warned one trainee, "*you come into the middle of a deal not knowing too much about PFI and it can be difficult to get your head round the deal structure. And then you've also got to realise there are a huge number of parties and all the parties are trying to look after their own interests.*" In this field, Shadbolt has been involved in many major deals, some of them purely domestic (Colchester Garrison MoD Project; Stoke Mandeville and Manchester Royal Infirmary PFI Hospitals), others based abroad (the Thessaloniki PPP submerged toll road tunnel, which enables traffic to bypass Greece's second city, and the €700 million Bucharest Bypass). All are big, complicated and require sophisticated legal advice. Said one source: "*One benefit of advising construction clients*

*is that most of them are clued-up and know the law, so they can spot a good piece of advice. You are certainly kept on your toes.*"

Several of the firm's traditional construction clients now look to it for corporate, property, employment and general litigation advice. One example is the firm's representation of a large American aircraft leasing company in an action against Buzz Stansted in respect of six Boeing 737 aircraft. In another case, the firm has been representing a company in a multimillion-dollar claim against an Indian manufacturer of valves used in the petrochemical industry. This diversification translates into different seat options for trainees, yet trainees are aware that these "*satellite*" departments are "*smaller and not able to absorb as many NQs as construction. When it comes to the crunch, qualification choices are reasonably limited compared to broader-based firms.*" That may well be so, but in 2005 all five of the firm's qualifiers chose to stay on at Shadbolt, entering a variety of departments.

## confidence boost

International work is fundamental to any analysis of Shadbolt. "*In my case it was the reason why I came here,*" reported one fairly typical source. "*Shadbolts continues to chase international work and we have an associate office in Tanzania, an office in Paris and one in Greece.*" Unsurprisingly there are travel opportunities, especially for qualified lawyers. "*One guy went over to Germany for a few weeks and has now been there for about six months... he does come home at weekends though!*" Even in the UK, certain partners' practices are predominantly international.

For trainees who speak French the three-partner Paris office will beckon. Two French partners deal with company commercial work and an English partner handles large arbitrations at the International Court of Arbitration. "*You're dealing mainly with construction contracts with arbitration clauses in them and academic aspects of English law. Foreign clients can sometimes be more flamboyant, particularly when thinking about what legal argu-*

# the true picture

ments will work, so you're doing research on the likeli-hood of different legal arguments." Back in the UK, secondments to construction companies are available to those whom the firm regards as suitable. Someone who'd taken up such a position recalled: "*I was dealing with commercial contracts and construction documents such as parent company guarantees, collateral warranties and tender documents; non-contentious work reviewing the documents, suggesting amendments and helping with negotiations.*" Depending on which company you go to, there may also be property litigation, personal injury claims and employment issues. "*You name it, I did it. You get an awful lot of independence and you're forced to do all the groundwork and then make decisions. It's a real confidence boost because you're not forced to make a decision as a trainee and on secondment you learn that you've got to be confident that your advice is 100% right.*"

The odd trainee comes to Shadbolt after working in the construction industry in some capacity, however most are completely inexperienced. What you need is "*the intellectual capacity for the work,*" "*a good understanding of contract law and to be outgoing and confident.*" An induction at the beginning of the training contract is supplemented throughout the two years and partners take time out and sit down and explain things through a good programme of in-house training sessions on contemporary subjects. "*Plus the fact that you can approach a partner for one-on-one training on a specific subject.*"

## the surreyal life

As one of only a handful of trainees "*your work is valuable and you can be an important part in the process. Friends of mine in big City firms are gobsmacked to learn I am drafting things they would only be photocopying.*" Our sources spoke of the excitement of being at a firm with something to achieve. Said one: "*The idea of being in a firm with 300 partners simply was not appealing.*" Yet here, "*many of the partners are from the big firms and they brought the*

culture with them – the culture of no messing around, get the work done, give a good service and keep the client happy.*"

Reigate, where it all started, is a pretty Surrey town, just a manageable commute from south London. Most trainees live in London though and their preference for working in the firm's Blackfriars office was clear. "*I like working in London but not in Reigate,*" said one interviewee. "*There's the travel issue, but also the two offices are run entirely differently. The cultures are so different it's like two separate firms. It's evident from simply looking at the buildings: Reigate is old and stuffy... you have to come in at the right time, wear a tie and are expected to be polite at all times.*" Another source painted a picture of an office that was "*quite conservative with a reasonably rigid hierarchy.*" By contrast, another source described the London office as "*more modern and better laid out. It is more flexible and no one really watches what time you come and go. The only thing that matters is getting the work done, and you can easily get by without wearing a tie or a suit.*" "*In London you have more leeway and there's more banter and room to negotiate.*"

Reigate appeals more to the refugees from big City firms, "*people who like their comfortable existence while carrying out high-powered work... but there are also lawyers who don't suit the place and who leave the firm because of the location.*" With the growth of the London office obvious to even the most casual observer, it's a fair question to ask – is this a City firm or a provincial firm at heart? One has to assume that the partners are considering carefully whether to continue growing both offices or focus on the capital.

Trainees settle the issue in their own way over drinks on a Friday night at the 'half way' point of the Slug and Lettuce in Clapham. And while on the subject of non-work activities, we must congratulate the five-a-side footballers on their success in the spring of 2005 when they walked off with the trophy in a hotly contested Wetherspoons'-sponsored tournament.

## and finally...

International work, clients at the forefront of their industry and lawyers leading in their field, the consensus from our interviewees is that "*Shadbolts' training sets you up amazingly well.*" Just don't ignore the firm's focus.

# Shearman & Sterling LLP

## the facts

**Location:** London
**Number of partners/assistants:** 26/96
**Total number of trainees:** 16
**Seats:** 4x6 months
**Alternative seats:** Overseas seats
**Extras:** Pro bono – various legal projects

Strong in corporate/M&A and capital markets, the London office of this US giant provides an action-packed training centred on big deals, big money and big hours.

## a part in history

Shearman & Sterling prides itself on a history of excellence. Founded in New York in 1873, its progress is linked with the fortunes of the nation itself. Shearman lawyers were involved in litigation arising from the Civil War; they advised Jay Gould in the takeover of the Union Pacific Railroad; and have acted for the Ford Motor Company since the days of the Tin Lizzie. The firm is very much old-school East Coast, and commentators and rivals alike look to it as a role model for the invasion of the European legal market. As well as establishing itself in London, the firm has rolled out its operation in Rome, Munich, Frankfurt, Paris and the other usual suspects.

Quick into East Germany when the wall came down, and China when they threw open their doors, Shearman has a habit of turning up Zelig-style in some of the most important historical and political events of the day. During the Iranian hostage crisis in 1979, Iran initiated secret negotiations to free the 52 American captives through a Shearman partner rather than normal diplomatic channels. On winning its independence from France in 1954, Algeria nationalised its vast oil and gas reserves and the resulting state-owned oil and gas company still retains Shearman & Sterling to represent it. After the first Gulf War, Kuwait hired the firm to seek reparations for environmental damage inflicted by Iraq. The firm makes much of this on its website, but it's fair to say that as a trainee your work will probably be more mundane!

## power rangers

The London office opened in 1972 and started practising with dual UK/US capability in 1996 when the transatlantic economy was booming and a whole raft of US firms made the journey across the pond. To give you some flavour of the London work from the past year, the projects practice (which has members in Paris and Abu Dhabi as well as London) worked on the development and financing of water and power projects in Oman and Bahrain and on International Power/Mitsui's purchase of Edison Mission Energy's portfolio of power projects. It also advised on a joint venture between BG, Petronas and Petroplus in the development of a £250 billion LNG importation terminal at Milford Haven in Wales.

In corporate finance the firm holds its own against the London establishment. It advised Viacom and Vivendi Universal in their sale of UCI Multiplex to Terra Firma Investments, a huge deal which took in the UK, Ireland, Germany, Austria, Italy, Spain, Portugal and Brazil. It beat Freshfields to instructions from $O_2$ on its corporate reorganisation, and lawyers also advised Malcolm Glazer on his successul takeover of Man United. On the banking side, they represented ABN AMRO as financial adviser to Royal Dutch Petroleum in the proposed unification of Royal Dutch/Shell, and Northern Rock in relation to its interest in Banco Santander's acquisition of Abbey, which brought it head-to-head with magic circle firms. The London capital markets practice advised AngloGold on the issue of $1 billion 2.375% guaranteed convertible bonds due 2009, convertible into American Depositary receipts of Anglogold Ltd. This, in case you were wondering, was a Rule 144A/Reg S transaction involving four key jurisdictions.

Ramping up its operations in London and poaching big-name partners from magic circle firms, this year Shearman put aside an extra half mill for generous pay rises for UK-qualified lawyers. NQs take home a very healthy £60k per year, a benefit which all five of the September 2005 qualifiers are now enjoying. Clearly in a bullish mood, the London office has added a property group and the M&A team is recruiting again. "*As a firm we can absolutely compete with the magic circle,*" boasted one source.

## what's the deal?

Training follows a traditional four-seat pattern with all new recruits spending two seats in the core areas of banking/finance, projects and M&A. Contentious seats cover both international arbitration and commercial litigation (and for those who can tell their Vermeers from their Van Dycks, somewhere in the firm there's a fine art litigation specialist). Those with more transactional tastes can fulfil the contentious requirement of the contract by way of a two-week litigation course at the College of Law, attended by all Shearman trainees. The other seat options are tax, property, competition, financial services and structured finance. There are no client secondments for trainees, but overseas seats include Singapore, Abu Dhabi, Brussels and New York. Said one trainee: "*Everyone in my intake who wanted an overseas seat has got one.*"

On a guided tour of the seats, we first heard from someone who had undertaken "*advisory work in asset management, mainly advising hedge funds and helping draft agreements. I helped to start a precedent database.*" Another had worked on projects in Abu Dhabi, which involved "*drafting,*

*tailoring agreements for deals, and due diligence. There were client meetings and I had lots of responsibility – I even went to a client meeting in Qatar on my own.*" Tax is "*very research-based, I helped to prepare papers for publication and worked on a couple of transactions.*" In this academic seat, "*there's lots of cutting-edge stuff but there's also a lot of menial tax filings.*" The big seat, M&A, involves "*liaising with clients and drafting agreements. I put together board minutes and did proof-reading and helped with the transactions.*" A number of insiders confirmed that "*M&A is the busiest department, but if you have to put in long hours, they won't say, 'Make sure you're in for 9.30am'.*"

Assessing the firm's key strengths, trainees told us: "*The project finance team does well every year. In other firms it's seen as the poor man's banking or tends to involve un-sexy construction work. We do lots of work in the Middle East – it's sexy, big-money work.*" In leveraged finance and banking, "*there are now as many paralegals as trainees.*" But that's not always a good thing! "*Sometimes after a Thursday night out you'd kill to do a day of photocopying. I closed a deal by myself and was in charge of looking after a client – I got some grey hairs... even at my tender age!*"

## frontier spirit

Yet the ethos of the firm is more relaxed than some rivals would have you believe. The dress policy seems to change like the seasons, but generally it is suits just when clients come a calling; on Fridays, jeans and polo shirts are pretty much compulsory. Socially "*there are lots of American associates who have that work-hard, play-hard mentality, and they don't tend to know too many people here so they all go out together.*" The office Christmas party last year was held in the Waldorf – "*a black-tie dinner and casino, where you could win an iPod or a trip on the Eurostar.*" Each department also throws its own Christmas knees-up: "*M&A's this year was at the Ivy.*" Lord knows how they swung that! Probably those 'connections' the firm is so famous for. One trainee proudly told us: "*Shearman is well known for its social side, we certainly know how to let our hair down...* " It's not unheard of for trainees to be whisked away to the annual European Lawyers weekend; someone even got to go to Vietnam for the Asian Lawyers weekend. Transport arrangements for overseas jaunts are not always conventional. Said one trainee: "*My former boss – who is frankly insane – flies aeroplanes and wants to buy a fighter jet. He taught me how to fly his Cesna and took us over to Brussels in it.*"

Trainees told us: "*The partners respond better to people who are not intimidated by them. They are looking for people who have confidence.*" "*They don't take on wimps. You can be nice and fluffy on the outside but there is a tough element to everyone, and you do need it because you must be able to fend for yourself.*" With a sly smile, one trainee told us: "*My notes say you have to be 'a keen self-starter, ready to assume responsibility at an early stage' – that sounds very trite and I wouldn't put it on my CV, but it is true to an extent.*" Because of the American heritage, you will be treated more as an associate, which apparently "*works to our benefit because we are paid handsomely and treated accordingly. The downside is that there's nowhere to hide in such a small intake.*" Clearly the massive salary brings with it more responsibility than you might get elsewhere. In one of the better sound bites of the year, we heard that "*if you're willing to dance they're willing to watch you.*" We couldn't decide whether we should be thinking more in terms of Napoleon Dynamite or Patrick Swayze. The people who shouldn't apply are "*the types at law fairs who ask if we do human rights law. You don't need to be interested in corporate finance when you're in your second year at university, but you need to have an inkling that it might be for you. No one is au fait with things like high-yield bonds before they start, but it helps if you think that working with banks in the City might be for you.*"

Speaking to trainees we learned that the key to good networking is asking questions that require the answer 'Yes'. Apparently it puts people in a positive frame of mind. This is just the start of the skills training: "*We had a session on cultural awareness in which they taught us how to present business cards. If you're dealing with an Oriental client you have to give them your business card using two hands, with your name facing them. In Asia you should never give it with the left hand.*" When it comes to Shearman's own culture, just as the Pilgrim Fathers carved their own destiny, the beauty of Shearman's UK colony is that "*there's no real sense of history; the UK partners have come from other firms and bring different things with them... hopefully the best not worst.*" In short, the culture is "*not stuffy or suffocating.*" If you want a good caricature: "*It's not feet-on-desk cigar chomping, but it's a long way from stiff-upper-lip Englishness.*" The other side of the dime is that "*there is a tough work ethic and there's very little flexibilty if there's work on.*" In true American style trainees take a "*practical view.*"

## and finally...

Shearman & Sterling is a place for people who are both pioneering and pragmatic, but the working pattern that attaches to this kind of firm is demanding, so "*if you want the easy life don't come here.*"

# Shoosmiths

## the facts

**Location:** Basingstoke, Birmingham, Milton Keynes, Northampton, Nottingham, Reading, Solent
**Number of partners/assistants:** 82/190
**Total number of trainees:** 27
**Seats:** 4x6 months
**Alternative seats:** Secondments

After its period of latency known in the annals of the *Student Guide* as the NBD (Nice But Dull) years, national firm Shoosmiths is looking rather impressive. Don't believe us? Then take note of the flocking clients and swelling profits (a 67% hike last year, a 144% increase in the last three).

## shooper dooper

Once a champion of the lay-by, Shoosmiths was best known for its high-volume, low-value residential conveyancing, debt recovery and PI claims, most of it conducted in various warehouse-like offices beside England's motorways. While the firm still handles masses of this work, a string of well-chosen lateral hires at partner level have been the catalyst for growth in its more interesting commercial departments. This invigoration of the firm's commercial practice has gone hand in hand with the exploitation of new markets, and Shoosmiths' now three-year-old investment in Birmingham brings the branch total to seven.

Healthy financial returns, increased staff numbers and an ever-more-impressive track record of deals and cases "*seem to be filtering down to everyone in terms of benefits.*" The coco department has doubled in size; the pensions and employment department is blossoming – all in all it's "*an exciting time to be in Shoosmiths.*" Clearly clients agree. Eschewing the services of its old lawyers, Anglian Water Services has appointed Shoosmiths for all its self-insured public liability and property damage litigation. Reproaching big City firms for their lack of commerciality and value for money, Daimler-Chrysler recently chose to give £1 million of its yearly legal spend to Shoosmiths. For that it gets litigation and competition advice and the odd trainee on secondment. Other faithful clients include high street favourites Boots and WHSmith.

Almost a third of Shoosmiths' work is real estate, and in this area clients include the celestial Central Board of Finance of the Church of England and the divinely material IKEA. The firm also acts for the South East England Development Agency regarding the Medway sites due to be decontaminated prior to development for housing key-workers. If John Prescott gets his way, this will bring about the largest change to the English landscape since the post-war rebuild. Projects such as Bellway's redevelopment of the Hither Green Hospital site into an urban village will be overseen by Shoosmiths' lawyers.

## shoopercalifragilisitc…

So how do you get from NBD to Shoopersonic? According to trainees it's because "*there are no ivory towers*" at the firm and clients love the lawyers' commonsensible approach to their business needs. Unashamedly cost-conscious, the firm operates from business parks in four locations (the Northampton HQ, Basingstoke, Solent and Reading), with Birmingham and Nottingham being the only city-centre sites. Of course Milton Keynes is arguably just one large business park.

Trainee life begins with two weeks "*putting on two stone*" in the baronial Highgate House just outside Northampton. There recruits complete the PSC and other training designed to "*set you up for your two years at the firm.*" They also get to eat far too much and make friends with fellow recruits from the other offices. The Shoo people have but one chief common denominator – "*We're all normal,*" a source certified. Unfortunately when they added: "*We're here because we're here and because this is what we want to do,*" it all became a little too Alan Partridge.

The trainees are a solidly redbrick group with "*enthusiasm*" for their chosen career, so leave your cynicism at the door because what Shoosmiths wants is "*someone who is prepared to make an effort to fit in.*" The Shoosmiths trainee has few pretensions and no desire to become a City lawyer. Ask any of them why this is and they quickly tell you that they're not looking for excess in their working lives. Said one: "*All firms say they promote the work/life balance – that elusive thing – but Shoosmiths do.*" We also sense that for many it's a case of 'big fish, small pond' syndrome. Then again, what's wrong with that?

## … fedexpealedocious

Across the offices, and throughout their two years, trainees sit in an open-plan environment with their departmental training principal close at hand to provide the supervision they need. They take on tasks from all the fee earners in their teams, and "*everyone is available for you to speak to*" should they come a cropper. As to which seats they do, aside from the Law Society's basic requirements nothing is compulsory. But be warned: go to Northampton and your choice is wide, go to Reading, which has just four departments, and your choice is far more limited.

The Northampton and Milton Keynes offices operate as one for training purposes, and with space for one trainee, the Birmingham office can now also be regarded as a part of this training trio. Movement between offices is not the norm, however, and trainee traffic between these three branches is certainly the heaviest in the network. The Northampton HQ is situated at The Lakes, "*a pretty business park*" a short way outside town. The available seats are commercial property, finance and banking litigation, property litigation, IP, employment, coco, personal injury and one of Shoosmiths' specialities – regulatory law, which covers health and safety, public liability ("*both including food law*") and licensing. One day you can be looking after a client which is marketing a hangover-curing soft drink, the next you might be dealing with the cause of those thumping heads. When the recent Licensing Act came into force it meant "*weeks of staying late*" for trainees, who only had a busman's holiday to the local pub, The Cherry Tree, to console them. Offering "*more court time than elsewhere*," a seat in the regulatory department means working with partners who adopt the hand luggage approach to training. Said one source: "*My training principal took me everywhere*." Trainees may get to undertake the odd small court application alone, but when an explosive subsidiary of a chemical firm blows, prompting the Health & Safety Executive to prosecute, you'll watch the fireworks in court from a safe distance behind a barrister.

By the end of a six-month stint in Northampton's commercial litigation department trainees will be running their own files. Most likely these will be "*basic debt actions*" for clients such as worldwide courier company FedEx, or the biggest player in the UK's fastest growing industry, gambling giant Gala.

Gambling debts accrue in the oddest places it seems. Expecting a world of seedy bedsits and betting slips, our sources found themselves chasing debtors who had fled the country taking their dues into a jurisdictional maze. Said one trainee: "*I had to get proceedings served through the British consulate in Abu Dhabi – it was a freaky thing*." Less freakish are the long disclosure lists that are required for the "*massive contractual claims*" on which trainees also assist. In jumbo-sized disputes it is more economical for a trainee to manage the time-consuming information trawl, though they may also be lucky enough to draft a witness statement. Alongside a steady stream of large commercial cases, the department takes on contentious probate work and further litigation is to be found in IP. The past year brought an interesting dispute over the ownership of the Dr Martens' logo.

The Milton Keynes office occupies space in the same building as one of the firm's clients – BP Oil. It's all mod cons, including those essential "*slide-down videoconferencing do-dahs*." The office additionally displays paintings selected, and even created, by staff. "*I'm partly responsible for some of that dodgy artwork*," boasted one trainee. Employment is a favourite seat in MK. "*It's fantastic because there's so much law involved*" and the cases cover "*things you can get your head around*." Acting for blue-chip companies, as well as drawing up skeleton arguments for tribunals, you'll also see a lot of the advocacy as Shoosmiths keeps as much of it as possible in-house. Said one trainee: "*It's quite impressive seeing colleagues up before a judge*." However it's not all rosy, and our source admitted to having undertaken some of the dreaded bundling in the seat – "*but it's not like I thought, 'Oh Christ, all I've done is bundling.'*"

The third point of the Midlands triangle, Birmingham, currently offers seats in commercial property, planning, construction and "*possibly insolvency*," with "*more coming soon*" as the office is set to double in size. From September 2006 it will take two trainees of its own.

## smoke on the water

In Nottingham, the large property department always equates to a busy six months, and over in the corporate department (which trainees say is about half the size of property) there's a very varied seat. "*I really enjoyed it,*" one past occupant told us. "*I basically got four seats rolled into one – IP, competition, general commercial and corporate.*" In one of the department's most recent deals it acted for 3i in the £10 million MBO of Nottingham-based Pharmaceutical Profiles which was spun out of Nottingham University in the early 1990s to provide clinical trial services to pharmaceutical and biotech companies. Better known clients of the department include Abbey, Bank of Scotland, RBS, Open University and British Gypsum. The other two available seats are employment and property litigation. If you're worried that this list seems a little too short, just remember the breadth of experience you'll get in coco.

Fridays in Nottingham are brought to a close in The Navigation, a mere stone's throw away over the canal. "*It's a bit of an old man's pub with a smoky atmosphere you could cut with a knife.*" Trainees can also participate in various networking and marketing events, including those of Nottingham's Young Professionals Group – "*free drinks, balls, pub crawls and stuff with accountants.*"

## southern comforts

The Solent office in its Fareham business park is the least convenient of all in the network and so "*a car is a must.*" The four trainees here can chose between employment, coco, commercial property, residential development, and landlord and tenant. This last seat will see them assisting on contentious rent arrears claims and, on big cases, research tasks and drafting claim forms, instructions to counsel and "*lots of letters to managing agents.*" The Reading office, like that in Solent, has a limited range of seats: employment, dispute resolution, coco and commercial property. For trainees this means a straightforward choice-free contract in these four areas, unless they double up on one seat or take a seat elsewhere in the network. "*If you want to get a choice of IP or IT, go to Northampton; for pensions go to Milton Keynes,*" and so on. Most trainees in Reading undertake a litigation seat, which means a fair amount of time "*dabbling in spinal injury research*" on behalf of "*major household-name insurers*". Basingstoke is a one-seat stop-off point for trainees, although the branch looks to be "*growing its own trainees*" from internal promotions amongst its case handlers. The branch "*buzzes*" with work from legal expenses insurers, mainly "*an awful lot of RTAs and medical negligence claims.*" Seconded trainees become the frontline, taking "*claimant calls from often very distressed people*" and then drafting schedules of loss, witness statements and claim forms.

## russian shoolette

Shoosmiths' intranet, Channel 9 ("*someone piped up with the name at a meeting and it stuck*"), combined with brisk e-mail traffic means that all new news plus the oddest of requests ("*does anyone know anything about Icelandic law?*") ricochet between the trainees. Socially, inter-branch gatherings are infrequent, though pan-firm training weekends – "*which are basically lessons with added piss-ups*" – provide opportunities to steal the towels you didn't dare from Highgate House. Christmas is a branch-by-branch domino fall of dinners and parties. Northampton and Milton Keynes celebrate together in the MK Bowl – the previous year's Russian dancing and vodka having received a resounding "*Da!*" from all concerned, the last Christmas party took a germane African theme. On a more regular basis, partners are not averse to putting a credit card behind the bar when called upon to do so, and the social life in most offices sounds quite good. Whether go-karting, football, cricket or Pimm's drinking are your 'sport' of choice, Shoosmiths does it all.

In September 2005 seven of the ten qualifiers stayed with the firm, going into commercial departments up and down the network.

## and finally...

For those who want good-quality commercial work without having to move anywhere near the capital, Shoosmiths has several different options. A penchant for business-park working would seal the deal.

# Sidley Austin Brown & Wood LLP

## the facts

**Location:** London
**Number of partners/assistants:** 34/36
**Total number of trainees:** 13
**Seats:** Length and number varies
**Alternative seats:** None

Sidley Austin Brown & Wood = excellent finance-based training contract. The equation is simple, the work anything but.

## supersize you?

Everything is on a larger scale in America. The landscapes stretch on forever, the cars are V12 gas guzzlers, a medium fries contains a bushel of potatoes. Yep, excess is the name of the game and it's no different in the world of law firms. When we say that Sidleys is a big law firm we don't so much mean big as massive. In fact we mean Enormous with a capital E. The Chicago-based giant this year saw revenue increase by 11% to hit the momentous $1 billion-plus turnover mark, making it only the fifth member of a very exclusive US club. But unlike many Americans this firm definitely has a passport: over 1,500 lawyers spread across 14 offices covering North America, Europe and Asia make Sidleys a true legal titan.

Almost 100 lawyers make up the London slice of the international pie, and with 80% of them UK-qualified the filling is definitely bramley-apple-English. Indeed, our sources tell us that *"you do feel part of a bigger firm and structure, and work has a heavy international flavour, but the London office is quite contained."* It's fair to say that this feeling is most true at trainee level where *"it seems as though decisions affecting you are made in the London office."* Beyond this, *"all other decisions seem to come down from on high in Chicago."* The apron strings stretch no further than London for trainees; they don't get overseas seats, instead waiting until after they qualify *"when you get to New York or Chicago for the new associates meeting."* By contrast *"there are always lots of partners visiting from overseas offices and weekly updates about the firm internationally which does generate a broader community feel."*

At a local level, trainees value the *"intimacy and sense of community"* that a relatively dinky office brings, revelling in the contrast that *"we're one of the larger US law firms in London, but still smaller than many City firms."* That said, they were also big enough to admit that *"beyond the advantages of a friendly and informal atmosphere, it's not really that different to other big corporate firms."* What really got our sources excited about the firm was *"the work – it's the real clincher; Sidleys does amazing work."*

## picture this

More particularly, Sidleys of London does often innovative work in the fields of international finance and capital markets, and has a special flair for securitisations. With an Anglo-American team that is perfectly placed to handle the full range of capital markets transactions from the US securities side of things to UK capital markets work, including equity and debt financing, LSE listings and emerging markets transactions, Sidleys dominates this market. *"Basically the type of work we do is unique in its scale and complexity. It's often exploratory too. If you've got complex securities issues then you come to Sidleys."* And come they do: the firm's clients include commercial and investment banks, US and European companies and financing, leasing and insurance companies. Just to give an idea of what the firm does, Sidleys this year took a lead role on an innovative £20 billion securitisation programme for FTSE 100 lender Northern Rock. This involved the formation of a special purpose vehicle Granite Master Issuer, which will subsequently be used to launch a series of mortgaged-backed bonds. All well and good you ask, but what's innovative about that? Well, it makes Northern Rock the first European issuer to secure 'shelf' registration for securitized bonds from the US Securities and Exchange Commission, status which allows the vehicle to issue further bonds without individual US registration. And in a further neat twist, the programme is 'de-linked,' leaving the possibility for further offers of senior debt without directly corresponding subordinated debt. Genius!

Now if you've followed all of that, then you have our respect, but if you are feeling slightly confused then that's just normal for a Sidleys trainee. "*Basically securitisation is like a hidden subject,*" admitted one, "*the LPC and the CPE don't cover it so it's like nothing you've ever seen before.*" Others chimed in with similar yet hopeful thoughts: "*It does take a while to get your head around the deals, but once you've done a few transactions start to finish you're familiar with everything.*" We wondered if this was exactly true and probed further and will leave this exchange of words to speak for itself.

Trainee: "*Once you understand the basic principle of securitisation it's all easy.*"

Student Guide Researcher: Could you define it for our readers please?

Trainee: "*Yes, of course. Well, er...* [sound of shuffling]*... the thing is I usually like to explain it with a diagram, that's how they explained it to us on the first day.*"

Student Guide Researcher: Can you describe the diagram so I can draw it?

Trainee: "*Er, not exactly. Sorry.*"

## money talks

Clearly, if you're considering Sidleys you'll have an interest in international financial markets, a willingness to put your back into learning about them

and you'll be happy to undertake a specialist training. If this sounds like you then you're not alone. "*The specific expertise was a real attraction,*" said one trainee, "*I mean you do weigh up the pros and cons and wonder whether more litigation experience might be helpful, but specialisation is better than spreading yourself too thin. When you qualify you understand finance so well that you're practically an expert in any international finance or corporate deal work.*" To get them to this stage, trainee's spend nine months or more in the "*massive*" international finance group (IFG), with a stint in corporate another given. Other seat options include employment, property, tax and a new seat in the regulatory group. The absence of a litigation seat is countered by a short course at the London branch of Nottingham Law School.

Corporate is a growth area for the firm with recent deals including advising CIT Group Inc. in its $950 million acquisition of the vendor finance leasing business in West Europe of CitiCapital and an instruction from First Data International in its €206 million purchase of Delta Singular Outsourcing Services. The "*smaller size makes it more open and friendlier than IFG,*" sources told us of the corporate department, adding that it comes across as "*the department most detached from IFG: the others all fulfil heavy support roles.*" In the case of the real estate department, partners often find themselves working closely with IFG on matters such as Citibank's £130 million loan facility allowing Bondcare to acquire a portfolio of nursing homes, or Morgan Stanley's similar £47 million loan facility allowing Arkminster to refinance a shopping centre. It goes without saying that the tax lawyers have a crucial role within the firm, and trainees here engage their brains in "*research and complex calculations*" but also enjoy a part-time client secondment to a bank.

## fly by nights

"*IFG is deadline-orientated: when there's a closing you'll be up all night,*" trainees admitted, reflecting that although the working day "*averages 9ish to 8pm, some people have had terrible hours.*" The shadow of the office's core practice is long, but smart casual attire and "*a collegiate atmosphere*" lend a welcome degree of informality. "*Everybody here wants to see things done as well as they can be,*" so we imagine few people dart for the door leaving work undone. Nor does there seem to be a reason why you'd want to dash away given that "*we're a bunch of accommodating personalities, everyone's driven, self-confident and no one will take the short cuts; but there's absolutely no arrogance.*" What's more, the size of the firm and "*the mountain of responsibility you get*" mean "*you feel the pressure build as the deadlines approach and your team responds, even late hours fly by because you just enjoy it so much.*"

Our sources were honest enough to admit "*jumping in and out of deals can leave you a bit lost,*" "*you can sometimes get stuck diligising [v. to do due diligence] and then your understanding of the deal suffers.*" However, for every moment of drudgery, there are times when trainees can "*run deals under supervision.*" And for those moments when "*you just don't get what's going on*" help is always on hand in the form of "*partners whom you can speak to as if they were trainees.*" "*They might be incredibly busy, but they'll always make time to answer you questions, even the stupid ones.*" As in previous years we heard that partners can be "*somewhat distant socially,*" but in the office "*there's absolutely no class system.*" It is an ethos that filters down the ranks so that "*when new trainees arrive there is a real rolling mentor/tutor feel, you help them as you were helped before.*" Six of the seven qualifiers stayed on in September 2005, presumably ready to do their bit for those that have followed them to the firm.

Sidleys resides on the top three floors of Moorgate Exchange "*surrounded by windows looking out over St. Paul's cathedral and beautiful views.*" The only downside is that "*everyone outside can see you.*" A "*big atrium with a strange sculpture,*" a "*large roof terrace where we have parties in the summer*" and "*a

cafeteria with Starbucks and a gym downstairs*" make all that transparency worthwhile. Trainees can often be found with junior associates in the Corney & Barrow on a Thursday evening – "*we go there an astonishing amount.*" Other tastes are satisfied by trips to the theatre ("*we saw Julius Caesar at the Barbican recently*") or the cut and thrust of the softball team's progress through the summer season.

## and finally...

"*It's not the broadest-based training but if you want finance and capital markets it's the place to come.*" This succinct assessment of training is all you really need to know about Sidley Austin Brown & Wood.

# Simmons & Simmons

## the facts

**Location:** London
**Number of partners/assistants:** 101/219
**Total number of trainees:** 104
**Seats:** 4x6 months
**Alternative seats:** Overseas seats, secondments
**Extras:** Pro bono – Battersea Legal Advice Centre, language training

Signs are that Simmons & Simmons is recovering its killer instinct after a lethargic few years. Solid City work, some pretty big clients and a peppering of international seats have been the staple diet for an age, but greater profits and a new sector-driven approach are now also being revealed.

## not so fuzzy logic

Any outfit with a historical "*reputation for being more cuddly than the average City law firm*" can expect to be accused of trading a cutting business edge for fuzzy pleasantry. Just ask Cameron McKenna and Lovells. As an opinion, it's little more than a variation on the old adage that nice guys finish second, but in the case of Simmons there did seem to be some truth to the cliché. Having been particularly ravaged by the aggressive recruitment strategies of US firms opening up in London in the mid to late 90s, the years since the millennium have not produced the finest financial results for the firm. It was perceived to be dropping off the pace of the top 20 and lacking focus. Throughout the period, Simmons retained its lustre in the eyes of prospective trainees, to whom "*flexibility and a slightly more human approach*" and a regular place in the *Sunday Times'* '100 Best Companies to Work For' survey were obviously of greater importance than how fat the partners' bank balances were. Yet, everything we heard this year suggests the firm is "*streamlining, sanding off the cuddly edges*" and "*trying to get away from the fluffy image*." And guess what? Trainees like it!

In 2004 Simmons cast off a number of assistants and downgraded 11 of its equity partners, all in a bid to arrest declining profitability. More than simply stabilising the numbers, the tactic helped Simmons' profits shoot up 40%, while turnover increased by 10%. And that's only the beginning because "*charismatic and dynamic*" new managing partner Mark Dawkins has been ringing the changes with a newly internationalised executive committee, reflecting the fact that 50% of the firm's turnover is generated from its 20 overseas offices. He has also introduced a policy whereby greater emphasis is now placed on the three or four best-performing areas of Simmons' eight sector groupings, the aim being to focus more closely on specific industries. This is a strategy that has been adopted by several other top firms.

In practical terms, this has seen Simmons' excellent finance departments "*becoming more the drivers,*" and the firm "*wanting to become known as a finance outfit.*" The excellent private capital and hedge funds teams scored major points last year for developing the innovative accelerated IPO method used in the flotation and sale of Northumbrian Water. The firm then repeated the trick in helping Collins Stewart and Anker plc on similar financing

deals. The deals kept rolling in – Simmons advised BNP Paribas in connection with a €40 million acquisition finance facility for American buyout house Hicks, Muse, Tate & Furst, and British Land on the £2.08 billion refinancing of the Broadgate Estate. Its capital markets team's successes include advice to niche bank Singer & Friedlander on a £250 million Eurobond issue, whilst the asset finance team possesses significant expertise in military and civilian financings and has this year gained Mitsubishi Corporation, Gulf Air, Rabobank and Virgin Atlantic Airlines as clients, as well as continuing to act for the MoD on projects like the £13 billion Future Strategic Tanker Aircraft project.

It seems it is not just the finance bods who can hold their heads high. "*The firm is also pushing corporate work,*" particularly through its traditional TMT and energy expertises. As well as representing clients like Orange, Telewest and Network Rail on commercial TMT matters, Simmons this year demonstrated its international corporate capability by assisting on mobile content provider Forside.com's £179.6 million bid for iTouch, the largest ever UK bid by a Japanese corporation. In energy matters, the firm boasts BP and Ofreg amongst its satisfied customers, and as well as advising Spanish renewables generator EHN on transactions it has also completed its first corporate job for Royal Dutch/Shell. Add in a top-of-the-range employment department, well-regarded IP team and growing pharmaceuticals strength (clients include GlaxoSmithKline) and it is clear how a sector-driven approach could well be the spur for continued performance improvements. Whether it can push back into the top 15 or begin to take on some of the biggest work for its big-name clients remains to be seen, but Simmons has definitely shaken off its torpor.

## sitting pretty

A trainee's view of all these changes reveals that refocused ambition and features such as stringent new billing targets may have "*taken the polish off*"

# the true picture

Simmons' friendly glow, but few are complaining. "*We just got new IT systems which make billing easier, and everyone knows they've got to do their bit,*" admitted one source. Another noted that "*in the past, seeing negative stuff in the press was disheartening, but now there's a feeling of moving on positively.*" Summing up, we'd agree with the trainee who saw the matter in very simple terms – "*The difference is that everyone is really busy now, the work is there. It's good for morale and that creates a good vibe that people tap into.*"

As for the effect on trainee life, most sources felt that "*it won't make much difference to the nature of the work; if you're in corporate it's corporate work whether your clients are banks, industrial or telecoms.*" Undoubtedly, the new financial/corporate emphasis should be a warning to anyone heading to Simmons primarily for the stellar employment team or other niche work, but in reality competition has always been fierce for the small teams. "*In our year, so many people wanted to be employment lawyers that several didn't even get a seat there,*" revealed one trainee. Although getting seats and even NQ jobs in the department is not impossible, "*the firm is trying to underplay employment in recruitment and get more financial types in.*"

All in all, trainee life remains pretty much the same, with six-month seats to be taken in each of four separate groups. One grouping includes corporate and projects, another encompasses all the financial seats, a third incorporates the contentious teams (commercial dispute resolution, employment and IP among them), and the final group offers a choice of tax, pensions, private capital, environment and property. In theory, and mostly in practice, trainees take strictly one seat in each, although "*there is some flexibility, especially if you've a predilection for say, finance, corporate or capital markets.*" Being in the same group, the "*highly popular*" employment and IP departments cannot both be visited, and those wishing for a spell in either are advised "*to petition from the beginning.*" Out of the office, secondments to clients including ExxonMo-

bil, UBS and Barclays are "*excellent, and even if you don't get your first choice, you'll get one.*" A new Dubai office is the latest overseas seat added to the list of 11 opportunities, with Tokyo, Hong Kong and Paris unsurprisingly the most sought after.

## the humanity...

Despite the emergence of a more profit-centric streak, some trainees remain adamant that "*it is still a more human place than many other firms.*" Others dryly noted that "*it is as relaxed as any law firm could be.*" Certainly, trainees were aware of "*tolerance and a determination to train you,*" which apparently characterises supervisors' attitudes. Add in three-monthly appraisals and a mentor system (which trainees use more or less as suits them) and it is no surprise that our sources say: "*You always know exactly how you're doing.*" The only thing that fails to sooth is the artwork adorning the walls (including many Damien Hirst originals). "*A lot of it's controversial, not least because most people really dislike it!*"

Good print and secretarial staff mean, "*you get relatively little rubbishy work,*" our sources said, while also admiring the firm's capacity for "*feeding you more and more responsibility as you progress.*" Although "*litigation involves some inevitable bundling;*" corporate "*had me running a data room;*" finance "*sometimes involved a lot of proof-reading*" and capital markets can be "*fear-making – it's just an entirely different language, you have to do document checking just to begin to understand,*" our sources were satisfied that "*the good work outweighs the mundane.*" On the 'good' side of the equation, they relished "*being deeply involved on a big corporate transaction, feeling really appreciated and valued.*" They had "*drafted documents, assisted on deal completions and become immersed in the analytical side of regulatory advice*" in finance; "*handled smaller prof neg claims*" in litigation; and "*took a lead on specific and defined parts of a transaction*" in capital markets. Overall, we can only conclude that the people who really thrive are those who "*make the effort to go around the department and get work from *a variety of sources."* Not only does this *"help you get your face known,"* but also *"lets you see different people's very different stylistic and technical approaches to the same type of work."*

## ballunacy

Clearly *"conscientiousness"* and *"self-motivation"* are what mark the 'thrivers' out, but beyond this it is difficult to put your finger on what makes a typical Simmons trainee. At a push, one source suggested *"a pleasing lack of egos, especially when I remember what law school was like with big-mouth magic circle types!"* Whilst most arrive with minimum dallying on the road to training, there is genuine *"diversity in university backgrounds."* We also noticed a *"strong and supportive"* sense of community amongst trainees that is illustrated perfectly in a story about a trainee unfortunately celebrating a birthday with a marathon work session. They arrived early on the happy day after a few short hours of sleep to find an office full of balloons and fellow trainees helping take on the workload. Sweet.

On the hours front, *"9am-7pm is fairly normal,"* but *"things can get hectic especially in the transactional seats."* In truth, late nights are not uncommon, even if *"weekends are rare and you're not often truly crucified."* When they do leave the office at a reasonable hour, trainees will as often as not *"walk straight into the Corney & Barrow downstairs – there are always Simmons people in there."* With more than 40 in each year group, *"it's unlikely you'll go out often with everyone,"* though we did observe that friendship groups seemed larger and more inclusive here than at some of the very biggest firms. Perhaps it's a gesture of solidarity in response to the fact that *"the firm is a bit stingy about giving a budget for trainee events."* At least there's a wealth of other social opportunities (including sports teams from rugby to hockey to softball) and frequent departmental drinks. Once a month, everyone in the firm can pop in for drinks in the *"spacious"* atrium. It is a good time to make wider acquaintances, as is a trip to the *"excellent"* canteen for

lunch or supper. *"If you're working late on a deal, the whole team will stop at 8pm and go and eat together in the canteen, crack a few jokes, have a laugh, relax then go back to work."* Some 29 of the 43 qualifiers in September 2005 will continue in this vein, having accepted NQ jobs.

## and finally...

Simmons & Simmons offers a solid City training with international opportunities and maybe just a dash of added feel-good. Do keep reminding yourself of the focus on finance and corporate work, however.

# SJ Berwin

## the facts

**Location:** London
**Number of partners/assistants:** 128/270
**Total number of trainees:** 72
**Seats:** 4x6 months
**Alternative seats:** Overseas seats, secondments
**Extras:** Pro bono – Toynbee Hall law centre, death row appeals; language training

London outfit SJ Berwin is a turbo-charged, souped-up, low-slung Ford Escort XR3i of a firm that has roared into the top 20 during its brief 23-year existence. It has a clutch of international offices and average profits per equity partner topped a cool half million last year. If you're planning to stick your go-faster stripes here, expect to be driven to within an inch of your life.

## the full monty

Why an XR3i and not a Ferrari, Beamer or Jag you ask? Well, what car characterises the flash, brash, cash-based 80s' ethos better than this quintessential lad's motor. All dual exhausts, 0-60 mph in two seconds, metallic paint and pumping speakers, it was every boy's pin-up. And boy is SJ Berwin a child of the 80s. Formed in 1982, it was the brainchild of

Stanley Berwin, who saw a gap in the market for an American-style, service-oriented firm that possessed energy and drive. He set about hiring a diverse group of lawyers to bring bite to his new practice, creating a something-to-prove, individualistic-yet-client-pleasing, take-on-the-world approach that has left an indelible cultural stamp upon the firm. Even today, with the pc, eco-friendly 90s and the first half of the supposedly increasingly work-life balanced noughties behind it, our interviewees admitted SJB is still characterised by a certain *"dick-swinging, independent"* ethos that is pure Thatcher. Leaving aside the question of whether Maggie actually had male genitalia, our sources told us they work with *"young partners at the hungry age where they're eager to prove themselves, consolidate their practices and take a bigger bite."* To give that ambition context, the firm's mouthful of a client list includes the Laurel Pub Company, Royal Bank of Scotland, ABN AMRO Capital, Laura Ashley, Goldman Sachs and First Calgary Petroleums.

Make no mistake: this is a full-bore corporate training with a heavy-duty work ethic to match. SJ Berwin has raced to prominence through the achievements of its private equity practice – both transactional and funds-based – which flies the flag in the firm's *"determination to challenge the magic circle."* True, SJB did lose out to funds arch rival Clifford Chance on the establishment of Barclays Private Equity €1.65 billion European Fund this year, but there was plenty more to keep its pecker up. The firm secured appointment to the European arm of private equity giant Hicks, Muse, Tate & Furst on its split from its US parent, having first acted for the buyout house on its £101 million acquisition of a majority holding in celebrity shoe brand Jimmy Choo. Such work has been at the heart of the firm's expansion into mainland Europe where offices in Madrid, Paris, Brussels, Munich, Frankfurt and Berlin give the firm *"real clout in Europe."* If they possess the right language skills and want a seat overseas, trainees can go to any of these offices, while stay-at-homes may also *"benefit from work with an international bias."*

Having snared a Clifford Chance M&A partner this year, SJB has also been ramping up its M&A practice. Furthering its love of shoes, it advised Shoe Studio Group on a £140 million purchase of Rubicon Retail, owner of the Principles and Warehouse brands. Real estate is another core strength and here an impressive client roster includes British Land, Hilton Hotels, Marks & Spencer, Land Securities and Sainsbury's. This year's advice to British Land on its £52 million purchase of five Homebase sites is typical of the department's work, as is an instruction from Quintain on the redevelopment of the new infrastructure around Wembley Stadium.

## wherever i leave my hat

On considering this roll call of success, you might not immediately judge SJ Berwin to be a firm that has *"lost a little bit of direction."* However, the ever-articulate and always perceptive SJB trainees put their collective finger on a dilemma facing the firm, so over to them...

*"It's got to the stage where it's no longer a small growing firm that punches above its weight, but it isn't top tier in terms of internal systems, management structure or culture,"* said one trainee. Another added: *"It wants to challenge the magic circle and retain its identity, but it isn't sure quite how to do that."* We're told one response has been to *"consolidate and expand existing strengths,"* whereas *"an apparent move to build up new strength in commercial litigation"* is perhaps another. For the moment a move to new premises is *"the factor everyone's hanging their hat on."*

In autumn 2005, SJB left behind several unappealing premises in the wastelands south of Kings Cross and north of Grays Inn to move into a space age, newly fitted-out office right on the Thames at Southwark Bridge. *"There's a big focus on making every aspect of the office perfect in architecture and systems: lots of blue tooth telephony and plasma screens,"* oohed one trainee. Another, less easily impressed, commented: "*There's a lot of 'new mate-rials'... we've all seen loft conversions like it.*" Beyond the surface details, everyone recognises that being "*united under one roof*" and "*smack bang in the heart of the city*" should have a positive effect on the morale of the firm. "*Hopefully clients will be more inclined to come to us,*" said one trainee tellingly. Time will tell, but in the short term everyone we spoke to was highly excited about the roof terrace. "*Apparently it's the largest in London and it has views over the Thames!*" Will it be reserved for special parties or available for everyday lunches, we wonder?

## full corporation expected

The SJB training contract uses the standard four-seat template, and with the firm dominated by its corporate practice, trainees are obliged to take at least two seats in this division (although banking, tax, financial services and overseas seats also count). We'll let our interviewees spell out the truth about corporate seats. "*You work for a bunch of driven peo-ple who love what they do and expect the same of you;*" "*people who work hard, often to the detriment of other things outside work.*" Unsurprisingly, in these seats trainees are "*massively busy,*" whether it is "*drafting subscription agreements*" or "*drowning in due diligence and organisational work on MBOs.*" We did hear gripes from some quarters that "*the partners need to have their understanding of what trainees can do updated, we're more than just biblers,*" but most were reconciled to the fact that "*you have to accept what you're given. It's par for the course.*" Generally, trainees were nonchalant about the hours they often worked. Said one: "*Yeah, it can be 12-13 hours a day for a prolonged period, but if you feel miserable it is only because you're tired, it's never wrist-slittingly bad.*"

By contrast, the mighty real estate group is described as "*very friendly, sometimes chaotic, always busy and welcoming*" and involves far easier hours of 9am till 6.30ish. Trainees run "*licensing files start to finish,*" perhaps progressing to "*negoti-ating leases,*" they also "*assist senior assistants and*

partners on transactions for massive clients.*" Such exposure allows them to observe "*different negoti-ating styles*" and see the intersection of real estate, corporate transactions and finance at close quar-ters. This year's instruction from British Land on the £2.8 billion refinancing of the Broadgate Estates companies is just such a multidisciplinary matter.

If corporate seats can involve enforced long hours, then find yourself in a niche seat and "*you do 60-hour weeks through choice to make a good impression.*" Trying to get a seat in the most prized departments such as employment, IP and media (including film financing) can feel like panning for gold with a colander – exhausting and poten-tially futile. Trainees recognise that "*strategy is important,*" saying: "*if you want a specific seat you've got to gun for it from the start. Every time you make your choices, emphasise it.*" One source had attended training sessions in a desired department from week one, put it top choice at every seat rota-tion and had to wait until the fourth seat to get in. However with seats in litigation, reconstruction & insolvency, EU competition, commerce and tech-nology, construction, overseas seats, secondments and even a regular placement in Westminster with SJB partner and Conservative MP Jonathan Djanogly, there is certainly variety on offer. Over-all though, if you don't want a rigorous and exacting corporate-heavy training then don't pick SJB.

## hardy young things

On that note a few salutary anecdotes. "*The low point for me was getting half way home on a Sunday night at 3am and having to go back because the client wanted something else done.*" "*My high point was get-ting an email from a client that said, 'Thank you for your work'. It wasn't exactly satisfying, but I felt like I'd got the job done.*" Persistence, staying power and "*self-motivation*" are the qualities required at a firm which "*isn't a kindergarten, there's no hand-hold-ing,*" where "*it's good to work hard to be on people's* radars" and where "*you get as much responsibility as you prove you want.*" From the comfort and luxury of our fur-lined *Student Guide* work pods, we were exhausted just listening to all this talk of graft. We also noted that trainees may not always get much feedback on their efforts. "*It does depend on your supervisor... But you'll always be told if you've done something incorrectly,*" said one source. Most perceived this as just another feature of a trainee existence that breeds "*self-sufficiency,*" suggesting that "*if you ever learn something at your appraisal that you didn't already know, you haven't been working properly.*"

SJB trainees are hardy. They possess "*initiative, and are really confident but not overbearing.*" One mature trainee praised younger contemporaries as "*the keenest and most insightful bunch of people I have ever met, and that's quite a thing to say for a group in their 20s.*" What delighted our interviewees, who described themselves as "*a cohesive group,*" was that "*there is no one type.*" "*People come from different backgrounds and previous careers.*" It is a claim we hear not infrequently, though in the case of SJB it seems to be true. Whoever said that faint heart never won qualification was right, but in 2005, 23 out of 29 bold individuals put their name to paper and stayed on in NQ positions, with most departments taking at least one qualifier.

The trainees' social scene will undoubtedly be revolutionised by the office move and "*drinks on the roof terrace*" has become a much-anticipated event. There is some feeling that the firm has underestimated the importance of social functions of late, though what we heard of "*outlandishly drunken*" Christmas parties and a thriving sports scene (hockey, football, softball and cricket teams and an annual sailing weekend) made it sound like there is enough to sustain most. The major consequence of the move will be the loss of highly expensive SJB drinking hole Centros. A moment's silence ladies and gentlemen, whilst generations of future trainees' bank accounts are lifted from the shadow of debt.

## and finally...

This ambitious and unpretentious firm should fulfil the hungriest of trainee appetites and for someone made of the right stuff it is a cracking option. Some students should be more wary of SJ Berwin though: it is most definitely not the right place for anyone pursuing an easy life or that holy grail of work-life balance.

# Slaughter and May

## the facts

**Location:** London
**Number of partners/assistants:** 121/395
**Total number of trainees:** 185
**Seats:** 4x6 months
**Alternative seats:** Overseas seats
**Extras:** Pro bono – RCJ CAB, Islington and Battersea law centres; language training

The most urbane yet most misunderstood member of the magic circle, Slaughter and May's clever corporate conjury is an elusive art. We ventured behind the curtains to find out how it's done.

## abracadabra

Slaughters stagecraft is "*streamlined and slick.*" No matter how closely you watch, it's impossible to spot the sleight of hand; the firm is "*meticulous in everything;*" "*it's about getting everything perfect.*" Mammoth corporate deals are performed to exacting standards without grand flourishes or wand waving. There is "*not much wastage in what they are doing*" and certainly "*no gimmicks.*" However, imperious professionalism and cool reserve have earned the firm a reputation as "*quite standoffish*" and "*very dry.*" Our sources were acutely aware of the image of the firm as "*arrogant, conservative and fairly stuffy,*" and we sensed that many were slightly disappointed that most outsiders' understanding of their employer went no further than these pejorative terms. Trainees attribute this to the fact that

Slaughters is *"keen to do things their own way"* and is *"the last firm to react to trends."* We heard that *"everyone else has dress-down and we don't"* and that *"you're not thrown company benefits for no good reason."* Similarly, on the recruitment stage, while other City firms pull bunches of flowers and other freebies out of pockets, Slaughters simply *"depends on its name and reputation."* There is no need to hoop-jump through the recruitment process because at Slaughters a simple CV or form and a *"pretty free-rolling interview"* will do. One trainee pondered: *"I thought there was some great magic behind it and really there isn't. They just want to know they can sit in an office with you and not feel like throwing things at you."*

Of Slaughters' reputation, one trainee said: *"It can appear frosty because when criticised, or invited to criticise, the firm is just terribly polite, stiff upper lip, smiles all round."* Grace under fire, simplicity and excellence – it's a formula that works. Our parent publication *Chambers UK* reveals just how highly regarded Slaughters is for complex corporate finance transactions, and there are surveys that suggest this is the firm other law firm's partners would wish to be at if they had to choose another.

## last laugh

A cornerstone of *"the Slaughters Way"* is its differing attitude to world domination. When the other four magic circle firms busied themselves with opening scores of offices, Slaughters opted for a best friends policy. This sees it working out of just three of its own overseas offices (Brussels, Paris and Hong Kong), and in alliance with the best firms in other jurisdictions, for example Urìa y Menèndez in Spain and Hengeler Mueller in Germany. Said one trainee: *"I really liked that – it didn't impose itself as a conglomerate."* Until quite recently the firm's detractors *"openly mocked the best friends policy, but it has worked and they have gained more respect."*

One benefit of refusing to waste money launching expensive and unprofitable overseas offices, and then having to spend money closing them, is that Slaughters has remained the most profitable UK law firm. Its partners earn an average of £1 million per head per year – the likes of Clifford Chance don't even come close. How does it achieve this? It has more clients on the main list of the London Stock Exchange than any other, and acts for the likes of Shell, Cazenove and Diageo. And the deals? *"The size of transactions is pretty much as big as they come!"* In 2004 it advised on the largest recommended public takeover, Spanish Banco Santander's £8.9 billion offer for Abbey National; the largest hostile public offer, Philip Green's well-publicised approach to Marks & Spencer; and the largest private equity deal, Morgan Stanley Real Estate and Songbird's £5.2 billion offer for Canary Wharf Group. With such stellar performances on the corporate stage, we find ourselves inclined to agree with the source who concluded that *"there is a degree of truth in the reputation for arrogance: the work here is very good and the way we do it is the right way."*

## initial thoughts

So let's be clear: *"The majority of the work here is straight-down-the-line corporate."* One source explained the division of labour: *"There is a corporate hub in the middle, six or seven corporate groups, from M&A to general commercial stuff, then two financing groups outside that, and all the others are pretty much support."* With a minimum of two of your four six-month seats in a central corporate group, a Slaughters training is decidedly corporate in nature. That said, you must also bear in mind that the firm has a generalist approach and no one seat will be overly specialised.

Speaking of the different corporate groups, one source chuckled: *"I have friends at Freshfields who are part of 'Corporate Team 27'... it's so impersonal!"* Here *"everyone is known by their initials. If you're lucky you're given your own, though there may be an X or Y stuck in there."* Discussions about the corporate groups prompted such baffling comments as *"TAK isn't as popular as JEFR"* and *"NPB can be* quite intense." NPB takes its name from corporate legend Nigel Boardman and the team is "*hard-working and high profile... partly because of him.*" A seat here "*does have its nasty moments,*" and with vast, complex deals on the table, we were unsurprised to hear one trainee admit: "*When I turned up I had no idea what anything was.*" Another concurred: "*I just didn't have a clue, but I learnt very quickly.*" Working on "*acquisitions that you see on the front page of the FT,*" trainees soon realise they will get "*up to speed*" in the data room, not the boardroom. As one observed: "*You don't go to a lot of completion meetings as they don't like too many faces kicking around.*" Inevitably, "*some days are tedious as hell, just checking the cross-references and the amendments,*" but these days do not fill a seat from beginning to end. "*I don't feel that I spend a lot of my time doing stuff that you could get a chimpanzee to do,*" assured one source; others spoke of rewarding and detailed research into "*intricate points of law.*" A philosophical outlook certainly helps – "*some things are exciting when you look at them as a whole even though the bit you are assigned is quite mundane.*" Like the masterful magician's long-suffering assistant, a trainee may not enjoy being shoved in a box, sawn in half and pulled every which way, but it's still a pretty cool trick and the maestro always gets a huge round of applause.

The feast-or-famine nature of corporate practice means "*one day you're working your arse off, the next you're twiddling your thumbs.*" In quiet spells, a sensible 9.30am to 6pm day leaves plenty of time for departmental training sessions, language classes, pro bono work and a new finance and business course. One source was told by their supervisor not to stay late because "*a) I won't notice, and b) I'll think you're silly.*" In times of plenty it is a different story: the corporate teams "*do so much work – always late nights, always weekends – it kills people.*" Trainees are expected to shrug off this close shave with death and stay at work "*until stupid o'clock in the morning.*" Applicants must consider how they feel about this.

## roll out the barrel

The remaining one or two seats will be spent in a satellite department, perhaps TMT, financial regulation, commercial property or competition. Trainees submit their preferences before arriving at the firm, and on arrival should allocated seats not be to their taste, the firm is not averse to people doing swapsies. Competition and IP are currently popular, as is commercial property because it is "*the only chance you'll have to get your own pile of files.*" As in all satellite departments, "*there is an element of corporate support*" to the work. Lately lawyers assisted on Punch Taverns' £335 million acquisition of Innspired Group, one of many pub portfolio deals handled by the firm in recent years. As one trainee put it: "*Someone seems to be transferring hundreds of pubs around all the time!*"

Contentious experience can be gained during a spell in commercial litigation, IP/IT or employment and pensions. A litigation seat may be split into two, with three months spent in tax, and this is a blessing for some, a headache for others. "*You either love litigation or you hate it,*" but a quick show of hands revealed that these days "*it is massively popular.*" Litigation provides "*an incredible breath of fresh air*" in a "*charismatic*" and "*very bubbly*" team. Explaining this widespread enthusiasm, we heard that "*you're really asked to use your brain.*" There is also "*a lot of client contact, which is what people miss in the corporate groups.*" While vast, contorted cases can bring a welter of pagination, bundling and document checking, some trainees are lucky enough to attend court, even "*sitting at the front with counsel.*"

Most trainees stay in London for the entire two years. Overseas seats come from a pick 'n' mix counter offering 18 different locations, most with best friend firms, but we're told that "*if you definitely want to go abroad, Slaughters is not the right place.*" Some sources grumbled that the allocation of overseas placements was unclear and left them feeling short-changed when they charged their Oystercard for yet another six months. Those dead set on a specific location "*have to work the system,*" and "*the most sure-fire way of securing a seat is to get a partner who has an interest in work abroad to speak for you.*" You can improve your chances of getting away by being flexible – Stockholm, for example, is "*always undersubscribed.*"

## school's out

Even when pressured by a demanding young audience, Slaughters is not usually in the habit of showing its hand. From the allocation of overseas seats to qualification decisions, the Slaughters Way "*can be quite opaque.*" Even with formal appraisals at the end of each seat – and "*in theory an informal one after three months to give you a bit of guidance*" – some supervisors can be sparing with their words, leaving our sources sensing that at times they were missing the trick. One reported: "*I don't think we get enough feedback.*" Though mollycoddling is not Slaughters' style, "*they do look after their own.*" If problems arise there are "*infinite ways to sort things out.*"

There is an open-door policy, though one trainee confessed: "*It's a bit like going into the headmaster's office.*" Of course, for every supervisor who adopts the stern mathematics master approach ("*very keen on hierarchy and likes to be treated as the boss*"), there are others who fit the liberal young art teacher mould ("*treats you as a contemporary, even an equal, and asks you what you think*"). As one source observed: "*The partners are glittering stars and you are extremely careful with them.*" Another, less flattering, comment went something along the lines of "*they are old and have been around a lot. They deserve a bit of respect.*" Our advice? Tuck your shirt in and lose the gum.

After-class games include touch rugby, rounders, netball, sailing and softball, or for those with a sick note, there is a choice of the local Corney & Barrow, the St Paul's Tavern and the Artillery Arms. In keeping with the firm's no-frills approach, the extra-curricular programme is a slim-line volume and you won't find yourself rushing from art club to archery or choir to cadets. The firm's annual black-tie dinner at the Grosvenor, though not entirely sober, is certainly a civilised affair. Similarly restrained are Slaughters' offices on Bunhill Row. Despite "*marble everywhere, the partners have gone for the non-offensive approach.*" Art and design features go some way to lightening the atmosphere, particularly the three-inch-deep water feature that runs across the client reception floor and occasionally drenches the feet of unsuspecting visitors. Apparently "*the security guards are fitter for having to bound across and stop people walking into it.*" Presumably it was the same guards who escorted a gnome, complete with fishing rod, off the premises last April Fool's Day.

Perks are minimal. You won't need to fit a trip to the corporate masseur in between your corporate manicure and corporate nap in the corporate sleeping pods; instead, there are "*spotless shower rooms*" and a heavily subsidised canteen, verdicts on which are as follows. "*The food is brilliant for breakfast and lunch, and terrible in the evening. Dinner is basically what is left over.*" At any time of day you can have your steak cooked to order and there is "*usually a guy with a moustache in the corner making risotto.*" The canteen is also home to the corporate jukebox, "*a big flashing thing that plays every song on the planet.*" "*The story goes it was given to an old partner as a gift from a client, and his wife refused to have it in their nice Chelsea home so it was installed in the restaurant.*" Again this year trainees confirmed the sad news that "*you are not allowed to play it.*" Spoilsports.

## a love-hate relationship?

The current trainee group is described as "*eclectic*" and ranges from the "*public schoolboy who plays polo and has a yacht to the lad from Brum with broken knuckles.*" One source quipped: "*I have been surprised talking politics with individuals that there are a lot of really quite left-wing people!*" Another thought, however, that "*you've got to be generally conformist*" to fit in. Though "*the Oxbridge contingent does still exist,*" the firm's priority is to "*take* people who are the best at the job" and "people come from all over, including universities I haven't even heard of." Outstanding intellect, good insight and quick wit are commonplace, but there is still room for those with "brilliant minds and very few social skills... people who are very academic and don't necessarily have all those City business skills." Indeed, "if you are looking for more of a banking atmosphere, Slaughters isn't for you." Trainees suggest that "the atmosphere isn't overly aggressive," and they are "much more competitive with themselves than each other." For our part, we've always found the trainees a delight to speak to, perhaps because they are eloquent in speech, independent in their thinking and, importantly, at times extremely funny. Like the firm itself, they never try and oversell the training to us but still leave us convinced of its merits.

Outside "the core that is desperate for partnership," we encountered sage sources mindful that a glittering career at Slaughters can leave you "wedded to the firm." Regardless of their long-term aspirations, all seemed focused on building solid foundations to their career, yet they were also aware that time spent in non-corporate seats was rarely more than an interesting diversion from what is essentially a heavy-duty corporate training. Think anything else and you may end up disappointed on qualification. We suggest you heed this trainee's advice – "Be realistic about why you are coming here, and that's for big work for plcs." In September 2005, 51 of the 56 second-years chose to stay post-qualification.

## and finally...

Training with Slaughter and May should be a masterclass in breathtaking corporate magic. Definitely not for those who'd prefer more homespun hocus pocus. Or Debbie McGee cartwheeling down the corridor.

# Speechly Bircham

## the facts

**Location:** London
**Number of partners/assistants:** 51/77
**Total number of trainees:** 10
**Seats:** 4x6 months
**Alternative seats:** None

For a mid-sized City firm with a steadfast reputation for both commercial and private client work, Speechly Bircham offers the discerning trainee a solid training package without distracting whistles and bells.

## simplicity itself

We've got to say it: the name Speechly Bircham conjures images of a Dickensian snitch. You know the sort; pointy nose, frock coat, mincing steps, definitely up to no good. In reality the firm epitomises something entirely different – "an honest, good firm" that is "not trying to be something it's not." Viewed from another angle, "you get what you pay for... it is what you see." And what you see are core practice groups in property, corporate, litigation and private client, all undertaking solid work for respectable clients. Simplicity itself.

This unbefuddled approach permeates the training contract right from the start. "The application form was really straightforward; they just wanted to know the relevant things." Seat rotation is also handled in characteristically simple style. The first seat is chosen for you and you can express preferences for the remaining three. With two seats on offer at any one time in the larger departments, "in the main, people do get what they want" and, as in the past, "the only problem department is employment" where this year people were queuing up at the door. In typical fashion they did not revert to blackmail, bribery or other mischief, but "sorted it out between them."

## paint jobs

While other firms boast more frills than Keira Knightley in an Empire-line petticoat, Speechlys is simply dressed. With *"vistas over the City,"* its offices *"lean towards a more traditional, conservative style."* Certainly *"there is no large television in reception."* The inevitable practical problems of a utilitarian approach to décor (*"there are no numbers coming out of the lift"* and *"the floors all look the same"*) is addressed by cunning colour coding, each floor dressed in its own *"nice pastel shade."*

On the *"peuce"* first floor, trainees *"get thrown in at the deep end"* with property work. *"As long as you don't sink, it does give you confidence for later on,"* we heard. The team *"competes with firms that are very much bigger"* for work from a mix of investors, developers, banks and local authorities. It recently spring cleaned RBS' Manchester property interests, dusting away some 20 freehold and leasehold properties. On vast transactions, such as the £216 million disposal of the UK property portfolio of Israeli-quoted Alony Hetz, trainees handle *"more general co-ordination, helping to pull everything together"* and organise stamp duty forms and other *"post-completion stuff."* By running some of their own smaller files, trainees brush up on their drafting and file management skills. A stint in the smaller property litigation group brings *"work from everyone in the department."* The group handles rights of first refusal, leasehold enfranchisement matters, restrictive covenant disputes and all manner of nuisance issues including *"really strange stuff like light reflecting off buildings and damaging cars in a car park."*

## circus acts

In comlit, trainees balance *"huge disclosure exercises"* with a *"fair bit of variety,"* the highlights being taking *"sole responsibility for debt collections,"* drafting claim forms and defences, attending directions hearings and *"watching the barristers do their bit."* The firm's valued construction team shares the second floor with comlit. Unfortunately, here, *"because of the nature of the work, you are never going to be managing the files."* On the non-contentious side, the team is advising on the £150 million redevelopment of Drake Circus in Plymouth for P&O. On these big matters there is *"quite lot of research"* for trainees. On the contentious side, they draft witness statements, issue proceedings and attend mediations and case management conferences.

The corporate department (fourth floor, *"bluey tones"*) is another common stopover for trainees. *"It doesn't get the FTSE 100 clients,"* revealed one honest source, though there are a number of interesting names on the roster. Among them are Rothschild Trust Corp and Tell-Tale Productions, the creators and producers of The Tweenies. Trainees encounter *"a lot of the normal stuff,"* ie maintaining company registers, annual returns, shareholder resolutions, board minutes, data room duty plus small drafting exercises on commercial agreements. Essentially, *"you are the bottom rung of the ladder but the stuff you do, you see the point of."* It's not been all good news in the corporate department, however; in the summer of 2005 two partners left for an American law firm having spent only two years at Speechlys.

## private words

Though most of the firm's lawyers concentrate on commercial law, *"there is no question of private client being tucked away."* Quite the opposite. The team has taken on three new partners from rival firms this year to gain *"a bit more fire-power"* in relation to contentious trusts and probate, matrimonial matters and international work. Among Speechlys' notable clients are the Howard de Walden family, Alexander Thyssen and Lord Lloyd-Webber. It wasn't just the big names that were making an impression on our sources; one announced that *"out of all the departments, this was the one that impressed me the most in terms of their professionalism. They are just a very smart, stylish, classy outfit. A class act."*

# the true picture

Trainees gushed about the work on offer, telling us how "*the individual experience of each trainee is quite unique.*" Yes, "*there is a lot of helping out with fairly basic wills, liaising with the Inland Revenue on basic tax matters,*" but it is "*a great seat to go to in terms of things I learnt about dealing with clients.*" Partners think carefully about who trainees meet and work for; said one source: "*I fully understand why they don't want a trainee scaring off a well-known client.*" At least they get plenty of exposure to "*Mr and Mrs Joe Bloggs.*" One objective soul curbed their enthusiasm for the experience, saying: "*I don't want to overplay the private client department*" because in terms of size and work "*private client is balanced with property and commercial.*" However, if the warmth and respect with which our interviewees spoke of the team says anything, then other departments could learn a thing or two from it.

## posh nosh

Trainees are "*suited and booted every day,*" but with a heating/cooling problem so severe that the firm is now suing its landlord, it's probably best to dress in layers. Most getting in by 9am and leaving by 6pm, though property and corporate seats bring longer hours at times. Trainees share an office with their supervisor and "*as you get more established, the work comes in from everyone.*" Our sources described impressive levels of client contact (we even heard of someone who had been packed off to the Channel Islands on their own for a client meeting) and ample opportunities for advocacy. There were no real grumbles about grunt work, and photocopying tends to be done "*when I offer to do it*" or "*when I think it would be quicker to do it.*"

Mid-seat appraisals tend to "*iron out any problems*" leaving the more thorough starching for the end of each seat. While "*sometimes you do have to actively seek out the feedback,*" on whole supervisors "*want to be involved in what you are up to and know what you are doing.*" One source boasted: "*I can ask my supervisor anything, even silly questions.*" We suspect such questions are rare, having spoken to some pretty sorted-out interviewees. Recruits are drawn from "*state schools and private schools, north and south,*" and we learned of a couple of second-careerers, one a former accountant and the other a former BBC violinist. The obvious common thread was a vacation placement at the firm. In September 2005, three of the five qualifiers stayed on.

Speechlys' out-of-office life revolves around low-key trips to The Last on a Friday night, quiz nights, ice-skating at Somerset House, theatre trips and go-karting organised by the firm. In truth, it was descriptions of social events within the office that had our sources most excited. For all that Speechlys doesn't go in for corporate ballyhoo, on the food front there are plenty of creative flourishes. Chris, the office chef, is such a culinary wizard that one trainee confessed: "*I try and arrange my holidays around when there are staff lunches.*" Regular departmental training sessions for trainees are accompanied by plain-old sandwiches, seminars are accompanied by canapés ("*They aren't really canapés – there is so much food I don't need to eat when I get home*") and monthly fee-earners' lunches are a veritable feast of curries, risottos and the like. The boat is also pushed out for the Christmas party, the last one taking an Oscars theme. There were statuettes for the general office staff (Best Supporting Act), a red carpet and a dubiously accredited photographer whose shots now adorn office walls. At least these should help you figure out where you are in the building if you've forgotten the colour coding!

## and finally...

If you are hunting for a comprehensive training in a solid, straightforward commercial practice with a burgeoning private client team, sign up for the vac scheme and you'll be sure to know what you are getting.

# the true picture

## Stevens & Bolton LLP

### the facts

**Location:** Guildford
**Number of partners/assistants:** 25/37
**Total number of trainees:** 6
**Seats:** 4x6 months
**Alternative seats:** None

Stevens & Bolton's mission is to bring the Square Mile to Guildford. As missions go, this one has been anything but secret, and so far a considerable number of disaffected City lawyers and several FTSE 100 clients have been lured to the firm's door. Will the Surrey firm tempt you too?

### an incredible story

Clark Kent could turn himself into a super hero in seconds. Bruce Wayne needed just a few short minutes in the cave with trusty Alfred to slip into his bat things. S&B has taken slightly longer to bring about its transformation. It enjoyed a quiet existence for most of the time *"since the mid-19th century, when it started in Camberley and Farnham."* At one stage it was operating from as many as five small high street offices; then in the early 1980s the firm's management had a vision that the future lay with commercial work. Changing S&B's orientation meant closing branches to consolidate everything into a single site in Guildford. Remarking on S&B's evolution and its determination to become the hottest thing in Surrey, one trainee explained how *"the whole firm has been pulled up by a proactive management board."* They also revealed some interesting facts about the firm's pedigree: *"Our managing partner was the trainee of the senior partner, who was also a trainee. His father was senior partner before him."* And *"the firm has never merged; its growth is purely organic."*

It's a lovely story, but how relevant is it to a firm that is increasingly defined by the hotshot lawyers it recruits from the City? Not especially. *"Except perhaps for trainees who go around the whole firm and*

*get to see the different departments. In private client, for example, it doesn't seem irrelevant. You can be working on trusts where the documents date back to the 1960s"* and some of the private clients from the old days still use the firm.

### holy smoke, batman

Echoes from the old S&B may be audible in family, residential conveyancing and tax and trusts, but these days the loudest noise comes from the three main commercial departments – coco, litigation and property. Coco has *"slightly got the edge size-wise,"* and in 2004 it took a major scalp from London giant Simmons & Simmons – its head of corporate, Guildford resident Ken Woffenden. *"Ken started here a couple of months before me,"* one trainee told us, *"and people say he looks so much happier now than he did when he arrived."* New lawyers like Ken mean big new clients for the firm, for instance international tobacco giant Gallaher. As impressive as this is, we should point out that the client list is still dominated by regional and medium-sized companies.

*"Corporate has a reputation for working the hardest and for being the real heavyweights of the firm,"* reported one trainee. Among its recent deals are the following gems: the creation of the largest privately owned UK Burger King franchise; a merger that produced the largest independent contract caterer in the UK; and the acquisition of Pleasurewood Hills in Suffolk by a leading French theme park operator. The trainee's role in this type of deal is *"to check bundles of documents, read through disclosed documents and categorise the company's liabilities, draft letters of disclosure and attend completion meetings."* In other words, be Robin to Batman. One source saw the department as *"the most sociable"* despite the pressure, saying: *"To some extent it can make or break you, but you also have the best opportunity to shine and get to work with the most partners."*

Trainees all spend six months in each of coco, litigation, commercial property and private client.

In litigation "*I ran a few basic contract claims and helped out on a big matter,*" reported one source. With a steady stream of appearances in front of district judges over the road in Guildford County Court, the seat certainly has its appeal. As for the downside, there is the preparation of court bundles, which can swamp your days from time to time. "*At least it's not as if the partner just throws them down; it's more a case that you're totally involved. They always make sure they take you to court and conferences.*" The same can usually be said of trainee tasks in the property department, which has just experienced "*an absolutely stonking year!*"

Some trainees seem to have wangled split seats between tax and trusts and other options, be this employment (the department last year impressed everyone by recruiting guru Stephanie Dale from London firm Denton Wilde Sapte), family or a return visit to one of the three core commercial teams. Whatever the practice area, it is usual to sit with a partner and to work with others in the group. It is also usual to receive two appraisals and a further check-up from the HR manager and training partner Beverley Whittaker. This dynamic duo seem to have a clever gadget in their utility belts for all kinds of training issue.

## riddle me this

Surrey connection? We could barely find a trainee with one this year. "*So long as you've made a conscious decision to apply to S&B and not just picked it out of a directory at random*" that seems enough. Nevertheless, we were left wondering why it was that a twenty-something would choose to start their career in a commuter town with which they had no prior connection when the capital is so close by. And when we say close we mean anything between 30 and 45 minutes on the train depending on who you ask and whether there's a following wind. The most common response to our question claimed: "*The quality of work is no different to London but the hours are better... and it's just doesn't feel like London.*" Fair enough, but why then would many of the

younger staff – trainees among them – choose to live in London and "*reverse commute?*" Should we consider the many Clapham dwellers the exception to the rule that S&B types just don't see the appeal of the Big Smoke? It's baffling.

So you've chosen county living over Clapham. Perhaps you've rented a flat in Guildford and walk to work. Maybe you have set up home in a nearby village and drive. Neither route to work will take long (nor indeed would the 20-minute train journey from Clapham Junction to the station opposite the office). And it gets better still. On qualification all lawyers get an allowance of £500 per year to cover the cost of a space in the adjacent public car park. If you arrive by Shank's pony you get to pocket the cash. Wherever your preferred domicile, the working day will normally leave you with enough time to indulge in a personal life. "*It's not like the high street, where you're home every day at 5.30pm, but I'd say our average hours are until 6pm or 6.30pm, even though I've had my share of late nights.*" These late nights crop up most often in corporate, where "*the adrenaline really runs when it gets to midnight and you're negotiating the finer points of a deal.*"

## a sting in the tale

S&B occupies a converted warehouse abutting the River Wey in Guildford. "*We're literally right next to it so you can see the canoeists and a houseboat.*" We loved the tale of the supertrainee who ended up "*diving into the water to save someone from drowning.*" Though she managed to save the poor woman, "*she got completely covered in nettle stings as she climbed back up on to the bank.*" With only half a dozen trainees and all staff housed in one office, you get to know people easily. From the sounds of it, the staff are a loyal bunch and this is repaid by management being "*big on consultation – we have business planning meetings annually where they sit down and say where the firm is going. All the fee earners go to it.*" We asked the trainees to share their vision of the future with us and they obliged without hesitation. "*I really feel the firm is going somewhere and getting* good clients. Even since I started as a trainee, the quality of the work has increased." As for the physical expansion of the firm, *"we are getting too big for our offices and will have to move into outside space. The thing that is great is that there's not a high turnover of staff. People know they have it good."* In 2005, two of the three qualifying trainees stayed on with the firm.

There is a presumption that *"it is easier to transfer from a City firm and that qualifying into a regional firm will hold you back, but actually a lot depends on the exposure you've had to work,"* reasoned one source. *"My friends in the City have done much less than me."* We also ended up in a debate about the presumption that *"top-calibre students go to City practices." "Well, that's not the case here,"* we were told. Recruits come with *"the full suite of qualifications and experience"* – good universities, good degrees (Firsts among them) and ample legal work experience (including time spent in New York and Washington firms).

Perhaps because so many people drive to work or choose to spend their free time with family or other friends, S&B is *"not an extra-social firm"* and Friday night doesn't always mean frothing tankards in the local alehouse. There are some organised events: at a go-karting tournament between Surrey firms the S&B corporate and banking lawyers came third, and summer and Christmas parties are full-on fun. The real advantage to working at a firm of this type is that senior people get to know you in the office and learn to put their faith in you. It's probably far more useful in the long run than the odd free pint in the local boozer.

## and finally...

Many firms claim to have transported the best bits of the City experience to the countryside, yet in Stevens & Bolton's case canny management and a good long-term strategy allow the claim to stand up. If you genuinely crave a GU postcode over an EC one, start exercising your superpowers of persuasion for interview. And please remember to wear your pants underneath your trousers.

# Stephenson Harwood

## the facts
**Location:** London
**Number of partners/assistants:** 56/108
**Total number of trainees:** 34
**Seats:** 4x6 months
**Alternative seats:** Overseas seats, secondments
**Extras:** Pro bono – Hoxton and Camden law centres, language training

Situated within sniffing distance of the Thames, Stephenson Harwood excels in shipping finance and litigation, and also possesses a developing taste for aviation matters. On dry land, financial markets, commercial litigation and real estate complete the yarn.

## shaping up, shipping out

Puns and bad metaphors – just say no. The first few might be free, but habit becomes addiction and, once you're hooked, a downward spiral to misery is inevitable. At the *Student Guide* we know only too well the dreadful toll that is exacted – we've done pun cold turkey and dried out more times than we can count. But, when it comes to reviewing a firm with shipping work we're off the wagon faster than you can say shiver me timbers.

In recent years Stephenson Harwood has voyaged across the high seas (honk!) of a flagging economy and the perilous reefs (honk! honk!) of a complex merger that saw partners, qualifiers and assistants lost overboard or jumping ship (cymbal crash... aah thank you!). At one stage people wondered if it would founder on a business strategy that seemed to have moved too far from core strengths. But then last year *"the firm really began to turn the corner"* and now looks to be thriving under the careful stewardship of a new, young managing partner. He has, by all accounts, *"created the feeling of a new start"* whilst overseeing the firm's return to the carefully charted waters of its traditional practice strengths. It hasn't been plain sailing all the way: lateral hires at partner and senior assistant level in 2004 and 2005 have strengthened the finance practice with aviation, shipping and capital markets lawyers arriving, but the firm also lost a ship finance expert to a rival firm, Holman Fenwick & Willan and some litigators. Similarly, new employment, real estate and corporate lawyers added ballast and the firm delivered a 20% profit increase for 2004/5, yet overall turnover was down for the second year running. Nevertheless, in spite of crew changes, the indicators are that SH is on an increasingly even keel.

All eyes are upon the central banking and asset finance teams, which have delivered a substantial increase in income over recent years, suggesting that the refocus on core abilities is bearing fruit. Just as significantly, trainees told a similarly cheering story. Though they bore some scars ("*when I first joined morale was rock bottom, people kept leaving*"), all noted a growing "*feeling of real vibrancy.*" One enthused: "*There have been pay increases recently, the marketing events seem more lavish and everyone seems confident about the direction the firm is going in.*" Add in a refit of the firm's St Paul's Churchyard premises "*because the partners realise the post-merger refit skimped a bit and looks shabby now,*" and it seems the good ship SH is well primed for its forthcoming voyages.

## oh buoy!

When it comes to plotting their own course through the two years, trainees find themselves cruising along well-marked channels. One seat must be taken in either banking and asset finance (ship financing amongst other things) or shipping litigation. Though possible to spend time in both (if you really really love ships), anyone with a predisposition to seasickness will be relieved to learn that "*if you do one, you don't have to do the other.*" Beyond this there are no other compulsories so long as you fulfil the basic Law Society contentious/non-contentious requirements. There are seats available in real estate and commercial litigation (including

construction), corporate (including tax), and employment, pensions and benefits. For added excitement, overseas postings are offered in Hong Kong and Singapore. Reflecting on the available options, one source concluded: "*Our banking and finance is mainly asset finance, so we're almost more of a litigation firm with real estate and asset finance prongs.*" However they chose to define or classify the firm, trainees understood perfectly well that they were "*training under people who do excellent work.*"

Maritime and international trade is such a broad business sector that it occupies lawyers across the firm though trainees most frequently come into contact with matters maritime through the banking and asset finance (BAF) department. Known for its "*long hours,*" the department deals with work that is both international in scope and, at times, very high in value. To use one recent example, it advised various parties in the $900 million purchase of four oil tankers as part of the Qatargas II/III and Rasgas III projects in the Gulf – just one part of what is thought to be the largest ship-ordering bonanza ever, anywhere. Beyond the sea, an increasing emphasis on aviation has paid off in terms of new work. This year the BAF lawyers advised Bank of Scotland Aircraft Finance on an $11 million financing of a Boeing 757 by way of an operating lease to UK charter airline, Astraeus. A trainee's role in a BAF seat can involve "*a lot of bibling and form filling,*" although thankfully other more rewarding tasks exist too. General banking and PFI transactions such as the recent instruction from Royal Bank of Scotland on the Plymouth NHS LIFT project gave some trainees "*the opportunity for both client contact and a lot of research work.*"

## don't call me shirley!

SH possesses an excellent reputation for shipping litigation and commercial litigation. And seats are available in each. Like the shipping side of BAF, shipping litigation "*has a slightly more idiosyncratic atmosphere... quite macho and shouty.*" Depending on your disposition, this in turn is either "*invigorat-*

ing" or "*stressful.*" Shipping litigation ranges from claims against insurers for groundings, losses of cargo or detainment of vessels to complex matters such as the recent successful defense of a client in $24 million proceedings resulting from the collapsed financing of a bulk carrier fleet. Even those trainees who weren't immediately inclined towards this area told us: "*It's a very entertaining seat; I did the best work I've had there – working on the freezing of international assets in an oil dispute, going to court weekly and taking witness statements.*" On the commercial litigation side, lawyers have handled "*some very press-friendly matters*" of late, including the legal pursuit of Dame Shirley Porter's hidden cash-stash on behalf of Westminster City Council. Less newsworthy was a high-stakes claim by IXIS Corporate & Investment Bank against the arranger and lead managers of a £750 million securitisation transaction that went wrong. The department also counts Bank of America, Cadbury Schweppes and London Underground amongst its litigation customers, and trainees were pleased to report decent exposure, "*preparing witness statements and writing letters to clients.*" Some lucky people had also come into contact with "*the art-related cases that we do for a major auction house.*"

Real estate provides the third major slice of the firm's work; in fact between them real estate, litigation and BAF account for nearly two-thirds of business. Our sources had enjoyed "*being given 10-12 cases to run yourself and being the primary point of contact for clients.*" Responsibility comes especially "*when you're working for a supervisor who is the main contact for a big developer,*" though away from the excitement of new development projects, "*extensions of leases and property management issues*" are the stock-in-trade. At times there is "*an all-hands-to-the-pump mentality,*" but the payoff is seeing matters close up and feeling like an integral part of the crew. Time spent in real estate is valued as a first-seat experience, but as across the departments, our sources noticed that "*by your third seat you're effectively expected to be sending things out*

under your own steam and working much more proactively.*" If this prospect is an enticing one, so too is the knowledge that "*the support is there if you need it,*" and many of those we spoke to took confidence in the feeling that "*the partners are very good at telling whether you're suited to more responsibility, and they're not shy to give it.*"

Corporate plays a lesser role than it does in many similarly sized City firms. It is not that the firm isn't skilled in this area or lacks specialised knowledge – indeed it boasts a fine investment funds practice and acts for a number of institutions on their corporate investments – it's more that the emphasis lies elsewhere.

## art snubs

Trainees observed with slight puzzlement that part of the latest refit of their office includes, "*a whole bunch of modern art which is a very unStephenson Harwood bit of flashiness.*" Still, if the abstract shapes and provocative themes prove too much to bear, all they need do is look out of the window at "*the beautiful view of St. Paul's Cathedral.*" Situated practically on hallowed ground, the office is also close to the shops and cafés of Cheapside and Paternoster Square, and it's only a short hop across the Millennium footbridge to Tate Modern. As such "*the lack of a canteen*" doesn't weigh too heavily, with groups of trainees "*regularly meeting up for sandwiches by the river or in the square.*" Back in – or should we say on – SH HQ, "*the roof terrace is the real hub for firm socialising,*" playing host to regular drinks evenings, "*barbecues in the summer*" and any number of client events. The latter tend to be themed – "*lately we've had James Bond, Burns' night and midsummer night,*" and the excuse to dress up isn't the only enjoyable feature of these evenings – "*trainees get invited to marketing events a lot and you're expected to help host them so you really feel included and involved.*" Combine this with "*very decent*" hours of 9am to 6.30ish and it's not hard to see why "*everyone wanted to stay on this year.*" Unfortunately, one legacy of the recent past is a trainee population larger than the firm can currently support upon qualification, which explains why in September 2005 only six of the 11 qualifiers stayed on with the firm.

A business-casual dress code prevails when dinner suits and kilts are not required, and we sense that this style of dress is wholly appropriate for a firm that has a certain calmness and gentility to its nature. After work, sports teams help promote team spirit and, when not roof-bound, "*trainees and junior associates mix together a lot*" in local hostelries such as The Cock Pit and The Rising Sun. Trainees "*all get on well*," but with an average age of "*mid-to-late 20s,*" and the majority having had "*some experience other than the straight-through route,*" few live in each other's pockets. We noted graduates from a broad spread of universities among the trainee group – "*from Oxford, Manchester and Southampton to Hull, Brunel and De Montfort,*" and concluded that attempting to stereotype them was futile.

## and finally...

Stephenson Harwood excels in shipping, is rightfully proud of a great name in litigation and is making some notable inroads into finance areas beyond its established stomping ground of asset finance. An interest in any of these practice groups is definitely the best reason for choosing the firm, but our sources would string us from the yardarm if we didn't highlight the firm's pleasant nature as an equally compelling factor.

# Taylor Vinters

## the facts

**Location:** Cambridge
**Number of partners/assistants:** 28/40
**Total number of trainees:** 14
**Seats:** 4x6 months
**Alternative seats:** Brussels, secondments

Taylor Vinters' commitment to the Cambridge area is paying off. Dynamic industry sectors join with the east of England's Establishment to support a broad practice which spans corporate, property, IP/IT and life sciences, tax and trusts, family, personal injury, rural affairs, food law, bloodstock and equestrian law.

## racing forwards

This veritable star shower of skills is the result of the fusion "*50 odd years ago*" of Newmarket private client and agriculture firm Taylors with Vinters, a Cambridge-based commercial outfit. The result is a successful firm, with a "*full-service ideal*" and the capacity to handle clients' business, property and personal affairs... "*and then, of course, we can sort out the horses as well.*"

The most recent side effect of the Taylor Vinters chemical reaction is $T^2$, the firm's commercial and technology team. Undertaking a broad range of work for Cambridge's life sciences, hi-tech and biotech communities, $T^2$ has a prominent position on the firm's table of elements. Its focus on biopharmaceuticals is evident through clients such as Roche Diagnostics, Argenta Discovery, BioWisdom and Sareum. There is also superb IP work for clients such as Cambridge Silicon Radio and Xennia Technology, and commercial IT advice for clients including online booking services company Active Hotels and software components supplier Gissing Software. From trainees we heard that technology and IP work is "*really going to be pushed and pushed hard,*" the firm having "*essentially taken the entire Eversheds Cambridge team lock, stock and barrel*" in May 2005. Indeed, with the arrival of Eversheds' former national head of IP, Patrick Farrant, it certainly seems that this is where TV is set to make the biggest bang.

## a good turn every day

Through four seats, trainees are exposed to the full spectrum of TV's work and encounter clients ranging from Cancer Research UK to Wisdom

Toothbrushes, and the University of Cambridge to the Girl Guide Association. As is common elsewhere, "*second-years get first dibs on seats*" and "*in the first year you go where you are put.*" After this the firm tries hard to accommodate an individual's interests and "*if needs be, they will split a seat for you – they don't like doing it, but they want you to do what you want to do.*"

"*Chances are, you will do a PI seat in the first year*" and it is "*a really good seat to start in as it gets you used to the working environment, you are trained quite closely and you aren't thrown in at the deep end so much.*" The first-class team is known for its catastrophic brain and spinal injury work, particularly on claims arising out of accidents at work and on the road. While their mentors achieve awards valued in the hundreds of thousands of pounds, trainees work on much smaller matters, taking the lead on witness statements, drafting schedules of loss and interviewing clients. Even the most skeptical source admitted: "*I may have been put off applying if I had realised what a big PI firm it was, but it is not something that should put people off because the training in PI is very structured and valid.*"

"*The firm also tries to make sure all trainees do a property seat*" in rural services, planning and development, or commercial property. Deals such as the development of a £40 million cancer research centre at Addenbrookes Hospital for the University of Cambridge and the redevelopment of King's Parade in Cambridge City Centre for King's College attracts trainees to the department. One told us they really enjoyed their planning and development seat after "*starting to recognise all the different sites, and thinking 'That's my block of flats!'*" Or how about rural services for something "*a bit different?*" Here, trainees negotiate their own farm tenancies and small land sales and purchases; plus there is the added excitement of "*writing copious reviews of Farmers Weekly*" to keep colleagues up to date.

For commercially minded trainees there are two seats in corporate. The team acts for "*very small family businesses right up to AIM-listed plcs,*" so in

addition to "*assisting on bits and bobs*" there are "*smaller transactions that trainees can actually be involved in. It is fantastic from our perspective because the processes you go through are the same as for bigger transactions.*" In addition to decent responsibility and client contact across their seats, plus advocacy if you want it, there is also "*less grunt work than expected.*"

## the mussels from brussels

Lawyers usually adhere to a civilised 9ish till 6ish working day and our sources muttered about "*lots of that quality of life stuff.*" Obviously there will be longer days in busy departments, but "*if you enjoy working until 3am every day, it is not the place for you.*" If old-school formality is also your bag, you may want to look elsewhere: TV operates a "*fairly horizontal*" internal structure. A new committee gives secretaries, admin staff, junior lawyers and trainees a chance to have their say on anything from ideas about future strategy to which paperclips should be purchased. This year, trainees also participated in a business management game ("*Monopoly with knobs on*"), described as "*a glorified board game showing the foot soldiers how the partners earn their corn.*" For hands-on tuition in the art of earning a living, trainees need go no further than a desk close to their supervisor in the open-plan office. Relationships over the partitions are generally easygoing and "*there are always people around to answer your daft questions.*" Three-monthly appraisals "*basically come down to a chat with your supervisor*" and, more typically, TV's "*fairly informal*" approach means that any issues are dealt with as and when they arise.

Confident and bright, our sources were drawn from across the twenty-nothing-thirty-something divide and most had some pre-existing link with Cambridge, be this through family or uni. They left us in no doubt that this is where their career ambitions lay although one or two lucky trainees opt to spend a few months on an overseas placement with a firm in Brussels called Crosby Renouf. "*The trainee's job is to answer the hotline queries that come* through on random bits of European law," so for anyone with a developing interest in competition law, state aid and such like, a spell here is ideal. They also get to occupy a flat that "even the Clifford Chance and A&O trainees look upon with envy."

## the future's orange

In stark contrast to Crosby Renouf's location in a building shared with the German Embassy, TV's HQ is effectively a large grey bunker (codenamed "General Belgrano") on a business park on the Cambridge Science Park. One dry source told us: "Very big and very grey is quite a charitable description;" another said: "It sounds quite dismal really, doesn't it? It's not the most amazing building, but it does stand out and the location is really important to the firm." Indeed it is – across the road are a host of hi- and biotech ventures. In a bid to improve the offices, professional space planners were brought in to "produce all these fantastic graphs showing where we were at what times of day, and the temperature in the offices." One trainee announced: "I think I might have missed my vocation!" Mutterings about doing away with open-plan working and high hopes for a canteen are yet to be addressed so, for now, "the sandwich van across the road is the most successful business in the business park." The firm lays on lunch for its lawyers three Fridays a month.

TV's out-of-town location means "the amenities of Cambridge are a no-go" during the day but Q.Ton on the Science Park ("a sort of restaurant-cum-bar thing with the most improbable opening hours") is the local hangout when inclement weather precludes pub lunches by the river and in nearby villages. For years now, the Student Guide has played hunt the secret beer fridge. The secrecy of its location was always the most fascinating aspect of its existence and so you can only imagine how upset we were to learn that not only does everyone now know exactly where it is (in corporate), but "there has been a proliferation of beer fridges around the firm." Of course, "the original beer fridge is still the best." A social committee organises bowling,

karaoke, trips to the races plus summer and Christmas parties, last year's Christmas bash being held in King's College. Sports teams have "a fairly big presence in the firm" – football, hockey and rugby are all on offer, and when we called a cricket team had just returned from the Slovenian leg of its world tour.

Every year, TV celebrates the festive season with a pantomime. Trainees are more than welcome to join in the fun but are permitted to take only parts that befit their status. "In Snow White and the Seven Dwarves we were trees; in Charlie and the Chocolate Factory we were Oompa Loompas." Commenting on their festive humiliation, one source moaned: "After the Oompa Loompas, we are going to be unemployable anywhere else." Not a problem for this year's qualifiers – all five found golden tickets and jobs with the firm.

## and finally...

Taylor Vinters is unquestionably Cambridge-focused in its business plan, and if your interests are similarly so, it's an ideal choice.

# Taylor Wessing

## the facts

**Location:** London, Cambridge
**Number of partners/assistants:** 101/154
**Total number of trainees:** 44
**Seats:** 4x6 months
**Alternative seats:** Overseas seats, secondments
**Extras:** Pro bono – Blackfriars settlement Legal Advice Clinic; language training

Taylor Wessing is a mid-sized Anglo-German firm that excels in the IP and life sciences arena whilst also acquitting itself impressively in mainstream commercial work.

## the great fork debate

The last few years have seen the firm try on different labels in order to find the exact name and image that fits its aims and practice. A bid to develop stronger European focus was achieved decisively by the 2002 merger of Taylor Joynson Garrett with the German firm Wessing. That took care of the name. As for the image, the firm tried variations on a theme. First it was an IP/IT/life sciences specialist with full-service back up; then full-service firm with good IP/IT/life sciences lawyers. And now? We thought we'd quiz the trainees...

...who seemed no more clear than we were. "*Are we a multi-service firm with a healthy IP practice or a specialist IP firm which has a number of bolt-on commercial operations?*" asked one trainee. "*If we're holding a trump card, why aren't we playing it?*" reasoned another. The issue then is one of not only identity but also intention.

In the well-known land law case of Street v Mountford, Lord Templeman effectively said that a garden fork is a garden fork no matter what you call it. Taking this argument to its logical conclusion surely a law firm is a law firm no matter what you call it. Well, sort of. The thing is that a garden fork doesn't generally develop a business plan and nor does it rely upon the goodwill and self-image of its individual prongs. A law firm on the other hand needs to know what it is and how it wishes to develop. If this keeps changing – even if only ever so slightly – then its message and people can become confused. Moreover, when you're applying to train with a firm it's important to know where it is going and what it might become by the time you start working there. Basically, you want an assurance that the *Ground Force* team isn't waiting behind your gate to transform your garden while you pop out to the shops.

Having said all this, no one we spoke to had been duped into coming to TW on false promises. If anything, the debate as to what the firm sees when it looks in the mirror has enabled trainees to grasp the mantle in every seat they undertake. "*The firm appears to have a lot of growth areas at the moment, meaning plenty of possible career avenues for trainees.*" They should soon be able to feel the full benefit of the firm's recently stated desire to widen its European reach, as German and French seats are "*in the pipeline.*"

## spirit in the sky

TW runs a four-seat training with a compulsory stint in corporate. The seat allocation process won a hearty slap on the back from trainees. "*If you don't get what you want for your seat, the people in grad recruitment will make sure that you're well looked after next time around.*" Meetings at the beginning of the traineeship enable the HR people to gain a good idea of where you see yourself going and establish a preliminary seat plan. Nothing is so final that it can't be altered down the line should you discover a passion for something unexpected.

We encountered a raft of positive feedback when it came to individual seats. Said one source: "*The great thing about every seat has been the fact that as trainees we're not hidden away in the slightest; we do get to meet the big-name clients.*" Most acknowledged that the compulsory corporate seat is "*pretty hardcore*" and can involve "*a continuous stream of 18-hour days.*" A dramatic claim but you'll understand their basic point – at times the hours can feel hellish. Though the seat brings much of "*the donkey work that is inevitable for a trainee,*" our sources found the silver lining in the cloud. "*The late hours do lead to real team spirit,*" yawned one, while another proudly detailed the occasions when he'd worked solo on joint ventures and sale and purchase agreements.

The real estate team was universally commended as "*a really fun department to work in.*" There's no doubt that the firm is steadily increasing its market profile in this practice area, particularly in relation to large property finance transactions. Significantly, it advised the Bank of Scotland on a £650 million funding for the acquisition of six UK shopping centres and on the acquisition and financing of a £500 million sale and leaseback between the UK's largest independently managed pub operator, Spirit, and the joint venture set-up between West Coast Capital, Prestbury Investment Holdings and Bank of Scotland. The involvement of a (West Coast) US investor is not uncommon on TWs deals; the firm has developed a good reputation with this type of client. Real estate is the best seat for gaining practical experience, regular interaction with clients and running your own small files. The private client practice was equally well endorsed and "*you could do a lot worse than a seat in the pensions group.*"

## enigma variations

Most of those we spoke to freely admit the firm's IP reputation had governed or at least influenced their decision to join the firm. TW is a titan in this area of practice and sits right at the top of the league tables prepared by our parent publication *Chambers UK*. On the so-called 'soft' IP side the firm covers trade marks, copyright, passing off and other brands advice. The soft seat is "*the one that leads to the best dinner party conversations*" and is consequently extremely popular with trainees. The department has recently started advising Christian Dior on trade mark matters and counts as clients the authors Dick Francis and Terry Pratchett and the estates of composers Irving Berlin, Ira Gershwin, Delius and Elgar.

'Hard' IP is commonly reserved for the ex-scientists among the trainee group. Whilst professing an interest in scientific matters may swing you a seat in patent litigation, if you want to feel like you're actually being useful, specialist knowledge will prove invaluable and each year the firm recruits a number of trainees with extensive scientific and technical qualifications and/or experience in the knowledge that they can "*add value with [their] previous experience and expertise.*" The right kind of trainee can really be useful; one source attended a trial, helped to prepare experts' witness statements and cross-examinations, watched experiments and schmoozed clients. There is no guarantee that you'll see a trial because patent litigation can go on for years and your seat may bring you into the depart-

ment at a less dramatic stage of the litigation process. Among the firm's most recent major patent matters is the House of Lords pharmaceuticals case Kirin-Amgen v Transkaryotic Therapies. We should stress that not all IP work is litigious. Proving this point the firm has lately been advising Geron on a stem cell collaboration agreement.

Client secondments (BA, Toyota, Discovery Channel) continue to be extremely popular. "*It's a great way of making contacts and finding out what clients actually want from their lawyers,*" reported one of the lucky few who had experienced a six-month break from the firm. If you want to work with a particularly "*young and vibrant team,*" a corporate seat in the firm's smaller Cambridge office is also a possibility. In case you were wondering, the office was brought into the fold in 2002 when the old Andersen Legal network collapsed.

## river of dreams

Smart glass and steel offices on the north bank of the Thames provide superb views and allow "*a leisurely stroll along by the river during lunch or after work.*" Chances are you will actually get the time for that stroll because apart from the potential horrors of the corporate seat ("*when you gotta stay late, you gotta stay late*"), the working day is manageable. Full marks also for the facilities and support staff: "*We have everything we need, the library is well stocked, the IT guy is incredible and we even get our own laptops.*" A model of law firm efficiency? Well, that's the aim.

The seniority of supervisors varies according to the seat undertaken, a feature welcomed by trainees. "*Being exposed to different personalities and levels of seniority enables you to take a lot more on board,*" they told us. Interestingly, one or two of our sources felt the firm was rather partner-heavy, or to use their words: "*Too many chiefs and not enough Indians.*" Maybe this was the view of the management board. We understand that in the next couple of years it plans to trim down the number of equity partners. In general, the appraisal system operates successfully, although there were the usual murmurings about certain supervisors dragging their heels on completing and returning feedback forms. "*The idea is that the trainee has a mid-seat review after three months then a longer one at the end, although inevitably along the way the supervisor lets you know when you're going in the wrong direction.*" The trainees who qualified in September 2005 were clearly headed in the right direction: 13 of the 14 stayed with the firm.

## sunk by a preacher man

And so to important news concerning the trainees' social lives. It's official: after spending several years groaning on its deathbed, The Witness Box's last rites have been read. When Friday comes along, The Evangelist is now the pub of choice due to its "*potent blend of vibrancy and light.*" (!) When we spoke to trainees they were gearing up for TW's 'Angels and Devils' summer party at Tantra, which if anything like last year, should have been "*a wildly entertaining night out.*" A variety of sporting options are also available to the energetic trainee, and teams are entered in a host of different competitions across Europe, giving people the chance to dazzle clients with their footwork as well as their legal ability. Any reader who's into cricket and wondering why the name Taylor Wessing is so familiar, let us put you out of your misery – yes, this firm was one of the sponsors of the England v Australia Test matches.

## and finally...

If you're from a scientific background but want to keep your options open before committing yourself to an IP career, then this firm is an excellent choice. The inverse is true for any law or arts student who regrets putting down their conical flask at a young age.

# TLT Solicitors

## the facts

**Location:** Bristol, London
**Number of partners/assistants:** 51/91
**Total number of trainees:** 14
**Seats:** 4x6 months
**Alternative seats:** Secondments

An ever-growing firm, TLT is intent on strengthening its position as Bristol's 'number three'. Bristol's legal animal farm can now rival the city's zoo: Burges has its Salmon, Osborne Clarke parades a panther logo and now a greyhound graces TLT's website. Will the mutt try to take on the big cat? Will TLT leave other Bristol firms eating its dust? Which will become the official beast of Bristol?

## playing footsy 100

Five years ago when Trumps met Lawrence Tucketts it was love and the pairing produced a firm that proved dreams really can come true. The new firm targeted the local businesses overlooked by larger and less regionally focused rivals and the strategy paid off. TLT has grown plump and healthy. After consolidating this local client base, the firm recently took the decision to pack a handkerchief, sling it over a stick and set off for London town where it has found a new merger partner in the form of a small but established 11-partner firm with a healthy banking practice called Lawrence Jones. The merger has provided a clear signal of TLT's commitment to the expansion of its already substantial banking and finance department (HSBC, Lloyds TSB and RBS all use its services) and its awareness that a City base is the only realistic way to do this. For its part, Lawrence Jones brought a dowry of good clients including Allied Irish Bank and Banco Espirito Santo.

Away from the banking world, TLT's other primary interests are also commercial. It has beefed-up its retail and leisure, construction, financial services, technology and media departments in the past year and must have been particularly pleased when its licensing and property teams were joined by two partners from Osborne Clarke. Locally, TLT has found success with the Avon Rubber Group, Severn Delta and the charming characters at Aardman Animations. It has been working with the Wallace and Gromit creators since they climbed into the Wrong Trousers and strutted off to Cannes carrying 'The Curse of the Were-Rabbit.'

It's not all Wensleydale and cracker crumbs, however. The firm provides commercial and IT legal services to Imperial Tobacco, the world's fourth biggest tobacco manufacturer. As any local historian will tell you, it is perhaps only fitting that a tobacco giant sends business to Bristol, though just in case you're turned off by such unpleasantries, we'll add that, in all, some 11 FTSE 100 companies instruct the firm. Much of the time it is local enterprises that jostle for a trainee's attention. Most recently, Shakespeare at the Tobacco Factory – the premier bard company in the South West – sought advice from the firm when converting to a charity. Brimming with Bristolian pride, TLT has also given planning advice on a controlled preservation environment around Brunel's steamer SS Great Britain.

## monitored for training purposes

Trainees tell us that working in the banking and lender services department, which handles new loans and a lot of debt recovery cases, can sometimes feel like *"a call centre."* Debt recovery is often allocated to new arrivals, and that's probably the best time for a seat that effectively balances *"getting you into the thick of things"* with *"tight supervision for learning the ropes."* Sure, debt recovery work gives you immediate responsibility for your own cases and valuable court experience – trainees can appear alone before a district judge in their first week – but there is a sense that once you've done it a few times you're over it. Basically, you instantly become *"disciplined as a solicitor"* whether you like the work or not. Residential conveyancing is

another area in which trainees are *"let loose straight away"* on their own files.

Handling your own files does not have to mean staying late every night. Indeed, most of those we spoke to had only laboured after hours once or twice during their training and had been happy to do so when circumstances dictated. Longer hours are most likely to be clocked up in corporate where the experience differs greatly from the own-show deal of some other seats. Trainees assist on partners' work and learn to become their shadows. Our sources spoke of probing clients for information, helping to draft disclosure letters or other core documents, as well as producing board minutes and resolutions after meetings. It all adds up to a sense of having *"a lot of involvement."*

Though they have bags of choice in Bristol including seats in general commercial, construction and corporate defence, commercial property and commercial dispute resolution, the Lawrence Jones merger has opened up the prospect of spending six months in London and added a shipping seat to the list. Seats are allocated in meetings with the HR manager and, interestingly, one of the most sought-after options is to be found in the smaller, non-commercial part of the firm. TLT's private client limb contains a tax and trusts seat and a seat in its top-ranked family law department. Indeed, several trainees freely admitted to us that family law had been the thing that drew them to the firm in the first place. In this department trainees become *"involved in all aspects of family law,"* with cohabitation and divorce files mixed in with care proceedings. Most get to do at least one unsupervised meeting with a client and attend court for a variety of different hearings. Be aware that just one family seat is available at any one time so there is no guarantee you'll get it. Employment is another hot seat although this year the entrance of two newly qualified solicitors into the department meant it became unavailable to trainees for six months. One seat that is always open is property; indeed, according to trainees it is quasi-compulsory.

# the true picture

## smells like team spirit

A brief glance at TLT's training brochure sums up the mood of the firm. On one page, athletes strain on starting blocks, a trio of parachutists freefall upside-down on another; momentum and expectancy meet a team focus. Our sources' comments likewise teemed with *"teams." "Team players"* were everywhere, along with cricket teams, netball teams and a softball team (currently riding high in the Property Surveyors League – hurrah!). In short, *"people need to be a team"* and TLT's sporting life requires all to play along.

Ranked at number 96 in the *Sunday Times'* survey of '100 Best Companies to Work For', TLT by all accounts is an equally pleasant place to train. It's all about being embraced by the team, so *"don't come if you want a true City replica... you actually get your hands dirty."* Best of all, *"trainees are not put in a cupboard!"* Instead, they're out there meeting clients and making contacts at seminars and workshops organised by the firm. We take our hats off to the brain who comes up with the titles of these marketing-slash-education events – 'Asbestos: an inspector calls'. Pure genius!

TLT's Redcliff Street office is *"modern"* with *"modern art"* and a *"modern"* feel. To match its waterfront location, the chosen décor is *"beech and blue"* like the website. The open-plan office may be formal – and did we mention modern – but there is *"an inclusive culture and no department is avoided."* Supervisors, more often than not an associate rather than a partner, are close at hand, most trainees sitting with theirs. Individual feedback on work goes beyond the set three-monthly appraisals: supervisors are always prepared to go through trainees' efforts and explain what went wrong. Trainees described their relationship with partners as *"transparent,"* telling us this limpidity ensures that the steering of the firm is open for all to see. Certainly everyone we spoke to was fully aware of managing partner David Pester's mission to take TLT *"from a top-100 to a top-50 law firm." "It's really exciting to work for someone with a vision,"* effused

one source. It was disappointing to hear, then, that in September 2005 only one of the three qualifiers took jobs with the firm.

## bard drinkers

Older editions of the *Student Guide* lamented the demise of TLT's old drinking den, the Shakespeare. Alas, a new tavern has yet to be presided over by the Falstaffs of the firm, but this may be due to the efforts of an active social committee that has organised everything from jaunts to Amsterdam and Alton Towers, snowboarding at the Tamworth Ski Dome and a booze cruise to France. The most outlandish spree is the annual dragon boat race that draws TLT staff to the River Avon. Even the partners get involved. Don't always count on partner participation, however; they do seem to have a performance problem at the annual Christmas party and, as yet, have failed to rise to the occasion with a skit. The excuse this year was the pressure of the Lawrence Jones merger. Reliable as ever, trainees put on a mock awards ceremony to entertain the revellers. *"If you're a wuss the Christmas party is a horror,"* whispered one source. Let's hope next year the partners can at least manage to belt out an S-Club tribute.

## and finally...

Two key themes come out of TLT – the team and the vision. The current vision to expand is great news for prospective trainees, who will enter the firm at a time of growing opportunities.

# Teacher Stern Selby

## the facts

**Location:** London
**Number of partners/assistants:** 21/24
**Total number of trainees:** 10
**Seats:** 4x6 months
**Alternative seats:** None
**Extras:** Pro Bono – Toynbee Hall Legal Advice Centre

Teacher Stern Selby sits at the smaller end of 'medium-sized', has crafted itself an understated public profile, and undertakes a standard division of labour – property, coco and litigation. So far so mainstream, but this thirty-something success story can also carry off some highly contentious ensembles.

## occupying the middle ground

When explaining their reasons for choosing TSS, one trainee told us: "*I didn't want a massive firm, but I didn't want to go to one bloke and his brother; I didn't want to be the first trainee for five years or do the photocopying and make the coffee.*" Within such broad parameters, why opt for TSS over any other firm falling between the corporate monolith and Bloggs Bros? According to its trainees, TSS is "*very commercially minded. Partners are incredibly well versed in the legal aspects, but you don't do stuff because it is legal and clever, you do it to get the result for the client.*" We also heard that TSS is "*not staid, traditional or stuffy.*" Certainly, a brief glance at the firm's groundbreaking education negligence work and its superb media practice implies this. Think about it any longer and you have to conclude that any firm that advises on the alleged nocturnal rompages of Premiership footballers has to be "*open minded.*"

For trainees, the existence of the three key departments means six months spent in each of property, corporate and litigation before returning to a department of choice for the final six months. Time and again we heard how "*people are placed*

*where they want to be*" and "*the firm bends over backwards to accommodate you.*" If three compulsory seats sounds a little prescriptive, rest assured "*you really do get a mix of work.*" Within each seat, the bulk of a trainee's workload comes from their supervisor, so getting the right supervisor would appear to be the key to happiness. The firm is open to requests for particular supervisors in order to receive particular work, "*as long as it doesn't screw the system up too much.*"

## AIMing high

"*Definitely the largest department, with a lot of big deals,*" property is "*good to do for a first seat.*" It exposes trainees to the core of the firm and is excellent preparation for subsequent seats as "*a lot of the litigation can be property oriented and in coco things are often property driven.*" The team carries out residential and commercial transactions worth "*anything up to £100 million*" and is instructed by a broad mix of clients, including developers, investors, landlords and tenants, a number of them private companies and "*private individuals using their own capital.*" Trainees also noted a preponderance of shopping centre work and secured lending for UK clearing banks and building societies.

Though the classic cog-in-wheel analogy lends itself to the trainee's role on larger property transactions, our sources insisted they were "*a larger cog compared to what you would be at other firms.*" In addition to this supporting role, "*every trainee will do a file from start to finish.*" It may be a simple residential matter ("*mine turned out to be a bit of an exam question – you could just see someone thinking it up*"), but it gives the trainee a much-valued opportunity to "*do pretty much everything a normal solicitor would do.*"

A spell in coco exposes trainees to mergers and acquisitions, disposals, joint ventures and buyouts plus AIM listings. As "*a by-product of the property stuff,*" a chunk of the coco work involves tax-planning strategies for property deals, and there are also employment matters to manage and commercial transactions with elements of media, IP, IT and e-commerce. Instead of a spell of pure coco, some trainees are seated within the firm's small private client team. Not an ideal posting for a deal junkie, but if you'd rather be drafting wills and powers of attorney than board minutes and stock transfer forms, speak up.

## legal education

TSS' litigation department is *"split into quarters"* – property, commercial, media/entertainment and *"the medical and educational negligence bit."* The work available to trainees will depend on which supervisor they sit with, though *"most people, regardless of who they sit with, would do both property and commercial litigation."* Trainees accept that they are *"involved at a relatively low level"* but suggest *"you do end up further up the scale than you would at a larger firm."* And what could be higher up the scale than popping along to the High Court, Court of Appeal or House of Lords, as some of our sources had done. On these larger cases, standard tasks naturally include research and the inevitable bundle preparation. On the subject of boring admin, one voice of reason observed that *"you can't let your ego get in the way of the work."* Trainees additionally manage smaller debt claims and minor employment matters themselves, so there is at least some room for a little ego.

A six-month stint of medical and educational negligence under the tutelage of Jack Rabinowicz is *"very much a coveted seat."* His small but stellar practice has a national reputation for groundbreaking work for individual claimants. On the medical negligence side, there are cerebral palsy and birth defects cases, and in terms of educational negligence, *"some of it is for people who really have been screwed by the system; other clients are trying to fit into the system."* The firm takes on matters as diverse as *"the kid who has been expelled, and the kid who is at one school and wants to be somewhere else,"* plus cases of children whose special educational needs have not been met or who have been bullied. Currently it is challenging the Scottish Parliament's power to charge students from England, Wales and Northern Ireland more for university tuition than students from Scotland and other EU countries. It is also involved in the judicial review of a local education authority's refusal to contribute to a 14-year-old's private school fees on the grounds that her exceptional intelligence did not constitute a special educational need. Trainees lucky enough to spend time with Jack Rabinowicz encounter not only judicial review but also special educational needs tribunals. They are permitted to draft instructions to counsel, sit in at court and attend client meetings. It can be gruelling stuff – as one observed: *"This is people's lives: if you don't win the case, the kid can't go back to school. It is like criminal law – it is costly, and involved."*

Just as *"you have to sit with Jack to get education and medical negligence,"* so for media work *"you have to be in the right place at the right time."* The right place is somewhere in the vicinity of Graham Shear's desk, and the work revolves around defamation and reputation management for international celebrities and sports personalities. Shear's team has advised Dwain Chambers in respect of the athlete testing positive to THG and Rio Ferdinand following his failure to attend a drugs test. The team was also involved in protecting the identities of certain Premiership footballers embroiled in speculation regarding the alleged rape of a 17-year-old.

## viva las vegas

The firm's contemporary contentious work belies a good old-fashioned approach to training, including a valuable *"partner-led style"* that equally marks its approach to clients. A programme of lunchtime seminars for trainees, plus departmental meetings, supplement the knowledge gained day by day from supervisors who *"always fill you in on the deal and let you know what is going on."* Our sources told us: *"They take notice of what you have been doing"* and *"if you do something well they definitely praise you. You get a good feeling."* *"They explained a lot to me,"* one added. As well as quarterly appraisals, there are trainee meetings once a month *"just to make sure everything is ticking over."* The training partner *"keeps a close eye on us,"* informed one trainee.

Our sources praised the firm for not having a *"work-till-midnight ethos."* Apart from a smattering of late nights when needs must, a reasonable 9am to 6.30ish day is perfectly possible. Said one source: *"They are very understanding and appreciate that we all have lives outside of our jobs."* This is arguably a beneficial side effect of the firm's Jewish heritage. After hours, there is *"no regimented social life."* The firm organises occasional quiz nights and a drinks party on the last Friday of the month. Trainees have acquired a habit of hanging out in Starbucks at lunchtime, and on a Friday evening local pub, The Old Nick, has been known to waylay lawyers and staff. The Christmas party is a black tie affair, and last year took on a Las Vegas theme. Entertainment was provided by a Chinese Elvis and fancy dress was optional. Amazingly trainees were divided on this point. Said one: *"I think it's hideous!"* Another told us: *"I was definitely a part of the black-tie brigade."* And so it seems that while partners are more than happy to make appearances as Elton John or bunny girls, for trainees *"nothing is expected of you except not to get horribly drunk and barf all over the floor."* Hardly likely – our sources came across as a respectable, composed and mature group. All four qualifiers stayed with the firm in September 2005.

## and finally...

Whether you choose it for classic West End property experience, unique education and media expertise or general all-round commercial tutelage, Teacher Stern Selby is a wise choice among the small-to-medium-sized London options.

# Travers Smith

## the facts

**Location:** London
**Number of partners/assistants:** 56/138
**Total number of trainees:** 40
**Seats:** 4x6 months
**Alternative seats:** Paris
**Extras:** Pro bono – ICSL and Paddington law centres, death row appeals, language training

Travers Smith has long been regarded as a member of the 'Golden Circle': an elite band of smaller corporate firms producing 24-carat results for impressive clients through pure talent, rather than monumental mass.

## in the gutter, looking at the stars

For those who are seduced in equal measure by gleaming corporate work and the prospect of a bespoke training, a Travers apprenticeship is an alluring proposition. The hallmark of a Travers training is a room-sharing system that places trainees with both a partner and an assistant, to receive two-on-one tuition plus *"a wonderful insight"* into *"a real variety of work at all degrees of complexity and size."* In a system that retains elements of traditional private tutelage, trainees work under the careful supervision of partners who *"sit you down, explain what needs to be done and why, look at what you've produced then run through it with you again."* Not only does the system provide exceptional personal tuition, from an early stage *"you are close enough to get a picture of what is going on."* So, while a Travers trainee is unlikely to be whipping out his loupe on his first day to examine the intricate detail of the multimillion-pound corporate gem on the counter, he can at least lean over the shoulder of a master craftsman and squint. Certainly, he won't be elbowing his peers into the gutter to press his nose against the shop window.

On display in the Travers luxury goods shop this year are deals with billion-pound price tags. See in the corner that £1.25 billion acquisition of Coral Eurobet and just behind it the £1.27 billion sale of ntl's broadcast division? Ooh look! New client gems in the Travers setting include Hermes Private Equity, NM Rothschild, The Tussauds Group, Wagamama and Saga.

## a cut above

A four-seat system requires trainees to complete a corporate seat (private equity or corporate finance), a contentious seat (employment or litigation) and property or banking. Trainees are informed where they are going next as they progress through their training contract, and though they might feel inclined to *"put in a strongly worded request,"* the reality is that *"the team allocating the seats put you where they think you are needed, and would be strongest."* The nature of the fourth seat is the trainee's own choice. As in most firms *"employment is very popular, people are dying to do it when they come."* Others hanker after corporate recovery and litigation.

A seat in the pivotal corporate department can be a daunting experience: not only is the department *"where we have really shone in recent years, and where we are most highly thought of,"* but also as one source observed: *"It's not particularly tangible if you have no experience of the business world. When presented with the corporate structures of 300 companies on a sheet of paper the size of a wall, it is hard to get your head round it."* We sympathise. This year deals have included the £1.35 billion acquisition of Saga and the £101 million sale of Jimmy Choo. On such large matters trainees are kept on their toes drafting the minutes of board meetings and preparing Companies House filings; on smaller transactions they get to strut their stuff by *"setting up companies and swapping their ownership."*

The corporate department also offers French-speaking trainees a spell in the firm's Paris office. Here, the nature of the office's pan-European work means *"you don't see the overall deal structure as you would in London."* (Perhaps they don't make pieces of paper that big.) To compensate, if you are fortunate enough to work in Paris, before boarding the Eurostar *"you do one month in London to give you exposure to mainstream corporate work too."* What follows is a flat in Montmartre and a fair helping of responsibility in a *"linchpin office."* No wonder our sources described it as an opportunity to *"be in the middle of it all."*

In fact corporate must be considered 'the middle of it all'. Throughout our interviews we heard of *"corporate-support-type work"* being done in all the other departments, which *"dovetail with the corporate department."* Main stage it may be, but the corporate department is no bullring. Any *"cut and thrust"* is diluted by *"a sense of camaraderie"* and gentlemanly behaviour. Corporate work The Travers Way has an air of refinement: this is less the hunting ground of pinstriped Alpha males and more a bastion of good manners and good lawyering.

## man overboard

Travers' litigation team has of late worked on Enron-related issues for a large investment bank and the ongoing representation of the Mirror Group Pension trustees in Maxwell litigation. The team also acts for Tussauds Theme Park in proceedings arising from alleged noise nuisance at Alton Towers. On such large matters a trainee is involved at a low level, but the department's pro bono undertakings provide *"the opportunity to run with your own work."* The other advantage of pro bono work is that *"it moves a lot faster than some of our larger pieces of litigation."* If you need any convincing on this point, just consider the fact that while Mr Maxwell was slipping off the side of his gin palace and into his watery grave, the average trainee was still splashing around in inflatable arm bands. Perhaps Captain Bob should've worn some that fateful night.

By contrast, trainees in property can confidently *"jump in at the deep end"* with client contact from day one, files to *"pretty much run on your own"* and smaller projects to juggle. *"It's terribly nerve wrack-*

ing, but brilliant fun," one trainee enthused. As well as substantial commercial deals, the department handles planning and environmental matters plus financing. For trainees, work "ranges from very basic conveyancing – land searches and stuff – through to heading along to meetings alone with nothing but a brief case and a wodge of business cards."

IT, IP and competition are common choices for that fourth, wild card seat. Or how about trying the "incredibly diverse" pensions seat, which also includes employment and trusts work. Perhaps you'll be tempted by six months in tax where "it is quieter because people are sitting there thinking clever things." But don't think that silence means hitting the snooze button – this more scholarly work invariably means "at the end of the day you are tired in the head." Bless.

## not too posh to paper push

It may be indicative of the type of person Travers recruits that trainees revere the firm's more cerebral work as "what I imagined working here would be like – intellectually challenging and professionally rewarding." To cast our sources as intellectual elitists would be wrong, but there is no escaping the fact that at Travers, there are clear recruitment criteria: "first you need a good academic record" and then "after the academics, they ask if the person will fit in." As well as the "smattering of Oxford and Cambridge" grads, we spotted trainees from a number of highly regarded universities – Durham, Edinburgh, Bristol and "a little St Andrews enclave."

A dib-dib-dib, do-your-best attitude requires a "certain element of mucking in and being ready to turn your hand to all sorts of work." The trainee's lot is a mixed one, but Travers' deals are by and large "not so enormously vast that you are sucked into a data room for months." Several of our sources were pleasantly surprised that when working on a deal "the equivalent people on the other side are qualified." We feel inclined to agree with the interviewee who observed that these trainees "are less gruntish than most." Indeed they are among the most eloquent

and well mannered that we encounter on the *Student Guide*. Utterly charming, perfectly gracious and terribly, terribly mature, it is tempting to describe them as posh. But let's be clear, "it is a particular type of posh." Travers is "not at all 'rah'" but instead that "proper sort of pucker" that translates into warm affability and politeness. One source summed up: "We aren't all landed gentry – there are people who have funny regional accents – but we are good eggs." In September 2005, there wasn't too much of a scramble for jobs, with 12 out of the 13 qualifiers staying on with the firm.

## what am i bid?

The training programme maintains a rigorous rolling boil throughout the two years, with in-house seminars plus a "two-pronged" mid and end-of-seat appraisal system. Typical of a firm where "you would never get a slap on the back and a nudge," the appraisal system is "all done rather professionally." The first prod of the fork comes from your supervisor, while the second stab is from the training partners. The overall result is "ultimately quite constructive" and the system "reassuringly formal, but not intimidating." This is typical of a firm where sound traditional values have not reverted to the default setting of rigid hierarchy, starched collars and stiff upper lips. Our sources described "pretty easy communication between partners and trainees," and though a day in the office "is not Friday night at a comedy club, it is light hearted." That day can be an efficient 9.30am-6.30pm or can just as easily turn into longer days and even longer nights. As one brave soul put it: "If you are busy enough in your own project, the day flies by, and the night flies by too. It is not at all unpleasant."

The firm's offices ("not all plate glass and polished steel, but certainly not dark timber and Indian rugs") are a stone's throw from a host of cool bars in the area around Smithfield meat market. Yet, as in every year since time began, trainees continue to patronise a local boozer called The Bishop's Finger. Hearing us crestfallen at this lack of ingenuity and adventure, several sources assured us that "*there is a rebel element.*" Actually, too many of them boasted: "*I rather like to believe that I led it.*" Who to believe? Perhaps the trainee who told us: "*The classier people like to go to Betjemans, and there is Smiths – the occasional rebel faction go there, but you have to be terribly trendy.*" The sorry truth of it is "*we just don't cut the mustard on trendy... or classy.*" The Bishop's Finger it is then.

Other activities include rugby sevens, hockey and football, which are all "*taken terribly seriously.*" There is also the standard format Christmas party (this year at the Savoy), quiz nights and recently a charity auction where lots included dinner at the House of Lords, golfing holidays in St Andrews, and one of the trainees. For what purpose we dared not ask.

## and finally...

For a superb City training in an utterly respected firm, Travers Smith is a golden opportunity. Its training is so highly sought after that you'll have to pull out the stops on the application.

# Trowers & Hamlins

## the facts

**Location:** London, Manchester, Exeter
**Number of partners/assistants:** 79/143
**Total number of trainees:** 33
**Seats:** 4x6 months
**Alternative seats:** Overseas seats
**Extras:** Pro bono – Toynbee Hall Legal Advice Centre

So, you really enjoyed studying land law, but there's no denying that your racy alter ego quite fancies jetting off to a glamorous foreign location. Doomed by indecision? Not quite.

## very big mortgages

The foundations of City-based Trowers & Hamlins are underpinned by property work. Variations on the real estate theme include property litigation,

commercial property and projects and construction, but it is the firm's public sector and social-housing work that has the redoubtable reputation. Unsurpassed in the field, Trowers represents a host of registered social landlords (or RSLs), namely housing associations and co-ops, local authorities and trusts, on the purchase and sale of affordable homes. It also works on "*a lot of corporate and company-based stuff, stock transfers and PFI projects.*" To illustrate, the team is acting for Wakefield and District Housing in relation to a stock transfer comprising 32,000 homes. The venture involves an RSL investing over £700 million in homes and services over a period of ten years and it is being partly funded by a £420 million loan arrangement from the RBS, the largest ever loan awarded to a social housing provider. Equally, regeneration and development projects can run into hundreds of millions of pounds. To give one example, £400 million is being spent on the regeneration of West Hendon town centre, complete with children's facilities, a sailing club and around 2,000 new homes.

Though the firm's biggest UK matters are to be found in its stellar social housing practice, "*there is an awful lot of stuff that isn't social housing.*" A stint in commercial property exposes trainees to sales, purchases, leases and licences for "*more typical property clients – property companies, retailers etc.*" Construction clients cover a broad spectrum: HM Prison Service shares desk space with Manchester Airport and the company that owns the Eden Project; major contractors Sir Robert McAlpine and Willmott Dixon bunch up in the filing cabinet with the Berkeley Group and some of the biggest names in residential development as well as NHS trusts and a whole host of local authorities.

## court on the hop

Rest assured that training at Trowers will not mean a two-year exile in the bowels of the Land Registry or 24 months sorting title deeds. Though we were interested to hear that the firm has signed up to the

College of Law's litigation programme (something the *Student Guide* as become accustomed to hearing from magic circle or American firms with insufficient litigation capacity), those trainees who had undertaken property litigation seats described *"a lot of anti-social behaviour work with RSLs and possession claims against squatters,"* all of which involved *"a lot of running to court, sitting in on hearings and making applications."* But as one source rightly pointed out: *"As property is quite a big part of what we do, it would be strange to apply here if you hated it."*

So let's say you try it and you learn that *"you aren't massively keen on property."* Apparently *"it needn't dominate your training contract."* Indeed, trainees told us *"corporate is growing quite fast, employment likewise."* Trowers' corporate finance practice includes the niche but growing area of Islamic finance, a type of lending that does not fall foul of Sharia law. More typically for trainees, a stint in corporate involves regular M&A, share transfers and the like, necessitating *"lots of drafting of smaller documents such as board minutes and resolutions"* plus research, disclosure exercises and *"discrete tasks within larger matters."* At the other end of the scale is private client, a *"really bizarre little department"* offering seats that give *"exposure to a lot of different law"* and *"a lot of one-on-one client contact."*

Whether it is *"general stuff like conveyancing"* or rushing off to court for *"bits and pieces of on-the-hop advocacy,"* attending meetings and dealing with clients, where the nature of the work allows, trainees manage their own files. Even in a public sector seat where vast projects means that a *"fast-moving, very varied"* experience comes at the expense of autonomy, trainees were clear on how their *"little bit fits in to the wider picture"* and enjoyed knowing that *"someone is relying on your bit."* When it comes to taking on responsibility, *"the sky's the limit,"* an approach that treats trainees *"as more of a junior fee earner. "* It left one of our sources *"shocked, and concerned that I might make a serious mistake;"* however, the same source conceded that

*"after a while you appreciate it is an incredible way to learn quickly."*

Trainees generally share an office with an assistant solicitor and report to a partner. On the feedback front, a quick mid-seat appraisal is followed by a longer debrief at the end of each seat, when trainees can also give feedback on their supervisors. A trainee solicitors' committee exists to take care of any collective grievances, but perhaps it has become a victim of its own success as *"we never have anything to say."* Even seat allocation goes relatively smoothly: the first of a trainee's four seats is picked for them and thereafter they submit their preferences. The comment that *"a lot of work is put into seeing what you want to do"* explains why we couldn't find anyone disappointed with their lot. Trainees seem quick to cotton on to the firm's superior strengths so, although *"at the start they just want to do what they know from the LPC,"* two years down the line, *"housing is the most popular for applying for jobs."* In September 2005, 12 of the 13 qualifiers stayed with the firm, three going into housing and three into commercial property. One took up a post in Bahrain.

## moss side or pool side?

A spell at one of the firm's other offices is also popular. While the Exeter office is off-limits for trainees, *"you are encouraged to go to Manchester"* for property litigation or housing. Apparently up in Manchester there is *"a lot of anti-social stuff."* Little encouragement is required when it comes to filling seats on Emirates flight EK008 to Dubai International.

A network of successful offices in the Gulf means six-month placements in Abu Dhabi, Dubai, Bahrain and Oman. These offices expose trainees to *"real across-the-board work"* including *"large-scale oil, gas and telephone projects,"* banking and finance, corporate/commercial transactions and a smattering of property or litigation. Though the Gulf offices are considerably smaller than London, the size of the deals need not be and trainees *"learn a lot* about how to be a lawyer and how commercial decisions are made." More particularly they liaise and negotiate with government departments and get involved in marketing and networking. Work aside, a stint overseas includes "a good package – car, flat, extra pay... " plus desert trips, beaches, sunshine, palm trees... Yet even in the face of such temptations, Trowers harbours a hard core of homebodies. "The split is about half and half between those who wouldn't go and those who would." Dubai is the most popular destination, but even here, "if you really want to go and say so early on, you have a good chance."

So, how does Trowers reconcile regeneration in the urban centres of the UK with the glitz of The Palm project, World Islands and the Burj-Al-Arab Hotel? Our sources understood our confusion, saying: "It is quite strange. Just by chance those two have developed as the firm's fortes." Whether this makes the firm slightly schizophrenic or merely diverse in its interests seems to matter less than the fact that its pre-eminence in both fields offers trainees the opportunity to excel in either.

## school dinners

Trowers' London HQ is located close to the Tower of London on its very own traffic island. If this doesn't sell it to you, river views, nearby parks and excellent transport links may do the trick. Since last year when we reported that the firm canteen played Magic FM, a new catering company has been drafted in, along with a new CD collection, which one source admitted "must be passable – it hasn't stuck in my mind as bad." The food isn't bad either, and a recent School Dinners Day saw "all the old favourites on the menu." Jamie Oliver eat your heart out. Actually, Monday lunchtimes always have a scholarly theme, with "half an hour for lunch followed by a one-hour lecture." And to prove the point that Trowers is "very big on know-how," we're reminded that there are also departmental training sessions and "frequent internal and external seminars."

A typical day follows a civilised 9am to 6.30pm pattern. "And I always take lunch," iterated one source. Inevitably, "in corporate, people will occasionally work until nine or ten for a week or so." However there is some consolation. While the rest of the firm is suited and booted every day, "for some odd reason" the corporate department don't have to wear ties. Trainees tell us they are drawn from "a reasonable mix of schools," though "probably all from redbrick unis with a handful of Oxbridge." They struck us as cheerful, content and willing to give things a try... even if it's swapping a boob tube for a kaftan for six months. We concur with the source who told us that to fit in at Trowers "you've got to pitch in and do whatever, and do it with good grace."

Nearby St Catherine's Dock and Butler's Wharf have plenty of good places to while away the evenings. "At the moment, Bar 38 just up the road" is a favourite but Trowers trainees are a fickle bunch and we were unsurprised to learn of "a few renegades" who prefer The Assembly. All we can say is don't expect them to still be frequenting the same places when you arrive. The firm lays on karaoke, darts evenings, pool competitions and quizzes; there is football and rugby (for lads and ladies separately), netball (for both at once), squash and tennis (no gender stipulated). Christmas parties tend to be organised departmentally and the annual summer party brings the Exeter, Manchester and London offices together. At last year's party a chocolate fountain was "a bit of a highlight," scoring particularly well with the female trainees. Typical!

## and finally...

As if to prove that social housing lawyers with a taste for the Middle East are not such a rare breed, or that Trowers & Hamlins' offering is not such an unlikely combination, one source described the package as "a winner for me." We reckon that an interest in either side of the practice should be more than enough to make the firm your top choice.

# Walker Morris

## the facts

**Location:** Leeds
**Number of partners/assistants:** 44/110
**Total number of trainees:** 30
**Seats:** 6x4 months
**Alternative seats:** Occasional secondments

Since the 1880s, Walker Morris has been offering no-fuss legal advice to clients in Yorkshire and beyond. Over the years it has built up a superb reputation and it shows no sign of loosening its grip on the top end of the market.

## leeds united

Leeds' legal landscape is dominated by big national firms: Pinsent Masons, Eversheds, Addleshaw Goddard, Hammonds and DLA Piper. Together with our subject firm, they form the Leeds Big Six. The first thing you need to understand about WM is that it is the only truly independent firm to grace this hallowed cabal. The next is that its solidity, profitability and reputation are envied by many in the profession, and not just locally. We reckon there are plenty of partners in the national firms who would give their eye teeth for the independence and self-determination of this Leeds-only partnership.

WM is one of a small handful of sterling regional independents, among them Birmingham's Wragge & Co, Bristol's Burges Salmon and Newcastle's Dickinson Dees. The defining characteristics? Perhaps it is an element of conservatism in management, perhaps it is the level of profitability, or perhaps it is pulling power when it comes to talented lawyers and valuable clients. Yet "*unlike Wragges, who felt the need to open a London branch,*" WM trainees were in no doubt that the future of their firm lies solely in Leeds. Doubtless thinking of their rivals in the Big Six, one trainee declared: "*Some firms spread themselves too thin; we stand apart by holding on to a one-office, one-city mentality.*" To those who dismiss firms outside the Square Mile as

parochial, just look at the figures: WM's turnover of £44 million (up 11.4% since 2004) is testament to the commercial vitality of both the firm and its setting.

## very important people

A six-seat training system is popular with trainees for the usual reasons – they get to see more areas of the firm and if they don't gel with a supervisor or their work, they can move on to the next one far more quickly. Said one source: "*It's great when you know that if a seat isn't what you want it's only four months and not a quarter of your contract gone.*" All our sources had sat with either a senior associate or a partner, usually the latter. This is great for Q&As, but sometimes a problem for Ps&Qs because "*there are some characters amongst the partners and it is they who make or break a seat not the work or area of law.*" In the first half of the training contract, recruits have no choice as to which seats they do, taking up what is left over after second-years have made their choices.

A seat in property "*won't leave you swamped; they're good at gauging what you could handle.*" At first it will be a case of assisting on your supervisor's files – no mean feat when this amounts to "*due diligence on 400-odd properties.*" After poring over reports on leasehold and freehold buildings, looking for problems and loopholes, you might get to run some of your own files – "*small commercial conveyances and residential work for our VIP clients.*" VIP, eh? And who might they be? "*Not telling,*" came the reply. One thing sources weren't tight-lipped about was the prestige attached to WM's property department, something our parent publication *Chambers UK* confirms by ranking it top in Yorkshire. The department's client list goes some way to explaining its success: on the books are Debenhams, Starbucks, Footlocker, Monsoon, Evans, Trafford Centre, Bellway Homes, Taylor Woodrow, Persimmon and Bank of Scotland. You may have noticed a strong retail and residential theme to this list, but the department also acts for public sector clients, among them Wakefield Metropolitan District Council, which the firm assisted on the large-scale voluntary transfer of 32,000 properties. It has also advised on the purchase and development of over 20 sites for Travelodge recently, a fact that you will now remember every time you see one on the side of the road...

## kiwis can fly!

Equally well respected for its work is the insolvency litigation team, with whom you might spend your litigation seat. The person who told us the experience could be a tad "*boys' own*" might have been swayed by recent intense activity on the Leeds United administration. Typical trainee tasks include drafting instructions to counsel and attending client meetings with your supervisor. Debt collection files and small bankruptcies and liquidations also fall to the trainee. It's a seat of hustle and bustle and this is also the case in corporate, which is currently "*an extremely busy department.*" Described as "*hectic, but a really positive experience,*" trainees had nothing negative to say about coco seats, apart from the "*up-and-down*" hours. "*Sometimes you're out the door at 6pm and sometimes it's three in the morning.*" Due diligence, visiting clients, document collation and drafting ancillary transaction documents will all bring you to "*the big rush at the end when you're negotiating the last point.*" And if you think that sounds exciting, "*it's the trainee who usually has to point out to clients where to sign.*" Even if you're going home with the milk floats, the knowledge that "*everyone in the team is working for the same goal balances all the pressures.*" Among the firm's latest deals are the sale of leading laser eye surgery company Ultralase to Spanish purchasers for £30 million; the £328 acquisition by BUPA of a 44-home care provider; and the £17 million sale of Kent International Airport (nope, we'd never heard of it either) to a new Kiwi owner.

Having earned their wings in the first year, trainees finally get some choice as to their second-year seats. How about employment? One busy trainee uttered breathlessly: "*Can't talk – have about ten of my own files to get through... you're much more on your own here.*" Dealing with both claimant and respondent files means trainees see "*both sides of the coin: the poor fella who's been binned off and the renegade employee.*" Some trainees squeeze in a secondment, perhaps to a pharmaceutical client – unnamed "*because of the animal libbers.*" Secondments free trainees from the close supervision they receive in the office, although all our sources applauded partners and associates for their good judgement in knowing when to step back and give them more freedom. The trainee who is more interested in black letter law and complex structures designed to maximise tax savings will be eager to spend time with the WM tax bods. The work of the team is greatly valued not only by clients but also colleagues in corporate, property and other practice areas, leading to a constant influx of thorny problems and dilemmas from all over the firm.

## a game of two halves

Other seat options include banking insolvency, planning, construction, commercial, property litigation and commercial litigation. It is common to repeat a favoured seat and the second half of the training contract is definitely more within the control of trainees, which enables them to nudge their way towards the area that most interests them for qualification. As for how many NQs stay on with the firm, in September 2005 it was 13 out of 15.

We'll let you into a secret: the "*one-office*" ethos now hides a three-site operation in Leeds. WM's headquarters is an imposing brick building in the centre of the city's business district, though trainees reveal that it looks more prestigious from the outside than the inside, which "*needs a bit of renovation.*" A lead could be taken from WM's satellite offices: the property team's Bank House and the personal injury team's Cloth Hall Court outshine the main King's Court office. We understand the PI team has grown quite used to the luxuries on offer; the chill-out room and satellite TV are perfect for watching important week-day footie matches with colleagues and clients. Indeed, we noticed the firm has a penchant for the beautiful game. It has acted not only for Leeds United but also Bradford City, Huddersfield Town, Grimsby Town and Hull City. And when individual players sign up to sponsorship deals, the WM lawyers are ready to smooth things along. They recently advised PUMA on its sponsorship agreement with Manchester United defender Gabriel Heinze. Rugby and cricket get a look in too: on the client list are rugby league's Bradford Bulls, plus a number of sporting bodies – the Professional Cricketers Association and Professional Rugby Players Association among them. These bodies refer players with problems to the firm... but we probably ought not to tell you exactly who.

## let's talk turkey

After what will undoubtedly be a year of hard work, you'll want to eat a good Christmas dinner with colleagues – play your cards right and you could eat up to half a dozen of them at WM. You may wonder how such gastronomic feats could happen at a law firm outside Texas: "*It's down to the way Christmas parties are structured – you get team, departmental and trainee parties plus a firm-wide one.*" Then there's a summer bash with "*grand-scale*" eating, drinking and dancing. Last time it was held in Leeds' County Arcade shopping centre, an ornate piece of Victorian architecture. Trainees did find it a bit strange "*partying down amongst the posh shops*" but certainly enjoyed themselves.

The regular social scene never strays too far from the main office: "*Bar Work is the work bar.*" Two minutes from the back door, it is "*a pretty good craic*" on a Friday night – "*everyone is there: IT bods, secretaries, trainees, associates and partners.*" Yes, there is "*an element of hierarchy,*" but all partners are addressed by their first name and are "*up for a laugh*" when out after work. End-of-month drinks mean "*a few hundred quid behind the bar*" ... and a few trainees on the tiles, we imagine! Tri-annual team days out always go down well and have included things such as a treasure hunt in Ilkley,

"*home of the world-famous Betty's Tea Rooms.*" After the impressive amount WM trainees manage to ingest, it's a good job that they love nothing more than a good walk, waterski, football match, cricket match, etc.

To us this looks like a firm where you either throw yourself into things or get less than you ought out of the experience. This is a lesson that paralegals learn, and the best of them sometimes find they have earned themselves a training contract as a result.

## and finally...

Singular and full of character, Walker Morris is the ideal training ground for would-be solicitors seeking a commercial career that begins and ends in Leeds. The only caveat we'll add is that you must be prepared to ease out your belt by a notch or two.

# Ward Hadaway

## the facts

**Location:** Newcastle, South Shields
**Number of partners/assistants:** 53/61
**Total number of trainees:** 16
**Seats:** 4x6 months
**Alternative seats:** None

Ward Hadaway is a clear contender for a medal in the North East Legal Olympics, and it has got its eye on something other than the third-place end of the podium.

## the michael owen factor

Since taking the helm of the firm in 1999, managing partner Jamie Martin has presided over a 100% increase in turnover. Fee income has grown to £17.5 million and the plan is to keep growing. Clearly WH is a firm to watch and close rival Eversheds, for one, certainly has to be vigilant. Trainees also say regional heavyweight Dickinson Dees had better mind its step. Eversheds recently lost its Newcastle construction partner to the WH partner-munching machine (which also pulled in people from Pinsents to fatten the construction team). As well as importing new partners, WH has consistently retained all its trainees on qualification and made many external appointments. But it's not all one-way traffic and not too long before we went to press another rival, Watson Burton, nabbed one of the firm's corporate partners.

It's interesting for us softie Southerners to watch the North East legal market. The region's top firms have correctly identified the trend for winning better work from clients who are happy to give the high prices of London a wide berth. We have previously referred to a snowball effect up in Newcastle – better quality work attracting lawyers with greater experience and notable contacts; this in turn attracting more good work etc. Rather like the Magpies pulling in Michael Owen, Newcastle firms can now hire lawyers who might previously have ignored the city for jobs in Leeds or London.

## ward rounds

Ironically, "*aggressive*" expansion may mean a "*whittling down*" of the already small private client teams as WH consolidates its already significant commercial departments. An area in which WH gets gold is litigation, and here the firm has handled some very large and unique cases. Take the example of the 13 US Navy ghost ships intended to be towed over from the James River, Virginia for dismantling and recycling in Hartlepool's shipyards. Not a plan popular with either the general public or Greenpeace, but all in a day's work for WH's client Able UK. Or not, as it eventually turned out after a tussle in the courts. The partner-heavy commercial litigation department takes two trainees at a time and they soon learn that preparing case chronologies and summaries of background documents is labour-intensive work and some cases involve huge quantities of information. "*It is more difficult to charge a partner's time to assimilate information – it is better for the trainee to do it,*" one source explained. The plus side of this document-heavy labour is that you "*can get a good insight into larger claims.*"

In another area of litigation, clinical negligence, the firm has been chosen along with 11 others by the NHS Litigation Authority to defend hospitals and trusts from the ever-increasing number of claims from patients left dissatisfied, injured or worse following medical treatment. Big medical cases "*can give you a buzz,*" according to one source. As elsewhere in the firm, there are department-specific continuing education sessions, though we suspect you need a stronger stomach here than in, say, property. "*We had a guest speaker on oncology, it was fairly horrendous and there were pictures.*" As we always say: like our clocks, our tastes don't always run the same. An ability to work as part of a team "*on a small bit of a large NHS case*" is as useful a trait as an ability to cope with gory details. For trainees there are limelight moments, but in reality there's a good deal of research and trawling through medical records. At least this pays dividends when you need to flex your knowledge before clinical staff at hospital meetings.

## the house of wards

There is yet more litigation on offer in the realm of property. Here, service charge and dilapidation disputes bring trainees into contact with the surveyors employed to wrangle over the original state and condition of a building and help calculate recompense for landlords. If you're too squeamish for clin neg, this could be right up your street.

And while on the subject of landlords, there is nowhere better than a transactional property seat for trainees to get their own files and develop core skills. At first they try out smaller residential conveyances to get them used to the "*basic steps,*" following this with the "*bread and butter*" of lease renewals. When helping out partners on larger deals, they do attend some meetings to watch the masters at work, but the essence of the seat is "*classic legal work,*" which can mean poring over "*really* thick 60-page documents" in which "every word counts." Among the department's flagship transactions are more than £170 million worth of deals for the Church Commissioners, including the sale of its London Millbank Estate to the House of Lords for £65 million. The department has also been doing a lot of work for residential developers such as Barratt, Persimmon and Bellway. And in keeping with the firm's good reputation for health litigation, the property lawyers have been assisting on NHS LIFT projects that are renewing and developing primary care facilities in the north of England.

WH advises Newcastle City Council and has shown a keen interest in the city's renaissance. When we asked about the appeal of Newcastle for an aspiring young professional, one enthusiastic trainee echoed some of the managing partner's recently published words of wisdom: "We have the Centre of Life research venue, they made the first cloned human embryo y'know... Then there are all the universities here, too, so in IT and IP you get these cool projects." The firm's commercial wing has indeed been flapping hard to draw in technology clients – Zytronic Plc, Tanfield Group Plc, Romag Holdings Plc and many other profitable but lesser-known plcs are keeping the lawyers active and on their toes.

Trainees complete a four-seat circuit of the firm, with seats in coco, litigation and property all likely. As we've already seen, this in itself brings a good deal of variety in terms of the work on offer. In addition to those already mentioned, further seats are available in employment, banking, property lit, planning, IP/IT and private client.

## if a tree falls in the forest...

When interviewing WH trainees this year, we encountered one or two who had taken the firm's "aggressive" growth and ambitious business strategy as a model for personal development. Yet WH is certainly not populated entirely by corporate survivalists. Proof came from their position "half way down a list of 100" on the Kielder Challenge, a team-building endurance competition that separates the men from the boys... and girls. The first day of the two-day event is spent "spanning gaps and building things in the forest" – including your own overnight shelter. Who won? "Not us!" Aggression spoke with a whimper that night in the rain: there were "some real hardcore contingents there," remonstrated our source. "There were engineers... and even people from Coca-Cola." The full-fat, not the diet types, we're guessing. Of more concern to readers is the nature of the typical WH type and the ethos of the firm. Comparing the firm with its main competitors in legal Newcastle, one trainee pronounced their employer to be "young and progressive," not like old man Dickie Dees, who they love to characterise as "a bit stuffy and resting on [his] laurels a little." There is clearly "a friendly rivalry" between the two firms.

Corporate fun and games continue throughout the year with everything from football to an annual dragon boat race. The WH team is a dead cert in the football as it can deploy a semi-professional player, an asset which we agree is "really handy." Games tend to end in a bloody "8-1" to the warriors of Ward, though given their cowered performance in the forest, we only offered trainees 80-1 odds for a WH victory in its dragon boat. The firm holds a summer barbecue and a Christmas party at which the age-old plan of eating, drinking and merry-making is put into action. A fairly close-knit trainee community has its weave tightened further by the Newcastle Trainee Solicitors Group which organises plenty of events.

WH's home on the Quayside has fantastic views of the Tyne and Millennium bridges, as well as other new and refurbished riverside buildings including the old Baltic Flour Mills and the Sage. Rather like the city of Newcastle, Ward Hadaway is on the up, and it looks to have reached the stage where prospective trainees from around the country might be tempted to sign on the dotted line. Indeed, the current trainee group contains people who have no deep roots in the region, giving credibility to the claim that you need only "*prove you like the North East and have a reason to be there.*" In September 2005, six of the seven qualifiers took jobs with the firm, going into several departments.

## and finally...

If they gave out medals for energy, drive and ambition, Ward Hadaway would be weighed down with them. The type of trainee that would suit the firm is someone wholly committed to building a career in the North East and enthusiastic about playing their part in making the firm even more successful. If that sounds too trite for you then unfortunately you've just read the wrong feature.

## Watson, Farley & Williams LLP

### the facts

**Location:** London
**Number of partners/assistants:** 41/65
**Total number of trainees:** 22
**Seats:** 6x4 months
**Alternative seats:** Overseas seats
**Extras:** Language training

Intrigued by matters maritime but balk at getting drenched? As well as core work in shipping and asset finance, Watson, Farley & Williams has a broader portfolio of experiences for trainees to sample.

### all at sea?

"*Make sure people know they won't just do shipping,*" one source firmly ordered. And so we will. Since opening up for business 23 years ago, WFW has also delved into aviation, telecoms, asset finance, energy – heck they've even got media and entertainment lawyers. Yet shipping clients are important and have assisted with the growth and development of many of the firm's other areas of practice. For example, on the client list of WFW's

energy department, shipping clients like Teekay (which used the firm in its bid for three LNG carriers worth $468 million) mingle with energy clients like Guangdong Dapeng, the company behind a pioneering Sino-Australian deal to transport the fuel of CNOOC, China's biggest producer of natural gas.

### beer money

At WFW you get six seats for the price of four in the training contract. While this gives breadth of experience, trainees' choices must fit in with the following stipulations. Litigation is a must, as is "*corporate, and then either pure finance or shipping finance, although they prefer it if you do both.*" Many people also spend one seat abroad, usually around the middle of the training contract. The last seat will ideally be taken in the department into which you hope to qualify, so boosting your experience from four to eight months in that field. Seat allocation seems to work well, perhaps because "*there aren't so many people per intake and you have six seats, so you tend to get what you want.*"

Dealing with those compulsory seats one at a time, let's first visit litigation. The firm's work is most definitely international in scope and it is developing an excellent name in the world of arbitration. Among its arbitration clients is the Government of India. It called on the firm to mediate in one of the world's largest investment treaty arbitrations in which India slugged it out with Malaysian subsidiaries of multinational conglomerates GE and Bechtel over the Dabhol power project worth over $1.3 billion. You'll have to get used to figures like this – $1.1 billion was also at stake when T-Mobile clashed with Vivendi and its Polish subsidiary Elektrim Telekomunikacja in Europe's biggest telecoms dispute, concerning control of Central Europe's burgeoning mobile phone market. And in what is probably the best arbitration in the world, Carlsberg met with WFW's client Beer Chang from Thailand in a dispute over licensing worth $650 million.

# the true picture

On the very biggest cases mundane work may lie in store for trainees. Said one: "*[Being] involved in a huge arbitration makes everything more document and admin based*" because huge cases involve "*huge disclosure exercises.*" Trainees at least get assistance ("*the paralegal does the indexing*") and they never complete a seat without going before masters ("*nerve wracking the first time but not a problem after that*"). If lucky, a trip to the High Court will have them taking notes or even frantically passing hastily scribbled messages forward to a barrister in full flow. Not all cases are prohibitively supersized however; on some smaller shipping cases trainees spoke of "*drafting claim forms and witness statements – they don't just give you admin work.*"

Next stop corporate, a seat of "*huge variety*" where company flotations are a staple, AIM work a speciality and clients in the energy and natural resources, international trade, transport and travel/leisure sectors the target. We noted a string of Australian deals had kept lawyers busy. As well as advising Ballarat Goldfields (listed on the Australian Stock Exchange) on its fast-track admission to AIM, they assisted Eurogold Limited (also listed Down Under) on its admission and fund raising. In yet another Aussie deal, client Black Rock Oil & Gas (already AIM-listed) bought Wildlook Enterprises and raised funds through share placements and exercising warrants. Our sources spoke of becoming immersed in share transfers, taking notes at meetings, reviewing company prospectuses and verifying admission documents.

## it's a ship not a boat!

Neglected on law degrees, ignored at LPC level, shipping law is a mystery to most prospective trainees. "*I didn't know anything about it,*" confessed one source, "*but Britain's economy is so directed by what goes on in shipping.*" The uninitiated need not be put off taking the plunge. Treading water in an unfamiliar area of law is made easier with a life jacket and whistle in the guise of "*background lectures*" intended "*to show how a shipping transaction goes through.*" A ship

finance seat will have you working on tax-led structures, "*setting up companies to finance ships*" and dealing with the banking documentation. Due to the amounts involved, don't expect to manage files solo. In fact, a combination of the four-month seat, the relative unfamiliarity of shipping law and the magnitude of deals means you'll probably be limited to babysitting one aspect of a deal. Nevertheless, trainees hardly ever photocopy in finance seats – "*the admin staff do that.*" Instead their time is spent drafting, corresponding with the other side and attending and note-taking at meetings to set the terms of a deal.

Non-shipping finance seats bring a good deal of document management and a decent role on smaller transactions. One source told us about assisting on sale and leaseback transactions when assets are sold to raise cash and then leased back by the company. "*I had no files of my own but I was responsible for the conditions precedent element of transactions.*" Larger transactions are to be found in the projects seat, which revolves around "*finance for big infrastructure projects such as power stations and wind farms.*" Not only permitted to have a stab at the first drafts of documents, trainees report contacting clients by telephone and e-mail and attending meetings with partners. Initially you might just take notes but "*they encourage you to contribute too.*" On the drafting front, as the seat progresses, "*hopefully the supervisor wades in less and less.*"

You might fill one of your four-month slots with competition ("*The law changes so much so there's a lot of research, for example on the intricacies of merger cases in LNG and energy*") or property, tax or employment. One trainee who'd spent time doing the last spoke of getting "*enough work to keep you busy but not there until midnight.*" Given the international nature of the clientele, you'll likely encounter immigration issues as clients move staff around the world. Like so many of the other seats, in employment it's a case of "*assisting on files and doing smaller jobs, you have to build up to responsibility and not be scared by it.*"

## pacific heights

One of the main pulls at WFW must be the seat abroad and it should come as no surprise that among recruits a second language is "*a valued commodity*." If you're after New York or Roma, forget about it – "*there are no English partners there and according to Law Society requirements a trainee must be accompanied by one*." Instead, tickets to Bangkok, Singapore, Piraeus and Paris are all up for grabs. In Asia "*you'll be looked after well*," with five-star treatment doled out at your new home – the nearest five-star hotel. As with all secondments, you're relatively unconstrained in the small office where "*you get more responsibility*." In Singapore, you'll be elevated up the 37-storey Hitachi Tower and whisked into your own office overlooking the sea ("*although you'll spend most of your time with your back to it*"). The working day will be "*a totally different experience*," as the trainee is let loose amongst the office's solicitors and "*you work for the whole team*." "*Learning to time-manage and build up organisational skills*" becomes a priority. In Asia, travel opportunities abound and partners encourage the seconded trainee to take full advantage. "*They say, 'Make the most of it!' so you do*." A long weekend to Cambodia or Thailand is "*never frowned upon*."

In Paris you'll work on the Champs-Elysèes, your desk will face the Eiffel Tower and you'll live in the middle of Le Marais in earshot of Notre Dame. Work is split between shipping finance and projects, and you'll need to brush up on your French before you go. A seat in Piraeus is all shipping finance. Again, it comes with perks – "*trainees get the top floor overlooking Athens and the view is great!*" Who knows! An unconfirmed 'Wilkommen' may await future trainees in Hamburg. Opened in October 2005, this new office focuses on shipping and shipping finance; in keeping with the firm's overall bent, it additionally plans to create energy, general finance and corporate teams.

## a warm reception

Back in London, every four months trainees air their views at a meeting with the relevant training honchos. A culture of warmth means there are rarely major issues to thrash out; in fact we hear the only frosty thing about WFW is the clever glass in the meeting room walls which turn opaque at the press of a button. Said one trainee of the firm's general culture: "*The working environment is very good. When you're starting out as a trainee and flapping around you need approachable people, and they are here*." Doubtless the eight qualifiers (out of ten) that stayed with the firm in September 2005 remembered this when the new intake of trainees arrived.

Sadly, trainees were remarkably tight-lipped about their social lives back in London. We know that Christmases mean flash parties at The Savoy or Claridges, though for love nor money we couldn't glean any detail other than – as with all parties of that ilk – "*black-tie things are very good fun*." More routinely, trainees organise nights out amongst themselves, although when it comes to drinks after work, we regret to inform readers that "*our local got knocked down so now it is All Bar One*."

## and finally...

Watson Farley & Williams always strikes us as a firm that has a lot to offer trainees, not just in terms of the number and variety of seats, but also in terms of its internal culture. All that and four months in the sun.

# Wedlake Bell

## the facts

**Location:** London
**Number of partners/assistants:** 39/42
**Total number of trainees:** 12
**Seats:** 4x6 months
**Alternative seats:** None

London firm Wedlake Bell has a diverse offering, ranging from a solid private client team through excellent corporate and property work to some jazzy media and IP matters.

## mown down

This firm looks ideal for any trainee hunting down a rounded commercial experience and maybe a sniff of private client work. Trainees select their seat preferences for the entire two years well in advance, and at the start of the training contract the firm delivers a full two-year order with all the timeliness and accuracy of an Ocado van. If you're not happy with the contents of your delivery, *"there is scope to change"* but only if *"you can swap with someone else and they can rejig it."* Though no seat is compulsory, the staples in a Wedlake Bell basket are corporate and property as these are the largest departments and take two trainees at any one time.

The client list is a gloriously mixed bag. *"Sometimes there's a plc"* (Dairy Crest Group and DHL), but more commonly clients are either listed on AIM or mid-market private companies. We rather like the sound of Hayter, the manufacturers of the Royal lawnmower, which Wedlake Bell advised when it was bought out by a US company. Working on corporate deals, *"you generally assist in the background."* However, in a compact firm such as this, there are fewer people to hide behind and the responsibility of running due diligence and verification on AIM flotations, aiding M&A negotiations and meeting clients caused one source to conclude: *"I was effectively dealing with people about three years PQE on other side."*

## bowled over

The popular property team *"has a buzz about it"* and a seat here exposes trainees to commercial property, property finance, construction, property litigation and cricket. The firm's crack eleven is mainly composed of property lawyers (you may be asked to join) and the department also acts for Surrey County Cricket Club. In a straight commercial property seat, *"at any one time you could be dealing with up to 20 files of your own,"* which means leases

to negotiate plus searches, exchanges and completions to juggle. It's a similar story in property litigation where the team has doubled in size and turnover in the past year. Here trainees get to draft claims and defences and build up plenty of contact with clients and counsel on adverse possession cases, problematic lease renewals, injunctions and dilapidation claims.

The respected construction group provides *"a very good, rounded seat."* This small team also advises Surrey County Cricket Club and recently helped it with its new £20 million stand at The Oval which included a 'living screen' to protect the good people of SE11, SW8 (and perhaps also SW9 if Kevin Pietersen is batting) from straying balls. Lord Denning would turn in his grave. The seat offers *"a good mix of contentious and non-contentious work,"* and a stint here will undoubtedly find you manning the phones of the National Specialist Contractors Council helpline which provides free legal advice to the council's members. Helpline duty translates into *"giving on-the-spot advice"* on *"lots of different queries including parking fines."* Trainees say: *"It is quite daunting for the first month; you have to keep your wits about you."* Fear not, if it's a million-pound question you are entitled to ask a friend and then phone the caller back; in fact, *"they like that – they then think theirs must be quite a taxing problem."*

## faked

According to trainees, Wedlake Bell's respected private client department *"earmarks them as a traditional firm."* We suspect the firm's other departments may like to take to one side the trainee who said *"private client is Wedlake Bell,"* but there is no denying that the team does carry weight, especially since the bolt-on of private client boutique Beattie & Co in May 2005. The team operates out of Guernsey and London, but don't pack your bucket and spade just yet, a seat in private client gets about as close to the beach as, well, Holborn. The firm handles everything from complex offshore tax structures and trusts to more humdrum affairs including wills and residential conveyancing. Wealthy clients include *"celebrities, landed gentry, lots of Lords and Ladies and entrepreneurs."* While there is little scope for autonomy, trainees in private client seats are not sent below stairs.

Adding a *"modern twist"* is the *"really quite modern and brilliant"* MIPCOM. Not a curious sub-department of MI5, the CIA or anyone else for that matter, MIPCOM stands for media, intellectual property and commercial litigation. Sadly this means no Pierce Brosnan in a DJ and no Clooney in camouflage gear, though from the way one source cooed: *"Ooh! I love MIPCOM!"* you'd never realise. For trainees, MIPCOM brings *"lots of responsibility"* and a few of their own matters, including *"bits of media, bits of IT, lots of IP and of course commercial stuff."* Occasionally they encounter celebrity clients (*"quite famous, well, not mega mega famous"*) and there are many dazzling brands to choose from, including the distributor of Lacoste, Stone Island and Fake. On the subject of fakes, contentious IP work has included a successful action against the former UK distributor of Fantasy Tan and the successful defence of copyright infringement claims brought by the publishers of *Ideal Home* against the publishers of *Home* magazine. Commercial litigation is a more sober proposition with the work tending to revolve around breaches of contract and fiduciary duty, fraud and business recovery.

## dressed up

Confirming our suspicions that a faint whiff of mothballs lingers in more than just the private client department, we heard that Wedlake Bell is *"quite modern in lots of outlooks, but in things like dress it wants to keep it traditional for its clients."* That said, one source was quick to qualify the firm's approach by saying: *"It is not necessarily old-school, but has traditional values."* Traditional values means a visible chain of command although *"on a Friday night there are general office boys and the senior partner all drinking together."* The trainees we spoke to found it *"quite comforting that there isn't a super-*

*long hours culture"* and reported an 8.45am to 6.30pm day as standard, adding that even busy spells *"don't spill out over the weekend."* Despite gripes about grunt work in past years' interviews, one source said: *"In all honesty, I have had some bits here and there but no more than is to be expected. Everyone is expected to do photocopying, whether a trainee or a partner. You just get on with it."* Overall our conversations revealed a thorough training that includes the excitement of advocacy and exposure to work from across teams under the watchful eye of a supervisor, bolstered by a *"very instructive"* system of appraising trainees every month.

## stripped down

In 2004, Wedlake Bell moved from Covent Garden to a Georgian building on Bedford Row. Despite being *"quite traditional on the outside,"* the building has been *"stripped down within"* and oak panelling has been replaced by the usual mod cons, glass walls and *"quasi-marble floors"* – excellent news for the trainee who told us: *"I didn't really want to go to a bigger firm where you can quickly disappear into the woodwork."* Taking their fresher image seriously, an Art Committee has been formed with a remit to replace the oil paintings that were *"here, there and everywhere"* in the old offices. Trainees also report on *"several people coming in and out trying to get their flower arrangements right."* All that said, there is *"nothing over the top"* – the leather sofas remain and the height of corporate frippery is a telly and toaster in the new Break Out room. A side effect of the move from Covent Garden was the loss of The Lamb and Flag as the favoured local, and moves to cultivate relations with the good people of The Old Nick are still in the early stages. Trainees told us woefully: *"The Lamb and Flag was an institution in itself. The Old Nick hasn't really established itself at that level yet."* Wedlake Bell certainly seems to take its hostelries seriously; for other pursuits the pickings are lean, though we do like the nostalgic ring of the firm's netball team – the Wedlake Belles.

Our sources viewed the office move as *"a mas-*

*sive step up"* for Wedlake Bell and an opportunity for the firm to progress and expand. We hear that *"there are some seats to fill"* in the building but that the firm is *"not trying to take over the world."* Our sources liked the snug fit of a firm where *"you could actually help in something constructive,"* and ventured to suggest that anyone flexing rippling corporate biceps may find Wedlake Bell a little on the small size. Similarly, those who cannot hold their own in the pub may stumble on the firm's coattails. While trainees assert that *"there generally isn't any common denominator"* among the group, we feel inclined to disagree. All those we spoke to were measured and mature, and claim the ability to *"put [themselves] out there."* Thereafter, the firm makes room for a mix of personalities. In 2005, two of the five qualifiers ended up staying on with the firm.

## and finally...

Take heed of the trainee who told us: *"I did look at smaller firms and larger firms, and thought this one had it just right."* For a decent work, a good old-fashioned training and lots of drinking partners, Wedlake Bell may be your perfect fit.

# Weil, Gotshal & Manges LLP

## the facts

**Location:** London
**Number of partners/assistants:** 25/80
**Total number of trainees:** 18
**Seats:** 4x6 months
**Alternative seats:** Overseas seats, secondments
**Extras:** Pro bono – RJC CAB, FRU, Bar Council and Solicitors pro bono units

With just ten years of UK living under its belt, American law firm Weil, Gotshal & Manges may not be quite ready for British citizenship, but its London office is its largest outside New York. State-

side, the firm has an unparalleled reputation for insolvency and reconstruction work; in London, admiring glances are usually reserved for its corporate practice. If you're looking for an alternative to the magic circle, you ought to consider this one.

## big weil world

Weil Gotshal has played a role in the aftermath of the largest corporate crash-and-burns of recent years – Enron, WorldCom, Global Crossing, Federal Mogul and United Airlines. Vast experience and expertise led the firm to involvement in two of the most significant pan-European restructurings of 2004 – Parmalat and Eurotunnel. London lawyers, too, handle their share of insolvency-related matters, but they have also developed a distinctive and UK-specific reputation for big-money corporate finance, particularly private equity work.

The London office takes its inspiration from *"the huge figurehead of [its managing partner] Mike Francies... he drives a lot of what the firm does here."* Weil UK has solid working relationships with a number of investment companies – GE Capital, KKR and Doughty Hanson, for example. Its most important relationship, however, is with US leveraged buyout house Hicks, Muse, Tate & Furst, which the London office advised on both the £527 million IPO of grocery supplier Premier Foods and the £640 million take-private of Weetabix. Lawyers also assisted various banking consortia on some of the largest M&A and buyout transactions of the past twelve months, including the £5.4 billion take-private of Canary Wharf, the €2.4 billion take-private of women's healthcare specialist Warner Chilcott, and the €2.3 billion take-private of European retailer Royal Vendex.

If distinctive practice strengths make this American beast a *"pretty Anglicised"* specimen in the UK, trainees were quick to point out some universal defining characteristics, the main one being *"the ethos of inclusiveness – it is multicultural, multiracial here."* They freely admitted: *"Being big on diversity is a very American thing,"* but took pride in a culture which relies on the efforts of lawyers in 20 offices worldwide from Silicon Valley and Shanghai to Boston and Budapest. "*You're just as likely to deal with lawyers in China or Germany as New York. It makes you feel like you're in one firm.*" Our sources estimated their work was "*75% international, 25% UK-based.*" Said one: "*I get shedloads more cross-border work than anyone else I know; my knowledge of cross-border law is up there with associates at other firms.*"

## a good caffeine buzz

Seat rotation involves a compulsory six months in corporate and a compulsory stint in litigation (although "*people who are less interested in this can do a split seat of only three months*"). A finance or securitisation seat is "*encouraged but not absolutely required*" and there are several other seat options including real estate, competition, tax, technology, restructuring, securitisation and capital markets. Regular opportunities to take a corporate seat in New York or an IP seat in Silicon Valley, together with the possibility (if you speak French) of a seat in Paris, all serve to reinforce a world-without-bounds mentality. But why travel when the world comes to you? "*In two months on a major acquisition I had four or five work streams across about 26 jurisdictions and was liaising with 15 lots of local counsel,*" one trainee explained.

The scale and scope of the corporate department's work means that "*the atmosphere is more pressured than in some others,*" and its success has made it "*slightly less maverick and innovative, more hierarchical than it once was.*" For trainees, "*there is a lot less drafting, more organisational work and company secretarial-type things,*" but the sense of drama and glamour is undeniable. Yes, "*you're often absolutely screwed on hours;*" nonetheless, the thrill of "*working on the biggest deals all the time*" even makes "*certifying signatures at 3am a buzz.*" Well, we say that, but "*maybe not always!*"

Litigation can be similarly "*all-hours*" if a court deadline is approaching. One source regarded it as "*a fantastic seat*" and recalled "*drafting skeleton arguments and witness statements, meeting clients and working with nearly every member of the team.*" Trainees never run short of court visits and, perhaps because of this, claimed the team was run "*very much like a barristers' chambers.*" It certainly has an impressive client list, which includes Weil's big-name customers – Enron, Hicks Muse and Premier Foods. Lawyers are also advising the likes of Oxfam on a pro bono basis. This connection recently saw them helping on the set up and launch of Progreso, Oxfam's new fair-trade coffee shop chain, and there is a regular trainee secondment to the charity. As you might imagine this is not only good for the soul but offers "*fantastic in-house experience on everything from contractual analysis to potential litigation.*"

## risky business

The "*complex technicalities*" of securitisation mean that "*even though everyone works very hard to involve you, and supervisors are good at explaining things,*" it's the sort of work that you have to grow into. Just accept that little will make sense on day one and "*there is a limit to what you can do as a trainee.*" At least the relative tedium of administrative work is lightened by "*plenty of drafting of deeds of charge*" and the rush you get from deal closures. More hands-on experiences are available in banking, real estate and the "*very popular*" restructuring seats. A lot of the work of the real estate team is tied to the deals handled over in corporate – the Canary Wharf financing was the perfect example of this – and invariably corporate support roles mean "*lots of due diligence, lease reviews and certificate verifications.*" Standalone work is usually more rewarding because "*you get your own mini files on which you are maintaining ongoing leases and doing the correspondence.*"

Over in banking and restructuring there is "*loads of research and tonnes of drafting on cross-border matters.*" Restructuring is particularly popular because trainees like "*working in a small team with good exposure to associates and a lot of client contact.*"

One satisfied source told us: "*I was given a leading role working with the company and proposed administrators on a major potential restructuring. I even led sections of the meeting with the clients.*" The other "*smaller, very business-oriented*" departments offer divergent experiences, and we particularly enjoyed hearing about "*the virtual A-level geography lesson I had in competition.*" How so? "*It was a proposed chemical industry takeover so we laid a map out and pinned out where factories were, where jurisdictions changed and where potential problems might occur.*" Sounds like a game of Risk to us.

## water feet-ures

Weil Gotshal occupies three floors of a "*spacious and pleasant*" building near Moorgate. It has a Starbucks upstairs and an M&S store downstairs so at least you'll be covered for good grub and lattes. The other notable features are "*some very odd orange and green artwork on the walls*" and a third-floor atrium with "*a shallow, floor-level pond-thing*" that "*someone is supposed to have stumbled into at some point during a drinks party.*" Most socialising takes place in the nearby Corney & Barrow or Sosho Match, and quite often takes place "*at lunchtimes*" or is linked to the activities of the sports teams. From the sounds of it, "*people don't over-socialise together outside work.*" Exceptions are made for the annual Christmas and summer parties, departmental events, charity quiz nights ("*where everyone lets their hair down... people can be hilarious*") and the European fee earner gathering every two years. "*The last one was in Cannes with no expense spared!*" We hear the goodie bag contained a Weil Gotshal-branded beach towel and flipflops.

The heavy demands of the job can often times put the kibosh on the social scene, so for example: "*The week before 20 people will have signed up for something and then suddenly everyone's busy.*" Trainees say the firm's reputation for working lawyers hard is well deserved, telling us: "*You can work late for large blocks of time.*" At least the close proximity of the M&S store makes buying a clean shirt easy, and "*the firm is good about you getting time off in lieu.*" In general, however, our sources expected no sympathy, recognising that "*you can't get the quality of experience if you're not prepared to take the hours.*"

Such a pragmatic view was characteristic of our interviewees. They define themselves as "*diligent, ambitious, friendly,*" and came across as a sparky and intelligent bunch. The attraction of international work had clearly played a major part in their choice of training but they also cited "*ready access to high-quality, high-profile work;*" "*closeness to the partners;*" and a desire to work alongside "*go-getting staff with a relaxed and friendly outlook.*" For them, it had been important to plot a career path that avoided the magic circle with its vast armies of trainees and ingrained bureaucracy. Working in smaller teams and in a smaller office, trainees could point to constant client contact and stressed how "*every single person is out to please the client and we pull out all the stops to do it.*" They acknowledge that training at the larger firms has certain advantages. "*When it comes down to it the magic circle must be doing something right... whether we get a better formal training I don't know, but we do get plenty of hands-on work and a steep learning curve.*" This is a firm for the type of person who wants "*to roll [their] sleeves up and get stuck in,*" learning on the job rather than in a classroom set-up. For this reason, trainees accept that "*being here might not suit every personality type.*"

"*Being self-starting and proactive*" is important, and although regular appraisals serve their purpose well, the greatest satisfaction we detected was "*when you've been given responsibility, you've got on with it and it is recognised that you've pulled it off.*" Who wouldn't enjoy "*doing today, what associates were doing yesterday?*" But as for becoming associates themselves, it's a confused picture. Previously 100% every time, trainees have found in the last two years NQ retention has dropped off. In 2005, eight of the 12 qualifiers stayed with the firm. The work preferences of the others did not match with what was on offer at the end of the contract. If you can't honestly say that the firm's corporate and capital markets work interests you – or is likely to – you should think again about your motivation for applying. But even if you give it a go and something else turns out to be your thing, you may end up agreeing with the departing trainee who told us: "*I can honestly say that I wouldn't have done my training contract anywhere else – it's been fantastic.*"

## and finally...

Weil Gotshal & Manges is a firm with a great pedigree. If you want excellent hands-on training with masses of client contact and international work – and a weighty salary to boot – then it is an excellent choice. However, let nothing distract you from the fact that you'll work very hard here.

# White & Case

## the facts

**Location:** London
**Number of partners/assistants:** 45/145
**Total number of trainees:** 50
**Seats:** 4x6 months
**Alternative seats:** Overseas seats
**Extras:** Pro bono – eg war crimes tribunal work, Justice in Exile (Guantanamo), language training

White & Case may pay top dollar, but that's the most American thing about it. A pan-continental practice spanning 26 nations makes it a definitively international practice. As they say on TV, never underestimate the power of local knowledge.

## don't dilly dally

Though you won't find partners in the London office trading cocker-ney banter and following the vaahn home, it has to be said that W&C has not diverged from its policy of developing a genuinely home-grown feel to every office it opens. Established in 1971, the W&C London office is now as

English as a bank holiday on Southend Pier and the vast majority of lawyers are UK-qualified. "*Naturally there are some US lawyers, but there are just as many other overseas lawyers,*" vouched one source. Another was quick to tell us: "*It feels more an international firm than US firm – energetic, young and can-do but not all the clichès about incredibly aggressive US firms with manic workers.*"

Traditionally recognised as banking and finance experts the firm has inveigled its way into the workings of many nations through a 'sovereign practice' that represents governments worldwide. Its own stated aim – to be "*the pre-eminent global law firm*" – smacks a little of world domination, but thus far reports that the managing partner has ordered the construction of a giant laser to melt the sun are unsubstantiated. Though we jest, real evidence for the firm's ambition is found in the recent growth of the London office. Numbers of lawyers in the capital have increased from 89 in 2001 to over 240 in 2005, giving White & Case the largest presence of any imported 'US firm' in the City. Turnover and profits have also skyrocketed in this period, not least because of stellar performances in the banking and EPAS (energy and projects) groups.

## going mainstream

Rapid growth has changed the office, and the trainees we interviewed had all observed a shift in the identity and work focus of the firm from the days of their applications several years previously. "*Coming here used to be a very outside-the-box choice, a bit of a leftfield option for people who wanted magic circle work without the magic circle lifestyle, but it's become more conventional of late.*" With the rapid increase in the numbers of fee earners, and also trainees, it isn't surprising that the "*defined sense of community*" has "*dissipated a bit.*" The expansion has largely focused around finance, with project finance and capital markets "*all ramped up.*" This shift was particularly noted by trainees with an eye for non-contentious and support departments. Their advice is to consider carefully if W&C is the right firm for you "*if you primarily want to do IP, employment or even litigation these days – the main focus is transactional and getting seats in those departments is very, very hard.*" The good news for those who are attracted to transactional work is that "*project finance and capital markets – the flashy departments – are getting the quality work and pushing the magic circle.*"

In W&C's four-seat training, only finance and something contentious are compulsory. There is certainly a good spread of seats – as well as asset finance, project finance, structured finance, capital markets, banking and acquisition finance, there are also seats in corporate, tax, construction, real estate, employment and IP. Though the litigation department is well developed (and apparently still "*a core area in partners' minds*"), trainees confess that with their expanded numbers, "*getting a seat there is tricky and qualifying there next to impossible.*" One almost universal truth is that trainees will spend six months working at one of the firm's numerous European or Asian offices. Increased trainee numbers have made popular seats like Hong Kong "*even more competitive,*" but Stockholm and Johannesburg have recently been added to the pot, and "*if you don't get your first choice, you'll still go somewhere pretty cool.*" Again, if you have no real urge to take a seat abroad, the advice of trainees is to consider carefully whether W&C is the firm for you. It isn't just the six months spent in foreign parts that add international flavour to the training: even in London you'll be exposed to a wealth of cross-border transactions.

## deal me in

Whichever path they pick through the departments, trainees praise the firm's ability "*to get you meaningfully involved work.*" Their experiences do vary across the firm, not least due to "*the partners who run departments and the big role they play in setting the tone of work.*" Banking, for example, whether it be acquisition finance or asset finance, is "*a standout place for atmosphere*" and "*the partners*

are good fun but still put in serious work.*" Here, trainees find themselves "*thrown in*" and must "*hit the ground running.*" In acquisition finance, advice to the banks involved in Telewest's recent £1.8 billion refinancing are the order of business. On big deals such as this, our sources reported on their graduation from "*admin-based work and company searches to minor drafting.*" In asset finance the story is the same: "*filing and menial work*" turns into more challenging assignments and "*associates will involve you in transactions from beginning to end.*" Asset finance relates to anything from planes to ships to industrial machinery, with last year's advice to Vietnam Airlines on a $150 million purchase of three Airbus aircraft quite typical.

Over in projects the scale of work can be gargantuan, which is perhaps what led one trainee to describe it as "*a powerhouse department*" and another to whisper of "*a certain air of arrogance that they make or break the firm.*" The $11.2 billion Qatargas II project on which W&C represented ExxonMobil and Qatargas Petroleum is the sort of deal that ensures "*the atmosphere is extremely hectic.*" In this environment, as you'd expect, trainees resign themselves to "*helping out with whatever needs doing.*"

Corporate seats place trainees in smaller teams, which means "*fantastic*" exposure to deals. Said one source: "*I had lots of responsibility on a share purchase and saw the whole transaction through.*" Of late, the corporate lawyers have acted on some pretty big deals, including advice to a group of multinationals on a transaction structured as a steel offtake supply arrangement worth around £3.6 billion, and assisting the Government of Greece on the part sale of its national gas distribution network. We spoke to corporate trainees in quiet times when "*a lot of filing and indexing*" dominated but we did hear that "*those there at Christmas worked all hours.*" Interestingly, we also learnt of "*a more formal and hierarchical atmosphere*" with "*a lesser culture of feedback.*" Similarly, a seat in capital markets can be "*tough.*" Just as in corporate, whilst "*people are friendly socially, in terms of the work it's more hierar-chical and trainees are expected to do the grunt work."* The scale of deals (eg advising Credit Suisse on the $100 million debut Eurobond issue by a leading Ukrainian bank) often means *"irregular hours," "hard work"* and *"a lot of proof-reading and adding changes to documents,"* with *"associates running the deals and delegating discrete tasks."*

## winning formula

Away from transactional work, the commercial liti-gators have also built up relationships with banks and have been acting for a group of lenders attempting to gain complete control of the Formula One business. Despite the undeniable glamour of such cases, trainees end up with a back-seat role and it looks as if more fun is had by the lucky few that do their contentious seat in either IP or employment. Both of these niche departments are described as *"incredibly informal"* and possess a culture of *"con-tinuous feedback."* Employment in particular offers *"client meetings every week, drafting of agreements and running your own little cases."* Other smaller departments such as tax or real estate are also *"informal and very relaxed, but much less social."*

Across the seats, what characterises the two years is *"training that is not based on classroom-style learn-ing so much as being proactive and getting your hands dirty."* Our sources appreciated that *"information is there for you to digest, but you're not spoon-fed"* and preferred participation in *"training sessions that are for all fee earners"* not just trainees. Everyone had experienced *"being given work you don't understand or the context it fits into"* which served to remind them that *"you're at the bottom of the food chain,"* but they also enjoyed *"less bureaucracy, a great deal of individual attention from supervisors and good levels of responsibility."* Even if there is some sense that *"as numbers increase, the firm needs to keep working on the way it communicates with trainees,"* in most departments trainees felt *"pretty comfortable that you know how you're doing and how partners or asso-ciates view you and your work."*

## flat pack

The firm's move to a *"light, airy, all glass and space"* single-site office near Bank was an important one. After years of working on several sites, staff revel in *"an air of cohesion," "seeing people you never knew existed"* and *"feeling like one firm."* The new des res has not altered the *"flat hierarchy"* we've grown used to hearing about, and neither has the super-relaxed dress code been tightened up. Features like *"the cen-trum with glass lifts floor to ceiling"* and an *"excellent canteen"* are much appreciated as a sign of the new, but one hangover of the old remains unchanged – *"the hours can be terrible."* There's really no way around this issue except that *"in the quieter times you leave at 6pm if you're done."* If that doesn't prove consolation enough, trainees can always reflect on their whopping salaries, which are among the high-est in London.

Each month the firm throws a drinks party in the office (*"an African theme last time"*) and a welter of the usual sorts of sports teams aid social cohe-sion. Unfortunately, trainees couldn't pin down exactly what defines a W&C type, though they could tell us this – *"None of us have that corporate face, the deluded sense of self-grandeur or the inclina-tion to stab each other in the back."* If by implication they mean pleasant, articulate and driven within reason, then we'd have to agree. In September 2005, 19 of the 20 qualifiers stayed with the firm to fur-ther enjoy the company of their peers (and possibly to gloat about their NQ salaries).

## and finally...

*"A more personal, learning-on-the-job experience"* and a route to the top which circumvents the magic circle – White & Case has much to offer a budding City type.

# Wiggin LLP

## the facts

**Location:** Cheltenham, London
**Number of partners/assistants:** 12/18
**Total number of trainees:** 6
**Seats:** 4x6 months
**Alternative seats:** Secondments

Wiggin LLP is an unusual thing – a top-ranked boutique media firm specialising in film, music, sport, gaming, publishing and broadcasting. What makes it even more unusual is that it is based in Cheltenham.

## in the wiggining...

Once upon a time in the not-so-dim-and-distant past, the world was a different place. There were only four TV channels, a mobile phone was one with a very long flex, the only places you had windows were on your house and car, and being a 'media lawyer' meant you listened to the 'Today' programme on the way to work. But times change and so do law firms. In 2003, lawyers specialising in media work at Cheltenham firm Wiggin Osborne Fullerlove demerged from their private client brethren, giving birth to one of the few dedicated media practices in the UK.

Those trainees we interviewed were the very last to spend time on the WOFL floors of the shared Cheltenham Promenade premises, and could see exactly where the newly streamlined and "*ambitious*" Wiggin is heading. "*WOFL is old school, smaller and quieter, their logo is black and white. Wiggin is dynamic, forward thinking and moving to embrace its expertise as a premier niche media firm.*" Apparently the "*flamboyant*" and "*colourful new look*" now sported by the Wiggin website is part of a conscious attempt to draw a line under a post-merger process that has seen the two firms "*gradually diverging.*" The site is emblazoned with the new slogan "Think Media. Think Brighter. Think Wiggin." It's a bold pronouncement also on view across the Cheltenham and London offices, which have been made over in the same spirit – "*TVs in the receptions, eight-foot high film posters and that sort of thing.*" Trainees are the first to admit that it is a look you'd sooner expect in "*trendy media Soho*" than sleepy Georgian Cheltenham, but recognise with glee that "*it's what the clients expect and you've got to meet their expectations.*"

## wiggin' out

Ah yes, the clients. If the new image is only just kicking in, don't imagine that Wiggin is taking its first tentative steps into the world of media practice. If you're a budding media lawyer and of a nervous disposition, then you might want to take a calming drink of water before you read the next few lines. The firm predominantly represents businesses and organisations (usually London-based) rather than talent, but that doesn't make the client roster any less dizzying. In alphabetical order: Al Jazeera, BBC Films, British Phonographic Industry, Channel 4, Condé Nast, Emap, Five, HBO, Hutchinson 3G, ITV, Macmillan, Napster, Paramount Pictures, Telewest, Time Warner Books, Trinity Mirror, Twentieth Century Fox Film Corp and Warner Brothers have all been satisfied customers of Wiggin in recent years, and that's only the half of it.

Feeling calm? There isn't space to do justice to the full range of Wiggin's media talents in this feature, but suffice it to say that if it's in the media then the firm probably have a hand in it. Television and digital carriage are a particular strength and in the last year lawyers advised top UK racecourses on the termination of a £308 million Attherace Media Rights agreement and the establishment of the new 31 channel 'Racing UK', including UK and international rights agreements and all related EPG, carriage, conditional access and data contracts. Getting even more technical, the firm also received instruction from ITV on both its archive library output deal with ITN and on a ten-year digital-carriage agreement with Teletext, whilst Flextech

# the true picture

Television turned to Wiggin in a dispute with Universal concerning the quality of programming delivered, specifically the *Jerry Springer Show* on taste and decency issues.

Wiggin is also handy when it comes to online or mobile data matters, having advised Littlewoods on the agreements for the acquisition of betting and gaming software for web and digital TV usage, as well as helping GWR in a complex negotiation regarding licensing for point-of-presence network technologies for the handling of on-air requests and interface with on-air playlists. In fact, Wiggin seems happiest wherever the convergence of media technologies throws up legal issues and is not only currently advising the British Phonographic Industry in a litigation against the CD WOW internet retail business, but also the UK Record Industry in proceedings concerning the use of peer-to-peer networks like KaZaA and Grokster.

But so much for the digital age, how about the good old-fashioned magic of the movies? Well, courtesy of two partners with a background as film studio executives in the States – making them unique in the UK – Wiggin advises big US studios on all aspects of film making from script development and purchase, to financing arrangements, production, distribution and selling popcorn in the foyer. Okay, we made the last bit up, but lest you doubt our claims, the firm this year advised Paramount in connection with production related work on feature films 'Aeon Flux' and 'Mission: Impossible III', and Warner Bros in connection with the sale and leaseback transaction for 'The Phantom of the Opera.' It doesn't get more showbiz than that.

## earwiggin'

But just how much exposure will the average trainee get to such work? The answer should prick up your ears: *"A lot!"* The small size of the firm coupled with its specialist expertise means every single seat involves *"very focused media work."* Whilst contemporaries at larger firms strain every sinew to spend six months in a niche seat, Wiggin trainees enjoy the option of *"media, which is in two sections, broadcasting and technology,"* and media litigation (*"music and defamation"*), property, employment and corporate (*"which includes film"*). What's more, there is also a regular secondment to the British Phonographic Industry. With only four six-month slots to fill they seem almost spoilt for choice, but *"because each area is heavily media focused, there isn't one seat that is fiercely competitive."* Property and employment, for example, *"exist to serve the media clients,"* so you're never too far from the action, but if you have a specific focus in mind, then trainees tell us it is also possible to specialise. *"Someone did three seats of focused music broadcasting and technology work."*

The basic trainee experiences are common across departments with *"an emphasis on client contact,"* a *"policy of giving you lots of responsibility"* and a minimal amount of the less desirable tasks because *"we don't really do bundling or pagination, there's an outside firm for that."* But what is really music to the ears of trainees is that *"you're often on cases at the cutting edge of technology and legal issues, helping to make decisions that haven't been made before."* In the media department trainees find themselves *"doing a lot of broadcasting matters, regulatory stuff regarding Ofcom"* or by contrast *"drafting terms and conditions for online gaming companies."* Media lit sees them assisting on *"defamation matters, mainly in terms of publishers and magazines, although there are a few high-worth individuals too."* This is also the department handling the UK Record Industry and BPI matters, so trainees can expect *"lots of contact with major record labels and queries from the music industry,"* and the BPI secondment is a chance to get an *"even closer experience of anti-music-piracy work in an in-house context."* Time in corporate on the other hand allows trainees to assist on TV and film financing and production matters as well as other media transactions.

# the true picture

## cotswold life

The work that Wiggin trainees enjoy is a clear reason to come to the firm, but what about that Cotswold location? And why is it there if the London office facility is *"constantly full of Wiggin lawyers, and there are even drivers to take the partners to and from the City."* As we talked to trainees – none of whom had a connection with the area before commencing their contracts – it became quite clear why *"it would take a massive impetus to make the firm move."*

Wiggin is based in a beautiful building where appropriately a cinema once stood. It is *"right in the heart of Cheltenham, on the poshest shopping street, The Promenade"* opposite a rather grand fountain. Getting to work, taking a lunch break or popping out for a post-work drink is a matter of pleasure rather than *"a scramble like in London."* If moving to the area was initially *"an effort,"* once in situ our sources had found that *"initially your social life revolves around the firm, and you have a stronger connection with work people than you might do in London,"* but *"there's a lot to do in Cheltenham and most people develop connections outside work quickly."* What's more, we heard of several people who maintained London-based love lives and most people find the Cotswold location proves remarkably popular for *"mates in London at big firms who want to escape at the weekends."* Add in Wiggin's *"substantial wages"* and the lower cost of living in Cheltenham and the whole picture begins to look highly appealing. Probably exactly what went through the mind of the new corporate tax partner who arrived from Ashurst earlier in 2005.

Common characteristics of Wiggin trainees are a *"sociable, robust attitude"* that is *"invaluable in client meetings."* The firm has *"a deceptively relaxed atmosphere"* but no lack of intensity in its work. At times you will be *"gritting yourself to work all night"* and normal hours are *"typically 8.30am to 7.30 or 8pm,"* which is definitely long for a regional firm, but perhaps not so terrible when

considered in the context that *"we're basically a London firm in terms of expertise."* After work it is just a short hop to the *"masses of restaurants and bars,"* usually The Residence in Montpellier or *"other expensive wine bars."* A Friday evening drinks trolley helps keep the wallets heavy and the *"firm's social atmosphere ticking over,"* before the truly brave go off to sample the local nightlife. *"Subtone is a trainee haunt. It is... er... well, the catchment area is all of the rural Cotswolds so it's a phenomenon!"* A game of football, a country walk, or even a *"Cotswold pub crawl"* are common ways to clear the passages at the weekend and the lifestyle evidently suits most. Normally two of the three qualifiers stay on with the firm each year, and in 2005 it was one out of two. Whether they stay or go, trainees recognise the value of *"top-drawer media experience that means you're well placed to go to any other firm in the field."*

## and finally...

Fantastic experience, all the benefits of a London training in the comfort of the Cotswolds – you're probably not the only one thinking that an application is a must, so make it a good one.

# Withers LLP

## the facts

**Location:** London
**Number of partners/assistants:** 58/81
**Total number of trainees:** 26
**Seats:** 4x6 months
**Alternative seats:** Overseas seat
**Extras:** Language Classes

At Withers, traditional private client work does not come at the expense of a modern outlook. In addition to stellar private client and family teams, the firm cuts a dash as a sophisticated international outfit with designs on the commercial market.

## distant horizons

"*If you're interested in family and private client, there is an elite of firms that are good at it.*" Withers is one of them, with over half the firm's annual turnover generated by work for private clients. Although faithful to a core client base of "*landed estates, older-money clients and lots of lords and ladies,*" the firm is not content to sit back and smugly survey its estate. "*There is a huge drive towards new, younger, money-eyed clients.*" Such as? "*Entrepreneurs, owners of high street chains, arty, publishing and writing-related clients*" plus "*normal City people and people you read about who made a fortune last year doing this or that.*" The firm's London client base includes 15% of the *Sunday Times*' Rich List. Withers is by no means UK-centric though. A 2002 merger with US partnership Bergman Horowitz gives the firm the largest private client team in the world, with 100 specialists in London, New York and New Haven. As one trainee observed: "*We are definitely cornering the market as far as I can see.*"

Withers is also eyeing up the commercial market and "*gunning for slightly bigger projects on the property and corporate side.*" The rationale is clear: "*When a private client is brought into the building we want them to be attracted to the commercial side too.*" Some clients already are: a considerable amount of the firm's commercial work is cross-referred from private client lawyers. Activity revolves around small-scale banking and finance, advising companies that have grown to the point at which they contemplate a listing on AIM, and the preparation of commercial contracts for "*cool esoteric clients.*" Think "*the kind of people who have concessions in Harvey Nicks,*" for example Lulu Guinness Ltd, which recently acquired a majority shareholding in Cath Kidston Ltd. On the charitable front, the firm has been advising Macmillan Cancer Relief on fundraising, sponsorship and constitutional issues, and on the sporting front it has renegotiated a sponsorship agreement for the Renault Formula One team. A rapidly growing IP team has recently started taking a trainee to help on its work for a swathe of fashionable names including Julien Macdonald, Ghost, Philip Treacy and Moschino.

As is fitting for such a fashion-conscious firm, Withers has a well-established Italian connection and an office in Milan which from September 2005 will provide one overseas corporate seat. In June 2005, it announced the opening of another office in Geneva, a sensible move given that some 30% of the world's overseas-held private wealth is managed there. There are also plans to open a third US office, in Greenwich, Connecticut, in 2006. No wonder trainees described "*a feeling of optimism*" and "*a culture of change.*" Don't be surprised – Withers may be "*conservative with a small c,*" but it was also an early subscriber to LLP status and one of the first leading UK firms to appoint a female senior partner.

## private properties

The size and profile of the private client practice ensures this work will account for one of your four seats. Beyond this, trainees exercise their preferences and, despite "*a huge fight for family,*" feel they are "*treated very well in terms of getting what we want.*" Trainees share an office with a supervisor but are "*allowed to go out and get work elsewhere.*" This can be especially handy in private client where a seat may focus on one field, say domestic estates, entrepreneurs or probate.

Private client's subdivisions are indicative of work so specialist that, as a fresh-faced trainee, "*often when you go into a meeting you have no idea what is going on.*" Hence the need for close supervision and detailed departmental training ("*sometimes three times a week*") on everything from "*budget updates to the finer points of trust law.*" Trainees find it possible to not only learn the basics, but also to "*really concentrate on the interesting stuff.*" A probate seat may give trainees "*a very narrow view*" of the firm's broadest department, but it does afford autonomy. Here, "*you really do get your own files and are pretty much allowed to deal with clients directly.*" By contrast, in a seat in estate planning "*they can be a little reticent in letting trainees*" *loose on long-standing clients."* This may be a blessing in disguise as the firm's wealthiest clients require *"amazingly complex structures"* and *"bizarre tax advice."* One dumbfounded trainee exclaimed: *"I couldn't believe the first time I saw a will that was 35 pages long!"*

## money can't buy you love

Withers' family department is legendary and trainees are certainly aware of its top-notch reputation. They compared the experience to that in the private client by telling us it was *"so completely different it is untrue!"* How so? For starters, the work is often highly contentious and cases can be *"massive, high in value, convoluted and years and years old."* Despite this, there is heaps of client contact for trainees. Among the people who use the family lawyers are *"huge celebrities"* (sadly trainees were tight-lipped), though *"mostly they are just very wealthy people with a complete inability to agree with each other."* One trainee smitten with family law gushed about the department's work: *"It is so impressive and quite fast-paced – I worked harder here than in corporate!"* When asked what it was that kept trainees so busy, another exclaimed: *"Goodness! A whole range of things – lots of client contact including initial meetings, drafting documents, attending hearings and conferences with counsel, taking notes, drafting letters of advice to clients, doing research..."* With so much to do, it is little wonder that *"you really feel part of a case,"* but the flipside of *"meaty work"* is that *"there is a lot of bundling to be done."* Our sources were philosophical on this point; one even admitted: *"Sometimes it is quite nice as you can actually read into the case."* Furthermore, *"you tend to find that you start off doing bundling and end up doing drafting."* Ultimately, you'll even end up running your own small files and dashing off to court to make applications before district judges.

## hardly model behaviour

The property lawyers' work includes everything from Benetton's acquisition of retail sites to advice to landed estates on *"grazing and fishing licences and selling off fields."* Trainees spend part of their time helping out on larger commercial deals by researching and drafting, and part running their own residential sales and purchases. The seat means *"a lot of responsibility and less supervision, for better or for worse."* Though they are not handed the keys for properties with a £20 million price tag, they do take control of a fair number of deals. Said one source: *"Arriving to find 20 files on my desk meant the first week was a week of deep breaths and trying to stay on top of things."*

For heaps of court time and engrossing research, try litigation. Cases span employment and property problems, commercial disputes and contentious probate. A spell in the latter promises exposure to matters such as the recent case of Sherrington v Sherrington, where adult children challenged the validity of their (solicitor) father's will after he left his £5 million estate to his second wife. In commercial litigation, *"you can have a really small file and help on an absolutely enormous case that takes three people working for two years."* Among the most interesting matters on the books lately was the defamation claim brought against the BBC on behalf of companies in the Elite model group following allegations made by TV's undercover supersleuth Donal MacIntyre.

*"For stereotypical corporate work, this is not the place to come,"* announced one source. Instead trainees encounter charity clients, referrals from the private client and family departments, *"bits of odd tax advice"* and *"quite fiddly but quite interesting bits of drafting."* We're told corporate *"would like to be seen as more than just an extension of the firm,"* and moves to build up the department may explain the longer hours trainees have worked lately. Otherwise, across the firm an average 9am to 6.30pm day will usually only be extended in family seats.

## loving your work, stefan

Withers' Old Bailey office has a "*grandiose listed frontage*" which belies "*a snazzy interior*" of glass and chrome. Our sources cooed over an "*understated, trendy and tasteful*" décor, referring to silk-clad walls in a reception area that is stocked up with more copies of Vogue, Tatler and Country Life than a Chelsea newsagent. The decor is apparently "*what you would expect if you were dining somewhere really nice.*" Perhaps the Withers canteen, where in-house chef Stefan provides "*modern British cuisine with a Mediterranean twist.*" There are also home-made cookies in meeting rooms, "*fabulous eats and classic cocktails*" for client parties, and fish and chips wrapped in the Law Society's *Gazette* for firm quiz nights.

We were thrilled to hear that trainees continue to find their way round the firm's peculiar two-limbed building by imagining it as a pair of trousers and referring to various offices by way of their position along the two legs. One source proudly admitted: "*Yes, I am sitting in the crotch!*" Such a comment was indicative of the easy humour and confidence of our interviewees. As for who these people are, though "*there seem to be a hell of a lot of Oxbridge people coming through,*" others are drawn from universities including Bristol, Birmingham, Durham and the LSE. In September 2005 nine out of 13 qualifiers stayed on with the firm.

Socially, Withers' trainees are "*quite understated.*" This is not the place to come if your idea of a great night out includes a gallon of Smirnoff Ice, Las Ketchup, the 'bab van and a gutter. Imagine instead "*a lot of flair, a lot of style and fabulous parties.*" Our sources helped us visualise Pimm's, a chocolate fountain and the courtyard of Gibson Hall for this year's summer bash. At other times, trainees can join a book group, departmental excursions (ice-skating, day trips to France, family picnics and boat trips), football and netball teams, and when we rang we heard there were plans for a Summer Olympics on Hampstead Heath. To ease aching limbs or tight shoulders, Withers brings a masseur into the office, although many people find that nipping over to Corney & Barrow or the Magpie & Stump after work is just as good for loosening up.

## and finally...

Withers' superb private client and family work will always mark it out from the crowd. If this side of the law attracts you and your tastes are more Kensington High Street than Camden High Street, you have to apply.

# Wragge & Co LLP

## the facts

**Location:** Birmingham, London
**Number of partners/assistants:** 105/400
**Total number of trainees:** 48
**Seats:** 4x6 months
**Alternative seats:** Secondments
**Extras:** Pro bono – College of Law and other advice schemes; language training

Birmingham's Wragge & Co is the undisputed big daddy in the Midlands. Its client list is as illustrious as its reputation for staff satisfaction is impressive. Training here has got to be a great start to a legal career.

## blowing bubbles

One of the first things you have to appreciate about Wragges is its superb client base. The names couldn't be better: BA, National Grid, Powergen, the DTI... Given the number of blue-chip, giant-sized names serviced by the firm you could be forgiven for thinking it was a leading London firm. The firm landed new client BT earlier last year, and soon after the BT bonus it went into top gear when a rebuked Eversheds lost its place on Honda's legal panel. This new trophy client sits on the mantelpiece between other carmakers Ford and Toyota. And there was yet more vroom when the firm's pensions department landed instructions from MG Rover's pension

# the true picture

trustees.

In other news, Wragges is now assisting on the MoD's £3 billion purchase of twin aircraft carriers – regally christened HMS Queen Elizabeth and HMS Prince of Wales – and there was a ringing endorsement of its IP practice, when it was instructed to represent $O_2$ in one of the key cases of the past year after Hutchison 3G (now known as 3) dared encroach upon $O_2$'s blue bubble imagery. Unfortunately, the Court of Appeal saw things from 3's perspective. Brands aplenty flock to Wragges' IP team, among them Microsoft, Marks & Spencer, Ordnance Survey, HJ Heinz and fellow Brummies Cadbury Schweppes.

## going for gold

Wragges has discovered that the patronage of top-grade clients and work makes it far easier to recruit and retain high-quality lawyers at all levels, both into its Birmingham base and its second office in London. Under the Wragge & Co banner, lawyers have been running some impressively large deals including, in property, some key work undertaken by a new 'Regeneration Team'. Acting for Sanctuary Housing Association it advised on a £300 million large-scale voluntary transfer of council homes in the London Borough of Tower Hamlets, with a seven-year programme of refurbishment, demolition and construction of 2,300 homes in Stepney. The team also advised the Greater London Authority on the 2012 Olympic bid.

On the corporate front, the firm advised on numerous private equity deals including Robert Dyas' £61 million sale of its 75-store hardware business. It also advised RAC on the disposal of its Isuzu Truck import business and Japanese investment bank Nomura International on its £245 million acquisition of Earls Court & Olympia's exhibition centres. Busy clients such as Nomura represent the way forward for Wragges, because the Earls Court deal, although not insubstantial, is by no means the biggest the bank undertakes. Back in 2003, Nomura instructed Wragges on its whopping £2.5 billion bid

for Scottish & Newcastle's retail division.

While it is all systems go on the commercial front, the firm's 15-strong private client team found itself surplus to requirements and decamped to Mills & Reeve last year. We see this as evidence of Wragges' desire to concentrate on commercial work and to slough off its less profitable areas. Indeed, if we were to find an Achilles' heel it is that profitability is not as high as it could be. We suspect the firm's management has every intention of working on this.

## gypsies, tramps and ceo's

Of more immediate concern to our readers is the nature of the training on offer at the Midlands giant. First things first, all trainees are recruited to the Birmingham office and are given the option of taking seats in London, where IP, private equity, real estate and employment/pensions teams are ready to welcome them. Property seats are mandatory for all, though the practice area is a diverse one encompassing both commercial and residential matters. Property management assignments involve negotiating leases for both landlords and tenants, so enabling the trainee "*to see things from both sides of the fence.*" Even those fresh from their LPC will run their own files on relatively simple leases, which, as one source pithily surmised, is all about getting to know one word very well – 'reasonable'. "*On a basic level, if favouring the landlord take all the 'reasonables' out of the lease, and if acting for a tenant, amend and add 'em in.*"

A first seat in the residential development group equals "*a few weeks of panic with a stack of letters waiting to go out.*" The frequent client contact and speedy drafting will inure you to life in law; in a snap you'll be negotiating with councils over access roads leading to new housing estates. The retail and leisure team will give you "*up to 30 files of your own.*" From the initial letter to polishing off the lease agreement, a trainee will see plenty of pubs and clubs tenanted by the time their six months are up. "*Writing threatening macho letters is fun*" in property litigation, "*the flipside of which is the necessary grunt work.*" The time spent preparing court bundles will be worth it, however, when you get to go to hearings and trials with supervisors. Trainees also take charge of some of the straightforward evictions, serving notice on defaulting tenants and acting on "*the removal of travellers and squatters.*"

Corporate, too, is compulsory but rather than "*plonk you in*" (as in property), a week's worth of induction greets the trainee upon their arrival in the department. "*It's responsibility all the way at Wragges,*" so you won't be tucked behind a photocopier. "*I dealt with clients, even directors,*" reported one source. Obviously "*you can't have a trainee leading a multimillion-pound deal,*" so expect to draft ancillary documents, directors' appointments, Companies House forms, board minutes, etc. And of course there will be "*lots of document management.*"

The third '*option seat*' is when trainees get to sample something more specialist. Employment and pensions is the most sought-after choice. If lucky enough to get the posting, trainees spend three months sitting with the employment team and three with the people in pensions. In employment, you'll be constantly researching and keeping fee earners abreast of "*changes in the rules and regulations for tribunals on sex, race and disability.*" When not poring over statutes, you'll learn to review and draft contracts of employment as well as negotiate settlements and compromise agreements. The trick apparently is to be fully prepared to have the first few efforts "*either corrected or completely rewritten by your supervisor.*" Some of the time will be spent assisting on corporate deals, "*where employment issues are part of a merger or acquisition.*" In both the employment half and the pensions half, "*you'll get good work and you won't be there until 8pm every night.*"

## smart moves

Wragges consistently charts in the *Sunday Times'* 'Best Companies to Work For' survey, last year ranking 24th. Internally, the firm has long been defined by a consultative approach and boasted multitude of staff think-tanks and committees. The trainees have their own forum, which "*sometimes just handles the social events budget and sometimes doubles as a way for trainees to have their say.*" Trainees tend to be aware of the firm's plans, telling us: "*The general strategy is quite clear.*" Previously renowned for a touchy-feely approach, things "*may be less so in the future,*" as there is "*a slight shift in emphasis – we're geared more to profitability.*" "*I think this reflects trends in the legal world,*" opined one source; besides, "*it's a law firm, not a hippy commune!*"

A hotchpotch of business buzzwords has bewitched the partners. "*You have to comply with these strategic imperatives, and then there's the high-performance culture thingie,*" one trainee informed us. We thought this was the year of the rooster, but no, "*this is the Year of Excellence*" in which "*a high-performance culture*" will cohere with "*an inclusion culture*" to create a "*24/7 client service.*" And then there's "*SMART*" – "*Something Achievable Realistic Timed Oriented... I can't remember what it means.*" Hurrah for Google! SMART stands for Specific – Measurable – Achievable – Realistic – Time bound. Business gobbledegook aside, communication at the firm is still as good as it ever was and the move to open-plan working is in part responsible. Said one trainee: "*You can pipe up if you know something and get to chat about things you're working on.*"

## organised chaos

England's second city plays host to a healthy legal community and has gone through something of a renaissance in recent years. "*The new Bull Ring is excellent and Brum is really nice,*" beamed one source who just seconds earlier had poured scorn on Brum's alias the Venice of the North. Like Birmingham itself, Wragges' Colmore Row HQ is an unkempt hive of activity. Its interiors display "*chaos-decor*" and "*there aren't many windows – you're lucky if you get natural light.*" "*Filing cabinets are everywhere and our tidy desk policy is not strictly*" adhered to." Cramped conditions mean "*the long-term plan is to acquire another nearby building.*" In London the firm occupies space in the old Prudential building in Holborn. It is "*old on the outside, new on the inside*" and considerably roomier than the premises in Birmingham. "*It's quite chilled,*" one source told us. "*It has the feel of a smaller firm.*" Wragges also shares an office in Brussels with "*a German partner-friend-company.*" There's no seat here, but trainees do get to pop over "*if needed in the European competition group.*"

As for the people it recruits, we encountered a confident and articulate group in our interviews. The firm displays a tendency towards "*redbricks, Durham, Exeter, London and Oxbridge,*" although good academic credentials alone aren't enough. According to one source: "*You need a bit of nous because commercial law is 90% business and 10% law.*" Once welcomed into the fold, Wragges likes to keep people. NQ retention rates for 2003 and 2004 were 100%; in September 2005 the firm was slightly less successful yet still beat most other firms, keeping 15 of its 17 qualifiers.

## those pesky kids

Week by week, out of hours, trainees are not averse to fun. The Walkabout is the gateway to Birmingham's chav boulevard, Broad Street, where "*there's always a fight.*" Usually the Wragges recruits steer clear and head for more civilised venues such as Aprés, Digress and Chi ("*good lunches, takes forever to get served though*"). They're not above high jinks and general naughtiness, however. Last year after a night at Brindleyplace some trainees found themselves canalside with the urge to untie a boat. "*We didn't know people actual lived in those things,*" one of the culprits admitted. On board, a light came on and an irate boat dweller emerged: "*He chased us all the way past Bobby Browns!*"

Various events are organised by the Birmingham Trainee Solicitors' Society, but none can beat the firm's own Christmas extravaganza, which unusually takes place in January (apparently for budgetary reasons). Last time, it involved the creation of a fairground within the International Convention Centre and ended up with "*two people falling off the hired carousel.*" Said carousel was later a casualty of an unsafe mix of "*free booze and candyfloss.*" It all sounds like a lot of fun and with a £1,000 cash prize up for grabs, Lady Luck can turn the Christmas bash into a nice little earner for one member of staff.

## and finally...

The Wragge & Co name on your CV is the ultimate bonus in a training experience that takes you through all the basics via a superb client base. Though we sense a shift to a more profit-driven culture, this is still one of the most desirable firms to work for in the UK.

# solicitors a-z

# Addleshaw Goddard

150 Aldersgate Street, London, EC1A 4EJ
Sovereign House, PO Box 8, Sovereign Street, Leeds LS1 1HQ
100 Barbirolli Square, Manchester, M2 3AB
Tel: (0161) 934 6000 / (020) 7606 8855
Fax: (0161) 934 6060 / (020) 7606 4390

## firm profile

As a major force on the legal landscape, Addleshaw Goddard offers extensive and exciting opportunities to all its trainees across the entire spectrum of commercial law, from employment and banking to real estate, corporate finance, entertainment, PFI and litigation. Ranked 16th largest law firm in the UK with a fee income in 2004/5 of £139 million, the firm was voted UK Firm of the Year at the Legal Week Awards 2004 and as a trainee with this firm, you'll be a key member of the team from day one. Whether based in the Leeds, London or Manchester office (or out on secondment), you'll work closely with blue-chip clients within a supportive yet challenging environment, and be part of a structured training programme designed to ensure your success - now and in the future.

## main areas of work

The firm has four main business divisions: finance, contentious and commercial, corporate, and real estate. Within these divisions as well as the main practice areas it also has specialist areas such as sport, media and entertainment and private client services such as family and trust and tax.

## trainee profile

Graduates who are capable of achieving a 2:1 and can demonstrate commercial awareness, motivation and enthusiasm. Applications from law and non-law graduates are welcomed, as are applications from mature students who may be considering a change of direction.

## training environment

During each six-month seat, there will be regular two-way performance reviews with the supervising partner or solicitor. Trainees have the opportunity to spend a seat in one of the firm's other offices and there are a number of secondments to clients available. Seated with a qualified solicitor or partner and working as part of a team, enables trainees to develop the professional skills necessary to deal with the demanding and challenging work the firm carries out for its clients. Practical training is complemented by high-quality training courses provided by both the in-house team and external training providers.

## sponsorship & benefits

CPE and LPC fees are paid, plus a maintenance grant of £4,500. Benefits include corporate gym membership, season ticket loan, subsidised restaurant, pension and private healthcare.

## vacation placements

Places for 2006 - 75; Duration - 2 weeks; location - all offices; Apply by 10 February 2006.

| Partners | 170 |
| Associates | 500+ |
| Trainees | 89 |

**contact**
The Graduate Recruitment Team
grad@addleshawgoddard.com

**selection procedure**
Interview, assessment centre

**closing date for 2008**
31 July 2006

**application**
Training contracts p.a. **50**
Applications p.a. **2,000**
% interviewed **10%**
Required degree grade **2:1**

**training**
Salary
1st year
Manchester/Leeds **£20,000**
London **£28,000**

2nd year
Manchester/Leeds **£22,000**
London **£30,000**

Holiday entitlement
25 days
% of trainees with
a non-law degree p.a. **45%**

**post-qualification**
Salary
Manchester/Leeds **£33,000**
London **£48,000**
(under review)
% of trainees offered job
on qualification (2005) **78%**

**other offices**
Leeds, London, Manchester

# Allen & Overy LLP

One New Change, London EC4M 9QQ
Tel: (020) 7330 3000  Fax: (020) 7330 9999
Email: graduate.recruitment@allenovery.com
Website: www.allenovery.com/careeruk

## firm profile

Allen & Overy LLP is an international legal practice, comprising Allen & Overy LLP and its affiliated undertakings, with 4,800 people in 25 major centres worldwide. The practice's client list includes many of the world's leading businesses, financial institutions, governments and private individuals.

## main areas of work

Corporate, finance, dispute resolution, real estate, tax, employment and private wealth management and charities.

## trainee profile

You will need to demonstrate a genuine enthusiasm for law, and both energy and initiative. The practice looks for creative, problem-solving people who can quickly identify salient points without losing sight of detail. As an international commercial practice, business awareness and an international outlook are prerequisite, as is the ability to work closely with others.

## training environment

Allen & Overy offers a training contract characterised by flexibility and choice. The practice's training programme is widely regarded as the best in the City and continues throughout a career with Allen & Overy. Given the strength of the practice's international Finance and Corporate departments, trainees spend 12 months working in these areas. They also spend time in Dispute Resolution or Employment gaining contentious experience. There are opportunities to undertake international and client secondments. By working closely with trainers and colleagues, trainees develop practical experience and enjoy a high level of early responsibility. A positive, open and co-operative culture is encouraged both professionally and socially and a wide range of sporting and social activities are available.

## benefits

Private healthcare scheme, private medical insurance, season ticket loans, subsidised restaurant, gym membership, six weeks unpaid leave upon qualification.

## vacation placements

Places for Christmas 2005 (final year students and graduates all disciplines): 20; Duration: ten days; Remuneration: 250p.w.; Closing date: 31st October 2005. Places for summer 2006 (penultimate year students all disciplines): 75; Duration: 3 weeks; Remuneration:£250 p.w.; Closing date: 31st January 2006. Places available in London.

## sponsorship & awards

GDL and LPC fees paid. Maintenance grants: LPC - £7,000, GDL - £6,000 in London, £5,000 elswhere.

---

| | |
|---|---|
| **Partners** | 440* |
| **Associates** | 1858* |
| **London Trainees** | 247 |
| *Denotes world-wide number | |

**contact**
Graduate Recruitment

**method of application**
Online application form

**selection procedure**
Interview

**closing date for 2008**
GDL candidates
**End Jan 2006**
Law candidates **End Aug 2006**

**application**
Training contracts p.a. **120**
Applications p.a. **2,700**
% interviewed p.a. **12%**
Required degree grade **2:1**

**training**
Salary
**1st year (2005) £29,000**
**2nd year (2005) £33,000**
Holiday entitlement **25 days**
% of trainees with a
non-law degree p.a. **45%**
% of trainees with a
law degree p.a. **55%**
No. of seats available
in international offices
**32 seats twice a year and 8
client secondments**

**post-qualification**
Salary (2005) **£51,000**
% of trainees offered job
on qualification (as at
31/3/05) **90%**
% of partners (as at
31/1/05) who joined as
trainees **32%**

**international offices**
Amsterdam, Antwerp, Bangkok, Beijing, Brussels, Bratislava, Budapest, Dubai, Frankfurt, Hamburg, Hong Kong, Luxembourg, Madrid, Milan, Moscow, New York, Paris, Prague, Rome, Shanghai, Singapore, Tokyo, Turin, Warsaw

# asb *law*

Innovis House, 108 High Street, Crawley, West Sussex RH10 1AS
Tel: (01293) 601422  Fax: (01293) 601450
Email: louise.nicholas@asb-law.com
Website: www.asb-law.com

## firm profile

asb law, a top-100 law firm and one of the largest in the south east, provides legal services to a diverse range of clients including high net worth individuals, businesses, financial institutions, government and public sector bodies. The firm's prestigious clients and the range of the services provided demonstrate that it is possible to enjoy a challenging and rewarding career without the grind of a daily commute to the City. asb has offices in Brighton, Crawley, Croydon, Horsham and Maidstone.

## main areas of work

Principal types of work are banking, corporate finance, commercial, commercial litigation, commercial property/planning, employment, environment, technology/e-commerce, insolvency and recovery, intellectual property, licensing, personal injury - claimant and defendant, family, residential property, tax, trust and probate.

## trainee profile

The firm is looking for strong intellectual ability, drive and initiative in people who are client-focused and commercially minded with strong interpersonal skills. You should relish the prospect of early responsibility and contact with clients in a supportive environment.

## training environment

The programme is divided into four six-month seats, tailored to your strengths/interests. Training is structured to empower you to learn, take responsibility and interact with clients from an early stage and includes workshops/seminars as part of the firm's professional development programme. Some flexibility is required as seats can be in any of the five offices. A structured career path from trainee to partner is in place for the right candidates. asb law is proud of its history of retaining trainees on qualification.

## sponsorship & benefits

An interest-free loan is available for the LPC, repayable over the period of the training contract.

| Partners | 40 |
|---|---|
| **Vacancies** | **5** |
| **Total Trainees** | **10** |
| **Total Staff** | **260** |

**contact**
Louise Nicholas
Tel: (01293) 601422

**method of application**
Application form downloaded from firm's website

**selection procedure**
2 interviews and a written exercise

**closing date for 2008**
31 July 2006

**application**
Training contracts p.a. **5**
Applications p.a **1,000**
% interviewed **5%**
Required degree grade **2:1**

**training**
£18,000 (2005)

**offices**
Brighton, Crawley, Horsham, Croydon, Maidstone

# Ashurst

Broadwalk House, 5 Appold St, London EC2A 2HA
Tel: (020) 7638 1111  Fax: (020) 7638 1112
Email: gradrec@ashurst.com
Website: www.ashurst.com

## firm profile

Ashurst is a leading international law firm advising corporates and financial institutions, with core businesses in mergers and acquisitions, corporate and structured finance. The firm's strong and growing presence in Europe and elsewhere is built on extensive experience in working with clients on the complex international legal and regulatory issues relating to cross-border transactions.

## main areas of work

Commercial; corporate; energy, transport and infrastructure; EU and competition; international finance; litigation; real estate; and tax.

## trainee profile

To become an Ashurst trainee you will need to show common sense and good judgement. The firm needs to know that you can handle responsibility because you will be involved in some of the highest quality international work on offer anywhere. The transactions and cases you will be involved in will be intellectually demanding, so Ashurst looks for high academic achievers who are able to think laterally. But it's not just academic results that matter. Ashurst wants people who have a range of interests outside of their studies. And they want outgoing people with a sense of humour who know how to laugh at themselves.

## training environment

Your training contract will consist of four seats. For each, you will sit with a partner or senior solicitor who will be the main source of your work and your principal supervisor during that seat. Seats are generally for six months. Anything less than that will not give you sufficient depth of experience for the responsibility Ashurst expects you to take on. The firm asks trainees to spend a seat in a contentious area of practice and one in a transaction-based department. You are free to choose your remaining two seats, subject to availability.

## benefits

Private health insurance, pension, life assurance, interest-free season ticket loan, gym membership and 25 days holiday per year during training.

## vacation placements

Places for 2006: A two-week Easter placement scheme primarily aimed at final-year non-law undergraduates and all graduates. Two three-week summer placement schemes primarily aimed at penultimate-year law undergraduates. Remuneration £250 p.w. Closing date 31 January 2006.

## sponsorship & awards

CPE and LPC funding plus maintenance allowances. LPC Distinction award of £500. Language tuition bursaries.

| | |
|---|---|
| **Partners** | 162 |
| **Assistant Solicitors** | 470 |
| **Total Trainees** | 95 |

**contact**
Stephen Trowbridge
Graduate Recruitment Manager

**method of application**
Online

**selection procedure**
Interview with 1 assistant followed by interview with 2 partners

**closing date for 2008**
31 July 2006

**application**
Training contracts p.a. **45-50**
Applications p.a. **2,500**
% interviewed p.a. **15%**
Required degree grade **2:1**

**training**
**Salary**
(2005)
**First six months**
**£28,000**
**Second six months**
**£29,000**
**Third six months**
**£31,000**
**Fourth six months**
**£32,000**
Holiday entitlement **25 days**
% of trainees with a non-law degree p.a. **45-50%**
Number of seats abroad available p.a. **8**

**post-qualification**
Salary (2005) **£48,000**
% of trainees offered job on qualification (2004) **90%**

**overseas offices**
Brussels, Dubai, Frankfurt, Madrid, Milan, Munich, New Delhi, New York, Paris, Singapore, Tokyo

# Baker & McKenzie LLP

100 New Bridge Street, London EC4V 6JA
Tel: (020) 7919 1000  Fax: (020) 7919 1999
Email: london.graduate.recruit@bakernet.com
Website: www.ukgraduates.bakernet.com

## firm profile

Baker & McKenzie is a leading global law firm based in 69 locations across 38 countries. With a presence in virtually every important financial and commercial centre in the world, our strategy is to provide the best combination of local legal and commercial knowledge, international expertise and resources.

## main areas of work

Corporate; commercial; dispute resolution; banking and finance; EC, competition and trade; employment; intellectual property and information technology; pensions; tax; projects; property. In addition the firm has cross-departmental practice groups, such as media and communications, insurance and reinsurance, business recovery and environmental law.

## trainee profile

The firm is looking for trainee solicitors who are stimulated by intellectual challenge and want to be 'the best' at what they do. Effective communication together with the ability to be creative and practical problem solvers, team players and a sense of humour are qualities which will help them stand out from the crowd.

## training environment

Four six-month seats which include corporate and a contentious seat, usually within the firm's highly regarded dispute resolution department. There is also the possibility of a secondment abroad or to a client. At the start of your training contract you will have a meeting to discuss individual seat preferences and during each seat you will have formal and informal reviews to discuss your progress. Your training contract commences with a highly interactive and practical induction programme which focuses on key skills including practical problem solving, interviewing, presenting and the application of information technology. The firm's training programmes include important components on management and other business skills, as well as seminars and workshops on key legal topics for each practice area. There is a Trainee Solicitor Liaison Committee which acts as a forum for any new ideas or raises issues which may occur during your training contract. Trainees are actively encouraged to participate in a variety of pro bono issues and outside office hours there is a varied sporting and social life.

## benefits

Permanent health insurance, life insurance, private medical insurance, group personal pension, subsidised gym membership, season ticket loan, subsidised staff restaurant.

| Partners | 76 |
| Assistant Solicitors | 183 |
| Total Trainees | 70 |

**contact**
Jane Austin

**method of application**
Online application form

**selection procedure**
Candidates to give a short oral presentation based on the facts of a typical client problem, interview with two partners, meeting with a trainee

**closing date for 2008**
Non-law **18 Feb 2006**
Law **31 July 2006**

**application**
Training contracts p.a. **30**
Applications p.a. **2,000**
% interviewed p.a. **10%**
Required degree grade **2:1**

**training**
Salary
**1st year (2005) £29,000 +
£3,000 'joining bonus'
2nd year (2005) £32,000**
Holiday entitlement **25 days**
% of trainees with a
non-law degree p.a.
**Approx 50%**
No. of seats available
abroad p.a. **Variable**

**post-qualification**
Salary (2005) **£50,000**
% of trainees offered job
on qualification (2005) **88%**

495

# Baker & McKenzie LLP continued

## vacation placements

**London Summer Placement** - Places for 2006: 30; Duration: 3 weeks; Remuneration (2005): £270 p.w.; Closing date: 31 January 2006.

**International Summer Placement** - Places for 2006: 3-5; Duration: 6-12 weeks divided between London and an overseas office; Remuneration (2005): £270 p.w.; Closing date: 31 January 2006.

## sponsorship & awards

CPE/GDL funding: fees paid plus £6,000 maintenance.
LPC funding: fees paid plus £7,000.

## additional information

As mentioned, trainees have the opportunity to spend three months working in one of the firm's overseas offices. Trainees have already been seconded to its offices in Sydney, Hong Kong, Frankfurt, Chicago, Washington DC, Brussels and Moscow. In addition, the firm also operates an Associate Training Programme which enables lawyers with 18-24 months pqe to spend between 6-24 months working in an overseas office.

## trainee comments

"I chose Baker & McKenzie because of the unique package it offers to potential trainees. On the one hand, it is a global firm that offers the opportunity to be involved in high calibre commercial work for large corporate clients. On the other, it has a relatively small trainee intake. This means that trainees can expect to take on a good deal of responsibility from the outset, whilst gaining experience of working with lawyers worldwide." Katherine Pawson [newly qualified]

"Baker & McKenzie was an obvious choice for me when I was looking for a training contract. I wanted to work in an international environment and my training contract has certainly provided that. I cannot recall working on a deal which did not have a cross border element to it. Given the size of the global firm, the trainee intake in London is relatively small. This translates into trainees getting a lot of early responsibility throughout, and I have often been the one responsible for liaising with our overseas offices on large multi-jurisdictional deals. It can be a steep learning curve to begin with, but somebody is always on hand with advice if you need it." Paul Lucas [newly qualified]

"Throughout my training contract, I have been given as much responsibility as I can handle and have been made to feel that I am an important part of the team. I have had lots of contact with clients and have worked with a range of lawyers both in the London office and in our offices around the world. The firm has lived up to my expectations both in terms of quality and variety of work and the relaxed and down to earth office atmosphere. This makes it easier to approach lawyers with any questions, meaning that I have never felt completely out of my depth, and it also makes coming to work a lot more enjoyable!" Virginia Allen [4th seat trainee]

### overseas offices

Almaty, Amsterdam, Antwerp, Bahrain, Baku, Bangkok, Barcelona, Beijing, Berlin, Bogotá, Bologna, Brasilia, Brussels, Budapest, Buenos Aires, Cairo, Calgary, Caracas, Chicago, Chihuahua, Dallas, Düsseldorf, Frankfurt, Geneva, Guadalajara, Hanoi, Ho Chi Minh City, Hong Kong, Houston, Jakarta, Juarez, Kuala Lumpur, Kyiv, Madrid, Manila, Melbourne, Mexico City, Miami, Milan, Monterrey, Moscow, Munich, New York, Palo Alto, Paris, Porto Alegre, Prague, Rio de Janeiro, Riyadh, Rome, St Petersburg, San Diego, San Francisco, Santiago, São Paulo, Shanghai, Singapore, Stockholm, Sydney, Taipei, Tijuana, Tokyo, Toronto, Valencia, Vienna, Warsaw, Washington DC, Zürich

# Barlow Lyde & Gilbert

Beaufort House, 15 St Botolph Street, London EC3A 7NJ
Tel: (020) 7247 2277  Fax: (020) 7643 8500
Email: grad.recruit@blg.co.uk
Website: www.blg.co.uk

## firm profile

Barlow Lyde & Gilbert is a leading international business law firm with more than 300 lawyers and 81 partners. The firm's principal office in the UK is in Aldgate in the City of London. BLG is particularly well known for its expertise in insurance law having first started to practise in this area in the 19th century. The firm has long been recognised as pre-eminent in all aspects of this field and it has formed the bedrock from which the firm has expanded into virtually all areas of business law. Today BLG is widely based with strong practices in corporate, financial and commercial law, as well as in all kinds of commercial litigation. The firm also has highly rated aerospace, shipping and international trade, information technology and employment teams.

## trainee profile

BLG recruits 16-18 trainees each year and looks for intelligent and motivated graduates with good academic qualifications and with the social skills that will enable them to communicate effectively and get along with their colleagues and clients.

## training environment

During your training contract you will have six-month seats in four different areas of the firm. The firm will always try to accommodate a trainee's preference for a particular type of work and there may be opportunities to spend time in its other offices, on secondment with clients or on exchange programmes with overseas law firms. A capable trainee will be given responsibility from an early stage in his or her training, subject of course to supervision, and will have to deal regularly with clients. Social activities play an important role for BLG and successful candidates can look forward to a variety of sporting and social events which ensure that people in different parts of the firm have a chance to meet and stay in contact with each other. Trainees are also encouraged to participate in the firm's various pro bono activities.

## vacation placements

An increasing number of BLG's trainees come to the firm through its vacation schemes. Whether you are a law or non-law student the firm will introduce you to a City practice. You will be given the opportunity to become really involved and you can even choose which department you want to spend time in. The closing date for applications is 31 January 2005. The firm also runs open days and drop in days throughout the year. Application is by way of a covering letter and application form.

## sponsorship & awards

Full payment of fees and a maintenance grant are provided.

| | |
|---|---|
| **Partners** | 81 |
| **Assistant Solicitors** | 195 |
| **Total Trainees** | 35 |

**contact**
Caroline Walsh
Head of Graduate
Recruitment & Trainee
Development

**method of application**
Online application form

**selection procedure**
Interview day

**closing date for 2007**
31 July 2006

**application**
Training contracts p.a.
**16-18**
Applications p.a. **2,000**
% interviewed p.a. **10%**

**training**
Salary
**1st year £28,000**
**2nd year £30,000**
Holiday entitlement
**5 weeks**

**post-qualification**
Salary **£47,000**
Trainees offered job
on qualification (2005)
**11 out of 15**

**other offices**
Hong Kong, Shanghai,
Singapore

BLG
Barlow Lyde & Gilbert

# Beachcroft Wansbroughs

100 Fetter Lane, London EC4A 1BN
Tel: (020) 7242 1011  Fax: (020) 2831 6630
Email: bwtrainee@bwlaw.co.uk
Website: www.bwlaw.co.uk

## firm profile
Beachcroft Wansbroughs provides an integrated and consistent national service capability across its strong regional office network and its major offices in the City of London. The firm offers contentious and non-contentious comprehensive legal services to clients in the corporate, commercial, financial, health, insurance and public sectors.

## main areas of work
The firm is managed in two divisions: Litigation and Commercial. These divisions cover a wide range of law including Injury Risk, Professional Risk, Property, Financial Services, Insolvency, Projects, Health, Public Law, Employment and many more.
The firm has created a partnership with a strong sense of purpose and shared value; client service is their guiding principle. They have cultivated a reputation for leading rather than following and this is evident in their IT applications and their approach to training.

## trainee profile
The firm looks for outgoing, commercially minded people preferably with 2:1 honours degree in any subject. You will need to be an excellent team player, possess a mind capable of analysing, interpreting and applying complex points of law.

## training environment
Training takes place over a two year period in London, Bristol, Manchester or Leeds, during which time you'll pursue a demanding study programme, whilst occupying 4 x 6 months seats in some of the key areas of commercial law. Responsibility will come early and the firm provides the supervision and support to enable you to develop and grow.

## benefits
The firm operates a flexible benefits scheme including holiday, pension and private healthcare.

## vacation placements
BW run a paid placement scheme for law and non law students each summer. The closing date is 1st May, please visit www.bwcareers.co.uk for further details.

## sponsorship & awards
Beachcroft Wansbroughs provides payment for GDL, LPC, and £3500 bursary.

| Partners | 139 |
| Assistant Solicitors | 259 |
| Total Trainees | 58 |

**contact**
Naomi Birch
Graduate Recruitment and
Development Officer
Admin Centre
PO Box 2048
One Redcliff Street
Bristol BS99 7UR
Email: bwtrainee@bwlaw.co.uk

**method of application**
Apply online at
www.bwcareers.co.uk for
an application form

**selection procedure**
Assessment centre and
panel interview

**closing date**
1 August each year

**application**
Training contracts per annum
30+
Required degree
2:1 preferred

**training**
Salary
1st year, regions-£20,000
pa
2nd year, regions-£22,500
pa
1st year, London-£28,000
pa
2nd year, London-£30,000
pa

**offices**
Birmingham, Bristol,
Brussels, Leeds, London,
Manchester, Winchester

# SJ Berwin LLP

222 Gray's Inn Road, London WC1X 8XF
Tel: (020) 7533 2268  Fax: (020) 7533 2000
Email: graduate.recruitment@sjberwin.com
Website: www.sjberwin.com/gradrecruit

## firm profile
Since its formation in 1982, SJ Berwin LLP has established a strong reputation in corporate finance. It also has a number of niche specialisms in areas such as private equity and film finance. Much work is international and clients range from major multinational business corporations and financial institutions to high net worth individuals.

## main areas of work
The firm has a wide range of departments, including corporate finance, real estate, litigation, intellectual property, employment, commercial, EU and competition, construction, banking, tax and financial services. Of these, corporate finance is the largest, generating around 45% of the annual turnover.

## trainee profile
The firm wants ambitious, commercially-minded individuals who seek a high level of involvement from day one. Candidates must be bright and determined to succeed. They should be likely to achieve a 2:1 or first.

## training environment
The traineeship is split into four six-month seats in a variety of departments, including two corporate seats. There are opportunities for seats in the firm's overseas offices. The firm has a dedicated training department and weekly training schedules, coupled with training designed specifically for trainees, allow a good grounding in legal and non-legal skills and knowledge.

## vacation placements
Places for 2006: 60; Duration: 2 weeks; Remuneration: £225 p.w.; Closing Date: 31 January 2006.

## sponsorship & awards
GDL and LPC fees paid and between £5,000 - £7,000 maintenance.

| | |
|---|---|
| **Partners** | **128** |
| **Assistant Solicitors** | **270** |
| **Total Trainees** | **70** |

**contact**
Graduate Recruitment Team

**method of application**
online application form

**selection procedure**
2 interviews (early September)

**closing date for 2008**
31 July 2006

**application**
Training contracts p.a. **38**
Applications p.a. **2,000**
% interviewed p.a. **10%**
Required degree grade **2:1**

**training**
Salary
**1st year £28,000**
**2nd year £32,000**
Holiday entitlement
**50 days over 2 years**
% of trainees with
a non-law degree p.a. **40%**
No. of seats available
abroad p.a. **8**

**post-qualification**
Salary **£50,000**
% of trainees offered job
on qualification (2005) **80%**
% of assistants who joined
as trainees **26%**
% of partners who joined
as trainees **12%**

**overseas offices**
Brussels, Frankfurt, Madrid, Berlin, Paris, Munich

# Berwin Leighton Paisner

Adelaide House, London Bridge, London EC4R 9HA
Tel: (020) 7760 1000 Fax: (020) 7760 1111
Email: traineerecruit@blplaw.com
Website: www.blplaw.com

## firm profile

Berwin Leighton Paisner is a top 15 City practice. It is a commercial law firm with expertise in many major industry and service sectors. The firm is a modern growing practice that puts a premium on commercial, as well as technical advice, client relations and transactional care. The firm is entrepreneurial and innovative. The firm was delighted to win The Lawyer Magazine award for 'Law Firm of the Year' 2004 and Chambers and Partners' UK Law Firm of the Year, 2005.

## main areas of work

Corporate finance; business & technology services; employment, incentives & pensions; competition, commercial real estate; planning & environment; regulatory; construction and engineering; banking and capital markets; property finance; asset finance; PFI/projects; and litigation and dispute resolution.

## trainee profile

The firm is looking for intelligent, energetic, positive and hard-working team players who have an interest in business and gain a sense of achievement from finding solutions.

## training environment

Training starts with an induction covering all the practical aspects of working in a law firm from billing to client care. Comprehensive technical education programmes have been developed for each department and trainees attend weekly seminars supplemented by trainee lunches and skills sessions. You will undertake a tailor-made Professional Skills Course which is run in-house. Trainees spend six months in four seats and your progress will be reviewed every three months. The office environment is relaxed and friendly and trainees can enjoy early responsibility secure in the knowledge that they are fully supervised.

## benefits

Flexible benefits package including permanent health insurance, private medical insurance, subsidised gym membership, 25 days holiday a year.

## vacation placements

Places for 2006: Assessment centres held during March and April at either university campus or the firm's London office, application by online application form before 28 February 2006. The assessment centres could lead to a two-week placement in the summer vacation. There are 50 places available on the summer placement scheme.

## sponsorship & awards

CPE/GDL and LPC fees paid and £4,500 maintenance p.a.

---

**Partners** 140
**Assistant Solicitors** 233
**Total Trainees** 70

**contact**
Debbie Berman

**method of application**
Firm application form online

**selection procedure**
Assessment day & partner interview

**closing date for 2008**
31 July 2006

**application**
Training contracts p.a. **35**
Applications p.a. **2,000**
% interviewed p.a. **5%**
Required degree grade **2:1**

**training**
Salary
1st year (2004) £28,000
2nd year (2004) £32,000
Holiday entitlement **25 days**
% of trainees with a
non-law degree p.a. **46%**
No. of seats available
abroad p.a. **0**

**post-qualification**
Salary (2004) **£50,000**
% of trainees offered job
on qualification (2005) **81%**
% of assistants who joined
as trainees (2005) **47%**
% of partners who joined
as trainees (2005) **30%**

**european offices**
Brussels, associated office in New York, Paris, Rome, Milan

# Bevan Brittan

35 Colston Avenue, Bristol BS1 4TT
Tel: (0870) 194 3050 Fax: (0870) 194 8954
Email: hr.training@bevanbrittan.com
Website: www.bevanbrittan.com

## firm profile
Bevan Brittan has firmly established itself as a truly national law firm and continues to attract high profile national and international clients and challenging, groundbreaking work. The firm is nationally recognised for its expertise in providing legal advice to clients in both the public and private sectors and is notable for being one of the very few practices whose work is equally strong in both sectors.

## main areas of work
The firm is structured around five primary areas of the UK economy: built environment, health, government, insurance and finance and commerce, industry & services. The firm operates in cross- departmental teams across these markets, harnessing the full range of skills and experience needed to provide top quality legal advice in the context of a specialist knowledge of both the sector concerned and the client's business. Areas of work covered include Claims; Commercial; Commercial Litigation; Construction; Employment; Real Estate, Planning, Projects, Banking.

## trainee profile
Bevan Brittan recognises that the firm's success depends upon a team of lawyers dedicated to service excellence. Its success is maintained by attracting and keeping enthusiastic, bright people with sound common sense, plenty of energy and the ability to work and communicate well with others. Language and IT skills are also desirable.

## training environment
During each six-month seat, the core of your training will be practical work experience in conjunction with an extensive educational programme. Together the training is aimed at developing attitudes, skills and legal and commercial knowledge which is essential for your career success. You are encouraged to take on as much work and responsibility as you are able to handle, which will be reviewed on a regular basis with your supervising partner. The firm is friendly and supportive with an open-door policy along with a range of social, sporting and cultural activities.

## vacation placements
Places available for 2006: 60 across the three offices. Closing date: 31st March 2006.

## sponsorship & awards
Bursary and funding for GDL and LPC.

| Partners | 68 |
| Total Trainees | 38 |

**contact**
HR and Training
(0870) 194 3050

**method of application**
Online application

**closing date for 2008**
31 July 2006

**post-qualification**
% of trainees offered job
on qualification (2005) **82%**

**other offices**
Birmingham, Bristol,
London

# Bircham Dyson Bell

50 Broadway, London SW1H OBL
Tel: (020) 7222 8044  Fax: (020) 7222 3480

## firm profile

Bircham Dyson Bell is one of the top 10 fastest growing law firms in the UK. Employing over 280 people, (with 45 partners), the firm has doubled its turnover within the last five years. In 2005 we were short listed for six awards (including Partner of the Year, Most Enterprising Law Firm of the Year, and Private Client Law Firm of the Year). The firm acts for many high-profile clients from a wide-variety of sectors, including real estate, public and private companies, charities, private clients, and public sector organisations. The firm enjoys a market-wide reputation for the quality of its people, their knowledge, and their pro-active approach to clients.

## main areas of work

Located in central London, Bircham Dyson Bell is recognised as having leading departments in the charity, private client, parliamentary, planning and public law fields. The firm also has strong company commercial, real estate and litigation teams.

## trainee profile

Applications are welcome from both law and non-law students who can demonstrate a consistently high academic record. The firm is looking for creative thinkers with a mature, confident and practical outlook who will thrive in a friendly, hard-working environment. Many of BDB's current trainees have diverse interests outside law.

## training environment

The firm's training is designed to produce its future partners. To achieve this they aim to provide a balance of both formal and practical training and will give early responsibility to those who show promise. The two-year training contract consists of 4 six-month seats during which you will work alongside partners and other senior lawyers, some of whom are leaders in their field.

As the firm practises in a wide variety of legal disciplines, trainees benefit from a diverse experience. Trainees undergo specific technical training in each seat in addition to the mandatory Professional Skills Course (PSC). Great emphasis is now placed on soft skills training and development.

## benefits

25 days' holiday, group health care, life assurance, health insurance and pension schemes.

## sponsorship & awards

Bircham Dyson Bell provides funding for GDL and LPC fees.

| Partners | 45 |
|---|---|
| Assistant Solicitors | 65 |
| Total Trainees | 15 |

**contact**
Neil Emerson, Training Principal
(020) 7227 7000

**method of application**
Please submit your CV with a covering letter via the firm's website,
www.bdb-law.co.uk

**selection procedure**
2 interviews with members of the Graduate Recruitment Team, comprising a number of partners and members of HR

**closing date for 2008**
31 July 2006 for autumn 2008

**application**
Training contracts p.a. **8**
Applications p.a. **450**
% interviewed p.a. **10%**
Required degree grade:
**2:1 degree preferred**

**training**
Salary
**1st year (1 October 2005) £27,500**
**2nd year (2005) £28,500**
Holiday entitlement
**25 days**

**post-qualification**
Salary **£44,000**
% of trainees offered job on qualification (2005) **50%**

# Bird & Bird

90 Fetter Lane, London EC4A 1JP
Tel: (020) 7415 6000  Fax: (020) 7415 6111
Website: www.twobirds.com

## firm profile

Bird & Bird is a sector-focused, fulls-service international law firm. They firm has 119 partners and over 750 staff (including 23 trainees) across offices in Beijing, Brussels, Dusseldorf, Frankfurt, The Hague, Hong Kong, Madrid, Milan, Munich, London, Paris, Rome and Stockholm. The firm is proud of its friendly, stimulating environment where individuals are able to develop legal business and interpersonal skills. The firm's international reach and focus on sectors will enable you to work across borders and for a variety of companies, many of which will operate at the cutting edge of the industries in which they operate. The firm has a leading reputation for many of the sectors on which it focuses: aviation and aerospace, banking and financial services, communications, e-commerce, information technology, life sciences, media and sport. From each of its ofices, they firm provides a full range of legal services to these sectors. This includes: commercial corpoate, dispute resolution, employment, EU & competition, finance, intellectual property, outsourcing, privacy and data protection, real estate and tax.

## main areas of work

Commercial, corporate, corporate restructuring and insolvency, dispute resolution, employment, EU & competition law, finance, intellectual property, outsourcing, real estate, regulatory and administrative, tax.

## trainee profile

The firm looks for high-calibre recruits – confident individuals capable of developing expert legal skills and commercial sense.

## training environment

Following an introduction course, you will undertake four seats of six months. The choice of final seat is yours and is normally the area into which you elect to qualify. Some seats may be spent in the firm's international offices. You will share an office with a partner or senior assistant solicitor who will guide and advise you. You will develop drafting and legal research skills and gain familiarity with legal procedures. The firm encourages you to make an early contribution to casework and participate in client meetings. External lectures are arranged to cover the Professional Skills Course. Trainees are encouraged to join the number of sports teams at the firm and to attend various social events.

## benefits

BUPA, season ticket loan, subsidised sports club membership, life cover, PHI, pension, childcare and eyecare vouchers.

## vacation placements

Places for 2006: 20; Duration: 2 x 3 weeks; Remuneration: £240 p.w.; Closing Date: 31 January 2006.

## sponsorship & awards

LPC and CPE fees paid and a yearly maintenance grant of £3,500.

---

**Partners** 119*
**Assistant Solicitors** 421*
**Total Trainees** 23*
*\* denotes worldwide figures*

**contact**
Lynne Walters
lynne.walters@twobirds.com

**method of application**
Online application form

**selection procedure**
Assessment mornings

**closing date for 2008**
31 July 2006 for law and non law students. Non law students can also apply before 10 March to be considered for the firm's April assessment week

**application**
Training contracts p.a. **14**
Applications p.a. **850**
% interviewed p.a. **8%**
Required degree grade **2:1**

**training**
Salary
**1st year (2005) £28,000**
**2nd year (2005) £30,000**
Holiday entitlement
**25 days**
% of trainees with a non-law degree p.a.
**Varies**

**post-qualification**
Salary (2005) **£45,000**
% of trainees offered job on qualification (2005) **75%**

**overseas offices**
Beijing, Brussels, Dusseldorf, Frankfurt, Hong Kong, London, Madrid, Milan, Munich, Paris, Rome, Stockholm, The Hague

# Boodle Hatfield

89 New Bond Street, London, W15 1DA
Tel: (020) 7629 7411  Fax: (020) 7629 2621
Email: hr@boodlehatfield.com
Website: www.boodlehatfield.com

## firm profile

Boodle Hatfield is a highly successful medium-sized firm who have been providing bespoke legal services for more than 275 years. They still act for some of their very first clients and are proud to do so. The firm has grown into a substantial practice, serving the full spectrum of commercial and private clients, both domestically and internationally.

## main areas of work

The ethos of facilitating private capital activity and private businesses underpins the work of the whole firm. The interplay of the skills between five major areas – tax and financial planning, property, corporate, litigation and family – makes Boodle Hatfield particularly well placed to serve these individuals and businesses.

## trainee profile

The qualities the firm look for in their trainees are commitment, flexibility and the ability to work as part of a team. Students with 2.1 or above and high A levels should apply.

## training environment

Trainees spend up to six months in up to four of the firm's main areas: Property, Corporate, Tax & Financial Planning and Litigation. Boodle Hatfield is well known for the high quality of its training. All trainees are involved in client work from the start and are encouraged to handle their own files personally as soon as they are able to do so, with the appropriate supervision. The firm's trainees therefore have a greater degree of client contact than in many firms with the result that they should be able to take on more responsibility at an early stage. Trainees are given formal appraisals every three months which are designed as a two-way process and give trainees the chance to discuss their progress and to indicate where more can be done to help in their ongoing training and development.

## benefits

Private healthcare, life assurance, season ticket loan, pension scheme, private health insurance, conveyancing grant.

## vacation placements

Two week placement between June and September, for which 10 students are accepted each year. Applicants should apply via the application form on the website at www.boodlehatfield.com from 1 January 2006.

## sponsorship & awards

LPC and GDL/CPE plus maintenance grant.

| | |
|---|---|
| **Partners** | **27** |
| **Assistant Solicitors** | **39** |
| **Total Trainees** | **10** |

**contact**
Emma Turner
020 7079 8133

**method of application**
Online application

**selection procedure**
Interviews with the Training Principal, a Partner and the HR Director plus an ability test in verbal reasoning

**closing date for 2008**
31 July 2006

**application**
Training contracts p.a. **6-8**
Required degree grade **2:1**

**training**
Salary
**1st year £27,500**
**(Sept 2005)**
**2nd year £29,500**
Holiday entitlement
25 days

**post-qualification**
Salary **£44,000**
% of trainees offered job on qualification (2005) **100%**

**regional offices**
Oxford

BOODLE
HATFIELD

BESPOKE LEGAL SERVICES

# B P Collins

Collins House, 32-38 Station Road, Gerrards Cross SL9 8EL
Tel: (01753) 889995  Fax: (01753) 889851
Email: jacqui.symons@bpcollins.co.uk
Website: www.bpcollins.co.uk

## firm profile

B P Collins was established in 1966, and has expanded significantly to become one of the largest and best known legal practices at the London end of the M4/M40 corridors. At its main office in Gerrards Cross, the emphasis is on commercial work, including company/commercial work of all types, commercial conveyancing and general commercial litigation. Alongside this there is a highly respected private client department specialising in tax planning, trusts, charities, wills and probates, and an equally successful family law team.

## main areas of work

Company/commercial, employment, IT/IP, civil and commercial litigation, commercial conveyancing, property development, private client and family law.

## trainee profile

Most of the partners and other fee-earners have worked in London at one time or another but, tired of commuting, have opted to work in more congenial surroundings and enjoy a higher quality lifestyle. Gerrards Cross is not only a very pleasant town with a large number of high net worth private clients but it is also a convenient location for serving the extremely active business community at the eastern end of the Thames Valley including West London, Heathrow, Uxbridge, Slough and Windsor. The firm therefore looks for trainees who are likely to respond to this challenging environment.

## training environment

The firm aims to have six trainee solicitors at different stages of their training contracts at all times. Trainees serve five months in four separate departments of their choice. The final four months is spent in the department in which the trainee intends specialising. The firm has a training partner with overall responsibility for all trainees and each department has its own training principal who is responsible for day to day supervision. There are regular meetings between the training principal and the trainee to monitor progress and a review meeting with the training partner midway and at the end of each departmental seat. The firm also involves its trainees in social and marketing events including golf and cricket matches, and other sporting and non-sporting activities.

| | |
|---|---|
| **Partners** | 20 |
| **Assistant Solicitors** | 28 |
| **Total Trainees** | 6 |

**contact**
Mrs Jacqui Symons

**method of application**
Handwritten covering letter & CV

**selection procedure**
Screening interview & selection day

**closing date for 2007/8**
30 June 2006

**application**
Required degree grade **2:1, A & B 'A' level grades.**

**training**
Salary
**1st year £19,000**
**2nd year £20,000**

# Brabners Chaffe Street

1 Dale St, Liverpool L2 2ET
Tel: (0151) 600 3000 Fax: (0151) 227 3185
Brook House, 70 Spring Gardens, Manchester M2 2BQ
Tel: (0161) 236 5800 Fax: (0161) 228 6862
7-8 Chapel Street, Preston PR1 8AN
Tel: (01772) 823921 Fax: (01772) 201918
Email: trainees@brabnerscs.com
Website: www.brabnerschaffestreet.com

## firm profile
One of the top North West commercial firms, Brabners Chaffe Street, in Liverpool, Manchester and Preston, has the experience, talent and prestige of a firm that has a 200-plus-year history. Brabners Chaffe Street is a dynamic, client-led specialist in the provision of excellent legal services to clients ranging from large plcs to private individuals.

## main areas of work
The firm carries out a wide range of specialist legal services and Brabners Chaffe Street's client base includes plcs, public sector bodies, banks and other commercial, corporate and professional businesses. Brabners Chaffe Street is organised into five client-focused departments: corporate (including commercial law); employment; litigation (including media); property (including housing association and construction); private client.

## trainee profile
Graduates and those undertaking CPE or LPC, who can demonstrate intelligence, intuition, humour, approachability and commitment.

## training environment
The firm is one of the few law firms that holds Investor in People status and has a comprehensive training and development programme. Trainees are given a high degree of responsibility and are an integral part of the culture of the firm. Seats are available in the firm's five departments and each trainee will have partner-level supervision. Personal development appraisals are conducted at six-monthly intervals to ensure that trainee progress is valuable and informed. The training programme is overseen by the firm's Director of Training and Development, Dr Tony Harvey, and each centre has a designated Trainee Partner. It is not all hard work and the firm has an excellent social programme.

## sponsorship & awards
From 2006 assistance with LPC funding will be available.

| | |
|---|---|
| Partners | 46 |
| Associates | 26 |
| Assistant Solicitors | 31 |
| Fee Earners | 23 |
| Total Trainees | 18 |

contact
Liverpool office:
Dr Tony Harvey
Director of Training and
Risk Management

method of application
Application form (please request by email, fax or post only)

selection procedure
Interview & assessment day

closing date for 2008
Apply by 31 July 2006 for training contracts commencing in September 2007/8

application
Training contracts p.a. 7
Required degree grade
2:1 or post-graduate degree

training
Salary
1st year (2006) £19,000
Holiday entitlement 25 days

offices
Liverpool, Manchester, Preston

# Brachers

Somerfield House, 59 London Road, Maidstone ME16 8JH
Tel: (01622) 690691  Fax: (01622) 681430
Email: info@brachers.co.uk
Website: www.brachers.co.uk

## firm profile
Brachers is a leading firm in the South East with an established City office. The firm is principally involved in corporate and commercial work although it has a niche private client practice. The firm has a leading healthcare team, one of 14 on the NHSLA panel.

## main areas of work
Company/commercial, general litigation, medical negligence, commercial property, employment, private client and family.

## trainee profile
Candidates need to have a strong academic background, common sense and be team players. Both graduates in law and non-law subjects are considered as well as more mature candidates.

## training environment
Trainees have four six-month seats out of company/commercial, property, general civil litigation, defendant insurance, medical negligence, family, employment, and private client. Trainees have two appraisals in each seat. The firm has an open door policy and is committed to developing a long-term career structure. Social events are organised.

## sponsorship & awards
LPC/CPE £6,000 discretionary award.

| | |
|---|---|
| **Partners** | 21 |
| **Assistant Solicitors** | 28 |
| **Total Trainees** | 6 |

**contact**
Mary Raymont

**method of application**
Online application from
www.brachers.co.uk

**selection procedure**
Interview day with partners

**closing date for 2008**
31 July 2006

**application**
Training contracts p.a. **6**
Applications p.a. **400**
% interviewed p.a. **7.5%**
Required degree grade **2:1**

**training**
Salary
1st year (2003) £17,400
2nd year (2003) £19,030
Holiday entitlement **23 days**

**post-qualification**
Salary **(2004)**
**£31,000**
% of trainees offered job
on qualification **90%**

**other offices**
London

# Bristows

3 Lincoln's Inn Fields, London WC2A 3AA
Tel: (020) 7400 8000  Fax: (020) 7400 8050
Email: info@bristows.com
Website: www.bristows.com

## firm profile

Bristows specialises in providing legal services to businesses with interests in technology or intellectual property. The firm acts for some of the largest companies in the world and helps protect some of the most famous brands. Its work reaches beyond intellectual property law to corporate and commercial law, property, tax, employment law and litigation.

## main areas of work

Intellectual property 54%; company/corporate finance/commercial 15%; IT 16%; commercial litigation (including employment) 10%; commercial property (including environmental) 5%.

## trainee profile

Bristows is looking for applicants with outstanding intellects, with strong analytical skills and engaging personalities. It is also looking for people who will contribute to the ethos of the firm. Bristows is a very friendly firm and believes that you get the best from people if they are in a happy and supportive working environment.

## training environment

The firm's training programme gives you the knowledge and skills to build on the extensive hands-on experience you will gain in each of its main departments. You will be working closely with partners, which will accelerate your training. Part of this training may also involve a secondment to one of a number of leading clients. With the international spread of its clients, the probability of overseas travel is high, especially upon qualification.

## benefits

Excellent career prospects, a competitive package, firm pension scheme, life assurance and health insurance.

## vacation placements

Schemes are run for one week during Christmas and Easter breaks, two weeks during the Summer break. Remuneration: £200 p.w.; Closing Date: Christmas –26 November; Easter/Summer – 28 February.

## sponsorship & awards

CPE/LPC fees plus £5,000 maintenance grant for each.

---

**Partners** 29
**Assistant Solicitors** 61
**Total Trainees** 15

**contact**
Graduate Recruitment Officer

**method of application**
Application form

**selection procedure**
2 individual interviews

**closing date for 2008**
31 January 2006 for February interviews,
31 August 2006 for September interviews

**application**
Training contracts p.a.
**Up to 10**
Applications p.a. **3,500**
% interviewed p.a. **6%**
Required degree grade
**2:1 (preferred)**

**training**
Salary
**1st year (2003) £26,000**
**2nd year (2003) £28,000**
Holiday entitlement
**4 weeks**
% of trainees with
a non-law degree p.a. **86%**

**post-qualification**
Salary (2004) **£43,000**
% of trainees offered job
on qualification (2004) **89%**
% of assistants (as at
1/9/01) who joined as
trainees **41%**
% of partners (as at 1/9/01)
who joined as trainees **53%**

# Browne Jacobson

Nottingham, Birmingham, London
Tel: (0115) 976 6000 Fax: (0115) 947 5246
Email: traineeapplications@brownejacobson.com
Website: www.brownejacobson.com

## firm profile

The firm is one of the largest in the Midlands, with regional and national reach through our offices in Nottingham, Birmingham and London. Operating as a full service commercial practice, they offer clients practical and creative solutions designed to meet their needs. Their clients and their people value the open, friendly and flexible nature of the firm's culture. Recent accolades include: voted one of the 10 best places to train in the UK (LEX magazine) for three years running third place in 2005 Managing Partners Forum European Practice Management Awards for Best Corporate Citizen. 2005 winner for Nottinghamshire Law Society Pro Bono and Charity Firm of the Year and Young Solicitor of the Year. Finalist in Trainee Solicitor of the Year category. Also recognised as an Investor In People.

## main areas of work

A complete legal service for commercial, insurance and public sector clients. Key areas include corporate finance, banking, trade and innovation, tax, financial planning, property, employment, pensions, construction, commercial and property litigation, planning, personal injury, fraud, local authorities, environmental, French inward investment, medical negligence, social housing and education. The firm has a national profile across many sector groups including countryside and environment, freight and logistics, professional indemnity, health and retail.

## trainee profile

You should be confident, enthusiastic, ambitious, committed and capable of placing client care at the centre of what you do. A straightforward approach along with the capability to prioritise, work well under pressure and to tight deadlines is also a must. You should be a team player and be able to take on responsibility from an early stage. The firm supervises their trainees but encourages and expects them to take a common-sense and commercial approach to solving their clients' legal and business problems and helping the firm meet its objectives.

## training environment

You will spend four periods of six months in some of the principle areas of the firm, gaining an overview of the practice. As part of your training you will work on your own cases, developing your skills with hands-on experience although appropriate support and supervision is readily accessible.

## sponsorship & awards

PGDL fees, LPC fees plus maintenance grant.

| Partners | 57 |
| Assistant Solicitors | 110 |

**contact**
Philippa Shorthouse
HR Advisor

**method of application**
Apply online at
www.brownejacobson.com
/trainees

**selection procedure**
Assessment Centre

**closing date**
31 July two years before
the training contract is due
to commence

**application**
Training contracts p.a. **10**
Applications p.a. **800**
% interviewed p.a. **5%**
Required degree grade **2:1**

**training**
Salary **£21,500**
Holiday entitlement **25 days**
% of trainees with a
non-law degree p.a. **36%**

**post-qualification**
Salary **Market Rate**
Holiday entitlement
**25 days**

brownejacobson

# Burges Salmon

Narrow Quay House, Narrow Quay, Bristol BS1 4AH
Tel: (0117) 902 2766 Fax: (0117) 902 4400
Email: katy.edge@burges-salmon.com
Website: www.burges-salmon.com

## firm profile
Burges Salmon is proof that law doesn't necessarily have to mean London.
Based in Bristol, the firm's turnover has more than tripled in recent years as they continue to win prestigious clients out of the hands of City rivals. Clients such as Orange, the Ministry of Defence and Mitsubishi Motors rely on their legal expertise and in doing so have helped cement the firm's reputation as creative, lateral thinkers. Burges Salmon's primary asset is its people. Trainees benefit from supervision by some of the best minds in the industry: lawyers who are leaders in their field with a formidable depth of experience. All this against the backdrop of Bristol: a city with a quality of life you would be hard pressed to find anywhere else in the UK.

## main areas of work
Burges Salmon provides national and international clients with a full commercial service through 6 main departments: Corporate & Financial Institutions (CFI); Commercial; Property; Tax & Trusts; Commercial Disputes & Construction (CDC); and Agriculture, Property Litigation & Environment (APLE). Specialist areas include: Banking; EU & Competition; Corporate Finance; Employment; IP & IT; and Transport. The firm is ranked top tier by Chambers and Partners for 17 of its practice areas.

## trainee profile
Burges Salmon's lawyers are intelligent, ambitious individuals who work hard to achieve their goals. Successful applicants demonstrate a high degree of commercial acumen coupled with a genuine enthusiasm for the law. They must possess a strong academic background and show evidence of achievement in non-academic pursuits which demonstrate an ability to build relationships with both clients and colleagues alike.

## training environment
Trainees play a vital role in shaping the future of the firm and Burges Salmon invests a great deal of time and resource into training and development. The firm is justifiably proud of its reputation for offering some of the best training in the profession: the Law Society recently accredited their training programme with seven points of good practice, where in previous years the maximum awarded to any firm was two. Training is personalised to suit each individual, and the six seat structure allows the opportunity to experience a wider range of practice areas before making a decision on qualification. This dedication to trainees is demonstrated by a high retention rate, which is well above the industry average.
Trainees are given early responsibility balanced with an open door policy for advice and guidance. Supervisors are partners or senior lawyers who are highly trained to ensure trainees gain as much as possible from every seat and will tailor the workload to fit with each individual's interests and abilities. There are many opportunities for trainees to take an active role in cases involving high profile clients as well as running their own files on smaller cases. The firm also encourages secondments which offer new perspectives on the profession and enable trainees to build relationships with clients.

| Partners | 62 |
|---|---|
| Assistant Solicitors | 171 |
| Total Trainees | 37 |

**contact**
Katy Edge, Graduate Recruitment Officer

**method of application**
Employer's application form available on website

**selection procedure**
Penultimate year law students, final year non-law students, recent graduates or mature candidates are considered for open days, vacation placements and/or training contracts

**closing date for 2008**
31 July 2006

**application**
Training contracts p.a.
**20-25**
Applications p.a. **1,500**
% interviewed p.a. **10%**
Required degree grade **2:1**

**training**
Salary
**1st year (2005) £21,500**
**2nd year (2005) £22,500**
Holiday entitlement **24 days**
% of trainees with
a non-law degree p.a. **50%**

**post-qualification**
Salary (2005) **£35,000**
% of trainees offered job on qualification (2005) **94%**
% of assistants who joined as trainees (2005) **60%**
% of partners who joined as trainees (2005) **25%**

# Burges Salmon continued

## benefits

Annually reviewed competitive salary, 24 days paid annual leave, bonus scheme, pension scheme, private health care membership, mobile phone, laptop, Christmas gift, corporate gym membership, sports and social club.

## vacation placements

Burges Salmon offers 40 two-week Vacation Placements during the summer. Individuals visit 2 departments of their choice supervised by a partner or senior solicitor, and attend court visits and client meetings. Current trainees run skills training sessions, sports and social events. Remuneration: £200 per week.

Selection for Vacation Placements is via Open Days which take place in February 2006.

## sponsorship and awards

The firm pays GDL and LPC fees at the institution of your choice. Maintenance grants of £4,500 are paid to LPC students, and £9,000 to students studying for both the GDL and LPC (£4,500 p.a.).

## comments

"The firm has managed to win work that other national rivals would kill for, and all without sacrificing quality on the altar of ambition. With client wins such as EMI Group, Reuters, and Coca Cola HBC, Burges Salmon has quietly built the elite firm outside London." A leading awards body.

"I particularly value Burges Salmon lawyers for their approachability, their interest in our business and their enthusiasm." Amanda Doyle, UK Group Counsel, Orange.

"To date, my training contract with Burges Salmon has been enjoyable and rewarding. The quality and variety of the work means that I look forward to coming into work, which is something I really value. The firm provides a comprehensive, focussed training programme and this is demonstrated by the high retention rate of trainees on qualification." Jonathan Eves, Trainee Solicitor

"The quality of work on offer was one of the main reasons I chose Burges Salmon and I have not been disappointed. The work I am involved in ranges from large, high profile deals to smaller cases where I am able to run my own files. Trainees enjoy a high level of responsibility because supervisors and other lawyers are always willing to answer questions and provide the support necessary for each case." Lucy Gray, Trainee Solicitor

# Capsticks

77-83 Upper Richmond Road, London SW15 2TT
Tel: (020) 8780 2211 Fax: (020) 8780 4811
Email: career@capsticks.co.uk
Website: www.capsticks.com

## firm profile
Rated as the country's leading healthcare law firm by the Legal 500 and other leading directories, Capsticks handles litigation, administrative law, employment, commercial and property work for a wide range of healthcare bodies, including almost 250 NHS Trusts, PCTs, Strategic Health Authorities, private sector health providers, health-related charities and regulatory bodies.

## main areas of work
Clinical Law 52%; Commercial 16%; Commercial Property 14%; Dispute Resolution 8%; Employment Law 10%.

## trainee profile
Successful candidates possess intellectual agility, good interpersonal skills and are capable of taking initiative.

## training environment
Six four-month seats, which may include clinical negligence/advisory; commercial property; commercial; employment; and dispute resolution. Trainees take responsibility for their own caseload as well as assisting on larger cases and work with clients from an early stage. There are also opportunities to contribute to the firm's marketing and management processes. There are numerous in-house lectures for all fee earners. There is an open door policy, and trainees receive informal feedback and supervision as well as regular appraisals. Despite the firm's rapid expansion, it has retained a friendly atmosphere and a relaxed working environment. There are frequent informal social and sporting activities.

## benefits
Bonus scheme, pension, PHI, death in service cover, interest-free Season Ticket Loan.

## vacation placements
Places for 2006: Yes; Duration: 2 weeks; Closing Date: 28 February 2006.

## sponsorship & awards
Scholarship contributions to GDL and LPC courses.

| | |
|---|---|
| Partners | 29 |
| Assistant Solicitors | 54 |
| Total Trainees | 9 |
| Other Fee-earners | 6 |

**contact**
Sue Laundy

**method of application**
Application form

**selection procedure**
Candidates are encouraged to participate in the firm's summer placement scheme. Final selection is by interview with the Training Principal & other partners

**closing date for 2008**
31 July 2006

**application**
Training contracts p.a. **4-5**
Applications p.a. **c.150**
% interviewed p.a. **c.16%**
Required degree grade
**2:1 or above**

**training**
Salary
**1st year TBA**
**2nd year TBA**
Holiday entitlement
**22 days p.a. (increased by 1 day p.a. to max 25 days)**
% of trainees with a non-law degree p.a. **22%**

**post-qualification**
Salary (2005)
**£41,500 + benefits**
% of trainees offered job on qualification (2005) **65%**
% of assistants (as at 1/9/05) who joined as trainees **43%**
% of partners (as at 1/9/05) who joined as trainees **10%**

# Charles Russell

8–10 New Fetter Lane, London EC4A 1RS
Tel: (020) 7203 5000 Fax: (020) 7203 5307
Website: www.charlesrussell.co.uk

| | |
|---|---|
| Partners | 93 |
| Other fee-earners | 197 |
| Total trainees | 28 |
| Total staff | 560 |

## firm profile

Charles Russell is one of the UK's top 50 firms, providing a full range of services to UK and international companies and organisations, while its renowned private client and family practices continue to thrive. It has regional offices in Guildford, Cheltenham and Oxford. The practice is known for its client care, high quality, expertise and family approach. The strategy is simple – to help clients achieve their goals through excellent service. Many lawyers are ranked as leaders in their field. Experienced in carrying out cross-border corporate and commercial work, the practice also provides clients with access to 150 recommended law firms across the world as part of the two major legal networks, ALFA International and the Association of European Lawyers. The pratcice's lawyers and staff are highly motivated and talented people. The practice's commitment to training and development and strong team spirit is a key ingredient to being known as a friendly practice to work with and work at.

## main areas of work

75% of the practice's work is commercial. Principle areas of work include media and communications, employment and pensions, charities, private client/family, corporate/commercial, intellectual property, dispute resolution, real estate and insurance/reinsurance.

## trainee profile

Trainees should be balanced, rounded achievers with an excellent academic background.

## training environment

The practice recruits a small number of trainees for its size each year. This allows trainees to undergo the best possible training. Trainees usually spend six months in four of the following training seats – dispute resolution, corporate/commercial, real estate, private client, family, employment/pensions and intellectual property. Secondments to clients are also often available. Wherever possible the practice will accommodate individual preferences. You will be seated with a partner/senior solicitor. Regular appraisals are held to discuss progress and direction. Trainees are encouraged to attend extensive in-house training courses. The PSC is taught both internally and externally. Trainees are encouraged to take on as much responsibility as possible. A social committee organises a range of activities from quiz nights through to sporting events.

## benefits

BUPA; PHI and Life Assurance: pension plan; season ticket loans; 25 days holiday plus additional day for house moves; dress-down Fridays; dry cleaning collection service; croissants and muffins are available between 8:00am and 9:00am each Friday in London.

## sponsorship & awards

The practice pays for course fees whilst you are at law school and also offers a grant of £4,500 per annum to London & Guildford trainees and £3,500 p.a. to Cheltenham trainees.

### contact
graduaterecruitment@
charlesrussell.co.uk

### method of application
Online application

### selection procedure
Assessment days to include an interview & other exercises designed to assess identified performance criteria

### closing date for 2008
31 July 2006

### application
Training contracts for 2007: **16**
Applications p.a.
**Approx 2,000**
% interviewed p.a. **3%**
Preferred degree grade **2:1**

### training
Salary
**1st year (2005) £28,000**
**2nd year (2005) £30,500**
Holiday entitlement
**25 days + additional day for house moves**

### post-qualification
Salary (2005) **£46,000**

### regional offices
Also offers training contracts in its Cheltenham & Guildford offices. Applications are dealt with by the London office.

# A-Z Solicitors

# Cleary Gottlieb Steen & Hamilton LLP

City Place House, 55 Basinghall Street, London, EC2V 5EH
Tel: (020) 7614 2200 Fax: (020) 7600 1698
Email: lonlegalrecruit@cgsh.com
Website: www.clearygottlieb.com

## firm profile

Cleary Gottlieb is a leading international law firm with more than 800 lawyers practising in the world's major financial centres. Founded in 1946, the firm operates as a single, integrated partnership, serving a clientele comprising many of the world's largest multi-national corporations, financial institutions and sovereign governments, as well as small start-ups, private clients and charitable organisations.

## main areas of work

(In London) Mergers and acquisitions, corporate, capital markets and finance, tax, regulatory, competition/antitrust and intellectual property.

## trainee profile

Successful candidates must demonstrate exceptional academic ability together with evidence of extra-curricular achievement and must be enthusiastic about practising law in a challenging and dynamic international setting. Language skills are an advantage. Occasionally entrance is possible via a US LLM and the New York Bar exam. Such candidates start by spending nine months in the New York office.

## training environment

There are no departments at Cleary Gottlieb. Trainees sit with partners and senior solicitors and work on a mix of M&A, capital markets, finance, tax, regulatory, competition and intellectual property work. Seats change every six months. There are opportunities to travel, work in other offices and go on secondment to clients in the UK and abroad. Qualified solicitors are from time to time seconded to the New York and Hong Kong offices. Trainees may have the opportunity to take the New York Bar exam. Trainees are encouraged to take responsibility early and in most respects fulfil the same role as first year lawyers in other offices.

## benefits

Pension, health insurance, long-term disability insurance and health club membership.

## vacation schemes

The London office runs three vacation schemes, one at easter for two weeks, and two in summer for a period of three weeks. The closing date for the 2006 schemes is February 14, 2006.

## sponsorship & awards

LPC fees and £8,000 maintenance award.

| | |
|---|---|
| **Partners** | 15 |
| **Solicitors** | 48 |
| **Total Trainees** | 8 |

**contact**
Legal Recruitment

**method of application**
Cover letter and CV

**selection procedure**
Usually 2 interviews

**closing date for 2008**
July 31 2006

**application**
Training contracts p.a. up to **5**
Applications p.a. **2,250**
% interviewed p.a. **1%**
Required degree grade
**High 2:1 from a leading university and excellent A levels**

**training**
Salary
**1st year (2005) £35,000**
**2nd year (2005) £40,000**

**post-qualification**
Salary **£74,000**

**overseas offices**
New York, Washington DC, Paris, Brussels, Moscow, Frankfurt, Cologne, Rome, Milan, Hong Kong and Tokyo

CLEARY GOTTLIEB

# Clifford Chance

10 Upper Bank Street, Canary Wharf, London, E14 5JJ
Tel: (020) 7006 1000  Fax: (020) 7006 5555
Email: graduate.recruitment@cliffordchance.com
Website: www.cliffordchance.com/gradsuk

## firm profile

Clifford Chance is a truly global law firm, which operates as one organisation throughout the world. Its aim is to provide the highest quality professional advice by combining technical expertise with an appreciation of the commercial environment in which its clients operate.

## main areas of work

Banking and finance; capital markets; corporate; litigation and dispute resolution; real estate; tax, pensions and employment.

## trainee profile

Consistently strong academic profile (minimum 2:1 degree), a broad range of interpersonal skills and extra curricular activities and interests, commitment to the career, ability to communicate fluently and accurately.

## training environment

The Clifford Chance training contract has been devised to provide students with the technical skills and experience needed to contribute to the firm's success on a daily basis, to achieve your professional qualification and to progress to a rewarding career. The two year training contract consists of four six month seats. Most trainees spend a seat on a secondment at an international office or with a client. In each seat trainees will be working alongside senior lawyers. Trainees are encouraged to use initiative to make the most of expertise and resources available to the firm. Three-monthly appraisals and monitoring in each seat ensure trainees gain a range of work and experience.

## benefits

Prize for first class degrees and top performers on the Clifford Chance LPC, interest-free loan, private health insurance, subsidised restaurant, fitness centre, life assurance, occupational health service, and permanent health assurance.

## vacation placements

Places for 2005-2006: Christmas Workshops, vacation placements during Easter and summer break. There is a strong social element to the programme; Duration: 2 days for Christmas Workshops, 2-4 weeks for other schemes; Remuneration: £270 pw; Closing Date: 18 November 2005 for Christmas Workshops; 31 January 2006 for other schemes. A number of international placements will also be available during the summer. Selected candidates will have the opportunity to spend two weeks in London, followed by two weeks in one of the firm's European offices.

## sponsorship & awards

GDL and LPC fees are paid, and from September 2006 a maintenance grant of £7,000 will be paid to LPC students. £6,000 will be paid to GDL students studying in London, and £5,000 to those studying elsewhere.

| London office | |
|---|---|
| Partners | 222 |
| Lawyers | 681 |
| Trainees | 196 |

**contact**
Isabella Crocker
Resourcing Specialist

**method of application**
Online application

**selection procedure**
Assessment day comprising an interview with a partner & senior solicitor, a group exercise & a verbal reasoning test

**application**
Training contracts p.a. **120**
Applications p.a. **2,000**
% interviewed p.a. **25%**
Required degree grade **2:1**

**training**
Salary
**1st year £29,000
(Aug 2005)
2nd year £33,000**
Holiday entitlement **25 days**
% of trainees with
a non-law degree p.a. **45%**
No. of seats available
abroad p.a. **86**

**post-qualification**
Salary (Aug 2005) **£50,000**
% of trainees offered job
on qualification (2005) **90%**

**overseas offices**
Amsterdam, Bangkok, Barcelona, Beijing, Brussels, Budapest, Dubai, Düsseldorf, Frankfurt, Hong Kong, Luxembourg, Madrid, Milan, Moscow, Munich, New York, Padua, Paris, Prague, Rome, São Paulo, Shanghai, Silicon Valley, Singapore, Tokyo, Warsaw, Washington DC

# Clyde & Co

51 Eastcheap, London EC3M 1JP
Tel: (020) 7623 1244  Fax: (020) 7623 5427
Email: theanswers@clydeco.com
Website: www.clydeco.com/graduate

## firm profile

Clyde & Co's aim is to be the premier law firm in Insurance, Transportation, Trade and Natural Resources, providing a full service to an international client base from key strategic locations. The firm's dispute resolution practice is one of the largest in the UK. It has unsurpassed knowledge and experience in insurance and reinsurance, marine, aviation, transportation and trade & energy, offering a full corporate and commercial service in these areas and to businesses involved in international trade. Trainees are recruited to work in London and Guildford during their two-year training contract.

## main areas of work

Insurance/reinsurance, marine, transport & aviation, dispute resolution, international trade & energy, corporate/commercial, corporate recovery/insolvency, property, IT/IP and employment.

## trainee profile

The firm is looking for graduates with excellent academic records, outgoing personalities and keen interests. Trainees need to have the social skills that will enable them to communicate effectively and build relationships with clients and colleagues. The ability to analyse problems, apply common sense and provide solutions to situations are all qualities the firm seeks. Ultimately Clyde & Co recruits to retain and they are seeking candidates who will remain with the firm beyond qualification.

## training environment

Clyde & Co is a friendly and supportive environment and we encourage our trainees to take on responsibility from as early as possible. They offer four six-month seats in the London and Guildford offices, as well as opportunities for secondments to national and international clients. They are also able to offer trainees seats in overseas offices. Regular appraisals are held with your supervising partner to assess your progress, skills and development needs. With such a small number of trainees, they are usually able to accommodate individual preferences when it comes to choosing seats.

## benefits

Pension, life assurance, private medical insurance, subsidised gym membership, interest-free season ticket loan and restaurant.

## legal work experience

The firm runs two-week summer vacation schemes for 20 students. Please visit the website for the exact dates. Applications are made online and the closing date for the scheme is 31 January 2006.

## sponsorship & awards

GDL and LPC fees paid plus a maintenance grant.

---

| | |
|---|---|
| **Partners** | 146 |
| **Fee-earners** | 363 |
| **Total Trainees** | 44 |

**contact**
Kate Wild
Graduate Recruitment Officer

**method of application**
Online via website
www.clydeco.com/graduate

**selection procedure**
Assessment session with Graduate Recruitment followed by interview with 2 partners

**closing date for 2008**
31 July 2006

**application**
Training contracts p.a. **20**
Applications p.a. **1,200 +**
% interviewed p.a. **5%**
Required degree grade **2:1**

**training**
Salary
**1st year (2005) £28,000**
**2nd year (2005) £31,000**
Holiday entitlement **25 days**
% of trainees with
a non-law degree p.a. **60%**

**post-qualification**
Salary (2005) **£48,000**

**overseas offices**
Paris, Nantes, Piraeus, Dubai, Abu Dhabi, Hong Kong, Shanghai, Singapore, Caracas, Rio de Janeiro, Belgrade*, Moscow*, St Petersburg*
* Associated office

# CMS Cameron McKenna

Mitre House, 160 Aldersgate Street, London EC1A 4DD
Tel: (0845) 300 0491  Fax: (020) 7367 2000
Email: gradrec@cms.cmck.com
Website: www.law-now.com

| | |
|---|---|
| **Partners** | 136 |
| **Assistant Solicitors** | 641 |
| **Total Trainees** | 120 |

**contact**
Graduate Recruitment
Team  (0845) 300 0491

**method of application**
Online application form
www.law-now.com/gradrec

**selection procedure**
2 stage selection
procedure. Initial interview
and verbal reasoning test
followed by an assessment
centre

**closing date**
31 July 2006

**application**
Training contracts p.a. **60**
Applications p.a. **1,500**
% interviewed p.a. **35%**
Required degree grade **2:1**

**training**
Salary
**1st year (2005) £28,500**
**2nd year (2005) £32,000**
Holiday entitlement
**25 days + option of flexible
holidays**
% of trainees with
a non-law degree p.a. **40%**
No. of seats available
abroad p.a. **Currently 13**

**post-qualification**
Salary (2005) **£50,000**
% of trainees offered job
on qualification (2003) **90%**

## firm profile
CMS Cameron McKenna is a leading international law firm and an integral part of CMS, the alliance of European Law firms. They've earned a reputation for outstanding client service, acute business awareness and for being passionate about client relationships. They work for some of the worlds leading companies, helping to solve their problems so they can run their businesses more efficiently. The firm believes that to give the best advice, lawyers must clearly understand the industry, marketplace and concerns of their clients. All lawyers have a specialist interest in at least one major industry sector and are committed to building long- term relationships with their clients.

## main areas of work
The firm's clients benefit from an extensive range of tailored services, delivered through offices in the UK. Central Europe, North America and Asia. The firm's services include banking and international finance, corporate, real estate, commercial, energy projects and constructions, insurance and re-insurance.

## trainee profile
The firm looks for high achieving team players with good communication, analytical and organisational skills. You will need to show initative and be able to accept personal responsibility, not only for your own work, but also for your career development. You will need to be resilient and focused on achieving results.

## training environment
The firm is friendly and supportive and puts no limits on a trainee's progress. It offers four six months seats, three of which will be in the firm's main areas of practice. In addition, you may gain experience of a specialist area or opt for a secondment to a national or international client. In each seat you will be allocated high quality work on substantial transactions for a range of government and blue-chip clients. Regular appraisals will be held with your seat supervisor to assess your progress, skills and development needs. The three compulsory modules of the Professional Skills Course will be completed on a fast track basis during the trainee induction. This enables trainees to be effective and participate on a practical level as soon as possible. The Professional Skills Course is complimented by a comprehensive in house training programme that continues up to qualification and beyond.

## vacation placements
Places for 2005/2006: 55 Easter, Christmas and summer, Duration: 2 weeks, Remuneration: £225pw.

## benefits
Annual bonus, gym membership/subsidy, life assurance, pensions scheme with firm con- tributions, private healthcare, season ticket loan, confidential care line, subsidised restaurant and 25 days holiday with options to buy a further five days

## sponsorship & awards
GDL and LPC sponsorship is provided. The firm will cover the cost of all law school fees and provide you with a maintenance grant (£5,000 London, Guildford and Oxford and £4,500 elsewhere).

C/M/S/ Cameron McKenna

# Cobbetts

Ship Canal House, King Street, Manchester M2 4WB
Tel: (0845) 165 5045
Email: lawtraining@cobbetts.co.uk
Website: www.cobbetts.co.uk/graduate

## firm profile
Cobbetts is one of the UK's leading law firms with offices in the three key commercial centres of Birmingham, Leeds and Manchester. With a consistent reputation for innovation, quality and job satisfaction, the firm continues its tremendous growth, with clients to match. The firm's client base of regional, national and international clients includes PLC, mid-sized corporates, financial institutions and public sector / not for profit organisations, ensuring that trainees enjoy a breadth and depth of experience.

## main areas of work
Cobbetts has developed true national practice areas – property, corporate, commercial, banking, employment, litigation services, social housing and private capital – and key specialist expertise in fields including media, the public sector, planning and public markets, in particular on to AIM.

## trainee profile
Applications are encouraged from both law and non-law undergraduates who anticipate attaining a high class honours degree. Mature students and those wishing to change career are also encouraged to apply. Applicants must be personable with a determination to work hard and succeed.

## training environment
Four six-month seats are available. Typically these include one property, one litigation and one commercial/corporate seat. There is an opportunity for one trainee each year to spend three months in Brussels.

## benefits
Opportunity to join BUPA scheme after 4 months, gym membership, Social Club, pension scheme, travel loan, death in service, counselling service.

## sponsorship & awards
The firm offers financial assistance for the Graduate Diploma in Law and the LPC, will meet the cost of the Professional Skills Course and provides a maintenance grant which is currently £3,000.

| | |
|---|---|
| **Partners** | **146** |
| **Assistant Solicitors** | **117** |
| **Total Trainees** | **47** |

**contact**
Sally Driscoll
(0845) 165 5045

**method of application**
Online

**selection procedure**
Assessment days

**closing date for 2008**
14 July 2006

**application**
Training contracts p.a. **25-30**
Applications p.a.
**approx.1,000**
% interviewed p.a. **approx 10%**
Required degree grade
**2:1**

**training**
Salary for each year of training
**1st year** £21,000
**2nd year** £22,000
(both reviewed annually)
Holiday entitlement
**Starting at 23 days**

**post-qualification**
Salary NQ **£33,000**
Reviewed annually

% of trainees offered job on qualification **90%**

**other offices**
Birmingham, Leeds

# Coffin Mew & Clover

Fareham Point, Wickham Road, Fareham PO16 7AU
Tel: (01329) 825617  Fax: (01329) 825619
Email: sarajlloyd@coffinmew.co.uk
Website: www.coffinmew.co.uk

## firm profile
Founded more than a century ago, the firm has grown to become one of the larger legal practices in the Southeast with major offices located in the cities of Portsmouth and Southampton and just off the M27 Motorway at Fareham. The firm is in the enviable position of operating a balanced practice offering private client and business services in approximately equal volume and is particularly noted for a number of niche practices with national reputations.

## main areas of work
The firm is structured through eight core departments: corporate/commercial; employment; commercial litigation; personal injury; commercial property; family/crime; residential property; trust/probate. Niche practices include intellectual property; finance and business regulation; social housing and medical negligence.

## trainee profile
The firm encourages applications from candidates with very good academic ability who seek a broad-based training contract in a highly progressive and demanding but friendly and pleasant environment.

## training environment
The training contract is divided into six seats of four months each which will include a property department, a litigation department and a commercial department. The remainder of the training contract will be allocated after discussion with the trainee concerned. The firm aims to ensure that the trainee spends the final four months of his or her training contract in the department in which he or she hopes to work after qualification.

## sponsorship & awards
LPC funding available by discussion with candidates.

## vacation placements
Open week in July each year; application as per training contract. Closing date 31 March 2006.

| | |
|---|---|
| **Partners** | 20 |
| **Trainees** | 10 |
| **Total staff** | 204 |

**contact**
Mrs Sara Lloyd
Practice Manager

**method of application**
CV & covering letter

**selection procedure**
Interview

**closing date for Sept 2008**
31 July 2006 (can apply after January 1, 2006)

**application**
Training contracts p.a. **5**
Applications p.a. **400+**
% interviewed p.a. **5%**
Required degree grade
**2:1 (save in exceptional circumstances)**

**training**
Salary
**1st year**
**Competitive market rate**
**2nd year**
**Competitive market rate**
Holiday entitlement **20 days**
% of trainees with a
non-law degree p.a. **25%**

**post-qualification**
Salary (2005) **£29,000**
% of trainees offered job
on qualification (2005) **50%**
% of assistants who joined
as trainees **20%**
% of partners who joined
as trainees **60%**

# Covington & Burling

265 Strand, London WC2R 1BH
Tel: (020) 7067 2000 Fax: (020) 7067 2222
Email: graduate@cov.com
Website: www.cov.com

## firm profile

Covington & Burling is a leading US law firm, founded in Washington, with offices in London, New York, San Francisco and Brussels. The London office was established in 1988 and has continued to grow progressively since then.

## main areas of work

In London, the main areas of work are corporate & commercial, employment, insurance, tax, life sciences, litigation & arbitration, IP/IT, and competition. The firm is known worldwide for its remarkable understanding of regulatory issues as well as its depth and expertise in areas including IT, e-commerce and life sciences. In such work, the firm represents many blue-chip clients including Microsoft, Bacardi, Krispy Kreme, Business Software Alliance and Armani.

## trainee profile

The firm is looking for outstanding students who demonstrate genuine commitment to the legal profession and who have not only excellent academic ability, but also imagination, and the necessary practical and social skills required to respond to the evolving needs of its clients. In return, the firm can offer innovative and fascinating work in a stimulating and supportive environment.

## training environment

The firm offers a unique and personal training programme to suit the individual needs of each trainee. Following a comprehensive introduction, trainees will spend six months in each of corporate, litigation and arbitration, and IP/IT departments. The fourth seat will be spent in one of the life sciences, employment or tax practice areas. The firm encourages trainees to take early responsibility in order to get the most out of their training period and trainees will receive regular feedback to enhance their development.

## benefits

Penion, permanent health insurance, private health cover, life assurance and season ticket loan.

## vacation placements

16 places during summer vacation. Closing date for applications 28 February 2006.

## sponsorship & awards

GDL and LPC fees paid. Maintenance grant of £5,000 per annum.

| | |
|---|---|
| **Partners:** | 175* |
| **Associate Lawyers &** | |
| **Other Fee-earners:** | 350* |
| **Total Trainees:** | 8 |

*\* denotes worldwide figures*

**contact**
Graduate Recruitment Manager
(020) 7067 2089
graduate@cov.com

**method of application**
See website www.cov.com

**selection procedure**
1st & 2nd interview

**closing date for 2008**
31 July 2006

**application**
Training contracts p.a. **4**
Required degree grade **2:1**

**training**
Salary:
1st year £30,000
2nd year £33,000
(subject to review)

**overseas offices**
Brussels, New York, San Francisco, Washington

# Cripps Harries Hall LLP

Wallside House, 12 Mount Ephraim Road, Tunbridge Wells TN1 1EG
Tel: (01892) 506006  Fax: (01892) 506360
Email: graduates@crippslaw.com
Website: www.crippslaw.com

## firm profile
A leading regional law firm and one of the largest in the South East, the firm is recognised as being amongst the most progressive and innovative regional practices.
Although long-established, this is a young firm where the atmosphere is professional and forward-thinking while friendly and informal. The firm is regarded by many businesses, institutions and wealthy individuals as the natural first choice among regional law practices.
The firm achieved the Lexcel quality mark in January 1999, the first 'Top 100' firm to do so.

## main areas of work
Commercial 42%, dispute resolution 31%, private client 27%. Its associated company, Cripps Portfolio, provides financial services.

## trainee profile
Individuals who are confident and capable, with lively but well organised minds and a genuine interest in delivering client solutions through effective and pragmatic use of the law; keen to make a meaningful contribution both during their contract and long term career with the firm.

## training environment
The firm offers a comprehensive induction course, a well structured training programme, frequent one to one reviews, regular in-house courses and seminars, good levels of support and real responsibility.
The training programme is broader than most other firms and typically includes six seats in both commercial and private client areas. Trainees usually share a room with a partner and gain varied and challenging first hand experience.

## sponsorship awards
Discretionary LPC funding: Fees – 50% interest free loan, 50% bursary.

| | |
|---|---|
| **Partners** | **35** |
| **Assistant Solicitors** | **50** |
| **Total Trainees** | **14** |

**contact**
Annabelle Lawrence
Head of Human Resources

**method of application**
application form available
on website

**selection process**
1 interview with Managing
Partner and Head of
Human Resources

**closing date for 2008**
31 July 2006

**application**
Training contracts p.a. **7**
Applications p.a. **Up to 750**
% interviewed p.a. **6%**
Required degree grade **2:1**

**training**
Salary
**1st year (2005) £17,500**
**2nd year (2005) £20,000**
Holiday entitlement **25 days**
% of trainees with a non-law
degree p.a. **30%**

**post-qualification**
Salary (2005) **£31,000**
% of trainees offered job
on qualification (2005) **100%**
% of assistants/associates
(as at 1/5/05) who joined as
trainees **30%**
% of partners (as at 1/5/05)
who joined as trainees **20%**

CRIPPS HARRIES HALL LLP

# Davenport Lyons

30 Old Burlington Street, London W1S 3NL
Tel: (020) 7468 2600  Fax: (020) 7437 8216
Email: dl@davenportlyons.com
Website: www.davenportlyons.com

## firm profile
Davenport Lyons is a leading entertainment and media law practice and combines this work with strong company/commercial (including IP/IT), litigation, property and private client departments. The firm adopts a keen commercial and practical partner-led approach and builds on long-term partnership with its clients.

## main areas of work
Media/entertainment; music; litigation (defamation/IP/IT/contentious/property/general commercial/dispute resolution/insolvency/entertainment licensing); company and commercial (IP/IT); commercial/residential property; tax and trust; matrimonial; employment.

## trainee profile
2:1 or above; interesting background; business acumen; practical with breadth of interests; sociable; knowledge of foreign languages an advantage.

## training environment
Four seats of six months each. Three-monthly assessments. Supervision from within departments. Ongoing programme of in-house lectures and professional skills training. Davenport Lyons offers interesting hands-on training. Trainees are treated as junior fee-earners and are encouraged to develop their own client relationships and to handle their own matters under appropriate supervision.

## benefits
Season ticket loan; client introduction bonus; contribution to gym membership; discretionary bonus; 23 days holiday, life assurance.

## vacation placements
Places for 2006: 18; Duration: 2 weeks; Remuneration: £175 p.w.; Closing Date: January 2006.

## sponsorship & awards
The firm does not offer financial assistance.

---

**Partners** 35
**Assistant Solicitors** 44
**Total Trainees** 13

### contact
Marcia Mardner
HR/Training Manager
Michael Hatchwell
Training Partner

### method of application
CV & covering letter

### selection procedure
Interviews

### closing dates
Closing date for 2008
**31 July 2006**

### application
Training contracts p.a. **6**
Applications p.a. **2,000**
% interviewed p.a. **2%**
Required degree grade **2:1**

### training
Salary
**1st Year trainee**
**£28,000 - £28,666**
**2nd Year trainee**
**£29,332 - £30,000**
Holiday entitlement **23 days**
% of trainees with a
non-law degree p.a. **70%**

### post-qualification
% of trainees offered job
on qualification (2005) **80%**
% of assistants (as at 2005)
who joined as trainees **15%**
% of partners (as at 2005)
who joined as trainees **3%**

Davenport Lyons

# Davies Arnold Cooper

6–8 Bouverie Street, London EC4Y 8DD
Tel: (020) 7936 2222  Fax: (020) 7936 2020
Email: daclon@dac.co.uk
Website: www.dac.co.uk

| | |
|---|---:|
| **Partners** | 65 |
| **Total Fee-earners** | 110 |
| **Total Trainees** | 13 |
| **Total Staff** | 315 |

## firm profile
Davies Arnold Cooper is a commercial law firm. It has offices in the City of London, Manchester, Madrid and Mexico City. Its aim is to be recognised as a strong provider of legal services in two areas: commercial disputes, whatever their nature; and property, every aspect of it.

## main areas of work
Commercial disputes: 70%; property: 30%.

## trainee profile
If you secure a training contract with Davies Arnold Cooper you will most probably have a 2:1 degree, either in law or in another academic subject, as well as good A level grades. You will definitely be a self-starter with plenty of energy and common sense. What you've done with your life so far counts for much more than where you went to school/university. The firm likes maturity and in the past has awarded several contracts to those for whom the law is a second career: doctors, accountants, ex-public service and armed forces.

## training programme & environment
The firm encourages you to take on responsibility as soon as you join and will give you as much as you can handle, although you will always be supervised and never left alone to struggle. You will experience both contentious and non-contentious work and because the firm only takes on a handful of trainees every year, the chances are you will be able to select your preferred seats. There are five training contract positions available for September 2008. Applications should be made using the firm's application form which is available on request or from the website.

## benefits
Current first year salary is £26,000. 22 days holiday, private medical insurance and season ticket loan.

## sponsorship & awards
CPE and LPC fees paid plus maintenance grants.

# Dechert LLP

Times Square, 160 Victoria Street, London EC4V 4QQ
Tel: (020) 7184 7000 Fax: (020) 7184 7001
Email: lynn.muncey@dechert.com
Website: www.dechert.com

## firm profile
Dechert LLP is a leading international law firm based in 17 offices throughout the United States and Europe. Worldwide they employ over 1800 people, and their largest offices are in Philadelphia, New York and London. Their London practice has around 300 people, and was established in 1938. Dechert provides a full service to business clients. The firm's clients are major companies and individuals throughout the world. At the same time, as a medium-sized office in London, Dechert retains a friendly and sociable atmosphere where everyone knows each other.

## main areas of work – London
The firm's lawyers work across a wide spectrum of business, commercial property and litigation specialisations. For example, they have particular strengths in financial services, banking and securitisation, employment, defamation, intellectual property, insurance, property finance and tax. The firm represent clients from the United States and Continental Europe, alongside its UK client base.

## trainee profile
Candidates should be able to empathise with a wide range of people, as the firm's clients come from all walks of life. Dechert looks for enthusiasm, intelligence, an ability to find a practical solution to a problem and for powers of expression and persuasion. Also wanted are those with a desire and ability to promote the firm's business at every opportunity. Dechert wants people who will remain on after qualifying and make their careers with the firm. Dechert offers challenging and exciting work as well as a high-flying start to your career. If this sounds interesting to you and you have academic ability, excellent communication skills, and an ambition to play a pivotal role in the further growth and success of the firm, Dechert would like to talk with you.

## training environment
Dechert invests heavily in training with trainees having the opportunity to work on high-profile national and cross-jurisdictional projects. Unusually, training is divided into six four-monthly periods. The six seats are discussed with each trainee individually so that training reflects his/her own interests and needs. The greater number of seats makes it easier to accommodate requests to work in specific areas of the firm. Trainees are regularly seconded to the Brussels office, and also from time to time, to offices in the USA and Germany. The firm has a dedicated training programme managed by its Director of Training (a former Director of the College of Law, London). The PSC is provided in a tailored format by the firm, with many modules taking place in-house. That apart, there is an extensive training programme in which trainees are encouraged to participate (numerous aspects being particularly aimed at trainees).

The firm's award winning pro bono programme exposes their lawyers to a world of extraordinary work, from international human rights and community development through to prisoners' rights and charity work.

## benefits
Free permanent health care and life assurance, subsidised membership of local gym and interest-free season ticket loan.

---

| | |
|---|---|
| Partners | 34* |
| Assistant Solicitors | 82* |
| Total Trainees | 24* |

*denotes London figure

**contact**
Lynn Muncey

**method of application**
Online application form

**selection procedure**
Communication exercises & interviews with partners & assistant solicitors

**closing date for 2008**
31 July 2006

**application**
Training contracts p.a.
between 12 and 15
Applications p.a. Approx 1,500
% interviewed p.a. Approx 9%
Required degree grade 2:1 (or capability of attaining a 2:1)

**training**
Salary
1st year (2005) £28,000
2nd year (2005) £32,000
(to be reviewed September 2006)
Holiday entitlement 20 days
% of trainees with a non-law degree p.a. Varies
No. of seats available abroad p.a. 3 or 4 (plus shorter secondments to US offices)

**post-qualification**
Salary (2005) c.£50,000
(to be reviewed July 2006)
% of trainees offered job on qualification 75%
% of partners who joined as trainees 50%

**overseas offices**
Boston, Brussels, Charlotte, Frankfurt, Harrisburg, Hartford, Luxembourg, Munich, Newport Beach, New York, Palo Alto, Paris, Philadelphia, Princeton, San Francisco, Washington

# Dechert LLP continued

## vacation placements - 2 programmes
Dates: 3 - 14 July and 17 - 28 July; Places for 2006: up to 16 (8 on each programme);
Remuneration: no less than £225 p.w.; Closing Date: 28 February 2006.
**Assessment days:** one in April and one in October; Places: 20-30 on each

## number of vacancies
The firm recruits between 12 and 15 trainees per year (one intake in September).
Applications for 2008 will be considered between 1 June and 31 July 2006.

## sponsorship & awards
LPC fees paid and £7,000 maintenance.

## trainee comments
"When I started at the firm I was impressed that the trainee induction took place in Philadelphia, where we were truly welcomed to the whole firm. During my training contract I was also given the opportunity to spend four months with our competition team in Brussels. I was exposed to a different way of working life and was also able to appreciate the truly international nature of the work that the firm does. The firm also offers the opportunity for trainees to work in Munich with the private equity team there, in addition to a variety of client secondments and a judicial secondment. The firm is very keen to tailor the training to each trainee's interests and requirements. There is a flexibility here that my friends training at other firms envy. It helped ensure that my decision to qualify into Dechert's corporate department was the right one for me. Due to the smaller intakes and the six-seat rotation there is a much higher chance of being assigned to the seats that you really want to do. Dechert is a great place to work and I know that accepting a training contract here was the right decision. Be it in Brussels or London, or indeed during my short time in Philadelphia, I have been made to feel part of a team that both supports and challenges me." (Harriet Smith, Newly Qualified, read English Literature at Bristol)


"The great advantage of the Dechert six seat system is that it allows trainees to try a variety of seats without committing a full six months. The result is a freedom to experience seats which you may not have initially considered without fear of restricting options on qualification. Combined with the option to do multiple seats in any one department, this means that those trainees with a set preference can take full advantage of up to a year in their chosen department at Dechert, while those who are yet to decide can get a wider exposure and broader experience. Either way, the result is that the all important decision as to where to qualify is as informed and prepared as possible." (Daniel Hawthorne, Newly Qualified, read Law at Cambridge, Pembroke College)

# Denton Wilde Sapte

Five Chancery Lane, Clifford's Inn, London EC4A 1BU
Tel: (020) 7242 1212  Fax: (020) 7320 6555
Email: jo.wilson@dentonwildesapte.com
Website: www.dentonwildesapte.com

## firm profile
Denton Wilde Sapte is a large commercial law firm based in London with offices in Europe, the Middle East and the CIS. The firm's strengths lie in its sector focus, and its practice areas are as strong and diverse as its client list.

## main areas of work
Banking & finance; corporate; dispute resolution; EU & competition; employment & pensions; energy & infrastructure, real estate, tax; technology, media & telecommunications.

## trainee profile
The firm looks for candidates who are team players with a strong academic and extra curricular record of achievement.

## training environment
Four six month seats, including at least one transactional and one contentious seat. Most trainees also spend one seat in the Banking & Finance and/or Real Estate Department. The firm aims to offer trainees as much choice as possible with their seats, one of which may be spent in one of the international offices or with one of the firm's clients. You will be given as much responsibility as you can handle, working with the law, with the team and with clients in real business situations. The firm works hard to maintain a friendly and open working environment where ideas are shared and people work together to achieve goals.

## benefits
Flexible benefit scheme. Meal away from home allowance. Season ticket loan.

## vacation placements
Open days during December 2005 and summer schemes during June and July 2006. Closing date for applications for open days is 25 November 2005 and for summer schemes 10 February 2006.

## sponsorship & awards
GDL and LPC tuition fees covered plus £4,500 maintenance grant for each year of study, £5,000 if studying in London.

---

**Partners** 150
**Fee-earners** 530
**Total Trainees** 65

**contact**
Jo Wilson

**method of application**
Application form

**selection procedure**
First interview; selection test; second interview & case study

**closing date for 2008**
31 July 2006

**application**
Training contracts p.a. **30**
Applications p.a. **1,500**
% interviewed p.a. **10-15%**
Required degree grade **2:1**

**training**
Salary
**1st year £28,000**
**2nd year £31,000**
Holiday entitlement **24 days**
% of trainees with a
non-law degree p.a. **40%**
No. of seats available
abroad p.a. **Currently 8**

**post-qualification**
Salary (2004) **£48,000**
% of trainees offered job
on qualification (2005) **72%**

**overseas offices**
Abu Dhabi, Almaty, Cairo, Dubai, Gibraltar, Istanbul, Moscow, Muscat, Paris, Tashkent

# Devonshires

Salisbury House London Wall  London EC2M 5QY
Tel: (020) 7628 7576  Fax: (020) 7256 7318
Email: training@devonshires.co.uk
Website: www.devonshires.com

## firm profile
Devonshires has been in the City of London for more than 150 years. The firm prides itself on its reputation for providing all its clients - who are based throughout England, Wales, the Channel Islands and the Isles of Scilly - with expert, cost-effective advice. The firm is a recognised leader in the social housing market and currently advises over 220 registered social landlords. The firm also advises financial institutions and stock exchange listed debt issuers; charities; corporations; government - domestic and international; insolvency practitioners; NHS trusts; private clients; professional service providers; property developers and investors, including financial institutions.

## main areas of work
Property & conveyancing 50%; commercial 10%; PPP/PFI 10%; litigation 9%; finance 9%; employment 6%; construction 4%.

## trainee profile
The firm recruits high calibre trainees who are all-rounders. You don't have to be a law graduate - the firm welcomes applications from all disciplines and all universities. What you must have are keen commercial and technical qualities and proven academic abilities. You will also be able to show a demonstrable interest in a legal career and have a wide range of interests outside the office.

## training environment
Training usually involves four seats of six months each, working with partners and senior staff in departments such as banking (company and commercial), church/charity, construction, employment, family/matrimonial, housing management litigation, personal injury, litigation/dispute resolution, PFI and property. You will be required to cover a minimum of three practice areas and have a minimum of three months' contentious experience.

## benefits
Interest-free season ticket loans, healthcare scheme membership, trainee social group, subsidised health-club membership, dress down Fridays, life assurance, dental care.

## sponsorship & awards
Under review.

| | |
|---|---|
| **Partners** | **18** |
| **Total Number of Fee-earners** | **80** |
| **Total Trainees** | **11** |

**contact**
Human Resources Administrator
(020) 7628 7576

**method of application**
Online application form at www.devonshires.com only

**application**
Training contracts p.a. **4**
Applications p.a. **500**
% interviewed p.a. **5%**
Required degree grade
**2:1 and higher**

**training**
salary for each year of training
Year 1: **£25,500**
Year 2: **£26,500**
holiday entitlement **22 days**

**post-qualification**
Salary **competitive**
% of trainees offered job on qualification (2004) **80%**

# A-Z Solicitors

# Dickinson Dees

St. Ann's Wharf, 112 Quayside, Newcastle upon Tyne NE99 1SB
Tel: (0191) 279 9046  Fax: (0191) 279 9716
Email: graduate.recruitment@dickinson-dees.com
Website: www.trainingcontract.com

## firm profile
Dickinson Dees enjoys an excellent reputation as one of the country's leading commercial law firms. Based in Newcastle upon Tyne, the firm prides itself on the breadth of experience and expertise within the firm which enables it to offer services of the highest standards to clients. Whilst many of the firm's clients are based in the North, Dickinson Dees works on a national basis for national and internationally based businesses and organisations.

## main areas of work
The firm has 700 employees and is organised into four key departments (Company Commercial, Commercial Property, Litigation and Private Client) with 38 cross departmental units advising on specific areas. They also handle large volumes of high-quality work for a diverse client base.

## trainee profile
They firm is looking for intellectually able, motivated and enthusiastic graduates from any discipline with good communication skills. Successful applicants will understand the need to provide practical, commercial advice to clients. They will share the firm's commitment to self-development and teamwork and its desire to provide clients with services which match their highest expectations.

## training environment
Trainees are relatively few for the size of the practice. You are fully integrated into the firm and involved in all aspects of firm business. The training contract consists of four seats -one in each of the Commercial Property, Company Commercial and Litigation departments. You may be able to specialise for the fourth seat. Trainees sit with their supervisors and appraisals are carried out every three months. The firm has its own Training Department as well as a Graduate Recruitment Adviser and Graduate Programme Adviser. There are induction courses on each move of department with opportunities for trainees to get involved in the firm's training programme. The firm offers a tailored in-house Professional Skills Course which is run in conjunction with the College of Law. The working environment is supportive and friendly with the benefits of working in the vibrant, bustling city of Newcastle yet within 15 minutes from unspoilt countryside.

## vacation placements
Places for 2006: 40; Duration: 1 week; Remuneration: £125 p.w.  Our work placement weeks are part of the recruitment process and all applicants should apply online at www.trainingcontract.com.  Apply by 31 December 2005 for Easter vacation work placements.  Apply by 28 February 2006 for Summer vacation work placements.

## sponsorship & awards
GDL/LPC fees paid and £4,000 interest free loan.

| | |
|---|---|
| **Partners** | 65 |
| **Total Staff** | 700 |
| **Total Trainees** | 27 |

**contact**
Sally Brewis, Graduate Recruitment Adviser

**method of application**
Apply online at www.trainingcontract.com

**selection procedure**
Aptitude and ability tests, negotiation exercise, personality questionnaire, interview

**closing date for 2007**
31 July 2006

**application**
Training contracts p.a. up to **12-15**
Applications p.a. **800**
% interviewed p.a. **10%**
Required degree grade **2:1** in either law or non-law

**training**
Salary
**1st year (2005) £18,500**
**2nd year (2005) £19,500**
Holiday entitlement **23 days**
% of trainees with a non-law degree p.a. **40%**
No. of seats available abroad p.a. **2**
**(3-month secondments)**

**post-qualification**
Salary (2005) **£32,500**
% of trainees offered job on qualification (2004) **83%** **(10/12)**
% of partners (as at 1/9/05) who joined as trainees **32%**

**other offices**
Tees Valley
Brussels (associated office)

# DLA Piper Rudnick Gray Cary UK LLP

Victoria Square House, Victoria Square, Birmingham B2 4DL
Tel: (020) 7796 6677   Fax: (0121) 262 5793
Email: recruitment.graduate@dlapiper.com
Website: www.dlapiper.com

## firm profile

DLA Piper is one of the world's largest full service commercial law firms with UK offices in Birmingham, Edinburgh, Glasgow, Leeds, Liverpool, London, Manchester and Sheffield.

The firm now has more than 6,800 employees working from over 50 offices in 20 countries across Europe, Asia and the US and its clients include some of the world's leading businesses, governments, banks and financial institutions. This impressive client base coupled with emphasis on providing high quality service and teamwork, offers a challenging fast paced working environment.  For the fifth year running the firm has appeared in The Sunday Times survey of the '100 Best Companies to Work For' as well as holding the 'Investors in People' accreditation, demonstrating the firm's commitment to its employees and their ongoing development.

As well as taking care of its own people, DLA Piper has extensive Corporate Social Responsibility/Pro Bono programmes in place.  The firm feels that taking part in these programmes helps to broaden the perspectives of the DLA Piper people that take part. For trainees, pro bono work (for companies like The Princes Trust) means gaining valuable experience in running their own cases and experiencing a unique level of work and responsibility.

DLA Piper was voted 'Law Firm of the Year' at the Legal Business Awards 2005.

## main areas of work

DLA Piper has the following main areas of work: banking; business support and restructuring; commercial and projects; corporate; human resources; litigation; real estate; regulatory; and technology, media and communications.

## trainee profile

The firm is looking for individuals from either a law or non-law background who have a minimum of 3 Bs at A Level (or equivalent) and expect, or have achieved a 2.1 degree classification - but good academics are no longer sufficient.  DLA Piper looks for highly motivated and energetic team players with sound commercial awareness, outstanding communication and organisational skills, and, above all, an appetite for life!

There is no such thing as a 'standard' DLA Piper trainee, they do not want to recruit clones.  Trainees are encouraged to be themselves and, in that respect, be different.

As soon as future trainees are recruited DLA Piper does as much as possible to make them feel part of the firm, for example, writing to them regularly and organising social events where future trainees can meet one another as well as current members of staff.

| | |
|---|---|
| Partners | 1120 |
| Other lawyers | 1800 |
| Total Trainees | 171 |

**contact**
Sally Carthy, Head of Graduate Recruitment

**method of application**
Online application form

**selection procedure**
First interview, second interview, assessment afternoon

**closing date for 2008**
31 July 2006

**application**
Training contracts p.a. **85+**
Applications p.a. **2,500**
% interviewed p.a. **10%**
Required degree grade **2:1**

**training**
Salary (2005)
**1st year £29,000 (London)**
**£20,000 (Regions)**
**£16,000 (Scotland)**
**2nd year £32,000 (London)**
**£22,000 (Regions)**
**£18,000 (Scotland)**
% of trainees with a non-law degree p.a. **40%**

**post-qualification**
Salary (2005)
**£50,000 (London)**
**£34,000 (regional offices)**
**£30,000 (Scotland)**

**uk offices**
Birmingham, Edinburgh, Glasgow, Leeds, Liverpool, London, Manchester, Sheffield

**overseas offices**
Austria, Belgium, Bosnia-Herzegovina, China, Croatia, Czech Republic, Denmark, France, Germany, Georgia, Hong Kong, Hungary, Italy, Netherlands, Norway, Poland, Russia, Singapore, Slovakia, Spain, Sweden, Thailand, Ukraine, USA.

# DLA Piper Rudnick Gray Cary UK LLP cont'd

## training environment

From induction to qualification and beyond, DLA Piper ensures that its employees develop the necessary skills and knowledge to survive in a busy client-driven environment. Trainees complete four six month seats during the course of their training contract. If you want responsibility, they will give you as much as you can handle and your progress will be monitored through regular reviews and feedback. The compulsory Professional Skills Course is run in-house and is tailored to meet the needs of the firm's trainees. This combined with on-the-job experience, provides trainees with an excellent grounding on which to build their professional careers.

DLA Piper trainees are able to express a preference for their seats, and as much as possible is done to ensure that during the course of the training contract these preferences can be accommodated.

## vacation placements

DLA Piper runs summer vacation schemes across all of its UK offices. The scheme aims to give a thorough insight into life at the firm. Attendees shadow a fee-earner in two departments and are given a range of work to do, they are also allocated a trainee 'buddy' to help out with any queries. The scheme also includes presentations from departments and social events with the trainees.

Places for 2006: Approx 200; Duration: 2 weeks; Remuneration (2005 figures) £210 per week (London), £170 per week (regions and Scotland); Closing Date: 31 January 2006.

## sponsorship & awards

Payment of LPC and GDL fees plus maintenance grant in both years, is offered to future trainees who have yet to complete these courses.

## benefits

Trainees are entitled to join the firm's pension, private health cover, life assurance and permanent health insurance schemes. Holiday entitlement is 25 days per year.

## trainee quotes

"I was really impressed by the way the graduate recruitment team kept in contact with me while I was still at university and law school. There's regular contact, support and you receive letters, the firm's magazine and press releases. You actually feel part of the team from the outset and reassured knowing that you can always pick up the phone if you have any queries. It's a great way to start."

# DMH Stallard

100 Queens Road, Brighton BN1 3YB
Tel: (01273) 223703 Fax: (01273) 223711
Email: recruitment@dmhstalard.com
Website: www.dmhstallard.com

## firm profile

DMH Stallard is an approachable and innovative firm with an open culture which encourages personal development and provides its personnel with a high level of support in order to achieve this. The firm offers expertise and service comparable to City firms to a range of commercial organisations, non-profit institutions and individual clients. By focusing on the client's needs DMH Stallard provides practical and creative solutions. DMH Stallard operates from offices in Brighton, Crawley/Gatwick and London.

## main areas of work

Corporate/commercial; commercial property, planning and environmental; employment, intellectual property/IT; litigation; residential conveyancing; personal injury; private client; property litigation.

## trainee profile

The firm welcomes applications from motivated graduates from all backgrounds and age groups. Enthusiasm, a mature outlook and commercial awareness are as prized as academic ability, and good communication skills are a must. Ideal applicants are those with the potential to become effective managers or strong marketeers.

## training environment

Usually four six month seats taken from the following areas: employment, intellectual property/IT, corporate/commercial, planning and environmental, commercial property, commercial litigation, property litigation, personal injury, residential conveyancing and private client. Trainees are closely supervised by the partner to whom they are attached but have every opportunity to work as part of a team and deal directly with clients.

## vacation placements

Places for Summer 2007: Priority given to trainee interviewees with a limited number of unpaid places; Duration: 1 week; Closing Date: 31 January 2007.

| | |
|---|---|
| **Partners** | 46 |
| **Assistant Solicitors** | 22 |
| **Total Trainees** | 13 |

**contact**
Jessica Leigh-Davis

**method of application**
Application form

**selection procedure**: First interview and assessment day (March/April), work experience, then second interview and assessment day (August)

**closing date for 2008**
31 December 2006

**application**
Training contracts p.a. **6-7**
Applications p.a. **115**
% interviewed p.a. **20%**
Required degree grade **2:1**

**training**
Salary
**1st year (2005) £19,000**
**2nd year (2005) £21,000**
Holiday entitlement **23.5 days**
% of trainees with a non-law degree p.a. **33%**

**post-qualification**
Salary (2005) **£31,000**
(Brighton & Crawley)
% of assistants (as at 1/7/03) who joined as trainees **46%**
% of partners (as at 1/7/03) who joined as trainees **47%**

# Dorsey & Whitney

21 Wilson Street, London EC2M 2TD
Tel: (020) 7588 0800  Fax: (020) 7588 0555
Website: www.dorsey.com

## firm profile
Dorsey & Whitney is amongst the largest law firms in the world with more than 20 offices situated across three continents. The firm has over 650 lawyers worldwide. The London office of Dorsey & Whitney has over 40 lawyers and trainees. It continues to build on its traditional strengths in corporate law, litigation and intellectual property work through its wide range of practice groups.

## main areas of work
The London office offers the full range of legal services including corporate finance, cross border M&A, commercial litigation, tax, employment, real estate, intellectual property and competition law.

## trainee profile
Dorsey & Whitney is looking for 'self-starters', capable of meeting the intellectual and business challenges of a successful multi-national practice. Candidates should be committed team players who enjoy rewarding client work. An honours degree at 2:1 level or above and some relevant work experience is also required.

## training environment
The training contract is split into four individual 'seats' of six months each. Each trainee will be required to complete litigation and corporate seats. Secondments to major clients are available. All trainees are supplied with the encouragement and support necessary to maximise their potential. Through the mentoring, professional development and evaluation programmes, the firm strives to develop and retain the highest calibre lawyers.

## benefits
Non-contributory pension schemes; health insurance and life insurance.

| Partners | 12 |
| Assistant Solicitors | 28 |
| Total Trainees | 8 |

**contact**
Andrew Rimmington,
Partner (020) 7588 0800

**method of application**
Application by letter with a current curriculum vitae addressed to Andrew Rimmington.

**closing date for 2008**
30 September 2006

**application**
Training contracts p.a. **4**
(currently under review)

**training**
Salary
**1st year (2005) £28,500**
**2nd year (2005) £31,500**
Holiday entitlement **22 days plus public holidays**

**post-qualification**
Salary (2005) **£55,000**
Dorsey & Whitney aims to offer a qualified position to all candidates who have shown the appropriate level of performance during training, subject to the needs of the firm

# DWF

Centurion House, 129 Deansgate, Manchester, M3 3AA
Tel: (0161) 603 5000  Fax: (0161) 603 5050
Email: trainees@dwf.co.uk
Website: www.dwf.co.uk

## firm profile

DWF delivers a complete menu of legal services for businesses, providing innovative solutions and strategies - whatever and wherever the problem or opportunity. The firm possesses specialist technical know-how and industry sector expertise. It has a reputation for efficient and business-friendly service and for delivering outstanding value for money. DWF is a top tier law firm of choice for businesses based or operating in England and Wales, with a credible and effective national and international capability. Through its work with successful and growing businesses, DWF has become one of the fastest growing law firms in the UK.

## main areas of work

Services cover asset finance, banking, business recovery, commercial agreements, competition, construction, corporate, debt management, dispute resolution, employee incentive planning, employment law, food law, health safety and environment, insurance, intellectual property, internet and technology, legal training, licensing, pensions, planning, property and wealthcare. These services are delivered by specialist teams - including leading experts in their field. DWF has a client base covering a wide range of industries and is known for its service innovation as its DWF HR Horizons, and Advantage service demonstrate. Information about the industry sector groups and innovative services can be found at www.dwf.co.uk.

## trainee profile

DWF wants trainee solicitors to play a part in building on its success. The firm is looking for trainees who enjoy working as part of a busy team, respond positively to a challenge and have what it takes to deliver results for clients. The firm is looking for its partners of the future and in recent years virtually all of its qualifying trainees have been offered jobs.

## training environment

All trainees commence life at DWF with a welcome programme, designed to provide a clear picture of the firm and its services, before moving to their first seat. The firm provides a flexible seat rotation including employment, corporate, property, commercial litigation and insurance, with agreed options which focus on post-qualification aspirations. This is supplemented by general training as well as specific training relevant to the particular seat using in-house and external courses. Appraisals are carried out during each seat to review progress and development. Trainees will have the opportunity to join in the busy social life within the offices and with local trainee solicitors' groups.

| | |
|---|---|
| **Partners** | 67 |
| **Assistant Solicitors** | 119 |
| **Total Trainees** | 15 |

**contact**
Sarah Fielding
HR Officer
(Manchester address)

**method of application**
Online application

**selection procedure**
2 stage interview/selection process

**closing date for 2007/2008**
31 July 2006

**application**
Training contracts p.a. **8**
Applications p.a. **c.500**
% interviewed p.a. **23%**
Required degree grade **2:1**
**in any discipline**

**training**
Salary
**1st year (2005) £20,000**
Holiday entitlement
**25 days p.a. minimum +**
**option to buy & sell holidays**

**post-qualification**
% of trainees offered job
on qualification (2005) **100%**

**benefits**
Flexible benefits scheme
including insurance,
pension & other benefits

**vacation placements**
Summer vacation schemes

**sponsorship & awards**
LPC funding for tuition fees

# Eversheds

Senator House, 85 Queen Victoria Street, London EC4V 4JL
Tel: (020) 7919 4761  Fax: (020) 7919 4919
Application Form Online at www.eversheds.com
Email: gradrec@eversheds.com
Website: www.eversheds.com

## firm profile
Eversheds LLP has over 2,000 legal and business advisers providing services to the private and public sector business and finance community. Access to all these services is provided through the firm's international network of offices. Eversheds combines local market knowledge and access with the specialisms, resources and international capability of one of the world's largest law firms.

## main areas of work
Corporate, commercial, litigation and dispute management, real estate, human resources (employment and pensions) and legal systems group. In addition to these core areas each office provides expertise in a further 30 business and industry sectors.

## trainee profile
Eversheds' people are valued for being straightforward, enterprising and effective. The firm listens to its clients. It likes to simplify rather than complicate. It expects trainees to be business-like, unstuffy and down-to-earth. You will need to display commercial acumen, imagination and drive and, above all, you  will need to be results-driven. As a trainee you will get as much responsibility as you can handle and will benefit from the 'hands on, learning by doing' philosophy. The firm takes your training very seriously but expects it to be fun too.

## training environment
You will be encouraged to play a major part in the direction your training and development takes, with advice and supervision always available. In each department you will sit with a partner or a senior assistant and participate from an early stage in varied, complex and high-value work. Eversheds aims to retain as many trainees as possible on qualifying and many of the partners were trainees with the firm. A steep learning curve begins with a week of basic training followed by departmental seats – three of which will cover the firm's main practice areas. During your training you will also complete an Eversheds designed Professional Skills Course and, on qualification, follow a progressive career structure.

## benefits
Regional variations.

## vacation placements
Places for 2006: 250; Duration: 2 weeks in Summer, 1 week at Easter; Remuneration: regional variations; Closing Date: 31 January 2006.

## sponsorship & awards
GDL/LPC fees and maintenance grants in accordance with the terms of the firm's offer.

| Partners | 400+ |
|---|---|
| Assistant Solicitors | 2,000+ |
| Total Trainees | 180+ |

**contact**
gradrec@eversheds.com

**method of application**
Apply online at
www.eversheds.com

**selection procedure**
Selection days include group and individual exercises, presentations and interview

**closing date for 2008**
31 July 2006

**application**
Training contracts p.a. **80**
Applications p.a. **4,000**
% interviewed p.a. **20%**
Required degree grade **2:1**

**training**
Salary
**1st year London (2005)**
**£29,000**
**2nd year London (2005)**
**£32,000**
Holiday entitlement **25 days**
% of trainees with
a non-law degree p.a. **45%**
No. of seats available
abroad p.a. **Up to 12**

**post-qualification**
Salary London (2005)
**£50,000**
% of trainees offered job
on qualification (2005) **82%**

**offices**
Barcelona*, Birmingham, Brussels, Budapest*, Cambridge, Cardiff, Copenhagen, Doha** Ipswich, Kuala Lumpur*, Leeds, London, Madrid*, Manchester, Milan*, Munich*, Newcastle, Norwich, Nottingham, Paris, Rome*, Shanghai*, Singapore*, Sofia*, Stockholm*, Valladolid*, Vienna*, Warsaw*, Wroclaw*
* Associated office
** In co-operation

# Farrer & Co

66 Lincoln's Inn Fields, London WC2A 3LH
Tel: (020) 7242 2022  Fax: (020) 7242 9899
Email: graduates@farrer.co.uk
Website: www.farrer.co.uk

## firm profile
Farrer & Co is a mid-sized London law firm. The firm provides specialist advice to a large number of prominent private, institutional and commercial clients. Farrer & Co has built a successful law firm based on the goodwill of close client relationships, outstanding expertise in niche sectors and a careful attention to personal service and quality.

## main areas of work
The firm's breadth of expertise is reflected by the fact that it has an outstanding reputation in fields as diverse as matrimonial law, offshore tax planning, employment, heritage work, charity law, defamation and sports law.

## trainee profile
Trainees are expected to be highly motivated individuals with keen intellects and interesting and engaging personalities. Those applicants who appear to break the mould – as shown by their initiative for organisation, leadership, exploration, or enterprise – are far more likely to get an interview than the erudite, but otherwise unimpressive, student.

## training environment
The training programme involves each trainee in the widest range of cases, clients and issues possible in a single law firm taking full advantage of the wide range of practice areas at Farrer & Co by offering six seats, rather than the more usual four. This provides a broad foundation of knowledge and experience and the opportunity to make an informed choice about the area of law in which to specialise. A high degree of involvement is encouraged under the direct supervision of solicitors and partners. Trainees attend an induction programme and regular internal lectures. The training partner reviews trainees' progress at the end of each seat and extensive feedback is given. The firm has a very friendly atmosphere and regular sporting and social events.

## benefits
Health and life insurance, subsidised gym membership, season ticket loan.

## vacation placements
Places for 2006: 30; Duration: 2 weeks at Easter, two schemes for 2 weeks in summer; Remuneration: £240 p.w.; Closing Date: 31 January 2006.

## sponsorship & awards
CPE Funding: Fees paid plus £4,500 maintenance. LPC Funding: Fees paid plus £4,500 maintenance.

| | |
|---|---|
| **Partners** | 62 |
| **Assistant Solicitors** | 55 |
| **Total Trainees** | 17 |

**contact**
Graduate Recruitment Manager

**method of application**
Online via the firm's website

**selection procedure**
Interviews with Graduate Recruitment Partner and partners

**closing date for 2008**
31 July 2006

**application**
Training contracts p.a. **8-10**
Applications p.a. **800**
% interviewed p.a. **5%**
Required degree grade **2:1**

**training**
Salary
**1st year (2005) £27,500**
**2nd year (2005) £30,000**
The firm operates a performance related bonus scheme based on both personal and firm performance
Holiday entitlement **25 days**
% of trainees with non-law degrees p.a. **50%**

**post-qualification**
Salary (2005) **£43,000**
trainees offered job on qualification (2005) **100%**
% of partners (as at July 05) who joined as trainees **60%**

# Field Fisher Waterhouse

35 Vine Street, London EC3N 2AA
Tel: (020) 7861 4000  Fax: (020) 7488 0084
Email: graduaterecruitment@ffw.com
Website: www.ffw.com/careers

## firm profile

Field Fisher Waterhouse (FFW) is a mid-sized City law firm that provides a broad range of legal services to an impressive list of clients that range from small unlisted UK companies to multinationals and foreign corporations. They pride themselves on offering creative solutions and practical advice for clients in an ever-changing commercial world, and as part of The European Legal Alliance have a strong presence across 20 European cities.

## main areas of work

Throughout their Training Contract trainees have the opportunity to work within IP & technology, corporate and commercial, banking and finance, regulatory and real estate. They also offer trainee seats in a wide range of other areas including public sector, construction, litigation, employment and travel and aviation.

## trainee profile

The firm is looking to recruit trainees from both law and non-law backgrounds who have a strong academic background, excellent communication skills, enthusiasm and the ability to work as part of a team.

## training environment

FFW offers a six seat training contract and their range of practice areas enable them to offer outstanding opportunities for training. Trainees are treated as a valued part of the team and are encouraged to assume early responsibility. Practical training is complemented by a comprehensive programme of in-house seminars, workshops and external courses, accompanied by regular feedback and a formal assessment at the end of each seat. The firm invests highly in the development and training of all its trainees and provides good quality work within a friendly, relaxed and supportive working environment. You will also have additional support from your fellow trainees, a buddy and a mentor who is a senior solicitor. FFW believes this working environment is just one of the reasons that it has retained 100% of trainees upon qualification in 2005.

## sponsorship & benefits

Sponsorship and a £4,500 maintenace grant is paid for both the PgDL and LPC. Other benefits include: 25 days' holiday, life assurance, season ticket loan, medical insurance, GP service, and pension in addition to having two squash courts in our offices.

## vacation placements

Increasingly, trainees have come to the firm through the summer vacation scheme, which provides a useful way of getting an insiders view of FFW. The firm runs two two-week schemes during July where you have the opportunity to spend a week in two different departments and take part in a variety of work and social activities.
Please apply online for the Summer Vacation Scheme and Training Contracts, via the website at www.ffw.com/careers.
Deadline for 2006 Summer Vacation Scheme: 31 January 2006
Deadline for 2008 Training Contracts: 31 August 2006

| | |
|---|---|
| Partners | 87 |
| Assistant Solicitors | 134 |
| Vacancies | 17 |
| Total Trainees | 34 |

**contact**
Graduate Recruitment

**method of application**
Apply online via the firm website,
www.ffw.com/careers

**selection procedure**
Interviews and a written assessment

**closing date for 2008**
31 August 2006

**application**
Training contracts p.a. **17**
Applications p.a. **1,200**
Required degree grade **2:1**

**training**
Salary
**1st year £28,000**
**2nd year £31,000**
Holiday entitlement
**25 days**

**post-qualification**
Salary (2005) **£47,000**
% of trainees offered job
on qualification (2005) **100%**

**offices**
London

# Finers Stephens Innocent

179 Great Portland St, London W1N 6LS
Tel: (020) 7323 4000  Fax: (020) 7580 7069
Email: gradrecruitment@fsilaw.co.uk
Website: www.fsilaw.co.uk

## firm profile

Finers Stephens Innocent is an expanding practice based in Central London providing a range of high quality legal services to corporate and commercial clients. The firm offers a range of services focused to meet the requirements of its primarily commercial client base. The firm's philosophy includes close partner involvement and a commercial approach in all client matters. Dedicated teams create services that are supplied in a cost effective manner with a working style which is personable, client supportive and informal. The firm is a member of the Network of Leading Law Firms and of Meritas.

## main areas of work

Commercial property; litigation; media; employment; family; defamation; company/commercial; private client. See the firm's website for further details.

## trainee profile

The firm looks for academic excellence in applicants. It also looks for maturity, an interesting personality, strong communication skills, ability to think like a lawyer and an indefinable 'it' which shows that you have the potential to become a long-term member of the firm's team. Mature applicants are especially encouraged.

## training environment

After your induction programme, you will complete four six month seats, sharing a room with either a Partner or Senior Assistant. The firm has two Training Partners who keep a close eye on the welfare and progress of trainees. There are regular group meetings of trainees and an appraisal process which enables you to know how you are progressing as well as giving you a chance to provide feedback on your view of your training.

## benefits

20 days holiday, pension, private medical insurance, life insurance, long-term disability insurance, season ticket loan.

## sponsorship & awards

LPC and CPE course fees.

| | |
|---|---|
| Partners | 33 |
| Assistant Solicitors | 32 |
| Total Trainees | 9 |

**contact**
Personnel Department

**method of application**
CV & covering letter

**selection procedure**
2 interviews with the Training Partners

**closing date for 2008**
30 July 2006

**application**
Training contracts p.a. **5**
Applications p.a. **800**
% interviewed p.a. **3%**
Required degree grade **2:1**

**training**
Salary
**1st year**
**Highly competitive**
**2nd year**
**Highly competitive**
Holiday entitlement **20 days**
% of trainees with a non-law degree p.a. **0-50%**

**post-qualification**
Salary
**Highly competitive**
% of trainees offered job on qualification (2003) **40%**

# Fladgate Fielder

25 Noth Row, London W1K 6DJ
Tel: (020) 7462 2299  Fax: (020) 7629 4414
Email: trainees@fladgate.com
Website: www.fladgate.com

## firm profile
Fladgate Fielder is an innovative, progressive and thriving law firm based in the heart of London's West End which prides itself on its friendly and professional working environment.

## main areas of work
The firm provides a wide range of legal services to a portfolio of prestigious clients in the UK and overseas, including multinationals, major institutions and listed companies, clearing banks, lenders and entrepreneurs. Their lawyers have experience in most major areas of practice and we combine an accessible and responsive style of service with first class technical skills and in-depth expertise. They have a strong international dimension based on multilingual lawyers working in London and complemented by access to an extensive network of overseas lawyers. They operate international 'desks' which serve continental Europe (with an emphasis on the Germanic countries), Israel, the Asia-Pacific region, the US and the Middle East. The firm's three main departments comprise property (which includes separate planning, construction and property litigation teams), corporate (which includes tax and employment groups) and litigation. These are complemented by cross-departmental teams focusing on areas of sector specialisation including media, sports, intellectual property and technology, real estate, hotels and leisure, insurance, finance and lending, trusts and professionals.

## trainee profile
The firm seeks trainees with enthusiasm, leadership potential and excellent interpersonal skills. You must be able to work independently or in a team and will be expected to show common sense and initiative. Awareness of the commercial interests of clients is essential and you will ideally have a flair for marketing and business development. You will have a minimum of a 2.1 degree, although not necessarily in law, together with three excellent A levels or equivalent. The firm is keen to attract candidates with developed language skills.

## training environment
Typically, you will complete four six month seats. Each seat will bring you into contact with new clients and colleagues and you can expect to gain real hands-on experience of a variety of deals and projects, both large and small. In each seat you will work alongside senior lawyers who will supervise your development and ensure that you are involved in challenging and interesting work. In addition to on-the-job training, each department has a comprehensive training schedule of seminars and workshops covering a range of legal and skills training. The firm has a modern culture and an open-door policy where trainees are given early responsibility and encouraged to achieve their full potential

## benefits
Pension, permanent health insurance, life assurance, season ticket loan, sports club loan, bonus scheme.

| | |
|---|---|
| **Partners** | 39 |
| **Assistant Solicitors** | 35 |
| **Total Trainees** | 6 |

### contact
Mrs Annaleen Stephens, Human Resources Manager

### method of application
Please apply using the firm's application form. Further information and an application form are available at the firm's website www.fladgate.com

### selection procedure
Assessment day and interview

### closing date for 2007/8
31 July 2006

### application
The firm operates a biennial recruitment programme and will be recruiting for its 2007 and 2008 intakes in Summer 2006. Training contracts p.a. **3** Required degree grade **2:1**

### training
Salary **£27,000-£28,500** Holiday entitlement **20-21 days**

### post-qualification
Salary **to be confirmed** % of trainees offered job on qualification (2005) **100%**

# Foot Anstey

21 Derry's Cross, Plymouth PL1 2SW
Tel: (01752) 675000  Fax: (01752) 675500
Senate Court, Southernhay Gardens, Exeter, EX1 1NT
Tel: (01392) 411221  Fax: (01392) 685220
Email: training@foot-ansteys.co.uk
Website: www.foot-ansteys.co.uk

## firm profile
Foot Anstey is one of the leading full-service law firms in the South West and has a strong reputation and prominence in the region. With a growing national and international client base the firm is recognised for its expertise in many sectors.

## main areas of work
Commercial property, property litigation, commercial litigation, company and commercial, banking, employment, insolvency, clinical negligence, criminal advocates, family and childcare and private client. Niche areas include media, marine, charities, and e-commerce.

## trainee profile
The firm welcomes applicants from all law and non-law graduates who have a strong academic background, established communication skills and who are committed to achieving excellent standards of customer service. A strong team ethos is paramount to the firm. Trainees can expect to be welcomed into a friendly and supportive environment where they will find the quality and variety of work both challenging and rewarding.

## training environment
The wide range of legal services provided offers trainees opportunities in many areas of law, sitting in either the Exeter, Plymouth or Taunton offices. Trainees undertake four seats of six months and, excepting the first, trainees are normally able to select their seat. All trainees attend an induction course. Individual monthly meetings are held with supervisors and a quarterly group meeting with the training principal. Appraisals are conducted halfway through each seat. New trainees are given a second year buddy to help them find their feet. Regular communication between the trainees and supervisors ensures an open and friendly atmosphere. The PSC is taught externally. The firm holds Lexcel and Investors in People accreditations and has an excellent training and development programme.

## benefits
Contributory pension, 25 days' holiday.

## vacation placements
The deadline for the summer placement scheme is 31 March 2006.

## sponsorship & awards
£8,000 grant towards LPC and living expenses.

| Partners | 32 |
|---|---|
| Assistant Solicitors | 61 |
| Total Trainees | 20 |

**contact**
Richard Sutton
(01752) 675151

**method of application**
CV and covering letter to Richard Sutton at the Plymouth office address. Alternatively email it to: training@foot-ansteys.co.uk or apply online at www.foot-ansteys.co.uk

**selection procedure**
Assessment day

**application**
Training contracts p.a. **12**
Required degree grade **2:1 (preferred)**

**closing date for 2008**
31 July 2006

**training**
Salary
1st year (2005) **£16,750**
2nd year (2005) **£19,000**
Holiday entitlement **25 days**

**post-qualification**
Salary (2005) **£30,500**
% of trainees offered job on qualification (2005) **83%**
% of assistant solicitors who joined as trainees (as at 30/04/05) **31%**
% of partners who joined as trainees (as at 30/04/05) **23%**

**Other offices in Taunton & Bridgwater**

# Forbes

73 Northgate, Blackburn BB2 1AA
Tel: (01254) 580000  Fax: (01254) 222216
Email: graduate.recruitment@forbessolicitors.co.uk

## firm profile

Forbes is one of the largest practices in the north with 24 partners and over 350 members of staff based in nine offices across the north of England. The firm has a broad based practice dealing with both commercial and private client work and can therefore provide a varied and exciting training contract. The firm is however especially noted for excellence in its company/commercial; civil litigation; defendant insurer; crime; family and employment departments. It has a number of Higher Court Advocates and the firm holds many Legal Service Commission Franchises. Underlying the practice is a strong commitment to quality, training and career development – a commitment underlined by the fact that Forbes was one of the first firms to be recognised as an Investor in People and its ISO 9001 accreditation. For applicants looking for a 'city' practice without the associated hassles of working in a city then Forbes could be it. The firm can offer the best of both worlds - a large firm with extensive resources and support combined with a commitment to quality, people and the personal touch.

## main areas of work

Company/commercial, civil litigation, defendant insurer, crime, family and employment services.

## trainee profile

Forbes looks for high-calibre recruits with strong Northwest connections, good academic records, who are also keen team players. Candidates should have a total commitment to client service and identify with the firm's philosophy of providing practical straightforward legal advice.

## training environment

A tailored training programme involves six months in four of the following: crime, civil litigation, defendant insurer in Leeds or Blackburn, matrimonial, and non-contentious/company commercial.

| | |
|---|---|
| **Partners** | 24 |
| **Assistant Solicitors** | 50 |
| **Total Trainees** | 15+ |

**contact**
Graduate Recruitment Manager

**method of application**
Handwritten letter and CV

**selection procedure**
Interview with partners

**closing date for 2008**
31 July 2006

**application**
Training contracts p.a. **4**
Applications p.a. **350 plus**
% interviewed p.a. **Varies**
Required degree grade **2:1**

**training**
Salary
**1st year At least Law Society minimum**
**2nd year (2005) £17,720**
Holiday entitlement
**20 days pa**

**post-qualification**
Salary
**Highly competitive**
% of trainees offered job on qualification (2004) **100%**

# Ford & Warren

Westgate Point, Westgate, Leeds, LS1 2AX
Tel: (0113) 243 6601  Fax: (0113) 242 0905
Email: clientmail@forwarn.com
Website: www.forwarn.com

## firm profile

Ford & Warren is an independent, single office commercial law firm based in Leeds. Over the last 15 years the firm has sustained a rapid and generic growth without mergers or acquisitions so that it now occupies the whole of the prestigious Westgate Point office block in the heart of the commercial centre of Leeds. The firm has 21 partners, 92 solicitors and paralegals and a total staff of over 200. Ford & Warren has the following departments: Employment; Road and Rail; Transportation; Corporate; Commercial Litigation; Commercial Property; Insurance and PI; Tax and Inheritance; Matrimonial. The firm has a significant presence in the public sector particularly in health and education. The firm has areas of high specialisation where its lawyers have a national reputation and its client base includes the largest limited companies and PLCs. These areas include transportation and the licensed and leisure industries.

## main areas of work

Employment and industrial relations; road and rail transportation; corporate; insurance and personal injury; commercial property/real estate; public sector; tax and inheritance; matrimonial. The Dispute Resolution/Commercial Litigation Department has five sections: commercial dispute resolution, property litigation, finance litigation, insolvency and debt recovery.

## trainee profile

The firm is looking for hard working, self-reliant and enthusiastic individuals who will make a contribution to the firm from the outset. Applicants must have a strong academic background, a genuine enthusiasm for the law and the social abilities required to work effectively with colleagues and clients. The majority of lawyers practising at the firm joined as trainees.

## training environment

The firm offers seats in employment, commercial litigtion, corporate, insurance and personal injury, commercial property and private client. Usually, trainees will undertake four seats of six months, although split seats may sometimes be available. The final six months takes place in the department into which the trainee wishes to qualify. The firm has a comprehensive in-house training programme for all lawyers and the PSC is also provided internally.

## selection procedure

First interviews and exercise held with the Trainee Recruitment Manager and a Partner in September and early October. Successful candidates are invited to a second interview with the Managing Partner, including a further exercise and presentation.

| | |
|---|---|
| **Partners** | **21** |
| **Assistant Solicitors** | **92** |
| **Total Trainees** | **12** |

**contact**
Debra Hinde

**method of application**
Handwritten letter and CV or email

**selection procedure**
Interviews and exercise

**closing date for 2008**
31 August 2006

**application**
Training contracts p.a. **6**
Applications p.a. **700**
Required degree grade **2:1**

# A-Z Solicitors

# Forsters LLP

31, Hill Street, London W1J 5LS
Tel: (020) 7863 8333  Fax: (020) 7863 8444
Email: ajfairchild@forsters.co.uk
Website: www.forsters.co.uk

| Partners | 29 |
| Assistant Solicitors | 46 |
| Total Trainees | 8 |

**contact**
Alison Fairchild

**method of application**
Application form

**selection procedure**
First interview with HR Manager & Graduate Recruitment Partner; second interview with 2 partners

**training**
Salary
**1st year (2005) £26,000**
**2nd year (2005) £28,000**
Holiday entitlement **22 days**

**post-qualification**
Salary (2005) **£43,000**
% of trainees offered job on qualification (2005) **100%**

## firm profile

Forsters opened for business in 1998 with the 11 founding partners previously being partners of Frere Chomley Bischoff. The partnership now comprises 29. It is a progressive law firm with a strong reputation for its property and private client work as well as thriving commercial and litigation practices. The working atmosphere of the firm is friendly and informal, yet highly professional. A social committee organises a range of activities from quiz nights to sporting events as Forsters actively encourages all its staff to have a life outside of work!

## main areas of work

The firm has a strong reputation for all aspects of commercial and residential property work. The groups handle investment funding; development; planning; construction; landlord and tenant; property taxation and residential investment and development. Forsters is also recognised as one of the leading proponents of private client work in London with a client base comprising a broad range of individuals and trusts in the UK and elsewhere. The firm's commercial practice specialises in acquisitions and financing for technology, communication and media companies whilst its litigation group conducts commercial litigation and arbitration and advises on a broad spectrum of matters.

## trainee profile

Successful candidates will have a strong academic background and either have attained or be expected to achieve a good second class degree. The firm considers that factors alongside academic achievements are also important. The firm is looking for individuals who give a real indication of being interested in a career in law and who the firm feels would readily accept and work well in its team environment.

## training environment

The first year of training is split into three seats of four months in three of the following departments: commercial property, private client, company commercial or litigation. In the second year the four month pattern still applies, but the firm discusses with you whether you have developed an area of particular interest and tries to accommodate this. Second year seats might include construction, employment, family or property litigation. The training is very 'hands on' as you share an office with a partner or assistant who will give you real responsibility alongside supervision. At the end of each seat your progress and performance will be reviewed by way of an appraisal with a partner from the relevant department.

## sponsorship & benefits

22 days holiday p.a., season ticket loan, permanent health insurance, life insurance, subsidised gym membership. Fees paid for both PGDL and LPC.

# Freeth Cartwright LLP

Cumberland Court, 80 Mount Street, Nottingham NG1 6HH
Tel: (0115) 901 5504  Fax: (0115) 859 9603
Email: vicki.simpson@freethcartwright.co.uk
Website: www.freethcartwright.co.uk

## firm profile

Tracing its origins back to 1805, Freeth Cartwright LLP became Nottingham's largest firm in 1994 with successful offices now established in Derby and Leicester. Whilst Freeth Cartwright LLP is a heavyweight commercial firm, serving a wide variety of corporate and institutional clients, there is also a commitment to a range of legal services, which includes a substantial private client element. This enables it to give a breadth of experience in training which is not always available in firms of a similar size.

## main areas of work

Property and construction, commercial services, private client and personal litigation.

## trainee profile

Freeth Cartwright LLP looks for people to bring their own perspective and individuality to the firm. The firm needs people who can cope with the intellectual demands of life as a lawyer and who possess the wider personal skills which are needed in its diverse practice.

## training environment

Freeth Cartwright LLP is committed to providing comprehensive training for all its staff. The firm's training programme is based on in-house training covering technical matters and personal skills, supplemented with external courses where appropriate. The firm endeavours to give the best possible experience during the training period, as it believes that informal training on-the-job is the most effective means of encouraging the skills required in a qualified solicitor. One of the firm's senior partners takes responsibility for all its trainees and their personal development, overseeing their progress through the firm and discussing performance based on feedback. Normally, the training contract will consist of four six month seats in different departments, most of which are available in the firm's Nottingham offices, although it is possible for trainees to spend at least one seat in another location.

| | |
|---|---|
| Members | 59 |
| Assistant Solicitors | 67 |
| Total Trainees | 14 |

**contact**
Vicki Simpson

**method of application**
Online application form

**selection procedure**
Interview & selection day

**closing date for 2007**
31 July 2006

**training**
Starting salary (2005)
**£18,000**

**offices**
Nottingham, Leicester, Derby

Freeth
Cartwright
LLP

# Freshfields Bruckhaus Deringer

65 Fleet Street, London EC4Y 1HS
Tel: (020) 7936 4000  Fax: (020) 7832 7001
Email: graduates@freshfields.com
Website: www.freshfields.com/graduates

## firm profile
Freshfields Bruckhaus Deringer is a leading international firm with a network of 28 offices in 18 countries. The firm provides first-rate legal services to corporations, financial institutions and governments around the world.

## main areas of work
Corporate; mergers and acquisitions; banking; dispute resolution; joint ventures; employment, pensions and benefits; asset finance; real estate; tax; capital markets; intellectual property and information technology; project finance; private finance initiative; US securities; antitrust, competition and trade; communications and media; construction and engineering; energy; environment; financial services; restructuring and insolvency; insurance; international tax; investment funds.

## trainee profile
Excellent academic qualifications, a broad range of skills and a good record of achievement in other areas. Language skills are also an advantage.

## training environment
The firm's trainees receive a thorough professional training in a very broad range of practice areas, an excellent personal development programme and the chance to work in one of the firm's international offices or on secondment with a client in the UK or abroad. It provides the professional, technical and pastoral support necessary to ensure that you enjoy and make the most of the opportunities on offer.

## benefits
Life assurance; permanent health insurance; group personal pension; interest-free loan; interest-free loan for a season travel ticket; free membership of the firm's private medical insurance scheme; subsidised staff restaurant; gym.

## vacation placements
Places for 2006: 125; Duration: 2 weeks; Remuneration: £550 (net); Closing Date: 31 January 2006 but apply as early as possible after 1 December 2005 as there may not be places left by the deadline.

## sponsorship & awards
GDL and LPC fees paid plus from September 2006 maintenance of £7,250 for those studying the LPC and £6,250 for those studying the GDL.

---

**Partners** 519
**Assistant Solicitors** 1,613
**Total Trainees** 208
**(London based)**

contact
Maia Riley

method of application
Online application form

selection procedure
2 interviews and written test

closing date for 2008
31 July 2006

application
Training contracts p.a. **100**
Applications p.a. **c.2,000**
% interviewed p.a. **c.12%**
Required degree grade **2:1**

training
Salary
**1st year £29,500**
**2nd year £33,500**
Holiday entitlement **25 days**
% of trainees with a
non-law degree p.a. **c.45%**
No. of seats available
abroad p.a. **c.68**

post-qualification
Salary **£52,000**
% of trainees offered job
on qualification **c.95%**

overseas offices
Amsterdam, Barcelona, Beijing, Berlin, Bratislava, Brussels, Budapest, Cologne, Dubai, Düsseldorf, Frankfurt, Hamburg, Hanoi, Ho Chi Minh City, Hong Kong, Madrid, Milan, Moscow, Munich, New York, Paris, Rome, Shanghai, Singapore, Tokyo, Vienna, Washington DC

# Gateley Wareing

One Eleven, Edmund Street, Birmingham B3 2HJ
Tel: (0121) 234 0121  Fax: (0121) 234 0079
Email: wendyw@gateleywareing.com
Website: www.gateleywareing.com

| | |
|---|---|
| **Partners** | 30 |
| **Vacancies** | 6 |
| **Total Trainees** | 12 |
| **Total Staff** | 210 |

## firm profile

A 30-partner, Midlands-based practice, with an excellent reputation for general commercial work and particular expertise in corporate, plc, commercial, employment, property, construction, insolvency, commercial dispute resolution, banking and tax. The firm is expanding (210 staff) and offers a highly practical, commercial and fast-paced environment. The firm prides itself on its entrepreneurial style and its work hard, live life to the full reputation. The firm focuses on owner-led businesses, but also counts some household names and internationals amongst its clients.

**contact**
Mrs Wendy Warburton
HR Manager

**closing date for 2008**
Vacation placements:
11 February 2006
Training contracts:
31 July 2006

## trainee profile

Applications are invited from second year law students and final year non-law students and graduates. Applicants should have (or be heading for) a minimum 2.1 degree, and should have at least three Bs (or equivalent) at A-level. Individuals should be hard-working team players capable of using initiative and demonstrating commercial awareness.

**training**
Salary
**1st year £20,000**
**2nd year £22,000**

**post-qualification**
Salary **£33,000**

## training environment

Four six month seats with ongoing supervision and appraisals every three months. PSC taken internally. In-house courses on skills such as time management, negotiation, IT, drafting, business skills, marketing, presenting and writing in plain English.

**offices**
Birmingham, Leicester, Nottingham

## benefits

Current trainee offered as a 'buddy' - a point of contact within the firm, library available, invitation to summer party prior to joining.

## vacation placements

One-week placements over the summer. Deadline for vacation placement scheme is 11 February 2006 and for training contracts is 31 July 2006. Apply online at www.gateleywareing.com.

## sponsorship & awards

CPE/LPC and a LPC maintenance grant of £4,000.

# A-Z Solicitors

# Government Legal Service

GLS Recruitment Team, Chancery House, 53-64 Chancery Lane,
London WC2A 1QS
Tel: (020) 7649 6023
Email: glstrainees.tmp.com
Website: www.gls.gov.uk

## firm profile
The Government Legal Service (GLS) joins together around 2000 lawyers and trainees. They work in some 40 Government organisations, including major Departments of State and the regulatory bodies. A GLS lawyer's work is quite unique, and reflects the huge range of Government activities. GLS lawyers work in the public interest and have the rare opportunity to make a positive contribution to the well-being of the country. Many move around Government Departments as they progress, developing skills and acquiring knowledge of new areas of the law. Others choose to specialise in one area. Whatever route they take, they find the work hugely rewarding and stimulating.

## main areas of work
GLS lawyers have just one client – the Government of the day – and that client requires advice and support on a host of domestic and international matters. As a GLS lawyer, you could deal with ground-breaking cases in the courts, advise Ministers, work on a public inquiry or become involved in the passage of legislation through Parliament.

## trainee profile
As well as a good academic background, the GLS seeks analytical minds that can get to the root of a problem, along with good communications skills. Because GLS lawyers work as part of a team, people skills are important, as is the potential to become a good manager when you progress and take on further responsibility.

## training environment
The GLS provides a unique and varied training environment for trainees and pupils. Generally, trainee solicitors work in four different areas of practice over a two-year period in the Government Department to which they are assigned. Pupil barristers divide their time between their Department and chambers. The GLS prides itself on involving trainees and pupils in the full range of casework conducted by their Department. This frequently includes high profile matters and will be under the supervision of senior colleagues.

## benefits
These include professional development opportunities, excellent pension scheme, civilised working hours, generous holiday entitlement and subsidised canteen facilities.

## vacation placements
Summer 2006 vacation placement scheme; approx 60 places. Duration: 2-3 weeks. Closing date 31 March 2006. Remuneration: £200-£250 pw.

## sponsorship & awards
LPC and BVC fees as well as other compulsory professional skills course fees. Funding may be available for the CPE. They provide a grant of around £5-7,000 for the vocational year.

---

**Total Trainees** around 50

**contact**
glstrainees@tmp.com or visit www.gls.gov.uk

**method of application**
Online application form

**selection procedure**
Day at assessment centre to undertake a group discussion exercise, a written question and an interview

**closing date for 2008**
31 July 2006

**application**
Training contracts p.a. **22-30**
Applications p.a. **1,200+**
% interviewed p.a. **10%**
Required degree grade
**Min 2.2 (some Government Departments require a 2.1)**

**training**
Salary begins at over £20,000 in London and varies acording to Government Department. It is lower outside London.

Holiday entitlement 25 days on entry

**post-qualification**
Salary varies according to Government Department; the vacancies section of the GLS website will give a flavour of what to expect.

% of trainees accepting job on qualification (2004) at least **98%**

# Halliwells

St. James's Court, Brown St, Manchester M2 2JF
Tel: (0870) 365 9492  Fax: (0870) 365 9493
Email: lesley.morgan@halliwells.com

## firm profile

Halliwells is one of the largest independent commercial law firms in the North West. Over the last few years the firm has increased substantially in both size and turnover and now has in excess of 110 partners and 250 fee earners. During the last 12 months Halliwells has been recognised as the fastest growing law firm, continued growth that leads to an ongoing requirement for solicitors and has given rise to more internal promotions to partnerships.

## main areas of work

Real Estate; Dispute Resolution; Corporate; Corporate Recovery; Business Services and Trust & Estates.

## trainee profile

Candidates need to show a good academic ability but do not necessarily need to have studied law at university. They should demonstrate an ability to fit into a hardworking team. In particular, Halliwells is looking for candidates who will continue to develop with the firm after their initial training.

## training environment

Each trainee will have five seats in at least three separate departments. These will usually include commercial litigation, corporate and commercial property. Individual requests from trainees for experience in a particular department will be accommodated wherever possible. Requests for inter-office secondments are also encouraged. The trainee will work within one of the department's teams and be encouraged to assist other team members to help broaden their experience. Specific training appropriate to each department will be given and trainees are strongly encouraged to attend the firm's regular in-house seminars on legal and related topics.

A supervisor will be assigned to each trainee to support their development throughout the seat. Each trainee will be assessed both mid-seat and end of seat.

## benefits

A generous pension scheme plus a subsidised gym membership is available.

## vacation placements

60 summer vacation placements places will be available during summer 2006. We operate four schemes at our Manchester, London and Liverpool offices, each lasts for two weeks. Schemes commence first week in July. Remuneration £150 per week. Closing date for applications is 31 March 2006.

## sponsorship & awards

The firm pays GDL fees and LPC fees plus a £4,500 maintenance grant for each course.

| | |
|---|---|
| **Partners** | 115 |
| **Assistant Solicitors** | 190 |
| **Total Trainees** | 50 |

### contact
Lesley Morgan
(Graduate Recruitment Manager)
Lesley.morgan@halliwells.com

### method of application
Online application only

### selection procedure
Group exercise, presentation and interview

### closing date for 2008
31 July 2006

### application
Training contracts p.a.
**Manchester - 20**
**London - 5**
**Liverpool - 5**
**Sheffield - 1**
Applications p.a. **1,500**
% interviewed p.a. **8%**
Required degree grade **2:1**

### training
Salary
**1st year (2005) £22,145**
**2nd year (2005) £23,175**

### post-qualification
Salary (2005) **£34,000**
% of trainees offered job on qualification (2005) **90%**

# Hammonds

Rutland House, 148 Edmund Street, Birmingham B3 2JR
7 Devonshire Square, Cutlers Gardens, London EC2M 4YH
2 Park Lane, Leeds LS3 1ES
Trinity Court, 16 Dalton Street, Manchester M6O 8HS
Tel: (0870) 839 0000  Fax: (0870) 839 3666
Website: www.hammonds.com

## firm profile
Hammonds is one of Europe's largest corporate law firms and a member of the Global 100. In the UK alone, the firm advises over 25 FTSE 100 companies and over 50 FTSE all share companies. The firm has offices in London, Birmingham, Leeds, Manchester, Brussels, Paris, Berlin, Munich, Rome, Milan, Madrid, Turin and Hong Kong. The firm has 1,300 staff, including 202 partners, 518 solicitors and 80 trainees. It is regarded as innovative, opportunistic and highly successful in the markets in which it operates.

## main areas of work
Corporate; commercial dispute resolution; construction, engineering and projects; employment; EU and competition; finance law (including banking); intellectual property and commercial; media/IT; pensions; property; sports law; tax.

## trainee profile
Hammonds seeks applications from all disciplines for both vacation work and training contracts. It looks for three characteristics: strong academic performance, work experience in the legal sector and significant achievement in non-academic pursuits.

## training environment
Around 40 trainee solicitors are recruited each year who each carry out six four-month seats during their training contract. The firm ensures variety and broad-based experience. Fixed location contracts avaiable in Birmingham, Leeds, London and Manchester.

## benefits
Flexible benefits scheme which allows trainees to choose their own benefits from a range of options.

## vacation placements
Places for 2006: 64; Duration: 2 weeks; Remuneration: £230 p.w. (London), £180 p.w. (Leeds, Manchester, Birmingham); Closing Date: 31 January 2006.

## sponsorship & awards
PgDL and LPC fees paid and maintenance grant of £4,500 p.a.

---

| | |
|---|---|
| **Partners** | 202 |
| **Assistant Solicitors** | 518 |
| **Total Trainees** | 80 |

**contact**
The Graduate Recruitment Team

**method of application**
Online application form

**selection procedure**
Assessment and interview

**closing date for 2008**
31 July 2006

**application**
Training contracts p.a. **40**
Applications p.a. **1,200**
% interviewed p.a. **10%**
Required degree grade **2:1**

**training**
Salary
**1st year (2005)**
**£20,500 regional**
**£27,000 London**
**2nd year (2005)**
**£23,000 regional**
**£30,000 London**
Holiday entitlement **23 days**
% of trainees with a non-law degree p.a. **25%**
No. of seats available abroad p.a. **15**

**post-qualification**
Salary (2005)
**London £46,000**
**Other £34,000**
% of trainees accepting job on qualification (2005) **87%**

**overseas offices**
Brussels, Paris, Berlin, Munich, Rome, Milan, Turin, Hong Kong, Madrid

# Harbottle & Lewis LLP

Hanover House, 14 Hanover Square, London W1S 1HP
Tel: (020) 7667 5000  Fax: (020) 7667 5100
Email: kathy.beilby@harbottle.com
Website: www.harbottle.com

## firm profile

Harbottle & Lewis LLP is recognised for the unique breadth of its practice in the entertainment, media, travel (including aviation) and leisure industries. It undertakes significant corporate commercial and contentious work for clients within these industries including newer industries such as digital mixed media.

## main areas of work

Music, film and television production, theatre, broadcasting, computer games and publishing, sport, sponsorship and advertising, aviation, property investment and leisure.

## trainee profile

Trainees will have demonstrated the high academic abilities, commercial awareness, and initiative necessary to become part of a team advising clients in dynamic and demanding industries.

## training environment

The two year training contract is divided into four six-month seats where trainees will be given experience in a variety of legal skills including company commercial, litigation, intellectual property and real property, working within teams focused on the firm's core industries. The firm has a policy of accepting a small number of trainees to ensure they are given relevant and challenging work and are exposed to and have responsibility for a full range of legal tasks. The firm has its own lecture and seminars programme in both legal topics and industry know-how. An open door policy and a pragmatic entrepreneurial approach to legal practice provides a stimulating working environment.

## benefits

Lunch provided; season ticket loans.

## sponsorship & awards

LPC fees paid and interest-free loans towards maintenance.

| | |
|---|---|
| Partners | 24 |
| Assistant Solicitors | 40 |
| Total Trainees | 8 |

**contact**
Kathy Beilby

**method of application**
CV & letter by post or email

**selection procedure**
Interview

**closing date for 2008**
31 July 2006

**application**
Training contracts p.a. 4
Applications p.a. 800
% interviewed p.a. 5%
Required degree grade 2:1

**training**
Salary
1st year £25,900 (2005)
2nd year £26,900 (2005)
Holiday entitlement
in the first year 23 days
in the second year 26 days
% of trainees with
a non-law degree p.a. 40%

**post-qualification**
Salary (2005) £44,000

549

# Henmans

116 St. Aldates, Oxford OX1 1HA
Tel: (01865) 722181  Fax: (01865) 792376
Email: welcome@henmans.co.uk
Website: www.henmans.co.uk

## firm profile

Henmans is a well-established Oxfordshire-based practice with a strong national reputation, serving both corporate and private clients. Henmans' philosophy is to be extremely client focused to deliver exceptional levels of service. The firm achieves this through an emphasis on teamwork to ensure clients always have access to a specific partner with specialist support, and through an ongoing programme of recruitment and training to guarantee clients optimum advice and guidance. Henmans has invested heavily in IT and has implemented a case management system to enhance services and client care. Henmans' policy of bespoke services and controlled costs ensure that both corporate and private clients benefit from City level litigation standards at competitive regional prices. The firm is now accredited as an Investor in People.

## main areas of work

The firm's core service of litigation is nationally recognised. The personal injury and clinical negligence litigation is strong, as is professional negligence work. Professional negligence and commercial litigation: 29%; personal injury: 26%; property: 17%; private client (including family)/charities/trusts: 18%; corporate/employment: 10%.

## trainee profile

Commercial awareness, sound academic accomplishment, intellectual capability, IT literate, able to work as part of a team, good communication skills.

## training environment

Trainees are introduced to the firm with a detailed induction and overview of the client base. Experience is likely to be within the PI. Property, family, professional negligence/commercial litigation and private client departments. The firm values commitment and enthusiasm both professionally and socially as an integral part of its culture. The firm provides an ongoing programme of in-house education and regular appraisals within its supportive friendly environment.

| | |
|---|---|
| **Partners** | 23 |
| **Other Solicitors &** | |
| **Fee-earners** | 38 |
| **Total Trainees** | 6 |

**contact**
Viv J Matthews (Mrs)
MA CH FCIPD
Head of HR

**method of application**
Application form on website

**selection procedure**
Interview with Head of HR & partners; presentation and skills tests

**closing date for 2008**
31 July 2006

**application**
Training contracts p.a. **3**
Applications p.a. **450**

**training**
Salary
**1st year (2004) £17,750**
**2nd year (2004) £19,000**
Holiday entitlement **23 days + 2 firm days at Christmas. BUPA and pension also provided.**
% of trainees with a non-law degree p.a. **30%**

**post-qualification**
Salary (2004) **£31,000**
% of assistants who joined as trainees **28%**
% of partners who joined as trainees **15%**

# Herbert Smith LLP

Exchange House, Primrose Street, London EC2A 2HS
Tel: (020) 7374 8000  Fax: (020) 7374 0888
Email: graduate.recruitment@herbertsmith.com
Website: www.herbertsmith.com

## firm profile

Herbert Smith is an international legal practice with over 1,100 lawyers and a network of offices in Europe and Asia. In addition, it works closely with two premier European firms with whom it has an alliance - the German firm Gleiss Lutz and the Dutch and Belgian firm Stibbe.

The firm has a diverse, blue-chip client base including FTSE 100 and Fortune 500 companies, major investment banks and governments. What makes Herbert Smith stand out is its culture: a collegiate working environment, a pre-eminent market reputation in key practices and industry sectors and an ambition to be consistently recognised as one of the world's leading law firms.

## main areas of work

Corporate (including international mergers and acquisitions); finance and banking (including capital markets); international litigation and arbitration; energy; projects and project finance; EU and competition; real estate; tax; employment and trusts; construction and engineering; insurance; investment funds; IP; US securities.

## trainee profile

Trainees need a strong academic record, common sense, self-confidence and intelligence to make their own way in a large firm. They are typically high-achieving and creative thinking – language skills are an advantage.

## training environment

Structured training and supervision are designed to allow experience of a unique range of contentious and non-contentious work. You will be encouraged to take on responsibilities as soon as you join the firm. You will work within partner-led teams and have your own role. Individual strengths will be monitored, developed and utilised. On-the-job training will be divided into four six-month seats; one seat will be in the corporate division, one in the litigation division and you will have a choice of specialists seats such as IP or EU and competition, as well as an opportunity to go on secondment to a client, the firm's advocacy unit or an overseas office. Great emphasis is placed on professional and personal development and the firm runs its own legal development and mentoring programme.

## sponsorship & benefits

CPE/GDL and LPC fees are paid plus plus up to £7,000 maintenance grant p.a. Benefits include profit share, permanent health insurance, private medical insurance, season ticket loan, life assurance, subsidised gym membership, group personal accident insurance and matched contributory pension scheme.

## vacation placements

Places for 2005/06: 115. Winter 2005 (non-law students only), Spring and Summer 2005 (law and non-law students). Closing Dates: 11 November 2005 for Winter scheme; 31 January 2006 for Spring and Summer schemes. Opportunities in some of the firm's European offices.

| | |
|---|---|
| Partners | 210* |
| Fee-earners | 577* |
| Total Trainees | 170* |

*denotes worldwide figures

**contact**
Kerry Jarred, Graduate Recruitment Manager

**method of application**
Online application form

**selection procedure**
Case study and interview

**closing date for Sept 2008/Mar 2009**
31 July 2006

**application**
Training contracts p.a. up to **100**
Applications p.a. **circa 2000**
% interviewed p.a. **20%**
Required degree grade **2:1**

**training**
Salary
**1st year £29,000**
**2nd year £33,000**
Holiday entitlement
**25 days, rising to 27 on qualification**
ratio of law to non-law graduates is broadly equal

**post-qualification**
Salary (2005) **£50,000**
% of trainees offered job on qualification (Sept 2005)
**91% (based on no. of jobs offered)**

**overseas offices**
Bangkok, Beijing, Brussels, Hong Kong, Moscow, Paris, Shanghai, Singapore, Tokyo

**associated offices**
Amsterdam, Berlin, Frankfurt, Jakarta, Munich, New York, Prague, Stuttgart, Warsaw

# Hewitsons

42 Newmarket Road, Cambridge CB5 8EP
Tel: (01604) 233233  Fax: (01223) 316511
Email: mail@hewitsons.com (for all offices)
Website: www.hewitsons.com (for all offices)

## firm profile
Established in 1865, the firm handles mostly company and commercial work, but has a growing body of public sector clients. The firm has three offices: Cambridge, Northampton and Saffron Walden.

## main areas of work
Three sections: corporate technology, property and private client.

## trainee profile
The firm is interested in applications from candidates who have achieved a high degree of success in academic studies and who are bright, personable and able to take the initiative.

## training environment
The firm offers four six-month seats.

## benefits
The PSC is provided during the first year of the training contract. This is coupled with an extensive programme of Trainee Solicitor Seminars provided by specialist in-house lawyers.

## vacation placements
Places for 2005: A few placements are available, application is by way of letter and CV to Caroline Lewis; Duration: 1 week.

## sponsorship & awards
Funding for the CPE and/or LPC is not provided.

| | |
|---|---|
| **Partners** | 53 |
| **Assistant Solicitors** | 50 |
| **Total Trainees** | 15 |

**contact**
Caroline Lewis
7 Spencer Parade
Northampton NN1 5AB

**method of application**
Firm's application form

**selection procedure**
Interview

**closing date for 2008**
End of August 2006

**application**
Training contracts p.a. **10**
Applications p.a. **850**
% interviewed p.a. **10%**
Required degree grade
**2:1 min**

**training**
Salary
**1st year (2005) £18,000**
**2nd year (2005) £19,000**
Holiday entitlement **22 days**
% of trainees with a
non-law degree p.a. **50%**

**post-qualification**
Salary (2005) **£31,500**
% of trainees offered job
on qualification (2005) **50%**
% of assistants (as at
1/9/05) who joined as
trainees **54%**
% of partners (as at 1/9/05)
who joined as trainees **32%**

# Hill Dickinson

Pearl Assurance House, 2 Derby Square, Liverpool L2 9XL
Tel: (0151) 236 5400  Fax: (0151) 236 2175
Email: recruitment@hilldickinson.com
Website: www.hilldickinson.com

## firm profile

Hill Dickinson is one of the UK's leading commercial law firms with a widespread of national clients and expertise, and highly developed specialist practices and markets. The firm offers a comprehensive range of legal services from its offices in Liverpool, Manchester, London and Chester.
In February 2005, the firm was named the UK's Regional Law Firm of the Year 2005-06 at the prestigious annual Legal Business Awards and is first Official Sponsor and exclusive Official Lawyers to Liverpool 2008: European Capital of Culture.

## main areas of work

Hill Dickinson is recognised as national market leader for commercial property and related disciplines, and is widely regarded as a major force in financial services, including insurance, commercial litigation and NHS clinical negligence / health-related litigation. It has one of the leading shipping and transport practices in the UK, a flourishing corporate and commercial practice and a national reputation for being forward thinking and innovative.
Clients include corporates from all sectors, the public sector, insurance companies, banks and financial institutions. The firm advises logistics organisations and transport companies, health service providers and the NHS Litigation Authority. The firm also has one of the leading private client practices in the UK.

## trainee profile

Commercial awareness and academic ability are the key factors, together with a desire to succeed. Trainees are viewed as the partners of the future and the firm is looking for personable individuals with whom it wants to work.

## training environment

Trainees spend periods of six months in one of the Divisions and will be given the chance to specialise in specific areas. You will be given the opportunity to learn and develop communication and presentation skills, legal research, drafting, interviewing and advising, negotiations and advocacy. Trainees are encouraged to accept responsibility and are expected to act with initiative. The practice has an active social committee and a larger than usual selection of competitive sporting teams.

## vacation placements

One week structured scheme with places available for 2006. Apply by CV and covering letter to Phil Bradbury by April 2006.

| Partners | 115 |
|---|---|
| Assistant Solicitors | 114 |
| Total Trainees | 23 |

**contact**
Peter Barlow (North West)
Jamie Monck-Mason (London)

**method of application**
CV with supporting letter by email

**selection procedure**
Assessment day

**closing date for 2008**
31 July 2006

**training**
Salary
**1st year (2005) £19,500**
**2nd year (2005) £21,000**
**London weighting £5,000 (where applicable)**
Holiday entitlement
**4 weeks**

**post-qualification**
% of trainees offered job on qualification **100%**

**offices**
Liverpool, Manchester, London, Chester

# Hodge Jones & Allen

31-39 Camden Road, London, NW1 9LR
Tel: (020) 7482 1974  Fax: (020) 7267 3476
Email: hja@hodgejonesallen.co.uk
Website: www.hodgejonesallen.co.uk

## firm profile

Hodge Jones & Allen was founded in Camden Town in 1977. It is now one of the largest legal firms in north London, having grown from four to over 170 staff. Although the firm has private and commercial clients, it also has contracts with the Legal Services Commission in many areas of practice and is known as one of the leading, predominantly publicly funded law practices in the Country. The firm is led by one of its founding partners, Patrick Allen. It has been involved in a number of high profile cases including, the King's Cross fire, the Marchioness disaster, Broadwater Farm riots, Real IRA BBC-bombing trial, the second inquest into the New Cross fire, MMR vaccine litigation and Gulf War Syndrome. The firm is located in a single modern office next to the canal, in a lively and trendy part of Camden Town.

## main areas of work

Crime, personal injury, multi party actions, public law, police actions, miscarriage of justice claims, human rights, medical negligence, family, housing, mental health, property, wills and probate, prison law.

## trainee profile

Trainees will have an excellent academic record, enthusiasm and a positive approach, good communication skills and a commitment to access to justice for all, regardless of ability to pay.

## training environment

Trainees have a full induction on joining HJA covering the work of the firm's main departments, procedural matters and professional conduct. Training consists of four six-month seats and trainees normally share an office with a partner who assists them and formally reviews their progress at least once during each seat. The training is well structured and trainees have the benefit of a mentoring scheme. The firm provides good secretarial and clerking support so trainees can concentrate on legal work rather than administration. The firm has an excellent IT infrastructure and continues to invest heavily in IT to keep pace with innovation.

## benefits

Pension scheme, Life Assurance, disability insurance, quarterly drinks, summer outing and Christmas party.

| | |
|---|---|
| **Partners** | 19 |
| **Assistant Solicitors** | 37 |
| **Total Trainees** | 13 |

**contact**
HR Department

**method of application**
Application form (available online)

**selection procedure**
Interview with 2 Partners

**closing date for 2007**
26 August 2006 (apply one year in advance)

**application**
Training contracts p.a. **6-7**
Applications p.a. **500**
% interviewed p.a. **5%**
Preferred degree grade
**2:1 min**

**training**
Salary: £20,000
Holiday entitlement
20 days p.a.

**post-qualification**
Salary: £25,750
% of trainees offered job on qualification: **75%**

# Holman Fenwick & Willan

Marlow House, Lloyds Avenue, London EC3N 3AL
Tel: (020) 7488 2300  Fax: (020) 7481 0316
Email: grad.recruitment@hfw.co.uk

## firm profile
Holman Fenwick & Willan is an international law firm and one of the world's leading specialists in maritime transportation, insurance, reinsurance, energy and trade. The firm is a leader in the field of commercial litigation and arbitration and also offers comprehensive commercial advice. Founded in 1883, the firm is one of the largest operating in its chosen fields with a team of over 200 lawyers worldwide, and a reputation for excellence and innovation.

## main areas of work
The firm's range of services include marine, admiralty and crisis management, insurance and reinsurance, commercial litigation and arbitration, international trade and commodities, energy, corporate and financial.

## trainee profile
Applications are invited from commercially minded undergraduates and graduates of all disciplines with good A levels and who have, or expect to receive, a 2:1 degree. Good foreign languages or a scientific or maritime background are an advantage.

## training environment
During your training period the firm will ensure that you gain valuable experience in a wide range of areas. It also organises formal training supplemented by a programme of in-house seminars and ship visits in addition to the PSC. Your training development as an effective lawyer will be managed by the HR and Training Partner, Ottilie Sefton, who will ensure that your training is both successful and enjoyable.

## benefits
Private medical insurance, permanent health and accident insurance, subsidised gym membership, season ticket loan.

## vacation placements
Places for 2006: Dates: 26 June - 7 July/17 July -26 July; Remuneration (2005): £250 p.w.; Closing Date: Applications accepted 1 Jan - 14 Feb 2006.

## sponsorship & awards
GDL Funding: Fees paid plus £5,000 maintenance; LPC Funding: Fees paid plus £5,000 maintenance.

| | |
|---|---|
| Partners | 80+ |
| Other Solicitors & Fee-earners | 120+ |
| Total Trainees | 16 |

**contact**
Graduate Recruitment Officer - Rachel Frowde

**method of application**
Online application form

**selection procedure**
2 interviews with partners & written exercise

**closing date for 2008**
31 July 2006

**application**
Training contracts p.a. **8**
Applications p.a. **1,000**
% interviewed p.a. **5%**
Required degree grade **2:1**

**training**
Salary (Sept 2005)
**1st year £28,000**
**2nd year £30,000**
Holiday entitlement **22 days**
% of trainees with a non-law degree p.a. **50%**

**post-qualification**
Salary **£47,500** (Sept 2005)
% of trainees offered job on qualification (Sept 2005) **78%**

**overseas offices**
Hong Kong, Nantes, Paris, Piraeus, Rouen, Shanghai, Singapore

# Howes Percival

Oxford House, Cliftonville, Northampton NN1 5PN
Tel: (01604) 230400  Fax: (01604) 620956
Email: katy.pattle@howespercival.com
Website: www.howespercival.com

## firm profile

Howes Percival is a 34-partner commercial law firm with offices in Leicester, Milton Keynes, Northampton and Norwich. The firm's working environment is young, progressive and highly professional and its corporate structure means that fee-earners are rewarded on merit and can progress to associate or partner status quickly. The type and high value of the work that the firm does places it in a position whereby it is recognised as being a regional firm by location only. The firm has the expertise, resources, and partner reputation that match a city firm.

## main areas of work

The practice is departmentalised and the breakdown of its work is as follows: corporate 30%; commercial property 25%; commercial litigation 20%; insolvency 10%; employment 10%; private client 5%.

## trainee profile

The firm is looking for eight well-educated, focused, enthusiastic, commercially aware graduates with a minimum 2:1 degree in any discipline. Howes Percival welcomes confident communicators with strong interpersonal skills who share the firm's desire to be the best.

## training environment

Trainees complete four six month seats, each one in a different department. Trainees joining the Norwich office will remain at Norwich for the duration of their training contract. Within the East Midlands region, there is the opportunity to gain experience in each of the three East Midlands offices. Trainees report direct to a partner, and after three months and again towards the end of each seat they will be formally assessed by the partner training them. Trainees will be given every assistance by the fee-earners in their department to develop quickly and will be given responsibility as soon as they are ready.

## benefits

Contributory pension scheme. Private health insurance. LPC/CPE funding, maintenance grant.

## vacation placements

Vacation placements are available in June, July and August. Please apply in writing to Katy Pattle at the above address (enclosing your CV) indicating which location you would prefer. The closing date is 30 April 2006.

| | |
|---|---|
| Partners | 34 |
| Solicitors | 80 |
| Total Trainees | 12 |

**contact**
Miss Katy Pattle
HR Assistant

**method of application**
Online application form

**selection procedure**
Assessment centres

**closing date for 2008**
31 July 2006

**application**
Training contracts p.a. **8**
Applications p.a. **300**
% interviewed p.a. **10%**
Required degree grade **2:1**

**training**
Salary
**1st year £21,000**
**2nd year £23,000**
Holiday entitlement
**23 days p.a.**

**post-qualification**
% of trainees offered job on qualification (2005) **83%**
% of assistants who joined as trainees **52%**
% of partners who joined as trainees **9%**

# Hugh James

Hodge House, 114-116 St. Mary Street, Cardiff CF10 1DY
Tel: (029) 2022 4871  Fax: (029) 2038 8222
Email: training@hughjames.com
Website: www.hughjames.com

## firm profile
Hugh James is one of the leading law firms in the UK. It is a practice which provides a comprehensive range of commercial and private client services across the UK from its network of offices in South Wales. Hugh James recently won the Large Law Firm of the Year Award at the inaugural Welsh Law Awards. The firm is committed to providing modern innovative services and continues to develop its products and services to meet the needs of a diverse UK customer base.

## main areas of work
The practice is divided up into four divisions: business litigation (26%); business services (34%); claimant litigation (27%); public funded (13%). Specialist teams have been established to service niche areas of the law and the firm has a multidisciplinary and dynamic approach to the provision of legal services.

## trainee profile
Hugh James welcomes applications from law and non-law undergraduates with a good class degree. Candidates must possess first class legal knowledge and an ability to apply that with practical skills. In addition, good interpersonal and IT skills are required. The majority of trainees are retained upon qualification and are seen as an integral part of the future of the firm. Hugh James is proud of the fact that the vast majority of its present partners were trained at the firm.

## training environment
Trainees generally undertake four seats of not less than six months which may be in any of the firm's offices. Broadly, experience will be gained in all four main work categories. The breadth of work dealt with by the firm enables it to ensure that over-specialisation is avoided.

## benefits
Company contribution to stakeholder pension scheme.

## vacation placements
Available Summer 2006.

| Partners | 48 |
| Assistant Solicitors | 60 |
| Total Trainees | 16 |

**contact**
Diane Brooks
HR Manager

**method of application**
Application form available from HR Manager or website

**selection procedure**
Interview and presentation

**closing date for 2008**
31 March 2006

**application**
Training contracts p.a. **8**
Applications p.a. **500**
% interviewed p.a. **30%**
Required degree grade **2:1**
**or a good reason why a 2:2 was obtained**

**training**
Salary
**Competitive & reviewed annually**

**other offices**
Merthyr Tydfil, Blackwood

# Ince & Co

International House, 1 St Katharine's Way, London E1W 1UN
Email: recruitment@incelaw.com

## firm profile
From its origins in maritime law, the firm's practice today encompasses all aspects of the work areas listed below. Ince & Co is frequently at the forefront of developments in contract and tort law.

## main areas of work
Aviation, business and finance, commercial disputes, energy, insurance and reinsurance, shipping and trade.

## trainee profile
Hardworking competitive individuals with initiative who relish challenge and responsibility within a team environment. Academic achievements, positions of responsibility, sport and travel are all taken into account.

## training environment
Trainees sit with four different partners for six months at a time throughout their training. Under close supervision, they are encouraged from an early stage to meet and visit clients, interview witnesses, liaise with counsel, deal with technical experts and handle opposing lawyers. They will quickly build up a portfolio of cases from a number of partners involved in a cross-section of the firm's practice and will see their cases through from start to finish. They will also attend in-house and external lectures, conferences and seminars on practical and legal topics.

## benefits
STL, corporate health cover, PHI, contributory pension scheme.

## vacation placements
Places for 2006: 15; Duration: 2 weeks; Remuneration: £250 p.w.; Closing Date: 14 February 2006.

## sponsorship & awards
LPC fees, £4,750 grant for study in London, £4,000 grant for study elsewhere. Discretionary sponsorship for CPE.

| Partners | 72* |
|---|---|
| Assistant Solicitors | 94* |
| Total Trainees | 23* |

*denotes worldwide figures*

**contact**
Claire Kendall

**method of application**
Typed/handwritten letter & CV, containing full breakdown of degree results & A-level grades, with contact details of 2 academic referees

**selection procedure**
Interview with HR professional & interview with 2 partners from Recruitment Committee & a written test

**closing date for 2008**
31 July 2006

**application**
Training contracts p.a. **8-10**
Applications p.a. **1,500**
% interviewed p.a. **5%**
Required degree grade **2:1**

**training**
Salary
**1st year £27,000**
**2nd year £30,000**
Holiday entitlement **22 days**
% of trainees with a non-law degree p.a. **55%**

**post-qualification**
Salary **£47,000**
% of trainees offered job on qualification (2005)
**91.6%. All accepted!**
% of partners (as at 2005) who joined as trainees
**Approx 78.8%**

**overseas offices**
Hamburg, Hong Kong, Le Havre, Paris, Piraeus, Shanghai, Singapore

# Irwin Mitchell

Riverside East, 2 Millsands, Sheffield S3 8DT
Tel: (0870) 1500 100  Fax: (0870) 197 3549
Email: graduaterecruitment@irwinmitchell.co.uk
Website: www.irwinmitchell.com

| | |
|---|---|
| **Partners** | **84** |
| **Assistant Solicitors** | **182** |
| **Total Trainees** | **42** |

## firm profile

Irwin Mitchell is a rapidly expanding international practice with 84 partners and over 1800 employees. The firm's strong reputation for dealing with novel and complex areas of law and handling developmental cases such as: vibration white finger and CJD means that it can offer a broad range of experience within each of its specialist departments, giving trainees a high standard of training.

## main areas of work

Corporate services 24%; claimant personal injury 28%; insurance litigation 37%; private client 11%.

## trainee profile

The firm is looking for ambitious and well-motivated individuals who have a real commitment to the law and who can demonstrate a positive approach to work-life balance. Irwin Mitchell recruits law and non-law graduates and views social ability as important as academic achievement. Irwin Mitchell believes trainees are an investment for the future and endeavours to retain trainees upon qualification. In addition to the firm's training contract vacancies it also runs a work placement scheme giving potential training contract candidates a chance to experience what it is like to be a solicitor within the firm.

## training environment

Irwin Mitchell offers a week long structured welcome programme to trainees joining the practice. In addition regular training events are held throughout the firm. The Professional Skills Course is financed by the firm and is run in-house, being tailored to meet the needs of the firm's trainees. During your training contract you will be given as much responsibility as you can handle, giving you a real opportunity to work with the law, your colleagues and to develop your client relationship skills. Your development will be encouraged through frequent reviews and feedback.

## benefits

Healthcare scheme, contributory pension scheme, subsidised gym membership, away day and Christmas party.

## sponsorship & awards

Payment of PGDL and LPC fees plus a £3,000 maintenance grant.

### contact
Claire England,
Graduate Recruitment Officer
Tel: (0114) 274 4626

### method of application
Please visit the firm's website
www.irwinmitchell.com
for more details, from
1 December 2005

### selection procedure
Assessment centre &
interview

### closing date for 2008
31 July 2006

### application
Training contracts p.a. **20-25**
Applications p.a. **1,200**
% interviewed p.a. **50%**
Required degree grade:
**The firm does not require a
specific degree grade**

### training
Salary
**1st year £18,540**
**2nd year £20,600**
**(outside London)**
**reviewed annually in**
**September**
Holiday entitlement
**24.5 days**

### post-qualification
% of trainees offered job on
qualification **80%**

### Overseas/Regional Offices
Birmingham, Leeds,
London, Newcastle,
Sheffield, Marbella &
Madrid

# Jones Day

21 Tudor Street, London, EC4Y 0DJ
Tel: (020) 7039 5959  Fax: (020) 7039 5999
Email: recruit.london@jonesday.com
Website: www.jonesdaylondon.com/recruit

## firm profile

Jones Day operates as one firm worldwide with 2,200 lawyers in 30 offices. Jones Day in London is a key part of this international partnership and has around 200 lawyers, including around 40 partners and 40 trainees. This means that the firm can offer its lawyers a perfect combination - the intimacy and atmosphere of a medium sized City firm with access to both UK and multinational clients.

## main areas of work

Jones Day has five core departments: corporate; lending and structured finance; real estate; litigation and tax. There are specialist groups for competition, construction, environment, planning and insolvency, insurance, employment and pensions.

## trainee profile

The firm looks for candidates with either a law or non-law degree who have strong intellectual and analytical ability and good communication skills and who can demonstrate resourcefulness, drive, dedication and the ability to engage with clients and colleagues.

## training environment

The firm operates a unique, non-rotational system of training and trainees receive work simultaneously from all departments in the firm. The training is designed to provide freedom, flexibility and responsibility from the start. Trainees are encouraged to assume their own workload, which allows early responsibility, a faster development of potential and the opportunity to compare and contrast the different disciplines alongside one another. Work will vary from small cases which the trainee may handle alone (under the supervision of a senior lawyer) to larger matters where they will assist a partner or an associate solicitor. The firm runs a structured training programme with a regular schedule of seminars to support the thorough practical training and regular feedback that trainees receive from the associates and partners they work with.

## vacation placements

Places for 2005/06:
Christmas (non-law): 20 places; 2 weeks; £300; closing date 31 October.
Easter 2006 (non-law): 10 places; 2 weeks; £300; closing date 14 February.
Summer 2006 (law): 40; 2 weeks; £300; closing date 14 February.
Placements last for two weeks with an allowance of £300 per week. Students get to see how the firm's non-rotational training system works in practice by taking on real work from a variety of practice areas. They also get to meet a range of lawyers at various social events.

## benefits

Private healthcare, season ticket loan, subsidised sports club membership, group life cover.

## sponsorship & awards

CPE/PgDL and LPC fees paid and £8,000 maintenance p.a.

| | |
|---|---|
| Partners | 40 |
| Assistant Solicitors | 80 |
| Total Trainees | 40 |

**contact**
Lisa Holmes
Recruitment Manager

**method of application**
CV and letter online at
www.jonesdaylondon.com/
recruit

**selection procedure**
2 interviews with partners

**closing date for 2008**
31 August 2006 - please
apply by end of July to ensure
an early interview slot

**application**
Training contracts p.a. **15-20**
Applications p.a. **1,500**
% interviewed p.a. **12%**
Required degree grade **2.1**

**training**
Salary
**1st year (2005) £36,000**
**2nd year (2005) £40,000**
Holiday entitlement
**5 weeks**

**post-qualification**
Salary (2005) **£55,000**
% of trainees offered job on
qualification (2005) **100%**

**overseas offices**
Continental Europe, Asia,
North America

# Kendall Freeman

43 Fetter Lane, London, EC4A 1JU
Tel: (020) 7583 4055  Fax: (020) 7353 7377
Email: graduaterecruitment@kendallfreeman.com
Website: www.kendallfreeman.com

## firm profile
Kendall Freeman handles high value and complex matters for corporates, banks and clients in the insurance and reinsurance industry and public sectors. The firm was awarded the LCN/TSG 2004 award for Best Trainer at a Medium-Sized City Law Firm.

## main areas of work
Arbitration, ADR, banking, charities, commercial litigation, company and commercial, construction, corporate finance, corporate tax, employment, energy and offshore engineering, insolvency, restructuring, insurance/reinsurance, mergers and acquisitions and international law.

## trainee profile
The firm is small by City standards with 21 partners, but successfully competes and acts alongside the largest international and UK firms of solicitors in its work. It can therefore offer excellent training with high quality work in a more personal environment than the larger firms. The firm seeks energetic individuals with initiative and commercial sense who do not want to be one of a crowd. Trainees need to have a very strong academic backround and excellent people skills as they will have early client interaction.

## training environment
Trainees spend six months of their training contract in four of the firm's major practice areas and once a month are able to discuss their progress with a partner. Believing supervised, practical experience to be the best training, the firm soon gives trainees the chance to meet clients, be responsible for their own work and join in marketing and client development activities. Regular workshops in each seat help develop basic skills in the different practice areas. There is a trainee solicitors' committee which meets regularly and which is attended by two trainee representatives where any suggestions or concerns can be voiced. Each trainee is allocated a partner as a mentor.

## vacation placements
The firm runs a vacation scheme during July.

## sponsorship & awards
Full CPE/GDL and LPC funding and a maintenance grant of £5,000 (London) / £4,500 (outide London).

| | |
|---|---|
| **Partners** | 21 |
| **Assistant Solicitors** | 37 |
| **Total Trainees** | 17 |

**contact**
Graduate Recruitment
(020) 7556 4414

**method of application**
Firm's online application form
http://graduate.kendallfreeman.com

**selection procedure**
Assessment morning plus one interview with two partners

**closing date for 2008**
31 July 2006

**application**
Training contracts p.a. **8**
Minimum required degree grade **2:1**

**training**
Salary
**1st year £29,000 (Sept 05)**
**2nd year £32,500 (Sept 05)**

**post-qualification**
**Salary £50,000 (Sept 05)**

**summer placements**
10 p.a.
**open days**
3, accomodating 75 students
**closing date for summer placements**
28 February 2006
**closing date for open days**
12 May 2006

Kendall Freeman

# Kirkpatrick & Lockhart Nicholson Graham LLP

110 Cannon Street, London, EC4N 6AR
Tel: (020) 7648 9000  Fax: (020) 7648 9001
Email: traineerecruitment@klng.com
Website: www.klng.com

| | |
|---|---|
| **Partners** | 51 |
| **Fee Earners** | 123 |
| **Trainees** | 21 |
| **Total Staff** | 296 |

## firm profile
K&LNG is one of the largest Anglo-American legal combinations in history with approximately 1,000 lawyers practising across 12 offices, one in London and eleven in major cities throughout the US. The firm represents entrepreneurs, growth and middle market companies and leading global corporations both nationally and internationally.

## main areas of work
The firm has eight main areas of practice in London. These are, corporate finance, capital markets, real estate, banking, construction and engineering, corporate tax and VAT, litigation and dispute resolution, and intellectual property. K&LNG is also highly regarded in a number of specialised niche areas including employment, financial services, insolvency, music rights, planning and environment, private equity, sport, telecoms and travel and leisure.

## trainee profile
Highly motivated, intelligent graduates of any discipline.

## training environment
Trainees spend six months in four out of the six following seats: Company, Litigation, Intellectual Property, Construction, Tax and Real Estate. Each trainee sits with a supervisor and is allocated a mentor to ensure all-round supervision and training. K&LNG has a firmwide induction scheme and recently won awards for its career development programme. Trainees are encouraged to participate fully in all the activities of the firm. High importance is placed on the acquisition of business and professional skills, with considerable emphasis on client contact and early responsibility. The training programme consists of weekly legal seminars, workshops, and a full programme of skills electives. Language training is also available.

## benefits
Permanent health insurance, life assurance, season ticket loan, subsidised gym membership, pension, BUPA and 25 days holiday.

## vacation placements
The London office runs two schemes held during the month of July. Applications should be made online prior to the 15th February 2006.

## sponsorship & awards
CPE and LPC fees paid plus annual maintenance grant of £4,500.

**contact**
Tina Two

**method of application**
Online only

**selection procedure**
Interview 7 assessment

**closing date for 2007**
31 July 2006

**application**
Training contracts p.a. **20**
Applications p.a. **800**
% interviewed p.a. **10%**
Required degree grade **2:1**

**training**
Salary
1st year (2005) **28,000**
2nd year (2005) **31,000**
% of trainees with a non-law degree p.a. **Varies**

**post-qualification**
Salary (2005) **£49,000**
% of trainees offered job on qualification (2005) **90%**

**overseas offices**
Pittsburgh, Boston, Dallas, Harrisburg, Los Angeles, Miami, Newark, New York, Palo Alto, San Fransisco, Washington

# Lawrence Graham

190 Strand, London WC2R 1JN
Tel: (020) 7379 0000  Fax: (020) 7379 6854
Email: graduate@lawgram.com
Website: www.lawgram.com

## firm profile

Lawrence Graham is a London-based firm delivering a full range of commercial and legal solutions worldwide. Driven by its corporate and real estate practices, the key sectors in which the firm operates are financial services, real estate, insurance, hospitality & leisure, banking, IT, natural resources and the public sector. The firm has strong relationships with law firms around the world, particularly in the US and Asia, as well as a Monaco office.

## main areas of work

The firm's four core departments are: business & finance (including corporate/M&A, banking & finance, IT & outsourcing, investment funds, employment, insurance, pensions, EU/competition, housing & local government); real estate (commercial property, planning, construction, environment & health & safety, real estate litigation and finance); dispute resolution (commercial litigation, corporate recovery, insurance & reinsurance disputes, shipping, contentious trusts & estates, corporate investigations); and tax & private capital. Work is often international in its scope.

## trainee profile

The firm is looking for individuals from a variety of backgrounds with refined communication skills who can demonstrate a commitment to a career in the commercial application of law. A strong academic track record with a minimum 2.1 degree is a basic requirement. Also required is a good record of achievement in other areas - indicative of the ability to succeed in a demanding career - and evidence of team working skills and the ability to handle responsibility.

## training environment

Under partner supervision trainees will be given early responsibility. Training is structured to facilitate the ability to manage one's own files and interact with clients. In addition to the Professional Skills Course, there are departmental training and induction sessions. Training consists of four six-month seats: a real estate, business & finance and a contentious seat are compulsory. The final seat can be either in tax & private capital or a second in business & finance or real estate.

## benefits

Season ticket loan, on-site gym, life assurance.

## vacation placements

Places for 2006: 32; Duration: 2 weeks during Easter break and 3 x 2 weeks between June and July; Remuneration: £220 p.w; Closing Date: 31 January 2006.

## sponsorship & awards

GDL Funding: Course fees and £4,000 maintenance grant.
LPC Funding: Course fees and £4,000 maintenance grant.

| | |
|---|---|
| **Partners** | 93 |
| **Assistant Solicitors** | 109 |
| **Total Trainees** | 35 |

**contact**
Vikki Horton

**method of application**
Firm's application form.
For law **After 2nd year results**
For non-law **After final results**

**selection procedure**
Interview

**closing date for 2008**
31 July 2006

**application**
Training contracts **24**
Applications p.a. **800**
Required degree grade **2:1**

**training**
Salary
**1st year (2005) £28,000**
**2nd year (2005) £32,000**
% of trainees with a
non-law degree p.a. **45%**

**post-qualification**
Salary (2005) **£48,000**
% of trainees offered job
on qualification (2005) **70%**

# Laytons

Carmelite, 50 Victoria Embankment, Blackfriars, London EC4Y 0LS
Tel: (020) 7842 8000  Fax: (020) 7842 8080
Email: london@laytons.com
Website: www.laytons.com

## firm profile

Laytons is a commercial law firm whose primary focus is on developing dynamic business. The firm's offices in Bristol, Guildford, London and Manchester provide excellent service to its commercial and private clients who are located throughout the UK. The firm's approach to legal issues is practical, creative and energetic. The firm believes in long-term relationships, they are 'client lawyers' rather than 'transaction lawyers'. The key to its client relations is having a thorough understanding of businesses, their needs and objectives. Working together as one team, the firm is supportive and plays to each others' strengths.

## main areas of work

Corporate and commercial, commercial property (including land development and construction), dispute resolution, debt recovery, insolvency, employment, intellectual property, technology and media, private client and trusts.

## trainee profile

Successful candidates will be well-rounded individuals, commercially aware with sound academic background and enthusiastic and committed team members.

## training environment

Trainees are placed in four six-month seats, providing them with an overview of the firm's business, and identifying their particular strengths. All trainees have contact with clients from an early stage, are given challenging work, working on a variety of matters with partners and assistant solicitors. Trainees will soon be responsible for their own files and are encouraged to participate in business development and marketing activities. The firm works in an informal but professional atmosphere and its philosophy is to invest in people who will develop and become part of its long-term success.

## vacation placements

Places for summer 2006: 6. Duration: 1 week. Closing Date: 31 March 2006.

## sponsorship & awards

LPC and CPE funding: consideration given.

| Partners | 31 |
| Assistant Solicitors | 43 |
| Total Trainees | 18 |

### contact
Bill Brydon (Bristol)
Neale Andrews (Guildford)
Stephen Cates &
Lisa McLean (London)
Christine Barker (Manchester)

### method of application
Application form

### selection procedure
Usually 2 interviews

### closing date for 2008
31 August 2006 (although posts are filled as soon as suitable candidates are identified)

### application
Training contracts p.a. **8**
Applications p.a. **2,000**
% interviewed p.a. **5%**
Required degree grade
**1 or 2:1**

### training
Salary
**1st year (2005) Market rate**
**2nd year (2005) Market rate**
Holiday entitlement
**23 days per year**

### post-qualification
Salary (2005) **Market rate**
% of trainees offered job on qualification (2005) **63%**
% of assistants (as at 1/9/05) who joined as trainees **44%**
% of partners (as at 1/9/05) who joined as trainees **35%**

### regional offices
Training contracts are offered in each of Laytons' offices. Apply directly to desired office. See website for further details: www.laytons.com

# LeBoeuf, Lamb, Greene & MacRae

1 Minster Court, Mincing Lane, London EC3R 7YL
Tel: (020) 7459 5000  Fax: (020) 7459 5099
Email: traineelondon@llgm.com
Website: www.llgm.com

| | |
|---|---|
| Partners | 20 |
| Counsel | 5 |
| Associates | 40 |
| Total Trainees | 10 |

## firm profile

LeBoeuf, Lamb, Greene & MacRae is an international law firm with over 600 lawyers worldwide in offices across Europe, the US, Africa, Middle East and Asia. The London office, established as a multinational partnership in 1995 employs over 70 lawyers and is the hub office for the firm's European and international practice. The London office handles varied, interesting work and will suit people who want early responsibility in a relaxed but hard working environment.

## main areas of work

General corporate, litigation and dispute resolution, energy, corporate finance, project finance, capital markets, private equity, insurance, insolvency, real estate, tax, intellectual property, employment, trusts and estates.

## trainee profile

LeBoeuf, Lamb, Greene & MacRae is looking for outstanding people in the broadest possible sense. The firm welcomes applications from varied, non-traditional backgrounds. Interpersonal skills are very important: the firm likes bright, engaging people. Linguistic skills are useful (but not crucial). The firm wants proactive people who will contribute from day one and who will thrive in a diverse and cosmopolitan environment.

## training environment

Trainees spend six months in four seats. The firm's training programme is comprehensive and covers an induction programme, participation in internal seminars and training sessions and attendance at external courses, including the Professional Skills Course. You will be encouraged to act on your own initiative from an early stage. Trainees sit with a senior lawyer, often a partner, who can give ongoing feed back and guidance and progress is reviewed every six months. There are opportunities for placements in both Moscow and Paris.

## benefits

Firm contributes to health, life and disability insurance, season ticket loan, business casual year round.

## sponsorship & awards

Full payment of CPE/LPC fees and maintenance grant of £7,000 provided.

**contact**
Nicholas Jelf

**method of application**
CV & covering letter

**selection procedure**
2 interviews

**closing date for 2008**
31 July 2006

**application**
Training contracts p.a. **6**
Applications p.a. **700**
% interviewed p.a. **6%**
Required degree grade **2:1,**
**A,A,B 'A'Level Equivalent**

**training**
Salary
**1st year £33,000**
**2nd year £37,000**
Holiday entitlement **25 days**
% of trainees with a
non-law degree p.a. **50%**

**post-qualification**
Salary **(2005) £65,000 and**
**performance related bonus**

**overseas offices**
Albany, Almaty, Beijing, Bishkek, Boston, Brussels, Hartford, Houston, Jacksonville, Johannesburg, Los Angeles, Moscow, New York, Paris, Pittsburgh, Riyadh, San Francisco, Washington, D.C.

# Lester Aldridge

Russell House, Oxford Road, Bournemouth BH8 8EX
Tel: (01202) 786161  Fax: (01202) 786110
Email: juliet.milne@LA-law.com
Website: www.lesteraldridge.com

## firm profile
Lester Aldridge is a dynamic business providing both commercial and private client services across central southern England. The firm also operates in a number of niche markets nationally including asset finance, corporate finance, licensing, marine and retail. The effective corporate management structure ensures LA is focused on delivering pragmatic solutions to their clients. LA places great emphasis on a positive working environment, and the work/life balance, understanding that this will ultimately be of benefit to clients.

## main areas of work
Corporate, banking and finance 32%; litigation 30%; private client 21%; commercial prorerty 12%; investments 5%.

## trainee profile
Candidates should have strong intellectual capabilities, be commercially aware, resourceful and able to relate easily to other people. IT skills and a team approach are also required.

## training environment
Training consists of four six-month seats across the firm. About half way through each seat trainees discuss their preferences for the next seat and every attempt is made to match aspirations to the needs of the firm. Trainees have a training principal for the duration of the contract who will discuss progress every month. They receive a formal comprehensive appraisal from their team leader towards the end of each seat, and the managing partner meets all trainees as a group every three months.

## benefits
Life assurance and pension schemes.

## vacation placements
Places for 2005: 8; Duration: 2 weeks; Remuneration: £75 p.w.; Closing Date: 31 March 2006.

## sponsorship & awards
LPC.

---

| | |
|---|---|
| Partners | 40 |
| Total Trainees | 11 |
| Total Staff | 360 |

**contact**
Juliet Milne

**method of application**
Letter, CV & completed application form

**selection procedure**
Interview by a panel of partners

**closing date for 2008**
31 July 2006

**application**
Training contracts p.a. **10**
Applications p.a. **300**
% interviewed p.a. **5%**
Required degree grade **2:1**

**training**
Salary
Starting: **£16,500 at present, increasing by £500 after each seat**
Holiday entitlement **22 days**
% of trainees with a non-law degree p.a. **20%**

**post-qualification**
Salary (2004) **£31,000**
% of trainees offered job on qualification (2005) **100%**
% of assistants (as at 1/9/01) who joined as trainees **30%**
% of partners (as at 1/9/03) who joined as trainees **25%**

**offices**
Bournemouth (2), Southampton, Milton Keynes & London

# Lewis Silkin

12 Gough Square, London EC4A 3DW
Tel: (020) 7074 8000  Fax: (020) 7832 1200
Email: train@lewissilkin.com

## firm profile

Lewis Silkin is a commercial firm with 44 partners. What distinguishes them is a matter of personality. For lawyers, they are notably informal, unstuffy…well, human really. They are 'people people'; as committed and professional as any good law firm, but perhaps more adept at the inter-personal skills that make relationships work and go on working. They place a high priority on the excellent technical ability and commercial thinking of their lawyers and also on their relationships with clients. Clients find them refreshingly easy to deal with. The firm has a friendly, lively style with a commitment to continuous improvement.

## main areas of work

The firm has a wide range of corporate clients and provides services through five departments: corporate, employment & incentives, litigation, property and media, brands & technology. The major work areas are commercial litigation and dispute resolution; corporate services, which includes company commercial and corporate finance; defamation; employment; marketing services, embracing advertising and marketing law; property, construction and project finance; technology and communications, including IT, media and telecommunications. They are UK leaders in employment law and have a strong reputation within social housing and the media and advertising sectors.

## trainee profile

They are looking for trainees with keen minds and personalities, who will fit into a professional but informal team.

## training environment

The firm provides a comprehensive induction and training programme, with practical hands-on experience from day one. You will sit with either a partner or senior associate giving you access to day-to-day supervision and guidance. The training contract consists of four six-month seats. At least three will be in one of the main departments, with the possibility of the fourth being in one of the firm's specialist areas.

## benefits

These include individual and firm bonus schemes, life assurance, critical illness cover, health insurance, season ticket loan, group pension plan and subsidised gym membership.

## vacation placements

There are four vacation scheme sessions which take place during June and July. Two two-week placements and two one-week placements, giving 16 participants the opportunity to gain first-hand experience of life at Lewis Silkin. Applications should be made via the firm's application form between October 2005 and the end of January 2006.

## sponsorship & awards

Funding for LPC fees is provided plus £4,500 maintenance.  Funding for GDL fees is provided.

| | |
|---|---|
| **Partners** | **44** |
| **Assistant Solicitors** | **70** |
| **Total Trainees** | **13** |

**contact**
Lucie Rees
Graduate Recruitment
Manager

**method of application**
Application form

**selection procedure**
Assessment day, including an interview with 2 partners & an analytical exercise

**closing date for 2008**
31 July 2006

**application**
Training contracts p.a. **5**
Applications p.a. **800**
Required degree grade **2:1**

**training**
Salary
**1st year £29,000**
**2nd year £31,000**
Holiday entitlement **22 days**

**post-qualification**
Salary (2005) **£43,000**

# Linklaters

One Silk Street, London EC2Y 8HQ
Tel: (020) 7456 2000  Fax: (020) 7456 2222
Email: graduate.recruitment@linklaters.com
Website: www.linklaters.com/careers/ukgrads

## firm profile
Linklaters is a global law firm that advises the world's leading companies, financial institutions and governments on their most challenging transactions and assignments.

## main areas of work
The firm's work is divided into three main areas – Corporate, Finance & Projects and Commercial. While many law firms will have strengths in particular areas, Linklaters is strong across the full range of business law. This is one of the factors that makes Linklaters such a challenging and rewarding place to train as a lawyer.

## trainee profile
This is a firm that achieves exceptional things for clients, but it is also a supportive community in which individuals are encouraged to be themselves. Experienced people are generous with their time when supporting and coaching their less experienced colleagues. If you ask anyone from Linklaters what they most enjoy about the firm, the answer is usually the same: "It's the people".

## training environment
Linklaters recruits graduates in both law and non-law disciplines. Those graduates who don't have a law degree take the Graduate Diploma in Law conversion course (GDL), which involves a year at law college. The next step is the year-long Legal Practice Course (LPC) which all trainees have to complete before they begin their training contracts. The training contract itself is built around four six-month seats or placements. The seat system gives trainees front-line exposure to a range of practice areas. This develops versatile, well-rounded lawyers, but it also gives trainees a good idea of the kind of law they want to do when they qualify. There are also opportunities for client secondments or overseas placements as part of the training contract.

## sponsorship & benefits
GDL and LPC fees are paid in full, plus a maintenance grant. The LPC maintenance grant is £7,000 and the GDL maintenance grant is £6,000 in London and Oxford, and £5,000 elsewhere. Profit- and performance-related bonus schemes; 25 days' holiday; health and worldwide travel insurance; life assurance; pension scheme; interest-free season ticket loan; subsidised gym membership.

## vacation placements
Christmas scheme for 30 final year non-law students and three summer schemes for 80 penultimate year law students. Remuneration will be £275 pw. The four week summer schemes offer some students the opportunity to spend two weeks in another European office.

| | |
|---|---|
| **Partners** | 500 |
| **Associates** | 1,500 |
| **Trainees** | 250* |
| *(London) | |

**contact**
Charlotte Hart

**method of application**
Application form (available online)

**selection procedure**
Critical reasoning test, 2 interviews plus commercial case study (same day).

**application**
Training contracts p.a. **130**
Applications p.a. **4,000**
Required degree grade **2:1**

**training**
Salary
1st year (2005) **£29,700**
Holiday entitlement **25 days**
% of trainees with a non-law degree p.a. **33%**

**post-qualification**
Salary **£52,000 +**
**discretionary performance-related bonus**

**offices**
Amsterdam, Antwerp, Bangkok, Beijing, Berlin, Bratislava, Brussels, Bucharest, Budapest, Cologne, Frankfurt, Hong Kong, Lisbon, London, Luxembourg, Madrid, Milan, Moscow, Munich, New York, Paris, Prague, Rome, São Paulo, Shanghai, Singapore, Stockholm, Tokyo, Warsaw

# Lovells

Atlantic House, Holborn Viaduct, London EC1A 2FG
Tel: (020) 7296 2000  Fax: (020) 7296 2001
Email: recruit@lovells.com
Website: www.lovells.com/graduates

## firm profile
Lovells is one of the world's leading international law firms based in the City of London, with offices in Asia, Europe and North America. The firm's strength across a wide range of practice areas sets it apart from most of its competitors.

## main areas of work
The firm's core areas of practice are corporate, litigation, real estate and specialist groups (including EU/competition, intellectual property, media and telecommunications, employment, tax).

## trainee profile
High calibre candidates who can demonstrate strong academic/intellectual ability, ambition, drive, strong communication and interpersonal skills, professional/commercial attitude.

## training environment
Trainees spend six months in four different areas of the practice to gain as much experience as possible. They have the option of spending time in their second year of training in an international office or on secondment to the in-house legal department of a major client. A comprehensive part of the programme of skills training is run for trainees both in-house and externally, placing a particular emphasis on advocacy and communication. Trainees are offered as much responsibility as they can handle as well as regular reviews, six-monthly appraisals and support when they need it.

## benefits
PPP medical insurance, life assurance, PHI, season ticket loan, in-house gym, staff restaurant, access to dentist, doctor and physiotherapist, discounts at local retailers.

## vacation placements
Places for 2006: 90. Placements available at Christmas 2005 (closing date 11 November), Easter and Summer 2006 (closing date 10 February).

## sponsorship & awards
GDL and LPC course fees are paid, and a maintenance grant is also provided of £5,000 for London and Oxford and £4,500 elsewhere. From September 2006, the firm's maintenance grants will be £7,450 for all students reading the LPC and GDL in London and £6,450 for students reading the GDL elsewhere. In addition, £500 bonus on joining the firm; £1,000 advance in salary on joining; £500 prize for a First Class degree result.

| Partners | 329 |
| Assistant Solicitors | 1600 |
| Total Trainees | 145 |

**contact**
Clare Harris
Recruitment Manager

**method of application**
Online application form

**selection procedure**
Assessment day: critical thinking test, group exercise, interview

**closing date for 2008**
31 July 2006

**application**
Training contracts p.a. **90**
Applications p.a. **2,500**
% interviewed p.a. **20%**
Required degree grade **2:1**

**training**
Salary
1st year (2005) **£29,000**
2nd year (2005) **£32,000**
Holiday entitlement **25 days**
% of trainees with a
non-law degree p.a. **40%**
No. of seats available
abroad p.a. **22**

**post-qualification**
Salary (2005) **£50,000**

**international offices**
Alicante, Amsterdam, Beijing, Berlin, Brussels, Budapest, Chicago, Düsseldorf, Frankfurt, Hamburg, Ho Chi Minh City, Hong Kong, London, Madrid, Milan, Moscow, Munich, New York, Paris, Prague, Rome, Singapore, Shanghai, Tokyo, Warsaw, Zagreb

# Lupton Fawcett

Yorkshire House, East Parade, Leeds LS1 5BD
Tel: (0113) 280 2000  Fax: (0113) 245 6782
Email: hr@luptonfawcett.com
Website: www.luptonfawcett.com

## firm profile

Lupton Fawcett is a well-established yet dynamic and integrated practice. The firm offers a full range of legal services to both commercial and private clients alike on a quality-driven and client-led basis with the emphasis on providing first-class cost effective and practical solutions which exceed the clients' expectations. The firm was one of the first in Leeds to hold both Investors in People and the Law Society's Lexcel quality standard.

## main areas of work

The commercial division offers the chance to gain experience in corporate, commercial property, employment, intellectual property, insolvency and commercial and chancery litigation. On the private client side, opportunities are available in financial services, trusts and probate, family and residential conveyancing. Further specialist areas of the firm include employment, licensing and advocacy, IT and e-commerce, sports law, debt recovery, insurance litigation and specialist personal injury.

## trainee profile

Although strong academic achievements are required, the firm places a high value on previous experience and interests which have developed commercial awareness, maturity and character. Trainees will also be able to demonstrate enthusiasm, confidence, good interpersonal and team skills, humour, initiative, commitment and common sense.

## training environment

Training at Lupton Fawcett is normally split into four six-month seats. Trainees office share with the partner or associate with whom they are working and are an integral part of the team, assuming a high degree of responsibility. Appraisals following each seat take place to ensure that progress is monitored effectively. A full in-house training programme enables continual development as well as from training gained from excellent hands-on experience. Trainees will have the chance to meet clients and be responsible for their own work, as well as being involved in and actively encouraged to join in marketing and practice development initiatives. There is a full social programme in which the trainees are encouraged to participate as well as sporting events organised by the office and an excellent informal social culture.

## benefits

Health insurance, season ticket loans, interest free loans towards LPC funding available by discussion with candidates.

| | |
|---|---|
| **Partners** | 27 |
| **Assistant Solicitors** | 18 |
| **Associate Solicitors** | 13 |
| **Total Trainees** | 5 |

**contact**
HR Department
(0113) 280 2251

**method of application**
Online at
www.luptonfawcett.com

**selection procedure**
Interviews & assessment days

**closing date for 2008**
31 July 2006

**application**
Training contracts p.a. **2-3**
Applications p.a. **300**
% interviewed p.a. **10**
Required degree grade **2:1** preferred

**training**
Salary
**Competitive with similar size/type firms**
Holiday entitlement
(under review) **20 days**

**post-qualification**
Salary
**Competitive with similar size/type firms**
% of trainees offered job on qualification (2003-04) **90%**

# Mace & Jones

19 Water Street, Liverpool L2 0RP
Tel: (0151) 236 8989  Fax: (0151) 227 5010
Email: donal.bannon@maceandjones.co.uk
Pall Mall Court, 61-67 King Street, Manchester, M2 4PD
Tel: (0161) 214 0500  Fax: (0161) 832 8610
Website: www.maceandjones.co.uk

## firm profile
Mace & Jones is a leading regional practice in the North West and remains a full service firm while enjoying a national reputation for its commercial expertise, especially in employment, litigation/insolvency, corporate and property. The firm's clients range from national and multinational companies and public sector bodies to owner managed businesses and private individuals, reflecting the broad nature of the work undertaken. Sound practical advice is given always on a value-for-money basis.

## main areas of work
Commercial litigation/insolvency 15%; commercial property 15%; company/commercial 15%; employment 35%; personal injury/private client/family 20%.

## trainee profile
The firm seeks to recruit highly motivated trainees with above average ability and the determination to succeed. The right calibre of trainee will assume responsibility early in their career. The firm provides a comprehensive internal and external training programme.

## training environment
Trainees complete an induction course to familiarise themselves with the work carried out by the firm's main departments, administration and professional conduct. Training consists of four six-month seats in the following departments: company/commercial, employment, commercial litigation/personal injury litigation, property law, family law. Strenuous efforts are made to ensure that trainees are able to select the training seat of their choice. A trainee will normally be required to share an office with a partner who will supervise their work and review the trainee's progress at the end of the seat. The PSC is taught externally. The firm operates an open door policy and has various social events.

| Partners | 38 |
| Assistant Solicitors | 51 |
| Total Trainees | 8 |

**contact**
Donal Bannon
Liverpool Office

**method of application**
Online

**selection procedure**
Interview with partners

**closing date for 2007**
31 July 2006

**application**
Training contracts p.a. **varies**
Applications p.a. **1,500**
% interviewed p.a. **2%**
Required degree grade **2:1**

**training**
Salary
**1st year (2004) £16,000**
**2nd year (2004) £16,500**
Holiday entitlement **20 days**
% of trainees with a
non-law degree p.a. **40%**

**post-qualification**
Salary (2003) **Negotiable**
% of trainees offered job
on qualification (2005) **50%**
% of assistants (as at 1/7/03)
who joined as trainees **30%**
% of partners (as at 1/9/03)
who joined as trainees **25%**

# Macfarlanes

10 Norwich Street, London EC4A 1BD
Tel: (020) 7831 9222  Fax: (020) 7831 9607
Email: gradrec@macfarlanes.com
Website: www.macfarlanes.com

## firm profile
Macfarlanes is a leading City law firm practising at the forefront of many areas of commercial endeavour. The firm is instructed by major businesses, industrial enterprises and high net worth individuals who appreciate the distinctive benefits of working with a firm which offers a cohesive and focused approach. Much of their work has a significant international element.

## main areas of work
The firm's areas of practice are broadly defined under the four main headings of corporate; property; litigation and dispute resolution; and private client.

## trainee profile
It is Macfarlanes' belief that the strongest firm will be achieved by choosing a mix of people, reflecting different styles so as to meet the needs that they – and their varied range of clients – will have in the future. Macfarlanes does not just need its trainees to show intelligence and imagination, but also a high level of self-reliance, energy and enthusiasm.

## training environment
Anyone joining Macfarlanes cannot expect to lose themselves in the crowd. Because they recruit fewer trainees, each individual is expected to play their part and everyone's contribution counts. There are other benefits attached to working in a firm of this size: It helps retain an informal working atmosphere – people quickly get to know one another and are on first name terms across the board. There is the sense of community that comes from working closely together in smaller teams. Everyone at Macfarlanes has a vested interest in getting the best out of each other, including their trainees.

## benefits
A comprehensive benefits package is provided.

## vacation placements
Places for 2006: 36; Duration: 2 weeks; Remuneration: £250 p.w.; Closing Date: 28 February 2006.

## sponsorship & awards
CPE and LPC fees paid in full and a £5,000 maintenance allowance for courses studied in London, Guildford and Oxford and £4,500 for courses studied elsewhere. Prizes for those gaining distinction or commendation on the LPC.

| | |
|---|---|
| **Partners** | 65 |
| **Assistant Solicitors** | 126 |
| **Total Trainees** | 49 |

**contact**
Louisa Hatton

**method of application**
Online via website

**selection procedure**
Assessment day

**closing date for 2008**
31 July 2006

**application**
Training contracts p.a. **25**
Applications p.a. **1,000**
% interviewed p.a. **20%**
Required degree grade **2:1**

**training**
Salary
**1st year (2005) £29,000**
**2nd year (2005) £33,000**
Holiday entitlement **23 days**
% of trainees with a
non-law degree p.a. **50%**

**post-qualification**
Salary (2004) **£50,000**
% of trainees offered job
on qualification (2005) **93%**
% of partners (as at 1/9/05)
who joined as trainees **66%**

# Manches

Aldwych House, 81 Aldwych, London WC2B 4RP
Tel: (020) 7404 4433  Fax: (020) 7430 1133
Email: sheona.boldero@manches.com
Website: www.manches.com

## firm profile

Manches is a London and Oxford-based commercial firm with strengths across a range of services and industry sectors. The firm's strategy has seen a greater concentration and focus on the firm's core commercial industry sectors of technology and media, property, construction and retail, while continuing to be market leaders in family law. The firm offers 10 trainee places each September.

## main areas of work

**Industry Sectors::** Technology and media, property and construction.
**Legal Groups:** Corporate finance (emphasis in technology); commercial property; commercial litigation; construction; family; employment; intellectual property; information technology; biotechnology (Oxford office only); trusts and estates (Oxford office only).

## trainee profile

Manches looks for candidates with a consistently good academic record who are enthusiastic, committed and with an outgoing engaging personality. They should display a strong sense of commercial awareness, the ability to think for themselves and excellent interpersonal/social skills.

## training environment

The firm provides high quality, individual training. Trainees generally sit in four different seats for six months at a time (one of which is usually in a niche practice area). The firm's comprehensive in-house training structure enables them to take responsibility from an early stage, ensuring that they become confident and competent solicitors. Trainees have the opportunity to actively participate in departmental meetings and briefings and receive regular appraisals on their progress.

## benefits

Season ticket loan, BUPA after six months, permanent health insurance, life insurance, pension after three months.

## vacation placements

Places for 2006: 24 approx.; Duration: 1 week; Remuneration: £200/wk; Closing Date: 31 January 2006.

## sponsorship & awards

CPE/PgDL and LPC fees are paid in full together with an annual maintenance allowance (currently £4,000 p.a. - under review).

| | |
|---|---|
| **Partners** | **52** |
| **Assistant Solicitors** | **60** |
| **Total Trainees** | **20** |

**contact**
Sheona Boldero
sheona.boldero@manches.com

**method of application**
Application form (online)

**selection procedure**
1st interview with HR, second interview with 2 partners.

**closing date for 2008**
31 July 2006

**application**
Training contracts p.a. **10**
Applications p.a. **860**
% interviewed p.a. **10%**
Required degree grade **2:1**

**training**
Salary
**1st year (2005)**
**London £27,500**
**2nd year (2005)**
**London £31,000**
Holiday entitlement **24 days**

**post-qualification**
Salary
**London £45,000**
% of trainees offered job on qualification (2005) **90%**

# Martineau Johnson

No 1 Colmore Square, Birmingham B4 6AA
78 Cannon Street, London, EC4N 4NQ
Tel: (0870) 763 2000  Fax: (0870) 763 2001
Email: jennifer.seymour@martjohn.co.uk
Website: www.graduates4law.co.uk and www.martineau-johnson.co.uk

## firm profile

Martineau Johnson is an independent commercial law firm, with offices in Birmingham and London. It is also part of Multilaw, a worldwide network of associated law firms, giving national and international reach.

Martineau Johnson's greatest asset is its people. It has earned a reputation for caring for its lawyers and its support staff and their career progression, and encourages an open culture throughout the firm. This is evidenced by the firm's recent debut into the Sunday Times Top 100 Best Companies to Work For. The firm is also an accredited Investor in People.

Martineau Johnson also adopts a personal approach in its dealings with clients, aiming to deliver clear and concise advice, with an appreciation of clients' business needs and the environments in which they operate.

The firm's commitment to clients care and quality is endorsed by the ISO 9001 standard.

## main areas of work

Commercial 20%; corporate services 23%; commercial disputes management 14%; property 18%; private client 14%.

## trainee profile

Trainees are vital to Martineau Johnson's future and no effort is spared to give the best possible experience and support to them, whilst treating them as individuals. There is a very high retention rate at the end of training contracts, when trainees are generally offered roles in their preferred departments and specialisms.

## training environment

Martineau Johnson's aim is to work in partnership with trainees, providing them with mentoring, supervision, support and an exposure to the key areas of the firm's practice. Trainees are actively encouraged to be an integral part of the team delivering legal solutions to its clients whilst benefiting from quality work, flexible seat rotation in a small and friendly team environment. Generally, the firm's trainees are given experience in its chosen sectors: commercial, corporate services, commercial disputes management, property and private client – they are then given the opportunity to carry out further work in areas of their choice and specialism. There are opportunities for Birmingham-based trainees to be exposed to the London scene. Trainees benefit from a structured career training programme tailored to their personal development needs - and it covers not only legal technical matters, but also a business and commercial approach which have never been more central to successful professional careers. In giving training and offering experience that matches the best city firms, Martineau Johnson offers a rare opportunity for trainees to lay great foundations for their legal career in a fast-moving, ever-changing but caring environment.

| | |
|---|---|
| Partners | 39 |
| Assistant Solicitors | 99 |
| Total Trainees | 21 |

**contact**
Jennifer Seymour

**method of application**
Online application form
www.graduates4law.co.uk

**selection procedure**
Assessment centre - half day

**closing date for 2008**
30 July 2006

**application**
Training contracts p.a. **10-12**
Applications p.a. **500**
% interviewed p.a. **10%**
Required degree grade **2:1**

**training**
Salary
**1st year (2005) c. £20,000**
**2nd year (2005) c. £21,500**
Holiday entitlement **23 days**
% of trainees with a
non-law degree (2005) **30%**

**post-qualification**
Salary (2005) **£34,000**
% of trainees offered job
on qualification (2005) **87%**
% of assistants (as at 1/9/05)
who joined as trainees **38%**
% of partners (as at 1/9/05)
who joined as trainees **42%**

MARTINEAU JOHNSON

# Mayer, Brown, Rowe & Maw LLP

11 Pilgrim Street, London EC4V 6RW
Tel: (020) 7248 4282  Fax: (020) 7782 8790
Email: graduaterecruitment@mayerbrownrowe.com
Website: www.mayerbrownrowe.com/london/careers/gradrecruit

## firm profile

Mayer, Brown, Rowe & Maw LLP is among the 10 largest law practices in the world with over 400 partners and more than 1,300 lawyers worldwide. Mayer, Brown, Rowe & Maw works with its international clients from offices in seven US cities (Charlotte, Chicago, Houston, Los Angeles, New York, Palo Alto and Washington) and six European cities (Berlin, Brussels, Cologne, Frankfurt, London and Paris). The firm also uses a network of law firm contacts in Europe to advise on local law, and regularly works alongside a correspondent firm in Mexico City and associated firms in Shanghai and Beijing.

## main areas of work

In London, the practice advises a wide range of clients including multinational corporations, financial institutions, governments, partnerships, joint ventures, trade organisations and business start-ups. Much of its work is cross-border and multi-jurisdictional. The major emphasis in Europe is across industry sectors including financial services, chemicals, telecommunications, insurance and reinsurance, real estate, construction & engineering, energy and professional practice. Working within this framework core practice lines include corporate and securities (including M&A and corporate finance), litigation and dispute resolution, finance and banking, financial restructuring and insolvency, tax, environment and public law, employment, pensions, intellectual property, outsourcing, advertising, music and publishing, antitrust and international trade.

## trainee profile

The practice is interested in motivated students with a good academic record and a strong commitment to law. Commercial awareness gained through legal or business work experience is an advantage. Applications are welcomed from both law and non-law students.

## training environment

Students looking for a leading international law practice that offers exposure to a multitude of blue chip companies and a wide range of international work, combined with the confidence of knowing they have a place in its future, should contact Mayer, Brown, Rowe and Maw LLP. Trainees will participate in a lively, energetic and positive business culture, spending time in four six-month seats including the corporate and litigation departments. The practice's culture of getting immersed in a client's business means that there are excellent secondment opportunities. In addition to the Professional Skills Course, the practice offers an individual professional development and training programme. Three-monthly appraisals assist trainees in reaching their true potential.

## benefits

Benefits include 25 days holiday per annum, interest free season ticket loan, subsidised sports club membership and private health scheme.

## vacation placements

Places for 2006: 32; Duration: 2 weeks during Easter and Summer vacations. Experience in two of the principle work groups plus a programme of seminars, visits and social events.

## sponsorship & awards

GDL and LPC fees, plus a maintenance grant of £4,500 (£5,000 for London and Guildford).

| | |
|---|---|
| **Partners** | 97 |
| **Assistant Solicitors** | 143 |
| **Total Trainees** | 54 |

### contact
Maxine Lawrence,
Graduate Recruitment
Manager

### method of application
Online application form

### selection procedure
Selection workshops
including an interview, a
business analysis exercise,
a group exercise & an
online verbal reasoning test

### closing date for
**Sept 2008/March 2009**
31 July 2006

### application
Training contracts p.a.
**Approx 25-30**
Applications p.a. **850**
% interviewed p.a. **9%**
Required degree grade **2:1**

### training
Starting salary (2005) **£29,000**
Holiday entitlement **25 days**
% of trainees with a
non-law degree p.a. **42%**
No. of seats available
abroad p.a. **2**

### post-qualification
Salary (2005) **£50,000**
% of trainees offered job
on qualification (2005) **88%**
% of partners who joined
as trainees **35%**

### overseas offices
Berlin, Brussels, Charlotte,
Chicago, Cologne,
Frankfurt, Houston,
London, Los Angeles, New
York, Palo Alto, Paris,
Washington DC

# McCormicks

Britannia Chambers, 4 Oxford Place, Leeds LS1 3AX
Tel: (0113) 246 0622  Fax: (0113) 246 7488
Wharfedale House, 37 East Parade, Harrogate HG1 5LQ
Tel: (01423) 530630  Fax: (01423) 530709
Email: l.jackson@mccormicks-solicitors.com
Website: www.mccormicks-solicitors.com

| Partners | 12 |
| --- | --- |
| Assistant Solicitors | 29 |
| Total Trainees | 8 |

**contact**
Linda Jackson

## firm profile

McCormicks is a unique legal practice at the heart of a vibrant commercial region. With core traditional values of integrity, technical excellence and hard work, the firm is committed to deliver an unrivalled quality of service and innovation to its clients and quality of life to its people. McCormicks combines the full range and depth of skills across its entire practice with the firm's renowned fearlessness and ability to punch above its weight in order to deliver the best possible result.

**method of application**
Application form

**selection procedure**
Assessment Day &
Interview with two partners

**closing date for 2008**
28 July 2006

## main areas of work

With a diverse range of clients from private individuals to high profile international organisations its work is never dull. Trainees are exposed to all its practice areas including sports law, media and entertainment law, corporate and commercial, commercial property, commercial litigation, charity work, family, corporate crime, insolvency and intellectual property.

**application**
Training contracts p.a. **4**
Applications p.a. **500**
% interviewed p.a. **16%**
Required degree grade **2:1**

## trainee profile

Intellectual achievement, ambition, a sense of humour and commitment to hard work are crucial qualities of a McCormicks trainee. The firm will challenge you but support you at every step of the way.

**training**
Salary
**highly competitive**

## training environment

Trainees are assigned to one of six departments and supervised throughout by a mentor. The firm's training work will develop skills, knowledge and ambition within a friendly, progressive and supportive environment. Your development will be reviewed regularly by the mentor, team supervisor and the training partner. There is an open door policy and a great team spirit.

**post-qualification**
Salary (2005)
**Highly competitive**
trainees offered job
on qualification (2005) **4 of 4**
% of partners (as at 1/1/2005)
who joined as trainees **50%**

## vacation placements

Places for 2006: Available in summer vacation. Closing Date: Application forms by 24 February 2006.

# McDermott Will & Emery UK LLP

7 Bishopsgate, London EC2N 3AR
Tel: (020) 7577 6900  Fax: (020) 7577 6950
Website: www.mwe.com/london
Email: graduate.recruitment@europe.mwe.com

## firm profile
McDermott Will & Emery UK LLP is a leading international law firm with offices in Boston, Brussels, Chicago, Düsseldorf, London, Los Angeles, Miami, Milan, Munich, New York, Orange County, Rome, San Diego, Silicon Valley and Washington DC. The firm's client base includes some of the world's leading financial institutions, largest corporations, mid-cap businesses, and individuals. The firm represents more than 75 of the companies in the Fortune 100 in addition to clients in the FTSE 100 and FTSE 250. Rated as one of the leading firms in The American Lawyer's Top 100, by a number of indicators, including gross revenues and profits per Partner.
London Office: The London office was founded in 1998. It is already recognised as being in the top 10 of the 100 US law firms operating in London by the legal media. The firm has over 65 lawyers at present in London, almost all of whom are English-qualified. The firm provides business oriented legal advice to multinational and national corporates, financial institutions, investment banks and private clients. Most of the firm's partners were head of practice at their former firms and are recognised as leaders in their respective fields by the most respected professional directories and market commentators.

## main areas of work
Banking and finance; corporate, including international corporate finance and M&A; private equity, EU competition; employment, IP, IT and e-business; litigation and arbitration; pensions and incentives; taxation; telecoms and US securities. London is the hub for the firm's European expansions.

## trainee profile
The firm is looking for the brightest, best and most entrepreneurial trainees. You will need to convince the firm that you have made a deliberate choice.

## training environment
The primary focus is to provide a practical foundation for your career with the firm. You will experience between four and six seats over the two-year period and the deliberately small number of trainees means that the firm is able to provide a degree of flexibility in tailoring seats to the individual. Trainees get regular support and feedback.

## benefits
Private medical and dental insurance, life assurance, permanent health insurance, season ticket loan, subsidised gym membership, employee assistance programme, 25 days holiday.

## sponsorship & awards
GDL and LPC funding and mainenance grant.

| | |
|---|---|
| **Partners** | 585* |
| | 22 (London) |
| **Associate Lawyers &** | |
| **Other Fee-earners** | 427* |
| | 45 (London) |
| **Total Trainees** | 2 in 2004 |
| | 3 in 2005 |

*denotes worldwide figures*

**contact**
Áine Wood

**method of application**
CV & covering letter. See website for selection criteria

**selection procedure**
2 interviews with partners and written exercise

**closing date for 2008**
31 July 2006

**training**
Salary
1st year (2005) £31,500
2nd year (2005) £35,000

**post-qualification**
Salary (2005) £60,000

McDermott
Will & Emery

# McGrigors

5 Old Bailey, London, EC4M 7BA
Tel: (020) 7054 2500/2501
Email: graduate.recruitment@mcgrigors.com
Website: www.mcgrigors.com

## firm profile

McGrigors is a medium sized law firm with a turnover of £45 million and has an open and enthusiastic approach to everything it does. Clients range from small businesses to large household names. This allows trainees to work on and see large transactions for the well known organisations whilst at the same time gaining the practical, hands on experience of dealing with the smaller transactions. The firm's client base includes BP, Royal Bank of Scotland, O2 and Ufi and they continue to have a well established, best friends relationship with leading professional services firm KPMG.

## main areas of work

Practice areas include: banking and finance, commercial litigation, competition, construction procurement, contentious construction, corporate, dispute resolution, employment, human rights, IP & commercial, projects/PPP, public law, public policy, real estate, tax litigation, and telecoms.

## trainee profile

Principally, McGrigors seeks students who are not only intellectually capable but also commercially interested - trainees need to show that they are interested in business, not simply black letter law. The firm wants people who display ambition and enthusiasm in equal measure, who are confident in their abilities to meet a demanding job, and who are dedicated to completing the task at hand.

## training environment

McGrigors' training is based on the standard rotation of six-month seats in four main practice areas. The firm encourages their trainees to spend at least one six-month seat at one of the firm's other offices, to allow them to gain a breadth of experience of the firm and as broad a range of legal work as possible. The firm also actively encourages secondments to clients and in the last 12 months have seconded trainees to KPMG, O2, and RAB Capital.

## benefits

The firm offers private medical cover, life assurance, pension, a daily lunch allowance amounting to over £600 a year and income protection.

## sponsorship & awards

CPE and LPC fees are paid plus maintenance of £4,500 for each year in England.

---

**Partners** 54*
**Assistant Solicitors** 109*
**Total Trainees** 74*
*denotes firm wide

### contact
Georgina Bond
(020) 7054 2569 - London
Margaret-Ann Roy
(0141) 567 9551 -
Scotland/Belfast

### method of application
Online application form via firm website

### selection procedure
Half day assessment including interview, presentation and aptitude tests

### closing date
July 2006

### application
No. of training contracts p.a.
**10-15 in each office bar Belfast**
% interviewed - **15%**
Required degree grade - realistic estimate of 2.1 or higher

### training
Salary
London **1st year £28,000**
**2nd year £32,000**
Scotland **1st year £16,500**
**2nd year £19,500**
Holiday **33.5 days including bank holidays**

### post-qualification
Salary London **£48,000**
Scotland **£30,000**
% offered job **73%**

### overseas/regional offices
London, Edinburgh, Glasgow, Belfast

# Mills & Reeve

112 Hills Road, Cambridge CB2 1PH
Tel: (01223) 222336  Fax: (01223) 355848
Email: graduate.recruitment@mills-reeve.com
Website: www.mills-reeve.com

## firm profile

Mills & Reeve is one of the UK's leading commercial law firms, providing a comprehensive range of services to a mix of regional and national businesses, institutions and individuals in the UK and internationally. It operates from offices in Birmingham, Cambridge, London and Norwich.

## main areas of work

The firm offers a full range of corporate, commercial, property, litigation and private client services. Areas of work where trainees currently sit include: corporate, banking, corporate tax, education and public law, technology, real estate, planning & environment, PFI, construction, insurance, commercial disputes, probate & trust administration, agriculture and estates, private tax, employment, family & matrimonial, litigation, real estate disputes and regulatory defence.

## trainee profile

The firm welcomes applications from both law and non-law disciplines. Candidates should already have or expect a 2.1 degree or equivalent. Trainee solicitors should display energy, maturity, initiative, enthusiasm for their career, a professional approach to work and be ready to accept early responsibility.

## training environment

At Mills & Reeve trainees complete six four-month seats and are recruited to the Birmingham, Cambridge and Norwich offices. Subject to business needs, the firm is happy for those trainees with a desire to undertake a seat not practised in their base office to temporarily move to another office, including London, and supports the move with an accommodation allowance. During each seat trainees sit with a partner or senior solicitor and performance is assessed by a mix of informal reviews during the seat and a more formal review at the end of each seat. A full induction integrates trainees quickly into the firm and ongoing in-house lectures and training by Professional Support Lawyers support the PSC.

## benefits

Life assurance at two times pensionable salary, a contributory pension scheme, 25 days holiday, bonus scheme, discounted rate for BUPA, corporate gym membership, social club.

## vacation placements

Applications for two-week placements during the summer must be received by 1 March 2006.

## sponsorship & awards

The firm pays the full costs of the CPE/GDL and LPC fees and offers a maintenance grant.

| | |
|---|---|
| **Partners** | 79 |
| **Assistant Solicitors** | 203 |
| **Total Trainees** | 37 |

**contact**
Graduate Recruitment

**method of application**
Firm's application form

**selection procedure**
Normally one day assessment centre

**closing date for 2008**
31 July 2006 for training contracts
1st March 2006 for work placements

**application**
Training contracts p.a. **20**
Applications p.a. **Approx 600**
% interviewed p.a. **10%**
Required degree grade **2:1**

**training**
Salary
**1st year (2005) £21,000**
**2nd year (2005) £22,000**
Holiday entitlement
**25 days p.a.**
% of trainees with a non-law degree **45%**

**post-qualification**
% of trainees offered job on qualification (2005) 74%
% of assistants (as at 1/9/05) who joined as trainees 30%
% of partners (as at 1/9/05) who joined as trainees 20%

# Mishcon de Reya

Summit House, 12 Red Lion Square, London WC1R 4QD
Tel: (020) 7440 7198  Fax: (020) 7430 0691
Email: graduate.recruitment@mishcon.co.uk
Website: www.mishcon.co.uk

| | |
|---|---|
| Partners | 43 |
| Assistant Solicitors | 53 |
| Total Trainees | 15 |

**contact**
Human Resources Department

**method of application**
Application form

**closing date for 2008**
31 July 2006

**application**
Training contracts p.a. **6**
Applications p.a. **900+**
% interviewed p.a. **6%**
Required degree grade **2:1**

**training**
Salary
**1st year £27,000**
**2nd year £29,000**
Holiday entitlement
**25 days p.a.**
**Occasional secondments available**

**post-qualification**
% of trainees retained
(2004) **75%**
% of assistants who joined
as trainees **42%**
% of partners who joined
as trainees **15%**

## firm profile
Mishcon de Reya is a mid-sized central London law firm offering a diverse range of legal services for businesses and individuals. Their foundation is based upon a dynamic range of corporate clients that seek effective advice through close collaboration. Through their expertise and entrepreneurial spirit they deliver legal and commercial solutions to businesses of all sizes.

## main areas of work
Mishcon de Reya's expertise falls into four main areas: Corporate, Litigation, Property and Family. The firm also has a number of specialist groups including Banking & Debt Finance, Betting & Gaming, Brands & Rights, Corporate Recovery & Insolvency, Corporate Tax, Employment, Financial Services, Investigations & Asset Recovery, Immigration, IT, Media & Public Advocacy and Personal Tax, Trusts and Probate.

## trainee profile
Applications are welcome from penultimate-year law students, final year non-law students and other graduates wishing to commence a training contract in two years' time. The firm wants people who can meet the highest intellectual and business standards, while maintaining outside interests. Candidates should therefore be enterprising, enthusiastic and committed, and see themselves as future partners.

## training environment
Trainees have the opportunity to experience four different 'seats' of six months each. All trainees get exposure to at least three of the four core departments and are also able to gain experience in specialist groups during their time with the firm. Trainees share a room with a partner or assistant solicitor. Because of the relatively few training contracts offered, trainees can expect to be exposed to high quality work with early responsibility. In order to support this, the firm has a wide-ranging training programme and provides extensive internal training in addition to the Professional Skills Course. Quarterly appraisals and monitoring in each seat ensures trainees gain a range of work and experience.

## benefits
Medical cover, subsidised gym membership, season ticket loan, permanent health insurance, life assurance and pension.

## vacation placements
Places for 2006: 12; Duration: 2 weeks; Expenses: £200 p.w.; Closing Date: 15 March 2006.

## sponsorship & awards
CPE and LPC funding with bursary.

# Morgan Cole

Buxton Court, 3 West Way, Oxford OX2 0SZ
Tel: (01865) 262699  Fax: (01865) 262670
Email: recruitment@morgan-cole.com
Website: www.morgan-cole.com

| | |
|---|---|
| **Partners** | 50 |
| **Lawyers** | 179 |
| **Total Trainees** | 28 |

**Trainee Places for 2007:**

| | |
|---|---|
| Cardiff/Swansea | 5 |
| Oxford/Reading/London | 5 |
| Total | 10 |

**contact**
Janice Okuns

**method of application**
Apply online at
www.morgan-cole.com/careers

**selection procedure**
Assessment Centre &
interview

**closing date for 2007**
31 July 2006

**application**
Required degree grade
**Preferably 2:1**

**training**
Salary
**1st & 2nd year (2005)**
Competitive for the Thames
Valley and South Wales
regions which are reviewed
annually in line with market
trends

**other offices**
Cardiff, Croydon, London,
Oxford, Swansea

## firm profile

Morgan Cole is one of the leading commercial law practices in the country, providing a comprehensive service to both individual and corporate clients in both the public and private sectors. The firm has a reputation for excellence and therefore attracts the highest quality of staff from all fields. The firm enjoys strong connections throughout the UK and the USA and is a founder member of the Association of European Lawyers, one of five leading UK law firms responsible for establishing a network of English speaking lawyers throughout Europe. The firm's areas of work are covered by eight practice areas: commercial; corporate and banking; employment; insurance; private client; health; commercial property; and dispute management. As a modern practice, the firm strives to meet the legal needs of clients in all sectors of industry, but places a specific emphasis on four main sectors: insurance; energy; health; and technology. Within these practice areas the firm's work includes: acquisitions and disposals; technology and intellectual property work; corporate finance; employment; energy; information technology; joint ventures; landlord and tenant litigation; management buy-outs and buy-ins; partnerships; PFI; public law; commercial property; construction; environmental/ planning/health and safety; heath and social care (including medical negligence); commercial litigation; licensing; family litigation and alternative dispute resolution.

## trainee profile

Successful candidates should be commercially aware, self motivated individuals with drive and initiative who are able to apply a logical and common-sense approach to solving client problems. The firm is seeking applications from graduates/undergraduates in both law and non-law subjects, preferably with at least a 2:1 degree.

## training environment

Trainees spend six months in four different practice areas, and since each practice area handles a wide variety of work within its constituent teams, there is no danger of over-specialisation.

## open days

Four in total: two in Oxford and two in Cardiff, in April and July each year. Applications to be made online before 31 March 2006.

## sponsorship & awards

The firm offers full funding of fees for attendance on the CPE/PgDL and LPC as well as making a contribution towards maintenance.

# Nabarro Nathanson

Lacon House, Theobald's Road, London WC1X 8RW
Tel: (020) 7524 6000  Fax: (020) 7524 6524
Email: graduateinfo@nabarro.com
Website: www.nabarro.com

## firm profile
One of the UK's leading commercial law firms with offices in London and Sheffield. The firm is known for having an open but highly professional culture and expects its lawyers to have a life outside work.

## main areas of work
Company and commercial law; commercial property; planning; pensions and employment; corporate finance; IP/IT; commercial litigation; construction; PFI; environmental law.

## trainee profile
Nabarro Nathanson welcomes applications from undergraduates and graduates with law or non-law backgrounds. Candidates must be able to demonstrate strong intellectual ability through the achievement of at least an upper second at degree level or equivalent relevant experience. Applicants also need exceptional qualities including: enthusiasm, drive and initiative, common sense, strong interpersonal skills and team working skills.

## training environment
Trainees undertake six four-month seats which ensures maximum exposure to the firm's core practice areas (company commercial, commercial property and litigation). The firm aims to retain all trainees on qualification. In addition to the core seats, trainees have the opportunity to gain further experience by spending time in specialist areas (eg pensions, IP/IT, tax, employment), possibly in Brussels, or completing a further seat in a core area. In most cases trainees will return to the seat they wish to qualify into for the remaining four months of their contract. This ensures a smooth transition from trainee to qualified solicitor.

## benefits
Trainees are given private medical insurance, pension, 25 days holiday entitlement per annum, a season ticket loan, access to a subsidised restaurant and subsidised corporate gym membership. Trainee salaries are reviewed annually.

## vacation placements
Places for 2006: 60; Duration: 3 weeks between mid-June and end of August; Closing Date: 10 February 2006.

## sponsorship & awards
Full fees paid for GDL and LPC and a maintenance grant (London and Guildford: £5,000; elsewhere: £4,500).

| | |
|---|---|
| Partners | 115 |
| Assistant Solicitors | 225 |
| Total Trainees | 61 |

**contact**
Anna Roberts

**method of application**
Online application form

**selection procedure**
Interview & assessment day

**closing date for 2008**
31 July 2006

**application**
Training contracts p.a. **25**
Applications p.a. **1,500**
Required degree grade **2:1**

**training**
Salary
**1st year (2005)**
**London £28,000**
**Sheffield £20,000**
**2nd year (2005)**
**London £32,000**
**Sheffield £22,000**
Holiday entitlement **25 days**

**post-qualification**
Salary (2005)
**London £50,000**
**Sheffield £32,000**
(reviewed annually)

**overseas offices**
Brussels

# Norton Rose

Kempson House, Camomile Street, London EC3A 7AN
Tel: (020) 7283 6000  Fax: (020) 7283 6500
Email: grad.recruitment@nortonrose.com
Website: www.nortonrose.com/graduate

## firm profile

Norton Rose is a leading city and international law firm. They provide an integrated business law service from a network of offices located across Europe, Asia and the Middle East. The firm works primarily for international corporates and financial institutions on large, complex, cross-border transactions, offering them the full range of business legal services.

## main areas of work

Corporate finance; banking; dispute resolution; property, planning and environmental; taxation; competition and regulatory; employment, pensions and incentives; intellectual property and technology.

## trainee profile

Successful candidates will be commercially aware, focused, ambitious and team-orientated. High intellect and international awareness are a priority, and language skills are appreciated.

## training environment

Norton Rose operates an innovative six-seat system. The first four seats (16 months) include one seat in each of the firm's core departments - corporate finance, banking and dispute resolution - plus an optional seat in one of the firm's other, non-core departments - employment, pensions and incentives, tax, competition and EC, intellectual property and technology, or property, planning and environmental. The remaining eight months can be spent in the department in which you wish to qualify, or you can visit a different practice area for four months to help you to decide, and spend the last four months in your qualification seat. Alternatively, from your third seat onwards, you can elect to spend four months in one of the firm's international offices or apply for a client secondment. The firm's flexible seat system makes the transition from trainee to qualified solicitor as smooth as possible. The system has won the firm's trainees' approval, and from their point of view, develops associates with the adaptability and expertise the firm needs for its future.

## benefits

Life assurance (21+), private health insurance (optional), season ticket loan, subsidised gym membership.

## vacation placements

Places for 2005: 15 Christmas. Places for 2006: 45 summer and 15 Christmas; Duration: summer: Two weeks, Christmas: Two weeks; Remuneration: £250 p.w.; Closing Date: 31 October 2005 for Christmas 2005, 31 January 2006 for summer and 31 October 2006 for Christmas 2006. Five or six open days per year are also held.

## sponsorship & awards

£1,000 travel scholarship, £800 loan on arrival, four weeks unpaid leave on qualification. LPC/CPE fees paid plus up to £7,000 maintenance grant.

| Partners | 204* |
| Assistant Solicitors | 538* |
| Total Trainees | 129 |

*denotes worldwide figures*

**contact**
Ruth Edwards

**method of application**
Online only

**selection procedure**
Interview and group exercise

**closing date for 2008**
31 July 2006

**application**
Training contracts p.a. **60**
Applications p.a. **3,000+**
% interviewed p.a. **8%**
Required degree grade **2:1**

**training**
Salary
1st year **£28,500**
2nd year **£32,000**
Holiday entitlement **25 days**
% of trainees with a
non-law degree p.a. **40%**
No. of seats available
abroad p.a. **22 (per seat move)**

**overseas offices**
Amsterdam, Athens, Bahrain, Bangkok, Beijing, Brussels, Dubai, Frankfurt, Greece, Hong Kong, Jakarta,* London, Milan, Moscow, Munich, Paris, Piraeus, Prague, Rome, Singapore, Warsaw*
*Associated office*

# Olswang

90 High Holborn, London WC1V 6XX
Tel: (020) 7067 3000  Fax: (020) 7067 3999
Email: graduate@olswang.com
Website: www.olswang.com

## firm profile
Forward thinking and progressive, Olswang's ethos has always focused on realising the potential of its clients, of all of its people and the potential within every situation. The firm's aim is simple: to be the preferred law firm of leading companies in the technology, media, telecommunications and real estate sectors. Olswang knows the players, knows the business and above all, understands the issues. Established in 1981, the firm has a total staff of more than 500 and has offices in London, the Thames Valley and Brussels.

## main areas of work
Advertising; banking; bio-sciences; commercial litigation; corporate and commercial; media litigation; e-commerce; employment; EU and competition; film finance and production; information technology; intellectual property; music; private equity; real estate; sponsorship; sport; tax; telecommunications; TV/broadcasting.

## trainee profile
Being a trainee at Olswang is both demanding and rewarding. The firm is interested in hearing from individuals with a 2:1 degree and above, exceptional drive and relevant commercial experience. In addition, it is absolutely critical that trainees fit well into the Olswang environment which is challenging, busy, energetic, individualistic, meritocratic and fun.

## training environment
Olswang wants to help trainees match their expectations and needs with those of the firm. Training consists of four six-month seats in the corporate, media, communications and technology, litigation or real estate groups. You will be assigned a mentor, usually a partner, to assist and advise you throughout your training contract. In-house lectures supplement general training and three-monthly appraisals assess development. Regular social events not only encourage strong relationship building but add to the fun of work.

## benefits
Immediately: life cover, medical cover, dental scheme, subsidised gym membership, subsidised staff restaurant, season ticket loan. After six months: pension contributions. After 12 months: PHI.

## vacation placements
Places for 2006: June & July; Duration: 2 weeks; Remuneration: £250 p.w.; 17 students per scheme; Closing Date: 31 January 2006.

## sponsorship & awards
LPC and GDL fees paid in full. Maintenance grant of £4,500 (inside London), £4,000 (outside).

| Partners | 80 |
| Assistant Solicitors | 163 |
| Total Trainees | 39 |

**contact**
Victoria Edwards
Recruitment Manager

**method of application**
Online

**selection procedure**
Business case scenario, interview, psychometric test and written exercises

**closing date for 2008**
31 July 2006

**application**
Training contracts p.a. **20**
Applications p.a. **2,000**
% interviewed p.a. **4%**
Required degree grade **2:1**

**training**
Salary
**1st year (2004) £28,000**
**2nd year (2004) £32,000**
Holiday entitlement **24 days**
% of trainees with a non-law degree p.a. **50%**

**post-qualification**
Salary **(2004) £48,000**

**overseas offices**
Brussels

# Orrick, Herrington & Sutcliffe

Tower 42, Level 35, 25 Old Broad Street, London EC2N 1HQ
Tel: (020) 7562 5000  Fax: (020) 7628 0078
Email: mbartlam@orrick.com or lmacdonnell@orrick.com
Website: www.orrick.com

## firm profile

Orrick was founded in 1863 in San Francisco, California, and is now one of the world's leading international law firms. Orrick is known for its market-leading finance practices, as well as corporate, restructuring, intellectual property and litigation practices. The London office has particular expertise in structured finance, including securitisation, energy and project finance, global debt restructuring and corporate rescue, mergers & acquisitions, joint ventures, capital market transactions and general corporate matters, litigation & arbitration, real estate, tax, EU & UK competition law and employment. Much of Orrick's client work involves cross-border transactions which have increased substantially in recent years with the development of the firm's European network consisting of offices in London, Paris, Milan, Rome and Moscow.

## trainee profile

If you set your standards high, have a strong work ethic and are a bright, talented graduate of any discipline, early responsibility and broad-based experience is guaranteed. Applicants should have at least three A-level passes at grades A and B and a 2.1 degree.

## training environment

Orrick, Herrington & Sutcliffe is not a firm for every graduate: They value team players and reward collaboration over competition. They give individuals the opportunity to flourish in an unstuffy and lively work environment and encourage interaction among lawyers across international offices at every level of experience within the firm. They support learning through a steadfast focus on training and a mentoring programme that will provide you with the right foundation for building your legal career and for working with clients. There are regular appraisals throughout the two year training contract. Trainees work closely with fee earners and gain practical experience in research, drafting, procedural and client-related skills. The firm offers the benefits of a major international law firm providing leading practices in a variety of sectors with the opportunity for interaction in an informal office environment.

## benefits

Pension, health insurance, subsidised gym membership, season ticket loan, private medical insurance, and dental care.

## sponsorship & awards

PgDl: Funding: Fees paid plus £4,000 p.a. maintenance (discretionary).
LPC: Funding: Fees paid plus £4,000 p.a. maintenance (discretionary).

---

**Partners 17** (London)
**Assistants 24** (London)
**Total Trainees 6** (maximum)

**contact**
Martin Bartlam or
Lynda Macdonnell

**method of application**
Lettr & CV (by post or
email)

**selection procedure**
2 interviews with HR &
partners

**closing date for 2008**
31 July 2006

**application**
Training contracts p.a.6
Required degree grade 2:1

**training**
Salary (subject to review)
1st year: £28,000
2nd year: £32,000
Holiday entitlement 20 days

**Overseas offices**
London, Los Angeles,
Milan, Moscow, New
York, Paris, Pacific
Northwest, Orange
County, Rome,
Sacramento, San
Francisco, Silicon Valley,
Taipei, Tokyo and
Washington DC.

# Osborne Clarke

2 Temple Back East, Temple Quay, Bristol BS1 6EG
Tel: (0117) 917 4322
Email: graduate.recruitment@osborneclarke.com
Website: www.osborneclarke.com

| | |
|---|---:|
| **Partners** | 99 |
| **Solicitors** | 122 |
| **Trainee Solicitors** | 47 |
| **Total Staff** | 681 |

## firm profile

Committed to its clients' success, and with an energetic and unstuffy approach, Osborne Clarke is a European law firm that operates globally through its international network of legal businesses. The firm advises clients in a number of industry sectors: years of investment in gaining true insider knowledge across those sectors has enabled the firm to adapt its legal solutions to clients' business needs and to provide them with access to its envied networks. With traditional strength in transactions and advisory services, the firm's ability to operate as 'one office' across different locations enables it to offer contrasting capabilities: local focus and international expertise. One of the firm's defining features is its 'human touch': the open, collaborative and friendly working environment is what sets it apart, and is why the firm is commended for its individual approach.

## main areas of work

Corporate, finance and property transactions and the full spectrum of business law services, including commercial contracts, employment, outsourcing & dispute resolution. Industry sectors include: tech & telecoms; life sciences; natural resources; leisure & retail; business services; media.

## trainee profile

The firm recruits highly driven and motivated trainees who can demonstrate a clear commitment to a career in law. Candidates must have a high degree of commercial acumen, be able to demonstrate the ability to take on responsibility, and show initiative. The firm particularly values extra-curricular activities, which demonstrate effective communication and well developed teamwork skills. They look for a strong academic performance and candidates should have achieved, or expect to achieve at least a 2:1.

## training environment

The 2-year training programme is well structured and offers a blend of formal and practical on-the-job training. Trainees spend 6 months in 4 training seats, including one seat in corporate. This ensures that you gain a broad experience and exposure to different areas of law. Trainees will often undertake a seat in at least two of the firm's UK offices and may experience a secondment to the German or US offices. Training supervisors are assigned to each seat and provide day-to-day support through coaching, monitoring and the delegation of work. Regular three-month reviews are held with the training supervisor.

## benefits

25 days holiday entitlement, employers pension contributions, private healthcare cover, season ticket loan, permanent health insurance, group life assurance cover.

## vacation schemes

20 one-week placements in April or July, during which you will meet trainees, solicitors and partners, get involved with some real work and experience first-hand life at Osborne Clarke. Remuneration: £175 - £200 per week, depending on location. Applications should be made online by the 31 January 2006.

## sponsorship & awards

CPE/GDL and LPC course fees paid plus a maintenance grant for each, some conditions apply.

**contact**
Graduate Recruitment Team

**method of application**
Online application form

**selection procedure**
Assessment day: group & individual exercises, psychometric tests, partner interview and presentation exercise

**closing date for 2008**
31 July 2006

**application**
Training contracts p.a. **20**
Applications p.a. **1,000-1,500**
% interviewed p.a. **12%**
Required degree grade
**2:1**

**training**
Salary (2005/2006)
**1st year £28,000
London & Thames Valley,
£21,500 Bristol**
Holiday entitlement **25 days**
% of trainees with a non-law degree p.a. **Approx 40%**

**post-qualification**
Salary (2005/2006)
**£35,000 Bristol
£48,000 London
£43,000 Thames Valley**

**offices**
Bristol, Cologne, London, Munich, Silicon Valley, Thames Valley

**overseas offices**
Osborne Clarke Alliance Locations: Barcelona, Brescia, Brussels, Copenhagen, Helsinki, Madrid, Milan, Paris, Rome, Rotterdam, St Petersburg, Tallinn.

# Pannone & Partners

123 Deansgate, Manchester M3 2BU
Tel: (0161) 909 3000  Fax: (0161) 909 4444
Email: julia.jessop@pannone.co.uk
Website: www.pannone.com

## firm profile

A high profile Manchester firm continuing to undergo rapid growth. The firm prides itself on offering a full range of legal services to a diverse client base which is split almost equally between personal and commercial clients. The firm was the first to be awarded the quality standard ISO 9001 and is a founder member of Pannone Law Group – Europe's first integrated international law group. Pannone & Partners was voted 4th in the 'Sunday Times' 100 Best Companies to Work For in 2005 and is the highest placed law firm in the survey.

## main areas of work

Commercial litigation 19%; personal injury 31%; corporate 13%; commercial property 7%; family 8%; clinical negligence 7%; private client 9%; employment 6%.

## trainee profile

Selection criteria include a high level of academic achievement, teamwork, organisation and communication skills, a wide range of interests and a connection with the North West.

## training environment

An induction course helps trainees adjust to working life, and covers the firm's quality procedures and good practice. Regular trainee seminars cover the work of other departments within the firm, legal developments and practice. Additional departmental training sessions focus in more detail on legal and procedural matters in that department. Four seats of six months are spent in various departments and trainees' progress is monitored regularly. Trainees have easy access to support and guidance on any matters of concern. Work is tackled with gusto here, but so are the many social gatherings that take place.

## vacation placements

Places for 2006: 50; Duration: 1 week; Remuneration: None; Closing Date: Easter 27 January 2006, Summer 28 April 2006.

## sponsorship & awards

Full grant for LPC fees.

| | |
|---|---|
| **Partners** | 84 |
| **Assistant Solicitors** | 101 |
| **Total Trainees** | 25 |

**contact**
Julia Jessop

**method of application**
Online only

**selection procedure**
Individual interview, second interview comprises a tour of the firm & informal lunch

**closing date for 2008**
31 July 2006

**application**
Training contracts p.a. **14**
Applications p.a. **1200**
% interviewed p.a. **10%**
Required degree grade **2:1**

**training**
Salary
**1st year (2005) £21,000**
**2nd year (2005) £23,000**
Holiday entitlement **23 days**
% of trainees with a
non-law degree p.a. **30%**

**post-qualification**
Salary (2005) **£32,000**
% of trainees offered job
on qualification (2005) **80%**
% of assistants who joined
as trainees **35%**
% of partners who joined
as trainees **25%**

# Payne Hicks Beach

10 New Square, Lincoln's Inn, London WC2A 3QG
Tel: (020) 7465 4300  Fax: (020) 7465 4400
Email: lstoten@paynehicksbeach.co.uk
Website: www.paynehicksbeach.co.uk

## firm profile

Payne Hicks Beach is a medium-sized firm based in Lincoln's Inn. The firm acts for both private clients and businesses. It is highly rated for private client and matrimonial advice and also specialises in commercial litigation, property and corporate and commercial work.

## main areas of work

Private client 41%; matrimonial 22%; property 17%; commercial litigation 13%; corporate and commercial 7%.

## trainee profile

The firm looks for law and non-law graduates with a good academic record, an ability to solve practical problems, enthusiasm and an ability to work hard and deal appropriately with their colleagues and the firm's clients.

## training environment

Following an initial induction course, trainees usually spend six months in four of the firm's departments. Working with a partner, they are involved in the day to day activities of the department, including attending conferences with clients, counsel and other professional advisers. Assessment is continuous and trainees will be given responsibility as they demonstrate ability and aptitude. To complement the PSC, the firm runs a formal training system for trainees and requires them to attend lectures and seminars on various topics.

## benefits

Season travel ticket loan, life assurance 4 x salary, permanent health insurance, contribution to personal pension plan.

## sponsorship & awards

Fees for the CPE and LPC are paid.

| | |
|---|---|
| **Partners** | 28 |
| **Assistant Solicitors** | 21 |
| **Total Trainees** | 5 |

**contact**
Miss Louise Stoten

**method of application**
Letter & CV

**selection procedure**
Interview

**closing date for 2008**
1 August 2006

**application**
Training contracts p.a. **3**
Applications p.a. **1,000**
% interviewed p.a. **3%**
Required degree grade **2:1**

**training**
Salary
**1st year (2005) £27,500**
**2nd year (2005) £29,500**
Holiday entitlement
**4 weeks**
% of trainees with a
non-law degree p.a. **50%**

# Penningtons Solicitors LLP

Bucklersbury House, 83 Cannon Street, London EC4N 8PE
Tel: (020) 7457 3000  Fax: (020) 7457 3240
Website: www.penningtons.co.uk

## firm profile
Penningtons Solicitors LLP is a thriving, modern law firm with a 200-year history and a deep commitment to top quality, partner-led services. Today, the firm is based in London and the South East with offices in London, Basingstoke, Godalming and Newbury.

## main areas of work
In the business sphere, Penningtons advise on matters relating to all aspects of commercial property, intellectual property, management buy-outs and buy-ins, mergers, acquisitions and joint ventures, as well as dispute resolution. Advice is also given on information technology, business recovery, commercial contracts, agricultural and environmental law, and company secretarial services are offered. The firm also helps families and individuals with advice on property, tax and estate planning, family law, general financial management, the administration of wills and trusts, charities, personal injury, clinical negligence and immigration. Clients often ask Penningtons to advise on both their private and commercial affairs.

## trainee profile
Penningtons seeks high calibre candidates with enthusiasm and resilience. A high standard of academic achievement is expected: three or more good A level passes and preferably a 2:1 or better at degree level, whether you are reading law or another discipline.

## training environment
You will be given a thorough grounding in the law, spending time in three or four of the firm's departments - corporate and commercial, litigation, dispute resolution, property and private client. The firm ensures a varied training is given, avoiding too specialised an approach before qualification. Nonetheless, the experience gained in each department gives you a solid foundation, equipping you to embark on your chosen specialisation at the end of your training contract with the firm. Penningtons knows its trainee solicitors are happiest and most successful when busy with good quality work. The firm believes in introducing trainees to challenging cases. The value of giving its trainees responsibility, and allowing direct contact with clients is recognised. However, experienced solicitors are always ready to give support when needed.

## benefits
Life assurance, critical illness cover, pension, private medical insurance, 23 days holiday, interest free season ticket loan, sports and social events.

## vacation placements
The firm offers both summer vacation placements and information days. Applications are accepted from 1 December 2005 to 31 March 2006.

## sponsorship & awards
Full fees and maintenance for the LPC plus a maintenance grant of £4,000.

**Partners** 68*
**Assistant Solicitors** 120*
**Total Trainees** 26
*denotes worldwide figures

**contact**
Andrea Law

**method of application**
Online via firm's website

**closing date for 2008**
31 July 2006

**application**
Training contracts p.a. **12**
Applications p.a. **1,000**
% interviewed p.a. **5%**
Required degree grade **2:1**

**training**
Salary
**1st year (2005)**
£27,000 (London)
**2nd year (2005)**
£29,000 (London)
Holiday entitlement 23 days

# Pinsent Masons

30 Aylesbury Street, London, EC1R 0ER
Email: graduate@pinsentmasons.com
Website: www.pinsentmasons.com/graduate

| | |
|---|---|
| **Partners** | 260+ |
| **Lawyers** | 900 |
| **Total Trainees** | 110 |

## firm profile

Pinsent Masons is a top 15 UK law firm that is committed to sector-driven growth through an industry-recognised business model: the Chosen Markets Strategy. This strategy aligns the firm to specific business sectors to achieve market-leading positions. As a result, the firm has developed a successful and innovative approach to building strong, broad and deep corporate relationships. Client service is at the core of the firm and it works with a substantial range of FTSE 100, Fortune 500 and AIM quoted organisations as well as local and central government departments.

## main areas of work

Banking & Finance, Corporate, Dispute Resolution & Litigation, Employment, Insurance & Reinsurance, International Construction & Energy, Outsourcing, Technology and Commercial, Pensions, Projects, Property, Tax and UK Construction & Engineering.

## trainee profile

The firm welcomes applications from both law and non-law graduates with a good honours degree. In addition to a strong academic background, the firm is looking for people who can combine a sharp mind with commercial acumen and strong people skills to get to the very heart of their clients' businesses.

## training environment

Trainees sit in four seats of six months across the practices, and are supervised by partners or associates. There are also opportunities for trainees to be seconded to clients. There is a supportive team culture, with early responsibility and contact with clients encouraged.

In addition to the training required by the Law Societies, the firm offers a broad-ranging and custom-made training programme designed to deliver superb technical and management skills that link with the needs of the business. This is the first stage in the firm's focused development programme that supports individuals on the route to partnership.

The firm has an open-door policy and informal atmosphere with a positive focus on work-life balance.

## summer vacation placements

Places for 2006: 120; Duration: 2 weeks; Closing Date: 31 January 2006.

## sponsorship & awards

In England, a full sponsorship is offered for the CPE and LPC fees, as well as a maintenance grant. In Scotland, financial assistance is offered for Diploma fees.

**contact**
Kate Fergusson
Recruitment Hotline:
(0845) 300 3232

**method of application**
Online application form

**selection procedure**
Assessment day including interview

**closing date for 2008**
31 July 2006 (English offices) and 21 October 2006 (Scottish offices)

**application**
Training contracts p.a. **55**
Applications p.a. **2,000+**
Required degree grade **2:1**

**training**
Salary
1st year (2005) £28,000 (London)
2nd year (2005) £32,000 (London)
Holiday entitlement **25 days**

**post-qualification**
Salary (2005)
£48,000 (London)
% of trainees offered job on qualification (2005) **88%**

**UK offices**
London, Birmingham, Bristol, Edinburgh, Glasgow, Leeds, Manchester

Pinsent Masons

# Prettys

Elm House, 25 Elm Street, Ipswich IP1 2AD
Tel: (01473) 232121  Fax: (01473) 230002
Email: agage@prettys.co.uk
Website: www.prettys.co.uk

## firm profile

Prettys is one of the largest and most successful legal practices in East Anglia. The firm is at the heart of the East Anglian business community, with the expanding hi-tech corridor between Ipswich and Cambridge to the west, Felixstowe to the east and the City of London 60 minutes away to the south. The firm's lawyers are approachable and pragmatic. It provides expert advice to national and regional businesses.

## main areas of work

Prettys' broad-based practice allows it to offer a full-service to all its clients. Business law services: company, commercial, shipping, transport, construction, intellectual property, information technology, property, property litigation, employment, commercial litigation, insurance, professional indemnity, health and safety and executive immigration. Personal law services: French property, personal injury, clinical negligence, financial services, estates, agriculture, conveyancing and family.

## trainee profile

Prettys' trainees are the future of the firm. Applicants should be able to demonstrate a desire to pursue a career in East Anglia. Trainees are given considerable responsibility early on and the firm is therefore looking for candidates who are well motivated, enthusiastic and have a good common sense approach. Good IT skills are essential.

## training environment

A two-week induction programme will introduce you to the firm. You will receive continuous supervision and three-monthly reviews. Training is in four six-month seats. Trainees work closely with a partner, meeting clients and becoming involved in all aspects of the department's work. Frequent training seminars are provided in-house. The PSC is taken externally. The Law Society's Monitoring of Training Officer recently visited the firm and concluded "Prettys offers a very strong commitment to training within a supportive environment."

## additional information

One day placements are available (apply to Angela Gage).

## sponsorship & awards

Grants available to support LPC.

| Partners | 16 |
| Total Trainees | 10 |

**contact**
Angela Gage
Human Resources Manager

**method of application**
Application letter & CV

**closing date for 2008**
July 31 2006

**application**
Training contracts p.a. **5**
Required degree grade
**2:1 preferred in law or other relevant subject.**
**Good A Levels**

**training**
Salary
**Above Law Society guidelines**

Holiday entitlement **25 days**

**post-qualification**
% of trainees offered job on qualification (2004) **80%**

# Pritchard Englefield

14 New St, London EC2M 4HE
Tel: (020) 7972 9720  Fax: (020) 7972 9722
Email: po@pe-legal.com
Website: www.pe-legal.com

## firm profile

A niche City firm practising a mix of general commercial and non-commercial law with many German and French clients. Despite its strong commercial departments, the firm still undertakes family and private client work and is renowned for its ever-present international flavour.

## main areas of work

All main areas of commercial practice including litigation, commercial/corporate/banking (UK, German and French), IP/IT, property and employment, also estate and trusts (UK and off-shore), pensions, charities, personal injury and family.

## trainee profile

High academic achievers with fluent German and/or French.

## training environment

An induction course acquaints trainees with the computer network, online library and finance & administrative procedures and there is a formal in-house training programme during the first week. Four six-month seats make up most of your training. You can usually choose some departments, and you could spend two six-month periods in the same seat. Over two years, you learn advocacy, negotiating, drafting and interviewing, attend court, use your language skills every day and meet clients from day one. Occasional talks and seminars explain the work of the firm, and you can air concerns over bi-monthly lunches with the partners comprising the Trainee Panel. PSC is taken externally over two years. The Social Committee of the firm organises regular drinks parties, French film evenings, quiz nights and of course a Christmas party.

## benefits

Some subsidised training, monthly luncheon vouchers, and eligibility for membership of the firm's private medical insurance scheme as well as an interest free loan for an annual season ticket.

## sponsorship & awards

Full funding for LPC fees.

| | |
|---|---|
| Partners | 22 |
| Assistant Solicitors | 8 |
| Other Fee Earners | 12 |
| Total Trainees | 6 |

**contact**
Graduate Recruitment

**method of application**
Standard application form available from Graduate Recruitment or online

**selection procedure**
1 interview only in September

**closing date for 2008**
31 July 2006

**application**
Training contracts p.a. **3**
Applications p.a. **300–400**
% interviewed p.a. **10%**
Required degree grade **Generally 2:1**

**training**
Salary
**1st year (2004) £21,750**
**2nd year (2004) £22,250**
Holiday entitlement **25 days**
% of trainees with a non-law degree p.a. **Approx 50%**

**post-qualification**
Salary (2004)
**Approx £40,000**
% of trainees offered job on qualification (2002) **75%**
% of assistants (as at 1/9/03) who joined as trainees **50%**
% of partners (as at 1/9/03) who joined as trainees **40%**

# Reed Smith

Minerva House, 5 Montague Close SE1 9BB
Tel: (020) 7403 2900  Fax: (020) 7403 4221
Email: rgrewal@reedsmith.com
Website: www.reedsmith.com

## firm profile

Reed Smith is a leading international law firm and one of the 25 largest firms worldwide. The firm has grown rapidly over the past few years through a series of strategic mergers and lateral additions, with the result that it now has over 1,000 lawyers located in 17 cities throughout the United States, the UK and Europe. The firm has a strong presence on both the east and west coasts and its transatlantic capabilities mean it is strategically positioned to provide teams of US and UK lawyers who work together on major transactions crossing both continents.

## main areas of work

Its core services in the UK are European corporate, which encompasses a full corporate/commercial service including financial services, corporate finance, competition, M&A, reinsurance and corporate tax, litigation, employment and real estate.

## trainee profile

Enthusiastic, proactive, bright, commercially-minded graduates who want to work in a friendly atmosphere where personality, a sense of humour and a hands-on approach are encouraged.

## training environment

To help trainees build a strong career, the firm invests heavily in training (approximately one training session per week) covering a range of skills including advocacy, drafting and marketing. The firm provides an informal but fast-paced working environment where trainees are immediately given access to clients and fulfilling work, often with an international bias. Trainees who are fluent French and German speakers will be given opportunities to develop these skills. The firm has four seats available in European corporate, international litigation, real estate and employment.

## benefits

BUPA, IFSTL, life assurance, permanent health insurance & pension contribution.

## vacation placements

The summer placement programme is designed to offer graduates the chance to get a taste for life at Reed Smith. It is also an excellent opportunity for the firm to meet with prospective trainees in a relaxed and constructive environment and to provide them with a realistic representation of what trainee life may be like. The firm invites 12 students to experience mini-seats in European corporate, litigation and employment or real estate. Applicants should apply online before 31 January 2006. Places for Summer 2006: 12; Duration: 3 weeks (London), 2 weeks (Midlands); Remuneration: £600 (London), £300 (Midlands); Closing Date: 31 January 2006.

## sponsorship & awards

The firm will pay course fees for the CPE/GDL and LPC courses. A maintenance grant will also be provided to the value of £4,000 for CPE/GDL studies and £5,000 during LPC studies.

---

| | |
|---|---|
| **Partners** | **38** |
| **Assistant Solicitors** | **34** |
| **Total Trainees** | **14** |
| over 1,000 lawyers internationally | |

**contact**
Ms Rani Grewal
Recruitment Co-ordinator

**method of application**
Online

**selection procedure**
Assessment day:
2 interviews, aptitude test
& presentation

**closing date for 2008**
31 July 2006

**application**
Training contracts p.a.
**8 (London 6, Coventry 2)**
Applications p.a. **700**
% interviewed p.a. **3%**
Required degree grade **2:2**
**(any discipline)**

**training**
Salary
London
**1st year (2008) £28,000**
**2nd year (2008) £32,000**
**Coventry**
**1st year (2008) £19,500**
**2nd year (2008) £22,000**
Holiday entitlement **25 days**
% of trainees with a non-law
degree **25%**

**post-qualification**
Salary (2005) **£49,000**

# Reynolds Porter Chamberlain

Chichester House, 278-282 High Holborn, London WC1V 7HA
Tel: (020) 7242 2877  Fax: (020) 7242 1431
Email: training@rpc.co.uk
Website: www.rpc.co.uk/training

## firm profile

Reynolds Porter Chamberlain is a leading commercial law firm with approximately 250 lawyers. Based in central London, RPC is best known as a major litigation practice, particularly in the field of insurance and dispute resolution. They also have highly rated corporate, commercial property and construction deprtments. Their range of activities does not stop there however as another rapidly expanding part of the firm is its media practice. This handles defamation actions and has dealt with some of the biggest internet deals to date. In 2006, the firm's two London offices are coming together in one building near Tower Bridge.

## main areas of work

Litigation 60%; corporate 15%; commercial property 10%; construction 10%; media and technology 10%.

## trainee profile

The firm appoints 15 trainees each year from law and non-law backgrounds. Although proven academic ability is important (the firm requires a 2:1 or above), RPC also values flair, energy, business sense, commitment and the ability to communicate and relate well to others.

## training environment

As a trainee you will receive first rate training in a supportive working environment. You will work closely with a partner and be given real responsibility as soon as you are ready to handle it. At least six months will be spent in each of the three main areas of the practice and the firm encourages trainees to express a preference for their seats. This provides a thorough grounding and the chance to develop confidence as you see matters through to their conclusion. In addition to the internally provided Professional Skills Course the firm provides a complimentary programme of in-house training.

## benefits

Four weeks holiday, bonus schemes, private medical insurance, income protection benefits, pension, season ticket loan, subsidised gym membership, active social calendar.

## vacation placements

Places for Summer 2006: 18; Duration: 2 weeks; Remuneration: £250 p.w.; Closing Date: February 2006.

## sponsorship & awards

CPE/PgDL Funding: Fees paid plus £4,500 maintenance; LPC Funding: Fees paid plus £4,500 maintenance.

| | |
|---|---|
| **Partners** | 65 |
| **Assistant Solicitors** | 250 |
| **Total Trainees** | 22 |

**contact**
Kate Gregg
Graduate Recruitment
Officer

**method of application**
Online application system

**selection procedure**
Assessment days held in
September

**closing date for 2008**
11 August 2006

**application**
Training contracts  p.a. **15**
Applications p.a. **900**
% interviewed p.a. **6%**
Required degree grade **2:1**

**training**
Salary
**1st year  (2005) £28,000**
**2nd year (2005) £30,000**
Holiday entitlement **20 days**
% of trainees with a non-law
degree p.a. **Approx 25%**

**post-qualification**
Salary (2005) **£48,000**
% of trainees offered job
on qualification (2003) **80%**
% of assistants (as at
1/9/03) who joined as
trainees **30%**
% of partners (as at 1/9/03)
who joined as trainees **35%**

# Richards Butler

Beaufort House, 15 St. Botolph Street, London, EC3A 7 EE
Tel: (020) 7247 6555  Fax: (020) 7247 5091
Email: gradrecruit@richardsbutler.com

## firm profile
Established in 1920, Richards Butler is noted for the exceptional variety of its work. It has acknowledged strengths in commercial disputes, commodities, competition, corporate finance, energy law, insurance, media/entertainment, property and shipping, in each of which it has international prominence. Over two thirds of the firm's work has an international dimension.

## main areas of work
Banking/commercial/corporate finance 26%; insurance/international trade and commodities/shipping 28%; commercial disputes 30%; commercial property 16%.

## trainee profile
Candidates should be players rather than onlookers, work well under pressure and be happy to operate as a team member or team leader as circumstances dictate. Candidates from diverse backgrounds are welcome, including mature students with commercial experience and management skills.

## training environment
Four or five seat rotations enable Richards Butler to provide practical experience across as wide a spectrum of the law as possible. Trainees can also apply for secondment to one of the firm's overseas offices, Hong Kong, Paris, Abu Dhabi, Piraeus or to one of their client's in-house legal teams.

## benefits
Performance related bonus, life insurance, BUPA, interest-free season ticket loan, subsidised staff restaurant, staff conveyancing allowance.

## vacation placements
Places for 2006: 30; Duration: 2 weeks; Remuneration: £220 p.w.; Closing date: 31 January 2006. In addition, the firm offers overseas scholarships to Paris, Hong Kong, Abu Dhabi and Piraeus. The scholarship consists of a return airfare, accommodation, living expenses and two weeks of work experience. Please see website for further information.

## sponsorship & awards
CPE Funding: Fees paid plus £6,000 maintenance with effect from September 2006.
LPC Funding: Fees paid plus £6,000 maintenance with effect from September 2006.

---

| | |
|---|---|
| Partners | 104* |
| Fee-earners | 400* |
| Total Trainees | 64* |

*\* denotes worldwide figures*

**contact**
Mark Matthews

**method of application**
Online application form

**selection procedure**
Selection exercise & interview

**closing date for 2008/09**
31 July 2006

**application**
Training contracts p.a. **20**
Applications p.a. **2,000**
% interviewed p.a. **5%**
Required degree grade **2:1**

**training**
Salary
**1st year (2005) £29,000**
**2nd year (2005) £32,000**
Holiday entitlement **25 days**
% of trainees with a
non-law degree p.a. **25%**
No. of seats available
abroad p.a. **10**

**post-qualification**
Salary (2005
**£48,000 plus bonus**
% of assistants who
joined as trainees **59%**
% of partners who
joined as trainees **48%**

**overseas offices**
**Abu Dhabi, Beijing,
Brussels, Hong Kong,
Muscat\*, Paris, Piraeus,
São Paulo**
**\* Associated office**

# Salans

Millennium Bridge House, 2 Lambeth Hill, London EC4V 4AJ
Tel: (020) 7429 6000  Fax: (020) 7429 6001
Email: london@salans.com

## firm profile

Salans has an open and friendly culture with an informal, but hardworking environment. It is a multinational law firm with full-service offices in the City of London, Paris and New York, together with further offices in Almaty, Baku, Bratislava, Bucharest, Istanbul, Kyiv, Moscow, Prague, Shanghai, St Petersburg and Warsaw, and an affiliated office in Budapest. The firm currently has over 570 fee-earners, including 120 partners worldwide, with 30 partners residing in the London office. Salans was named East European Law Firm of the Year at the Chambers Awards 2004, and were runners-up in the Employment Team of the Year award at The Lawyer Awards 2005. Their Banking and Finance Team advised on the Trade Finance Deal of the Year 2004 which was announced summer 2005.

## main areas of work

**London Office:** Banking and finance; corporate; litigation; employment; real estate; insolvency and corporate recovery; information technology and communications; betting and gaming; and media and film finance.

## trainee profile

You will have high academic qualifications, including good A-Level (or equivalent) results, and the ability to approach complex problems in a practical and commercial way. The firm is looking for highly motivated, creative and enthusiastic team players. It looks to recruit trainees who make a difference, want early responsibility and live life in the fast lane of the ever-changing legal world. Relevant work experience demonstrating a desire to pursue a career in law will be viewed positively, and language and computer skills are also valued.

## benefits

Private healthcare, pension, life assurance, critical illness cover, season ticket loan.

## sponsorship & awards

LPC tuition fees paid.

---

**Partners** (Worldwide) 120
**Assistant Solicitors** (Worldwide) 280+
**Total Trainees** (London) 8

**contact**
Vicky Williams
HR Manager

**method of application**
Handwritten letter & CV

**selection procedure**
interview programme and selection workshop

**closing date for 2008**
31 July 2006

**application**
Training contracts p.a. **3-4**
Applications p.a. **500+**
% interviewed p.a. **3%**
Required degree grade **2:1**

**training**
Salary
**1st year (2005) £27,000**
**2nd year (2005) £29,000**
Holiday entitlement **25 days**
% of trainees with a
non-law degree p.a. **Variable**
No. of seats available
abroad p.a. **None at present**

**post-qualification**
Salary (2005) **Variable**
% of trainees offered job
on qualification (2005) **100%**

**overseas offices**
Almaty, Baku, Bratislava, Bucharest, Budapest*, Istanbul, Kyiv, Moscow, New York, Paris, Prague, Shanghai, St Petersburg and Warsaw

*affiliated office

# Shadbolt & Co LLP

Chatham Court, Lesbourne Road, Reigate RH2 7LD
Tel: (01737) 226277  Fax: (01737) 226165
Email: recruitment@shadboltlaw.com
Website: www.shadboltlaw.com

## firm profile
Shadbolt & Co LLP is an award-winning, dynamic, progressive firm committed to high quality work and excellence both in the UK and internationally. The atmosphere at the firm is friendly, relaxed and informal and there are various social and sporting activities for staff. The firm comprises a lively and enterprising team with a fresh and open approach to work. The firm's qualified staff have a high level of experience and industry knowledge and some are widely regarded as leading practitioners in their field.

## main areas of work
The firm is well known for its strengths in major projects, construction and engineering and dispute resolution and litigation with established expansion into corporate and commercial, employment, commercial property and IT and e-commerce. The firm provides prompt personal service and its client list includes some of the world's best known names in the construction and engineering industries.

## trainee profile
Applicants must demonstrate that they are mature self-starters with a strong academic background and outside interests. Leadership, ambition, initiative, enthusiasm and good interpersonal skills are essential, as is the ability to play an active role in the future of the firm. Linguists are particularly welcome, as are those with supporting professional qualifications. The firm welcomes non-law graduates.

## training
Four six month seats from construction and commercial litigation, arbitration and dispute resolution, major projects and construction, employment, corporate and commercial and commercial property. Where possible individual preference is noted. Work has an international bias. There are opportunities for secondment to major clients and work in the overseas offices. Trainees are treated as valued members of the firm, expected to take early responsibility and encouraged to participate in all the firm's activities, including practice development. The firm is accredited by the law society as a provider of training and runs frequent in-house lectures. The PSC is taught externally.

## sponsorship & benefits
Optional private healthcare, permanent health insurance, group life assurance, paid study leave, season ticket loan, discretionary annual bonus of up to 5% of salary, paid professional memberships and subscriptions, 50% refund of LPC upon commencement of training contract.

## vacation placements
Places for 2006: 6; Duration: 2 weeks; Remuneration (2005): £188 p.w.; Closing Date: 28 February 2006; Interviews: March 2006.

| Partners | 24 |
|---|---|
| Assistant Solicitors | 17 |
| Total Trainees | 10 |
| Total Staff | 119 |

**contact**
Andrea Pickett

**method of application**
Online application form

**selection procedure**
Interview (1) written assessment & group exercise

**closing date for 2008**
31 July 2006 (interviews September 2006)

**application**
Training contracts p.a. **4**
Applications p.a. **100**
% interviewed p.a. **20%**
Required degree grade **2:1 (occasional exceptions)**

**training**
Salary
**1st year (2005) £25,000**
**2nd year (2005) £29,000**
Holiday entitlement **20 days rising to 25 on qualification, with opportunity to 'buy' an additional 5 days holiday p.a.**
% of trainees with a non-law degree p.a. **50%**
No. of seats available abroad p.a. **1**

**post-qualification**
Salary (2005) **£43,000**
% of trainees offered job on qualification (2005) **100%**
% of assistants (2005) who joined as trainees **40%**
% of partners (2005) who joined as trainees **0%**

**other offices**
Reigate, City of London, Paris, Dar es Salaam, Athens

**Shadbolt & Co** LLP
Solicitors

# Shearman & Sterling LLP

Broadgate West, 9 Appold Street, London EC2A 2AP
Tel: (020) 7655 5000  Fax: (020) 7655 5500

## firm profile
Shearman & Sterling LLP is one of New York's oldest legal partnerships, which has transformed from a New York-based firm focused on banking into a diversified global institution. Recognised throughout the world, the firm's reputation, skills and expertise are second to none in its field. The London office, established in 1972, has become a leading practice covering all aspects of English and European corporate and finance law. The firm employs over 140 English and US trained legal staff in London and has more than 1,000 lawyers in 19 offices worldwide.

## main areas of work
Banking, leveraged finance and securitisation. Project finance. M&A. Global capital markets. International arbitration and litigation. Tax. EU and competition. Financial Institutions Advisory & asset management (legal and regulatory advice to financial instititions and infrastructure providers, both in a retail and wholesale context, and both on-line and off-line). Executive compensation & employee benefits (sophisticated advice on the design and implementation of compensation and benefits arrangements). Intellectual property. Real estate.

## trainee profile
The firm's successful future development calls for people who will relish the hard work and intellectual challenge of today's commercial world. You will be a self-starter, keen to assume professional responsibility early in your career and determined to become a first-class lawyer in a first-class firm. The firm's two year training programme will equip you with all the skills needed to become a successful commercial lawyer. You will spend six months in each of four practice areas, with an opportunity to spend six months in Abu Dhabi, Brussels, Hong Kong or Singapore. You will be an integral part of the London team from the outset, with your own laptop, Blackberry and mobile phone. The firm will expect you to contribute creatively to all the transactions you are involved in. The firm has an informal yet professional atmosphere. Your enthusiasm, intellect and energy will be more important than what you wear to work. The firm will provide you with a mentor, arrange personal and professional development courses and give you early responsibility. The firm wants to recruit people who will stay with it; people who want to become partners in its continuing success story.

## sponsorship & awards
Sponsorship for the CPE/PgDL and LPC courses, together with a maintenance grant of £5,000.

| | |
|---|---|
| **Partners** | 26 |
| **Assistant Solicitors** | 96 |
| **Total Trainees** | 17 |

**contact**
Kirsten Davies
Tel: (020) 7655 5082

**method of application**
Application form

**selection procedure**
Interviews

**closing date for 2008**
31 July 2006

**application**
Training contracts p.a. **15**
Required degree grade **2:1**

**training**
Salary
**1st year (2004) £35,000**
**2nd year (2004) £37,500**
Holiday entitlement
**24 days p.a.**
% of trainees with non-law degree p.a. **40%**
No of seats available abroad **4**

**post-qualification**
Salary (2005) **£60,000**
% of trainees offered job on qualification (2005) **100%**

**overseas offices**
Abu Dhabi, Bejing, Brussels, Düsseldorf, Frankfurt, Hong Kong, Mannheim, Menlo Park, Munich, New York, Paris, Rome, San Francisco, Sao Paulo, Singapore, Tokyo, Toronto, Washington DC

# Shoosmiths

The Lakes, Bedford Road, Northampton NN4 7SH
Tel: (0870) 086 3223  Fax: (0870) 086 3001
Email: join.us@shoosmiths.co.uk
Website: www.shoosmiths.co.uk/careers

## firm profile

Growing steadily, with seven offices across the country, 72 partners and 1,200 staff, Shoosmiths is one of the big players outside London. By joining the firm you can expect to experience a full range of interesting and challenging commercial work. In a demanding legal market, Shoosmiths has developed exciting, even radical, services helping it to exceed the highest expectations of its clients. The firm supports and encourages its people to develop exhilarating, balanced careers. Shoosmiths' workplace culture offers a stimulating environment, time for family and the opportunity to put something back into the community.

## main areas of work

Corporate/commercial; commercial property; dispute resolution; employment; planning; banking; financial institutions; private client; personal injury.

## trainee profile

You will be confident, motivated and articulate with natural intelligence and the drive to succeed, thereby making a real contribution to the firm's commercial success. You will want to be a part of a winning team and will care about the kind of service you give to your clients, both internal and external.

## training environment

You will be involved in 'real' work from day one of your training contract. Sitting with a Partner who will oversee your training and career development, you will have direct contact with clients and will draft your own letters and documents. Your experience will build through your daily, practical, workload complemented by the training you would expect from a leading national law firm. In addition to the compulsory Professional Skills Course, the firm offers a comprehensive internal training programme that includes managerial, legal and IT training as standard. Over the course of two years, you will complete four seats of six month duration to help you decide which area you would like to qualify into.

## benefits

Flexible holidays, pension (after 3 months service), life assurance, various staff discounts, Christmas bonus.

## vacation placements

Places for 2006: 30; Duration: 2 weeks; Remuneration: £230 p.w.; Closing Date: 28 Feb 2006.

## sponsorship & awards

LPC funding: £13,000 – split between fees and maintenance.

| | |
|---|---|
| **Partners** | 82 |
| **Assistant Solicitors** | 250 |
| **Total Trainees** | 28 |

**contact**
Sarah Woods

**method of application**
Application form via website

**selection procedure**
Selection centre - full day

**closing date for 2008**
31 July 2006

**application**
Training contracts p.a. **14**
Applications p.a. **1,000**
% interviewed p.a. **10%**
Required degree grade **2:1**

**training**
Salary
**Market Rate**
Holiday entitlement
**23 days + option to flex**

**post-qualification**
Salary **Market rate**

**offices**
Northampton, Nottingham, Reading, Solent, Milton Keynes, Basingstoke, Birmingham

# Sidley Austin Brown & Wood

Woolgate Exchange, 25 Basinghall Street, London EC2V 5HA
Tel: (020) 7360 3600  Fax: (020) 7626 7937
Email: itabraham@sidley.com
Website: www.sidley.com

## firm profile

Sidley Austin Brown & Wood is one of the world's largest full-service law firms combining the strengths of two exceptional law firms. With more than 1,550 lawyers practising in 13 offices on three continents (North America, Europe and Asia), the firm provides a broad range of integrated services to meet the needs of its clients across a multitude of industries. The firm has over 90 lawyers in London and is expanding fast.

## main areas of work

Corporate securities; corporate finance; investment funds; tax; banking regulation; securitisation and structured finance; corporate reconstruction; property and property finance.

## trainee profile

Sidley Austin Brown & Wood is looking for focused, intelligent and enthusiastic individuals with personality and humour who have a real interest in practising law in the commercial world. Trainees should have a 2:1 degree (not necessarily in law) and three A levels at A and B grades. Trainees would normally be expected to pass the CPE (if required) and the LPC at the first attempt.

## training environment

Sidley Austin Brown & Wood is looking to recruit six to eight trainee solicitors to start in 2008. The firm is not a typical City firm and it is not a 'legal factory' so there is no risk of being just a number. The team in London is young, dynamic and collegiate. Everyone is encouraged to be proactive and to create their own niche when they are ready to do so. Trainees spend a period of time in the firm's specialist groups: international finance, tax and property. Sidley Austin Brown & Wood in London does not have a separate litigation department, although some litigation work is undertaken. The firm does, however, organise external litigation training for all trainees. In each group trainees will sit with a partner or senior associate to ensure that students receive individual training that is both effective and based on a real caseload. In addition, there is a structured timetable of training on a cross-section of subjects and an annual training weekend.

## benefits

Healthcare, disability cover, life assurance, contribution to gym membership, interest-free season ticket loan.

## sponsorship & awards

CPE and LPC fees paid and maintenance p.a.

| | |
|---|---|
| **Partners** | 34 |
| **Assistant Solicitors** | 65 |
| **Total Trainees** | 13 |

**contact**
Isabel Tabraham, Legal and Graduate Recruitment Manager

**method of application**
Covering letter & employee application form

**selection procedure**
Interview(s)

**closing date for 2008**
28 July 2006

**application**
Training contracts p.a. **6-8**
Applications p.a. **500**
% interviewed p.a. **15**
Required degree grade **2:1**

**training**
Salary
**1st year (2005) £29,000**
**2nd year (2005) £33,000**
Holiday entitlement **25 days**
% of trainees with a
non-law degree p.a. **50%**

**overseas offices**
Beijing, Brussels, Chicago, Dallas, Geneva, Hong Kong, London, Los Angeles, New York, San Francisco, Shanghai, Singapore, Tokyo, Washington DC

# Simmons & Simmons

CityPoint, One Ropemaker Street, London EC2Y 9SS
Tel: (020) 7628 2020  Fax: (020) 7628 2070
Email: recruitment@simmons-simmons.com
Website: www.simmons-simmons.com

## firm profile

Simmons & Simmons is a leading international law firm with over 1,000 legal staff in 20 business and financial centres across Asia, Europe, the Middle East and the US. They believe it is their unique approach to their work that sets them apart from the competition - and led to them being the only law firm to be awarded the Queen's Award for Enterprise in the International Trade category.

## main areas of work

Their core practice areas are commercial, corporate, dispute resolution, EU & competition, employment, finance, IP, projects, real estate, and environment and tax.

## trainee profile

A strong academic track record is essential. Whether you have studied a law or a non-law degree, the firm will expect at least a 2:1 or its equivalent. And as they will be expecting you to fit in well and work closely with energetic, focused teams around the world, they will be looking for evidence of a well rounded set of skills and competencies.

## training environment

The firm has devised training programmes to develop you and enable you to attain the highest standards of excellence. They will give you experience in a range of areas of law to ensure that you take a balanced approach to gaining the knowledge, expertise and abilities you will need to qualify into the practice area of your choice.

## benefits

Include future trainees loan, season ticket loan, gym loan, group travel insurance, group accident insurance, death in service, medical cover, subsidised staff restaurant.

## vacation placements

Vacation scheme opportunities available. Deadline: 31 January 2006.

## sponsorship & awards

In the absence of local authority funding, the firm will cover your tuition fees at law school. The firm will also give you a maintenance allowance to help cover your expenses.

| | |
|---|---|
| **Partners** | 202 |
| **Assistant Solicitors** | 565 |
| **Total Trainees** | 172 |

**contact**
Vickie Chamberlain
Graduate Recruitment
Manager

**method of application**
Online application

**selection procedure**
Assessment days:
document exercise,
interview & written exercise

**closing date for 2008**
31 July 2006

**application**
Training contracts p.a. **50**
Applications p.a. **2,500**
% interviewed p.a. **15%**
Required degree grade **2:1**

**training**
Salary
1st year (2005) **£28,000**
2nd year (2005) **£32,000**
Holiday entitlement **25 days**
% of trainees with a
non-law degree p.a. **50%**
No. of seats available
abroad p.a. **26**

**post-qualification**
Salary (2005) **£50,000**
% of trainees offered job
on qualification (2005) **70%**

**overseas offices**
Abu Dhabi, Brussels,
Dubai, Düsseldorf,
Frankfurt, Hong Kong,
Lisbon, London, Madeira,
Madrid, Milan, New York,
Oporto, Padua, Paris,
Qatar, Rome, Rotterdam,
Shanghai, Tokyo, plus
Beijing opening later this
year.

# Slaughter and May

One Bunhill Row, London EC1Y 8YY
Tel: (020) 7600 1200  Fax: (020) 7090 5000
Email: grad.recruit@slaughterandmay.com (enquiries only)
Website: www.slaughterandmay.com

## firm profile

One of the leading law firms in the world, Slaughter and May enjoys a reputation for quality and expertise. The corporate, commercial and financing practice is particularly strong and lawyers are known for their business acumen and technical excellence. As well as its London office, in order that the firm provides the best advice and service across the world, it nurtures long-standing relationships with the leading independent law firms in other jurisdictions.

## main areas of work

Corporate, commercial and financing; tax; competition; financial regulation; dispute resolution; technology, media and telecommunications; intellectual property; commercial real estate; environment; pensions and employment.

## trainee profile

The work is demanding and the firm looks for intellectual agility and the ability to work with people from different countries and walks of life. Common sense, a mature outlook, the ability to communicate clearly and the willingness to accept responsibility are all essential. The firm expects to provide training in everything except the fundamental principles of law, so does not expect applicants to know much of commercial life. Trainees are expected to remain with the firm on qualification.

## training environment

Four or five seats of three or six months duration. Two seats will be in the field of corporate, commercial and financing law with an option to choose a posting overseas (either to one of the firm's offices or to a "best friend" firm), or competition or financial regulation. One seat in either dispute resolution, intellectual property, tax or pensions and employment is part of the programme and a commercial real estate seat is also possible. In each seat a partner is responsible for monitoring your progress and reviewing your work. There is an extensive training programme which includes the PSC. There are also discussion groups covering general and specialised legal topics.

## benefits

BUPA, STL, pension scheme, subsidised membership of health club, 24 hour accident cover.

## vacation placements - summer 2006

Places: 60; Duration: 2 weeks; Remuneration: £275 p.w.; Closing Date: 27 January 2006 for penultimate year (of first degree) students only.

## sponsorship & awards

CPE and LPC fees and maintenance grants are paid.

| | |
|---|---|
| **Partners** | 130 |
| **Associates** | 427 |
| **Total Trainees** | 185 |

**contact**
Charlotte Houghton

**method of application**
Online (via website) preferred or by posting to the firm a CV and covering letter

**selection procedure**
Interview

**application**
Training contracts p.a.
**Approx 85**
Applications p.a. **2,000+**
% interviewed p.a. **25%**
Required standard
**Good 2:1 ability**

**training**
Salary (May 2005)
**1st year £29,500**
**2nd year £33,000**
Holiday entitlement
**25 days p.a.**
% of trainees with a non-law degree **Approx 50%**
No. of seats available abroad p.a. **Approx 30-40**

**post-qualification**
Salary (May 2005) **£51,000**
% of trainees offered job on qualification (2005) **96%+**

**overseas offices**
Paris, Brussels and Hong Kong.

# Speechly Bircham

6 St Andrew Street, London EC4A 3LX
Tel: (020) 7427 6400  Fax: (020) 7353 4368
Email: trainingcontracts@speechlys.com
Website: www.speechlys.com

## firm profile
Speechly Bircham is a mid-sized City law firm with an excellent client base. Its strong commercial focus is complemented by a highly regarded private client practice. The firm handles major transactions as well as commercial disputes. It regularly handles work of a quality and complexity which is unusual for a firm of its size. Speechly Bircham's strengths lie in the synergy of the relationships between its four main departments: private client, corporate and tax, litigation and property.

## main areas of work
Corporate and tax 25%; property 25%; litigation 25%; private client 25%.

## trainee profile
Both law and non-law graduates who are capable of achieving a 2:1. The firm seeks intellectually dynamic individuals who enjoy a collaborative working environment where they can make an impact.

## training environment
Speechly Bircham divides the training contract into four six-month seats. Emphasis is given to early responsibility and supervised client contact providing trainees with a practical learning environment.

## benefits
Season ticket loan, private medical insurance, life assurance.

## vacation placements
Places for 2006: 12. The firm's summer placement scheme for students gives them the chance to experience a City legal practice. In a three-practice placement, students will be asked to research and present on a legal issue at the end of their placement; Duration: 3 weeks; Remuneration: £250 p.w.; Closing Date: 14 February 2006.

## sponsorship & awards
CPE and LPC fees and a maintenance grant.

| Partners | 51 |
| Assistant Solicitors | 77 |
| Total Trainees | 10 |

**contact**
Nicola Swann
Human Resources Director

**method of application**
Application form (available by request or online)

**selection procedure**
Interview

**closing date for 2008**
31 July 2006

**application**
Training contracts p.a. **6**
Applications p.a. **500**
% interviewed p.a. **25%**
Required degree grade **2:1**

**training**
Salary
**1st year**
£28,000-£29,000
**2nd year**
£30,000-£31,000
Holiday entitlement **20 days**
% of trainees with a non-law degree p.a. **50%**

**post-qualification**
Salary (2005) **£47,000**

603

# Stephenson Harwood

One St Paul's Churchyard, London EC4M 8SH
Tel: (020) 7809 2812  Fax: (020) 7003 8263
Email: graduate.recruitment@shlegal.com
Website: www.shlegal.com/graduate

## firm profile
Established in the City of London in 1828, Stephenson Harwood has developed into a large international practice, with a commercial focus and a wide client base.

## main areas of work
Corporate (including corporate finance, funds, corporate tax, business technology); employment, pensions and benefits; banking and asset finance; dry and wet shipping litigation; commercial litigation; and real estate.

## trainee profile
The firm looks for high calibre graduates with excellent academic records, business awareness and excellent communication skills.

## training environment
As the graduate intake is relatively small, the firm gives trainees individual attention, coaching and monitoring. Your structured and challenging programme involves four six month seats in areas of the firm covering contentious and non-contentious areas, across any department within the firm's practice groups. These seats include 'on the job' training and you will share an office with a partner or senior solicitor. In-house lectures complement your training and there is continuous review of your career development. You will have the opportunity to spend six months abroad and have free language tuition where appropriate. You will be given your own caseload and as much responsibility as you can shoulder. The firm plays a range of team sports, offers subsidised membership of a City health club (or a health club of your choice) and has privileged seats for concerts at the Royal Albert Hall and access to private views at the Tate Gallery.

## benefits
Subsidised membership of health clubs, private health insurance, BUPA membership, season ticket loan and 25 days paid holiday per year.

## vacation placements
Places for 2006: 18; Duration: 2 weeks; Remuneration: £250 p.w.; Closing Date: 17 February 2006.

## sponsorship & awards
Fees paid for CPE and LPC and maintenance awards.

Partners 70*
Assistant Solicitors 219*
Total Trainees 34
* denotes world-wide figures

contact
Caroline Thompson
(Graduate Recruitment)

method of application
Online application form only

selection procedure
assessment centre

closing date for
Sept/March 2008
31 July 2006

application
Training contracts p.a. 12
% interviewed p.a. 10%
Required degree grade 2:1

training
Salary
1st year (2004) £28,000
2nd year (2004) £32,000
Holiday entitlement 25 days
% of trainees with a
non-law degree p.a. 50%
No. of seats available
abroad p.a. 10

post-qualification
Salary (2004) £49,000
% of trainees offered job
on qualification (2002) 65%
% of assistants (as at
1/9/01) who joined as
trainees 37%
% of partners (as at 1/9/01)
who joined as trainees 46%

overseas offices
Paris, Piraeus, Singapore,
Guangzhou, Hong Kong,
Shanghai

associated offices
Greece, South Africa,
Kuwait, Croatia, France,
Bucharest

# Stevens & Bolton LLP

The Billings, Guildford, Surrey GU4 1YD
Tel: (01483) 302264  Fax: (01483) 302254
Email: gradrec@stevens-bolton.co.uk
Website: www.stevens-bolton.co.uk

| | |
|---|---|
| **Partners** | **25** |
| **Assistant Solicitors** | **37** |
| **Total Trainees** | **6** |

## firm profile

Stevens & Bolton is a leading law firm based in Guildford with a national reputation. The firm provides clients with a City-calibre service and offers its trainees a supportive culture and excellent training. This was recently recognised when the firm won two awards, in 2005 Best Recruiter and in 2004 Best Trainer (medium regional law firm) both awarded by LawCareers.net and the TSG. The firm has 25 partners and over 130 staff in total. The firm has grown rapidly in the past five years and is one of the major firms in the region, described recently by The Legal 500 as a 'regional heavyweight'. In March 2005 the firm was shortlisted by Legal Business for Regional Firm of the Year. The firm's work is over 80% commercial, the remainder being private client work advising medium and high net worth individuals. The firm acts for a diverse range of clients. These include FTSE 100 businesses, subsidiaries of major international groups and growing, owner-managed companies. The firm receives instructions from household names such as Gallaher Group plc, Hays plc, The BOC Group and Morse plc to name a few!

**contact**
Julie Bounden
(01483) 302264

**method of application**
Graduate application form and covering letter, available from the website or by request

**selection procedure**
Two interviews & other processes

**closing date for 2008**
30 September 2006

## main areas of work

Corporate and commercial, property, litigation and dispute resolution, employment and pensions, private client and family.

**application**
Training contracts p.a. **3**
Applications p.a. **250**
% interviewed **14%**
Required degree grade **2:1**
**& one grade A at 'A' Level**

## trainee profile

The firm requires a good academic record and individuals with interests such as music, sport, travel and who have a genuine enthusiasm to work in the law.

**training**
Salary
**1st year (2004) £23,000**
**2nd year (2004) £25,000**
Holiday entitlement **25 days**

## training environment

Usually you will sit with a partner who will act as your supervisor and you will get real responsibility early on. There is a comprehensive cross-departmental training programme and regular reviews of performance.

**post-qualification**
Salary (2004) **£39,000**
% of trainees offered job on qualification (2005) **70%**

## benefits

Private medical insurance, life assurance, pension, rail or car park season ticket loan, permanent health insurance and 25 days holiday.

**overseas/regional offices**
Guildford only

## sponsorship & awards

Providing no local authority grant is available, full fees for the GDL and LPC plus a £4,000 maintenance grant.

STEVENS & BOLTON LLP

# Tarlo Lyons

Watchmaker Court, 33 St John's Lane, London EC1M 4DB
Tel: (020) 7405 2000  Fax: (020) 7814 9421
Email: trainee.recruitment@tarlolyons.com
Website: www.tarlolyons.com

## firm profile
Tarlo Lyons is a modern London firm focused on delivering creative commercial solutions for technology-driven businesses. The firm has a leading reputation for its technology work and its expertise provides real benefits for its clients across a range of sectors.

## main areas of work
Tarlo Lyons continues to focus confidently on technology and other developments for our commercial clients. It has particular strengths in areas such as IT and outsourcing, hotels, leisure and gaming and financial services. Clients include global corporates, UK listed and unlisted corporates, entrepreneurial businesses and individuals. The main practice areas are commercial property, commercial technology, corporate, dispute resolution and employment and resourcing.

## trainee profile
Tarlo Lyons lawyers can be identified as smart, commercially savvy, fun and professional – they aren't defined by the school they went to or their examination results. The firm welcomes applicants who have taken a gap year or who have had work experience in business. It values the differences in skills, strengths and ideas each person brings.

## training environment
Opportunities for learning are provided throughout the training contract. You will gain work experience in most departments, including at least three months in the firm's Dispute Resolution Department, with the PSC taught externally. Your work experience will be interactive and varied and you will participate in a wide range of business development and marketing activities.

## benefits
Tarlo Lyons offers competitive compensation and your salary may be enhanced by a discretionary bonus payment. The firm's benefits package includes a 50% subsidy to a nearby gym, private health cover, death in service cover and participation in a pension plan.

## sponsorship & awards
LPC fees paid.

| Partners | 22 |
| Assistant Solicitors | 12 |
| Total Trainees | 6 |

**contact**
Trainee Recruitment
Co-ordinator

**method of application**
Application form available
from website

**selection procedure**
2 interviews

**closing date for 2008**
4 August 2006

**application**
Training contracts p.a. **3**
Applications p.a. **200**
% interviewed p.a. **10%**
Required degree grade **2:1**

**training**
Salary
**1st year (2004) £27,000
on average
2nd year (2004) £29,000
on average**
Holiday entitlement **25 days**
% of trainees with a
non-law degree p.a. **50%**

**post-qualification**
Salary (2004) **£42,000**
(Salary levels may
increase subject to
market conditions)

# Taylor Walton

28-44 Alma Street, Luton LU1 2PL
Tel: (01582) 731161  Fax: (01582) 457900
Email: luton@taylorwalton.co.uk
Website: www.taylorwalton.co.uk

## firm profile
Strategically located in Luton, Harpenden and St Albans, Taylor Walton is a major regional law practice advising both businesses and private clients. Its strengths are in commercial property, corporate work and commercial litigation, whilst maintaining a strong private client side to the practice. It has a progressive outlook both in its partners and staff and in its systems, training and IT.

## main areas of work
Company/commercial 15%; commercial property 20%; commercial litigation 15%; employment 10%; family 5%; private client 10%; residential property 20%; direct conveyancing 5%.

## trainee profile
Candidates need to show excellent intellectual capabilities, coupled with an engaging personality so as to show that they can engage and interact with the firm's clients as the practice of law involves the practice of the art of communication. Taylor Walton sees its partners and staff as business advisers involved in clients' businesses, not merely stand-alone legal advisers.

## training environment
The training consists of four six-month seats. The trainee partner oversees the structural training alongside a supervisor who will be a partner or senior solicitor in each department. The firm does try to take trainees' own wishes in relation to seats into account. In a regional law practice like Taylor Walton you will find client contact and responsibility coupled with supervision, management and training. There is an in-house training programme for all fee-earning members of staff. Trainees are given the opportunity to discuss their progress with their supervisor at a montly appraisal meeting. In addition, at the end of each seat there is a post seat appraisal conducted by the trainee partner. The PSC is taught externally. The firm is friendly with an open door policy and there are various sporting and social events.

## vacation placements
Places for 2006: 8; Duration: Up to 3 weeks; Remuneration: £176 per week; Closing Date: 30 March 2006.

## sponsorship & awards
September 2008: full LPC sponsorship.

| | |
|---|---|
| **Partners** | 24 |
| **Assistant Solicitors** | 32 |
| **Total Trainees** | 10 |

**contact**
Jim Wrigglesworth

**method of application**
CV with covering letter

**selection procedure**
First & second interview with opportunity to meet other partners

**closing date for 2008**
30 July 2006

**application**
Required degree grade
**2:1 or above**

# Taylor Wessing

Carmelite, 50 Victoria Embankment, Blackfriars
London EC4Y 0DX
Tel: (020) 7300 7000  Fax: (020) 7300 7100
Website: www.taylorwessing.com

## firm profile
Taylor Wessing is a powerful source of legal support for commercial organisations
doing business in Europe. Based in the three largest economies in Europe, Taylor Wessing
provides the full range of legal services to major corporations and growing
enterprises. Taylor Wessing boasts a strong reputation in the corporate, finance and
real estate sectors alongside in-depth experience across the full range of legal services
including property, tax, litigation & dispute resolution, employment & pensions and
private client.

## main areas of work
Corporate, intellectual property, finance & projects, real estate, litigation & dispute resolution,
employment & pensions and private client.

## trainee profile
High intellectual ability is paramount and the firm seeks a minimum of ABB grades at
A Level and at least a 2.1 degree in any discipline. The firm looks for team players who
have excellent communication skills, energy, ambition, an open mind and a willingness
to learn. You will also need to demonstrate a commitment to a career in law and a
genuine interest in business.

## training environment
As part of your training, you will spend six months in four different departments,
including a seat in the corporate department. There is also the possibility of a secondment
to another office or a client. Trainees work closely with a number of partners and
associates in the departments - so are directly involved in high-quality work from the
start. At the beginning of the training and throughout you have ongoing discussions
about your interests and how they fit in with the growth and needs of the departments.
There is support every step of the way, with regular feedback and appraisals in the middle
and at the end of each seat. Not forgetting the Professional Skills Course, which is
run in-house, along with other training courses as necessary during the two years.

## benefits
Private medical care, permanent health insurance, season ticket loan, subsidised staff
restaurant, non-contributory pension scheme.

## vacation placements
Places for 2006: 30 Duration: 2 weeks; Remuneration: £225 per week; Closing date: 10
February 2006.

## sponsorship & awards
GDL and LPC fees paid in full. Maintenance grant £4,500 per annum.

| | |
|---|---|
| **Partners** | 210 |
| **Fee-earners** | 574 |
| **Trainees** | 40 (UK) |

**contact**
Graduate Recruitment
Department

**method of application**
online application form

**selection procedure**
two interviews, one with a
partner, and psychometric
test

**closing date for 2008**
31 July 2006

**application**
Training contracts p.a. **20**
Applications p.a. **1,150**
% interviewed p.a. **8%**
Required degree grade **2:1**

**training**
Salary
1st year **£28,000**
2nd year **£31,000**
Holiday entitlement **25 days**
% of trainees with a
non-law degree p.a. **40%**

**post-qualification**
Salary (2005) **50,000**
% of trainees offered job
on qualification (2003-04)
**93%**

**overseas offices**
Berlin, Brussels, Cologne
Dusseldorf, Frankfurt,
Hamburg, Munich, Paris and
representative offices in
Alicante and Shanghai.
Associated office in Dubai.

# Teacher Stern Selby

37-41 Bedford Row, London WC1R 4JH
Tel: (020) 7242 3191  Fax: (020) 7242 1156
Email: r.raphael@tsslaw.com
Website: www.tsslaw.com

| | |
|---|---|
| **Partners** | 20 |
| **Assistant Solicitors** | 25 |
| **Total Trainees** | 10 |

## firm profile
A central London-based general commercial firm, with clientele and caseload normally attributable to larger firms. It has a wide range of contacts overseas.

**contact**
Russell Raphael

## main areas of work
Commercial litigation 24%; commercial property 40%; company and commercial 20%; secured lending 10%; private client 3%; clinical negligence/education/judicial review 3%.

**method of application**
Online

**selection procedure**
2 interviews

**closing date for 2008**
31 July 2006

## trainee profile
Emphasis falls equally on academic excellence and personality. The firm looks for flexible and motivated individuals, who have outside interests and who have demonstrated responsibility in the past.

**application**
Training contracts p.a. **3-6**
Applications p.a. **1,000**
% interviewed p.a. **5%**
Required degree grade
**2:1 (not absolute)**

## training environment
Trainees will spend between six and eight months in three departments (company commercial, litigation and property). Most trainees are assigned to actively assist a partner who monitors and supports them. Trainees are fully involved in departmental work and encouraged to take early responsibility. Trainees are expected to attend in-house seminars and lectures for continuing education. The atmosphere is relaxed and informal.

**training**
Salary
**1st year (2006) £25,000**
Holiday entitlement
**4 weeks**
% of trainees with a
non-law degree p.a. **50%**

## vacation placements
Places for 2006: Approximately 20 places to those that have applied for training contracts.

## sponsorship & awards
Will be considered.

**post-qualification**
Salary (2005) **£40,000**
% of trainees offered job
on qualification (2005) **100%**
% of assistants (who joined
as trainees **38%**
% of partners who joined as
trainees **44%**

# Thomas Eggar

The Corn Exchange, Baffins Lane, Chichester PO19 1GE
Tel: (01243) 813253
Email: mark.james@thomaseggar.com
Website: www.thomaseggar.com

| | |
|---|---|
| Vacancies | 8 |
| Partners | 58 |
| Trainees | 16 |
| Total Staff | 429 |

**contact**
Mark James BEM

**method of application**
Letter & CV

**selection procedure**
CV, assessment centre & interview

**closing date for 2008/2009**
1 August 2006

**training**
The firm aims to pay the going rate for a South Eastern regional firm. A London weighting is paid to those who undertake seats in the London office. The firm also pays a taxable travel allowance to all its trainees.
Required degree grade
**2:1 (any discipline)**

**other offices**
Chichester, Gatwick, London, Worthing

## firm profile

Thomas Eggar is rated as one of the top 100 law firms in the UK. Based in the South East, it is one of the country's leading regional law firms with a staff of over 400. The firm offers both private client and commercial services to a diverse range of clients, locally, nationally and internationally. It also offers financial services through Thesis, the firm's investment management arm, which is the largest solicitor-based investment unit in the UK.

## main areas of work

Apart from its strength in the private client sector, the firm handles property, commercial and litigation matters; among its major clients are banks, building societies and other financial institutions, railway and track operators and construction companies.

## trainee profile

The firm seeks able trainees with common sense, application and good business acumen, with a 2.1 degree in any discipline. Applications can be made up to 1 August 2006 for training contracts to commence in March/September 2008 and March 2009. Applications should be in the form of a CV and covering letter. You should give details of your attachment to the South East region in your covering letter.

## training environment

Trainees would normally have four seats covering commercial property, commercial, litigation and private client. In order to give good exposure to various specialisations, some of the seats are likely to be in different offices.

## vacation placements

There is a very limited summer placement scheme in July and August each year: this runs for five days, three days in the Gatwick office and two days in the London office. Applications should be made with CV and covering letter to Mark James by 31 March 2006. Please give details of your accommodation plans in your covering letter. Travel expenses are paid.

## sponsorship & awards

LPC 50% grant, 50% loan.

# Thomson Snell & Passmore

3 Lonsdale Gardens, Tunbridge Wells, Kent TN1 1NX
Tel: (01892) 510000  Fax: (01892) 549884
Email: solicitors@ts-p.co.uk
Website: www.ts-p.co.uk

## firm profile

Thomson Snell & Passmore continues to be regarded as one of the premier law firms in the South East. The firm has a reputation for quality and a commitment to deliver precise and clear advice which is recognised and respected both by its clients and professional contacts. It has held the Lexcel quality mark since January 1999. The firm is vibrant and progressive and enjoys an extremely friendly atmosphere. Its offices are located in the centre of Tunbridge Wells and attract clients locally, nationally and internationally.

## main areas of work

Commercial litigation 12%; corporate and employment 13%; commercial property 13%; private client 22%; personal injury/clinical negligence 20%; residential property 13%; family 7%.

## trainee profile

Thomson Snell & Passmore regards its trainees from the outset as future assistants, associates and partners. The firm is looking for people not only with strong intellectual ability, but enthusiasm, drive, initiative, strong interpersonal and team-working skills, together with good IT skills.

## training environment

The firm's induction course will help you to adjust to working life. As a founder member of Law South your training is provided in-house with trainees from other Law South member firms. Your two-year training contract is divided into four periods of six months each. You will receive a thorough grounding and responsibility with early client exposure. You will be monitored regularly, receive advice and assistance throughout and appraisals every three months. The Training Partner will co-ordinate your continuing education in the law, procedure, commerce, marketing, IT and presentation skills. Trainees enjoy an active social life which is encouraged and supported.

## sponsorship & awards

Grant and interest free loan available for LPC.

| | |
|---|---|
| **Partners** | **31** |
| **Assistant Solicitors** | **60** |
| **Total Trainees** | **8** |

**contact**
Human Resources Manager
Tel: (01892) 510000

**method of application**
Letter & application form available from website

**selection procedure**
Assessment interview

**closing date for 2008**
31 July 2006

**application**
Training contracts p.a. **4**
Applications p.a. **Approximately 500**
% interviewed p.a. **5%**
Required degree grade **2:1 (any discipline)**

**training**
Salary for each year of training
**Competitive regional salary**
Holiday entitlement **25 days**

**post-qualification**
% of trainees offered job on qualification **100% in 2005**

**overseas/regional offices**
Network of independent law firms throughout Europe and founding member of Law South

# TLT Solicitors

One Redcliff St, Bristol BS1 6TP
Tel: (0117) 917 7777  Fax: (0117) 917 7778
Email: graduate@TLTsolicitors.com
Website: www.TLTsolicitors.com

## firm profile

At the heart of TLT's strategy is a belief that great people make a great business. It is this attitude and strategy that has lead TLT to be listed in the Sunday Times 100 Best Companies to Work For in 2005 and has won the firm awards such as the Legal Business UK Regional Law Firm of the Year Award in 2004. These accolades reflect TLT's reputation which is built on an eagerness to understand its clients' businesses and a "whatever it takes" approach to client service.

## main areas of work

An impressive national and international client base ensures high quality work in a broad range of specialist areas: banking, capital markets, commercial dispute resolution, construction, corporate, employment, family, insolvency and business breakdown, intellectual property, lender services, mergers and acquisitions, partnerships, pensions, planning and environmental, property, tax, technology and media.

## trainee profile

Strong academic background together with commitment and drive to succeed.

## training environment

TLT's commitment to excellence will ensure that trainees benefit from a well developed and challenging training programme. Training is delivered through 4 seats of 6 months duration, chosen in consultation with the trainee. In each seat the trainee will sit with a lawyer although their work will be drawn from all members of the team in order to gain the widest possible experience. Regular monitoring and development planning ensures that trainees get the most out of their training and helps them to identify their long term career path from the varied specialisms on offer.

## benefits

Pension, private medical insurance, life assurance and subsidised sports/health club membership.

## vacation placements

12 paid summer placements available, each lasting 1 week.  Apply online by 31 March 2006.

## sponsorship & awards

CPE and LPC fees plus maintenance payment

| | |
|---|---|
| **Partners** | 51 |
| **Assistant Solicitors** | 226 |
| **Total Trainees** | 12 |

**contact**
Louise Chapman
Human Resources

**method of application**
Firm's application form online

**selection procedure**
Assessment Centre

**closing date for 2008**
31 July 2006

**application**
Training contracts p.a. **8**
Applications p.a. **500+**
% interviewed p.a. **10%**
Required degree grade
**2:1 prefered**
non-law degree p.a. **17%**

**post-qualification**
Market rate

# Travers Smith

10 Snow Hill, London EC1A 2AL
Tel: (020) 7295 3000  Fax: (020) 7295 3500
Email: graduate.recruitment@traverssmith.com
Website: www.traverssmith.com

## firm profile

A leading City firm with a major corporate and commercial practice. Although less than a quarter of the size of the dozen largest firms, they handle the highest quality work, much of which has an international dimension.

## main areas of work

Corporate law (including takeovers and mergers, financial services and regulatory laws), commercial law (which includes competition and intellectual property), dispute resolution, corporate recovery/insolvency, tax, employment, pensions, banking and property. The firm also offers a range of pro bono opportunities within individual departments and on a firm wide basis. In 2004, solicitors from the firm were awarded two separate national awards in recognition of their outstanding contributions to pro bono work.

## trainee profile

The firm looks for people who combine academic excellence with common sense; who are articulate, who think on their feet, who are determined and self motivated and who take their work but not themselves seriously. Applications are welcome from law and non-law graduates.

## training environment

Travers Smith has earned a phenomenal reputation in relation to its size. The work they undertake is exciting, intellectually demanding and top quality involving blue chip clients and big numbers. This means that their trainees gain great experience right from the outset.

The firm has a comprehensive training programme which ensures that trainees experience a broad range of work. All trainee solicitors sit in rooms with partners and assistants, receive an individual and extensive training from experienced lawyers and enjoy client contact and the responsibility that goes with it from the beginning of their training contract.

## benefits

Private health insurance, permanent health insurance, life assurance, corporate health club membership, subsidised bistro, season ticket loan.

## vacation placements

Summer 2006: 3 schemes with 15 places on each; Duration: two weeks; Remuneration: £250; Closing Date: 31 January 2006. The firm also offers a two week Christmas scheme for 15 students.

## sponsorship & awards

GDL and LPC paid in full plus maintenance of £5,000 per annum to those in London and £4,500 per annum to those outside of London.

| | |
|---|---|
| Partners | 56 |
| Assistant Solicitors | 138 |
| Total Trainees | 41 |

**contact**
Germaine VanGeyzel

**method of application**
CV and covering letter
online or by post

**selection procedure**
Interviews (2 stage process)

**closing date for 2008**
31 July 2006

**application**
Training contracts p.a. **Up to 25**
Applications p.a. **2,000**
% interviewed p.a. **15%**
Required degree grade **2:1**

**training**
Salary
**1st year (2004) £28,000**
**2nd year (2004) £32,000**
Holiday entitlement 20 days

**post-qualification**
Salary (2004) **£50,000**
% of trainees offered job
on qualification (2005) **92%**
% of assistants (as at 1/9/05)
who joined as trainees **68%**
% of partners (as at 1/9/05)
who joined as trainees **71%**

# Trowers & Hamlins

Sceptre Court, 40 Tower Hill, London EC3N 4DX
Tel: (020) 7423 8000  Fax: (020) 7423 8001
Email: gradrecruitment@trowers.com
Website: www.trowers.com

## firm profile

Trowers & Hamlins is a substantial city and international firm. Particular strengths include housing and housing finance, local government, UK and international projects, company commercial, construction, commercial property and public/private sector initiatives including private finance. Other specialisations include the health sector, environmental law, employment and charities.

## main areas of work

Property (housing, public sector, commercial) ; company and commercial/construction; litigation; private client.

## trainee profile

Personable, enthusiastic candidates with a good academic record and wide-ranging outside interests. The ability to work under pressure and with others, combined with versatility, are essential characteristics.

## training environment

Trainees will gain experience in four seats from: company/commercial, construction, property, international, litigation, employment and private client. Trainees are encouraged to learn from direct contact with clients and to assume responsibility. The training programme is flexible and, with reviews held every three months, individual preferences will be considered. A training officer assists partners with the training programme and in-house lectures and seminars are held regularly. There are opportunities to work in Manchester and the Middle East. The firm encourages a relaxed atmosphere and blends traditional qualities with contemporary attitudes. Activities are organised outside working hours.

## benefits

Season ticket loan, private healthcare after six months service, Employee Assistance Programme and discretionary bonus, Death in Service.

## vacation placements

Places for 2005: 25-30; Duration: 2 weeks; Remuneration: £225 p.w.; Closing Date: 1 March (Summer). Open Day: June/July.

## sponsorship & awards

CPE and LPC fees paid and £4,250-£4,500 maintenance p.a.

---

| Partners | 79 |
| Assistant Solicitors | 143 |
| Total Trainees | 32 |

**contact**
Graduate Recruitment Office

**method of application**
Letter, application form & CV

**selection procedure**
Interview(s), essay & practical test

**closing date for 2008**
1 August 2006

**application**
Training contracts p.a. **18**
Applications p.a. **1,600**
% interviewed p.a. **4%**
Required degree grade **2:1+**

**training**
Salary (subject to review)
**1st year £28,000**
**2nd year £30,000**
Holiday entitlement **25 days**
% of trainees with a non-law degree p.a. **40%**
No. of seats available abroad p.a. **Between 4-6**

**post-qualification**
Salary (2005) (subject to review) **£47,000**
% of trainees offered job on qualification (2003) **90%**
% of assistants (as at 1/7/05) who joined as trainees **44%**
% of partners (as at 1/7/05) who joined as trainees **34%**

**overseas offices**
Abu Dhabi, Dubai, Oman, Bahrain, Cairo

# Walker Morris

Kings Court, 12 King Street, Leeds LS1 2HL
Tel: (0113) 283 2500  Fax: (0113) 245 9412
Email: hellograduates@walkermorris.co.uk
Website: www.walkermorris.co.uk

## firm profile
Based in Leeds, Walker Morris is one of the largest commercial law firms in the North, with over 750 people, providing a full range of legal services to commercial and private clients both nationally and internationally.

## main areas of work
Litigation 40%; property 27%; company and commercial 26%; private clients 2%; tax 2%; other 3%.

## trainee profile
Bright, articulate, highly motivated individuals who will thrive on early responsibility in a demanding yet friendly environment.

## training environment
Trainees commence with an induction programme, before spending four months in each main department (commercial property, corporate and commercial litigation). Trainees can choose in which departments they wish to spend their second year. Formal training will include lectures, interactive workshops, seminars, interactive video and e-learning. The PSC covers the compulsory elements and the electives consist of a variety of specially tailored skills programmes. Individual IT training is provided. Opportunities can also arise for secondments to some of the firm's major clients. Emphasis is placed on teamwork, inside and outside the office. The firm's social and sporting activities are an important part of its culture and are organised by a committee drawn from all levels of the firm. A trainee solicitors' committee represents the trainees in the firm but also organises events and liaises with the Leeds Trainee Solicitors Group.

## vacation placements
Places for 2006: 45 over 3 weeks; Duration: 1 week; Remuneration: £170 p.w.; Closing Date: 28 February 2006.

## sponsorship & awards
LPC & PGDL fees plus maintenance of £4,500.

| | |
|---|---|
| Partners | 44 |
| Assistant Solicitors | 110 |
| Total Trainees | 30 |

**contact**
Nick Bates

**method of application**
Application form

**selection procedure**
Telephone & face-to-face interviews

**closing date for 2008**
31 July 2006

**application**
Training contracts p.a. **15**
Applications p.a.
**Approx. 800**
% interviewed p.a.
Telephone **16%**
Face to face **8%**
Required degree grade **2:1**

**training**
Salary
**1st year (2005) £20,000**
**2nd year (2005) £22,000**
Holiday entitlement **24 days**
% of trainees with a non-law degree p.a.
**30% on average**

**post-qualification**
Salary (2005) **£33,000**
% of trainees offered job on qualification (2005) **93%**
% of assistants (as at 1/7/05) who joined as trainees **60%**
% of partners (as at 1/7/05) who joined as trainees **55%**

# Ward Hadaway

Sandgate House, 102 Quayside, Newcastle upon Tyne NE1 3DX
Tel: (0191) 204 4000  Fax: (0191) 204 4098
Email: recruitment@wardhadaway.com
Website: www.wardhadaway.com

## firm profile

Ward Hadaway is one of the most progressive law firms in the North East and is firmly established as one of the region's heavyweights. The firm attracts some of the most ambitious businesses in the region and its client base includes a large number of plcs, new start-ups and well established private companies.

As a business founded and located in the North East, the firm has grown rapidly, investing heavily in developing its existing people, and recruiting further outstanding individuals from inside and outside of the region. The firm is now listed in the top 100 UK law firms, with an outstanding 25 lawyers recognised in the top 500 in the UK.

## main areas of work

Corporate Finance, Business Services, Commercial Property, Planning, Debt Recovery, Dispute Resolution, Technology, Intellectual Property, Healthcare, Employment, Construction, Licensing and Private Client Services.

## trainee profile

The usual academic and professional qualifications are sought. Sound commercial and business awareness are essential as is the need to demonstrate strong communication skills, enthusiasm and flexibility. Candidates will be able to demonstrate excellent interpersonal and analytical skills.

## training environment

The training contract is structured around four seats (property, company/commercial, litigation and private client) each of six months duration. At regular intervals, and each time you are due to change seat, you will have the opportunity to discuss the experience you would like to gain during your training contract. The firm will always try to give high priority to your preferences. You will share a room with a partner or associate which will enable you to learn how to deal with different situations. Your practical experience will also be complemented by an extensive programme of seminars and lectures. All trainees are allocated a 'buddy', usually a second year trainee or newly qualified solicitor, who can provide as much practical advice and guidance as possible during your training. The firm has an active Social Committee and offers a full range of sporting and social events.

## benefits

23 days holiday (26 after five years service), death in service insurance, contributory pension.

## vacation placements

Applications for summer vacation placements should be received by 28 February 2006. Duration one week.

## sponsorship & awards

CPE & LPC fees paid and £2,000 interest-free loan.

---

| Partners | 53 |
| Total Trainees | 18 |

**contact**
Carol Butts
Human Resources Manager

**method of application**
Application form &
covering letter

**selection procedure**
Interview

**closing date for 2008**
31 July 2006

**application**
Training contracts p.a. **10**
Applications p.a. **400+**
% interviewed p.a. **10%**
Required degree grade **2:1**

**training**
Salary
1st year (2005)  £18,500
2nd year (2005)  £19,500
Holiday entitlement **23 days**
% of trainees with a
non-law degree p.a. **Varies**

**post-qualification**
Salary (2005)
**£32,500 minimum**

# Watson Burton LLP

1 St James' Gate, Newcastle upon Tyne NE99 1YQ
Tel: (0191) 244 4444  Fax: (0191) 244 4500
Email: enquiries@watsonburton.com
Website: www.watsonburton.com

## firm profile

Watson Burton LLP is one of the top law firms in the North of England with almost 200 years' experience and a well-earned reputation for helping its clients succeed.
Over the last few years the firm has become one of the fastest-growing law firms in the country operating from offices in Newcastle and Leeds. The senior partner was recognised in The Lawyer's Hot 100. This is the definitive run down of the 'new breed' shaping the legal profession. And the firm as a whole has been recognised by The Lawyer Magazine as "Ones to Watch" and quoted as "the fastest organically growing UK practice" for the second year running.
For the firm's trainees, this represents an exciting time to join the firm, providing you with an opportunity to work across the full range of legal services for a leading law firm that is going places.

## main areas of work

Watson Burton LLP's business is mainly commercial and they have particular strengths in business advice, property services, employment, dispute resolution, debt recovery, professions and insurance, technology, IP and media, corporate finance, education and wealth protection. In addition to providing the full range of legal services, they have recently launched a brand-new sports law unit and they have the largest construction and engineering practice outside of London voted number one by The Legal 500.

## trainee profile

The firm seeks to recruit talented and bright law graduates with a flair for communication and a common sense approach to business. They value an approachable, down to earth attitude. This way they can continue their track record in first rate client service and can continue to put their clients first. Although law graduates are preferred, the firm's primary focus is on character and intellectual strength, and outstanding graduates of other disciplines are always considered. They have positions in both the Newcastle and Leeds offices and recruit separately to appoint trainees into these positions.

## training environment

The firm provides top-class training from modern office environments in both Leeds and Newcastle. They have the best technology and the right resources to provide a thorough and comprehensive introduction to the law. And they have a vast team of experienced lawyers who you can call on for assistance and guidance where needed. Watson Burton LLP's training programme includes both in-house and external seminars. Trainees are encouraged to assist in the firm's marketing from day one. Alongside careful and regular supervision, they offer trainees a high level of responsibility at an early stage.

## sponsorship & benefits

The firm provides ample study leave, offers paid professional memberships and subscriptions, and give full payment for LPC fees.

| | |
|---|---|
| **Partners** | **36** |
| **Assistant Solicitors** | **16** |
| **Total Trainees** | **5** |

**contact**
Margaret Cay
(0191) 244 4301
margaret.cay@watsonburton.com

**method of application**
Download & complete the application form on the website, return along with a covering letter, to Margaret Cay, stating which office you wish to be considered for.

**closing date for 2008**
31 July 2006

**application**
Training contracts p.a. **5**
Applications p.a.
around **1,000**
% interviewed p.a. **2%**
Required degree grade **2:1**

**training**
Salary
**£16,750** plus Leeds weighting for Leeds based trainees, rising by £1,500 over the two year training period, plus an annual cost of living increase and salary review in May of each year.

**post-qualification**
Salary
**Not less than £32,250**
% of trainees offered job on qualification (2005)
**100%**

**regional offices**
Newcastle & Leeds

# Watson, Farley & Williams LLP

15 Appold Street, London EC2A 2HB
Tel: (020) 7814 8000  Fax: (020) 7814 8017
Email: graduates@wfw.com
Website: www.wfw.com

## firm profile
Established in 1982, Watson, Farley & Williams has its strengths in corporate, banking and asset finance, particularly ship and aircraft finance. The firm aims to provide a superior service in specialist areas and to build long-lasting relationships with its clients.

## main areas of work
Shipping; ship finance; aviation; banking; asset finance; corporate; litigation; e-commerce; intellectual property; EU/Competition; taxation; property; insolvency; telecoms; project finance.

## trainee profile
Outgoing graduates who exhibit energy, ambition, self-assurance, initiative and intellectual flair.

## training environment
Trainees are introduced to the firm with a comprehensive induction course covering legal topics and practical instruction. Seats are available in at least four of the firm's main areas, aiming to provide trainees with a solid commercial grounding. There is also the opportunity to spend time abroad, working on cross-border transactions. Operating in an informal, friendly and energetic atmosphere, trainees will receive support whenever necessary. You will be encouraged to take on early responsibility and play an active role alongside a partner at each stage of your training. The practice encourages continuous learning for all employees and works closely with a number of law lecturers, producing a widely-read 'digest' of legal developments, to which trainees are encouraged to contribute. All modules of the PSC are held in-house. The firm has its own sports teams and organises a variety of social functions.

## benefits
Life assurance, PHI, BUPA, STL, pension, subsidised gym membership.

## vacation placements
Places for 2006: 30; Duration: 2 weeks; Remuneration: £200 p.w.; Closing Date: 24th February 2006.

## sponsorship & awards
CPE and LPC fees paid and £4,500 maintenance p.a. (£4,000 outside London).

| | |
|---|---|
| **Partners** | **62** |
| **Assistant Solicitors** | **150** |
| **Total Trainees** | **22** |

**contact**
Graduate Recruitment Manager

**method of application**
Online application

**selection procedure**
Assessment centre & Interview

**closing date for 2008**
30 July 2006

**application**
Training contracts p.a. **12**
Applications p.a. **1,000**
% interviewed p.a. **10%**
Required degree grade
**Minimum 2:1 & 24 UCAS points or above**

**training**
Salary
**1st year (2005) £28,500**
**2nd year (2005) £32,500**
Holiday entitlement **22 days**
% of trainees with a
non-law degree p.a. **50%**
No. of seats available
abroad p.a. **12**

**post-qualification**
Salary (2005)
**Not less than £50,000 at the time of writing**
% of trainees offered job
on qualification (2005) **80%**
% of assistants (as at 1/9/04) who joined as trainees **60%**
% of partners (as at 1/9/04) who joined as trainees **4%**

**overseas offices**
New York, Paris, Piraeus, Singapore, Bangkok, Rome, Hamburg*

*(opening Oct. 2005)

# Wedlake Bell

52 Bedford Row, London, WC1R 4LR
Tel: (020) 7395 3000  Fax: (020) 7395 3100
Email: recruitment@wedlakebell.com
Website: www.wedlakebell.com

## firm profile
Wedlake Bell is a medium-sized law firm providing legal advice to businesses and high net worth individuals from around the world. The firm's services are based on a high degree of partner involvement, extensive business and commercial experience and strong technical expertise. The firm has over 80 lawyers in central London and Guernsey, and affiliations with law firms throughout Europe and in the United States.

## main areas of work
**For the firm's business clients:** Banking and asset finance; corporate; commercial property; media, IP and commercial; internet and e-business; employment services; pensions and share schemes; construction; litigation and dispute resolution.
**For private individuals:** Tax, trusts and wealth protection; offshore services.

## trainee profile
In addition to academic excellence, Wedlake Bell looks for commercial aptitude, flexibility, enthusiasm, a personable nature, confidence, mental agility and computer literacy in its candidates. Languages are not crucial.

## training environment
Trainees have four seats of six months across the following areas: corporate, banking, construction, media and IP/IT, employment, pensions, litigation, property and private client. As a trainee the firm encourages you to have direct contact and involvement with clients from an early stage. Trainees will work within highly specialised teams and have a high degree of responsibility. Trainees will be closely supervised by a partner or senior solicitor and become involved in high quality and varied work. The firm is committed to the training and career development of its lawyers and many of its trainees continue their careers with the firm often through to partnership. Wedlake Bell has an informal, creative and co-operative culture with a balanced approach to life.

## sponsorship & benefits
LPC fees paid and £2,500 maintenance grant where local authority grant not available. During training contract: pension, travel loans, subsidised gym membership, health and life insurance.

## vacation placements
Places for 2006: 6; Duration: 3 weeks in July; Remuneration: £200 p.w.; Closing Date: End of February.

| | |
|---|---|
| **Partners** | **39** |
| **Assistant Solicitors** | **42** |
| **Total Trainees** | **14** |

**contact**
Natalie King

**method of application**
Application form

**selection procedure**
Two interviews

**closing date for 2008**
End of July 2006

**application**
Training contracts p.a. **7**
Required degree grade **2:1**

**training**
Salary
**1st year (2005) £26,000**
**2nd year (2005) £28,000**
Holiday entitlement
1st year **23 days,**
2nd year **24 days**
% of trainees with a
non-law degree p.a. **50%**

**overseas offices**
Guernsey

# Weightmans

India Buildings, Water Street, Liverpool L2 0GA
Tel: (0151) 227 2601  Fax: (0151) 227 3223
Email: hr@weightmans.com
Website: www.weightmans.com

| | |
|---|---|
| **Partners** | 76 |
| **Assistant Solicitors** | 125 |
| **Trainees p.a.** | 12 |

**method of application**
online with
www.weightmans.com

**closing date for 2008**
31 July 2006

**other offices**
Birmingham, Leicester,
London, Manchester

## firm profile
Weightmans is a national firm of solicitors, with offices in Birmingham, Leicester, Liverpool, London and Manchester. There are over 600 people in the firm's dedicated teams, including 76 partners. Weightmans is one of the largest defendant litigation practices in the UK as well as a thriving commercial practice, offering a comprehensive range of legal services.

## trainee profile
The firm looks to recruit twelve trainee solicitors each year. When considering training contract applications they look for applicants from a variety of academic backgrounds, who can demonstrate an ability to achieve results. Above all, the firm values well-motivated candidates with a practical and pragmatic approach, who can make a positive impact on a team.

## training environment
The firm want its trainees to feel that they are making a positive contribution to a team. You will have the opportunity to be involved in challenging and rewarding work from the very start through Weightmans' supportive and well structured training programme, which consists of four 'seats'. Towards the end of each six-month rotation, you will have a review meeting with your supervisor, where you will receive feedback on your progress. This will be followed by a meeting with one of the 'mentoring' partners from the specifically appointed Training Committee, at which you can feedback your comments and have input into the progression of your training contract and future rotations.

## application details
The application form can be found on the firm's website. You will then be contacted after the closing date of 31st July in respect of the outcome of your application.

## benefits
Weightmans pay a starting salary well above the minimum recommended by the Law Society and this is reviewed every year to ensure that it is competitive. They also offer an excellent benefits package, which includes a pension, health cover, life assurance and 25 days holiday. From the moment you accept a training contract with Weightmans, the firm pledges their support to you, paying all course/study fees for LPC and CPE and inviting you to be part of their team.

# Weil, Gotshal & Manges

One South Place, London EC2M 2WG
Tel: (020) 7903 1074  Fax: (020) 7903 0990
Email: graduate.recruitment@weil.com
Website: www.weil.com

## firm profile

Weil Gotshal & Manges is a leader in the marketplace for sophisticated, international legal services. With more than 1,200 lawyers across the US, Europe and Asia, the firm serves many of the most successful companies in the world in their high-stakes matters and transactions.

## main areas of work

Established in 1996, the London office now has over 130 lawyers. It has grown rapidly to become the second largest of the firm's 19 offices - it is the hub of the firm's European practice. Key areas are private equity, M&A, business finance and restructuring, capital markets, securitisation, banking and finance, litigation and tax. The firm's expertise covers most industries including real estate, manufacturing, financial services, energy, telecommunications, pharmaceuticals, retailing and technology. In the firm's work on private equity, leveraged finance and principal finance transactions, it advises clients on the acquisition, the raising of the requisite financing and on any subsequent high yield or equity offerings. Due to the international nature of the business, the firm's lawyers are experienced in working closely with their colleagues from other offices - this ensures a co-ordinated approach to providing effective legal solutions efficiently.

## vacation placements

Places for 2006: 12 in summer vacation. Closing date for applications by online application form: 14 February 2006.

| | |
|---|---|
| Partners | 25 |
| Assistant Solicitors | 80 |
| Total Trainees | 18 |

**contact**
Jillian Singh

**method of application**
online application form

**closing date for 2008**
31 July 2006

**application**
Training contracts p.a. **12**
Required degree grade **2:1**

**training**
Salary
1st year (2005) £35,000
Holiday entitlement **23 days**

**overseas offices**
Austin, Boston, Brussels, Budapest, Dallas, Frankfurt, Houston, Miami, Munich, New York, Paris, Prague, Silicon Valley, Singapore, Warsaw, Washington DC, Wilmington

# White & Case

5 Old Broad Street, London EC2N 1DW
Tel: (020) 7532 1000  Fax: (020) 7532 1001
Email: trainee@whitecase.com
Website: www.whitecase.com

## firm profile

White & Case is a global law firm with more than 1,900 lawyers worldwide. The firm has built a network of 38 offices, providing the full range of legal services of the highest quality in virtually every major commercial centre and emerging market. They work with international businesses, financial institutions and governments worldwide on corporate and financial transactions and dispute resolution proceedings. Their clients range from some of the world's longest established and most respected names to many start-up visionaries. The London office employs 240 lawyers who work on a variety of sophisticated, high-value transactions. Many of the legal matters we handle feature in the legal press worldwide as our clients achieve firsts in privatisation, cross-border business deals, or major development projects.

## main areas of work

Asset finance, banking and structured finance, capital markets, construction and engineering, corporate, dispute resolution, employment and benefits, energy, infrastructure and project finance, financial restructuring and insolvency, intellectual property, international arbitration, litigation, mergers and acquisitions, real estate, private equity, tax, telecommunications.

## trainee profile

Trainees should be ambitious, creative and work well in teams. They should have an understanding of international commercial issues and have a desire to be involved in high profile, cross-border legal matters.

## training environment

Trainees undertake four seats, each of six months in duration. As a leading global law firm, clients expect White & Case lawyers to have international knowledge and experience so the firm guarantees one of these seats will be in Asia, Europe or Africa. Regardless of where they work, trainees get a high level of partner and senior associate contact from day one, ensuring they receive high quality, stimulating and rewarding work. Trainees are encouraged to take early responsibility and there is a strong emphasis on practical hands-on training, together with plenty of support and feedback. The firm recruits and develops trainee solicitors with the aim of retaining them on qualification and an average retention rate of 93% proves the point.

## benefits

BUPA, gym membership contribution, pension scheme, season ticket loan, discretionary bonus scheme, welcome bonus.

## vacation placements

Places for 2006: 40-50; Duration: 2 weeks; Remuneration: £300 per week; Closing Date: 31 January 2006.

## sponsorship & awards

GDL and LPC fees paid and £5,500 maintenance p.a. Prizes for commendation and distinction for LPC.

| | |
|---|---|
| **Partners** | **45** |
| **Assistant Solicitors** | **145** |
| **Total Trainees** | **50** |

**contact**
Ms Emma Fernandes

**method of application**
Online application via firm website

**selection procedure**
Interview

**closing date for 2008**
31 July 2006

**application**
Training contracts p.a. **25-30**
Applications p.a. **1,600**
Required degree grade **2:1**

**training**
Salary
**£36,000, rising by £1,000 every 6 months**
Holiday entitlement **25 days**

**All trainees are guaranteed to spend a seat overseas**

**post-qualification**
Salary (2005) **£63,000**

**overseas offices**
Almaty, Ankara, Bangkok, Beijing, Berlin, Bombay, Bratislava, Brussels, Budapest, Dresden, Düsseldorf, Frankfurt, Hamburg, Helsinki, Ho Chi Minh City, Hong Kong, Istanbul, Johannesburg, London, Los Angeles, Mexico City, Miami, Milan, Moscow, New York, Palo Alto, Paris, Prague, Riyadh, Rome, San Francisco, São Paulo, Singapore, Shanghai, Stockholm, Tokyo, Warsaw, Washington DC

# Wiggin LLP

95 The Promenade, Cheltenham GL50 1WG
Tel: (01242) 224114  Fax: (01242) 224223
6 Cavendish Place, London, W1G 9NB
Tel: (020) 7612 9612  Fax: (020) 7612 9611
Email: law@wiggin.co.uk  Website: www.wiggin.co.uk

## firm profile

Wiggin LLP is recognised as a leading firm in the core areas of media and entertainment law including, music, film, sport, television and radio broadcasting, broadcast regulation, technology (both broadcast related and IT and software related), online and interactive gaming and betting, publishing, defamation, privacy and contempt, as well as corporate/commercial, property and commercial litigation. Based in Cheltenham and London, the firm continues to build upon its blue-chip client base both nationally and internationally.

## main areas of work

Media (including media litigation) 77%; Corporate 12%; Commercial Litigation 7%; Property 4%.

## trainee profile

If you can demonstrate a passion for media and the law then the firm is interested. If you can top that with strong academics and demonstrable commitment to success then Wiggin LLP definitely want to hear from you. The firm can offer you first-class training and experience and the opportunity to qualify at an exciting, friendly, cutting-edge firm, which has the ambition to be nothing less than the best.

## training environment

Training is divided into four seats. Trainees will be based in the firm's Cheltenham office and will be eligible to work in the company/commercial, non-contentious media (two seats), media litigation and property departments.  The firm also currently has a secondment arrangement with a key client on a rolling six month basis.  Trainees are encouraged to take an active role in transactions, assume responsibility and deal directly with clients. In-house lectures and seminars are held regularly and training reviews are held every three months. The firm offers the attraction of Cheltenham combined with technical ability and experience akin to a large City firm. Its relatively small size encourages a personal approach towards staff and client relations.

## benefits

Life assurance, private health cover, pension scheme, permanent health insurance, subsidised gym membership.

## sponsorship & awards

PgDL and LPC fees and £3,500 maintenance p.a.

| | |
|---|---|
| **Partners** | 12 |
| **Assistant Solicitors** | 18 |
| **Total Trainees** | 6 |

**contact**
Human Resources Manager

**method of application**
Online application only -
www.wiggin.co.uk

**selection procedure**
Two-day selection

**closing date for 2008**
31 July 2006

**application**
Training contracts p.a. **3**
Applications p.a. **500**
% interviewed p.a. **8%**
Required degree grade **2:1**

**training**
Salary
1st year (2005) **£26,500**
2nd year (2005) **£31,500**
Holiday entitlement **20 days
+ one day per annum up
to max 25 days**
% of trainees with a
non-law degree p.a. **50%**

**post-qualification**
Salary (2005) **£44,000**
% of trainees offered job
on qualification (2005) **100%**
% of assistants (as at 2005)
who joined as trainees **29%**
% of partners (as at 2005)
who joined as trainees **25%**

# Withers LLP

16 Old Bailey, London EC4M 7EG
Tel: (020) 7597 6000  Fax: (020) 7329 2534
Email: emma.macdonald@withersworldwide.com
Website: www.withersrecruitment.com

## firm profile

Withers LLP is the first international law firm dedicated to the business and personal interests of successful people, their businesses, their families and their advisers.
With offices in London, Milan, Geneva, New York and New Haven (Connecticut), the firm has unparalleled expertise in commercial and tax law, trusts, estate planning, litigation, employment and family law. The firm's status as the largest private client team in Europe and our outstanding reputation in family law sets us apart from other City firms.
The firm's international client base includes more than 15% of Britain's wealthiest citizens (based on the Sunday Times Rich List), at least 10% of the 50 wealthiest families based in Europe with US connections, and a significant number of the Forbes 400 list of Richest Americans.

## main areas of work

Agricultural property, banking, charities, company and commercial, employment and employee benefits, family, fraud and asset tracing, IP and IT, international trust litigation, insolvency, private client, professional negligence and property.

## training environment

Trainees complete four seats, each of six months' duration in Private Client, Family, Property, Litigation, IP and Corporate. Trainees often work in cross departmental groups thus gaining exposure to diverse areas of law.

## benefits

Bonus, 23 days holiday, interest-free season ticket loan, private medical insurance, pension, life assurance, social events and subsidized canteen.

## vacation placements

Easter and Summer vacation placements are available in the firm's London and Milan offices in 2006. Students spend two weeks in two different departments. The closing date for applications is 31 January 2006. In the London office there are 24 places available during the summer and 6 at Easter. It also has a number of places available throughout the year (except August) in its Milan office for fluent Italian speakers.

## sponsorship & awards

CPE/PgDL and LPC fees and £4,500 maintenance p.a. are paid. A cash prize is awarded for a distinction or commendation in the CPE/PgDL and/or LPC.

| Partners | 84 |
| Legal Staff | 222 |
| Total Trainees | 26 |

**contact**
Emma MacDonald
Senior Recruitment Officer

**method of application**
Application form (available online)

**selection procedure**
2 interviews incl. written exercise and presentation

**closing date for 2008**
training scheme:
31 July 2006
Closing date for 2006
vacation scheme:
31 January 2006

**application**
Training contracts p.a. **14**
Applications p.a. **1,000**
% interviewed p.a. **10%**
Required degree grade **2:1**

**training**
Salary
1st year (2005) **£28,000**
2nd year (2005) **£30,000**
Holiday entitlement **23 days**
% of trainees with a
non-law degree p.a. **50%**

**post-qualification**
Salary (2005) **£46,000**

**overseas offices**
Milan, Geneva, New York,
New Haven

# withers L

# Wollastons

Brierly Place, New London Road, Chelmsford, Essex CM2 0AP
Tel: (01245) 211211  Fax: (01245) 354764
Email: recruitment@wollastons.co.uk
Website: www.wollastons.com

## firm profile

Wollastons is a dynamic, regional law firm, widely recognised as the leading, commercial practice in Essex. Wollastons has a strong reputation as a forward-thinking and energetic organisation, offering high levels of service to both businesses and private clients. The firm's first-class resources, including sophisticated IT, and the lively atmosphere attracts high calibre lawyers, keen to work in a modern, professional environment. The Investors in People accreditation demonstrates a strong commitment to staff development and training at all levels.

## main areas of work

Main practice areas include corporate and commercial; commercial property; commercial disputes; employment; planning and property disputes; private client and family.

## trainee profile

Applications are welcomed from able and ambitious graduates with 300 UCAS points and a 2:1 degree. Candidates should have a commercial outlook, be confident, outgoing and able to demonstrate a wide range of interests. A link with the Essex area would be useful.

## training environment

Trainees have four six-month seats. These will normally include: company and commercial; commercial disputes; commercial property and employment. Trainees sit with a partner or a senior solicitor and form an integral part of the team. Trainees are fully involved in a wide range of interesting work and, although work is closely checked, trainees are encouraged to take responsibility from an early stage. The firm is very friendly and informal and trainees receive a great deal of individual attention and support. Progress is kept under constant review with mid-seat and end of seat appraisals.

## sponsorship & awards

LPC fees paid.

| | |
|---|---|
| **Partners** | 15 |
| **Fee-earners** | 44 |
| **Total Trainees** | 4 (2 p.a.) |

**contact**
Jo Goode - HR Manager
(01245) 211253

**method of application**
CV and application form,
see website for details

**selection procedure**
3 stage interview process

**closing date for 2008**
1 November 2006

**application**
Training contracts p.a. **2**
Applications p.a. **Approx 500**
Interviewed p.a. **Approx 50**
Required degree grade
**2:1 & 300 UCAS points**

**training**
Salary
**1st year £21,000**
**2nd year £22,000**

INVESTOR IN PEOPLE

# Wragge & Co LLP

55 Colmore Row, Birmingham B3 2AS
Tel: Freephone (0800) 096 9610
Email: gradmail@wragge.com
Website: http://graduate.wragge.com

## firm profile

Wragge & Co is a top 20 UK law firm providing a full-service to some of the world's largest and most successful organisations. Only by providing the highest quality of work and excellent client service can the firm list 33 of the FTSE 100 as its clients. With its main base in Birmingham and an office in London, over 70% of the firm's work is generated outside the Midlands and over 25% is international. Much has been said and written about the firm's culture. People who work at Wragge & Co will tell you it has a strong culture based on: (a) Integrity and honesty - in the firm's relationships by working to a set of values and commitments. (b) Working as a team - by ensuring everyone at Wragge & Co feels valued, can play a part in the firm going forward and act as a single team. (c) Making a commitment to its people - by communicating openly so they understand the business they are contributing to and can buy into the firm's overall aims. Wragge & Co encourage a balanced and flexible approach to work which results in lower stress levels and greater retention rates. Wragge & Co is a 'relationship' firm. The firm was 24th in The Sunday Times "100 best companies to work for 2005" and one of the best workplaces in the UK in a recent Financial Times survey. Wragge & Co was also voted "The Law Firm With the Best Training Environment" at a leading lawyer awards ceremony in 2003 and 2004.

## main areas of work

The firm has a national reputation in many areas, including dispute resolution, employment, tax, media, project finance and transport and utilities. It also has the UK's third largest real estate group and leading practices in corporate, construction, banking and intellectual property. Other "top five" areas include antitrust, public law and regulation and pensions. The quality of its work is reflected in the firm's client list, which includes AT&T, British Airways, Cadbury Schweppes, Cap Gemini Ernst & Young, Carlton UK Television, H J Heinz, HSBC, Marks & Spencer, McDonald's, Powergen, and Royal Bank of Scotland. The firm has over 1,000 employees, including 105 partners. While its main base remains in Birmingham the firm also has an office in London which deals with intellectual property, private equity, real estate and employment and pensions. You'll be given the opportunity to spend at least six months in the London office. More than a quarter of the firm's work is international and it is formally associated with German independent Graf von Westphalen Bappert & Modest. Many of its solicitors have broadened their experience and their language skills by undertaking international secondments in law firms across the world.

| | |
|---|---|
| **Partners** | 105 |
| **Assistant Solicitors** | 400 |
| **Total Trainees** | 48 |

**contact**
Julie Caudle,
Recruitment Manager

**method of application**
Applications are made online at http://graduate.wragge.com

**selection procedure**
Telephone discussion & assessment day

**closing date**
Sept 2008/March 2009: 31 July 2006. If you are a non-law student, please return your form as soon as possible, as the firm will be running assessment days over the forthcoming year

**application**
Training contracts p.a. 25
Applications p.a. 1,000
% interviewed p.a. 25%
Required degree grade 2:1

**training**
Salary Birmingham (Sept 2005)
1st year £21,500
2nd year £24,500
Salary London (Sept 2005)
1st year £28,500
2nd year £31,500
Holiday entitlement 25 days
% of trainees with a non-law degree p.a. Varies

**post-qualification**
Salary (2005)
Birmingham £34,500
London £49,000
% of trainees offered job on qualification
(2003 & 2004) 100%

# Wragge & Co LLP continued

## trainee profile

The firm is looking for graduates of 2:1 standard at degree level, with some legal or commercial work experience gained either via a holiday job or a previous career. You should be practical, with a common sense and problem solving approach to work, and be able to show adaptability, enthusiasm and ambition.

## training environment

The firm aims to transform its trainees into high quality, commercially-minded lawyers. You will spend six months in four different practice areas, usually including real estate, corporate and litigation, with a chance to specialise in a seat of your choice. From day one, you will work on live files with direct contact with clients and other solicitors, and be responsible for the management of the transaction and its ultimate billing. The more aptitude you show, the greater the responsibility you will be given. You will be supported by the graduate recruitment team, a partner who acts as a mentor to you throughout your training contract and a supervisor who will co-ordinate your work and give you weekly feedback. Introductory courses are provided at the start of each seat in addition to the professional skills course training requirements. This formal training complements "on the job" learning and it is more than likely that the firm's commitment to your development will extend well past the number of days recommended by the Law Society. Some of the courses will be residential, allowing you to reflect on your work practices, forge relationships and compare notes without the disturbances of your daily work. The firm's excellent trainee retention rates are the greatest testament to its training programme.

## benefits

Wragge & Co's benefits include prizes for 1st class degree and LPC distinction, £1,000 interest free loan, pension scheme, life insurance, permanent health insurance, 25 days holiday a year, travel schemes, private medical insurance, sports and social club, independent financial advice, corporate gym membership rates and a Christmas gift.

## sponsorship

The firm will provide your tuition fees for LPC and GDL (where relevant) and a maintenance grant of £4,500 for each year of study for LPC and GDL.

## vacation placements

Easter and summer vacation placements are run at Wragge & Co. As part of its scheme, you will get the opportunity to experience different areas of the firm, attend client meetings and get involved in real files. There are also organised social events with the firm's current trainees. Again, you can apply on-line at http://graduate.wragge.com (paper application form available on request). The closing date for applications is 31 January 2006.

Wragge & Co LLP is a Limited Liability Partnership

contacts

# contacts

**The Law Society**
113 Chancery Lane,
London WC2A 1PL
Tel: 020 7242 1222
E-mail: info.services@lawsociety.org.uk
www.lawsociety.org.uk

**Education and Training Department**
Tel: 0870 606 2555
E-mail: legaled@lawsociety.org.uk
www.training.lawsociety.org.uk

**Trainee Solicitors Group**
The Law Society
113 Chancery Lane,
London WC2A 1PL
Helpline: 08000 856 131
E-mail: info@tsg.org
www.tsg.org.uk

**The Bar Council**
289-293 High Holborn
London WC1V 7HZ
020 7242 0082
www.barcouncil.org.uk
For all other departments including the Education
and Training Department and the Equality and
Diversity Committee contact the main switchboard.

**Gray's Inn, Education Department**
8 South Square. Gray's Inn,
London WC1R 5ET
Tel: 020 7458 7800
www.graysinn.org.uk

**Inner Temple, Education & Training Department**
Treasury Building, Inner Temple,
London EC4Y 7HL
Tel: 020 7797 8250
www.innertemple.org.uk

**Lincoln's Inn, Students' Department**
Treasury Office, Lincoln's Inn,
London WC2A 3TL
Tel: 020 7405 0138
www.lincolnsinn.org.uk

**Middle Temple, Students' Department**
Treasury Office, Middle Temple Lane,
London EC4Y 9AT
Tel: 0207 427 4800
www.middletemple.org.uk

**The Institute of Legal Executives**
Kempston Manor, Kempston,
Bedfordshire MK42 7AB
Tel: 01234 841000
E-mail: info@ilex.org.uk
www.ilex.org.uk

**Government Legal Service**
Chancery House,
53-64 Chancery Lane,
London WC2A 1QS
Tel: 020 7649 6023
E-mail: glstrainees@tmp.com
www.gls.gov.uk

**Crown Prosecution Service**
50 Ludgate Hill,
London EC4M 7EX
Tel: 020 7796 8053
www.cps.gov.uk

**The Law Commission**
Conquest House, 37-38 John Street,
Theobalds Road,
London WC1N 2BQ
Tel: 020 7453 1220
E-mail: communications@lawcommission.gsi.gov.uk
www.lawcom.gov.uk

**Citizens Advice Bureaux**
Head Office, Myddelton House,
115-123 Pentonville Road,
London N1 9LZ
Tel: 020 7833 2181
Volunteer Hotline: 08451 264264
www.citizensadvice.org.uk

**Legal Services Commission**
Head Office, 85 Gray's Inn Road,
London WC1X 8TX
Tel: 020 7759 0000
www.legalservices.gov.uk

**Chartered Institute of Patent Agents**
95 Chancery Lane,
London WC2A IDT
Tel: 020 7405 9450
E-mail: mail@cipa.org.uk
www.cipa.org.uk

**Institute of Trade Mark Attorneys**
Canterbury House, 2-6 Sydenham Road, Croydon,
Surrey CR0 9XE
Tel: 020 8686 2052
www.itma.org.uk

Institute of Chartered Secretaries
and Administrators:
16 Park Crescent,
London W1B 1AH
Tel: 020 7580 4741
www.icsa.org.uk

The Law Centres Federation
Duchess House,
18-19 Warren Street,
London W1T 5LR
Tel: 020 7387 8570
E-mail: info@lawcentres.org.uk
www.lawcentres.org.uk

Free Representation Unit
6th Floor 289-293 High Holborn
London WC1V 7HZ
Tel: 0207 611 9555
Email: admin@freerepresentationunit.org.uk
www.freerepresentationunit.org.uk

The Bar Lesbian & Gay Group
Email: info@blagg.org
(BLAGG) www.blagg.org
Lesbian & Gay Lawyers Association
www.lagla.org.uk

The Society of Asian Lawyers
c/o Saima Hanif
4-5 St Gray's Inn Square
Gray's Inn
London WC1R 5AH
Email: info@societyofasianlawyers.com

The Society of Black Lawyers
9 Winchester House, 11 Cranmer Road
Kennington Park Road
London SW9 6EJ
Tel: 020 7735 652

The Association of Muslim Lawyers
PO Box 148 High Wycombe
Bucks HP13 5WJ
Email: aml@aml.org.uk
www.aml.org.uk

The Association of Women Barristers
Jane Hoyal 1 Pump Court Temple
London EC4Y 7AB
Email: Janehoyal@aol.com
www.womenbarristers.co.uk

Group for Solicitors with Disabilities
c/o Judith McDermott
The Law Society, 113 Chancery Lane
London WC2A 1PL
Tel: 020 7320 5793
Email: secretary@gsdnet.org.uk
www.gsdnet.org.uk

LPC Central Applications Board
P.O. Box 84, Guildford,
Surrey GU3 1YX
Tel: 01483 301282
www.lawcabs.ac.uk

CPE Central Applications Board
P.O. Box 84, Guildford,
Surrey GU3 1YX
Tel: 01483 451080
www.lawcabs.ac.uk O)

Online Pupillage Application System
Technical Assistance Helpline: 01491 828918
E-mail: pupillages@gtios.com
www.pupillages.com

Career Development Loans
Freepost, Warrington WA4 6FB
Tel: (freephone) 0800 585505
www.lifelonglearning.co.uk/cdl

# notes

# barristers

# barristers timetable

| | law students – penultimate undergraduate year | non-law students – final year |
|---|---|---|
| Throughout the year | Start thinking about getting some relevant work experience. Do plenty of research into chambers/mini pupillages | |
| By the end of January | | Apply for the CPE |
| By the end of April | Apply for a pupillage under the year early scheme on Olpas | |
| May | | Apply for a CPE scholarship from an Inn of Court. If successful, join that Inn |
| June to September | | Do pre-CPE mini-pupillages |
| September/October 2006 | Start final year of degree | Start CPE |
| November | By November apply through BVC Online for the BVC. Apply to an Inn of Court for a scholarship | |
| During final year/CPE | Apply for pupillage to non-OLPAS sets. Do mini pupillages | |
| April | Before 30th April apply for pupillage through OLPAS | |
| June | Apply for Inn membership | |
| September 2007 | Start the BVC. Apply through the September tranche of OLPAS; make further pupillage applications to non-OLPAS sets | |
| April | If unsuccessful last year, apply for pupillage before 30th April | |
| June | Finish BVC | |
| September | Apply for pupillage through OLPAS if you have yet to be successful | |
| October 2008 | Start pupillage | |
| Summer | Be offered tenancy at your pupillage chambers or apply for tenancy or a 3rd siv elsewhere | |
| October 2009 | Start tenancy | |
| 2039 | Be appointed to the High Court Bench | |
| 2049 | Get slapped on the wrist by DCA for falling asleep in court | |

# So you want to be a barrister...

## barcode

Don't let the often curious terms used at the Bar confuse or intimidate you!

**barrister** – a member of the Bar of England & Wales.

**bench** – the judiciary

**bencher** – a senior member of an Inn of Court. Usually silks and judges, known as masters of the bench

**brief** – the documents setting out case instructions

**bvc** – the Bar Vocational Course. Currently, its successful completion entitles you to call yourself a barrister in non-legal situations (ie dinner parties), but does not of itself give you rights of audience. Moves are afoot to require part of pupillage to have been completed before the title is conferred.

**bvc online** – the application system through which applications to Bar school must be made.

**cab-rank rule** – self-employed barristers cannot refuse instructions if they have the time and experience to undertake the case. You cannot refuse to represent someone because you find their opinions or actions objectionable.

**call** – the ceremony whereby you become a barrister

**chambers** – a group of barristers in independent practice who have joined together to share the costs of practising. Chambers is also the name used for a judge's private office.

**circuit** – The courts of England and Wales are divided into six circuits: North Eastern, Northern, Midland & Oxford, South Eastern, Western, and Wales & Chester circuits.

**clerk** – administrator/manager in chambers who organises work for barristers and payment of fees, etc

**counsel** – a barrister

**cracked-trial** – a case that is concluded without a trial. This will be because the defendant offers an acceptable plea or the prosecution offers no evidence. Cracked and ineffective trials (where there is a lack of court time or the defendant or a witness does not attend) frustrate the bench and are considered a waste of money.

**devilling** – (paid) work done by a junior member of chambers for a more senior member

**employed bar** – some barristers do not engage in private practice at chambers, but are employed full-time by a company or public body.

**first and second six** – pupillages are divided into two six-month periods. Most chambers now only offer 12-month pupillages, however it is still possible to undertake the two sixes at different sets.

**inns of court** – ancient institutions that alone have the power to 'make' barristers. There was a time when there was a proliferation of them but now there are only four: Gray's Inn, Inner Temple, Lincoln's Inn and Middle Temple.

**junior** – a barrister not yet appointed silk. Note: older juniors are known as senior juniors

**junior brief** – a case on which a junior is led by a senior. Such cases are too much work for one barrister alone and may involve a lot of research or run for a long time. Ordinarily, junior counsel will not conduct advocacy.

**keeping term** – eating the dinners in hall required to be eligible for call to the bar

**mini-pupillage** – a short period of work experience spent in chambers

**olpas** – the Online Pupillage Application System

**pupillage** – the year of training undertaken after Bar school and before tenancy.

**pupilmaster** – a senior barrister with whom a pupil sits and who teaches the pupil. The Bar Council is encouraging the term pupil supervisor.

**QC** – one of Her Majesty's Counsel, formerly appointed by the Lord Chancellor. The system fell into abeyance in 2004 and has now been revived with a new, more open appointments system.

**set** – as in a 'set of chambers'

**silk** – a QC, so named because of their silk robes

**supervisor** – the new name for a pupilmaster.

**tenant/tenancy** – permission from chambers to join their set and work with them. A 'squatter' is someone who is permitted to use chambers' premises, but is not actually a member of the set. A 'door tenant' is someone who is affiliated with the set, but does not conduct business from chambers' premises

## reality check

A career at the Bar offers intellectual satisfaction, variety and autonomy. The question is will you ever make it past the first hurdle? Any number of people will tell you to reconsider your chosen career path and train as a solicitor. "It's a dying profession," they'll tell you. "You'll never get pupillage." "You'll never get tenancy." "You didn't go to Oxbridge." "You'll never see your family and you'll become an alcoholic." None of these statements is wholly true, even if all are worthy of consideration.

Prospective barristers must prepare themselves for the most challenging game of musical chairs they have ever played. Roughly one in five people who enrol on the BVC end up with a lasting career at the Bar. If you're not familiar with the figures then turn to page 642. If you're back with us then you have passed the first test.

And FYI, the early years aren't necessarily what you'd call a money-spinner. The CPE is quite expensive, the BVC is painfully expensive, and a poorly funded pupillage year can be equally expensive. The Bar Council requires all pupillages to be funded to the tune of £10,000, and many criminal and common law sets think that's adequate. The position is very different at the top commercial and civil sets, where awards are more akin to those of trainee solicitors at commercial firms. Indeed some sets, such as 4 New Square, guarantee enviable earnings for the first three years of tenancy. If undertaking a minimally funded pupillage check with your Inn to see what scholarships and awards are available.

If you thought the Bar was a way in which you could both serve your community and earn a fortune, take note. The remuneration for publicly funded work has always been pretty bad. Andrew Hall QC, Chairman of the Bar Council's Remuneration Committee, said: "*The criminal legal aid system is in a bad state of disrepair and crumbling due to failure to invest in its payment systems. Rates are ten years out of date and growing more intolerable. We are rapidly approaching a position in which it is at risk of catastrophic collapse.*" The government has frozen publicly funded barristers' pay for the last eight years in cases lasting between one and ten days – these account for more than 95% of Crown Court trials. The Bar Council's number crunchers calculate this to be a cut of 23% in real terms since 1997. The extent of criminal barristers' discontent is evidenced by the 'strike' planned for the week we went to press.

There are now proposals to reduce the rates paid for trials lasting more than ten days. A review into the procurement of advocacy services has been commissioned and is expected to be completed in 2006. There is little expectation of much relief, however. While this may look rather interesting if observed from the safety of a desk in a commercial or Chancery chambers, for those just starting out on a publicly funded career – or contemplating one – it means that you need to get a decent pupillage followed by tenancy at a good set unless you are prepared to risk a life of relative pauperdom.

If we're honest, we don't expect this to have put too many readers off. It is perhaps the one thing that all wannabe-barristers have in common – a breathtaking belief that if anybody is going to succeed why shouldn't it be them. We salute your chutzpah, but it is time to take a good hard look at yourself. Does you CV show a strong, if not impeccable, academic background? Does it suggest you have the potential to be a good advocate and prove your commitment to the Bar?

## the basics

Get a diary, make a pledge to yourself to note every key date in it and then keep it close at hand. Good time management and a well-planned strategy are crucial. In any event, if you're really committed to this career path you might as well get used to this way of thinking. If you're still at university there's plenty to be getting on with. If there is anything a little *outré* about your CV – you're mature or you have poor A-levels, for instance – getting a First is a really good idea. 2:1s are two a penny and as for 2:2s, well, if you end up with one of these you'll have to be pretty remarkable in some other respect to persuade a recruiter to give you a try. In general, chambers are much more interested in your undergraduate performance than what you can muster up at Bar School, and for the record we have it on excellent authority that good pupillages can be secured with the scantiest of passes on the CPE/GDL. That said, 'Very Competent' grades proliferate on the BVC, so why be awkward and get a 'Competent'?

## mini adventures

Let's look a little closer at your commitment to the Bar. The best way to demonstrate that you possess any is to carry out some mini-pupillages. Remember, mini-pupillage is just high-falutin' barristerspeak for work experience. They come in two flavours: assessed and unassessed. During an unassessed mini you will observe a barrister in his or her chambers and probably also in court. How much you will be involved in proceedings varies hugely. In the course of a good mini you will sit in on a pre-trial conference, with the client's permission, and will be included in discussions about the law. One person we spoke to was invited to spend nearly every moment from fry-up to nightcap with their supervising barrister, though we suspect this is not the norm. Another reported turning up at chambers on the appointed day only to be told by a clerk to go to a particular court; after finding the court and sitting in the public gallery for a while, they eventually tracked down their putative supervisor in the robing room where they were greeted with something between bemusement and indifference. It is not unheard of for mini-pupils at commercial sets to go days at a time without seeing the inside of a court. Don't become fixed on the idea of spending a whole week with chambers as you may find it easier (and more beneficial) to get a couple of days here and there. Arguably the benefits are the same and you'll be able to compare your experiences.

Many sets will only recruit those that have undertaken an assessed mini-pupillage with them. This will be a more formal experience and will keep you on your toes the entire time. The most likely scenario is that you'll be given a set of papers to analyse and then be asked to produce a piece of written work. Our best advice is to take constant notes throughout your mini-pupillage and don't be afraid to ask your supervisor questions at appropriate moments if you see or read something you don't fully understand. Shortly after it finishes, take a couple of hours to write up what you saw and learned about the place and the work you did. Think particularly about the quality of any advocacy you observed and what you thought about the lifestyle in general. This will be helpful when completing application forms and chatting with recruiters at interviews. In fact, approach all relevant 'experience' from now on mindfully and with a pen.

## how do i get one?

Not all chambers offer mini-pupillages, so start off by checking chambers websites and making a list of potentials. A set's website will tell you the format your application should take and the person to whom it should be addressed. In general, chambers will want a CV and covering letter.

As with everything else in this game, demand for mini-pupillages is high so apply as you would Calamine lotion on a rash – liberally and at the first sign of an itch for the Bar. This is when personal contacts really come into their own. People get pupillage through whom they know less than some people would have you believe, but getting a mini is different. Speak to any barristers you know and make your intentions clear. If Uncle Eddie dated some woman at 17 Ramshackle Row back in the 80s, get him to contact her again. Most barristers are flattered by the idea of some youngster wanting to follow in their wake and are genuinely willing to help. If your little black book isn't reading like a copy of the *Times Law Reports* then create your own contacts. Apply to an Inn of Court to be assigned a sponsor; and if you've started dining, stop hiding in the corner and schmooze already.

The question as to how many mini-pupillages you should do is not that easy to answer except to say that less than one is too few but reach a dozen and all you're demonstrating is that you've nothing else going on in your life.

## extra-curricular activities

So you are well on the way to getting a great degree and you've done a handful of mini-pupillages. It's high time you thought about doing some pro bono work (that's legal advice given for free to people who can't really afford to pay). You will be required to do a certain amount on your BVC anyway, but anything you do off your own bat will always have added value. There are plenty of ways to get involved in pro bono work.

What else should you do? "*Everything you can*," was the advice of one QC. In a nutshell this means getting involved with every debating and mooting opportunity that crops up. At law school you'll have the chance to enter mock trial competitions. And you might also want to keep an eye out for essay competitions. Further, the scholarships offered by the Inns should be thought of not only as a way of funding your education, but also as a way of adding weight to your CV. Don't underestimate the capacity of a prize or award to mark you out from all the other well-qualified candidates out there.

## olpas: getting a foot in the door

The Online Pupillage Application Service has been up and running since 2001. It is not compulsory for chambers to participate in the scheme, but every pupillage provider is required by the Bar Council to advertise its vacancies on the Olpas website, www.pupillage.com. The same information is also produced in the Pupillages and Awards Handbook, published to coincide with the opening of the online system and the National Pupillage Fair held in March. Olpas has

two seasons: summer and autumn. The closing date for summer season applications is 30 April, allowing three months for interviews, with offers made after 31 July. The autumn season opens at the end of August and closes on 30 September, with just a month for interviews and offers made after 31 October. A set of chambers may participate in one or other season.

Students may apply for a pupillage through Olpas during as many seasons as they like, but are limited to 12 sets in each. Most LLB students apply during the final year of their degree course, although some of the top commercial sets encourage students to apply in their penultimate year in an attempt to snap up the best candidates. Twelve-month pupillages are the most common and convenient option for students, although six-month pupillages are also offered by some sets and there is nothing unusual about undertaking a 'first six' and a 'second six' in different sets.

The 'beauty' of Olpas is that all correspondence regarding interviews, offers and rejections is sent via e-mail, which is supposed to be time-saving and efficient. However, it will make you obsessional about checking your inbox, which in turn can become annoying to everyone around you. A number of sets show a healthy disdain for the whole shebang and choose to call on that old-fashioned contrivance, the mobile telephone.

## perfect pitch

Think carefully when choosing where to apply. If you know you're top dollar and that's what you're after then off you go. If you're not sure of your calibre take a look at the CVs of chambers' latest recruits. This will give you some indication of the kind of person the set wants. If you didn't go to one of 'those two' universities, why apply exclusively to sets whose members are all dyed-in-the-wool Oxbridge types?

Be consistent. Chambers won't see which other sets you are applying to but the way the Olpas form is designed, they will see the list of practice areas that you have chosen. Think about it from their point of view: when all candidates are equally well educated and fully rounded why bother with the guy that says he is interested in construction, crime and intellectual property? Don't hedge your bets; put down the barest minimum and limit the potential for awkward interview questions.

## an exercise in form filling?

Keep it personal. Put nothing on the form that you cannot talk about for a good four minutes. Take FRU – who isn't commencing/currently under-taking/about to complete their FRU training? If you haven't actually signed out a case then a mention of FRU can look like desperate filler material. Anchor your spiel in your own experiences and your application will be more persuasive.

Keep it pithy. Shakespeare once said brevity is the soul of wit. It should also be the spirit of an Olpas form. For each section you can write no more than 150 words and this should help your cause as long sentences can be tedious and you're chances of getting an interview are greatly improved if the recruiter stays conscious.

Avoid being trite. You'll be asked to explain why you want to be a barrister. That a career at the Bar offers an attractive combination of academe and practicality is a given. Here you run most danger of getting lost in the crowd. Think what the obvious answer is and write something more meaningful.

Write proper. For instance, 'practice' is the noun; 'practise' is the verb. If you haven't learnt this already, now is the time. As one senior QC put it: "Given that this is a job in which a strong command of the English language is paramount, we are often amazed at some of the fundamental errors that crop up in the Olpas applications."

Don't make silly mistakes. Your mantra should be: "Save, print, check. Save, print, check." With some of the best sets getting around 500 applications, they are itching for a reason to put your form in the bin. Don't give them this one.

## non-olpas sets

Olpas is not the only way to secure a pupillage. One student told us they had made "12 applications through Olpas and not a single sniff; two non-Olpas applications – one pupillage! Olpas just didn't work for me." Securing pupillage outside of Olpas can save a lot of heartache, as a veteran of the non-Olpas circuit told us: "Not only did I get security early on, which was nice, but I avoided the huge amount of stress and pressure that Olpas gen-erates." A set's decision not to be part of the online scheme says nothing about its quality.

The application process at each set will be dif-ferent and will operate on a different timetable. Some use the Olpas calendar but many don't, and this can bring its own problems. One pupil cautioned: "The exploding offer phenomenon is a real difficulty. Shortly before my first Olpas inter-view I was made a very attractive offer from a non-Olpas set that I just couldn't pass up. They are a great chambers and I'm really happy to be there but it did stop me from trying my hand elsewhere." Research things well in advance to make sure you don't miss any deadlines. As one interviewee counselled: "Applying to non-Olpas sets requires a great deal of motivation. There are a lot of them out there and many of them are very good. They should be taken very seriously." If nothing else, keeping your eyes peeled for advertisements and checking your diary to see which sets' deadlines are looming will afford some diversion through-out the year. And remember, all pupillages must be clearly notified on the Olpas website.

## expect the spanish inquisition

So you've got an interview? Well done. Firstly, dress like you're going to court not the set of Ally McBeal. A good handshake and an engaging smile will do wonders. First interviews should be rea-sonably painless. The panel want you to stand out and they will want to like you. You can make it easy for them by leaving the bells and whistles at home, but also reminding yourself that serious is not the same as solemn. Most chambers will be grading you on standard criteria that incorporates attributes from intellect to personality. Check their website and see if this is published.

Expect your first interview to involve a discussion of the hottest topics in your prospective practice area and some gentle investigation into your application form. It is possible that the first Olpas round you do will coincide with the end of term. Tough. Start preparing for your interviews as soon as your hangover has worn off. When the interview invitations do come through, you may not be left with much time to get out your *Nutshells*. And get them out you must. Read *The Times* every Tuesday and keep your subscription to *Counsel* up to date. As well as being abreast of current legal issues you should also stay clued-up on current affairs. And when we say clued-up what we really mean is develop an opinion. "Oh yes, *terrorism*, isn't it awful," is never going to cut it.

Finally, think about what isn't on your CV and how you can account for anything missing or a little embarrassing. It is probably best to approach these things with honesty rather than creativity, but whichever you go for if you got a 2:2 you need to offer a reason why. Oh, and learn a joke.

For second interviews expect a larger panel made up of a broader cross-section of people from chambers. While the format of the interviews may vary between sets, the panel will always want to assess the depth of your legal knowledge, your advocacy potential and your mettle. Weaknesses on you CV will be sniffed out and pursued with tenacity, and you will be pressed to the extent of your knowledge and intellect. Don't let them push you around; if you believe in your position then stick to it. Resolve is just as necessary for a career at the Bar as receptivity, and the panel will want to know when push comes to shove that you can fight your corner.

Criminal and mixed sets will commonly give you an advocacy exercise, such as a bail application or a plea in mitigation (their basic structures will fit on a post-it, so why not note them down and keep with you at all times). Most, if not all, sets will pose a legal problem, with the amount of preparation time you are given ranging from ten minutes to a week. Don't panic. You'll never feel prepared enough and no one else will either. If you can be trusted not to use all your time flicking through the index, take an appropriate textbook or practitioner's text.

A second interview is often the time when ethical questions raise their ambiguous heads. There is rarely a correct answer to these questions. However, you can do yourself a favour by reading the Code of Conduct, which is available on the Bar Council's website. It's a real page turner.

A second interview will be less fun than the first, but hang on to the fact that you've done marvellously to get this far and keep it together.

## dust yourself off and try again...

What if you have finished the BVC and you still don't have pupillage? You are not alone. This enforced year out can be a grim and daunting prospect. However, this time can be used to improve your CV. Complete your FRU training and do some tribunals. Ask yourself how you can become more marketable. The answer you'll probably come up with is paralegalling or outdoor clerking. This will earn you valuable experience and chambers love the idea that you might bring work with you. Earn some money and maybe have some fun. Remember that if all goes according to plan this will be the last opportunity you get to spend three months farming llamas. If that rings your bell...

## and the fat lady sings

It is not right to approach this game as one of many possible careers: you need to believe that it is this or nothing. That said, you should give yourself a time limit in which to secure pupillage and perhaps make it a little shorter than the seven years for which your BVC is valid.

# the inns of court

Like Yorkshire pudding and cricket, the four ancient Inns of Court are great British institutions that have withstood the sands of time. Bearing a striking similarity to Oxbridge colleges, with the customary chapel, hall and library, the Inns were originally places of residence and learning for young barristers. The Inns still perform some important functions: they alone have the power to 'call' a person to the Bar. Before you can be called you must 'keep term' by attending dinners or other qualifying sessions.

## brideshead regurgitated?

All four Inns offer mooting, whether it be at internal, inter-Inn or national competition level. Those in need of careers advice can take advantage of mentoring schemes and the Inns also run a marshalling scheme giving students the opportunity to spend a week sitting alongside a judge, observing the proceedings and discussing the case at the end of the day. Advocacy workshops and seminars are held at Cumberland Lodge in the heart of Great Windsor Park (pack your waxed jackets for that one) and the Inns' various students' associations all have active social calendars.

Students must join an Inn by the June before they start their BVC, but the earlier they join the earlier they can make the most of everything.

## lining your pockets

All four Inns offer scholarships for the CPE, BVC and pupillage. You don't have to be a member of the Inn to apply for these, but you must undertake to join in the event that you are successful. The highly competitive selection process includes an interview. There is normally money reserved to help students from the regional BVC institutions meet their costs when visiting the Inn, and to pay for qualifying sessions. Many of the Inns offer awards for overseas internships. For specific details of the amounts on offer, students should contact the Inns directly or check their websites.

## lincoln's inn

**www.lincolnsinn.org.uk**

Lincoln's Inn is an oasis of calm amid a sea of chaos. The biggest Inn, it boasts some 'A' list celebrities including Cherie and Tony. Students recommend the Inn for its "*free-flowing wine and the great atmosphere*." As well as the usual activities, the Inn organises an annual trip to visit the European Court of Justice, the Court of Human Rights and the Hague Tribunals. Lincoln's is known for its international membership.

## inner temple

**www.innertemple.org.uk**

From Chaucer to Charlie Falconer, this Inn has more history than we've had hot dinners. It is a place for firsts: the first female barrister was a member, as was the first female Treasurer, Dame Elizabeth Butler-Sloss. Its Students Association packs a busy social diary and the mooting society is a regular contender in international competitions.

## middle temple

**www.middletemple.org.uk**

As former member Charles Dickens put it, the Middle Temple has "*something of a clerkly monkish atmosphere, which public offices of law have not disturbed, and even legal firms have failed to scare away*." Debating is a particular forte and the 'Christmas Revels' are notorious. Students recommend lecture nights for "*copious amounts of food and wine and excellent guest speakers*."

## gray's inn

**www.graysinn.org.uk**

The smallest and most traditional of the Inns. At dinners, toasting is the order of the day, particularly on Grand Day when a communal chalice of wine is passed down the table in "*pious memory of Good Queen Bess*." Students say, "*you get to know other students and Benchers really quickly, and there are always familiar faces at dinner*.

# pupillage and the tenancy decision

Pupillage is a game of two halves: in the first six months, pupils will be assigned to a supervisor whom they will shadow and assist. This will involve attending court, carrying out legal research and drafting paperwork. Many chambers will also run their own in-house advocacy training in addition to the compulsory training organised by the Inns of Court.

Expect to spend your first six under the supervision of more than one supervisor; the purpose of the year is to give you as wide an experience of chambers' work as possible. After six months, pupils who have obtained 'second sixes' in a different set will pack their bags. Those who remain in their original set will notice a few changes. In the second six pupils can usually handle work in their own right (though under the 'L' plate of their supervisor's insurance policy). In a criminal set, pupils will attend the magistrates' court on a regular basis, whereas in commercial sets the opportunity to do work entirely alone will be less regular (or sometimes entirely absent).

As well as learning the tools of the trade, pupils must worry about the looming tenancy decision. We've reproduced the Bar Council's statistics for you because, as you're probably aware already, securing a pupillage does not guarantee you a job at the end of the year. Exactly what chambers look for in a new tenant varies from set to set, and pupil supervisors will no doubt give their pupils a few hints along the way. Generally, however, all sets value certain basic skills and attributes, so we hope the following tips will stand you in good stead.

Try to establish a good relationship with the clerks.

They are the people that will be pushing work in your direction, and senior clerks often have an influential voice when it comes to the tenancy decision. Especially in the second six, try to give instructing solicitors a good impression. Word of how you perform and your bedside manner will get back to chambers via them. Barristers' chambers are businesses, and if a firm of solicitors is suitably pleased with you and wants to instruct you again, it's all good news.

It is easy to see yourself as being in competition with the other pupils in chambers. In some sets this is definitely not the case; in others...well, yes you probably are. Either way, there is more to be gained by providing each other with mutual support and encouragement than there is from tying their shoelaces together when they aren't looking!

Those who end up without an offer of tenancy will find clerks and members of chambers are normally happy to help pupils secure tenancy or a further period of pupillage elsewhere. Many chambers will allow pupils to stay on for a third six months of pupillage. Squatting is often another possibility. Unfortunately for some pupils, despite persistence and hard work, becoming a tenant in private practice just doesn't happen. This doesn't mark the end of your legal career as there are still plenty of career opportunities for qualified barristers in employed practice, whether it be in local or central government, or as an in-house lawyer in the private sector. Furthermore, the solicitors' side of the profession is increasingly employing those who come from the Bar, whether or not they wish to requalify as solicitors.

| | 98-99 | 99-00 | 00-01 | 01-02 | 02-03 | 03-04 | 04-05 |
|---|---|---|---|---|---|---|---|
| BVC applicants | 2,696 | 2,370 | 2,252 | 2,119 | 2,067 | 2,570 | 2,883 |
| BVC enrolments | 1,459 | 1,490 | 1,407 | 1,386 | 1,332 | 1,406 | n/a |
| Students passing the BVC | 1,238 | 1,201 | 1,110 | 1,182 | 1,121 | 1,251 | n/a |
| First six pupils | 706 | 681 | 695 | 812 | 586 | 518 | 571 |
| Second six pupils | 694 | 704 | 700 | 724 | 702 | 557 | n/a |
| Pupils awarded tenancy | 541 | 511 | 535 | 541 | 698 | 601 | n/a |

# practice areas at the bar

## chancery

The Chancery Division of the High Court has traditionally heard cases with an emphasis on legal principles, foremost among them the concept of equity. Chancery work epitomises legal reasoning; it is an area for those who love the law and love to grapple with its most complex aspects. The tools of the Chancery practitioner's trade are legal arguments and their skills lie in the application of these tools to real-life situations. Chancery practice may have ancient roots, but as Catherine Addy at Maitland Chambers was keen to point out: *"You are often looking at ancient principles but will be applying them to modern situations and, of course, the principles themselves often evolve over time. It is not at all uncommon to be referring, in the same case, to authorities from the nineteenth century as well as those handed down in 2004."*

### type of work
Chancery can be divided into 'traditional' (trusts, probate, real property, charities, mortgages) and 'commercial' (company law, shareholder disputes, partnership, banking, pensions, financial services, insolvency, professional negligence, tax, media, IP). Most Chancery sets will undertake both, albeit with varying emphases. Furthermore, the division between Chancery practice and commercial practice is less apparent than before. Barristers at commercial sets can frequently be found on Chancery cases and vice versa, though some areas, such as tax and IP, often beg specialisation.

At first, small commercial and property-related cases (eg possession proceedings) will see you in and out of county courts up and down the country. You can also expect your fair share of winding up applications in the Companies Court and appearances before the bankruptcy registrars. In the more prominent sets, you might be brought in as second or third junior on larger, more complex cases – possibly even an overseas case.

Your lay client could be anyone from a little old lady to the finance director of a blue-chip company. *"Variety is the spice of life,"* Catherine reminded us. *"Sometimes it's nice to have a human side to a case."* The thing to remember is that although advocacy will be a core element of your work, you will spend the majority of your time in chambers, perusing papers, considering arguments, drafting pleadings, skeletons and advices, or conducting settlement negotiations. While some instructions fly into chambers, need immediate attention and then disappear just as quickly, others can rumble on for years – although not quite as long as the infamous case of Jarndyce and Jarndyce in Dickens' blockbusting Chancery saga, *Bleak House*.

### skills needed
Invariably, Chancery lawyers are pretty hot in the brains department; they are high fliers with a real affinity for the law. Catherine thinks that when trying to find your *"inner Chancery persona,"* you should consider whether you are most interested in equity, trusts, company and insolvency law. She also ventures that you'll enjoy the analytical process involved in constructing an argument and evaluating the answers to legal problems. *"Of course, quite often there isn't a straightforward answer, and that's why you end up in court trying to find one."*

Solicitors will come to you with complex and puzzling cases. Once you've unravelled and analysed them you'll then need to explain legal arguments and principles in such a way that the solicitor and lay client both understand the advice you are giving. You also need to be able to present your argument to the judge in a persuasive and sophisticated manner. Far from being a legal boffin, you need to be a master of communication and practical in the legal solutions you offer.

Unlike your peers practising crime, your weekly agenda won't be set by last-minute briefs for next-day court appearances. Instead, you'll need self-discipline and an instinctive sense of exactly how much time and energy you need to devote to each of the instructions on your desk.

## prospects

This is a highly competitive area of practice to break into. An excellent academic record is a must; most pupils in leading sets will have a First-class degree, although this is certainly not a pre-requisite, and do bear in mind that this need not be in law. You should also demonstrate an aptitude for public speaking and, if a law under-grad, this should include mooting experience. You should also be able to show that you've completed at least a couple of mini-pupillages – with or including Chancery sets. The Chancery Bar seems to be fairly immune to the bad-news stories about shrinking work and tumbling brief fees. This is the Rolls-Royce end of the Bar and it continues to attract not only plenty of domestic work, but also a considerable amount of offshore and cross-border instructions.

## commercial

The commercial Bar handles business disputes in a range of industry sectors. In its purest definition, commercial cases are heard by the Commercial Court or one of the Mercantile Courts or Business Lists. A broader definition includes matters dealt with by both the Queen's Bench and Chancery Divisions of the High Court, and the Technology and Construction Court (TCC). Many commercial disputes are arbitrated, which is similar to litigation, but a little more flexible and conducted in private. Also, alternative methods of dispute resolution, such as mediation, are becoming more popular as they can have the advantage of preserving commercial relationships that might otherwise have been destroyed by the litigation process.

## type of work

We spoke to Sean O'Sullivan, a tenant at 4 Pump Court, about the nature of the job. Likening commercial litigation to playing "*a giant game of chess*," he spoke about guiding the client through the litigation process, and selecting the most appropriate manoeuvres to put them in a better position with their opponent. The role blends advice and paper advocacy with courtroom advocacy. Sean explained how the client positions itself through statements of case, witness statements, and interlocutory skirmishes. In this sense, life as a commercial barrister is a far cry from that of a criminal practitioner, who might be in court every day. As the majority of disputes settle, "*it's all about assessing the prospects of success...and then doing a deal which reflects or exceeds that assessment.*"

Very junior barristers will, at least in some commercial sets, get to handle their own small cases – perhaps initially including common law cases such as road traffic, PI or employment disputes – while gaining exposure to larger commercial cases by assisting more senior colleagues. As a 'second junior' they will carry out research and prepare first drafts of documents to assist the first junior and the QC leading the case. Just as importantly, they will have the opportunity to observe silks in action in court, learning how to cross-examine witnesses and how best to present arguments. Then, in time, their own cases will increase in value and complexity: claims relating to shipping, insurance and reinsurance, commodities, banking, and general contractual matters are all standard fare. At seven years' call, Sean has handled all these types of case, as well as professional negligence, shipbuilding and entertainment industry disputes.

The fundamentals of almost all matters are contract and tort, and the area remains rooted in common law, although domestic and European legislation is also important. Commercial barristers' incomes now reflect the popularity of the English courts with overseas litigants, and cross-border issues including competition law, insolvency and conflicts of laws are all increasingly relevant.

## skills needed

You need to be very bright to stand a chance at the commercial Bar and you'll have to work long hours, often under pressure. Sean suggested that: *"The real skill is in spotting the argument that most people won't see or identifying the argument that is most likely to be persuasive."* Written skills are just as important as oral advocacy, possibly more so. And yet, brainpower is only half of the story: *"You can't necessarily expect to have developed any commercial acumen as a student, but you will need to pick it up quickly in practice; you'll have to understand the client's business objectives in order to see how you can help them to achieve them."* Your service standards must be impeccable and your style user-friendly: *"This means putting yourself out for solicitors and clients,"* Sean explained. *"Sometimes they'll send you something in a hurry and you have to pick it up and run with it, even if it isn't in the form you would prefer. And if they call you late in the evening or at weekends, you take the call. The commercial firms of solicitors don't want pomp and ceremony. They are not instructing barristers because they are impressed by the wigs, they just want to get the job done. If you are going to help them do that, great; if not, they will find someone who will."*

## prospects

Much has been said about shrinking small-end work but overall the commercial Bar is faring well. Get yourself into a good set and there's nothing to stop you making an exceedingly good living. Consciously or not, most barristers tend to specialise to a degree by building up expertise on cases for a particular industry sector, for example shipping or banking. It gives them the added value that solicitors look for when deciding who to instruct.

Competition for pupillage at the commercial Bar is as tough as it gets. A First-class degree is commonplace and you'll need to offer ample evidence of mooting and debating. You'll also need impressive references and a willingness to work extremely hard.

## common law

English common law derives from the precedents set by judicial decisions rather than from the contents of statutes. Most of the cases run by common law barristers turn on principles of tort and contract, and are dealt with in the Queen's Bench Division (QBD) of the High Court and the county courts. At the edges, this type of practice blurs into both Chancery and commercial law.

## type of work

As any junior in a common law set will tell you, one of the major attractions is the variety of work that lands on their desk: employment, PI, inquests, crime, landlord and tenant, small commercial and contractual disputes – it's all there for the taking. According to Akash Nawbatt from Devereux Chambers: *"Employment and PI are your bread and butter, but you get to cover different areas of the law and each case has its different facts. This is both challenging and interesting."* Common law barristers tend to carry on practising on a full range of cases throughout their careers, but there is an opportunity to begin to specialise between five and ten years' call.

Prospects for advocacy are good, and on average you could expect to be in court two to three days per week. As Akash says: *"Most people come to the Bar to be on their feet and arguing cases."* Not only can pupils expect to have their own cases during their second six, but also their pupilmasters or senior barristers could select them to be a junior on a more complex case. It is undeniable that a recent drive towards mediation has reduced the number of cases going to court, and that some solicitors have made strides in advocacy, but on the whole the role of the barrister is still valued. Solicitor advocates may frequently attend directions hearings, but are still rarely seen at trial. Legal Aid cutbacks and conditional fee agreements – especially for PI claims – both affect remuneration, but if you can get tenancy at a good set, you'll still be able to earn a pretty good living.

## skills needed

Akash observes: *"Personal skills cannot be underestimated. Often the client won't have been to court before and will be very nervous. It's your responsibility to put them at ease, so a good bedside manner is crucial. They may be expecting someone older than you, so you have to inspire confidence at an early stage."*

As you will be dealing with a variety of cases, you will need a nimble mind to assimilate the factual details of each one, and a good long-term memory when it comes to the law itself. You must be flexible in your working practices: *"At the junior end the work comes in at very short notice, but you have to be able to meet your deadlines. The night before the case you may have to read a lever arch file and digest what's important."* On the downside, this means it is difficult to plan too far ahead, and your friends may have to get used to you bailing out on them at short notice. On the upside, the chances of you ever growing bored are minimal.

## prospects

The market is fiercely competitive at the junior end and you have to make your mark to secure your next set of instructions. If you want to specialise in a certain area, make sure that you have thoroughly researched the sets you apply to for pupillage. As ever, mini-pupillages are advised.

# crime

Such is the number of TV shows portraying criminal briefs that the general public could be forgiven for assuming that the entire Bar practises crime. It's an area that cries out for individuals of a certain disposition and specific talents though...

## type of work

Pupils cut their teeth on motoring offences, committals and directions hearings in the magistrates' courts. Things progress quickly and by the end of their second six, pupils should be instructed in their own right. In the early years junior tenants will be exposed to the entire gamut of cases: initially trial work is restricted to smaller offences such as common assault, but this soon turns into ABH, robbery and possession of drugs with intent to supply. Perform well and this could lead to a role as a junior on a major Crown Court trial.

Apply to be included on the CPS list so that you can prosecute as well as defend. Oliver Blunt QC from Furnival Chambers notes that, apart from a regular source of income, *"working on both sides of the street tends to make you a better advocate."*

Joining the criminal Bar will ensure you have ample opportunity to develop your nascent advocacy skills. According to Oliver: *"Advocacy skills are the same for the minor cases as the major ones. Indeed, convincing a hard-core bench of cynical justices can be more difficult than a credulous jury."* Many advocates start off their careers reading from a script, only much later feeling sufficiently confident in their oratory flair to improvise their performance. But even the most skilful advocate knows that success rests on effective case preparation, and never forgets that the law and sentencing policies evolve constantly.

## skills needed

Arguably criminal barristers need an appreciation for theatre and an innate sense of dramatic timing. Oliver told us: *"Defence work appeals to the iconoclast – the prosecution attempts to create an impenetrable edifice, and you have to smash a hole in the side. In a sense you have a captive audience in the jury, and the impact of a closing speech can swing the result either way."* Criminal barristers must be able to relate to people, whether they are defendants, witnesses, victims, judges or members of a jury. They must also impress the instructing solicitor and gain their trust, particularly when still a junior looking to build a practice. Sometimes dealing with defendants requires a great deal of patience. Oliver explained: *"You have to be receptive to your client's arguments, even if you have no faith in them. You need to be prepared to explain the ramifications of what they are seeking, and sometimes make it clear that their application really is hopeless."*

A good team ethic is important – pupils and juniors are effectively kept afloat by the relationships that their seniors have built with instructing solicitors' firms. Oliver has a simple piece of advice: *"Although it is important to market yourself, don't denigrate others or get a reputation as a 'diary watcher'. This always gets back to the clerks."*

## prospects

The criminal Bar tends to provide more pupillages than other areas, but these don't necessarily translate into tenancies, because the market is so competitive. It is also worth noting that life at the junior Bar is becoming more demanding than ever before: the inception of graduated fees (paid by the Legal Services Commission) and the rise of solicitor advocates have both had a negative effect. However, if you're willing to accept the more limited financial rewards, the allure of the stage could still prove irresistible.

# employment

*"Employment legislation is blooming."* These words from Littleton Chambers junior Eleena Misra help to explain the good fortune of employment barristers. It's also true that people are more aware of their employment rights than ever before as *"cases are more widely reported now. People see a Metro headline: 'Chef wins £10,000 from employer' and they think it's worth having a bash."* Legal representation is not required in an employment tribunal, and only rarely will there be a costs penalty for the unsuccessful party, so there are fewer barriers to bringing a case. *"And consider the effect of the internet,"* Eleena added. *"You can even issue a claim online!"* True, accessibility is one of the aims of the employment tribunal system; however, cases are often of such complexity that specialist legal advice is absolutely essential.

## type of work

Few juniors limit themselves solely to employment practice – most will also undertake civil or commercial cases. Eleena's set is known for its employment expertise, and she spends up to 75% of her time on this type of work. Few juniors nail their colours to the mast, only acting for applicants (employees) or respondents (employers). However, at senior level this changes a bit because respondents can generally afford to pay higher legal fees.

Straightforward tribunal claims, such as unfair dismissals, discrimination cases and relatively low-value contract claims are interspersed with more complex matters such as whistleblowing, injunctions to prevent the breach of restrictive covenants, and cases that cross over with company law actions that involve shareholders. Eleena is *"frequently dealing with redundancy dismissals and race and sex discrimination claims."* Other forms of discrimination claims are coming on stream as a result of new EU legislation concerning age, religion and sexual orientation.

Most advocacy takes place in an employment tribunal or the Employment Appeals Tribunal, as opposed to the courts, and the atmosphere and proceedings in each are deliberately less formal. *"Hearings are conducted with everyone sitting down,"* Eleena explained. *"They follow the basic examination-in-chief, cross-examination and closing submissions, so even though you're not on your feet, you're still advocating."* A barrister has to modify his or her style when appearing against someone who is unrepresented, as *"no tribunal likes to see a barrister intimidating an applicant in person."*

## skills needed

Of course you've got to love advocacy, but beyond that there are skills and personality traits that a good employment lawyer will possess and develop. They say no one expects the Spanish Inquisition, but equally, no one can predict what they'll encounter in a tribunal. As Eleena rightly points out: *"The majority of people spend more time in the workplace with colleagues than they do with their nearest and dearest. The situations and conflicts that can arise have endless, endless variations."*

The cases she's worked on have ranged from *"the very, very sad and distressing to the hilarious."* One case involved an investigation into the throwing of a Cadbury's Creme Egg while another required a site visit to a public house in Mayfair. And then consider for a moment how distressing it must be to cross-examine someone with a disability about sensitive medical issues. *"You have to do your job but it's never pleasant to see someone burst into tears,"* Eleena admitted.

Keeping abreast of developments in the law is crucial because sometimes you'll have precious little time to prepare your case for trial. Furthermore, with new directives, regulations and cases appearing all the time, you'll be forever having your cases stayed while others with similar points are being heard on appeal.

## prospects

The future looks pretty bright for employment lawyers, and there are many good sets that offer the work as a part of the pupillage package. Look up the people at the Free Representation Unit (see page 25) sooner rather than later – they have a lot to offer students and pupils by way of first-hand experience.

# family

Packed with emotionally charged issues, family law is a demanding practice area for a barrister, who is likely to be involved only in the most complex or combative cases. A huge amount of court time is allotted to divorce, separation, adoption, child residence and contact orders, financial provision and domestic violence. However, increasingly mediation is used to resolve disputes in a more efficient and less unsettling fashion. The family Bar had been concerned that this, and an increase in solicitor advocates, would lead to a downturn in work;

yet, with the exception of children's cases in which solicitors have always been encouraged to do their own advocacy, instructions for the Bar appear to have continued largely unabated.

## type of work

Barristers learn the ropes on simple county court matters, progressing to complex matters in the Family Division of the High Court. In the early years, there will be a lot of private law children work (disputes between parents), small financial cases and injunctions in situations of domestic violence.

Ellen Saunders at One Garden Court, explained how financial arrangements and *public and private law children's work* each offer their own challenges. In the former it helps to have an interest in understanding pensions and shares and a good grounding in the basics of trusts and property. Meanwhile, private law children's cases can sometimes involve serious allegations between parents and require the input of child psychologists; the public law counterpart (care proceedings between local authorities and parents) invariably includes detailed and often harrowing medical evidence. Ellen advises checking the orientation of a set before applying for pupillage, though she also cautions against narrowing your options too early.

The legislation affecting this area is comprehensive, but there's also a large and flourishing body of case law. You must keep abreast of all new decisions because while no two families are identical, the basics remain the same in relation to the problems they experience. The job is, therefore, more about negotiating general principles than adhering strictly to precedents.

## skills needed

Ellen believes that *"you can't be someone who needs predictability,"* as *"what your client wants at 5pm is often different to what they wanted at 9am."* The emotional subtext calls for communication, tact and maturity in abundance. *"You have to develop empathy for clients and personal resilience in equal measures.*" Inevitably, the work involves asking clients for intimate details of unpleasant aspects of their private life, and breaking devastating news to the emotionally fragile. As Ellen explained: "*In most cases, this is a once-in-a-lifetime experience for your client and they rely on you to hold their hand throughout, even when you have to give them advice that they don't want to hear.*"

The end result of these cases will have a truly significant impact on each of the lives touched by it, so it is crucial to find the most appropriate course of action for each client. The best advocates are those who can "*differentiate between a case and client requiring a bullish approach, and those which cry out for settlement and concessions to be made.*"

## prospects

We're told that one in three marriages breaks down in the UK, yet the family Bar is quite small and competition for pupillage is hot. "*Going straight into family law from university, it can seem daunting to advise on mortgages, marriages or children when you've never experienced these things yourself.*" As such, those embarking on a second career, or those who have delayed a year or two and acquired other life experiences, may have an advantage. Ellen stressed that pupillages don't always go to those with starred Firsts, saying: "*No one will get in on exam results alone.*" Improve your chances by doing at least one mini-pupillage in a family law set and consider how working with a voluntary organisation that deals with family and relationship issues might benefit you. Finally, bear in mind that family cases are not the most lucrative as legally aided work is generally poorly paid, but the satisfaction to be gained from assisting a client at such a crisis point in their life can be incalculable.

## public law

Public bodies operate within statutory constraints and are bound by the principles of public law. Their decisions may be challenged on procedural or other public law grounds: maybe they haven't considered the relevant facts in reaching their decisions; have made an unreasonable decision; perhaps the body or officer didn't have the authority to make the decision in the first place; or they won't reveal to you how and why they have made a decision. If you are a pioneer for justice and the advancement of the law, read on.

### type of work

For those not yet happy to plump for a pigeonhole and sit in it, public law interlocks with an array of different areas of law, such as competition, European, employment or general common law. Maya Lester at Brick Court Chambers explained how "*most chambers doing public law have other specialisms too: some have a criminal emphasis, and others a more commercial emphasis, some focus on employment law or human rights.*" Remember, some sets that do not profess to be public law specialists undertake judicial review work. For example, criminal barristers will often handle issues relating to prisoners or breaches of procedure by police. And a set concentrating on commercial work might handle judicial reviews of DTI or other regulatory decisions. Accordingly, cases can range from "*pro bono or legal aid work for an individual, to commercial judicial review for magic circle firms, or government instruction*s."

Barristers with a local authority clientele act for a number of different departments on a range of work, sometimes relating to planning, housing or environmental matters and education, health, prisons and children. There has been a recent spate of cases concerning community care issues and the provision of social services by local authorities. Judicial reviews of immigration decisions also make up a significant chunk of the

Administrative Court's case list, and at the other end of the spectrum sit some high-profile and contentious cases, such as that of Jodie and Mary the conjoined twins, whose surgeons applied for judicial review in respect of the decision to prosecute if they were to separate them.

Where an event is of great public importance, inquiries are sometimes commissioned by the Government and then operate independently. The Bloody Sunday Inquiry and the Hutton Inquiry into the death of David Kelly illustrate well the different types of issue that come under scrutiny. The Human Rights Act has undoubtedly affected public law and, as Maya explains: "*Its first few years have shown that many areas still need to be sorted out; for example, issues relating to privacy are arising all the time but the law is still not clear.*"

With such a variety of work falling under the public law umbrella, it is unsurprising that "*everyone has a different experience*" but the split between advisory work and advocacy is quite distinct. About half of Maya's time is spent giving opinions rather than doing oral advocacy, and she stresses that "*you won't be getting on a train to go to court every day. A lot of your life will be spent in chambers on written advocacy, drafting skeleton arguments and opinions, advising public bodies on the implications of the Human Rights Act, or whether their structures comply with public law principles.*" That said, there will be opportunities to get stuck into advocacy early on in your career. The preliminary permissions stage of judicial review proceedings provides the junior barrister with "*a short 30-minute hearing that they can do alone.*" Perfect.

Public international law appeals to many students, but openings in relevant chambers are limited. Traditionally it's been the preserve of academics – the leading names are predominantly sitting or ex-professors at top universities, but also include Foreign Office veterans and the occasional more senior barrister. Governments want tried-and-tested counsel and will expect those they instruct to be recognised, published authors. This is not an area of work you'll fall into by accident, nor is it one you're likely to get into until you're much more experienced. If the academic route is not for you, good luck in your search for pupillage specialising in public international law.

## skills needed

...a desire to battle through red tape...genuine interest in the fundamental laws by which we live...knowledge of administrative and constitutional law...familiarity with EU and international law...creativity...common sense...rationality... keen intellect...

If you are interested in the academic legal arguments but want to apply them practically, public law provides the forum for debating those issues. Maya says: "*You can get a real sense that you are helping people – there is a human interest.*" But providing real remedies for real people demands a very practical mind and a broad perspective combined with common sense. "*You have to be able to stand back and look at the broader implications of what you are saying.*" Both applicants and public bodies have "*an equally valid interest in proper decision-making processes, and you have to be able to see both sides of the coin.*"

The Administrative Court is one of the most inundated branches of the High Court, so you'll need to develop an efficient style of advocacy. Long and dramatic performances are rarely well received; you must learn how to cut to the chase and deliver the pertinent information, draw on the relevant case law or statutory regulations and present your arguments promptly. Importantly though, while an inquiring and analytical mind is essential, public law is "*not as precise a science as commercial law or tax...it requires using the principles of reasonableness, fairness, rationality. It is a more discursive thing, and is as much about finding interesting and creative arguments rather than a precise answer.*"

# the bar

## prospects

Studying constitutional law subjects is one way of demonstrating your enthusiasm for public law practice. However, Maya warns against closing your mind to everything else because "*your practice will probably be mixed with other areas of the law.*" Get a few mini-pupillages under your belt, do as much mooting as possible and read quality newspapers to familiarise yourself with the public law issues raised in them. Maya "*wouldn't discourage anyone from doing something else, such as a Masters degree, before going to the Bar – people should take the opportunity, while they can, to become a broader lawyer.*" Lastly, don't forget to look at the opportunities available within the Government Legal Service.

## chambers UK bar practice areas tables 2005-6

### Administrative & Public Law: General
#### London

| | QCs | Jrs |
|---|---|---|
| **1** **Blackstone Chambers** | | |
| (Mill QC & Beazley QC) | 7 | 8 |
| **2** **Brick Court Chambers** | | |
| (Sumption & Hirst ) | 4 | 4 |
| **Doughty Street Chambers** | | |
| (Robertson QC) | 4 | 4 |
| **39 Essex Street** | | |
| (Davies & Wilmot-Smith) | 4 | 4 |
| **11 King's Bench Walk** | 4 | 2 |
| **Landmark Chambers** | 3 | 3 |
| **Matrix** | 5 | 3 |
| **3** **1 Crown Office Row** | | |
| (Robert Seabrook QC) | 2 | 2 |
| **Garden Court Chambers** | | |
| (Davies & Griffiths) | 1 | 3 |
| **4-5 Gray's Inn Square** | | |
| (Appleby & Straker) | 1 | 3 |
| **3 Hare Court** | | |
| (James Guthrie QC) | 2 | 1 |
| **1 Temple Gardens** | 1 | 1 |

### Banking & Finance
#### London

| | QCs | Jrs |
|---|---|---|
| **1** **Fountain Court** (Brindle/Lerego) | 8 | 8 |
| **3 Verulam Buildings** | | |
| (Symons/Jarvis) | 8 | 7 |
| **2** **Brick Court Chambers** | | |
| (Sumption/Hirst) | 4 | - |
| **Essex Court Chambers** | | |
| (Pollock) | 4 | 1 |
| **One Essex Court** (Grabiner) | 7 | 3 |
| **3** **Erskine Chambers** (Cone) | 1 | - |
| **20 Essex Street** (Milligan) | 1 | - |
| **Serle Court** (Bladen) | 2 | 1 |
| **3/4 South Square** | | |
| (Crystal/Weedon) | 6 | 1 |

### Chancery: Commercial
#### London

| | QCs | Jnrs |
|---|---|---|
| **1** **Maitland Chambers** | | |
| (Lyndon-Stanford/Aldous/Driscoll) | 8 | 7 |
| **2** **Serle Court** | | |
| (Lord Neill of Bladen QC) | 7 | 6 |
| **4 Stone Buildings** (Bompas) | 4 | 5 |
| **3** **XXIV Old Buildings** | | |
| (Mann/Steinfeld) | 3 | 4 |
| **3/4 South Square** | | |
| (Crystal/Weedon) | 5 | 3 |
| **Wilberforce** (Nugee) | 5 | 2 |
| **4** **Enterprise** (Weatherill) | – | 2 |
| **New Square** (Purle) | 2 | - |
| **3 Stone Buildings** (Vos) | 2 | - |
| **11 Stone Buildings** (Cohen) | - | 1 |

### Chancery: Traditional
#### London

| | QCs | Jnrs |
|---|---|---|
| **1** **Wilberforce** (Nugee) | 6 | 7 |
| **2** **5 Stone Buildings** (Harrod) | 5 | 6 |
| **3** **Eleven New Square** (Marten) | 2 | 4 |
| **Maitland Chambers** | | |
| (Lyndon-Stanford/Aldous) | 4 | 2 |
| **New Square** (Purle) | 1 | 3 |
| **10 Old Square** (Price) | 1 | 4 |
| **11 Old Square** (Waters) | 1 | 5 |
| **Serle Court** | | |
| (Lord Neill of Bladen QC) | 2 | 3 |
| **4** **XXIV Old Buildings** | | |
| (Mann/Steinfeld) | 1 | 3 |
| **9 Stone Buildings** (Chapman) | - | 4 |

### Competition/EU Law
#### London

| | QCs | Jnrs |
|---|---|---|
| **1** **Brick Court Chambers** | | |
| (Sumption/Hirst) | 7 | 8 |
| **Monckton Chambers** | | |
| (Lasok/Parker) | 8 | 8 |
| **2** **Blackstone Chambers** | | |
| (Mill/Beazley) | - | 1 |
| **11 King's Bench Walk Chambers** | | |
| (Tabachnik/Goudie) | - | 2 |
| **Matrix** | 1 | 2 |

### Commercial (Litigation)
#### London

| | QCs | Jnrs |
|---|---|---|
| **1** **Brick Court Chambers** | | |
| (Sumption & Hirst) | 13 | 7 |
| **Essex Court Chambers** | | |
| (Gordon Pollock QC) | 10 | 9 |
| **One Essex Court** | | |
| (Lord Grabiner QC) | 13 | 9 |
| **Fountain Court** | | |
| (Brindle & Lerego ) | 9 | 6 |
| **2** **Blackstone Chambers** | | |
| (Mill & Beazley) | 4 | 7 |
| **3 Verulam Buildings** | | |
| (Symons & Jarvis) | 8 | 12 |
| **3** **20 Essex Street** | | |
| (Iain Milligan QC) | 5 | 7 |
| **7 King's Bench Walk** | | |
| (Kealey & Flaux) | 4 | 1 |
| **Serle Court** | | |
| (Lord Neill of Bladen QC) | 5 | 3 |
| **4 Stone Buildings** | | |
| (George Bompas QC) | 4 | 3 |
| **4** **Erskine Chambers** | | |
| (John Cone) | 3 | 1 |
| **Maitland Chambers** | | |
| (Lyndon & Aldous & Driscoll) | 3 | 3 |
| **XXIV Old Buildings** | | |
| (Mann & Steinfeld) | 2 | 3 |
| **3/4 South Square** | | |
| (Crystal & Lord Alexander) | 3 | 2 |

# the bar

## Information Technology
### London
| | QCs | Jnrs |
|---|---|---|
| **[1] 4 Pump Court** | | |
| (Friedman/Moger) | 2 | 2 |
| **11 South Square** (Floyd) | 3 | 2 |
| **[2] Atkin Chambers** (Akenhead) | 4 | 1 |
| **[3] Henderson Chambers** | | |
| (Henderson) | 2 | 1 |
| **Hogarth Chambers** (Morcom) | 1 | 2 |
| **Three New Square** (Watson) | 1 | 1 |
| **8 New Square** | 1 | 2 |

## Crime
### London
| | QCs | Jnrs |
|---|---|---|
| **[1] 2 Bedford Row** | | |
| (William Clegg QC) | 8 | 9 |
| **Doughty Street Chambers** | | |
| (Robertson QC) | 10 | 4 |
| **2 Hare Court** | | |
| (David Waters QC) | 4 | 7 |
| **Hollis Whiteman QEB** | 8 | 6 |
| **6 King's Bench Walk** | | |
| (Roy Amlot QC) | 12 | 6 |
| **3 Raymond Buildings** | | |
| (Clive Nicholls QC) | 8 | 7 |
| **[2] 25 Bedford Row** | | |
| (Rock Tansey QC) | 6 | 5 |
| **9-12 Bell Yard** | | |
| (Lord Carlile of Berriew QC) | 4 | 3 |
| **23 Essex Street** | | |
| (Charles Miskin QC) | 3 | 2 |
| **18 Red Lion Court** | | |
| (David Etherington QC) | 5 | 3 |
| **[3] Atkinson Bevan Chambers** | | |
| (Atkinson QC) | 2 | 3 |
| **7 Bedford Row** | | |
| (David Farrer QC) | 4 | 1 |
| **9 Bedford Row** | | |
| (Anthony C Berry QC) | 5 | 2 |
| **Charter Chambers** | | |
| (Stephen Solley QC) | 4 | 2 |
| **Furnival Chambers** | | |
| (Andrew Mitchell QC) | 4 | 4 |
| **Garden Court Chambers** | | |
| (Davies & Griffiths) | 5 | 4 |
| **Matrix** | 4 | 2 |
| **2-4 Tudor Street** | | |
| (Richard Ferguson QC) | 2 | 5 |
| **[4] 2 Dyers Buildings** | 1 | 2 |
| **187 Fleet Street** | 2 | 1 |
| **Nine Lincoln's Inn Fields** | | |
| (David Nathan QC) | 2 | 3 |
| **5 Paper Buildings** | | |
| (Carey QC & Caplan QC) | 3 | 1 |
| **Tooks Chambers** | | |
| (Michael Mansfield QC) | 2 | 2 |

## Employment
### London
| | QCs | Jnrs |
|---|---|---|
| **[1] Blackstone Chambers** | | |
| (Mill/Beazley) | 3 | 9 |
| **11 King's Bench Walk Chambers** | | |
| (Tabachnik/Goudie) | 7 | 13 |
| **Littleton Chambers** | | |
| (Kallipetis) | 4 | 13 |
| **[2] Cloisters** (Langstaff/Allen) | 2 | 9 |
| **Devereux** (Edelman) | 2 | 9 |
| **Matrix** | 2 | 6 |
| **Old Square** (Hendy) | 4 | 14 |
| **[3] Essex Court** (Pollock) | 1 | 2 |
| **Fountain Court** | | |
| (Brindle/Lerego) | 1 | - |
| **Outer Temple** (Mott) | - | 4 |

## Family/Matrimonial
### London
| | QCs | Jnrs |
|---|---|---|
| **[1] 1 Hare Court** | | |
| (Anthony Hacking QC) | 7 | 11 |
| **One King's Bench Walk** | | |
| (Anthony Hacking QC) | 9 | 10 |
| **Queen Elizabeth Building** | | |
| (Andrew Moylan QC) | 3 | 7 |
| **[2] 29 Bedford Row Chambers** | | |
| (Nicholas Francis) | 4 | 12 |
| **One Garden Court** | | |
| (Platt QC & Ball QC) | 4 | 3 |
| **4 Paper Buildings** | | |
| (Jonathan Cohen QC) | 2 | 4 |
| **[3] Coram Chambers** | | |
| (Roger McCarthy QC) | 1 | 2 |
| **1 Crown Office Row** | | |
| (Robert Seabrook QC) | 2 | - |
| **14 Gray's Inn Square** | | |
| (Forster & Brasse) | - | 2 |
| **22 Old Buildings** | | |
| (Benet Hytner QC) | - | 5 |
| **Renaissance Chambers** | | |
| (Setright QC & Jubb) | 1 | 1 |

## Human Rights
### London
| | QCs | Jnrs |
|---|---|---|
| **[1] Blackstone Chambers** | | |
| (Mill/Beazley) | 4 | 6 |
| **Doughty Street** (Robertson) | 5 | 8 |
| **Matrix** | 5 | 8 |
| **[2] Brick Court Chambers** | | |
| (Sumption/Hirst) | 2 | 2 |
| **39 Essex Street** | | |
| (Davies/Wilmot-Smith) | 2 | 1 |
| **Garden Court Chambers** | | |
| (Davies/Griffiths) | 2 | 2 |
| **[3] 1 Crown Office Row** | | |
| (Seabrook) | 1 | - |
| **11 King's Bench Walk Chambers** | | |
| (Tabachnik) | 1 | 1 |
| **Tooks Chambers** (Mansfield) | 1 | 1 |

## International Arbitration: General Commercial & Insurance
### London
| | QCs | Jnrs |
|---|---|---|
| **[1] Essex Court** (Pollock) | 9 | 4 |
| **[2] 20 Essex Street** (Milligan) | 6 | 1 |
| **[3] One Essex Court** (Grabiner) | 2 | - |
| **7 King's Bench Walk** | | |
| (Kealey/Flaux) | 3 | - |
| **[4] Brick Court Chambers** | | |
| (Sumption/Hirst) | 1 | 1 |
| **Littleton Chambers** | | |
| (Kallipetis) | - | - |
| **Matrix** | 2 | 1 |
| **Quadrant Chambers** (Teare) | 5 | - |

## Construction
### London
| | QCs | Jnrs |
|---|---|---|
| **[1] Atkin Chambers** | 11 | 11 |
| (Akenhead) | | |
| **Keating Chambers** (Ramsey) | 12 | 16 |
| **[2] 4 Pump Court** | | |
| (Friedman/Moger) | 4 | 6 |
| **[3] Crown Office Chambers** | | |
| (Edwards-Stuart) | 4 | 2 |
| **39 Essex Street** | | |
| (Davies/Wilmot-Smith QC) | 3 | 3 |
| **[4] Four New Square** | | |
| (Justin Fenwick QC) | 2 | 4 |

# the bar

## Immigration

### London

| | QCs | Jnrs |
|---|---|---|
| [1] **Garden Court Chambers** | | |
| (Davies & Griffiths) | 2 | 12 |
| [2] **Blackstone Chambers** | | |
| (Mill QC & Beazley QC) | 2 | 3 |
| **Doughty Street Chambers** | | |
| (Robertson QC) | 1 | 6 |
| **Matrix** | 1 | 2 |
| **Tooks Chambers** | | |
| (Michael Mansfield QC) | - | 7 |
| [3] **39 Essex Street** | | |
| (Davies & Wilmot-Smith) | - | 2 |
| **6 King's Bench Walk** | | |
| (Sibghat Kadri QC) | 1 | 2 |
| **Renaissance Chambers** | | |
| (Setright QC & Jubb) | - | 2 |

## Intellectual Property

### London

| | QCs | Jnrs |
|---|---|---|
| [1] **Three New Square** | | |
| (Watson) | 6 | 7 |
| **8 New Square** | 7 | 12 |
| **11 South Square** (Floyd) | 4 | 8 |
| [2] **One Essex Court** (Grabiner) | 1 | 3 |
| **Hogarth Chambers** (Morcom) | 2 | 7 |
| **Wilberforce Chambers** | | |
| (Nugee) | 1 | 1 |

## Insurance

### London

| | QCs | Jnrs |
|---|---|---|
| [1] **Brick Court Chambers** | | |
| (Sumption & Hirst) | 9 | 4 |
| **Essex Court Chambers** | | |
| (Gordon Pollock QC) | 7 | 4 |
| **7 King's Bench Walk** | | |
| (Kealey QC & Flaux QC) | 7 | 3 |
| [2] **Fountain Court** | | |
| (Brindle QC & Lerego QC) | 3 | 1 |
| **3 Verulam Buildings** | | |
| (Symons QC & Jarvis QC) | 3 | - |
| [3] **Devereux Chambers** | | |
| (Colin Edelman QC) | 1 | 1 |
| **20 Essex Street** | | |
| (Iain Milligan QC) | 2 | 2 |
| **4 Pump Court** | | |
| (Friedman QC & Moger QC) | 2 | 2 |

## Media & Entertainment

### London

| | QCs | Jnrs |
|---|---|---|
| [1] **Blackstone Chambers** | | |
| (Mill/Beazley) | 3 | 6 |
| [2] **8 New Square** | 3 | 3 |
| [3] **Essex Court Chambers** | | |
| (Pollock) | 2 | 1 |

## Real Estate Litigation

### London

| | QCs | Jnrs |
|---|---|---|
| [1] **Falcon Chambers** | | |
| (Gaunt/Morgan) | 7 | 19 |
| **Maitland Chambers** | | |
| (Lyndon-Stanford/Aldous) | 7 | 15 |
| [2] **Landmark Chambers** | 3 | 6 |
| **Wilberforce** (Nugee) | 5 | 3 |
| [3] **Enterprise Chambers** | | |
| (Weatherill) | - | 4 |
| **Henderson Chambers** | | |
| (Henderson) | - | 2 |
| **Selborne Chambers** (Tager) | - | 5 |
| **Serle Court** | | |
| (Lord Neill of Bladen) | 1 | 5 |
| **Tanfield Chambers** (Hughes) | - | 7 |

## Public International Law

### London

| | QCs | Jnrs |
|---|---|---|
| [1] **Essex Court Chambers** | | |
| (Gordon Pollock QC) | 3 | 2 |
| **20 Essex Street** | | |
| (Iain Milligan QC) | 4 | - |
| [2] **Blackstone Chambers** | | |
| (Mill QC & Beazley QC) | 2 | 1 |
| [3] **Matrix** | 2 | - |

## Shipping & Commodities

### London

| | QCs | Jnrs |
|---|---|---|
| [1] **Essex Court Chambers** | | |
| (Gordon Pollock QC) | 6 | 5 |
| **20 Essex Street** | | |
| (Iain Milligan QC) | 6 | 7 |
| **7 King's Bench Walk** | | |
| (Kealey QC & Flaux QC) | 6 | 6 |
| **Quadrant Chambers** | | |
| (Nigel Teare QC) | 8 | 13 |
| [2] **Stone Chambers** | | |
| (Steven Gee QC) | 4 | 2 |

## Personal Injury

### London

| | QCs | Jnrs |
|---|---|---|
| [1] **39 Essex Street** | | |
| (Davies & Wilmot-Smith) | 5 | 6 |
| **12 King's Bench Walk** | | |
| (Andrew Hogarth QC) | 6 | 8 |
| [2] **Outer Temple Chambers** | | |
| (Philip Mott QC) | 3 | 4 |
| **2 Temple Gardens** | | |
| (Andrew Collender QC) | 4 | 4 |
| [3] **Crown Office Chambers** | | |
| (Edwards-Stuart QC) | 1 | 4 |
| **Devereux Chambers** | | |
| (Colin Edelman QC) | 1 | 4 |
| **Farrar's Building** | | |
| (Patrick Harrington QC) | 3 | 2 |
| **9 Gough Square** | | |
| (John Foy QC) | 1 | 4 |
| **Old Square Chambers** | | |
| (John Hendy QC) | 3 | 2 |
| [4] **1 Crown Office Row** | | |
| (Robert Seabrook QC) | 2 | 1 |
| **Doughty Street Chambers** | | |
| (Robertson QC) | 1 | 2 |
| **No. 1 Serjeants' Inn** | | |
| (Edward Faulks QC) | 1 | 2 |

## Tax

### London

| | QCs | Jnrs |
|---|---|---|
| [1] **Gray's Inn Tax Chambers** | | |
| (Milton Grundy) | 4 | 5 |
| **Pump Court Tax Chambers** | | |
| (Thornhill QC) | 6 | 4 |
| [2] **11 New Square** | | |
| (John Gardiner QC) | 3 | - |
| [3] **One Essex Court** | | |
| (Lord Grabiner QC) | 1 | - |
| **Monckton Chambers** | | |
| (Lasok QC & Parker QC) | - | 2 |
| **15 Old Square** | | |
| (Rex Bretten QC) | 2 | - |
| **3 Temple Gardens Tax Chambers** (Bramwell) | 1 | 2 |

# Chambers Reports

Although barristers' chambers are catching up with law firms in terms of the information they provide about pupillage, making an informed choice about where to apply is still a tricky process for most students. Working out the practice area in which you want to specialise is difficult enough, but then having to fathom which set you're likely to fit in at, and which is likely to be interested in you, can be really difficult. Even with improvements in many chambers' websites, the only way of really knowing what's what is by having a look around the set.

Because it's impossible to do mini-pupillage in every set that takes your fancy, the *Student Guide* has visited some of the country's best sets for you. We spent the summers of 2004 and 2005 nosing round the 44 sets listed on the next page, speaking with pupils, tenants and clerks so that you don't have to. We tried to cover as many different types of set as possible, though we should stress that our selection does not comprise a UK Top 40. Such a list would be impossible to compile because of the variety of work undertaken at the Bar. What we can say is the following featured sets are all very highly regarded for both pupillage and in general by clients and others in the legal profession.

Our tour took us from the grandeur of the Chancery Bar to the more modest surroundings of sets conducting mainly publicly funded work. Among the 44 sets there should be something to suit all tastes, be they commercial, common law, criminal, family, IP, tax, regional or otherwise. Given that most sets (and pupillages) are based in London, the majority of those covered are in the capital. This year we also took up an invitation to visit Liverpool and have profiled Exchange Chambers in addition to the three Manchester sets we popped along to in 2004.

Whichever you do choose, be reassured that the prime aim of recruiters is to find talented applicants and to then persuade them to accept an offer. They do not expect ready-formed barristers to turn up at their door for interview, and gladly make allowances for candidates' lack of knowledge or experience on specific subjects. Much has been said and written about how awful pupillage interviews can be, and how pupillage itself amounts to little more than a year of pain and humiliation. From what we can tell, this is not the norm. Sure, interviews can be challenging, but they are designed to get the best out of candidates. As for pupillage, it is in a set's best interest for the year to be a useful and rewarding experience for pupils.

The itinerary for our visits included conversations with members of the pupillage committee, pupilmasters or supervisors, the senior clerk, junior tenants and, most crucially, current pupils. The aim was not merely to get the low down on pupillage at each set but also to learn something about chambers life and to pick up tips for applicants. To this end we drank endless cups of tea, munched our way through five kilos of biscuits and took numerous guided tours, checking out artwork and libraries along the way. If we've communicated the qualities that make each set unique then we've done our job and it's over to you to make your choices.

# the chambers reports sets

| no. | set | location | head of chambers | (qcs/juniors) |
|-----|-----|----------|------------------|---------------|
| 1 | 2 Bedford Row* | London | William Clegg | 63 (15/48) |
| 2 | Blackstone Chambers | London | Mill/Beazley | 63 (27/36) |
| 3 | Brick Court Chambers | London | Sumption/Hirst | 64 (26/38) |
| 4 | Cloisters | London | Langstaff/Allen | 44 (4/40) |
| 5 | Crown Office Chambers | London | Antony Edwards-Stuart | 77 (15/62) |
| 6 | Devereux Chambers | London | Colin Edelman | 45 (6/39) |
| 7 | Doughty Street Chambers | London | Geoffrey Robertson | 85 (16/69) |
| 8 | Erskine Chambers | London | John Cone | 25 (8/17) |
| 9 | Essex Court Chambers | London | Gordon Pollock | 74 (29/45) |
| 10 | One Essex Court | London | Anthony Grabiner | 57 (21/36) |
| 11 | 20 Essex Street | London | Iain Milligan | 45 (15/30) |
| 12 | 39 Essex Street* | London | Davies/Wilmot-Smith | 64 (19/45) |
| 13 | Falcon Chambers | London | Gaunt/Morgan | 34 (8/26) |
| 14 | Fountain Court | London | Brindle/Lerego | 59 (21/38) |
| 15 | Furnival Chambers* | London | Andrew Mitchell | 68 (8/60) |
| 16 | One Garden Court* | London | Platt/Ball | 47 (6/41) |
| 17 | Garden Court Chambers | London | Davies/Griffiths | 87 (8/79) |
| 18 | Government Legal Service* | London | n/a | n/a |
| 19 | 2-3 Gray's Inn Square* | London | Porten/Scrivener | 50 (9/41) |
| 20 | 2 Hare Court* | London | David Waters | 49 (11/38) |
| 21 | Hogarth Chambers | London | Christopher Morcom | 26 (4/22) |
| 22 | 7 King's Bench Walk | London | Kealey/Flaux | 42 (11/31) |
| 23 | 11 King's Bench Walk* | London | Tabachnik/Goudie | 49 (12/37) |
| 24 | Maitland Chambers | London | Lyndon-Stanford/Aldous/Driscoll | 64 (14/50) |
| 25 | Matrix | London | n/a | 52 (13/39) |
| 26 | Monckton Chambers* | London | Parker/Lasok | 38 (11/27) |
| 27 | Four New Square* | London | Justin Fenwick | 57 (11/46) |
| 28 | Old Square Chambers* | London | John Hendy | 57 (10/47) |
| 29 | Pump Court Tax Chambers* | London | Andrew Thornhill | 25 (8/17) |
| 30 | 4 Pump Court* | London | Friedman/Moger | 49 (12/37) |
| 31 | Quadrant Chambers* | London | Nigel Teare | 46 (12/34) |
| 32 | Queen Elizabeth Building | London | Andrew Moylan | 29 (3/26) |
| 33 | 3 Raymond Buildings* | London | Clive Nicholls | 47 (14/33) |
| 35 | 3 Serjeants' Inn* | London | Francis/Grace | 41 (7/34) |
| 34 | Serle Court | London | Lord Neill of Bladen | 47 (12/35) |
| 36 | 3/4 South Square | London | Crystal/Alexander | 45 (16/29) |
| 37 | 4 Stone Buildings | London | George Bompass | 24 (5/19) |
| 38 | 2 Temple Gardens* | London | Andrew Collender | 46 (7/39) |
| 39 | 3 Verulam Buildings | London | Symons/Jarvis | 56 (19/37) |
| 40 | Wilberforce Chambers | London | Edward Nugee | 44 (15/29) |
| 41 | Exchange Chambers | L'pool/Manchester | Turner/Braithwaite | 85 (11/74) |
| 42 | Deans Court* | Manchester | Stephen Grime | 61 (9/52) |
| 43 | Kings Chambers* | Manchester/Leeds | Frances Patterson | 62 (8/54) |
| 44 | St Johns Buidings* | Manchester | Michael Redfern | 105 (10/95) |

*These sets were visited during 2004. All others were visited 2005.*

# chambers reports

## 2 Bedford Row

**Chambers UK rankings:** Crime,
fraud: criminal

There's something inherently serious about 2 Bedford Row. Perhaps it's the photograph of blindfolded Justice – sword in one hand, scales in the other – on chambers' website. Perhaps it's chambers' waiting room, on the walls of which hang two large and imposing court artist's sketches depicting scenes from the bewigged hall of fame that is chambers' past. However you judge it, serious crime is what this set excels at. Wipe the dust from your first-year criminal law textbook, take a look at the Table of Cases, and you will soon discover that 2 Bedford Row has featured heavily in a good number of them. R v Brown, The Herald of Free Enterprise, Kebeline v DPP, Prosecutor v Tadic – it's all there.

Since the day the set was founded in 1983 by current head of chambers and much sought after defence lawyer William Clegg QC, solicitors, defendants, the Crown and statutory bodies have relied on the courtroom skills of 2 Bedford Row's barristers. Whether prosecuting for the Health & Safety Executive or defending the perpetrators of alleged war crimes in the International Criminal Tribunal for Former Yugoslavia, they have the necessary gravitas and experience. In every field of criminal law, they are unashamedly good at what they do.

A pupillage with this set concentrates primarily on crime, though chambers is involved in public inquiry work and sports disciplinary matters. Pupils start their careers swimming with the bigger fish in chambers, and as such the first six is, as one pupil explained, a process of *"learning by osmosis."* Spending the vast majority of their time with a single pupilmaster, they feel *"like a spare part at times,"* but the important thing is to soak it all up. *"You learn so much just by watching how counsel interact with each other in the robing room,*

*and by seeing them deal with solicitors or the CPS."* What pupils actually encounter depends on the luck of the draw. While one junior tenant spent the entirety of his first six assisting in the preparatory stages of a complex fraud trial, another did the rounds of London's Crown Courts, observing much shorter *"knock-about, three to four-day trials."* Everyone agrees that it is advisable to take on work for other members as a way of getting your face known, particularly as when you undertake legal research for a senior member *"it's not uncommon for you to be invited along to court to see the fruits of your labour put into action. That's very satisfying."*

The set's standing is reflected in the kind of work pupils see in their second, practising six months. *"As a pupil here, you'll get your hands on the kind of work that you just wouldn't expect to see in other sets,"* we were told. One pupil recalled her first appearance in court – a baptism of fire that consisted of prosecuting a defendant for breach of a Community Punishment Order in front of an Old Bailey judge. If you're worried about being asked to run before you can even walk, rest assured there will also be plenty of standard-fare magistrates' court work, though this in itself may feel like a hundred-metre sprint with little time to catch your breath. As we were warned by a young pupil who'd just got back from court: *"It's a gruelling schedule. I'm usually in one court in the morning and another in the afternoon, then it's back to chambers to prepare for the next day."* For those who are not fortunate enough to be taken on as a tenant at the end of the year, this *"nuts-and-bolts"* experience becomes invaluable.

For those who do achieve a qualifying time in the pupillage race and progress to tenancy the change in pace is an *"exponential"* one. The baby junior we interviewed observed that *"before you know it, you'll go from facing three lay magistrates to standing up in front of three Lord Justices arguing an appeal against sentence... it really does happen that quickly.*" The tenancy decision is made in September by a committee of all members. There is no formal assessment programme during the pupillage year; instead, *"pupils are encouraged to apply to solicitors who have instructed them for references."* Effectively, the assessment takes place in the field.

Despite 2 Bedford Row's success and standing, this is not a place in which senior members *"go around flaunting their egos."* Indeed, on our brief visit we found the atmosphere unstuffy and understated. We also sensed that while there is a reasonable social scene, people like to get their heads down and work hard during the day. *"We're definitely workaholics; we're sociable with it, but the job itself is all-consuming."* Easy and understated are words that would best describe the relationship between clerks and juniors. First-name terms are the norm, and those at the junior end of the food chain told us they were perfectly happy discussing their career ambitions with the senior clerks, who in any event *"know our practices inside out."*

If you want your application form to be plucked from what is always a pretty big pile, you'll need to be hard-working too. You must also show a firm commitment to criminal practice. It wouldn't appear to matter where your degree is from, though anything below a 2:1 and you should be very impressive in other aspects. On top of all this, you'll also need to have *"something a bit different from the norm."* A brief glance at the CVs of current members bears out one junior tenant's observation that *"we don't fit the traditional mould of a barrister."* One pupil had been a tabloid journalist before changing career, and several members had experiences outside the law. No one is suggesting that a first career is prerequisite, but it clearly helps if you have experience of the real world beyond academia. In the words of one pupil: *"You need to be lucid and intelligent, but you also need to have that human touch, and be on the same wavelength as your client. It's through being able to understand your client that you get decent instructions from them."*

A good application form will only get you so far; what these recruiters are really interested in is how you perform at interview. There's a two-round process, the first interview being a fairly brief chat, usually with a topical/legal theme, and the second incorporating an advocacy exercise handed out four hours in advance. If you're one of the lucky ones that gets this far, don't worry if you come out of the interview room feeling utterly harangued. The job is all about thriving under pressure, so the interview is designed to reflect this. We chatted to one pupil who was convinced he'd flunked the whole thing after a *"grilling."* Obviously not!

We'll end with the endorsement of the junior tenant who told us: *"It's true that pupillage can be stressful and hard work, but if you revel in that pressure, and in the fact that for the first time you're doing the job for real, then you'll love it here."*

## Blackstone Chambers

**Chambers UK rankings:** Admin & Public Law, commercial litigation, competition/European law, employment, environment, financial services, fraud: civil, human rights, immigration, media & entertainment, professional discipline, public international law, sports law

"This is the world of the Temple: the fountain, the chambers, the quad; where Brick Court speaks only to Blackstone and Blackstone speaks only to God." Normally we are resistant to such poetic praise but there is no mistaking the reverence in which the 63 members (27 of them silks) of this set are held. Leaders in pretty much every area in which the set decides to dip its toes, *"anything short of excellence is just not acceptable,"* according to one seasoned tenant.

It would probably take less space and time to detail the high-profile matters that members of Blackstone haven't appeared in than to provide an exhaustive list of all the set's notable cases but just as a taster, how about Stephanie Villalba's £7 million sexual discrimination, unfair dismissal and unequal pay claim against Merrill Lynch, challenges to human fertilisation, or the successful representation of the former Fulham football manager Jean Tigana in High Court proceedings against his old club? As you can see, Blackstone Chambers has its fingers in a lot of pies. Apparently a few years ago, in a particularly memorable chambers meeting the clerks asked the members whether they wanted to be the best-paid members of the Bar or just well-paid but with the most interesting workload. They chose the latter.

The set moved to Blackstone House in 1998, having previously resided at 2 Hare Court. The change of location is credited with galvanising the set into a more forward-thinking entity and led the way for younger members to take the reins with a mandate to innovate. Everyone knows about the set's pre-eminence in public law, employment and human rights but in recent years members have found themselves at the forefront of new practice areas such as sport and media, as well as taking a lead role in the trend for mediation.

The road to pupillage at Blackstone is a tough one and to get there you're going to have to mark yourself out as someone who is "*capable of sustained academic brilliance.*" Careful though: "*A fat Oxbridge First will not be enough on its own to get an interview.*" Candidates who make it through the paper cut will have shown unquestioned commitment to the Bar. For the most part this will mean mini-pupillages and voluntary work, but given that the set prides itself on the quality of its advocacy, it is also worth accumulating significant public speaking experience through mooting or debating. At interview you're going to have to be completely on top of the legal issues of the day. Candidates are supplied with a list of topical questions half an hour beforehand and are expected to be able to discuss and defend when under extreme questioning (although we were assured that "*any*

*attack is done in a good-natured way*"). One recent example asked whether libel laws offer too much protection to celebrities. Clarity of presentation and speed of thought are the key attributes recruiters want to see. "*We're not so bothered with the candidate's depth of knowledge on the issue. The question is whether they are able to argue elegantly and eloquently.*" If you've impressed and haven't already completed a mini-pupillage with Blackstone, you will be invited to undertake one so members can take a longer look at you. Make the most of it as the second round of interviews will focus on your experiences within chambers. "*The people who have made it through to the second round will have passed with flying colours. What we're trying to work out is whether they really want to come to Blackstone or not.*"

Pupillage is split into spells with four pupil-masters in different areas of practice. As it is rare to find a Blackstone barrister with just one core specialisation this leads to exposure to a wide range of work. The matters encountered will often receive considerable media attention: one pupil's first day involved accompanying his pupilmaster to address a nine-member panel of the House of Lords on whether the imprisonment of suspected terrorists at Belmarsh prison was unlawful.

Pupils only work for their PMs and do no paid work in their second six; the key thing is to make a good impression with every PM and score highly in the monthly videoed advocacy exercises. "*Yes, it's pressurised, but the fact that it's on videotape means that you can be sure the whole process is pretty objective.*" Every pupil receives a formal letter after six months detailing how they're getting on and identifying areas for improvement. The tenancy committee collates this information and places it before a chambers meeting in July when decision is made as to who gets taken on. Although we were told that it is possible for every pupil to get tenancy, recent history suggests that about half make it. And those that don't? "*Blackstone pupils don't get turned down when they knock on doors.*"

Blackstone is very much the set that pioneered a relaxed dress code and while "*no one wanders around in their underwear*" the tenants we met did look pretty comfortable on the sweltering day that we visited them. Then again, the pupils we met were wearing suits, so perhaps it is the case that true comfort at work can only be achieved after pupillage is over. As befits a set that is very consciously progressive, the decor is highly contemporary and a stroll around different members' rooms revealed furniture worlds apart from the dark brown mahogany we so often encounter on our visits. Readers will also be pleased to know that the gold-fish stationed in the middle of the clerks' room that so struck us on our last visit to Blackstone are all alive and well and have managed to breed prolifically. With picturesque views of the Thames the pièce de résistance is chambers' roof garden, which weather allowing plays host to Friday evening drinks. It was also the setting for last year's Christmas party. Continuing the social theme, chambers has a softball team that can often be found playing against various firms of solicitors in Hyde Park.

The eighteenth-century English jurist William Blackstone once remarked on how "the public good is in nothing more essentially interested, than in the protection of every individual's private rights." Although barristers at this set work both for individuals and the state, ultimately their ideals reflect those of their namesake.

## Brick Court Chambers

**Chambers UK rankings:** Admin & Public Law, aviation, banking & finance, commercial litigation, competition/European law, environment, civil fraud, human rights, insurance, international arbitration, professional negligence, sport

This 64-member set is a giant at the commercial Bar, but that's just the start of it. It also leads in the fields of European Union law and public law.

Beyond the English courts, the set's EU specialists appear at the Competition Appeal Tribunal, as well as the Court of Justice and Court of First Instance in Luxembourg. Public law specialists are familiar with the European Court of Human Rights in Strasbourg and various other international forum. Sheer variety of activity could alone be regarded as Brick Court's greatest selling point. In fact, it is the quality of legal advice and the strength of its advocates that make chambers stand out.

Of the 26 silks in chambers, key names include the likes of Jonathan Sumption and Sir Sydney Kentridge, and their track records bear testimony to a phenomenal work ethic. No wonder a handful of the top guys earn a million or more each year. Sumption lately acted for the government in the claim brought by Railtrack shareholders, Kentridge in the case challenging the legitimacy of the hunting ban. Both had a big hand in the long-running Three Rivers litigation. Draw in other members' achievements and you have a pretty impressive portfolio of top work. Christopher Clarke QC was Counsel to the Tribunal in The Bloody Sunday Inquiry (and was recently appointed as a High Court judge); David Lloyd Jones joined Sumption in The Hutton Inquiry, and various members have been participating in the Equitable Life litigation, EU competition wrangles on behalf of Microsoft, and an international dispute between Trans-world Metals and a Russian oligarch concerning a smelting plant in Kazakhstan. Some of chambers' other cases have things other than money at stake – members were involved in controversy concerning the Greek Olympic sprinters and various right-to-life cases. Knowing all this, you begin to get a sense of why Brick Court is such a colossus.

By the sounds of things, pupillage at Brick Court is "*a steep learning curve and a real shock to the system.*" Fortunately, there are no hidden agendas: "*It's quite simple; if your work is up to scratch then you'll make the grade.*" (Though, naturally, 'up to scratch' means damned good.) Chambers took on none of its pupils in 2004. However 2005 was a different story, with two of the four now happily ensconced as tenants. "*At the end of the day, it's all about ability. That's not to say that the people we don't take on aren't able, it's just that they haven't reached our absolute magical standard.*"

The nine gruelling months leading up to the tenancy decision in July are spent with three separate pupilmasters, and attempts are made to ensure that pupils see a good spread of the different types of work on offer. PMs do allow their charges to carry out work for others in chambers, but the pupillage committee has a definite view on pupils not needing to hawk themselves around chambers impressing all and sundry. The pupil we spoke to had spent her time working in each of the set's three major areas – public, EU and general commercial law, observing "*highly cerebral matters right from the off.*" The option of spending a week in the set's annex in Brussels is taken up by some, and one pupil who had done so described it as "*a nice change of scene and great from an EU law awareness point of view.*"

Besides "*working prodigiously hard,*" the best tip for a Brick Court pupil is to "*imagine every piece of work is your own. Putting your name to something has to be like a stamp of quality.*" Also, when doing work for your PM, "*look at the bigger picture... it's about picking the right points, not all of them.*" This definitely isn't the place to come if you intend to pack up and head home at 6.02pm every day because the standard to which you are aiming inevitably requires late nights and weekends spent working. Another factor in the equation is the series of monthly assessed advocacy exercises that see pupils slug it out with each other in front of a panel of eminent members. "*It's not a gladiatorial trial,*" we were assured; indeed, pupils actually seemed to find solace in having their compatriots beside them. "*It's more fun staggering through the waterfall with everyone else. We all go for a drink afterwards.*" Real-life advocacy is available in the second six, via small matters such as social security

and possession hearings, which the clerks secure through relationships that are deliberately cultivated with a view to building up pupils' experience.

The tenancy decision is made in July, after the pupillage committee makes its recommendations to the entire set. By this stage the pupils should have an inkling as to how things will go, if only because they'll have had an appraisal of their prospects at the six-month stage. Almost all choose to stay for a full 12-month pupillage, appreciating what it can do for them, even if they must look elsewhere for tenancy.

How do you get onto the Brick Court pupillage shortlist? Although the set does participate in Olpas, this really is little more than a final sifting stage. An assessed mini is a prerequisite for interview (although, confusingly, you have to interview for the mini-pupillage as well). The running theme of a successful candidate's application will be "*sustained academic excellence;*" at the interview stage this must be backed-up by evidence that they can "*articulate, process and analyse.*" The panel's questions will be demanding and intense, much like the style of advocacy in the commercial court. "*We find it exhilarating answering incisive questions in court and we expect those we take on will find it the same.*" In addition to a pre-prepared problem question, expect to discuss a topical legal matter. In 2005, interviewees were asked to discuss the decision to allow Roman Polanski to give evidence in his libel trial via video-link.

We felt duty-bound to ask about the supposedly austere atmosphere within chambers. Does it really exist? "*We've probably got that reputation because we're quite an introverted set and less concerned with outward appearances than some of our competitors,*" came the answer. "*Once people get here, the myth soon dissipates.*" There's still a sense of hierarchy. Clerks still call seniors Mister and Sir, while a pupil confessed: "*There are members that I wouldn't address because I'd have no idea what to call them.*" One of the juniors probably had it spot-on when they told us: "*Yes, there is a degree of respect and deference, but these characters have more than earned it. It's an absolute meritocracy and everyone is happy with that."* The plush Essex Street premises have a certain majestic quality to them, with the fifth-floor roof garden offering a magnificent vista over the city. This choice spot is the setting for various marketing events with solicitors' firms, and as the senior clerk told us: *"You can sometimes see the Blackstone crew launching a book or something."*

Brick Court attracts true high-fliers, those prepared to make sacrifices in order to succeed. The pupil we spoke to had obviously enjoyed pushing herself to her legal limits – her opinion on the year: *"It was the easiest money I've ever earned because every day was just so interesting."* You have to ask, if it is such a demanding place, why would anyone choose pupillage at Brick Court? Again, the answer is simple. If you want to be at the best set for commercial work, or public law, or EU law, you have to put it right at the top of your shortlist. Brick Court does have equally good competition – in commercial cases it's the likes of Fountain, Essex Court and One Essex; in EU law it competes with Monckton; on the public law side it has rivals in Blackstone, Doughty Street, 11 KBW and a few others – but no other set achieves the same degree of excellence in all of them.

# Cloisters

**Chambers UK rankings:** Clinical negligence, employment, product liability

Fifty-three years old and counting, the Cloisters juggernaut shows no signs of putting on the brakes. Its 44 practitioners continue to handle headline cases, more often than not on the winning side. Recent matters have included Harrygate (the unfair dismissal case of former Eton art teacher Sarah Forsyth); Saudi torture victims; appearances on behalf of members of the public who had made allegations of electoral fraud against three Labour councillors in Birmingham; the case of Ross v Ryanair (in which a disabled man was charged a fee for taking a wheelchair from check-in to the departure gate) and the public inquiry into the racist murder of Zahid Mubarek at Feltham Young Offender Institution. Evidently the Pump Court-based set is as committed as ever to its founding values of "fighting for the individual." Given this motto, you might think that members would appear primarily for claimants, but we learn that in the employment sphere, approximately 50% of the set's work is now respondent-based. Inevitably, justifications are advanced for this: you can only know your enemy by working for him and the social conscience work has to be financially supplemented by the respondent work.

As these cases indicate, Cloisters has its fingers in a number of pies. In all areas of practice within chambers, members have taken on landmark challenges. In employment, agreement was finally reached in Wilson v North Cumbria Acute hospitals NHS Trust, a widely reported equal pay matter that has resulted in the largest ever settlement in the UK. The case involved 1,500 women represented by UNISON and may pave the way for further equal pay cases against the NHS. Members have additionally won permission to take the UK's leading age discrimination case to the House of Lords. In sport, a member has acted in a landmark case in the Court of Arbitration for Sport in Lausanne concerning the football transfer market. In human rights, although ultimately not successful, members tried to bring a case for unlawful exile on behalf of thousands of Chagossians removed from the island of Diego Garcia in 1965. In personal injury, clinical negligence and product liability, the set is conducting leading litigation, one recent case involving a young woman who contracted listerial meningitis as a week-old infant and hydrocephalus which remained undiagnosed for a year. Left with severe learning difficulties and physical problems, she received an out-of-court settlement of £3.9 million. In another case a leukaemia victim who was rendered paraplegic following an injection which was administered intrathetically rather than intravenously received a settlement of £1.5 million. The presence of high-profile and unusual work in so many areas ensures considerable scope for any young barrister or pupil. The set's four silks, Brian Langstaff, Simon Taylor, Arthur Davidson and Robin Allen, have each built a strong name, both in court and out. Allen is actively involved in advisory work on the drafting of employment legislation, providing Cloisters' juniors with excellent opportunities for research, and was recently appointed as a trustee of the London Bombings Relief Charitable Fund, set up to assist the victims and families affected by the terrorist attacks on 7 July 2005.

A wide range of solicitors instruct the set, the niche operators and campaigning firms mingling with big City firms specialising in commercial law. This is perhaps a testament to chambers' quality of service and a strong streak of realism as well as idealism. Regardless of who you act for, certain qualities will always stand you in good stead at Cloisters: "*You need resilience and you need to be able to pick yourself up and dust yourself down for the next big fight.*"

Pupils spend at least three months in each of chambers' two core areas – employment and personal injury. In the first six, their work will consist of drafting opinions and pleadings, attending conferences and preparing cross-examinations for their pupil supervisor. They'll have a fair idea of how well they're performing as the feedback is "*incredibly useful because they go into so much depth.*" The second six is a different experience entirely. Gone are the regular 9am to 6pm days as the supervisor's shadow. They are still allocated a supervisor but a pupil's working rhythm will vary according to the size and nature of their own caseload. That's right, *their* caseload. Towards the end of pupillage, second sixers are on their feet for

clients in employment tribunals and county courts. Naturally their work is initially fairly basic, simple employment claims or small civil claims, but the set has close links with various pro bono organisations which means that some quite interesting cases trickle through. Another thing to note is that the pupillage award has grown considerably in recent years, which means that pupils can focus on getting the widest possible experience without worrying too much about their finances.

Nailed to the end of the year is a series of assessed exercises to test pupils' advocacy, research and drafting skills. The results are used in conjunction with a final interview with the tenancy committee to determine whether the set will offer tenancy. If a pupil reaches a specified standard (80%), tenancy is a given. In this process there is minimal scope for subjectivity, a degree of consideration being paid to the input of the pupil supervisors. "*We're consciously trying to minimise the 'if your face fits' approach to tenancy selection,*" proclaimed one member. "*But it's certainly not a complete free-for-all;*" in recent years one or two pupils have been granted tenancy each time. We sensed that pupils are not usually overly competitive with each other. "*I feel insulated from the typical popularity contest that goes on between pupils. The objective nature of the system means we're more likely to confide than compete,*" revealed one pupil. The only fly in the ointment in this exquisitely fair system is the fact that the decision is not made until September, meaning that the unfortunates who don't get taken on can be disadvantaged when trying to locate a third six.

Getting pupillage at Cloisters is no cakewalk and if you don't show evidence of commitment to the set's core values on your Olpas form then you're unlikely to be invited to interview. "*We want to root out the absolute mercenaries, but at the same time we're not looking to attract complete zealots.*" Throw in a demonstrable aptitude for a career at the Bar plus sterling academic credentials and the chances are you'll be among the 70 or so hopefuls who are summoned for first interview. Here, you'll be given half an hour to prepare a contract or tort-based problem question and the key element the panel is looking for is an ability to order things clearly in your mind. In other words, you've got to *"get to grips with the problem and not get bogged down with the irrelevant stuff. The candidate who structures their answer well always scores highly."* The second interview is longer with much of the discussion centred on another problem question, but this time you will have had a week to prepare (and bite your fingernails to the quick).

Though Cloisters is well into middle age, there is a sense of youth and energy about the place. After our last visit we referred to the set's nickname 'Bolly Chambers', earned as a result of members' desire to crack open the champagne at every available opportunity. Nothing much has changed it would seem. *"Every time there's a birthday, engagement or anniversary, we make sure we celebrate it. We're certainly a chambers that comes together for a party."* A relaxed dress code is illustrative of the set's informal nature – *"pomp and circumstance is not the Cloisters way."* Something that is 'the Cloisters way' is an informal commitment by every member to do at least five days of pro bono work each year. This is just one part of a set of collective values that defines and binds chambers together but – we're happy to say – doesn't overwhelm it.

## Crown Office Chambers

**Chambers UK rankings:** Clinical negligence, construction, personal injury, product liability, professional negligence, professional negligence: construction

With 77 practitioners, Crown Office Chambers comfortably holds the title of London's largest common law set. In May 2005 Anthony Edward-Stuart QC took over the reins from previous joint heads of chambers Michael Spencer QC and Christopher Purchas QC, who had steadied the ship since the merger between One Paper Buildings and 2 Crown Office Row in 2000. The point of the merger was to fuse two first-class insurance-led sets into one superset that could better ride the ups and downs of the market. A sort of 'if you can't beat 'em join 'em' merger, if you like. Though not quite a unified body in geographical terms just yet, there is certainly a commonality of purpose at COC. That commonality is insurance litigation, the thread that runs through even the specialist areas of practice. COC can justifiably boast expertise in six key areas: construction, insurance, health and safety, product liability, professional negligence and personal injury. It is also developing an impressive education practice. This spread of expertise has placed it in various notable cases including a number of work-related stress matters heard in the Court of Appeal following the House of Lords decision in Barber v Somerset County Council; class action litigation in relation to MMR, tobacco and oral contraceptives; and representation at public and judicial inquiries into major rail crashes and the racist murder of Zahid Mubarek at Feltham Young Offender Institution.

The list of solicitors that instruct the set is long and features leading firms from around the country including Halliwells, CMS Cameron McKenna, Pinsent Masons, Beachcroft Wansbroughs, Berrymans Lace Mawer, Lovells, Morgan Cole and Vizards Wyeth. Again, the common denominator for many is their insurance clientele. Although it varies according to each member's practice, the majority (roughly 70/30) of the work undertaken at COC is on the defendant side, typically insurance companies disputing liability and/or quantum. Is it difficult, when defending claims brought by injured individuals, to have as a principal aim the minimisation of insurance companies' financial outlay? Not a bit. *"There is no monopoly on virtue in a PI claim,"* countered one junior tenant. Indeed, the public backlash against ambulance chasers and the compensation culture lays the path open for the argument that it is the defendant barristers who actually have the moral high ground. Having said this, our sources had to concede that the client contact on offer in claimant work "*does get the old adrenaline flowing a lot more than when you're doing defendant work.*"

As with many sets, the first three-month segment of pupillage is a bedding-in period, with a little more required of you in the second three. All up, the first six is split between time in chambers learning to draft pleadings etc. and accompanying your supervisor or another practitioner to court a couple of times each week. This is an opportunity to see the nuts and bolts of common law advocacy and the other court skills that will be required of you in practice. One pupil recalled the buzz of seeing one of the most eminent silks in chambers tearing strips off an expert witness in cross-examination. "*It was a highly inspirational experience. When you see people of that quality doing their stuff and then get the chance to talk with them afterwards, you feel very privileged indeed.*" Our thanks go to the seasoned campaigner who gave us the lowdown on what it takes to be a successful common law practitioner. "*You need to be exceptionally strong at fact management. Being able to work out which facts undermine and which facts help is an integral part of what we do.*"

The second-six pupil is a busy animal. In addition to doing work for their pupil supervisor and appearing in court three or four times a week on CMCs, infant settlement approval hearings and some small claims trials worth under £5,000, after a little practice they progress to fast-track claims (worth up to £15,000). Most hearings at this level tend to be within the M25 although travelling further afield is certainly not unheard of. As well as court hearings you'll do paperwork for other members of chambers too. Fortunately supervisors are on hand to act as gatekeepers, ensuring that you don't make promises you can't keep. Certain members hold more sway than others in the

tenancy decision meeting and, knowing this, supervisors will gently nudge you in their direction from time to time so you get your chance to impress. Another important tip is to make sure you're always courteous to your instructing solicitors because the feedback they give to the clerks will be factored into the tenancy decision in July. Supervisors at COC are a conscientious bunch and clearly concerned with their pupils' welfare. Said one: "*We're not a 'good morning, good night' sort of set. We like to engage with the pupil.*" We have to say, in the money-driven world of insurance, it's refreshing to find a set that is as intent on developing pupils' professionalism and ethical responsibilities as it is their commercial nous and courtroom skills. And supervisors aren't the only port of call for problems; the most junior tenants take the role of aunts and uncles to the pupils, and because they don't get a say in the tenancy decision "*you don't have to worry about what you say and how stupid you sound.*"

As a non-Olpas set, all applicants need to complete COC's own application form. This is your opportunity to show off an excellent academic record and an extensive knowledge of what the set is all about, whilst also demonstrating outside interests. Jump through this particular hoop and you'll find yourself at a first interview. But be prepared for some off-the-wall questioning – one recent example required candidates to explain an iPod to a Martian. The recruiters are looking for a blend of "*articulacy, assertiveness and aptitude;*" the candidate who is able to "*argue unattractive positions without preparation*" will score highly.

The reality is that if you make it to pupillage, you'll never get to know everyone in chambers given its size. It got us wondering whether the presence of such a large number of barristers had a negative or positive impact on the set's self-image and social life. We learned that weekly drinks in one of the conference rooms are "*always well attended*" and that Chez Gerard and The Gaucho Grill provide the setting for spontaneous drinks when the junior end of chambers is in the mood. Pupils are invited to all of these events and the supervisor we spoke to makes a point of ending each of his pupil's sojourns with lunch in the restaurant of their choosing. Cricket matches with solicitors firms feature in the summer's entertainment programme, the idea being "*to lose competitively so that the firms continue to instruct us.*" Surely it's not that simple!

## Devereux Chambers

**Chambers UK rankings:** Employment, insurance, personal injury.

If it's a busy mix of cases and a convivial atmosphere you're after and you rather like the northern edge of the Temple, Devereux Chambers is absolutely your set. Okay, so it is not top dog in any one area of practice but its members do have a habit of cropping up in the rankings for an impressive number of areas. In addition to three core specialisations of employment, personal injury and commercial, members have a presence in health and safety, telecommunications, sports law, education, environment, professional negligence and even tax. Head of chambers Colin Edelman QC has an excellent name for insurance and reinsurance. He has acted in several notable cases recently, including one dealing with 9/11 compensation. On the employment side, where there is an even balance of applicant and respondent work, chambers has been involved in cases that have attracted considerable media attention, particularly in the realm of high-value discrimination and bullying claims against big international banks. In a case where employment meets PI, one member of chambers, Oliver Hyams, acted for the employee in the recent House of Lords matter McCabe v Cornwall County Council which defined the conditions in which an employee can sue an employer for stress-related personal injury.

The story of how Devereux became a jack of many trades is quite interesting. Until the mid-seventies, it operated happily on a diet of crime and personal injury. Then, in a classic case of right place, right time, members became involved in a number of high-profile trade union matters which in turn led to the set developing a growing reputation in the employment sphere in the 1980s. Gradually the criminal work died away and was replaced by an increasingly commercial caseload. Throw in the fact that this was where Alan Moses QC (now a senior Court of Appeal judge) once plied his trade and you can see how the set has managed to upgrade the quality of its work over the years. Top-level work doesn't lead to top-level stuffiness however. "*Even though we're a bit more specialised these days we've managed to retain that common law set ethos which means that no one's up their own arse.*" This is also a set with advocates who enjoy their time in court. "*We're not court jesters but it's definitely true that well-deployed wit can produce many benefits in the courtroom.*"

The way to navigate a successful course through pupillage at Devereux is to show proficiency in each of the set's core areas by impressing a different pupil supervisor every three months. Whether this bar has been cleared will become apparent in a vote by all tenants in a July meeting. If at least two-thirds of members are on-side then you're in. A tip: put in maximum effort when doing personal injury work as this is the biggest group in chambers. In addition to the report sheets filled in by supervisors there are also a number of assessed advocacy exercises to be taken throughout the year. The constant feedback pupils receive is not only extensive, it can be critical and "*you get the feeling that they are always trying to encourage and not undermine confidence.*"

Typically pupils will research an aspect of a case and write an opinion. The temptation to try and impress your PM with all the law you can muster should be avoided as Devereux prides itself on providing clear and concise practical advice to clients – not bamboozling them with spurious exceptions to the rule. In your second six, you're on your feet from the word go with instructions including RTAs and relatively straightforward employment tribunal claims.

If you set your heart on pupillage at Devereux, be prepared to go the extra mile to get an interview. It's not just what you write on your application but the way you write it. "*Even the most mundane detail can be written in an interesting way.*" A consistently high level of academic achievement is important but most of all the recruiters are looking for "*people who are on their way up.*" The candidate's motivation for applying to Devereux is also key: "*If they can show that they would be a good fit with the set we take that into account.*" The first interview is a getting to know you session with a discussion on any interesting aspects of the candidate's CV. Fair play to them, our sources were happy to confirm that extreme examples of altruism are not the deciding factor here. "*Everyone seems to have dug a well in Namibia these days, we're on the lookout for the candidate who grabs our attention.*" Display the requisite combination of articulacy, poise and humour and you'll probably be back for a second interview when you'll be presented with a problem question half an hour before proceedings. This is your chance to demonstrate your ability to give structured answers in a fluent manner with minimal preparation time. "*The successful candidates are those who are able to organise their minds and engage the panel. Everyone who gets to the final stage is manifestly very bright, but some can't cope with pressure.*"

After the second interview candidates can have a confidential chat with a baby junior and "*ask as many stupid questions as [they] like.*" This is the perfect opportunity to get the low-down on chambers whilst also finding out the correct answer to the problem question they have just tackled. The new tenant we spoke to saw this gesture as pivotal in influencing her decision to choose Devereux over other sets. "*It gave the impression of an open, friendly, supportive set and I can honestly say nothing I've seen since has altered that impression.*"

As is increasingly common in the Temple, a lack of space in chambers has resulted in approximately half of the 45 members moving to Queen Elizabeth Building overlooking Middle Temple Gardens. We wondered whether this led to a slightly polarised atmosphere – not a bit, "*everyone comes up from QEB most days to have a bit of a gossip.*" Although we are always wary of extensive claims of friendliness and camaraderie within sets, we have to say that our visits to Devereux more than substantiate the assertion. There's no formal chambers tea at Devereux, just "*ad hoc sandwich sessions in a conference room depending on who is about.*" If there is a major sporting event during the week, the set will normally reserve seats in a local pub so people can go and watch it. A netball team has been formed ("*it puts everyone on a level playing field*") and the clerks-v-barristers football match "*always proves entertaining.*" Evidently there is a thriving social scene, though our sources stressed "*there is no assessment on social interaction, we don't make judgements on who's going to be the best drinking buddy.*"

As we left Devereux, before navigating our way back down the alleyways towards the RCJ, we paused to admire the colourful geraniums and fuchsias on show in the window boxes. They seemed an apt reflection of the barristers on show at Devereux – vibrant, natural, cheerful.

# Doughty Street Chambers

Chambers UK rankings: Admin & public law, clinical negligence, crime, defamation/privacy, fraud: criminal, human rights, immigration, personal injury, police law, product liability

Many people say they want to make a difference, few actually do so. We'd venture that Doughty Street has more than its fair share of the kind who are not only motivated to fight the good fight but actually climb into the ring eager for the sound of the bell. Ranked by *Chambers UK* in more 'worthy' areas of practice than you can shake a stick at, the set plays host to practitioners who battle to protect and develop human rights. Doughty Street's website sets out its collective values and, in short, these boil down to "defending freedom and citizens' rights" and running chambers according to principles of "equality, respect and diversity."

Imagine you're a man who has been imprisoned for 25 years following a conviction for the attempted murder of a nine-year-old boy. Imagine you were just 15 years old and living in care when you were accused of the crime and you were never told of your right to consult a solicitor. Imagine you're a gypsy unable to stay on a site you've come to regard as your home. Imagine you're one of 417 prisoners sitting on death row in Uganda, praying that your sentence will be commuted to life imprisonment. These are situations embraced by Doughty Street lawyers.

Long involvement in criminal and immigration law is complemented by high-level expertise in areas such as press freedom and personal injury cases connected with, for example, Gulf War Syndrome and forces' post-traumatic stress disorder. This is the place to go if you want to rub shoulders in the library with real big hitters such as Helena Kennedy QC, Edward Fitzgerald QC and Keir Starmer QC, whose clients include the McLibel two and MI5 whistleblower David Shayler.

Putting 85 barristers together in a relatively small Georgian terrace inevitably means space is at a premium. As pupils and junior tenants are often in court this isn't an insurmountable problem, but we do suggest you put aside any notions of having your own magnificent office complete with mahogany desk and grandiloquent bookcase stacked with law reports. Pupils tend to be based in the less glamorous confines of the set's civil and criminal libraries in the basement where they have access to chambers' extensive computer facilities.

No one pretends pupillage at Doughty Street is easy. It is in fact "*a year-long interview, with a seemingly endless parade of assessments and hurdles to clear.*" Before kicking off, pupils are provided with a list of all the potential supervisors and invited to select the one with the practice that most appeals. Depending on the area in which they want to specialise, their first six is spent with either a civil or a criminal practitioner. Naturally enough, the criminal pupils spend the majority of their time in court while their civil counterparts are more likely to be found in the basement researching or preparing written work. Regardless of this distinction, when it comes to the second six all pupils take to their feet for their own magistrates' court criminal cases as well as occasional immigration and asylum hearings. Pupils are automatically provided with the cost of Zones 1-2 travel and additional travel costs are immediately reimbursed.

The race for tenancy is very much an open competition between four pupils. Doughty Street isn't one of those 'we'll take on everyone if they're good enough' places; the set takes on one new tenant from among its pupils each year and one only. Pupils earn their stripes through a combination of written and oral assessments and the mountainous pile of report sheets prepared by their supervisors throughout the year. No feedback is offered on these set pieces of work, meaning that until the tenancy announcement in October, it can be hard for a pupil to gauge how things are going. What did become clear from our discussions with pupils past and present is that the element of the unknown leads to esprit de corps between the pupils, which in turn makes the process a lot more bearable.

One of those we interviewed sagely commented that "*someone who was determined to shaft everyone else wouldn't be here anyway; that would run totally against the ethos of the place.*" The pupils appear to have no complaints about the nature of the decision-making process, saying: "*We went into this with our eyes wide open, everyone has been com-*

pletely up front about it from day one." The objective nature of the system means "*there's none of that paranoia about what work other pupils have got or who they are chatting to in the library.*"

The "*militantly fair*" rules that apply to the tenancy decision are also in play when it comes to pupillage applications. Olpas applications are scrutinised by at least two members of chambers who apply strict criteria in assembling a list of candidates for first interview. This is not the place to apply to on a whim, and unless you can demonstrate a genuine commitment to the welfare of others in addition to strong intellect and high motivation, you'll waste the time of all concerned. Although it was stressed that attempts are made to ensure that the 21-year-old LLB student and the 41-year-old candidate with bags of life experience are competing on a level playing field, it was telling that the youngest pupil we spoke to was in their late twenties. With regard to academic qualifications, nothing suggests that any particular institution is preferred, and the focus – such that it is – rests purely on your results. Applicants with less than a 2:1 must ensure they have sufficiently impressive non-academic achievements to make a compelling case for an interview. The sort of thing that will tick this commitment box may include working in a Law Centre or for a charitable organisation. Bear in mind that Doughty Street's recruiters are looking for evidence of long-term commitment so it pays to get involved with such organisations as early as possible.

First-interview candidates are given a problem question on something topical just ten minutes before meeting a panel of two barristers. In recent years questions have concerned animal rights and the right to privacy for paedophiles. The candidate must present their case persuasively and anticipate potential stumbling blocks. The panel looks for "*someone who demonstrates potential as both a barrister and a future colleague,*" so try to find a perfect blend of authority and personality. The second interview shortens the field to 20 hopefuls and follows a similar format, just with a larger panel and questioning that is noticeably more rigorous.

Doughty Street attracts people of a certain political and philosophical persuasion and there are no prizes for guessing that the underlying emphasis is somewhat anti-establishment. Said one source: "*Of course we're all political animals, you don't do this type of work without having cultivated some sort of social conscience.*" That said, we didn't get the impression that pupils are obliged to have their Amnesty International membership badges on display at all time. "*No one in chambers is impressed with political tub-thumping. The chances are if you've got something to say you'll act on it.*"

Informality is the order of the day and if members aren't due in court, chances are they'll be dressed casually. Don't mistake this informal vibe for laziness – everyone works phenomenally hard. The work demands it. Whether it's a senior QC involved in a highly publicised international war crimes case or an anonymous immigration matter conducted by a baby junior, barristers here are conscious of "*dealing with matters of major humanitarian significance*" and, as such, must always apply "*absolute commitment to the cause.*"

Although it's a set where "*everybody does their own thing outside of work*" there is ample interaction between members during the week and pupils assured us that "*no one, whatever their seniority, is too busy to offer advice if asked to do so.*" Friday evenings always involve drinks in chambers' reception room or the garden, and those not rushing back to family commitments will inevitably be drawn to nearby pub The Duke. When we visited, plans were afoot to mark the set's 15th anniversary with a garden party at one of the silks' homes.

You won't end up at Doughty Street by accident or mere good fortune; you have to be the sort of person who has a real desire to be at the sharp end of the law and work hard to stay there. In short, this set remains the destination of choice for those who wish to stay true to the ideals that got them interested in law in the first place.

# Erskine Chambers

**Chambers UK rankings:** Banking & finance, commercial litigation, company, insolvency/corporate recovery

Highly professional, highly committed and highly respected, Erskine Chambers is the natural destination for the pupil whose boat is rocked by shareholder disputes, takeovers and mergers. No other set gets near Erskine for the quality and depth of its company practice. Although it sounds like a narrow branch of law, company law actually impacts on a wide range of commercial disputes. Regulars on the pink pages, members are always in the mix on the biggest and bitterest takeover fights – think Philip Green's aggressive bid for M&S and the scrap for control of the Canary Wharf Group. Those drawn to long-running litigation can't fail to be impressed with Erskine's involvement in the Equitable Life case and the 'Spice Wars' dispute between members of the Pathak family who were battling over their shareholdings and control of the family's multimillion-pound pickle business. Insolvency also features large and highly publicised matters have included Marconi and MyTravel.

Having resisted the urge to get involved in the merger mania among commercial sets at the beginning of the decade, Erskine has cemented its independence by moving to brand new Chancery Lane premises in January 2004. It has proved a big hit with all concerned. In a previous edition we noted how the set had a very private feel to it with closed doors the norm. The increase in size means that every tenant now has a huge room and enough space to pile up huge quantities of files; as a consequence open doors are now very much par for the course. That's not to say that the set has metamorphosed into a place where everybody indulges in endless conversations in the corridor but there is certainly a more open feel than when we last visited. One thing that hasn't changed is that (as is perhaps inevitable with a top specialist

set) a significant number of cases end up being conducted against other members of chambers.

Let's get one thing straight: Erskine barristers are remarkably talented but they don't boast about how great they are. The typical barrister has earned a reputation for "*meticulous measured advocacy*" and epitomises quiet authority. We doubt that it was coincidence that everyone we spoke to had a cool, calm, grounded air. "*Someone with a large ego would be at a real disadvantage here. We have a tough audience, a combination of astute business people and the best commercial solicitors in the country. These aren't the sort of people who appreciate being talked down to.*"

The set would like to be a little larger but it appears that any future expansion is to be carried out in a characteristically cautious manner. "*We're not going to compromise on quality in order to beef up the head count.*" Indeed, in recent years, any growth has been organic. By the same token, those who leave Erskine rarely do so in order to join another set; the call is either to the bench or retirement. The net result of all this is that if a pupil does gain tenancy at Erskine, it's because the set sees them as someone who will still be with chambers in 30 years' time. If you suffer from any sort of commitment phobia, maybe this isn't the place for you. Among the set's eight QCs is star name and head of chambers Robin Potts. He follows in the wake of company law oracle Richard Sykes whose opinions were treated almost as gospel in both private sector and government circles.

An applicant's academic record is going to have to be pretty strong to snag an interview at Erskine. The ideal candidate should be able to demonstrate a high degree of self-discipline because: "*We're looking for evidence of time-management skills, someone who has managed to excel academically but also do other things at the same time. A commercial practitioner needs to be able to keep a number of projects on the go at one time and devote enough time to each of them.*" Naturally enough, a further prerequisite for a successful application is a demonstrable interest in company law. "*We don't expect anyone to have an A-Z knowledge of the subject, just a genuine interest in it.*" A final piece of advice for your application form: "*Be succinct and accurate. We like applicants who say in one sentence what others say in three.*" When it comes to interview, "*the ability to think coherently and clearly and be willing to stand up and defend your position*" is highly prized, as are "*people who can be amicable and articulate.*"

The pupillage year is split up into three-month segments spent with four different pupilmasters and mistresses whose practices can have either litigation or advisory leanings. In view of the fact that company law matters can be long-running, strenuous efforts are made to ensure that pupils are kept up to speed with the progress of cases on which they have worked earlier in the year. "*It's important a pupil gets to see the twists and turns every case can take.*" At first glance, pupillage at Erskine appears to be less stressful than at other commercial sets. For the first three months "*the pupil is not in the spotlight, it's more of a bedding-in process.*" Don't get used to the easy life though because after Christmas "*things step up a gear or two*" and over the next six months pupils must complete written work (a mixture of opinions and pleadings typically) for every member of chambers. This work can come back to haunt them at a later stage as it is largely what influences the tenancy decision in July. Nonetheless, the requirement was seen as "*a great opportunity to interact with everyone and show what you are capable of on an individual basis.*" Pupils' hours are not excessively long: the one we spoke to was always away by 6.30pm and, in view of the fact that he had no security key-tag, there was no way he could physically be in the building past 7pm.

The learning experience doesn't stop at the end of pupillage; those who do get taken on as tenants often go on six-month secondments to City firms such as Slaughter and May or US practice Skadden Arps, all of which paints a picture of a set

that is supportive of its younger practitioners.

This isn't a Friday-drinks-in-the-clerks-room sort of operation: "*We're not that type of set, we work hard here but those who do play hard, tend to do it outside of chambers.*" The social scene – such as it is – tends to revolve around chambers tea, the ideal moment to bounce ideas and legal concepts off others. The pupil we spoke to was "*never made to feel afraid to chip in*" and praised the event as "*extremely enlightening.*"

We were left with the impression of a set that is supremely comfortable with itself and equally clear about where it wants to go. Anyone thinking about joining its ranks must have the ability and the will to learn to uphold high standards. What the set can promise is excellent quality work, excellent earning potential and unquestioned respect from others at the Bar and beyond.

# Essex Court Chambers

**Chambers UK rankings:** Agricultural & rural affairs, banking & finance, commercial litigation, employment, energy & natural resources, fraud: civil, insolvency/corporate recovery, insurance, international arbitration, media & entertainment, public international law, shipping

A child of the 1960s, Essex Court Chambers was formed by a group of five ambitious young barristers eager for fame and fortune. They quickly established themselves and Essex Court is now one of the elite magic circle sets at the commercial Bar. For many years it was principally fêted for its expertise in shipping and insurance law, although recently other areas have been developed, with a number of members building respected practices in fields such as banking and finance, or media and entertainment. Epitomising this multi-tasking approach is head of chambers Gordon Pollock QC, who is ranked in an impressive six different practice areas in *Chambers UK*. If you think chambers rests on the reputation of one or two giants, forget it – Essex Court has a total of 29 silks within the 74-strong membership and there are highly respected figures at every turn. For example, VV Veeder is a king in international arbitration, Andrew Hochhauser steals the show in employment and Sir Christopher Greenwood is a bona fide big hitter for public international law. The set generates instructions from a wide range of solicitors, though it has developed especially good links with firms such as Clyde & Co, Holman Fenwick & Willan and Ince & Co. Major work of recent times has included the BCCI litigation and various shipping cases including that relating to the oil tanker *Prestige* which sank off the coast of Spain and caused considerable pollution. Proving that members are certainly not restricted to shipping cases, one of them represented Michael Jackson in an action relating to the now infamous documentary Martin Bashir made for Granada television, and another took on a VAT dispute concerning mobile phone company 3G. A third worked on a dispute relating to the Iraq Oil for Food programme.

One of the first things to note about pupillage at Essex Court is that it could all be over very quickly. Unusually for the commercial Bar, the tenancy decision is made after just six months, and although the unfortunates are not immediately booted out of the door, it normally works out best for all parties if a second six is undertaken elsewhere. Those we spoke to saw the early decision date as a real advantage. "*It means you can get on with the learning side of things in the second six without the distraction of having to impress everyone.*" As to how many pupils succeed in getting tenancy, "*the bar is set high, but if you clear it then you're in. There are no other considerations like space or work.*" In 2005 the set took on three of its five pupils; the year before it was two out of four.

Whilst "*not fast and furious,*" the first three months of pupillage are an important time as pupilmasters are "*running the rule over the pupil's character,*" if only because they are required to produce written reports on pupils' progress at the end of their period of supervision. The key period is undoubtedly the first three months after Christmas. The pupil we spoke with may have been slightly understating things when he described the experience as "*short but hard.*" Five successive fortnights are spent with five different senior practitioners (three silks, two senior juniors) who sit on the pupillage committee, and the pupil carries out an array of exercises for each one. Some may watch over your every move and give you small tasks to complete daily, others may set you one large challenge and tell you to come back in ten days with the finished article. Admittedly, you'll pick up some useful experience during this period, but pupils are left in no doubt that this stage of pupillage is "*all about assessment. You have to excel in all areas in order to clear the barrier.*" Feedback is only given at the end of the process and not during, meaning that pupils are "*completely in the dark about how things are going*" until the tenancy decision is made just before Easter. It's only fair to say that while much is demanded of pupils, much is given in return. Attention is lavished on them at "*tremendously instructive*" tuition sessions delivered weekly by silks.

Essex Court prides itself on being a "*very caring set*" that places a high priority on pastoral care for pupils. Clerks were compared to housemasters by virtue of the way they "*look after you and make sure that you're headed in the right direction.*" From what we can tell, the clerks are in no small part responsible for the learning-based approach to the second six. In essence, the pupil is able to dictate the direction of their future practice through indicating the areas in which they would like to specialise. With this in mind they can then tailor their second six in order to augment their knowledge in their chosen field. By way of example we heard about secondments to solicitors firms, lecturing appointments and pupils accompanying eminent silks to international courts. The senior clerk underlined the set's approach to junior tenants: "*We're interested in the bigger picture, we want to map out everyone's career a long way in advance.*"

Contrary to what one might expect from a set bursting with silks, there is considerable interaction between members: "*We're not at all toffee-nosed,*" claimed a pupil. "*Everyone is down-to-earth and exceptionally well-grounded. Arrogance just wouldn't be tolerated here.*" The weekly Friday chambers lunch is always well attended and provides "*an ideal opportunity to get your feet under the table.*" Juniors can often be found in the nearby Seven Stars chewing the cud over the day's events, but the important dates on the social calendar are the summer party and the Christmas do, which last year was at The Reform Club.

"*Academic excellence is merely the starting point*" for an application to Essex Court. If you haven't got a First or a particularly compelling reason for not having earned one you won't even get a shoelace in the door, let alone a foot. "*There is a highly intellectualised collegiate feel about the place,*" said one member. "*Academic debate is strongly encouraged.*" Something well illustrated by the annual student mooting competition chambers has run for over 30 years. Recruiters are equally keen on candidates who can show a nascent commercial focus. With this in mind, vacation schemes at solicitors firms and a master's degree in something pertinent to commercial litigation are looked upon favourably. It helps to be a winner as well – the CVs of recent recruits are littered with scholarships and prizes. Throw in a bit of public speaking ("*we have cultivated a strong reputation for the quality of our oral advocacy*") and you've got every chance of being among the 40 or so invited to the single round of interviews. After navigating the obligatory problem question where the panel are looking for the candidate who "*presents the relevant arguments clearly and concisely,*" the "*probing yet good-natured*" questioning then focuses on your experiences in an attempt to avoid the "*formulaic stock responses which every candidate has in their repertoire.*"

Although they're all competing with one another for the best pupils and the top work, each of the four magic circle sets has its own individual characteristics. Essex Court has 45 years of tradition on its side yet is not afraid to be forward thinking when needs be. Its move out of the Temple in 1994 to its swish premises at 24-28 Lincoln's Inn Fields is a clear example of that... despite the fact that none of the others followed!

# One Essex Court

Chambers UK rankings: Banking & finance, commercial litigation, company, energy & natural resources, fraud: civil, intellectual property, international arbitration (general commercial), professional negligence, tax

One Essex Court is 40 years old in 2006 and, as it approaches middle age, it has plenty of reasons to feel proud. Firmly established in the magic circle of commercial sets, it hosts a squad of big-name silks including Mark Barnes, Ian Glick, Nick Strauss, younger star Laurence Rabinowitz and legendary head of chambers Lord Grabiner, who gets pulled in on 'bet the company' cases.

The OEC juggernaut really got up and running in the 1970s when Sam Stamler QC, along with two pupils (Strauss and Grabiner) formed strong links with the corporate law firm Slaughter and May. Stamler's measured approach became a blueprint for high practice standards, which continue today, and clerks were encouraged to be up front with solicitors about different practitioners' availability to ensure that double booking never became an issue. The set is able to operate in this cautious manner by virtue of the scale of its charges. "*We're expensive, but our clients know that we're worth it in the end,*" we were told. Also important to note is the generalist nature of OEC's practitioners; they are perfectly able to "*turn their hand with aplomb to any type of commercial dis-*

*pute."* The list of firms that now instruct the set reads like a Who's Who of major litigation, and there is a certain inevitability about the high-profile nature of the cases on which members act. The multi-billion pound Equitable Life jamboree; post-Enron claims including Mahonia Ltd v West LB; and the international banking litigation involving Sumitomo and Crédit Lyonnais are all evidence of the set's claim to be a number one choice for commercial and banking cases. And sometimes, even if the claim doesn't run to billions, clients simply want the best advocates. Earlier in 2005, Lord Grabiner found himself arguing in court over the provenance of a £2 million Louis XV urn sold at auction by Christies.

Quality advocacy is a hallmark of this set. Those in charge of pupils believe they can hone an individual's skill and performance, provided the nuts and bolts are there in the first place. *"There's no such thing as a born advocate,"* a pupilmaster told us, *"but if you don't have that sense of self-assurance then you'll never be convincing."* Don't interpret this as arrogance: *"The commercial barrister with a God complex will never be regularly instructed on the big cases. Who'd want to put up with that for two years?"* Which brings us on to the other attributes you'll need to thrive at OEC. First, commercial awareness – can you recognise the business needs of your client and answer the questions that are important to them? This may require more than legal knowledge. Second, you'll need to be a problem-solver with real attention to detail because: *"Any mistake you make has the potential to cost your client millions. You have to be prepared to go over everything with a fine-tooth comb."*

Pupillage at OEC is apparently *"a long but enjoyable slog."* Expect a change of pupilmaster every three months, each one having a relatively broad commercial practice. If you do have leanings towards the tax and IP spheres though, feel free to bring it up and efforts will be made to accommodate your wishes. Although most of your time is spent in chambers researching and drafting, you will get a few days in court to observe the advocates in action. You will effectively become the property of your first two pupilmasters and they will only allow you to take work from other members if they think you can handle it. Having them act as gatekeepers cuts out the otherwise unavoidable sense of awkwardness that comes when you have to turn people down. As and when first six pupils do work for other members, it will usually be limited to research. Unsurprisingly, *"accuracy is the buzzword,"* and at times it can be nerve-wracking working for some of the big names. The second six also brings advocacy and paid work. Whatever, wherever: it's all good experience.

Working the occasional weekend or series of late nights is a hazard of the job for a commercial practitioner and OEC isn't one of those sets that shoos pupils out of the door if they're still in chambers after 6pm. The pupils we spoke to expected to be in by 9am and still working until at least 7pm on an average day. When things get hairy, reach for the Red Bull. On the plus side, after gaining tenancy, decent breaks between cases more than make up for long hours, and as one member explained: *"If you get really into an interesting case you don't feel the time flying by."* A hard-working atmosphere inevitably leads to a quiet-to-moderate social scene, though a group of regulars can often be found lunching at the unofficial 'chambers table' in Inner Temple's dining hall. There are also drinks for an hour or so on Friday evenings and showing up won't do your tenancy prospects any harm. The dress code for tenants is relatively informal, but pupils are best advised to stick to suits to be on the safe side. Apparently when it comes to conduct, appearance and demeanour, *"the test is what would some mythical elderly member of chambers think?"*

In the recent past chambers has taken on three brand-new tenants per year. Life as a baby junior is a mix of very small cases which can be run alone, and positions as second or third junior on larger cases. The earning potential is fantastic.

OEC practitioners tend to be measured individuals who don't waste their words. That's not to say the flamboyant or garrulous individual won't survive here, rather that the focus is on substance not bluster. To that end, your academic credentials are going to have to be highly impressive to get yourself an invitation to interview. Anything less than a First in your degree and you'll need to plump up your Olpas form with a grand slam of extra-curricular achievements. This is also the time to show an "*intelligent appreciation of what life as a commercial barrister entails.*" At interview you'll be presented with a practical legal problem and a copy of *Chitty on Contracts* 90 minutes prior to meeting the panel. Here's your opportunity to display that hallowed problem-solving ability we mentioned. The panel members will also be asking themselves how well you engage with them and "*will we have confidence in this person with our hard-earned client base?*"

Every year the OEC competes fiercely with the other magic circle sets to snag pupils from the two handfuls of crème de la crème candidates. Every year the set is convinced that it comes out a winner, but what marks it out from the competition? "*It's a serious set, but at the same time there is a refreshing lack of pomposity,*" explained one member. "*You don't sense that there's any agonising about where the set wants to be. There is no identity crisis. It's exactly where it wants to be and that's the sign of good management.*" Which brings us to the set's recently retired senior clerk Robert Ralphs, who has been in chambers since the 1960s and a major influence on the set. Ralphs, who still works as a consultant to the set, has been the custodian of Sam Stamler's original approach to accepting instructions and conducting work – quality conscious and extremely rigorous; ample time in which to provide the highest calibre of advice. Knowing that the set has no room for second best, the question you need to ask is simple: do you see yourself as a top-flight candidate?

# 20 Essex Street

**Chambers UK rankings:** Banking & finance, commercial litigation, insurance, international arbitration, public international law, shipping

20 Essex Street is a bastion of excellence in shipping and international law and has been for quite some time. Nobody we spoke to knew exactly the year of chambers' birth although we were able to trace it back as far as 1926, which still makes it an old-timer. Evidently, the set is conscious of its shipping heritage – much of the art on display around chambers has a nautical theme and the key firms that instruct members include the established big-hitters on all matters maritime: Holman Fenwick & Willan, Clyde & Co, Richards Butler, Ince & Co – you'd be hard pressed to find a major name in shipping that hasn't come knocking on its door for advice in recent years.

As we sat in chambers' waiting room before our interviews, we glanced over at the usual newspapers and latest editions of various legal magazines. Among the literature was a copy of the brochure recording the highlights of the *Chambers Global Awards* which took place in May 2005. At this glitzy event – the Oscars of the profession, some might say – 20 Essex Street won the prime award for UK barristers: 'Commercial Set of the Year'. And it's not hard to see why. Head of chambers Iain Milligan has been one of the key players in the monolithic Equitable Life litigation; other members have been involved in film finance litigation (HIH v Chase Manhattan) as well as the EC competition dispute over the cost of replica football kit (Allsports, JJB, Manchester United and Umbro v Office of Fair Trading). The set's reputation may be closely linked with the sea but these days general commercial cases are as much the meat and potatoes of its work. Beyond this, individual members have developed other specialist areas; for example, an Article 6 Human Rights Act argument was advanced on behalf of the defendants in the Guinness fraud trial (R v Lyons, Saunders and others), whilst one junior worked with Birnberg Peirce to ensure the leader of the Kurdish resistance avoided the death penalty (Ocelan v Government of Turkey). Throw in the set's heavyweight status in public international law (eminent figures Sir Elihu Lauterpacht and Sir Arthur Watts loom large) and a panel of 18 arbitrators (including Dr Julian Lew – a recent steal from Herbert Smith) and you can see why a pupillage should not be regarded as purely an introduction to shipping law and practice. Naturally, the set attracts a number of applications from people who are keen to get involved in public international law matters, but the reality is that this type of work is rarely accessible to anyone who hasn't already made a name for themselves in the field, usually as an academic.

Even though a junior member admitted "*the obvious intelligence of certain members can be intimidating for a pupil,*" the atmosphere in chambers is not overly academic and "*certainly not at all stuffy.*" The set is not looking for "*someone who would squirrel themselves away in the library all day,*" and pupils are "*positively discouraged from working after 6pm.*" However, we doubt the pupil we spoke to was exaggerating when she described the year as the "*steepest learning curve of [her] life.*"

The year is divided into four equal parts, each being spent with pupilmasters of differing seniority. The majority of the work a pupil undertakes is 'live' so there is "*the novelty of actually feeling useful from time to time.*" A pupil's role will typically require them to prepare research notes for conferences or arbitrations and draft skeleton arguments. The cases undertaken will inevitably be weighty commercial matters, but no matter how senior their pupilmaster, pupils are unlikely to get stuck on a particularly paper-heavy case, as chambers views it as "*important that the learning process continues at all times – we like our pupils to see lots of different work.*" It was also stressed that "*pupils are certainly not used as fodder for menial tasks.*"

Advocacy exercises kick in after Christmas.

These normally see two pupils duking it out on a matter previously argued in court by a member of chambers. The advantage of this is that afterwards "*you find out who really won and can see if anything you argued had any practical value.*"

Six months into the year, all members of chambers meet to discuss the pupils' progress. If things are not working out for one or more of them, then it's cheerio and onto somewhere else for a second six. Show "*potential for outstanding performance*" and the journey continues until the final tenancy decision is made in July, again by all members of the set. With four pupils recruited each year, the claim that all will be awarded tenancy if they reach the required objective standard is a bold one. Evidence shows that usually two get the nod each year. Our junior sources cried fair, not foul, saying: "*You certainly feel like you are getting a fair crack of the whip and that's all you can really ask for.*" Those who are successful are then given the opportunity to augment their advocacy exposure by carrying out road traffic cases towards the end of pupillage on the basis that any court time is good court time. Once installed as a tenant they tend to balance their workload between acting as a second or third junior on a big case and building up their own practice with small commercial cases.

Although seasoned veterans admitted that the daily chambers tea is "*not as well attended as it once was,*" it still remains a useful occasion to "*get yourself known by other members.*" Outside of working hours, the junior end of chambers is fairly sociable, and whilst there isn't one favourite venue, members are known to frequent Daly's Wine Bar and The Edgar Wallace. On a sporting note, in addition to football and cricket matches, there is a chambers golf day. One year a pupil won the event and, in spite of committing such a horrendous faux pas, still managed to get taken on as a tenant.

We visited the set around the same time as it was conducting pupillage interviews and managed to visit the designated interview room to sample the atmosphere encountered by hopefuls. Bizarrely enough, the modular table had been specially shaped into something resembling a maple leaf. Sadly not some tilt of the hat towards Canada, the reasoning behind this layout was to make the candidate "*feel more at ease*" with the assembled interview panel. Don't get too comfortable though, and don't be fooled by the fact that there is only one round of interviews. If you haven't done a mini-pupillage prior to applying then your application for pupillage will double up as one for an assessed mini to be carried out during June and July. The point to make here is that the assessment process is far more in-depth than it might first appear. The interview itself lasts 30 minutes and also requires the candidate to analyse a problem question 15 minutes beforehand. The recruiters are not "*testing knowledge of the law, or of specific authorities, but are instead looking to see how the candidate responds to a lively debate.*"

This is a highly polished, intellectually rigorous set, fully aware of the esteem in which its members are held throughout the commercial world. It follows then that once admitted as a pupil you're going to have to work very hard to develop whatever potential recruiters saw in you.

## 39 Essex Street

**Chambers UK rankings:** Admin & public law, clinical negligence, construction, environment, human rights, immigration, local government, personal injury, planning, professional discipline, professional negligence

Whether by design or by coincidence, 39 Essex Street has built itself a profile not dissimilar to that of, dare we say it, Blackstone Chambers. So much so that the two could be sisters, though we express no opinion as to which one is the better looking. As the former home of civil liberties guru and director of Liberty, Shami Chakrabarti, the set has long been

known as a heavyweight in the fields of administrative and public law, human rights and immigration. But chambers is becoming equally at home in the fields of commercial law, employment, media, sports and professional negligence among other things. A pupillage here will inevitably be split between the public and private arenas, and for this reason it makes an ideal choice for anyone unwilling to put too many eggs in one basket.

The cosy, lamp-lit Victorian charm of Essex Street stops at the front door of No.39, where a trad exterior gives way to a modern and businesslike interior. It's smart, it's tidy and it is spacious. Words that could apply equally to chambers' website, which as well as being easy to navigate does a very thorough job of flagging up the recent activities of members, including their landmark cases, publications and other achievements. This is probably in no small part due to the fact that 39 Essex has complemented the traditional clerking system with a management team, bringing in not only a chambers director but also a practice development manager.

39 Essex likes to move its pupils around chambers during their 12 months. In order for them to see as much work as possible, they are assigned to four different supervisors, spending three months with each. Inevitably that means swapping from public to private law work, which pupils say is "*mentally challenging*" because "*you have to get your head around a whole new area of law.*" When not observing their supervisors in court, pupils attempt first drafts of the paperwork for a case and conduct legal research. Sometimes supervisors will actually use their pupils' work, though "*this depends entirely on the pupil supervisor that you are with.*" We're also told that it's not unheard of for a pupil to come up with a point that their supervisor hadn't thought of before, and for that point to be adopted in a legal argument in court.

Opportunities for advocacy do arise in a pupil's second six, though because of the nature of public law proceedings – being conducted almost entirely in the High Court – *"you're not going to be doing your own judicial review applications."* Instead, expect the odd small claim here or case management conference there. Pupils do not undertake work for other members of chambers on an ad hoc basis; the pupillage committee takes the view that it is better for them to follow the same person for *"a sustained amount of time"* so as to *"build up a rapport"* with them. To expose pupils to other members, a body that is ominously named the 'Shadow Pupillage Committee' has been established. Pupils must complete four *"quite intensive"* pieces of written work for the committee during their second six, and these form a not insubstantial part of the formal assessment for the tenancy decision, which is made in July.

Chambers has developed close working relationships with a number of local authorities and it is common for pupils and juniors to be seconded to their legal departments. The management also has other tricks up its sleeve for promoting its junior members to clients. In fact, we got the impression that becoming a junior tenant here is rather like being one of those poor stage-school kids, dragged from audition to audition by their pushy mother. In his first year in chambers, one junior tenant had (on top of his ordinary workload) drafted a series of consultation paper responses for Liberty, advised on a pro bono basis on the presentation of evidence to the Soham Inquiry (also for Liberty), contributed to two leading texts for a legal publisher and appeared in three episodes of Casualty. Okay, that last one was a joke, but you get the point – chambers is serious about getting juniors' careers off to a flying start.

If we've made life at 39 Essex Street sound full on, we should qualify our report by saying that chambers enforces a strict 9am 'til 6pm policy for pupils (including an hour for lunch). One junior recalled how, when working late in the library one evening, he was discovered by a senior QC who, staring at him in disbelief, asked what he was doing so late. We heard no complaints of pupils being chained to the photocopier or lugging books about, and first-name terms are the norm amongst most members. There's a smart but casual dress code, so long as you keep a bat suit for meeting clients or going out to court. This seems in keeping with the way that 39 Essex tenants – at the junior end at least – see themselves as *"modern and forward looking."* To bring everyone together, there are either lunches or drinks on alternate Fridays, which are well attended *"from the most junior clerks to the most senior silks."* The pupils tell us that at these events even such household names as Richard Clayton QC (whose accolades include acting for Cold War spy George Blake in AG v Blake) are amenable to having their ears bent on difficult human rights points.

There's no point in beating about the bush: to stand a chance of getting into 39 Essex Street your CV needs to be pretty hot...okay, very hot. Take a look on the website at the sort of experiences recent tenants gained before arriving in chambers. One had worked as an assistant for a leading public international lawyer helping to prepare submissions for the International Court of Justice in the case of Croatia v Yugoslavia. Another had spent a few months as an intern at the European Court of Human Rights. As everyone we spoke to agreed: *"If there's one thing that we've got in common, we've nearly all done other things before we came here."* Pro bono work is highly valued too. The head of chambers is a trustee of the Free Representation Unit, and most members commit at least 20 hours a year to pro bono activities.

A mini-pupillage is highly recommended. Chambers runs a season of week-long assessed minis from January to June to coincide with the Olpas recruitment process. As well as accompanying barristers to court, mini-pupils will undertake formally assessed written work and a group advocacy exercise, which this year took the form of a hearing before a mock Court of Appeal. The deadline for applications falls in the November of the previous year so apply early, because while a mini-pupillage is not strictly speaking a precondition for pupillage selection, it is clear that chambers places great weight on the process. The good news is that if you make it through the pupillage application paper-sifting stage, there will only be one interview, including the customary legal problem. The verdict on the interview? *"It was an argument with five barristers...not exactly heated, but everything that I said was challenged."* We reckon if you manage to get as far as a pupillage interview here, a small challenge like that will be water off a duck's back.

# Falcon Chambers

**Chambers UK rankings:** Agriculture & rural affairs, real estate litigation

Climb a spiral staircase in the quiet no man's land between Middle and Inner Temple just behind Temple Church and you will chance upon the country's leading property set. Go through its front door and you enter a waiting room more in keeping with a vodka bar than that of a barrister's chambers. Frosted glass partitions lit by coloured spotlights, chairs clearly the work of a hip Swedish designer called Inge and an array of abstract art more suited to a Hoxton PR agency. This set moved to its current ab fab location in the early 90s, having previously resided at 11 King's Bench Walk. Back in those days, in addition to strength in real property matters, the set also had major specialisations in construction and engineering law. When numbers reached a point of critical mass, the decision was made to split into two specialist chambers: consequently Keating and Falcon were born. With 26 out of 34 members ranked in *Chambers UK* for property litigation, it is clear that the latter houses the majority of the leading property lawyers in the country. Members author or co-author most of the leading land law texts – *Woodfall's Law of Landlord and Tenant, Megarry & Wade,* and the landlord and tenant section of *Halsbury's Laws.* Major matters handled recently have included the landmark gay tenancy rights case of Ghaidin v Godin-Mendoza in the Court of Appeal and Bakewell v Brandwood, a case concerning the rules behind acquisition of prescriptive rights of way. Classic stuff.

So what makes a successful property barrister? Those we spoke to stressed the need for strong analytical skills. *"So much of our work involves the construction of contracts. You need to able to analyse every word in detail in order to get the right result for the client."* Specialising in one area of law can bring its own challenges. *"It's important to be enthusiastic about your work in a niche set as there are no other areas of law to escape to."* The client base is certainly varied; practitioners might one day be acting for a farmer in a restrictive covenant case and then advising a multinational company on the interpretation of a lease the next. Barristers have ample opportunity to strut their stuff in court, and although it's not quite adrenaline advocacy it does occasionally produce suitable dinner party anecdotes. One junior tenant regaled us with an amusing tale of how he acted as a human shield between his landlord client and three irate squatters.

Every law student knows that land law is like Marmite – you either love it or hate it. But what if you forget what you learned before pupillage? Anticipating this danger, in the July prior to pupillage the set lays on a comprehensive introduction to landlord and tenant law. This is the ideal opportunity for pupils to meet their future pupilmasters over lunch and inch their feet under the table. In pupillage proper, recruits sit with a different PM every three months and the subject matter tends to be pretty much the same whoever you end up with. It tends to be the pupilmasters who have the most influence in the tenancy decision and, consequently, the majority of a pupil's work will be done for these members rather than others in chambers.

One of the great advantages of being a property barrister is that the cases never last too long and are certainly nowhere near as lengthy as some of the major fraud and pensions cases the courts have seen of late. One silk told us that the longest he'd ever spent in court on one matter was two weeks. As a result, "*pupils get to see a wide range of matters and aren't just stuck on one boring case for the duration.*" In the second six, when the clerks decide pupils are ready, they may start taking their own work, typically undefended possession hearings ("*the staple diet of any pupil doing real estate work*") and small injunction applications. This progresses on to defended possession hearings in the first years of tenancy.

The pupil we spoke to admitted to being rather surprised that his year had been "*remarkably stress-free*" compared to the experiences of contemporaries at other Chancery sets. "*Although it's been taxing from an intellectual point of view, the social side of things has been the exact opposite of all those horror stories that you often hear.*" The chambers institution of tea and toast in the afternoon probably contributes to this. Why toast? "*Everyone got a bit fed up with biscuits, it's nice to mix things up with jam and marmalade.*" There is also the weekly lunch every Friday where all members congregate in the library to catch up and perhaps discuss recent cases. Beyond the law, members find common ground socially, some play cricket together and a keen sailing contingent meet for weekends at the coast. Closer to home The Old Cock on Fleet Street is the local watering hole ("*by proximity not choice,*" muttered one tenant darkly), or if people are feeling a little more energetic they may visit The Seven Stars on Carey Street. Pupils are always invited along to these impromptu get-togethers and it's worth attending just so you can catch up with all the chambers gossip.

The decision-making process vis-à-vis tenancy is not as transparent as we have seen at many other sets. Pupils do get detailed feedback on the work they do for each PM, but their knowledge of their tenancy prospects tends to operate on a 'no news is good news' basis. If after five months tenancy looks unlikely, the tenancy committee will have a quiet word and suggest the pupil finds a second six elsewhere. If, however, the pupil has heard nothing, it goes to a chambers meeting in June or July, when every member has a vote. In a further twist, at the six-month point the committee makes a decision as to whether to also advertise externally for new tenancy applications. Obviously, if it does open up the field to all comers in this way it can make the Falcon pupil feel as if their future in chambers isn't looking too rosy.

The best advice we can give to prospective pupils is that displaying "*real fizz*" at interview will impress the panel, as will demonstrating a "*clear ability to marshal the facts*" and "*superior powers of analysis.*" Most of those interviewed have Firsts or a very high 2:1 from... well let's just say it is business as usual for the more prestigious universities. As one source freely admitted: "*The majority of people we take on are from Oxbridge but over the years we have been known to take on individuals from places like Durham and Bristol.*" There is no particular Falcon personality type and the best we could muster by way of descriptions were "*someone we'd be happy to go out to supper with*" and "*if you're not a gregarious type then you're going to struggle.*"

Falconry is the art of training falcons to hunt and return. The legal eagles at this set are more gatherers than hunters as their reputations are such that work comes to them. This has got to be good news for any pupil who can convince the set's recruiters to make space for them up in the eyrie.

# Fountain Court

**Chambers UK rankings:** Aviation, banking & finance, commercial litigation, employment, civil fraud, insurance, product liability, professional negligence

In the leafy surroundings of the Temple sits a fountain that is part of both legal and literary folklore. In *Martin Chuzzlewit,* Charles Dickens described the Temple fountain as a welcome fixture in the dry and dusty channels of the law and used it as a meeting place for Ruth Pinch and her brother Tom. Rumour has it that Fountain Court Chambers' main building, which backs onto Essex Street, was occupied by prostitutes in the eighteenth century when Covent Garden was the hub of London's nightlife. These days it's a more serious breed of commercial practitioner that inhabits the building. Think of any major commercial case in living history and the chances are that a Fountain Court barrister will have played a part. Think landmark litigation moments like BCCI, Three Rivers and, more recently, Equitable Life and then you're starting to get the idea. Any set that numbers the Attorney General (Lord Goldsmith), the Lord Chancellor (Lord Falconer) and a past Master of the Rolls (Lord Bingham) amongst its former members is always going to be a quality outfit. And with big-hitting silks such as Bankim Thanki, Michael Brindle, Anthony Boswood and Nicholas Stadlen on board, the set shows no signs of releasing its grip on top work.

With such pre-eminent names both past and present, it is understandable that a new pupil might feel somewhat daunted. Chambers recognises this and tries to make the first three-months as relaxed as possible. "We take the view that pupils will only show what they're made of if they're comfortable in their surroundings and so the first three is a bedding-in process," a member of the pupillage committee told us. The pupil we spoke to certainly thought life had initially felt a little less full-on compared to her peers at other major commercial sets. But the pressure does ramp up and the work schedule can become "intense." As a set, Fountain has a reasonably broad commercial practice, and among the generalists there are also some specialists, for example in the fields of insurance, aviation, employment and sports law. Pupils usually sit with generalists unless they have a particular practice area preference that can be accommodated.

After the first three months of what is essentially shadowing, pupils are given bite-sized chunks of whatever is occupying their pupilmaster's time, whether it's producing a skeleton argument, preparing for a conference, writing an opinion or drafting pleadings. The level and depth of feedback given to pupils is pleasingly high: "They go into so much detail it can make your head hurt. You can't fail to learn from this sort of attention." From the second three onwards pupils can also undertake work for other members of chambers, fully conscious of the fact that their performance will influence the June tenancy decision. Although strong advocacy skills are sought through the recruitment process, don't expect to be putting them to use during pupillage. "In truth," confessed one source, "it's all about paperwork, and depending on who you're with, weeks can pass by between court appearances." The second six continues in much the same vein. Two more PMs give you the benefit of their expertise but you will also spend time with some of the junior practitioners just so you get a taste of what's to come.

If you want to be constantly on your feet in court in your second six look elsewhere. Pupillage is in essence a long-haul exercise. Just as commercial cases can go on for considerable periods of time, requiring the set's barristers to maintain a steady pace and consistency of performance, so pupillage is all about gradually developing the right techniques and style to appeal to the leading firms of solicitors that will provide them with instructions in years to come. There's no scrimping or corner-cutting allowed at the big-money end of the commercial Bar.

We started off our tour of chambers in the waiting room, "a blend of the modern and the traditional," we were assured. Since we last visited, the wall between Fountain Court and 35 Essex Street had been knocked through with the result that you can become a bit disoriented when wandering around. The grandeur of the rooms varies according to the seniority and taste of their inhabitants, but actually the communal staircases alone are magnificent enough to underline chambers' wealth. Further evidence of success comes in the form of a gym in the basement. Continuing the sporting theme, chambers organises a series of cricket matches amongst members and staff each year and sometimes also plays against magic circle firms of solicitors. It sounds as if they're not too bad at the beautiful game either – we spotted the 2005 inter-chambers football trophy proudly on display in the clerks' room. They'll hate us for saying this but we suspect the winning of the cup had more to do with the clerks than the barristers. There is a chambers tea but it tends to be frequented by the older end of the set and it's certainly not obligatory for a pupil to attend. Lunchtimes provide the best opportunity for getting your face known. Members typically either grab a sandwich together or head off to lunch in hall.

Just one look at the CVs of the junior tenants should tell you that getting a foot in the door as a pupil will be impossible without seriously impressive academic credentials. Finding the junior tenant who hasn't got a starred First from Oxbridge in this intellectual set is a tricky business. Recruiters favour those applicants who have clearly researched career opportunities within the legal profession, so for example, they tell us: "We're reassured when we see that someone has done a vac scheme at a firm of solicitors, as it shows that they've actually made an informed decision on coming to the Bar." Other pieces of application advice: "Avoid bullshit! It's easy to spot people quoting the website at you. Also, avoid ridiculous phrases like 'I relish the challenge.' The simpler the language the better as far as we're concerned." The first round of pupillage interviews is relatively relaxed, with the focus being on aspects of your CV. The second outing is much more formal and involves a quasi-legal problem which comes with 15 minutes of preparation time. Having made a five-minute presentation, the eight (yes eight) members of the panel will then pepper you with questions in order to ascertain whether you've got what it takes to hold your own in the commercial courts. "We're certainly not after automatons, above all we want someone with a bit of vigour."

Fountain Court prides itself on being a member-driven set. The rationale behind this is simple – "There's little point in being self-employed if you've got someone telling you what to do all the time." This certainly fits in with the impression we formed of the place – it knows it has the pick of the yearly crop at its disposal and it will often be the first choice for the driven and intellectually astute young practitioner. Newtonian principles of gravity dictate that water shot out of a fountain will eventually come down. Fountain pupils, it seems however, can continue an upward trajectory.

# Furnival Chambers

**Chambers UK rankings:** Crime

Founded in 1985, this leading criminal set of 68 barristers specialises in all kinds of serious crime, including a niche in the growing field of asset confiscation. Senior members of chambers have appeared in some of the most publicised criminal trials in recent years, not least among them the Millennium Dome diamond heist, which achieved widespread media attention when the Old Bailey judge nodded off during the closing speeches. Other well-known cases include the Sarah Payne murder and the 'Beauty in the Bath' appeal.

Chez Furnival there's not an oil on canvas or chaise longue in sight: chambers has a modern, light and airy feel to it, which seems to go hand in hand with the set's ethos. As one barrister told us: "Furnival Chambers is far from being stuffy; we pride ourselves on being informal, but at the same time professional." New recruits will be disappointed if they're expecting a rigid hierarchy, and can expect to be welcomed into chambers life from the very beginning of pupillage. QCs make a habit of showing pupils around on their first day, and all newcomers have a reception thrown in their honour. "Everyone makes a real effort to get to know you."

Once the welcome drinks and tour are over, pupils *"knuckle down to some hard work."* Everyone agrees that the pupillage year is a tough one, and that what you see is what you get. The first six is spent with a single pupilmaster, though there is also a compulsory two-month secondment to the asset forfeiture team. Expect to be exposed to serious crime and hope you have the stomach for it. There will be plenty of paperwork, including writing written advices on sentencing or appeal, drafting skeleton arguments and summarising the evidence in trial bundles. If a pupilmaster has a lengthy trial on the circuits, chambers *"won't waste pupils' time by sending them along too if there isn't much to be done,"* but will instead turn to others to find alternative work. This is a good way for pupils to get their faces known.

A 40-hour in-house advocacy course runs throughout the first six and covers the kind of situations likely to be encountered in the early years of practice. Pupils and juniors agree that this training is *"very, very thorough, and really worthwhile."* In addition to their pupilmaster, pupils will also be assigned a junior tenant to act as godparent, another point of contact, who usually proves to be an invaluable source of advice and guidance. It works so well because the godparents are entirely detached from the tenancy decision.

We were particularly impressed with the *Hi-De-Hi!*-style tannoy used by the clerking team to announce the availability of new work. Yet a second six is no holiday, and pupils must zip up their boots for a dawn 'til dusk trawl of London's magistrates' courts. In court every day, it's not uncommon for them to get through nine or ten different clients in a single morning's work. Ever heard the motto, 'Pupil barristers: love the jobs you hate'? Furnival's pupils know it well, and are expected to take part in a Saturday court duty rota. There really is no rest for the wicked! And as you'd imagine, there will be challenging and unpredictable clients to deal with from the word go. One pupil told us of a client (one of her first) who,

when asked to plead guilty or not guilty to a minor offence, caused a disruption. Needless to say he was taken down to the cells pretty sharpish. Her advice: *"It can be pretty devastating when things go wrong, but it's a real learning curve...and if you really don't know what to do next, there will always be someone from chambers available on the end of the phone to guide you through it."*

With all those briefs flooding into their pigeonholes, surely these pupils must be raking it in. Not so, we were told; *"in the second six, you've got to be prepared to go at least two to three months without getting paid a thing. When you get your chambers grant, save some of it for the later months."* The good news is that the fees do eventually trickle in, and during the latter months of the second six, pupils start getting Crown Court briefs in their own name for routine work like sentences and 'mentions'.

For anyone considering tenancy here, a third six is considered a must. In a job where being excellent on your feet in court is everything, *"six months of advocacy experience just isn't long enough to see what you're made of."* For those who make the grade, the dial is turned up a notch and *"you start to build up a practice of your own."* Furnival won't offer third sixes to pupils unless they consider them to have a realistic prospect of tenancy, so make it through to a third six and it's a really good sign. To quote one pupil: *"I feel like here they are really trying to mould you into a future tenant."*

So who would fit the Furnival mould? When we probed into the backgrounds of the barristers and pupils we met, we found a complete absence of academic snobbery – this is not an Oxbridge-only set. What everyone did have in common was a certain fieriness, and we sensed they were the sort who'd definitely give you a really good fight in court. Chambers looks for applicants who can perform well under pressure. As we were told by one member of the pupillage committee: *"There's a complete cross-section of personalities here...academic ability is only worth so much, and we place a lot of emphasis on how candidates perform at interview."*

First-round interviews are short and sweet. To try and make things as fair as possible, everyone is asked the same five questions, often including an ethical or legal topic. Be prepared to fight your corner and to argue things from an alternative point of view as well as the one you hold instinctively. Make it through to the second round and you'll note that the interview panel likes to *"do a bit more heckling."* There will also be an advocacy exercise to prepare, usually a plea in mitigation or a bail application. Applicants who are still at university are at no disadvantage because *"it's not the content that's being judged, it's the style and the delivery that we're interested in."* You'll also be required to give a three-minute speech on the topic of your choosing. Apparently, previous topics have included 'bog snorkelling on my gap year' and 'why playing poker is a skill not a game of chance.' In other words, you've got free rein to talk about anything under the sun as long as you can engage and persuade your audience. Despite sounding like a mediaeval trial by ordeal, everyone we interviewed spoke positively about the interview experience: *"The process was well structured, and I knew what to expect. I think that brought the best out in me."*

We think that if you're bright and outgoing, are good at putting together a persuasive argument and have a passion for criminal law, Furnival Chambers will bring out the best in you too.

## One Garden Court

**Chambers UK rankings:** Family

Turn your back to Middle Temple Hall, dive between the roses and sneak through the narrow doorway: One Garden Court is unassuming from the outside, and within there is little to remind you of the grandeur of the Temple. The set spares its visitor all the self-conscious trappings of a chambers determined to wow with stylish sofas and interesting artwork. Instead, it chooses to impress by relying on its successes in the family law courts. One Garden Court can trace its roots back to family and civil set Lamb Building, established in the 1950s; however, in 1989 an *"ideological schism"* led to the departure of a family law contingent. The breakaway group blossomed into what is now the largest set of chambers in which all members specialise in family law.

Chambers' 47 tenants cover *"a healthy dose of ancillary relief and care work,"* plus adoption, child abduction, international children's law, mediation, human rights issues and family-related crime. Our colleagues on *Chambers UK* inform us that the set's four silks are all expert in children's work (including tough-end care cases) and that its reputation for ancillary relief work has also grown in stature, with many juniors very well regarded in this field. The client base is as diverse as the work: *"There are two different faces – the posh, moneyed clients and the care clients. They have a variety of professional needs."*

Sitting with four pupilmasters for three months each ensures that pupils are *"exposed to the full spectrum within the narrow field of family law,"* including both publicly and privately funded work, ancillary relief, contested divorces, care work and private children's work. Pupils generally stick close to their PMs, though *"if you have a spare moment you can do work for others too."* Inevitably, both their workload and their autonomy grow as the months pass. *"In the first six they kick you out by 6.30pm, but you then get busier with your own practice,"* so that *"by the end of the second six months you barely see your pupilmaster."* You won't be left to flounder around though; *"you really can phone members at home, and late at night, to cry for help."* With PMs, *"feedback comes if you specifically ask for it,"* and *"if you screw up, it's okay – everyone knows it takes a while to get into family practice."* While there are *"no gold stars for excellence,"* *"you will get invited for coffee to go over stuff."*

Over the course of the year, pupils "*definitely do money, and care, and a seat with a more junior junior with a broader practice, plus another seat to mop up and make sure you've seen everything.*" A cracking case-a-day schedule sees second six pups cutting their teeth on Family Law Act (domestic violence) and children's cases, with the agenda including non-molestation orders, contact hearings and removals from the jurisdiction. Pupils enthused about "*quite juicy stuff*" that puts them "*on the frontline from the start.*" This pattern continues in the early years of tenancy, when "*as a junior, care work keeps you busier.*" Money cases, it seems, come later on.

Chambers has a space problem, so members shoehorn themselves behind desks and tuck themselves into cupboards under stairs, stoically remarking: "*It's fine – there's plenty of room for me and my laptop!*" The cheerfulness with which members bunk up and knuckle down is indicative of "*a real camaraderie, and sense that you are all part of the gang.*" Possibly this feeling stems from the nature of family practice, the clientele and the type of people attracted to the work.

Various people took pride in telling us how chambers is "*not traditional for the sake of it.*" One interviewee described it as "*open to change;*" another as "*more liberal*" than most and "*a grown-up, co-operative affair.*" However, any suggestion that family practice equates to little more than highbrow social work is dismissed with a reminder that a human touch does not mean a soft touch. Chambers' style artfully combines the requisite good bedside manner with a "*straight-down-the-line, no-messing-around*" approach.

But this is where any sense of authority or old school ends; "*there's none of that Mister-Miss-Madam stuff*" and "*no standing on ceremony.*" Furthermore, between barristers and clerks there is "*a mutual respect,*" with neither taking the upper hand. "*It is a very democratic place, right down to the tenancy decision.*"

The set has an annexe in Exeter, which for those of a few years call may provide a desirable "*lifestyle option.*" Back in the Temple, the lifestyle is caffeine fuelled. The formal post-court afternoon tea ritual plays no part here and is viewed as just another "*horror story from Chancery.*" Instead, "*you just go for coffee with the people you like*" ...unless it's been a particularly harrowing day at court, in which case Daly's wine bar is close to hand. A self-confessed "*loose-knit community,*" members are "*not cloyingly sociable*" and assured us that "*we don't live in each other's pockets*" (possibly because they live in each other's desk drawers). Our thanks to the wit who said: "*We recognise new arrivals and we recognise retirements, and if there's been nothing to recognise for a while, we recognise that.*"

The set takes on three pupils every two years. The interview is a relaxed affair and "*there is no grilling on the law; we just want to put people at ease and relax them to give them a chance to show themselves.*" Those who had been through the process said: "*They were interested and asked questions I could respond to, rather than presenting me with an ethical dilemma with no answer.*" One sensed "*a genuine empathy*" from the interviewers. Leaving academic standards to one side, the set seeks out those who will fare well in the family law context, because "*you are putting yourself quickly on to a very narrow track.*" It wants pupils who can "*click into the service orientation,*" and those who are "*clued up about life, able to ask the right questions and able to talk to people.*" Aware of the value of a little life experience, the set welcomes those with previous careers just as much as those who have fast-tracked through academia. And with a varied client base demanding differing approaches, we can see why "*there is no magic formula.*"

The tenancy committee makes its decision based on a more rigorous procedure involving a mock brief and interview, plus written reports from all pupilmasters and other interested parties. The committee's recommendation is then put to a full vote of the members and so "*anyone too aloof wouldn't get on – you need to make yourself known.*"

Pupils are not linked up to chambers intranet (by which votes are cast), and although this is "*not an insurmountable problem,*" it does act as a reminder that one's position is temporary.

While heavily glossed fire doors and magnolia walls took us back to our school days, and some of those we met reminded us of the type of well-meaning and chatty teacher who always made themselves accessible, there's no sense of pupils being tested, examined or league-tabled. Then again, we did learn of a spelling test, which has been taken by all members at one stage or another. The ten-word test has been devised by one of the barristers (just for fun) and includes words like "*miniscule, supersede, moccasin and fuchsia.*" A written note is made of all scores!

After a long day in court and a cross-examination from us, we left our sources to put the kettle on and reach for the dictionary to mug up on a few tricky words.

# Garden Court Chambers
## (formerly Two Garden Court)

**Chambers UK rankings:** Admin & public law, crime, human rights, immigration, police law, social housing

In 1974 a crack commando unit of six young barristers set up in practice with the aim of ensuring representation for those who most need it. Today, still true to their founding values, they survive as soldiers of fortune. If you have a problem, if no one else can help, and if you can find them, maybe you can hire a Garden Court barrister. You might consider our comparison of a group of 87 well-respected barristers with The A-Team to be flippant; after all, practitioners at this set deal with such crucially important societal issues as immigration, housing and crime. By comparison Hannibal et al were more concerned with welding tanks and flamethrowers together in the three

minutes before Colonel Decker burst in with the military police to arrest them for the crime they didn't commit. Look closer though and you'll see that the two teams are not so different – both came into existence to protect the vulnerable.

And just in case you're confused by the set's name, Garden Court Chambers was until recently known as Two Garden Court. It made the change following its move away from the confines of the Temple to larger, plush premises at 57-60 Lincoln's Inn Fields, incidentally a former abode of Spencer Percival, the only Prime Minister ever to be assassinated (in 1812).

The typical clients for these barristers tend to be those from the outer edges of society who would be most at risk without representation. If you want specifics then how about the successful defence of Westminster anti-war protester Brian Haw in various criminal proceedings arising out of his long vigil opposite Parliament. Members were also involved in the Mubarek Inquiry (the racist murder of an Asian prisoner at Feltham Young Offenders Institute) and the gay tenancy rights case of Ghaidan v Godin-Mendoza. This is the set where big-name silks such as Courtenay Griffiths, Laurie Fransman and Ian Macdonald reside and, consequently, the work is very much A-grade.

Pupillage at Garden Court is undoubtedly a demanding yet enriching year. One pupil spoke admiringly of the "*full and thorough training*" that he had received, commending the strong level of guidance that had been offered in comparison to that experienced by friends at other legal aid sets. The year is divided into four equal parts, each being spent with a different supervisor. Pupillage will definitely entail spells in crime and immigration as these are the practice areas in which the majority of GC barristers ply their trade. Beyond this you could express your interest in another practice area or a specific supervisor and the pupillage committee will take this into account before the allocation process gets underway.

In addition to working for your own pupillage

supervisor, perhaps drafting advices, skeleton arguments and judicial review claim forms, you can also approach any member of chambers for additional work. In fact, pupils recommend this as "*a great way of broadening your experience.*" After a first six by your master's side, most of your second six will be spent on your feet in the magistrates' courts undertaking summary trials, or in the Crown Court for first appearances, mentions and sentencings. In addition there will also be appearances at immigration tribunals. It's not all in-the-field training; pupils also attend a series of seminars covering advocacy, courtroom etiquette, substantive law and legal developments.

As for your chances of gaining tenancy, things are looking up in comparison with recent years. When we visited chambers, the PTC (pupillage and tenancy committee) was in the process of changing its policy concerning recruitment from within. It used to be the case that any tenancy vacancies would be advertised externally and opened up to all comers, with the result that (in the interest of fairness) the Garden Court pupil's application was treated no differently from anybody else's and in effect they had to regard pupillage as more of a training than a route into tenancy. It may have been fair to outsiders, but it was not a system that particularly benefited pupils. GC's new plan will see one or two pupils being taken on after 12 months in much the same way as you would expect elsewhere. Those who do not make it tend to fare well at other sets and GC has been known to allow people to squat for a further six months until they find another set.

Chambers' recruiters acknowledge that cutting the approximately 700 applications down to about 30 interviewees "*always feels quite brutal and can mean that the young fresh-faced law student is at a distinct disadvantage.*" How so? "*We want more than declarations of intent; we want proof of commitment to social justice. It's going to be hard to compete with ten years of experience in an international aid charity for example.*" The mes-

sage: look at the stats and do the maths. If your CV is not screaming social conscience then it's most likely going to be a wasted application. Those who do make it to interview are still advised to take care, as one of the biggest turn-offs for the set's interviewers is a lack of general social awareness. "*We've interviewed people who are obviously extremely clever and doubtless have the potential to be successful barristers, but they haven't seemed like they really cared about the Garden Court ethos.*" If you're in any doubt as to the types of individual that have succeeded in making a home in chambers you need only look at the members' profiles on the set's website.

Make it to interview and you will undertake an advocacy exercise, invariably on a criminal theme such as a plea in mitigation or bail application, and then answer a number of questions designed to test your knowledge and commitment to publicly funded work. It's best to display a genuine and motivated attitude at this point because "*this isn't the set for those with a cynical, laid-back attitude. We want to see drive and passion in our pupils.*"

In view of the fact that a large number of pupils (eight when we visited) all sit together in one room in chambers, it is inevitable that a social scene quickly develops among them. The Devereux and Refreshers Bar proved to be popular with those we met but inevitably the move to Lincoln's Inn Fields will dictate a change of allegiance. Pupils are very much included in the various functions within chambers, many of these organised by the different practice groups. "*They're certainly not treated like a different breed,*" said a supervisor. "*We try to make sure that they are invited to everything.*" The set's Christmas party, held at a Soho nightclub, is famed throughout the Bar.

In many ways Garden Court has been the scruffy older brother of other 'cool' sets like Matrix and Doughty Street. It started the social conscience ball rolling and showed how it was possible for a set to be united under a shared ethos. Perversely, it is the set's strong egalitarian values which may have proven to be its undoing in recent years as many of its former pupils now ply their trade at competitor sets, frustrated that their pupillage at Two Garden Court did not lead to anything more substantial. It is to be hoped that the move to larger premises, coupled with the implementation of a new, more pupil-friendly policy on tenancy decisions will ensure it can grow from within. And we love it when a plan comes together...

Chambers' motto is "Do right, fear no one." If you're made of the stuff Garden Court wants to see then that probably sums you up too.

## Government Legal Service

There was a time when becoming a barrister meant finding a home in chambers as a self-employed practitioner and nothing else. In fact, not so long ago, the very idea of a barrister being 'employed' would have had senior judges and barristers choking on their sherry. A pupillage in the Government Legal Service (GLS) provides an alternative to the orthodox route of a 12-month pupillage in chambers. The GLS employs about 2,000 lawyers, around a third of whom are barristers, and of the 25 people lucky enough to make it through the GLS recruitment process each year, a small handful of them will train as pupil barristers. We asked a few of them to shed some light on what, for us, was undiscovered territory.

The GLS recruitment process gets going a full two years in advance of the start of pupillage. Whether you want to be a solicitor or a barrister, the procedure is the same: shortlisted candidates are called to spend a day at the GLS assessment centre. During an individual interview applicants are asked to discuss pre-prepared topics, both legal and non-legal. There is also a group problem-solving exercise. The pupils we spoke to confirmed that this process compared very favourably with their experiences of interviews in chambers. Said one: *"The pupillage panel is chaired by a non-lawyer with human resources training. While it was certainly challenging, I felt that the panel brought the best out in me, and I didn't feel under attack, as in some pupillage interviews."*

For applicants who impress on the assessment day, the next hurdle is being accepted by a government department. Just like trainee solicitor applicants, potential GLS pupils can look on the GLS website to see which departments have vacancies for pupils. As with a conventional pupillage, GLS pupils normally spend their first six months in chambers, a placement that is usually organised by the sponsoring department (though it is also possible for applicants to arrange their own first six independently with the agreement of their department). In some cases, is might also be possible to arrange three sets of four months so that the first and last four months are served within the department, thus enabling pupils to spend part of their practising second six in chambers. If you're wondering why a set would want to take on a pupil in full knowledge that they would be leaving after six months, bear in mind that there's probably something in it for them too. After all, government work often makes up a substantial proportion of the work of some chambers. While a pupil in chambers, you should see the full range of your supervisor's work in line with the Bar Council Common Checklist, and be treated in exactly the same way as any other pupil. It's also worth noting that whilst in chambers, GLS pupils are not in competition with their peers, as they don't have to fight tooth and nail for tenancy. As one GLS pupil told us: *"It made my relationship with the other pupils and my experience in chambers much more relaxed knowing that I wasn't a part of the competition."*

In the second six, GLS pupils make the transition from the world of private practice to the world of an employed government lawyer. In line with *"the GLS mantra that you must never stay in your comfort zone for too long,"* this will often mean that you are exposed to a very different area of law to the one you saw in your first six. A predominantly civil first six might well be followed by a second six in a department whose work is heavily prosecution based.

The second-six experience will vary from one department to another. Some departments conduct a lot of their own litigation from beginning to end, giving pupils the opportunity to get on their feet in court. A typical week for a pupil in the Department of Trade and Industry might well include everything from making decisions to prosecute and drafting indictments to actually prosecuting regulatory offences under the Companies Act in a magistrates' court. The role of a barrister in other departments (the Home Office or the Department of Constitutional Affairs being good examples) is more likely to be entirely advisory. Here, you might be asked for your opinion on the compliance of a new piece of legislation with the Human Rights Act or the legality of a new immigration policy.

Wherever you go, you will be given a significant amount of responsibility. Take the experiences of a pupil in the Solicitors Office of HM Revenue & Customs. *"In my first week, I was given complete control over a VAT Tribunal appeal involving points of human rights law and EU law."* Though pupils say that they *"appreciate being trusted with important work,"* they also say that *"there is a very high level of support from training supervisors throughout pupillage, and work always gets checked before it is sent out."*

There are subtle differences in the way that GLS pupils work as lawyers within a government department. Unlike their colleagues in private practice, who will often only meet their clients at the door of the court, barristers in the GLS have much more direct contact with the 'client', who will ordinarily be a civil servant within their department. Like it or lump it, as a lawyer there will always be bureaucracy to deal with, and in the GLS, chambers bureaucracy gets replaced by civil service bureaucracy. There are no clerks to deal with,

meaning that your workload will be assigned by a 'line manager' instead. No briefs being dumped on your desk at 6 o'clock on a Friday night here though – the pupils tell us that *"the system for allocating work is much more regularised."* That means that it's usual to know what you'll be doing from one day to the next, and regular office hours are the norm. We also noticed a structured approach to pupils' training. At the start of training, pupils sit down with their supervisors and agree *"measurable objectives"* against which they will be assessed throughout the year. As well as informal day-by-day feedback, there are formal written appraisals at the middle and end of the pupillage.

If donning a wig and gown on a daily basis is part of your game plan, the GLS probably isn't for you. Though several government departments handle their own litigation, *"in longer, more complicated cases, it's seen as more cost effective to instruct counsel from the Treasury Panel."* In other words advocacy experience in the higher courts is going to be limited. No one we spoke to had gone into the job for the advocacy. As one pupil told us: *"I've really enjoyed the advocacy that I've done, but it's not part of my overall career plan."* Instead, both had been attracted to the job by the prospect of being able to get their hands on high-quality work that involved a regular exposure to public and EC law, which *"is incredibly difficult to get into in private practice."* But did they regret not having the same autonomy as their self-employed contemporaries in chambers? Apparently not, and in fact, it seems that at the early stages of their careers at least, GLS pupils are able to exercise a fair degree of choice as to the type of work they do. As a case in point, the pupil that we interviewed in Revenue & Customs had chosen to specialise in civil work at an early stage, whereas, by contrast, many of her colleagues at the same stage of their careers in chambers found themselves *"at the whim of their clerks."* A caveat though: for those who see themselves specialising in the long term, think again. GLS barristers are kept on their toes, and it's certainly the norm to move from one department to another after a couple of years. It remains possible for GLS pupils to cross the boundary from public to private later on in their careers, in the event of a change in heart, as the completion of pupillage leads to a full practising certificate from the Bar Council.

If you are looking for a practice that is largely advisory, the GLS is well worth serious consideration. While there's no guarantee of being taken on at the end of the year, and your supervisors will expect high standards, it's clear that the GLS recruits pupils with a view to retaining them. The pupils we spoke to clearly felt less uncertain about the future and less insecure than the majority of those we encountered in chambers. With a salary and a pension scheme to boot, it's little wonder.

# 2-3 Gray's Inn Square

**Chambers UK rankings:** Consumer law, health and safety, licensing, local government, planning

It was a typical summer's day when we strolled across the lawns of Gray's Inn Square towards numbers 2 and 3 – brilliant sunshine the one minute, torrential downpour the next. The freshness in the air gave clarity to the sights and sounds of the Inn. Upon leaving chambers we couldn't help but reflect on the aptness of this backdrop to a set where an awareness of heritage and tradition is retained, even as the breeze of modernity wafts through. Whilst it is happy to be celebrating its 150th birthday this year, nostalgic myopia has no place at this set; it is "*clear sighted about where it wants go to*" and aware that "*there is no set quite like us.*"

Criminal practice has been important "*since the year dot*" and remains so through the expertise of senior members like chambers head Anthony Scrivener. But his parallel stature in planning law reflects the other traditional pillars that support "*a very diverse set,*" which "*has an increasing sense of corporate identity*" and "*a definite business plan.*" The set is highly regarded for public and local government law, planning, consumer law, health and safety and civil litigation, serving over 300 local authorities, government departments and private companies. Licensing and environmental work are also strong suits.

Consolidating and strengthening expertise in these areas of practice has been at the heart of chambers expansion from 34 to 50 members in the last two years, but the set has its wits about it. Changes in licensing law have prompted the recruitment of two barristers and a solicitor in the last year "*to expand and diversify the practice.*" And not just any solicitor; no less than Jeremy Phillips, former head of licensing at Eversheds and Osborne Clarke. He might as well have written the book in the subject and, in fact, he has: "*He's the author of 'Phillips on Licensing.'*"

Chambers recruits pupils carefully. An initial meeting is followed by a longer second-stage interview at which applicants face an advocacy test and general grilling from a panel of up to eight people. The set looks for types with "*hunger and the ability to get on with people, a must given our diverse client base.*" As our sources were quick to admit, there's no easy handle on the work – "*We're no Doughty Street human rights set.*" So should you claim a life-long obsession with planning and local authorities? "*No, we'd frankly view that with suspicion. We like to see that people have taken the trouble to find out and understand what we do, in as much as you can.*" That's easier for some than others. There are former local authority employees and town planners at the set, but chambers takes on just as many recent graduates, and the advice to this type of applicant is that "*you should feel able to discuss the major issues in government and planning, but don't obsess about the particulars.*"

As for why the uninitiated might find chambers' work attractive, one source reflected that "*the variety appealed to me from the beginning, but across the board the public-personal element of work*" *is what engages and challenges.*" True, we observed a less ideological commitment to the law than one might expect at, say, Doughty Street. Nonetheless it was universally agreed that "*if you're full-on commercial, you wouldn't be happy here.*"

Juniors cover a lot of bases. "*There's a lot of written and court work at the junior end, whether it's county court, civil or criminal work, and plenty of briefs from seniors.*" Pupils find themselves "*doing minor local residents' issues, or even small inquiries in planning,*" "*RTAs, social security tribunals and repossessions,*" and "*a lot of applicant immigration work.*" If you're not sure what local authority instructions will entail: it's anything and everything "*from employment to elections, health and safety enforcement to finance, education to community care.*" Getting the picture? As one pupil enthused: "*One of the joys of the set is the challenge of suddenly being given work on an area of law you know nothing about.*"

Another "*major attraction*" is chambers' insistence that "*pupils are on their feet in court four to five days a week in the second six.*" It makes for "*a very difficult six months, balancing out your own work with your responsibilities to others as you're approaching the tenancy decision.*" Pupils reported working an increasing number of weekends in the second six, but insist that "*supervisors and the chambers director are protective of you getting overloaded.*" One supervisor concurred, saying: "*We try to provide a lot of support before and after court, to be proactive in discussing issues and to be aware that even the simplest matter can hold hidden terrors.*"

Pupils move between supervisors three times, "*partly for maximum exposure to members, partly for breadth of experience, partly to satisfy their preferences.*" Each sits with the same three supervisors so as to create a level playing field. This is typical of "*a very open chambers that gives you the chance to improve and doesn't leave you in the dark with your paranoias and insecurities for company!*" Seniors confirmed that mistakes "*are expected, not just tolerated,*" with emphasis placed on a

pupil's subsequent reaction. Halfway through their time together pupil and supervisor share informal feedback, and at the end of their cohabitation the supervisor writes a review, which the pupil is allowed to read and respond to. Together with "*reports from anyone else you've worked for*" and even "*letters of praise from solicitors,*" these reviews form the bedrock of the pupillage committee's recommendations for tenancy. "*Often 20-30 pages long*" and structured around "*strict criteria that ask, 'Is this candidate outstanding?'*" all our sources were confident there were "*no hidden surprises and you'd understand the final decision.*" The set is genuinely "*supportive if you don't get tenancy.*" One pupil was allowed to stay on until she found other work. Another was even luckier – "*Chambers recognised the ability of the candidate, but felt that the maturity wasn't quite there. The pupil agreed to stay on for a further six, and at the end of that period was accepted into chambers and is now very successful.*"

A senior told us: "*One of the great things is the culture of putting your pen down if someone needs help. A junior pupil or tenant can always have an informal discussion with a 20-to-30-year called.*" Wondering how easy that might feel at the junior end, we quizzed a pupil on the point. "*Well, my supervisor told me to take a licensing point to the resident expert, and obviously I felt like a nervous idiot, but it ended up in him explaining what it would have taken me three days to work out.*" Support can be found in all quarters of the chambers, and everyone is on "*first-name terms throughout.*" There is always an exception that proves the rule though. The one person who is not referred to by first name is Malcolm Spence QC. But it's not because he's an ogre or a staunch traditionalist, rather he's "*a wonderful grandfather figure who lives in the flat upstairs and comes down twice a day. You just couldn't call him Malcolm!*"

Tales of treats from Konditor & Cook ("*Fabulous cakes...the sort you'd make yourself if only you had the time, inclination and energy*" –

Nigella Lawson, *Vogue*) and "*5pm gatherings at the fax machine in reception*" give an insight into the almost cosy side of chambers life. One source even admitted: "*Coming back after court feels like coming home to a family. You can moan or boast about the day.*" In terms of its social scene, chambers "*doesn't pressure you to go out at all; in fact, it could do with being ramped up.*" Although relieved that "*it's not like a criminal set where you're judged on the strength of your bladder and liver,*" pupils and juniors do recognise the value of socialising together, "*so we're trying to organise more casual events more often to improve connections and communication.*"

We started out by saying that 2-3 Gray's Inn Square values both tradition and modernity, and we think it balances these two aspects of its character well. Despite huge growth in the ranks of members, there has been "*an increasing sense of loyalty to the set over recent years.*" Chambers has a clear idea of where it is going, and it's going there come rain or shine.

# 2 Hare Court

**Chambers UK rankings:** Crime, fraud: criminal

The site upon which 2 Hare Court is built has long been associated with crime and punishment. It was here that former Lord Chief Justice and Lord Chancellor Judge Jeffreys, otherwise known as the hanging judge of the bloody assizes, kept his chambers during the 17th century. In modern times, 2 Hare Court has also earned a reputation as a leading set for serious crime, though whilst an impressive 14 of the senior members have taken up judicial appointments, we have it on good authority that none has a penchant for hanging.

Having been invited to take a seat on the (almost too) comfortable brown leather sofa, we took the time to soak up the atmosphere in the busy reception area. It's a well-turned-out gaff, and whoever calls the shots here is careful to ensure that the generous vases of fresh cut flowers complement the tastefully decorated interior. There are some grand finishing touches, including a marvellous fireplace in the main conference room.

Chambers' style is reflected again in the design of its brochure, which closely resembles the cocktail menu of a smart hotel bar. We ordered Orlando Pownall QC followed by a sweet sherry, but unfortunately he wasn't on the menu that day, and so we busied ourselves with interviewing the pupils instead. Definitely a mixed bag of people, all of them had gone down the CPE route and boasted first degrees that included sociology and computer sciences. As for their universities, well, all of them were well known, but there certainly wasn't a hint of elitism. All three of the pupils we met were slightly older than the norm, which they felt gave them a distinct advantage as criminal practitioners – "*It's probably a good thing in this job to come across as being closer to 30 rather than 20. It makes dealing with clients that bit easier.*"

The road to tenancy at 2 Hare Court requires pupils to complete the standard 12 months of pupillage and, in common with many criminal sets, a further third six for those that show the potential to become future tenants. Each pupil sits with three different supervisors to expose them to as much of chambers' work as possible. As one of the supervisors told us: "*The first few months of pupillage are about giving pupils a cradle-to-grave guide to criminal practice. We teach them the skills necessary to master a brief, we teach them how to get all the important issues out of their client in conference, and we try to guide them through the court process from beginning to end.*" As you might expect in a busy criminal set, there will always be plenty of people looking for a spare pair of hands to help with important or time-consuming cases, and these are allocated to pupils on a rota basis to ensure that everyone gets a bite of the cherry. There is also an opportunity to shadow a judge (usually a former member of chambers) for a week.

The second six brings plenty of court work. One pupil recalled her second day in the magistrates' court: *"A senior member of chambers sat down with me beforehand and we went through the brief together, making a checklist of the most important issues."* The second six also means a good deal of travelling: though 95% of chambers' work is in London, it is not unheard of for pupils to be sent to places as exotic as Wantage and the Isle of Wight. On the plus side, the clerks *"don't generally accept the kind of briefs that are just there to abuse pupils,"* and chambers will pay pupils' travel expenses, so that the financial return for, say, a Norwich Crown Court mention (worth about £45) is not swamped by the train fare. The second six also includes a two-week secondment to the CPS, during which pupils can expect up to three trials per day.

Once the official 12-month pupillage is up, chambers asks people to complete a further six months before applying for tenancy. Pupils are automatically considered for a third six *"unless we don't think that they have a hope of getting a tenancy at the end of it."* The tenancy decision is made after a lengthy consideration of written work, performance in court (yes, that man sat in the public gallery dressed as Groucho Marx was a spy!) and feedback from instructing solicitors and judges.

The three pupils we met were just coming to the end of their second six when we spoke to them. Each reflected positively on their time at 2 Hare Court, and certainly there were no horror stories of endless days of menial chores. They had been given full access to the chambers intranet and their own electronic diaries in their second six months; *"we feel that we're respected as professionals, and as part of the team,"* they told us. Their early days in court had been helped along by *"approachable and practical"* clerks, who regularly offer feedback via instructing solicitors. All up, though it was a tough year, they agreed it had not been all hard work and no play. The social scene, particularly at the junior end, is active and on most nights of the week you'll find 2 Hare Court tenants haunting at least one of the local bars. Chambers operates an informal, but rigorously enforced, policy of never allowing a pupil to buy the drinks, and at Christmas it treats them to a slap-up meal and drinks in a swanky restaurant. Pupils also go to solicitors' parties in order to do some of that all-important networking. Remarkably, given all the canapés they must have eaten, they looked in pretty good shape.

What recruiters are looking for is *"an appropriate level of dedication and a real determination to succeed."* Importantly, your application will not be thrown in the bin if you came out of university with a 2:2, so long as you can show that you didn't waste your time in the pub. *"Sometimes academic high-flyers don't make great advocates. We're looking for people with a personality too."* The first interview allows the panel to check that the candidate who looks brilliant on paper is right in the flesh. The second is more rigorous with a legal problem or two thrown in for good measure. Tips? It would be a good idea to brush up on your first-year criminal law, and keep up to date with current affairs. Couple that with *"a bit of self-confidence and a bit of charm,"* and don't forget to take a look at that cocktail menu we mentioned!

# Hogarth Chambers

**Chambers UK rankings: Information technology, intellectual property**

As all you legal historians will be aware, celebrated 18th century painter and satirist William Hogarth caused considerable upheaval when he had the nerve to suggest that artists' work should be protected from other people passing it off as their own. He felt so strongly about this that he successfully petitioned Parliament to introduce a copyright bill. And so the foundations for successive generations of intellectual property lawyers were laid down...

When One Raymond Buildings and 5 New Square merged in 2001, Hogarth was deemed an apt figurehead for their alliance. A further merger with 19 Old Buildings in 2004 brought more IP practitioners on board. High-profile cases such as Arsenal v Reed (where a man selling Arsenal merchandise outside the stadium was prosecuted for breach of copyright) and Douglas v Hello! (where a man and a woman got upset at a magazine taking pictures of them eating cake) have cemented the set's strong reputation in IP and related fields. Nonetheless, there are still enough pure Chancery practitioners knocking around in Hogarth Chambers to ensure pupils are exposed to a variety of work. As one junior practitioner commented: *"We're still a commercial set at heart, it's just that our IP practice is becoming increasingly pre-eminent."*

The fact that the set takes only one pupil per year enables it to tailor the whole experience according to the pupil's needs and practice preferences. In theory, the pupillage is split into four three-month periods spent with different pupil supervisors; in practice this can vary depending on whether a pupil has particular strength in a given area such as copyright or data protection. It's certainly not uncommon for a pupil to be away from their supervisor for a number of weeks to assist another member on a case in an area in which they have expressed interest. The idea is that *"the pupil has the opportunity to excel."* Recent recruits were quick to salute the efficacy of the system, saying: *"It stops you feeling like a spare part when you're able to contribute in an area that you actually know something about."* New for 2006 is the possibility of a pure IP pupillage, which will encompass the full range of both 'hard' and 'soft' work. The reason for offering it is simple – chambers wants to ensure that those fully intent on specialising in IP from the outset are not put off by the thought of months spent on Chancery matters.

A pupillage at Hogarth won't give you much advocacy experience. The majority of a pupil's time is spent in chambers researching and then producing written work, ie opinions and pleadings. Although some of the subject matter can be a little dry, (corkscrew patents, anyone?) there is ample glamorous 'soft' IP work on offer. *"The sort of person who thrives here has the ability to analyse material in considerable depth and then explain it clearly and concisely."* With a varied client list that includes drugs companies, manufacturers and elements of the artistic community, it is vitally important to be able to maintain a real handle on the facts to ensure that your advice is accessible yet comprehensive.

So how do you become the intellectual property of Hogarth, for a year at least? Chambers expects a hand-written covering letter with typed CV. It's hard to tell whether this is an attempt to thwart the copy-and-paste approach to covering letters or if they just want to see how close you sat to the front in calligraphy class; either way it undoubtedly gives candidates the chance to *"make their case for interview clearly."* What the recruiters look for above all is *"strong academic credentials,"* and whilst the briefest glance at the CVs of junior tenants might indicate that the best place to establish these credentials is Oxbridge, it is worth noting that the two most recent pupils studied elsewhere. *"We're after people who aren't afraid to engage with a complex subject in real depth,"* noted one member, and the more a candidate can demonstrate this the better their chance of being invited to a first interview. An assessed mini-pupillage is *"a good foot in the door."* Do well and you've probably just doubled your chance of pupillage interview. The set also values good interpersonal skills as *"when you're dealing with a wide-ranging client base including blue-chip companies such as Nike and Microsoft you need people who are able to press the flesh and inspire clients with confidence."*

At interview the emphasis is on a candidate's ability to think quickly and *"fight their corner well."* With the interview panel attempting to pick holes in your argument, *"your back is against the* wall and it's very much a case of sink or swim." If you stay afloat through to the second round, expect more of the same, but also be on the look out for increasingly bizarre questions. One of our sources was asked to describe a spiral staircase without using the words 'spiral' or 'staircase'...

Whilst a few members of chambers reside in the annexe at 19 Old Buildings, everyone else is at 5 New Square. The fourth floor is home to many junior tenants and is the driving force behind chambers' social life. Friday evenings might see people amble down to the Seven Stars or go for drinks at someone's home. A not-to-be-missed event – especially if you see yourself as a bit of a Freddie Flintoff – is the annual cricket match against patent and trademark attorneys Marks & Clerk which "*always leads to quality banter.*" Indeed, getting known by solicitors, patent attorneys and trademark agents is essential in the early years; to this end junior practitioners are encouraged to get involved with seminars and write articles on new developments.

The daily ritual of chambers tea does not seem to be too much of an ordeal for pupils. Admittedly no one portayed it as the most fun you can have without laughing, but it is "*a good opportunity to get everyone on side.*" Attendance at tea is not compulsory but pupils tend to "*go with the flow of their pupil supervisor*" so removing the anxiety of the decision about whether to pop in for a cheeky digestive. One non-culinary reason for attending is the chance to look at the portrait of Sir Joseph Swan, accredited with the invention of the light bulb, on display in the room where tea is served. Before making any bright comments about the voluminous nature of Sir Joseph's beard, bear in mind that he is an ancestor of Christopher Morcom QC, the head of chambers, in whose room you are standing.

We're not sure if we quite agree with the person who described the set as having "*a magical vibe to it*" as the dominant characteristics of those we spoke to were more connected to intelligence, hard work and ambition than hocus-pocus and abracadabra. More Hogarth than Hogwarts then, and we think that's just the way they like it.

# 7 King's Bench Walk

**Chambers UK rankings:** Commercial litigation, insurance, international arbitration, professional negligence, shipping

Seven King's Bench Walk has the kind of history people write books about. In fact we're surprised the BBC hasn't produced a Sunday evening drama about the goings on in this part of the Temple. The set's own website is a fascinating read, and we're sure it won't mind us giving you a taster...

In 1666, the buildings on the walkway to the office of the Court of King's Bench were destroyed in the Great Fire of London, so the premises occupied by our subject set date back only to 1685. Since then it's been one legal inferno after another due to the prominence of successive residents. In 1819, Serjeant Wilde defended and saved Queen Caroline's honour and life in the face of an accusation of adultery; in the mid-19th century Lord Halsbury occupied rooms here with crack prosecutor Sir Harry Bodkin Poland, and together they defended a former Governor of Jamaica on a murder charge.

The last 40 years have less to do with sex scandals and death and everything to do with breeding masterful judges. Lords Denning, Brandon, Goff, Hobhouse and Mance were all members of the modern-day 7KBW, which formed in 1967 through an amalgam of two sets. With its origins in shipping, latterly the set has been less reliant on this area of practice. It had a major breakthrough into the insurance world with the mammoth Lloyd's litigation in the 90s, and since then has driven up its reputation in the field, with members taking core roles in both the Barings cases and the recent swathe of film finance litigation. Other cases include the insurance liabilities for breast implants and asbestos-related illnesses. Shipping cases now amount to just a quarter of the set's work; insurance accounts for another 60% or so and the remainder is made up of general commercial cases. Some barristers do more shipping and others more insurance and reinsurance work, but whatever their orientation, their caps are set at "*top-end work not knock-about work.*" Such instructions beg "*excellence in performance,*" and 7KBW's instructing solicitors (Cyde & Co, Ince & Co, BLG, Richards Butler and other top firms) expect – and are prepared to pay for – nothing less.

"*Honesty and excellence,*" is how one source described this small set's core principles; another told us: "*We're regarded as academic and technically rigorous on the law...we're trusted to put the case straight.*" Concepts of integrity and not pushing the boundaries of the law fit with a style that is "*not particularly flamboyant; rather conservative.*"

Pupils sit with five supervisors over the course of the year. The first will supervise the pupil for three months, the second for two and the other three will take six-week turns. "*Some are more talkative, some quieter. Some give you more academic research, some more practical procedural things.*" If you're writing an opinion on the merits of a case, it may take a few days to read through several A4 files before you can start, or you may be asked to make some notes on a point of law which takes just a few hours. Either way, you will spend most of your time doing paperwork. The learning curve is described as "*almost vertical*" and the work "*complicated,*" with issues and facts "*expressed in obscure terminology.*"

Quite separately, month by month, five QCs acting as 'pupillage assessors' and the joint heads of chambers give each pupil a set piece of work. Additionally, from Christmas onwards any member who has suitable work is encouraged to request pupils' assistance. Before the end of the first six, pupils are given an indication of whether they have a real shot at building a career at 7KBW. It seems hard to predict – in 2003 none of the

pupils were ultimately taken on; in both 2004 and 2005 one made the grade.

The second six of most pupillages is a time for getting on your feet in court and earning; here, pupillage is a full 12 months of learning. One of the youngest juniors extolled the virtues of this approach, saying: "*It's important to be somewhere where you become good at what you do.*" The instructions he'd received had all been directly relevant to his future practice, so there had been no winding up applications or treks to Wolverhampton for mortgage repossessions. The clerks hadn't fed him scraps just to give him court time; they'd secured low-end work (often direct instructions from P&I Clubs) that was "*pertinent to the reality of practice.*" He was currently handling his own carriage of goods case in Norwich, while also assisting more senior members of chambers as a second junior.

The work requires barristers to apply black letter law to contractual situations and to be "*very practical and think about what the parties to the contract wanted. Law is very academic, but as barristers we are required to be practical and pragmatic.*" And if you ever begin to lose sight of the practical side of things, sometimes the paperwork you'll receive on a shipping case will include pictures of the vessels in question.

Describing the people she worked with, the pupil told us: "*They are very, very clever,*" yet "*not arrogant or pretentious. Even if you're working for a silk, they'll take you seriously (although I imagine the temptation is not to). As pupils we can't expect to be on a level as we don't have the experience, but they lay a lot of emphasis on the fact that you'll improve.*" Simply put: 7KBW looks for pupils who can meet its exacting standards of intellectual ability and technical accuracy. It's fitting, then, that the problem question students must tackle at a pupillage interview (eg preparing a skeleton argument for an appeal to the House of Lords on a reported Court of Appeal case) is sent to them a week beforehand, allowing ample time to consider and draft a high-quality response. It's not about showmanship or proving you can wing it on short notice; "*you've got to get to the right answer. All the oral advocacy in the world is not going to help you if you've got the answer wrong.*"

At 7KBW there's no formal constitution, no chief exec and the management committee has a light touch. It's not overrun with subcommittees and full meetings of members are rare; if there is a meeting, it will most likely be for the July tenancy decision. One member told us there was surprisingly little in the way of politics: "*We're too busy getting on with our own practices.*" Another added: "*There's an expectation you'll give it your all.*"

While actively discouraged from attending chambers tea (it can make them feel "*awfully uncomfortable*") pupils are welcome at a monthly buffet lunch. Clerks are after-hours allies and drinking companions in The Witness Box, although this might not feel the case the morning after the traditional clerks-and-pupils night out "*on the lash.*"

Conventional in so many ways from its location in the Temple, to its traditional-to-a-tee decor and its long history of sending QCs to the Bench, 7KBW is your classic barristers' chambers. We rather like conducting our interviews in barristers' rooms, amongst the piles of papers and the invitations to garden parties. It made our visit less clinical than they can sometimes seem in the sterile surrounds of sleek meeting rooms, where our interview notes are written with chambers' own-brand pens on their own-brand paper. We're not so sure 7KBW has commissioned items so peripheral to legal practice. This is the commercial Bar straight up, no cocktail umbrellas (or parties for that matter) and no marketing spiel. What you see is what you get and 7KBW isn't planning to change any time soon.

# 11 King's Bench Walk

**Chambers UK rankings:** Admin & public law, competition/European law, education, employment, human rights, local government

1981 was an important year. In the USA it heralded the appointment of the first female justice in the Supreme Court. In the UK 11 KBW was launched. Among its founder members were a future Lord Chancellor (Derry Irvine) and a future prime minister (Tony Blair).

Whilst not exactly operating on a law for law's sake manifesto, there is little doubt that this is the place for those who want to fully engage with the theoretical side of the law. "*Debate is strongly encouraged; the sort of work we're involved in means that there is no such thing as a spurious point.*" Further evidence of the academic esteem that the set generates becomes clear when you tot up the number of legal textbook authors housed within chambers; almost half the set contribute to Tolley's Employment Handbook, a practitioner's bible often cited in tribunals. But it's not all intellectualising and there is a practical significance to the work undertaken. Members have recently been involved in the challenges to the new Hunting legislation and have been contributing to the ongoing debate on how to treat suspected terrorists.

Chambers has all the usual trappings and trimmings: mahogany desks, bookcases crammed with law reports and case papers strewn over busy practitioners' rooms. The set's communal space has a number of colourful Philip Sutton works (Derry's a fan of this Slade School artist apparently) adorning the pale cream walls. Lack of space dictates that some members operate from the ultra-modern Temple Chambers on nearby Tudor Street whilst the basement of No.10 KBW houses an extensive law library and No.9 provides a few more rooms for members. We were assured that plans are afoot to try and enable all members to gather and work under one roof.

In general, 11 KBW has grown from within, with the exception of a few years ago when barristers from 4-5 Gray's Inn Square (Cherie Booth's old set) joined around the same time as Matrix formed. In spite of all its connections the temptation to paint the set as a bastion of New Labour should be resisted. 11 KBW is a political animal only in that it handles government instructions; one senses that this is because of the advanced and interesting legal appeal of the work and not because the set has any particular political affiliations.

For a pupil the first three months are a low-key experience; it's not until the second and third quarters that they start doing work for members of chambers other than their supervisor. This is also when the "*scrupulously fair tenancy system*" kicks in and each piece of work is double-marked and filed away until July when the decision is made. The required standard is that of a new tenant. Hit that consistently and the pupil will be welcomed with open arms. To give pupils an indication of the way things are going, after six months there is a formal review with the head of the tenancy committee. If things have not gone as well as hoped this may be the point where it is gently suggested that the pupil should move on somewhere else for a second six.

Typical workload involves drafting opinions, skeleton arguments or cross-examinations and research notes for conferences. Pupils complete a minimum of six of these every three months, treating every piece like an exam problem question where they have to explore all the areas, no matter how tenuous they seem, in order to get the top marks. "*The stuff we work on ends up getting argued in the House of Lords or the Court of Appeal so there will always be very clever people on the opposite side going through everything with a fine toothcomb in order to find a weakness.*" Nothing less than perfect will do by the sounds of things.

Not that there's any danger of a pupil here lacking a ferocious work ethic, but just in case they do, three months are spent with 'Treasury Devil' Philip Sales, who "*works so hard it's like sitting next to a Tasmanian Devil; he's just a blur of activity from nine 'til seven.*" Sales' position as the Treasury Solicitor means that he has an incredibly varied caseload and, as such, his pupil is exposed to some impressive matters. Lately he was acting in the case concerning the death of Iraqi civilians held in custody by British forces in Iraq, and the case of British American Tobacco UK Ltd and others v Secretary of State for Health concerning the validity of legislation banning tobacco advertising.

Having endured 12 months of predominantly paper-based activity, the focus shifts dramatically for new tenants who are instantly on their feet in employment and education tribunals. To prepare prospective tenants in the last three months of pupillage they ride shotgun with new tenants. Nonetheless, it's clear that the jump from theory to practice is quite a shock to the system. The first year of tenancy is rent-free so as to allow you to fill the coffers after years of relative hardship.

As well as exceptionally strong academic credentials applicants must have an ability to express ideas cogently because "*it's no good someone having prodigious intelligence if they can't communicate it to the client.*" The way to jump ahead of the pack is to bag yourself an assessed mini-pupillage. One pupil felt it gave him the edge: "*Having already done work for them meant that I knew what to expect and what they were looking for.*" The academic nature of the set is apparent in the sort of questions you're sent a week prior to the single-round interview. Typically, there will be a couple of cases to read through and comment on. The interview panel isn't just concerned with what you say, it's also the way that you analyse things that is important. "*It's not enough to come out with brilliant-sounding assertions. Showing how you get to them is key.*"

Make no mistake, this is a seriously demanding pupillage and its paper-based nature means that it can be quite solitary at times. Most days a group of people go for lunch at Inner Temple, but don't expect to be part of a conga line wending its way to the Witness Box or Pegasus Bar every night. The chances are you'll be working late in the library and in early the next day. The flip side of this is that you are at a set that is at the vanguard of public law and you'll never be short of intellectual stimulation.

## Maitland Chambers

**Chambers UK rankings:** Agriculture and rural affairs, Chancery: commercial, Chancery: traditional, charities, commercial litigation, company, insolvency/corporate recovery, partnership, professional negligence, real estate litigation

Created in 2001 out of the merger of 13 Old Square and 7 Stone Buildings, in 2004 Maitland also incorporated 9 Old Square and now has 64 barristers – the "*perfect number*" for a commercial Chancery set apparently. Among the 14 QCs are many leading names including Catherine Newman, Charles Aldous, Michael Lyndon-Stanford and Christopher McCall. It excels in both traditional and commercial Chancery, and the 9 Old Square arrivals brought with them an extremely strong property practice. Maitland is the doyen of the contentious Chancery world: members were involved in the House of Lords case of National Westminster Bank Plc v Spectrum Plus Ltd & Ors, which rewrote many of the rules on insolvency and naturally enough they are also involved in the huge Equitable Life dispute that is lumbering through the courts. Other matters of interest and intrigue have included advice to the Beckhams in the privacy dispute with their former nanny, and the Barings and BCCI cases. When not in court, members are busy contributing to or editing legal texts, among them *Snell on Equity*, Hill & Redman's *Law of Landlord & Tenant* and *Halsbury's Laws*.

The first three months of pupillage are a time for "*bedding in*" and, as such, supervisors are more lenient with mistakes. After Christmas "*the hon-*

*eymoon is over*" and the pupillage transforms into a "*highly intense environment*" where "*you are aware that every error is harmful to your tenancy prospects.*" If you think this sounds overly harsh, remember, clients pay top whack for the best advice possible and in this undoubtedly tough world, a "*huge amount of industry and diligence*" is required at all stages of one's career. Chancery practice attracts "*intellectually disciplined*" individuals with accurate judgment; those who are adept at legal reasoning and readily come up with coherent justifications for their conclusions. As one junior put it: "*You can't wing it in the Chancery courts.*" It is because the necessary skill and knowledge doesn't come about overnight that "*you need to be prepared to put in the hours in order to get to the required standard.*"

In an effort to put pupils on a level playing field, they all sit with the same group of pupil supervisors. This additionally ensures exposure to several of the areas of specialisation on offer within chambers, including company, insolvency and professional negligence. Supervisors are keen to fully utilise their pupils' talents, reasoning that "*an able pupil is a real asset to your practice.*" The payback is that there's no skimping on feedback; "*when they go through your work they really go to town, the red pen is well and truly out in force!*" During the year, there are five advocacy exercises judged by eminent members. Besides being quite nerve-wracking, "*they improve your case management skills*" and they stand as a substitute for actually getting on your feet in court during the second six.

Due to the merger with 9 Old Square, Maitland had five pupils when we visited, which may have exacerbated the somewhat competitive atmosphere we encountered. Nevertheless, any set which lets its pupils know how far up the pecking order they sit after six months is hardly discouraging competition. We weren't entirely surprised to hear stories of pupils working at weekends in order to create a good impression. The crunch comes at the tenancy decision in June when all members meet. When we visited, four out of the five pupils had made it past the six-month stage and two had just been taken on as tenants.

Chambers tea at Maitland is one of those occasions when it's best to be seen but not heard. One pupil didn't feel deprived of the opportunity to take centre stage, telling us: "*To be honest, it's a relief to be able to veg out and not worry about trying to say anything too intelligent!*" If pushed we'd have to say one gets the impression that at Maitland you're best advised to mind your ps and qs during pupillage and "*there is the feeling that senior members of chambers are keeping an eye on things.*" That said, Thursday nights in a local pub are an opportunity to unwind with juniors. The venue is dependant on the whims of one of the set's most important committees – Pubco – which convenes to make a decision on a Thursday afternoon. Usually they plump for somewhere like the White Horse or Tooks Court.

When a set becomes as large as Maitland, especially if it has grown through mergers, attempts to promote cohesion are important. Chambers sprawls across four separate premises in Stone Buildings and Old Square, with its main hub at 7 Stone Buildings. The calmness of the traditional waiting room belies the intensity of labour and firepower within chambers. Make no mistake, this is a seriously talented, extremely polished and remarkably well-managed collection of lawyers. It's a style and standard that is sought out by the pupillage committee each year. To impress them on paper you must show "*a first-class academic record*" (look at the CVs of members on the website). Make the paper cut and there are effectively three rounds of interviews. The first is a "*challenging chat*" during which it will become clear to the panel whether you've got "*the 'it' factor.*" This will be ascertained via a question on something fairly topical, such as that asked in 2004 – whether the English cricket team were right to visit Zimbabwe. Make it through to the second interview and

there's another problem question, this time with 30 minutes of preparation beforehand. The question will involve some sort of contractual or lease interpretation, and this is your chance to show an ability to spot problems and come up with practical solutions; in other words, to display the shoots of the "*commercial pragmatism*" that is so sought after in the top sets. Perform well and you're onto the final challenge – an assessed mini-pupillage lasting two days. Make it through all three stages and we reckon you deserve that pupillage!

As befits a set that is named after a legal historian, Maitland wants to make legal history itself by not only securing a king of the hill position on mainstream Chancery work, but also going toe-to-toe with a number of niche and commercial practices. The ambition and drive of members and managers makes this an exciting place to be right now.

## Matrix

**Chambers UK rankings:** Admin & public law, competition/European law, crime, defamation/privacy, education, employment, environment, fraud: criminal, human rights, immigration, international arbitration, police law, public international law

Hatched in the innocence and optimism of the new millennium, it is no exaggeration to say that Matrix has tried to revolutionise the ways of the Bar. The idea is to "*change attitudes by changing terminology*" so the old terms 'pupil', 'tenant' and 'clerk' have been consigned to the waste paper bin and replaced by 'trainee', 'member' and 'practice manager.' Although not alone in professing to live by core values, Matrix prides itself on ensuring that these beliefs are actually upheld in day-to-day practice. Those core values in full then: independence; client care and quality of service; teamwork and co-operation; practice diversity; public service ethos; innovation; a democratic structure; efficiency in administration and management; promotion of equality of opportunity; and closer links between practising and academic lawyers. Every angle is covered by the looks of things. Active links with the community also mean that more and more people are being exposed to the progressive end of the Bar, and just in case there were any doubt as to Matrix's intentions, it has deliberately taken on premises that look more like an ad agency than barristers chambers.

So, aside from the vocabulary and mission statements, what's different about Matrix? Let's start with the absence of any noticeable hierarchy. There is no head of chambers (instead a perpetually changing management committee) and the names of the 52 members are displayed alphabetically on the board outside, meaning that the most respected silks like Clare Montgomery, Philippe Sands and Rabinder Singh are afforded no more acclaim than their lesser known junior counterparts. The thing that really catches the eye, however, is the range and calibre of the work undertaken. Matrix has been highly successful in balancing considerable amounts of 'worthy' work with a thriving civil caseload. "Not everyone is hankering after the sexy cases," we heard. "As a set we're aware of the need to maintain a broad practice." Rankings in ten practice areas in Chambers UK add weight to this contention, but you can only really appreciate the magnitude of chambers' achievement when you look at some of the big cases on which members have worked. If you like your cases 'sexy' then look at Ben Emmerson QC as one of the key protagonists in the House of Lords Belmarsh detainee case and Antony White acting for Naomi Campbell in her successful appeal against Mirror Group Newspapers for damages for breach of confidence. Rabinder Singh led the call for a judicial enquiry into the legality of the war in Iraq. On a more commercial note, members acted for the National Association of Health Food Stores in challenging a European Directive on food supplements in the ECJ, whilst Cherie Booth QC acted for the trade union Amicus in its challenge to the government's implementation of European Directives on discrimination on the grounds of sexual orientation. Many Matrix practitioners are active on the academic side of the law, highlighting the fact that the set has an academic approach rather than simply a moral approach to human rights.

We say forget the terminology entirely and accept that a Matrix traineeship works much like pupillage elsewhere. There are three three-month stints with practitioners in different fields, and then the decision as to whether you get taken on as a member in June. One seat will inevitably be spent with someone with public law/human rights leanings "as that, deep down, is at the core of the set's work," though trainees are allowed input as to the nature of their other seats. Naturally, if you're with a criminal practitioner, much of your time will be spent in court, preparing cross-examinations and observing first hand the extent of your supervisor's advocacy powers. Time spent with a civil practitioner will involve considerably more paperwork – pleadings, opinions, skeleton arguments or judicial review applications. The trainee we spoke to recounted how she had observed and been copied into everything: "I heard every telephone call and saw every piece of written work that my trainee supervisor produced. It's the only way to learn the right habits."

Regardless of the practice area you work in, certain attributes will stand you in good stead when the membership decision is made. "There's no soft landing here. You need to be intellectually astute from the word go." Equally, the ability to produce written work of a "consistently high standard" will always stand you in good stead. In addition to work for other members, a trainee's capabilities are assessed by written and oral exercises throughout the year. One area of traineeship that Matrix is conscious it needs to increase is the amount of advocacy available to trainees in the second half of the year. At the moment it can feel like "*a big leap into the unknown*" when a trainee becomes a full member. The sort of matters undertaken by trainees during this period vary according to which practice area they've steered themselves towards; eg those interested in employment undertake any low-level tribunal claims that come into chambers.

Although it was admitted that the raft of well-known members can be "*quite intimidating*" before the traineeship begins, one young barrister we spoke to recalled how "*any feeling I had of walking on eggshells disappeared very quickly.*" As one would expect from such a self-consciously forward-thinking organisation, everyone is on first-name terms and there is "*certainly no deference to seniority.*" A trainee is encouraged to work a 9am to 6pm day, although must accept that weekends may be impinged upon "*whenever you need to finish off a piece of important work.*" On the social side, "*things have picked up in the past 12 months and we're definitely coming together as a set,*" hence (or perhaps because of) the introduction of Thursday lunches and fortnightly chambers drinks. The Christmas party is apparently a good one, if only because "*watching the silks strutting their stuff on the dance floor is always entertaining!*" And speaking of showy moves, a group of members popped to the local cinema to see the screening of 'The Matrix 3: Revolutions' when it came out. It was unavoidable, we suppose.

The application process for traineeships is typically transparent. Points are awarded to applicants for academic ability, advocacy experience, voluntary work and demonstration of 'Matrix values.' Reach the required number of points and you'll be invited to a first-round interview. This lasts for 15 minutes with discussion tending to focus on a recent topical case, though you do also have the opportunity to make a good impression by "*steering things in the direction of your interests.*" The second-round interview is longer and confronts you with a tricky legal question designed to "*stretch your problem-solving*

*capabilities to the hilt.*" Remember, the recruiters are looking for the sort of candidate who is able to take a knock in their stride and won't despair if things don't appear to be going well. With almost 500 applications per year for traineeship, it's clear that the set is not attracting any one particular breed of applicant. The single characteristic that is bound to unite all successful candidates will be an "*absolute drive and commitment to becoming an accomplished barrister.*"

The Matrix brand has undoubtedly become an important and successful one in a short space of time but we'd venture to suggest that it means different things to different people. Some prefer the way that "*independence and autonomy are respected within the set,*" whilst others cite the lack of tradition as "*enormously liberating.*" One junior member did confess that he had started to refer to chambers as 'the office'. We're not convinced it will catch on. Matrix will always be at the forefront of developments in the law but we imagine that as it gets older it may become a little less self-aware and the work alone will be able to speak for the set.

# Monckton Chambers

**Chambers UK rankings:** Competition and European law, tax

Monckton Chambers traces its roots back to the 1930s, when it was headed by two-time cabinet minister and valued adviser to Edward VIII, Sir Walter Monckton. After a career as a barrister and all-round good guy (penning the King's abdication speech among other things), Sir W became chairman of Midland Bank and eventually earned the title of Viscount. In Gray's Inn since the sixties, the set only adopted the Monckton moniker in 1998. But more of that later.

The most important thing to understand about Monckton is its practice profile: this is a go-to set for European law issues, competition and

VAT. *Chambers UK* speaks of the intellectual fire-power of members, and only one other set – at best, two – competes at this level. The next most important thing to know is that a lot of work comes from government departments, an aspect of chambers' business that dates from the mid-80s and a QC called Christopher Bellamy who forged good relations with the Treasury Solicitor. All Monckton's juniors now aim to get on one or more of the government's lists of approved counsel. A knock-on effect, according to one member, is that "*it's important for us to remain apolitical.*"

Government departments have a different agenda from private sector clients, who are primarily "*concerned with winning and costs.*" By contrast, "*the government is more sensitive to doing the right thing*" and "*establishing precedents.*" Ultimately, "*if they lose, they can change the law,*" but wherever necessary they want the law on a particular point to be well defined and, of course, decided in their favour. No barrister would admit that winning isn't important to them, but at Monckton we also concluded that establishing legal precedent is as important...to some at least.

"*We have a reputation for being thorough, detailed and conscientious,*" a pupilmaster told us, adding: "*What we look for in pupils is attention to detail.*" They need it in spades because the work is frequently "*intricate.*" He reminded us (not that we needed him to) that there were "*no end of pedants at the Bar,*" yet if you're in the business of making or establishing law and your client wants "*certainty,*" perhaps a dose of pendantry is healthy. No one actually blushed when they said the word, but almost all our sources at Monckton referred to the set as having a "*cerebral*" quality. "*It's an intellectually challenging place,*" one of the two pupils conceded. The other nodded in agreement. We rather liked the fact that they could sit together without eyes like daggers – competitive sensitivities were absent between them...even though the July tenancy decision was just weeks away. Each felt confident that chambers hadn't recruited two pupils with the deliberate intention of offering just one tenancy. And they were right to be confident as both now have tenancy.

Monckton's pupillage isn't advocacy-heavy, yet we mustn't give the impression you'll never go to court. One of the pupils told us about a number of one-day judicial review hearings he'd been taken along to and was soon to sit in on a 15-day trial. Nonetheless, advisory work and legal research define the year, with a typical instruction being to advise on how the competition authorities would view a merger of two companies. Over the year, you'll sit with four different PMs and work for many other members of chambers. Reflecting on her pupillage, the newest tenant said: "*I wasn't just a research assistant; I was drafting opinions and pleadings...even though they were crawled over by my pupilmaster or whoever I worked for.*" In the second six, you can push for some of your own cases, maybe acting for the VAT Man on an appeal from someone who's been caught with bootleg alcohol.

The real drama is to be found in the set's big competition cases. The replica football kit case is a great example. Its complexity is demonstrated by the multitude of parties in the action brought by the OFT against Manchester Utd, the FA and several retailers, which it claimed had entered into a price-fixing arrangement. In all, some seven members of chambers acted for four different parties, so underscoring the set's standing in competition law while at the same time highlighting the need to maintain Chinese walls between members. With fines of £18.6 million at stake, it was no surprise that the OFT's decision was referred to the Competition Appeals Tribunal (CAT), so setting in motion its first ever witness trial. Both of the 2003/4 pupils sat with one of the key barristers on the case. The first met witnesses, read their statements and attended strategic meetings with the OFT. After three months, he went to sit with a different PM and the other pupil took his place. The temperature of the case rose as it progressed towards trial, and our second pupil found himself tackling parts of the first draft of the cross-examination script and then attending the trial itself. Not wanting to miss out, the first pupil also attended parts of the trial.

We uncovered no painful or archaic traditions to make their lives a misery, and established that they don't suffer the embarrassment of being called Mr or Miss by the clerks, who reserve such formality for the most senior members. We were assured that Monckton was a *"democratic set; at chambers meetings, juniors' voices are listened to. There's not a couple of autocrats at the top saying like it or lump it."* Many of the juniors choose to dress casually when not seeing clients or going to court; one chap was in cropped combats and sandals when we met him. After work on Thursdays or Fridays, people slip into the local pub and there's even a social programme of sorts, although it can probably be best described as ad hoc.

If you make it to a pupillage interview, the panel won't be so interested in digging around in your CV; instead it will engage in some *"rigorous questioning"* on a problem question. It looks for *"academically confident people who can express themselves in a coherent manner...we want to see if the points made are sensible and that someone can hold their own."* Interestingly, we heard: *"We're not keen on overly pushy pupils."* Academic excellence (commonly a First, though not necessarily an Oxbridge degree) is paramount, yet in only a minority of cases do pupils fly through academia on autopilot and straight into practice. One of the current crop had spent a year at the Law Commission; the other had worked at the Lord Chancellor's Department. A previous year's pupil qualified at Freshfields as a competition solicitor and worked as a référendaire at the ECJ. Two new tenants joined the set in the summer of 2004 – one had been the legal secretary to the president of the Competition Appeals Tribunal and the other a référendaire at the ECJ. This sort of thing impresses the clients.

Monckton has been very strategic: back in the late 90s it took on its first practice manager and has since developed roles for PR and business development managers. It also coined the distinctive Monckton name. Since embracing professional managers, members' earnings have headed skywards.

In the autumn of 2004 chambers settled into stylish, additional premises at Nos. 1 and 2 Raymond Buildings, which just like the base at No 4 have sash windows that bring the gardens of Gray's Inn right into chambers. On the day we visited Monckton, the temperature soared to 32°C. Sunbathers packed the lawns, doubtless many of them observing that day's astronomical phenomenon – a transit of Venus. Who knows, in 2012 when Venus next transits the sun, you might be climbing through the sash window of your own room and onto the lawns. If so, don't forget your special glasses.

# Four New Square

**Chambers UK rankings:** Construction, financial services, product liability, professional negligence, prof. neg.: construction

In 1999, professional negligence supremo Four New Square upped sticks from the Temple and moved to the heart of Chancery territory – Lincoln's Inn. Its intention was simply to move into better, roomier accommodation, but it ended up developing a hitherto unexplored area of practice. Though the set originally drifted into Chancery work, it has given legs to the drift by recruiting a few Chancery practitioners. *"Our location has definitely influenced our work profile,"* we were told. However, professional indemnity cases of all types (though predominantly solicitor-related) still account for 60% of business.

Professional indemnity instructions come from litigation stalwarts such as Barlow Lyde &

Gilbert, Kennedys and Reynolds Porter Chamberlain, leading provincial and national firms and the in-house legal teams of large insurers such as Zurich and St Paul. Beyond this, chambers holds its own in construction, general insurance and reinsurance, general commercial litigation and product liability. In the latter area, members have been involved in litigation concerning vCJD, tobacco, BSE, MMR and numerous pharmaceutical products. Additionally, a few barristers pursue more specialist practices, including financial services and clinical negligence.

Each pupil has three supervisors: the first until Christmas, the second until Easter and the third with a looser grasp on their time in the second six. "*People expect anyone who does pupillage here to have done professional indemnity,*" though because all supervisors do a range of other work, pupils' experiences are reasonably broad. We also learned that "*pupillage will be studded with unique experiences*" whenever the opportunity arises. We had to chuckle when someone said: "*Pupillage can be a bit like running for office for a year,*" but at least at Four New Square you don't have to shake the hands and kiss the babies of every member of chambers. Or try and work for them all. As one supervisor said: "*It's not helpful for silks to come along and poach pupils.*"

Pupils tend to stick close to their supervisors, sharing their rooms and shadowing their practices. Said one supervisor: "*The pupil will do a piece of written work, e-mail it to me and then we'll go through it together.*" It's a time for absorbing necessary skills and techniques, for learning the law and developing a good manner with solicitors and other members of chambers. "*Getting the law right is the base starting point; commercial nous grows over time.*" The year is spent drafting skeleton arguments and pleadings, and preparing notes on obscure points of law; basically feeling "*pretty involved*" and even "*jointly responsible for what is going on.*"

After three months you'll receive an informal appraisal and after six a full-on review with the chair of the pupillage committee, who'll have collected written reports from your supervisors. Also marked on the calendar are a week's marshalling in the High Court and three moots, the last of which takes place in the High Court in front of former member of chambers Mr Justice Jackson. With anything up to three-quarters of chambers coming along to watch you perform, it's acknowledged to be "*a pretty bizarre form of torture.*" We wondered if the moots added to a sense of competition between pupils, but one of them assured us that while these tests were "*emotional,*" "*there have been no bad tempered or difficult periods between us.*"

Pupils are allowed to earn in the second six, as part of the guaranteed earnings scheme. They usually get to court once or twice a week on something pretty simple, such as an application to set aside a judgment in default, a debt claim or a small RTA hearing. The progression into the first year of tenancy appears seamless. "*Clerks will deliberately seek out small work for pupils and juniors,*" including employment cases, which are excellent for cross-examination experience. In the early days as a junior you'll encounter contract claims, building disputes ("*dodgy double glazing, for example*"), PI and mortgage possessions amongst other things. Your own prof neg cases will be "*phased in*" – at first just arguments about quantum rather than liability, and drafting pleadings. In this field, cases rarely get as far as trial.

There's no need to worry about striking out on your own straight away, because for the first three years you'll have your own mentor. They will be someone you've chosen yourself, not the loser in a game of buggins' turn. Juniors also undertake placements with solicitors to see how mammoth litigation matters are managed and experience "*life inside a solicitors firm.*"

At the interface between solicitor and barrister is the clerk, and an examination of a set's clerking style and function informs on so much. Four New Square operates a team clerking system, with each clerk having their own PA. You only have to meet the senior clerk for a few minutes to realise that claims of "*sympathetic clerking*" don't ring hollow. "*It's all about understanding what a barrister wants from his or her life,*" she told us, "*and being honest about someone's suitability and availability.*" If all this makes life in chambers sound easy, take note: after speaking to several people, we were left in no doubt that they work extraordinarily hard.

As well as being hardworking, chambers is run with determined efficiency. "*The head of chambers is quite strong and decisive,*" we heard. And unusually for a barrister, "*he's a fantastic businessman.*" We're not suggesting he's managing chambers – there are staff for that – but having a clued-up head gives the right lead. The set as a whole is "*conscious of the importance of marketing and having a brand.*" Accordingly, it is not averse to a spot of judicious socialising with solicitors and insurers, nor organising lectures and seminars for them. As a pupil put it: "*You get a sense of a growing chambers in terms of reputation and standards.*"

Set against a backdrop of good relations all round, where "*there's no big divide*" between members and staff, twice each year there are big parties. At Christmas it's a champagne reception, and in the summer a family day with a magician, bouncy castle and face painting (presumably for the kids, though we can't be certain). A couple of members are really into horse racing and have invested in a runner called Wasted Costs, which sports Sunderland FC colours. Several other members have also been dragooned into the venture; "*some have just a 2% stake...probably just a nostril!*" On the subject of horses we prised a bit more information from a pupil, who told us one of her PM's was an amateur jockey. Unfortunately, as a tall man, he has to keep his weight to a minimum: "*I always felt very guilty eating my lunch in front of him.*" She had no lunchtime dilemmas with a different PM though; he bought her a sandwich every day. Except on the days he and other PMs took all three pupils out to lunch.

If Four New Square interests you, you must apply for a week-long assessed mini pupillage. Do well and you'll be invited to a formal pupillage interview at a later date, which amounts to a short advocacy exercise ("*no more than five minutes*") and a discussion about what you did in your mini. The chair of the pupillage committee told us: "*I want to see if they can express themselves confidently and clearly,*" though he warns: "*there's no point in acting like an old-fashioned barrister.*" To understand the full significance of this statement you probably need to understand that here a great deal of weight is placed on commercial and strategic advice – "*getting the law right is just stage one, then it's a case of developing a focus on what to do next and why.*" In this set, the emphasis is "*half court work and half strategic advice.*" It sounds as if most pupils grasp this principle, as usually two out of three get tenancy each year, and "*there's no shilly-shallying around about the decision, it's all very fair.*"

You can form a fair impression of Four New Square within moments of walking into its light and spacious reception. Imagine Heals does Georgian in a subtle, contemporary, mushroomy kind of way, then add an infectiously chirpy receptionist who's juggling three phones while charming a steady stream of clients. It looks effortless, though we doubt it is.

## Old Square Chambers

**Chambers UK rankings:** Employment, environment, health & safety, personal safety

When we pitched up at Old Square Chambers and saw our contact decked out in jeans and sweater, it became immediately clear that hidebound conservatism is inimical to this set. Its members were unanimous that "*we are very far from a traditional set of chambers,*" stressing "*we're informal, unpretentious, very focused, very driven.*" Chambers never allows the dust to settle: not long in its current, utterly business-like digs, it is hoping to move again to larger premises in 2006 to allow for further expansion. The set also has 11 tenants in a second base in Bristol, located in "*breezy premises, very close to solicitors.*" All in all, this is a mobile set, ready and willing to adapt to changing times and proud of its recently attained Legal Services Commission Quality Mark, which demands "*high standards in everything from equal opportunities to complaints procedures.*"

Back in the late 70s, chambers took a long hard look at itself and jettisoned its crime practitioners, leaving a common law practice that became defined by its claimant PI, applicant employment work and strong trade union links. More recently it has "*achieved a balance between applicant and respondent work,*" and developed environmental, product liability, clinical negligence and public enquiries expertise. While holding onto relationships with unions, the set now also receives instructions from the in-house legal teams of Ford and Rover, and solicitors firms from Lovells to Farrer & Co. We were unsurprised to hear how "*some departments run the way a modern business should, and overall we are run how a modern set should be run.*" Nevertheless, whilst "*there's a strong idea of who we are as a corporate entity,*" clerks and tenants alike stressed: "*People are individuals, there are blends of interests, tastes, desires and ambitions.*"

In terms of work, individuals can control the composition of their practice; we even heard of a pupil who asked for, and got, only employment matters. In terms of the set's composition, there's a good gender balance and a refreshing diversity that can only have resulted from an open recruitment process. When one senior on the pupillage committee told us: "*We don't recruit people in our mould,*" it clearly wasn't hot air – members' past lives include accountancy, academia and trade union work. However, would-be pupils would be well advised to show "*a demonstrable interest in our specialist work.*" Pupillage interviews mean 30-

35 minutes in front of a slender three-person panel because "*we like to let the person relax into the process.*" A verbal reasoning section assesses "*potential as an advocate,*" but the emphasis is on a candidate's ability to justify his or her thoughts; "*it often doesn't matter if the answer itself is wrong as long as there's a clear line of thought.*"

Pupils can expect a supportive 12 months at Old Square, and both they and their supervisors happily agreed that "*it's not a year-long interview.*" The set encourages all eligible members to become accredited as supervisors, and with pupils changing supervisor four times over the year, every last one is required. Spending three months per supervisor, pupils gain exposure to different aspects of practice. Said one: "*Of my two employment supervisors, one did discrimination and the other commercial employment.*" The system aims to "*cater to peoples' interests,*" but also allows the open-minded pupil "*a broad range of work.*"

Whilst everyone else is free to dress as they choose, pupils wear suits at all times in case of unexpected client contact. In the first six, there's a steady stream of calls from court requiring research, skeleton arguments and advices to be drafted. Pupils said: "*The good thing is that your work actually gets used.*" And they didn't feel as if they were in last chance saloon over getting things right: "*You're always given development points, given a chance to improve.*" This is not least down to the efforts of the pupil supervisors, who offer "*guidance, feedback and mentoring, identifying people the pupil needs to work for who haven't seen the pupil's work.*"

Second-six pupils are restricted to two or three court attendances per week to ensure they keep on top of things. Supervisors liaise with clerks to make sure their charges don't get overloaded; after all, "*it could affect people's impressions if work starts coming late.*"

The past year's pupil traditionally hands over his or her phone number, creating the safety net of "*someone to phone and ask the idiot questions.*" The large volume of small PI and employment work makes for "*good knockabout advocacy experience*" at tribunals and county courts, contrasting with "*coming back and working on much more cerebral issues.*" Whether it's unfairly dismissed celebrities or recently fired joe bloggs, slip-and-trip PI claimants or work for trade unions or local authorities, "*an ability to relate to people and express yourself clearly*" is important.

The clerks emphasised "*the deluge of good-quality work for pupils,*" mentioning particularly that applicant trade union PI or employment work could offer excellent experiences "*because they don't want to pay full whack for a top-end barrister.*" It sounds good on paper but be sure you're ready for the reality. Said one pupil: "*I turned up at tribunal and was facing a silk – what a nightmare!*" The set also sends pupils along to observe specialist cases when they arise. Having recently included product liability cases for Sainsbury's and L'Oreal, and public inquiries such as the Ladbroke Grove Rail Crash and a major organ-retention scandal, the attraction for pupils is obvious.

When it does come to tenancy, the set is thorough in its decision making. No gut instincts here! The number of vacancies is decided in April, each of the pupils then makes a formal application and goes through an interview process in June that incorporates a written appraisal and an advocacy test. The panel also takes into consideration feedback from members above seven to eight years' call before recommending its findings to the entire set. At least one person each year is given tenancy, and the early decision in June gives those not selected the chance to look elsewhere.

Pupils generally work a reasonable 9am-6.30pm and "*one weekend in four,*" but things rapidly get busier upon gaining tenancy. For all its non-traditional feel, this is a "*committed and hardworking*" set. Nevertheless we found plenty of evidence to suggest a convivial atmosphere. First names are used throughout and the notion of afternoon tea was scoffed at – "*we just don't have

it!*" Summer and Christmas drinks parties are "*very relaxed and normally at someone's house,*" and pupils are welcomed along to regular drinks with juniors at various Gray's Inn locals. It is definitely not an all-encompassing social scene, but mature working and personal friendships are all part of chambers' balanced environment. One member told us: "*We're very supportive of each other; I'll go along to a colleague's book launch even though there's nothing in it for me,*" whilst another reflected: "*I've got a lot of friends in chambers.*"

These last two comments sum up Old Square Chambers well – balanced, modern and businesslike with a sense of community.

# Pump Court Tax Chambers

**Chambers UK Rankings:** Tax

As Benjamin Franklin said: "In this world nothing is certain but death and taxes." There can be no place where the latter is more certain than at Pump Court Tax Chambers. As the set's senior clerk told us: "*We cover every area of tax going.*" When instructions stray into insurance or company law, "*we don't touch them;*" on trusts matters, however, Pump Court is in direct competition with Chancery sets. It was interesting for us to hear that "*because everyone here does the same thing there is a sense of collective identity.*"

This is a small, tight-knit, QC-heavy set. It is in the fairly unique position of receiving the lion's share of its work from accountants rather than solicitors; indeed some of its members started life as accountants themselves. At least 60% of business comes from the big four and smaller accountancy firms, or direct from industry from companies such as Diageo. According to one member, with such professionals "*you can be more interactive, have closer relationships...less formal ones even. *In that sense the barrister - professional client relationship breaks down and you can just talk to them as a person and build up a rapport."* The government, too, seeks advice from Pump Court, and chambers currently provides the First Chancery Junior to the Inland Revenue as well as barristers on the B and C panels.

As for the solicitors firms that instruct the set, these range from the giants of the magic circle to one-man bands in the provinces. With the exception perhaps of the smallest law firms, all who instruct are themselves well versed in tax law. It follows then that what they expect from a barrister is a highly sophisticated service – not something that can be developed with ease or speed, and certainly not in a single year. Pupils at Pump Court take no paid work and new junior tenants are embargoed for a year from taking their own instructions. As a pupilmaster put it: *"You're in a vicious circle at the start of practice. The law is very complicated and/or there's a huge amount of money involved. The client wants a safe pair of tried-and-tested hands...so how do you get onto the bottom rung of the ladder?"* The answer is by devilling for more senior members. A baby junior admitted the system left them feeling *"shielded,"* but that compensation lay in the fact that *"you learn so much more by devilling for silks and senior juniors."* Certainly, one must be patient because there's no getting around the fact that *"tax law has a longer incubation period."* At least juniors pay no chambers rent until their income reaches £75,000 pa. At senior level, however, and particularly on the corporate tax side, the per-head income is way above the average in commercial sets.

It sounds to us as if tax lawyers play a lifelong game of chess against the Chancellor of the Exchequer. *"Every year the finance bill cuts off a piece of our work and we have to look for other sources."* Luckily, finance bills have a habit of changing tax regimes and opening and closing loopholes. The other thing that strikes you when you talk to a tax lawyer is that their work is anything but abstract.

*"We're not working in a vacuum,"* explained one; *"we're advising on the tax consequences of family trusts or big tax avoidance schemes."* For example, members of chambers recently advised Debenhams and other retailers on VAT liability on credit card payments.

Alas, *"tax is not perceived as sexy"* and Pump Court receives surprisingly few pupillage applications. A PM analysed the problem for us, saying: *"There's a perception that tax is all about numbers, and for the majority of students it's an unknown quantity. Compare it with shipping, which is applied tort and contract – charter parties and ships crashing into each other – students will be applying existing knowledge. Most people haven't studied tax as an option, but that doesn't matter to us."* A young junior agreed: *"They told me not to worry about having no prior knowledge."* Nevertheless, she added: *"It's been a steep learning curve...reading everything and trying to understand it. Thankfully pupilmasters gave me enough guidance."*

Light on facts and evidence, heavy on law and its interpretation – that's how the work of a tax lawyer looks to us. *"Sometimes instructions come in and they're just a page long: here's the facts now how does this piece of legislation apply? We are asked to give statutory interpretation; our work amounts to very pure legal problem solving."* This couldn't be more different from the work on offer in commercial sets where instructions can sometimes be accompanied by rooms full of boxes of evidence. As one barrister put it: *"The nice thing about tax is that you are arguing about law not fact."*

What does it take to be a tax lawyer? Attention to detail and the ability to think around a problem. Sloppiness is disastrous, but pupillage should help you to tie down your thinking. *"It's all very well to vaguely feel what the answer is, but you have to know exactly how, step by step, you get to that answer."* As one pupil so charmingly put it: *"There is no woolly half ground in tax opinion."*

Another thing you should appreciate is that in tax practice there is far less advocacy, and if a matter litigates then it does so at a very high level. Yet, "*if there were no advocacy at all, ever, there would be no point in being a barrister.*" In the early years, advocacy comes in the shape of VAT tribunals, either before the Special Commissioners (legislative interpretation) or the General Commissioners (cases turning on facts). You might end up in tribunal because Customs alleges a restaurateur hasn't paid his VAT, or in a county court hearing where Customs is enforcing a payment due from a building company. But remember: the majority of your career will be spent in chambers, albeit that Pump Court's full programme of seminars for clients could give you a taste for public speaking!

Pupils are assigned to several PMs, the first for three months, the others for two months each. This gives them as much exposure as possible to different work and "*ensures no single person is playing God in relation to someone's career...it safeguards against a clash in personalities.*" The same group of PMs see the work of each pupil, and the pupils each undertake the same two pieces of assessed work, submitting it anonymously. These assignments are copied to every member of chambers and play a significant role in the tenancy decision, which is made in July. Reports from PMs and a general sense of how the pupil interacts with other members are also considered. Here, as in many sets, if things are not going well in your first six, you'll be advised to cut and run to another area of practice for your second.

Pupils sit together (presently in the library) rather than with their PMs, but this is in no way due to any unwillingness to include them in chambers life. The presumption, rarely rebutted, is that if something's going on pupils are invited – seminars, lunches (not always in hall as "*hall is a bit stuffy and full of barristers*"), drinks and a recent concert in Middle Temple church followed by a garden party. Pump Court's own version of chambers tea is morning coffee at 11am, and for pupils it's the perfect opportunity to find out who's who.

They aren't expected to chip in with conversation, and frankly they'd be unable to as it is limited to esoteric tax points. Pupils always remove the trolley at the end of the break; according to one of them it provides a reason to stay without worrying about when is the polite time to leave. Aside from the obvious comedy value of the tradition, it does sound a bit antiquated; indeed from where we sat in the trad-as-they-come premises we sensed it could be easy to stereotype Pump Court as old school. Yet all those we spoke to assured us: "*There's no stiffness about the place.*" And for the antidote to the leather-bound, wood-panelled Bedford Row building, all you need do is slip through the small courtyard to the rear and into a modern and stylish annexe.

Clearly it takes a particular kind of person to suit tax law, yet we left Pump Court wondering if too many students are writing off the idea before giving it sufficient thought. A mini-pupillage is definitely the way forward.

## 4 Pump Court

**Chambers UK rankings:** Construction, information technology, insurance, professional negligence, professional negligence (construction).

Can a leopard change its spots? It seems so. If we'd written about 4 Pump Court 15 years ago, you'd now be reading a feature on criminal and family practice. It's remarkable how complete the change in this set's activities has been; practice now rests on four sturdy pillars: construction, insurance, technology and professional negligence. More than this, 4 Pump Court has pushed its way to the top of the rankings for technology cases, and many of the set's dozen QCs sit as deputy judges in the High Court or in the Technology and Construction Court. Yet chambers hasn't forgotten its roots; junior members learn their trade on humble RTAs and sale of goods cases, fully aware that their seniors had also cut teeth in the county and magistrates' courts. No one here is too proud to talk of such matters; indeed they take pride in a strong legacy of advocacy.

It can be no coincidence that changes in the set's orientation have occurred under the watch of the current chambers director, who as well as having provided continuity for the last 14 years used to be a partner in a law firm. It is beyond doubt that her experiences on the other side of the professional fence have ensured that the benefits of modern commercial management came to this set earlier than most. Having established a new direction, we heard how *"aggressive but low-key marketing has paid dividends – we're not sitting on our laurels."*

Pupillage is equally well managed, though the system deliberately avoids the clinical objectivity to be found at certain other sets. The chairman of the pupillage committee sat on the Bar Council's pupillage review panel and chambers has been funding its pupils since the 1980s. Stressing that the set wishes to grow from the bottom up and by recruiting tenants from amongst it own pupils, several people reminded us that in 2003 three of the four pupils gained tenancy. The harvest is not always so plentiful, but each year the set does welcome four pupils, who follow a carefully planned routine that is designed to offer breadth and practical experience.

The first six is split into two equal parts, with the pupil sitting with two pupilmasters who each specialise in one or other of the four main pillars of practice. Bearing in mind that the PMs will be instructed on reasonably complex cases, time with them is largely chambers based. That said, if a barrister is embarking on a very large case, they will not be allocated a pupil until they are once again able to supply an interesting mix of smaller matters. We spoke with one PM about how she involved her pupil in construction matters. *"If I have a case management conference,"* she said, *"I*

make them write the skeleton argument beforehand. Or they'll do the notes for a conference with a client, advices and pleadings if they are not too big and legal research for a break."* If you're thinking of applying here, don't underestimate the importance of written work, because these days *"there is much more emphasis on paper advocacy...skeletons are so important, and therefore it is also so important that pupils can write."* Each of chambers' four pillars represents a different world, but in construction, as in technology and insurance work, the barrister must effectively be two experts in one. Knowing the law is not enough; one has to also become embedded in the industry sector, interact easily and confidently with expert witnesses, specialist solicitors and their lay clients. As many of the cases involve mountains of technical information and evidence, pupils must have an appetite for detail.

Pupils are set a series of four exercises (two written, two advocacy) to assess how they are developing and to prime them for a much more hands-on second six. *"We aim to give them feedback within a week of each exercise...positive and negative."* *"Of course you go in nervous to the pit of your stomach,"* one baby junior recalled the experience, adding that in his experience pupils had not become overly competitive with each other, preferring instead to have *"preliminary discussions to chat about points of law."*

Given the set's commitment to continual feedback, pupils shouldn't be shocked by sudden bad news: *"I can't remember anyone leaving us at the six-month stage,"* the pupillage committee chair told us. A brief period of shadowing the most junior members of chambers marks the halfway stage and allows pupils to see first-hand what their second, practising six will hold. Pupils have their own clerks for the second-six and a single PM acts more as a guardian than a tutor. Soon enough they are dealing with a flurry of small instructions, usually county court PI matters such as one-day fast track trials or infant settlements. Because "*your work is entirely dependent on the clerks,*" it's easy to see the importance of the rule that insists the first thing pupils must do every day is pop into the clerks' room to say good morning and have a chat. It's patently clear that "*they are keen to get us into court at the junior end.*" As for what it takes to cope, "*it requires personal responsibility and confidence, because you are the one who has to talk to the solicitors – people who have been doing their job for years – and you have to give them a steer as to where you think the case is going.*"

The tenancy decision is made by a committee, not the entire set; indeed, as one silk told us: "*I can't remember the last time we had a full meeting of all members.*" New tenants always share a room with someone slightly more experienced, but also find any number of people are willing to sit down and talk them through things. "*If I have a few bankruptcy hearings,*" one baby junior said, "*I go and see the king of bankruptcy. People here have a sense of duty...obligation to help others in chambers.*"

There's ample opportunity to chat on a Friday night over drinks in the waiting room (unfussy, clean lines, TV usually on). Sometimes after work, a few people will slip into The Devereux or Daly's, and because several members have caught the sailing bug, there's always a voyage or regatta to plan. Look at the set's website and you'll see the yacht it sponsors. We'll weigh anchor on this point for a moment because it says much about chambers. Just as on a boat you don't wave cheerily as one of your fellow crew members tumbles overboard, at 4 Pump Court you don't allow your colleagues to drown...or, worse still, push their head underwater as you struggle to rise above the waves.

Seeking permission to come aboard? Here's the drill. References are sought and considered for every applicant. About 10% are called for a thorough but not unpleasant interview at which they tackle a problem and are expected to chat intelligently on a current legal topic. No prior construction, technology or insurance industry experience is necessary and non-law graduates fare

equally well. In truth, there's nothing especially unique about the ideal candidate for chambers; 4 Pump Court wants exactly the same type of pupil as the other good quality commercial sets. One's background seems unimportant so long as it is replete with academic success, and one's personality need not conform to a chambers mould, though we'd suggest that chambers wants to perpetuate the good conduct and care it has always shown towards the Bar, courts and clients alike.

You can't help but leave 4 Pump Court with the idea that it is a happy ship, and seeing as we've already sunk to the use of clichés, we might as well add that the decks are nicely scrubbed, the crew financially healthy and the navigators running a wise course.

## Quadrant Chambers

**Chambers UK rankings:** Aviation, international arbitration, shipping, commodities, travel

Known as 4 Essex Court until 2004, Quadrant Chambers has moved into what is undoubtedly the most spectacular accommodation known to the Bar. Four Grade II listed buildings on Fleet Street opposite the Royal Courts of Justice and backing onto the Temple have been drawn together and linked by a modern atrium. To secure the move, Quadrant had to compete with other sets and convince the landlord, Middle Temple, of its good prospects. The new address looks likely to boost and broaden the set's profile, if only because it contains an extensive suite of fully kitted-out meeting rooms suitable for ADR proceedings or as a base for out-of-town solicitors with business in the RCJ or the Commercial Court. An abundance of space will allow Quadrant to grow at a self-dictated pace, though for now members are happy to rattle around their new home.

As befits a set with roots in shipping and insurance, two of the four component buildings started life as 17th-century coffee houses. In time they developed grand Georgian dining rooms, frequented by judges, solicitors and barristers. As we craned our necks up towards the ornate ceiling in Quadrant's library, we imagined conversations between long-dead counsel rolling around the room in a rich fog of coffee fumes and pipe tobacco smoke. Yet what is most striking about chambers' new home is that it juxtaposes perfectly the trappings of past success and the symbols of a bright future.

Away from its adopted bricks-and-mortar history, Quadrant does have a past of its own. Numbers 1-4 Essex Court had long housed shipping barristers, and at Number 2, the set's founder Barry Sheen QC developed a wet shipping practice after quitting the navy at the end of WWII. In 1978 he was appointed as a judge in the Admiralty Court, so starting a tradition of sending senior QCs to the Admiralty Bench. He was followed by Sir Anthony Clarke QC (now the new Master of the Rolls) and Sir David Steel QC, who between them moved chambers into the thick of the insurance world via Lloyd's of London. Traditionally, chambers' business has centred on international trade and shipping claims, pretty much all of which are insurance-related; however, in the late 90s it acquired new members from niche aviation law set 5 Bell Yard. As well as developing this field, Quadrant has also been encouraging more general commercial instructions.

The house style is not overly academic or abstract; it's more of a "*sleeves-rolled-up approach.*" "*We're known for our integrity,*" one barrister remarked, "*and for playing with a straight bat.*" The aim is simply to give "*concise and helpful assistance to the client,*" using a "*Commercial Court style...there's no room for grandstanding at all.*" For what it's worth, after visiting the set we concluded that these comments were equally applicable to pupillage and "*the pups,*" as the chambers director so endearingly called them. Much of chambers'

work turns on the construction of contract terms and statutes. But this is only part of the equation: a barrister here must also have the knack of "*untangling the factual issues in a case*" as well as "*the ability to wrestle with jurisprudential issues.*"

As an acknowledgement that they may not have studied shipping or insurance law in any detail, new pups undergo a 12-part induction. Then, over the course of the year, they sit with four pupilmasters (the term 'supervisor' drifts in and out of Quadrantspeak), each of whom produces a written report on the pupil, who can in turn comment on its content. A moot in the second three months will usually involve a fairly short summary judgment application based on a real set of papers. The assessment regime is an open one and almost all pupils sail through the six-month break period to complete a full year's training. To stand a chance in the July tenancy decision, they must demonstrate that "*on picking up a set of papers, they can confidently and persuasively argue a point of view,*" even if their PM, playing devil's advocate, chooses to see things differently.

Nothing about Quadrant led us to conclude that pupillage was a particularly unpleasant process. Typically a 9am to 6.30pm routine, the demands of the working day didn't strike us as overly rigorous either. As one pupil quipped: "*They're trying to train you up not kill you!*" During the second six, pupils are allowed to do pieces of work for other members of chambers, though it is not policy to provide them with paid work. "*We don't view them as unpaid devils but pupillage is all about educating and training the pupil, and it takes a full 12 months to get them fully up to speed.*" Chambers has a large pool of potential supervisors to call upon, the more experienced of whom will be assigned to the pupils who need the most help. The basic idea is that pupils see at least two distinct areas of practice, so no one drowns in a sea of shipping cases.

Always remember that here, as in any other commercial set, most of your time will be spent on paperwork. "*It's not the sort of practice for someone who doesn't like looking at things in the library,*" someone said. "*You've got to like black-letter law...it's technical, intricate and detailed.*" A young junior estimated 75% of her time was spent in chambers, much of it drafting pleadings for disputes over charter parties and bills of lading – good old-fashioned spats over cargo damaged onboard ships or consignments of rotten grain. To boost her time in court, she had also been instructed on banking matters and consumer credit cases. "*It's all good court experience!*" she told us.

Towards the end of pupillage and in the early part of tenancy, "*you've got to be exceptionally organised because you'll be working for a lot of people.*" You have to be sensible about what you take on and perhaps also take guidance from the real professionals in chambers – the practice managers. Musing on this, a young junior said: "*You have to have a very personal relationship with your practice manager. For example, they've got to know what's going on at home...it's not that they pry, but it's useful for them to know if you are having a terrible time.*" In the first couple of years, juniors handle a broad range of commercial work and only then see where their practice is going and what they most enjoy. If at any time they need a few words of wisdom, their 'Godfather' (usually a senior junior) is the first port of call for pastoral care. "*Even when they're really busy, they have to help you.*"

If you make it to the two-stage pupillage interview, you'll find that much the same will be demanded of you as in any other commercial set. However, it is worth bearing in mind all that we have said about chambers' style of advocacy and the value it places on common sense.

The social scene is characterised by close circles of friends and in summer months the pavement opposite Daly's wine bar ("*which does very well out of us!*") is positively staked out. Pupils, barristers and staff all attend a monthly chambers lunch, which pupils say is great for getting to know people. "*We all rub along very well*

*together,*" one PM revealed. He also considered the set to be "*egalitarian and meritocratic...and the seniors are not stuffed shirts, they don't stand on ceremony.*" Something perhaps typified by a refusal to countenance rituals such as chambers tea. Finally coming together in one building has increased the likelihood of bumping into people in the normal course of the day, and reinforced "*a general feeling of corporate care.*" Practice managers, who once suffered in silence in grim rooms in separate buildings, now "*feel more a part of the new corporate image*" – an image in which it is hoped that "*our history will be less obvious*" so "*people will no longer see us as just a shipping set.*"

Chambers has long suffered from "*poor-relation*" syndrome in comparison to the magic circle commercial sets. "*When we had grubby premises, we had a difficult job arguing against that,*" one barrister admitted. Nowadays all you need do is take one look inside 10 Fleet Street to be left in no doubt as to Quadrant's vision of the future.

# Queen Elizabeth Building

**Chambers UK rankings:** Family

Within sight of Queen Elizabeth Building the Thames runs seawards and traffic inches along the Embankment to Blackfriars Bridge. Inside the Middle Temple chambers of this 100+-year-old, top-drawer family set, walls hung heavy with oil paintings of robed judges and a pervading decorous air combine to suggest a strong current of conservatism. Though the building was constructed less than 50 years ago, QEB has made a home that feels considerably older. But perhaps this is only fitting for a set defined by "*a sense of pride in the institution,*" whose people place "*value on loyalty*" and where people are "*very aware of a long-standing reputation for excellence.*" Whilst it may not be moving at a million miles an hour, we heard: "*It has changed incredibly in the last 14 years,*" *losing the Eton-Harrow-Oxbridge feel."*

QEB possesses a keen sense of a heritage of excellence, reflecting its long-held status as one of the – if not *the* – best family sets. Top-ranked by *Chambers UK* for family law, QEB has for many years represented the well-off, the powerful, the famous and even the notorious as their marriages unravel. Beyond this it has continually acted on law-making matters. Earlier highlights include the divorces of Charles and Diana, Sir Bob Geldof and Paula Yates, Mick Jagger and Jerry Hall. In the law-making category are cases like White v White and Cowan v Cowan.

Equally important in the QEB psyche is a tradition of senior members moving on to judicial appointments. The roll call includes Sir Harry Philimore (Nuremberg War Trials/Lord Justice of Appeal), Sir Roger Ormerod (CA) and latterly Dame Florence Baron, who now sits in the High Court. Whilst the prestige of such a record is undoubted, it tends to leave QEB a little short of QCs with just three currently in situ. That said, chambers is happy to be *"small and self-contained"* and has *"no plans to increase beyond the 29 of us here at the moment."* This comment puts the tenancy decision in context – up to four pupils per year chasing one or two tenancies per year.

*"Becoming a judge isn't necessarily a burning career ambition at the forefront of pupils' minds but it's definitely a good career progression."* The upshot of excellence past and present is that QEB is a no-brainer for those seeking a family law pupillage. *"There just wasn't any contest, I wanted family and it's top of the tree,"* confirmed juniors and pupils alike. Lest you worry that your lack of detailed family law knowledge will see you fail to score even an interview, rest assured that chambers considers the likely inexperience of some applicants. *"Some people do have a feel for the discipline, others not and whilst we look for evidence of interest in the form of work experience at family law sets or solicitors, it's not a requirement,"* recruiters told us. Nevertheless, at interview you could be asked to discuss recent

reported cases so do some homework.

But homework can only prepare you so much for life in chambers and pupils tell us *"no Bar course really gives a feel for ancillary relief. The first six months involve a massive learning curve."* The first six is *"the time to ask stupid questions and get all the help you can, because it's harder to get help when you're up and running."* Pupils train under three supervisors for four months each, observing them on what can only be described as top-grade work. They are in the enviable position of seeing high-value and often high-profile cases, frequently possessing an international aspect. The specific approach of a supervisor will dictate the pupil's experience but all were reported to be good at *"checking your work and giving feedback,"* whilst one even *"insists that you do all his work before he does it to help you understand."* It should be emphasised that the core work is *"rich people's divorce,"* with cases involving children much less frequent than financial matters. Inevitably this means carving up large country estates rather than care proceedings on council estates. Although some members' have practices that include PI and clinical or professional negligence, such work is a sideline. All pupils are assigned a buddy from among the juniors and in the first six will accompany them to court to get a feel for what will follow.

Second six pupils and juniors find that *"at the bottom end you get non-family-related possessions and bankruptcies,"* and delusions of glamour are dispelled by being sent out *"to crappy cases at god-knows-where-court."* Typical instructions for a junior range from *"small money cases for council tenants on legal aid to ancillary relief for those in the middle-income bracket."* It is essential that *"you are able to deal well with a wide variety of clients who are all likely to be going through a period of upheaval in their lives."* And this is a very important point – as members were keen to point out to us, chambers possesses a good balance of *"aggressive advocates and sensitive types."*

A key attraction of family law is *"the all-round*

*challenge.*" Said one source: "*I didn't want to work for a faceless company; here you have the dual responsibility of dealing firmly and sensitively with emotional clients, whilst keeping your eye on the legal ball.*" The benefit of pursuing these challenges at a top set like QEB is that "*the family law articulates with almost every aspect of business life, includes pensions and trusts and also embraces social issues like civil marriage and human rights.*" In other words, commercial acumen and "*high intellectual standards*" are just as important tools of the trade as social skills.

QEB has the highest of expectations and its July tenancy decision means that pupils "*enter what is effectively a nine-month assessment process.*" Younger sources were keen to stress that "*you have to pace yourself,*" while those further up the ladder pointed to the importance of being "*exact and precise.*" In addition to formal advocacy and written tests, clerks and supervisors "*do their best to ensure that you have worked for everybody in chambers,*" so that when members meet to take the tenancy decision all are well informed. While no one pretends that getting tenancy isn't a competitive business, those with whom we spoke were adamant that "*although there is an expectation of excellence, mistakes aren't held against you.*" One junior we interviewed recalled when, as a pupil, she slept in and in so doing missed a court appearance with the head of chambers by several hours. "*But when I called in apologising profusely, everyone acted as though my alarm clock had betrayed me!*" Lucky.

Senior clerk Ivor Treherne has held the post for over 25 years and is described as "*paternal but with authority*" or, more baldly, "*God for pupils.*" Though he has neither a beard nor apparently a sense of Old Testament justice, he is seemingly omniscient when it comes to scheduling. "*Ivor always seems to know just what you can handle in your timetable, whether you can take on extra work or if you're making trouble for yourself.*" This oversight can be valuable at a time when pupils are trying to impress as many members of chambers as possible.

However full the days become – they seem to average 8.30am-6pm for pupils and anything from two to four days a week in court – there is always time for afternoon tea. Tea lady Tina is at the heart of this set-defining event, providing biscuits and chocolate which prove the downfall of many a vow of abstinence. "*If I go I end up eating 25 biscuits,*" said one source, "*...so many calories in one room.*" Tea offers "*a break in the day where you can bounce ideas off people, ask for advice or just have a chat.*" Otherwise, the social life in chambers is relatively quiet, though "*juniors do invite pupils out for drinks and lunches,*" giving them opportunity to "*ask the silly questions.*" There is also a party to welcome new pupils and chambers meals or drinks events "*to mark the big occasions.*" At such events old members might pop in for a chinwag.

Overall, QEB genuinely seemed to us to be a "*good-humoured*" place defined by "*a cohesive sense of identity*" that still leaves some room for the individual touch. Recent pupils hailed from backgrounds as diverse as performance, journalism and higher study, though in all those we met we noted a certain single-minded determination to succeed... or as one source put it: "*Ambition and a hard-working attitude.*" This is not a set for those with crusading tendencies or a habit of rocking the boat. QEB knows what it is and sees no need to change. And who can blame it when the formula is a winning one?

## 3 Raymond Buildings

**Chambers UK rankings:** Crime, fraud: criminal, licensing.

Three Raymond Buildings is home to many a big name at the criminal Bar, and since its formation in 1926 it has lent its name to many of the most notorious criminal trials and extraditions. Matrix Churchill, Jonathan Aitken, the Carl Bridgewater

Appeal and Pinochet's removal to face charges in Chile are just a few of its claims to fame. Think serious blue and white collar crime and then mix it with a complementary medley of extradition and regulatory work including licensing, judicial review and police law.

Spread over four floors of a Victorian terrace overlooking Gray's Inn Fields, 3 Raymond Buildings is exactly as you imagine barristers chambers ought to be. We were led in through a sturdy front door, via the lobby and into a tastefully furnished drawing room complete with a regulation-issue French-polished table. Clearly no one had been shopping at Ikea lately. In such elegant surroundings, you expect barristers to be dressed in regulation-issue pinstriped suits. Instead (with the exception of the pupil who had just got back from a morning in court) the young and up-beat juniors we met were dressed in smart but casual summer wear. Their ensembles, they advised us, were in keeping with chambers' policy of cultivating a *"relaxed, open and friendly atmosphere."*

A 12-month pupillage at 3 Raymond Buildings should give most pupils an introduction to a good range of chambers' work. The year is divided equally into three, with pupils spending time with a trio of supervisors. In the first six, they spend a substantial amount of their time in court observing and assisting their supervisor. There will also be written work, starting with small pieces of legal research, and moving on to noting briefs and more substantial pieces of legal drafting. As one pupil explained: *"You're really encouraged to go and do written work and research for other members of chambers. It's been a good way to meet members of chambers and make my face known."* Another good way is through the in-house advocacy exercises that take place throughout the year.

In their second six, pupils are up on their feet from the get-go and in court most days, sharpening their advocacy claws on routine magistrates' court work and local authority comittee hearings for licensing applications. As the months progress,

they don wigs and gowns for pleas in mitigation and short preliminary hearings at the Crown Court. The briefs for these normally arrive the afternoon before, so it's not unusual to have to stay up late to prepare for the hearing. On the plus side, most of chambers' work is in London, so nasty 10am appointments in Swindon tend to be the exception rather than the rule. It all sounded very pleasant, but what we really wanted was a good horror story and so we got a pupil to tell us about one of his first ever court appearances. *"It was a plea in mitigation prior to sentence,"* he said. *"I had never met my client before and it was my job to tell the judge what a thoroughly nice guy he was. When he emerged from the cells, I noticed that he was brandishing a tattoo reading 666 on the back of his head."*

The junior tenants we met were all very positive about their formative years at the criminal Bar. One had been led by QCs on three occasions in the House of Lords and had also made trips to the Court of Appeal and the High Court. As she explained: *"You soon get an idea of where you want to specialise. I was interested in extradition and public law, and the clerks and other members of chambers were really pleased to help foster me in the right direction. There's a huge support network here."* Apparently senior members provide more than just a support network; they also operate a round-the-clock ethics Batphone for young lawyers in distress. No matter where you are in the country, you can always count on the silky tones of a QC at the other end of the line, talking you through that professional conduct nightmare. Readers: don't go getting any ideas – the service is for 3 Raymond Buildings' pupils and members only.

Advocacy exercises aside, there is no formal assessment process throughout the year, but pupils do get feedback on all written work and each member who receives work from a pupil will report back to the tenancy committee. The grand finale takes the form of an advocacy assessment in front of the committee, followed by an 'informal' interview. The entire membership then cast their votes and may, or may not, take up the recommendations of the committee. The unlucky souls who aren't taken on are often allowed to squat or do a third six.

Chambers has a social dimension, which (certainly amongst the juniors) is alive and kicking. The highlight is a monthly drinks party, affectionately known as the Last Thursday Club... for obvious reasons. Pupils are not reduced to serving canapés or doing the washing-up; as one of the pupilmasters was keen to stress: "*There's no real delineation here. If you are a pupil, we treat you as an adult and as a member of chambers.*" Old habits die hard and clerks still refer to their barristers as Mr and Miss, though more junior members are called by their first names "*as long as solicitors and clients aren't around.*"

As well as a commitment to becoming a criminal advocate, successful pupillage applicants must demonstrate "*an ability to communicate to people on all levels. We're looking for people with charm, intelligence, persuasion and above all, level-headedness.*"

Applicants' forms are read by two different people, both of them applying uniform criteria. If they disagree on a candidate, the application will be read and vetted by a third. First-round interviews consist of general questions followed by a discussion of a topical issue, usually on a legal theme and notified to the interviewee half an hour beforehand. Make it through to the final 15, and you'll be invited to a rigorous second interview which tests candidates' ability to think on their feet and respond to a challenge with only 30 minutes' preparation.

If you're wondering whether you're cut out for 3 Raymond Buildings, apparently there is no particular 'type' in chambers. These people see themselves as an "*eclectic and diverse bunch of people.*" Certainly the contrast between the top and bottom ends of chambers would seem to suggest that this is the case. The combination of "*landed gentry*" at the more senior end with the bright young things at the junior end must make for some interesting dinner party conversations.

# 3 Serjeants' Inn

**Chambers UK rankings:** Clinical negligence, police law, professional discipline

Excuse the tasteless surgical gag, but 3 Serjeants' Inn really is at the cutting edge of medical law. A brief perusal of the Lloyd's Medical Law Reports and the popular press will reveal that members of this set have been recurrent players in the litigation that has shaped the modern law of medicine. *Bland, Re A (Conjoined Twins: Separation)*, *Sidaway*, the Bristol Royal Infirmary Inquiry and the Harold Shipman murders have all involved tenants from 3 Serjeants' Inn in one capacity or another.

It's not all doctors and nurses though. In recent years, the set has also developed a leading practice in police law, in which it acts predominantly for police authorities. Typically this work involves defending police in civil actions, judicial reviews and disciplinary proceedings, or pursuing court orders on behalf of the police in applications to, say, close down a crack den or get an anti-social behaviour order. Chambers also has a small, but nonetheless significant, team of construction and commercial lawyers.

The move from more modest premises in the Temple to the set's current home on Fleet Street gives 3 Serjeants' Inn an appearance of grandeur that most other chambers lack the space to pull off. Indeed, at first glance, visitors could be forgiven for thinking that they'd arrived at the wrong building. Occupying the premises of an old bank, the open-plan reception area-cum-clerks' room is spacious and high-ceilinged with solid brass lanterns descending on chains, faux stone columns and a collection of rather gaudy frescoes depicting lusty scenes from classical mythology. The overall impact? A bit like Quadrant Chambers after a surprise ambush by Lawrence Llewelyn-Bowen.

Pupillage follows a three by four-month programme and where a pupil has a particular interest, they can normally expect to spend at least part of the year working in that area. The nature of chambers' specialisation ensures exposure to a variety of tribunals. As well as standard-fare clinical negligence actions in the High Court, it's not uncommon for members to be involved in *"life or death"* telephone applications for 'without notice' injunctions in emergency treatment decisions.

Unsurprisingly for a predominantly civil set, there's a heavy emphasis on drafting. Practice makes perfect, and chambers is beginning to adopt a uniform way of giving feedback to its pupils. For a typical piece of work like, say, drafting a statement of case, the pupil's finished draft is returned to them by e-mail with additions and corrections marked clearly in red, accompanied by an additional page of commentary at the end. According to the pupils this system works very well: *"The feedback is always constructive"* and *"expectations are built up gradually."* The development of pupils' written work is an important factor in the tenancy decision, but that said, one pupil told us: *"Everyone emphasised that it's okay to make mistakes as you're learning... as long as you don't make the same mistake twice."*

Advocacy skills are also considered *"a major thing,"* and these barristers are *"known for being tough trial advocates."* Pupils are eased into things gradually, and to use a clinical analogy, the first few months will be more about practising sutures than full-on brain surgery. At the time of writing, there was no formal in-house advocacy training over and above that provided by the Inns, though there were suggestions that it might be introduced in the near future. However, it sounds as if there's no shortage of opportunities to practice. Chambers is particularly fortunate in that it enjoys a steady stream of instructions from one of its probation service clients to prosecute breaches of community sentences in the Crown and magistrates' courts. This work has become a staple for second six-pupils, who describe it as *"a fantastic opportunity to develop advocacy skills."*

When it comes to work, it's a case of 'have brief, will travel'. From Norwich to Newcastle, the pupils we met had certainly done the rounds. From time to time, the value of the brief is outstripped by the cost of travel, which means pupils are effectively *"paying for the privilege of doing a piece of work,"* but our sources accepted this as a necessary evil in the very early stages of practice. And anyway, the competitive pupillage award should certainly take the sting out of the tail.

Pupil supervisors enforce a nine-till-six policy rigidly... in the first six at least, and pupils say that socially they feel very much a part of chambers and are welcomed along to the regular and informal lunches, as well as drinks on a Friday. Pupils also told us that, on their arrival, juniors made a real effort to take them under their wing. Each was allocated their own aunt or uncle to act as a mentor, and a sounding board for niggling concerns.

The dreaded tenancy decision is made a little later than in most other sets, coming at the beginning of October. 3 Serjeants' Inn believes that *"twelve months' pupillage should mean twelve months' pupillage,"* and so that is what pupils are assessed on. If, for whatever reason, tenancy isn't on the cards, people are allowed to squat while they plan their next move. Once your name is on the door, the clerking team won't waste a moment in promoting it to clients. Personal letters and profiles are sent out to instructing solicitors, and juniors are encouraged to take part in regular seminars and lectures. The style of clerking here is hands-on, with the senior clerk making it his business to know about all the barristers on his books. He sits down with each new tenant in order to ascertain their expectations in terms of income and their desired specialisation. Juniors say that in the early years of practice, *"the clerks are more than happy to steer you in the direction that you want your career to take."*

While we are always assured on our various visits to different chambers that there is no one type of person whose face fits, we're damned if we don't come out finding something that brings a set together. What we noticed in everyone we met at this set was a real sense of ambition coupled with a desire to deliver the goods. These barristers are driven towards getting their hands on better and better instructions, and then producing the best work possible. As one pupil supervisor put it: *"You need to have a certain passion for doing well and working smart. It's about attention to detail, determination and a desire to really do your best."*

Apply to this set and you'll need to provide a good reason for wanting to specialise in its chosen areas of practice. If you find that you are about to write 'I am applying to this set because I'm really interested in clinical negligence' but you don't have anything to back that up with, your CV probably needs a shot of Botox. It's definitely a good plan to apply to this set, and others with similar areas of specialisation, for mini-pupillage. If that doesn't work out, seek out some other relevant experience. You could try, for example, a work experience placement with the police, CPS or an NHS Trust. A 2:2 needn't prevent you from applying here, and in fact a few senior (and highly successful) members of chambers didn't quite manage to bag a 2:1 themselves. But you will need to persuade the person reading your application that there are other things about you that will make you a good pupil/tenant. As for the interview, it will come in either one or two rounds, depending on how many candidates come through the initial screening process. There will certainly be some form of legal problem to tackle, as well as a discussion of something of topical interest. No shrinking violets please: the pupils' advice was to *"be prepared to demonstrate your reasoning and hold your corner."*

If you do go under the knife at 3 Serjeants' Inn and come out the other end with a pupillage, we think that you'll have done pretty well.

# Serle Court

**Chambers UK rankings:** Banking & finance, Chancery: commercial, Chancery: traditional, commercial litigation, company, civil fraud, insolvency/corporate recovery, partnership, professional negligence, real estate litigation

The Serle Court story is one of élan, innovation and no little foresight. In 2000, the Chancery set at 13 Old Square merged with the commercial set at 1 Hare Court, leading to the creation of an entity with genuine expertise in both the Queen's Bench and Chancery divisions of the High Court. This has enabled the set's 47 practitioners (12 silks among them) to attain recognition in an impressive spread of practice areas. The most notable exponent of this jack-of-all-trades approach is *Chambers UK's* leading Star at the Bar, Michael Briggs QC, who is ranked in the guide in a staggering 11 areas of practice. Serle Court members have acted in much of the biggest commercial Chancery litigation in recent years: head of chambers Lord Neill of Bladen QC and Dominic Dowley QC represented the liquidators in BCCI, whilst other members were heavily involved in the cases of Sumitomo and Spectrum.

Pupillage is split into four three-month periods spent with different pupilmasters. Attempts are made to ensure that both pupils share the same PM to ensure some degree of uniformity of assessment. The sort of work they encounter can vary from highly specialised Chancery areas such as partnership law to general *"knockabout commercial"* work. According to those we spoke to, pupillage at Serle Court is *"all about learning not earning."* Pupils don't undertake their own work during the year, but this shouldn't put anyone off applying as the size of the pupillage award ensures no one is forced to live off the minimum wage. Chambers' thinking is simply that it makes more sense for a pupil to fully benefit from the experience and guidance of those at the top of their profession than to "*flounder around on your own for a couple of months taking on low-grade work.*" The commitment to providing top-level training is exemplified by the assessed advocacy exercise that takes place halfway through pupillage. In recent years, the judging panel has been headed by Michael Briggs QC and featured other big hitters from within chambers. As one pupil reasoned: "*These people's time is extremely valuable. If chambers is prepared to free them up for a couple of hours for our benefit then it shows they mean business.*"

So, if it's not the place to aim for if you want to be on your feet straight away in pupillage, what about the period straight after? "*The key thing in the first few years of practice is producing a consistently high standard of paperwork.*" Interestingly, most of the work you secure during the first couple of years of tenancy will stem from the contacts you made during pupillage. A very junior tenant described his pupillage year as "*a bit of a marketing exercise; it's not just about impressing people so that they take you on, you want to get passed work in the future as well.*" Initially the advocacy a junior might experience will be small-scale (eg bankruptcy petitions and consent orders), but it does grow in time. Another thing to note is that Serle's excellent reputation for offshore work can also mean that juniors are sometimes needed in exotic locations such as the Cayman Islands. Talk about hardship!

We certainly got the feeling that we were in the company of some highly intelligent individuals though it's less a case of off-the-cuff brilliance and more to do with measured excellence. Perhaps this is borne out by the type of work encountered by commercial Chancery barristers. As one seasoned tenant put it: "*Jury advocacy is not the key skill for practitioners here. When we do actually get into court we're concerned with placing reasoned arguments in front of judges and anticipating questions. It's never about winging it.*" Our visit leads us to conclude that those who apply here should have "*an enquiring mind.*" That is to say, apply if you're someone who is consistently "*thinking outside of*

*the box.*" As with the other leading sets in commercial and Chancery work, the emphasis is on intellectual ability, and the member of the pupillage committee we spoke to was fairly candid when discussing how to demonstrate this. "*The vast majority of people we interview have Firsts, and a significant amount of them have been to Oxbridge. It just happens that way.*" Once at interview, you need to present yourself as someone who is able to "*fully engage with and then answer the questions we ask.*" Seasoned debaters beware: "*Having an answer for everything will only impress if the answer has substance. The candidate who takes a deep breath and actually thinks about the question before answering will score more highly than the one who plays for time with obviously pre-prepared spiel.*"

The tenancy decision is made in July, and the factors taken into consideration include the work you've done for other members, how much you've impressed your PMs and your performance in an assessed advocacy exercise that takes place after six months. Your chances of being taken on are good. As one tenant explained it: "*The presumption is that you'll be a tenant here. We just need to see if you've been able to get from A to B in the learning curve quick enough.*"

Recognising the need to cast aside the crusty old image of the Chancery Bar, Serle Court is not alone in wanting to portray itself as a modern and progressive set. A couple of years ago it went to the trouble of commissioning a respected architect in order to attain a contemporary feel in its New Square premises. Gone are the wooden name boards that sit proudly outside other Lincoln's Inn sets; gone are the landscape paintings hanging in the waiting room. Walk in to Serle Court and you have to agree that designer chap did a pretty good job. Readers of our last report may remember reading about three yellow plastic ducks that had been launched by some enterprising prankster into the pigeon netting above the courtyard behind chambers. We're pleased to report that the ducks are alive and well and showing no signs of waddling off. Not even to the set's annexe nearby on Chancery Lane, where 14 members ply their trade. Serle Court practitioners can justifiably claim to be a sporty bunch; its football and cricket teams lead the way in igniting inter-chambers competition. On a marginally less energetic note, the social life at Serle Court is also thriving. Thursday drinks at the Gaucho Grill are always well attended, and the chambers tradition of never letting pupils put their hands in their pockets for anything ensures that each year's batch is well looked after. Sometimes clerks will address pupils in formal terms *"but that's only to impress solicitors"* confided one source.

We have to concur with the individual who described pupillage at Serle Court as *"very civilised – nowhere near as barbaric as elsewhere."* If it's modernity and meritocracy that you're after, then you'll find it here.

## 3/4 South Square

**Chambers UK rankings:** Banking & finance, Chancery: commercial, commercial litigation, company, fraud: civil/ insolvency/corporate recovery

Ever thought about why some people are so fascinated by other people's misfortune? Witness the gawping crowd that gathers around a traffic accident or the glee of the tabloids when lurid tales emerge and bring down a celebrity. We're not accusing 3/4 South Square of this ugly addiction, but by their own admission, *"wherever something collapses we're there."* A self-styled *"broad and modern set"* that *"prides itself on its commercial and business knowledge,"* this chambers is widely regarded as *the* insolvency practice in the UK. As such, it loves a good corporate collapse. When the mighty fall, odds are that one of the set's 16 silks or 29 other tenants are helping to pick through the rubble. They had prominent involvement in the

biggest cases of the last ten years – BCCI, Maxwell, Polly Peck, Lloyd's of London, Barings, Enron, Railtrack, Marconi, ntl, TXU and Spectrum Plus.

While chambers has a not unreasonable desire to be seen as *"a rounded commercial set,"* it is also wholly justified in its claim that *"no one else in the world has such a collection of insolvency experts."* Giving proof to the claim is a well-developed network of *"loose associations with overseas law firms"* from Paris to Hong Kong, South Africa to Singapore. This means chambers *"often functions like an international call centre, referring work to our contacts."* And, yes, the process is two-way, so that *"around 45% of work litigates here but is driven by overseas clients."* To illustrate this point, members of the set have been involved in the UK end of the Italian Parmalat bankruptcy, as well as matters in the Cayman Islands and at the ECJ. Emphasising chambers' diversity, we also learned that some hard-core overseas shipping arbitration has recently been handled.

With work pouring in from across the world, and not forgetting that time and insolvency wait for no man, 3/4 South Square *"is practically a 24-hour practice."* Whether it is (head of chambers) Michael Crystal or a junior tenant, *"someone is always working through the night."*

Run strategically by a *"steering committee, which meets regularly with barristers,"* 3/4 has developed a sense of purpose and identity that it is impossible to ignore. The people we spoke to were well aware that chambers is frequently compared with a small law firm. Certainly, the set *"doesn't like to sit around and wait for the ball."* Instead, practice managers, silks and juniors will *"go out, to the Caymans say, to meet prospective clients."* Discreetly branded and with a website packed with helpful Big Smoke advice for international or non-London visitors, a lot of thought has gone into positioning 3/4 in its marketplace. On our previous visit to the set's home in Gray's Inn, one of its buildings was receiving a makeover; two years later and the adjoining premises were getting the same *"light and open," "clean and commercial"* touch.

If you're attracted to the set's style but have no idea what insolvency practice entails, then apply for a mini-pupillage. You'll get to see the barristers work and all parties get to *"look each other up and down."* There are a limited number available and they *"by no means guarantee a better chance of pupillage."* What they will do is allow you to fast-track to the second round of interviews, should you decide to go further. Given that of the 200 who apply each year, 50 make it to the first round and only 20 to the second, this sounds like some advantage.

No matter how you get there, by round two you'd better have some clear ideas about insolvency. *"Of course we'd be suspicious of anyone claiming a passionate interest in it,"* said one member of the pupillage committee, *"but we're nevertheless keen for people to show an interest in developing a career in our core areas of work."* *"Sound commercial sense"* and *"good reasoning and analytical skills"* are sought beyond the obvious good academic grades. And *"if you've had the opportunity to take insolvency topics on the BVC but haven't, we'd want to know why."* Combined with *"rigorous standards,"* the fact that chambers ideally *"takes pupils on with a view to them becoming tenants"* means *"we sometimes don't fill all the pupillage places."*

The quality that defines successful applicants is *"the ability to take a commercial view on theoretical matters."* It is also described as *"the key"* to continuing good performance in an area that *"demands a practical approach"* to the problems of clients who *"expect you to fight tooth and nail for them."* It's not the same as family or crime practice where clients may lose their liberty or access to their children, nonetheless company insolvencies – and certainly personal bankruptcies – involve the collapse of livelihoods. As such, *"black letter expertise alone isn't enough."* As one pupil supervisor put it: *"It's all about a sound grasp of the business law environment. You're grap-*

*pling with the technical, legal issues and you're also almost guaranteed a dust-up in court."* Accordingly, pupils must quickly grasp the essentials of several modes of working.

At the end of the first six, *"feedback is gathered from every pupil supervisor and the pupillage committee grades the pupil."* Grade A means *"super talented,"* B means *"a good chance of tenancy,"* and C signifies *"slim prospects."* The C-grade pupil will be recommended to pursue a second six elsewhere. No one is forced to leave before the year is up, but *"we find it's fairest all round... no one is labouring under illusions."* Accordingly, *"the pressure is on from day one"* and pupils do their level best to impress. However, a system of rotating between supervisors every six weeks ensures *"pupils have lots of chances to make a good impression"* as well as exposing them to a broad range of work and people. The dominance of insolvency work leads to a certain continuity of experience. Said one junior tenant: *"We all basically do about 60% insolvency and 40% spin-offs from insolvency."*

Researching and composing written advices, *"drafting letters to clients and preparing for conferences"* are all standard tasks, as is getting used to *"the principles of real court work; the need to absorb relevant facts and research the law."* Variety emerges from the differing characteristics, seniority and training methodology of supervisors. *"Some are superb advocates,"* while *"others have an incredible eye for detail,"* observed one pupil. A junior recalled *"different training styles – some give you daily training, you do their work and go over it. Others give you a broader area to study, which you then discuss. Several give you mock applications to prepare and present."* The system involves practically every eligible member. Chambers additionally defines its training by way of *"heavy involvement for pupils"* and *"constant feedback, not just letting people sit in the dark."* The year is undoubtedly hard, but those who *"shine and impress"* are received well, especially if they possess "*a talent for inquiry, the ability to ask the right questions.*"

"*The incredibly complex nature*" of insolvency work means those who stay for a second six are "*rarely on their feet in court.*" They continue to watch and learn, "*observing mediations and advocacy*" and "*assisting in the drafting of skeleton arguments.*" The wait is worthwhile for those who make the grade, and a July tenancy decision is made in much the same way as the end-of-first-six cut. "*By late July, August and September, pupils start to take their own briefs;*" once in the swing of junior tenancy they are "*continuously in and out of court*" with Companies' Court applications and winding-up petitions. Said one source: "*I see our junior tenants and they've got smiles on their faces. Their brains are being pushed and they're advising everyone from small clients to the senior partners of law firms.*"

Members enjoy "*friendly working relationships,*" although "*we're not constantly in each other's pockets.*" Despite the cohesion of the set's external identity, a characteristic self-sufficiency leads individuals to "*work hard, but each in our own way.*" There is no afternoon tea, but "*there are regular Friday night drinks*" and an "*array of dinners*" as well as "*a convivial summer party in the Gray's Inn Walks.*" Pupils don't find it too hard to get involved, especially because "*supervisors take them along to everything with a professional angle, even if it is meals out with clients.*" All in all, we took away an impression of a modern, confident and self-assured set that is comfortable with its reputation. If you've a penchant for business or a nose for corporate disaster, this is the place for you.

# 4 Stone Buildings

**Chambers UK rankings:** Commercial litigation, company, financial services, fraud: civil, insolvency/corporate recovery

Size isn't everything and here is the set that proves it. With just 24 members, 4 Stone Buildings is a relative pygmy, yet that hasn't stopped it achieving the distinction of earning top slot in the table in the latest edition of *Chambers UK* that measures the ratio of individual rankings to size of set.

Originally a Chancery specialist, chambers' focus on company and commercial law kicked off in the 1970s with the arrival of eminent silk Peter Curry from leading commercial law firm Freshfields. His arrival also signalled the development of supplementary expertise, notably in insolvency, but also financial services and civil fraud. As any of you with half an eye on the commercial world will know, these strands have each proved to be rich seams of quality work. Today's crop of stellar QCs includes the likes of Robert Miles and head of chambers George Bompas, and the pedigree of the cases on which they worked is unquestioned. Their activities additionally demonstrate how the set's unofficial maxim of 'quality not quantity' continues to pay off. Members have been working on the BCCI litigation and, as in keeping with other top commercial sets, Equitable Life. Chambers also receives a considerable amount of overseas work, with the Bahamas and Hong Kong proving to be particularly common destinations for barristers looking to build up their Air Miles.

With insolvency matters at the core of chambers' business, the set's client base is typically composed of liquidators, administrators, bankers, company directors and accountants. For all these 'professional' clients, the ability to comprehend extremely technical concepts and then present reasoned conclusions in a clear and concise manner is crucial in the barristers they instruct. It's a similar story with the specialist company law instructions, who work in the realm of mergers and acquisitions, reorganisations of share capital, and company shareholder disputes including petitions under section 459 of the Companies Act. "*The days of clients coming humbly to barristers in their ivory towers are long gone,*" stressed one member. "*More than anything, you need commercial awareness to thrive in today's market.*"

Pupillage at 4 Stone Buildings is paper-heavy and you should expect far less face-to-face interaction with clients than your peers at common law sets. "*You have to be the sort of person who is happy to sit and read papers for hours at a time,*" confided a baby junior, so it is clearly not suitable for someone with a short attention span. The first six months are split between two pupilmasters, and the work involves the usual skeleton arguments and research projects. During this time other members of chambers may borrow you for assistance on cases, the idea being that "*you're exposed to as many differing viewpoints and styles as possible.*" It seems that pupils do have their uses – one very junior tenant recalled the sense of pride he felt when his skeleton argument was quoted verbatim by a judge. One of the undoubted highlights of pupillage is the time spent with Treasury Devil Jonathan Crow, who only takes instructions from government sources. "*The work is so interesting and of such monumental importance it's like you're a secret agent,*" said one excited pupil.

Pupils say their working hours are not unduly onerous, with 9am until 6.30pm the norm. We also noted that the assessment regime is considerably lighter than at some other top sets, the raison d'être being that the pupil is there to learn, not jump through hoops. As they are only guaranteed a first six, pupils are advised to arrange a second six elsewhere, although ideally they will acquit themselves well and be invited to extend their stay for a full twelve months. Should this be the case, the second six continues in much the same vein as the first because the work undertaken is relatively specialised and pupils will rarely be able or permitted to take their own instructions. This being the case, advocacy must wait until after pupillage when baby juniors are introduced to winding-up applications and other minor matters via the set's relationships with smaller and regional firms. Although there are no hard and fast rules, the set

tends to offer just one tenancy per year after a meeting of all members in July.

The recruitment of pupils operates with the same deadlines as, but outside of, the Olpas system. Having looked at the set's own application form we can tell you that it is quite minimalist in its approach. We are also able to advise that you should take care to convey a sense of "*clarity and articulacy*" when writing about your interests and motivations. On the academic front, there is no stated preference for a First over a 2:1 and equally it seems that the institution you attended is not the be-all and end-all. It is equally admirable that chambers telephones the referees of every single applicant for pupillage. An unassessed mini pupillage with chambers is advised but not mandatory.

If you are among the lucky 30 selected for the single round of interviews you will be presented with a problem question and given an hour's worth of preparation time before facing a panel that includes the influential senior clerk David Goddard (or "God" as he is occasionally referred to by established members). The question is company law-based – in recent years it has included the analysis of a balance sheet – although the recruiters are not looking for a candidate who merely parrots the law; they want someone who is able to "*digest the relevant facts quickly and then formulate an appropriately structured response that holds up under intense questioning.*" Make no mistake, the questioning will be intense, though a member of the pupillage committee emphasised that "*it's not an exercise in humiliation, we will only push you if we think you're on track. The harder the questions, the better you are probably doing.*" As well as showing grace under fire, it is "*mental agility and fluency*" that will tip the balance for the successful candidate. Do well in interview and you will be invited to spend a couple of days in chambers if you have not already undertaken a mini-pupillage with the set.

In spite of all the typical barristerial trappings of huge desks, carriage clocks and copies of *Coun-*

*try Life* in the waiting room, we left 4 Stone Buildings and its elegant setting within Lincoln's Inn with an underlying impression of informality. We believed the person who told us that *"anyone who takes themselves too seriously won't fit in here – we are the antidote to the pompous and stuffy Chancery sets that one tends to associate with Lincoln's Inn."* This could be because of the size of the set – *"everybody knows everybody else and there aren't any of those imposing factions that you find in the big sets."* It could equally stem from the thriving social scene within chambers. Afternoon tea is well attended (even though the tea itself continues to be *"treacle-like"*), and once a week it is held in the set's annexe at No. 6, just so everyone feels included. Outside working hours, members seem to enjoy each other's company and have been known to go ice skating together at Somerset House. Everyone congregates at the head of chambers' house for summer parties, although we suspect those who still need the Air Miles look forward most to the annual day trip to Paris for lunch.

Chambers prides itself on being *"a user-friendly set that punches above its weight"* and it is hard to disagree. The pupil who manages to display that hallowed combination of intelligence, business sense and amiability will fit in nicely at 4 Stone Buildings. Make it to tenancy and the future looks very bright indeed.

## 2 Temple Gardens

**Chambers UK rankings:** Clinical negligence, personal injury, professional discipline, professional negligence

Don't allow the chunky pupillage award offered by 2 Temple Gardens to leave you thinking that this set will occupy a magic circle law firm-style glass and steel palace. From outside it's more a case of blink and you'll miss it. Tucked away at the end of Middle Temple Lane, the way in is certainly

understated. Sure, the interior is smart, modern and airy, but there's nothing boastful about the décor. Yet, given that this leading common law set is among the top players in at least four different practice areas, there is plenty to boast about.

If you are looking for a pupillage that will give you an all-round experience of civil practice, 2tg is worth serious consideration. Chambers is organised into ten different practice groups. On the one hand, there is a commercial edge to the practice, with groups specialising in banking, construction, insurance and reinsurance, and on the other there's a strong common law base that includes, among other things, clinical and professional negligence, personal injury and an expanding employment team. The practice groups have become quite close knit, and we got the feeling that, although self-employed, these barristers see themselves as part of a wider team and are keen to work together to steer chambers forwards. As one of the practice managers explained: *"There's a real sense of cohesion within the different groups, and senior QCs will often organise training weekends for more junior members of chambers."*

Within a twelve-month pupillage, every pupil will be guaranteed time in at least three practice groups, the year being split into three four-month 'seats'. The pupil we met was in the twilight hours of her pupillage and had just been offered a tenancy at 2tg. She had begun the year shadowing a clinical negligence practitioner: *"As well as going to the High Court, I saw disciplinary proceedings in the General Medical Council and went to the Privy Council on an appeal."* Being a civil practice, there will be plenty of paperwork, whether it be drafting letters of claim (the kind of letter you don't want to get in the post), statements of case or written advices. The approach at 2tg is 'I'll show you mine, if you show you yours'. Pupils have a stab at a first draft of a piece of written work, and then sit down with the pupilmaster to compare it with the boss's version.

In the second, practising six the paperwork continues as before, but the difference is that some of it will start getting sent out to real clients. There will also be some court work. In an average week, pupils can expect to see the inside of a courtroom around three times, usually for quite straightforward things to start off with – small claims arising out of road traffic accidents or short interim applications in cases belonging to other members of chambers. To prepare pupils for D-Day, they all get the opportunity to go out and about with a junior tenant for a week. There are also three advocacy exercises to prepare, in which a 2tg QC sits as 'judge'. As a member of the pupillage committee explained: "*The advocacy exercises are there to help pupils. Their performance wouldn't be taken into account when making the tenancy decision, unless the pupil hadn't been doing well in other things, and their advocacy was especially good.*"

When it came to real advocacy, the pupil we met had her own set of top tips for the first appearance in court. First, "*get there early;*" second, "*bring plenty of photocopies of anything that you need to rely on;*" and finally, if all else fails, try "*winking at the judge.*" And they say that flattery will get you nowhere…

Of course, flattery won't get you a tenancy at 2tg. The tenancy decision is arrived at after a strict and comprehensive analysis of the work pupils have done for their PMs or others in chambers, and we were left in no doubt that the committee discounts remarks made by members unless they are based upon a piece of work.

As for getting your foot in through the door as a pupil, the recruitment process is similarly rigorous in its assessment of candidates' potential. The first round of the selection process brings together the 40 people who looked best on paper for something not dissimilar to a corporate weekend away. Spread over a whole Saturday, the lucky 40 will be invited to chambers, where, under close scrutiny, they will be divided into small groups and asked to perform a *Crystal Maze*-style challenge. Don't worry, there's nothing physical or gloopy involved and not a barmy host in sight – 2tg is interested

only in applicants' grey matter. Though we are under strict instructions not to say any more, what we are permitted to reveal is that there are also individual written tests and a series of talks by barristers and clerks. Oh, and a free lunch! The purpose of the day is to whittle the crowd down to 15 people, who will be subsequently be given an individual interview with an attendant legal problem to discuss. Apparently, those who are relatively new to the study of law shouldn't lose any sleep as the important thing at this stage is not simply regurgitating reams of statute and case law, but showing your potential to think like a barrister. Our source on the pupillage committee expanded on this point, telling us the panel was interested in "*an applicant's ability to see, in massive amounts of detail, what is relevant and what isn't.*"

So what makes a potential 2tg barrister? Obviously, the potential to become a great advocate is important. Think precision and detail rather than wowing the jury with your best Perry Mason because "*a Commercial Court judge is far more interested in someone who can master a bundle and get to the point really quickly.*" There's no doubt that "*raw intellectual grit*" is valued too, and we couldn't help but notice a heavy preponderance of Firsts from Oxbridge amongst the last ten junior tenants, but character will also take you a fair distance. 2tg is not simply looking for brainboxes, they're also looking for someone who is "*self-aware, personable and friendly.*"

Like many sets, 2tg has become streetwise about marketing itself to solicitors. As a pupil, you can guarantee that you'll be packed off for a week to one of the many leading firms that regularly instruct chambers in order to provide them with an extra pair of hands (and showcase your talents and general appeal). As the practice managers told us: "*It's certainly important for solicitors to get to meet people at the junior end of chambers.*" The various practice groups also run series of seminars for solicitors that all pupils are encouraged to attend. To facilitate chit-chat afterwards, there are usually drinks and a finger buffet at which the smart pupil will grab a pinwheel sandwich and network like crazy!

It's not all about impressing potential clients; these barristers know how to let their wigs down too, and regular Friday night drinks in chambers allow pupils, members and clerks to mingle. When asked to describe the atmosphere at 2tg, pupils and juniors agreed on this: *"It's not like some chambers where everyone keeps their doors shut, or some chambers where everyone is all over each other. It's a happy medium."* Happy medium it may be, middle of the road it is not.

# 3 Verulam Buildings

**Chambers UK rankings:** Banking & finance, commercial litigation, financial services, fraud: civil, insurance, professional negligence

After our last visit to 3VB we noted that the set appeared to have designs on entering the elite 'magic circle' of commercial sets. Judging by what we've heard it's almost there and although it hasn't quite joined the club yet, the application form has pretty much been filled in, put in an addressed envelope and is on the verge of being posted. If the membership decision was determined on the numbers of runners and riders each set had in the Equitable Life litigation then 3VB would be a shoo-in – various members are acting for both Ernst & Young and the executive directors. Members also played a big part in the film finance litigation that has been kicking around the courts. In addition to finance disputes – an area in which it is one of the two leading sets – chambers is historically strong on insurance and civil fraud, having been involved in cases of such magnitude as Polly Peck, Maxwell and Grupo Torras.

A respected stable of 56 barristers (of which 19 are silks) reside in the spacious premises on the eastern perimeter of Gray's Inn. In some ways, it would probably be more accurate to name the set 2-5 Verulam Buildings given that chambers occupies the lion's share of the short terrace, but we must concede that '3VB' does have a certain edge to it. The interior design now reflects this, as does the super-efficient team of practice managers that ensure the smooth running of day-to-day affairs.

Chambers has tried out a number of addresses and activities in its time. The modern-day banking and commercial focus can be traced back to former head of chambers Andrew Leggatt QC who got this side of things going in the 1970s. Since then chambers has had more than its fair share of prominent players. The silks that loom large in chambers today include the current head of chambers Christopher Symons and two Blairs, Bill and Michael (who are not related to each other but Bill is the PM's brother). Coming up through the ranks are a clutch of good names (among them Ali Malek, Andrew Sutcliffe, Adrian Beltrami and Sonia Tolaney), and it is a widely held view that the presence of real talent at all levels will stand the set in good stead in years to come.

A broad range of experiences are on offer to the 3VB pupil. Although the set is best known for its work in banking and insurance, individual practitioners are increasingly recognised for their expertise in areas such as media and entertainment and professional negligence. Abandon ideas of spending much time in court, especially in the early years of practice, because the 3VB barrister is *"not primarily an oral advocate."* The job is more about *"getting to grips with vast amounts of paper"* – in other words a lot of pleadings, skeleton arguments and opinions for the pupil to draft. It is for this reason that people who are able to be *"precise, meticulous and methodical"* flourish at the commercial Bar.

Pupils develop these attributes under the tutelage of four pupilmasters, who each guide them for three months. As an extra measure designed to maximise exposure to the entire range of work on offer in chambers, pupils are additionally allocated 'shadow' PMs, who provide a taster of the work more typical at the junior end. The second six does bring opportunities for pupils to undertake their own work, usually small-end matters such as masters' appointments and small claims. *"It's a real buzz finally appearing in front of a real judge after all the training,"* revealed a pupil.

This is clearly a set that tries to look after its pupils. Said one recruiter: *"We don't believe in the school of hard knocks. Everyone remembers how tough pupillage is so we have no intention of adding to the stress."* PMs and shadows acknowledge a duty to create an environment in which pupils perform to the best of their ability. *"We want to be able to sit back at the end of the year and feel that each pupil has had a fair crack of the whip."* Tenancy is decided in July, the membership basing its decision on reports produced on each pupil by their pupilmasters and anyone else who has seen their work during the year. The set prefers to make its judgement on the basis of how you get on with 'live' work as opposed to a series of contrived assessments. The evidence of recent years shows that pupils have taken their chances well, with a decent number being taken on as tenants.

The set's recruiters were frank about the sort of applicants that they're looking for. *"We're battling with the other commercial heavyweights for the same top characters,"* one admitted. 3VB currently offers the highest pupillage award at the Bar, no doubt in an attempt to let the brightest applicants know how seriously it wants them. Yet still, chambers finds itself making some shrewd calculations when offers are about to be made in August – *"there's no point making offers to people that you know are not going to accept."* The way of ensuring that you don't suffer the fate of being overlooked by virtue of your seemingly super candidate status is to ensure that you develop a personal rapport with the recruiters through a mini-pupillage. This three-day experience is not assessed as such but will result in the production of a slim report that is pushed in the direction of the pupillage committee should you decide to apply. You will be invited

to discuss your mini-pupillage experiences at first interview, so it's probably a good idea to keep your eyes open and make detailed notes about what you've seen and learned about chambers. The second interview is more formal, and discussion will centre on a pre-prepared problem that you are sent three days prior to proceedings. The candidate who is able to display evidence of *"structured thought and clarity of expression"* will edge ahead as this is most definitely a set that values logic and articulacy above most other characteristics.

Pupils are encouraged to attend the vast majority of chambers' social functions throughout the year, although when we enquired as to the reason for not inviting pupils to the Christmas dinner, the answers were uncharacteristically hazy. A desire to ensure that the pupil *"doesn't feel on edge"* was the stock response when we really pressed the point, but we can't help suspecting that it's more to do with the events of a couple of years ago when a pupil is alleged to have overdone it on the wine and in one fell swoop managed to administer a near-fatal blow to their tenancy chances. A more established venue for indulging in a few drinks is the Yorkshire Grey on Gray's Inn Road where the junior tenants take the pupils once a month.

3VB is recognised throughout the profession as a highly successful commercial outfit, and one that is particularly renowned for its standards of client service. We're of the opinion that pupillage here represents a tremendous opportunity for a young barrister to learn the commercial ropes, yet not be exposed to the stuffiness and pomp more readily associated with some of its competitors.

# Wilberforce Chambers

**Chambers UK rankings:** Chancery: commercial, Chancery: traditional, intellectual property, pensions, professional negligence, real estate litigation

# chambers reports

We suppose it had to happen at some point but it still doesn't make it any less of a surprise. The Chancery Bar has shed its crusty image, in favour of a sleeker, more modern approach to business. Presumably designed to wow the big commercial firms that bring the most valuable cases through the door, the change in style was a necessary response to the fact that the boundary between commercial cases and commercial Chancery cases was no longer as clear and the strict demarcation as to which sets handle each has been crumbling. To take some examples, barristers of both Chancery and non-Chancery persuasions have been involved in many of the major cases of recent times such as Barings, BCCI and Gruppo Torras. Similarly, Wilberforce barristers have encroached on the territory of the commercial sets, bringing (according to *Chambers UK*) an "intellectually rigorous," "formidable" and "incisive" style of advocacy to a variety of commercial cases. Although the set's image might be evolving, there is no mistaking the old-school pedigree of silks such as Edward Nugee, Jules Sher, David Lowe, Michael Barnes, Terence Mowschenson and Michael Bloch. Though members do stray into the QBD, it should be noted that the set's workload is still predominantly Chancery-based, with a considerable number of cases in the property, professional negligence and banking spheres. Members were extensively involved with the landmark undue influence case of Etridge that went all the way to the House of Lords and are acting for one of the defendant directors in the ongoing Equitable Life litigation.

The fact that Wilberforce retains its status as the leading set for traditional Chancery work (good old-fashioned trusts, probate, real property and that kind of thing) might excuse it for being set in its ways, yet Wilberforce seems happy to change many things. In a move that would have been unheard of in the old days, it has breached the traditional solicitor-barrister divide by adding a couple of partners from magic circle law firms to its list of members. One such is Anna Carboni, former IP chief at Linklaters. Her arrival has boosted the set's reputation in the IP field, where it was already involved in many of the leading cases. In trademarks and passing off, there was Mars v Nestlé (scraps over the shape of the POLO mint and the registrability of the slogan 'Have a Break') and on the patent side, the ICC arbitration Oxford Gene Technology v Affymetrix.

Most members of chambers are housed at No.8 New Square in the leafy surrounds of Lincoln's Inn, that bastion of Chancery practice and the setting for the opening scenes of Dickens' Bleak House. Its neighbours include several other Chancery sets and what can probably be described as a cluster of fairly traditional solicitors firms. Inside No.8 huge rooms with imposing desks and even more imposing bookcases are the norm on the lower floors where more senior members sit. As you climb the broad wooden staircase the rooms get smaller and smaller until only suitable for the humblest new tenant. From time to time a couple of the QCs bring their dogs into work – last time we visited, Terence Mowschenson's two King Charles Spaniels sprawled by the fireplace in his room. So far, so quaint. Cross over New Square to the modern building at No.16 and things are entirely different. Built on the site of 'The Boghouse' – toilets that dated back to 1693 – it is generously equipped with state-of-the-art conference facilities. The new clerks' room, complete with CCTV screens depicting all the comings and goings at number 8, is also up to the minute.

At Wilberforce the tenancy decision is made after six months. "*We don't believe in mucking people around or raising false hopes. We think six months gives a pupil enough time to make their mark.*" Jump through the hoop at this stage and then you can relax for a while. "*The emphasis is on learning in the second six, you've proved yourself by then, so it's not all about end product.*" If you're not successful at this point then you need to find a second six elsewhere sharpish, but chambers will do what it can to make the process easier. As for the set's track record for taking on pupils: in 2004 all three made the grade, in 2003 no one was taken on and the year before that one person came up with the goods.

Although it's undeniably a bonus to know where you stand early on, the flipside of the coin is that you have to hit the ground running in order to impress. The crucial period is split into three two-month spells with different supervisors. The tenancy decision will be largely based on their opinion of your performance, as they will be the providers of the vast majority of your work. Typically this will include writing opinions, drafting statements of case, producing skeleton arguments or preparing cross-examinations. The road to success at a top Chancery set is not always easy. As one practitioner put it: "*Chancery work is more intellectually challenging than the other branches of the law. You need to love the law in order to get the most out of it.*" This fondness must also extend to research-based activity in the library, as, unfortunately, the brilliant points made by your pupil supervisor in court will not just be plucked out of thin air. Although most of your time will be spent in chambers, the second six will provide the occasional county court hearing in which to hone your advocacy skills and thus ease the transition into tenancy.

If you're hoping to be recruited as a Wilberforce pupil you can choose one of two routes. Option one involves filling in chambers' own pupillage application form and trying to get on the list for a first interview. Option two bypasses the first interview stage, replacing it with a week-long assessed mini-pupillage. Whichever avenue you pursue, certain qualities will serve you well. "*The search is always for someone who is unflappable, self-assured and confident.*" In addition to impeccable academic credentials – incidentally chambers readily admits to liking CPE applicants and the pupil without a First is very much in the minority – a further judgement is made as to how well the candidate will get on with solicitors and clients. "*They may well have buckets of intelligence but do they have the ability to be articulate and forthcoming with everyone?*"

Members of similar vintage tend to stick together. More often than not, it is the set's numerous marketing events that bring all members together after work. The regular time for gathering is the "*universally popular*" fortnightly chambers lunch. "*Everyone makes an effort to attend and we try and ensure that the conversation doesn't just centre on the latest Chancery developments.*"

With its CCTV, sleek brochures and solicitor hires, Wilberforce makes a convincing argument that it has blown away the cobwebs associated with Chancery practice. The process of modernisation is what has kept Wilberforce at the forefront of its traditional areas of strength and it is what will enable it to develop a name in other chosen fields such as IP.

## Exchange Chambers

**Chambers UK rankings:** Commercial litigation, local government, personal injury, police law

With a ticket to ride in one pocket and a host of outdated stereotypes in the other we boarded the 9.18 from Euston to Liverpool's Lime Street and wondered what to expect from our visit to Exchange Chambers. What we found was a regional superset with a wide practice and some high-profile cases.

Exchange takes its name from its previous location at Exchange Flags outside Liverpool Town Hall. The set moved to Derby Square about 14 years ago and is now right on the doorstep of Liverpool Crown Court. There are a whopping 85 members, the majority in Liverpool and 25 or so in Manchester, where Exchange set up an annexe a few years back. Among the members are 11 silks, an impressive tally for a set outside London.

It is probably overstating things to describe the happenings of the past few years as a revolution, but there's little doubt that the make-up of the set's practice has changed considerably. Due in part to the excellence of former head of chambers John Kay QC (later Lord Justice) it was once the case that criminal work dominated. Now work is roughly split into three different areas: criminal, personal injury and commercial/Chancery. It is this last area that has grown the most of late, with the set now taking instructions on matters that might previously have been sent down to one of the London sets. This increased prominence is exemplified by instructions to act for opera singer Russell Watson in his management dispute, and instructions in relation to follow-on litigation arising out of the Enron insolvency.

The criminal team, meanwhile, hosts big name players such as Tim Holroyde QC and David Turner QC, the latter heavily involved in defending one of the directors of the company that employed the Chinese cockle pickers who died in the Morecambe Bay tragedy. In the personal injury group at Exchange, the presence of spinal injury specialist Bill Braithwaite QC is enough to ensure a valuable and varied caseload. As one would expect of a set with a long list of specialist barristers, the list of instructing solicitors is equally long – Exchange barristers work for Addleshaw Goddard, Halliwells, Burton Copeland and Pannone & Partners to name but a few. The set is also active prosecuting cases for HM Revenue & Customs, the Health and Safety Executive and the DTI.

Our magical mystery tour of chambers enabled us to cover every inch of the large single floor that accommodates the set's Liverpool-based practitioners. Step through from the hotel-like exterior and you're in the hub of chambers – in the main reception area with its potted plants and photos of members of the judiciary adorning the walls, barristers, clerks and admin staff bustle around. Separate waiting rooms prevent *"that embarrassing situation where company directors and alleged child molesters are sat next to each other; each thinking that the other is in the same situation."* Along the striking red corridors, barristers occupy rooms painted in various bold shades. Whether it's because of space limitations or simply that they're a sociable bunch, each room is shared by as many as six of them, often from differing practice groups.

The long and winding road to pupillage at Exchange Chambers starts with the Olpas form. When we visited plans were in the air to outsource the paper-sifting stage, and given that the set attracted nearly 600 applications last year you can see why. No matter who ends up looking at the form, a strong academic record will be the first consideration for the recruiter. Next, the question is whether the applicant has clearly researched the set or not. *"We want people who know what we're all about, a generic reason for choosing us will not impress."* It's a two-stage interview process here: showing that you possess *"leadership, presence and poise"* in the first 30-minute interview will improve your chances of being invited back to the second test of endurance. This lasts for two days and provides the opportunity to meet most members of chambers whilst also undertaking a series of different advocacy exercises. At the end of day one, you get the chance to 'unwind' by going out for a meal with some members. Go easy on the wine though, your social skills are being assessed.

A day in the life of an Exchange pupil is undoubtedly a demanding one. *"Beneath all of the banter and all the fun, we work really hard and expect the same from our pupils,"* confided one source. Whilst you're not quite working eight days a week, you evidently have to be prepared to adopt the *"ferocious work ethic"* shared by members if you want to be a success. A common law pupil has one pupil supervisor and two deputies who specialise in differing practice areas. The pupil drafts claims and writes opinions for his or her supervisor and is expected to be up to scratch within about six months. During this period, work will also be undertaken for other members of chambers in order to ensure every section on the Bar Council checklist is ticked off. In the second six, pupils can take on their own work and end up travelling a fair amount. By all accounts it is "*a terrifyingly pure adrenaline rush*" when you're on your feet for the first time. Let's hope it's addictive because you'll be doing a lot of it as the years go by. On the criminal side, work tends to be a mixture of bail applications, mentions and summary trials. There is also the chance to practise pure commercial law if that's the route that appeals to you. This route requires a six-month stay in Manchester as this is where a number of the commercial practitioners are based. If you want to go down this route, you should flag it up in your Olpas form.

Regular review meetings are held with the pupil's supervisor and the chambers director and this is the opportunity to "*highlight any problems and underline all the positives.*" At Exchange, it seems nobody is afraid to ask for a little help from their friends when the need arises. "*We're always sharing problems with each other.*" Nonetheless, the ability to think for yourself is highly prized: "*If a pupil shows initiative, then we're very happy.*" Tenancy prospects are remarkably healthy for pupils at this set. To not get taken on "*you're going to have to do something pretty awful*" and this might well explain the degree of rigour when recruiting pupils. The supervisor we spoke to summed it up as "*equality of effort,*" saying: "*We've obviously seen some potential in the pupil and we feel that we've failed if we don't allow it to be fulfilled.*"

It seems that the legendary Scouse wit is alive and well at Exchange Chambers. Members of all levels of seniority eat lunch together in one of the larger rooms, and joint head of chambers David Turner QC, who has a reputation for being "*a bit of a wag,*" is especially adept at bringing pupils out of their shells with his "*wicked sense of humour.*" Friday night drinks at a local bar are always "*a bit of a laugh*" and have been known to end up as "*a bit of a session.*" Chambers' Christmas party involves a group lunch and then "*it descends from there.*" Speaking of descents, it has been known for a group of members to jump an Easyjet flight for a weekend of Alpine skiing.

Everyone we spoke to loved Liverpool and its way of life. Exchange Chambers is very much the big noise in town right now and it has ambitions to be *the* set in the North West. In order to thrive here, your commitment to the city and to the work must go further than being able to whistle 'A Hard Day's Night.'

## Deans Court Chambers

Chambers UK rankings: Crime, family, health & safety, personal injury

For ten points, what links footballer and impromptu kung fu legend Eric Cantona with mass-murderer Harold Shipman? You guessed it: their criminal trials both involved barristers from Deans Court chambers (defending Cantona and prosecuting Shipman, in case you wondered). High-profile work is something this leading Manchester set is well accustomed to receiving, which is understandable given its pedigree. With a history that goes back a good hundred years, chambers has produced its fair share of silks over the decades and, in turn, sent its fair share of them to the senior judiciary. At the time of writing, there were three former members sitting on the High Court Bench, including Mr Justice Ryder who we understand to be a bit of a spring chicken as judges in the Family Division go.

As the name suggests, chambers used to occupy premises within the confines of Deans Court, close to the law courts. However, gradual expansion (currently there are 61 tenants) led to a move to roomier accommodation in the legal enclave of St John's Street. We get the feeling that, when it comes to painting and decorating at least, there's a certain amount of keeping up with the Joneses amongst the residents of the street. Rather than Vera Duckworth stone cladding, the look is a subtle blend of the modern with the traditional. The smart glass tablet bearing the names of the tenants blends in discreetly with the grand, columned Georgian entranceway. Inside, the theme continues, comfortable leather furniture mingling with linear vases, garnished with giant Linda Barker twiglets. A solicitor coming here for the first time would instantly recognise a set doing rather well for itself.

For anyone looking for a pupillage that will give them a taste of both civil and criminal work, this is a good place to apply; though as the senior clerk was eager to stress, members see themselves as *"multidisciplinary specialists rather than generalists."* Deans Court is divided into a series of practice groups, including civil litigation (PI being a particular forte), family, crime, and health and safety and regulatory, which is apparently a booming area at the moment. Win a pupillage here and the assumption is that you are here to stay unless something pretty unexpected happens: in the last decade, all pupils have been given tenancy. With this in mind, the pupillage committee *"tends to recruit pupils with a view to filling a space within a particular practice area,"* and so it is advisable to check that the spaces available at the bottom end of the members' list match with your career aspirations before putting in an application.

Pupils will normally spend the pupillage year with just one common law pupil supervisor, but throughout the first six, they will also be seconded to the family and criminal groups for a month each. Chambers also tries to accommodate individual's interests where possible. One of the pupils we met had followed the CPE route to the Bar: *"I knew that crime interested me but I hadn't had much exposure to civil work."* He was allowed to split his time between a civil and a criminal supervisor.

This is a year of metamorphosis. Your supervisor will of course help you to develop the bare bones of your drafting skills and expose you to plenty of advocacy, but being a barrister is about much more than this, and *"the interpersonal dynamic is important too."* You may have achieved a double First from Oxford, but can you strike up a good relationship with instructing solicitors and clerks? At Deans Court, pupillage is just as much about learning to be commercially minded and client-focused as it is about honing legal skills. To quote one of the supervisors: *"The barrister that solicitors keep coming back to will be the one who they, and ultimately their client, can get on with."*

Once the second six comes, *"they keep you on your toes;"* indeed the clerks *"would have you on your feet every day if they had their way!"* Pupils usually have a second six practice that is predominantly civil or predominantly criminal, though it's common for them to undertake a bit of both if required. There's no such thing as a typical week here: you could be in the Crown Court in the morning doing a plea in mitigation, then off to the county court in the afternoon to deal with a PI small claim. What makes the experience of Manchester pupils different from their London counterparts is the sheer volume of available court work, even for pupils who undertake a largely civil training. So much so that *"on occasion, we have to ask the clerks to take us out of court for a day or so, so that we can get the paperwork done."*

On gaining tenancy things change, and the baby juniors will normally become a part of one or more of the closely knit practice groups. The work gets progressively more demanding so that, instead of handling interim applications for other peoples' cases, juniors are given small trials of their own. An acknowledgement that there is still much to be learnt, baby juniors will be led by more senior members of chambers on more complex cases. And whenever a QC picks up a particularly interesting case, *"the clerks will try to find time out for juniors so that they can sit in and observe."*

There are plenty of formal and informal opportunities for young barristers to market themselves, whether this is through giving seminars at solicitors firms or through the regular dinners and quiz nights held for solicitors, which we are told *"regularly descend into debauchery."* We didn't dare ask for details.

While pupils and junior tenants alike agree that they managed to maintain a social life as well as a working life, some supervisors will inevitably crack the whip harder than others, including one who makes a point of *"shaking the student hangover out of his pupils."* Be prepared to convert that student hangover into a barrister's hangover at times though, because *"the Northern Circuit is a very sociable place to be."* The Manchester Bar is nowhere near as vast as the London Bar and the 40 or so Mancunian pupils maintain contact throughout the year, frequently getting together in the pub to swap notes. There are also formal social events organised by chambers, such as the annual Christmas meal, and the practice groups regularly organise Friday night trips to the pub. Apparently, for the criminal group *"any night of the week will do."*

If you're serious about applying to Deans Court, a mini-pupillage is highly recommended. We noticed that the academic backgrounds of many of the tenants betray a rather northern flavour, and whilst Oxbridge is certainly represented, its presence is well in proportion to other universities. In recent years, many recruits have opted for Manchester Metropolitan BVC, and it's probably fair to say that studying at MMU will provide students with a good opportunity to expose themselves (and their advocacy skills) to members of chambers, many of whom lecture there from time to time. We should also point out that there are people here who have no direct connection with Manchester at all. Understandably though, chambers expects applicants to be able to show that they are committed to the idea of living in the area and working on the Northern Circuit.

We can see the draw of the Manchester Bar. A lower cost of living and practising in a city that now gives London a run for its money in terms of entertainment and culture; the opportunity to rise up the ranks to the dizzy heights of the High Court – it's a miracle that the London Bar hasn't upped and left. Indeed that's exactly what one of Deans Court's pupil supervisors had done. Born and bred in Manchester, he first knocked on the door of chambers (that's how it used to be done) for some work experience when he was still in short trousers. He then went to London to seek his fortune, but the draw of the North, and with it a more varied practice, became irresistible. Now, some 20 years after being called, he's back to stay. We say, why wait the 20 years?

## Kings Chambers

**Chambers UK rankings:** Chancery, clinical negligence, commercial litigation, environment, insolvency, local government, partnership, planning

As they say at Old Trafford: if you can see the Pennines it's going to rain, and if you can't it's already raining. The day we visited Manchester's most up-market set, Kings Chambers, it was bucketing down. Thankfully (and appropriately), the set shares King Street with Armani, Pink's, Whistles and a score of other lovely retailers with terribly convenient doorways in which to 'shelter' from the downpour.

Before settling in King Street, Kings Chambers tried several Manchester addresses on for size over the 60-odd years since it was established by Charles Norman Glidewell just after WWII. Town and country planning legislation was, of course, one of the new initiatives introduced by the post-war government, and CNG and his colleagues wasted no time in getting involved and developing a name as a specialist planning set. Practice has broadened over the years to incorporate all manner of local government work – public inquiries, education (including school expulsions), highways, residential care homes and environmental prosecutions. Today, around a third of chambers' business falls into this category.

Some 40% of business falls within the commercial/Chancery sphere and emanates from big national firms of solicitors (DLA, Eversheds, Addleshaws etc) right down to sole practitioners. The set also receives instructions from London firms with business in the Manchester District Registry. The remaining quarter of chambers' work is made up of common law matters. To clarify, no one handles family or crime work so, effectively, chambers operates exclusively in the privately funded arena. It's a deliberate policy and one that marks Kings Chambers out from the majority of Manchester sets. The plan for the future is to boost the commercial and Chancery work and to continue building a reputation for PI – all through organic growth and individual lateral hires. Said the senior clerk: "*We may not be the biggest in Manchester, but we are the strongest. Though we don't want to be a megaset.*"

Yet chambers is a sizeable set with eight silks among its 62 members. It is also worth noting that chambers additionally has premises at 5 Park Square in Leeds; "*everyone is expected to work in both places and people can voluntarily physically locate themselves in Leeds.*" Its three practice groups operate quite distinctly. Members generally only work in one field, though frequently they share rooms with colleagues from another practice group. Pupils are recruited only after the needs of each group have been assessed and all pupillages are specialist. When we visited, chambers had just one pupil, who was being trained as a commercial and Chancery practitioner. While there is no guarantee of tenancy at the end of the year, no pupil has been disappointed in the past seven years. "*If we take three pupils, it's because there is room for three tenants,*" said one of chambers' recruiters; "*it means pupils can support each other and not worry about showing weakness to each other.*" As for bidding farewell to a pupil showing slower progress in their first six, we were told by one pupilmaster: "*I've seen people turn around after fairly shaky first sixes and become great on their feet.*"

Recruits are allocated to two PMs for six months each. In the first six, it sounds as if the pupil is looked after very well; "*they're not like a puppy you get for Christmas and put in a shoebox!*" Indeed, the current pupil told us: "*My first six pupilmaster made a lot of sacrifices for me: not having holidays and picking me up in the mornings before going to court...I felt like my pupilmaster was in loco parentis.*" As he or she will be in court most days, so will you. The rest of the time you'll have a stab at the PM's written work and generally be "*housetrained.*" One explained her approach: "*I set the pupil some work at the beginning of the week, having made an assessment of the time they'll have available. I'm really hot on encouraging them to learn to time-manage and work to deadlines.*" As for accompanying her to court, "*they see all the papers and then I'll set them an exercise to summarise the key points of the case or to prepare a written piece outlining the cross-examination. After the hearing we'll have a debrief and I'll explain to them that's why I did what I did.*" She continued: "*We make sure they maintain absolute, utmost propriety, because if you don't have your reputation...*" Well indeed, but what exactly is this set's reputation? "*We're seen as the big swots; a bit geeky!*" A certain degree of aloofness stems from the fact that "*we've the biggest turnover and because we don't do crime, we're not sitting around in the robing room chatting for three hours with other barristers.*"

Towards the end of the first six, pupils are encouraged to go to court and conferences with baby juniors in order to experience small claims hearings, case management conferences, fast track trials and any kind of district judge's appointment. Second six pupils gain independence (though they still sit with and are guided by a PM) and begin to earn their own living. We asked the current pupil how he'd spent the previous week and his response might surprise someone in a London second six. Monday had been spent on half a dozen winding-up applications and a directions hearing. On Tuesday he'd resisted an application for the stay of a warrant for possession of a residential property. On Wednesday a multi-track trial had been scheduled, though it settled; on Thursday he'd applied to set aside a judgement in default concerning the enforcement of a guarantee on a loan, and then he finished up the week with a bankruptcy and a small claim. "*The difference between London and Manchester at the junior end,*" he told us, "*is that we're in court on at least a daily basis.*"

The pace is certainly frenetic and "*you'll prepare things the night before.*" This means long hours. "*Chambers won't tolerate anything that is not excellent – that's the benchmark and that's what chambers is built on.*" He also thought that while the first six was all about teaching him "*clarity of thought,*" his second-six PM was intent on teaching him a "*combative and competitive*" style and "*imbuing me with resilience.*"

Everyone uses first names around chambers (clerks too), and when work allows there are visits to the pub and five-a-side football matches. "*People have always got time for each other and there are no door-slammers.*" We're told chambers has "*a mixed bag of members,*" which makes for "*interesting debates at lunch.*" These relate to everything from "*Coronation Street, football and gossip to stories about judges...there's a great oral tradition on the Northern Circuit.*" Pupils are more than welcome to join in, and as a matter of fact, they have central role in the lunchroom – making the tea. The idea is that it helps them to get to know people, but we dare say it's a chore no one misses after the pupillage year is out.

The first step for any student hopeful is to attend the set's annual 'mini-pupillage fair', a three-day event for around 25 students. Everyone in

chambers is involved and students are put in groups for court visits, advocacy workshops, guest speakers (a district judge, the local law society, the old head of chambers telling circuit stories), tea with each practice group and a night in the pub. When we suggested it sounded like the legal version of Glastonbury, no one disagreed. "*There's no drugs though!*" Make it to a pupillage interview and you can expect a gentle chat about your CV, more testing questions about the area of law in which you're interested and some questions on current issues. "*We want people who are personable and have a real interest in chambers and the area of law they're applying for. And they need a bit of backbone; they must be able to justify their position.*"

One other day you'll need a bit of backbone is the day chambers holds its Christmas lunch. At 11am, members and staff decamp to a restaurant in Chinatown, leaving the pupils "*home alone*" to man the phones. Every year without fail the partygoers play pranks on them. The current pupil had taken a call from a Court of Appeal judge's clerk who sounded suspiciously like the senior clerk. After their ordeal, pupils join their colleagues to eat, drink and sing karaoke. What more could you ask for?

# St Johns Buildings

**Chambers UK rankings:** Clinical negligence, crime, family, personal injury

Guarded at one end by Deansgate and pouring into one of the few inner-city parks at the other is St John Street, a pocket of legal Manchester that's full of Georgian charm. Our subject set plays a distinct and noteworthy part in this microcosm of the Bar. Having folded three and a half chambers into one superset in the last four years, it is now the largest in Manchester. Some 105 members (including ten silks) handle common law, crime, family, mental health and commercial cases.

A quick romp through SJB's history informs much. The rump of the set was originally formed in the late 1940s at No.28 by a group of Jewish barristers, frustrated at not being able to find tenancy elsewhere. Their legacy can be seen today in SJB's diversity of membership and belief in the importance of fairness and respect. Now that many other parts of the Bar have discovered such concepts, there's less need for chambers to be defined by these traits. However, any reader concerned about whether they are male enough, white enough, straight enough, or had passed through a sufficiently established school or university, should stop worrying. As one source said: "*No.28 had an equal opportunities policy before the phrase was ever devised.*" Yet from quirky, nonconformist beginnings, 28 grew into an establishment set and delivered more than its fair share of senior members to the bench, including the first female High Court judge, Dame Joyanne Bracewell.

In 2002, No.28 merged with its next-door neighbour at 24a, a set that came into existence a quarter of a century earlier. Forget any notions of 70s' idealism, we were left concluding that "*hungrier*" crime-heavy 24a had more in common with Thatcher's ambition-driven 80s than the philosophical liberalism of the preceding decade. Two years on from the first coupling, the doors opened to Merchant Chambers' commercial barristers and in September 2005 another ten practitioners came over from Queen's Chambers. What has resulted is a well-structured organisation with distinct clerking teams and formalised practice groups. In the civil group there are around 35 members (some of whom only handle employment law); the family group has more than 20; crime weighs in at around 40 members and the commercial group has ten. The mergers were not based merely on practice considerations but also on a belief that, culturally, the three sets could mesh together.

SJB is nothing if not well managed...masterminded even. The relationship between barrister and senior clerk is always an intriguing one, and SJB's Chris Ronan is clearly one part business heavyweight and one part agony aunt. Every month pupils climb on to his metaphorical couch for a deconstruction of their progress and goals, and it doesn't stop when they gain tenancy. One barrister was quite happy to admit: "*Chris rules your life...he shows you all the feedback, what you did and what you billed.*" We heard no complaints. There's also a safety net in the shape of the practice groups – "*You are never on your own as you work in teams, and you're constantly up against each other in court. In the Salford robing room, you'll see five, six or even seven other members of chambers...you could almost hold a meeting.*"

Believing that attempting anything other than a specialised pupillage would be nonsensical, SJB recruits pupils only after assessing the business needs of each practice group and matching the recruit's character to the particular pupilmaster to whom they'll be assigned. This approach stems from a fundamental principle that every pupil should secure tenancy. The chair of the pupillage committee couldn't remember when someone had last been refused it, and told us: "*If someone goes off the rails in pupillage, it's our job to get them back on...if they are here, we want to look after them and develop them, inculcating them with chambers' ethos.*"

Which leads us nicely to the subject of what SJB now believes in after its transformation into a superset. Using members' own words, it goes something like this: "*Absolutely proper preparation, consistency every time you turn out for a client, careful marshalling of thoughts, always checking the law, aspiring to the highest standards, being non-judgmental about the people you meet.*" And for pupils, "*recognising that everyone [at court] has more experience than you...including the lady behind the sandwich counter.*" SJB runs a two-stage pupillage interview process, and those who make the "*dispiritingly long*" shortlist for the first interview will be sent a problem to prepare. Make it to the second stage and, an hour before facing the interview panel, you'll be handed a mock brief for, say, a plea in mitigation. With experience as a recorder, the chair of the pupillage committee is perfectly placed to play the judge. "*I'm looking for good logical analysis,*" he told us; "*someone who can identify a good point from a bad one. If I challenge people, I like someone to know when to push a point and when to stop.*"

When we visited SJB, two pupils were midway through tornado-like second sixes, one specialising in civil matters and the other in crime. We spoke with the latter about life on the first rung of the ladder and a second six with more court time than your average tearaway teenager. "*I have worked every day,*" he said; "*mostly mags' work and two thirds of it prosecuting for the CPS, which is a lot of work in a short space of time and good experience for fact management and time management.*" You'll get into court for 10am having had the papers for just a couple of hours. "*You've an early start because there's a lot to do,*" although the magistrates' court is notorious for defendants or witnesses not showing up. If you have seven sets of instructions and all but two are no shows, "*you could be done by 11am.*" Much of the time you're up against a solicitor who could have had the case for a year, and you have "*maybe 12 minutes to read the file and then be ready to fight against this person and conduct a cross-examination.*" Everything about the first six is designed to prepare you for the onslaught of the second. "*I was in court every day then too, the majority of the time with my pupil-master, although I also got time with other criminal practitioners.*" First-six pupils must all experience some work outside their chosen field; in the case of a crime pupil this might mean two weeks spent with a civil practitioner working on personal injury cases.

A young junior specialising in family law (with a bit of crime thrown in for good measure) talked of an equally full-on schedule. "*I am in court every day...I have to ask if I want days out.*" You really have to drive, because your patch is extensive: "*You could

be in Preston for a hearing and you'll get a call asking 'Can you go to Lancaster for a bench warrant?' Or you'll be asked to do an ex parte domestic violence injunction when you've just put your bag down after a day in court.*" Sometimes you'll end up scribbling down directions on the back of a paper towel and tearing off to arrive at the next venue, where you'll be handed the file just as the bench comes in. In what can only be described as an understatement, our source said: "*You've got to be adaptable!*"

Will a career at the Manchester Bar ringfence you into the Northern Circuit? Apparently not. Although for our pupil, Manchester was big and crime-ridden enough to keep him in the city's courts most of the time, a family law QC told us he'd also appeared in Derby, Nottingham, Birmingham and London in the past year. Yet the strength of their desire to be in Manchester was obvious in all those we met. The silk spoke of "*a village atmosphere where most barristers know each other.*" He also felt that, in a city of Manchester's size, better relationships could be made with the wider professional community – "*You get to know most of the paediatricians, solicitors and social workers.*" Our junior told us: "*I would have gone to London if I thought for one moment that being in Manchester would have impeded me.*" She readily admitted: "*I am ambitious,*" but after joining SJB, "*I knew I would spend 40 years here without having to move.*" From up north, the London Bar isn't something to aspire to.

In the basement of SJB is a room with a large red table. It is no ordinary table. It is the epicentre of everything. Here at this table, you and your lunchtime sandwich will make friends and grow comfortable with your seniors. You will be initiated into the fine traditions of black humour and general gossip. You will become accepted as a colleague. Your mission, should you be awarded pupillage, is to find that table on your first day and to sit and eat. The rest of your career will unfold from there...

# barristers a-z

# Blackstone Chambers (I Mill QC and T Beazley QC)

Blackstone House, Temple, London EC4Y 9BW   DX: 281
Tel: (020) 7583 1770   Fax: (020) 7822 7350
Email: pupillage@blackstonechambers.com
Website: www.blackstonechambers.com

| | |
|---|---|
| **No of Silks** | 27 |
| **No of Juniors** | 38 |
| **No of Pupils** | 4 (current) |

**contact**
Miss Julia Hornor
Practice Manager

**method of application**
OLPAS

**pupillages (p.a.)**
12 months **4-5**
Required degree grade
**Minimum 2:1**
**(law or non-law)**

**income**
Award **£35,000**
Earnings not included

**tenancies**
Junior tenancies offered
in last 3 years **50%**
No of tenants of 5 years
call or under **10**

## chambers profile
Blackstone Chambers occupies modern, fully networked premises in the Temple.

## type of work undertaken
Chambers' formidable strengths lie in three principal areas of practice: commercial, employment and public law. Commercial law includes financial/business law, international trade, conflicts, sport, media and entertainment, intellectual property and professional negligence. All aspects of employment law, including discrimination, are covered by Chambers' extensive employment law practice. Public law incorporates judicial review, acting both for and against central and local government agencies and other regulatory authorities, all areas affected by the impact of human rights and other aspects of administrative law. Chambers recognises the increasingly important role which mediation has to play in dispute resolution. Three members are CEDR accredited mediators.

## pupil profile
Chambers looks for articulate and intelligent applicants who are able to work well under pressure and demonstrate high intellectual ability. Successful candidates usually have at least a 2:1 honours degree, although not necessarily in law.

## pupillage
Chambers offers four (or exceptionally five) 12 month pupillages to those wishing to practise full-time at the Bar, normally commencing in October each year. Pupillage is divided into four sections and every effort is made to ensure that pupils receive a broad training. The environment is a friendly one; pupils attend an induction week introducing them to the Chambers working environment. Chambers prefers to recruit new tenants from pupils wherever possible. Chambers subscribes to OLPAS; applications should be made for the summer season.

## mini pupillages
Assessed mini pupillages are available and are an important part of the application procedure. Applications for mini pupillages must be made by 30 April; earlier applications are strongly advised and are preferred in the year before pupillage commences.

## funding
Awards of £35,000 per annum are available. The pupillage committee has a discretion to consider applications for up to £9,000 of the pupillage award to be advanced during the BVC year. Since Chambers insists on an accessed mini pupillage as part of the overall application procedure, financial assistance is offered either in respect of out of pocket travelling or accommodation expenses incurred in attending the mini pupillage, up to a maximum of £200 per pupil.

# Cloisters

Cloisters, 1 Pump Court, Temple, London, EC4Y 7AA
Tel: (020) 7827 4000  Fax: (020) 7827 4100
Email: clerks@cloisters.com
Website: www.cloisters.com

| | |
|---|---|
| **No of Silks 1** | 3 |
| **No of Juniors** | 40 |
| **No of Pupils** | 3 |

**contact**
pupillage@cloisters.com

**method of application**
via OLPAS

**pupillages (p.a.)**
3 for 12 month

## chambers profile
Cloisters is a leading set with particular expertise in employment, equality, discrimination and human rights, personal injury and clinical negligence, media and sport, and public and regulatory law. Cloisters is known for its legal excellence, approachability, superb customer service and cost-effectiveness. It recruits only barristers who can offer these qualities.

## type of work undertaken
Cloisters acts for both applicants and respondents in all its specialist areas. Cloisters in 2003 was the first barristers chambers to ever win the The Lawyer 'Employment Team of the Year' award. In 2005, Cloisters appears in 19 of the 50 cases to watch chosen by the respected employment commentator Michael Rubenstein. The Cloisters Personal Injury Team had a very strong 2004, appearing in many landmark cases. One of their specialisms is in cases involving occupational stress or bullying at work, which contains elements of both personal injury and employment law. Members of the clinical negligence team brought in more than £60m for claimants last year. They handle a full range of cases, including cases worth more than £5m. The Cloisters sport practitioners handle disciplinary regulations, consultative work, litigation, non-professional sporting activity cases and matters arising from sports cases such as employment or contractual issues.

## pupil profile
Chambers welcomes applications from outstanding candidates from all backgrounds and academic disciplines, including lawyers coming late to the bar.

## pupillage
Chambers offers 3 twelve month pupillages to those wishing to practise full-time at the bar, normally commencing in October each year. Each pupil is supervised and the supervisor changes every 3 months to show the pupil different areas of practice. Second six pupils will be allocated work by clerks subject to availability of work and pupil ability.

## mini-pupillage
Applications should be made in writing to Anna Beale with accompanying CV.

## funding
Cloisters offers three funded pupillages each year. Each pupil will receive an award (currently £25,000 per year). Pupils can also ask for an advance.

# A-Z Barristers

# Furnival Chambers

Chambers of Andrew Mitchell QC
32 Furnival Street, London EC4A 1JQ
Tel: (020) 7405 3232 Fax: (020) 7405 3322
Website: www.furnivallaw.co.uk

## chambers profile
Furnival Chambers was established 1985. It is an energetic and progressive leading criminal set and the leading set in the field of asset forfeiture and confiscation.

## type of work undertaken
Chambers undertakes serious criminal cases across the board but enjoys particular expertise in:

**Asset Forfeiture & Confiscation:** The asset forfeiture team specialises in money laundering prosecutions, mutual assistance and confiscation proceedings in the criminal courts, and injunctive and receivership work in the civil courts. Members of the team include the authors of the leading practitioners' textbook and regularly conduct cases in Commonwealth and Caribbean jurisdictions.

**Extradition:** Representing both individuals and foreign states. Members have advised and appeared in proceedings relating to Enron and the Madrid train bombings.

**Serious & Complex Fraud:** Members have advised and appeared in Guinness, Blue Arrow, BCCI, Goldman Sachs and many other significant SFO trials.

**Terrorism:** Members appeared in the trial of the Gloucester shoe bomber, the first Al Qa'eda funding prosecution post 9/11, the Afghan Stansted hijacking, the "Ricin" conspiracy and significant IRA trials.

**Sexual Offences:** Members appeared in the Deep Cut trial and R v Mohammed Dica.

## pupil profile
Pupils will spend two months during their first six months with the asset forfeiture team. Applicants are expected to have excellent academic qualifications and an ability to absorb complex documentary material.

## pupillage
Further information regarding Chambers' pupillage policy is available on the Chambers website. Chambers operate a compulsory in-house advocacy course which pupils must pass before being permitted to practise in their second six months. Pupils can, therefore, expect to be well prepared for an exceptionally busy second six.

## mini pupillages
Assessed mini-pupillages are available. Applications should be made in writing to Clara Milligan (Chambers Administrator) with accompanying CV.

contact
Clara Milligan
(Chambers Administrator)
pupillage@furnivallaw.co.uk

method of application
OLPAS summer season
2006 for 2007

income
1st 6 months
£7,500
2nd 6 months
£7,500

tenancies
6

# 2 Hare Court

2 Hare Court, Temple, London EC4Y 7BH
Tel: (020) 7353 5324   Fax: (020) 7353 0667
Email: clerks@2harecourt.com
Website: www.2harecourt.com

| | |
|---|---|
| No of Silks | 11 |
| No of Juniors | 36 |
| No of Pupils | 2 |

**contact**
Jeremy Benson QC

**method of application**
OLPAS (summer)

**pupillages (p.a.)**
Two 12 month pupillages
Minimum degree 2:1

**tenancies**
According to ability

**annexes**
None

## chambers profile
2 Hare Court is well established as one of the leading sets specialising in criminal law. Members of Chambers defend and prosecute at all levels in London, throughout England and Wales and overseas, and are experienced in advising parties from the commencement of the investigation, including issues arising from international judicial assistance. Chambers has a strong tradition of representation both on the Bar Council and Criminal Bar Association.

## type of work undertaken
Chambers has considerable experience in high profile cases involving murder, corporate manslaughter, terrorism, police corruption, drug trafficking, sexual offences and internet pornography as well as those involving child witnesses and has increasingly specialised in commercial fraud and international money laundering. Individual tenants also provide specialist expertise in associated fields including immigration, licensing and health and safety.

## pupil profile
Chambers select as pupils articulate and well motivated individuals of high intellectual ability who can demonstrate sound judgement and a practical approach to problem solving. Candidates should have at least a 2.1 honours degree.

## pupillage
Chambers normally offers two 12 month pupillages starting in September. The year is divided into two six month periods although pupils are assigned to a different pupil master for each of the four months to ensure experience in different areas of crime. Chambers pays for the "Advice to Counsel" course and runs their own in-house advocacy training.

## mini pupillages
The programme runs throughout the year with one mini pupil taken each week and two each week in the summer. Applicants must be at least 18 years old and either be studying for Higher Education qualification or on or about to start CPE or BVC course. Please see the website for further details of the scheme, the application process and to download an application form.

## funding
12 month pupils will be sponsored through a combination of an award scheme, guaranteed earnings and additional earnings. No clerks' fees or deductions are taken from earnings.

2 HARE
COURT

Community
Legal Service

Quality Mark - Legal Services
Accredited Chambers

# Maitland Chambers (incorporating 9 Old Square)

7 Stone Buildings, Lincoln's Inn, London WC2A 3SZ
Tel: (020) 7406 1200   Fax: (020) 7406 1300
Email: clerks@maitlandchambers.com
Website: www.maitlandchambers.com

## chambers profile
Chambers UK has rated Maitland as the pre-eminent commercial Chancery litigation set every year since its merger in 2001.

## type of work undertaken
Chambers is instructed on a very wide range of cases – from major international litigation to county court disputes. Much of the work is done in London, though the set frequently advises and appears for clients in other parts of the United Kingdom and abroad. Members are recommended as leaders in their field in commercial Chancery, company, charities, insolvency, media and entertainment, traditional Chancery, property litigation, partnership, pensions, banking, energy, tax, agriculture and professional negligence.

## pupil profile
Academically, Maitland Chambers looks for a first or upper second. Pupils must have a sense of commercial practicality, be stimulated by the challenge of advocacy and have an aptitude for and general enjoyment of complex legal argument.

## pupillage
Pupils sit with at least three different barristers but spend their first few months with one supervisor in order that the pupil can find his or her feet and establish a point of contact which will endure throughout the pupil's time in chambers. Pupils also undertake a structured advocacy training course which consists of advocacy exercises conducted in front of other members of chambers.

## mini pupillages
Applications are considered twice a year with a deadline of 30 April for the period June to November, and 31 October for December to May. Applications should be made with a covering letter and cv (listing university grades) to the Pupillage Secretary.

## funding
Chambers offers up to three, 12-month pupillages, all of which are funded (£40,000 for pupils starting in October 2006). Up to £10,000 of the award may be drawn down in advance during BVC year.

| | |
|---|---|
| No of Silks | 14 |
| No of Juniors | 52 |
| No of Pupils | up to 3 |

contact
Valerie Piper
(Pupillage Secretary)
pupillage@
maitlandchambers.com

method of application
See chambers website from January 2006. Application deadline for pupillage in 2007-08 is 6 February 2006.

pupillages (p.a.)
Up to 3 funded

income
£40,000 p.a.

tenancies
7 in last 3 years

maitland
CHAMBERS
INCORPORATING
9 OLD SQUARE

# Quadrant Chambers (Nigel Teare QC)

Quadrant House, 10 Fleet Street, London EC4Y 1AU
Tel: (020) 7583 4444  Fax: (020) 7583 4455
Email: pupillage@quadrantchambers.com
Website: www.quadrantchambers.com

## chambers profile

Quadrant Chambers is one of the leading commercial chambers. Chambers offers a wide range of services to its clients within the commercial sphere specialising particularly in maritime and aviation law. Quadrant Chambers is placed in the first rank in both specialisms by Chambers Guide to the Legal Profession. In shipping law, seven silks and nine juniors were selected by Chambers, and Chambers concluded that 'these highly commercial barristers are at the forefront of the aviation field'. In both these areas the set had more 'leaders in their field' selected than any other set of chambers. Quadrant Chambers advises on domestic and international commercial litigation and acts as advocates in court, arbitration and inquiries in England and abroad.

## type of work undertaken

The challenging and rewarding work of chambers encompasses the broad range of commercial disputes embracing arbitration, aviation, banking, shipping, international trade, insurance and reinsurance, professional negligence, entertainment and media, environmental and construction law. Over 70% of chambers work involves international clients.

## pupil profile

Quadrant Chambers seeks high calibre pupils with good academic qualifications (at least a 2.1 degree) who exhibit good written and oral skills.

## pupillage

Chambers offer a maximum of four funded pupillages of 12 months duration (reviewable at six months). Pupils are moved amongst several members of Chambers and will experience a wide range of high quality commercial work. Outstanding pupils are likely to be offered a tenancy at the end of their pupillage. Further information can be found on the website.

## mini pupillages

Mini pupillages are encouraged in order that potential pupils may experience the work of Chambers before committing themselves to an application for full pupillage.

## funding

Awards of £35,000 p.a. are available for each funded pupillage – part of which may be forwarded during the BVC, at the Pupillage Committee's discretion.

| | |
|---|---|
| No of Silks | 12 |
| No of Juniors | 35 |

**contact**
Secretary to Pupillage Committee

**method of application**
Chambers' application form

**pupillages (p.a.)**
1st 6 months **4**
2nd 6 months **4**
12 months
**(Reviewed at 6 months)**
Required degree
**Good 2:1+**

**income**
1st 6 months
**£17,500**
2nd 6 months
**£17,500**
Earnings not included

**tenancies**
Current tenants who served pupillage in Chambers **19**
Junior tenancies offered in last 3 years **6**
No of tenants of 5 years call or under **7**
Income (1st year)
**c. £50,000**

# Serle Court

Serle Court, 6 New Square, Lincoln's Inn, London WC2A 3QS
Tel: (020) 7242 6105   Fax: (020) 7405 4004
Email: pupillage@serlecourt.co.uk
Website: www.serlecourt.co.uk

## chambers profile

'...outstanding commercial chancery set...' Chambers & Partners Guide
2005. Serle Court is one of the leading commercial chancery set with 44 barristers
including 12 silks. Widely recognised as a leading set, Chambers is recommended in 17
different areas of practice by legal directories. Chambers has a stimulating and inclusive work environment and a forward looking approach.

## type of work undertaken

Litigation, arbitration, mediation and advisory services across the full range of
chancery and commercial practice areas including: administrative and public law,
banking, civil fraud, commercial litigation, company, financial services, human rights,
insolvency, insurance and reinsurance, partnership, professional negligence, property,
regulatory and disciplinary, trusts and probate.

## pupil profile

Candidates are well-rounded people, from any background. Chambers looks for
highly motivated individuals with first class intellectual ability, combined with a practical approach, sound judgment and the potential to become excellent advocates. Serle
Court has a reputation for 'consistent high quality' and for being 'responsive and able
team members' and seeks the same qualities in pupils.

## pupillage

Pupils sit with different pupil supervisors in order to experience a broad a range of
work. Two pupils are recruited each year and Chambers offers: an excellent preparation for successful practice; a genuinely friendly and supportive environment; the
opportunity to learn from some of the leading barristers in their field; a real prospect
of tenancy.

## mini-pupillages

About 30 available each year. Apply with CV to pupillage@serlecourt.co.uk.

## funding

Serle Court offers awards of £40,000 for 12 months, of which up to £12,500 can be
drawn down during the BVC year. It also provides an income guarantee worth up to
£100,000 over the first two years of practice.

| No of Silks | 12 |
| No of Juniors | 34 |
| No of Pupils | 2 |

**contact**
Hugh Norbury
Tel (020) 7242 6105

**method of application**
Chambers application
form, available from
website or Chambers.
Not a member of OLPAS

**pupillages (p.a.)**
Two 12 month pupillages

**tenancies**
Up to 2 per annum

serle court

# 3/4 South Square

3/4 South Square, Gray's Inn, London WC1R 5HP
Tel: (020) 7696 9900 Fax: (020) 7696 9911
Email: pupillage@southsquare.com
Website: www.southsquare.com

| | |
|---|---|
| No of Silks | 16 |
| No of Juniors | 28 |
| No of Pupils | 3 |

**contact**
Pupillage Secretary
Tel (020) 7696 9900

**method of application**
CV with covering letter

**pupillages (p.a.)**
Up to four, 12 month pupil-lages offered each year

## chambers profile
Chambers is an established successful commercial set, involved in high-profile interna-tional and domestic commercial litigation and advice. Members of Chambers have been centrally involved in some of the most important commercial cases of the last decade including Barings, BCCI, Lloyds, Maxwell, Railtrack, TXU and Enron.

## type of work undertaken
3/4 South Square has a pre-eminent reputation in insolvency and reconstruction law and specialist expertise in banking, financial services, company law, professional negli-gence, domestic and international arbitration, mediation, European Union Law, insurance/rein-surance law and general commercial litigation.

## pupil profile
Chambers seek to recruit the highest calibre of candidates who must be prepared to com-mit themselves to establishing a successful practice and maintaining Chambers' position at the forefront of the modern Commercial Bar. The minimum academic qualification is a 2:1 degree.

## pupillage
Pupils are welcomed into all areas of Chambers' life and are provided with an organ-ised programme designed to train and equip them for practice in a dynamic and challenging environment. Pupils sit with a number of pupil supervisors for periods of six to eight weeks and the set looks to recruit at least one tenant every year from its pupils.

## mini pupillages
Chambers also offers funded and unfunded mini-pupillages – please see the set's web-site for further details.

## sponsorship & awards
Currently £37,000 per annum (reviewable annually).

# 4 Stone Buildings

4 Stone Buildings, Lincoln's Inn, London WC2A 3XT
Tel: (020) 7242 5524   Fax: (020) 7831 7907
Email: d.goddard@4stonebuildings.com

| | |
|---|---|
| **No of Silks** | 5 |
| **No of Juniors** | 20 |
| **No of Pupils** | 2 |

**contact**
David Goddard
(020) 7242 5524

**method of application**
On Chambers own
application form

**pupillages (p.a.)**
2 x six months

**tenancies**
At least 1 per year

**annexes**
None

## chambers profile
An established friendly company/commercial set involved in high profile litigation and advice.

## type of work undertaken
4, Stone Buildings specialise in the fields of company law, commercial law, financial services and regulation and corporate insolvency.

## pupil profile
Candidates are expected to have first class, or good second class degrees. But mere intellectual ability is only part of it: a successful candidate must have the confidence and ambition to succeed, the common sense to recognise the practical advice a client really needs, and an ability to get on well with clients, solicitors and other members of Chambers - and the clerks.

## pupillage
The set aim to give all pupils the knowledge, skills and practical experience they need for a successful career at the Bar. They believe that it is important for all pupils to see as much as possible of the different kinds of work in Chambers. This enables pupils to judge whether their work suits them, and enables different members of Chambers to assess the pupils. Each pupil therefore normally spends time with two or more pupil-masters within any six month period. If other members of Chambers have particularly interesting cases in Court, pupils will be encouraged to work and attend Court with them. All pupils work in their pupil masters' rooms, read their papers, attend their conferences, draft pleadings and documents, write draft opinions and accompany their pupil masters to Court. Pupils are treated as part of Chambers, and are fully involved in the activities of Chambers while they are with 4 Stone Chambers.

## mini pupillages
Up to 20 mini-pupillages offered per year of up to a weeks duration. Application by letter and cv.

## sponsorship & awards
£17,500 per six months.

## funding
As above.

# 3 Verulam Buildings (Christopher Symons QC/John Jarvis QC)

3 Verulam Buildings, Gray's Inn, London WC1R 5NT  DX: LDE 331
Tel: (020) 7831 8441 Fax: (020) 7831 8479
Email: chambers@3vb.com
Website: www.3vb.com

## chambers profile
3 Verulam Buildings is a large commercial set with a history of expansion by recruitment of tenants from amongst pupils. Over the past 10 years, on average, two of its pupils have become tenants every year. Chambers occupies recently refurbished, spacious offices overlooking Gray's Inn Walks with all modern IT and library facilities. Chambers prides itself on a pleasant, friendly and relaxed atmosphere.

## type of work undertaken
A wide range of commercial work, in particular banking and financial services, insurance and reinsurance, commercial fraud, professional negligence, company law, entertainment, arbitration/ADR, as well as other general commercial work. Members of Chambers regularly appear in high profile cases and a substantial amount of Chambers' work is international.

## pupil profile
Chambers looks for intelligent and ambitious candidates with strong powers of analysis and reasoning, who are self confident and get on well with others. Candidates must have at least a 2:1 grade in an honours subject which need not be law.

## pupillage
Chambers seeks to recruit three or four funded 12 months pupils every year through OLPAS. Each pupil spends three months with four different members of Chambers to gain experience of different types of work. Chambers also offers unfunded pupillages to pupils who do not intend to practise at the Bar of England and Wales.

## mini pupillages
Mini pupillages are available for university, CPE or Bar students who are interested in finding out more about Chambers' work. Chambers considers mini pupillage to be an important part of its recruitment process. Candidates should have, or expect to obtain, the minimum requirements for a funded 12 month pupillage. Applications are accepted throughout the year and should be addressed to Matthew Parker.

## funding
In the year 2006-07 the annual award will be at least £42,000, up to £15,000 of which may be drawn during the BVC year.

| | |
|---|---|
| No of Silks | 19 |
| No of Juniors | 37 |
| No of Pupils | 4 |

**contact**
Mr George McPherson (Pupillage)
Mr Christopher Harris (Mini Pupillage)

**method of application**
OLPAS & mini pupillage CV & covering letter stating dates of availability

**pupillages (p.a.)**
12 months **4**
Required degree grade **2:1**

**income**
In excess of £42,000 (which was the award for 2006-07) Earnings not included

**tenancies**
Current tenants who served pupillage in Chambers **Approx 41**
Junior tenancies offered in last 3 years **8**
No of tenants of 5 years call or under **9**

# Wilberforce Chambers

8 New Square, Lincoln's Inn, London WC2A 3QP
Tel: (020) 7306 0102   Fax: (020) 7306 0095
Email: pupillage@wilberforce.co.uk
Website: www.wilberforce.co.uk

## chambers profile

Wilberforce Chambers is a leading commercial chancery Chambers and is involved in some of the most commercially important and cutting edge advice and advocacy undertaken by the Bar today. Most members are recognised as leaders in their field by the key legal directories. Instructions come from top UK and international law firms with a complex and rewarding range of work for international companies, financial institutions, sports and media organisations, private individuals and well-known names. While clients demand high intellectual performance and client care standards the rewards are a successful career at the Bar. The atmosphere in Chambers, which is guarded with great care, is one of a united and friendly 'family'.

## type of work undertaken

Practices include commercial litigation, company, financial services and banking, insolvency, intellectual property and information technology, pensions, private clients, trusts and taxation, property litigation, planning, professional negligence, sports and media and charities.

## pupil profile

You should possess high intellectual ability, strong motivation and excellent communication skills. You need to have maturity and confidence and have the ability to work with others and analyse legal problems clearly, demonstrating commercial and practical good sense. Wilberforce Chambers looks for people who possess real potential to join Chambers as a tenant at the end of their pupillage with them and a 2:1 degree (in law or another subject) is a minimum requirement. The set has a track record of taking CPE students.

## pupillage

Chambers operates a structured pupillage programme with continual assessment aimed at giving you a broad experience of commercial chancery practice under several pupil supervisors with whom you are able to develop your skills. It offers 2 x 12-month terminable pupillages and aims to reach a decision about tenancy after the first six months pupillage. Application forms are available from the website at www.wilberforce.co.uk.

## mini-pupillages

Chambers encourages prospective pupils to have a mini-pupillage with them, though this is not a prerequisite for pupillage. The mini-pupillage programme is for one week and is an opportunity to learn how Chambers operates, to meet members of Chambers and to see the sort of work that they do. Chambers runs three separate mini-pupillage weeks (two in December and one in July). Please visit the website for further information.

## funding

The award for 2007/2008 is £40,000 pa (£20,000 for a six-month pupillage). The award is paid monthly. A proportion of the pupillage award (up to £13,500) can be drawn-down during the BVC year.

| | |
|---|---|
| **No of Silks** | 15 |
| **No of Juniors** | 28 |

**contact**
Pupillage Secretary
(020) 7306 0102

**method of application**
Online via website

**pupillages (p.a.)**
Two x 12 months

**mini-pupillages**
Total of 21 places

**minimum qualification**
2:1 degree

**tenancies in last 3 years**
7

WILBERFORCE CHAMBERS